ℰNVIRONET LINKS

EnviroNet Links direct students to useful environmental science sites on the Net. The links enhance and reinforce the material presented in the text and offer "real-world" examples of environmental science concepts. Jones and Bartlett constantly monitors the links to ensure there will always be a working and appropriate site at the other end of the link.

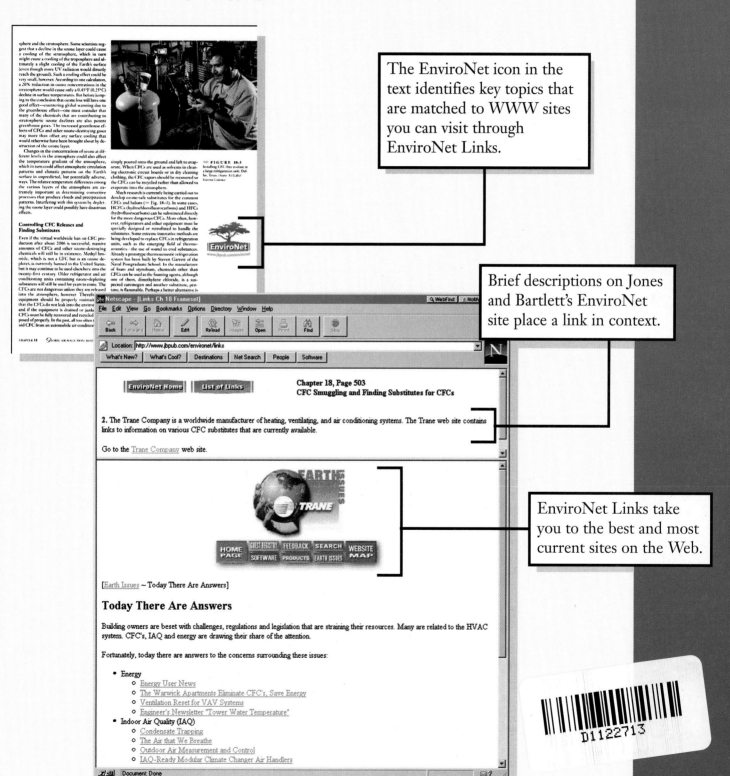

The EnviroNet icon in the text identifies key topics that are matched to WWW sites you can visit through EnviroNet Links.

Brief descriptions on Jones and Bartlett's EnviroNet site place a link in context.

EnviroNet Links take you to the best and most current sites on the Web.

EnviroNet
www.jbpub.com/environet

INTEGRATED SECTION EXERCISES

Integrated Section Exercises require students to synthesize the material presented in several chapters. The activities are designed to enhance critical thinking and research skills.

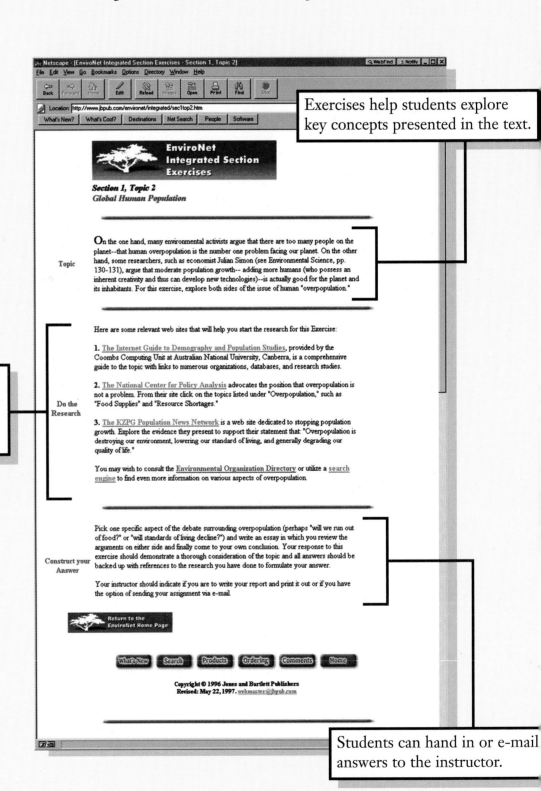

Exercises help students explore key concepts presented in the text.

Students can research each issue through the web sites or use Internet search tools to find their own sources.

Students can hand in or e-mail answers to the instructor.

EnviroNet

On-Line Updates provide summaries of recently published articles on current environmental science topics. Instructors might print out and distribute these updates in class or students can read the updates for research, reference, or personal interest.

A brief summary of a current issue.

Updates are based on current journal articles.

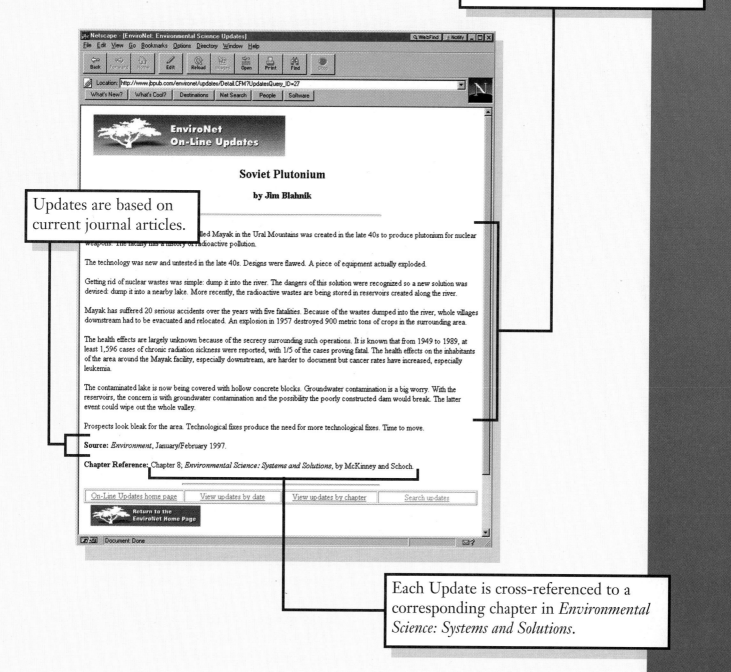

Each Update is cross-referenced to a corresponding chapter in *Environmental Science: Systems and Solutions*.

EnviroNet
www.jbpub.com/environet

The Environmental Organization Directory lists many of the key organizations involved in environmental affairs and provides searching and direct linking capabilities. By contacting these organizations, students can learn more about environmental issues and get involved.

Each listing provides contact information for the organization, including e-mail and web site addresses, if available.

Each entry includes a brief description.

The directory is grouped by Government Agencies and Nongovernmental Organizations, with links to other directories of environmental science organizations. The directory may be browsed or searched by keyword.

Netscape - [EnviroNet: Environmental Science Newsletter]

File Edit View Go Bookmarks Options Directory Window Help

Back Forward Home Edit Reload Images Open Print Find Stop

Location: http://www.jbpub.com/environet/orgs/Detail.CFM?EnviroOrgs_ID=4

What's New? | What's Cool? | Destinations | Net Search | People | Software

EnviroNet Environmental Organization Directory

Rainforest Action Network
450 Sansome Street, Suite 700
San Francisco, CA 94553
Phone: 415-398-4404
Fax: 415-398-2732
E-mail: rainforest@ran.org
URL: http://www.ran.org/ran/

The Rainforest Action Network (RAN) works to protect the Earth's rainforests and support the rights of their inhabitants through education, grassroots organizing, and non-violent direct action.

Nongovernmental Organization

Back to Environmental Organizations home page

Return to the EnviroNet Home Page

What's New | Search | Products | Ordering | Comments | Home

Copyright © 1996 Jones and Bartlett Publishers
Revised: . webmaster@jbpub.com

Netscape

The On-Line Survey asks students to think through environmental issues and express their opinion on-line. Controversial, thought-provoking questions expose students to a wide variety of opinions from around the globe.

A brief recap of a key topic from the text.

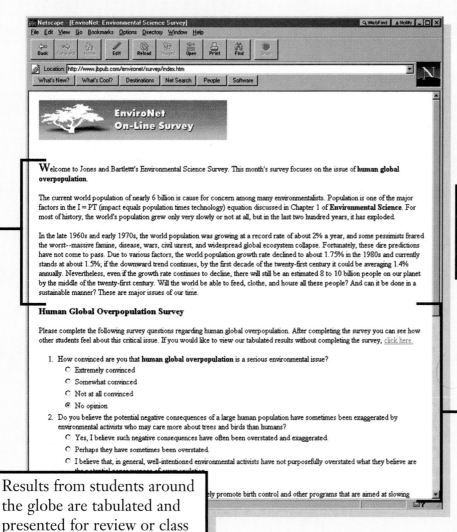

Here students anonymously answer and submit 5-10 opinion questions about the topic.

Results from students around the globe are tabulated and presented for review or class discussion.

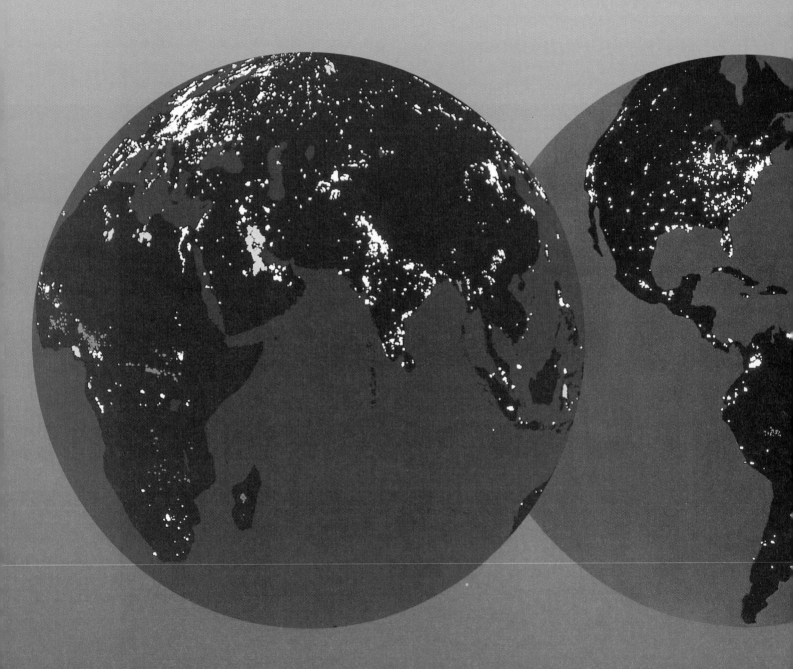

*S*atellite images of the Earth at night, as recorded by the visible/infrared Operational Linescan System on board a Defense Meteorological Satellite Program (DMSP) spacecraft. The white patches indicate city lights, and thus the extent of urbanization around the world. Red areas indicate large-scale burning of vegetation (such as in tropical forest regions of equatorial Africa). Yellow areas are due to the burning of natural gas flares associated with oil fields (for instance, around the Persian Gulf). (*Sources:* Eastern Hemisphere (at left): NASA GSFC/Science Photo Library/Photo Researchers; Western Hemisphere (at right): NASA/Mark Marten/Science Photo Library/Photo Researchers.)

Environmental Science

SYSTEMS AND SOLUTIONS

Web Enhanced Edition

MICHAEL L. McKINNEY
UNIVERSITY OF TENNESSEE,
KNOXVILLE

ROBERT M. SCHOCH
BOSTON UNIVERSITY

JONES AND BARTLETT PUBLISHERS

Sudbury, Massachusetts

BOSTON

LONDON

SINGAPORE

Editorial, Sales, and Customer Service Offices

Jones and Bartlett Publishers
40 Tall Pine Drive
Sudbury, MA 01776
978-443-5000
info@jbpub.com
http://www.jbpub.com

Jones and Bartlett Publishers International
Barb House, Barb Mews
London W6 7PA
UK

Production Credits

DEVELOPMENTAL EDITING
Dean DeChambeau

COPYEDITING
Patricia Lewis

INTERIOR DESIGN
Diane Beasley

ARTWORK
GRAPHS AND CHARTS
John and Judy Waller, Scientific Illustrators
MAPS
Alice and Will Thiede, Carto-Graphics
SCHEMATICS
Precision Graphics

INTERIOR ELECTRONIC PAGE LAYOUT
David J. Farr/ImageSmythe, Inc.

WEB SITE DESIGN
Andrea Wasik

WEB ICON & WALK-THROUGH
Greg and Carolyn Duffy, ArtScribe, Inc.

COMPOSITION
Parkwood Composition

COVER DESIGN
Greg and Carolyn Duffy, ArtScribe, Inc.

COVER IMAGE
Image copyright © 1998 by PhotoDisc, Inc. All rights reserved.

PRINTING AND BINDING
Banta Company

Chief Executive Officer: Clayton E. Jones
Chief Operating Officer: Donald W. Jones, Jr.
Executive Vice President and Editor-in-Chief: Tom Walker
Director of Sales and Marketing: Rob McCarry
Marketing Manager: Rich Pirozzi
Senior Managing Editor: Judith H. Hauck
Acquisitions Editor: Brian L. McKean

Library of Congress Cataloging-in-Publication Data

McKinney, Michael L.
     Environmental science / Michael L. McKinney. Robert M. Schoch.—
  Web enhanced ed.
       p. cm.
     Originally published: Minneapolis/St. Paul: West Pub,. ©1996.
     Includes bibliographical references and index.
     ISBN 0–7637–0613–2
     1. Environmental sciences. 2. Pollution—Environmental aspects.
  3. Environmentalism. I. Schoch, Robert M. II. Title.
  IN PROCESS
  363.7—dc21   97–40642
                                                                              CIP

Commitment to the Environment

As a book publisher, Jones and Bartlett is committed to reducing its impact on the environment. This and other Jones and Bartlett titles are printed using vegetable-based inks and recycled post-consumer paper. We purchase our paper from manufacturers committed to sustainable, environmentally-sensitive processes. We employ the Internet and office computer networks technology in our effort toward sustainable solutions. The new communication technology provides opportunities to reduce our use of paper and other resources through on-line delivery of instructors' materials and educational information. And of course, we recycle in the office.

Printed in the United States of America
03 02 01 00 99 98 97   8 7 6 5 4 3 2 1

 TEXT IS PRINTED WITH SOY INK ON 10% POST CONSUMER RECYCLED PAPER

 PRINTED WITH SOY INK

C ONTENTS

SECTION 1 — ENVIRONMENTAL PRINCIPLES — 1

CHAPTER **1**

$\mathcal{I}$ NTRODUCTION TO ENVIRONMENTAL SCIENCE 2

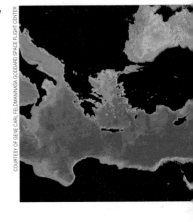

CHAPTER **2**

$\mathcal{T}$ HE PHYSICAL ENVIRONMENT 30

CHAPTER 3

𝒯HE BIOSPHERE 59

CHAPTER 4

ℰNVIRONMENT: AN INTEGRATED SYSTEM OF FOUR SPHERES 94

CHAPTER 5

𝒟EMOGRAPHY 112

SECTION 2 PROBLEMS OF RESOURCE DEPLETION 145

CHAPTER 6

𝒫RINCIPLES OF RESOURCE MANAGEMENT 146

CHAPTER 9

ALTERNATIVE ENERGY SOURCES AND ENERGY CONSERVATION   226

U.S. DEPARTMENT OF ENERGY

CHAPTER 10

MINERAL RESOURCES   257

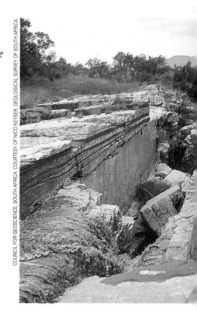

COUNCIL FOR GEOSCIENCE SOUTH AFRICA, COURTESY OF NICO KEYSER, GEOLOGICAL SURVEY OF SOUTH AFRICA

CHAPTER **13**

$\mathscr{F}$EEDING THE WORLD   352

SECTION 3   PROBLEMS OF ENVIRONMENTAL DEGRADATION   387

CHAPTER **14**

$\mathscr{P}$RINCIPLES OF POLLUTION CONTROL   388

CHAPTER 17

AIR POLLUTION: LOCAL AND REGIONAL 463

CHAPTER 18

GLOBAL AIR POLLUTION: DESTRUCTION OF THE OZONE LAYER AND GLOBAL WARMING 493

CHAPTER 19

$\mathcal{M}$UNICIPAL SOLID WASTE AND HAZARDOUS WASTE   525

SECTION 4   SOCIAL SOLUTIONS   561

CHAPTER 20

$\mathcal{E}$NVIRONMENTAL ECONOMICS   562

CHAPTER 22

$\mathcal{H}$ISTORICAL, SOCIAL, AND LEGAL ASPECTS OF THE CURRENT ENVIRONMENTAL CRISIS 606

REFACE

The critical importance of environmental science and environmental studies cannot be disputed as we enter the twenty-first century. Virtually everyone is aware of environmental issues—be they global warming, the depletion of the ozone layer, the controversy over nuclear power, or the continuing problems of water pollution and solid waste disposal. Politicians who once focused primarily on such issues as economic productivity and national security now increasingly acknowledge that environmental sustainability is a necessary prerequisite if we are to ensure our survival. The United Nations Conference on Environment and Development (popularly known as the "Earth Summit"), held in Rio de Janeiro in June 1992, was the largest international summit ever held, attracting delegates from over 175 countries including more than a hundred heads of state. No citizen of the Earth can afford to be ignorant of environmental issues.

We wrote this book to provide a comprehensive overview and synthesis of environmental science. *Environmental Science: Systems and Solutions* provides the reader with the basic factual data necessary to understand current environmental issues. But to know the raw facts is not enough. A well-informed person must understand how various aspects of the natural environment interconnect with each other and with human society. We thus use a systems approach as a means of organizing complex information in a way that highlights connections for the reader. The systems approach allows the reader to take in the information without feeling overwhelmed, as often happens when large amounts of information are presented in a disorganized fashion. With a subject as diverse as environmental science, it is easy to get lost in the details. We have always kept the "big picture" in mind.

All too often environmental discussions become bogged down in partisan rhetoric or "gloom and doom" tactics. Our intention is not to preach, but to inform. Accordingly, in approaching what is often an extremely controversial subject, we have adopted an objective and practical perspective that tries to highlight what is going right in dealing with modern environmental problems.

A key concept among modern environmentalists is sustainability. In this book we have adopted the sustainability paradigm: we focus on sustainable technologies and economic systems and the ways that sustainable development can be implemented around the world. Our emphasis is on specific examples that can give concrete meaning to the concept: sustainable technological and social solutions to environmental problems are discussed throughout the book. We hope to inspire the reader to move beyond simple awareness of current environmental problems to become an active promoter of sustainable solutions to those problems.

WEB ENHANCEMENT

Environmental Science: Web Enhanced Edition provides students with Web-integrated activities and direct links to World Wide Web resources. The starting point is *EnviroNet*, Jones and Bartlett's own extensive environmental science home page. Students reach the *EnviroNet* home page by entering the URL **http://www.jbpub.com/environet** into a World Wide Web browser such as Netscape Navigator or Microsoft Internet Explorer.

EnviroNet icons in the text's margins identify important topics that are matched to WWW sites the students can visit through *EnviroNet*. The authors provide brief descriptions to place the links in context *before* the student connects to the site. Jones and Bartlett constantly monitors the links to ensure there will always be a working and appropriate site on line.

At *EnviroNet*, Web-integrated exercises provide the students with an opportunity to use the Web and their own critical thinking skills to better understand concepts from the text. Each exercise sends the students to diverse Web sites to help them in their research, or they can use the linked Internet search tools to find their own sources. *EnviroNet's* On-line Updates, written by Jim Blahnik of Lorain County Community College, gives monthly synopses of articles from popular magazines and science journals that discuss new success stories and emerging concerns in the rapidly changing, and often controversial, field of environmental science. The Environmental Organization Directory is a searchable database of many environmental organizations. If the organization has a web site, the directory provides a link whenever possible. Each month, *EnviroNet's* On-Line Survey gives students a chance to respond anonymously to a series of questions on environmental issues that could be expected to cause strong polarization between opposing groups. The students will be able to see how their responses compare to those of other students from across the country who have already taken the survey.

ORGANIZATION

The book is divided into four basic sections. Section 1, *Environmental Principles* (Chapters 1–5), describes how natural systems work, including both physical systems (Chapter 2) and biological systems (Chapter 3). The systems approach is introduced in Chapter 1, reinforced in Chapter 4, and expanded throughout the rest of the book. The final chapter of the first section focuses on the increasing impact that the growing human population has had on all natural systems.

Section 2 (*Problems of Resource Depletion*) deals with issues surrounding the use of natural resources by human society. Chapter 6 introduces the broad principles of resource management. The following chapters address energy use, mineral use, water use, and the use of biological resources (including agriculture and soil resources). A major theme is that humans have been rapidly depleting many of these resources and that we must begin using them in a sustainable manner if we are to survive and flourish in the future.

Section 3 (*Problems of Environmental Degradation*) concentrates on various forms of pollution and waste—the results of dumping large amounts of the by-products of human society into the environment. Chapter 14 introduces the principles of pollution control while subsequent chapters deal with toxicology, pesticides, water pollution, air pollution, global warming and the destruction of the ozone layer, municipal solid waste, and hazardous waste. Every chapter includes discussions of how we can limit or mitigate the effects of excessive pollution, especially by limiting production of pollutants in the first place, as well as by increased efficiency, reuse, recycling, and substitutions.

A major emphasis of the book is on solutions to the current "environmental crisis." Woven throughout the text are discussions and examples of environmentally friendly technological, legal, and economic solutions. We firmly believe that sustainable and realistic solutions must be implemented and that the root causes of the environmental problems we now face must be addressed. Such problems cannot be solved using science and technology alone; the human aspect must also be taken into account. Therefore, even though this is primarily an environmental science text, we have devoted the final section (Section 4, Chapters 20–22) entirely to *Social Solutions*. This section includes explicit discussions of social, economic, legal, and ethical issues and solutions to current environmental problems.

USING THIS BOOK FOR A COURSE IN ENVIRONMENTAL SCIENCE OR ENVIRONMENTAL STUDIES

This book was designed to be accessible to introductory non-major students, but it has enough depth and breadth to be used in a majors course. It can be adapted to either an environmental science course or an environmental studies course, and it can be utilized for either one or two semesters. Also, the book was designed so that the chapters need not necessarily be used in the order in which they appear. In particular, depending on the nature and emphasis of a particular course, an instructor may choose to use the social solutions chapters at either the beginning or end of the course or to omit certain chapters entirely.

Assuming a standard 15 full weeks for a semester (usually about a week is lost due to holidays, exams, and the like), the chapters of this text might be assigned according to one of the following schedules:

For a comprehensive environmental science and studies course:

- Week 1   Chapters 1 & 2
  Introduction and Physical Environment
- Week 2   Chapters 3 & 4
  Biosphere and Integration of the Physical and Biological Environments
- Week 3   Chapter 5
  Demography
- Week 4   Chapters 6 & 7
  Resource Management, Fossil Fuels, and Hydroelectric Power

- Week 5   Chapters 8 & 9
  Nuclear Energy, Alternative Energy Sources, and Energy Conservation
- Week 6   Chapters 10 & 11
  Mineral and Water Resources
- Week 7   Chapter 12
  Natural Biological Resources
- Week 8   Chapter 13
  Food and Agriculture
- Week 9   Chapters 14 & 15
  Pollution, Toxicology, and Pesticides
- Week 10   Chapter 16
  Water Pollution
- Week 11   Chapter 17
  Local and Regional Air Pollution
- Week 12   Chapter 18
  Global Warming and Destruction of the Ozone Layer
- Week 13   Chapter 19
  Municipal Solid Waste and Hazardous Waste
- Week 14   Chapters 20 & 21
  Environmental Economics and Ethics
- Week 15   Chapter 22
  Historical, Social, and Legal Aspects of Contemporary Environmentalism

For a basic environmental science course:

- Week 1   Chapters 1 & 4
  Introduction and Integration of the Physical and Biological Environments
- Week 2   Chapter 5
  Demography
- Week 3   Chapter 6
  Resource Management
- Week 4   Chapters 7 & 8
  Fossil Fuels, Hydroelectric Power, and Nuclear Energy
- Week 5   Chapter 9
  Alternative Energy Sources and Energy Conservation
- Week 6   Chapter 10
  Mineral Resources
- Week 7   Chapter 11
  Water Resources
- Week 8   Chapter 12
  Natural Biological Resources
- Week 9   Chapter 13
  Food and Agriculture
- Week 10   Chapter 14
  Pollution Control
- Week 11   Chapter 15
  Toxicology and Pesticides

- Week 12   Chapter 16
  Water Pollution
- Week 13   Chapter 17
  Local and Regional Air Pollution
- Week 14   Chapter 18
  Global Warming and Destruction of the Ozone Layer
- Week 15   Chapter 19
  Municipal Solid Waste and Hazardous Waste

For a general environmental studies course (emphasizing social and historical aspects):

- Week 1   Chapters 1 & 4
  Introduction and Integration of the Physical and Biological Environments
- Week 2   Chapter 21
  Environmental Ethics
- Week 3   Chapter 22
  Historical, Social, and Legal Aspects of Contemporary Environmentalism
- Week 4   Chapter 5
  Demography
- Week 5   Chapter 18
  Global Warming and Destruction of of the Ozone Layer—examples of the impact humans are having on the environment
- Week 6   Chapter 6
  Resource Management
- Week 7   Chapter 7
  Fossil Fuels and Hydroelectric Power
- Week 8   Chapters 8 & 9
  Nuclear Energy, Alternative Energy Sources, and Energy Conservation
- Week 9   Chapter 12
  Natural Biological Resources
- Week 10   Chapter 13
  Food and Agriculture
- Week 11   Chapters 14 & 15
  Pollution, Toxicology, and Pesticides
- Week 12   Chapter 16
  Water Pollution
- Week 13   Chapter 17
  Local and Regional Air Pollution
- Week 14   Chapter 19
  Municipal Solid Waste and Hazardous Waste
- Week 15   Chapter 20
  Environmental Economics

If this book is used for a two-semester course, some of the lengthier chapters should be used over a longer period than one week. In particular, we recommend that the following chapters be split as indicated and extended over two weeks:

- Chapter 2   General Physical Environment/ Natural Hazards
- Chapter 7   Fundamentals of Energy/Fossil Fuels and Hydroelectric Power
- Chapter 9   Alternative Energy/Energy Conservation
- Chapter 12   Biodiversity/Public Lands
- Chapter 13   Food/Soil Resources
- Chapter 18   Destruction of the Ozone Layer/Global Warming
- Chapter 19   Municipal Solid Waste/ Hazardous Waste
- Chapter 22   Historical and Social Perspectives/Environmental Law

If these chapters are used as suggested, then chapter or subchapter readings from the text will easily fit into a two-semester (approximately 30 full weeks) schedule.

$\mathcal{P}$EDAGOGICAL FEATURES

Each chapter uses the same basic organizational format. Following an opening photograph and an outline of the contents, the chapter begins with a Prologue that is intended to draw the reader into the subject matter of the chapter.

The text is written so as to be interesting and accessible to the average reader and is profusely illustrated with color diagrams demonstrating basic concepts and key ideas. Additionally, numerous charts, tables, drawings, and photographs enrich the basic text. Throughout the text key terms denoting important concepts are in boldface type. Each chapter contains a number of "Issues in Perspective" boxes that focus on current aspects and major controversies pertaining to the subject matter of the chapter. Most chapters feature "Case Studies" with thought-provoking questions to promote critical thinking.

The end-of-chapter material includes a comprehensive summary, a list of the chapter's key terms, and two kinds of questions. The Study Questions test objective knowledge and require fairly short answers; in most chapters the last two study questions include a quantitative component. Answers to the odd-numbered Study Questions are in Appendix F at the end of the book. The Essay Questions require more analytical and crit-

ical thinking skills. Finally, at the end of each chapter, a list of Suggested Readings directs the reader to recent, widely accessible books on related topics.

This book includes several special features. Inside the back cover is a map of North America showing the physical geography and political boundaries of all the states and provinces of the United States, Mexico, and Canada. This map will serve as a handy reference guide for the reader when various states, provinces, and countries are mentioned in the text.

The appendixes include discussions of common measures of energy and power, English/ metric conversion tables (throughout the text we have used a dual system of English/metric units), selected major pieces of U.S. environmental legislation, selected pieces of international environmental legislation, a list of selected environmental organizations and government agencies, and finally the answers to odd-numbered Study Questions. These appendixes should be useful to students as they peruse the text or decide to delve deeper into environmental issues.

The book concludes with a glossary of key terms and a detailed index.

$\mathcal{A}$NCILLARY MATERIALS

To assist you in teaching this course and supplying your students with the best in teaching aids, Jones and Bartlett Publishing Company has prepared a complete supplemental package available to all adopters:

- The comprehensive instructor's manual and test bank, prepared by Jay Templin, includes teaching ideas, chapter overviews, learning objectives, discussions of common student misconceptions, answers to the even-numbered Study Questions in the text, audiovisual and multimedia sources, Internet sources, and the test bank containing approximately 2,000 multiple-choice, true/false, fill-in-the-blank, matching, short-answer, analogy, and quantitative questions.
- Jones and Bartlett's Instructor's Resource CD-ROM provides a complete electronic lecture presentation package using Persuasion, the instructor's manual, and the entire test bank. The presentation package, prepared by Charles Olmsted of the University of Northern Col-

orado, provides electronic slides of text outlines, graphs, and artwork for each chapter of *Environmental Science*. Some of the presentations include animations. The presentations are available for Macintosh and for Windows. The package comes with a Persuasion player. The entire test bank is also provided on diskette.

- A slide set and full-color transparency acetate set provide clear, effective illustrations of 150 of the most important pieces of artwork and maps from the text.

- *Outlooks: Readings in Environmental Literacy*, edited by Michael McKinney and Parri S. Shariff, is a collection of 51 current articles to supplement materials that students will encounter in their course work. The articles come from a variety of general interest and science magazines. Jones and Bartlett can make this supplement available with the text as a set, or it can be purchased separately.

- *Case Studies in Environmental Science* is a collection of 60 case studies prepared by Robert Schoch. Each case study explores controversial issues in environmental science and is followed by questions that emphasize critical examination of the issues and the impact poor ethical decisions can have on the environment. At the same time, the questions show that there are no easy answers to environmental issues. Each case study includes source references.

- A study guide, written by Jim Blahnik of Lorain County Community College, is closely tied to the main text. The guide provides an overview of each chapter, learning objectives, exercises to test the students on key terms, chapter concept questions, table and graph interpretation exercises, quantitative exercises, and a practice exam consisting of multiple-choice, true/false, fill-in-the-blank, and matching questions. The study guide also includes resource material on "What You Can Do" in the form of specific suggestions, activities, resources available to students, and "green" career ideas that cover science and nonscience positions.

- A Student Note Taking Guide contains printed copies of all of the art that is used in the electronic slide presentation package. Bound with perforated, three-punched pages, it allows students to take notes as the slides are shown in lecture.

 # ACKNOWLEDGMENTS

As authors, we are ultimately responsible for the content of this book, but dozens of people have provided help, encouragement, and advice. In particular, we are grateful for the advice of many teachers and practitioners of environmental science. Due to its depth and breadth, environmental science contains far more information than only two people can master, and we drew heavily on the expertise of people who have specialized in its many subfields. We therefore wish to express our deep appreciation to the reviewers of the book manuscript:

Clark E. Adams
Texas A & M University

David A. Adams
North Carolina University

John W. Adams
University of Texas, San Antonio

Michael Albert
University of Wisconsin, River Falls

Sara E. Alexander
Baylor University

Gary L. Anderson
Santa Rosa Junior College

Richard D. Bates
Rancho Santiago College

Mark C. Belk
Brigham Young University

Charles F. Bennett
University of California, Los Angeles

Keith Bildstein
Winthrop College

Gerald Collier
San Diego State University

Harold Cones
Christopher Newport University

Carl F. Chuey
Youngstown State University

Lorraine Doucet
University of New Hampshire, Manchester

Nicholas P. Dunning
University of Cincinnati

L. M. Ehrhart
University of Central Florida

George W. Hinman
Washington State University

Gary J. James
Orange Coast College

Robert L. Janiskee
University of South Carolina

Michael G. King
College of the Redwoods

Clifford B. Knight
East Carolina University

Cindy M. Lee
Clemson University

Jack Lutz
University of New Hampshire

Timothy F. Lyon
Ball State University

Theodore L. Maguder
St. Petersburg Junior College

Kenneth E. Mantai
SUNY, Fredonia

Heidi Marcum
Baylor University

Priscilla Mattson
Middlesex Community College

W. D. McBryde
Central Texas College

Richard L. Meyer
University of Kansas

Henry R. Mushinsky
University of South Florida

Muthena Naseri
Moorpark College

Arnold L. O'Brien
University of Massachusetts, Lowell

Charles E. Olmsted
University of Northern Colorado

Nancy Ostiguy
California State University, Sacramento

Richard A. Paull
University of Wisconsin, Milwaukee

Adrienne Peacock
Douglas College

Charles R. Peebles
Michigan State University

R. H. Pemble
Moorhead State University

Chris E. Petersen
College of DuPage

Dennis M. Richter
University of Wisconsin, Whitewater

Gordon C. Robinson
University of Manitoba

C. Lee Rockett
Bowling Green State University

Paul Rowland
Northern Arizona University

David B. Scott
Dalhousie University

Ray Sumner
Los Angeles Valley College

R. Bruce Sundrud
Harrisburg Area Community College

Peter G. Sutterlin
Wichita State University

S. Carl Tobin
Utah Valley State College

Jerry Towle
California State University, Fresno

Lee B. Waian
Saddleback College

Linda Wallace
University of Oklahoma

Joel Weintraub
California State University, Fullerton

Frank Williams
Langara College

Richard J. Wright
Valencia Community College

Craig ZumBrunnen
University of Washington

We would like to thank the people at Jones and Bartlett Publishers behind this web enhanced edition. They include Brian L. McKean, senior biology editor; Judy Hauck, senior managing editor; Mary Hill, senior production editor; Mike Campbell, director of internet technology; Andrea Wasik, web designer; Kathryn Twombly, project editor; and Amy Bartok, editorial assistant.

Very special thanks are due to Jerry Westby, the college editorial manager for West Educational Publishing during the original edition's long years from conception to production. He was a prime motivator, catalyst, and source of reason and understanding. Dean DeChambeau, the developmental editor first at West and now at Jones and Bartlett, was also closely involved with the book. He offered invaluable advice on making the information more "reader friendly." His hard work ranged from reading many revisions of the chapters to finding and even taking photographs for the book. Also, it would be very difficult to find better production editors than Barbara Fuller and Laura Nelson of West Publishing Company. They are consummate, dedicated professionals who greatly improved the final product; it was a pleasure working with them.

This book was initially conceptualized and begun by M. L. M., but given the magnitude of the undertaking, he invited R. M. S. to help him complete the book. In the final analysis, both authors are equally responsible for the entire book. Both pored over the manuscript many times, writing and rewriting so the book would speak with a single voice.

M. L. M. thanks Deb Tappan for her hard work in helping with the extensive retyping that was sometimes needed in a short time frame. Tina Rolan and Jane Ansley helped with reading, editing, and many production chores. Special thanks to Vickie McKinney for chasing down reluctant permission requests. Finally, thanks to my hundreds of students in environmental courses through the years. Your curiosity and interest inspire me.

R. M. S. thanks his wife, Cynthia, and sons, Nicholas and Edward, for their patience during the writing and production of this book. Furthermore, Cynthia often helped by reading and informally reviewing various chapters and sections. R. M. S. also extends his appreciation to his parents, Milton and Alicia Schoch, and his parents-in-law, Robert and Anne Pettit, who offered continued encouragement and support during this project.

Michael L. McKinney, Knoxville, TN
Robert M. Schoch, Attleboro, MA

LEARNING GUIDE

Before you become absorbed in this textbook, take a moment to look over the next few pages. We've provided an overview of the built-in learning devices you'll find throughout the book. Becoming familiar with these unique features can make your navigation through the material much easier.

GETTING STARTED
Chapter outlines will get you started with a quick overview of what topics you can expect to cover.

Prologues open each chapter. These interesting short stories provide a fascinating glimpse into a number of diverse subjects. Interesting and dynamic photos, such as the elephant you'll find opening Chapter 12, tie into the prologues.

PROLOGUE *How Much Is That Ivory in the Window?*

In the contiguous United States, the bald eagle has rebounded from 400 nesting pairs in the 1960s to over 3000 pairs today. A flock of 20 whooping cranes has grown to 200. Bison have gone from just under 1100 to over 20,000. Even more important are success stories in tropical countries, which are the cradle for most of the world's biological diversity. But in these countries, which are beset by overpopulation and poverty, merely passing laws prohibiting killing does not work as well as it has in the United States. The most successful strategies in the tropics have fought extinction by removing economic incentives to kill species. An example is elephant survival.

Once home to millions of elephants, Africa had fewer than 700,000 by the late 1980s and was projected to have fewer than 25,000 by the early twenty-first century. Richard Leakey, son of the famed anthropologist and director of Kenya's Wildlife Services, had seen poachers reduce Kenya's elephant population by 70% in 10 years, killing them at the rate of three per day.

Leakey took action. Game wardens were issued new vehicles, automatic weapons, and surveillance aircraft, with orders to shoot poachers on sight. Within weeks, elephant killing dropped dramatically, from three per day to one per month. More importantly for the elephants' long-term survival, Leakey joined with many other conservationists in calling for a global ban on sales of ivory. In 1989, over 80 member nations of the Convention on International Trade in Endangered Species (CITES) agreed to this ban. It has been enormously successful. Before the ban, ivory in Africa sold for about $100 per pound. By 1990, the price had plummeted 20-fold to $5 per pound, and the elephant decline had slowed by 80%. Many bans had been instituted before, but the key difference here was the widespread resolve by people in many industrialized nations to stop buying ivory billiard balls, carved ivory, and other items. By removing the economic incentive to kill elephants, potential buyers of ivory did much more to stop the killing than armies of game wardens could accomplish.

But what of the poachers? Leakey realized that the local poverty would be magnified without the income formerly provided from ivory. He therefore turned to the growing market for "ecotourism," where tourists visit rainforests and go on safaris. By providing employment as hotel workers, guides, and many other local jobs, ecotourism provides incentives to maintain the pristine natural environment. (continued)

BEAUTIFUL AND DYNAMIC

The text's illustration program and page layout were carefully developed to convey critical information in an attractive fashion. As you look through the text, you'll notice the consistent use of vibrant colors. Not only are the colors beautiful to look at, but they also make for clearer and more informative illustrations.

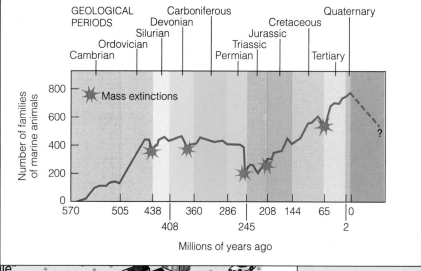

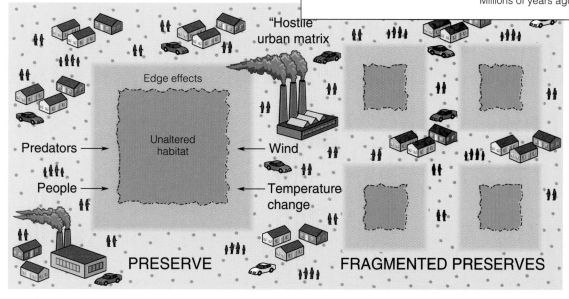

Buffer zones are another important preserve characteristic (Fig. 12–20). Buffer zones are areas of moderately utilized land that provide a transition into the unmodified natural habitat in the core preserve where no human disturbance is allowed. For example, campgrounds and limited cattle grazing may be permitted in the outermost buffer zone, with hiking in the innermost buffer zone. Buffer zones are a major departure from traditional preserves that were viewed as "islands" of natural habitat in a hostile "matrix" of agricultural or urban landscape.

NOW WHERE WAS I?

You just spent a few minutes studying an illustration and now you can't remember where you left off reading. This little gold box appears next to figure references within the text. It's a little feature, but a real time-saver.

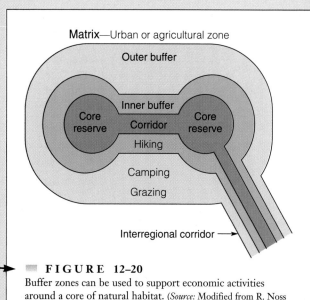

FIGURE 12–20
Buffer zones can be used to support economic activities around a core of natural habitat. (*Source:* Modified from R. Noss and A. Cooperrider, *Saving Nature's Legacy* [Washington, D.C.: Island Press, 1994], p. 148.)

The "Miner's Canary": Decline of Songbirds

In the 1980s, amateur birdwatchers began to notice a pronounced decline in the abundance of many different songbird species in North America. A number of statistical studies have confirmed the birdwatchers' observations. Table 1 shows the results of a study comparing bird sightings in the 1940s and in the 1980s in the Washington, D.C., area.

The loss of songbirds is alarming in many ways. One reason is the obvious reduction in quality of life to people who enjoy their beauty and singing. But more alarming to some is that songbirds are sensitive to many environmental changes. They are like the "miner's canary": these birds were kept in mines because they were more sensitive than people to bad air. A sick or dying bird was a warning.

Nor are songbirds declining only in North America. In 1994, the Worldwatch Institute reported that two-thirds of the songbird species of the world were experiencing a decline in abundance.

What is causing such declines? As usual, all the causes of extinction probably play at least some role: loss of food species and introduction of predators are clearly involved with some songbird losses. But John Terborgh of Duke University and many other bird experts have suggested that habitat loss and fragmentation are key factors in the decline. Indeed, songbirds are hit with a "one-two" punch of habitat loss. Many migrate from North America to the tropics, and they are losing habitat in both places. Species that spend winters in the tropics are declining faster than those that do not. One reason is that tropical defor-

TABLE 1 *Sightings of Songbird Species in Rock Creek Park, District of Columbia*

Species	MEAN NUMBER OF PAIRS SIGHTED		Percentage Change
	In 1940s	In 1980s	
Migrants			
Red-eyed vireo	41.5	5.8	−86.0
Ovenbird	38.8	3.3	−91.5
Acadian flycatcher	21.5	0.1	−99.5
Wood thrush	16.3	3.9	−76.1
Yellow-throated vireo	6.0	0.0	−100.0
Hooded warbler	5.0	0.0	−100.0
Scarlet tanager	7.3	3.5	−52.1
Black-and-white warbler	3.0	0.0	−100.0
Nonmigrants			
Carolina chickadee	5.0	4.3	−14.0
Tufted titmouse	5.0	4.5	−10.0
Downy woodpecker	3.5	3.0	−14.3
White-breasted nuthatch	3.5	3.1	−11.4

(*Source:* Reprinted by permission of the National Audubon Society.)

estation is removing their wintering sites.

But even songbirds that stay in North America all the time are declining. Here the reason is apparently habitat disruption in North America, especially from forest fragmentation. Investigations since the early 1980s have shown that fragmented forests can greatly hinder songbird reproduction because of edge effects. Nest predators, such as raccoons, opossums, and housecats, take a much greater toll where forest fragmentation produces edges that allow easier access to nests. Nests that are deep in the forest and thus less exposed are less preyed upon.

Furthermore, cowbirds destroy more eggs through nest parasitism when the forest is fragmented. Cowbirds lay eggs in songbird nests, and the songbirds raise cowbird chicks instead of their own. Cowbirds prefer disturbed farmland, so loss of forests promotes the spread of cowbirds and opens up songbird habitat to access by these nest parasites.

Learning Guide

CASE STUDY

Are Habitat Conservation Plans the Answer?
The California Gnatcatcher Example

In 1982, Congress passed an amendment to the Endangered Species Act that was intended to meet some of the main criticisms of the original act. Opponents had charged that the act (1) interfered with economic growth, (2) emphasized saving species rather than whole ecosystems, and (3) waited until a species was on the verge of extinction before protecting it. The amendment created a new approach designed to make the act more flexible, reduce economic costs, and protect many species before they are near extinction.

The new approach is called a habitat conservation plan (HCP). Under an HCP, some of the habitat of an endangered species can be destroyed (called an "incidental take") as long as a plan is drawn up to reduce future losses. An HCP usually evolves as a compromise from discussions among landowners, developers, environmental groups, local governments, and the U.S. Fish and Wildlife Service, which eventually must approve the HCP. Ideally an HCP will protect all current or potentially endangered species in an area, while simultaneously permitting human use of nearby lands as deemed necessary by social consent.

By 1994, 7 HCPs had been approved and another 60 were under discussion from California to Key Largo, Florida. Each HCP is unique and some are more successful than others. California has the most HCPs to have been approved. The first was at San Bruno Mountain south of San Francisco, which emerged as a compromise between housing developers and environmentalists wanting to save the mission blue butterfly. In fact, this conflict at San Bruno led to the legislation creating the HCP concept.

A good example of the complexities an HCP can encounter involved the coastal sage scrub habitat of southern California. This

FIGURE 1
The California gnatcatcher has generated national controversy. (*Source:* Anthony Mercieca/Photo Researchers.)

habitat includes some of the nation's most expensive real estate in prime locations around Los Angeles, San Diego, and nearby areas. But it is also home to a rare songbird called the California gnatcatcher (Fig. 1). Only 2600 pairs remain, with 70–90% of the habitat already destroyed. In 1993, after three years of discussion among developers, environmentalists, and government officials, Interior Secretary Bruce Babbitt announced that the gnatcatcher would be listed as "threatened" instead of "endangered" as proposed by the U.S. Fish and Wildlife Service. The less urgent "threatened" status allows officials to work out the details of an HCP that may permit development on some of the remaining scrub habitat. But the HCP will also call for establishing up to 12 reserves that will benefit as many as 40 other coastal sage scrub species that are also in jeopardy from this disappearing habitat.

Questions

1. Many environmentalists strongly dislike the HCP concept because they believe it is "giving away" species and habitat to development. Can you think of a better way to resolve habitat versus development conflicts? Explain.
2. Since "extinction is forever," why would anyone ever approve of the HCP concept? How could development ever be justified over the irreversible loss of species? Explain.
3. Would you approve of an HCP that permitted one species to go extinct, but allowed 5 other species to survive? If it allowed 10 others to survive? Twenty others? Explain your reasoning.

STUDY QUESTIONS

1. Is species richness at local scales related to species richness at regional scales? Explain and give an example.
2. What is the "bottom-up" approach? How are buffer zones, ecotourism, and sustainable harvesting related to this?
3. What is a species-area curve? What does it predict if 90% of a habitat is destroyed?
4. What is biological impoverishment? What causes it?
5. How many mass extinctions have occurred before now? What was the average extinction rate before humans? How much higher is the rate now?
6. Name and describe two key reasons why habitat fragmentation is one of the most destructive ways of disrupting habitat.
7. Name the four main causes of extinction.

Which are biological? Do most extinctions involve just one cause?
8. What is an extinction vortex? What are two basic causes of an extinction vortex? What is the minimum viable population?
9. Where are exotic species an especially important cause of extinction? Why? Give examples.
10. Are diverse communities more easily disturbed? Explain.
11. Are all species equally important? Give two major examples. Where do unique species fit in?
12. How are genetic patent rights important in promoting biodiversity conservation? Give specific examples. What is chemical prospecting?
13. What is a hot spot? How can hot spots be used in selecting the location of preserves?

14. What are two widely suggested solutions to the national park funding problem?
15. Compare and contrast selective cutting and clear-cutting.
16. If you estimate that 50 species per day are going extinct, how many species will be extinct in a year? In 100 years? What percentage of all species will be extinct in 100 years, if there are 10 million species on Earth?
17. If you estimate that 100 species per day are going extinct, how many species will be extinct in a year? In 100 years? What percentage of all species will be extinct in 100 years, if there are 10 million species on Earth?

ESSAY QUESTIONS

1. Why is biodiversity important? Discuss some of its many values, and indicate the ones you favor the most.
2. What are the characteristics of a well-designed preserve? How are they related to "edge effects" and minimum viable population sizes?
3. What is "ecotourism"? Discuss its advantages and disadvantages in saving species.
4. Are marine species being threatened? By what? Discuss possible solutions.
5. Discuss the pros and cons of the U.S. Endangered Species Act. Is it a failure? A success? How should it be improved?
6. Discuss the problems of the U.S. Forest Service and those of the National Park Service. What differences and similarities do you see in the problems of the two agencies?

SUGGESTED READINGS

Baker, R. 1993. *Environmental management in the tropics*. Boca Raton, Fla.: CRC Press.

Berger, J. J. 1990. *Environmental restoration*. Washington D.C.: Island Press.

Fiedler, P. L. and S. Jain, eds. 1992. *Conservation biology*. New York: Chapman & Hall.

Frome, M. 1992. *Regreening the national parks*. Tucson: University of Arizona Press.

Jacobs, L. 1992. *Waste of the West: Public lands ranching*. Tucson: Lynn Jacobs.

Jordan, C. F. 1995. *Conservation*. New York: Wiley.

Jordan, W. R., M. Gilpin, and J. Aber. 1987. *Restoration ecology*. Cambridge: Cambridge University Press.

Meffe, G. K., and C. R. Carroll. 1994. *Principles of conservation biology*. Sunderland, Mass.: Sinauer.

Norton, B. G., ed. 1986. *The preservation of species*. Princeton: Princeton University Press.

Noss, R., and A. Cooperrider. 1994. *Saving nature's legacy*. Washington, D.C.: Island Press.

O'Toole, R. 1987. *Reforming the forest service*. Cov-

elo, Calif.: Island Press.

Primack, R. B. 1993. *Essentials of conservation biology*. Sunderland, Mass.: Sinauer.

Terborgh, J. 1992. *Diversity and the tropical rain forest*. New York: W. H. Freeman.

Tobin, R. J. 1990. *The expendable future: U.S. politics and the protection of biodiversity*. Durham, N.C.: Duke University Press.

Wilson, E. O. 1992, *The diversity of life*. Cambridge, Mass.: Harvard University Press.

BUILT-IN STUDY AIDS

Need a quick memory refresher for an upcoming exam? You'll find a chapter summary at the end of each chapter.

Extirpation? Ecotourism? Buffer zones? Important key terms are listed at the ends of each chapter. For more complete definitions, flip to the glossary in the back of the book. It's easy to find—there's a colored band on the edge of each glossary page so you can open right to it.

Study questions and essay questions are a great way to test your knowledge of the subject matter. They can really help you prepare for an upcoming exam.

Want to know more? A list of suggested readings tells you where you can find more information on a wide variety of environmental topics.

ADDITIONAL RESOURCES FOR STUDENTS

We've put together a few additional resources that you may wish to purchase to help you in your environmental science class. They will also come in handy should you decide to pursue further environmental studies. Check with your college bookstore to see if any of these items are available.

STUDENT STUDY AND ACTION GUIDE
This combination study and action guide provides study tips, environmental suggestions for your own life, and "green" career ideas for both science and nonscience majors. It also includes chapter overviews, learning objectives, quantitative exercises, table and graph exercises, concept questions, group learning exercises, and practice exams.

STUDENT NOTE TAKING GUIDE
This guide includes copies of all electronic transparencies provided to instructors. They are printed on paper with space for you to take lecture notes. Saves you from having to copy everything off the transparencies.

BOOK OF READINGS
Outlooks: Readings in Environmental Literacy contains 51 articles. Each article begins with an introduction and ends with questions for discussion.

ABOUT THE AUTHORS

MICHAEL L. McKINNEY is an associate professor in the Department of Geology and in the Department of Ecology and Evolutionary Biology at the University of Tennessee, Knoxville. Since 1985 he has taught a wide variety of courses, focusing especially on environmental science and biodiversity issues at the undergraduate level.

Dr. McKinney received his Ph.D. in geology and geophysics from Yale University in 1985. He is the author of the introductory text *Evolution of Life*, several technical books on ecology and evolution, and more than 40 technical articles. Many of these technical publications involve his research on extinction and biodiversity loss. He is also known for his work on how species evolve by changes in developmental stages, including the evolution of childhood. Dr. McKinney has received a number of teaching awards for establishing and teaching environmental science courses for nonscience majors at the University of Tennessee.

With Dr. Schoch, he shares the belief that environmental knowledge is only a first step toward what should follow next: informed and pragmatic environmental advocacy. Dr. McKinney is president of the Foundation for Global Sustainability, a "grassroots" environmental advocacy group in Knoxville that sponsors "eco-fairs" for children, runs a speaker's bureau, and operates many other activities to educate the general public about local environmental issues ranging from endangered species in the Smoky Mountains to water pollution in urban creeks.

ROBERT M. SCHOCH is an associate professor of science and mathematics at the College of General Studies, Boston University, where he has specialized since 1984 in teaching undergraduate science, including physical science, biology, geology, geography, and environmental science courses. Dr. Schoch always includes a strong environmental component in all of the courses he teaches. He is a recipient of his college's Peyton Richter Award for interdisciplinary teaching.

Dr. Schoch received his Ph.D. in geology and geophysics from Yale University in 1983 and is the author of several technical books and numerous articles on various aspects of paleontology and geology. In honor of his paleontological contributions, the fossil mammal genus *Schochia* was named after him in 1993. In some circles, however, Dr. Schoch is better known for his work in Egypt. Correlating ancient environmental changes with surface and underground weathering features, he concluded that the base of the Great Sphinx was initially carved more than two thousand years earlier than had been generally believed. This research has been the subject of many articles in the professional and popular archaeological and Egyptological literature and has also been featured in several television documentaries aired around the world. Understanding past environmental changes is important as we face future challenges.

Besides his academic and scholarly studies, Dr. Schoch is an active environmental advocate who stresses a pragmatic, hands-on approach. In this connection, he helped to found and served as president of a local community land trust devoted to protecting land from harmful development. Likewise, Dr. Schoch takes an active part in "green" politics (in 1995 he was elected to the local city council).

Dr. Schoch lives in Attleboro, Massachusetts, with his wife, Cynthia, and their two sons, Nicholas and Edward.

ENVIRONMENTAL PRINCIPLES

Science alone does not have and never will have solutions to the fundamental environmental problems of our time, which are religious in the largest sense of the word, dealing as they do with values and the human spirit. If we remember this at all times, our science will then be freed to play the part that is expected of it in the battle to save the life on this planet.

DAVID EHRENFELD, biologist and writer

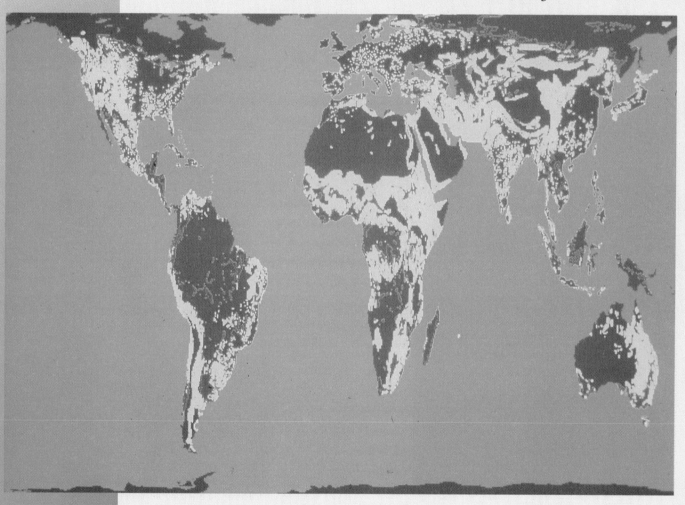

PHOTO   *Much of the world's land area has been disturbed by humans. In this photo, red indicates land that is greatly altered and yellow shows the partially altered land area. Only the green area remains in a relatively natural state, and it is disappearing rapidly.* (*Source:* Lee Hannah, Conservation International.)

INTRODUCTION TO ENVIRONMENTAL SCIENCE

PROLOGUE *People Making a Difference*

One of the most common sayings in environmentalism is "think globally, act locally." Its key message is that while we should keep the "big picture" in mind, we should not become overwhelmed by the large scale of many environmental problems. Global warming, ozone deple-

PHOTO *Norris McDonald has organized cleanups of the Anacostia River. (Source: © 1995 Robert Rathe.)*

tion, overpopulation, hazardous waste, extinctions, and many other problems are so great that we may conclude that individual actions cannot make a difference. But this is not true. Global environmental problems are the result of the local actions of many individuals, so the problems can only be solved if we change these many local actions. For example, the 7.7 to 8.8 billion tons (7 to 8 billion metric tons)* of carbon (the equivalent of 28.2 to 32.3 billion tons [25.6 to 29.3 billion metric tons] of CO_2, since carbon becomes carbon dioxide when combusted), added to the atmosphere each year are contributing to global warming. Much of this carbon comes from gasoline burned by individuals driving trillions of miles each year. Simple measures by each individual, such as car pooling or buying more fuel-efficient cars, could reduce the carbon addition by millions, even billions, of tons. Such local actions by each of us can save water, reduce pollution, reduce extinctions, and help solve many other environmental problems.

Working to solve these problems not only helps preserve the environment for future generations, it also makes you feel better. As this book will show, you yourself can do thousands of things that will make a difference. Indeed, you may already be doing so. Here are three examples of how individuals have made a difference.

With more than 2800 miles (4500 km) of shoreline to monitor, local officials lacked the funding to adequately enforce pollution laws around Puget Sound in Washington. As a result, levels of water pollution were increasing. Concerned citizens formed the Puget Sound Alliance, a watchdog coalition that formed volunteer groups to look for polluters. Led by former sailing ship skipper Ken Moser, some 200 volunteers now regularly patrol areas of Puget Sound in kayaks, small boats, and on foot. By 1994, these pollution fighters had stopped the flow of contamination from at least 12 industrial sites, with more than $150,000 in fines charged to polluters.

The Anacostia River of Washington, D.C., was labeled the city's "refuse pit" by the *New York Times* because it was rich in sewage, street pollution, and other refuse. Norris McDonald started a campaign to focus attention on the river and clean it up. McDonald organizes cleanup days, leads river walks, conducts water tests, and persuades businesses to "adopt" stretches of the fouled suburban streams that feed, and pollute, the river. McDonald's efforts are among the few devoted to solving the environmental problems of African Americans, who often live near the Anacostia River. McDonald also founded the Center for Environment, Commerce, and Energy, an environmental organization that focuses on a number of environmental problems affecting African Americans.

Ballona Lagoon in Los Angeles is one of the last remnants of a vast saltwater wetland system that once covered hundreds of acres along the coast of southern California. Although the lagoon contains only 16 acres (6.5 hectares), it provides valuable habitat for over 20 species of migratory waterfowl, shorebirds, and dozens of species of plants, fishes, crabs, and clams. When Iylene Weiss learned that a developer planned to dredge Ballona Lagoon into a boat marina, she organized a grassroots campaign to teach the local community about the ecological importance of the lagoon. The Ballona Lagoon Watch Society was able to use scientific information provided by the developer's environmental impact statement to defeat the developer's plan. Next, the society convinced the Coastal Commission and the U.S. Environmental Protection Agency (EPA) to provide more than $100,000 in grants toward restoring the lagoon to better health. Today, work is underway to improve the tidal circulation that flushes pollutants from the lagoonal waters, and Ballona Lagoon is once again alive with a variety of flowering native plants.

*Unless otherwise noted, *tons* refers to short tons (2000 pounds).

INTRODUCTION

Concern about the environment is a worldwide phenomenon. The results of a recent poll, shown in  Figure 1–1, reveal that most people in both industrialized and developing nations have at least some concern about environmental problems. As we will see throughout this book, environmental problems are global in scope because humans and our technology have become so widespread and so potent. Our planet has existed more than four billion years, yet never before has one species dominated the Earth and other species so completely (Fig. 1–2). Few people doubt that humanity now stands at a unique crossroads. In all likelihood, the next few decades will drastically change the Earth and its inhabitants. It is up to individuals to try to influence the outcome so that the wel-

FIGURE 1–1

Percentages of respondents in different nations who express a "great deal" and a "fair amount" of concern about the environment. (*Source:* R. E. Dunlap, G. H. Gallup, Jr., and A. M. Gallup, *Health of the Planet* [Princeton, N. J.: George H. Gallup International Institute, 1993, p. 11]. Reprinted with permission from The George H. Gallup International Institute.)

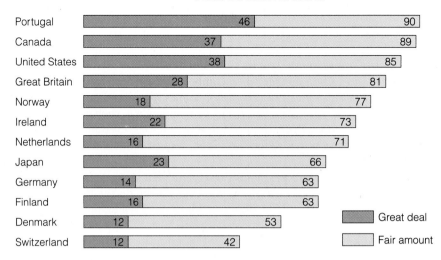

Portugal 46 90
Canada 37 89
United States 38 85
Great Britain 28 81
Norway 18 77
Ireland 22 73
Netherlands 16 71
Japan 23 66
Germany 14 63
Finland 16 63
Denmark 12 53
Switzerland 12 42

■ Great deal
□ Fair amount

DEVELOPING NATIONS

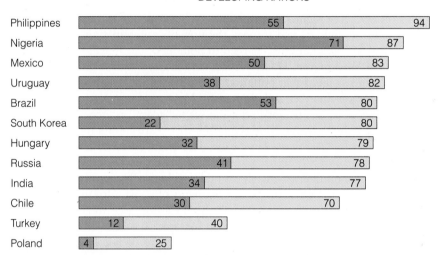

Philippines 55 94
Nigeria 71 87
Mexico 50 83
Uruguay 38 82
Brazil 53 80
South Korea 22 80
Hungary 32 79
Russia 41 78
India 34 77
Chile 30 70
Turkey 12 40
Poland 4 25

FIGURE 1–2

Even parts of Antarctica, shown here, have become dumping grounds for human waste. (*Source:* William E. Larose/Greenpeace.)

fare of both humans and the environment is best served.

While this book will present many important facts, it also has two larger goals. One is to help you sort through the huge amount of environmental information available and focus on important issues. The second goal is to show how this information can be used effectively to help society make the fundamental changes needed to build a world that can sustain many generations of people, with a decent standard of living, while minimizing human impact on the natural environment.

Beyond "Information Overload": Environmental Wisdom

One of the challenges we face today is how to cope with information overload. Newspapers, radio, and television bombard us daily with data

FIGURE 1-3
Henry David Thoreau was an early and articulate American naturalist. (*Source:* The Granger Collection, New York.)

and statistics. Feeling overwhelmed, most people react by "tuning out."

But rather than quit trying to assimilate this information, we might recall Henry David Thoreau's advice to "simplify! simplify!" Thoreau has become a hero to many environmentalists because he long ago predicted many of the problems that we now face (Fig. 1–3). His advice to simplify was a response to what he saw as a tendency for civilization to become increasingly more complex and removed from the natural world that nourished it. This, he said, led to anxieties and spiritual impoverishment despite material wealth.

We can heed Thoreau's advice by mentally stepping back and keeping our priorities set on what we think is important. In this way, we can focus on the information that we can use, instead of trying to learn it all (which no one can do). Ideally, we can strive to seek what might be called **environmental wisdom.** Wisdom is the ability to sort through facts and information to make correct decisions and plan long-term strategies. Wisdom is gained through education and practical experience, so environmental wisdom takes time to develop. Wisdom also means that we take a broad view in solving problems and weigh all kinds of information, social and economic as well as technical. Environmental science is often called **holistic,** meaning that it seeks connections among all aspects of a problem.

Lack of environmental wisdom is costly in many ways. It is costly to other species, to our quality of life, to future generations, and often to

human happiness itself. But the most easily measured costs are economic. A good example is Figure 1–4, which shows that money is often poorly spent on environmental problems in the United States. Problems that pose substantial risks such as ozone depletion receive less money than hazardous wastes and other problems that are less threatening. Such spending inefficiencies occur because people often lack adequate information about the true risk of environmental problems. And when they do have this information, they fail to take a holistic approach and ignore such aspects as long-term global impacts. Lack of environmental wisdom also makes us, as individuals, susceptible to increasingly common "eco-scams" and "greenwashing" marketing that unscrupulously seek to profit from environmental concerns (see Issues in Perspective 1–1).

Beyond Bumper Stickers: Building a Sustainable World

Many environmentalists now point out that past efforts have tended to be "Band-Aids," focusing on short-term, emergency actions rather than long-term solutions. Examples of this approach include cleanup of wastes and pollution after they are produced (Fig. 1–5) and trying to save species only when they are nearly gone. Besides being less effective, such piecemeal, late-acting remedial solutions are almost always the most expensive way to solve environmental problems.

FIGURE 1-4
The actual risk of a hazard compared to the amount of public concern about that risk. There is often little correlation between the risk and the concern. As a result, large amounts of money (size of "dot") are spent on small risks while large risks, such as global warming, get less money. (*Source:* Environmental Protection Agency.)

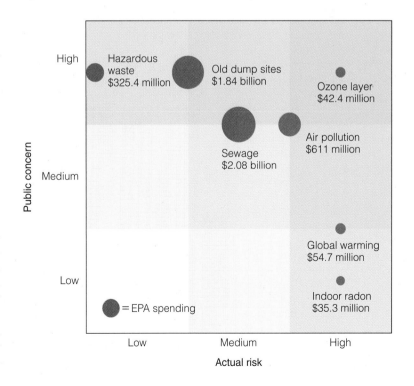

Environmental Insanity and Pseudoscience: Perils of Ignorance

One of the paradoxes of modern life is that technology permits people to live in unprecedented comfort while remaining in unprecedented ignorance of the natural physical and biological systems that support their lifestyles. Many modern citizens, preoccupied with their daily concerns, have become mentally isolated from the natural environment that supports them (Fig. 1). Some writers and social scientists consider this isolation to be a form of insanity. Science historian Gerald Holton, for example, says: ". . . persons living in this modern world who do not know the basic facts that determine their very existence, functioning, and surrounding, are living in a dream world. Such persons are, in a very real sense, *not sane.*"

This ignorance of natural science has greatly impaired society's ability to solve the growing number of environmental problems. When people lack even a basic understanding of science, they can be easily swayed by politicians, interest groups, and many others who use "scientific" data to influence public opinion for their own purposes. For example, the late Dixy Lee Ray wrote two books, *Trashing the Planet* (1990) and *Environmental Overkill* (1993), arguing that public debate on environmental issues is dominated by unqualified alarmists. Many environmental groups and certain political groups, she argued, have used such issues as global warming to further their own agendas. Moreover, these groups allegedly use dubious data and poorly trained "experts" to scare an unknowing public.

Ironically, Dr. Ray was herself a well-known politician of strong convictions. Her own books have subsequently been criticized as being highly biased in their selective use of scientific data and poorly qualified "experts" to argue against various environmentalist claims. Nevertheless, Ray's main point is certainly valid: an ignorant public will always remain at the mercy of people who use scientific claims to influence them. Such people include not only politicians seeking votes, but also businesses. "Greenwashing" is a new fad in marketing that seeks to sell products by making environmental claims. Often, these claims are greatly exaggerated; gullible consumers spend extra money, but the environment does not benefit.

Aside from such marketing scams, environmental ignorance causes money to be wasted in another way: spending priorities for environmental problems may be distorted. Consider how the U.S. Environmental Protection Agency (EPA) spent its nearly $7 billion 1993 budget. As Figure 1–4 shows, the EPA often spent the least money on environmental problems that pose the highest risk: ozone depletion, global warming, and indoor radon. The agency spent the most money on problems that have much lower risk, such as old dump sites and sewage, which kill far fewer people each year.

Why does such inefficient spending occur? Much of the reason is that the EPA's spending priorities simply reflect the concerns of the taxpaying public it serves. As the graph illustrates, the public is more worried about sewage and old dump sites than about indoor radon and global warming. The implication is that if the public were better educated about the environment, money would be spent more wisely.

What can be done? Two actions need to be taken to solve the problem of public ignorance. First, citizens must try to become better informed about basic science, especially environmental sciences, by taking a college course in the subject or similar measures. But the educational process continues throughout life, so everyone must also keep up with environmental news in newspapers, magazines, and books. It is important to focus on the factual information available and reach your own conclusions, instead of relying only on opinions of others.

Second, more scientists should actively participate in the public debates on environmental issues. Traditionally, scientists have avoided the public arena for many reasons: (1) professional scientific organizations reward time spent on research and offer no recognition (or even chastisement) for public service; (2) the frustration of dealing with biased ideologues; (3) the difficulty of communicating complex arguments in an era of "sound bites" and information oversaturation; and (4) the inability of science to resolve questions of social values, which are the cause of many environmental disputes. Nevertheless, valid scientific information is desperately needed, so reluctant scientists must be persuaded to join the debate.

FIGURE 1

City-dwellers throughout the world often live in little or no contact with the natural environment. (*Source:* Francois Perri/Gamma Liaison.)

FIGURE 1–5
Cleaning up toxic waste is an expensive "band-aid" approach. It is much cheaper to design methods that produce less waste. (*Source:* Paul Bierman/Visuals Unlimited.)

The United States has spent more than $1 trillion on pollution cleanup since 1970.

In the last few years, the rising cost and inefficiency of cleaning up pollution after it is produced have led to a search for better approaches to solving environmental problems. Generally, holistic approaches have been able to solve problems more cheaply and efficiently. By examining society and the environment as an interconnected system, we can often solve many problems at once. As Figure 1–6 shows, environmental problems arise from (1) resource depletion and (2) pollution. Past efforts at pollution control were largely "end-of-pipe" solutions, cleaning up waste after it was produced. But as the figure shows, pollution can also be controlled by reducing the flow of material through society. Such **input reduction,** which conserves resources and reduces pollution at the same time, is now widely accepted by environmental economists (Chapter 20) and others as a better solution to most environmental problems. Input reduction illustrates the kind of fundamental change needed to build a society that can be maintained for many years without degrading the environment.

Figure 1–6 also identifies the two basic causes of environmental problems, population and traditional industrial technology. Both need to be addressed if long-term solutions are to be achieved. Population and traditional industrial technology have both led to increased resource consumption and pollution. Two key solutions are therefore to reduce population growth and develop environmentally "friendly" technologies. Many newer technologies, such as solar and wind power, are much less harmful to the environment than the traditional, resource-intensive, highly polluting technologies of the industrial age.

Fossil fuels, for example, are a rapidly disappearing, nonrenewable resource and a major cause of most forms of air pollution. The World Bank estimates that building a world economy based on

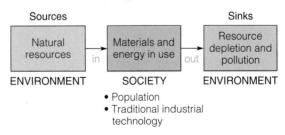

FIGURE 1–6
Environment is a source and a sink for matter and energy that flow through society. Population and traditional industrial technology accelerate the flow, leading to resource depletion and pollution. (*Source:* Modified from D. H. Meadows, D. L. Meadows, and J. Randers, *Beyond the Limits* [Post Mills, VT.: Chelsea Green, 1992, p. 7]. Reprinted from *Beyond the Limits,* Copyright © 1992 by Meadows, Meadows, and Randers. With permission from Chelsea Green Publishing Company, White River Junction, Vermont.)

solar, wind, and other renewable, less-polluting fuels would cost about $20 trillion, or about twice the amount of money spent by the United States and the former Soviet Union on the Cold War. To put it another way, the cost is almost equal to the $21 trillion gross world product, the goods and services produced by the world economy in one year. The United States could switch away from fossil fuels for an estimated $2 trillion, which is the amount we spend on the military in eight years.

What Is Environmental Science?

Environmental science is the application of all fields of natural science toward solving environmental problems. Biology, geology, chemistry, physics, meteorology, and many other disciplines are included in a basic environmental science text such as this. In addition to presenting scientific concepts, the book also discusses social solutions to environmental problems. These are included because many of us who teach environmental courses have found that people (understandably) become discouraged and pessimistic if we talk only about problems. Laws, ethics, economics, and other aspects of human behavior will play a key role in solving environmental problems.

Environmental science courses at both the basic and the advanced level are the most rapidly growing courses at many colleges in the United States and in many other nations. Individual disciplines are developing environmental chemistry, environmental biology, environmental geology, and many similar courses to address society's changing needs. Many colleges now recognize majors in environmental science, and some schools are even establishing departments of environmental science.

$\mathcal{H}$ISTORY OF ENVIRONMENTAL IMPACT AND ENVIRONMENTAL MOVEMENTS

Considering the age of the Earth and even the human species, the massive environmental impact of humans is a very recent development. Indeed, our relationship with the environment has evolved as we and our technology have evolved.

Environmental historians often identify five basic stages in this evolution, as shown in Figure 1–7. These stages are largely determined by the economic activity in which humans engage using the technologies available. This activity, in turn, affects how humans impact the environment.

1. *Hunting and gathering.* Early humans were largely at the mercy of their environment, so they generally viewed it in adversarial terms. Weather, predators, food shortages, and disease were constant threats.

2. *Agriculture and conservationism.* The shift from hunting and gathering to cultivating food is one of the most profound milestones in human evolution. It allowed a great increase in population size and permitted people to settle down in large towns and cities. But agriculture also had a major impact on the environment. People began to view land as a resource to be exploited wherever needed. As land was cleared and cultivated, however, the wilderness vanished. Toward the end of the agricultural stage, the loss of wilderness became so great that alarmed citizens began conservation movements to set up preserves for the remaining wilderness. In the United States, this happened in the late nineteenth century and is often associated with President Theodore Roosevelt (Fig. 1–8). Today many developing countries still have agricultural economies, and their vanishing wilderness, especially tropical rainforests, has stimulated the growth of conservationism.

3. *Industry and environmentalism.* The Industrial Revolution began in England around 1800. As nations industrialize, population grows faster, and the environment is perceived more and more as a place to dispose of the concentrated waste by-products of industry. The result is a rapid increase in air and water pollution, as well as problems with solid and hazardous waste disposal. Toward the end of this stage, pollution becomes so widespread that antipollution social movements emerge. In the United States, these social movements began in the early 1960s and peaked in the 1970s. When people talk about "environmentalism," this antipollution movement is often what they mean. Several early books heralded this new awareness including *Silent Spring* (1962) by Rachel Carson, which warned of pesticide pollution; *The Population Bomb* (1968) by Paul Ehrlich; and *The Limits to Growth* (1972) by Donella H. Meadows and others. As Table 1–1 shows, the antipollution movement added litigation and citizen activism to the lobbying tactics used by the conservationists. These efforts and rising public concern led to the passage of landmark environmental legislation by the U.S. Congress:

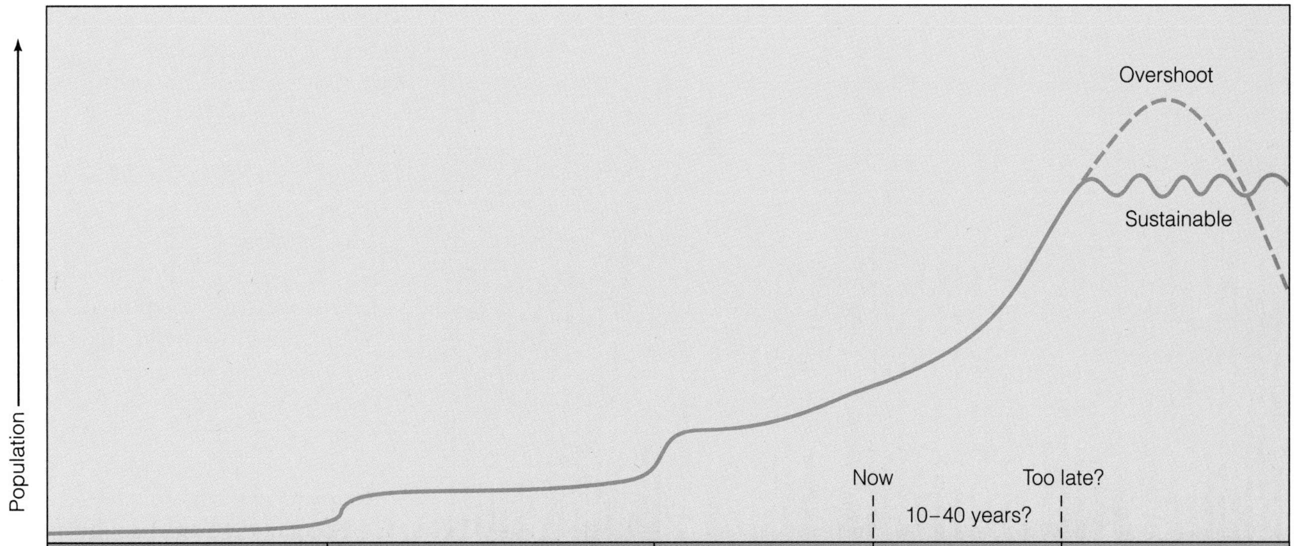

Economic activity / Perception / Impact / Response / Examples table:

	Hunting and gathering	Agriculture	Industry	Transition	Postindustrial
Economic activity	Hunting and gathering	Agriculture	Industry	Transition	Postindustrial
Perception of environment	Adversary	Resource	Dumping ground	Awareness of limits	Spaceship or wasteland
Environmental impact	Minimal	Vanishing wilderness	Pollution	Widespread degradation	Minimal or massive
Environmentalist response	—	Conservation movement	Environmental movement	Sustainability movement	—
Examples	—	Game preserves, parks	Clean Air, Water, Waste Acts of 1970s	Market-based incentives	—

Time ⟶

- **1970** **NEPA:** National Environmental Policy Act requires environmental impact studies before land development projects.

  EPA: Environmental Protection Agency created.

  CAAA: Clean Air Act Amendments.

- **1972** **CWA:** Clean Water Act reduces pollution of lakes and rivers.

  CZMA: Coastal Zone Management Act begins cleanup of coastal ocean waters.

- **1973** **ESA:** Endangered Species Act enacted to preserve endangered species.

- **1974** **SDWA:** Safe Drinking Water Act requires EPA to set and enforce drinking water standards.

- **1976** **TSCA:** Toxic Substances Control Act helps limit the amount of poisonous chemicals made and sold in the United States.

- **1980 CERCLA:** Comprehensive Environmental Response, Compensation, and Liability Act, or "Superfund," began systematic cleanup of large waste sites.

Many more federal, state, and local laws and amendments have been passed since these. The United States now spends about $115 billion per year, over 2% of the gross national product (GNP), to clean up pollution. This figure is expected to rise to $170 billion (or 2.6% of GNP) by the year 2000. The efforts to clean up pollution have been highly successful in some areas, including lakes and rivers, toxic waste dumps, and ocean dumping.

4. *Transition and sustainability.* Although some forms of pollution have been reduced, many other environmental problems have increased. In the United States, for example, species of wildlife are becoming imperiled at increasing rates as habitat is destroyed. Groundwater contamination has worsened, and there are many thousands of hazardous and radioactive waste sites that will likely not be cleaned up for centuries. Despite recycling and precycling efforts, the amount of solid waste produced per person continues to climb. Globally, the EPA has cited global warming, ozone depletion, and increasing species extinction as the greatest

FIGURE 1-7
Population and traditional industrial technology have increased the human impact on the environment in exponential fashion. Environmentalists have responded with the conservation movement, the environmental movement, and the current sustainability movement. Many people believe that we are currently in a transition stage and that humans have 10–40 years to prevent "overshoot" and attain sustainability.

FIGURE 1–8
Theodore Roosevelt (left) and
John Muir in Yosemite. (*Source:*
Theodore Roosevelt Collection/
Harvard College Library.)

environmental threats to future generations. These problems are caused in large part by rapidly increasing population in developing countries, which also leads to local food shortages and the loss of billions of tons of soil to erosion each year.

We are currently in this fourth stage—the transition. Environmental problems have become so widespread that they demand large-scale solutions that involve many aspects of society. Beginning in the early 1980s, a sustainability movement has emerged to try to deal with these problems. Unlike the conservation and antipollution movements of the past, which emphasized specific problems, this movement seeks long-term coexistence with the environment. **Sustainability** means meeting the needs of today without reducing the quality of life for future generations. This includes not reducing the quality of the future

environment. Sustainability is achieved through sustainable ("green") technologies that use renewable resources such as solar power and recycle many materials. These technologies allow a **sustainable economy** that produces wealth and provides jobs for many human generations without degrading the environment.

The sustainability movement uses three approaches not attempted by previous environmental movements. First, it focuses explicitly on trying to reduce society's use of all resources. Emphasis is thus on input reduction, as opposed to end-of-pipe solutions. *Waste is viewed as a symptom, not a cause, of the environmental crisis.*

Second, the sustainability movement is more holistic. It realizes the necessity of addressing the social, and especially economic, causes of environmental degradation. This has led to an increasing appreciation of the role of poverty and other economic factors that cause people to deplete resources and pollute. Market-based solutions are becoming more popular, and less emphasis is placed on the legal solutions used in the past. For example, many experts now agree that it is often more effective and cheaper for society to tax coal, gasoline, and other polluting substances than to pass laws specifying how much pollution may be emitted. The higher gasoline prices encourage people to drive less or buy fuel-efficient cars, for instance. Such economic approaches acknowledge that, far from being anti-environmental, business can greatly benefit the environment. It is what people produce and sell that can cause environmental problems, not the acts of producing and selling in themselves. Producing and selling furniture made from tropical rainforest timber will harm the environment whereas brazil nuts, rubber, and many other rainforest products may be extracted and sold with little or no long-term damage.

Third, the sustainability movement has encouraged the growth of thousands of local community action groups, as opposed to the national groups that dominated the conservationism and environmentalism periods. As Table 1–1 shows, most of the major environmental organizations arose before 1980, during the conservationism and environmentalism periods. Since the Love Canal toxic dump (1978) and the Three Mile Island nuclear accident (1979), residents of communities have become increasingly active in addressing local environmental problems. Vocal debates over

TABLE 1–1 *Major Environmental Organizations in the United States*

LOBBYING ORGANIZATIONS				NONLOBBYING ORGANIZATIONS			
Era/Organization	Year Founded	1990 Membership[a] (Thousands)	1990 Budget ($ Million)	Type/Organization	Year Founded	1990 Membership[a] (Thousands)	1990 Budget ($ Million)
Progressive era				**Direct action**			
Sierra Club	1892	560	35.2	Greenpeace USA[b]	1971	2300	50.2
National Audubon Society	1905	600	35.0	Sea Shepherd Conservation			
National Parks and				Society	1977	15	0.5
Conservation Association	1919	100	3.4	Earth First!	1980	(15)	0.2
Between the wars				**Land and wildlife preservation**			
Izaak Walton League	1922	50	1.4	Nature Conservancy	1951	600	156.1
The Wilderness Society	1935	370	17.3	World Wildlife Fund	1961	940	35.5
National Wildlife Federation	1936	975	87.2	Rainforest Action Network	1985	30	0.9
				Rainforest Alliance	1986	18	0.8
Post–World War II				Conservation International	1987	55	4.6
Defenders of Wildlife	1947	80	4.6				
				Toxic waste			
Environmental era				Citizens' Clearinghouse			
Environmental Defense Fund	1967	150	12.9	for Hazardous Waste	1981	7	0.7
Friends of the Earth	1969	30	3.1	National Toxics Campaign	1984	100	1.5
Natural Resources Defense							
Council	1970	168	16.0	**Other major organizations**			
Environmental Action	1970	20	1.2	League of Conservation			
Environmental Policy Institute	1972	NA[c]	NA	Voters	1970	55	1.4
				Sierra Club Legal Defense			
				Fund	1971	120	6.7
				Cousteau Society	1973	264	16.3
				Earth Island Institute	1982	32	1.1

[a]Membership data are for individual members. Data in parentheses are estimates.
[b]Greenpeace created a sister lobbying organization, Greenpeace Action, in 1988. Membership overlaps considerably between the two organizations.
[c]Not a membership group.
(*Source:* "Major Environmental Organizations in the U.S.," from *Encyclopedia of the Environment*, edited by Ruth A. Eblen and William R. Eblen. Copyright © 1994 by Houghton Mifflin Company. Reprinted with permission of Houghton Mifflin Company. All rights reserved.)

incinerators, landfills, land development, and many other environmental issues now often dominate the local news (▨ Fig. 1–9). Such local participation is often called **grassroots activism.** Recently, grassroots groups with common interests have begun to network by establishing regional and national newsletters and computer nets. By the mid-1990s, many of the national organizations listed in Table 1–1 had begun to experience a decline in membership. Although some people suggest that this decline means environmental interest is waning in the United States, others argue that it simply reflects the transfer of environmental allegiance from national to grassroots organizations.

All three characteristics of the sustainability movement arose from the desire to find better ways to solve widespread environmental problems. Grassroots activism is often the best way to deal with local issues. The rise of input

reduction and economic approaches reflects the need to reduce social costs. While litigation and lobbying are still used, the sustainability movement also uses direct action and lifestyle changes. In keeping with its more holistic approach, this movement is also ecocentric ("environment-centered") instead of anthropocentric. In other words, the sustain-

▨ **FIGURE 1–9**
Citizen protest is an effective and growing way to promote local environmental sustainability. (*Source:* Reuters/Bettmann.)

ability movement seeks to preserve nature for reasons beyond simply improving the quality of human life. Nature is viewed as having a high "intrinsic" value that is not related to human needs.

5. *Postindustrial stage—sustainability or overshoot?* The current stage is called the transition because it will almost certainly determine the long-term fate of the environment for many future generations. Environmental degradation is now occurring so fast and on such a large scale that, according to most estimates, the Earth will reach the fifth, or postindustrial, stage, when the outcome will be irreversible, in 10 to 40 years.

As Figure 1–7 shows, this outcome will be one of two possible alternatives. One is a sustainable future, where population stabilizes and technology becomes less environmentally harmful. The second alternative is **overshoot,** where population climbs so high and technology is so harmful that the environment is degraded to the point that relatively few people can be supported, at least with a decent standard of living.

What can be done to avoid overshoot at this critical transition time? Let us begin by taking a closer look at what is meant by "environmental impact," and why humans cause it.

W HAT IS ENVIRONMENTAL IMPACT?

Environmental impact refers to the alteration of the natural environment by human activity (■ Fig. 1–10). Figure 1–6 identified two basic types of environmental impact: resource depletion and pollution. In other words, there is too much input (resources) and too much output (pollution). Input reduction seeks to slow both depletion and pollution, while output reduction just slows pollution.

Figure 1–6 also showed that population and traditional industrial technology are the two main forces accelerating resource depletion and pollution. The following equation is a simple way to remember this:

$$\text{Impact} = \text{population} \times \text{technology, or}$$

$$\text{I} = \text{PT}$$

It is easy to see why the number of people affects impact. Traditional industrial technology has historically tended to increase the effect of each person. For example, a baby born in the United States has many times the impact of a baby

born in a developing country because over a lifetime the U.S. baby has historically consumed many more resources, such as fossil fuels, and produced much more pollution.

Both population and traditional industrial technology have been increasing very rapidly worldwide. This has led to an extremely rapid increase in environmental impact. This section briefly examines both of these factors.

Exponential Growth of Human Population

The world population is currently 5.8 billion. For millions of years, relatively few humans were on Earth at any given time. As technology improved, so did human control over the environment. Fossils show that humans began to hunt larger game animals and migrated from Africa into other parts of the world over 500,000 years ago. Both inhabiting new environments and exploiting new foods such as larger game allowed human populations to increase. Nevertheless, the total human population on Earth remained quite low until the development of agriculture. Even then, population growth did not become explosive until the 1900s when it was aided by the global spread of industry and modern medicine (■ Fig. 1–10), especially the great reduction in infant deaths. Each year the world population experiences a net gain of about 95 million people, the equivalent of about one-third of the population of the United States.

Exponential Growth

Exponential growth of any kind is caused by multiplicative processes. It occurs in population growth because biological reproduction is inherently multiplicative: by producing offspring, we "multiply." Exponential growth usually has an initial "lag phase" of slow growth followed by a period of increasingly accelerated growth (see Fig. 1–7). This pattern occurs because, initially, small numbers are being multiplied together; as larger numbers are multiplied, the rate of growth increases "explosively." Consider, for example, a pond where the algae cover starts from a single algal cell and doubles in size each day. For a long time, you would see nothing happening. Once larger areas were covered, however, the algae would spread extremely fast: one day, the pond would be only half covered; the next day, it would be completely covered.

How long will human population growth continue before it encounters environmental limitations? The answer depends on how many people the Earth can support, a question that is much

EnviroNet
www.jbpub.com/environet

(a)

(b)

 **FIGURE 1–10**

Human impact on the Catskill Mountains is seen in these paintings by Thomas Cole, created just six years apart. Note the deforestation between 1837 (a) and 1843 (b). (*Sources:* (a) Thomas Cole, *View on the Catskill, Early Autumn* (1837). The Met-

ropolitan Museum of Art, Gift in memory of Jonathan Sturges by his children, 1895. Copyright © 1979/80 by the Metropolitan Museum of Art.. (b) Thomas Cole, *River in the Catskills* (1843). Gift of Mrs. Maxim Karolik for the M. and M. Karolik Collection of American Paintings, 1815–1865. Courtesy of Museum of Fine Arts, Boston.)

debated, in part, because the answer depends on how high a standard of living one assumes. However, many estimates predict that the Earth can adequately and sustainably support between 6 and 8 billion people (Chapters 5 and 13). If true, population growth clearly must decline very soon if overshot is to be avoided. Unfortunately, almost all population projections by the United Nations, the World Bank, and other organizations indicate that world population will probably not stabilize until it exceeds 11 billion, sometime in the middle to late twenty-first century.

Exponential Growth of Technology

The second basic factor in our impact equation, $I = PT$, is technology. Traditional industrial technology has increased the overall environmental impact by increasing the impact per person:

$$\text{Overall impact} = \text{population} \times \text{technology}$$
$$= \text{number of individuals} \times$$
$$(\text{impact/individual})$$

As ▰ Figure 1–11 shows, this impact per person occurs through an increase in both resource depletion and pollution.

Traditional industrial technology has tended to increase per capita resource use and pollution for many types of resources and pollutants. ▰ Figure 1–12a illustrates the fact that solid waste output has grown dramatically in the United States in the last few decades.

But technology need not have this harmful effect. Traditional industrial technologies, such as

the internal combustion engine, were developed during a period of rapid industrial growth, when resources were abundant and pollution was of little concern. As we see later in the chapter, many new sustainable or "green" technologies are being developed that can greatly reduce individual impact. More efficient technologies, such as fuel-efficient cars, use fewer resources and produce less pollution when an individual uses them. Alternative technologies can eliminate many impacts altogether. Replacing coal-burning machines with solar-powered machines conserves nonrenewable fossil fuels and eliminates many air pollutants released by burning coal. Many people are reducing their reliance on any kind of modern technology and learning the benefits of "living more simply." Examples include using fewer household appliances and fewer chemical pesticides and fertilizers on lawns.

▰ **FIGURE 1–11**

Traditional industrial technology (T) has increased the throughput per person. This is multiplied by the number of people (population or P) to obtain the total resource depletion and pollution produced by a society.

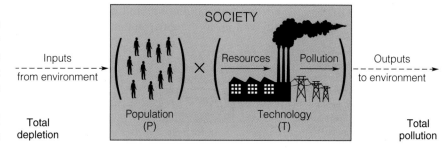

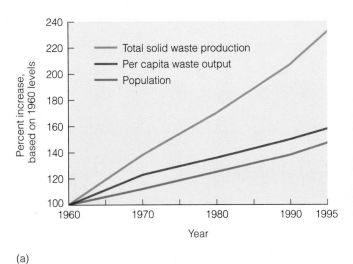

(a)

(b)

FIGURE 1–12
(a) Trends in U.S. total solid waste production, output per person, and population.
(b) Greenpeace protesters on a New York garbage barge.
(*Sources:* (a) Based on data from the U.S. Environmental Protection Agency and the U.S. Bureau of the Census. (b) Dennis Capolongo/Greenpeace.)

Exponential Growth of Environmental Impact

The exponential increase of population and traditional industrial technology have caused an exponential increase in environmental impact, I. For example, Figure 1–12a shows how the overall impact of municipal solid waste of U.S. society has grown as a result of both increased population and increased waste per person.

The increase in total solid waste in Figure 1–12a is typical of the pattern seen in many other kinds of pollution. A society that produces such waste is likely to be consuming many resources that ultimately generate the waste. For example, global consumption of fossil fuel has risen exponentially due to the growing world population and the spread of technologies that use fossil fuels (increasing per capita use of fuels). As more fossil fuels are burned, not only are resources depleted but more pollution is generated, including the carbon that contributes to global warming. Figure 1–13 illustrates this correlation between depletion and pollution. As technology and population grow, more materials and energy move through society. This accelerates the depletion of environmental resources. In addition, the materials and energy that move through society must have somewhere to go when society is finished with them. Solid waste, air and water pollution, and other outputs usually end up in the environment. The movement

of materials and energy through society is often called **throughput.** Environmental resources are referred to as **sources** of throughput, and environmental reservoirs that receive throughput are called **sinks.** This "throughput" model is the basis for many "systems approaches" that attempt to link social systems such as the economy to natural systems. For instance, it is the basis for many important concepts in environmental economics (Chapter 20). The throughput model is discussed in a number of important books such as *Beyond the Limits* (1992) by Donella Meadows and others. In the fossil fuel example, fossil fuels are the sources showing consumption impact, and the atmosphere is the sink showing pollution impacts of carbon, leading to global warming. Carbon is the material whose throughput is being accelerated by growing population and technology.

Acceleration of throughput to increase both depletion and pollution in industrialized societies is evident by almost any measure:

1. Developed nations have only 22% of the world's population, but consume 88% of the world's natural resources and 73% of the world's energy.
2. The United States consumes far more meat, fossil fuels, and pesticides per person than the vast majority of other nations, while producing more solid waste per person than almost any other nation.

FIGURE 1–13
Throughput of matter and energy depletes and pollutes the environment. (*Source:* Modified from D. H. Meadows, D. L. Meadows, and J. Randers, *Beyond the Limits* [Post Mills, Vt.: Chelsea Green, 1992, p. 7]. Reprinted from *Beyond the Limits.* Copyright © 1992 by Meadows, Meadows, and Randers. With permission from Chelsea Green Publishing Company, White River Junction, Vermont.)

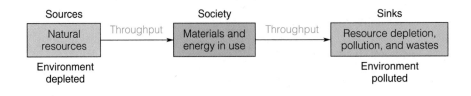

Is Human Impact on the Environment the Same as Cancer?

Many observers have described the human species as a kind of planetary disease, namely, cancer. They see the growth of civilization as a malignancy that is destroying the global ecosystem. Although this analogy may seem preposterous at first, it is remarkably accurate in a number of ways. If we consider humans to be the cancer and the environment healthy tissue, the history of human activities exhibits all four major characteristics of a malignant process.

1. Rapid, uncontrolled growth
2. Invasion and destruction of adjacent tissue (environment)
3. Metastasis (colonization and urbanization)
4. Undifferentiation (homogenization of global culture)

Furthermore, mathematical models show that the details of the spread of civilization are strikingly similar to the spread of cancer. ▬ Figure 1 shows the growth of London from 1880 to 1955, but you can find similar pictures in medical texts that illustrate the growth of cancer cells.

The cancer analogy even fits well with the impact equation, $I = PT$. The growth of civilization has witnessed both an increase in the number of people and the growth of technologies that have increased T, the rate of depletion and pollution per person. Similarly, many kinds of cancer cells use more nutrients and produce more waste than slower-growing normal cells.

Let us hope that the analogy with cancer does not extend to its final trait: The ultimate fate of all cancer cells is to die when they kill their host. Cancer cells obviously cannot think, and we can hope that humans can find a way to build a soci-

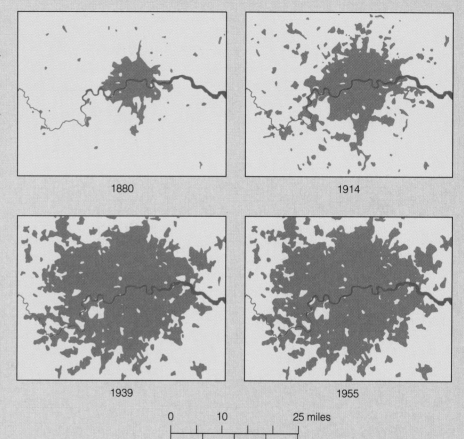

1880   1914

1939   1955

0   10   25 miles

0   10   40 km

▬ **FIGURE 1**

The growth of London from 1880 to 1955. (*Source:* Reprinted with permission from James H. Johnson, *Urban Geography* (1967), p. 124.)

ety that more closely resembles healthy tissue, which has no net growth and less-wasteful cells. We could accomplish this in two ways:

1. Reducing P. We could replace uncontrolled population growth with replacement turnover (each cell is replaced as it dies) so there is no net growth.
2. Reducing T. We could replace resource-consumptive and highly polluting technologies with efficient ones that use fewer (and renewable) resources and pollute less. This reduces per capita impact.

3. The United States has about 5% of the world's population but produces nearly 20% of the world's greenhouse gas pollution (and many other air and water pollutants) and between 33% and 50% of the world's solid waste (estimates vary).

In summary, there are two basic kinds of environmental impacts, depletion and pollution. Both have increased because growing consumption of resources increases pollution as throughput is accelerated. The main causes of increased throughput have been the growth of (1) population and (2) traditional "industrial" technology. This human impact on the environment has even been compared to cancer (see Issues in Perspective 1–2).

WHY DO PEOPLE DEPLETE AND POLLUTE? THE ENVIRONMENT AS A COMMONS

In 1968, the biologist Garrett Hardin wrote a famous essay called "The Tragedy of the Commons." He argued that property held in common by many people will be destroyed or at least overused until it deteriorates. He gave the example of a pasture where each herdsman in the village can keep his cattle. The herdsman who overgrazes the most will also benefit the most. Each cow added by a herdsman will benefit the owner, but the community as a whole will bear the cost of overgrazing. Because the benefit of adding another cow goes to the individual and the cost of overgrazing goes to the community, the "rational" choice of each individual is to add cows. The commons thus rewards behaviors that lead to deterioration, such as overgrazing, and punishes individuals who show restraint. Those who add fewer

cows will simply obtain fewer benefits while the commons itself deteriorates anyway because of the individuals who continue to add cows. This problem with common property was known long before Hardin's eloquent essay. For instance, the ancient Greek philosopher Aristotle noted that "what is common to the greatest number has the least care bestowed upon it."

Hardin's pasture exemplifies the problems that arise when any part of our natural environment is treated as common property. Unless there is some kind of regulation, overexploitation will likely occur via both input and output impacts:

1. Commonly held resources, such as the pasture, will become depleted through excessive consumption.
2. Commonly held environmental sinks will be overwhelmed by pollution.

Many local, regional, and global environmental problems illustrate this view of the commons as a source or a sink:

	PROBLEM
■ Atmosphere as global common sink	Global warming, ozone lost
■ Atmosphere as regional common sink	Acid rain
■ Atmosphere as local common sink	Urban smog
■ Ocean as global common sink	Ocean pollution
■ Ocean as global common resource	Many fish species overfished
■ Rainforest as common sink	Global warming promoted by deforestation
■ Rainforest as common resource	Biodiversity reduced by deforestation

Notice that some of these commons are shared by many nations. The international nature of many environmental problems adds greatly to the complexity of solving them because international agreements are required. Consider the Mediterranean Sea. A confined shallow ocean basin surrounded by many nations, this sea is one of the most overfished and polluted large bodies of water on Earth (■ Fig. 1–14).

SAVING THE COMMONS: REDUCING THROUGHPUT BY PAYING TRUE COSTS

If we are to save the environmental commons, the throughput of matter and energy through all soci-

FIGURE 1–14
A computer-enhanced image of pollution in the Mediterranean Sea. Red, yellow, and orange areas are concentrations of plankton growth promoted by discharge of raw sewage. (Blue indicates clear water.) Most coastal cities lack sewage treatment. (*Source:* Courtesy of Gene Carl Feldman/NASA Goddard Space Flight Center.)

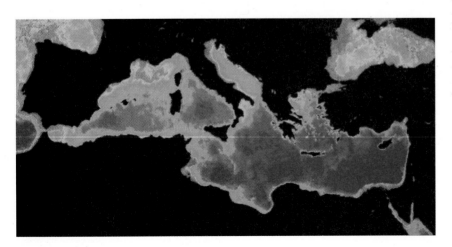

eties must be reduced. This will slow both depletion and pollution. Increased impact (I) has been driven by increasing population (P) and traditional industrial technology (T), so their growth must be reduced.

The economic forces that promote population growth and the use of environmentally harmful technology have arisen because the environment has been *undervalued* in the past. The true costs of using the environment as both a source and a sink have not been incorporated into global economic activity. Traditional economics has considered the environment as a "free" commodity, such as the atmospheric sink, or a source of very cheap materials, such as cheap timber or ores. This view has led to technologies that are inefficient, wasteful, and highly polluting. It has also contributed greatly to the rapid population growth of developing nations. Poverty is strongly correlated with high population growth rates, and people in resource-rich tropical developing nations are often underpaid for their resources (as compared to prices in many developed nations) (Fig. 1–15).

Reducing Technological Impact: Defusing the Bomb of the North

Rapid population growth is often described as a "time bomb" that will greatly degrade the environment in coming years. While population growth is especially rapid in the Southern Hemisphere, the industrialized nations of the Northern Hemisphere are also contributing to environmental degradation through their widespread use of traditional industrial technologies developed during a time of abundant resources. Traditional industrial technologies are not only wasteful and polluting, but they also tend to rely on nonrenewable resources. Thus, technology impact may be viewed as the environmental "time bomb" of the North. The solution is to reduce technological impact, or T in the impact equation I = PT.

There are two basic ways to reduce technological impact. Neither needs to involve painful self-sacrifice and a lower quality of life. To the contrary, both methods of technology reduction can improve quality of life in many ways by improving human health and the environment.

- *Use less technology.* One way to reduce technology impact (T) is simply to try and use less technology. Long before Thoreau, many people observed that machines can have detrimental effects on humans. Riding bicycles to work (instead of cars), buying products with fewer

artificial chemicals, and using fewer appliances are but a few ways that people have reduced their reliance on technology.

- *Use sustainable technology.* The second way to reduce technology impact is to use technologies that are much more "environmentally friendly" than the fossil fuel–based, industrial technologies of the past. **Sustainable technology** permits humans to meet their needs with minimum impact on the environment. It produces a sustainable economy that provides jobs for many generations without degrading the environment.

There are many kinds of sustainable technologies, ranging from direct solar and wind power to recycling. While advances in pollution cleanup technologies are often heralded, true sustainability results from input reduction: slowing resource depletion also slows pollution. Figure 1–16 illustrates the three basic ways that sustainable technologies achieve input reduction, or conservation: (1) efficiency improvements, (2) reuse and recycle, and (3) substitution.

Efficiency improvements reduce the flow of throughput by decreasing the per capita resource use. The United States, more than almost any other country, uses technologies developed during times of abundant resources. As a result, it generates much waste, providing enormous opportunities to save many resources by relatively simple changes in existing technologies. The amount of waste is so great that, in many cases, the large amount of resources saved will more than compensate for the cost of investment to make the change.

Let us again use the example of energy, which drives all economies. Each year, the United States spends about 10–11% of its national wealth to pay for the energy needed to produce that wealth. In contrast, Japan spends only about 5–6% of its national wealth on energy because it uses energy about twice as efficiently as the United States. For example, more efficient machines, often designed to be lighter and smaller, perform the same tasks but use less energy. It is estimated that changes in U.S. technology, ranging from high-mileage cars to superefficient heating and cooling systems to new lighting technologies could reduce overall energy consumption by up to 80%. A simple illustration of the amount of waste is the widely used incandescent lightbulb that wastes 95% of the electricity used by converting it to heat instead of light.

Many other resources in the United States could also be utilized much more efficiently. To list just a couple of examples:

1. *Wood.* The United States converts only about 50% of raw timber directly into furniture and other refined timber products, compared to 70% in Japan.
2. *Water.* The United States uses over twice as much water per person as most other nations on Earth. The average U.S. farmer could easily cut water use by more than half by adopting water conservation measures such as microirrigation that pipes water to crops instead of using evaporation-prone irrigation ditches.

Reuse and recycling are the second best way to accomplish input reduction (Fig. 1–16). **Reuse** refers to using the same resource over and over in the same form. An example would be soda bottles that are returned, sanitized, and refilled. **Recycling** refers to using the same resource over and over, but in modified form. The soda bottles, for instance, could be melted to produce new glass bottles. Wastewater, paper, plastics, and many other resources can also be recycled. In general, reuse is less costly than recy-

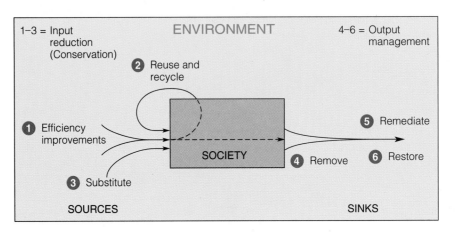

FIGURE 1–16
Three ways to reduce inputs are efficiency improvements, reusing and recycling, and substitution. Three ways to manage outputs are "end-of-pipe" removal, remediation, and restoration.

Simply switching to compact fluorescent bulbs, which are much more efficient, would allow the United States to shut down all the nuclear power plants in the nation. This example shows how conservation can reduce environmental damage.

In addition to reducing environmental damage, efficiency improvements have two immediate economic advantages. First, as noted, the improvement usually pays for itself. The cost of a technological change that increases efficiency is usually recovered within a few years, and sometimes almost immediately. A 1993 study by the Aluminum Corporation of America found, for instance, that reducing the weight of aluminum cans by just 1% will save about $20 million per year in aluminum. Also, increased efficiency tends to produce many more jobs than wasteful technologies. The energy industry, such as oil, coal, and nuclear, is much less labor-intensive than the energy conservation industry that designs and maintains many kinds of energy conservation equipment.

cling because the resource is not modified. Both measures are often less costly than extracting "virgin" resources, such as aluminum ore or cutting trees for paper, because they usually consume less energy and fewer natural resources than making products from virgin materials. Recycling aluminum cans, for example, can save up to 95% of the energy cost of cans from newly mined aluminum. Recycling and reuse are thus less costly in both economic and environmental terms than using natural raw materials.

Reuse and recycling are also labor-intensive so they create many new jobs. Increasing the recycling rate of aluminum in the United States from 30% to 75% would create an estimated 350,000 new jobs. For every 15,000 tons (13,600 metric tons) of solid waste recycled, nine jobs are created; incinerating that waste creates two jobs.

Substitution of one resource for another can benefit the environment in a number of ways. A renewable resource can be substituted for a nonrenewable one, or a less-polluting resource can substitute for a highly polluting resource. Often the newly substituted resource provides both benefits. Substituting renewable, cleaner alternative fuels such as solar and wind energy for fossil fuels is an example. Another example is making products from paper instead of plastics, which are made from fossil fuels and last longer in the environment. Like conservation, reuse, and recycling, substitution also often yields economic benefits. Studies routinely show that substitution of solar and wind power technologies for the fossil fuel energy now consumed in the United States would produce three to five times as many jobs as now exist in fossil fuel industries.

*Promoting Sustainable Technology:
Paying True Costs*

Some people are surprised to learn that many sustainable technologies were invented centuries ago. Wind and water power are examples. The solar cell was invented in the 1950s. These technologies have failed to become widespread largely for social and economic reasons, not technical ones. When nonrenewable resources are cheap, they will be wasted because people have no incentive to increase efficiency, recycle/reuse, and substitute renewable resources. ▪ Figure 1–17a shows the situation when resources are cheap and sinks are free and are treated as "commons." Note that there is much throughput, which leads to high rates of resource depletion and pollution.

For instance, many private and government studies show that the price of gasoline is at least $3.50 per gallon when all environmental costs are included. These environmental costs include smog and other urban air pollutants, global warming, contamination of groundwater by leaking underground oil tanks, oil spills, and many other well-known impacts of gasoline use. Yet the price of gasoline in the United States has remained far below $3.50 (averaging less than $1.50 per gallon), although most other industrial nations have higher prices.

When market prices do not reflect all the true costs of a product or service, economists call this a **market failure** (also called an "externality"; see Chapter 20). Many environmental problems can ultimately be traced to market failures. To list just a couple of examples:

1. Electricity from nuclear energy does not include the cost of disposing of nuclear waste; electricity produced by coal burning omits the cost of most air pollution.
2. Water used by many U.S. farmers does not reflect the fact that the groundwater is being

depleted much faster than it is being replenished by rainfall.

Most economists suggest society can correct market failures by adjusting the costs of products and services to include environmental costs. Figure 1–17b shows how fees can be imposed at many locations of throughput to make these adjustments. Such fees are often called **green fees.** Fees that increase the price of a resource are particularly effective because they promote conservation of the resource and also reduce pollution by reducing throughput. For example, higher user fees on federal land for timber and ore deposits would encourage more efficient use of those

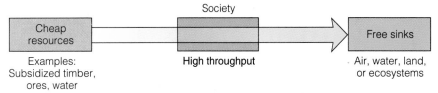

(a) Environmental costs excluded

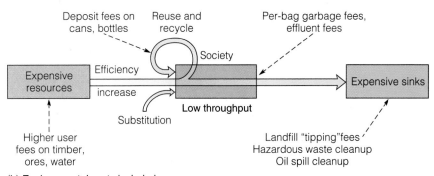

(b) Environmental costs included

resources and reduce solid waste. Similarly, fossil fuels taxes, such as a "gas tax" or "carbon tax" covering all fossil fuels, would encourage reduced and more efficient use of these fuels.

Other green fees include deposits, such as on cans or bottles, to encourage recycling (Fig. 1–17b). Charging for garbage by the bag and effluent (pollution) fees on factories are other examples. These fees motivate people to reduce the waste they produce. Other fees can be imposed for using sinks, such as "tipping fees" for landfill use or making polluters pay for cleanup (Fig. 1–17b).

Another benefit of green fees is that they may improve the environment at lower monetary costs than simply passing regulations and arresting violators. ▪ Figure 1–18 compares the effect of regulatory efforts to reduce carbon emissions with two different carbon (fossil fuel) taxes, one phased in slowly, the other phased in rapidly. All three

▪ **FIGURE 1–17**
(a) Excluding environmental costs by allowing cheap resources and free sinks promotes high throughput (and therefore much depletion and pollution). (b) Including environmental costs by imposing user fees and deposit fees promotes an increase in efficiency, recycling, and all other forms of input reduction.

FIGURE 1–18
Effects on economic growth of three methods of cutting greenhouse gas emissions. Under Policy A, international carbon taxes are phased in slowly. Policy B also uses taxes, but they are phased in rapidly. Policy C relies on government regulations phased in rapidly. (*Source: The Economist*, July 7, 1990, p. 22. Copyright © 1990 The Economist Newspaper Group, Inc. Reprinted with permission. Further reproduction prohibited.)

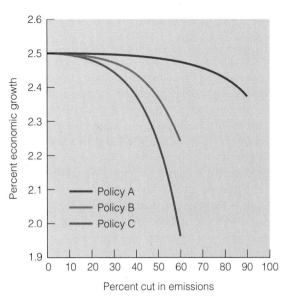

policies reduce greenhouse gas emissions, but carbon taxes, especially when phased in slowly, may have less negative impact on economic growth.

Although the United States is the world's largest resource consumer and polluter (by most measures), it unfortunately lags far behind most of the industrialized world in the use of green fees and other economic incentives to conserve resources and reduce pollution. The general trend has been the continuation of cheap resources and free sinks. In fact, in many cases the United States actively discourages conservation and encourages pollution by subsidies that reward these activities (as opposed to green taxes that discourage them). A 1993 study by the Alliance to Save Energy found that 58% ($21 billion) of federal energy subsidies went to fossil fuels and 30% ($11 billion) to nuclear energy; only 3% went to energy efficiency projects and 2% to renewable energy projects.

Figure 1–19 shows an example of great importance, the cheap cost of oil in the United States since the early 1980s, which has led to a reversal of the previous trend toward more fuel-efficient cars. Nevertheless, many observers think that a "greener" economy is inevitable because of

consumer demand for environmental quality and the economic benefits of sustainable technologies such as increased efficiency, reduced resource imports, and more jobs. As Issues in Perspective 1–3 describes, there are many signs that U.S. business is indeed becoming greener. This trend has been accompanied by increased discussion of green fees and the removal of government subsidies on timber, grazing lands, ore deposits, and oil companies (Chapters 6, 20, 22).

Reducing Population: Defusing the Bomb of the South

Over 90% of world population growth occurs in developing nations. Most developing nations are in the Southern Hemisphere, so this cause of throughput is especially important there. To defuse this so-called **population bomb,** we must address its central causes, which are often economic. Figure 1–20 shows how population growth is often driven by poverty. Poor people tend to have more offspring for a variety of reasons, including lack of education about birth control, lack of economic opportunities for women, and the need for children to perform chores and care for the aged (see Chapter 5). The result is a "vicious circle" in which population growth leads to poverty because too many people reduce the standard of living. Furthermore, the growing population reduces the amount of money available for investment in education, equipment, and other needs for economic growth.

Can this "poverty-population-environment cycle" of human misery and environmental destruction be broken? Decades of experience show that the economic causes of this cycle must be addressed. Poor people often have little interest in such abstract ideas as global warming or animal rights because they are trying to survive. Many people still subscribe to the **fallacy of enlightenment,** or the idea that education will solve the problem. But education is not enough; realistic solutions that remove the root causes of the problem must be found. Attempting to protect the environment by legal means, such as creating game reserves, is often not effective either because desperate people will break laws. Eliminating poverty will not only reduce many causes of population growth, but it will reduce environmental degradation as well.

FIGURE 1–19
Price of oil per barrel in the United States (in 1994 dollars). (*Source:* U.S. Department of Energy.)

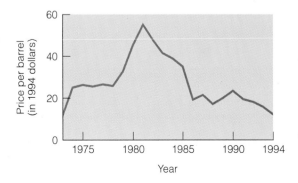

Reducing Population Growth by Paying True Costs

It has long been known that the economic woes of the developing nations must be solved. In 1961,

Business Is Green: The Jobs versus Environment Myth

In his book *The Environmental Economic Revolution* (1993), economist Michael Silverstein discusses how widespread interest in environmental quality is radically changing both the world economy and the discipline of economics. The rapid growth of the environmental cleanup and antipollution industries are the most obvious indicators. The United States alone will spend between $1.2 to $1.5 trillion on waste cleanup in the 1990s; worldwide, the estimate is $3–4 trillion. Antipollution and cleanup technologies have been among the fastest growing industries.

Silverstein argues, however, that the environmental revolution is affecting much more than the cleanup and antipollution industries. He contends that virtually all sectors of the U.S. and world economy are becoming "greener," and often profiting from it. His examples include:

1. *Travel industry.* The rapid growth of "eco-tours" that promote appreciation of nature (but must be done correctly to minimize harm).
2. *Recycling industry.* The rapid growth of recycling of many materials, from wood products to metals to plastics.
3. *Efficiency design industries.* The rapid growth of industries that design more efficient technologies that use fewer resources to accomplish the same task: low-flush toilets, energy-efficient machinery and cars, and so on (Fig. 1).
4. *Chemical industry.* The rapid growth of research into and production of chemicals that are less toxic and less persistent in the environment.

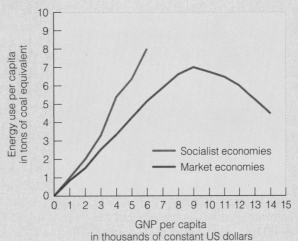

FIGURE 1

The low-flush toilet is just one of many new products that benefit the environment and the economy. (*Source:* Burrows/Gamma Liaison.)

Silverstein identifies two forces that are driving these changes in industrialized nations. One is public demand for goods and services that are less environmentally harmful. The other is that increased competition in the global economy demands that companies become efficient and

FIGURE 2

Energy use in socialist versus capitalist economies. (*Source:* From *Resources, Environment, and Population: Present Knowledge, Future Options,* edited by Kingsley Davis and Mikhail S. Bernstam. Copyright © 1991 by the Population Council, Inc. Reprinted by permission of Oxford University Press, Inc.)

reduce waste. U.S. companies have traditionally been very wasteful of energy and materials.

As a result of this ongoing environmental economic revolution both the economy and the environment are benefiting. Economic benefits include increasing profits for "green" companies both because consumers prefer their products and because such companies are more efficient. Also, as discussed in the text, "green" activities tend to create more jobs than depleting or polluting activities. In part, this is because recycling, making solar cells, installing insulation, and other environmentally friendly activities rely more on human labor than on machines. But it is also because these activities sustain the resources they rely on and therefore employ people for longer times. Loggers and miners, for example, often find themselves unemployed when the local trees or ore deposits are gone.

Most economists think that moderately free market economies are better at promoting environmentally friendly economic growth than socialist, or planned, economies. Poland, and many of the other formerly communist countries, are among the most polluted in the world. Socialist economies are much less energy efficient than market economies and therefore produce much more waste and depletion, as shown in Figure 2. The reason is that free markets tend to provide incentives for individuals to do the right things, and property rights help reduce abuse of an environmental commons. But, as noted in the text, a completely free market can lead to environmental degradation, too. Green taxes, laws, and other forms of regulation are then used to correct such market failures.

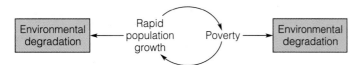

Poverty-population-environment cycle

the United Nations General Assembly pledged that developed nations would donate 1% of their gross national product (GNP) to developing nations. The model was the U.S. Marshall Plan, which provided money to help rebuild Europe and Japan after World War II. But instead of improving, the economies of most developing Southern Hemisphere nations have declined. Indeed, the gap in wealth between the developed and developing nations has widened at an increasing rate (Chapter 20). By the early 1990s, per capita wealth was nearly 20 times greater in high-income countries such as those of western Europe than in the developing countries.

This gap continues to grow because developing countries now pay a huge amount of interest on money that was lent to them many years ago. Developing countries now owe over $1.3 trillion. As a result of interest on this debt, the *net flow of money has been from South to North* since 1982. Rich countries now receive more money from poor countries (over $50 billion per year) than they transfer to them. This is sometimes called the **debt bomb.**

Some people argue that the solution to the debt bomb is increased foreign aid. They note that the 1% of GNP pledged in 1961 to developing nations has never been achieved. In 1994, the United States spent about $10 billion on foreign aid, which is about 0.17% GNP or slightly more than is annually spent on lawn care in the United States. It is also much less than the approximately $270 billion spent on national defense even though refugees from developing nations may be a bigger threat to national security than large-scale warfare.

Some economists argue that foreign aid to poor countries should not be viewed as charity. They note that these poor but resource-rich nations would not need charity if they were paid the true costs for their resources. This view is becoming increasingly common among the people living in the Southern Hemisphere. They maintain that if people in the developed Northern Hemisphere wish to save rainforests, they should pay for the environmental goods and services the forests produce. This would mean paying much

higher prices for tropical forest products (such as fruits) and services such as the trees' absorption of carbon dioxide to slow global warming. Although it is very difficult to estimate the true environmental costs in most cases, nearly all estimates indicate that developing nations are greatly underpaid for their resources (Chapters 6 and 20).

Appropriate payment for environmental goods and services could help eliminate poverty, probably much more effectively than foreign aid donations. These payments would break the vicious cycle and reduce population growth as well. A key necessity is that this increased wealth be used to buy sustainable technologies that focus on efficiency, recycling/reuse, and renewable resources. This proposal contrasts with older views that saw "modernization" of developing countries following the same developmental pathway as Europe, North America, and Japan.

𝒯HE ROLE OF THE INDIVIDUAL

The writer Wendell Berry said that the roots of all environmental problems ultimately lie in the values of the individuals who comprise society. Or, as the writer Paul Hawken put it, the environment is not being degraded by corporate presidents; it is being degraded by popular demand. By this he means that companies only produce things that people buy, and they cause depletion and pollution only as long as society permits such behavior to be profitable. For example, we have just seen how green fees, such as a carbon tax, could be used to correct the market failures that cause pollution. Yet these strategies are rarely applied in practice. People have generally voted down proposals to add green taxes, even where income and other taxes would be reduced to compensate.

A good example is the "gas tax." In the early 1990s, the Clinton administration initially conceived of a gasoline tax of up to a few dollars per gallon. As gasoline was only about a dollar per gallon, this would have raised gasoline costs close to the estimated true environmental cost of $3.50 per gallon. The goal of the tax was to promote fuel conservation and alternative fuels and reduce air pollution including carbon dioxide. The United States signed an international agreement, pledging to reduce carbon dioxide to slow greenhouse gas emissions (the United States produces nearly 20% of such emissions). But after extensive congressional debate, a gas tax of only about four cents was imposed rather than the two or three dollars originally conceived.

Values on the Here and Now: Why We Avoid True Costs

Why do individuals have values that lead to environmental degradation by "popular demand"? Many writers have argued that most large-scale problems arise because individuals are not good at dealing with problems beyond their own immediate situation. We tend to focus on the "here and now" of current time and local space. We think most about things we can see around us and things that have just recently happened to us or will soon happen to us.

This focus on the "here and now" is why people have been reluctant, especially in the United States, to pay true costs for goods and services that deplete or pollute the environment. Economists call this "discounting the future" and "discounting by distance." **Discounting the future** results from focusing on the "now": Environmental costs of our actions on future generations are not fully paid. Cheap gasoline and minerals, for instance, lead to rapid depletion of these nonrenewable resources making them unavailable to future generations. These resources are cheap because their current cost does not incorporate their value to future generations. Nor does the cost include the future effects of their use, such as global warming or other pollution hazards. **Discounting by distance** results from focusing on the "here": Environmental costs of our actions on people living in another area are not fully paid. Cheap ivory, imported animals, and tropical timber, for instance, lead to rapid depletion of those tropical resources, thereby degrading the environment for the people who live there. These resources are so cheap because their cost does not incorporate their full value to their local environment.

From an individual viewpoint, being preoccupied with immediate concerns has been a good survival trait. In our evolutionary and historical past, individuals needed to be aware of activity in their immediate vicinity to avoid predators and other dangers. However, modern technologies have led to problems that occur on far larger scales of time and space; their effects are global and last many centuries. Such problems require long-range planning that will span many generations and involve international cooperation. In their book *New World, New Mind* (1989), Robert Ornstein and Paul Ehrlich state that they believe our minds have a "putting out fires" approach to problems; another term might be "Band-Aid" approach. They indicate that only recently, with the sustainability movement, has there been widespread interest in addressing the systematic causes that underlie these problems.

A Solution: Values beyond the Self

It can be argued that the single greatest obstacle to building a sustainable society is this tendency of the human mind to focus on the here and now. It limits our ability to make the systemic social changes needed to solve regional and global problems. This is why David Ehrenfeld, in *The Arrogance of Humanism* (1981), warns that history shows that humans have never successfully managed anything for very long. How can we expect to solve global environmental problems with such limitations?

Figure 1–21 shows how people can extend their sphere of concern, beginning with close relatives and progressing through other social groupings to include all people. Ultimately, all living things can be included, as in the well-developed philosophy of "deep ecology" (Chapter 21). All of us initially begin with the self because infants and young children are preoccupied with their own needs. Some people remain very selfish throughout life, while other people develop some or all of the spheres of concern in Figure 1–21. If we are to place a higher value on the environment of the future and in other parts of the world, such extended spheres of concern are needed. If many people adopt this view, society will be more willing to pay green taxes, vote for politicians who favor sustainable lifestyles, and, in general, promote the solutions outlined here that require looking beyond the here and now.

Most sociologists believe that the trend has been in the opposite direction until now. The growth of modern civilization has promoted individualism that has progressively shrunk the sphere of

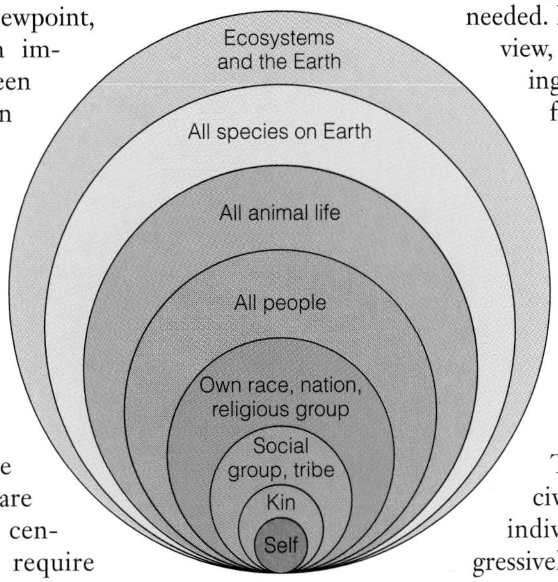

Ecosystems and the Earth

All species on Earth

All animal life

All people

Own race, nation, religious group

Social group, tribe

Kin

Self

FIGURE 1-21
An ethical sequence in which the individual concerns extend outward beyond self to progressively more inclusive levels. (*Source:* R. Noss, "Essay: Issues of Scale," in P. L. Fiedler and S. Jain, eds., *Conservation Biology* [Chapman & Hall, 1992, p. 240]. Reprinted by permission of Chapman & Hall.)

What Are Your Values? Would You Decline $600,000 to Save a Rainforest?

Although many of us say we are pro-environment, we never really know how strong our values are until we are asked to make personal sacrifices for them. For example, in this chapter, we have said that the environment of future generations is often discounted, or devalued. Most of us would like to change that situation, but just how much are we willing to sacrifice?

Consider the case of Miguel Sanchez, a subsistence farmer in Costa Rica. He was offered $600,000 for a piece of land that he and his family have tended for many years. This land consists of spectacular old-growth rainforest and a beautiful black sand beach in an area where land is rapidly disappearing to

development. The money was offered by a hotel developer. Sanchez declined, knowing that this was more money than he, his children, and his grandchildren would ever accumulate. Sanchez explained his decision: "I have no desire to live anywhere else. Money can be evil. People will ask me for money."

Miguel knows that cleared forest means less rain, less water in the rivers, less escape from the blazing tropical Sun. But he is reluctant to talk about his decision. Hundreds of other farmers and fishermen in his area feel the same way and are fighting development.

(*Source:* Adapted from A. Carothers, "Letter from Costa Rica," *E Magazine*, September 1993.)

Questions

1. How does Miguel's sacrifice compare to sacrifices you have made to promote long-term environmental health? What would you do if you were in Miguel's position?

2. Comment on this statement from writer Andre Carothers: America has "a skewed moral universe, where people regularly swoon over each other's negligible acts of charity." The writer's point is that we make a big deal about recycling cans, buying organic foods, and giving tiny donations to environmental funds. Is this a fair criticism or unjustified cynicism?

---

concern. Large cities have fostered a loss of community and the fragmentation of social groups, including even families. Can this trend be reversed? No one knows, but some encouraging signs have appeared. For example, the grassroots activism of the current sustainability movement is based on community concerns. There are also many examples of exceptional unselfishness in individuals, especially in developing countries where preserving the environment often prolongs one's poverty. Would you turn down $600,000 to preserve rainforest as the person in the Case Study did?

TOWARD A SUSTAINABLE WORLD

While no one knows if sustainability will be attained, there is certainly no shortage of debate and speculation. At one extreme are **cornucopians** who argue that human ingenuity has always overcome environmental limitations. They suggest that such inventions as genetic engineering could make agriculture more productive, for example, so that the planet will be able to support many more people at a high standard of living. At the other extreme are **cassandras** who argue that

humans have always altered the environment and managed things poorly; they insist that exponential growth of populations and technology will finally degrade the environment so much that it will lead to overshoot (see Fig. 1–7). Cornucopian and cassandran views have been common, in various forms, throughout history.

As is often the case, extreme views can be counter-productive. Too much optimism, such as a cornucopian view, can lull people into inactivity because they think the future will take care of itself. Too much pessimism, such as a cassandran view, can cause despair, which leads to inaction because people think that the future is bleak no matter what they do. Many writers therefore suggest a more moderate view that acknowledges that urgent environmental problems exist. These problems need to be addressed within the next few years, or at least decades, or they may lead to large-scale environmental degradation and overshoot. This moderate view relies on the **precautionary principle,** which says that, in the face of uncertainty, the best course of action is to assume that a potential problem is real and should be addressed. In other words, we are "better safe than sorry." The worst that can happen with this approach is that society will become more efficient, less wasteful, and less polluting, even if environmental problems are not as bad as some people argue. On the other hand, the results can be disastrous if the precautionary principle is not used and problems are indeed as urgent as some people say.

Assuming that a person wishes to rely on the precautionary principle, which specific environmental problems should be of most concern? The rest of this book seeks to answer this question. But you can gain some idea by looking at ● Table 1–2, which presents a priority list of environmental risks that was produced by a panel of distinguished scientists and published by the U.S. Environmental Protection Agency in 1990. The table lists four high-risk problems: habitat loss, species extinction, ozone depletion, and global climate change. These problems are high risk because they are global in scale and can affect our descendants for many future generations. Toxic pollutants and acid rain are medium-risk problems, followed by oil spills and other low-risk problems. Such a list is very tentative because collecting the data needed for a precise assessment of large-scale, long-term risks is difficult. But it does provide a starting point for thinking about priorities.

Visualizing a Sustainable World

Recall that sustainability means meeting the needs of today without degrading the environment for future generations. ● Table 1–3 summarizes many of the changes that are necessary to create a sustainable society. Most of these changes will be discussed later in the book, but for now some major points can be noted. First, many aspects of society are affected: scientific paradigms, role of the human, values toward nature, land, and people. Second, many social institutions are affected: religion, education, political systems, and economic systems. Third, technology and agriculture are affected. Fourth, many of these changes are ultimately based on increasing the importance of the community, from encouraging community values among individuals to creating decentralized, community-based economies and political systems.

The need for such pervasive changes is reflected in academic disciplines such as the social sciences and humanities, which once focused almost entirely on society as an entity distinct from the natural environment. For example, economics once focused almost exclusively on the flow of goods through society, ignoring the costs of depletion and pollution that the flow imposed on the environment. Similarly, the environment

TABLE 1–2 *Setting Priorities*

HIGH-RISK PROBLEMS

- Destruction and alteration of habitats (rainforests, wetlands)
- Species extinction
- Stratospheric ozone depletion
- Global climate change

MEDIUM-RISK PROBLEMS

- Herbicides and pesticides
- Toxic chemicals and other pollutants in surface water
- Acid rain
- Airborne toxics (mainly from factories but also from trucks, cars, buses)

LOW-RISK PROBLEMS

- Oil spills
- Groundwater pollution, mainly from landfills and toxic-waste sites
- Airborne radioactive particles
- Acid runoff from farms and industry
- "Thermal pollution" (activities of civilization that artificially heat the air and water)

(*Source:* Environmental Protection Agency.)

was studied as a largely separate entity by other disciplines such as ecology. The new field of environmental economics is a more holistic discipline that includes both society and the environment. It studies not just the flow of goods within society but also the effects on the environment.

Other socially oriented disciplines are also rapidly developing an interest in studies that incorporate the environment. Findings from such fields are incorporated throughout this book, and some receive separate chapters at the end.

𝒜BOUT THIS BOOK

The purpose of this book is to provide you with an overview of the natural environment and the way humans are increasingly affecting it. ▬ Figure 1–22 shows how the book is subdivided into the following four sections, which reflect the input-output, or throughput, processes that describe the environment, how environmental problems arise, and their solutions:

- Section 1: *Environmental Principles.* Earth and life form an interconnected system based on

TABLE 1–3 *Transition from the Industrial to the Ecological Age*

Some of these may be considered speculative attempts to understand the personal and humanistic aspects of sustainable living.

	INDUSTRIAL AGE	SUSTAINABILITY OR ECOLOGICAL AGE
Scientific paradigms	Mechanistic	Organismic
	Earth as inert matter	Gaia: Earth as superorganism
	Determinism	Indeterminacy, probability
	Atomism	Holism/systems theory
Role of the human	Conquest of nature	Living as part of nature
	Individual versus world	Extended sense of self
	Resource management	Ecological stewardship
Values in relation to nature	Nature as resource	Preserve biodiversity
	Exploit or conserve	Protect ecosystem integrity
	Anthropocentric/humanist	Biocentric/ecocentric
	Nature has instrumental value	Nature has intrinsic value
Relation to land	Land use; farming, herding	Land ethic: think like mountain
	Competing for territory	Dwelling in place
	Owning "real estate"	Reinhabiting the bioregion
Human/social values	Sexism, patriarchy	Ecofeminism, partnership
	Racism, ethnocentrism	Respect and value differences
	Hierarchies of class and caste	Social ecology, egalitarianism
Theology and religion	Nature as background	Animism: everything lives
	Nature as demonic/frightening	Nature as sacred
	Transcendent divinity	Immanent divinity
	Monotheism and atheism	Pantheism and panentheism
Education and research	Specialized disciplines	Multidisciplinary, integrative
Political systems	Nation-state sovereignty	Multinational federations
	Centralized national authority	Decentralized bioregions
	Cultural homogeneity	Pluralistic societies
	National security focus	Humans and environment focus
	Militarism	Commitment to nonviolence
Economic systems	Multinational corporations	Community-based economies
	Competition	Cooperation
	Limitless progress	Limits to growth
	"Economic development"	Steady state, sustainability
	No accounting of nature	Economics based on ecology
Technology	Addiction to fossil fuels	Reliance on renewables
	Profit-driven technologies	Appropriate technologies
	Waste overload	Recycling, reusing
	Exploitation/consumerism	Protect and restore ecosystems
Agriculture	Monoculture farming	Poly- and permaculture
	Agribusiness, factory farms	Community and family farms
	Chemical fertilizers and pesticides	Biological pest control
	Vulnerable high-yield hybrids	Preserve genetic diversity

(*Source:* From Ralph Metzner, "The Emerging Ecological World View," in Mary Tucker and John Grim, eds., *World Views and Ecology* [Cranbury, New Jersey: Associated University Presses, 1993]: 170–71. Reprinted with the permission of Associated University Presses.)

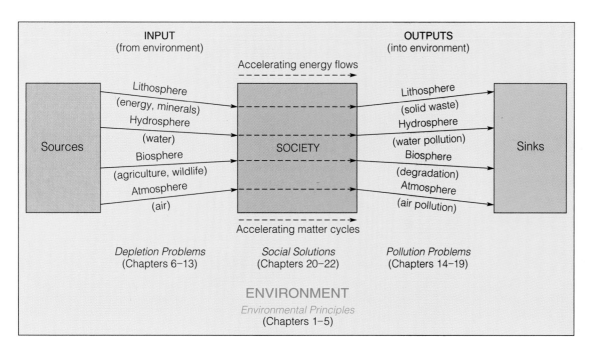

FIGURE 1–22

An overview of the book, showing the topics covered in each section.

INPUT
(from environment)

OUTPUTS
(into environment)

Accelerating energy flows

Sources

Lithosphere
(energy, minerals)

Hydrosphere
(water)

Biosphere
(agriculture, wildlife)

Atmosphere
(air)

SOCIETY

Lithosphere
(solid waste)

Hydrosphere
(water pollution)

Biosphere
(degradation)

Atmosphere
(air pollution)

Sinks

Accelerating matter cycles

Depletion Problems
(Chapters 6–13)

Social Solutions
(Chapters 20–22)

Pollution Problems
(Chapters 14–19)

ENVIRONMENT
Environmental Principles
(Chapters 1–5)

energy flow and matter cycles. Study of these natural systems includes the disciplines of geology, biology, chemistry, and many other natural sciences. Learning these principles permits a better understanding of how natural systems are disturbed.

- Section 2: *Problems of Resource Scarcity.* Depletion of environmental resources is one of the two basic types of environmental disturbance. It includes depletion of water, minerals including fossil fuels, soils, wildlife, and many other resources.

- Section 3: *Problems of Pollution.* Discharging waste into the environment is the other basic type of environmental disturbance. It includes pollution of air, water, land, and biological communities.

- Section 4: *Social Solutions.* Technological solutions are insufficient unless society is willing to employ them. Social solutions are interwoven throughout this book, but these chapters at the end allow us to focus on specific social institutions, and their legal, economic, and ethical aspects.

SUMMARY

Every day we receive vast amounts of information on the environment. To sort through it all, we need to develop environmental wisdom. Environmental science, a subject of growing concern, uses a holistic approach to realize the interconnected aspects of environmental problems and apply solutions.

As human existence has been relatively short compared to the age of the Earth, human and technological impacts on the environment have only recently occurred. Human-environment interactions evolve through five basic stages: hunting and gathering; agriculture; industry; transition; and the postindustrial stage. Environmen-

talist social movements arose during the agriculture, industry, and transition stages because of environmental degradations. Currently, we are in the transition stage, which has produced the sustainability movement. This movement uses three approaches not widely found in earlier environmental movements. First, it focuses on reducing societal consumption of resources. Second, by taking a holistic approach, the movement seeks to solve the structural social causes of environmental problems such as poverty. Lastly, it relies more on grassroots activism. The postindustrial stage will likely witness either sustainability or catastrophic overshoot of human civilization.

Environmental impact, the alteration of the natural environment by human activity, ultimately involves either resource depletion or pollution. Impact is promoted by population and traditional industrial technology:

Impact = (population)(technology)

The population of the world continues to increase by about 95 million people a year, increasing the environmental impact dramatically. Traditional, resource-intensive industrial technology has also increased exponentially. Impact is often measured as throughput, which is the movement of materials and energy through society.

Because the environment is a "commons," a commodity possessed by all, it is subject to the "tragedy of the commons." Commonly held resources are depleted through over-consumption, and commonly held environmental sinks are overwhelmed by pollution. The growth of both population and traditional industrial technology must be reduced in order to save environmental commons.

Environmental economists contend that in the past, the environment has been undervalued, giving rise to economic forces that promote increased population and environmental impact. In the Northern Hemisphere, the location of the majority of developed nations, the increase in harmful traditional industrial technologies is the greatest threat to the environment. However, by promoting efficiency improvements, reuse, recycling, and substitution, "green" or sustainable technology can reduce depletion and pollution. Economic incentives such as green fees can also be used to reduce throughput. By paying the true environmental costs of resources and sinks, exploitation and pollution can be discouraged. Until now, the opposite has been true in the United States, which has undervalued resources and used environmental sinks for waste disposal at little or no cost.

The Southern Hemisphere, which contains most of the developing nations, is responsible for 90% of the world's population growth. A vicious cycle exists in which population growth leads to poverty, which leads to environmental degradation. This cycle can be broken by building sustainable economies with sustainable technologies.

Industrial society has traditionally had values that lead to environmental degradation because they focus mainly on the "here and now." These values may be the single greatest obstacle to building a sustainable society. Whether society will succeed in building a sustainable world is highly debatable. Some people take the deeply pessimistic "cassandran" view while others take the other extreme, the blindly optimistic "cornucopian" view. Many people have more moderate views, such as those embodied in the "precautionary principle," which assumes that we are "better safe than sorry." People who hold this principle acknowledge that environmental problems are real, and seek long-term realistic solutions without being overly pessimistic or optimistic.

KEY TERMS

cassandras
cornucopians
debt bomb
discounting by distance
discounting the future
efficiency improvements
environmental science
environmental wisdom

fallacy of enlightenment
grassroots activism
green fees
holistic
input reduction
market failure
overshoot
population bomb
precautionary principle

recycling
reuse
sinks
sources
substitution
sustainable economy
sustainable technology
sustainability
throughput

STUDY QUESTIONS

1. Name several costs of a lack of environmental wisdom.
2. What is the most expensive way to solve environmental problems?
3. What is throughput?
4. Why is input reduction a good solution to many environmental problems?
5. Name the two basic causes of environmental problems.
6. Why was the cultivation of food such an important development in human technological evolution?
7. Name three pieces of landmark environmental legislation enacted by Congress and briefly describe each.
8. Define *sustainable technology* and a *sustainable economy*.
9. What is the difference between conservation movements of the past and the movements of the current transition stage?
10. What is a green fee? The "debt bomb"?
11. What is "discounting the future"?
12. How do environmental problems illustrate the tragedy of the commons?
13. What percentage of GNP did the United States pledge to developing nations in 1961? How much did the United States spend on foreign aid in 1994?
14. If the current world population is 5.8 billion, what will it be if it increases by 75% in 50 years?
15. If the current world population is 5.8 billion, what will it be if it increases by 50% in 50 years?

ESSAY QUESTIONS

1. Identify and describe the fourth stage of human and technological evolution. How does the environmental movement that emerged during this stage differ from previous environmental movements?
2. What is environmental impact? Identify two basic types of environmental impact and explain their causes.
3. Name and describe the three ways technological improvements can achieve input reduction, thereby decreasing environmental damage.
4. Describe the difference between the environmentalism of the 1970s and current environmentalism. What problems were associated with early environmentalism?
5. Why is the economic gap between the developed and developing countries increasing?

SUGGESTED READINGS

Brown, L., *et al.* Published annually. *Vital signs.* New York: W. W. Norton.

———Published annually. *State of the world.* New York: W. W. Norton.

Eblen, R., and W. Eblen, eds. 1994. *The encyclopedia of the environment.* Boston: Houghton Mifflin.

Harrison, P. 1992. *The third revolution.* New York: I. B. Tauris.

Meadows, D. H., D. L. Meadows, and J. Randers. 1992. *Beyond the limits.* Post Mills, Vt.: Chelsea Green.

Piel, G. 1992. *Only one world.* New York: W. H. Freeman.

World Resources Institute, 1994. *The 1994 information please environmental almanac.* Boston: Houghton Mifflin.

EnviroNet
www.jbpub.com/environet

THE PHYSICAL ENVIRONMENT

PROLOGUE   *The Year without a Summer*

*I*n New England 1816 was known as "the year without a summer." During June of that year average temperatures were 7 degrees Fahrenheit (F) below normal, ranging from a chilly 35°F (1.7° Celsius, or C) to a high of 88°F (31°C). Typical temperatures that summer were in the low 60s°F. Many crops failed and their prices rose. Since there was no feed for the hogs and cattle, livestock was sold off at record rates, causing the meat markets to collapse.

But the problems were not limited to New England; the story was the same in many parts of the world. Western Europe experienced similar cold weather, resulting in crop failures, food shortages, and famines. There were even food riots; armed bands raided and looted farms, bakeries, and grain warehouses looking for anything to eat. Europe suffered a typhus epidemic in 1816–1819, perhaps fostered by the widespread famine that left many people in a weakened state.

PHOTO   *The 1993 floods along the Mississippi and Missouri Rivers brought devastation to many areas, including Portage Des Sioux, Missouri, as can be seen in this photograph. (Source: Robert Visser, Greenpeace.)*

The year of 1816 was also a time of natural wonders. The Sun seemed to rise and set through a red cloud or veil of dust and vapor. Snows were very strange—they were colored. Brown, blue, and red snows fell in Maryland, brown snow in Hungary, and red and yellow snows in Taranto in southern Italy. In Taranto any snow is unusual, but red and yellow snow was actually alarming.

The strange weather of 1816, and its consequences, are attributed to a simple geological event: a volcanic eruption that had occurred the previous spring and summer (April through July 1815) at the mountain of Tambora on the island of Sumbawa in Indonesia. Tambora is the largest volcanic eruption recorded in modern historical times, and one of the largest in the past 10,000 years. An estimated 24 cubic miles (100 km³) of rock and debris were ejected from the volcano. Sulfur dioxide and small dust particles entered the stratosphere and blocked the light from the Sun, causing cold temperatures worldwide. The sound of the explosion could be heard a thousand miles away. Reportedly, only 26 of Sumbawa's 12,000 inhabitants survived. Forests and settlements were leveled in the tremendous explosion; lava covered the island and poured into the sea.

Tambora was a huge volcanic explosion by human standards, but geologically there have been much larger ones—even in the relatively recent past. Another eruption in Indonesia, which goes by the name of Toba, ejected an estimated 240 cubic miles (1000 km³) of rock and debris (10 times the volume of Tambora) in about 73,000 B.C. Our physical Earth is still a young and evolving planet. We, as small creatures crawling on the surface of the globe, are still subject to the mercies of nature in many respects even as we tamper with the global ecological balance. We must never forget we cannot totally isolate ourselves from our physical surroundings on this small world.

ℐNTRODUCTION

The environment is everything that surrounds you, including the air, the land, the oceans, and all living things. For convenience; the **natural environment** can be subdivided into two parts: (1) the **physical environment**, which includes nonliving things, and (2) **the biological environment**, which includes all life-forms. The physical environment can be further subdivided into the three basic states of physical matter: solid, liquid, and gas. This division creates four "spheres" that compose the natural environment. The three physical spheres are called the **lithosphere** ("lithos" = rock), **hydrosphere** ("hydro" = water), and **atmosphere** ("atmos" = vapor). The biological environment is called the **biosphere** ("bios" = life).

Figure 2–1 shows how the four spheres form the outermost layers of the planet Earth. They are underlain by a very thick molten layer of rock belonging to the **mantle** and a heavy metallic **core**.

Three major points about Figure 2–1 should be stressed. First, these four spheres make the Earth a dynamic planet. The lithosphere creates rocks as hot magma, generated by the "internal heat engine" of radioactive minerals. Sometimes this magma erupts onto the surface in the form of volcanoes such as Tambora. The atmosphere erodes the rocks with chemically reactive gases. The hydrosphere also erodes rocks as well as transporting them as sediments that are often ultimately deposited in ocean basins. The moving lithosphere then carries these sediments to great depth where they are reheated and remelted into magma, beginning the cycle anew. The life of the biosphere inhabits parts of the other spheres, relying on the cycling of chemicals through all of the spheres. Life also effects the other spheres by altering the cycling of chemicals, such as oxygen. Many rocks (for instance, most limestones) are the result of direct biological activity, and recent studies have discovered anaerobic bacteria living in rocks over 9000 feet (2740 m) below the Earth's surface.

Second, the figure illustrates that the spheres closely interact with one another. Matter is transported both within and between the spheres in various kinds of cycles. For instance, gases are expelled from the lithosphere (by volcanoes) and the biosphere (by plants and animals) into the atmosphere. Similarly, water vapor moves from the oceans to the atmosphere and back again. Moreover, there are also numerous cycles within each sphere. For example, new rocks are now being created in the lithosphere while simultaneously older rocks are being eroded away (the "rock cycle," discussed later). Thus, the Earth is an active, integrated system, with many cycles that

FIGURE 2–1

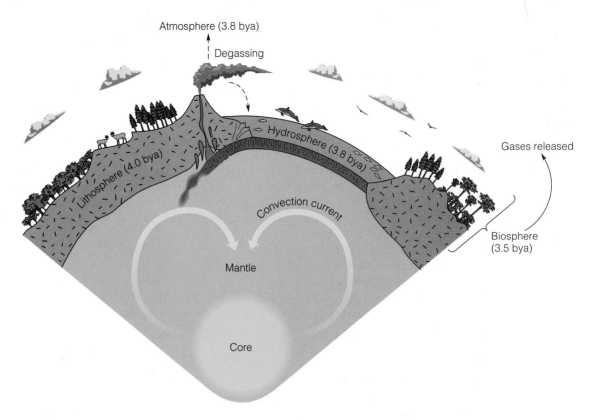

Spheres of the environment. The dates given in billions of years ago (bya) are approximate times when each of the major spheres of the environment originated: lithosphere 4.0 bya, atmosphere and hydrosphere 3.8 bya, and biosphere 3.5 bya. Note that the Earth is a dynamic planet and that all of the spheres have evolved and changed since its origin.

constantly transport matter both within and between the spheres at various rates.

Third, these dynamic and interactive spheres have evolved through time. Figure 2–1 depicts the environment as it exists today, but the Earth is about 4.6 billion years old. The current lithosphere, forming from a molten layer on the hot, young Earth, probably originated some 4 billion years ago. The oceans and atmosphere date back to at least 3.8 billion years ago, and the earliest known fossils (single-celled microbes) representing the biosphere are at least 3.5 billion years old. The evolution of the four spheres is discussed in this chapter (physical environment) and Chapter 3 (biosphere).

The Earth has evolved from a relatively homogeneous collection of particles (cosmic dust) to form a well-differentiated, complex, dynamic, recycling machine. Our planet may seem eternal and unchanging, yet it was very different 4 billion years ago, and it will continue to evolve and change. From a human perspective, such changes are slow and gradual, taking hundreds of millions of years. We must have a clear understanding of the delicate, and in many ways fortuitous, development of the present state of the Earth to fully comprehend just how fragile our environment really is.

WORKINGS OF PLANET EARTH TODAY

Earth and Its Neighboring Planets

Earth is the third planet out from the center of the solar system, but it is very different from the other planets.* Unlike its two immediate neighbors, Venus and Mars, which both have atmospheres that are 95–97% carbon dioxide, Earth has an atmosphere composed of about 78.1% nitrogen, 20.9% oxygen, and only 0.03% carbon dioxide. As a result, much of the sunlight and heat reaching the Earth is scattered back into space, and Earth has an average surface temperature of 59°F (15° Celsius, or C). At this temperature water can exist in a liquid state (water quickly evaporates on the hot surface of Venus and remains frozen on Mars), making it possible for life to be maintained on Earth. As far as we are aware, no other planet has anything resembling life.

The gases surrounding the Earth (▬ Fig. 2–2) and the liquids (primarily water) on its surface are continually swirling and moving, causing the degradation, erosion, and destruction of

---

*Moving out from the Sun, the planets are: Mercury, Venus, Earth, Mars, Jupiter, Saturn, Uranus, Neptune, and Pluto.

topographic highs such as mountains. The surface of our Moon is pockmarked with craters (Fig. 2–2) due to the lack of an atmosphere to weather them away. There are very few craters on Earth because they quickly erode away. Why then does the Earth's surface have any relief at all? The reason is that the Earth has an "internal engine."

The Earth's interior is seething and churning. Rocks slide and move plastically around one another. The interior is very hot, and at breaks and cracks, molten rock erupts at the surface as volcanoes. In other areas ancient rock is dragged back toward the center of Earth only to be reheated, melted, and rejuvenated. The vast majority of the Earth's surface is relatively young rock. In comparison, some of Earth's close neighbors—the Moon, Mercury, and Mars—are relatively inactive. The Moon and Mars show no evidence of plate tectonic activity, and their surfaces are covered with very ancient rocks, dating back more than 3 billion years. Mars has large volcanoes, including Olympus Mons, which rises 17 miles (27 km) high and is 340 miles (550 km) in diameter at the base, but shows no evidence of true plate tectonic activity. Of the planets close to Earth, only Venus shows some evidence of limited crustal movements comparable to the plate tectonics seen on Earth. But any tectonic movement on Venus appears to have been relatively limited; most of that planet's geological activity seems to be in the form of active volcanoes situated over stationary "hot spots" where molten rock wells up from the interior.

Present-Day Deep Structure of the Earth

In order to understand natural processes on the surface of the Earth, we must have a clear understanding of the structure of the Earth. The internal make-up of the Earth accounts for volcanoes and earthquakes. It even affects the composition of the atmosphere, oceans, and ultimately the nature of life on the Earth.

If we could cut a slice through the Earth, we would see that it is formed of concentric rings of differing constitutions—similar to the layers of an onion (▪ Fig. 2–3). From the outside, the first

major layer is the Earth's gaseous envelope or atmosphere. It extends in rarefied form for hundreds of miles above the Earth's surface, although almost the total mass is contained within the bottom 12 to 13 miles (20 km). The Earth's surface is covered with seawater or dry land (including land that contains freshwater lakes or ice patches) in a ratio of about 7 to 3. If all water were removed from the surface, we would observe two basic terranes: ocean basins, which average about 3 miles (5 km) depth below sea level and are floored with basaltic-type rocks, and continents and continental islands, which on average rise several hundred feet (a few hundred meters) above sea level, and are founded on granitic-type rocks. Actual ocean basins cover only about two-thirds of Earth's surface; in places the oceans lap onto the shallow continental margins.

The thin crust under the oceans averages only about 3 miles (5 km) thick. It is composed of about 50% (by weight) silicon dioxide (perhaps most familiar as the mineral quartz) and contains higher amounts of iron, magnesium, and calcium

▪ **FIGURE 2–2**
The Earth seen from the Moon. The Earth is a "living planet" with an active atmosphere and an internal heat engine driving many geological processes. In contrast, the Moon is a "dead planet" (our Moon is larger than Pluto and nearly as large as Mercury) with virtually no atmosphere or active geological processes on its surface. As a result, the Moon's surface is pockmarked with craters that have not eroded away. (*Source:* NASA.)

▪ **FIGURE 2–3**
Schematic section through the Earth.

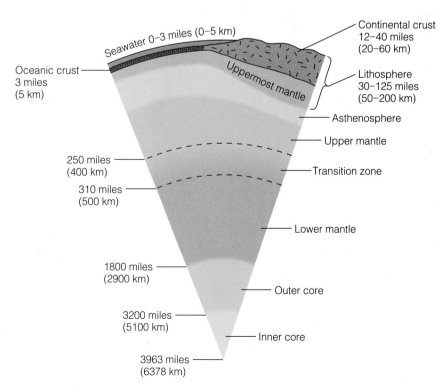

Seawater 0–3 miles (0–5 km)

Oceanic crust 3 miles (5 km)

Uppermost mantle

Continental crust 12–40 miles (20–60 km)

Lithosphere 30–125 miles (50–200 km)

Asthenosphere

Upper mantle

Transition zone

Lower mantle

Outer core

Inner core

250 miles (400 km)

310 miles (500 km)

1800 miles (2900 km)

3200 miles (5100 km)

3963 miles (6378 km)

than are generally seen in continental crust. The continental crust, ranging from about 12 miles to 40 miles (20 km to 60 km) thick, is about two-thirds silicon dioxide.

Below the crust, extending to a depth of about 1800 miles (2900 km), is the mantle, which is composed of about 45% silicon dioxide and 38% magnesium oxide. The relatively rigid upper layer of the mantle with its attached crust is known as the lithosphere. The lithosphere is the major unit of movement in plate tectonics (discussed below). Below the lithosphere lies another layer of the mantle, the relatively weak and soft **asthenosphere** (literally, weak or glassy sphere; see Fig. 2–3).

Beneath the mantle is the Earth's core. The outer core extends from a depth of about 1800 to 3200 miles (2900 to 5100 km) and consists of a liquid iron-nickel (mostly iron) alloy. Movements within the outer core probably are responsible for generating the Earth's magnetic field. The inner core, extending from a depth of about 3200 miles (5100 km) to the Earth's center (3963 miles [6378 km] deep), is composed of a solid iron-nickel alloy.

Plate Tectonics

If you look carefully at a map and imagine that the continents are pieces of a jigsaw puzzle, you will notice that the east coasts of North and South America appear to fit into the west coasts of Europe and Africa. This simple observation, and a wealth of other data, led to the hypothesis of drifting continents, first proposed by the German scientist Alfred Wegener in about 1912. Today a variation of the theory of continental drift, known as **plate tectonics**, is accepted by virtually all earth scientists. Indeed, plate tectonics forms the unifying theory for most of the geological structures observed on the surface of the planet. It is the active process of plate tectonics that not only moves continents, but also raises mountains, creates new sea floor, destroys and recycles old sea floor, and causes volcanoes to erupt and earthquakes to occur. Plate tectonics plays a major role in natural biogeochemical cycles on Earth—cycles which are now being disrupted by human activities (Chapter 4).

Today the Earth's lithosphere is divided into about eight major tectonic plates and numerous

FIGURE 2–4
The Earth's tectonic plates. The plates are in continuous motion relative to one another. Notice the relationship between plate boundaries, intense earthquakes, and major volcanic eruptions.

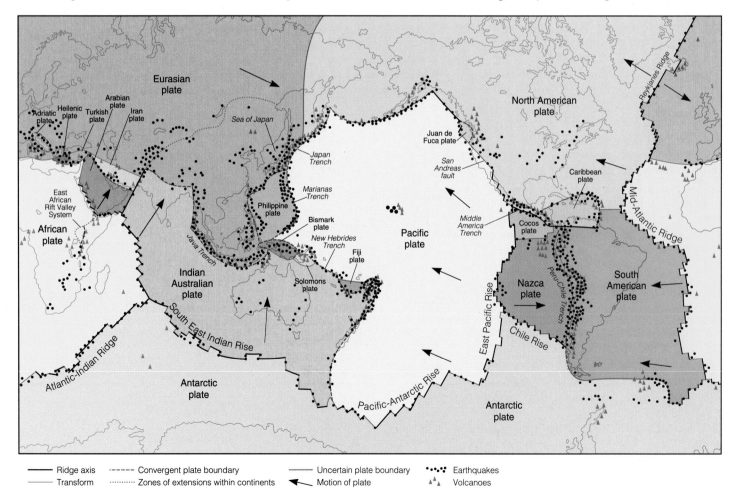

smaller ones (Fig. 2–4). These plates are in continuous motion, sliding past one another, colliding, or pulling apart from each other. Essentially, the continents are carried on the tops of the plates. The plates do not move very fast from a human perspective, about 0.8 to 12 inches (2 to 30 cm) a year, but this is fast enough to have caused major changes in the positions of the continents over the last few hundred million years (Fig. 2–5).

Prior to about 2.5 billion years ago, the Earth's surface was probably covered by small, rapidly moving "platelets," which slowly coalesced into larger, thicker plates. Only in the last 800 million years has the crust been characterized by modern-style, large, thick plates. About 240 million years ago, all of the continental landmass formed a single supercontinent, Pangaea, which has since split up into the present-day continents.

What causes the plates to move? This has been a topic of heated discussion over a number of years. Today most scientists believe that convection currents in the molten mantle move the lithospheric plates (Fig. 2–6). Heat continually flows out from the hot center of the Earth. As in a pot of cooking soup, the hot liquid rises to the surface and flows there for some distance; as the liquid cools, it sinks below the surface, only to be heated up and start the cycle once again. This is known as a **convection cell**. Giant convection cells are believed to exist in the liquid mantle, and as they cycle, the flowing mantle drags the overlying, rigid lithosphere plates along. As the Earth cools over time, the rates of motion of the plates are decreasing, and they are continuing to enlarge and thicken.

At divergent plate boundaries, places where two lithospheric plates are moving away from each other, a gap or void is left in the solid crust (Fig. 2–7). Initially, the rock in this area may start to collapse, forming a rift valley, but as the plates move apart, hot molten rock from the mantle wells up to fill the void and form new oceanic crust. This process is often referred to as sea-floor spreading. The classic example of a divergent plate boundary is the Mid-Atlantic Ridge, which runs roughly north-

south through the Atlantic Ocean.

Along deep-sea rift zones, hot water (about 660°F, or 350°C) emanates from hydrothermal vents. These vents often support unique ecological communities that are based on geothermal energy rather than the solar energy most ecosystems require (Fig. 2–8). Bacteria use the energy found in hydrogen sulfide (H_2S) and similar

(a)

(b)

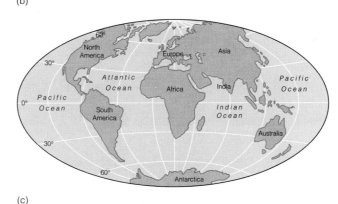

(c)

 FIGURE 2–5
Continental movements over the last 240 million years. (a) The Earth about 240 million years ago. (b) The Earth about 70 million years ago. (c) The modern Earth.

chemicals emanating from the vents to produce organic molecules from inorganic molecules. Crabs, clams, tube worms, and fishes then feed on the bacteria. Thus these vents dramatically illustrate the interrelationships between geological processes and living organisms.

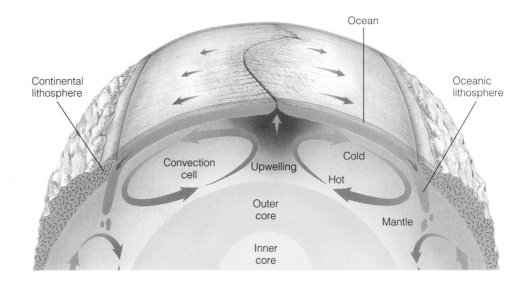

FIGURE 2-6
Convection cells in the Earth's mantle.

In some places, convergent plate boundaries occur where two lithospheric plates converge or collide (see Fig. 2–7). If the colliding edges of the two plates both bear oceanic crust, either plate may be forced, or subducted, under the other plate. A subduction zone is formed under the leading edge of the plate that remains on top. On the surface, where the plates are downwarped, a deep trench forms. As the subducted plate moves down into the hot mantle, it melts, and the lighter rock components rise to the surface, forming volcanoes. New continental crustal material, formed from the recycled oceanic crust, collects behind the trench. The northern and western edges of the Pacific Ocean (known as the "ring of fire" for their numerous volcanoes) are lined with convergent plate boundaries (see Fig. 2–4).

If the leading edge of one colliding plate contains continental crust and the leading edge of the other plate contains heavier oceanic crust, the plate with oceanic crust will always be subducted under the plate bearing lighter continental crust, which "floats" on top. If leading edges of colliding lithospheric plates both contain continental crust, neither can be subducted because they are both relatively light. Instead, the continents crash into one another, crumple, and deform, often raising imposing mountain ranges. The mighty Himalayas are the result of two continental landmasses crashing into one another. Eventually, the plates lock and relative motion between them stops.

Finally, two plates may slide past one another; their edges grind and slip against each other along what are commonly termed transform

FIGURE 2-7
Principal types of plate boundaries.

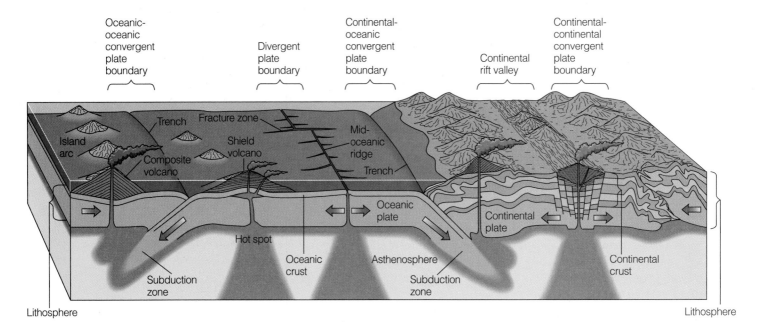

*E*NVIRONMENTAL PRINCIPLES   SECTION 1

faults. This is the least dramatic type of relative plate motion in that it usually does not involve either volcanoes or mountain building. Earthquakes are common along transform faults, however, as is well known by residents of California, where the Pacific plate slides north past the North American plate. The surficial rocks do not flow past one another slowly and smoothly, but tend to "hang up." Pressure builds, and then is suddenly released—the rock "jumps" and an earthquake occurs.

The Composition of Matter on the Earth

Rocks are by far the most common substances on the Earth's surface. Indeed, everything is rock or made primarily of materials that were once components of rocks. A clear understanding of rocks and the rock cycle (discussed later) are necessary in order to understand the cycling of matter through the environment (Chapters 1 and 4). Rocks themselves are composed of minerals, which in turn are composed of elements.

Minerals are naturally occurring, inorganic solids that have a regular internal structure and composition—they are said to be crystalline. Some well known minerals include quartz, diamond, garnet, and pyrite. In all, over two thousand different minerals are known. Minerals are composed of combinations of atoms of elements.

The **elements** such as iron, hydrogen, oxygen, mercury, and gold are the fundamental substances of our world. An element cannot be broken down chemically into other elements. There are close to 90 naturally occurring elements found in measurable amounts on Earth today, and additional elements have been artificially synthesized under laboratory conditions.

Atoms are the smallest units of an element that retain the physical and chemical properties of the element. When combined together, substances composed of different elements can take on new properties. Water, for instance, is a **compound** composed of atoms of the elements hydrogen and oxygen. Atoms themselves are divisible into even smaller particles. In the center of each atom is a nucleus composed of protons and neutrons (Fig. 2–9). Protons carry positive charges and neutrons are electrically neutral. Most of an atom's mass is contained in its nucleus, where the number of protons determines to what element the atom belongs. For example, all atoms of hydrogen have only one proton in their nucleus, whereas all atoms of gold have 79 protons in their nucleus. The number of protons in the nucleus is referred to as the atom's atomic number and is characteristic of the atoms of a particular element.

The number of protons and neutrons in the nucleus is the atom's atomic mass number. Atoms of the same element can have varying numbers of neutrons in their nucleus. In nature one can find carbon atoms with atomic mass numbers of 12, 13, or 14. These variants are known as isotopes of the element carbon. Some isotopes are unstable and undergo radioactive decay by emitting particles spontaneously so as to change into a more stable form of atom (see Chapter 8).

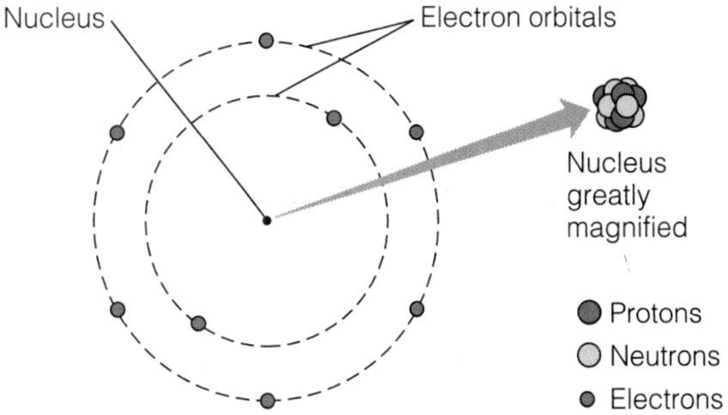

FIGURE 2–8
A deep-sea hydrothermal vent and its unique biotic community, which is based on geothermal energy rather than the solar energy most systems require. Bacteria use the energy found in hydrogen sulfide and similar chemicals to produce organic molecules. Crabs, clams, giant tube worms, and fishes then feed on the bacteria. (*Source:* Science VU–WHOI, D. Foster/Visuals Unlimited.)

FIGURE 2–9
The basic structure of an atom.

Properties of Atomic Particles

Particle	Charge	Mass	Location	Symbol
Proton	Positive	1.673×10^{-24}g	Nucleus	p
Neutron	Neutral	1.675×10^{-24}g	Nucleus	n
Electron	Negative	9.110×10^{-28}g	Orbitals	e

Orbiting around the protons and neutrons of the atom's nucleus are electrons (Fig. 2–9), small negatively charged particles that electrically balance the protons in an electrically neutral atom. If an atom has more electrons than protons, it will be a negatively charged ion. If it has fewer electrons than protons, it will be a positively charged ion.

Single atoms are much too small for us to perceive in isolation. Substances that we are familiar with are composed of tremendous numbers of atoms, which are almost always bonded together in various arrangements. Depending on how the atoms are arranged, we refer to states of matter composed of atoms as solids, liquids, or gases.

Rocks—Their Origin and the Rock Cycle

Most rocks are composed primarily of minerals and are classified into three basic categories: igneous, sedimentary, and metamorphic (■ Fig. 2–10).

Igneous rocks formed, or crystallized, from extremely hot molten rock known as magma ("igneous" = fire-rock). The lava that flows out of a volcano and hardens into rock is a well-known type of igneous rock. Igneous rocks that formed from lava flows or volcanic ash ejected from a volcano are known as extrusive igneous rocks. Most igneous rocks, however, form deep underground as liquid magma slowly cools and crystallizes; such rocks are known as intrusive igneous rocks. Typical intrusive igneous rocks include basalt, gabbro, and granite. Igneous rocks are the most common rocks, forming the vast bulk of the Earth's crust and all of its rocky inside (where it is not molten). On the surface of the Earth, however, igneous rocks are often covered by a blanket of sediments or sedimentary rocks.

Having formed deep inside the Earth, most igneous rocks are inherently unstable at the surface. Over time, the rocks weather, broken down by both mechanical (running water, ice, or wind) and chemical agents (such as acids and solvents found in nature—for instance, the ubiquitous carbonic acid of rainwater), and disintegrate into fragments. These fragments are known as sediments;

FIGURE 2–10
The three basic types of rocks—igneous, sedimentary, and metamorphic—and the rock cycle.

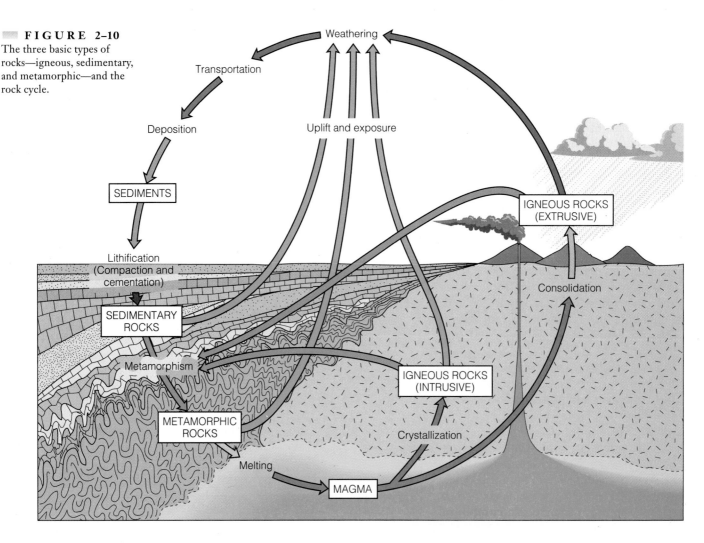

they generally consist of either small pieces of rock or single mineral grains, and come in various sizes—such as gravel, sand, silt, or mud. The sediments are physically transported from higher to lower elevations by running water, wind, or ice flows (glaciers), until they are deposited in a resting place. As piles of sediments accumulate, they become compacted and cemented together, or even crystallized. Minerals may precipitate between the sediment grains, binding them tightly together to form a **sedimentary rock** (Fig. 2–10). Sedimentary rocks cover approximately 75% of Earth's surface. Among the most common sedimentary rocks are sandstones and shales.

Not all sedimentary rocks are formed from the weathered remains of other rocks. Many limestones, for example, are formed from sediment that consists entirely of the old calcium carbonate shells or skeletons of sea organisms. Fossils, the remains of ancient organisms, are almost always found encapsulated in sedimentary rocks such as limestones, sandstones, and shales. Peats, coals, oils, and other fossil fuels, formed of the fragments of many plants and other organisms, are components of some sedimentary rock layers. Other types of sedimentary rocks are formed from the precipitation, or "sedimentation," of substances out of an aqueous solution, perhaps as it evaporates. For instance, large deposits of rock salt (halite) often form in this way.

Like igneous rocks, sedimentary rocks weather and break down. The sediments formed from sedimentary rocks can then be recycled to form other sedimentary rocks. The next generation of rocks may weather and the resulting fragments be recycled again, with the pattern occurring over and over.

The remaining class is **metamorphic rocks** ("metamorphic" = change of form). Metamorphic rocks are made when rock—igneous, sedimentary, or in some cases another metamorphic rock—is subjected to great temperature (but not hot enough to completely melt the rock) or pressure, or both (Fig. 2–10). The rock undergoes some combination of mineralogical changes (certain minerals are turned into other minerals) and/or textural changes (mineral grains may grow in size). In some cases the metamorphic rock may be produced by hot fluids released at the edge of a molten rock body that penetrates preexisting rock. Some common metamorphic rocks include slate (produced from the metamorphism of shale or mudstone), marble (produced from limestone), quartzite (produced from quartz sandstone), and various schists and gneisses (produced by the extreme metamorphism of various other types of igneous, sedimentary, and metamorphic rocks).

Geologists often refer to the **rock cycle** (Fig. 2–10). Effectively, all rock/earth material on the Earth's surface begins as igneous rock. Initial crystallization takes place at a rift zone where two lithospheric plates diverge. This new rock may weather directly into sediments or become metamorphosed, but perhaps most often it gets carried to a subduction zone where it is remelted, rises toward the surface, and eventually is added to the continental crust. From here it may be metamorphosed or remelted again, or it may be weathered at the surface, with the fragments eventually forming sedimentary rocks. The sedimentary rock may be weathered, broken into fragments, and made into other sedimentary rocks, or more sediments may be piled on top of it, until it is buried deep below the surface. With increasing temperatures and pressures, the sediments may be metamorphosed and eventually find themselves in a setting where they actually melt. If so, they will form genuine igneous rocks upon cooling and crystallization, thus continuing the rock cycle.

By human standards, the rock cycle is very slow, taking on the order of millions to hundreds of millions of years. Furthermore, it is not a complete or closed cycle. Once continental (granitic type) material is formed, it remains continental material, even if it cycles from igneous to sedimentary, to metamorphic, back to igneous, and so on. As described in the section on plate tectonics, continental material is too light to be subducted back into the mantle; thus, it is not recycled in that sense. More continental crustal material is in existence today than ever before in Earth history.

The Surface of the Earth: Hydrologic and Atmospheric Cycles; Climate and Weather

The Earth's surface is almost entirely covered with water—not just the seas and oceans, but numerous lakes, ponds, swamps, and even morning dew on the "dry" land. It is enveloped in an atmosphere composed predominantly of nitrogen, or N_2 (78.1%), and oxygen, or O_2 (20.9%). It is also bathed in radiation—energy in the form of heat (infrared radiation) and light—from the Sun. All of these components work together to make the surface conditions of our planet very active and constantly changing.

The Earth's atmospheric envelope is divided into layers, distinguished mainly by the changing temperature gradient encountered as one moves up into the atmosphere (Fig. 2–11): the troposphere, stratosphere, mesosphere, and ther-

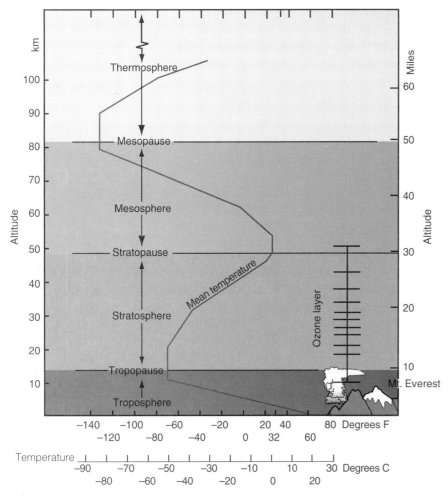

The structure of the Earth's atmosphere. The tropopause, stratopause, and mesopause are the boundaries between the troposphere and stratosphere, stratosphere and mesosphere, and mesosphere and thermosphere respectively.

mosphere. The changing temperature gradient is the result of the interplay of the energy received directly from the Sun, the gaseous constitution and density of the atmosphere at different levels, and the distance the energy (heat) reflected and emitted from the Earth's surface reaches into the atmosphere.

The density of the atmosphere decreases exponentially going away from the Earth's surface. An estimated 80 to 85% of the mass of the atmosphere is in the troposphere; 99% is found in the troposphere and stratosphere combined. Except for water vapor and ozone (O_3), the gross composition of the atmosphere (78.1% N_2 and 20.9% O_2, along with trace gases) is fairly constant up into the bottom of the thermosphere. Virtually all the water in the atmosphere is found in the troposphere, the region of the phenomena we call weather.

In terms of energy flow, the Earth's surface is an open system: it constantly receives energy from the Sun, and it continuously loses most of this energy to space. Approximately 30% of the incoming solar energy that reaches the upper atmosphere is immediately reflected back to space, and another 20% is absorbed by water vapor in the atmosphere, so only about 50% reaches Earth's surface. Very little (less than 1%) of the Sun's energy that reaches Earth goes into photosynthesis, and thus the direct support of living organisms. The vast majority of the energy that reaches Earth goes into evaporating surface waters; it thus reenters the atmosphere and is eventually dissipated into space as heat (electromagnetic radiation in the infrared range).

The movement of water about the surface of Earth, driven by energy from the Sun, constitutes the **hydrologic cycle** (▪ Fig. 2–12). Approximately 97.4% of the water on or near the Earth's surface is found in the seas and oceans, 1.98% is bound up as ice (primarily in the polar ice caps), 0.59% is stored temporarily as groundwater, only 0.014% is found in freshwater lakes and streams, and a mere 0.001% takes the form of atmospheric water vapor at any one point in time. The shifting of water over the globe through the hydrologic cycle redistributes heat and generally makes for more equitable climates. The hydrologic cycle also plays a prominent role in the rock cycle through the weathering and decomposition of rocks. Together with the atmospheric cycles, the hydrologic cycle is also responsible for **weather**, or the short-term, daily perturbations in the atmospheric/hydrologic cycles. **Climate** is the average weather over time ranges of decades to millennia to hundreds of millions of years.

Based on large-scale **atmospheric cycles**, the Earth's surface is divided into several major climatic belts that roughly correspond to latitudinal changes (north and south). Working out from the equator, one finds the rainforest belt (centered about the equator), the desert belts (centered about 30° north and south), the temperate regions, and the polar regions.

Convection cells form in the atmosphere similar to those believed to occur in the mantle. The rays of the Sun fall most directly on the equator, making the equatorial regions hotter than the rest of the Earth's surface. The hot air rises, carrying with it large quantities of water vapor (warm air can hold more moisture than cool air). The rising air leaves a relative void, and cooler, drier air closer to the surface flows in from the north and south to fill the void (▪ Fig. 2–13). This new cool air heats up, picks up moisture, and then itself rises from the equator. The rising air quickly cools, however, and loses its capacity to hold moisture. Consequently, vast quantities of water are released in the vicinity of the equator producing the tropical rainforests. As the air con-

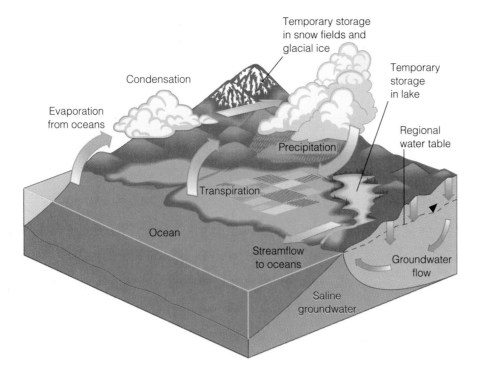

FIGURE 2-12
The hydrologic cycle.

tinues to rise and cool, it moves either north or south, continues to lose moisture, and eventually begins to sink as dry air in the region of 25 to 35° latitude north and south, giving rise to the subtropical high-pressure zones that produce some of the world's great deserts. Once the cool air approaches the surface, it flows south or north toward the equator. On reaching the equator the air again heats and absorbs moisture, and the cycle continues. Not all of the air sinks at the subtropical high pressure zones, however. Some of the air continues toward the poles where it eventually sinks and takes part in polar atmospheric cycles. Cold surface winds tend to blow from the poles toward the equator.

Of course, the atmospheric cycle is not quite that simple. Two effects in particular modify it. First, the Earth spins on its axis, causing the air in the convection cells to cycle at an angle rather than directly north and south. This is known as the Coriolis effect. To understand the Coriolis effect, imagine yourself standing on the geographical North Pole. The Earth is rotating toward the east. If you throw a ball, it will land to the west of where you aimed it—the Earth turns under it as it travels through the air. This effect produces the trade-winds that once carried sailing vessels across the oceans.

Second, the Earth's topography— the positions of its mountains, valleys, lakes, and oceans— greatly modify both weather and climate. The **oceans** that cover much of the surface contribute

greatly to the overall climate (Fig. 2–14). Moving air masses create ocean currents, which are then modified by the Coriolis effect and the continental landmasses that the currents bump into. Due to the great capacity of water to absorb and retain heat, ocean currents play an important role in distributing heat over the Earth's surface.

FIGURE 2-13
General circulation in the Earth's atmosphere.

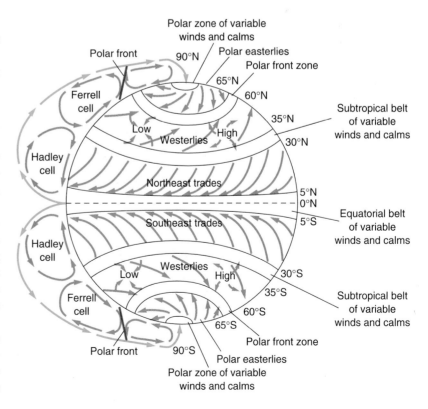

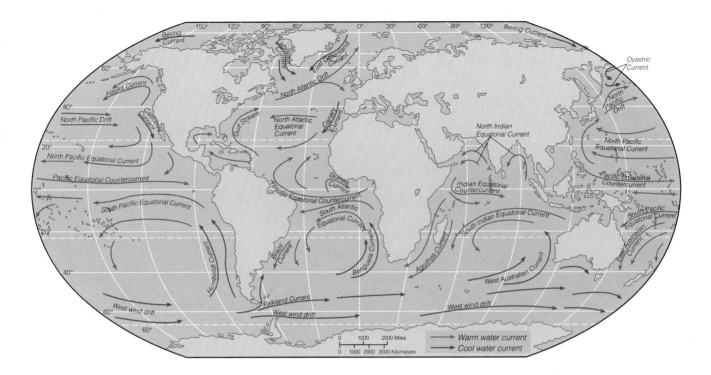

FIGURE 2–14
Global surface ocean currents.

On land the topography greatly influences weather patterns. For example, mountains may create rainshadows causing deserts to form on their leeward sides. When a warm moist air mass encounters a mountain, the air begins to sweep up the mountain's windward side. In so doing, the air rises, cools, and loses much of its moisture as precipitation. Once across the mountain, the now dry air flows down the other side, becoming warmer as it reaches lower elevations. Because the air has left its moisture on the other side of the mountain, a desert is created. In North America a rainshadow effect produces deserts east of the Sierra Nevada, and in South America the Andes Mountains are responsible for the extremely dry deserts found along the western coasts of Peru and Chile.

Local and global temperature and climate are also influenced by the albedo, or the proportion of the incoming solar radiation that is reflected back to space by various surfaces. Large, vegetation-free deserts and blankets of ice or snow have a large reflective capacity—a high albedo. Oceans and other large bodies of water, which have the ability to absorb heat, as well as areas covered with thick vegetation, have a low albedo.

Dust in the atmosphere can also have a high albedo and reflect significant amounts of radiation including heat back into space. As the Prologue described, the dust and ash emitted by the volcano Tambora had worldwide ramifications for the weather. The impact of a huge meteorite, could throw up blankets of dust and particulate matter that would have the same effect. Conversely, other additions to the atmosphere can lead to higher temperatures. Various greenhouse gases, most notably carbon dioxide, when added to the atmosphere (either artificially or naturally) create a blanket that allows radiation to enter, but blocks the escape of heat (see Chapter 18), thus leading to global warming.

Rotation, Orbits, and Seasons

In addition to its short-term, day-to-day fluctuations, weather is seasonal, changing on an annual basis. These cyclical variations in the weather are due to changes in the orientation of the Earth's axis. As you know, the Earth rotates on its axis once a day as it orbits around the Sun once a year. The Earth's axis of rotation is not perpendicular to the plane of its orbit, but rather is inclined at an angle of about 23.5°. Consequently, as the Earth follows its orbit, different parts of the surface are exposed to more direct rays from the Sun (▬ Fig. 2–15). In the Northern Hemisphere during the summer, the axis is tilted toward the Sun, causing sunlight to fall more directly on this part of the world. During the winter months, when the axis is tilted away from the Sun, the sunlight reaches the surface at an oblique angle. The seasons create fluctuating surface temperatures that stay within a moderate range. Without the seasons, large amounts of heat might be permanently trapped at the equator, and huge regions of permanently frozen wasteland would exist at moderate and high latitudes.

ORIGIN AND PHYSICAL DEVELOPMENT OF THE EARTH

The Earth is not a stagnant, unchanging planet. Since its origin around 5 billion years ago, our planet has been progressively developing and evolving. Atmospheric composition, climate and weather, continental and ocean positions, surface topography, sea level heights, and many other factors have varied in the past.

Therefore, if we are to evaluate the modern environment in a holistic context (taking into account the functional relationships between the parts and the whole), we need to take an historical perspective. For instance, to evaluate the current concentration of greenhouse gases and the predictions of global warming, we need to consider the changing composition of the atmosphere through geologic time and the oscillations in climate that have occurred over the past few million years (see Chapter 18). Similarly, we must compare present extinction rates of species to extinction rates over the last 500 million years (see Chapter 12).

Origin of the Solar System and Earth

The present universe is believed to be between 8 and 20 billion years old. Our little bit of the universe—our Sun and solar system—is very much younger, though. The Sun, Earth, and solar system originated about 5 billion years ago when a gas and dust cloud in our region of the galaxy began to collapse and coalesce. The material rotated more and more swiftly around its center, flattening the cloud into a disc shape and causing the accretion and condensation of particles of matter.

In the middle of the disc, the proto-Sun (the material that would become our Sun) condensed, and at various distances from the center eddies concentrated particles in clusters that formed planetesimals (small planet-like bodies). Through gravitational attraction and accretion, these bodies eventually became our familiar planets. By about 4.6 or 4.5 billion years ago, the Sun ignited, giving off tremendous heat and light. The influence of the Sun may have produced the basic arrangement of the planets we observe today, with the innermost planets being the "rocky" planets (Mercury, Venus, Earth and its Moon, and Mars) that can withstand the higher temperatures closer to the Sun, and the outer planets (Jupiter, Saturn, Uranus, Neptune, and Pluto) being frozen, gassy or icy planets.

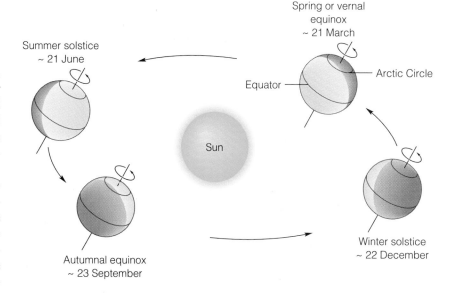

FIGURE 2–15
Rotation of the Earth around the Sun.

On the Earth, a period of intense heating caused the various components to melt and to separate into layers of heavier and lighter components. The dense iron-nickel components sank to the core while the lighter silicates rose and formed the mantle and crust. Many sources for the heat that led to this differentiation have been suggested, such as the impact energy of meteorites and asteroids, but in all likelihood, the main source was the radioactivity of elements trapped within the planet.

Origin of the Oceans

By about 4 billion years ago, the Earth probably had an ocean. We can assign an approximate date because among the oldest known rocks, formed some 3.8 billion years ago, are sedimentary rocks that show evidence of water weathering and erosion. But where did the water come from? Various hypotheses have been proposed. Many scientists believe that during the early accretion of the Earth, much water (initially in the form of water vapor) and large amounts of other gases were released by volcanoes. Modern volcanoes also spew out water, although much of their output may actually be recycled seawater. A significant amount of water may also have been deposited by icy comets that collided with the primitive Earth.

Over time, the oceans have accumulated salts as weathered material from the rocks of the continents has washed into them. The oceans contain ions, or salts, of such elements as sodium, magnesium, and chlorine along with smaller amounts of calcium, silica, potassium, and various dissolved gases including oxygen, carbon dioxide, and sulfur dioxide.

Origin of the Atmosphere

The earliest atmosphere of which we have any direct evidence, that of about 3.5 to 4 billion years ago, was very different than the atmosphere of today. It almost certainly originated from the Earth's interior as the planet underwent melting and segregation into a core, mantle, and crust. This early atmosphere probably contained large amounts of nitrogen gas, appreciable amounts of carbon dioxide, some methane and ammonia, and virtually no molecular oxygen.

So where did the present atmosphere's oxygen come from? Two basic processes are known to produce oxygen gas in some abundance in the natural world: (1) the breakdown of water into hydrogen gas and oxygen gas by ultraviolet radiation and (2) plant photosynthesis, the process of using the energy of sunlight to combine carbon dioxide and water into carbohydrates, giving off free oxygen gas as a by-product. The latter process is much more efficient at producing oxygen.

Currently, photosynthesis produces an estimated 22 billion tons (20 billion metric tons)* of oxygen per year. Many scientists believe that the high oxygen level of our current atmosphere is largely the result of photosynthetic organisms dumping this once lethal toxic waste into the environment over the last 3 billion years. As the levels of oxygen in the atmosphere increased, organisms evolved the ability to utilize oxygen in an efficient form of metabolism known as aerobic respiration; ultimately these changes allowed the evolution of very complex, multicellular life-forms.

NATURAL HAZARDS

Humans have always had to deal with "unpredictable" **natural hazards**—earthquakes, volcanic eruptions, floods, avalanches, droughts,

---

*Unless otherwise noted, *tons* refers to short tons (2000 pounds).

fires, tornadoes, hurricanes, and so forth (● Table 2–1). For most of human history such phenomena were beyond human control: they were neither caused by humans, nor was there much humans could do to predict their occurrences or mitigate (make less severe) their consequences.

Although many acts of nature still cannot be controlled, we have learned to better predict their occurrences and mitigate their effects. Furthermore, we have come to understand that some types of phenomena have a large anthropogenic (produced or caused by humans) component. Flash floods and avalanches may be caused, or at least exacerbated, by human deforestation in hilly regions. Abnormal droughts, storms, and other unusual weather phenomena may be caused or magnified by human interference with the atmosphere, such as the emission of high levels of greenhouse gases. Earthquakes, at least on a local level, may be caused by the pumping of fluid wastes into rocks lying deep below the surface.

As the Earth's human population increases, the damage done by naturally occurring, periodic "disasters" is magnified. A coastal area may be hit by a major storm once every century, a river may swell over its "normal" banks covering the floodplain only once every few centuries, or a naturally set forest fire may periodically burn off dead underbrush and litter on the forest floor. Viewed on a temporal scale of millennia (thousands of years), such events form an integral part of the natural ecosystem cycle; from a natural, holistic perspective, they are not disasters at all. But when dense human populations inhabit a coastal area or a river's floodplain and depend on a forest for lumber products or for scenic beauty, these events are perceived as terrible disasters—and so they are from a human perspective. But they are disasters that, given a little knowledge of the natural world, should have been easily anticipated. In this section, we briefly introduce some of the basic types of natural hazards that civilization must face as we continue to live in a natural environment.

TABLE 2–1 *Estimated Deaths Due to Major Natural Hazards 1960–1995*

HAZARD TYPE	ESTIMATED TOTAL DEATHS	EXAMPLES OF MAJOR EVENTS	DEATHS
Tropical cyclones	800,000	East Pakistan (Bangladesh) 1970	500,000
Earthquakes	600,000	Tangshan, China 1976	250,000
Floods	46,000	Vietnam 1964	8,000
Avalanches, mudslides	38,000	Peru 1970	25,000
Volcanic eruptions	35,000	Colombia 1985	23,000

Earthquakes and Volcanoes

Earthquakes and volcanic eruptions are geological phenomena that humans may be able to predict (though not always), but can virtually never control. With few exceptions, earthquakes and volcanoes are due to processes that take place deep within the crust and mantle. Volcanic eruptions are usually accompanied by at least minor to moderate earthquakes, but very large earthquakes can occur in the absence of volcanic activity. As we have already discussed, earthquakes and volcanic activity are associated with the boundaries of the lithospheric plates (refer to Fig. 2–4), and can be explained in terms of moving and/or subducting plates. But earthquakes (and less commonly volcanoes) can also occur in the middle of plates; indeed, no place on the surface of Earth is immune to earthquake activity.

Earthquakes

Earthquakes are essentially shock waves that originate when large masses of rocks suddenly move relative to each other below the Earth's surface. For instance, along a plate boundary where two lithospheric plates are sliding past each other, the plates may "hang up," allowing strain (frictional drag) to accumulate until it is finally relieved by rock movement—causing an earthquake. Earthquakes can originate up to 450 miles (700 km) below the surface. When the sudden rock movement occurs, various types of shock, or seismic, waves are transmitted through the Earth, causing the shaking or trembling felt by humans on the surface. A large earthquake may be detectable around the world.

Earthquakes are a constant threat to human life and well-being in some areas. Perhaps the most devastating set of earthquakes occurred near Shensi, China, in 1556 killing an estimated 830,000 people. A dozen earthquakes that caused the death of 100,000 people or more, have been recorded. Estimates are that, on average, earthquakes kill at least 10,000 people a year and cause about $500 million in property damage. Japan, a nation always at risk for earthquakes, suffered devastating consequences in 1995 when a quake hit the Kobe area killing over 5000 people, injuring another 25,000, and initially leaving over 300,000 homeless (Fig. 2–16).

The intensity, magnitude, or strength of an earthquake is commonly measured either on the Richter scale (in North America) or the Mercalli scale (in Europe). The Richter scale (see Issues in Perspective 2–1) is based on the amplitude of the seismic waves recorded by seismographs (instruments that record the motions of the Earth's surface) coming from a particular earthquake. The Richter scale is a logarithmic scale so that every unit corresponds to a 10-fold increase in the amplitude of the seismic waves. Thus a 7.0 earthquake is characterized by seismic waves with an amplitude of 100 times that seen in a 5.0 earthquake. Theoretically, the Richter scale has no upper limit, but some of the largest recorded earthquakes (such as the Lisbon earthquake of 1755 immortalized in Voltaire's *Candide*) have been ranked at about 8.9–9.0 (Table 2–2).

 FIGURE 2–16
The 1995 Kobe earthquake killed more than 5000 people and disrupted the lives of hundreds of thousands more.
(*Source:* Bunyo Ishikawa/ Sygma.)

Forget the Richter Scale?

Most members of the American public automatically associate an earthquake's size with a number on the "Richter scale." But, in fact, the original Richter scale, devised by Charles Richter in 1935 to measure the magnitude of southern California earthquakes using a then common—but now obsolete—seismograph, is outdated and virtually never used (Fig. 1). Indeed, Richter originally devised his scale not for scientific purposes, but as a way to express the relative sizes of earthquakes to inquiring journalists. Over the years, seismologists have continued to devise various scales to measure parameters such as the magnitude of earthquake waves passing through the Earth's crust, waves passing through the planet's interior, and long-period vibrations that measure the energy released at the earthquake's source (often known as the "moment magnitude").

Journalists in the popular press may refer to any of these scales as a "Richter scale," and for any particular earthquake, the magnitude that is measured may vary depending on the scale used. Another complication is that one unit of magnitude on a Richter–style scale originally corresponded to 10 times more "shaking" of the ground a certain distance from the earthquake as recorded on a certain type of seismograph. Yet seismographs (as well as people) stationed closer to or further from the epicenter may detect a different set of frequencies and vibrations or

"shaking." And 10 times more shaking does not correspond to ten times more energy released by the earthquake; on a typical Richter–style scale, a magnitude 7.0 quake will release about 33 times as much energy as a 6.0 quake and 1000 times as much as a 5.0 quake. Thus, the use of the term "Richter scale" has led to widespread confusion. A recent trend in the

FIGURE 1
Charles Richter, inventor of the "Richter Scale," standing next to an old seismograph. (*Source:* UPI/Bettmann.)

popular press is simply to use the generic term "magnitude" to refer to the relative size and strength of an earthquake; such magnitudes are often based on moment magnitudes.

But if the Richter scale has outlived its usefulness, what will replace it? Professional seismologists compare different earthquakes using seismic moments, which are calculated on the basis of such factors as the length of the fault rupture, the amount of rock movement, and the stiffness of the rock, but these are considered too complex for the public. The long-established Mercalli scale measures the intensity of earthquake damage—which may be what most people are concerned about. Another suggestion is that the energy released by earthquakes might be converted into atomic bomb or TNT equivalents. Thus, a magnitude 5.0 earthquake is equivalent to the detonation of approximately 1000 tons of TNT while a magnitude 6.0 earthquake releases about the same amount of energy as was released by the atomic bomb dropped on Hiroshima. Another possibility is to describe earthquakes in terms of the ground's acceleration as it shakes, perhaps using the unit "g" (the acceleration due to gravity on the surface of Earth, which is equal to 32 ft/sec² [9.8 m/sec²]). An earthquake that results in ground shaking in excess of 0.2g (20% of the force of gravity) may cause structural damage to many buildings.

The Mercalli scale (Table 2–3) is more qualitative, based primarily on observations of the effects caused by an earthquake close to its origin. This scale classifies earthquakes into a dozen basic categories, from instrumental (earthquakes so small that they can be detected only on seismo-

graphs) to catastrophic (earthquakes where local destruction is virtually total). The Mercalli scale is easily related to the Richter scale in an approximate way (Table 2–3).

Much research has recently gone into devising ways to predict earthquakes in both the long term and the short term. Some work has attempted to discover long-term earthquake cycles, based on the movements of the lithospheric plates and also perhaps correlated with such phenomena as meteoritic impacts, variations in the Earth's geomagnetic field, sunspot activity, and variations in the length of the day. Such work is very difficult to pursue, and no method has been able to predict long-term earthquake events with any degree of accuracy.

As for the short term, researchers have identified several precursors that often signal the probability of a major earthquake in earthquake-prone areas. The most commonly utilized precursors are unusual land deformation, seismic activity, geomagnetic and geo-electric activity, groundwater fluctuations, and natural phenomena such as animal behavior and unusual weather conditions (see Issues in Perspective 2–2 on page 49).

Although we usually do not think of earthquakes as being caused by human activity, some earthquakes are indeed anthropogenically induced (caused by humans). Earthquakes have been induced by nuclear blasts, conventional blasting, mining activities, fluid injection and extraction from rocks deep underground, and the building of dams and reservoirs. A now classic example of human-induced faulting and seismic activity occurred near Denver in the early 1960s, when nerve-gas waste was disposed of by pumping it down a well to great depths where it would be below groundwater supplies. Pumping the waste down the well at high pressures triggered a series of earthquakes. Since then it has been verified experimentally in oil fields that pumping fluids into the ground (and in some cases extracting them, such as the pumping out of oil) can induce seismic activity.

The most important cause of human-induced earthquakes seems to be the construction of large dams and reservoirs. In the case of at least six major dams around the world, including Hoover Dam on the Colorado River, earthquakes of a magnitude greater than 5 on the Richter scale (moderately strong earthquakes, capable of minor damage) have apparently been induced by the impounding of water in large reservoirs. Over 1000 earthquakes of various magnitudes have been felt since Hoover Dam was constructed in 1935; before 1935 the area was not known for earthquake activity. Worldwide dozens of dams have been associated with seismic phenomena. It is thought that water in the reservoir may penetrate the underlying bedrock and cause rock slippage that generates earthquakes. The

TABLE 2–2 *Some of the Largest Earthquakes, by Magnitude on the Richter Scale*

YEAR	LOCATION	MAGNITUDE
1755	Lisbon, Portugal	9.0
1906	Andes (Colombia)	8.6
1906	Valparaiso, Chile	8.4
1906	San Francisco, United States	8.25
1911	Tienshan, China	8.4
1920	Kansu, China	8.5
1923	Tokyo, Japan	8.2
1933	Japanese trench	8.5
1950	North Assam, India	8.6
1960	Chile	8.3–8.9
1964	Alaska	8.6
1976	Tangshan, China	8.2
1977	Sumba, Indonesia	8.9
1977	Argentina	8.2
1979	Indonesia	8.1
1985	Mexico City, Mexico	8.1
1994	Bolivia	8.2

huge mass of water in the reservoir also exerts tremendous pressures on the underlying rocks, and this can cause downwarping and subsidence of the land's surface.

Given that humans have inadvertently caused earthquakes, some people suggest that in the future we might be able to intervene to control natural earthquake activity. Perhaps, in an active earthquake zone, we could selectively induce a series of small earthquakes by either injecting or extracting fluids from the rocks. The small, relatively harmless earthquakes might relieve the strain on the rocks and thus allow us to avoid a single large, very destructive earthquake.

Volcanoes

Volcanoes are basically spots in the Earth's crust where hot, molten rock (magma) wells up to the surface (▪ Fig. 2–17). Active volcanoes are found almost exclusively in three geologic settings: at convergent plate margins where one lithospheric plate subducts under another, melting the rock which rises to the surface as volcanoes (for instance, in Indonesia and elsewhere along the Pacific rim); at divergent plate margins where magma wells up to the surface as two lithospheric plates pull apart from each other, forming a rift (as in the middle of the Atlantic Ocean); and over mantle hot spots, areas that lie over a hot mantle plume that breaks through the crust and spews molten rock onto the Earth's surface (as in the Hawaiian Islands).

TABLE 2–3 *The Mercalli Scale of Earthquake Intensity*

SCALE	INTENSITY	DESCRIPTION OF EFFECT	MAXIMUM ACCELERATION (MM SEC^{-2})	CORRESPONDING RICHTER SCALE
I	Instrumental	Not felt except by a very few under especially favorable circumstances.	<10	
II	Feeble	Felt only by a few persons at rest, especially on upper floors of buildings. Delicately suspended objects may swing.	<25	
III	Slight	Felt quite noticeably indoors, especially on upper floors of buildings, but many people do not recognize it as an earthquake. Standing automobiles may rock slightly. Vibration like a passing truck.	<50	<4.2
IV	Moderate	During the day felt indoors by many, outdoors by few. At night some awakened. Dishes, windows, doors disturbed; walls make cracking sound. Sensation like heavy truck striking building. Standing automobiles rock noticeably.	<100	
V	Slightly strong	Felt by nearly everyone, many awakened. Some dishes, windows, etc., broken; a few instances of cracked plaster; unstable objects overturned. Disturbances of trees, poles, and other tall objects sometimes noticed. Pendulum clocks may stop.	<250	<4.8
VI	Strong	Felt by all, many frightened and run outdoors. Some heavy furniture moved; a few instances of fallen plaster or damaged chimneys. Damage slight.	<500	<5.4
VII	Very strong	Everybody runs outdoors. Damage negligible in buildings of good design and construction; slight to moderate in well-built ordinary structures; considerable in poorly built or badly designed structures; some chimneys broken. Noticed by persons driving automobiles.	<1000	<6.1
VIII	Destructive	Damage slight in specially designed structures; considerable in ordinary substantial buildings, with partial collapse; great in poorly built structures. Panel walls thrown out of frame structures. Fall of chimneys, factory stacks, columns, monuments, walls. Heavy furniture overturned. Sand and mud ejected in small amounts. Changes in well water. Persons driving automobiles disturbed.	<2500	
IX	Ruinous	Damage considerable in specially designed structures; well-designed frame structures thrown out of plumb; great in substantial buildings, with partial collapse. Buildings shifted off foundations. Ground cracked conspicuously. Underground pipes broken.	<5000	<6.9
X	Disastrous	Some well-built wooden structures destroyed; most masonry and frame structures destroyed with foundations destroyed; ground badly cracked. Rails bent. Landslides considerable from river banks and steep slopes. Shifted sand and mud. Water splashed (slopped) over river banks.	<7500	<7.3
XI	Very Disastrous	Few, if any (masonry) structures remain standing. Bridges destroyed. Broad fissures in ground. Underground pipelines completely out of service. Earth slumps and land slips in soft ground. Rails bent greatly.	<9800	<8.1
XII	Catastrophic	Damage total. Practically all works of construction are damaged greatly or destroyed. Waves seen on ground surface. Objects are thrown upwards into the air.	>9800	>8.1

(*Source:* United States Geological Survey.)

Predicting Earthquakes

The careful periodic surveying of known benchmarks on the Earth's surface can lead to the detection of movement within the crust. Benchmarks may have moved relative to each other, suggesting possible faulting. In some areas where an active fault zone has been identified, accurate surveys across the fault zone can detect very slight movements (on the order of millimeters) that may be precursors of larger earthquake activity to come. In known earthquake-prone areas, instruments called tiltmeters can be used to monitor the surface of the Earth; if the surface starts tilting rapidly, an earthquake is usually imminent.

Daily monitoring of seismic activity is useful in an earthquake–prone area. Changes in the background seismic activity, especially increases in activity (sometimes referred to as foreshocks), can herald a major earthquake. The Earth's surface is characterized locally by magnetic fields and electric currents flowing through the rocks. Anomalous geo-magnetic and geo-electric activity may be detectable months, days, or hours before an earthquake strikes. Another technique that has been used very successfully in China is to monitor groundwater levels in wells. Fluctuations in normal water levels may precede an earthquake by hours to over a week. Radon levels in groundwater may increase for years before a major earthquake; this is probably due to the movement of water through new cracks that open up in the rocks before the onset of an earthquake.

Some of the most interesting and useful predictors are also extremely low-tech and poorly explained from a scientific perspective (indeed, they almost verge on superstition): namely, the behaviors of various animals in the days and hours before an area experiences an earthquake. The Japanese have observed that catfish exhibit unusual behavior before an earthquake, becoming very active and even jumping out of the water (▪ Fig. 1). All kinds of domestic animals become restless and exhibit odd behaviors prior to an earthquake: dogs bark, pigs become very aggressive, horses refuse to go into their stables, and so forth. Wild animals also show unusual behavior: burrowing animals leave the ground, rats run around randomly, snakes attempt to leave the area, and worms crawl from the ground to the surface in large numbers. In the San Francisco area, the behavior of zoo and marine animals is monitored daily as part of the local earthquake prediction system.

Possibly, certain animals are sensitive to vibrations (or ultrasound) generated by small earthquakes undetectable to humans that precede a major earthquake. Perhaps some animals are extremely sensitive to the smell of methane that may leak from the ground prior to an earthquake. Another possibility is that electrostatic particles may be coming from the ground; furry and feathered animals, such as mammals and birds, are generally very sensitive to electrostatic charges.

Reports of unusual weather before major earthquakes have often been dismissed as nonsense. However, some researchers have suggested that degassing of methane and other gases from below the Earth's surface may precede a major earthquake and could account for unusual weather phenomena such as strange mists, glowing skies, and flashes of light. If electrostatic particles are released prior to an earthquake, this also might help explain unusual weather phenomena.

All in all, predicting earthquakes is still a tricky business, perhaps more art than science. But China in particular has a very good track record; the Chinese have been able to predict a number of major earthquakes in time to evacuate cities before they were hit. Although substantial financial losses may still be unavoidable, by removing people from the area, the death toll can be kept at a minimum.

▪ FIGURE 1

The Japanese have used catfish behavior as a predictor of earthquakes, and according to Japanese legend earthquakes are caused by the movement of a giant catfish. This antique illustration shows people attempting to subdue the giant catfish that causes earthquakes. (*Source:* Katsuhiko Ishida.)

FIGURE 2-17

Volcanoes can be classified according to whether they extrude predominantly basaltic or andesitic magma. Volcanoes at divergent plate boundaries and hot spots tend to produce basaltic magma which is relatively silica-poor and originates from the mantle. Andesitic magma contains a higher percentage of silica and is generally formed from the remelting, differentiation, and recrystallization of previously existing crustal or mantle material. Thus andesitic volcanoes are commonly found in subduction zones where rock is remelted.

Basaltic magmas are hotter and much less viscous than andesitic magmas, which tend to contain a much higher percentage of gases (often predominantly water vapor). Consequently, whereas lava may flow smoothly out of the crater of a basaltic volcano, andesitic volcanoes tend to be much more explosive, shooting out steam and other gases, rock fragments of various sizes, and volcanic ash.

Volcanic eruptions can affect hu-

FIGURE 2-18
Seen here are the remains of St. Pierre, a once thriving city of 30,000 on the island of Martinique, that was destroyed by the 8 May 1902 eruption of Mount Pelée. (*Source:* USGS.)

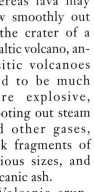

mans on both a local and a global scale. On a local level, volcanic eruptions can destroy local towns and cities. In A.D. 79 ash falls and mudflows triggered by the eruption of Mount Vesuvius in Italy buried the towns of Pompeii and Herculaneum. The eruption of Mount Pelée on Martinique in 1902 destroyed the city of St. Pierre, killing some 30,000 people in a span of two minutes (Fig. 2–18). As we have seen, large volcanic eruptions can have worldwide effects by spewing dust, ash, and gases (including material that can form acid rain) into the atmosphere, affecting global weather patterns. For example, the 1883 eruption of Krakatoa, a volcano in the Sunda Straits between Sumatra and Java, spewed 4 cubic miles (18 km³) of rock, ash, and other debris into the atmosphere to heights of 50 miles (80 km). The materials initially reduced the amount of incoming solar radiation reaching the Earth's surface by an estimated 13%. Even two years later, the amount of incoming solar radiation over France was still 10% below normal.

The eruption of Krakatoa also set off tsunami that caused damage throughout the Pacific basin. Tsunami (Japanese for "harbor wave") are huge waves, sometimes caused by explosive volcanic activity in or near the oceans or by large undersea earthquakes (usually registering higher than 6.5 on the Richter scale) or landslides. Fortunately, tsunami are relatively rare; however, they can be extremely destructive. The waves can range in height from less than 3 feet (1 m) to nearly 200 feet (60 m).

In 1692 an earthquake destroyed Port Royal, Jamaica, and the resulting tsunami threw harbored ships inland over two-story buildings. The Lisbon earthquake of 1755 sent a wave across the Atlantic Ocean that temporarily raised the sea by 10 to 13 feet (3–4 m) in Barbados.

Even with modern technology and knowledge, predicting future volcanic activity is extremely difficult. Although we know where to expect active volcanoes relative to lithospheric plates and can determine if a volcano is active or dormant (based on the time since its last eruption), we cannot predict exactly the timing and intensity of future eruptions. Researchers use many of the same techniques used for predicting earthquakes. Seismic activity, land deformation, geomagnetic and geo-electric parameters can be monitored. Any anomalous behavior, like a change in seismic activity or active deformation of the sides of a volcano, can herald an imminent eruption. But estimating the strength and type of eruption that will occur is difficult. The analysis of gases given off by volcanoes holds some promise for predicting volcanic activity, at least in the short term. But sampling gases being vented from an active volcano that may be near eruption can be very difficult and dangerous.

Land Instability

A very widespread form of natural geologic hazard, usually brought on by human ignorance of the principles of geology and soil mechanics, is the collapse of soil or weathered rock material. Landslides, rockfalls, and avalanches may bury roads, buildings, and other human structures. Soils may fail to support buildings, thus causing them to collapse. Such phenomena may occur simply because humans erect structures in areas that are geologically unstable and thus unsuitable for building. Human activity, such as clear-cutting a mountainside, may induce land instability. Of course, natural phenomena such as earthquakes and volcanic eruptions may also induce landslides, rockfalls, avalanches, surface subsidence, and so forth.

Weather Hazards

Hurricanes, typhoons, tornadoes, droughts, floods, heat waves, wind storms, dust storms, and other "irregular" weather patterns can wreak havoc on human settlements. Full discussion of this large and complex topic is beyond the scope of this book, but here we will briefly mention some major types of storm hazards. Due to possible global warming brought on by the greenhouse effect (see Chapter 18), some researchers expect a dramatic increase in irregular weather patterns, particularly the number of violent storms, in the relatively near future.

Tropical Cyclones

Tropical **cyclones** are intense storms that develop over warm tropical seas ( Fig. 2–19). When they occur in North America, tropical cyclones are generally referred to as hurricanes; when they occur in Southeast Asia, they are known as typhoons. Approximately 100 to 120 tropical cyclones develop worldwide every year, and many of them travel far inland as well as posing hazards

to coastal areas. Every five years or so, a hurricane along the east coast of North America crosses the Appalachian Mountains and enters the Great Lakes region.

In terms of deaths, tropical cyclones are among the worst natural hazard that humans currently face. Between 1960 and 1995 approximately 800,000 people died as a result of tropical cyclones compared with 600,000 people killed by

FIGURE 2–19
Tropical cyclones, more commonly known as hurricanes and typhoons, are among the most destructive of natural hazards. Here we see Cutler Ridge, Florida, after being hit by Hurricane Andrew, August 1992. (*Source: B. Wisser/Gamma Liaison.*)

earthquakes. Of the people who died in tropical cyclones, however, 500,000 lost their lives in a single event—when a cyclone hit Bangladesh (then East Pakistan) in 1970. The death rate was so high because Bangladesh is immensely overcrowded and people live in a low-lying deltaic area that, given the regularity of storms, is virtually unsuitable for human habitation. In addition, the islands of the delta were swamped with salt water that damaged or destroyed over 990,000 acres (400,000 hectares) of rice paddies; about a million head of livestock were killed; and over 50 million people were significantly affected by the storm (the total population of Bangladesh is over 115 million). Bangladesh was hit by another tropical cyclone that caused 100,000 deaths in 1985 and by yet another that killed 140,000 people in 1991.

Realistically, humans can do very little about tropical cyclones, or most natural climatic hazards, except to take preventive measures long before the disasters hit. For instance, areas prone to tropical cyclones should not be heavily settled. Early predictions of impending storms can help the public take proper precautions, such as evacuating low-lying areas that will be hardest hit. Unfortunately, in countries like Bangladesh many people have no place to live except areas that are prone to tropical cyclones, and even when an imminent cyclone is detected, evacuating hundreds of thousands to millions of people at once is virtually impossible.

Tornadoes and Other Strong Wind Phenomena

Tornadoes are a classic American phenomenon; about 80% of all tornadoes occur in the United States, mostly in the Great Plains (about 600 a year in this area). The typical tornado consists of a rapidly rotating vortex of air that forms a funnel (Fig. 2–20); tornadoes may be associated with hurricanes, but not necessarily. A tornado may be relatively harmless as long as the funnel does not touch the surface of the Earth. But when they do touch down, tornadoes are among the most intense and destructive phenomena found in nature. As a result of winds of 250 to 300 miles per hour (400 to 500 km/hr) or greater and changes in air

FIGURE 2–20
A vortex of rotating air, with wind speeds as high as 300 miles an hour (500 km/hr), a single tornado can cause incredible destruction in a small area.

pressure found within the funnel, tornadoes can lift objects weighing hundreds of tons. A tornado that moves over water can suck in millions of tons of water, perhaps temporarily draining a river or lake.

Despite their destructive force, tornadoes that touch the surface of the Earth are fairly localized phenomena. Their contact with the ground generally lasts only half an hour or less; at most the ground path of a single tornado might be 1100 yards (1 km) wide and 10 or 20 miles (a few tens of kilometers) long.

Although most humans associate tornadoes with trouble, in actuality tornadoes serve a number of important geological and ecological functions. They transport large quantities of clay and silt particles from one area to another. They also serve as an important biotic dispersal mechanism; tornadoes have been proposed as the primary mechanism by which various species are dispersed extremely rapidly over fairly large areas. Seeds, pollen, microorganisms, insects, and even such animals as fishes, frogs, toads, and turtles can be transported alive for a few hundred miles (several hundred kilometers) in a tornado. Tornadoes may explain how aquatic species could migrate between unconnected lakes in parts of North America.

Tornadoes are not the only weather phenomenon associated with strong winds that pose a hazard for humans. Much more important, in terms of their frequency and worldwide extent, are dust storms. In historic times, there have been some very major dust storms indeed. In 1901 a dust storm carried approximately 165 million tons (150 million metric tons) of dust from the Sahara in Africa to western Europe and the Ural Mountains. In 1928 a dust storm removed an estimated 16.5 million tons (15 million metric tons) of soil from Ukraine and deposited it in Romania and Poland. The dust storms that occurred in the midwestern United States during the 1930s are legendary. Over 2.5 million acres (1 million hectares) of agricultural land were severely damaged by the resulting loss of topsoil.

Floods

A **flood**, quite simply, is a high flow of water that overruns its normal confinement area and covers land that is usually dry. Natural floods are a normal part of the physical environment, but because they often seem "unusual" from a human perspective—occurring irregularly over periods of decades, centuries, or millennia—they may take us by surprise. Cumulatively, floods are among the most destructive of all natural hazards. In China flooding along the Yangtze and Yellow Rivers has taken the lives of millions of people over the last century and a half (many were drowned or died of flood-associated diseases or flood-caused starvation when crops were destroyed); in the United States floods have caused billions of dollars worth of damage and killed hundreds of people. The human losses due to floods are greatly exacerbated by the fact that riverfront properties are often considered prime real estate, many towns and farms are located in natural floodplains, and large cities are often situated along rivers.

Other than storm surges, where the sea level rises locally relative to a low coastal area (such as during a hurricane), two basic types of floods can be distinguished: riverine floods and flash floods. Riverine floods occur along major streams or rivers when particularly heavy rainfalls or the rapid melting of snow causes a large amount of water to flow through the drainage basin. Riverine floods may also occur when dams, either natural or human-made, break due to the strain imposed by high water levels and flood conditions or to other causes. Flash floods generally occur in drainage basins containing small, shallow, or ephemeral (periodically dry) streams when heavy rainfall overloads the system with water.

In the natural environment, rivers and streams are generally short-term phenomena. Rivers continually change their course and flood their banks; the flooding serves to transport and redistribute sediments and nutrients carried by the water. The annual floods of the Nile, bringing fresh nutrients to restore the fertility of the land, were the lifeblood of the ancient Egyptian civilization. Flooding can thus be viewed as a small part of the larger hydrologic and rock cycles.

When humans develop a drainage basin, however, they tend to build permanent structures as if the rivers and streams are permanent, sedentary features of the landscape. All too often humans do not properly consider the natural periodic occurrence of floods. Consequently, when the occasional major flood does occur (perhaps only once every hundred or thousand years), the toll in human life and property loss can be immense. To make matters worse, many human activities inadvertently promote flooding. Farming, overgrazing, deforestation, paving large expanses, and other aspects of development limit the ability of water to seep into the ground (infiltration). As a result, there will be more runoff—more water will travel overland when it rains—which can

promote flooding. Mining, construction, and other human activities can cause stream channels to become filled with sediment, hindering their ability to carry water quickly, and this too promotes flooding.

Even human activities that are specifically directed at controlling or avoiding flood conditions can actually promote flooding. Dams built to control flood surges may burst and cause even more flooding. Furthermore, even a properly maintained dam will eventually collect silt, ending its usefulness. Water reservoirs behind dams may flood large tracts of forest or agricultural land, and as these artificial pools sit stagnant, they may become a breeding ground for disease vectors and pests (see the discussion in Chapter 7). Dams also disrupt stream flow, causing areas downstream to undergo abnormal erosion due to sediment starvation (the sediments once carried by the stream are trapped behind the dam). Of course, some forms of aquatic wildlife can be severely disrupted by artificial dams.

Channelization, the artificial straightening of a stream or river to increase its capacity to carry large amounts of water quickly downstream, has been used in some areas as a flood control measure. Such channelization often damages the natural aquatic life in the stream, and it can further exacerbate flooding conditions downstream by carrying even more water at a faster rate. Likewise, for thousands of years, humans have built dikes, levees, and flood walls to keep a stream in its channel and avoid flooding. But if, or when, the levees or dikes are breached, the resulting flood can be devastating. All the evidence points to the conclusion that artificial containment structures can only be a temporary measure at best; ultimately, they are bound to fail. In 1927 a breach in an Army Corps of Engineers' levee allowed the Mississippi River to flood over 2.3 million acres (nearly a million hectares) of land despite the efforts of 5000 workers to repair the levee. In China the Yellow River has been artificially contained by levees and dikes for hundreds of years; periodically, they break (for instance in 1887 and 1939), flooding up to 10,000 square miles (26,000 km^2) of land at a time.

Today, rather than emphasizing engineering works such as the construction of dams and levees to control flooding, many authorities are advocating stricter zoning laws and better floodplain management policies. Ultimately, development may need to be strictly limited in flood-prone areas (see Issues in Perspective 2–3).

The Great Midwestern Flood of 1993

During the summer of 1993, the Mississippi and Missouri river system experienced unusually high floodwaters that resulted in widespread devastation. Natural and human-made levees broke, and water spilled over the banks of the rivers, flooding 8 million acres (3.24 million hectares) outright and soaking another 12 million acres (4.36 million hectares) to the point where the land was too wet to grow crops. Farmland was damaged, crops were lost, and buildings were turned into soggy messes. Some towns were completely enveloped for a short time by the waters. Many people lost everything they owned, including their livelihoods. Estimated damage was in the range of $12 billion. Nearly 70,000 people were left homeless, but fortunately, only 50 lost their lives. Over four hundred counties in Illinois, Iowa, Kansas, Minnesota, Missouri, Nebraska, North Dakota, South Dakota, and Wisconsin were declared federal disaster areas.

Many factors combined were responsible for the extent and nature of the 1993 floods. The phenomenon known as El Niño, a body of warm water that develops in the eastern Pacific every few years, released moisture into the atmosphere that was carried by the jet stream to the Mississippi valley. This, along with other somewhat unusual weather conditions, such as a very dry high pressure system that

occurred in the eastern United States during the spring and summer of 1993, resulted in massive rainfalls in the Midwest.

But massive rainfalls do not necessarily result in destruction of the magnitude that took place during the 1993 floods. Many human-built structures, from factories, to homes, to entire towns, were destroyed simply because they were in the natural floodplain of the river. In most cases this was not the area that the river floods annually, but rather the hundred-year floodplain, an area that will be flooded approximately once a century. It is questionable whether humans should be building or occupying such flood-prone areas.

Some scientists believe that human attempts to control and channel the Mississippi River system also contributed to the floods. A major flood took place in the lower Mississippi valley in 1927, killing 214 people. In response, Congress instructed the U.S. Army Corps of Engineers to undertake a massive building program to contain and control the rivers so that such disasters would not happen in the future. Over the next 60 years, hundreds of dams and thousands of miles of artificial levees and flood walls were built along the Mississippi River and its tributaries to channel the water. But when the river is confined to relatively narrow channels during flood conditions, the water

rises quicker and higher and flows with increasing speed and force. Under natural conditions, the river will spread widely over the natural floodplain, dissipating its energy and not rising so high. If a levee breaks, as occurred in many areas in 1993, the damage caused by the floodwaters can be much more extensive and severe than if there had never been a levee in the first place. If a levee holds, then an increasing volume of water flows in the channel, and flood conditions are worsened downstream.

What can or should be done to mitigate flood damage in the future is a topic of intense debate. Should humans attempt to control and channel natural rivers? It has been suggested that many artificial levees should be dismantled so that the rivers can flow freely along their preferred courses. Should humans be allowed to live in flood-prone areas? Perhaps entire towns and communities should be moved to higher ground. Is it right for people who live in an area known to be subject to floods to collect from government-subsidized flood insurance, or apply for federal disaster relief, only to rebuild in the same flood-prone area again? Or should they be forced to relocate to a safer area? Some people argue that people who insist on living in a flood-prone area should be solely responsible for the consequences if they or their property are damaged by floodwaters.

Droughts

Droughts—periods of abnormally low rainfall over an extended period of time in a particular area—can have devastating effects. Due to drought, agricultural productivity may drop dramatically, and even drinkable water for humans may be in short supply. Droughts, and likewise periods of abnormally high rainfall that may cause flooding, are a typical aspect of the climate in the long run. But in the short run, humans may

settle in an area based on abnormally good (perhaps moister than usual) weather conditions, which may last for decades, and then be hard hit when drier weather conditions set in again. Changing human land-use patterns, especially the destruction of tropical forests and human-induced desertification, may affect circulation patterns globally, increasing local droughts. Additionally, it is possible that global warming due to the human-induced greenhouse effect may shift precipitation patterns, causing once well-watered areas to become drier.

Major droughts have been experienced in recent years in a number of places around the world, in particular, Ethiopia, Sudan, and especially the Sahel region (Chad, Niger, Mali, Burkina Faso, Mauritania, Senegal, and Gambia) south of the Sahara in Africa ( Fig. 2–21). This area is instructive, for prolonged dry conditions have been exacerbated (made worse) by human practices. The declining rainfall in the area has led to reduced plant growth, which reduces the amount of evapotranspiration (water given off from the soil by evaporation and water given off from plants by transpiration), which decreases the local moisture content of the atmosphere, which further decreases the amount of rainfall locally. Over time the soil dries out and heats up. The lack of vegetation allows the wind to carry more dust into the lower atmosphere, which can add to the heating of the air higher up in the troposphere, contributing to atmospheric instability and reducing the amount of dew that forms at night. All of these factors enhance and accelerate drought conditions in the Sahel region. Furthermore, human overpopulation has exacerbated the situation. Shrubs and trees are cut down and burned as fuel or fed to animals. Virtually all of the arable land (land fit to be cultivated or tilled) is under cultivation, often utilizing inappropriate Western plowing, which leads to progressive destruction of the soil structure and erosion of the topsoil. A hard crust remains on the surface of the land, preventing water from infiltrating the soil on the rare occasions when rain occurs. Together these factors are causing severe desertification in the once semiarid Sahel region.

Fires

Fires are a natural part of many ecosystems; particularly severe natural fires may be the result of drought conditions and lightning. Since prehistoric times, humans have set fires—some of which invariably get out of control. Forest fires, grassland fires, and bushfires are particularly feared in the United States and Australia, but they pose a threat to forests around the world. Major fires in the past include the 1871 forest fires that destroyed 4.2 million acres (1.7 million hectares) of forest in Wisconsin and Michigan and killed 2200 people and the 12 million acres (4.8 million hectares) of forest that burned during 1980 in Canada. The Ash Wednesday fires of 16 February 1983 in South Australia and Victoria (southern Australia) destroyed over 1.2 million acres (over half a million hectares) of land, including urban areas (nearly two dozen towns were destroyed), forest, and pasture; killed over 300,000 sheep, 18,000 cattle, and 76 people; and injured another 3,500 people. By far the greatest known fire incident was the Great Siberian fire of 1915, which burned 390,000 square miles (1 million km³) of land in Siberia following a severe drought. Huge amounts of smoke were injected into the atmosphere blocking incoming solar radiation and suppressing ground temperatures.

For the past century, a basic principle of U.S. wilderness management has been to fight fires, whether they are set by humans or occur naturally. Timber interests saw fighting fires as preserving a resource; people interested in recreation or preservation saw the prevention of fires as a way to protect the wilderness.

But by the 1940s, some foresters had begun to question the wisdom of suppressing all natural forest fires. Slowly, they came to realize that fires play a critical role in nature. Fires promote the decomposition of some forest litter (dead leaves, branches, and so on) and are an essential component of the biogeochemical nutrient cycle. Periodic fires increase the biotic diversity (the range of different organisms) of an area because they maintain more open habitats necessary for

 **FIGURE 2–21**
The Sahel region of Africa has experienced extreme droughts in recent years, yet the people continue to attempt to farm the land in an effort to survive. (*Source:* Alain Nogues/Sygma.)

FIGURE 2–22

The unconsolidated sediments found along many coasts can spell disaster for the local homeowner when a major storm strikes, as demonstrated by this house on the Norfolk coast of England. (*Source:* Hodson/Greenpeace.)

some species, especially certain birds and larger mammals. Certain plants need periodic fires as part of their life cycle; for example, the seeds of the giant sequoia (California redwood) and the jack pine must be exposed to the heat of a fire before they will germinate.

Coastal Hazards

Coastal regions along the oceans and larger lakes are among the most sought-after places for human occupation; in the United States, over half of the population lives on or near such coasts, and the same holds true around the world. Yet geologically, coastal areas can be very unstable and prone to change. Natural erosional processes are ongoing along many coasts, and human habitation may accelerate the process, for instance, by destroying wild plants that help stabilize soils and sands. In the United States approximately 25% of the coastline experiences severe erosion. The shifting sand dunes and unconsolidated sediments found on many coasts provide a poor foundation for homes or other buildings. Wave action and moderate storms can cause a shore to recede (in some cases at a rate of 60 feet [20 m] a year), leaving structures dangling on the edge of cliffs or eventually collapsing into the water (Fig. 2–22).

Storm surges—sudden local rises in sea level caused by hurricanes and typhoons—pose particular threats to coastal regions. Likewise, tsunamis can wreak havoc on coastal areas. Yet despite the risks, coastal areas remain popular places of residence and recreation.

S UMMARY

The natural environment is an integrated system composed of four spheres: the lithosphere, hydrosphere, atmosphere, and biosphere. The physical environment, composed of the first three spheres, closely interacts with the biosphere.

Our physical environment, the planet Earth, has been continuously evolving for the last 4.6 billion years, culminating in the world we experience today. But even now Earth continues to develop; it is a young, active planet characterized by shifting continents, mountain building, erosional processes, and atmospheric cycles. A cross-section through the Earth shows a concentric layered structure (core, mantle, lithosphere, and atmosphere). The Earth's crust is made out of rocks that are in turn composed of elements and compounds. Much of

the Earth's surface is covered with water, and the entire planet is surrounded by an atmosphere composed of about 78% nitrogen and 21% oxygen. The Earth rotates around the Sun and spins on its axis. These movements give rise to the daily cycle of day and night and the yearly cycle of seasons. Incoming solar radiation drives the hydrologic and atmospheric cycles.

The crust and lithosphere are divided into giant tectonic plates that move relative to one another, creating and destroying crustal material and causing natural earthquakes and volcanic activity. Natural radioactive fission reactions power the tectonic cycle. The rock cycle is a result of a combination of tectonic inputs (heating and melting rocks) and atmospheric inputs (weathering and eroding rocks on the Earth's surface).

Our solar system had its origins nearly 5 billion years ago when a huge gas and dust cloud collapsed and coalesced. The early Earth was very different from the present-day Earth, with less continental material and an atmosphere that lacked free oxygen. Over time the modern oceans and atmosphere developed, and the continents grew.

Our physical environment can be hospitable and indeed is absolutely necessary for humankind's continued survival. At the same time, the natural environment presents many hazards. Hazards associated with tectonic activity include earthquakes and volcanoes; hazards associated with weather cycles include tropical cyclones, tornadoes, floods, and droughts. Ultimately, humans may still find themselves at the mercy of nature.

asthenosphere
atmosphere
atmospheric cycle
biological environment
biosphere
climate
compound
convection cell
core
cyclone

earthquake
element
flood
hydrologic cycle
hydrosphere
igneous rock
lithosphere
mantle
metamorphic rock
mineral
natural environment

natural hazard
ocean
physical environment
plate tectonics
rock cycle
sedimentary rock
tornado
volcano
weather

STUDY QUESTIONS

1. Name the four spheres of the natural environment.
2. How does planet Earth compare to its nearest neighbors in the solar system?
3. If one could cut a slice through the Earth, what would be encountered?
4. Describe modern plate tectonic theory.
5. What is the composition of matter on Earth?
6. What are the differences and similarities among sedimentary, igneous, and metamorphic rocks? Where does each form and occur?
7. What is the importance of the hydrologic cycle?
8. What are the major reservoirs of water on Earth?
9. What happens when warm, moisture-laden air rises?
10. Explain the causes of the seasons.
11. Describe the basic structure and composition of the atmosphere.
12. How did our solar system originate?
13. What are some of the most dangerous natural hazards?

14. When an earthquake occurs in the Earth's crust, caused by a rupture of the rock along a fault, seismic (shock) waves are released. Various types of seismic waves are generally recognized, including primary P-waves (compressional waves) and secondary S-waves (shear waves). P-waves travel faster than S-waves; in a certain context, P-waves may travel at a speed of 4.8 miles per second, and S-waves at a speed of 2.7 miles per second. Given this information, then the time, T_S (in seconds), that S-waves require to travel a certain distance (D) in miles from the epicenter (the point on the Earth's surface at, or immediately above, the rupturing fault that caused the earthquake; the epicenter is generally most damaged by the shock waves) to a seismograph can be expressed as follows:

$$T_S = D/2.7$$

Likewise, the time P-waves require to arrive can be expressed as

$$T_P = D/4.8$$

The difference in arrival time between the S-waves and the P-waves is

$$T_S - T_P = (D/2.7) - (D/4.8)$$
$$\text{or}$$
$$T_S - T_P = (2.1D)/13$$

Therefore, the distance (in miles) from the earthquake's epicenter to the seismograph is

$$D = 13(T_S - T_P)/2.1$$

Using this equation, if the difference in arrival time between S-waves and P-waves for a certain earthquake is 6 minutes and 23 seconds at a particular seismograph station, how far away is the epicenter of the earthquake from this seismograph station?
15. Using the equation in Question 14, if the difference in arrival time between S-waves and P-waves for a certain earthquake is 4 minutes and 16 seconds at a particular seismograph station, how far away is the epicenter of the earthquake from this seismograph station?

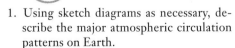

ESSAY QUESTIONS

1. Using sketch diagrams as necessary, describe the major atmospheric circulation patterns on Earth.
2. Briefly summarize some key events in Earth history over the last 4 billion years.
3. What approaches have scientists used in their attempts to predict future earthquake and volcanic activity?
4. Describe some of the more important weather hazards. What, if anything, can humans do to prepare for such disasters?
5. After a major flood, should people whose homes and businesses were destroyed by the flood be allowed to rebuild in the floodplain? If so, under what conditions and who should pay for the rebuilding (insurance companies or the federal government)? If you feel people should not be allowed to rebuild, why not? Justify your answer.

Archer, A. A., G. W. Luttig, and I. I. Snezhko, eds. 1987. *Man's dependence on the Earth*. Paris: UNESCO.

Bryant, E. A. 1991. *Natural hazards.* Cambridge: Cambridge University Press.

Ernst, W. G. 1990. *The dynamic planet*. New York: Columbia University Press.

Friday, L., and R. Laskey, eds. 1989. *The fragile environment*. Cambridge: Cambridge University Press.

Goudie, A. 1990. *The human impact on the natural environment*, 3d ed. Cambridge, Mass.: MIT Press.

Mannion, A. M. 1991. *Global environmental change: A natural and cultural history*. New York.: John Wiley.

Margulis, L., and L. Olendzenski, eds. 1992. *Environmental evolution*. Cambridge, Mass.: MIT Press.

Monroe, J. S., and R. Wicander, 1995. *Physical geology: Exploring the Earth (second edition)*. St. Paul: West Publishing Company.

Officer, C., and J. Page. 1993. *Tales of the Earth: Paroxysms and perturbations of the blue planet*. New York: Oxford University Press.

Pipkin, B. W., 1994. *Geology and the environment*. St. Paul: West Publishing Company.

Robinson, A. 1993. *Earth shock: Hurricanes, volcanoes, earthquakes, tornadoes and other forces of nature*. London: Thames & Hudson.

Turner, B. L., II, W. C. Clark, R. W. Kates, J. F. Richards, J. T. Mathews, and W. B. Meyer, eds. 1990. *The Earth as transformed by human action*. Cambridge: Cambridge University Press.

Van Andel, T. H. 1985. *New views on an old planet: Continental drift and the history of the Earth*. Cambridge: Cambridge University Press.

THE BIOSPHERE

PROLOGUE   *Restoring the Biosphere by Applying Ecology*

e are privileged to live at a time when the diversity of life on Earth is about the richest it has ever been. Since the first microscopic life originated more than three billion years ago, the number of species on Earth has slowly climbed, as evolution has produced new kinds of adaptations. The 5 to 50 million species present today are many more than Earth held at the time of the dinosaurs, for instance. This richness makes the current "extinction crisis" all the more lamentable.

PHOTO   *Restoration ecology seeks to return natural habitats, such as the tall-grass prairies, to their original state. (Source:* Ron Klataske.)

By some estimates, as many as 100 species are becoming extinct every day. Many people recognize the importance of saving biodiversity and understand that preserves of native habitat must be set aside if we are to save species. The new fast-growing science of conservation biology seeks to discover the best ways of designing preserves. What is the best size for a preserve? The best shape? Exactly which species are most at risk of extinction? Such questions do not have simple answers, but the science of biological preservation has made enormous strides over the last few years.

Furthermore, one subfield of conservation biology seeks to go beyond preserving species before they go extinct. This subfield, called restoration ecology, seeks to restore entire ecosystems and biological communities to their former state. The tall-grass prairie, on which buffalo once fed, was reduced to a few tiny fragments around railroad tracks and other undeveloped areas in the American Midwest. Restoring this prairie has involved gathering the seeds and plants of remnant species and replanting them in carefully watched plots of land. But this is just the first step. Interactions among the native plants and animals, such as insect pollinators, must be established if a true biological community is to be re-created. Native grazing animals, birds, and many other prairie natives must ultimately be established if the tall–grass prairie is to live again. Doing this will be difficult, time-consuming, and expensive. So will be the task of restoring the Kissimmee River and Everglades of Florida and many other areas of the United States where restoration ecology is being applied. But to people who value biodiversity, the potential benefits are enormous. Instead of simply preserving remnants of biodiversity, we have the possibility of restoring whole ecosystems that we would otherwise never see again.

$\mathcal{I}$NTRODUCTION

In Chapter 2, we saw that the Earth is a dynamic entity that gave rise to life over 3.5 billion years ago when the first microbes appeared. Since that time, life has co-evolved with the Earth's atmosphere, hydrosphere, and lithosphere to create an integrated "living planet." Living things help cycle the elements and sustain an oxygen atmosphere while the Earth provides a habitable environment for life. In this chapter, we examine the fundamentals of ecology, which is the science of how organisms interact with each other and with the physical environment. These ecological principles have great practical value in determining just how much humans are disturbing biological systems and how this disruption can be minimized.

$\mathcal{E}$ VOLUTION OF THE BIOSPHERE

The very early appearance of life on Earth implies that natural processes readily produce life under appropriate conditions. Beginning in the early 1950s with the work of Stanley Miller and Harold Urey, scientists have shown that complex molecules possessed by all living things are readily produced under laboratory conditions that duplicate early environments on Earth. As ■ Figure 3–1 shows, the early atmosphere is thought to have been composed of ammonia (NH_3), methane (CH_4), water vapor (H_2O), and other gases. When these are subjected to electricity, which simulates lightning and sunlight, chemical reactions occur that produce **amino acids**. Amino acids are complex molecules that are the "building blocks" of proteins. Proteins make up enzymes and many other components of life such as muscles, hair, and skin.

Of course, protein molecules alone are not living things. Organisms are composed of molecules organized in very complex ways. The basic organizational unit of life is the cell. Remarkably, in the late 1950s, Sidney Fox found that heated amino acids can form cell-like structures sometimes called **protocells**. These structures are not true cells but have many cell-like properties such as being semi-permeable to certain materials.

Producing amino acids and protocells in the lab is far from creating life in the lab. Even the simplest bacteria are vastly more complex than these protein and protocellular building blocks. Nevertheless, the readiness with which these first steps toward life occur, combined with the fossil record, support the idea that life readily arose through natural processes.

Diversification of the Biosphere

Evolution through Natural Selection

Once life originated, it began to diversify into different kinds of organisms through biological evolution. As Charles Darwin first documented in

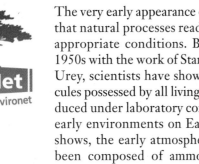

www.jbpub.com/environet

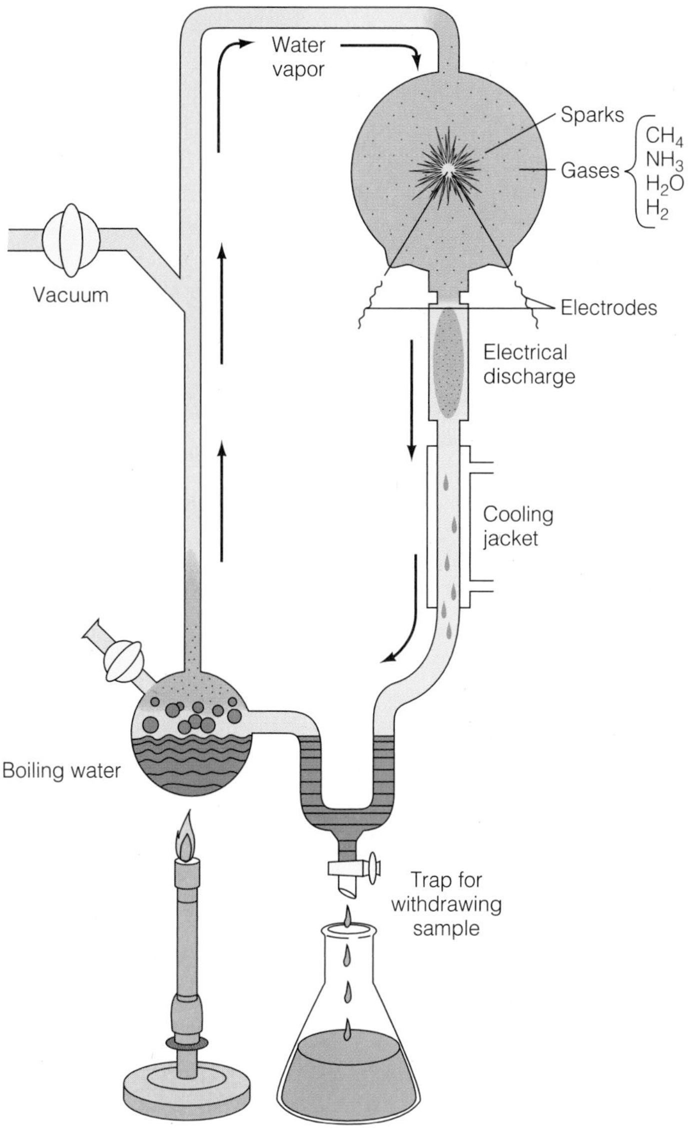

FIGURE 3–1
Experimental apparatus that
Miller and Urey used to show
that organic molecules could
be produced from the
chemical components of the
Earth's early atmosphere.

1859, biological evolution occurs from **natural selection** of individual variation:

1. Nearly all populations exhibit variation among individuals.
2. Individuals with advantageous traits will tend to have more offspring.
3. Advantageous traits will therefore become widespread in populations.

Variation in neck length in giraffes is an example. We know from fossils that early giraffes had relatively short necks. A few individuals, however, had slightly longer necks. In some localities, these giraffes had a feeding advantage because they could browse on leaves in taller trees. Consequently, in populations living where tall trees were common, longer-necked giraffes tended to have more offspring so that longer necks became more common.

If this process occurs with many traits over a long period of time, the population will eventually become very different from other populations and will create a new species. ▬ Figure 3–2 shows how isolation of populations promotes speciation. The different populations are exposed to different environments, which favor different traits, causing the populations to diverge through time. But when do two different populations become two different species? Biologists generally define a **species** as a group of individuals that can interbreed to produce fertile offspring (this definition applies only to sexual organisms; the issue of defining nonsexual species is a matter of debate in biological circles). A new species is therefore formed when members of a diverging population can no longer successfully mate with populations of the ancestral species. Closely related species, which have often diverged relatively

FIGURE 3-2
(a) Reduction of habitat may leave small isolated populations, called peripheral isolates. (b) Barriers may form to isolate small populations. (c) Out–migration to an isolated area may form small separated populations. In all cases (a–c), the small populations can evolve into new species. Isolated by thousands of miles of ocean, the Hawaiian honey-creeper has evolved into many forms, including species with short (d) and long (e) beaks. (*Source for (d) and (e)*: Jack Jeffrey.)

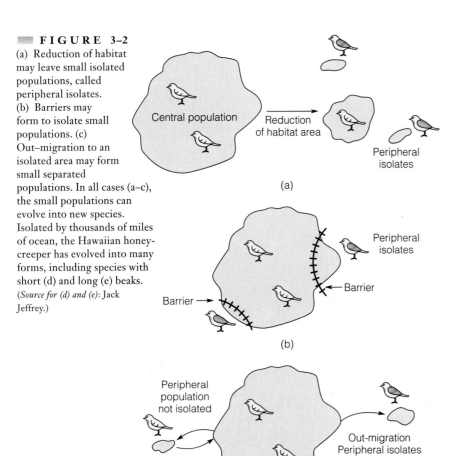

(d)

(e)

recently, are grouped together within the same genus. Similar genera are then grouped together within the same family. This method of classifying species according to hierarchically nested categories is a form of **taxonomy**. Applying this traditional system to humans, we have the following:

Kingdom Animalia

Phylum Chordata

Class Mammalia

Order Primates

Family Hominidae

Genus *Homo*

Species *H. sapiens**

Where does individual variation come from? This question is crucial because without the ini-

---

*Note that a species name must always be associated with a genic name or abbreviation (in this case *H.* for *Homo*). Thus humans are the species *Homo sapiens*; it is incorrect to call humans simply *sapiens*.

tial variation in the population, natural selection would have nothing to act upon. This question troubled Darwin himself because he was not aware of the work of Gregor Mendel who is credited with discovering the laws of inherited variation in 1865. Indeed, Mendel's work was not well publicized and was not rediscovered by scientists until the early 1900s. Mendel discovered that traits are passed on by **genes**, which are the basic units of heredity. Humans, for instance, have an estimated 50,000 to 100,000 genes that determine our traits. Variation in a population, or "gene pool," occurs because individuals possess different sets of genes that produce different traits. But how do different sets of genes arise? Reproduction is one way. Genes are shuffled when sperm and egg cells are fused causing offspring from the same parents to have different genes. A second cause of genetic variation is **mutation**, which is a spontaneous change in a gene. Genes are composed of **DNA** molecules, and mutations occur when DNA molecules are altered. Mutation is the ultimate source of all genetic variation.

Patterns of Diversification

Evolution through natural selection has produced an increasingly diverse biosphere, with the total number of species becoming greater through time. Initially, evolution was relatively slow. The right side of ▪ Figure 3–3 summarizes the evolution of life on Earth. For about 2 billion years after the first appearance of fossils, relatively few species of simple single-celled organisms, such as various bacteria and cyanobacteria (formerly known as blue-green algae), appear in the fossil record. A major change occurred about 1.5 billion years ago when more complex cells, called **eukaryotes** evolved. These cells had a true nucleus, chromosomes, and specialized cellular organelles such as mitochondria. Apparently, such complex cells were a main cause of increasing rates of evolution. Multicellular organisms, including sponge-like and jellyfish-like creatures, appeared in the oceans by at least 1 billion years ago. These probably evolved from colonies of single-celled eukaryotes, such as protozoa, that became progressively more specialized and integrated.

About 570 million years ago, the fossil record shows a rapid diversification sometimes called the **explosion of life**, when most of the major groups of animals first appear. Note in Figure 3–3 that this "explosion" corresponds to the time when modern oxygen levels were attained in the atmosphere. This permitted the evolution of more complex animals, which have a greater metabolic need for oxygen.

Following the explosion of life, living things diversified into new environments. As shown in Figure 3–3, life colonized the land (lithosphere) and the air (atmosphere) during the Paleozoic Era, which began with the explosion of life and ended with a global mass extinction. The Mesozoic Era, sometimes called the "age of dinosaurs," was the second major era, and it also ended with a mass extinction. The third and last era is the Cenozoic Era, sometimes called the "age of mammals." Although catastrophes, especially from global climate change, have temporarily caused species numbers to decrease at very rare intervals through mass extinctions, the overall trend throughout these eras is toward increasing numbers of species as life has adapted

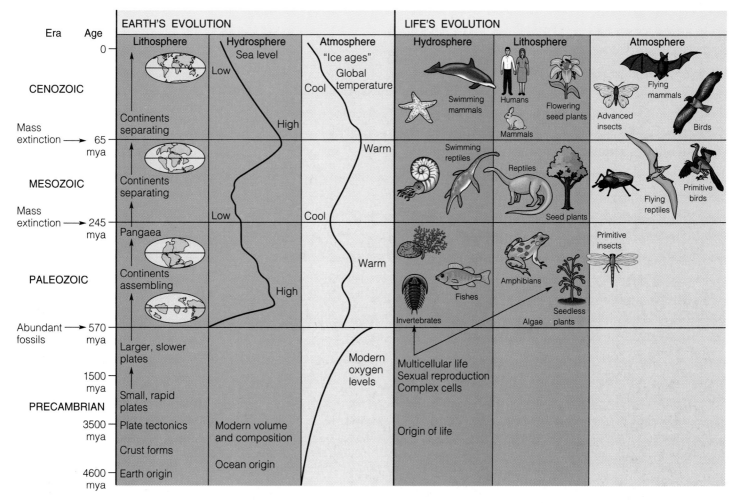

What Is "Ecology"?

The term "eco-" is derived from the Greek word *oikos*, which means "home." Since *logia* means "study of" in Latin, *ecology* is the "study of home." The word *economics* has the same derivation: *nomos* is Greek for "managing" so *economics* means "managing the house." Ironically, these two words—ecology and economics—which derive from the same word, are often thought to represent opposing interests. Even more ironically, "studying" the home and "managing" the home seem to have resulted in very different sets of priorities about how the home (that is, our environment) should be treated.

Henry David Thoreau was apparently the first to use the word *ecology* in one of his letters in 1858, but he did not give it a specific definition (and possibly Thoreau's *ecology* was simply a misspelling for some other intended word). Instead, the German biologist Ernest Haeckel is generally credited with introducing, in 1866, the word (originally spelled "oecologie") as it is now used in biology to mean the study of organisms and their interactions with each other and their physical environment.

Although scientists still use this technical definition, ecology has come to mean many other things, especially to nonscientists. As environmental awareness has risen over the last few decades and environmental issues have come to be discussed in social rather than scientific contexts, ecology has taken on new meanings. Thus, many people who express concern about the environment call themselves "ecologists" and are interested in "ecology." This label has even been extended to political ideologies that reflect these concerns. Thus, the political scientist William Ophuls has said that "ecology is a profoundly conservative doctrine in its social implications."

The confusion arises when ecology is expanded beyond its restricted meaning as a branch of biology that studies natural environments ("ecosystems") to refer to the social and political ideas of people who are actively concerned with preserving those natural environments ("ecosystems"). For reasons of clarity, we might do better to use *environmentalist* as a general term for someone who actively wants to *preserve* the natural environment, while reserving *ecologist* for scientists who *study* it. (Of course, a person can be, and often is, both an ecologist and an environmentalist.) Ophuls should say that *environmentalism* is a con-

servative doctrine because the "study" of something is not a doctrine at all: a doctrine is a system of beliefs.

In addition to being expanded to mean social and political environmental action, ecology has also been generalized as an academic term. Many students, perhaps even yourself, have enrolled in ecology courses expecting to learn about water pollution, solar power, and many other aspects of environmental problems. They are often surprised to find that the course focuses on the study of natural communities, unaltered by humans. While the study of natural laws governing such communities is basic to understanding how humans affect them, many students desire a broader perspective that includes pollution and other ways that humans modify the natural world. Environmental science, such as the course you are enrolled in now, has arisen in recent years to fulfill this need. Because environmental science is such a broad area of study, it is taught in a variety of traditional science departments, including biology, geology, chemistry, and geography. College courses labeled "ecology" are often primarily for students in biology or with interests in the specific study of natural communities.

to new environments and found "new ways of doing things" through mutation and natural selection. Ironically, we now live in a biosphere that is one of the most diverse in life's long history, although this will not be true in a few decades if current rates of species extinction continue (Chapter 12).

BIOSPHERE INTERACTIONS: POPULATIONS

The biosphere today, as in the past, is hierarchical: organisms, composed of atoms, molecules, and cells, are grouped into populations. Popula-

tions form communities, which then form ecosystems. Finally, ecosystems, when considered together, form the biosphere which subsumes all life on Earth (Fig. 3–4). This figure illustrates the interconnectedness of life because each level is composed of the units in the level below. Furthermore, the hierarchy is not static. Each level is dynamic, with many interactions occurring among its units. For instance, the organisms that compose populations interact in many ways, as do the populations that compose communities.

Ecology is the study of how organisms interact with each other and their physical environment. Because interactions occur at many levels in the hierarchy of life, ecology is very complex and often yields generalities and predictions that are less precise than we might wish. Partly because of this complexity, ecology has come to have a somewhat different meaning in popular usage (see Issues in Perspective 3–1).

The science of ecology, however, has advanced far since its formal origin over a century ago to provide us with a general understanding of how interactions in the hierarchy of life occur. Interactions among coexisting populations are among the most fundamental, so let us begin with them.

Population Dynamics

A **population** is a group of individuals of the same species living in the same area. There is no limit on the size of the area so a population may be all the bass in a lake or all the black bears in Alaska. Whatever the species or area, all populations undergo three distinct phases during their existence: (1) growth, (2) stability, and (3) decline (Fig. 3–5).

Growth occurs when available resources exceed the number of individuals able to exploit them, such as when a population is first introduced into an area. Individuals tend to reproduce rapidly, and death rates are relatively low because of the relatively abundant resources. Stability occurs when population growth levels off, as the environment becomes saturated with individuals of that population. However, stability is usually preceded by a population "crash" because the rapidly growing population abruptly exceeds the resources, causing an "overshoot" (Fig. 3–5; also Chapter 1). Even stable populations fluctuate, sometimes wildly, so stability does not mean that population abundance is unchanging. Usually, stability is the longest phase by far. Decline refers to the inevitable decrease in abundance that leads to extinction of all populations in the long term. Each of these three phases is affected by many factors; the study of how these factors interact is called population dynamics.

Growth of Populations

Nearly all populations have one key trait in common: they will grow exponentially if left unchecked (Chapter 1). This exponential growth occurs because individuals usually produce many more than one offspring in their lifetime. Furthermore, each of those offspring can, in turn, have many more. As a result, most populations have the potential to increase very rapidly. The potential for increase in a given population is called the **intrinsic rate of increase**, symbolized by r.

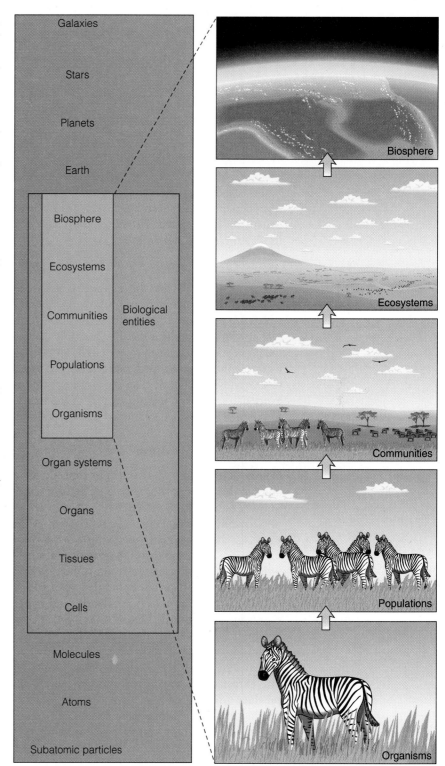

FIGURE 3–4

The cosmos can be depicted as a hierarchy from subatomic particles up through galaxies. Life, or biological entities, is at an intermediate level, ranging from cells through the biosphere.

FIGURE 3-5

Initially, a population will sometimes undergo exponential growth until it exceeds the capacity of the environment to support it, causing "overshoot." This phase is sometimes followed by a period of relative stability and eventually by decline.

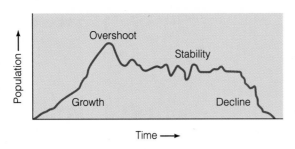

The exact intrinsic rate varies among populations depending on several factors, many of them genetically determined. Two of the most basic are the birth rate and death rate:

Intrinsic rate of increase = birth rate – death rate

This equation shows that the net rate of increase in a population is governed not only by the rate at which the population can multiply, but also by the rate at which individuals die. For example, bacterial populations have birth rates of millions per day while elephants have a birth rate of only one every few years. But bacteria also die by the millions every day so the net, intrinsic rate is dramatically lower than if it were determined by births alone.

Life History and Population Growth

Reproductive traits such as age at reproduction and number of offspring are major determinants of birth rate and thus intrinsic rate of increase. A population of organisms that reproduce at an early age and have many offspring will produce many more offspring through time than a population whose organisms delay reproduction and have only a few offspring. Ecologists refer to age of sexual maturation, age of death, and other events in an individual's lifetime that influence reproductive traits as the individual's **life history**.

Ecologists have traditionally depicted life history and population growth on a continuum. At one extreme are organisms that grow fast, reproduce quickly, and have many offspring per reproduction. At the other extreme are organisms that grow slowly, reproduce at a late age, and have few offspring per reproduction. For example, one reason bacteria have such a high intrinsic rate of population increase relative to elephants is that individual bacteria reproduce much more quickly. Many organisms have life history traits that fall into the intermediate range.

Age Structure and Population Growth

Population growth is also strongly influenced by the proportion of individuals of reproductive age.

Age structure refers to the relative proportion of individuals in each age group in a population. An age structure where most individuals are of reproductive and prereproductive age has a much greater potential for population growth than one that has more older individuals. Thus, a pyramid-shaped age structure has mostly individuals that have yet to reproduce while one that is narrower at the bottom has mostly individuals that have already reproduced (Fig. 3–6). Stable populations that maintain roughly constant abundances tend to have similar proportions of reproductive and prereproductive individuals. These patterns have enormous implications for human populations. As we will see in Chapter 5, developing countries often have pyramid-shaped population age structures so that their already strained economies are in danger of becoming even more burdened by future rapid population growth.

Population Stability: Regulation of Growth

Common sense tells us that nothing grows forever, and this is certainly true of populations. Growth is limited by a complex interaction of many factors, including other species.

The simplest way to examine abundance limits is to consider a species of microbe in a glass container (but the same analysis can be applied to any biological population, such as sheep on an island). When a few individuals are first admitted to the container, they will likely experience rapid population growth for the reasons we have just discussed. At some point, however, the limited space and food in the container will cause the multiplicative growth phase to enter a slower growth phase as net reproduction slows. Growth continues to slow until the population size stabilizes; that is, the population remains roughly constant, fluctuating around some average size. This average abundance where the population levels off is the **carrying capacity**, or the maximum population size that can be sustained by an environment for a long time. As noted earlier, the carrying capacity is usually briefly exceeded by an "overshoot" phase before the population levels off in the stability phase.

Four Basic Abundance Controls

What causes population size to level off and stabilize? Clearly, the ultimate cause is to be found in the environment: factors external to the population must be limiting the rate at which indi-

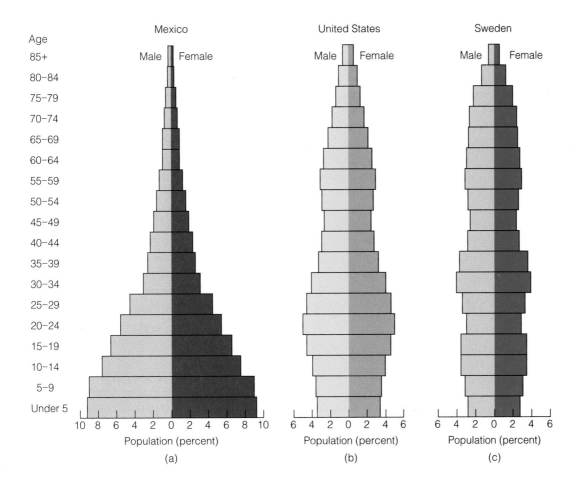

FIGURE 3–6
Three possible population age structures. (a) Mexico's age structure profile is typical of a rapidly growing population; (b) the profile of the United States indicates slower growth than for Mexico; and (c) Sweden's profile indicates a stable population.

viduals can reproduce and survive. Ecologists typically divide these environmental factors into two basic categories, the (1) physical and (2) biological environment. Within the biological environment, we can identify three subcategories of biological interactions that can limit population growth:

1. Physical environment
   - Physical limitations

2. Biological Environment
   - Competition
   - Predation
   - Symbiosis

Limitations of the physical environment include a vast number of constraints such as water supply, space availability, or soil and light in the case of plants. All constraints of the physical environment are determined by the population's **habitat**, which is the place where it lives. For example, the remaining Florida panther population currently lives in a wetland habitat including the Florida Everglades.

It only takes one aspect of the physical environment to limit population growth. For instance,

even if light, soil, temperature, and many other resources can support more plants, population abundance may be constrained far below that limit if a single resource, water, is scarce. This observation, which was made famous by the German botanist Justus Liebig in 1840, has come to be called the **law of the minimum**: growth is limited by the resource in the shortest supply.

Competition occurs when organisms require the same limited resource. Competition can take many forms, but two of the most important are exploitative and interference competition. Exploitative, or "scramble," competition occurs when both competing populations have equal access to the resource: the population that exploits the resource the fastest is the "winner." Interference competition occurs when one of the competitors prevents the other from gaining access. For instance, many plants secrete toxins that wash into surrounding soil to prevent other plants from encroaching and taking sunlight and soil nutrients.

A basic determinant of any competition is the organism's **niche**, which is often defined as the organism's "occupation" or how it lives. The niche includes what the organism eats, how it eats, and

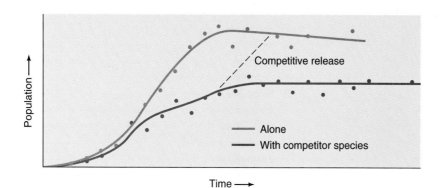

FIGURE 3–7

FIGURE 3–7
The population abundance of a *Paramecium* species increases when it is not raised with a competing species.

what eats the organism. The degree to which the niches of competing species overlap indicates the extent of similar resources required and therefore the strength of the competition between the species. **Competitive exclusion** occurs when niche overlap is very great and competition is so intense that one species eliminates the second species from an area. Although competitive exclusion has received much theoretical attention, some ecologists think it is relatively rare in nature. In contrast, species often compete for only one or a few resources. For example, foxes and owls in a forest may compete for mice, but each will also eat other prey that the other usually does not pursue. Such cases of minor niche overlap do not result in complete competitive exclusion. Instead, each competitor merely limits the abundance of the other. When the single-celled eukaryote *Paramecium aurelia* is raised alone, its population size is nearly twice as large as when it must share resources with a second species (Fig. 3–7).

An important result of competitive exclusion is that if one of two competing species is removed, the remaining species may increase in number. Thus the population of *P. aurelia* nearly doubles when the competitor is removed (Fig. 3–7). This is often called **ecological release** because the species is "released" from one of the factors limiting its abundance. In this case, some ecologists

would call it "competitive release," specifying release from competition. Humans often cause ecological release by selectively exterminating unwanted species; as a result, abundance controls are upset, and competitor species experience population booms. When farmers spray pesticides on crops, for example, they often find that another species increases its population numbers.

Predation occurs when organisms quickly kill and consume other living organisms. Predators can be divided into (1) carnivores, which prey on animals, and (2) herbivores, which prey on plants. As with competition, the extent to which predation limits abundance of prey varies considerably. In the most extreme cases, a predator drives the prey species to extinction. Many of the known cases of extinction have occurred when humans introduced a predator into a new area, especially an island. Much more commonly, predators simply limit abundance and do not drive the prey to extinction.

But why don't predators reproduce until they have eaten all the prey? At least three major reasons have been identified. For one thing, prey species have often evolved protective traits, such as camouflage, poisons, spines, large size, and so on. In addition, prey species often flee to refuges such as burrows and tree-tops where predators cannot reach them. Experiments have shown that an insect or microbe predator population in a container will consume the prey population unto extinction unless the prey can escape to a refuge. Finally, predators tend to engage in prey switching. When one prey species becomes scarce, predators switch to another prey, thereby allowing the first prey species to rebound in numbers.

Ecological release is also seen in predation control of abundance. When predator populations are greatly reduced by disease or other causes, or when prey populations move to an area without major predators (such as islands), the prey species may exhibit "predatory release" and expand in the same way populations expand when experiencing competitive release. Today, humans are a major cause of predator release both by killing off predators, such as mountain lions, and by introducing species into areas without major predators.

Symbiosis (*sym* = "together"; *biosis* = "life") encompasses many kinds of interactions, sometimes including competition and predation. As Table 3–1 shows, these interactions can be classified according to whether they benefit or inhibit one or both populations that are interacting. **Mutualism** benefits both species. An example of mu-

TABLE 3–1 *A Symbolic Classification of Symbioses*[a]

FORM OF SYMBIOSIS	SPECIES A	SPECIES B
Mutualism	+	+
Predation and parasitism	+	−
Commensalism	+	0
Competition	−	−
Amensalism	0	−
Neutralism	0	0

[a] + = benefit, − = detriment, 0 = no effect

FIGURE 3-8
Parasites, such as this leech, often do not kill their hosts. (*Source*: Visuals Unlimited/© Glenn Oliver.)

FIGURE 3-9
Commensal organisms, such as these barnacles, derive benefits from the turtle without harming it. (*Source*: Visuals Unlimited/© Neville Coleman.)

tualism is the coexistence of algae within the tissue of the tiny animals that build coral reefs. The algae are provided with a protected living space while the coral animals are supplied with nutrients from the algae's photosynthesis. Similarly, a lichen is actually a fungus and algae growing together symbiotically. Mutualism is thus a factor regulating the abundance of certain types of algae because their numbers are influenced by the abundance of coral or fungal hosts.

Parasitism is similar to predation in that one species benefits while harming the other species (Fig. 3–8). The main difference is that parasites act more slowly than predators and do not always kill the prey (host). **Commensalism** occurs when one species benefits and the other is not affected. For example, Spanish moss (a lichen) hangs from trees for support but causes the trees no great harm or benefit. Barnacles attach to crab shells in a similar way, deriving food from the surrounding water (Fig. 3–9). **Amensalism** occurs when one population inhibits another while being unaffected itself. Harm to one species is simply an incidental by-product of the actions of another. For example, when elephants crash through vegetation, they often have a detrimental effect on it, while gaining relatively few benefits (of course, the elephants get where they want to go).

The Real World: Complex Interaction of Abundance Controls

Our brief description of the various controls on abundance (physical fluctuations, competition, predation, and symbioses) has greatly oversimplified by discussing each control separately. In reality, most natural populations are governed not by a single control, but by several controls often acting simultaneously. When two populations of

beetles interact in the laboratory, for example, competition leads to a high abundance of one species and a very low abundance of another. When a third species, a parasite, is introduced, the formerly abundant species becomes the rarer one because it is more susceptible to the parasite (Fig. 3–10).

Now consider that natural communities are often composed of hundreds to many thousands of species. Any single population will often have many competitors, predators, and symbionts such as commensals. Abundance changes in any of these could have a major influence on the abundance of that population. At the same time, changes in physical conditions could also influence any of the populations, with each responding differently to a physical change. This complex interaction of abundance controls in natural ecosystems means that small changes in one control, such as the abundance of a prey species, can have a cascading domino effect throughout the ecosystem, causing other changes in the abundance of other species. Abundance of all species is therefore nearly always fluctuating in response to natural fluctuations in physical conditions and in other species.

Physically versus Biologically Controlled Systems

For over 60 years, ecologists have debated which of the abundance controls, if any, is the most important. Some have argued that physical factors play the major role. This is sometimes called

FIGURE 3–10
(a) With two competing species of beetles, the superior competitor can drive the other to a very low abundance. (b) The addition of a parasite can drive the formerly abundant species to rarity and allow the formerly rare species to increase. (*Source*: Modified from T. Park, *Ecological Monographs* 18 [1948]: 265–308. Reprinted with permission of Ecological Society of America.)

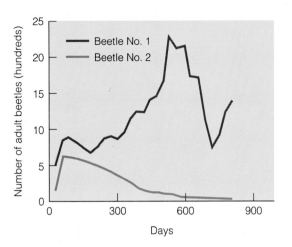

(a) Parasite absent

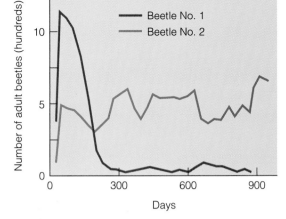

(b) Parasite added

density-independent regulation because physical processes usually operate independently of the present abundance. For example, a severe drought or storm can drastically reduce abundance of populations regardless of how many individuals exist when it strikes. Similarly, a volcanic eruption might kill all individuals on an island, whether there are dozens or millions. Other ecologists argue that biological interactions, especially competition and predation, are the major controls. This is sometimes called **density-dependent regulation** because current abundance plays a role in determining population change. For instance, the effect of a predator in reducing a prey species's abundance depends greatly on how many prey there are. As noted earlier, if a prey species's population becomes too low, the predator may switch to another prey.

Most ecologists now recognize that, in reality, population abundance is regulated by both physical and biological constraints, although one type of constraints may dominate in certain environments. We can depict environments on a continuum as in Figure 3–11. At one end are environments that are often subjected to physical disturbances or stress. An example is a beach, where wave action from storms and hurricanes can often cause great disturbances. At the other end are environments, such as the offshore tropical waters of a coral reef, where disturbances are rarer. Rapid changes in physical parameters such as water energy and temperature are neither common nor severe, so biological interactions are the major determinant controlling the abundance of the many reef species. But even in these extremes, many factors still interact to control abundance. For instance, even though physical processes may be the dominant regulators of abundance in beach environments, competition, predation, and other biological interactions are still occurring, affecting abundance.

Population Decline

While even stable populations rise and fall in abundance during fluctuations, given enough time, eventually most populations decline to zero and become extinct. Extinction is the elimination of all individuals in a group. In a local extinction, all individuals in a population are lost, but a new population can be reestablished from other populations of that species living else-

FIGURE 3–11
Population abundance is regulated by both physical and biological processes. In some environments, such as a beach, physical processes may play a much larger role than in other environments, such as a coral reef.

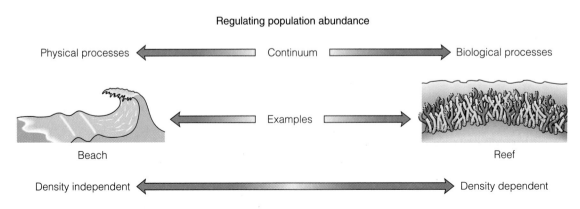

*E*NVIRONMENTAL PRINCIPLES   SECTION 1

where. Species extinction occurs when all populations of the species become extinct.

The inevitability of population decline is clear when we consider that over 99% of all species that have ever existed are now extinct. The vast majority of these became extinct before humans, so decline and extinction are natural processes. Ultimately, decline and extinction are caused by environmental change: one or more of the abundance controls becomes altered leading to an abrupt or gradual decline in abundance. For instance, many extinctions in the fossil record resulted largely from physical changes such as cooling temperatures. Similarly, the fossils reveal cases where competition from new groups apparently caused decline, such as when placental mammals invaded South America and replaced most marsupials.

Human Impact on Population Growth and Decline

Increasing human population and technology have caused progressively greater disruption in natural populations. Pollution, agriculture, and many other kinds of human alterations of the environment have destabilized populations by affecting the various abundance controls. Depending on the population, humans may cause (1) population growth by removing previous limitations or (2) population decline by imposing new limitations.

Human Impact on Population Growth

Populations grow when there is an excess of resources relative to the number of individuals available to exploit them. Humans commonly contribute to population growth in the four ways listed in ● Table 3–2; each involves removing a control on abundance.

Increase of available resources can be planned or unplanned. Agriculture and animal domestication are obvious examples of how humans can greatly increase the populations of plants and animals that they favor. We do this by providing far more food and other resources than those organisms would find in their natural state. The effect of humans on cat numbers provides a striking example. In England alone, domestic cats occur in such numbers that more than 300,000 cats must be destroyed each year. Yet before humans began to domesticate them a few thousand years ago (to catch mice in grain storage areas), the small, wild ancestors of our pet cats were relatively rare and were probably limited to the Middle East and Europe, a relatively small area compared to their present range. Similarly, corn,

potatoes, and many other domesticated organisms had much smaller ancestral ranges.

Unplanned increases in available resources by humans also have major effects. Pollutants, for example, generally represent unplanned releases of substances into water or air. These substances are often nutrients that are in short supply. Recall from Liebig's law of the minimum that growth is limited by the resources in shortest supply. Phosphorus and nitrogen are very often the two most limiting nutrients for plants in water or on land. When fertilizers rich in these nutrients are carried into rivers and lakes, the result is often runaway plant growth. This enrichment of nutrients in waters is called eutrophication. Eutrophication is a classic example of "too much of a good thing" because the decomposition of the accumulating plants uses up increasing amounts of oxygen, causing fishes and other organisms to suffocate.

Competitive release is common when humans try to eliminate a population of one species, allowing its competitors to increase in numbers. The most economically important examples occur when farmers try to eradicate pests from crops with pesticides. Because poison tolerance varies among species, some pests will not be killed by the poisons and will actually increase in numbers

TABLE 3–2 *Four Ways That Humans Cause Population Growth*	
	EXAMPLES
Increase available resources	Agriculture
	Nutrient pollution in lakes
Competitive release	Poisoning of insect pests
Predator release	Overhunting of large carnivores
Introduce to new areas	Game releases

when their competitors are gone. This is called a "secondary pest outbreak." A dramatic example occurred in Central America where cotton crops were sprayed in 1950 to kill boll weevils. The effort was highly successful until 1955, when populations of cotton aphids and cotton bollworms soared. When a new pesticide was used to remove them, five other secondary pests emerged. Such experiences have led to new methods of pest control (Chapters 13 and 15).

Predator release is common where humans hunt, trap, or otherwise reduce populations of predators, allowing the prey species's population to increase. For example, large mammalian predators such as wolves and panthers have long been the target of ranchers and farmers because they

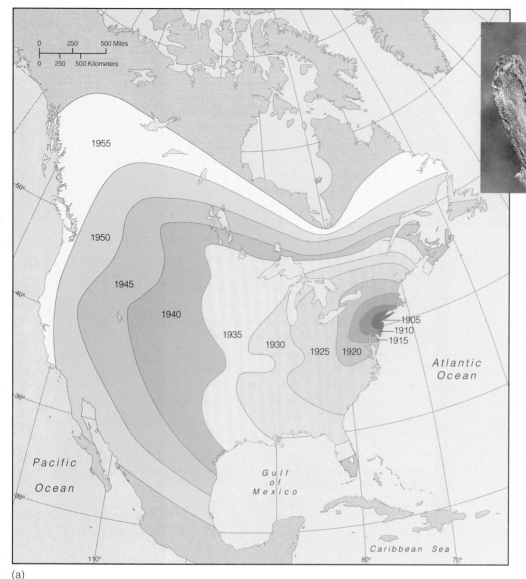

(b)

24 families of fishes have been successfully introduced into North America. The extent of this introduction is even more impressive considering that the vast majority of populations die out when initially introduced. A recent analysis of ballast water in a tanker revealed that it contained the live larvae of 367 species of marine organisms carried from Japan to the Oregon coast. Such ballast waters are routinely discharged. Once an organism is introduced and established, expansion can be quite rapid. The European starling covered North America in just a few decades after it was introduced in New York for a Shakespearean play in the early 1900s (■ Fig. 3–12).

■ **FIGURE 3–12**
(a) This map shows the rapid migration of the European starling across North America after its introduction in New York. (b) The European starling is now one of the most common birds in North America. (*Sources*: (a) C. B. Cox and P. Moore, *Biogeography* [Cambridge, Mass.: Blackwell, 1993], p. 62. Reprinted by permission of Blackwell Science, Inc.; (b) Harold Hoffman/Photo Researchers.)

prey on domesticated animals. The result has been a rapid increase in the predators' natural prey. Deer have shown an especially spectacular rise. Indeed, most experts estimate that more deer are now living in the United States than were here before Europeans arrived. Unfortunately, the excess populations often lead to overgrazing and death by starvation. For this reason, game hunting by humans is a justifiable activity, at least based on ecological criteria. By prudently culling deer and other prey, humans are essentially carrying out the role of predators that no longer exist.

Introduction of nonnative (also called "exotic") species into new areas may be the single greatest alteration of nature carried out by humans so far. Few people realize the enormous scale on which humans have, either accidentally or purposely, transferred organisms from one area to another. For example, more than 1500 insect species and

Human Impact on Population Decline

Humans are causing the decline and extinction of species at thousands of times the natural rate in nearly all parts of the biosphere. We will examine the causes of extinction in more detail in Chapter 12, but note here that humans alter the environment in four basic ways that cause population decline (● Table 3–3). All are directly related to the abundance controls. Habitat disruption occurs when humans disturb the physical environment in which a population lives. This disturbance can range from minor, such as mild chemical changes from air pollution, to major, such as total destruction of a forest by bulldozers or fire.

As Table 3–3 shows, humans change the biological environment in three ways that cause population decline. As we have seen, many new species have been introduced in various parts of the world. Introduced species are competitors, predators, or symbionts (including diseases and parasites) in the native biological system. Island species are especially susceptible to introduced species. An example of competitive decline in island species is the introduction of rabbits to Australia; the voracious appetite and rapid reproduction of rabbits led to decreased abundance of many native marsupials.

Human overkill is the shooting, trapping, or poisoning of certain populations, usually for sport or economic reasons. It is very difficult for humans to cause the extinction of "pest" species, such as roaches or mice, in this way because they are so abundant and reproduce so rapidly. However, overkill has been very effective in eliminating populations of large animals because they are much fewer and reproduce much more slowly. Leopards, elephants, rhinos, pandas, and many other large animals comprise a disproportionate number of threatened and endangered species in the world (Chapter 12). Secondary extinctions occur when a population is lost due to the extinction of another population on which it depends, such as a food species.

It is not necessary for these environmental changes to reduce a population to zero in order to cause extinction. Even if many individuals survive, the population may never recover if it becomes too small. Small populations are beset by many breeding problems, such as inbreeding and lack of mates, and are also more likely to become extinct from environmental fluctuations

such as hurricanes, droughts, and so on. Ecologists often refer to "minimum viable population" (MVP): if population abundance drops below the MVP, the population will probably never recover (Chapter 12).

Population Range

In addition to varying through time, abundance may vary geographically. Populations tend to have a maximum abundance near the center of their geographic range, which is the total area occupied by the population (Fig. 3–13). This central

TABLE 3–3 *Four Ways That Humans Cause Population Decline and Extinction*

The actions are listed in approximate order of importance in causing extinctions. In other words, habitat disruption causes the most extinctions today; secondary extinctions cause the least.

	EXAMPLES
Change physical environment:	
1. Habitat disruption	Draining a swamp, toxic pollution
Change biological environment:	
2. Introduce new species	New predator
3. Overkill	Big-game hunting
4. Secondary extinctions	Loss of food species

FIGURE 3–13
Organisms tolerate a range of conditions but thrive in an optimum range.

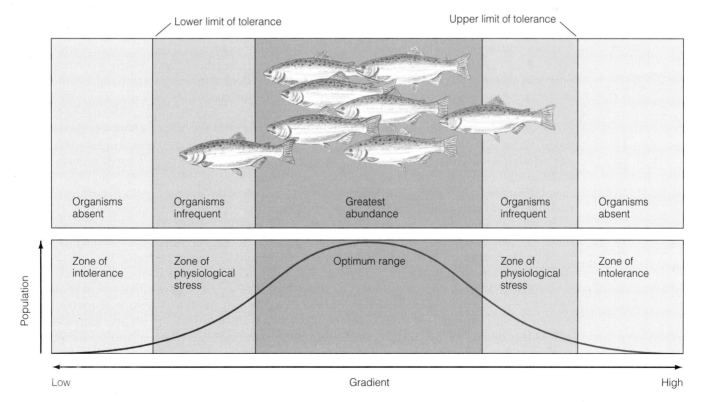

Lower limit of tolerance / Upper limit of tolerance

| Organisms absent | Organisms infrequent | Greatest abundance | Organisms infrequent | Organisms absent |

| Zone of intolerance | Zone of physiological stress | Optimum range | Zone of physiological stress | Zone of intolerance |

Population

Low   Gradient   High

FIGURE 3–14
The giant panda, which eats only bamboo, is an example of a specialized species. Such species are easily pushed to extinction. (*Source*: Jany Sauvanet/Photo Researchers.)

very patchy environment, individuals are commonly clumped together with gaps in between.

The size of the geographic range of populations also varies among species. **Endemic species** are localized and may have just one population that inhabits only a small area. This pattern is especially common in tropical organisms and in organisms that are highly specialized to live on resources with limited distributions or that have narrow environmental tolerances ( Fig. 3–14).

Human Impact on Population Ranges

Humans have both decreased and expanded the geographic ranges of populations. On the one hand, range decrease has commonly accompanied declining populations and extinction. Habitat destruction such as cutting down trees can also reduce a population's range. If the habitat disappears, the population's geographic range can be reduced to zero. This is a major reason why tropical extinctions are particularly destructive; with the high number of endemic populations, it does not take much habitat destruction to reduce the geographic range to zero. On the other hand, we saw how humans have often expanded geographic range by domesticating and introducing wild species into new areas (see Fig. 3–12).

ℬIOSPHERE INTERACTIONS: COMMUNITIES AND ECOSYSTEMS

A **community** consists of all populations that inhabit a certain area. The size of this area can range from very small, such as a puddle of water, to large regions encompassing many hundreds of square miles (or thousands of km²). The extent of a community thus depends on the size of the area one wishes to denote. An **ecosystem** is the community plus its physical environment. Therefore, ecosystems can also be delineated at many spatial scales.

Because ecosystems include both organisms and their physical environment, the study of ecosystems often tends to focus on the movement of physical components, such as the flow of energy and the cycling of matter, through the "system." This approach is often called the "functional" view. In contrast, because communities consist only of organisms, one can focus on describing how organisms are distributed in communities through time and space: this approach is called the "structural" view. We turn first to the community, or structural, view.

maximum occurs where the physical and biological factors that control abundance are the most favorable. As one moves away from this central optimum into the zone of physiological stress, abundance generally begins to decline. This decline is usually gradual because both physical and biological limiting factors tend to follow a gradient. Physical conditions such as temperature and salinity usually change gradually geographically, as do biological limits such as the abundance of competitors and predators. Eventually, the zone of physiological stress grades into the zone of intolerance, where the population is absent. The zone of intolerance occurs because some limiting factor has become so great that the species can no longer survive.

Abundance is almost never uniformly distributed throughout a population's geographic range because the environment is rarely uniform enough to follow perfect gradients. Instead, many irregularities occur; ecologists call this the patchiness of the environment. In populations that inhabit a

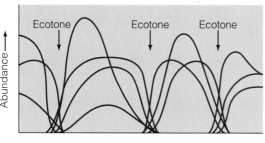

(a) Closed communities

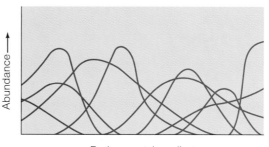

(b) Open communities

FIGURE 3-15
Each curve represents the abundance of a single species. (a) In closed communities, the species boundaries tend to coincide. (b) In open communities, the species boundaries are more randomly distributed. (*Source*: R. E. Ricklefs, *Ecology*, 3d ed. [New York: W. H. Freeman, 1990], p. 659. Copyright © 1990 by W. H. Freeman and Company. Used with permission.)

Community Structure

Populations are not randomly distributed in communities. Indeed, discovering the various spatial patterns by which species are distributed has been one of the major accomplishments of ecology over the last century. Two of the most important patterns are the open structure of communities and the relative rarity of most species in communities.

Open Structure of Communities

A key question about community structure is whether the populations that comprise a community have about the same geographic range and abundance peaks. Proponents of *closed community* structure argued that populations in most communities had similar range boundaries and abundance peaks. A closed community was thus a discrete unit with sharp boundaries called **ecotones** (Fig. 3–15a). In contrast, proponents of open communities argued that most communities had populations with highly varied abundance peaks and range boundaries. Open communities were said to have populations distributed more-or-less randomly relative to one another (Fig. 3–15b).

Decades of data collection have finally resolved this debate, showing that most communities are indeed open. For example, populations of the many plants comprising a typical forest community have highly varied ranges that almost appear randomly distributed. In the case of forests, tolerance to moisture is a major determinant: some species do best in wetter areas while others thrive in a wide range of moisture. As a result, population ranges very often overlap to various degrees depending on how similar the populations' tolerances to moisture are. Areas where drastic changes occur in the physical environment are the major exception to the generally open structure of communities. In such areas, boundaries between communities can be sharp because population tolerances are abruptly exceeded. A beach where land and sea come together, producing an ecotone, is an example. Because changes in the physical environment are usually more gradual, population abundance between communities also changes gradually.

The fact that communities are not closed makes their study more complicated because it is difficult to characterize, describe, and even name a community when it changes gradually in nearly every geographic direction. Ecologists often use advanced statistical methods, such as gradient analysis, to quantitatively describe the spatial changes in species composition. At any point along the gradient, the community is usually assigned a name on the basis of the most common species. One might refer to an oak-hickory forest community or a barnacle–blue mussel tidal zone community.

Another major implication of open communities is that communities are not tightly integrated assemblages of organisms that can be destroyed in an all-or-nothing fashion. Some ecologists once argued that communities were closed, highly-integrated units forming a "superorganism." They maintained that if we destroyed just one or a few populations, the whole superorganism would die, just as an organism dies if a key organ is removed. The fact that species come and go in communities, however, means that communities are generally not as integrated as the superorganismic concept said. This point is significant because many nonscientists still hold the superorganismic concept of biological communities.

Most Species Are Rare in Communities

A second basic population pattern is the relatively low abundance of most populations in communities. As we have seen, populations tend to have their peak abundance near the center of their range, where optimum conditions prevail. In the example of the forest community above, optimum moisture level seems to be a primary determinant of abundance. At any given point on the gradient, however, a large percentage of the individuals belong to just a few tree species. Even at their maximum abundance, most populations are much less abundant than a few dominant populations such as beech, maple, oak, and pine.

This high population abundance of only a few species is found in nearly all natural communities and in many kinds of organisms. From deep-ocean to mountain communities, populations of just a few species almost always dominate in abundance, with many species being represented by only a few individuals. The result is a logarithmic pattern because when we plot the number of individuals per species, the number of species with few individuals rises rapidly.

What causes this abundance dominance by a few species? This question is currently being debated among ecologists, but most agree that the general cause is related to resource partitioning. In any environment, a limited amount of resources is available. Because of their evolutionary history, individuals of only a few species are best able to exploit a large part of the available resources. These species were the first to evolve the ability to obtain and eat a common food in the community. Other species must partition the remaining resources and are therefore less abundant. A species that is very rare in one community, however, may be very abundant in a nearby community if conditions are different enough that the species's particular adaptations are more effective in exploiting the resources there.

Kinds of Communities

Many thousands of communities exist on the Earth. Rather than describe each in detail, we will examine the basic categories into which communities can be grouped.

The most basic distinction is between terrestrial (land) and aquatic (water) dwelling communities. The terrestrial group is often considered to include six major types of biomes (■ Fig. 3–16); the aquatic group includes two:

1. *Terrestrial.* Tundra, grassland, desert, taiga, temperate forest, tropical forest (including tropical rainforests).
2. *Aquatic.* Marine, freshwater.

A **biome** is a large-scale category that includes many communities of a similar nature.

Both terrestrial and aquatic biomes (and thus the communities within them) are largely deter-mined by climate, especially temperature. Climate is so important because it affects many aspects of the physical environment: rainfall, air and water temperature, soil conditions, and so on. Many secondary factors such as local nutrient availability, are also important, however. In all cases, biomes illustrate the key point that species will often adapt to physical conditions in similar ways, no matter what their evolutionary heritage. For instance, a desert biome in the western United States looks similar to a desert biome in North Africa even though the plants have different ancestries.

Terrestrial Biomes

● Table 3–4 describes six basic land biome types. The tundra and desert biomes represent adaptations to the extreme conditions of very low temperature and low water, respectively. Not surprisingly, communities in these biomes tend to have the least number of species because organisms have difficulty adapting to the extreme physical conditions. In contrast, the tropical rainforests tend to be richest in species, in part because the tropics have the most moderate conditions.

■ Figure 3–17, page 79, shows the distribution of the major land biomes, by altitude and latitude. This figure demonstrates the importance of temperature, which decreases with both increasing altitude and increasing latitude; similar changes result in both cases. The more detailed global view in ■ Figure 3–18, page 80, shows some of the true complexities of the latitudinal pattern. For example, tropical forests are not always neatly confined to equatorial areas, and there are various types of tropical forests, such as tropical scrub and tropical rainforests.

Aquatic Biomes

In general, conditions in water are much less harsh than those on land. Water experiences many fewer temperature fluctuations and provides more buoyancy as support against gravity. All of these differences occur because water, as a liquid medium, is much denser than the gaseous air. Most important perhaps, living in water eliminates the danger of drying out, whereas water is often scarce on land. Not surprisingly, then, life originated in the oceans and took many millions of years to adapt to land. Yet even though water covers about 71% of the Earth's surface, most of it contains relatively little life; most of the open ocean is a vast aquatic desert with few nutrients.

EnviroNet
www.jbpub.com/environet

(a)

(b)

FIGURE 3-16
Six major terrestrial biomes
(clockwise from top left):
(a) Canadian tundra; (b)
natural grassland in South
Dakota; (c) the Mojave desert;
(d) taiga forest in Canada; (e)
temperate forest in the Great
Smoky Mountains; (f) tropical
rainforest in Australia.
(*Sources*: (a) Joe McDonald/
Visuals Unlimited; (b) Ron
Spomer/Visuals Unlimited; (c)
Simon Fraser/Science Photo
Library/Photo Researchers; (d)
Dean DeChambeau; (e) Dick
Poe/Visuals Unlimited; (f) D.
Cavagnaro/Visuals Unlimited.)

(f)

(c)

(d)

(e)

TABLE 3-4 *Six Major Land Biomes*

The biomes are listed in approximate order going from the equator to the poles.

1. *Tropical rainforest.* The most complex and diverse biome, containing over 50% of the world's species while occupying only 7% of the land area. This high diversity is largely due to the relatively constant temperatures at all times: daily and seasonal changes (fluctuations) are usually less than a total of 9°F (5° C). Rainfall is very heavy, over 80 inches (200 cm) annually. Major plants include deciduous trees that form a multilayered canopy, including understory trees. Herbs and shrubs that tolerate intense shade form the ground flora. Insects are extremely abundant; perhaps 96% of insect species are found here.

2. *Grasslands.* Rainfall is scarce, about 10–30 inches (25–75 cm) per year, causing grasses to be the most prominent plants. Fires are common. Major animals include grazers, such as the bison in North America. Economically, this is the most important biome, providing grazing land for sheep, cattle, and other food animals, as well as the richest cropland in the world. The rich soils are formed by the relative lack of rain and held in place by grass roots.

3. *Deserts.* Rainfall is very scarce, less than 10 inches (25 cm) per year. Temperatures can be very hot or very cold. Desert plants are widely spaced to allow maximum moisture per plant. Plant adaptations to arid conditions include (1) storage of water as in cacti, (2) shedding leaves in dry periods by deciduous shrubs, and (3) rapid growth and reproduction during rare rainy periods. Animal adaptations are similar to plants, with some storing large amounts of water (such as camels) and others exhibiting rapid growth and reproduction after rains (such as desert toads).

4. *Temperate forests.* Rainfall is abundant, 30–60 inches (75–150 cm per year), with distinct seasonal change. Deciduous trees dominate, such as oak and hickory (western United States) and beech and maple (north-central United States). Ground cover of shrubs and herbs. These forests lack the spectacular diversity of tropical forests, but are still more diverse than coniferous forests. Animals include deer, foxes, squirrels, raccoons, and many other familiar forms.

5. *Taiga.* Also called coniferous forests, these occur in a broad belt in northern North America and Asia. Diversity is relatively low. Plants are dominated by conifers (evergreens), which are tolerant of dry, cold conditions. Prominent types of evergreens include spruce, firs, and pines whose needles conserve water and withstand freezing better than leaves. Animals include moose, snowshoe hare, wolves, and grouse. Due to acidic, thin soils, cleared taiga makes poor cropland.

6. *Tundra.* An extensive treeless plain whose topsoil is frozen all year except for about 6 weeks in summer. Below this is permafrost soil, which is frozen all year long and poses a hazard for building. During the brief summer thaw, life grows and reproduces rapidly. Lichens (algae and fungi symbionts), grasses, and small shrubs are dominant plants. Prominent animals include caribou (reindeer), arctic hare, arctic fox, and snowy owl. Many migratory birds arrive for the rich summer growing season, characterized by billions of insects, bright flowers, and marshy conditions.

Aquatic communities do not divide into distinctive biomes like those found on land because the liquid state of water makes nonclimatic conditions more important in determining what can live in a particular environment. Water is a powerful solvent and also readily carries many substances in suspension; these substances, which range from toxins to nutrients, influence life locally. Furthermore, water readily transports heat so warm currents, such as the Gulf Stream, can warm large areas even near the poles. This prevents a simple latitudinal gradient from forming. Therefore, ecologists often designate only two aquatic biomes: the marine biome and the freshwater biome.

Marine waters differ from fresh waters in containing more dissolved minerals (salts) of various kinds. On average, marine waters have about 3.5% salt, mainly sodium chloride, and many other materials as well. The marine biome is the largest biome by far (over 70% of the Earth's surface), but can be subdivided relatively easily into (1) **benthic** (bottom-dwelling), and (2) **pelagic** (water column) zones (Fig. 3–19, page 81). Benthic communities are further subdivided by depth: littoral (shore), continental shelf, and abyssal (deep-sea, including the hydrothermal vent communities mentioned in Chapter 2). Benthic organisms include burrowers (such as worms), crawlers (such as snails), and stationary filter-feeders (such as barnacles). Pelagic organisms include (1) planktonic organisms (floaters) and (2) nektonic organisms (swimmers). The **photic zone** is the upper part of the biome where light penetrates; usually, this zone extends to about 150 feet (46 m) below the water surface. The photic zone is the main zone of photosynthesis and therefore is crucial to life in the

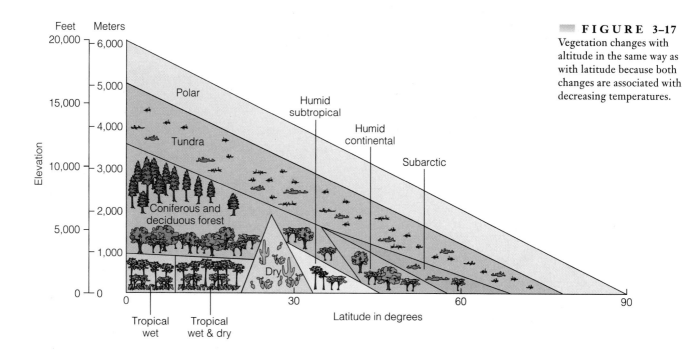

biome. The photosynthesizing plants, which form the base of the marine food pyramid, are mainly tiny planktonic organisms, such as diatoms. Much of the ocean is too deep for light to penetrate and drive the photosynthetic food base, though, so life is largely absent. Another reason why much of the ocean is a "biological desert" is that many nutrients in the ocean flow in from land and consequently are found only close to shore.

The freshwater biome can be subdivided into two zones: running water, such as rivers and streams, and standing water, such as lakes and ponds. Rivers and streams are not sharply delineated from lakes and ponds. In general, rivers and lakes are larger and more permanent than streams and ponds. The faster motion of running waters tends to keep them more highly oxygenated and more difficult to pollute. The slower motion of water in lakes and ponds leads to *stratification* of the water: the uppermost layer of water has plenty of oxygen while the oxygen decreases with depth. The uppermost layer is also much warmer during the summer and cooler during the winter than the lower layers. Most of the mixing between the uppermost and deeper layers occurs during seasonal changes known as spring and fall overturn. Like the marine biome, the freshwater biome has benthic (bottom-dwelling) and pelagic (swimming and planktonic) organisms and communities. Most of these have relatives in the marine realm (clams, snails, fishes, and plankton, for example), where the groups originated hundreds of millions of years ago.

Community Diversity

Diversity refers to how many kinds of organisms occur in a community. Diversity is therefore often expressed in terms of species richness, or the number of species in a community. Many factors influence diversity, and the importance of any single factor varies with the particular community. Nevertheless, most of these factors can be summarized by two diversity trends. The **latitudinal diversity gradient** describes how species richness in most groups steadily decreases going away from the equator. Consequently, richer communities are found in tropical areas. For instance, 2.5 acres (1 hectare) of tropical forest typically contain from 40–100 tree species. In contrast, a typical temperate zone forest has about 10–30 tree species while a taiga forest in northern Canada has only 1–5 species. Furthermore, the number of insect species living on those trees increases with the kinds of trees (resources) available to exploit, so tropical forests also have vastly more kinds of insects and other animal species per acre. As a result of this richness, habitat destruction in tropical countries generally leads to many more extinctions per acre than destruction elsewhere (Chapter 12).

Ecologists generally agree that this gradient is largely due to three interrelated factors: (1) environmental stability, (2) community age, and (3) length of growing season. Greater environmental stability in equatorial areas means that communities are exposed to less environmental change on a daily, seasonal, and even hundred-

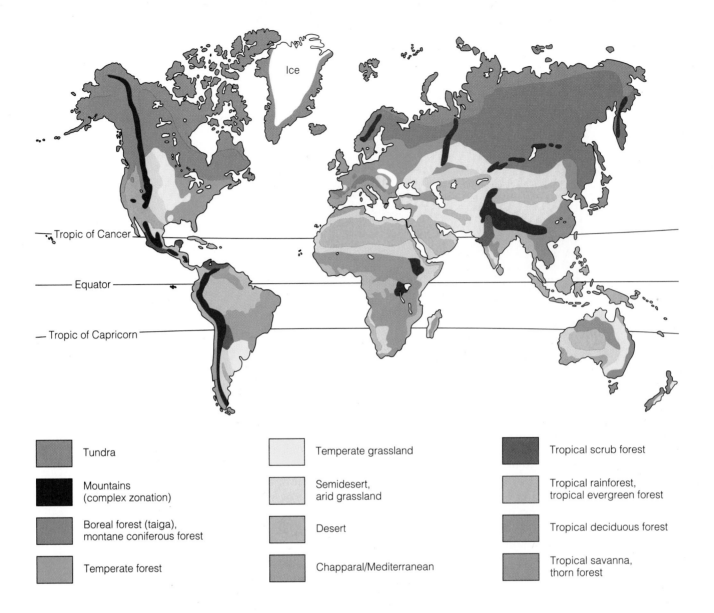

	Tundra		Temperate grassland		Tropical scrub forest
	Mountains (complex zonation)		Semidesert, arid grassland		Tropical rainforest, tropical evergreen forest
	Boreal forest (taiga), montane coniferous forest		Desert		Tropical deciduous forest
	Temperate forest		Chapparal/Mediterranean		Tropical savanna, thorn forest

FIGURE 3–18
Major terrestrial biomes of the world.

year basis. This stability allows more kinds of species to thrive because high disturbance or stress generally reduces diversity. Equatorial communities are older because they have been less disturbed by advancing ice sheets and other climatic changes over the long span of geologic time. Hence evolution has had more time to create new species. The longer growing season in equatorial areas leads to more photosynthesis and plant growth, which forms the food base for all life. As we will see, higher plant productivity supports a greater diversity of organisms that depend on the plants.

The second important diversity trend is the **depth diversity gradient** found in aquatic communities. This gradient shows how species richness increases with water depth, down to about 6560 feet (2000 m) deep, and then begins to decline. This gradient is due to (1) environmental stability and (2) nutrients. Environmental stabil-

ity increases as one moves away from the higher water energies of the beach and shoreline. As we have seen, stability allows more species to thrive. Similarly, as one moves offshore, the amount of nutrients from land runoff begins to diminish. Thus, even though deep water is very stable, it contains insufficient nutrients to permit the high productivity seen in shallower waters. Marine life depends especially on land runoff to supply limiting nutrients such as phosphorus.

To summarize, four major factors may increase diversity in any community: increasing environmental stability, age, growing season, and nutrients. Stability provides an accommodating environment for diversity to proliferate, age provides the time, and the last two factors provide the energy and nutrients to supply many types of organisms. In general, the more of these factors that a community has, the more species-rich it will be.

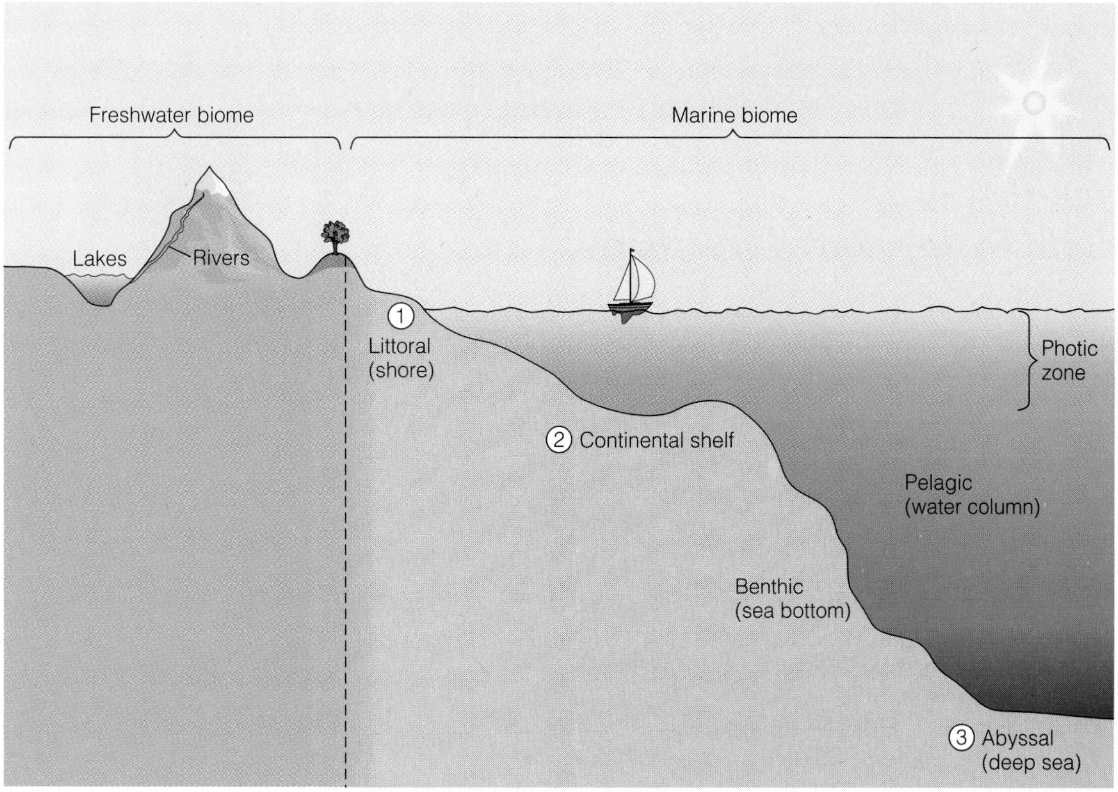

FIGURE 3–19
The two aquatic biomes are
freshwater and marine. The
marine biome can be divided
into benthic and pelagic
zones.

Community Change through Time

Biological communities change through time. This is not surprising since the physical environment that ultimately supports life is always changing. Whether we perceive change as "fast" or "slow" depends almost entirely on the time scale we are using. Two time scales are particularly useful for examining change in communities: ecological time and geological time. Ecological time focuses on community events that occur on the order of tens to hundreds of years. These events are most relevant to our own human time scale. Geological time focuses on community events that are longer, on the order of thousands of years or more, such as evolution.

Community Succession

Community succession is the sequential replacement of species in a community by immigration of new species and the local extinction of old ones. Community succession is initiated by a disturbance that creates unoccupied habitats for colonizing species. These colonizers usually have a hardy nature and are adapted for widespread dispersal and rapid growth, characteristics that enable them to become the first species to appear and thrive (see Issues in Perspective 3-2). This initial community of colonizing species is called the **pioneer community**. Eventually, other species migrate into the community. These new species are usually poorer dispersers and slower growing than the colonizers, but they are more efficient specialists and better competitors and therefore begin to replace the colonizers. This process continues, as still newer species migrate in, until the **climax community** is reached. The climax community, continues to change, although at a much slower pace.

Succession has been most fully documented in forest communities (█ Fig. 3–20, page 83). Pioneering plant species include lichens, mosses, and herbs, which give way to shrubs, small trees, and finally large trees in the climax community. Various animals, such as the bird and mammal species shown, also appear in sequence. The animal sequence is determined largely by the appearance of the plants they rely on.

Succession is characterized by a number of trends (● Table 3–5, page 84). One of the most basic is the decrease in productivity. Pioneering plants tend to be smaller in size and exhibit rapid growth that maximizes productivity. In later stages, as more specialized, slower-growing species begin to migrate in, productivity declines. As these later species immigrate, diversity increases because the more specialized species more finely subdivide the resources. In addition, the later species generally have larger size and longer life cycles. Together, these trends result in

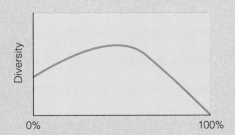

Can Destruction Be Good?
The Intermediate Disturbance Hypothesis

Most of us intuitively think of environmental disturbances as undesirable, negative events. Pollution, forest fires, the introduction of exotic species, and many other events that destroy organisms are regarded as invariably bad. Yet many ecologists are concluding that, in the long run, such disturbances can be beneficial for the diversity of biological communities.

How can destruction promote diversity? Consider an environment where there is little or no change. After a long time, the community often becomes dominated by a relatively small number of species. Some may be better competitors, such as toxin-secreting plants; others may be better at evading predators, such as speedy animals. For these and other reasons, some species will eventually disappear from the community.

In contrast, if the environment is disturbed, the dominant species may be removed from the disturbed area. Perhaps a fire destroys a few acres of forest. Such a

disturbance "cleans the slate" and opens up the area for species that might otherwise have been excluded by the more competitive and dominant species. Pioneer species, which are adapted for colonizing disturbed areas, are likely to be the first inhabitants after the disturbance (Fig. 1a). Eventually, these pioneers may be excluded by the dominants if no further disturbances occur and community succession takes its course. But if another disturbance occurs nearby, the pioneers can move on.

But just as too little disturbance is bad for diversity, so is too much disturbance. If the fire or other destruction occurs over too wide an area, it could wipe out many species, including both dominants and pioneers. Thus, ecological disturbances, like most things in life, are perhaps most beneficial in moderation (Fig. 1b). This concept has been encapsulated in the intermediate disturbance hypothesis of ecology: maximum diversity in an area is promoted when relatively small, localized

disturbances occur in parts of the area. These disturbances allow dominant species to persist in undisturbed parts and colonizing species to live in the newly disturbed parts. The net diversity of the whole area is therefore greater than if the environment were completely unchanging or completely disturbed (Fig. 2).

FIGURE 2

Moderate disturbances may promote greater diversity than either no disturbance or total disturbance.

FIGURE 1

(a) Forest fires, such as this one in Yellowstone, will often kill many species. (b) But such disturbances create new opportunities for other,

"disturbance-adapted," species. (*Source*: (a) © *Seattle Times*/Gamma Liaison; (b) © Nathan Farb/Gamma Liaison.)

(a)

(b)

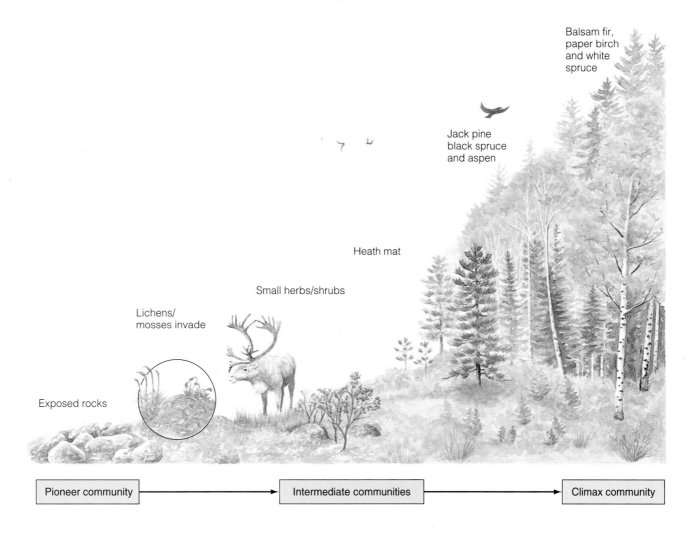

Balsam fir, paper birch and white spruce

Jack pine black spruce and aspen

Heath mat

Small herbs/shrubs

Lichens/ mosses invade

Exposed rocks

| Pioneer community | → | Intermediate communities | → | Climax community |

FIGURE 3–20
Ecological succession occurs when biological communities become established in a sequence, from pioneer through climax communities.

more biomass in later stages because living tissue accumulates. **Biomass** is the total weight of living tissue in a community. Finally, later stages tend to have populations controlled mainly by biological or density-dependent controls such as competition and predation. In contrast, early stages mainly show physical or density-independent controls, such as physical disturbance. Some communities, such as a beach, are generally in a constant state of physical disturbance so early-successional populations become permanent dwellers.

Succession occurs because each community stage, from pioneer to climax, prepares the way for the stage that follows. Soil conditions, nutrient availability, temperature, and many other environmental traits are altered by each preceding community. For example, the pioneering stage of a forest stabilizes the soil of a bare patch of land, begins to accumulate nutrients in the soil, attracts pollinating insects, retains water, and provides ground shade, among many other processes that make the environment more livable for later stages. The process of "preparation"

is ironic in the sense that species in each community often bring about their own demise. Yet these early species are adapted by evolution to be colonists and can nearly always migrate to other, newly disturbed areas that permit them to persist. Thus, nearly all natural landscapes (including sea-bottom areas) consist of a mosaic of undisturbed patches intermixed with patches that are disturbed to varying degrees. Ecologists think that this "patchiness" of the natural environment is crucial for maintaining diversity because it allows species from different stages of succession to exist simultaneously.

Community Evolution

Since communities are composed of populations of species, communities must also evolve. A comparison of a typical community from the Paleozoic Era, about 500 million years ago, with a typical community from the Cenozoic Era, living today, would reveal not only that the species composition of the communities differs, but that the present-day community contains more species.

TABLE 3–5 *Trends in Ecological Succession*

	STAGE IN ECOSYSTEM DEVELOPMENT	
ATTRIBUTE	Early	Late
Biomass	Small	Large
Productivity	High	Low
Food chains	Short	Long, complex
Species diversity	Low	High (?)
Niche specialization	Broad	Narrow
Feeding relations	General	Specialized
Size of individuals	Smaller	Larger (?)
Life cycles	Short, simple	Long, complex
Population control mechanisms	Physical	Biological
Fluctuations	More pronounced	Less pronounced
Mineral cycles	Open	More or less closed
Stability	Low	High
Potential yield to humans	High	Low

(*Source*: Adapted from R. Smith, *Elements of Ecology and Field Biology* [New York: Harper & Row, 1977]. Table 8–9: Trends in Ecological Succession from *Elements of Ecology and Field Biology* by Robert Leo Smith. Copyright © 1978 by Robert Leo Smith. Reprinted by permission of HarperCollins Publishers, Inc.)

The main reason why the global diversity of life has increased through time (Chapter 12) is that organisms have evolved "new ways of doing things." For instance, there were fewer burrowers on the Paleozoic sea floor because evolution had not yet produced organisms, such as clams with enhanced digging muscles, capable of burrowing to great depths in the sediment. As species become more specialized and find new ways to exploit resources in the physical environment, evolution produces communities with more species per unit area, a development called species packing.

Human Disturbance of Communities

Community structure is determined by species distributions, so whenever species distributions change, the structure is altered. We have seen that humans change natural species distributions in many ways from introducing new predators into pristine ecosystems to outright annihilation of large areas of habitat. However, the basic effect of nearly all human activity is community simplification: the reduction of overall species diversity (number of species).

In many cases, humans simplify communities on purpose. The farmer's agricultural and the suburbanite's horticultural communities of plants, insects, and other animals are common examples. In such cases, we seek to grow only certain species, creating a much lower diversity than normally is found in that area. The extreme case is called **monoculture**, meaning that only one particular species is grown. An example is a wheat field. Monocultures and other forms of extreme community simplification are very susceptible to diseases and other forms of destruction, such as the Irish Potato Famine. It is interesting to note that most of the plant species we cultivate for food and pleasure are species from pioneering communities. For example, corn, wheat, and many other plants are grasses that were originally adapted to colonizing disturbed areas. Humans favor them as food because they are fast-growing, rapidly reproducing organisms.

In other cases, humans inadvertently simplify communities. Construction, road building, pollution, and many other aspects of "development" act as disturbances that simplify communities. It is important to note that such stressed communities are simplified not only by having fewer species, but also by having some species that are superabundant. Although most species cannot tolerate the stressful conditions, some find the new conditions beneficial. For instance, some organisms thrive in highly polluted waters and even use the pollutants as food. Even in these inadvertent disturbances, we often favor early-successional species. Whether we are building roads, farms, cities, or lawns, one of our first actions is to bulldoze or otherwise remove the climax community. Because colonizing disturbed environments is what early-successional species are adapted to do, they have tended to thrive as we have expanded. Indeed, the term *weed* is virtually synonymous with early-successional species, which also include "weedy" animals, such as some mice and many insects. Issues in Perspective 3–2 discusses the possibility that disturbances may sometimes be beneficial.

Ecosystems and Community Function

Although communities vary in structure, certain basic processes, or functions, unite them all. The most basic processes are (1) energy flow and (2) matter cycling. All organisms must eat (take in energy and matter) to stay alive, causing energy and matter to move through the community. All energy and matter ultimately come from, and return to, the physical environment. We must therefore observe the ecosystem (community plus physical environment) to understand the complete process.

As Chapter 4 will discuss in detail, energy flows and matter cycles through all four of the environmental spheres. The movement of energy and matter through ecosystems represents move-

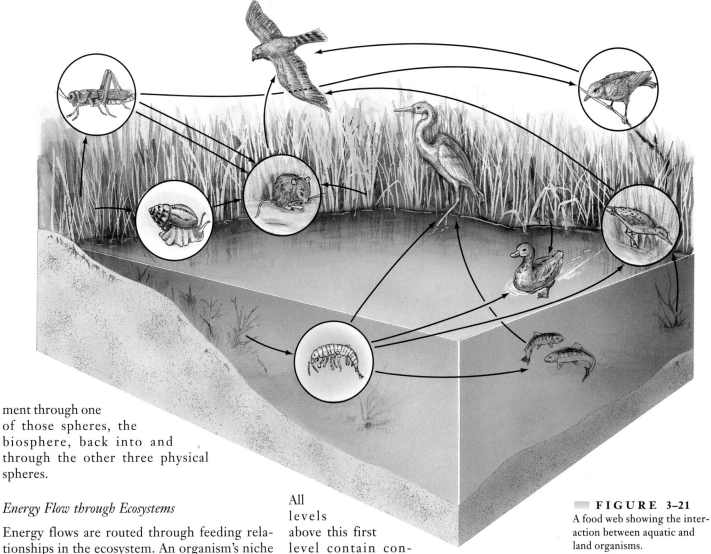

ment through one
of those spheres, the
biosphere, back into and
through the other three physical
spheres.

Energy Flow through Ecosystems

Energy flows are routed through feeding relationships in the ecosystem. An organism's niche ("occupation") in the ecosystem is closely associated with feeding. Energy flow through any ecosystem can be represented by the food web and the biomass pyramid. The **food web** describes the complex interrelationships by which organisms consume other organisms. The food web in ▬ Figure 3–21 illustrates how even aquatic and land organisms prey on each other.

Although food webs are adequate for graphically depicting the feeding relationships in any given ecosystem, the **biomass pyramid** provides a more basic understanding of energy flow (▬ Fig. 3–22). Biomass is the weight of living matter. The first trophic (feeding) level consists of the producers in the ecosystem, which produce the food used by all other organisms. Usually, the producers are plants, producing the food by photosynthesis; in a few deep-sea ecosystems, organisms produce food by chemosynthesis based on heat energy and compounds from underwater hydrothermal vents instead of the Sun's energy.

All levels above this first level contain consumers. First-order, or primary, consumers are herbivores that directly consume the producers, deriving energy from the chemical energy stored in the producers' bodies. As a marine example, first-order consumers include the crustaceans and other organisms that eat the phytoplankton. In a forest ecosystem, first-order consumers include deer and other plant eaters. Above the first-order consumers are the second-order (or secondary) consumers, which feed on the first-order consumers. In a marine ecosystem, second-order consumers may consist of fishes, lobsters, and other species. In a forest ecosystem, second-order consumers include wolves, panthers, and other meat eaters (carnivores) that eat the deer and other first-order consumers (▬ Fig. 3–23). Third-, fourth-, and even higher-order consumers can occur in some ecosystems. Decomposers are a special type of consumer. Decomposers, such as many bacteria, consume the tissue of dead organisms from all lev-

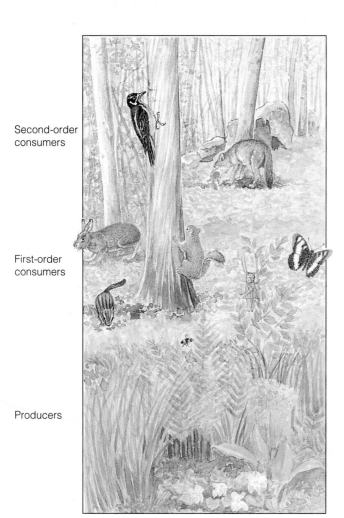

Second-order consumers

First-order consumers

Producers

Biomass	
Biomass of third trophic level	= Total combined weight of all carnivores
Biomass of second trophic level	= Total combined weight of all herbivores
Biomass of first trophic level	= Total combined weight of all producers

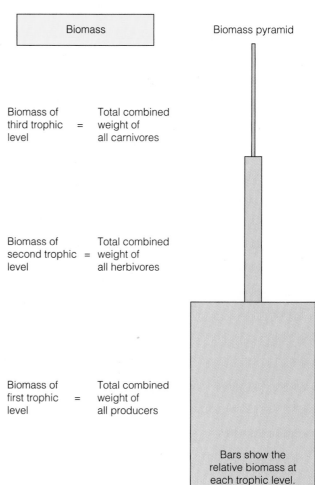

Biomass pyramid

Bars show the relative biomass at each trophic level.

■ FIGURE 3–22 (above)
A biomass pyramid. In most land food webs, biomass decreases from one feeding (trophic) level to the next highest.

■ FIGURE 3–23 (at right)
The gray wolf is a predator high on the biomass pyramid. (*Source:* Art Wolfe/Tony Stone Images.)

els of the food pyramid. Although they are inconspicuous, decomposers are extremely important in energy flow; in virtually all ecosystems, they consume the largest part of the energy flow.

Why does the biomass pyramid form? Biomass declines with each higher trophic level because progressively less food is available. Much of the food an animal consumes is not passed on to the animal that eats it. Instead, much of the food is (1) lost as undigested waste, or (2) "burned up" by the animal's metabolism to produce heat (■ Fig. 3–24). For example, a deer excretes about 25% of its ingested calories as undigested waste. Of the 75% that is digested, most is lost as metabolic waste products (such as urine) and, especially, body heat generated from movement and other kinds of maintenance. Thus, of all the calories eaten by the deer, less than 20% are converted into the deer's body tissue, which can be eaten by wolves or other animals that feed on the deer. Other organisms are more energy-efficient. Insects and other cold-blooded organisms can convert ingested calories into tissue much more ef-

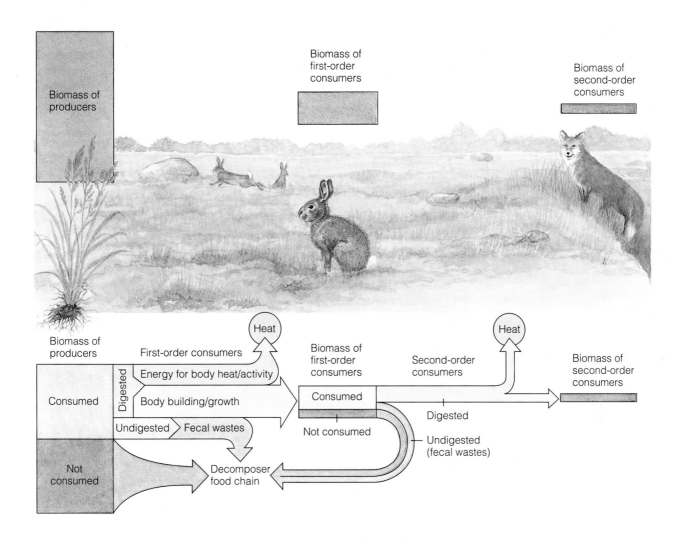

Biomass of producers

Biomass of first-order consumers

Biomass of second-order consumers

Biomass of producers

First-order consumers

Heat

Energy for body heat/activity

Digested

Consumed

Body building/growth

Undigested Fecal wastes

Not consumed

Decomposer food chain

Biomass of first-order consumers

Consumed

Not consumed

Second-order consumers

Heat

Digested

Undigested (fecal wastes)

Biomass of second-order consumers

FIGURE 3–24
Flow of biomass and energy through a food pyramid. Note that much of the biomass is consumed by decomposers.

ficiently than mammals because they have slower metabolisms. Even so, these organisms convert less than 50% of ingested calories into tissue. The result is a "leakage" of energy between each feeding level. This inefficiency is why feeding relationships form a pyramid. In general, about 80-95% of the energy is lost in the transfer between each level, depending on the organisms involved. Because so little energy is left, very few ecosystems have food pyramids with more than five levels. This is also why large carnivores are rare: they are the organisms at the top.

Ecosystem Productivity

The amount of food generated by producers at the base of the food pyramid varies greatly among ecosystems. Productivity is the rate at which biomass is produced in a community. **Net primary productivity (NPP)** is the rate at which producer, usually plant, biomass is created. Among the most productive terrestrial ecosystems are tropi-

cal forests and swamps (● Table 3–6), which produce plant biomass (NPP) at many times the rate of deserts. Temperate communities such as grasslands and temperate forests have intermediate productivities. The main reason for this pattern is that productivity on land increases where the growing season is longer. As ▬ Figure 3–25 shows, productivity tends to increase toward the equator where winters are milder and shorter. Deserts are the exception to this trend because lack of water limits growth, even though the growing season is long.

In terms of productivity per unit area, among the most productive aquatic ecosystems are estuaries and reefs, which may be up to 10 times more productive than certain other freshwater or marine ecosystems (Table 3–6). By this measure, the open ocean is the least productive by far. This point is crucial because the open ocean constitutes about 90% of the ocean. Therefore, 90% of the ocean, which is over half of the Earth's surface, is essentially a "marine desert"

TABLE 3-6 *Ecosystems and Productivity*

ECOSYSTEM TYPE	AREA (10⁶ km²)[b]	NET PRIMARY PRODUCTIVITY, PER UNIT AREA (g/m² or t/km²)[a] Normal Range	Mean	WORLD NET PRIMARY PRODUCTION (10⁹t)[c]
Tropical rainforest	17.0	1000–3500	2200	37.4
Tropical seasonal forest	7.5	1000–2500	1600	12.0
Temperate evergreen forest	5.0	600–2500	1300	6.5
Temperate deciduous forest	7.0	600–2500	1200	8.4
Boreal northern forest	12.0	400–2000	800	9.6
Woodland and shrubland	8.5	250–1200	700	6.0
Savanna	15.0	200–2000	900	13.5
Temperate grassland	9.0	200–1500	600	5.4
Tundra and alpine	8.0	10–400	140	1.1
Desert and semidesert shrub	18.0	10–250	90	1.6
Extreme desert, rock, sand, and ice	24.0	0–10	3	0.07
Cultivated land	14.0	100–3500	650	9.1
Swamp and marsh	2.0	800–3500	2000	4.0
Lake and stream	2.0	100–1500	250	0.5
Total continental	149		773	115
Open ocean	332.0	2–400	125	41.5
Upwelling zones	0.4	400–1000	500	0.2
Continental shelf	26.6	200–600	360	9.6
Reefs	0.6	500–4000	2500	1.6
Estuaries	1.4	200–3500	1500	2.1
Total marine	361		152	55.0
Full total	510		333	170

[a] t/km² = g/m² = metric tons/km² = approximately 2.85 tons per square mile.
[b] 10⁶ km² = approximately 386,000 square miles.
[c] 10⁹ t = 1 billion metric tons = approximately 1.102 billion tons.

(*Source*: M. Begon, J. Harper, and C. Townsend, *Ecology*, 2d ed. [Cambridge, Mass.: Blackwell, 1990] Reprinted by permission of Blackwell Science, Inc.)

in terms of productivity per unit area. Due to the size of the open ocean, however, it does make a significant contribution to the world's net primary productivity (Table 3–6). Reefs and estuaries are highly productive ecosystems despite their small areas. Unlike terrestrial ecosystems, the productivity of these nearshore areas is not strongly determined by the length of the growing season. Instead, nutrient availability tends to be the main limiting factor in marine ecosystems. The open ocean is relatively "starved" for some nutrients, especially phosphorus, because the source of the nutrients is runoff from land. Zones of upwelling can be highly productive, however, because the upwelling currents often carry many nutrients that have settled and been swept up from the ocean bottom. The upwelling zones west of Peru, which support a great fishing industry, are an example.

Net secondary productivity (NSP) is the rate at which consumer and decomposer biomass is produced. In other words, NSP includes all biomass except plants. A general rule of ecology is that primary and secondary net productivity are correlated: communities that have high primary productivity almost always have high secondary productivity. If the base of the food pyramid is producing much biomass, the organisms that consume and decompose plants will usually produce more biomass, too.

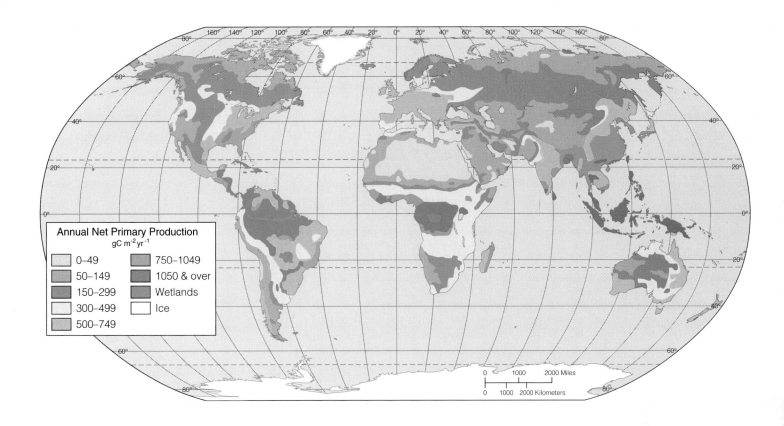

Annual Net Primary Production
gC m⁻² yr⁻¹

	0–49		750–1049
	50–149		1050 & over
	150–299		Wetlands
	300–499		Ice
	500–749		

Human Disturbance of Energy Flow and Productivity

The extent to which humans have altered ecosystem energy flow is demonstrated by a startling statistic: nearly 40% of the potential terrestrial NPP and about 2% of the oceanic ecosystem NPP is directly used, diverted, or lost (such as when forests are paved over to construct shopping malls) due to the activities of humans. This means that nearly half of the energy potentially converted by land plants is largely not available to species in natural ecosystems. Instead of trickling upward into the natural food pyramids, the energy flow is either "re-channeled" for human needs, such as directly feeding ourselves, feeding our pets, running our factories, or simply lost due to human activities (such as when we destroy tropical rainforests). This energy loss to nature is particularly striking considering that up to 90% of all species on Earth live on land. If we add the NPP of the aquatic food pyramid to that of the land pyramid, humans redirect an estimated 25% of global NPP.

Another way humans disturb productivity is by causing extinctions. Issues in Perspective 3–3 discusses evidence that humans not only "usurp" natural productivity, but also reduce what ecosystems can produce.

Matter Cycling through Ecosystems

The second basic ecosystem function, matter cycling, occurs because, unlike energy, matter is not always converted into less useful forms when used. Dozens of elements are cycled through ecosystems in biogeochemical cycles, which carry the elements through living tissue and the physical environment such as water, air, and rocks. An example is the biogeochemical cycle of carbon, which has a major influence on global climate (Chapter 4).

Most of the elements that cycle through ecosystems are trace elements, used in small amounts by organisms. Living things use carbon, hydrogen, oxygen, nitrogen, sulfur, and phosphorus in large amounts, however. Because organisms both metabolize and store these elements, ecosystems exert great control over how fast elements cycle. Some elements cycle in a matter of days while others may be buried for millions of years. For example, carbon may spend millions of years underground stored in fossil fuels such as coal and oil or as limestone (Chapter 4).

Ecosystems are generally very efficient in cycling matter, in that most matter is cycled over and over within the ecosystem itself (Fig. 3–26). For instance, the carbon atoms in a plant will be incorporated into a deer. These, in turn, will be incorporated into the tissue of a

FIGURE 3–25
Annual net primary productivity (NPP) on the Earth's land surface. In photosynthesis plants extract carbon from the atmosphere and utilize the carbon to form biomass. Therefore, one way to measure NPP is in terms of the amount of carbon converted into biomass per unit area per year. In this figure NPP is measured using the units grams of carbon per square meter per year (g C m⁻² yr⁻¹). [1 gram C per m² per year is approximately 0.029 ounce C per yd² per year.] Note that productivity is high in tropical forests and very low in arid regions. (*Source:* J. M. Melillo, *et al.,* *Nature* 363 [1993]: p. 237. Reprinted with permission from *Nature.* Copyright © 1993 Macmillan Magazines Limited.)

Does Extinction Reduce Ecosystem Productivity? How "Experimental Ecology" Answers Key Questions

*I*f an ecosystem loses plant species, is its primary productivity reduced? After all, the ground could be completely covered with just one species. Some ecologists, however, have argued that the more plant species in an ecosystem, the more biomass it can produce because they provide buffers against seasonal and other environmental changes. If one species suffers from cold, for instance, another can take over the photosynthetic processes.

After years of debate, evidence is accumlating that plant diversity does indeed tend to increase primary productivity. John H. Lawton and his colleagues at the Imperial College in England have performed a series of experiments that measured productivity of ecosystems under environmentally controlled laboratory conditions. As Figure 1 shows, their general finding was that plant productivity remained relatively high during the initial loss of species in very species-rich communities. But as the number of species continued to decline, productivity began to decrease until species-poor communities, with 1–5 plant species, showed significantly lower productivity. Much further work is needed to verify this finding, but it shows how experimental methods can answer crucial environmental questions that otherwise become embroiled in fruitless debates.

Another series of experiments conducted by David C. Tilman of the University of Minnesota produced another key finding: Increased diversity also increases ecosystem resistance to disturbance. Figure 2 shows that in Minnesota grasslands, species-poor communities produce much less relative biomass during drought years than species-rich communities. Apparently, having more species helps buffer the ecosystem against disturbances because some species can tolerate the disturbance better than others. By having more species, an ecosystem is more likely to have at least some species that can tolerate a disturbance and continue to produce biomass.

FIGURE 1

Declines in the number of species ultimately lead to declines in productivity.

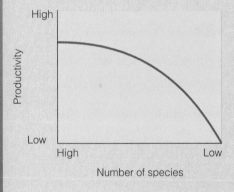

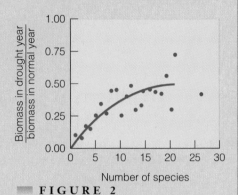

FIGURE 2

Communities with more species produce relatively more biomass in drought years than communities with fewer species. (*Source*: Redrawn from J. Lockwood and S. Pimm, "Do Species Matter?" *Current Biology* 4 [1994]: p. 456. Reprinted with permission from Current Science.)

The studies by Lawton and Tilman illustrate how ecological experiments can answer crucial questions about how extinction is impacting the environment. Species loss not only diminishes our world aesthetically and economically, it apparently impairs (1) ecosystem functioning such as biomass production and (2) ecosystem resistance to disturbance. A species-poor ecosystem has lower productivity during normal years, and this reduced productivity is even more drastically lowered during times of stress.

wolf that eats the deer. When the wolf dies, decomposers will incorporate the same carbon atoms. All of these changes take place within the ecosystem. Nevertheless, a small amount of matter will be lost from the ecosystem over time. Leaching from rainfall will carry off carbon in the form of decaying organic matter, leaves, and so on. In undisturbed ecosystems, this output loss is roughly balanced by an equal input gain of the same matter. For instance, carbon enters the ecosystem via weathering of rocks and is carried into the ecosystem by rainwater. In undisturbed natural ecosystems, both the input and the output are small relative to the amount of matter "locked up" and recycled within the biomass of the ecosystem itself (Fig. 3–26).

Both the rate and efficiency of matter cycling vary between ecosystems. The cycling of matter

Matter input
(rock weathering, rain)

Matter

Ecosystem

Matter output
(runoff, leaching)

Excess input,
disturbance
(such as eutrophication)

Excess output
(such as slash and burn
agriculture)

(a)

(b)

FIGURE 3–26
(a) A healthy ecosystem cycles
most of its matter over and
over through the food web.
Excess input and excess output
are symptoms of an unhealthy
ecosystem. An example of
excess input, where too much
matter enters into the system,
is fertilizer or nutrient excess.
An example of excess output is
the rapid loss of matter caused
by slash and burn agriculture.
(b) Slash-and-burn farming of
the rainforest releases nutrients normally stored in plant
biomass. (*Source*: (b) Jacques Jan-
goux/Tony Stone Images.)

is generally faster in tropical ecosystems, such as tropical rainforests and coral reefs, because biochemical reaction rates tend to increase with temperature. Matter cycling is also especially efficient in tropical ecosystems, where high rainfall will leach elements from the soil unless plants incorporate them quickly and efficiently into their tissue. Similarly, coral reefs thrive mainly in nutrient-poor tropical waters, so the elements in the nutrients must be utilized quickly and recycled very efficiently into the tissues of the marine life.

Human Disturbance of Matter Cycling

Matter cycling in the ecosystem is disturbed when humans alter the balance between the input and output of matter by creating (1) excess output, or (2) excess input (Fig. 3–26). Excess output occurs when humans suddenly release the large quantity of matter retained in the biomass of the ecosystem. For instance, in **slash and burn agriculture,** trees are cut down and burned. The burning releases the nutrients into the soil for agriculture. Unfortunately, the nutrients are quickly leached out of the soil where rainfall is heavy, as in the tropics where slash and burn techniques are common. This massive output of matter from the ecosystem is not fully replaced by input for many hundreds or perhaps thousands of years. During this time, the area can sustain only a relatively barren ecosystem with a fraction of its former diversity. In the meantime, farmers must move on and burn another area of tropical forest to produce arable land. This practice is contributing to massive tropical deforestation worldwide. Another example of excess output is the massive burning of fossil fuels. Billions of tons of carbon are released into the atmosphere annually from the burning of the tropical forests and other ecosystems. These emissions are contributing to the likelihood of global climate change (Chapter 18).

Disturbance by excess input commonly occurs when runoff from agricultural activity carries large amounts of fertilizer, organic waste, and other nutrients into natural ecosystems. This also destroys diversity because the excess nutrients cause eutrophication, leading to unrestrained growth of some organisms, such as algae in a lake. When the algae die, the decay of their now-abundant bodies by bacteria uses up so much oxygen that fish and many other organisms die.

SUMMARY

The very early appearance of life on Earth implies that natural processes readily produce life under appropriate conditions. The components of the early atmosphere are thought to have been ammonia, methane, water vapor, and other gases. When these are subjected to electricity, which simulates lightning and sunlight, chemical reactions occur that produce amino acids, complex molecules that are the building blocks of proteins. Proteins make up enzymes and many other components of life. The basic organizational unit of life is the cell.

Once life originated, it began to diversify into different kinds of organisms through biological evolution. Biological evolution occurs from natural selection of individual variation. Isolation of populations promotes speciation. Among sexual organisms, a species is a group of individuals that can interbreed to produce fertile offspring. Traits are passed on by genes, which are the basic units of heredity. Variation in a population, or "gene pool," occurs because individuals possess different sets of genes that produce different traits, as well as by mutation, which is spontaneous change in a gene.

The biosphere is hierarchical: organisms, composed of atoms, molecules, and cells, are grouped into populations. Populations form communities, which then form ecosystems. Ecosystems, when considered together, form the biosphere, which subsumes all life on Earth. Ecology is the study of how organisms interact with each other and their physical environment. A population is a group of individuals of the same species living in the same area. All populations undergo three distinct phases during their existence: (1) growth, (2) stability, and (3) decline. The potential for increase in a given population is called the intrinsic rate of increase. The intrinsic rate of increase = birth rate – death rate. Four basic abundance controls can limit population growth: (1) physical limitations, (2) competitors, (3) predators, and (4) symbiosis. Eventually, all populations become extinct. The ultimate cause of decline and extinction is environmental change.

Human alterations of the environment have led to destabilization of populations by affecting the various abundance controls. The result has often been either (1) population growth as previous limitations are removed or (2) population decline as new limitations are imposed.

Diversity refers to how many kinds of organisms occur in a community. The latitudinal diversity gradient describes how species richness in most groups steadily decreases going away from the equator. Thus, richer communities are found in tropical areas. The second important diversity trend is the depth diversity gradient found in aquatic communities: species richness increases with water depth down to a point about 6560 feet (2000 m) deep and then begins to decline. This gradient is caused by (1) environmental stability and (2) nutrients.

Although communities vary in structure, they all experience certain processes. The most basic of these processes are (1) energy flow and (2) matter cycling. All organisms must eat (take in energy and matter) to stay alive, causing energy and matter to move through the community. All energy and matter ultimately come from, and return to, the physical environment.

The food web describes the complex interrelationships by which organisms consume other organisms. The biomass pyramid provides a more basic understanding of energy flow. Biomass can be thought of as the weight of living matter. The first trophic level consists of the producers in the ecosystem, which produce the food used by all other organisms. All the levels above the first level contain consumers. First-order, or primary, consumers are herbivores that directly consume the producers, deriving energy from the chemical energy stored in the producers' bodies. Above the first-order consumers are the second-order consumers, which feed on the first-order consumers. Third-, fourth-, and even higher-order consumers can occur in some ecosystems. Decomposers consume the tissue of dead organisms from all levels of the pyramid. Decomposers are extremely important in energy flow, consuming the largest part of the energy flow in virtually all ecosystems. Humans now divert or redirect, for their own use, about 40% of the net primary productivity of all land plants on Earth.

Matter cycling occurs because, unlike energy, matter is not converted into less useful forms when used. Dozens of elements are cycled through ecosystems in biogeochemical cycles, which carry the elements through living tissue and the physical environment such as water, air, and rocks. Most of the elements that cycle through ecosystems are trace elements, used in small amounts by organisms. Living things do use carbon, hydrogen, oxygen, nitrogen, sulfur, and phosphorus in large amounts, however. Matter cycling is disturbed when humans alter the balance between input and output of matter through ecosystems by creating (1) excess output, or (2) excess input.

KEY TERMS

age structure
amensalism
amino acids
benthic
biomass
biomass pyramid
biome
carrying capacity
climax community
commensalism
community
competition
competitive exclusion
DNA (deoxyribonucleic acid)
density-dependent regulation
density-independent regulation

depth diversity gradient
ecological release
ecology
ecosystem
ecotones
endemic species
eukaryotes
explosion of life
food web
genes
habitat
intrinsic rate of increase
latitudinal diversity gradient
law of the minimum
life history
monoculture
mutation

mutualism
natural selection
net primary productivity (NPP)
niche
parasitism
pelagic
photic zone
pioneer community
population
predation
protocells
slash and burn agriculture
species
symbiosis
taxonomy

STUDY QUESTIONS

1. What is the basic organizational unit of life?
2. What is a protocell? What cell-like properties do protocells have?
3. What is a species?
4. What was Mendel's discovery? Explain.
5. What is the ultimate cause of all genetic variation?
6. What is the suggested reason for the "explosion of life"? Why would this promote life?
7. What are the three phases during a population's existence?
8. What is biomass? Monoculture?
9. What is the intrinsic rate of increase? What is its symbol?
10. Define age structure. Explain the meaning of the three diagrams in Figure 3–6.
11. What is the latitudinal diversity gradient?
12. What is the abundance control in the physical environment? What are the three abundance controls in the biological environment?
13. Explain the law of the minimum.
14. If a population doubles each day and begins with two individuals, what will the population be in five days?
15. What is the intrinsic rate of increase in a population with a birth rate of 100 per day and a death rate of 98 per day?

ESSAY QUESTIONS

1. Describe the process of evolution by natural selection. How has the physical environment affected the history of life?
2. Compare and contrast density-independent regulation and density-dependent regulation.
3. How do humans affect the biosphere? Include the following in your discussion: population growth, population decline, population ranges, communities, the energy flow and productivity, and matter cycling.
4. Discuss the difference between closed and open structure communities. Why are most communities open structure? What is an exception to this?
5. List and briefly describe six major land biomes and two major aquatic biomes.

SUGGESTED READINGS

Begon, M., J. Harper, and C. Townsend. 1990. *Ecology*, 2d ed. Cambridge, Mass.: Blackwell.

Cox, G. W. 1993. *Conservation ecology*. Dubuque, Iowa: W. C. Brown.

Freedman, B. 1989. *Environmental ecology*. New York: Academic Press.

Odum, E. P. 1993. *Ecology and our endangered life support system*, 2d ed. Sunderland, Mass.: Sinauer.

Primack, R. B. 1993. *Essentials of conservation biology*. Sunderland, Mass.: Sinauer.

Ricklefs, R. E. 1990, *Ecology*, 3d ed. New York: W. H. Freeman.

Smith, R. L. 1990. *Elements of ecology and field biology*, 4th ed. New York: Harper & Row.

CHAPTER 4

ENVIRONMENT: AN INTEGRATED SYSTEM OF FOUR SPHERES

OUTLINE

PROLOGUE   *Stardust and Caesar's Last Gasp*

A song about the famous Woodstock concert of the late 1960s said, "we are stardust, we are golden." Artistic metaphors aside, this is at least half true: all of us—and indeed all living things—are stardust. Many of the atoms in our bodies were forged by nuclear reactions in ancient stars over five billion years ago. The original Big Bang produced a universe containing only the two simplest elements, hydrogen and helium. Carbon, phosphorus, and all the heavier elements that comprise not only life but the Earth itself were formed from nuclear reactions produced by stars. Our "spaceship Earth" condensed, along with the rest of our solar system, from the remains of an exploded star.

The stardust that composes us and our global environment is always moving, always cycling. Because Earth is a relatively isolated island in space, the same matter is cycled over and over in ourselves and in our environment. Many of the atoms that composed your body as

PHOTO   *The Earth is an ancient entity. The air, land, sea and life have evolved together.* (*Source:* Frederic Edwin Church, *Cotopaxi* (1862). Oil on canvas, 48 in. x 7 ft. 1 in. Copyright © The Detroit Institute of Arts, Founders Society Purchase with funds from Mr. and Mrs. Richard A. Manoogian, Robert H. Tannahill Foundation Fund, Gibbs-Williams Fund, Dexter M. Ferry, Jr. Fund, Merrill Fund, and Beatrice W. Rogers Fund.)

a child are long gone, having been lost as new cells replaced dead cells. Atoms move through the environment in a similar fashion. A single oxygen atom that starts in molten magma may become an oxide molecule in a rock. A chemical reaction may release this atom into the atmosphere to form the oxygen we breathe. A famous chemical calculation illustrates the amazing extent of this "atomic recycling." Less than one-tenth of a cubic inch (one cubic centimeter) of air contains more than a billion billion molecules. Virtually every time you breathe, you may inhale some of the same air molecules contained in Julius Caesar's last gasp because the trillions of molecules he exhaled have had many hundreds of years to diffuse and mix into the global atmosphere.

We are recycled ancient stardust living out a tiny life span on an island of stardust that is five billion years old. When our lives are over, our atoms will once again join the dynamic, complex chemical web of our environment, and our descendants will inhale the atoms that we breathed.

NTRODUCTION

Everything in the universe is either matter or energy. The four spheres (atmosphere, hydrosphere, lithosphere, and biosphere) are composed of matter in the gaseous, liquid, or solid states. Energy is what makes matter move. One of the most basic laws of physics is the **law of conservation of matter and energy**, which says that matter and energy cannot be created or destroyed. However, matter and energy can be *transformed* into different kinds of matter and energy. For example, gases condense to become liquid; oxygen reacts with iron to form "rust" (iron oxide). The amount of matter on Earth is finite, but it is constantly being recycled, changing from one form to another. Any matter in our environment, from resources to wastes, simply represents a temporary storage of matter in one place and in one form. Ultimately, physical processes (such as evaporation) or chemical processes (such as oxidation) will cause the matter to be transported or change its chemical environment in the Earth's dynamic system of cycles.

approximately 90 elements that occur naturally on Earth, these six comprise the vast majority of atoms in the tissue of all living things. As ● Table 4–1 shows, oxygen alone accounts for more than 62% of the weight of the human body and more than 77% of the weight of the alfalfa plant. Carbon and oxygen together account for more than 80% of the weight of a human.

● Table 4–2 shows the relative abundances of the most common elements in the Earth's crust. Oxygen is the most abundant, just as it is most common in the human body. But the second most common human element, carbon, is hundreds of times rarer in the crust. Instead, silicon, which is virtually absent from the human body, is extremely abundant in the crust. You can see other major discrepancies by comparing Tables 4–1 and 4–2. These discrepancies illustrate how life is chemically distinct from its environment. Without biogeochemical cycles to transport and store temporary concentrations of matter for food and other uses, life could not survive.

Biogeochemical Cycles: An Introduction

When observing the cycles of matter such as water, rocks, nutrients, and other substances within and among the spheres, scientists often find it useful to focus on the cycles of chemical elements that compose those substances. This approach can be used to simplify our models of environmental cycles because just a few basic elements participate in many of the most important cycles on Earth. These cycles of chemical elements through the atmosphere, lithosphere, hydrosphere, and biosphere are called **biogeochemical cycles**.

Among the most important biogeochemical cycles are the six cycles that transport the six elements most important to life: carbon, hydrogen, oxygen, nitrogen, phosphorus, and sulfur. Of the

● **TABLE 4–1** *Atomic Composition by Weight of Three Representative Organisms*

ELEMENT	HUMAN	ALFALFA	BACTERIUM
Oxygen	62.81%	77.90%	73.68%
Carbon	19.37	11.34	12.14
Hydrogen	9.31	8.72	9.94
Nitrogen	5.14	0.83	3.04
Phosphorus	0.63	0.71	0.60
Sulfur	0.64	0.10	0.32
Total	97.90	99.60	99.72

TABLE 4–2	*The Relative Abundance by Weight of Some Chemical Elements in the Earth's Crust*

ELEMENT (CHEMICAL SYMBOL)	RELATIVE ABUNDANCE
Oxygen (O)	46.6%
Silicon (Si)	27.7
Aluminum (Al)	8.1
Iron (Fe)	5.0
Calcium (Ca)	3.6
Sodium (Na)	2.8
Potassium (K)	2.6
Magnesium (Mg)	2.1
Phosphorus (P)	0.07
Carbon (C)	0.03
Nitrogen (N)	Trace

Each of the many biogeochemical cycles has different pathways of transport and temporary storage reservoirs. The **carbon cycle** in Figure 4–1 is a typical biogeochemical cycle. Like many cycles, the carbon cycle, appears at first glance to be quite complex with many pathways (arrows), but closer inspection shows that these pathways are based on just two processes: withdrawal from and addition to the atmosphere.

1. *Withdrawal* of carbon is largely driven by **photosynthesis** whereby plants take carbon out of the atmosphere where it resides as carbon dioxide. The CO_2 is combined with water (H_2O) to form biochemical molecules such as sugars (CH_2O), and oxygen. Photosynthesis is conveniently written as:

$$CO_2 + H_2O + energy \longrightarrow CH_2O + O_2$$

This reaction is called photosynthesis because it requires energy from the Sun (*photo* = light; *synthesis* = combine).

Figure 4–1 also shows two "loops" of photosynthesis. Loop 1 illustrates the pathway of "living" carbon in the ongoing photosynthesis of modern plants. Loop 2 shows how "fossil" carbon forms. Fossil carbon is carbon that has been temporarily withdrawn from use by living organisms by becoming buried and stored. Carbon is temporarily stored in the lithosphere, when plants, such as tiny plankton in marine and fresh waters, die and sink to the bottom. After millions of years of burial, these dead plants, and the carbon in them, can become fossil fuels such as petroleum. Similarly, clams and other ocean shellfishes withdraw carbon for use in constructing their shells. When the shellfishes die, their shells contribute to the vast amounts of limestone (Fig. 4–2). Indeed, the large majority of the Earth's carbon now resides in the ocean. As Figure 4–3 shows, the ocean stores much more carbon than is found in the other three sinks—the atmosphere, lithosphere (geologi-

FIGURE 4–1
The carbon cycle. Loop 1 is "living" carbon that is still actively circulating among living organisms and their environment. Loop 2 is "fossil" carbon; it consists of carbon that is bound in molecules such as coal deposits that are deeply buried until released by burning or some other process. Combustion (and respiration) and photosynthesis ultimately cause carbon to move through both cycles.

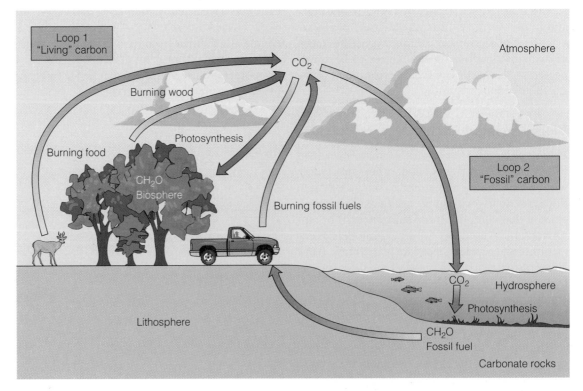

*E*NVIRONMENTAL PRINCIPLES   SECTION 1

FIGURE 4–2
Limestone, such as the white cliffs of Dover, is formed from shells of clams and other marine life. (*Source:* Laguna Photo/ Gamma Liaison.)

cal), and living organisms on land (terrestrial biosphere).

2. *Addition* of carbon to the atmosphere often occurs from combustion. As Figure 4–1 shows, combustion or "burning" is essentially the reverse of photosynthesis; oxygen (O_2) is combined with plant matter (CH_2O) to release CO_2 and H_2O:

$$CH_2O + O_2 \longrightarrow CO_2 + H_2O + energy$$

Setting fire to either living matter (loop 1) or fossil fuel (loop 2) will therefore release carbon dioxide. Similarly, when we digest food, we are carrying out combustion: our bodies take the oxygen we inhale and use it to break down the biochemical molecules we eat, such as plant foods. We then use the energy given off to move around, grow, and maintain our bodies. The carbon dioxide produced is exhaled into the atmosphere (loop 1). This process of biological combustion is called **respiration**.

Biogeochemical Cycles: Major Features

The biogeochemical cycles as a group can be analyzed in terms of a number of important features. These features include the cycles' pathways, their rates of cycling, and the degree to which they are being disturbed by human activities.

A Variety of Pathways

Each biogeochemical cycle has *many different pathways*: many chemical and physical processes help to cycle each atom. For instance, the carbon cycle transports carbon through all four spheres. From the atmosphere, the carbon dioxide (CO_2 molecule) dissolves in water in the hydrosphere, where plankton use the carbon to build body tissue (CH_2O molecule), thereby moving the carbon into the biosphere. When the plankton are buried and converted to fossil fuel, the carbon is converted to complex hydrocarbon molecules such as oil and becomes part of the lithosphere. When the oil is burned, the carbon is released back into the atmosphere where it may recycle through a different set of pathways. For instance, the CO_2 gas may be absorbed by a tropical tree the next time instead of by plankton.

Of course, each element has a different set of potential biogeochemical pathways. For example, unlike carbon, phosphorus generally does not cycle through the atmosphere because it does not easily form a gas. During its cycle, phosphorus often combines with different atoms than carbon does and therefore forms different molecules and undergoes different chemical reactions.

Variable Rates of Cycling

Biogeochemical cycles vary in their *rate of cycling*. Figure 4–4 shows the average amount of time

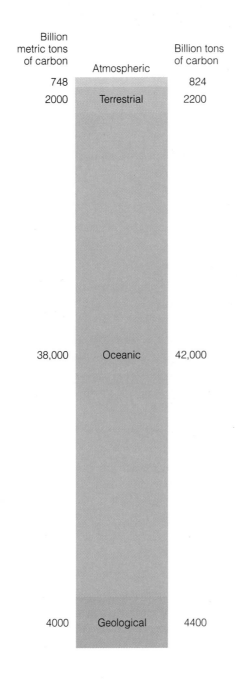

FIGURE 4–3

Major reservoirs of the carbon cycle, in billion tons of carbon. The oceans are the largest reservoir by far. (*Source:* W. M. Post, *et al.*, "*The Global Carbon Cycle*," American Scientist 78 [1990]: 315. Reprinted by permission of *American Scientist.*)

Billion metric tons of carbon		Billion tons of carbon
	Atmospheric	
748		824
2000	Terrestrial	2200
38,000	Oceanic	42,000
4000	Geological	4400

Why do substances cycle at such different rates? Two major determinants are (1) the *chemical reactivity* of the substance and (2) whether it has a *gas phase* (occurs in the atmosphere) somewhere in the cycle. The high chemical reactivity of carbon causes it to participate in many chemical pathways and is a main reason why it cycles so quickly. In addition, carbon is abundant as the gas carbon dioxide. Because gas molecules move much more quickly than more tightly bonded molecules in liquids or solids, the existence of a gas phase allows the substance to be transported more rapidly.

Although oxygen and water cycle more slowly than carbon dioxide, they actually cycle at relatively fast rates compared to many other substances. Like carbon dioxide, oxygen and water are chemically reactive and have a major gas phase. For instance, the average water molecule has a **residence time** of 10 days in the atmosphere, where it may move thousands of miles (thousands of kilometers) before traveling back to Earth as a liquid.

Thus, to find a substance that has an extremely slow cycling time, we should look for one that has no gas phase and is also relatively unreactive in natural systems. Phosphorus is a good example because it not only has a very slow cycling rate but is one of the six most important elements of life and is therefore of much interest and very well studied. Because of its chemical and physical properties, phosphorus does not form a gas and does not readily combine with other substances. Its main mode of transport is water, which moves much slower than air, and even in water phosphorus is relatively insoluble. As ■ Figure 4–5 shows, large amounts of phosphorus become "locked up" in storage for long periods of time as sediments in the deep ocean and the Earth's crust. Only relatively slow and rare events, such as upwelling ocean currents from the deep sea or weathering of phosphorus rich rocks, recycle the phosphorus.

Instead of the few hundreds to few millions of years typical of cycles with a gas phase, phosphorus requires many tens of millions of years to complete its biogeochemical cycle. This slow cycling rate drastically reduces the availability of this critical nutrient with profound effects for the biosphere. Phosphorus is usually the nutrient in shortest supply in most ecosystems and is therefore labeled the **limiting nutrient**. As we saw in Chapter 3, sudden availability of limiting nutrients in natural systems causes rapid growth.

water, oxygen, and carbon dioxide molecules take to make a complete cycle through the four spheres. Clearly, cycling rates can vary drastically over many orders of magnitude. Carbon takes only hundreds of years to cycle whereas water takes about two million years. These times are only approximate because specific molecules may cycle much more rapidly or slowly depending on the pathway they follow. A small number of carbon atoms (fewer than 1 in 10,000) in the active, living loop, for instance, may be stored as oil deposits for over 200 million years and cycle through the much slower fossil loop.

The Effects of Human Activity

Biogeochemical cycles are crucial to all life, but are being *greatly disturbed by human activity*. As human population and technology rapidly increase, huge quantities of materials are extracted through mining and other means and redistributed through all the spheres. The net result has been the disturbance of nearly all biogeochemical cycles. The most common type of disturbance is acceleration of the cycles: materials are being rapidly mined and otherwise extracted from storage reservoirs (sources) and, after use, are rapidly deposited back into the environment (sinks). This increased rate of cycling from source to sink leads to the two basic environmental problems: depletion and pollution (Chapter 1). Indeed, a basic definition of pollution is a temporary concentration of a chemical above levels that normally occur in its biogeochemical cycle.

No one really knows just how drastic or dangerous this acceleration of natural cycles will ultimately prove to be. No one doubts that major consequences will occur, however, and because biogeochemical cycles are global in nature, many of these consequences will occur on a global scale. Carbon provides a prominent example of how humans are actively disturbing a major cycle, with potentially drastic consequences. The burning of

fossil fuels, such as coal, petroleum, and natural gas, has released increasing amounts of carbon dioxide into the atmosphere. Figure 4–6a shows how global release of carbon has increased exponentially from about 1.1 billion tons (1 bil-

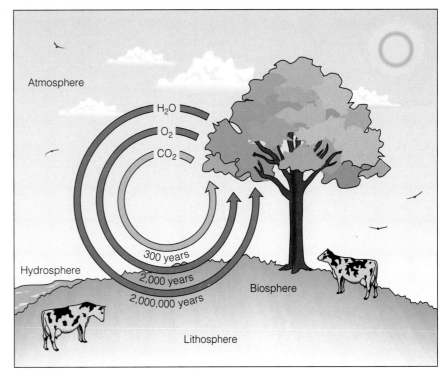

FIGURE 4–4
Recycling rates of water, oxygen, and carbon dioxide through the four spheres. (*Source:* L. Laporte, *Encounter with the Earth* [San Francisco: Canfield, 1975], p. 22. Modified by permission of Leo F. Laporte.)

FIGURE 4–5
(a) The global phosphorus cycle. The amount that flows on Earth is much smaller than the amount stored in rocks and sediment. (b) Phosphate is mined in Florida, and other areas, where ocean waters deposited phosphorus-rich sediments. (*Source:* (a) Adapted from D. Botkin and E. Keller, *Environmental Science: Earth as a Living Planet* [New York: Wiley, 1995], p. 63. Copyright © 1995 by John Wiley & Sons, Inc. Reprinted by permission of John Wiley & Sons, Inc.; (b) David Woods/The Stock Market.)

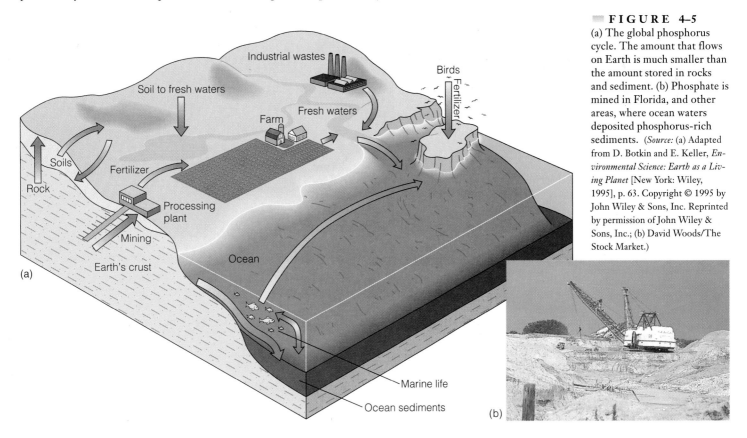

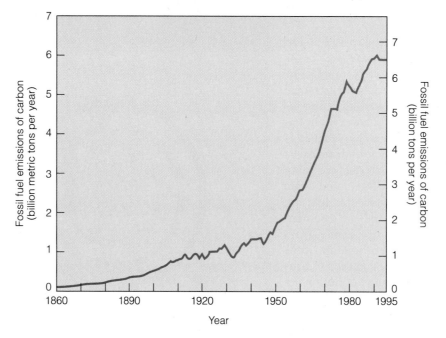

(a)

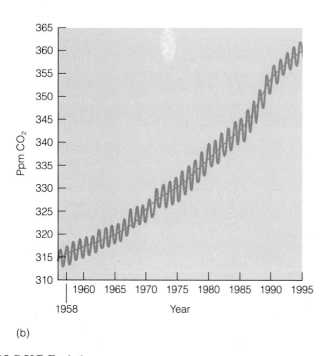

(b)

(c)

lion metric tons)* per year in 1940 to an estimated 6.6 billion tons (6 billion metric tons) per year in the 1990s. It is estimated that about half of this 6.6 billion tons per year is absorbed by plant life and the oceans, but the remainder is accumulating in the atmosphere in the form of carbon dioxide (Fig. 4–6b).

This accumulation of atmospheric carbon dioxide has many potential global consequences. For example, many studies have shown that the rate of plant growth will generally increase from increasing photosynthesis. The most publicized

_____
*Unless otherwise noted, *tons* refers to short tons (2000 pounds).

consequence is global warming. Carbon dioxide is a "greenhouse gas," meaning that it increases the ability of the atmosphere to trap heat. How much carbon dioxide can be added to the atmosphere before significant global warming will occur is much debated.

Figures 4–6c and 4–6b show that average global temperature has tended to increase along with carbon dioxide concentration, but conclusively proving that this is a simple cause-and-effect relationship is difficult. Nevertheless, many models project that major global warming will occur in coming decades under various scenarios. For instance, as developing countries industrialize, the global release of carbon will increase to an estimated 13.2 billion tons (12 billion metric tons) per year by the early twenty-first century if no attempt is made to switch to alternative (nonfossil) fuels, such as solar energy. Indeed, if all the fossil fuels (such as petroleum and coal) on Earth were burned, the atmospheric carbon dioxide concentration would increase by an estimated 10 times, or 1000%, its current level. So far, atmospheric carbon dioxide has risen only 30–40% above its level in the early nineteenth century. We will see in Chapter 18 why global warming is a matter of much concern: it can have profound effects on agriculture, sea level, and many other aspects of life.

Although the consequences of disturbing the carbon cycle are especially dramatic, all of the many dozens of biogeochemical cycles are increasingly being disturbed by humans. Some examples include excess phosphorus, which causes runaway plant growth in natural waters; nitrogen emissions, which contribute to smog; and sulfur emissions, which cause acid rain. These and other disturbances are discussed in detail in later chapters.

Energy Flows

The **first law of thermodynamics** says that energy cannot be created or destroyed, but can be transformed. The **second law of thermodynamics** says that when energy is transformed from one kind to another, it is degraded, meaning that the energy becomes less capable of doing work. For example, only about 30% of the chemical energy in gasoline is converted to the energy of motion in a car. Similarly, photosynthesis uses solar energy to create food from carbon and other atoms. Food represents chemical energy, which is stored in the bonds between atoms, so photosynthesis is a transformation from solar to chemical energy. As ▬ Figure 4–7

shows, this transformation is far from 100% efficient. Most of the incoming energy is "lost" as heat. Heat is considered to be low-quality energy and is capable of doing less work than high-quality energy.

Entropy refers to the amount of low-quality energy in a system. If entropy is very high, matter will tend to disorganize to simpler states. The second law of thermodynamics is sometimes called the *law of entropy* because all energy transformations will increase the entropy of a system unless new high-quality energy, such as sunlight, enters the system to replenish it. Later in the chapter we discuss how the Earth and all living things rely on such replenishment to resist entropy and maintain high levels of organization.

Some energy transformations are more efficient than others. By carefully refining our technology, humans have managed to achieve much greater efficiencies. For example, the best solar (photovoltaic) cells convert as much as 30% of sunlight to electricity. Other examples of energy conversion are the use of nuclear energy to generate electrical energy and the conversion of gasoline (chemical energy) into mechanical energy ("energy of motion"). In each of these and all other energy transformations, however, engineers long ago accepted that no matter how advanced our technology, some loss of usable energy will always occur, if only a few percent.

Because of this loss, energy cannot be recycled like matter. Ultimately, all the energy in a system will become relatively useless (transformed to heat) unless new energy flows into the system. Thus, we say that matter cycles, but energy must flow from one source to another. On Earth, the vast majority of new energy flows from the Sun. This energy originates with nuclear reactions at the Sun's core and travels as light energy across

▬ **FIGURE 4–7**
The two laws of thermodynamics. The first law is illustrated by the conversion of Sun energy (a) to food (chemical) energy (c). The second law dictates that heat loss (b) during conversion causes the amount of usable food (chemical) energy to be less than the Sun energy. In this case, it is much less. (*Source:* E. P. Odum, *Ecology and Our Endangered Life Support Systems* [Sunderland, Mass.: Sinauer 1989], p. 70. Reprinted by permission of Sinauer Associates, Inc.)

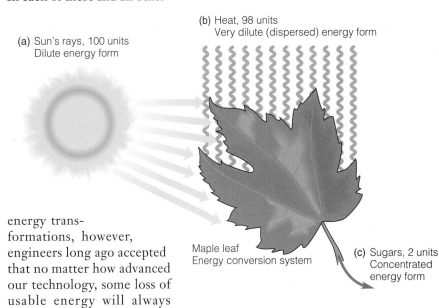

(a) Sun's rays, 100 units
Dilute energy form

(b) Heat, 98 units
Very dilute (dispersed) energy form

Maple leaf
Energy conversion system

(c) Sugars, 2 units
Concentrated energy form

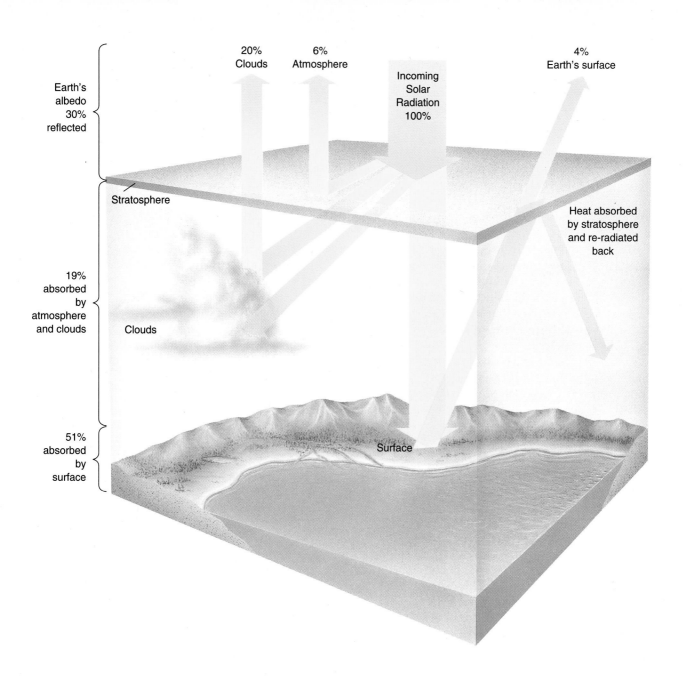

20%
Clouds

6%
Atmosphere

Incoming
Solar
Radiation
100%

4%
Earth's surface

Earth's
albedo
30%
reflected

Stratosphere

Heat absorbed
by stratosphere
and re-radiated
back

19%
absorbed
by
atmosphere
and clouds

Clouds

51%
absorbed
by
surface

Surface

▦ FIGURE 4–8
Thirty percent of the solar radiation striking the Earth is immediately reflected back into space; 51% is absorbed and radiated into space as heat. The remaining energy creates wind and drives the water cycle, photosynthesis, and other processes.

93 million miles (150 million km) to strike the Earth. Upon striking the Earth, the energy is transformed in many ways, depending on where it strikes. Collectively, the various flow pathways of all energy on Earth are called the Earth's **energy budget** (▦ Figure 4–8). Thirty percent of the incoming light is directly reflected back into space, especially by white clouds. Another 51% is absorbed and reradiated back into space as heat. The remaining energy powers the hydrologic cycle by evaporation, generates wind, powers photosynthesis, and in general drives many of the cycles within and between the spheres that we discussed earlier. Photosynthesis, for all its importance in sustaining most life on Earth, including humans, uses a tiny fraction, just 0.06% of solar radiation. And given the inefficiency of photosynthesis, much of this is wasted.

Actually, not all of the Earth's energy comes from the Sun. A small fraction comes from two other sources. One is the Moon's gravitational pull, which causes tides in the ocean. This tidal energy is thousands of times less than the amount of energy provided by the Sun. The second source of energy is the Earth's own internal geothermal energy, which is generated by radioactive minerals deep within the Earth. The heat diffuses outward to the Earth's surface and melts rocks to drive the tectonic cycle of the lithosphere and the emission of volcanic gases into the atmosphere. It also produces the heat that creates deep-sea vents in the ocean floor, where hot magma provides nutrients and energy to rich marine communities.

Human Use of Energy Flows

Humans are using ever-greater amounts of the energy flows on Earth. Modern civilization is built upon fossil fuels, which are fossilized plant materials that store solar energy from millions of years ago as chemical energy. Because they take so long to form, fossil fuels are called **nonrenewable resources**. If rates of use continue to rise, most estimates indicate that the world supply of oil will be used up within the next 100 years and world coal supplies within 300–400 years. Besides depletion, another problem with fossil fuels is the release of pollutants. Almost *all major air pollution*, including acid rain, smog, carbon monoxide, and greenhouse gases, is caused by burning fossil fuels. Although many of these pollutants can be controlled by smokestack devices, fuel cleansing, and other technical solutions, there is no economical way of removing the carbon because so much is produced. Burning just a gallon (3.785 liters) of gasoline produces over 20 pounds (9 kg) of carbon dioxide, and coal produces even more. Fossil fuels also cause many other pollution problems, such as seepage from storage tanks into groundwater and ocean spills.

Instead of using "fossilized" solar energy, it would be less damaging to use the solar energy flow as it strikes the Earth today. Because the Sun will last about five billion more years, solar energy will not soon be depleted, and the potential supply is vast. In just one month, the Earth intercepts more energy from the Sun than is contained in all the fossil fuels on the planet. Solar energy, along with tidal energy, is a form of **renewable energy**.

$\mathcal{O}$ VERVIEW: THE ENVIRONMENT AS A SYSTEM

As we have seen, the environment consists of four spheres, and matter cycles and energy flows through these spheres. A system approach will provide a convenient overview of this information.

What Is a System?

A **system** is technically defined as a "set of components functioning together as a whole." A system view allows us to isolate a part of the world and focus on those aspects that interact more closely than others. For example, a cell in the system we call a human body generally interacts much more closely with other cells in the body than with the outside world. By focusing only on those cells that function in digestion, we confine our view further, to the digestive system. The key point here is that most systems are *hierarchical:* they are composed of smaller sets of systems made of smaller interacting parts.

Three Key Traits of the Environmental System

We can analyze the global environment in terms of three system traits: openness, integration, and complexity.

Openness refers to whether a system is isolated from other systems. An **open system** is not isolated in that it exchanges matter or energy with other systems. A **closed system** is isolated and exchanges nothing.

The law of entropy means that energy cannot be recycled. Therefore, any system that does not have a renewing supply of energy from outside will eventually cease to exist. Not surprisingly then, the Earth is an open system in terms of energy. Figure 4–9 shows how energy flows from the Sun and is often radiated back into space. In contrast, the Earth is a closed system in terms of matter. If we discount the relatively tiny amount of matter added from meteorites and other space debris, the Earth contains all the matter it will ever have. Driven by energy from the Sun, this matter cycles over and over among the four spheres, often moving back and forth among the gas, liquid, and solid states, and participating in the metabolism of living things. Issues in Perspective 4–1 describes an attempt to create a closed system that would imitate the Earth.

Integration refers to the strength of the interactions among the parts of the system. For instance, the human body is a highly integrated system whose cells are interdependent and in close

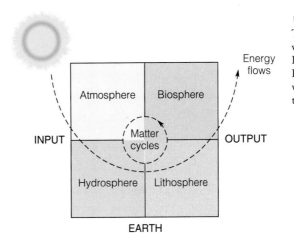

Biosphere 2: A Microcosm of Earth

In September 1991, the experimental Biosphere 2 project was colonized for the first time by a team of four women and four men. Located outside Tucson, Arizona, in the Sonoran Desert, this self-contained closed ecosystem was the first facility of its kind designed to simulate Biosphere 1—our Earth. Its goal, simply put, was to create a "working substitute" of our world (Fig. 1).

The double-laminated, glass-and-steel complex, described as "like an octopus with lumps," reaches 85 feet (26 m) at its highest point and encompasses five biomes including rainforest, desert, marsh, and ocean. Its colonists or "biospherians" were to reside in Biosphere 2 for a period of two years. During that time, they were to perform the duties necessary to maintain their environment as well as conduct research into the complex interactions found there. The plan called for large-scale recycling, with the biomes removing carbon dioxide and pollutants from the "atmosphere" in addition to releasing oxygen into the "atmosphere." All waste water was to be recycled as well. Within the 3.15-acre (1.27-

hectare) complex, the biospherians planned to grow a wide variety of food crops. Designed to be totally self-sustaining, Biosphere 2 proved to be more complex than anticipated.

One of the first problems to arise was an overabundance of carbon dioxide with a subsequent decrease in oxygen levels in Biosphere 2's atmosphere. Later determined to be due to the oxidizing bacteria in the compost-rich soil, the problem forced one of the biospherians to use an oxygen mask almost nightly, and a carbon dioxide scrubber had to be installed. This addition was controversial because Biosphere 2 was supposed to be a closed system. The team also had to cope with a decline in productivity of their agricultural crops that caused all eight biospherians to lose weight. On average, the male biospherians lost in excess of 25 pounds (11 kg) in six months. The decline in productivity was attributed largely to more cloud cover than had been expected and pest-related crop damage. In addition, the biospherians had to spend more time than anticipated maintaining the health of the biomes. Difficulties

ranged from an overgrowth of algae on the ocean reef to "rogue species" consuming ocean species or choking terrestrial plant species. Additionally, the plant pollinators began dying off; forcing, the biospherians to assume the role of pollinator as well. All in all, they had little time left for scientific research.

The shortage of scientific research coming out of Biosphere 2 aroused considerable controversy within the scientific community. The main area of contention was whether the project should be viewed holistically so as not to "test for effects individually," as was currently the method; or whether "a detailed, laid-out plan" of hard science should be used. Those who favored the "holistic" approach said Biosphere 2 should be allowed to "evolve" on its own while observations were made of its progress. Those wanting a more systematic research plan felt that the project's full potential as a living laboratory was being wasted. Finally, Edward P. Bass (underwriter of this $150 million project) and his co-planners opted for a more rigid scientific approach; they replaced the Bio-

communication. The loss of certain cells, such as those composing the heart or brain, can result in death of all the other cells in the system (the whole organism) because the cells are so interdependent. At the other extreme are systems with very weak integration, such as the cells in a colony of single-celled organisms (like the green algae, *Volvox*). Removal of many cells will have little effect on the remaining cells because they are less dependent on each other.

The degree of integration of the global environmental system is under debate. At one extreme are scientists who argue that the global system is a *superorganism*: the lithosphere, hydrosphere, atmosphere, and biosphere are intimately interconnected by many complex pathways. According

to this **Gaia hypothesis**, the Earth is similar to an organism, and its component parts are so integrated that they are like cells in a living body. Many scientists, however, believe that the global environment is less integrated than the Gaia hypothesis argues. This does not mean that the environment is "unconnected" or even as weakly connected as a colony of cells. We have already seen that many kinds of matter cycles and energy flows interconnect the spheres and cycle within the spheres as well. As Figure 4–10 shows, the true level of integration in the global system is probably somewhat less than a "superorganism" but considerably more than a loose collection of independent parts, such as a sponge (a sponge can be considered a colony of semi-independent

sphere 2 management team in August 1994 and initiated a new non-profit joint venture with Columbia University's Lamont-Doherty Earth Observatory. The operation would be headed by such renowned scientists as Wallace Broecker, a critic of the prior management team as well as a Lamont-Doherty geochemist.

Despite their problems, the biospherians could point to some major accomplishments. During the initial two-year period, Biosphere 2 lost only 9% of its atmosphere per year, 100% of the waste and water was recycled, and the biospherians produced 80% of their food supply. Upon review, such biomes as the marsh, coral reef, and ocean were found to be healthy.

In early March 1994, a second team of biospherians entered the Biosphere 2 facility. Based on their predecessors' results,

the new team made a few changes. This time, oxygen is being continually added to the system. Special plant species, which have a higher capacity to absorb carbon dioxide, have been added, as have shade-tolerant food crop species and pest-control species (toads and geckos) to make the agricultural plots more productive.

Problems and controversy aside, the Biosphere 2 project illustrates the intricate complexity of a closed system. It has implications for our own unique Biosphere 1—the Earth.

cells). Because the system is so vast and the interconnections so complex, the exact position of the Earth system on the "integration gradient" of Figure 4–10 will probably be the topic of much debate for many years.

Complexity is often defined as how many kinds of parts a system has. This definition conforms to our intuition: a tiny insect seems more complex to us than a large rock because it has many more "parts." The insect has more complex molecules, and these are used to construct cells and organs. This example also illustrates that complexity is often hierarchical, with smaller components being used to construct larger ones.

As you would expect, the environment is enormously complex. The four spheres, with their

matter cycles and energy flows, have trillions of different components operating at many spatial and temporal scales. Organisms, soils, rainwater, air, and many other components interact in complicated ways. Even the individual spheres are complex. Even with advanced computers, no one has been able to predict the weather, or even climate, very far in the future because the atmosphere is so complex. Indeed, the many interactions make unpredictability a basic characteristic of complex systems. This inability to predict how the environment will respond to changing conditions is perhaps the major reason for so much controversy and inaction over environmental problems. Issues in Perspective 4–2 examines some methods for studying complexity.

The four spheres are not a loose collection of living and nonliving things, as a cell colony can be (on the right). But neither are the four spheres a tightly integrated "superorganism." Instead the four spheres and the Earth system are somewhere between these two extremes (perhaps analogous to a jellyfish), with a moderate degree of interdependence (toward the left).

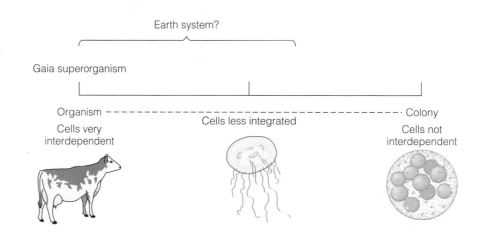

Major Obstacles: Delayed and Unpredictable Impacts

Unfortunately, social responses to environmental problems are greatly hindered by two of the key traits of the environmental system: its moderate integration and high complexity. Any system that is integrated, such as the environment, can transmit disturbances from one part of the system to another (■ Fig. 4–11). Integration results from connectedness so that resource depletion or pollution of one part of the environment can have cascading, or domino, effects into other parts. For example, removal of one species in an ecosystem will often affect the abundance of many other species, such as those that prey on or compete with it. Burning sulfur-rich coal affects the atmosphere as air pollution, but it also affects the hydrosphere when it falls as acid rain to acidify lakes. The biosphere is also affected because aquatic organisms in the lake can die from the more acidic lake water. The burning coal can even affect the lithosphere when the acid rain dissolves limestone and other alkaline rocks to form caves and sinkholes. This example shows how just one activity, burning coal, can affect all four spheres of the environment. Such wide-ranging cascading effects are anything but rare as we will see in later

■ **FIGURE 4–11**

The Mississippi River illustrates many delayed, unpredictable impacts by humans. Building of dams, for instance, has greatly reduced sediment flow into the Gulf of Mexico leading to beach erosion in many areas. (*Source: Science VU/Visuals Unlimited.*)

Systems and Chaos Theories: Ways to Study Complexity

Studying complex systems can be difficult because they have many parts that often interact in different ways. Over the last few decades, researchers have developed several methods of studying complexity. Systems theory and chaos theory, for example, try to produce general "laws" of complexity. Such laws would not only make complex systems more understandable, but they would allow us to predict more accurately how these systems will behave. Think how important such predictions could be in a complex system like the stock market or the weather!

Unfortunately, none of these theories has been entirely successful in providing a complete understanding of complexity or producing accurate predictions of how any complex system will behave. For example, despite thousands of studies and computer models, no one knows what exactly will happen to the stock market or the biosphere on a certain day in the future. Nevertheless, these theories have provided a better idea of how complex systems will generally behave under a given set of conditions. Thus, we have a general understanding of how a lake ecosystem will respond to excess nutrients even though we cannot specify every event.

Systems theory (or general systems theory) was one of the first widely used attempts to find "laws" of complex systems. It grew rapidly in the late 1940s during the boom in automation and information technology, so it has traditionally focused on how systems are regulated and become unregulated. Systems theory treats a complex system as a "black box" with inputs and outputs (as in Chapter 1). Such a system is kept at equilibrium by negative feedback processes, defined as processes that counteract perturbations. An example is a thermostat that turns a furnace on to produce heat when a house is cold and turns on air conditioning when it is hot. In contrast, positive feedback processes amplify perturbations. For example, a cooling global climate can cause more snow to remain on the ground, which leads to more global cooling because the snow reflects sunlight back into space. This causes yet more snow, and so on (a snowball effect).

Systems theory has been widely used as a convenient scheme to classify processes, such as positive feedback. However, it has often been criticized as too general or vague because by treating a system as a "black box," the theory omits many of the details of how the system operates. Therefore, more recent efforts to study complex systems have focused on more mathematical, rigorous descriptions of them. One theory that has received much attention is chaos theory. A chaotic system is one whose workings are extremely sensitive to even the slightest change: just the slightest perturbation can become greatly amplified through positive feedback. The classic example is the weather, as first described by E. Lorenz who helped discover chaos theory in the early 1960s. Lorenz created a set of equations that precisely described atmospheric conditions and showed how even tiny changes in one of the parameters could cause a massive alteration of the weather in a few days. This is often called the "butterfly effect" by analogy with the idea that a butterfly flapping its wings in South America could eventually affect the weather in North America (Fig. 1). By creating tiny changes in atmospheric turbulence, which in turn create cascading effects on larger air flows, the butterfly could have a major impact. (Of course, the chances that it actually will produce such a major impact are extremely low.)

Chaos theory's most important finding so far is that even simple systems, such as several atoms, often have chaotic properties. Consequently, predicting their precise behavior very far into the future is nearly impossible. How can we make predictions when a minute unseen change, as in the butterfly effect, can have cascading effects? Many theorists think it will always be impossible to accurately predict precise future behaviors in complex systems, which have even more potential for chaos than simple systems. Nevertheless, by applying chaos theory, patterns of regularity can be discerned and studied.

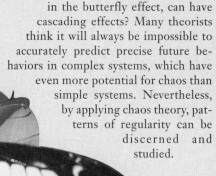

FIGURE 1
Can a butterfly in the rainforest affect the weather in North America? (*Source:* Kjell B. Sandved/Visuals Unlimited.)

■ FIGURE 4–12
"We can never do merely one
thing." Whenever we do
something, we cause a cascade
of impacts. These impacts
become less predictable with
time.

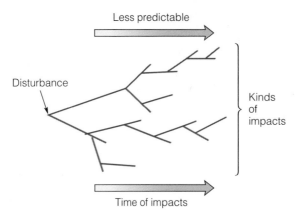

chapters. This connectedness of the environment means that virtually any action has a number of consequences, many of which are unforeseen and unintended. Such cascades are so important that the biologist Garrett Hardin has formulated the **first law of ecology**: "We can never do merely one thing." This is often called the "law of unintended consequences."

That the environment is only moderately integrated ("loosely connected") greatly hinders our ability to observe, and thus correct, the unintended consequences of our actions. The indirect connections and interactions in the environment create delays, or long lag times, before cascading effects become visible (■ Fig. 4–12). Returning to the acid rain example, it may take many years of coal burning before fish populations in lakes are affected. In other cases, the impacts can be delayed for centuries, millennia, or even longer. Global environmental impacts will usually take an especially long time to occur. Many decades and probably centuries will pass before the full effects of added atmospheric carbon dioxide on global temperature are observable. This lag time is one of the main reasons for the debate over global warming.

As we have seen, the complexity of the environment leads to unpredictability, which hinders social responses to environmental problems. As Figure 4–12 shows, the unintended cascades we cause not only take a long time, but occur as unexpected, complicated chains of events. Consider the Case Study, which discusses how global warming will likely change the distribution of diseases affecting human populations on Earth. How many people associate global warming with disease? Very few.

In addition to having many interactions, complex systems are unpredictable because some of the interactions exhibit **positive feedback**. Positive feedback occurs when part of a system responds to change in a way that magnifies the ini-

tial change. For example, evidence indicates that a slight increase in average global temperature can cause a further increase by melting some of the glaciers and snow that reflect sunlight back into space. Instead of reflecting light, more of the Earth's surface becomes available to absorb heat. Another example is poverty in developing countries that results from overpopulation; the poverty leads to high reproductive rates and thus still further overpopulation. In nontechnical terms, positive feedback is often called a snowball effect or vicious circle.

Society in the Environmental System

■ Figure 4–13 shows that modern society is embedded within the environment, being dependent on it for the materials and energy needed to maintain civilization. It also shows how industrialized society accelerates the cycling of matter and the flow of energy through itself and the four spheres.

In Chapter 1, we saw that all environmental problems involve either depletion (consumption) of sources or pollution (waste) of sinks. Thus, we can measure the net environmental impact of society by these two processes. As Figure 4–13 shows, depletion occurs when the accelerated cycling and flow remove matter and energy faster than they are being renewed by natural processes. Conversely, pollution occurs when the accelerated cycling and flow are discharged

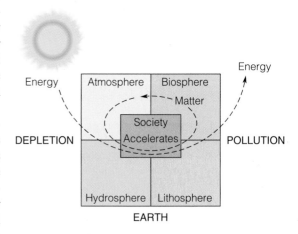

■ **FIGURE 4–13**
Society accelerates the cycling of matter through the four spheres, which depletes resources (matter inputs to society) and causes pollution (matter outputs by society). This acceleration is increasing due to increasing population (P) and traditional, nonsustainable technologies (T) (see Chapter 1). These technologies also increase the flow of energy by burning fossil fuels. Slowing population growth and using sustainable technologies will reduce this acceleration (Chapter 1).

Global Warming and Disease: Personal Choices, Collective Problems

A major theme of this chapter is that the complex connectedness of environmental systems leads to unpredictability of human impacts. Our individual actions can accumulate to have unseen consequences that are not evident for many years.

A good example is a 1995 landmark study released by the World Health Organization on the effects of global climate change on human health. The vast majority of research on global climate change has focused on physical impacts, such as a rise in sea level. But there are growing signs that the potential effects on human health are no less serious. This possibility came to public attention in 1993 when a controversial paper was published in the medical journal *The Lancet* (volume 342, p. 1216) concluding that the 1991 cholera outbreak in South America was related to localized warming of Pacific Ocean waters from global climate changes. The paper argued that the warming had caused the rapid growth of plankton that harbor the cholera bacterium leading to thousands of deaths (Fig. 1).

Though the causes of the cholera incident are still being debated, a number of new studies have identified other potential health impacts of global warming. One predicted impact is that many cities will experience "killer

FIGURE 1
Burial of cholera victims in Peru. (*Source:* Kit King/Gamma Liaison.)

heat waves" that will increase death from bronchitis, asthma, and many other ailments. Many other models show that the incidence of tropical diseases will increase significantly. Global warming is expected to have the most deadly effect on tropical developing nations, which are already suffering from poor sanitation. Epidemiologists (disease experts) predict increased rates of malaria, sleeping sickness, and the many other diseases shown in Table 1. Each year these diseases afflict more than 500 million people, killing over 2 million.

With global warming, the tropical carriers of these diseases, such as mosquitoes, will

spread as tropical conditions, including swamps, expand their ranges. An estimate published in the journal *Environmental Health Perspectives* in 1995 projected that a global temperature increase of 5.4°F (3°C) in the next century could result in 50–80 million new malaria cases per year. A natural "experiment" provides data that supports such projections: In 1987, the average annual temperature was 1.8°F (1°C) above normal; this increase was linked to a 337% rise in malaria that year in Rwanda.

Questions

1. How many people do you think are aware that a trip to the market in their car could contribute to an increase in malaria? Does this knowledge have any impact on your personal choices for transportation?

2. If major wide-scale problems, such as global warming, result from the accumulation of millions of personal choices each day, how can such problems be solved?

3. Does a nation such as the United States, which contributes more than its "fair share" of greenhouse gases to the atmosphere, bear any responsibility to help treat increased incidences of malaria and other diseases in developing countries?

TABLE 1 *Major Tropical Diseases Likely To Spread With Global Warming*

DISEASE	VECTOR	POPULATION AT RISK (MILLIONS)	PREVALENCE OF INFECTION	PRESENT DISTRIBUTION	LIKELIHOOD OF ALTERED DISTRIBUTION WITH WARMING[a]
Malaria	Mosquito	2100	270 million	(sub)tropics	+++
Schistosomiasis	Water snail	600	200 million	(sub)tropics	++
Filariasis	Mosquito	900	90 million	(sub)tropics	+
Onchocerciasis (river blindness)	Black fly	90	18 million	Africa/Latin America	+
African trypanosomiasis (sleeping sickness)	Tsetse fly	50	25,000 new cases/year	Tropical Africa	+
Dengue	Mosquito	Estimates unavailable		Tropics	++
Yellow fever	Mosquito	Estimates unavailable		Tropical South America and Africa	+

[a]As assessed by the World Health Organization: + = likely, ++ = very likely, +++ = highly likely.
(*Source:* Reprinted with permission from "If the Mercury Soars, So May Health Hazards." *Science* 267 [17 February 1995]: 957. Table from *The Lancet*. Copyright © 1995 American Association for the Advancement of Science.)

FIGURE 4-14
Pollution occurs when natural purification processes are overwhelmed, such as by large amounts of nutrients or poisons. (*Source:* Robert Visser/Greenpeace.)

FIGURE 4-14
Pollution occurs when natural purification processes are overwhelmed, such as by large amounts of nutrients or poisons. (*Source:* Robert Visser/Greenpeace.)

into the environment, overwhelming the local natural purification processes (Fig. 4-14).

Disturbing the Four Spheres

Problems of environmental depletion and pollution both exhibit the delayed and unpredictable impacts we have discussed. The remainder of this book is about these problems. Figure 4-15 outlines the rest of the book, showing which chapters examine each of the four spheres and the effects of depletion and pollution on each.

FIGURE 4-15
This is a modified version of Figure 1-22, presenting a detailed overview of the book. The diagram indicates which chapters discuss environmental depletion and pollution problems, and social solutions.

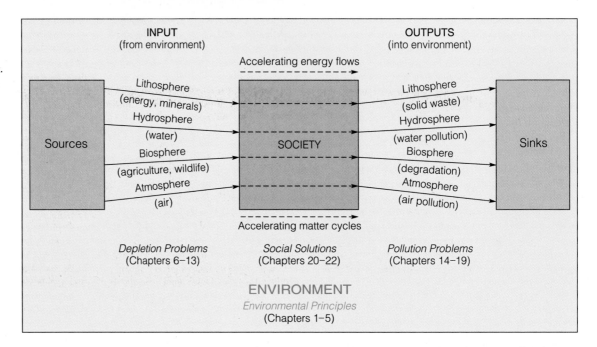

SUMMARY

Everything is either matter or energy. Although matter is finite, it is constantly being recycled in one of the Earth's many cycles. These cycles carry energy and matter through the Earth's four spheres. These spheres are the biosphere, which includes all life, and the atmosphere, hydrosphere, and lithosphere, which are the three physical spheres. The three physical spheres represent three states of matter: gas, liquid, and solid.

The biogeochemical cycles transport the elements important to life through all four spheres. The six most important elements for living organisms are carbon, hydrogen, oxygen, phosphorus, nitrogen, and sulfur. Biogeochemical cycles (1) feature many different pathways between the atmosphere, hydrosphere, and lithosphere; (2) have varying rates of cycling, depending on chemical reactivity, the occurrence of a gaseous phase, and residence time; and (3) are being disturbed by human activity. Most commonly, the cycles are accelerated by disturbance. For example, carbon is the product of fossil fuel burning. The increasing use of fossil fuels has led to an increased depletion of fuels and increased atmospheric carbon dioxide, promoting global warming.

Energy cannot be created or destroyed, but is capable of transformation, according to the first law of thermodynamics. The second law of thermodynamics says that during transformation, some useful energy is lost as "heat," producing entropy. This means that energy cannot be recycled like matter; rather, it must be renewed, with the main source of new energy coming from the Sun. Unfortunately, most traditional industrial technology does not rely on renewable energy from the Sun. It relies on fossil fuels (nonrenewable resources), which cause most major kinds of air pollution.

The environment, working as a system, has three key traits: (1) openness with a constantly renewing outside supply of energy; (2) integration among the four spheres; and (3) complexity, which causes unpredictability, hindering social responses to environmental problems.

KEY TERMS

biogeochemical cycles
carbon cycle
closed system
complexity
energy budget
entropy
first law of ecology

first law of thermodynamics
Gaia hypothesis
integration
law of conservation of matter and energy
limiting nutrient
nonrenewable resources
openness
open system

photosynthesis
positive feedback
renewable energy
residence time
respiration
second law of thermodynamics
system

STUDY QUESTIONS

1. Name the six elements most important to life.
2. What is a system?
3. Where is the majority of carbon stored?
4. Why do different substances cycle at different rates?
5. Why do large amounts of phosphorus become locked up?
6. What is the limiting nutrient in most ecosystems?
7. List several examples of disturbed biogeochemical cycles.

8. How is energy different from matter? How is it similar?
9. Why can energy not be recycled like matter?
10. Why are renewable energies much less polluting?
11. Name two alternatives to the Sun for the Earth's source of energy.
12. How much solar radiation does photosynthesis use?
13. What two traits of environmental systems hinder social responses?

14. If plants are only 2% efficient in using sunlight that they capture, and they capture less than 0.1% of all sunlight striking Earth, what is the total percentage of sunlight striking Earth that plants actually use?
15. According to some estimates, it would take about 20 centuries to melt all the ice on Earth and raise sea level by over 300 feet (92 m). How many human generations are 20 centuries? Assume that each generation is 25 years.

ESSAY QUESTIONS

1. Discuss the two "loops" of the carbon cycle.
2. Describe the major features of biogeochemical cycles.
3. What are the sources of the Earth's energy?
4. Name and describe the three key traits of the environmental system.
5. What are the two laws of thermodynamics? What is entropy?

SUGGESTED READINGS

Begon, M., J. Harper, and C. Townsend. 1990. *Ecology*, 2d ed. Cambridge, Mass.: Blackwell.

Gleick, J. 1987. *Chaos: Making a new science.* New York: Viking.

Myers, N., ed. 1993. *Gaia: An atlas of planetary management.* New York: Anchor Books.

Odum, E. P. 1993. *Ecology and our endangered life support system*, 2d ed. Sunderland, Mass.: Sinauer.

Post, W. M., *et al.* 1990. The global carbon cycle. *American Scientist* 78: 310–26.

Ricklefs, R. E. 1990. *Ecology*, 3d ed. New York: W. H. Freeman.

Schlesinger, W. H. 1992. *Biogeochemistry: An analysis of global change.* San Diego: Academic Press.

Smith, R. L. 1990. *Elements of Ecology and Field Biology*, 4th ed. New York: Harper & Row.

*D*EMOGRAPHY

PHOTO   *A street scene in Dhaka, the capital of densely populated Bangladesh. (Source: AP/Wide World Photos.)*

The current world population of more than 5.8 billion is cause for concern among many environmentalists. Population is one of the major factors in the I = PT (impact equals population times technology) equation that we discussed in Chapter 1. For most of history, the world's population grew only very slowly or not at all, but in the last two hundred years, it has exploded. In the late 1960s, the world population was growing at a record rate of about 2% a year, and some pessimists feared the worst—massive famine, disease, wars, civil unrest, and widespread global ecosystem collapse. Fortunately, these dire predictions have not come to pass. Due to various factors, the world population growth rate declined to about 1.75% in the 1980s and currently stands at about 1.6–1.7%. Nevertheless, even if the **growth rate** continues to decline, there will still be an estimated 8 to 10 billion people on our planet by the middle of the twenty-first century (Fig. 5–1). Will the world be able to feed, clothe, and house all these people? And can it be done in a sustainable manner? These are major issues of our time.

The United Nations has held major intergovernmental conferences on world population every 10 years since 1974. The first conference suggested that the solution might be the rapid industrialization of the developing nations where most of the rapid population increases were occurring. The participants reasoned that since fertility rates in Europe dropped to or below replacement level after the Industrial Revolution, the same should occur as developing nations industrialize and modernize. Researchers have since questioned whether industrialization really causes a population to stabilize. Correlation does not necessarily mean causation. Furthermore, could the world sustain the potential ecological destruction that might be involved in fully industrializing all of the developing world?

The 1984 United Nations population conference emphasized increasing access to modern family planning technologies and information, including contraceptives. To a large extent, such methods have paid off with results. Worldwide contraceptive use increased from 30% in 1970 to 55% in 1990, and the average family size dropped from 4.9 to 3.5 children. Yet it is unclear how much progress can be made via increased access to family planning information and modern contraceptives.

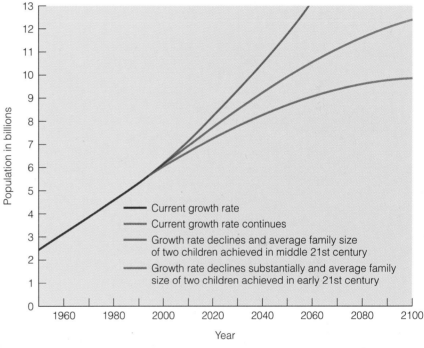

Furthermore, these are emotionally, politically, and religiously charged issues. Many people associate modern family planning, rightly or wrongly, with advocacy of abortion, a practice seen by some as morally repugnant. At the 1984 conference, the U.S. government, under the Reagan administration, objected to any kind of family planning that might include the possibility of abortion and cut off funding of international groups that provided abortion counseling (funding was restored in 1993 by the Clinton administration). The Vatican opposes any forms of contraception or abortion, as do many fundamentalist Islamic groups.

Indeed, such objections made headlines during the 1994 world population conference in Cairo. The Roman Catholic church objected to much of the original language in draft documents associated with the conference, and Islamic religious leaders and scholars called for a boycott of the conference. In fact some Muslim countries, such as Saudi Arabia, Lebanon, and Sudan, withdrew their delegations.

Still, productive ideas came out of the population conference, as the interrelationships among population, poverty, inequality among individuals and nations, environmental decay, and sustainable development were discussed. No longer can population, or overpopulation, be viewed simply as a cause of environmental destruction; rather it must be viewed as a major symptom of

FIGURE 5–1

World population projections into the twenty-first century. (*Source:* Based on U.N. data and projections found in World Resources Institute, *World Resources 1992–1993* and *World Resources 1994–1995* [New York: Oxford University Press, 1992, 1994].)

underlying social, economic, and environmental issues. Poverty, high fertility, and environmental degradation go hand in hand, each reinforcing the other. Studies in developing countries have demonstrated that as natural resources are depleted, people perceive a need for more children to help gather increasingly scarce fuel wood, obtain clean water, or perform other necessary tasks; consequently, birth rates rise. But as a result, there are fewer resources to go around, and the people are trapped in a downward spiral. Educating women, decreasing poverty, conserving resources, and reversing environmental degradation all have the effect of depressing population growth rates. A major focus of the 1994 population conference was women's education and status. In recent years, researchers have confirmed that as women's literacy rate and social status increase in many developing regions, the fertility rate decreases.

The United Nations has stated that the low status of women is the "root cause" of population growth and poverty in many developing countries. As women's access to education increases, so does their value in the workplace and their social status. Rather than having more children, many women use their newfound education and status to improve the quality of life for the children they have. And educating the women of the world is relatively inexpensive. Estimates are that raising the education level of all women in developing nations to at least equality with men would cost only $6.5 billion per year, less than is spent on lawn care annually in the United States, and much less than is spent on video games each year in the industrialized nations.

 NTRODUCTION

Currently, approximately 5.8 billion people are inhabiting the face of our planet. Over 10,000 people are added each hour, over a quarter million persons a day. The global population is increasing by approximately 90 to 100 million persons a year. **Demography** is the study of the size, growth, density, distribution, and other characteristics of human populations.

Earth is now a very crowded planet. Only about 4.9–9.9 billion acres (2–4 billion hectares) of the Earth's approximately 37 billion acres (15 billion hectares) of land surface are potentially suitable for human cultivation, the rest being too cold, too wet, or too dry for human purposes. In actuality, only about 3.7 billion acres (1.5 billion hectares) are cultivated. Given our current population, this means only about 0.64 acre (not even a third of a hectare) of cropland is available per person. Furthermore, the amount of land per person is declining yearly as the human population increases, cultivatable lands are eroded and destroyed, forests are cleared, and grazing land is overworked.

Human overpopulation is one of the central issues in environmental science. As noted in Chapter 1, high population levels increase both major types of environmental problems: (1) resource use and (2) pollution and waste. For example, our species alone utilizes, either directly or by diverting it from other uses, an estimated 40% of the world's terrestrial green plant production. The other 60% is divided among the remaining 5 million to 50 million terrestrial species with which we share the globe.

In this chapter we will review the early development of human society, trace the initially slow and subsequently **exponential growth** of the human population, and begin to explore the ways in which human population pressure has progressively modified the environment. We will also briefly discuss what is being done to address the current "population crisis."

WORLD POPULATION CHANGES OVER TIME

As discussed in Chapter 3, natural animal populations often exhibit an "S-shaped" growth curve—slow growth ("**lag phase**"), then rapid growth ("exponential phase"), then slowing down as limits are reached, and finally leveling out. The same curve can be applied to human populations. On a global scale, the human population is still in the rapid growth phase.

Starting Slow: The "Lag Phase"

About one million years ago, the total human population was only some 125,000. From this small size, the population slowly increased until by about 8000 B.C., it numbered about 5 to 10 million (Fig. 5–2). This slow increase was due to (1) the invention and development of tools

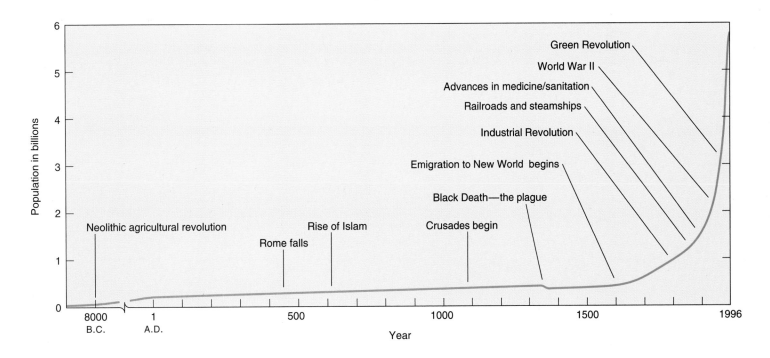

The graph shows Population in billions on the vertical axis (0 to 6) and Year on the horizontal axis (8000 B.C. / 1 A.D. to 1996). Labeled events include: Neolithic agricultural revolution, Rome falls, Rise of Islam, Crusades begin, Black Death—the plague, Emigration to New World begins, Industrial Revolution, Railroads and steamships, Advances in medicine/sanitation, World War II, Green Revolution.

■ **FIGURE 5–2**
World population changes over time.

which enabled food and other necessities to be procured more efficiently and thus allowed more people to be supported in the same area, and (2) migration to new areas, as from the Old World to the Americas. Although we tend to focus on chipped stone tools because they are most readily preserved in the archaeological record, many organic tools (woven nets, baskets, clothing, tents and other shelters) also were invented. Also "discovered" and used during this period was fire—to heat, cook food, and scare away potentially harmful predatory animals.

Before 10,000 years ago, humans had spread through most of the world, reaching all of the mainland landmasses except Antarctica and the islands of the Caribbean, Polynesia, Madagascar, and New Zealand, all of which were colonized subsequently. This simple spread of people to new areas allowed the world population to increase.

The extent to which early humans impacted and permanently modified their environments remains a hotly debated topic. Some researchers believe that through overhunting and competition for environmental resources, the Upper Paleolithic hunters of Europe, Africa, Asia, and the Americas were responsible for global patterns of extinction among large mammals, such as the woolly mammoth and the woolly rhinoceros, during the later Pleistocene (around 100,000 to 10,000 years ago).

In relatively small, isolated ecosystems, such as those found on islands, it is now well documented that gatherer and hunter cultures can cause a number of species to go extinct. Within a few

hundred years of the settlement of Madagascar by gatherers and hunters, a pygmy hippopotamus and a large flightless bird had gone extinct. The orginal colonists of New Zealand, also a gathering and hunting people, drove several dozen birds to extinction within 600 years of entering the island.

Another way that early humans may have modifed their environments was by setting fires. Setting forests on fire could both have made hunting easier by clearing the brush and also increased the populations of hunted herbivorous mammals, which would have thrived on the new growth of plants that would sprout up in cleared areas. Over the course of time, periodic fires would greatly modify the vegetational types in the area.

Thus, human modification of the environment is nothing new; many habitats that we think of as "natural" may in fact be the product of human intervention over tens of thousands of years. What is new in the late twentieth century is the extent, degree, and rate at which humans are modifying their environment—much quicker than we or the rest of nature can adapt to the new conditions.

The Agricultural (Neolithic) Revolution: Beginning Exponential Growth

The advent of domestication and agriculture about 10,000 years ago led to a sharp rise in the human birth rate for reasons discussed below. Though often referred to as the **agricultural (Neolithic) revolution**, this was actually a gradual process that extended over eight or more millen-

The Plague

In the mid-fourteenth century Europe, as well as much of Asia and Africa, was devastated by an outbreak of plague, which contemporaries called the Black Death (Fig. 1). The disease actually took three forms: bubonic plague, pneumonic plague, and septicemic plague (all caused by the bacterium variously known as *Pasteurella pestis* or *Yersinia pestis*). It is estimated that at least 25 million, and perhaps as many as 75 million, of Europe's population of 100 million died between 1347 and 1351. As the plague raged, the social structure of Europe was destroyed. Contemporary accounts report that government and law enforcement, religious ceremonies, and medical practice disappeared in areas where the plague was worst. In an ecological sense, the plague can be viewed as a classic case of a density-dependent mechanism that served to limit the population. Six and a half centuries later, it should serve as a warning to us as we continue to overcrowd our world.

Modern research suggests that the fourteenth-century plague may have originated among the wild rodents that live in the Kirghiz Steppes of Asia, one of several apparently permanent reservoirs of plague (others are in China, India, the southern

■ FIGURE 1

Victims of the Black Death appear in this fourteenth-century French fresco. A physician lances a plague-caused bubo (a swollen and inflamed lymph node) on a woman's neck; on the left is another victim with an enlarged bubo under his arm. (*Source*: The Granger Collection, New York.)

former Soviet Union, and the western United States). Under normal conditions, the plague does not spread beyond these reservoirs, but occasionally it does—with devastating effects. In the early fourteenth century, a major outbreak ravaged China,

nia and occurred independently at different rates in different parts of the world. Full domestication of many plants and animals seems to have been established in the Old World by 8000–5000 B.C. Once agriculture and domestication were entrenched, the delicate near balance between births and deaths, which had apparently held for hundreds of millennia, was broken, and the world's human population began to increase dramatically (see Fig. 5–2). By A.D. 1 the world population had increased to between 150 million and 300 million, and cities such as Rome had populations as high as one million. By contrast, the world population

had taken a million or more years to reach a total of, at most, 10 million people.

The dramatic increase in human population has been attributed to several factors: (1) Settlement on farms may have allowed women to bear and raise more children for, without the nomadic lifestyle, they no longer had to carry young offspring for great distances. Previously, women may have chosen to raise fewer children, perhaps using natural contraceptives and practicing primitive forms of abortion or infanticide to get rid of unwanted offspring. (2) Children are more useful in agricultural communities than in hunter and

India, and other eastern and Middle Eastern populations, killing millions. The plague spread west, and rumors of the terror spread even more quickly.

In the mid-fourteenth century, the city of Genoa in Italy controlled the Crimean port of Caffa on the Black Sea, which was attacked by Mongolian Tartars (Tatars) who had traveled west across Asia from the Kirghiz Steppes. While laying siege to Caffa, the Tartars began to die of a strange disease, characterized by fever, delirium, pneumonia, and in some cases enlarged, pus-filled, lymph nodes (buboes) that opened to the skin and drained spontaneously. The Tartars decided to withdraw, but before leaving, they catapulted the bodies of their dead comrades into the city —an early and particularly gruesome instance of biological warfare. The inhabitants of Caffa subsequently contracted the plague, and when infected Genoese returned to Italy in 1347, they carried the disease to Europe.

Medieval Europeans had no idea what caused the plague or how to control it. It is now known to be caused by a bacterium that can be carried by rodents, such as rats and squirrels, and is transmitted from rodents to humans by a flea. For tens of thousands, or even millions, of years, populations of *Yersinia pestis* have been living in the guts of fleas that feed on rats and infect them with the plague. Once the rat dies, the fleas seek another host, carrying with them the plague bacilli. Eventually, the plague-carrying flea also dies, but often not before it has infected other mammalian hosts and thus indirectly other fleas that feed on the same host. In the case of Caffa, rats probably fed on the bodies of the dead Tartars and became infected, fleas fed on the rats, and the fleas subsequently bit and infected humans.

Even today bubonic plague is not well understood—and isolated cases and small outbreaks continue to occur among humans. Why does it remain contained among rodent colonies for centuries, then suddenly and unexpectedly spread at an alarming rate among the human population? And why does the outbreak subside? Do only individuals who have some type of natural resistance to the plague remain? Are reservoirs of plague perhaps always in waiting, ready to spread when conditions are right? Unfortunately, we may not know what those "right" conditions are.

We should remember that, even with our advanced medical knowledge and technology, we could conceivably find ourselves again facing an unknown or poorly understood, but rampant and devastating, disease. Some would even suggest that the current AIDS (Acquired Immune Deficiency Syndrome) crisis is a roughly analogous situation. In fact, a 1994 report compiled by the U.S. Census Bureau's Center for International Research predicted that AIDS could have a significant impact on death rates and population sizes in many countries, including Uganda, Zambia, Zaire, Brazil, Haiti, and Thailand. For instance, according to the center's projections, if AIDS did not exist, Uganda, Thailand, and Brazil would be predicted to have populations of 49.8 million, 76.6 million, and 210.5 million, respectively, in 2020, but incorporating AIDS mortality their respective populations are expected to reach only 34.1 million, 62.9 million, and 197.5 million in 2020. Moreover, AIDS could devastate the economies of some poorer nations. Increased resources will need to be directed toward caring for people with AIDS, and as AIDS continues to spread, the productivity of the workforce will decrease.

gatherer cultures and therefore more highly valued. This would have increased the incentive to have more children. (3) Agriculture and domestication may have made softer foods available, which allowed mothers to wean their children earlier. Thus women could bear additional children over the course of their lifetimes. (4) Agriculture and domestication, by their very nature, allowed and promoted higher densities of people. Indeed, with farming one family or group of persons could raise more food than they personally needed. This surplus led directly to the rise of cities and civilization because it allowed people to develop and concentrate on manufacturing, trading, and other specializations. In a classic example of positive feedback, this in turn led to rapid advances in technology, art, and other innovations.

After late ancient times, the world's population slowly but steadily increased, except for a slight decline in the fourteenth century due to the plague (see Fig. 5–2 and Issues in Perspective 5–1), until the mid-seventeenth century when it totaled approximately 500 million. Since about 1650, the human population has grown at an ever increasing rate, reaching 800 million around 1750, 1.2 billion in 1850, slightly over 2.5 billion in 1950, 4.08 billion in 1975, and 5.8 billion today. Recent United Nations projections estimate that the world population will be 6.25 billion in the year 2000 and 8.5 billion in 2025. But such estimates are based on many uncertain variables, such as how quickly modern birth control methods will spread, and fertility rates drop. Current expectations are that the global population may not stabilize until it reaches 11 or 12 billion toward the end of the twenty-first century. And this is assuming that continued advances are made in decreasing global fertility rates and increasing global use of contraceptives!

Carrying Capacity

As we discussed in Chapter 3, many natural populations of organisms increase very rapidly when invading a new area, but then population growth slows as the upper limit of the number of individuals that the area can support is approached. Eventually, an equilibrium population size is reached. This pattern can be conceptualized in terms of the **carrying capacity** (represented by K; see Issues in Perspective 5–2 for details) for the particular population of organisms in a given area. K is the equilibrium limit of the population, or the carrying capacity, and can be thought of as the number of individuals of a certain population that can be supported in a certain area for a prolonged period of time given the resources of that area.

Applying these generalizations to human world population growth, we can ask, What is the carrying capacity of Earth relative to humans? This question has yet to be satisfactorily answered. Some believe that humans have already exceeded the world's carrying capacity (see Issues in Perspective 5–3 for an early proponent of this idea). How could this be? Remember that many people alive today are unable to meet their basic nutritional requirements. When a species lives within its carrying capacity, it does not degrade the resources upon which it depends. While degrading our resources (for example, through topsoil erosion and the pumping of underground water for irrigation faster than it is renewed), we produce enough food globally to feed a population of 5.8 billion, but more than 800 million of those people are undernourished. Given current global food production, it has been estimated that about 6 billion could be fed adequately if everyone kept to a vegetarian diet.

On the other hand, some persons believe we have not even begun to approach the physical limits on human population size. With appropriate technology and distribution systems for foodstuffs and other necessities, some argue that Earth might be able to support 40 to 50 billion humans (although for how long is another issue). The human carrying capacity also depends on the standard of living that is acceptable for the average human. To a certain extent, we can conceptually increase the world's carrying capacity by lowering the standards at which we are willing to exist.

One can argue that the world's human carrying capacity has systematically changed over time. Although physical and biological factors, such as the withdrawal of the ice and general global warming at the end of the Pleistocene (end of the Ice Ages) and the evolution or introduction of new plant or animal species, may have allowed human densities to increase, the prime factor increasing the human carrying capacity has probably been our increasingly advanced technology and culture.

As we described earlier, the development of stone tools, the harnessing of fire, and especially agriculture and domestication allowed humans to increase in population size from the hundreds of thousands to the hundreds of millions. Essentially, humans increased the carrying capacity of Earth for themselves.

Consider the last several hundred years. Specific developments that have increased the human population since the mid-seventeenth century include advances in agriculture, such as growing legumes, which replace nitrogen in the soils. This allowed fields to be cultivated continuously, rather than having to lie fallow every third year; the result was increased food production that could support a growing population. Also important was the development of modern theories of disease (the "germ theory") and sanitation, which decreased **infant mortality** and increased **life expectancy**. Vaccines for diseases were developed. Food preservation and storage were vastly improved. And, of course, the **Industrial Revolution** allowed the cheap and efficient mass production of necessary commodities. Since the mid-nineteenth century, we have seen continued improvements in mass production of food and goods, increasing advances in medical fields, and the so-called Green Revolution of the mid-twentieth century, which allowed greatly increased crop yields (see Chapter 13). All of these developments have not only increased the world's theoretical human carrying capacity, but they have also promoted the actual growth of the world population.

In the last few decades, though, major environmental changes, such as the buildup of greenhouse gases and the destruction of the ozone

Human Population Equations and Statistics

The basic equation describing the growth of a population (the change in the size of a population, represented by ΔN, that takes place over some interval of time, represented by Δt) is $\Delta N/\Delta t = rN$, where N is the population size, t is time, and r is the intrinsic rate of increase of the population (birth and recruitment rate minus death and emigration rate). If we are discussing the global human population as a whole, there is no recruitment or emigration, so the intrinsic rate of increase is simply the birth rate minus the death rate.

In discussing human populations, the following basic statistics are commonly used:

- *Crude birth rate.* The number of births per year per 1000 members of a population. The crude birth rate is commonly determined by dividing the total number of births in the given population by the midyear population size (which gives the number of births per individual per year) and then multiplying by 1000.

- *Crude death rate.* The number of deaths per year per 1000 members of a population. The crude death rate is calculated in a manner comparable to the crude birth rate.

- ***Rate of natural increase*** *(essentially* r*).* The crude birth rate minus the crude death rate. The rate of natural increase can be expressed in terms of number of additional humans per 1000 members of the population at midyear. Thus, a rate of natural increase of 20 per 1000 (= .02) means that the population is increasing overall by 20 individuals per 1,000 members of the population each year. A population of 10,000 at the midpoint of one year would grow to a population of 10,200 by the midpoint of the following year. When the rate of natural increase is a negative number, the population is decreasing in size over time rather than increasing.

- ***Percent annual growth*** *(or change) of a population.* The rate of natural increase expressed as a percentage of the given population. For example, if the rate of natural increase is 20 per 1000 (20/1000 = 0.02), the percent annual growth is 2%.

- ***Doubling time*** *of a population.* The amount of time that a population of a given size at time zero, increasing at a fixed rate, will take to double in size. Essentially, the annual growth rate of a population is equivalent to the compounding of interest on money in the bank; that is, as dollars of interest added to the account will themselves earn interest, so too will persons added to a population give birth to more people. To demonstrate, if the annual growth rate is 1.0%, then the doubling time will be 70 years (rather than 100 years as it would be if "interest" were not compounded). Likewise, the doubling times of populations with growth rates of 2.0, 3.0, or 4.0% per year are 35, 24, and 17 years, respectively. The doubling time of a population can be calculated roughly by dividing the percent annual growth into 70. For example, a population with a percent annual growth of 2.0 will double in size in about 35 years (70/2.0 = 35).

- *General fertility rate.* The total number of births in a population in any given year as a function of the total number of women in their reproductive years, variously defined as from age 15 to age 44 or 49. Often the general fertility rate is expressed in terms of number of births per 1000 women in their reproductive years and thus is calculated similarly to the crude birth and death rate, except that the number of births for a given year is divided only by the midyear number of reproductive-aged women in the population.

- *Total fertility rate (TFR).* Basically, the number of children a woman of a given population will have, on average, during her childbearing years. Replacement level is generally considered to be approximately 2.1 children per woman. (Women must replace not only themselves, but their male partners as well. All other factors being equal, more males tend to be born than females—about 105.5 male births for every 100 females born—and not all children make it to their reproductive years.)

- *Infant mortality rate.* The number of babies that die before their first birthday, given that they are born alive. Babies that are born but die shortly thereafter are included in both the crude birth rate and the crude death rate.

- *Life expectancy at birth.* The average number of years that a typical newborn baby can expect to live when it is born. Life expectancy can change over time; for instance, in certain populations the biggest hurdle to the newborn may be to survive for its first five years.

- *Carrying capacity.* The equation $\Delta N/\Delta T = rN$ maps an exponential J-shaped curve (see the discussion in Chapter 3) of population growth. This equation predicts astronomical population sizes after relatively short periods of time, and it does not take into account any factors that may limit the growth of a population. The equation for the J-shaped curve can be modified as follows:

$$\Delta N/\Delta t = rN \left[(K - N)/K \right]$$

where K is the equilibrium limit of the population, or the carrying capacity. This gives an S-shaped curve. The population size increases, but eventually levels out as factors that limit population growth take effect—such as lack of food, space to live, and so forth.

Thomas Malthus, the Original Population Pessimist

The English political economist Thomas Robert Malthus (1766–1834) is generally credited with being the first modern pessimistic thinker concerning population growth rates and the overpopulation problem. Indeed, the term **neo-Malthusian** is often used to refer to those who believe that the modern rapid increase in human population is extremely detrimental. Neo-Malthusians generally believe that we will run out of resources and seriously damage or destroy our environment unless we can control our breeding.

In his *An Essay on the Principle of Population, as It Affects the Future Improvement of Society* (1798, revised and enlarged in 1803), Malthus suggested that while the size of a population increases geometrically or exponentially, the means that support the population tend only to increase arithmetically; thus, increasing populations invariably outstrip their resource bases (Fig. 1). As this occurs, the poor get poorer and more desperate, leading to misery and vice. If humans do not intervene of their own accord, such as through "moral restraint" (restraint in breeding),

■ **FIGURE 1**
A "Malthusian view" of an overcrowded London of the future is shown in this 1851 George Cruikshank etching. (*Source:* The Granger Collection, New York.)

then the population increase will ultimately be checked by natural means, such as widespread famine, disease, and possible warfare. Although Malthus did not necessarily advocate direct birth control, he did suggest that early marriages should be avoided and self-restraint should be cultivated. Most neo-Malthusians are strong proponents of accessible birth control and family planning services.

Since his *Essay* first appeared, Malthus's ideas have been widely discussed—both admired and heavily criticized—and have greatly influenced subsequent generations. The effects of his writings have been profound in economic, political, social, and biological circles. It was from reading a version of Malthus's *Essay* that Charles Darwin hit upon the idea of natural selection and "survival of the fittest" as the major mechanism underlying biological evolution.

---

layer, have been taking place on a global level. Some observers have interpreted these changes as indicating that we have finally reached, and perhaps begun to exceed, Earth's carrying capacity for humans.

Growth Rate and Doubling Time of the World's Human Population

Many demographers are concerned that the human population growth rate has generally been increasing; the doubling time for the human population has been getting smaller and smaller. Between 10,000 years ago and A.D. 1650, the **annual growth rate** was less than 0.1% a year for a doubling time of over 1000 years. Between 1650 and 1850, however, the human population doubled again, reaching one billion in the mid-

dle of the nineteenth century. This was a doubling time of only 200 years, or an average annual growth rate of about 0.35%. In the next 80 years or so, the population doubled again, giving an average annual growth rate approaching 0.9%. In the late 1960s and into the 1970s, the annual growth rate hovered around 2.0%, and thus the doubling time was about 35 years. An annual growth rate of 2.0% may seem small, but it is enormous—especially in comparison with the annual growth rate during the vast majority of human history and prehistory. The human species has been adding more and more individuals at a faster and faster pace (study Figure 5–2 closely).

During the 1970s and 1980s, the annual rate of growth of the world's population began to decrease slightly, from about 2.0% per year to approximately 1.7% in 1987. For 1988, however, the annual growth rate rebounded to nearly 1.8%. For the period 1985 to 1990 (the latest for which accurate statistics exist), the average annual growth rate was 1.74%. Currently, it may actually be as low as 1.6%.

Today the world population stands at 5.8 billion, and opinions differ as to where it will stand in the future. In 1988 the United Nations predicted a global human population of 6.25 billion in the year 2000. If the growth rate continues at about 1.7%, there will be over 28 billion humans on Earth by the end of the twenty-first century. On the other hand, current projections, based on a declining growth rate, suggest that the world population will be approximately 8.5 billion in 2025. If we could stabilize at two children per family by 2015, then the world population might stabilize at about 9.3 billion in 2095. If it takes until 2060 to arrive at an average of two children per family, then the world population will perhaps stabilize at about 14.2 billion in the year 2120. Considering the current status of global family planning, and extrapolating what advances can be reasonably expected over the next century, many demographers have recently suggested that the global human population may top out at 11 or 12 billion sometime around the year 2100.

EnviroNet
www.jbpub.com/environet

$\mathcal{D}$ ISTRIBUTION OF THE EARTH'S HUMAN POPULATION

The present human population is distributed somewhat unevenly over the Earth (Fig. 5–3) —even more so in terms of access to and use of resources. A select few tend to be moderately to very well off, while the many lead mediocre, marginal, or substandard existences. Likewise, such basic statistics as infant mortality, **crude birth** and **death rates**, longevity, and so on vary widely from country to country.

Of the 5.8 billion people on the planet in 1996, 59.7% live in Asia (exclusive of the former Soviet Union), 13% in Africa, 9% in Europe, 7.3% in North and Central America, 5.5% in South America, 5% in the former Soviet Union, and 0.5% in Oceania (including Australia and New Zealand). More important perhaps is that in 1996 approximately 1.2 billion people live in **more developed countries** or **MDCs** (basically the countries of North America, Europe, Japan, Australia, New Zealand, and the former Soviet Union), whereas the remaining 4.6 billion people live in **less developed countries** or **LDCs**. As Figures 5–4 and 5–5, page 123, show, past and predicted future changes in population size are unevenly distributed among the continents and between the MDCs and LDCs. Whereas the population growth curve for Europe is essentially flat, it is sharply rising for Asia and Africa.

The population of the MDCs as a whole is increasing only very slightly; indeed, Austria, Belgium, and Italy have achieved zero population growth, and the populations of Germany and Hungary are declining. As a whole, the industrialized countries of the world have about a 0.4% growth rate. In contrast, the population of the LDCs is surging; as a whole, the developing world has a 2.0% growth rate. If the UN projections are correct, the world population will reach some 8.5 billion by 2025; of the 3.2 billion increase between 1990 and 2025, over 3 billion will be added to the LDCs (Table 5–1). Furthermore,

	POPULATION (MILLIONS)					PERCENT SHARE OF WORLD POPULATION				
Region	1950	1970	1990	2000	2025	1950	1970	1990	2000	2025
World total	**2516**	**3698**	**5292**	**6261**	**8504**	**100.0**	**100.0**	**100.0**	**100.0**	**100.0**
Industrialized countries	832	1049	1207	1264	1354	33.1	28.4	22.8	20.2	15.9
Developing countries	1684	2649	4086	4997	7150	66.9	71.6	77.2	79.8	84.1
Africa	222	362	642	867	1597	8.8	9.8	12.1	13.8	18.8
North America	166	226	276	295	332	6.6	6.1	5.2	4.7	3.9
Latin America	166	286	448	538	757	6.6	7.7	8.5	8.6	8.9
Asia	1377	2102	3113	3713	4912	54.7	56.8	58.8	59.3	57.8
Europe	393	460	498	510	515	15.6	12.4	9.4	8.1	6.1
Oceania	13	19	26	30	38	0.5	0.5	0.5	0.5	0.4
Former Soviet Union	180	243	289	308	352	7.2	6.6	5.5	4.9	4.1

TABLE 5–1 *Population Size and Projections for Major World Regions, 1950–2025*

(*Source:* World Resources Institute, *World Resources 1992–93* [New York: Oxford University Press, 1992], p. 76. Copyright © 1992 by The World Resources Institute. Reprinted by permission of Oxford University Press, Inc.)

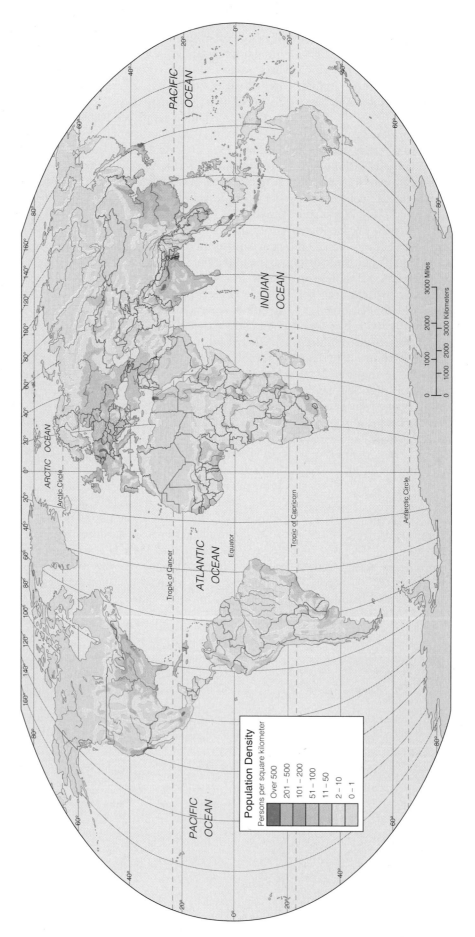

■ **F I G U R E 5-3**
Map of world population densities. Note that one square kilometer equals approximately 0.386 square mile, thus a population density of 10 persons per square kilometer equals approximately 26 persons per square mile.

Population Density
Persons per square kilometer

Over 500
201 – 500
101 – 200
51 – 100
11 – 50
2 – 10
0 – 1

PACIFIC OCEAN

INDIAN OCEAN

ARCTIC OCEAN

ATLANTIC OCEAN

PACIFIC OCEAN

Arctic Circle

Tropic of Cancer

Equator

Tropic of Capricorn

Antarctic Circle

0   1000   2000   3000 Miles
0   1000   2000   3000 Kilometers

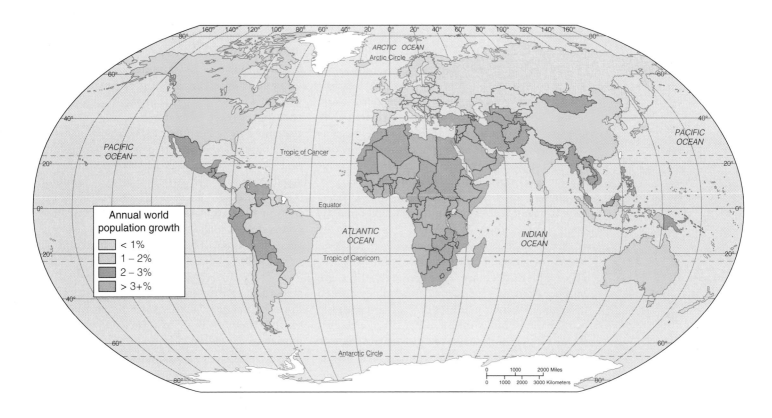

FIGURE 5–4

Average annual population growth rates around the world in the 1990s. (*Source:* Based on data from World Resources Institute, *World Resources 1994–95* [New York: Oxford University Press, 1994], Table 16.1, pp. 268–269.)

much of the estimated growth in the developed world will occur in the United States.

In 1996, 77% of the world's population lives in LDCs; in 2025, 84% will live in LDCs. These numbers are not incompatible with the estimate that currently only 16% of the world's people live an affluent American-like lifestyle, while 50% do not have adequate food or other necessities, and 34% live in extreme poverty. Such disparities may increase in the future.

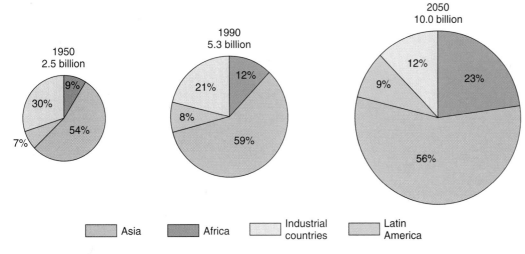

FIGURE 5–5

The shifting balance of the world's population by region, 1950–2050. Note that virtually no growth in the population of the present industrial countries is predicted between 1990 and 2050, yet the size of the world's population will continue to increase. Therefore, people of those industrial countries will account for a much smaller percentage of the world's population in 2050. In contrast, the populations of Asia and Africa will increase sharply, with the highest growth rates occurring in Africa. In 2050 the number of Asians could be greater than the number of all people on Earth in 1990. (*Source:* Reprinted with permission from Wade Roush, "Population: The View from Cairo." *Science* 265 [August 26, 1994]: 1166. Copyright 1994 American Association for the Advancement of Science.)

𝒜GE STRUCTURES

When comparing populations between different countries and regions, one must consider the **age structures** or the population **age profiles**. The age structure of a particular population is essentially a frozen profile of the population at any one instant (▬ Fig. 5–6); the age structure of a population will often change over time.

There are two common patterns in age structures. A typical Western industrialized country, which is an example of an MDC, has a relatively flat or uniform age structure profile (Fig. 5–6a); that is, in each age category from about age 0 to 30 or older, there are approximately the same number of people (of course, as people get much older than 50, their numbers drop off dramatically as they die of old age). In comparison, a typical LDC (Fig. 5–6b) has an age profile that is strongly skewed toward the younger categories, indicating that there are many more younger people than older people. The United Nations currently projects that in the year 2025, 18% of the populations of the MDCs will be under age 15, and 19% will be over 64, so the ratio of young to old will be about 1 to 1. In 2025, the LDCs will have 26% under age 15, and only 8% over 64, setting the ratio of young to old at 3.25 to 1.

In absolute numbers, a population that is skewed toward the young will continue to grow even as the birth rate falls. In fact, the **fertility rate** of a population can drop to, or below, the re-placement fertility rate (approximately 2.1 children per woman; see Issues in Perspective 5–2), yet the population will continue to increase in size for some time. As the population ages, more women will reach their reproductive years (generously regarded as 15 to 49 years in many UN statistics) and bear offspring. Thus, even as each woman, on the average, may have fewer children, many more women will be having children. In contrast, a flat age structure profile combined with replacement fertility will result in stable population numbers. As individuals age and move from one age category to the next, and ultimately to death, they will be replaced by equal numbers of individuals being born.

It is useful to take two-dimensional age structure profiles and plot them into three-dimensional graphs, the third dimension representing time (▬ Fig. 5–7). Such a diagram summarizes the major trends in a population over the period of time it covers. A three-dimensional age structure chart also helps us to visualize earlier population events and see how they may affect later events. Note that a diagonal on such a chart (see Fig. 5–7) represents a single cohort (or group born within the same time period); as the members of a given cohort age, they move to higher age groups. In other words, individuals who fall in the 0–5-year age interval at one particular time will be the individuals who will compose the 6–10-year age interval 5 years later, the 11–15-year age interval 10 years later, and so on. Figure 5–7 presents selected three-dimensional

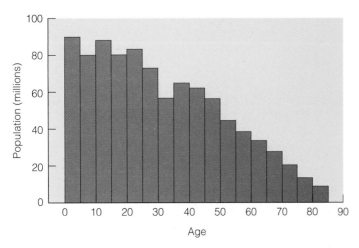

(a) More developed regions

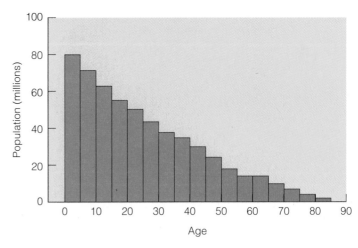

(b) Less developed region

▬ **FIGURE 5–6**

Examples of age structure profiles in two dimensions: (a) a typical more developed region; (b) a typical less developed region, such as Latin America. An age structure profile for a particular population records the relative numbers of people in different age categories, in these cases by five-year intervals (0–5 years, 6–10 years, 11–15 years, 16–20 years, and so on). (*Source: World Resources Institute, World Resources 1990–91* [New York: Oxford University Press, 1990], p. 50. Copyright © 1990 by The World Resources Institute. Reprinted by permission of Oxford University Press, Inc.)

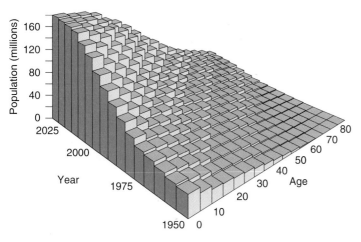

(a) Africa

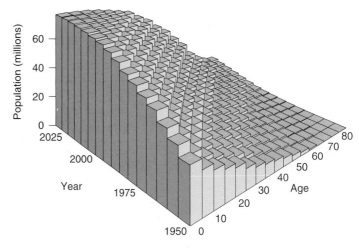

(b) Latin America

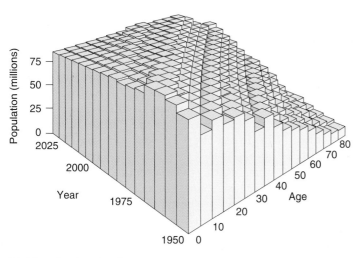

(c) More developed regions

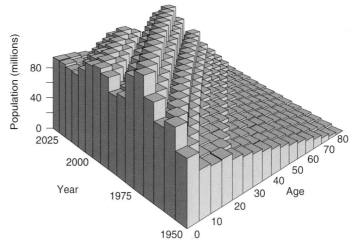

(d) China

age structure profile diagrams for various parts of the world, and ▀ Figure 5–8 shows the age structure profiles for the world as a whole in 1995 and the year 2050 (estimated projection).

$\mathcal{T}$HE CONSEQUENCES OF OVERPOPULATION

Rapid population growth and overpopulation have many far-reaching effects ecologically, economically, and societally. The increasing population is putting a greater and greater burden on the Earth's natural resource base and environment. As Paul Ehrlich (1988, p. 305) points out:

> One can think of our species as having inherited from Earth a one-time bonanza of nonrenewable resources. These include fossil fuels, high-grade ores, deep agricultural soils, abundant groundwater, and

the plethora of plants, animals, and microorganisms. These accumulate on time-scales ranging from millennia (soils) to hundreds of millions of years (ores) but are being consumed and dispersed on time-scales of centuries (fuels, ores) or even decades (water, soils, species).

Most people readily acknowledge that fossil fuels, such as oil and coal, are nonrenewable. However, many fail to realize that, from the human perspective, soils and much fresh water that is pumped from underground aquifers are also nonrenewable resources (see Chapters 11 and 13). Topsoils are being eroded at a tremendous rate, and in many regions the water table is being drawn down to alarmingly low levels. Another example is phosphorus, an extremely important element that is mined from nonrenewable rock deposits primarily in order to make modern fertilizers. A 1971 study concluded that known supplies of phosphorus would be exhausted by

 FIGURE 5–7
Three-dimensional age structure diagrams for various regions, 1950–2050. (a) Africa; (b) Latin America; (c) more developed regions; (d) China. (*Source:* World Resources Institute, *World Resources 1990–91* [New York: Oxford University Press, 1990], pp. 52, 53, 54. Copyright © 1990 by The World Resources Institute. Reprinted by permission of Oxford University Press, Inc.)

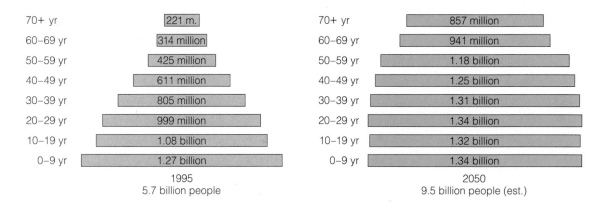

	1995
70+ yr	221 m.
60–69 yr	314 million
50–59 yr	425 million
40–49 yr	611 million
30–39 yr	805 million
20–29 yr	999 million
10–19 yr	1.08 billion
0–9 yr	1.27 billion

1995
5.7 billion people

	2050
70+ yr	857 million
60–69 yr	941 million
50–59 yr	1.18 billion
40–49 yr	1.25 billion
30–39 yr	1.31 billion
20–29 yr	1.34 billion
10–19 yr	1.32 billion
0–9 yr	1.34 billion

2050
9.5 billion people (est.)

FIGURE 5–8
Age structure profiles of the world as a whole in 1995 and 2050 (estimated projection). (*Source: U.S. News and World Report*, September 12, 1994, p. 58. Copyright, Sept. 12, 1994, *U.S. News & World Report*.)

2100, and that without phosphate fertilizers the Earth can support only one to two billion people.

Not only are we very quickly depleting resources, but we are also destroying ecosystems (as exemplified by deforestation and desertification), causing massive species extinctions, and irretrievably altering our environment by dumping greenhouse gases into the atmosphere (Chapter 18) and destoying the Earth's ozone layer. Later chapters will examine the consequences of these actions in detail.

Such ecological damage is not solely a function of more people. Given the discrepancies in affluence and technology among the Earth's peoples, not everyone impacts equally on the environment (remember the equation I = PT from Chapter 1). Persons in rich, industrialized countries (the MDCs) typically cause much more ecosystem damage per capita than persons in poor, nonindustrialized countries (LDCs). Based on such considerations, Paul Ehrlich has suggested that one new American baby and 250 new Bangladeshi babies pose an equal threat to the environment. The United States contains less than 5% of the world's population, yet consumes approximately 25% of the world's energy resources and produces about the same percentage of the world's pollution. Likewise, U.S. citizens consume approximately 12 times as much energy per capita as the average citizen in a developing country.

Generally, a country's quality of life decreases as its birth rate increases. Overpopulated countries and nations with quickly expanding populations tend to be characterized by low gross national product (GNP) per capita and high infant mortality rates. The poorest nations tend to have the highest population growth rates, but are least equipped to deal with increasing numbers of people. For example, a nation with a population growth rate of 3% (typical of some LDCs) will double its numbers in about 24 years. Simply to maintain the meager standard of living of its citizens, such a country must double its physical in-

frastructure (buildings, factories, roads, sewers, energy grids, and so on), as well as its production, agricultural output, medical and social services, and employment opportunities within the same amount of time. That would be a very difficult task for a rich nation, much less for an LDC. The inevitable result is that as the population increases, the per capita standard of living is lowered.

How does one measure quality of life? Widely applied criteria include single statistics such as the GNP per capita and the infant mortality rate. Other indices include the **Physical Quality of Life Index (PQLI)** and the **Human Suffering Index (HSI)**.

The PQLI, which was developed by the Overseas Development Council in the late 1970s, rates a country on the basis of the average life expectancy, infant mortality, and literacy rates of its citizens. Countries with low birth rates tended to have high PQLI rankings, whereas countries with high birth rates typically fell low on the PQLI scale.

More comprehensive is the HSI developed by the Population Crisis Committee in the 1980s. This index is the summation of a number of different ratings, such as the GNP per capita, food sufficiency, inflation, accessibility of clean drinking water, literacy, energy consumption, growth of the labor force, urbanization, and political freedom. The HSI scale ranges from 0 to 100, such that a rating of 0 to 25 is the minimal "human suffering" range, 25 to 50 indicates moderate suffering, 50 to 75 high suffering, and 75 to 100 indicates extreme suffering. Figure 5–9 shows the HSI for various nations; note that the higher the annual population increase, the higher the HSI. It is important to note that approximately 70% of the world's population lives in countries in Asia, Africa, or Latin America with suffering indices of 50 or higher and average annual population increases of 2.8%.

Rapid population growth and overpopulation lead to increased urbanization, increased unem-

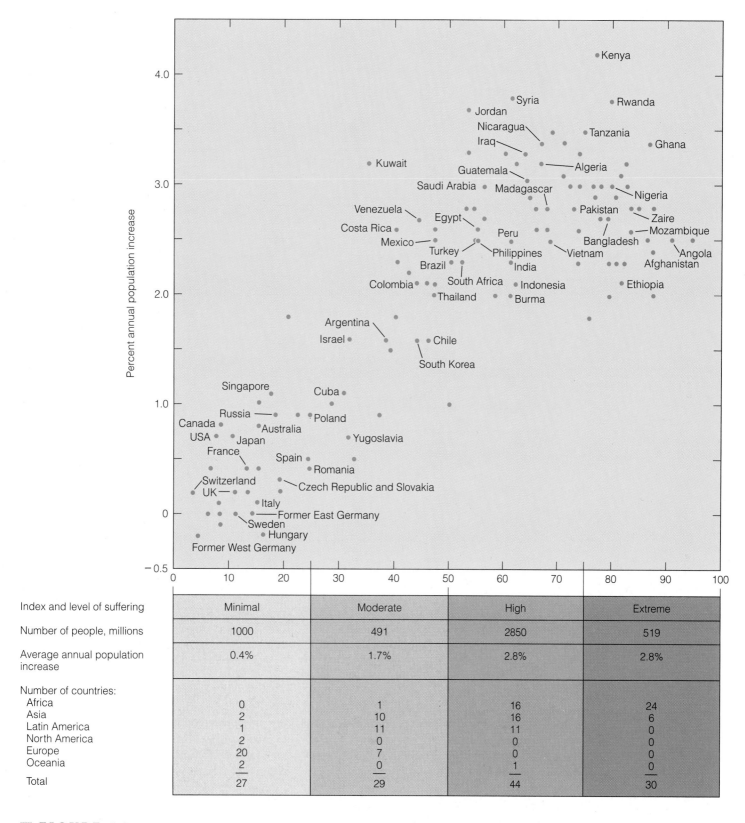

Index and level of suffering	Minimal	Moderate	High	Extreme
Number of people, millions	1000	491	2850	519
Average annual population increase	0.4%	1.7%	2.8%	2.8%
Number of countries:				
Africa	0	1	16	24
Asia	2	10	16	6
Latin America	1	11	11	0
North America	2	0	0	0
Europe	20	7	0	0
Oceania	2	0	1	0
Total	27	29	44	30

FIGURE 5–9

Population growth and human suffering. There is a strong correlation between the level of human suffering and the rate of population growth. Unfortunately, over half of the world's people live in countries characterized by high or extreme human suffering. (*Source:* S. L. Camp and J. J. Speidel, *The International Human Suffering Index* [Washington, D.C.: Population Crisis Committee, 1987]. Reprinted with the permission of Population Action International [formerly Population Crisis Committee].)

Urbanization

The last two hundred years have seen a strong global trend toward **urbanization**. In about 1800, only 3% of humanity could be classified as urban. By 1950 this number had risen to approximately 30%, and in 1990, 43% of all people lived in cities. Some commentators refer to this movement from country to city as the "urban revolution." In some developed nations, almost everyone can be classified as "urban." In the former West Germany in 1990, for example, the urban portion of the population constituted 94% of the total. Although the majority of the world's people are still rural dwellers, if present trends continue, soon the urbanites will overtake the ruralists; it is projected that in 2025 the urban population will amount to 60% of the world's total population.

Although the first genuine cities arose about 8000 to 6000 years ago and some ancient cities such as Rome at its height had populations as large as a million, large cities were rare until the twentieth century. Even as late as the year 1900, only 13 cities had populations of over one million (Chicago, Philadelphia, New York, London, Paris, Berlin, Vienna, St. Petersburg, Moscow, Beijing, Shanghai, Calcutta, and Tokyo; see ■ Fig. 1). Today over two hundred cities contain more

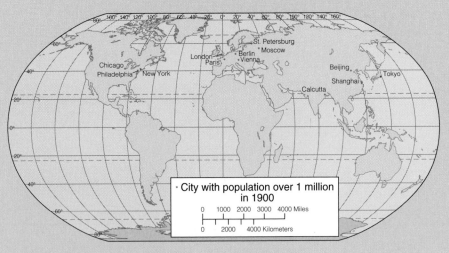

■ **FIGURE 1**

Major cities with populations over 1 million in 1900.

than a million people (■ Fig. 2), and by the end of the century, more than two dozen are expected to exceed 10 million. One of the largest is Mexico City with a 1990 population of over 20 million and a projected population of nearly 28 million for the year 2000.

The **megacity** with a population of more than 10 million people is a twentieth-century creation. As a city's population grows, it spreads out along the edges into the surrounding countryside,

giving rise to **suburban** sprawl. Lower land prices on the edge of the city may attract commuters who still go into the city center daily for employment. Slowly, residential suburbs push further and further away from the city center, and shopping centers and malls, theaters, and medical facilities, not to mention schools, churches, and post offices, are built to service the suburban residents. Soon people living in the suburbs may rarely venture into the heart of the city at all; they can find every-

ployment, and spreading poverty. Projections indicate that 60% of the world's population will live in urban areas by 2025 (see Issues in Perspective 5–4). In the developing world, many cities are growing at phenomenal rates and to phenomenal sizes (● Table 5–2, page 130), but much of the growth is in the form of slums, shanty towns, and squatter settlements that lack such necessities as adequate housing, safe drinking water, and proper sanitation systems.

Increasing population pressures lead to political instability and political and civil rights abuses. Population growth leads invariably to competi-

tion for limited resources, often culminating in outright armed conflict. This may take the form of increasing local crime and violence, particularly among various ethnic and racial groups, some of whom may have voluntarily migrated or been forcefully displaced due to increasing population pressures. Sometimes the conflict escalates to actual warfare, primarily domestic civil wars. There have been more than 20 million war-related deaths in the world since 1945, and over 75% of these came in domestic civil wars. The majority of these deaths have occurred in highly populated countries. Bangladesh, with one of the highest

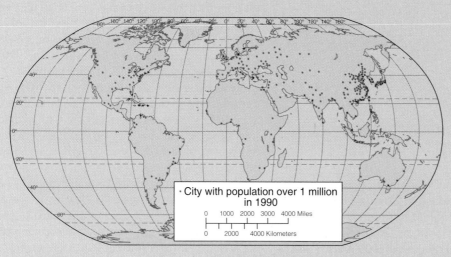

FIGURE 2

Major cities with populations over 1 million in 1990.

thing they need without leaving suburbia. As the suburbs of large cities expand outward, adjacent cities and their suburbs may meet and begin to merge, forming a vast network of adjacent urban and suburban communities (sometimes referred to as a conurbation), until they become a single vast urban area, the **megalopolis**. The term *megalopolis* was first coined to describe the almost continuous urban and suburban sprawl in the northeastern United States from Boston, through New York City and Philadelphia, down to Washington, D.C. Examples of megalopolises can now be found throughout the world; for instance, in the Netherlands, Amsterdam, Leiden, The Hague, Rotterdam, and Dordrecht all run together, and in Japan the Tokyo-Yokohama complex forms a megalopolis.

Cities may rise and fall. Some cities grow slowly, progressing from the village stage, to the town stage, to the small city stage, and gradually grow larger until they reach international status. An example is Rome, which since its humble origins nealy three thousand years ago has exerted a major influence on much of Western history as both the capital of the Roman Empire and the city that houses the Vatican (an independent city-state within the city of Rome), home of the head of the Roman Catholic church. For two thousand years, Rome has been a major center of culture and learning. Other major cities have been planned virtually from scratch and therefore never went through the stages of village, town, and small city. An example is Canberra, the capital of Australia. Its outlines were designed by the American Walter Burley Griffin (1888–1937) as a "garden city" emphasizing public open space. Although officially inaugurated in 1911, much of Canberra was not constructed until the 1950s and later.

City centers may decline as the suburbs develop and expand. As the population moves away from the center, the core of the city may deteriorate until eventually low land prices attract businesses and developers once again. A large city may go through stages of growth, stagnation, and rejuvenation.

---

population densities in the world, accounts for 1.5 million of these deaths. Likewise, since 1994, hundreds of thousands of people have died as a result of civil strife in Rwanda.

THE POPULATION OF THE UNITED STATES AND CANADA

The current population of the United States is approximately 270 million, just under 5% of the world's population. Although the total fertility rate is currently about 2.1 (as described in Issues in Perspective 5–2, 2.1 is generally accepted as **replacement level** fertility) and the average completed family size is 1.9 children, the population is still growing by approximately 2.5 million every year, in part due to **immigration**. During the first half of the 1990s the U.S. annual growth rate averaged slightly over 1%, faster than that of most industrialized countries. In fact, the most recent data indicate that the United States may be undergoing a small baby "boomlet."

The continued growth of the U.S. population is primarily attributable to two factors: (1) The current age structure of the population is such

TABLE 5-2 *Selected Examples of Rapid Population Growth in Cities Located in Developing Countries*

| | POPULATION IN MILLIONS | | |
City	1950	1991	Projection for 2000
Mexico City	3.05	20.9	27.9
São Paulo	2.7	18.7	25.4
Bombay	3.0	12.1	15.4
Jakarta	1.45	9.9	12.8
Cairo	2.5	10.1	12.5
Delhi	1.4	8.8	11.8
Manila	1.78	10.2	12.8
Lagos	0.27	8.0	12.5
Bogatá	0.61	5.9	7.9

(*Source:* Based on data from *The World Almanac and Book of Facts, 1995,* [Mahwah, N.J.: Funk & Wagnalls Corporation, 1994], p. 840.)

that a large number of women are now in or entering their reproductive years and bearing children; consequently, the birth rate is appreciably higher than the death rate. (2) Large numbers of immigrants, legal (about 600,000 a year) and illegal (numbers unknown), continue to enter the country—some 6 million immigrants entered the country legally during the 1980s, along with an estimated 2 million undocumented immigrants. The proportion of U.S. population growth attributable to immigration has risen by more than 20% since World War II. Often foreign-born women in the United States have higher fertility rates than do American-born women; this factor may also be contributing to the current baby boomlet.

In 1940 the U.S. population stood at 132 million, in 1960 at 180.7 million, in 1990 at 249.2 million, and in 1995 at 265 million; it is projected to reach approximately 322 million in 2025. That the U.S. population is growing faster than those of most of the industrialized nations of the world is worrisome, not only for the citizens of the United States but for the Earth. Remember that the United States consumes much more than its share of world resources and produces an equivalent amount of pollution and waste; this inordinate consumption will only get worse as the U.S. population increases.

Even within the borders of the United States, the increasing population pressure will undoubtly carry serious consequences. The infrastructure and social services will be further stressed. Dump sites for waste, both hazardous and nonhazardous, are in short supply. Freshwater supplies are already pressed; periodical water shortages have been reported around the country, and these will only increase. The agricultural capacity of the United States is decreasing, even as its population is increasing, due to the conversion of an estimated 3 million acres (1.2 million hectares) of agricultural land each year to other uses.

Canada, although much less densely populated than the United States, has an even higher population growth rate than the U.S. (Canada averaged 1.38% per year during the first half of the 1990s). In 1950 the Canadian population stood at 13.74 million, in 1960 at 17.9 million, in 1990 at 26.64 million, and in 1995 at 28.54 million. It is projected to reach 38 to 39 million in 2025. Geographically, Canada is a vast country, with an area slightly greater than the entire United States (including Alaska and Hawaii). Yet large portions of Canada, such as the Arctic regions, are inhospitable to dense human habitation. Consequently, over three-quarters of all Canadians are urban-dwellers. The majority of Canadians live within about 200 miles (322 km) of the U.S. border, many being concentrated in the metropolitan areas of Toronto, Montreal, and Vancouver.

IS POPULATION GROWTH REALLY A PROBLEM? THE ALTERNATIVE POINT OF VIEW

Widespread public concern over Earth's growing human population dates back to the late 1960s and early 1970s, aroused at least in part by the publication of two influential works: *The Population Bomb* (1968) by Paul Ehrlich and *The Limits to Growth* (1972) commissioned by the Club of Rome (written by Meadows and others). In the last 20 years, however, there has been an increasingly vocal opposition to the "doomsday" scenarios outlined by some of the population alarmists. One of the most vocal supporters of the pro-population movement is the economist Julian Simon.

Simon, in such books as *The Ultimate Resource* (1981) and *The Resourceful Earth: A Response to Global 2000* (with Herman Kahn, 1984), suggests that rather than being detrimental, moderate population growth is actually an asset. Essentially, Simon believes that "more people is better." The ultimate resource, according to Simon and like thinkers, is the human mind. Given human creativity, combined with high technology and cutting-edge science, virtually anything is possible. As population pressures increase, humans invariably find ways to produce more (Fig. 5–10), accomplish tasks more efficiently, and find substitutes for diminishing resources. Summarizing this view, Simon has stated that

> Taken in the large, an increased need for resources usually leaves us with a permanently greater capacity to get them, because we gain knowledge in the process. And there is no meaningful physical limit—even the commonly mentioned weight of the earth—to our capacity to keep growing forever (From *Discover* magazine, April 1990, pp. 47–48).

Simon bases his views on past history. Humankind has survived and proliferated up until now. Despite the dire warnings of the population alarmists, the world has not collapsed. Earth's human population continues to expand, perhaps with a few negative repercussions, but not the drastic consequences that some would have had us believe were inevitable. On the other hand, Simon's view is not the only way to look at the changes that have occurred in the last few decades. Although huge population-induced catastrophes have not yet occurred with the force to catch Simon's attention, this does not guarantee they will not occur. In some cases, short-term gains, provided by science, technology, and the one-time use of nonrenewable resources, may stave off disaster temporarily; but inevitably, many argue, we will reap the consequences of our actions.

INNOCUOUS POPULATION GROWTH—APPARENTLY

With Simon, some people argue that the Earth's human population has been increasing slowly but steadily for a long time with no apparent detrimental consequences to the environment. Since the world has survived for many years with a growing population, they conclude that there is no connection between increasing population and environmental damage.

These analysts reject the argument that we must limit our population growth to avoid running out of many nonrenewable resources. In their view, this argument is now obsolete. Not only have substitutes been found for some materials, but new technology has made many materials obsolete. Nonrenewable resources are no longer a limiting factor to the expansion of the human population and its culture.

However, we must consider the so-called renewable resources, such as animals in the wild, soils

and forests, natural fisheries, and so on. Renewable resources are only renewable if they are not over-exploited. For example, if only a few mature fish are taken from a lake, the fish population will not be adversely affected because a comparable number of additional young will reach maturity and replace those caught by humans. If too many fish are harvested, however, the reproductive potential of the fish may be adversely affected. Whereas human consumption is, all other things being equal, a simple linear function of the number of people, the impact on an ecosystem is nonlinear. Beyond a certain threshold value of harvesting, the resource will be damaged (becoming nonrenewable) if further harvesting continues. Such a threshold value can be reached very suddenly and passed by very quickly, resulting in damage or destruction of the once-renewable resource.

Dr. Nathan Keyfitz (Andelot Professor of Sociology and Demography, Emeritus, Harvard University) suggests, in agreement with many biologists, that one cannot naively extrapolate into the future using simplistic models based solely on past trends. For instance, using the model of fish in a lake, just because we have been able to increase our catch by 2% each year for 10 years does not mean that we can increase our catch by this amount indefinitely. At some point, if we continue to increase our catch by 2% per year, we will reach the threshold beyond which sustainable harvesting cannot be maintained, and the biological system will be severely damaged or possibly collapse totally.

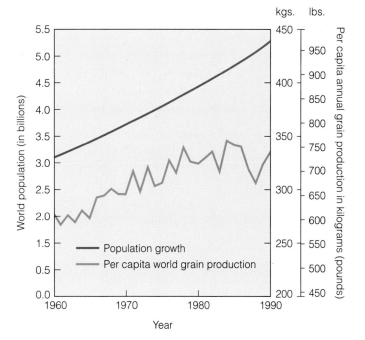

FIGURE 5–10
Graphs similar to this one appear periodically in the popular press in connection with discussions of the "population crisis." The point is that even as our world population has grown, the world's food supply has also increased. Some commentators believe data such as these constitute evidence that there is no global population problem—at most, there may be problems in the distribution of food and other resources. (*Source:* Based on data from the United Nations and the U.S. Department of Agriculture.)

SOLVING THE WORLD'S POPULATION PROBLEM

Industrialization, Economic Development, and the Demographic Transition

How do we solve the world's population problem? Many people have subscribed to the following proposition, as recently restated by Dr. Nathan Keyfitz (1991, pp. 39–40):

> The one thing that we know for sure about population is that people in the developed condition do not have many children; whatever problems the rich countries face, rapid population growth is not one of them. Hence, all that is needed is for the poor countries to develop and they too will be spared the troubles arising from rapid population growth.

This is the theory of **demographic transition**—essentially, that as a nation undergoes technological and economic development, its population growth rate will decrease. According to this theory, early in its history a nation will be characterized by both high birth rates and high death rates, and population growth will be relatively slow. With initial economic and technological development, the death rate will drop, while the birth rate remains high. Usually, this trend is ascribed to better nutrition, increased and advanced medical technology, more adequate shelter, and the like. Cultural norms are modified more slowly, however, and parents continue to produce large families, even though they do not "need" to because a higher percentage of their offspring survive and reach adulthood. Also, with intial economic and technological development, children will be in less demand as a labor force and will no longer be an economic asset. Still, because children continue to be produced at high rates, the nation will undergo rapid population growth, and the size of the population will increase dramatically.

Finally, industrial, technological, and economic development will mature and peak, and the culture will change to meet the new conditions. Parents no longer produce as many children as did previous generations. Why this is the case is still under investigation. As nations industrialize, many of the attributes and nuances of the indigenous culture are progressively lost. In many westernized societies, children are no longer needed as a form of "social security" to support the parents in their old age. High-technology material goods are in demand, the dietary intake tends to include more meat, and having a large number of children is deemphasized (▇ Fig. 5–11). In terms of a cost-benefit analysis, having more children is an economic burden. Until they are adults, children produce little, if anything. In one way or another, consumer goods appear to substitute for children. At any rate, values and cultural norms change, and the birth rate falls until it approximates the death rate; during this time, the nation's population growth rate slows down, perhaps even reaching zero or a negative number.

Problems with the Demographic Transition Model

The demographic transition model seems to describe well the population histories of some technologically advanced nations, especially in Europe. But does this model hold the key to the world's population problem? This is now being seriously questioned. Countries in Africa, Asia, and Latin America, for instance, have been heavily affected by westernization. Their death rates have been lowered, but their birth rates remain high. Consequently, their populations are growing at staggering rates. These nations are partly, but not fully, industrialized. With partial industrialization, their environments and resources are being destroyed, but they do not have the money to industrialize further. The longer a nation remains stuck halfway through the demographic transition, with high birth rates and low death rates, the larger its population will become. The larger the population becomes, the poorer the nation will be, the more poverty will manifest itself, and the harder it will be to end the cycle. A partial developmental program seems to be much worse than no developmental program at all; partial development has a very strong destabilizing effect. As Jodi Jacobson has pointed out, "slower economic growth in developing countries plagued by debt, dwindling exports, and environmental

▇ **FIGURE 5–11**
Increasing GNP (gross national product) per capita correlates with decreased birth rates (crude birth rates per 1000 members of the population), based on a study of 107 countries. (*Source:* From H. R. Pulliam and N. M. Haddad "Human Population Growth and the Carrying Capacity Concept." In *Bulletin of the Ecological Society of America* [September 1994, pp. 141–157].)

degradation means that governments can no longer rely on socioeconomic gains to help reduce births" (Jacobson, 1988, p. 151).

The demographic transition model has also been criticized on another, related issue. The industrialized, highly developed nations of the North reached their current level of development and affluence not only by degrading their own immediate environments, but also by exploiting the territory of the developing nations in the Southern Hemisphere. For example, for every acre (or hectare) of land farmed in the United Kingdom, another two acres (or two hectares) of land are farmed elsewhere in the world in support of the United Kingdom. Perhaps the classic example is the Netherlands, with a very dense population of nearly 1200 people per square mile (or nearly 450 people per km²); in contrast, the United States has a density of about 70 people per square mile (27 per km²). The Netherlands can support such a dense population only by importing massive amounts of foodstuffs and other resources. Essentially, the argument is that it would be impossible for the entire world to consist of only developed countries; without the developing countries, the developed countries could not exist at their present population densities and levels of affluence. In order for a would-be developing country to become a fully developed country, it needs suitable developing countries to exploit.

It is also highly questionable whether the correlation between development, industrialization, and lower fertility seen in Europe and the United States is a causal relationship. Not only are fertility rates lower in the industrialized nations, but so are rates of malnutrition, infant mortality, and illiteracy. This evidence suggests that fertility declines are caused primarily by rising levels of education, nutrition, and infant survivorship rather than by industrialization and development per se. A case in point would appear to be Costa Rica, which cut its fertility rate by 53% between 1960 and 1985 without major industrial development or a major effort in family planning. Instead, Costa Rica promoted education and health issues and waged a war on poverty.

Another factor that must be considered is that as the growth rate of a particular population declines, the age structure profile of the population will change. For example, the typical LDC currently has an age structure profile that is skewed toward the younger age groups. But as population growth rates decline, and birth rates approximate death rates, the population will "mature" and have many more persons in the older age categories than previously. Such a shift in age structure can seriously affect the culture and society. More adults in their prime will need jobs, and the elderly, who were once relatively rare, will demand a larger proportion of the resources with fewer younger people to support them.

Another consideration is the effect industrialization and rapid economic growth can have on indigenous cultures. Issues in Perspective 5–5 explores the issue of **cultural extinction.**

Contraceptives, Abortion, and Reproductive Rights

An obvious way to address the population problem is to continue and expand family planning services, the distribution of contraceptives (**birth control** devices; see ▬ Fig. 5–12), and the availability of safe, legal **abortions**, while promoting the "reproductive rights" of women (essentially the right to be able to choose not to bear children) throughout the world. Indeed, much progress has been made in these areas, but it is also a highly sensitive, emotionally charged subject. **Contraception**, abortion, and **reproductive rights** in general go against the grain of some major religions and cultural values. Some people in devel-

(a)

(b)

▬ **FIGURE 5–12**
(a) Contraceptive use by women strongly correlates with decreased fertility rates (based on a study of 50 countries). (b) Women attending a family planning class in India. (*Sources:* (a) From H. R. Pulliam and N. M. Haddad, "Human Population Growth and the Carrying Capacity Concept." In *Bulletin of the Ecological Society of America* [September 1994, pp. 141–157]. (b) Robert Nickelsberg/Gamma Liaison.)

Global Overpopulation, Yet Cultural Extinction

Even as the world population grows, the diversity of cultures is dropping. Around the world, tribal peoples and indigenous cultures are going extinct (known as **cultural extinction**) (■ Fig. 1). To cite a few examples, a third of the North American native languages and cultures and two-thirds of the indigenous languages and cultures of Australia have disappeared over the last two hundred years. In this century almost a hundred tribes have gone extinct in Brazil. Today virtually no native or indigenous peoples do not have some contact with the outside world. As a result, both passively and actively, by subtle indoctrination, by explicit education, and at times even by force, these peoples are being assimilated into the mainstream cultures of large nations; as this happens, the indigenous cultures are lost forever.

Generally, indigenous peoples are considered to be descendants of the original human inhabitants of an area, as opposed to later settlers of the region and their descendants. Indigenous people typically have their own language and distinct culture, often including their own religion. An estimated 4000 to 5000 indigenous cultures still survive (● Table 1). Some of these cultures have only a few dozen surviving members, whereas others have hundreds of thousands. But by global standards, all are minorities. Only 190 million to 625 million people belong to indigenous cultures (the range of estimates is partly a function of different definitions of "indigenous people").

Does it matter if the rarer cultures of the world go extinct? Certainly, many indigenous peoples themselves do not want to lose their cultures and languages. Around the world, indigenous peoples are organizing efforts to maintain their own ways and the integrities of their cultures, languages, and lands. Just as most people recognize the rights of an individual to exist, so too the rights of a culture and people to exist are being more widely acknowledged.

Land is a major issue in the maintenance and integrity of an indigenous culture. Typically, an indigenous people lived sparsely scattered throughout a particular geographic region. When invaders entered, they usually took the land from the natives. Thus, modern controversies surrounding the preservation of indigenous cultures often focus on the preservation of homelands occupied primarily by indigenous people. Such homelands must be of adequate size and quality for an indigenous people to survive and prosper. Of course, the same land that indigenous peoples feel is theirs is the land that members of the mainstream culture desire.

From an ecological and environmental perspective, indigenous peoples often tread lightly on their land. Many indigenous peoples follow a nomadic gatherer and hunter lifestyle, are herders, or practice forms of shifting cultivation. They usually have a subsistence economy and have learned

■ **FIGURE 1**

Ishi, the last surviving member of the North American Yahi-Yana tribe, was "discovered" in the foothills of Oroville, California, in 1911. He was the object of studies by anthropologists until his death in 1916. In this 1914 photograph he demonstrates a traditional call used to lure rabbits. (*Source:* The Phoebe A. Hearst Museum of Anthropology, University of California at Berkeley.)

TABLE 1 *Remaining Indigenous Peoples of the World in 1992*

REGION	INDIGENOUS PEOPLES
Africa and Middle East	Great cultural diversity throughout continent; "indigenous" share hotly contested. Some 25–30 million nomadic herders or pastoralists in East Africa, Sahel, and Arabian peninsula include Bedouin, Dinka, Masai, and Turkana, San (Bushmen) of Namibia and Botswana and pygmies of central African rainforest, both traditionally hunter-gatherers, have occupied present homelands for at least 20,000 years. (25–350 million indigenous people overall, depending on definitions; 2000 languages)
Americas	Native Americans concentrated near centers of ancient civilizations: Aztec in Mexico, Mayan in Central America, and Incan in Andes of Bolivia, Ecuador, and Peru. In Latin America, most Indians farm small plots; in North America, 2 million Indians live in cities and on reservations. (42 million; 900 languages)
Arctic	Inuit (Eskimo) and other Arctic peoples of North America, Greenland, and Siberia traditionally fishers, whalers, and hunters. Sami (Lapp) of northern Scandinavia are traditionally reindeer herders. (2 million; 50 languages)
East Asia	Chinese indigenous peoples, numbering up to 82 million, mostly subsistence farmers such as Bulang of south China or former pastoralists such as ethnic Mongolians of north and west China. Ainu of Japan and aboriginal Taiwanese now largely industrial laborers. (12–84 million; 150 languages)
Oceania	Aborigines of Australia and Maoris of New Zealand, traditionally farmers, fishers, hunters, and gatherers. Many now raise livestock. Islanders of South Pacific continue to fish and harvest marine resources. (3 million; 500 languages)
South Asia	Gond, Bhil, and other adivasis, or tribal peoples, inhabit forest belt of central India. In Bangladesh, adivasis concentrated in Chittagong hills on Burmese border; several million tribal farmers and pastoralists in Afghanistan, Pakistan, Nepal, Iran, and central Asian republics of former Soviet Union. (74–91 million; 700 languages)
Southeast Asia	Tribal Hmong, Karen, and other forest-farming peoples form Asia ethnic mosaic covering uplands. Indigenous population follows distribution of forest: Laos has more forest and tribal peoples, Myanmar and Vietnam have less forest and fewer people, and Thailand and mainland Malaysia have the least. Tribal peoples are concentrated at the extreme ends of the Philippine and Indonesian archipelagos, Island of New Guinea—split politically between Indonesia and Papua New Guinea—populated by indigenous tribes. (32–55 million; 1950 languages)

(*Source:* A. Durning, "Supporting Indigenous Peoples," in L. R. Brown *et al.*, *State of the World 1993* [New York: W. W. Norton, 1993], p. 82. Reprinted with permission of Worldwatch Institute, Washington, D.C., Copyright © 1993.)

to live sustainably within their environment. They know intimately the numerous plants and animals found within their territory and preserve this biodiversity. To put it simply, indigenous peoples preserve and maintain their ecological heritage, whereas once the land is taken from them, it is often degraded very quickly by the mainstream conquering culture. On a global basis, the places where the most cultural diversity is found (that is, the greatest numbers of indigenous peoples remain) are also typically the places where the most biological diversity is found. Preserving indigenous cultures—preserving cultural diversity—contributes to the preservation of biological and ecological diversity. A strong case can be made for the assertion that maintaining indigenous cultures is good for the global environment as a whole.

oping countries view family planning as genocide, for the developed, industrialized nations are encouraging the undeveloped and developing nations to curtail their populations. Many African governments have traditionally opposed family planning in the belief that curtailing population growth would hurt them economically; without people, leaders of these countries felt they could not reach their full economic potential. But this view is changing.

Birth Control Methods

● Table 5–3 summarizes the estimated use of effective birth control methods worldwide, including abortion as a separate category (after-the-fact birth control). Here effective refers to methods that, when used properly and regularly,

have a high chance of successfully avoiding an unwanted pregnancy.

Notice that female sterilization is extremely common in developing countries; IUDs are also used extensively, especially in China. In contrast, condoms and oral contraceptives, followed by abortion, are among the most popular forms of birth control in the industrialized nations. As these data illustrate, different types of contraceptives are suited to different cultures. Use of oral contraceptives is difficult, for instance, in a society that lacks good distribution networks for medicines.

The birth control methods that are probably best suited to the needs of developing countries include injectable contraceptives that can last for one to several months and hormonal implants that can help a woman avoid pregnancy for several years. Although many such methods are still in the laboratory stage, the hormonal implant NORPLANT shows potential. NORPLANT, which was approved for use in the United States in 1990, consists of small rods containing time-released hormones that are planted under the skin of the upper arm; they will protect the woman from unwanted pregnancy for up to five years. At any time the implant can be removed and the fertility of the woman restored. NORPLANT has no proven serious side effects (there have been complaints of headaches, weight gain, anemia, and other symptoms).

Problems with Contraceptive Use

Worldwide only 55% of couples at risk of pregnancy use contraceptives. Although some couples are not practicing birth control because they desire to have children, many simply are not informed about modern birth control methods and/or have limited or no access to contraceptives.

A major problem is that modern contraceptives are too expensive for many couples to afford. According to a 1991 study by the Population Crisis Committee, in about three-fourths of the developing nations, the average family cannot afford modern birth control methods. In some countries, the relative cost of birth control is exorbitant: 30% of the average annual income for a year's supply of birth control pills or condoms in Ethiopia, or 7% of the average annual income for condoms and 37% for birth control pills in Kenya. This means that from a practical standpoint, contraceptives must be regarded as a "luxury" to be indulged in only after such basic needs as food, clothing, and shelter are satisfied—unless they are supplied free or at reduced cost by

---

TABLE 5–3 *Estimated Use of Effective Birth Control Methods*

The estimates in the table are only approximate and are based on late 1980s data. It is very difficult to acquire and compile reliable statistics on contraceptive use and abortions, but the numbers presented here are representative.

Birth Control Method[a]	China	Other Developing Countries	Industrial Countries	World
	(million)			
Female sterilization	53	45	15	113
Intrauterine devices	59	13	11	83
Oral contraceptives	9	28	27	64
Condoms	5	12	28	45
Male sterilization	17	18	8	43
Other effective methods[b]	3	8	13	24
Total Users	146	124	102	372
Total Couples at Risk[c]	200	463	197	860
	(percent)			
Contraceptive prevalence (users as share of those at risk)	73	27	52	43
	(million)			
Abortions	12	16	26	54

[a]Effective or modern methods exclude natural family planning (rhythm), withdrawal, abstinence, and breastfeeding.
[b]Includes diaphragms, sponges, injectables, and implants.
[c]Number of married couples of reproductive age at risk of pregnancy; does not include those currently pregnant or sterile for other than contraceptive reasons.

(*Source*: J. Jacobson, "Planning the Global Family," in L. R. Brown *et al.*, *State of the World 1988* [New York: W. W. Norton, 1988], p. 161. Reprinted with permission of Worldwatch Institute, Washington, D.C., Copyright © 1988.)

governmental or private agencies or the United Nations.

Even in the United States, contraceptives are relatively expensive; a year's supply of birth control pills cost 1.1% of per capita income on average, for example. In contrast, a year's supply of birth control pills costs only 0.2% of per capita income in France. Such differences in cost can have a very real effect on fertility rates and unwanted pregnancies. The pregnancy rate among U.S. teenage women (15 to 19 years old) is approximately twice that among comparable young women in Denmark, where national health insurance makes contraceptive services universally available.

Abortion: A Major Issue of Our Time

Where contraception is unavailable, inadequate, fails, or simply goes unused, women may resort to abortion to terminate unwanted pregnancies. The number of abortions currently performed each year worldwide is uncertain, but estimates range from 40 to 60 million (see also Table 5–3, which estimates the number of abortions in 1986 at 54 million). Worldwide approximately one induced abortion occurs for every two to three live births. It is estimated that one-third to one-half of all women of reproductive age have at least one

abortion during their lives. In Brazil and Bangladesh, for example, about 20–35% of all pregnancies are aborted; and due to the general lack of effective contraceptives in the former Soviet Union, the typical woman had between five and seven abortions during her reproductive years.

The legality of abortion (▬ Fig. 5–13) and the ease of acquiring an abortion vary from country to country (● Table 5–4). In some countries, abortions are either totally illegal (such as Iran and Ire-

FIGURE 5–13
Birth control, family planning, reproductive rights, and especially abortion are highly sensitive, emotionally charged issues for many people. Even in the United States, where abortion is legal, many find it morally repugnant and wish to make it illegal. (*Source:* Mark Richards/PhotoEdit.)

● **TABLE 5–4** *Conditions Under Which Abortions Are Allowed, Selected Countries* ●

LIFE ENDANGERMENT[a]	OTHER MATERNAL HEALTH REASONS[b]	SOCIAL AND SOCIO-MEDICAL REASONS[c]	NO MANDATED CONDITIONS[d]
Bangladesh	Costa Rica	Argentina	Canada
Brazil	Egypt	Germany	China
Chile	Ghana	India	Czech Republic
Colombia	Israel	Peru	France
Indonesia	Kenya	Poland	Italy
Ireland	Morocco	United Kingdom	Netherlands
Lebanon	Zimbabwe		Russia
Mexico			Slovakia
Nigeria			Sweden
Pakistan			Tunisia
Philippines			United States
Sudan			

[a]When a woman's life would be endangered by carrying the child to term: some countries in this category prohibit abortion without exception.
[b]Such as a threat to the woman's overall health, and sometimes in the case of fetal abnormality, rape, or incest.
[c]Social factors, such as insufficient income, poor housing, or marital status, may be considered in evaluating a "threat" to the woman's health, or may be deemed sufficient conditions in and of themselves to warrant termination of a pregnancy.
[d]Countries in this category have liberal abortion laws, commonly known as "on request," which indicates the lack of legal obstacles to abortion but not necessarily the lack of social or administrative ones.

(*Source:* J. Jacobson, "Coming to Grips with Abortion," in L. R. Brown *et al.*, *State of the World 1991* [New York: W. W. Norton, 1991], p. 115. Reprinted with permission of Worldwatch Institute, Washington, D.C., Copyright © 1991.)

land) or legal only under very narrowly defined circumstances. According to recent surveys, about 25% of the world's population lives in nations that have very restrictive abortion laws (primarily in countries in Africa, Muslim Asia, or Latin America).

Abortions are carried out whether they are legal or illegal, however. Indeed, estimates are that almost half of all abortions performed each year are illegal. Thus, restricted access to safe, legal abortions does not result in fewer abortions being performed, but simply in more maternal deaths and injuries as a result of unsafe, illegal abortions. Whatever the legal status of abortion, abortion rates tend to rise as countries go through the demographic transition. As a nation modernizes and industrializes, the preferred family size drops. Abortion rates thus rise, especially if contraceptives are not widely used or available. Typically, however, rates of both contraceptive use and abortion will rise; then the abortion rate will peak and decline. In fact, Jodi Jacobson (1991, p. 121) reports that "the incidence of abortion has declined most rapidly in those countries where legalized abortion has been included as part of truly comprehensive voluntary family planning services—among the few to note are Denmark, France, Iceland, Italy, and the Netherlands."

Female Education and Status

One of the best ways to decrease the growth rate of a particular population is to increase the average educational level and societal status of women (Fig. 5–14). Female education is so successful in decreasing fertility rates for several reasons. Women typically apply their knowledge to improving the home situation of their families—for instance, by assuring better nutrition, health care, sanitation, and so on. Rates of infant and child mortality decline as a result, causing the population to become more receptive to the notion of smaller families. Educated women are also more likely to be willing and able to use contraceptive methods effectively. Finally, through education women can gain status and prestige in ways other than through bearing numerous offspring. Educated women can choose to pursue career opportunities that do not involve staying home and having children.

Unfortunately, the status of women is relatively low in many nonwesternized societies, including Islamic societies, traditional Latin America, and traditional African societies. In many traditional African societies, for example, women carry a large economic and labor burden, yet have almost no legal independence or rights. A groom buys his wife from the bride's family and pays a high price in the expectation that she will be fertile and produce many offspring to help with the chores. As long as a woman's social and economic status is tied to the number of children she bears, little headway can be expected in the area of decreasing fertility rates.

Another sign of the generally low status of women in developing countries is the low priority placed on women's health. An estimated 494,000 women of reproductive age die in the developing counties each year due to complications of pregnancy, childbirth, and abortion—20–40% of the deaths are due to unsafe abortions and an

FIGURE 5–14
(a) Increased average education levels correlate with decreased fertility rates, based on a study of 105 countries. This correlation holds at all levels, among both males and females, and at all ages. Particularly important for decreasing the growth rate of a population, however, is the education of women. [Note that UNESCO (United Nations Education, Scientific and Cultural Organization) defines the school enrollment ratio as total enrollment, regardless of age, divided by the population of the age group that typically corresponds to a specific education level (thus if enough younger or older children or adults are enrolled in school the ratio can go over 100%).]
(b) Women attending class, Jalālābād, Afghanistan.
(*Sources:* (a) From H. R. Pulliam and N. M. Haddad, "Human Population Growth and the Carrying Capacity Concept." In *Bulletin of the Ecological Society of America* [September 1994], pp. 141–157.
(b) Robert Nickelsberg/Gamma Liaison.)

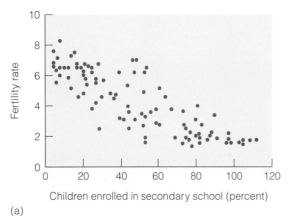

(a)

(b)

even higher percentage to unsafe childbirths. A 1991 Worldwatch Institute report estimates that 60% of these deaths could be avoided by spending approximately $1.50 a year on each woman in those countries.

Of course, educating women and improving their status will irrevocably alter these traditional societies. Some have questioned whether it is "right" for Westerners to interfere in the natural development and order of non-European cultures.

Economic Incentives, Disincentives, and Government Regulation of Childbearing

Private organizations and national governments have attempted to control population growth through voluntary programs, such as increasing the accessibility of modern birth control without mandating its use. But as the overpopulation problem has intensified, many governments have decided they must regulate childbearing.

To encourage their citizens to voluntarily limit the number of offspring, governments have offered a variety of economic incentives for using contraceptives, being sterilized, or limiting the number of children in a family. For example, in parts of Taiwan during the 1970s, families that had two children or less received annual payments, and in Thailand some families who utilized contraceptives could rent a team of water buffalo at a reduced rate. South Korea and Pakistan allow income tax deductions for families with two children or less. The government of Singapore has withheld employment benefits, housing subsidies, and preferred school admissions from families with more than three children. In extreme cases, such as in China and India (see the next section), sterilizations and abortions have allegedly been performed without the full consent of the individual concerned.

Many people question whether such policies are appropriate. For one thing, bribes and payoffs offered may be most attractive to the poor, and some people may not fully understand what sterilization entails. In addition, the case has been strongly argued that childbearing is, and should remain, a private family matter. But given the nature of the world today, childbearing is no longer a "private" matter; the number of children a couple bears affects more than that couple and their immediate family. As Ehrlich and Ehrlich (1990, p. 207) state:

> One must always keep in mind that the price of personal freedom in making childbearing decisions may be the destruction of the world in which your children or grandchildren live. How many children a

person has now has serious social consequences in all nations, and therefore is a legitimate concern of society as a whole.

Therefore, one might conclude that it is legitimate and even necessary for governments to be actively involved in the issue of childbearing and population growth. Most governments of developing countries now acknowledge the need for family planning, and according to the United Nations, only Cambodia, Iraq, Laos, and Saudi Arabia actively restrict access to family planning services.

Population Control around the World

Government efforts to curb birth rates have met with notable successes, as well as some failures. Great strides have been made in contraceptive use and availability; 9% of the world had access to contraceptives during the period 1960–1965, but by 1991 this percentage had risen to an estimated 51% and was perhaps as high as 55% in 1995. Yet this is not enough. The United Nations estimates that if we are to achieve a stable world population, 75% of all couples worldwide will need to use contraception. Contraceptive use is also very unevenly distributed (see Table 5–3); for instance, contraceptive use is close to 70% in the United States and about 73% in China, but only 4% in West Africa. This is part of the reason why 95% of global population growth is projected to take place in the developing nations of Africa, Asia, and Latin America during the next 35 years.

In the early 1990s, the average completed family in the developing nations excluding China had four or five children (and in some cases, especially in East Asia, three or less). Although this number represents a drop from the six children of the early 1960s, a recent United Nations Population Fund report observed that cutting the fertility rate from four children to two will prove more difficult than reducing it from six to four. We cannot expect contraceptive use to continue to increase, and fertility rates and average completed family sizes to decrease, at the same rates they have in the past couple of decades. But, of course, it is just this cut in fertility rate—from four to two—that is essential if we are to eventually stabilize the world's population.

Now let us briefly review how two nations, India and China, have attempted to deal with their overpopulation problems.

India

India, which is the world's second most populous nation, has had, and continues to have, enormous

■ FIGURE 5–15
India's population continues to increase at an extraordinary rate. Shown here are people bathing in the Ganges river at Vārānasi (Benares). (*Source:* Cathlyn Melloan/Tony Stone Images.)

population problems (■ Fig. 5–15). In 1960 India's population stood at 442 million; in 1990 it was 853 million, and it is projected to be more than 1.4 billion in 2025. Between 1960 and 1995, the average annual population growth rate dropped from 2.28 to 1.9%, but it is expected to remain near the latter number through 2025; thus India's population continues to increase at an alarming rate, doubling in 30 to 40 years. India accounts for approximately 16% of the world's population crowded onto about 2.42% of the world's landmass.

India was the first nation to acknowledge that it has an overpopulation problem. In 1952 the government instituted a family planning program, but it made little real progress. The program was reorganized in 1965, but by 1975 the growth rate had fallen by only 0.3%, and the population had reached some 600 million.

Perceiving the continued growth as a crisis, the government turned to what some considered extreme measures. In 1976 Indira Gandhi's government pressured all government employees to be sterilized after having a third child and for a short time even authorized compulsory sterilization for persons who had three or more children. These laws were extremely unpopular and helped

to force Gandhi from office in 1977. During that time, however, some 8 million people were sterilized, about 90% of them women. Since that time, India has used less drastic, more conventional measures, primarily the promotion of contraceptive use.

Despite decades of effort, India has still not made satisfactory progress in controlling its population growth. Part of the problem may simply be the enormous number of people that any population control program must reach. About 40% of Indian couples use birth control devices, but it is estimated that 75% should be doing so if India is to achieve a stable population. The Indian population continues to increase in size, and the country suffers from food shortages and problems with the distribution of food and other necessities.

China

With an estimated population of over 1.2 billion, China is the most populous nation on Earth (■ Fig. 5–16). Its population has nearly doubled since 1960, and despite an intensive population control program, its population continues to grow at about 1.4% a year, adding over 15 million new individuals annually.

China is a dictatorship; it has a high literacy rate, an emphasis on female education and equal rights, a relatively homogeneous culture, and a well-implanted basic health care system. Over the last two decades, the Chinese government has been actively involved in controlling population growth. The Chinese seem to have few qualms about using any available birth control methods from various types of contraceptives to essentially forced sterilizations and abortions. All of these factors have greatly aided China's efforts to control its numbers. The average annual population increase dropped from 2.61% for the period 1965–1970 to 1.45% for the period 1985–1990—a significant improvement. This was only accomplished through very extensive, intensive, and rigid methods, however.

In the early 1970s, the national government strongly promoted late marriages, well-spaced births, and limiting family size to two children per couple. To encourage such behavior, the government used all types of incentives, such as free child care, paid maternity leave, paid leave for abortions and sterilizations, better housing and education for children of small families, and so on. Peer pressure was also used to a considerable extent, and many decisions relative to marriage and planning births were made by governing councils of local communes or work brigades. Nonetheless, at the end of the 1970s, the country discovered that the population had reached approximately one billion.

The Chinese government decided that strong measures were in order and that the goal should be to stabilize the population at about 1.2 billion, then allow it to actually decrease in size. A one-child-per-family plan was promoted with strong economic and other incentives; those who had more than one child were subject to harsh fines and social ostracism. In time the policies became stricter and more coercive—compulsory sterilization and abortion were utilized in the cases of couples who already had two children, and there have been continuing reports of female infanticide.

In fact, data from China's 1990 census indicate that approximately 5% of the infant girls that it is estimated should have been born are not accounted for. It has been suggested that, because many Chinese prefer boys to girls (boys carry on the family name, earn their keep more easily, and support their parents in old age), they do not wish to "waste" their allotment of one child on a girl. Therefore, if a girl is born she may be drowned and registered as a stillbirth or not registered at all. In many remote villages where children are

FIGURE 5–16
The People's Republic of China is the most populous nation on Earth. Here a Beijing couple, with their only child, stand in front of a billboard encouraging only one child per family. (*Source:* Owen Franken/Sygma.)

born at home, such female infanticide might easily escape detection.

However, it is far from certain that female infanticide takes place on any large scale in China. Other explanations for the discrepant boy/girl ratios are also possible. Rather than being killed, the unwanted baby girls may be put up for adoption, be raised by relatives, or simply be raised by their parents without being officially registered (and thus counted in the census). Supporting the suggestion that many of the infant girls are not officially registered and counted is the fact that some population surveys find more five-year-old girls (as they enter school) than there were registered female births five years previously.

Unfortunately, the Chinese population control program has not been an unbridled success—indeed, it has not even reached its explicit goals. The one-child policy has encountered much resistance, especially in rural areas, and the program has been somewhat relaxed. Also, the introduction of a limited capitalism among farmers has made offspring more valuable, and the birth rate has increased. China's population continues to grow and is projected to be more than 1.5 billion by 2025 at current growth rates. China may face major problems in attempting to feed its people, and the country already suffers from severe pollution and environmental degradation.

SUMMARY

The Earth's human population has grown explosively in the last few centuries, and particularly over the last few decades, reaching a current total of 5.8 billion people. Depending on whether or not the world growth rate (currently at 1.6–1.7% a year) decreases substantially, there could be 8 to 12 billion people by the end of the next century. Furthermore, population growth is not distributed evenly over the globe; the greatest increases are occurring in the developing countries, which are least equipped to handle increasing numbers of citizens. In some Western industrialized countries, such as in Europe, the population has stabilized or is even declining. The United States has a high population growth rate compared to other developed countries, but part of the increase in population is due to immigration.

Humanity has a long history, and for hundreds of thousands or millions of years, our ancestors subsisted as gatherers and hunters at very low population levels. Major increases in human population came with the agricultural revolution (about 10,000 years ago) and the Industrial Revolution (in the last 250 years). Population is one of the major factors in the $I = PT$ equation (impact equals population times technology) and thus is a major concern of environmentalists. Yet much controversy surrounds the human population "crisis." What is the carrying capacity of Earth for humans? Is the problem that the Earth has too many people or that resources are not distributed fairly? Has human population growth essentially been innocuous so far, or are humans detrimentally and irreversibly impacting the natural environment?

When human population, or overpopulation, is acknowledged as a problem, many different solutions are offered. Some researchers believe that increased industrialization and economic development will force a demographic transition and thus halt population growth in developing countries. Others emphasize increasing medical care, family planning services, and the use of contraceptives. But some people are morally opposed to artificial contraceptive use as well as to abortions. Still another approach is to increase the educational level and social status of women in particular; studies indicate that there is a positive correlation between women's educational levels and decreased fertility rates. In some cases, governments have used voluntary (such as economic incentives and disincentives) and mandatory (allegations of forced contraceptive use, sterilizations, and abortions) means to regulate population growth. Numerous moral and ethical issues surround such practices.

The subject of human population is a complex, emotionally charged issue. The potential ramifications of increasing human numbers are a continuing theme that will recur in every chapter of this book.

KEY TERMS

abortion
age structure profile
agricultural (Neolithic) revolution
annual growth rate
birth control
carrying capacity
contraception
crude birth rate
crude death rate
cultural extinction
demographic transition

demography
doubling time
exponential growth
fertility rate
growth rate
Human Suffering Index (HSI)
immigration
Industrial Revolution
infant mortality rate
lag phase
less developed country (LDC)
life expectancy

megacity
megalopolis
more developed country (MDC)
neo-Malthusian
percent annual growth
Physical Quality of Life Index (PQLI)
rate of natural increase
replacement level
reproductive rights
suburb
urbanization

STUDY QUESTIONS

1. What approaches have been emphasized at the three United Nations intergovernmental conferences on world population that have been held every ten years since 1974?
2. What effects did early humans have on their environments?
3. Briefly summarize the history of human population growth over the last million years.
4. Explain how the agricultural revolution spurred human population growth.
5. List some factors involved in the exponential growth of the human population over the last two centuries.
6. Where is the highest rate of population growth taking place today? The lowest rate?
7. Describe several alternative scenarios for global population growth through the year 2100.
8. Compare and contrast the age structure profiles of populations in developing ver-

sus industrialized countries.

9. Briefly discuss how the equation I = PT relates to the problem of global human overpopulation.

10. Why has there been a trend toward increasing urbanization during the last few centuries?

11. List some of the reasons why many indigenous cultures are going extinct.

12. Describe the concept of the demographic transition model. What criticisms has this model received?

13. How does the education of women bear on the issue of global population?

14. If the population of Nigeria was 126.93 million at the midpoint of 1995 and had increased to 130.77 by the midpoint of 1996, what was Nigeria's percent annual growth over this period? At this annual growth rate, approximately how long will Nigeria's population take to double? (For information on population equations and statistics, see Issues in Perspective 5–2.)

15. If the population of El Salvador was 5.77 million at the midpoint of 1995 and had increased to 5.88 million by the midpoint of 1996, what was El Salvador's percent annual growth over this period? At this annual growth rate, approximately how long will El Salvador's population take to double?

ESSAY QUESTIONS

1. What are some of the potential consequences of global overpopulation?

2. Discuss the thesis that there is no such thing as human "overpopulation."

3. Describe some of the controversies surrounding various methods of birth control and abortion.

4. Discuss the appropriateness of voluntary versus mandatory government regulation of childbearing.

5. Compare and contrast the ways India and China have attempted to deal with their population problems. Do you approve of the approaches these countries have used? If you were an adviser on population policies to the Indian government or the Chinese government, what recommendations would you make?

SUGGESTED READINGS

Back, K. W. 1989. *Family planning and population control: The challenges of a successful movement.* Boston: Twayne Publishers.

Durning, A. 1993. "Supporting indigenous peoples." In L. R. Brown *et al., State of the world 1993,* pp. 80–100. New York: W. W. Norton.

Easterbrook, G. 1995. *A moment on the Earth: The coming age of environmental optimism.* New York: Viking.

Ehrlich, P. R. 1968. *The population bomb.* New York: Ballantine.

———. 1988. "Populations of people and other living things." In H. J. deBlij, ed., *Earth '88: Changing geographic perspectives,* pp. 302–15. Washington, D.C.: National Geographic Society.

Ehrlich, P. R., and A. H. Ehrlich. 1990. *The population explosion.* New York: Simon & Schuster.

Famighetti, R., ed. 1994. *The world almanac and book of facts, 1995.* Mahwah, N.J.: Funk & Wagnalls Corporation.

Hardin, G. 1993. *Living within limits: ecology, economics, and population taboos.* New York: Oxford University Press.

Jacobson, J. 1988. "Planning the global family." In L. R. Brown *et al., State of the world 1988,* pp. 150–169. New York: W. W. Norton.

——— 1991. "Coming to grips with abortion." In L. R. Brown *et al., State of the world 1991,* pp. 113–131. New York: W. W. Norton.

Keyfitz, N. 1991. "Population growth can prevent the development that would slow population growth." In J. T. Mathews, ed., *Preserving the global environment: The challenge of shared leadership,* pp. 39–77. New York: W. W. Norton.

Meadows, D. H., D. L. Meadows, and J. Randers. 1992. *Beyond the limits: Confronting global collapse, envisioning a sustainable future.* Post Mills, Vt.: Chelsea Green.

Meadows, D. H., D. L. Meadows, J. Randers, and W. W. Behrens III. 1972. *The limits to growth.* New York: Universe Books. This book, based on a two-year study undertaken at the Massachusetts Institute of Technology, was commissioned by the Club of Rome (a group of distinguished government officials, business executives, and scientists).

Ophuls, W., and A. S. Boyan, Jr. 1992. *Ecology and the politics of scarcity revisited: The unraveling of the American dream.* New York: W. H. Freeman.

Ponting, C. 1992. *A green history of the world.* New York: St. Martin's Press.

Short, J. R., ed. 1992. *Human settlement.* New York: Oxford University Press.

Simon, J. 1981. *The ultimate resource.* Princeton, N.J.: Princeton University Press.

Simon, J., and H. Kahn, eds. 1984. *The resourceful Earth.* New York: Basil Blackwell.

World Resources Institute. 1994. *World resources 1994–95.* New York: Oxford University Press.

PROBLEMS OF RESOURCE DEPLETION

Once we see our place, our part of the world, as surrounding us, we have already made a profound division between it and ourselves. We have given up the understanding. . . that we and our country create one another, depend on one another, are literally part of one another; that our land passes in and out of our bodies just as our bodies pass in and out of our land. . . It is for this reason that none of our basic problems is ever solved. WENDELL BERRY, poet, essayist, and social commentator

PHOTO   *Offshore oil platform near Louisiana at sunset.* (*Source:* Bob Thomason/Tony Stone Images.)

PRINCIPLES OF RESOURCE MANAGEMENT

P R O L O G U E *A Town that Pioneers Sustainability*

*A*rcata, California (population 16,000), which was founded in the mid-1800s, began in the usual way: an economy based on rapid exploitation of local resources. Gold fields in nearby mountains and lumber camps in the surrounding forests provided jobs and money for residents. For many decades, these and other natural resources were extracted, processed, and sold to the outside world. Often such rich natural bounty is eventually used up, and logging towns like Arcata

PHOTO *Recycling is a labor-intensive job that can potentially employ many more people than mining or extracting resources.* (Source: Phil Degginger/Tony Stone Images.)

tend to disintegrate like the mining "ghost towns" of the Old West. But Arcata continues to thrive today because it has broken the traditional cycle of dependence on virgin natural resources. Instead of extracting and processing only virgin materials, many local businesses are generating sizable profits and many jobs by reprocessing used and discarded materials. Cascade Forest Products, for example, employs about 35 people to make soil additives such as compost from discarded wood from local sawmills; Cascade's 1993 sales totaled $3.3 million. Another company, Fire & Light Originals, turns recycled glass cullet collected by Arcata Community Recycling Center into decorative tiles. Along with increased efficiency, this switch to manufacturing with recycled materials is one of the foundations of a sustainable economy and society. Instead of depleting the natural resources of future generations, the economy prospers by recycling materials that have already been extracted. Arcata illustrates how environmental concern can promote economic as well as ecological health.

INTRODUCTION

In this chapter, we take an overview of the nature of resources and how to better manage them. As Figure 6–1 shows, many natural resources, from all four spheres, suffer from depletion. Depletion occurs when a resource is utilized faster than it is replaced by natural processes. An oil deposit that took millions of years to form, for example, may be extracted and burned in just a few years, or a species that took many thousands of years to evolve may be driven to extinction in a few years.

The ideal goal of much resource management is sustainable resource use, which seeks to "conserve" or *slow down* the rate of resource exploitation to the point where the resource can be replaced by nature. Tree harvesting and ocean fishing are examples. In other cases, if the re-source is in immediate threat of disappearing, sustainable management must go farther and actually "preserve" the resource by *stopping* its current exploitation. Endangered species and endangered ecosystems, for instance, must often be preserved immediately, or they will disappear in a few years.

Recall (Chapter 1) that stopping or slowing down the rate of resource use not only slows depletion but usually has the added benefit of reducing pollution. A sustainable society would have "throughput" reduced to the point where exploited resources (inputs) are being renewed by natural processes and pollution (outputs) can be safely absorbed by natural processes. Historically, resource management has *not* achieved this goal of sustainable use because of social, economic, and

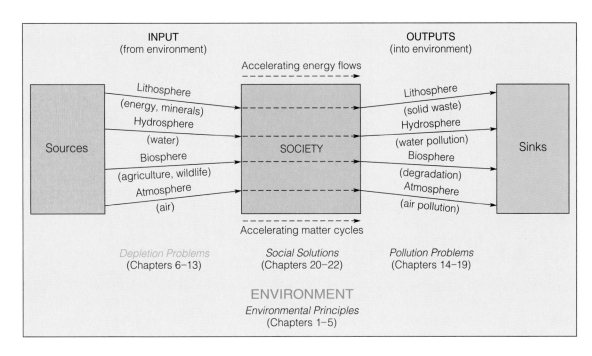

FIGURE 6–1
A major environmental problem with natural resources is their rapid depletion. This occurs when the movement of matter and energy through society is accelerated.

INPUT
(from environment)

OUTPUTS
(into environment)

Accelerating energy flows

Sources

Lithosphere
(energy, minerals)
Hydrosphere
(water)
Biosphere
(agriculture, wildlife)
Atmosphere
(air)

SOCIETY

Lithosphere
(solid waste)
Hydrosphere
(water pollution)
Biosphere
(degradation)
Atmosphere
(air pollution)

Sinks

Accelerating matter cycles

Depletion Problems
(Chapters 6–13)

Social Solutions
(Chapters 20–22)

Pollution Problems
(Chapters 14–19)

ENVIRONMENT
Environmental Principles
(Chapters 1–5)

political pressures that emphasize rapid exploitation of resources.

THE NEED TO MANAGE RESOURCES

EnviroNet
www.jbpub.com/environet

To some people, the concept of resource management reflects human arrogance. They argue that viewing the natural environment as a "resource" is a very narrow anthropocentric (human-centered) approach to nature. Another objection is that the concept assumes that humans not only should manage environmental resources but are able to manage them effectively. Both of these are very questionable assumptions. Many debates in environmental ethics revolve around whether humans have a right to "tamper" with nature, and if so, how much tampering is justified. Ethics aside, the assumption that humans are able, as a practical reality, to effectively manage nature is not shown in human history. Recall (Chapter 1) that David Ehrenfeld (in his book *The Arrogance of Humanism*) and many others have argued that humans have never effectively managed anything for very long.

In spite of these valid concerns, the need for resource management is inescapable. As human populations and technologies grow, inevitably pressures to exploit the environment will increase. Proper management can help minimize environmental damage. Careful planning of water use, for instance, could spare water for native ecosystems that would have been used for agriculture. Furthermore, management can help undo past damage. Elimination of alien (introduced) species, for example, is a common management strategy for some biological communities. Thus, although resource management is not an attractive concept in some ways, it is preferable to the alternative, which is uncontrolled resource exploitation. Global society will be facing many difficult environmental challenges in the future, and making informed decisions about how to use resources is essential for success.

WHAT IS RESOURCE MANAGEMENT?

Increasing resource use tends to be "bought" with increasing environmental costs. Mining, for example, tends to degrade the land more than tourism. But increasing resource use also tends to provide high short-term economic benefits. The history of the United States demonstrates that the economy has generally rewarded those entrepreneurs who most rapidly exploited natural resources. This process seemed justified to most people because modern society has traditionally ignored most environmental costs (Chapter 1). For instance, **benefit-cost analysis (BCA)** is a method of comparing the benefits of an activity to its cost. When the benefits (calculated in a dollar amount) are greater than the costs (calculated in a dollar amount), there is said to be a net benefit to society. If you ignore most environmental costs, any short-term economic benefits of resource use will seem worthwhile: when environmental costs are very low (artificially), the benefit will be greater than the costs. For example, clear-cutting a virgin forest could yield enormous profits (benefits) in the short term.

A more realistic way to analyze resource use is to include the long-term economic benefits of not using them. When this is done, less resource use often translates to greater economic benefits. The total economic value of a rainforest, for instance, is usually greater if the forest is utilized over a long time span for tourism, pharmaceuticals, native foods, and other uses then if it is cut down for a one-time short-term gain in lumber that leaves the forest unusable for decades or centuries. The total value of the rainforest is enhanced even more if extremely long-term environmental benefits are included, such as the value of the forest to future generations (Chapter 1).

RESOURCE MANAGEMENT: PRESERVATION, CONSERVATION, AND RESTORATION

Proper resource management is based on the recognition that less resource use can lead to long-term economic benefits and reduced environmental costs. Such management, while recognizing that some resource use is unavoidable, thus seeks to minimize use where possible. There are three basic options that resource management can apply to minimize resource use: preservation, conservation, and restoration.

Preservation refers to nonuse. A "preserve," national park, or wilderness area is an ecosystem that is set aside and (in theory at least) protected in its pristine, natural state. **Conservation** (input reduction) attempts to minimize the use of a natural resource. As discussed in Chapter 1 and later in this chapter, use can be minimized through efficiency improvements, recycling or reuse, and substitution of other resources. Finally, **restoration** seeks to return a degraded resource to its original state. For example, attempts are being made to redirect the Kissimmee River of Florida into the original path that is followed before it was altered by humans. The rapidly growing field of restoration ecology is attempting to return many ecosystems, such as tall-grass prairies and wetlands, to their original state.

A Brief History of Preservation, Conservation, and Restoration

When the national parks and national forests were being established in the early 1900s under Theodore Roosevelt, there was a lively debate over how much public land should be allotted to preservation and how much to conservation. By prohibiting most forms of resource use except tourism, national parks are an example of preservation (▬ Fig. 6–2). In contrast, national forests (and most other federal lands) permit timber cutting, mining, grazing, and other uses. The promoters of conservation won the debate, and most federal land has permitted these resource uses. In theory, such uses represent "conservation" because the resources are supposed to be closely managed in a way that minimizes damage to the land. This is rarely realized in practice, however, and many federal and state public lands have suffered extensive damage from overuse. As a result, many environmental groups have argued for setting aside more land as "designated wilderness" and other areas of preservation. Others, especially the Nature Conservancy, buy such land and set it aside as private preserves.

Restoration, the newest type of resource management, has become much more common in the 1990s. Aquifers, ecosystems, lakes, soils, and many other environments are being restored by a growing number of restoration specialists. Preservation and conservation are more cost-effective than restoration, which can be extremely expensive. Nevertheless, because so many environments are highly degraded from past abuses, restoration will undoubtedly become increasingly common.

Restoration is most effective at the *landscape level*. It does little good to restore a lake acidified from mining runoff to its normal chemistry unless the surrounding land is treated to help reduce acidic runoff. Similarly, reintroducing wolves into a small forest is unlikely to be successful unless the natural ecosystem for the entire region is prepared to support them. A small forest is not large enough for a self-sustaining wolf population (Chapter 12).

WHO CARES? THE MANY VALUES OF NATURAL RESOURCES

Up to this point, we have talked about the value of resources in economic terms. But as ▬ Figure 6–3 shows, people can place at least five values, sometimes called the **five e's**, on natural resources. One of the e's, ethical value, is what philosophers call an **intrinsic value**.

▬ **FIGURE 6–2**
The U.S. national park system represents an attempt to preserve nature. This scene shows the pristine beauty of Grand Teton National Park. (*Source:* Steve Bly/Tony Stone Images.)

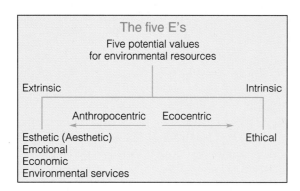

This is the value of a resource unto itself, regardless of its value to humans. Does a mountain have as much right to exist as you do? Does a worm? If you say "yes," then you place a high intrinsic value on these natural resources (Chapter 21). Intrinsic values are "ecocentric" (environment-oriented).

The other four e's are what philosophers call **extrinsic values** (Fig. 6-3). These are values that are external to a resource's own right to exist, referring instead to the resource's ability to provide something for humans. Such values are "anthropocentric" (human-oriented). Extrinsic values are more utilitarian, or practical, than intrinsic values and therefore tend to be more widely discussed in political and economic debates on resource management. Esthetic (aesthetic) value is the value of a resource in making the world more beautiful, more appealing to the senses, and generally more pleasant. The value you place on a mountain hike in the cool morning air might be an example. Some people place no value on this and would pay nothing for it. Others find it indispensable. Emotional values include the value of a resource beyond sensory enjoyment. Some people, for example, develop very strong emotional bonds to certain natural areas or certain plant or animal species. This is sometimes called a "sense of place." Many psychologists consider nature to be important for mental health, especially in children.

Economic values are directly involved with tangible products that can be bought or sold: food, timber, energy, and so on. As we previously discussed, society needs to focus more on long-term economic values, which actually provide more income over the long run. The value of resources for tourism, native fruits, or other sustainable products is ultimately much greater than the value of their destructive uses. Environmental service values are the value of resources in providing intangible "services" that allow humans (and other life) to exist on Earth. Plants help purify air and produce oxygen, and plant roots and soil microbes purify water; ultimately, all food relies on a variety of environmental services.

Some people place all five values on all environmental resources. How many values would you place on the forest shown in ▬ Figure 6–4? How many on a beach? Many people would place only economic values on such resources. Logging, mining, and other types of harvesting that destroy the resources are called **direct values**. Most environmental problems arise when resources are appreciated for only their direct value. Placing only "direct," short-term economic value on natural resources artificially "discounts" their true value to society and to future generations. For example, four of the five e's—esthetic, emotional, environmental services, and ethical values—are not direct values. They represent what economists call **indirect values**, meaning that they are valued in ways that do not involve direct mining, harvesting or other destruction of the resources. If resource prices incorporated both indirect values and long-term direct values, the prices would reflect the resources' true environmental cost. Consider the following comparison:

SHORT-TERM VALUE	LONG-TERM VALUES
Short-term economic value	Long-term economic value
	+ Esthetic value
	+ Emotional value
	+ Ethical value
	+ Environmental service value

While the short-term economic value of resources provides immediate financial rewards, harvesting the short-term value often destroys (1) the long-term economic value and (2) many or all of the indirect values. If society included all the values in the right hand column in its calculations of the value of existing natural resources, it would encourage less destructive harvesting of them. A major problem is that such values are subjective and very difficult to calculate, but estimates can be made (Chapter 20). Including these long-term values would motivate society to preserve resources and conserve them. More sustainable uses of resources, such as extractive forestry and ecotourism, will be encouraged and rewarded. As long as only short-term values are considered, overuse and exploitation will be encouraged and rewarded.

KINDS OF RESOURCES

A **resource** is a source of raw materials used by society. These materials include all types of matter and energy that are used to build and run society. Minerals, trees, soil, water, coal, and all other naturally occurring materials are resources. **Reserves** are the subset of resources that have been located and can be profitably extracted at the current market price. Raw materials that have been located but cannot be profitably extracted at the present time are simply called resources, as are those raw materials that have not been discovered.

Renewable resources can be replaced within a few human generations. Examples include timber, food, and many alternative fuels such as solar power, biomass, and hydropower. **Nonrenewable resources** cannot be replaced within a few human generations. Examples include **fossil fuels**, such as oil and coal, and ore deposits of metals. The phrase a "few human generations" is necessary because some resources are replaceable on very long, geologic time scales. Oil, coal, soils, and some metallic mineral deposits may form again if we wait for thousands to hundreds of millions of years. However, these rates of renewal are so many thousands of times slower than the rates of use that, for all intents, they are nonrenewable on a human scale. In contrast, solar energy is actually supplied faster than we can use it.

The concept of renewability is sometimes blurred. Very old groundwater in deserts may take centuries or even many thousands of years to replace, while groundwater in rainy tropical areas may be replaced in a few days. Thus, deep groundwater in deserts, sometimes called "fossil groundwater," is essentially a nonrenewable resource. Although nonrenewable resources cannot be replaced through natural processes on a human time scale, some (such as certain metals) can be recycled many times.

PATTERNS OF RESOURCE DEPLETION

Recall from Chapter 4 that there are two basic inputs from the environment, matter and energy. Matter constantly cycles through society and the environment whereas energy primarily has a one-way flow. Because of this difference, matter and energy are depleted differently.

How Matter Resources Are Depleted

Matter resources are depleted by being "lost" or dispersed. Ore deposits are unusually concentrated deposits of minerals that are normally

found in more dilute form in the Earth's crust. When we mine and process the ore into metals to build cars and other refined products, the atoms may be eventually dispersed (such as when gears wear down grinding against one another) or lost to further human use when we dispose of the products in landfills and elsewhere (of course, the "urban ore" of a landfill may later be mined for its metal content). Similarly, rapid erosion depletes soil not because the nutrients and minerals in the soil are destroyed, but because the soil is dispersed, ultimately into the oceans.

These examples are nonrenewable matter; when dispersed, molecules of metals and soils will stay dispersed unless we spend much energy and money to reconcentrate them. In the case of re-

FIGURE 6–4
What is the monetary value of a forest? Is it worthless? Is it priceless? The answer varies greatly from person to person. (*Source:* Michael Busselle/Tony Stone Images.)

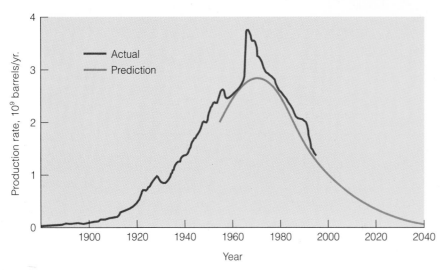

FIGURE 6–5
Predicted U.S. oil production by M. King Hubbert and actual U.S. oil production until 1991. Both curves peak around 1970. (*Source*: Modified from S. Judson/M. Kauffman, *Physical Geology*. Copyright © 1990, p. 372. Reprinted by permission of Prentice Hall, Upper Saddle River, NJ.)

newable matter resources, dispersal still occurs, such as when we build houses from timber, but we can regenerate the timber relatively quickly. Renewable matter resources are often biological resources that can be regrown.

How Energy Resources Are Depleted

Energy has a one-way flow through society because it is transformed to an unusable form, "waste heat," when we use it (Chapter 4). Energy resources are therefore depleted when they are transformed this way. This is a key difference from some forms of "lost" matter, which could be recollected and reconcentrated if society had enough cheap energy. In contrast, once energy is transformed, it is lost forever; waste heat can never be reconcentrated. If we burn oil or coal to release their chemical energy to drive an engine, that energy can never be reused.

We do have a major source of renewable energy, however: the Sun. This source of renewable energy could potentially keep society run-

ning for many millions of years. Examples of the Sun's energy include direct solar power, biomass, hydropower, and wind (Chapter 9).

Bubble Pattern of Depletion

Unsustainable use of many resources exhibits a bubble pattern of depletion. The best-known example is the so-called **Hubbert's bubble** of oil depletion. This was named after M. King Hubbert who accurately predicted the bubble pattern of oil depletion in the United States. Since the 1950s when his predictions were first made, they have proven to be strikingly accurate. U.S. oil production peaked around 1970 and has been declining since, as the richest reserves are steadily depleted (Fig. 6–5).

The bubble pattern has two main causes: exponential exploitation and exponential depletion. Because both use and exhaustion are exponential, they tend to form a mirror image. The left, or exploitation, side of the bubble is exponential because resources are exploited very quickly once society discovers their utility. The underlying cause of this exponential use is the exponential growth of human populations and the technology that uses resources (Chapter 1). Figure 6–6a shows that the exponential growth stage continues as long as supply exceeds demand. But because all resources on Earth are finite, limits to growth eventually occur, and demand begins to exceed supply. During this time, society usually intensifies its efforts to obtain more of the resource through further exploration and increased technological applications. However, these efforts usually soon encounter what economists call the **law of diminishing returns**, meaning that increasing efforts to extract the resource produce progressively smaller amounts. The result is shown in the right, or depletion, side of the bub-

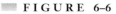 **FIGURE 6–6**
(a) Exponential exploitation occurs as long as the supply of a resource exceeds demand. Exponential decline occurs when demand exceeds supply. Switching to a new resource just perpetuates the "bubble" cycle of unsustainable use.
(b) England followed this pattern, switching from wood to coal when the forests were gone and from coal to oil when the easily extracted coal was exhausted, making oil relatively cheaper.

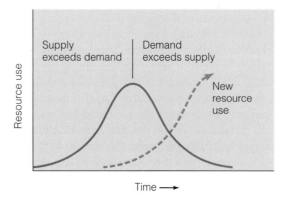

(a) Cycle of unsustainable use

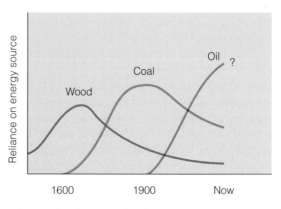

(b) Unsustainable use in England

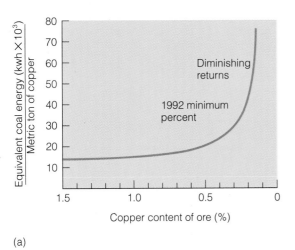

(a)

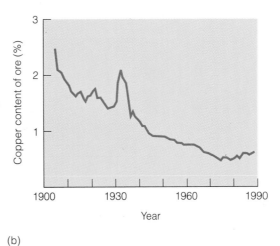

(b)

FIGURE 6–7
(a) The energy used to extract copper from ore increases exponentially when the ore's copper content is below about 0.5%. (b) Since 1905, the quality of copper ore mined in the United States has declined from 2.5% to about 0.5%. (*Source* for *a* and *b*: U.S. Bureau of Mines.)

ble. Production declines exponentially because the most easily extracted concentrations of the resource become exhausted.

As supplies of the resource decline, prices rise, sometimes leading to unemployment and other unpleasant changes. Historically, society has responded to the increase in resource prices by switching to another resource. Figure 6–6b shows how England switched from wood to coal as an energy source when the forests were decimated and more recently to oil because it is cheaper. Unfortunately, the series of bubble patterns shown for England has often been repeated elsewhere and with other resources as societies have tended to switch from one unsustainable resource to another. The only way to break this "cycle of unsustainable use" is to switch to sustainable uses, as discussed later in this chapter.

PROBLEMS WITH PAST RESOURCE MANAGEMENT

Society can respond to a diminishing supply of a resource in two ways: (1) intensify efforts to extract more of the resource or (2) reduce the need for the resource. Until recently, the first response was much more common. The usual result was a bubble pattern as depletion accelerated when supplies ran low. The mining of lower-grade, high-volume materials also led to pollution problems. Nevertheless, two influential concepts were advanced to justify these past intensification efforts.

Net Yield of Nonrenewable Resources

Intensified extraction of nonrenewable resources is based on the concept of **net yield**, which holds that a resource can continue to be extracted as long as the resources used in extraction do not exceed the resources gained. For example, at the current market price of copper, copper ore that is as low as 0.5% by weight copper content in the rock can profitably be mined. The price society is willing to pay for the copper is higher than the energy costs of mining it (Fig. 6–7a). Notice that the curve in Figure 6–7a is not straight, indicating that the energy used in mining increases exponentially after a certain point. The amount of waste rock and pollution also increases exponentially. This is a good example of the law of diminishing returns in that at some point more intense efforts begin to yield fewer rewards. In the United States, this point has already been reached for most oil and mineral deposits and for many other resources such as soils that require many tons of fertilizer.

Because energy prices have been relatively low over the last 90 years, it has been relatively easy to cope with the law of diminishing returns. For example, miners have simply switched to lower-grade deposits when high-grade deposits were depleted (Fig. 6–7b). This greatly increases the available supplies because nearly all nonrenewable resources are characterized by an *inverse quality curve*: higher-grade deposits of coal, oil, minerals and other resources are much rarer than lower-grade deposits.

The past pursuit of net yield has incurred great environmental costs by accelerating both depletion and pollution. Depletion accelerates because increasingly lower grade ores must be mined and more energy and other resources must be expended to extract the ore. Pollution accelerates because increasing amounts of waste rock are produced when lower-grade ores are mined (Fig. 6–8). The Goldstrike mine of Nevada, for example, the

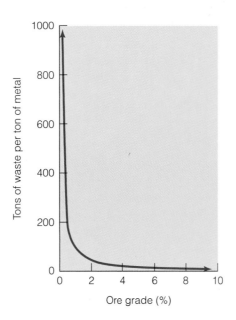

largest gold mine in the United States, moves 325,000 tons (295,00 metric tons)* of rock and waste to produce just over 100 pounds (45 kg) of gold. In 1991, globally 990 million tons (898 million metric tons) of copper ore was mined to produce about 9 million tons (8 million metric tons) of copper. In the past some geologists worried that eventually humans might run out of ores to mine. Many environmentalists now feel that the bigger issue is mining-related environmental degradation. Mining may have to be curtailed due to the pollu-

———————

*Unless otherwise noted, *tons* refers to short tons (2000 pounds).

tion generated by metal extraction rather than because the ores are actually depleted.

Maximum Sustainable Yield of Renewable Resources

Another very influential concept in resource management has been the **maximum sustainable yield (MSY)**, which holds that the optimum way to exploit a renewable resource is to harvest as much as possible up to the point where the harvest rate equals the renewal rate. As an example, a person could withdraw as much groundwater as needed up to the point where the withdrawal rate equaled the recharge rate from rainfall. Taking less could be considered underutilization and taking more would lead to depletion.

MSY has been especially influential in the management of renewable biological resources such as commercially important fishes and wildlife. The basic principle was that fishes, game, and other populations could be harvested up to the point where the population's ability to reproduce itself was impaired. For instance, individuals could have trouble finding mates if the population was overharvested. MSY actively encourages limited harvesting, because it holds that if population abundance becomes too high, further population growth is inhibited by crowding and competition (███ Fig. 6–9a). Thus, MSY aims at a balance between too much and too little harvesting to keep the population at some intermediate abundance.

Figure 6–9 shows that the MSY population level is usually about one-half of the carrying ca-

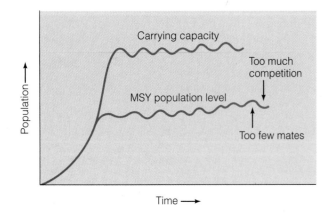

(a)

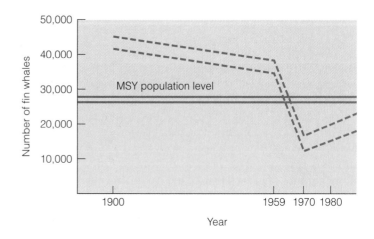

(b)

███ **FIGURE 6-9**

(a) Maximum sustainable yield (MSY) occurs at population levels around one-half of the carrying capacity. (b) Fin whales declined to levels well below MSY population levels during the 1960s (dashed lines show the range of estimated population sizes), but are slowly climbing back. The difference be-

tween the two solid lines at MSY population level is about 1200 individuals = MSY harvest per year. (*Source*: Diagram [b] modified from A. Beeby, *Applying Ecology* [Chapman & Hall, 1994], p. 138. Reprinted by permission of Chapman & Hall.)

*P*ROBLEMS OF RESOURCE DEPLETION   SECTION 2

pacity. Note that the number of individuals actually harvested is only a small fraction of the total MSY population. Fin whales, for example, have been overexploited well below their estimated MSY population (Fig. 6–9b). Current estimates are that fin whales could rebound to MSY population levels of about 28,000 individuals in 8–16 years. At those levels, an estimated 1200 individuals, or about 4.3% of the MSY population, could be harvested (1200 ÷ 28,000 = 4.3%).

Although it is widely practiced by state and federal government agencies regulating wildlife, forests, and fishing, MSY has come under heavy criticism by ecologists and others for both theoretical and practical reasons. An important theoretical shortcoming is that MSY does not take large environmental fluctuations into account: a bad winter or some other natural catastrophe could reduce the population unpredictably. More important perhaps are the many practical problems with MSY. Calculating the point at which population growth begins to slow from competition is very difficult. Indeed, in many cases such as marine fishes, just estimating the population size can be difficult. Consequently, estimating MSY with certainty is virtually impossible, although more sophisticated methods, such as refined statistical sampling models for estimating population size, are improving the calculations. Still, the decline in commercial fishing in many areas indicates that humans are harvesting far more than the MSY (see Issues in Perspective 6–1).

Despite these and other problems, many agencies continue to rely on MSY. A variation on the MSY concept known as the optimum sustainable yield (OSY) is also gaining popularity with some resource managers. It states that the optimum harvestable rate for a renewable resource must consider many factors, not just the maximum yield. How will harvesting affect other species in the ecosystem? How will it affect other human uses of the ecosystem, such as recreation? When such additional benefit-cost questions are included, managers usually find that the harvests recommended by OSY are less than the MSY.

CONSERVATION: REDUCING THE NEED FOR RESOURCES

The basic problem with net yield and maximum sustainable yield is that their main goal has been to maximize resource use. Their focus was on short-term economic gain. But as we noted earlier, long-term economic and other gains (such as

esthetic, emotional, and environmental services) are greater if the emphasis is shifted to reducing resource use. This can be done in three ways: preservation, conservation, or restoration of what has been degraded. Instead of maximizing resource use, the focus should be on accomplishing more with the resources that are used.

Conservation, or input reduction by lowering resource use, will thus be a fundamental part of a sustainable society. Recall from Chapter 1 that conservation (1) slows depletion of resources, (2) reduces pollution by slowing the flow of matter and energy (throughput) through society, and (3) saves money. For example, burning less coal by increasing a power plant's efficiency not only saves coal but produces less acid rain and other pollution. It is also often cheaper to design power plants to burn less coal than to pay for all the pollution control devices needed to trap the air pollution in the smokestack and then dispose of the trapped pollutants. Until recently, supplies of most resources were so abundant, especially in the United States, that little attention was paid to input reduction; as a result, depletion rates were high, and pollution was controlled by scrubbers and other forms of output, or "end-of-pipe," reduction.

Ways to Conserve: Efficiency, Recycling, and Substitution

Figure 6–10 shows three basic ways to conserve, or reduce the need for a resource: efficiency improvements, reuse/recycling, and substitution.

FIGURE 6–10
Input reduction (= conservation) can be achieved by efficiency improvements, reuse/recycling, and substitution. All three methods reduce the flow of materials and energy (throughput) into and out of society, slowing both depletion and pollution.

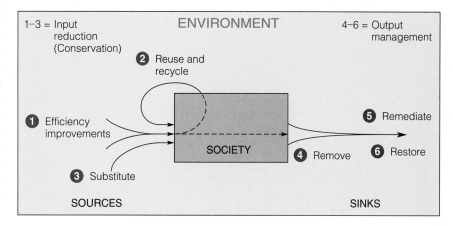

Efficiency improvement is generally most effective and economically cheapest because many technologies and activities are wasteful and inefficient. Different resources will require different methods of input reduction, however. It is very difficult, for example, to find affordable substitutes for water in many of its uses, such as agriculture and drinking, so increased effi-

How to Exceed Maximum Sustainable Yield: Overfishing in New England

In 1981, the United States declared a 200-mile (322 km) boundary around its shores, banning most foreign trawlers that had fished U.S. waters. The ban was an attempt to save the beleaguered New England fishing industry. The measure worked until Americans themselves began overfishing. Encouraged in part by a federal loan program, they began building more boats, equipping them with powerful fish-finding electronics. They lobbied to remove quotas on catches. And, for a while, they caught a lot more fish. But the trawler catch in New England peaked in 1983 and has since fallen sharply (Fig. 1). Stocks of flounder and haddock are near record lows. The cod population is down. Bluefin tuna and swordfish have been depleted. There have been booms and busts before, but scientists say that this time is different. The fleets are so big and the technology so advanced that fish no longer have anywhere to hide.

In 1983, the trawler catch reached 410 million pounds (186 million kg), up 66% from 1976. In 1990, the haul had declined to 282 million pounds (128 million kg). Although this was up from the low of 234 million pounds (105 million kg) in 1989, marine scientists say the increase was achieved by catching huge numbers of juvenile fish that had just reached the minimum size. Many of

FIGURE 1
New England fishermen are struggling to make a living because of the decline of many species. (*Source:* Tom Stewart/The Stock Market.)

the fish hadn't had a chance to spawn. They are being fished out faster than they are reproducing.

Some people in the fishing industry say they can't back off. They have to keep the boats going nonstop to make enough to survive. But others and conservationists insist that current measures, such as minimum net mesh sizes and occasional closures of overfished waters, simply are not enough. Strict catch quotas, trip limits, even moratoria on new boats are needed, or more people will be forced out of the business in the long run. Legislation has been introduced to reduce the size of the New England fleet by buying out vessels with money from a tax on the diesel fuel the fishing boats use. Some have suggested that the government should subsidize the fleets by meeting mortgages for those who do not fish a certain number of days. And severe restrictions are being placed on fishing in some areas, such as the once-fertile Georges Bank ecosystem off the coast of Massachusetts. Some way of rationally allocating fishery resources is needed to guarantee that the industry remains intact.

This is a classic example of the "tragedy of the commons." The oceans are used by many individuals and nations. Thus, many nations must agree on laws that govern access to ocean resources, and, perhaps more difficult, these laws must be enforced in ways that prevent overfishing.

ciency and reuse/recycling of wastewater are common.

Efficiency Improvements

Efficiency improvements occur when the same task is accomplished with fewer resources (Chapter 1). An example would be lighter, more fuel-efficient cars to conserve fuel and building materials. Between 1973 and 1992, the average efficiency of cars made in the United States doubled from 14 to 28 miles per gallon (6 to 12 km per liter). Such cars perform the same tasks as less fuel-efficient cars but use fewer resources in doing so. As another example, about two-thirds of the water used in irrigation is lost to evaporation. Using "micro-irrigation" where water is carried by pipes and sprayed through small holes reduces water loss to less than 20%.

Japan in particular and the European countries are leaders in devising technologies that improve efficiency. The **energy intensity index**, which equals energy consumption/gross national product, measures how much energy is used to produce the same unit of wealth (see Chapter 9). The index for the United States in the early 1990s was about 14.5 billion BTUs consumed per $1 million GNP (approximately 0.015 petajoules per $1 million GNP). In contrast, the index for Japan was about 5.7 billion BTUs per $1 million GNP (0.006 petajoules per $1 million GNP). Japan uses less than half the energy to produce a given amount of wealth, from manufacturing cars to heating hotel rooms. Material efficiency indexes, which indicate usage of other resources, show a similar pattern of waste for the United States. For example, Japanese technologies convert about 70% of raw timber into finished wood products while in the United States only about 50% is converted.

The relative inefficiency of resource use in the United States is a direct result of its historical endowment of abundant resources. Costs for energy and other resources were low, so efficiency was not encouraged. Ultimately, however, inefficiency is costly to any economy. According to many experts, energy inefficiencies account for at least 50% of U.S. energy use. With such inefficiency, money invested in energy-saving technologies would more than pay for itself by reduced energy costs. The Worldwatch Institute estimates that U.S. electricity could be reduced by 70% through efficiency gains, at *no* net cost because energy savings would equal the investment needed to make the changes. Increased efficiency leading to conservation of minerals and other resources would achieve similar savings.

Besides the economic savings, environmental savings from efficiency increases are also enormous. Less depletion saves more resources for future generations. Less resources extracted means less degradation of the land. Pollution control from reduced processing and usage can also be significant. To continue with the energy example, the pollutants released by the burning of fossil fuels are reduced when efficiency is increased. A major 1992 study in the journal *Science* concluded that national investments in energy conservation would not only save from $10 billion to $110 billion per year, but would reduce greenhouse gas (global warming) emissions up to 40%.

Reuse and Recycling

Reuse occurs when the same resource is used again in the same form, such as refilling soda bottles (Chapter 1). Recycling is similar, but the resource is not reused in the same form. The soda bottles, for instance, may be remelted to make new bottles or other glass containers. Like improved efficiency, reuse/recycling reduces depletion of resources and pollution from resource extraction and use (Fig. 6–10). Reuse/recycling is useful in reducing solid waste, which is important because landfills are being permanently closed at the rate of about two per day. Many areas of the United States, especially in the Northeast, are running out of space and few new landfills are opening up. Because about 33% of U.S. garbage consists of packaging, **precycling**, which is the reduction of packaging material by manufacturers, is becoming more important. Concentrated foods, for example, can often be packaged in smaller containers. Precycling is not recycling, but is conservation by increased efficiency; the same task is accomplished but fewer resources are used. Despite such efforts, the amount of solid waste in the United States continues to grow (Chapter 19).

The technological and economic aspects of recycling can be very complex. A simplified recycling scheme begins with **virgin resources**, which are the original natural resources being extracted. Both extraction, such as mining, and processing during product manufacture usually create pollution. The **recycling loop** begins before the purchased product is discarded; the discard is reprocessed into the same or perhaps another product. Note that, unlike the reuse loop, the reprocessed product does not have to be the same as the original. For example, while paper is often recycled into more paper, car tires are often recycled into road asphalt, shoes, playground structures, and many other products. As long as the discard is being used in place of a virgin resource, recycling occurs. Unfortunately, some manufacturers claim their products are recycled even though they do not meet this criterion of being used instead of a virgin resource (see Issues in Perspective 6–2).

The recycling loop is closed when someone buys a product containing recycled material (Fig. 6–11, page 160). This slows depletion of virgin resources and reduces pollution in two basic ways. Most obviously, it reduces the amount of solid waste that would have been discarded into landfills, incinerators, and other means of disposal. In addition, recycling reduces the pollution

EnviroNet
www.jbpub.com/environet

Is This Recycled or Not?

Since Earth Day 1990, many products touted as "environmentally friendly" have entered the market. Sometimes called green marketing or "greenwashing," promoting products as green can be very successful because of increasing concern over the environment. Unfortunately, green marketing has been plagued by misunderstandings and even false claims. A main reason is the lack of clear definitions. For example, what exactly does it mean when a product is advertised as being biodegradable or recycled (Fig. 1)?

The definition of biodegradability came to widespread public attention when "biodegradable" trash bags were found to degrade only under laboratory conditions, and not under those found in landfills. As a result, the company had to remove this claim, and the term *biodegradable* is now reserved for products that decompose under natural conditions. Another problem is that decomposition must involve true chemical destruction of the product into harmless components and not just reduction into smaller particles, such as smaller plastic pieces. But even if we define biodegradable as chemical decomposition in natural conditions, there is still plenty of room for vagueness. What are natural conditions? What if decomposition takes five years? Ten years?

The definition of a "recycled" product is perhaps even more difficult to specify. Many kinds of products are recycled in many ways, and the remanufactured products are often only partly composed of recycled material. Yet buying recycled material is essential to close the recycling loop. Paper recycling is a key illustration of the difficulties because it is so important: Paper is the largest component of municipal solid waste, composing over 40% of landfill volume. But the United States has no national legal standards defining recycled paper. As a result, some paper that is sold as recycled actually contains only a tiny fraction of recycled paper. Furthermore, even this recycled paper can be *preconsumer*, meaning that it is wastepaper generated by papermills, such as cuttings, scraps, and flawed batches. Such preconsumer waste is often not as desirable as recycling *postconsumer* waste, which is discarded by consumers; recycling postconsumer waste is more helpful to the environment because that is the source of so much landfill waste.

The lack of clear meaning for product environmental claims is harmful to nearly everyone. Consumers suffer when they pay extra for a product that is not what they think; companies that really try to produce environmentally friendly products suffer when they are undersold by companies that market more harmful products as environmentally friendly; and the environment suffers when we use harmful products when we think we are not.

The solution to such problems is to create clear definitions for envi-

FIGURE 1

Three types of recycling symbols commonly used in the United States. (a) This symbol simply means that the object is potentially recyclable, not that it has been or will be recycled. (b) This symbol indicates that a product contains recycled material, but it does not indicate how much recycled material is in the product (it could be only a very small amount). (c) This symbol states explicitly the percentage of recycled content found in the product.

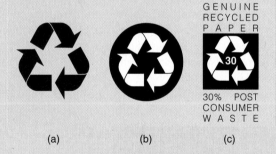

GENUINE
RECYCLED
PAPER

30% POST
CONSUMER
WASTE

(a)   (b)   (c)

that would have been produced from the extraction of the virgin resources.

Unfortunately, the recycling loop is *often not closed* because, even though people are willing to sort and return recyclable waste, there is often little consumer demand to purchase the recycled product. The reasons for this are usually economic: when products made from virgin resources are cheaper, the loop goes unclosed. If the costs of products made from virgin resources were increased to reflect their true cost to the environment, the price differential would disappear, and the loop could be closed.

Substitution

Substitution occurs when one resource is used instead of another (Chapter 1). Substitution can also help reduce both depletion and pollution problems. It helps with depletion because when one resource is being depleted, a more common substitute can be used at a cheaper price. For in-

ronmental marketing claims. Those who falsely make such claims can then be legally prosecuted, or at least conscientious consumers can avoid the products. Currently, some standards have been established by state and local laws and nonbinding agreements between consumer groups and companies. Unfortunately, these vary from place to place. Therefore support is growing for a single set of federal guidelines that would apply all over the United States. For example, the Environmental Protection Agency (EPA) currently has a paper guideline specifying that recycled paper should contain at least 50% recycled fiber. But companies are not required to use this definition, which also omits how much of the recycled fiber must be postconsumer. In 1992, the EPA invited the U.S. Office of Consumer Affairs and the Federal Trade Commission to join in developing voluntary guidelines for the use of environmental terms on product labels.

Until enforceable federal regulations are established, consumers and private organizations must educate themselves about what is being marketed. Two private nonprofit organizations, Green Cross Cer-

FIGURE 2

The "Green Cross" is a seal of approval that indicates a product promotes environmental sustainability. (*Source:* Roy Morsch/The Stock Market.)

tification Company and the Green Seal, test products and affix "seal of approval" logos if the product passes the tests (Fig. 2). Similar organizations also exist in other countries, such as the West German Blue Angel program, Canada's Environmental Choice, and Japan's Eco-mark. Unfortunately, certification by the Green Cross and Green Seal is largely voluntary: many companies never submit products for certification.

Consumers should also be aware that

many recycling logos on boxes and cans don't mean very much. For example, consider the familiar logo with arrows in a triangle that appears on many food and paper products. The arrows alone indicate that the product is recyclable; arrows within a circle mean "made from recycled materials." But this logo alone does not indicate the amount of recycled material, how easily recycled the product is, or other key information. For example, many products are recyclable but are never recycled because the manufacturer does not repurchase its own recycled material. The recycling loop remains "unclosed."

If you want to be a green consumer, here are a few basic rules: avoid needless shopping (conservation is always the "greenest" activity you can do); avoid vague environmental claims such as "environmentally safe"; where possible, try to buy products certified by the Green Cross or Green Seal; seek out minimal packaging and reusable containers; and look for specific information that a company may provide such as "made from 30% postconsumer recycled fiber" (this is preferable to a product made of, say, 10% postconsumer recycled fiber).

stance, aluminum, a very common metal in the Earth's crust, can sometimes be substituted for the much rarer and more expensive copper in making alloys, equipment, and other uses. Substitution helps with pollution problems when the extraction, processing, or disposal of the substituted resources produces less pollution. For example, many plastics last for 50 to 100 years in the environment before they significantly decompose. Also, plastics are made of a nonrenewable resource, petroleum, whereas trees are renewable.

Such considerations have led to the substitution of paper for plastic in many items, such as drinking cups and food containers.

Although it can be useful in reducing resource depletion, substitution is often less desirable than efficiency improvements or reuse/recycling. Instead of reducing overall resource depletion, substitution often simply switches depletion from one resource to another. This can be satisfactory if the new resource is renewable, as in paper, or very abundant, as with glass made from

■ **FIGURE 6-11**
Pens and many other products can be made from recycled tires. (*Source:* Photographed by Pat Toth-Smith, Aesthetic Images, for the catalog of Green Earth Office Supply, Redwood Estates, California.)

sand. Also, substitution often does not reduce pollution, solid waste, or other output problems. For instance, the use of paper products offers many environmental advantages over plastic, but it may do little to solve landfill space problems. Indeed, paper is already the largest component of city garbage.

ℛESOURCE ECONOMICS

All environmental problems are closely intertwined with economic causes. This is especially true of resources because their extraction and use are directly determined by their profitability.

Resource Overuse: Ignoring Environmental Costs

A basic reason why resources are overused is that they are too cheap. The price paid for metals, timber, petroleum, and many other virgin natural resources does not reflect their true environmental costs (Chapter 1). These true costs would include all five e's—esthetic, emotional, environmental services, and ethical values and long-term economic values. The price paid by consumers for natural resources now usually omits many of

these. The price of metals, for instance, rarely incorporates many of the environmental costs of mining: costs of water pollution on nearby aquatic ecosystems, esthetic loss from a cratered landscape, and so on. In Chapter 1, we saw how many environmental economists suggest that green fees, such as taxes, can incorporate environmental costs into natural resource use. Mining companies, manufacturers, and consumers all respond to higher prices by increasing efficiency, reusing/recycling more, and substituting more.

Another way to incorporate long-term and indirect values is to use basic market principles: consumers can demand sustainable products such as those made with recycled materials. When the profit made from such sustainable activities exceeds the profit made from destruction of resources, sustainable activities will be rewarded. At present, this is rarely the case, and unsustainable activities are more profitable.

Economics of Recycling

Recycling is an excellent example of the key role that economics plays in promoting resource conservation. Although about 80% of U.S. household garbage can be recycled as compost, aluminum, paper, and many other components, only about 13% of municipal solid waste was being recycled in 1992 because the economic incentives were lacking. Returning used items for collection is not enough. The recycling loop is closed only if collected items are used again to make a product that is repurchased. The loop will often go unclosed if products made from recycled materials cost more than products made only from virgin resources. Consumers will often choose to buy the cheaper product, and the waste people thought they returned for recycling will be taken to landfills because no one will buy it.

Widespread recycling is unlikely to occur until it is economically feasible, even though the number of U.S. communities requiring recycling has risen dramatically such that currently nearly half of all U.S. communities now have recycling programs in place. As many communities have learned, simply passing laws requiring recycling is not enough. Seattle, Washington, which resolved to recycle 60% of its garbage by 1998, is a good example. By 1993, Seattle had the highest rate of recycling of any major U.S. city, with 42% of its garbage being recycled and 90% of all single-family homes participating. By charging an extra fee for each barrel of garbage left out for pickup, the city encouraged people to sort their waste and deposit it in recycling containers.

Unfortunately, the city has had difficulty closing the loop on some materials, such as glass and paper, which were sometimes sent to landfills. Even though the average price of used newspapers dropped from $20 to $5 per ton (0.907 metric tons) in 1991, it was still often cheaper to make paper from trees, so no recycler would buy them. More recently, however, the price of paper has risen and the demand for recycled paper has increased especially since the federal government now requires all its offices to use recycled paper.

Why is recycled material sometimes more expensive than virgin material? A major reason is the cost of energy, including the energy of human labor. The cost of **embodied energy,** or the energy used in producing a product, is often the main factor determining the product's retail cost. The energy consumed in recycling some materials is much less than the energy consumed in processing virgin material. For example, mining and processing aluminum and many other metals is very energy-intensive. Because recycling aluminum uses much less energy, there is a strong cost incentive to reprocess it and close the loop. In everyday terms, recycling just one aluminum can saves enough energy to run a television set for three hours. The aluminum recycling industry is one of the fastest growing industries in the United States; it earns approximately $1 billion annually and recycles an astounding 50 billion aluminum cans per year, equal to 200 cans per U.S. citizen. This example shows how both the environment and jobs can benefit from recycling.

Recycling other materials, such as newspaper and glass, saves considerably less energy than recycling aluminum, however. When the costs of human energy, such as collecting and sorting the newspaper and glass, are added on, the slim profit margin may disappear, and the loop may sometimes be unclosed as in the Seattle example.

The problem of closing the recycling loop has many possible solutions. One option is to appeal to consumers to purchase recycled products, even if they cost more. For instance, some students buy recycled notebook paper even though it is more expensive because they want to encourage recycling. To encourage such buying on a wide scale, society can levy higher "green taxes" on virgin resources to boost the price of products made from them. If the taxes are high enough, the recycled product will be cheaper, and the loop will be closed through consumer demand. Lastly, human ingenuity and innovation may devise new recycling processes that lower costs or new products that appeal to consumers. For example, the growing problem of recycling

used tires has led to dozens of products that incorporate them, from sandals to tennis shoes and asphalt. When products that people want are created, there is an economic incentive to close the loop. Many businesses are finding new uses for plastics, such as stuffing for ski jackets and even "lumber" to build benches, fences, and playground equipment.

JOBS AND LIFE IN A SUSTAINABLE WORLD

A sustainable world meets today's needs without reducing the quality of life of future generations (Chapter 1). Modern resource exploitation is not even close to being sustainable. ▬ Figure 6–12 shows how the consumption of virgin raw materials such as minerals has increased much faster in the United States than population. Since 1900, materials consumption increased about *six times* faster than population growth. The average American today consumes six times more resources than the average American in 1900.

▬ Figure 6–13 shows that many jobs in the U.S. high-throughput society are concentrated at both ends of the flow of materials through society—in resource extraction and waste cleanup. This leads to unsustainability because resources are being used at a vastly higher rate than they are being replaced by natural processes.

Figure 6–13 also shows what an economy could look like in a low-throughput, sustainable world. Virgin resources would be more costly, re-

FIGURE 6–12
Consumption of materials in the United States has grown much faster than population. (Note that one metric ton = approximately 1.102 tons.) (*Source*: U.S. Bureau of Mines.)

FIGURE 6–13
(a) Cheap resources and environmental sinks promote an unsustainable, high-throughput economy with jobs concentrated in resource extraction and waste cleanup. (b) Expensive resources and environmental sinks promote a low-throughput, sustainable economy with jobs concentrated in resource conservation (input reduction) activities.

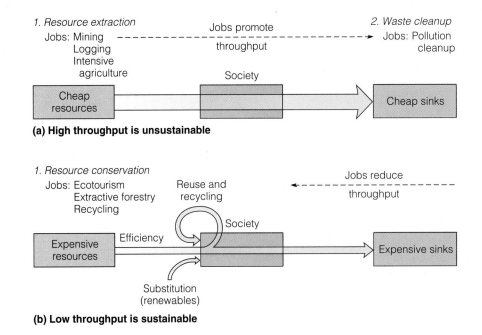

1. Resource extraction
Jobs: Mining
        Logging
        Intensive
        agriculture

Jobs promote throughput

2. Waste cleanup
Jobs: Pollution
        cleanup

Society

Cheap resources → Cheap sinks

(a) High throughput is unsustainable

1. Resource conservation
Jobs: Ecotourism
        Extractive forestry
        Recycling

Reuse and recycling

Jobs reduce throughput

Society

Expensive resources — Efficiency → Expensive sinks

Substitution (renewables)

(b) Low throughput is sustainable

FIGURE 6–14
"Solar farms," such as this one in California, can potentially provide many high-tech careers. *(Source:* Robert Visser/Greenpeace.)*

flecting their true long-term value and promoting highly efficient use of resources, reuse/recycling, and substitution of more abundant and more renewable resources. Jobs would be concentrated at the input end of the throughput flow and would involve sustainable resource management activities such as ecotourism, recycling, and the renewable energy industry (Fig. 6–14). These, and similar activities, reduce throughput and slow nonrenewable resource depletion and pollution. In contrast, in a high-throughput society today, jobs actively promote nonrenewable resource depletion and pollution.

In many cases, sustainable activities produce more jobs than unsustainable ones. Extracting resources often produces few jobs. For each person in the United States employed in logging timber, more than 25 people are employed in making furniture from it. Collecting used material and making furniture, or any item, from recycled or reused material would employ many more people than logging. Similarly, mining metals in the American West, for example, employs just 0.1% of all workers there. Tourism, a much cleaner industry, employs a much larger proportion of workers. Employment in the U.S. automobile manufacturing industry increased only 3% between 1980 and 1990. But employment in the auto repair industry increased by 50%, growing nearly 17 times faster. Auto repair is a form of efficiency improvement because it lets society accomplish the same task (car driving) with fewer resources (fewer new cars). Indeed, designing more durable and repairable products is an important step toward reducing throughput and curing the "throwaway" mentality. ● Table 6–1 shows many other specific opportunities for jobs to make society more sustainable.

TABLE 6–1 *Some Suggestions for Creating a Sustainable Society*

Environmentally harmful (unsustainable) activities can be solved in many ways. All of these solutions use efficiency, recycling, and substitution promoted by economic incentives to reduce throughput.

HARMFUL ACTIVITY	EXAMPLE	SOLUTIONS
Extraction	Mining high-grade ore—and then moving on to a new site because the land is artificially cheap, while ignoring lower-grade ore on the already-disrupted site	Higher land prices (through elimination of subsidies and addition of full costs of environmental disruption) would increase incentives to use more efficient extraction technologies, reducing the area of land disrupted.
Manufacture	Making paper from 90–100% virgin wood fiber	Most paperboard, paper packaging, and office paper can be made with less than 50% virgin input with no loss of quality, potentially saving millions of trees each year.
Product design	Designing "discount" products—from umbrellas to televisions to houses—that compete for low retail prices but do not last	Design emphasizing durability and reparability would reduce the number of times the consumer has to replace the product, and would thus reduce materials consumption.
Community development	Planning communities in which residences are far from workplaces and services	Planning that puts people closer to what they need and that makes efficient use of already-developed land would reduce the use of cars and thus the need for materials-intensive construction projects such as roads and bridges.
Direct consumption	Stressing immediate convenience of consumption and disposal as the ultimate good, without considering the prospects for sustainable consumption	Making changes in our consumption patterns to promote a culture of conservation—copying on both sides of the page, using canvas shopping bags, reading books from the library instead of buying new copies, taking public transportation—could ultimately save both money and materials.

(*Source:* Modified from Worldwatch Paper #121, *The Next Efficiency Revolution* by John E. Young and Aaron Sachs, with permission of Worldwatch Institute, Washington, D.C. Copyright © 1994.)

SUMMARY

The need for resource management is inescapable. Such management is required to minimize future environmental damage as human populations grow rapidly and nations become industrialized. Preservation seeks to shelter natural resources from any harmful, direct exploitation such as logging or mining. Conservation permits some types of direct exploitation, but seeks to minimize the amount of harm and degradation to the natural resource. Restoration is a type of resource management that seeks to undo past environmental damage. Restoration is becoming increasingly common because there are so many highly degraded environments from past misuse.

Resources are valued for more than their economic value. The intrinsic value of a resource is its ethical value, that is, its value without respect to how humans value it. Extrinsic values include emotional, esthetic, economic, and environmental service values. These four, plus ethical value, have been called the five e's, representing the five potential values for natural resources.

Resources are sources of raw materials used by society. Resources are renewable if they can be replaced within a few human generations. Resources such as fossil fuels, which take many millions of years to form, are nonrenewable. Matter resources are depleted by dispersion. Energy resources are depleted by a one-way flow through society in which the energy is transformed to an unusable form. Hubbert's bubble is a pattern of depletion typical of many resources in which unsustainable use causes rapid exploitation, followed by peak use, and then rapid exhaustion.

As resource supplies diminish, the response is either to expand and intensify extraction efforts or to find ways to reduce the need for the resource. In the past, intensification was the main response, in part, because of two influential concepts: net yield of nonrenewable resources and maximum sustainable yield of renewable resources. Both of these incur many environmental costs and focus almost solely on short-term economic gain. To have a sustainable society, we must rely on preservation and conservation. Conservation promotes input reduction by lessening resource use.

There are three basic ways to conserve: efficiency improvements, reuse/recycling, and substitution. Efficiency improvement is often the most effective and cheapest of these three methods. The United States does not use resources as efficiently as many other nations such as Japan. For example, the energy efficiency index shows that the United States uses over twice as much energy to perform the same tasks as is used in Japan. Reuse involves reusing a product in the same form. Recycling occurs when the product is remade into a useful but different product such as a sandal made from tires. A major problem in recycling today is the "unclosed loop": recycled products are often more expensive than products from virgin resources. There is thus less demand for the recycled product. One solution is to use "green fees" and other measures that make producers pay the true environmental cost of virgin resources. Substitution, although helpful in reducing depletion of one resource, may just result in the switching of depletion from one resource to another.

All three types of input reduction—efficiency improvements, reuse/recycling, and substitution—are promoted by making natural resource exploitation reflect its true environmental costs. Although these are very difficult to estimate, it is clear that in many, if not most cases, natural resources have been greatly underpriced. This philosophy of "cheap" abundant resources has encouraged wasteful, rapid exploitation. More costly pricing of resources will not only slow down their depletion, but often creates more jobs. Sustainable activities such as ecotourism and recycling tend to employ many more people than exploitative jobs. Furthermore, unsustainable jobs, such as logging pristine forests, often do not last long because the resource is soon gone.

KEY TERMS

benefit-cost analysis (BCA)
conservation
direct values
embodied energy
energy intensity index
extrinsic value
five e's

fossil fuels
Hubbert's bubble
indirect values
intrinsic value
law of diminishing returns
maximum sustainable yield (MSY)
net yield
nonrenewable resources

precycling
preservation
recycling loop
renewable resources
reserves
resource
restoration
virgin resources

STUDY QUESTIONS

1. At what level is restoration most effective?
2. What does conservation seek to minimize?
3. In the past, how has modern society treated environmental costs in estimating benefit-cost ratios of resource usage? How has this affected the ratio?
4. Distinguish between extrinsic and intrinsic values. Give examples of both.
5. Distinguish between indirect and direct values. Give examples of both.
6. Distinguish between reserves, resources, renewable resources, and nonrenewable resources.
7. How is depletion of matter resources different from depletion of energy resources? Give examples.

8. How has the past pursuit of net yield incurred environmental costs?
9. What are the two main causes of the bubble pattern?
10. Distinguish between optimum sustainable yield and maximum sustainable yield.
11. Maximum sustainable yield (MSY) seeks to keep the harvest rate equal to what? How is MSY related to carrying capacity?
12. What happens to throughput in a sustainable world? What kind of jobs are promoted?
13. What happens to throughput when virgin resources are made more costly by "green fees"? What kind of jobs are promoted?
14. Packaging accounts for 33% of U.S.

household garbage. It is projected that the average American will soon be discarding 4.5 pounds (2 kg) of garbage per day. How many pounds of this 4.5 pounds will be packaging? How much of the 4.5 pounds would be packaging if we reduced packaging to 20%?
15. Assume the U.S. gross national product remained constant, but U.S. energy consumption was reduced by 50%. How much would the U.S. energy intensity index be reduced? To what value would the current index of 14.5 billion BTUs per $1 million GNP (0.015 petajoules per $1 million GNP) be reduced?

ESSAY QUESTIONS

1. What are the five e's? Which are indirect values and why?
2. What are the criticisms of "maximum sustainable yield"?
3. Explain the various parts of the recycling loop. Why is it often not closed?
4. Give an example of a commonly recycled material in the United States. What materials are rarely recycled? Explain the economic factors that determine why one material is recycled more than another.
5. How does one calculate the "energy intensity index"? What does it mean? What is the historical reason why the United States has a much higher index than Japan?

SUGGESTED READINGS

Costanza, R., ed. 1991. *Ecological economics: The science and management of sustainability.* New York: Columbia University Press.

Daly, H. E., and J. Cobb. 1989. *For the common good: Redirecting the economy toward community, the environment, and a sustainable future.* Boston: Beacon Press.

Daly, H. E., and K. Townsend, eds. 1993. *Valuing the Earth: Economics, ecology, ethics.* Cambridge, Mass.: MIT Press.

Ehrlich, P. R., and A. H. 1991. *Healing the planet.* New York: Addison-Wesley.

Hawken, P. 1993. *The ecology of commerce.* New York: Harper Collins.

Jordan, C. F. 1995. *Conservation.* New York: John Wiley.

Meadows, D. H., D. L. Meadows, and J. Randers. 1992. *Beyond the limits.* Post Mills, Vt.: Chelsea Green.

Naar, J. 1990. *Design for a livable planet.* New York: Harper & Row.

World Bank. 1995 (issued annually). *World development report 1995.* Oxford: Oxford University Press.

Young, J. 1990. *Sustaining the Earth.* Cambridge, Mass.: Harvard University Press.

CHAPTER 7

FUNDAMENTALS OF ENERGY, FOSSIL FUELS, AND HYDROELECTRIC POWER

PROLOGUE *Increasing Electrical Efficiencies in the 1990s*

For the first two decades after Thomas Edison opened the first electric power company in New York in 1880, plant efficiencies were consistently under 10% (meaning that better than 90% of the energy in the fuel, such as coal, was being released as waste heat rather than being turned into useful electricity). Low plant efficiency means that many times more fuel has to be burned than would be necessary with more efficient plants, increasing not only the cost of the electricity produced, but also the potential damage to the environment in the form of greenhouse gases that may promote global warming and ground-level air pollution that may damage human

PHOTO   *Union Pacific oil pumps, Long Beach, California.* (*Source:* Robert Visser/Greenpeace.)

health. Furthermore, fossil fuels, which were and still are the primary energy source used worldwide to generate electricity, are a limited, nonrenewable resource.

All of these considerations (with localized air pollution and cost being primary concerns in the late nineteenth and early twentieth centuries) spurred engineers to develop improved plant and engine designs that resulted in a steady increase in efficiencies from the 1880s to about 1960 (■ Fig. 7–1). But by the early 1960s, efficiencies appeared to have peaked at between 35 and 40% efficiency. Some researchers doubted that large-scale plant efficiencies could ever be significantly increased. Larger and potentially more efficient power plants were inordinately expensive to build and were prone to shutdowns and other problems. An impasse seemed to have been reached.

Then in the late 1980s and early 1990s, engineers stopped thinking in terms of huge, old-fashioned steam-driven turbines and turned to the jet engine. Although jet engines were developed to power airplanes, they can also be used to drive a turbine and

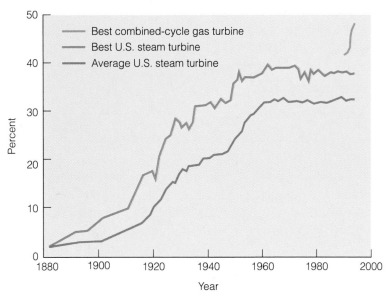

FIGURE 7–1
Electrical efficiency of fossil fuel power plants, 1882–1993. (*Source*: C. Flavin and N. Lenssen, *Powering the Future: Blueprint for a Sustainable Electricity Industry*, Worldwatch Paper 119 [Washington, D.C.: Worldwatch Institute, 1994], p. 22. Reprinted with permission of Worldwatch Institute, Washington, D.C., Copyright 1994.)

generate electricity. Modern gas turbines, derived from jet engine technology, use a pressurized mixture of natural gas (a fossil fuel) and air to drive an electric generator. A combined-cycle plant not only has a gas turbine, but uses excess heat to heat water and power a steam turbine. Together the turbines can reach approximately 50% efficiencies. These new combined-cycle turbine plants can be built relatively quickly and inexpensively (at about half the cost of a conventional coal plant of similar capacity). In addition, natural gas burns much cleaner, with less sulfur dioxide, carbon dioxide, nitrogen oxides, and other emissions than conventional coal-burning plants. In the short term, natural gas appears to be relatively abundant, and gas turbines can also run on gasified coal as well as gasified agricultural or forestry residues (biofuels). Thus, combined-cycle turbine plants may help us make the transition away from our current heavy reliance on fossil fuels to more environmentally sustainable and friendly energy technologies.

ℐNTRODUCTION

Human society is dependent upon a continuous flow of energy (■ Fig. 7–2); indeed, all living organisms require energy (for a discussion of exactly what energy is, see Issues in Perspective 7–1). Without energy life could not exist. One of the prime concerns of any nation is to ensure that its citizens have ready access to the energy they need, whether that energy takes the form of food, heat for a home, power to drive machinery, electricity to run appliances, or gasoline to fuel an automobile. As technology has advanced the amount of energy utilized by humans has increased dramatically. Energy consumption per capita in a technologically developed society today is at least a hundred times what it was when humans

first evolved and about six times what it was less than two hundred years ago (● Table 7–1). Of course, more people are living on the Earth today than at any one time in the past, so total energy use has increased even more dramatically than per capita energy use: today the world as a whole uses 70 times as much energy as it did in 1865.

Energy is necessary for industrial development; thus, most of the world's energy flow historically has been through industrialized countries. Crude estimates indicate that the typical European uses 10 to 30 times as much energy as the typical individual in a developing country, and the average North American uses 40 times as much energy

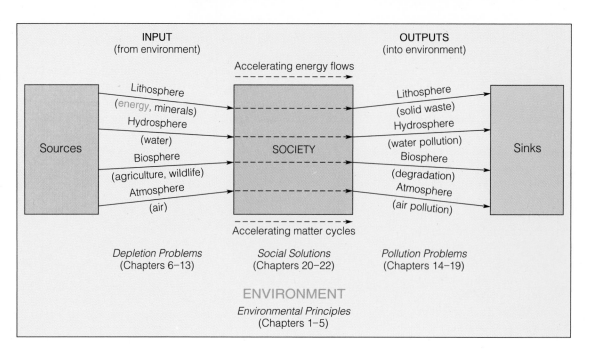

as the average person in the less-developed world. Certainly, this massive use of energy has brought material prosperity to the industrialized world, but at a substantial cost. The more energy humans use, the greater their detrimental impact on the environment. One could argue that virtually all our en-

TABLE 7–1   *Daily Per Capita Human Energy Consumption through Time*

TIME	DAILY PER CAPITA ENERGY CONSUMPTION	MAIN SOURCES	USE	ENVIRONMENTAL IMPACT
1,000,000 B.C.	2,000 kcal	Food, human muscle	Daily life	Minimal
100,000 B.C.	4,000–5,000 kcal	Food, fire, simple tools	Heating, cooking, hunting	Local and short term, mainly vegetation destruction and reduction of animal population
5000 B.C.	12,000 kcal	Animals, agricultural produce	Transportation, cultivation, construction	Local and longer term, mainly in agricultural areas; natural vegetation replaced by cultivated crops; aquatic environment altered; beginnings of soil degradation
A.D. 1400	26,000 kcal	Wind, water, coal, windmills, water wheels	Mechanical operations, pumping water, sawmilling, grinding grain, transportation	Local and longer term or permanent; natural vegetation removed; urban air pollution already common
A.D. 1800	50,000 kcal	Coal, steam engine	Mechanical operations, industrial processes, transportation	Local and regional; permanent major landscape changes begin; air and water pollution common in industrial areas
A.D. 1980	300,000 kcal	Fossil fuels, nuclear energy, internal combustion engine, electricity	Mechanical operations, industrial processes, transportation, social and cultural development	Local, regional, and global; permanent and perhaps irreversible air, water, and soil deterioration on global scale; acid rain; enhanced greenhouse effect; ozone depletion; increased atmospheric turbidity

(*Source*: D. Kemp, *Global Environmental Issues: A Climateological Approach* [London: Routledge, 1990], p. 3. Reprinted with permission from Routledge.)

Fundamentals—Energy, Work, Power, and Thermodynamics

ENERGY, WORK, AND POWER

What is energy? To a physicist *energy* is simply the ability to do work. But what is work? **Work** (W) is defined as a force (F) applied to a material object times the distance (d) that the material object is moved. This is expressed in the equation:

$W = Fd$ (Work equals force times distance)

A commonly used unit of force is the newton (named after Sir Isaac Newton), which is defined as the force that will accelerate a mass of one kilogram one meter per second per second (in a vacuum with no frictional resistance). Distance can be expressed in meters. A force of one newton times one meter is the unit of work known as the **joule** (**J**). Energy has the same units as work; thus, the energy that makes it possible to do a joule of work is a joule of energy.

Energy, the capacity to do work, can take many different forms and be stored in many different ways. Mechanical energy involves objects, their motion, and position. One form of mechanical energy is known as potential energy—energy stored by virtue of the position of an object. A brick raised over your head before you drop it has potential energy, as does the wound spring of a watch or the water behind a hydroelectric dam built across a river. When you drop the brick or the water is released from the dam, the potential energy is turned into kinetic energy, or the energy of motion. The water dropping from the dam can be used to turn the blades of a turbine. When the turbine is connected to a generator, it will convert the mechanical energy to electrical energy. Electrical energy involves the forces of charged particles, such as electrons, acting upon one another.

Energy can take the form of heat, which is the random motion of atoms and molecules in a substance. As the brick you drop hits the ground, or the water of a waterfall hits bottom, the brick and the ground, or water, will heat up—the macroscopic kinetic energy will be converted to energy at an atomic and molecular level. You can demonstrate this convincingly by pounding hard on a nail with a steel hammer and then immediately feeling the heat radiating from the nail's head.

Often energy of any form is expressed in units based upon heat energy. One **calorie** (also known as a gram-calorie, and commonly abbreviated cal) is the quantity of energy that, when converted completely to heat, will warm one gram of water by one degree Celsius (or centigrade, commonly abbreviated °C). A kilocalorie (or kilogram-calorie, commonly abbreviated kcal) is equal to 1000 calories; sometimes the term Calorie (with a capital C) represents a kilocalorie, as in the rating of foods by energy content. One kilocalorie is equal to 4184 joules of energy. Another commonly used energy unit is the British thermal unit (**BTU**). One BTU is the amount of energy that, when converted to heat, will raise the temperature of one pound of water one degree Fahrenheit (°F). One kcalorie is equal to 3.968 BTU.

When discussing energy consumption or production on a national or global scale, very large-scale units are used. Some of the more common units are listed in Appendix A. Two frequently used units are the **"quad,"** or quadrillion BTU (Q), and the **petajoule** (1×10^{15} joules, abbreviated PJ). One quad is equivalent to approximately 1054 petajoules. As an example, in 1989 the United States consumed approximately 34 quads worth of petroleum, or the equivalent of about 36,000 petajoules of oil (this represents about 880 million tons [800 million metric tons] of oil—the numbers are staggering).

Other forms that energy takes include the energy stored in the chemical bonds of substances (such as the energy in the food you eat or the gasoline that fills the tank of an automobile), the energy of light (electromagnetic radiation), and the energy that binds the particles composing the nucleus of an atom.

Energy is the capacity to do work, but this is not the complete story. How fast work is done—how fast energy is converted from one form to another—is the concept of power. **Power** is defined as work (requiring energy) divided by the time period over which the work is done:

Power = work/time (Power equals work divided by time)

A common unit of power is the **watt,** defined as one joule of work (or energy) per second. A kilowatt (kW) is equal to 1000 watts; a **megawatt (MW)** is equal to 1000 kilowatts, or 1,000,000 watts; a **terawatt (TW)** is equal to one billion (10^9) kilowatts, or 10^{12} watts. The unit horsepower is equal to three-quarters of a kilowatt, or 750 watts. Thus, a one-horsepower electric motor can convert 750 joules of electrical energy into mechanical energy per second. If we multiply a unit of power by time, we arrive at another unit for energy. For example, a one-kilowatt motor running for one hour will convert 1000 joules of electrical energy per second into mechanical energy; since there are 3600 seconds in an hour, it will convert 3,600,000 joules of energy in a kilowatt-hour (kWh). In other words, one kilowatt-hour is equal to 3,600,000 joules, or approximately 860.4 kilocalories (since 1 kilocalorie is equal to 4184 joules).

THE LAWS OF THERMODYNAMICS

In order to study energy and energy conversions, one must know the laws of ther-

(continued)

modynamics (the term *thermodynamic* means "heat movement").

The first law of thermodynamics is the law of the conservation of energy. Energy can be neither created nor destroyed—it is simply changed from one form to another (of course, it has been demonstrated that matter can be converted into energy, and vice versa, in nuclear reactions). Within an isolated (closed) system, the total quantity of energy will always be the same. However, not all energy is equivalent from a human perspective. One must take into consideration not only the quantity of energy, but also its form or quality. As energy is transformed from one type to another—for instance, from mechanical to electrical energy—the transformation will not be 100% efficient (some of the energy will be lost as waste heat). This leads to the second law of thermodynamics, which states that heat or energy cannot be transformed into work with 100% efficiency, and heat will always flow spontaneously from an object of higher temperature to an object of lower temperature. Another way of considering the second law of thermodynamics is to note that highly organized energy (such as electricity or mechanical energy) always ultimately degenerates into disorganized

energy (such as heat). **Entropy**, the concept of the amount of disorder or randomness in a system, always increases. For example, a liter of gasoline represents a relatively ordered, low-entropy system. The large, complex organic molecules in the gasoline store much high-quality energy. When this gasoline is burned in a car, some of the stored energy is converted into high-quality, usable mechanical energy. But much of the original energy is transformed into low-quality, high-entropy heat, and the gasoline is reordered into simple combustion products such as carbon dioxide, carbon monoxide, and water—randomness and entropy are increased in the system.

According to the laws of thermodynamics, entropy in the universe as a whole is continually increasing. In certain situations, entropy may decrease locally, but only at the expense of increasing entropy somewhere else. Living systems create and maintain order where there was previously disorder, but only by utilizing vast quantities of energy. Plants convert sunlight—a form of energy—into complex biological molecules that contain high-quality energy. These organic molecules are the high-quality energy reservoir upon which virtually all other life depends. Hu-

mans, in their quest for energy, are currently highly dependent upon the high-quality energy stored in the fossil fuels (oil, coal, natural gas) formed from the organic molecules of countless organisms over millions of years.

As described by the second law of thermodynamics, no energy transformations are 100% efficient. But from a pragmatic point of view, just how efficient (or inefficient) are our machines that transform energy from one form to another?

Efficiency is the useful work that is performed relative to the total energy input of a system. Thus, an engine that is 25% efficient will convert one-quarter of the energy contained in its fuel to mechanical work. In any engine some energy is lost as heat because of friction. Furthermore, a power plant or any other heat engine usually achieves the most efficient transformations of energy at a slower rate than humans desire. We prefer to have our energy converted quickly, so that we can drive faster or heat more houses within a specific timeframe, even if this takes a heavy toll on the efficiency of the energy exchange, meaning that we use considerably more fuel.

vironmental problems can be traced back to energy use (or overuse). The use of **fossil fuels** (**oil, coal,** and **natural gas**) is the major source of air pollution, acid rain, and greenhouse gases. Mining for coal or pumping oil can destroy vast tracts of land. Dams necessary for hydroelectric power production can wreak havoc on natural ecosystems and spread disease. Mining and processing of uranium to fuel nuclear power plants is fraught with hazards. Finally, conventional fossil fuel sources—upon which we rely most heavily— are nonrenewable and are being rapidly depleted.

Thus, energy consumption by humans raises two basic concerns: (1) Where will the energy

come from in the future as we deplete the most convenient, high-quality supplies of fossil fuels upon which much of modern industrial society is based? (2) How can we avoid the environmental degradation so often associated with the levels of energy consumption that characterize modern civilization?

We can take two basic approaches to these energy problems: we can address the supply side or the demand side. We can view energy as a commodity that we produce, and then attempt to maximize production of useful energy (such as refined oil or usable electricity); furthermore, we would use energy to solve any environmental problems that energy use may cause. Or we can consider energy to be a valuable resource and attempt to minimize its consumption, such as by increasing the efficiency of our energy-consuming devices, and thus minimize any detrimental environmental effects that energy use may entail.

Traditionally, energy problems have been addressed simply by harnessing more energy—increasing the usable energy supply. This strategy involves both increasing the rate at which current technologies can produce energy and developing new energy-producing technologies. Some people believe that the ultimate solution to the world's energy problems lies along the latter path. In the late 1950s and early 1960s, for example, some people thought that nuclear fission power plants would produce so much electricity so inexpensively that it would be "too cheap to meter." Furthermore, they envisioned nuclear energy as a safe, pollution-free source of power. As we will see in Chapter 8, because of unexpected costs and concerns, this vision never materialized. Currently, however, some advocates of nuclear fusion power hold essentially the same dream. Other people believe that our energy problems will be solved by the development and widespread use of environmentally benign "alternative" energy sources, such as solar power, wind power, and geothermal energy (see Chapter 9).

The other way to address the world's energy concerns is from the demand side. Why do we need energy anyway? We do not need it for its own sake, but for what it can accomplish. We need energy to cook our food, heat our homes and offices, run our refrigerators and televisions, power our factories, fuel our vehicles, and on and on. Thus, we can attempt to deal with our energy problems by lessening our energy needs and instituting energy-saving measures. Many people equate energy conservation with discomfort (turning down the thermostat in the winter), inconvenience (always having to turn off the lights when leaving the room), and even hardship (rationing of gasoline or high gas taxes that make it impossible to drive at will). But attacking the demand side of energy use need not lead to a reduction in living standards and a change in lifestyle for the worse. Rather, the current emphasis is on developing new technologies that produce and utilize energy more efficiently, such as automobiles that go farther on a gallon, or liter, of gas. Ways to promote energy conservation are discussed at the end of Chapter 9.

In this chapter and the following two, we explore the topic of energy. We observe the current global energy situation, discuss various methods of energy production, and explore the ways that the world's growing energy demands might be resolved.

𝓜ODERN SOCIETY'S DEPENDENCE ON ENERGY

Until about three hundred years ago, the vast majority of humans' energy needs were supplied by "traditional" energy sources: agriculture, human and animal labor, biomass (fuelwood and other burnable organic matter, such as agricultural waste, dung, peat), relatively small amounts of coal, wind power (windmills and sailing ships), and water power. Biomass and coal were used primarily for cooking, heating, and small-scale industrial processes such as metal refining or pottery production; wind power was utilized for transportation and small-scale processing and manufacturing; and water power was traditionally used for agriculture and manufacturing (for instance, irrigation, sawmills, and machine shops). But with the coming of the Industrial Revolution in Europe during the late eighteenth and early nineteenth centuries, the intensity of energy use increased. Water power remained important, but the use of fossil fuels—initially, coal—greatly increased. Coal power fueled the early Industrial Revolution. Then, in the latter half of the nineteenth century, petroleum products (oil, gasoline, and natural gas) began to be used on a major scale, not only to drive industry but also to heat and light homes; by the turn of the century, petroleum was being used to power the newly developed private automobile. By the end of the nineteenth century, electrical power was also becoming more widespread. The development of the electrical utility industry in the twentieth century has further added to our overall energy consumption and caused a dramatic shift in the mix of energy sources used by Western society (see the Case Study).

An Overview of the Current Global Energy Situation

In general, worldwide consumption of energy has increased steadily over the last two decades (Fig. 7–3, page 174), although it may now have temporarily stabilized at early 1990s levels. Between 1971 and 1991, worldwide energy consumption increased by approximately 45%. The World Energy Conference recently predicted that if current trends in population and capital growth continue, world energy demand could increase by

CASE STUDY

The United States—Sources and Consumption of Energy

ven today much of the world, especially in developing countries, depends on the traditional forms of energy used for centuries. But modern industrialized Western society seems inconceivable without the intensive energy use to which North Americans and Europeans have grown accustomed. As an example of energy sources and consumption in a modern industrialized nation, let us take a look at the United States.

The United States is both the leading producer and consumer of primary energy in the world. Currently, the United States produces approximately 19.5% of the world's energy, but it consumes approximately 24% of the world's energy; thus, the United States consumes about 23% more energy than it produces. The next two largest producers and consumers of energy are Russia (producing 13.3% of the world's energy, but consuming just 9.5%) and China (producing 8.8% and consuming 8.5%). Saudi Arabia is the world's fourth leading energy producer (accounting for 6% of world production), yet its energy consumption is just under 1% of the world total.

Energy production and consumption in the United States have generally increased over the last 35 years (Fig. 1), but consumption has grown faster than production. This means that energy imports (principally, oil and other petroleum products and natural gas) have substantially increased over the decades.

For example, consider 1989, a typical year and the latest for which a reasonably accurate and complete analysis is available (since 1989, U.S. energy consumption has increased by about 5–10%). In that year, the United States consumed some 79.9 quads of energy and energy materials (that is, electricity and fossil fuels; see Fig. 2). Of this 79.9 quads, 74.9 quads went directly toward energy uses such as heating homes, running machinery, and fueling vehicles. A quad is one quadrillion BTUs (approximately 1054 petajoules) or the equivalent of about 171–172 million barrels of oil. So in 1989 the United States consumed the equivalent of nearly 13 billion barrels of oil (the equivalent of over 50 barrels of oil for every man, woman, and child in the

United States). In addition, as shown in Figure 2, another 5 quads worth of oil and natural gas (the equivalent of over three barrels of oil per person in the United States) went toward nonfuel uses (such as oils for lubrication and hydrocarbons used as raw materials for the petrochemical industry).

Of the 74.9 quads of energy consumed in 1989, 20.1 quads, or over 25%, were lost during electrical transmission. Transmitting electrical power through standard power lines is very inefficient. Over twice as much electrical power is lost during transmission from large, centralized power plants as is delivered in useful form to consumers. Of the remaining 54.8 quads used, 16.4 quads (approximately 30%) went for residential and commercial use, such as heating, air conditioning, and lighting; 16.2 quads (approximately 30%) went to industry; and 22.1 quads (slightly over

40%) went to transportation. Note that if we include the energy lost during electrical transmission in our total, then transportation accounts for approximately 30% of all energy use in the United States (22.1 quads out of a total of 74.9 quads).

Inspecting Figure 2 further, we notice that our modes of transportation are relatively inefficient. We waste three times as much energy as we actually use. This is due in large part to the notoriously inefficient motor vehicles that we drive; with their low gas mileages, compared to the efficiencies that could be achieved even with today's technology, these vehicles waste most of the energy value of the gasoline. Most environmentalists advocate a major effort to increase the fuel efficiencies of cars and other vehicles (see Issues in Perspective 9–3 of Chapter 9). After energy lost during transmission through power lines,

FIGURE 1

U.S. energy production and consumption, 1960–1993. Notice that in 1960 the United States produced almost as much energy as it consumed, but since then the trend has been for consumption to outpace production. Today more than 20% of the energy consumed in the United States is imported. (*Source:* Data from *The World Almanac and Book of Facts, 1995* [Mahweh, N.J.: Funk and Wagnalls Corporation, 1994].)

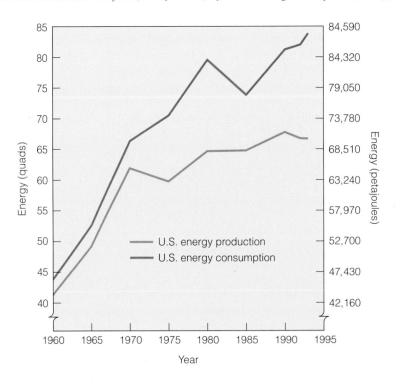

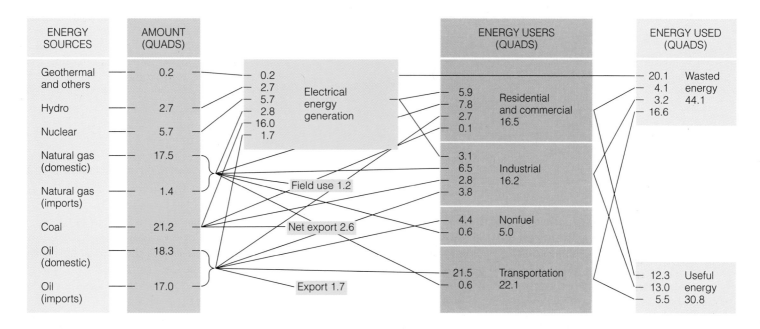

■ **FIGURE 2**

U. S. energy sources and consumption, 1989. Note that numbers do not necessarily add up exactly due to rounding and estimations, and also because various stored stocks, strategic reserves, and unaccounted crude oil (cumulatively totaling perhaps as much as two quads) have not been factored in. Due to many uncertainties and discrepancies in statistical compilations, it is very difficult to carry out a precise and thorough analysis of the energy sources and consumption of a large country like the United States. However, this analysis is certainly representative of current source and consumption patterns. One quad equals approximately 1054 petajoules. (*Source*: Lawrence Livermore National Laboratory, Livermore, California. Used with the permission of the University of California, Lawrence Livermore National Laboratory, and the U.S. Department of Energy.)

the inefficiency of our motor vehicle fleet is the largest single drain on the nation's energy budget.

Twenty-five percent of the energy used to heat, cool, and light our commercial and residential buildings, run our televisions and small appliances, and so forth is lost. Better insulation, more efficient refrigerators, and the like, could help decrease the energy losses in this sector. In addition, as we shall discuss further in Chapter 9, energy needs could be considerably reduced through the increased use of old and new technologies, such as passive and active solar heating, compact fluorescent lightbulbs, and many other energy conservation methods. The industrial sector uses energy with the greatest efficiency in the United States, but even so about one-fifth of the energy is wasted.

Looking at the supply side of Figure 2, about 40% of our energy comes from oil, an-

other 25% comes from coal, and more than 20% comes from natural gas. Thus, some 85 to 90% of our energy comes from fossil fuels; currently, then, the United States is truly dependent on fossil fuels. The remainder comes from hydroelectric power, nuclear power, and to a very small extent alternative energy sources (geothermal power, wind power, solar power, and so on). For its single largest energy source, oil, the United States is heavily dependent on imports (approximately half the oil we use is imported).

Q uestions

1. Some people feel that the United States has a "moral obligation" to the rest of the world to cut down on its energy consumption, especially since the United States consumes substantially more energy than it produces. What is your

opinion on this matter? If the United States suddenly slashed its energy consumption by 30% and stopped the importation of all fossil fuels, how would global trade relations be affected? How would a 30% cut in U.S. energy consumption benefit the environment?

2. If you were a cabinet member and the president charged you with promoting the reduction of U.S. energy consumption, which user sector in Figure 2 would you address first? Where do you think the most gains in energy savings can be made in the short term? In the long term?

3. Japan is the world's fourth largest consumer of primary energy, using approximately 5.5% of the world supply. Yet Japan produces just under 1% of the world's primary energy. Thus, in global energy matters, Japan could be seen as the inverse of a country like Saudi Arabia. Why does the world need both "Japans" and "Saudi Arabias," or does it? How does this either support or counter the argument that every nation should be energy self–sufficient?

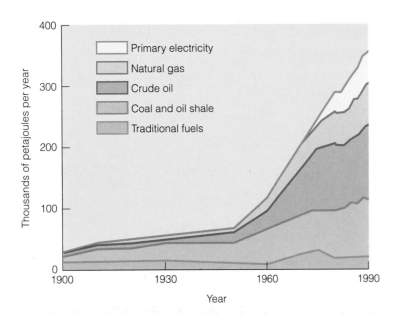

FIGURE 7–3
World energy use, 1900–1990. Notice how quickly energy use has increased since about 1950. (*Source:* Data from United Nations. Reprinted from *Beyond the Limits* copyright © 1992 by Meadows, Meadows, and Randers. With permission from Chelsea Green Publishing Co., White River Junction, Vermont.)

another 75% by the year 2020. In 1991, the most recent year for which accurate statistics are available, worldwide commercial energy consumption totaled 321,430 petajoules (approximately 10.2 terawatt-years [TW-yr] or 305 quads); of this total, more than 25% was consumed in North America (● Table 7–2), and 73% was consumed by the industrialized countries. Commercial energy consumption includes the use of petroleum products, coal, hydroelectric power, nuclear power, geothermal power, wind power, and so on. Besides commercial energy consumption, 19,942 petajoules (18.9 quads) of traditional fuels, such as fuelwood, charcoal, and animal and plant wastes, were consumed in 1991. Thus, traditional fuels supplied only about 6% of the world's energy consumption in 1991. The largest per capita consumptions of traditional fuels are in South America and Africa.

On a global scale, various sources of commercial energy play different roles (Table 7–2). Oil (liquid petroleum products generally) is the single largest source of commercial energy, accounting for 37% of world consumption in 1991. Next in importance is coal (including peat and oil shale), accounting for 29% of world consumption, closely followed by natural gas (24% of world consumption). The remaining 10% of commercial consumption is supplied by hydroelectric power, nuclear power, geothermal power, wind power, solar power, and other technologies.

Locally and regionally, the energy mix may differ significantly from that of the world as a whole. In many developing countries, for instance, coal is a more important energy source than oil, whereas in the industrialized nations in recent years, the use of natural gas has equaled or surpassed the use of coal.

The preceding discussion is based on statistics compiled primarily by the United Nations and published by the World Resources Institute. Another approach to the analysis of global energy patterns is to extrapolate from individual rates of energy use to a global level. Taking such an approach, Ehrlich and Ehrlich (1991) have estimated that the world was using energy in the early 1990s at a rate of approximately 13.1 terawatts (13.1 terawatt-years per year, which equals 13.1 TW). This rate of energy consumption is equivalent to consuming 413,960 petajoules (393 quads) of energy each year. The Ehrlichs' figure is somewhat greater than the 341,372 petajoules (324 quads) estimated by the United Nations, but the two figures are within approximately 20% of each other and probably bracket the true value of global energy consumption.

The variation in energy use between the industrialized countries and the developing world is remarkable. The richest 25% of the world's population use over 60% of the world's energy—and cause most of the environmental degradation associated with such energy use. The average rate of energy use in rich countries is 7.5 kilowatts (kW) per person versus 1.0 kW per person in developing countries. Individual countries may differ significantly from these averages. Canadians use energy at an average rate of about 13 kW per person, and Americans a bit more than 11 kW per person. In contrast, in parts of sub-Saharan Africa, the per capita energy consumption is less than 0.2 kW (and perhaps as low as 0.08 kW), meaning that the average American uses better than *55 times* (and perhaps as much as 137 times) as much energy as his or her fellow human in sub-Saharan Africa. Since intensity of energy use correlates fairly well with global environmental degradation, one can argue that the typical American does 55 to 137 times as much damage to the global environment as does the typical sub-Saharan African. (Remember the equation $I = P \times T$ [Impact equals Population times Technology] introduced in Chapter 1.)

Energy Scenarios of the Future

It seems inevitable that global energy use will increase in the future as the human population continues to grow at about 1.6–1.7% annually (mostly in the developing countries; see Chapter 5), and the developing countries strive to give

TABLE 7–2 *Commercial Energy Production and Consumption by Region and by Fuel (in Petajoules), 1991*

Region	LIQUID Production	LIQUID Consumption	GAS Production	GAS Consumption	SOLID Production	SOLID Consumption	PRIMARY ELECTRICITY Production Nuclear	PRIMARY ELECTRICITY Production Hydro	PRIMARY ELECTRICITY Consumption	TOTAL Production	TOTAL Consumption
World	132,992	119,178	76,275	76,315	93,689	93,947	22,669	9,311	31,990	334,890	321,430
Developing countries	78,715	31,471	15,147	11,872	37,736	36,870	857	3,231	4,007	135,686	84,290
Oil-exporting developing	65,156	12,603	11,125	7,927	1,140	564	33	566	589	78,020	21,683
OPEC	50,862	7,568	8,934	6,088	525	304	0	198	196	60,519	14,156
Non-OPEC oil-exporting	14,293	5,035	2,191	1,839	615	260	33	368	394	17,501	7,528
Oil-importing developing	13,559	18,868	4,022	3,945	36,596	36,306	824	2,665	3,488	57,666	62,607
Africa oil-importing	625	988	14	62	4,115	2,917	46	151	199	4,951	4,167
Asia and Oceania oil-importing	9,170	13,002	2,730	2,530	31,671	32,638	678	1,290	1,965	45,539	50,135
Latin America oil-importing	3,764	4,878	1,277	1,353	810	751	101	1,224	1,323	7,176	8,305
Industrialized countries	54,195	86,072	61,093	64,328	56,334	56,558	21,427	6,058	27,527	199,107	234,485
OECD industrialized	31,969	67,978	31,482	37,894	37,331	38,789	18,513	5,048	23,610	125,343	168,271
North America	21,875	34,562	23,883	23,987	23,704	20,730	7,609	2,716	10,339	79,787	89,618
Western Europe	8,829	22,928	7,490	10,911	9,002	12,868	8,575	1,698	10,308	32,594	57,015
Pacific	1,265	10,488	1,108	2,996	4,625	5,191	2,329	635	2,963	9,962	21,638
Non-OECD industrialized	22,226	18,094	28,611	26,434	19,003	17,769	2,915	1,009	3,917	73,764	66,214
Central Europe	514	2,367	1,199	2,595	6,284	5,695	602	162	827	8,761	11,484
Former Soviet Union	21,712	15,727	27,412	23,839	12,719	12,074	2,313	847	3,090	65,003	54,730

Note that "Liquid" fuel is essentially oil and related petroleum liquids; "Solid" fuel is essentially coal, peat, oil shale burned directly, and related substances; "Hydro" includes geothermal and wind energy. "Nuclear" energy is calculated in terms of the energy used to generate electricity at a rate of 30% efficiency; if expressed in terms of electricity actually generated, in order to make it comparable to "Hydro" in the table, "Nuclear" would be approximately 6800 petajoules, somewhat less than the 9311 petajoules included under "Hydro." OPEC = Organization of Petroleum Exporting Countries; OECD = Organization for Economic Co-operation and Development. Totals of all columns and rows do not add up exactly due to rounding and other minor inconsistencies; thus, for instance, in the last column the breakdown for energy consumption by regions totals to only 318,775 petajoules compared to 321,430 petajoules for the total world consumption (318,775 is 99.174% of 321,430 so the discrepancy is relatively small). For comparison with Figures 1 and 2 in the Case Study, there are approximately 1054 petajoules to one quad.

(*Source*: World Resources Institute, *World Resources 1994–95* [New York: Oxford University Press, 1994], p. 166. Used with the permission of The World Resources Institute.)

their citizens a "better" quality of life (which generally entails substantial increases in per capita energy consumption). Already, the environmental impact of our energy use is straining—and perhaps has exceeded—the capacity of natural systems to maintain themselves. Already, many researchers have provided data that indicate that our profligate energy consumption is irrevocably degrading the natural environment. Possibilities to stem this energy-induced environmental destruction include cutting back on energy consumption (perhaps through increasingly efficient technology) and increasing the use of **alternative energy** sources that cause less environmental degradation (for instance, replacing fossil fuels with cleaner energy sources). But just how much energy will the world need in the future? Al-

though no one can predict the future with absolute accuracy, we can explore some possible energy scenarios.

If the global human population were to increase to about 11 billion by the year 2030 (which could happen at recent rates of growth), and the average per capita energy usage were 5 kW (less than half of the present typical American energy use), then the global energy use would be some 55 TW—that is, over four times current energy consumption. Such massive energy production would be virtually impossible utilizing the current mix of energy sources, wherein most of the world's energy is derived from fossil fuels. The general consensus is that relying on conventional fuel sources to produce so much energy would be all but impossible due to the environmental damage their use would entail, independent of the finite supplies of such fuels. Such massive use of energy could only occur by using energy sources that are environmentally benign.

John Holdren of the University of California, Berkeley, has developed a future energy scenario that is both "optimistic" and also potentially realistic. In Holdren's scenario, the rich nations of the world would decrease their per capita energy use by about 2% per year from 1990 until 2025, lowering it from an average of 7.5 to 3.8 kW. This might be possible through the development of more efficient means of energy transmission and end-use applications, as well as through the further development of decentralized "alternative" energy sources. Over the same period, the population of the rich nations is expected to increase slightly—from 1.2 billion to 1.4 billion. Thus, in 2025 the rich nations would consume only 5.3 TW as compared to their current 9.0 TW. Meanwhile, over the same period, the developing nations would raise their per capita energy consumption by about 2% annually, so that by 2025 it would average 2.0 kW. At the same time, the population of the developing countries is predicted to increase from 4.1 billion to 6.8 billion people. Thus, in 2025 the developing countries would consume 13.6 TW. In total, then, Holdren's scenario predicts that in 2025 there will be 8.2 billion people on the planet using energy at the rate of 18.9 TW. Projecting further into the future, Holdren suggests that by the end of the next century the world population may peak at 10 billion people, and the per capita energy use of both industrialized and developing nations may converge at 3.0 kW, giving a total energy consumption of 30 TW—still over twice the rate of energy use today.

Notice that Holdren's scenario makes a number of assumptions. The population of the Earth will peak rather than continue to grow indefinitely. Per capita energy use in the industrialized nations will drop sharply, and the developing nations will be satisfied without reaching the former per capita energy consumption of the industrial nations. Of course, this does not mean that standards of living in industrialized countries have to drop, simply that energy will have to be used much more efficiently. Even so, the Holdren scenario predicts the need for substantially more energy than is currently being used worldwide. The only way to meet these energy requirements without totally destroying the planet will be to develop and utilize to an ever greater extent alternative energy technologies that are less damaging to the environment.

Power Plants—Supplying the People with Electricity

In modern, industrialized societies like the United States, a major form of energy consumption is the burning of fossil fuels to power vehicles and machinery directly or to heat buildings. Another large portion of the energy sector consists of producing **electricity,** which is then distributed to consumers for running electrical appliances, lighting, heating (to some extent), air conditioning, and so forth. Although at present electricity provides only about 13% of the world's end-use energy (about 17% in industrialized countries), it is often viewed as indispensable to modern society. Electricity is most often generated at electrical **power plants**, usually operated by private or semipublic utility companies, and then distributed to consumers.

Commercial power plants can take many forms, some of which are described in more detail later in this chapter and in the next two chapters. At present, electricity is most commonly generated by using a **turbine** to drive a **generator** that transforms mechanical energy into electrical energy. A turbine is simply a machine, something like an old-fashioned water wheel, that can convert the lateral motion of a flowing fluid (such as water, steam, or some other gas) into the rotational or turning motion of a shaft or axle. This turning motion can then be used to turn the generator that transforms mechanical energy into electricity.

The more common types of commercial power plants are mainly distinguished by the source of the energy that drives the turbine (● Table 7–3). In hydroelectric power plants, water falling from a dam drives the turbine. In wind-powered plants, the turbines are driven by wind—indeed, they take the form of huge windmills. In geothermal power plants, hot steam and other gases originating from the interior of the Earth may be used to drive the turbine. Most commonly, however, large power plants use artificially created steam. Water is heated to extremely high temperatures (600°F or higher/over 300°C), and the resulting pressure of the expanding steam is used to turn the turbines. The fuel that the power plant consumes provides the heat for generating the steam. In the United States, the most common fuel is coal. A coal-fired power plant (▬ Fig. 7–4) is, in the simplest sense, a huge furnace used to turn water into steam. Another common way to turn water into steam is by harnessing the tremendous amounts of heat given off by nuclear reactors—this method of generating electricity is commonly referred to as nuclear power. Other methods of heating water to produce steam, and ultimately electricity, include burning wood or other biomass, burning oil, burning natural gas, or using the focused energy of the Sun to heat water to high temperatures.

An internal combustion engine or turbine can also be connected to a generator. An internal combustion turbine is essentially an engine that burns oil or natural gas; rather than heating water first, it uses the hot gases from the burned fossil fuel directly to turn the turbine. Conventional steam-generating power plants, whether coal burning or nuclear fired, are typically large. They are extremely expensive, costing billions of dollars each, and take many years or even decades to build and put on line. Once built, these large plants are relatively efficient in converting fuel into electrical energy. Conversely, standard internal combustion turbines are smaller, less expensive to purchase, and can be placed into operation more quickly. The drawback is that they are much less fuel-efficient than larger plants, and the fuel they burn—oil or natural gas—is usually more expensive than the fuel (such as coal or uranium) of larger, steam-based power plants. However, newly developed gas turbines and combined-cycle plants (see the Prologue) are greatly increasing realized efficiencies.

Utilities that produce electrical power must have a considerably larger generating capacity than they actually need at most times. In fact, to ensure reliable production, the local grid of power plants usually must be able to generate ap-

TABLE 7–3 *World Electricity Generation, by Energy Source, 1971 and 1991*

SOURCE	1971		1991	
	Terawatt-Hours	Percent of Total	Terawatt-Hours	Percent of Total
Coal	2,142	40.3	4,671	38.8
Renewables[a]	1,241	23.4	2,290	19.0
Nuclear	111	2.1	2,106	17.5
Natural gas	714	13.5	1,594	13.2
Oil	1,102	20.8	1,376	11.4
Total[b]	5,311	100.0	12,037	100.0

[a]Primarily hydroelectric.
[b]Columns may not add to totals due to rounding.

The most important aspects of this table are the percentages given for each year; thus, we see that nuclear energy, for instance, is substantially more important in the 1990s than it was 20 years ago. The absolute values are given in terawatt-hours; one terawatt-hour is equivalent to 3.6 petajoules or approximately 0.0034 quads of energy. Due to differences in sources and methods of estimating energy production and consumption, the absolute numbers shown in this table are not identical to those shown for "Primary electricity" in Table 7–2. (*Source*: C. Flavin and N. Lenssen, *Powering the Future: Blueprint for a Sustainable Electricity Industry*, Worldwatch Paper 119 [Washington, D.C.: Worldwatch Institute, 1994], p. 14. Reprinted with permission of Worldwatch Institute, Washington, D.C., Copyright 1994.)

FIGURE 7–4
A coal-fired power plant, Shawville, Pennsylvania. (*Source*: Michaud Grapes/Photo Researchers.)

proximately 20% more electricity than is normally used at any one time. This extra generating capacity is known as the reserve capacity. Electricity is not used at an equal rate throughout the day or the year. Depending on the area, more electricity may be used during the day when businesses are operating and, in hot climates, when air conditioners are running at maximum capacity. The amount of electricity needed at the time of highest demand is known as the **peak load**. With current technology, it is very difficult to store electricity, and it is also not possible to turn large electrical power plants off when temporarily not needed. As a result, utilities must be able to satisfy peak load requirements, even if this means generating more electricity than is needed at other times of the day or year.

Another reason that utilities need to maintain a substantial reserve capacity is that at any one time more than 10% of the generating capacity may be shut down for repairs, routine maintenance, or changing the fuel (in nuclear plants). When a plant shuts down temporarily, power is supplied to its customers from the reserve capacity of other plants owned by the utility and connected to the same power grid (the set of power lines that connect power plants to their customers and to each other). Different electrical utility companies may purchase power from each other if their power lines interconnect. Even with interconnecting lines, however, transporting electricity over long distances is extremely inefficient and expensive because much of the electrical energy is lost in transit (although superconducting technology may help to alleviate this problem; see Issues in Perspective 9–2 in Chapter 9).

When the capacity of a utility's power plants is exceeded, **brownouts** and **blackouts** can occur. In a brownout, demand is only a few percent above the generating capacity of the utility; the voltage the consumers receive is inadequate with the result that the lights often dim. Blackouts are often associated with major breakdowns, either of a power plant or in the grid that distributes power. In a classic blackout, a region served by the utility is left without electricity for an extended period of time. Localized blackouts can also occur if demand significantly exceeds the utility's capacity to generate electricity. In such an instance, the utility may have to institute a rolling blackout—the utility stops and later restores electrical service to a sequence of neighborhoods in turn, each losing electricity for an hour or two during the day. Such a rolling blackout forcibly reduces the consumption of electricity.

Needless to say, brown-outs and blackouts are very disruptive to modern societies that are extremely dependent upon electricity.

Hard versus Soft Energy Technologies

Large, modern electricity-generating power plants have been characterized by physicist and energy consultant Amory B. Lovins as **"hard" technologies**. Hard energy technologies depend on large-scale plants that are complex, expensive, and centralized. The energy they generate, such as electricity, is of a very high-grade form and must be distributed to consumers through an elaborate system of hardware, such as power lines. Large coal-burning or oil-burning electrical power plants, major hydroelectric plants, and nuclear power plants are all classic examples of hard technologies. Another example would be petroleum production and refinement facilities connected to consumers by an elaborate system of pipes. Vast infusions of money are necessary to establish a hard technology and its accompanying infrastructure. Due to the substantial investments required, it can be very difficult to modify or abandon a hard technology once it is in place.

As Lovins points out, however, the end-uses of the high-quality energy delivered by a hard technology may be extremely low-grade applications, for instance, heating water or open space in buildings. Rather than burning oil or coal at a power plant to generate electricity and then transmitting the electricity to the consumer who uses it to generate heat, it is much more efficient to burn the oil or coal on site to generate heat directly. Or better yet, passive solar systems might be used to heat (and even cool) a building.

The alternative to hard energy technologies are **"soft" technologies**, such as using passive solar energy, burning wood or coal in a stove, using an on–site windmill or small water wheel, and even increasing energy efficiencies and promoting conservation measures. Soft technologies are small-scale, local (thus they do not require elaborate distribution systems), and usually much more environmentally friendly than hard technologies. Soft energy technologies are often relatively inexpensive to install and operate, and they deliver energy that is of the appropriate grade—such as high-grade electricity from photovoltaic cells to run computers and other electronic devices, and low-grade heat for space or water heating. Examples of both hard and soft technologies are discussed in this chapter and in Chapters 8 and 9.

$\mathcal{T}$ HE FOSSIL FUELS

Currently, the primary sources of commercial energy worldwide are, in order of decreasing importance, oil, coal, natural gas, and finally hydropower and nuclear power (see Table 7–2 and Fig. 7–3). In this portion of the book (Chapters 7 through 9), we will take a brief look at each, beginning with those that currently contribute the most to the human global energy budget, the fossil fuels and secondarily hydropower—the subjects of the remainder of this chapter. Nuclear power has, depending on the commentator, the potential to solve all of our energy problems or the potential to cause untold environmental damage. Accordingly, Chapter 8 is devoted to nuclear power. Finally, Chapter 9 covers "alternative" energy sources (such as solar power, wind power, biomass fuels, tidal power, and geothermal power) and also includes a discussion of energy conservation measures.

The Origin of Fossil Fuels

The fossil fuels are coal, oil (**petroleum**), and natural gas—fuels that formed over geologic time from the remains of plants and animals buried under layers of sedimentary rock. Fossil fuels are continuing to form today, but their formation is an extremely slow process. Humans are consuming fossil fuels millions of times faster than they are forming, so for all practical purposes fossil fuels, like most geological resources (see Chapter 10), constitute a nonrenewable resource. At present about 90% of all commercial energy worldwide is generated by burning fossil fuels.

Coal is formed primarily from the remains of dead plants. In fact, you can actually see the imprints of leaves and stems in some coal and associated rocks. Whenever dead vegetation collects on the ground in a forest or field or in the water of a swamp, microorganisms break down the organic matter. In most cases the decayed litter is eventually either washed away by running water or incorporated into the local soil and recycled once again into living plants. In some situations, however, especially in swamps, the plants may grow and die so quickly that dead plant material accumulates rapidly. Partially decayed and rotted material becomes buried under fresher layers of dead plant debris, and the deeper layers are cut off from a fresh oxygen supply. Without oxygen the decomposers cannot do their job, and the partially decayed plant material is preserved.

A thick accumulation of partially decayed plant material, usually found buried under other decaying plant material or sediment and thus cut off from the oxygen in the atmosphere, is known as **peat**. Peat is usually a brown-colored mass of plant material. It is rich in carbon, hydrogen, and oxygen—the main elements that make up the bulk of plant tissue—and it can be burned. In some countries, such as Scotland, peat bogs are actively mined as a source of fuel.

Peat is actually the first stage in the formation of coal. As the peat becomes buried under an increasingly thick layer of debris and sediment, it is compressed and the temperature rises. The water and some of the hydrogen and oxygen are driven away from the peat, so it becomes drier and relatively richer in carbon. Peat becomes compressed into **lignite**, a soft, dark brown, coaly material, and thence into **bituminous coal** (also known as soft coal), and finally into **anthracite** (or hard coal). Typical anthracite is about 95% carbon, contains few impurities, and burns with the highest heat value of any coal. All grades of coal, but especially lignite and bituminous coal, can contain many impurities such as iron sulfide, which produces sulfur dioxide, promoting acid rain and acid deposition (see Chapter 17) when the coal is burned.

Coal was formed in massive quantities during the course of past geological history. During the period from about 360 to 285 million years ago, such massive amounts of coal were formed that this is known as the Carboniferous Period (since coal is essentially an organic sedimentary rock composed primarily of carbon). Much coal has also formed since then. As coal formed, it acted as a long-term sink (or storage place) for carbon that would otherwise most likely have taken the form of carbon dioxide in the atmosphere. As humans mine and burn millions of years worth of accumulated coal and other fossil fuels, we are releasing more carbon dioxide than can be reabsorbed by the Earth. This imbalance may have drastic effects on the global temperatures and life support systems of the Earth (see Chapter 18 for a discussion of the "greenhouse effect" and other issues related to increased carbon dioxide concentrations in the atmosphere).

Oil (technically known as petroleum) is also formed from organic debris, but in the oceans rather than on land. Plant litter is carried by streams and rivers to the oceans, where it is deposited on the continental shelves and slopes. In addition, many organisms live in the surface waters of the oceans, including innumerable tiny to microscopic plants and animals, and as they die,

EnviroNet
www.jbpub.com/environet

their bodies may sink and accumulate on the sea bed. As the organic debris becomes buried by sediments, it is compressed and also heats up. Between about 122 and 212°F (about 50 and 100°C) the organic debris is converted to tiny droplets of liquid petroleum dispersed among the sediments. To be economically valuable, the dispersed oil must be naturally concentrated.

Oil is usually brought to the surface in liquid form by means of oil wells, but sometimes very heavy oil that is too thick and viscous to flow at normal surface temperatures is found in sand deposits. Tar sands, as they are commonly known, sometimes occur at shallow depths and can be mined using open-pit techniques. The oil is separated from the sand (using steam or by otherwise heating the sand), and the cleaned sand can be returned to the pit. The Athabasca Field in Alberta, Canada, profitably yields oil from tar sands.

The material in which the petroleum originates, usually an organic- and clay-rich sediment, is known as the source rock. As the source rock is buried and heated, not only do the organics convert to oil, but the clay is converted to a mudstone or shale. Oil can rarely be removed from the source rock directly because the mudstones and shales are relatively impermeable.

To form a commercially productive oil deposit, the petroleum must migrate from the source rock into a more porous and permeable reservoir rock, such as a sandstone, limestone, or (rarely) a fractured igneous rock. Petroleum, being less dense than rocks and water, will naturally tend to rise and migrate through the rock and fill voids in a higher, more porous rock. But this is still not sufficient to form an economic deposit of oil. The oil must be funneled and trapped in a confined area in the reservoir rock so that it does not continue to rise and disperse further, perhaps even reaching the Earth's surface. To prevent the oil from escaping, there must be an impermeable cap rock above the reservoir rock, forming an oil trap. Impermeable shale is a typical cap rock.

Oil traps can form deep below the surface through geologic activity as rocks are bent, folded, faulted, or otherwise deformed such that an appropriate cap rock lies above a reservoir rock, creating a confined space that will contain oil. Of course, there must be oil in still deeper rocks to migrate into the oil trap. Some perfectly good oil traps come up dry when they are drilled into simply because there was an inadequate amount of source rock in the area. Salt domes are often associated with oil fields. Because salt is less dense than other rock types, layers of salt (perhaps originally deposited on the bottom of a shallow sea) often rise through the surrounding rocks and form salt domes. As the domes form, they distort and bend the surrounding rocks, in some cases creating ideal oil traps.

Just as oil traps can form under natural conditions, so too can they be destroyed. During uplift or mountain-building processes, the cap rock may be breached or eroded away, and the petroleum will escape to the surface and decompose. Most commercial oil wells occur in relatively young rocks—rocks formed in the last hundred million years. This does not necessarily mean that substantially less oil was formed earlier in the Earth's history. Rather, oil deposits that formed over a hundred million years ago have had that much more time to be destroyed by natural processes.

Natural gas, composed primarily of methane, CH_4, is closely related to petroleum. As the petroleum is subjected to elevated temperatures beneath the Earth's surface, it is converted to natural gas. The gas is lighter than the liquid petroleum and therefore migrates to the top of an oil trap. Many oil deposits have a layer of natural gas above the liquid oil. In some instances the natural gas may leave the oil trap altogether and become concentrated in a separate natural gas trap and reservoir.

Besides thermogenic methane, produced by heat and pressure acting on buried organic matter as described above, methane is also produced in other ways. Biogenic methane is given off by microorganisms, such as decomposers, during metabolism. In a swamp or marsh, one may observe bubbles of gas rising to the surface of the water; most likely, this is biogenic methane, often called swamp gas or marsh gas. Some bacteria can live in the pores between rocks near the surface of the Earth; the methane they produce may become trapped in small deposits. Some geologists believe that methane may also be formed deep within the Earth through nonorganic processes, such as chemical reactions between graphite (a mineral composed of almost pure carbon) and water (H_2O) to form methane and oxygen (O_2). Unfortunately, much of this nonorganically produced methane may be trapped too deeply within the Earth, and perhaps distributed too diffusely in the crust, to be readily accessible to humans.

Human Use of Fossil Fuels

As has already been pointed out, the fossil fuels are currently the primary sources of commercial energy used worldwide. This is due to many factors. Historically, fossil fuels have been available in a plentiful supply that was easy to mine or otherwise obtain. Fossil fuels provide a form of high-grade, concentrated energy that is easily transported and can be put to many different uses. And at present, generating electricity using fossil fuels (specifically, natural gas and coal) is typically much less expensive (Table 7–4) than using competing technologies such as nuclear power plants, solar thermal, or wind power.

Oil

Oil is the most widely used form of commercial energy. It remains relatively cheap, is easily transported, and can be put to a variety of uses—from heating buildings and running machinery to (in modified form) fueling vehicles. Indeed, worldwide more than half of all oil is used for transportation.

Crude oil is an assortment of many different organic compounds. As it comes out of the ground, it is often a dark, viscous liquid that must be refined for use. Crude oil can range in color from black, brown, or amber to various shades of green. Crude oils also vary widely in their weight per given volume (specific gravity), viscosity, and content of salts, metals, sulfur, and other impurities. Some oils are highly corrosive as they come out of the ground and have a high sulfur content—these are known as "sour crude" and are often found in the Middle East. "Sweet crudes," such as are found in Libya, Nigeria, and Louisiana, are relatively noncorrosive and have a lower sulfur content. In the refining process, crude oil is turned into automobile gasoline, heating oil, jet fuel, tar for roads and roofs, motor oil, and innumerable other substances. Oil forms the raw materials to manufacture various plastics, fertilizers, medicines, and many products indispensable to the industrialized world. However, oil is a nonrenewable resource. Oil reserves are being used up quickly; the vast majority of the remaining reserves are found in the Middle East (Tables 7–5 and 7–6). The Gulf War of 1991 was effectively a battle over oil supplies. On a worldwide scale, if we continue to use oil at our current rate, the proven oil reserves will be completely used up by the middle of the twenty–first century.

Some proponents of the use of fossil fuels, such as oil, contend that current known reserves are a poor measure of how much oil actually still exists. They note that estimates of proven oil reserves, as well as coal reserves and natural gas reserves, have often been revised upward as more oil is

found. This is true to a certain extent, but it is also true that in general over the past two decades the new sources of fossil fuels that have been discovered have been smaller and of lower quality than past discoveries. Also, because of their inaccessibility, some proven reserves are much more expensive (in terms of dollars and energy) than others. For instance, it can cost five to ten times as much to produce a barrel of oil from Alaska or the North Sea as it does to produce a barrel of oil in the Middle East.

In 1955 the geologist M. King Hubbert predicted that U.S. oil production would peak about 1970, and decline thereafter; basically, Hubbert was correct (Fig. 7–5). Even if we can stretch our use of fossil fuels by a few decades, either by finding new sources (such as undiscovered oil fields) or by utilizing lower-quality sources (such as oil shale or forcing the remaining oil out of "depleted" wells; see Issues in Perspective 7–2, page 183), the fact remains that fossil fuels are a finite, nonrenewable resource. They will run out eventually. Before our fossil fuel resources are completely depleted, however, they may become

TABLE 7–4	Cost of Electric Power Generation in the United States (in 1993 Cents per Kilowatt-Hour), 1985, 1994, and 2000		
TECHNOLOGY	1985	1994	2000
Natural gas	10–13	4–5	3–4
Coal	8–10	5–6	4–5
Wind	10–13	5–7	4–5
Solar thermal[a]	13–26	8–10	5–6
Nuclear	10–21	10–21	*[b]

[a]With natural gas as backup fuel
[b]No plant ordered since 1978; all orders since 1973 subsequently canceled.
(*Source*: C. Flavin and N. Lenssen, *Powering the Future: Blueprint for a Sustainable Electricity Industry*, Worldwatch Paper 119 [Washington, D.C.: Worldwatch Institute, 1994], p. 32. Reprinted with permission of Worldwatch Institute, Washington, D.C., Copyright 1994.)

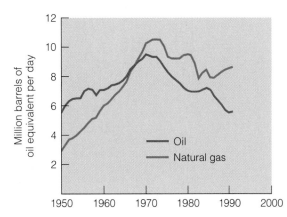

FIGURE 7–5
Natural gas and oil production in the continental United States, 1950–1991. (*Source*: Data from U.S. Department of Energy.)

TABLE 7–5 *Proven Commercial Energy Reserves (in Petajoules), 1990*

REGION	COAL Hard Coal Reserves	COAL Soft Coal Reserves	COAL R/P Years	OIL Reserves	OIL R/P Years	NATURAL GAS Reserves	NATURAL GAS R/P Years	TOTAL RESERVES
World	**19,841,141**	**4,582,845**	**209**	**5,639,794**	**45**	**5,004,802**	**52**	**34,578,702**
Developing countries	**6,711,060**	**734,799**	**163**	**5,030,292**	**68**	**2,358,035**	**96**	**14,344,306**
Oil-exporting developing	296,158	336,743	911	4,780,005	78	2,058,015	106	6,982,042
OPEC	247,255	335,696	1,511	4,397,271	91	1,904,014	116	6,394,357
Non-OPEC oil-exporting developing	49,903	1,047	164	382,734	30	154,001	50	587,684
Oil-importing developing	6,413,902	398,055	152	250,287	19	300,020	58	7,362,264
Africa oil-importing	1,724,503	56	341	14,864	24	27,017	827	1,766,440
Asia and Oceania oil-importing	261,766	1,494	333	43,017	12	44,153	28	350,432
Latin America oil-importing	4,427,631	396,506	123	192,405	22	228,849	65	5,245,391
Industrialized countries	**13,130,081**	**3,848,046**	**239**	**609,502**	**12**	**2,646,768**	**37**	**20,234,397**
OECD industrialized	8,205,121	1,907,746	231	264,443	10	507,729	14	10,885,039
North America	5,983,709	485,668	242	179,204	10	304,933	11	6,953,513
Western Europe	826,610	836,790	144	77,531	10	178,443	21	1,919,375
Pacific	1,394,802	585,287	358	7,708	7	24,353	21	2,012,150
Non-OECD industrialized	**4,924,960**	**1,940,300**	**252**	**345,059**	**14**	**2,139,039**	**62**	**9,349,358**
Central Europe	989,650	544,300	161	10,099	15	21,094	13	1,565,143
Former Soviet Union	3,935,310	1,396,000	300	334,960	14	2,117,945	65	7,784,215

The "R/P Years" ratio is the ratio of proven reserves to production rate, or the number of years that a particular proven reserve will last if the production rate is maintained at 1990 levels. Compare this table to Table 7–2.

(*Source*: World Resources Institute, *World Resources 1994–95* [New York: Oxford University Press, 1994], p. 167. Used with the permission of The World Resources Institute.)

so valuable as a source of the hydrocarbons used in manufacturing plastics, fertilizers, and so forth that the price will rise to the point where they will no longer be economically feasible as fuels. Furthermore, even before our last supplies of oil, coal, and gas are depleted, we may be forced to switch to non-carbon-emitting, non-fossil fuels due to the deleterious effects of greenhouse gas accumulation, acid precipitation, and ground-level air pollution (see Chapters 17 and 18). Both the sources of fossil fuels (the absolute amount of fossil fuels that occur on Earth) and the sinks for fossil fuels (the ability of the Earth to successfully absorb the waste products of the burning of fossil fuels) are already limiting their use. Currently, the burning of oil releases about 2.64 billion tons (2.4 billion metric tons)* of carbon per year into the atmosphere, over 30% of all carbon emissions. Additionally, burning oil releases such atmospheric pollutants as nitrogen oxides, sulfur dioxide, and various hydrocarbons.

Besides its contribution to atmospheric pollution, a particular concern with oil is that its use routinely results in huge amounts of raw oil

TABLE 7–6 *World Oil Reserves and Production (Billion Barrels), Selected Regions and Nations*

REGION OR NATION	CUMULATIVE PRODUCTION TO 1988	1988 PRODUCTION	KNOWN RESERVES	ESTIMATED UNDISCOVERED RESERVES
World	610.1	21.3	922.1	275–945
Middle East	160.2	5.1	584.8	66–199
Soviet Union	103.6	4.5	80.0	46–187
United States	152.7	3.0	48.5	33–70
Asia and Pacific	36.8	2.2	42.8	37–148
Africa	46.4	2.0	58.7	20–92
South America	57.9	1.4	43.8	18–86
Western Europe	15.7	1.4	26.9	11–56
Mexico	15.7	0.9	27.4	15–75
Canada	14.3	0.5	7.0	9–57
Eastern Europe	6.8	0.1	2.0	1–4

(*Source*: Data from D. H. Meadows, D. L. Meadows, and J. Randers, *Beyond the Limits* [Post Mills, Vt.: Chelsea Green Publishing Company, 1992], p. 71. Reprinted from *Beyond the Limits* Copyright © 1992 by Meadows, Meadows, and Randers. With permission from Chelsea Green Publishing Co., White River Junction, Vermont.)

*Unless otherwise noted, *tons* refers to short tons (2000 pounds).

Oil Shale and "Depleted" Oil Wells

You may have heard of **oil shale**. It is a rock (usually a shaley limestone) that contains not oil, but the organic precursors of oil known as kerogen—a waxy solid. Essentially, oil shale is a potential source rock for petroleum that has not yet been subjected to the correct geological environment to produce oil. If oil shale is mined and then heated in the correct manner, the kerogen can be artificially converted to oil. In better grades of oil shale, some 21 gallons (80 liters) or more of petroleum can be extracted from a ton (0.91 metric ton) of rock.

The United States has an abundance of oil shale, with major fields located in Wyoming, Utah, and Colorado. In the past some people viewed oil shale as at least a partial solution to our energy crisis. It has been estimated that the U.S. oil shale reserves contain the energy equivalent of anywhere from 2 to 5 trillion barrels of oil. Based on typical U.S. consumption rates of recent years, this means that conceivably oil shale could supply 350 to 900 years worth of energy. Such a conclusion is fallacious, however, because it ignores certain important facts. Using current techniques, many of the poorer deposits would require more energy to mine, refine, and convert the kerogen to oil than the final product would contain. Mining such low-grade oil shale would be counter-productive from an energy-use point of view. (It might be feasible in the future, though, if the desired product were not the energy contained in oil, but the petroleum per se, which could be used as a lubricant or as raw material for the petrochemical manufacturing industry.) Given this fact, a realistic estimate of the net energy potentially recoverable from oil shale would be 75 years worth at recent U.S. consumption levels. On a global scale, major oil shale deposits are rarer than in the United States, so it is very unlikely that they could ever supply a significant percentage of the global energy budget.

Moreover, the economics of oil shale mining and extraction do not favor such activities at the moment, although if crude oil prices doubled, exploiting oil shale might be commercially feasible. Before advocating such an undertaking, however, one must consider the environmental damage that will surely be entailed in mining and processing large amounts of rock to extract oil.

Another potential source of oil is previously pumped "depleted" wells. During normal pumping operations, only half or less of the oil in the reservoir rock is actually pumped to the surface. The rest of the oil remains trapped in the rock. In the United States, an estimated 300 billion barrels of crude oil remain underground below wells that have been exhausted using conventional means. Various techniques are being developed to extract this oil, such as pumping water, a water-detergent mixture, or superheated steam under high pressure into a depleted well to mobilize the remaining oil and flush it out. Of course, such methods have drawbacks. Energy is needed to heat steam or separate oil from an oil-detergent mixture, thus reducing the net gain of energy. Such techniques may also entail unanticipated environmental damage, such as the contamination of aquifers with pollutants.

being dumped into the environment. Some of this happens accidentally, as during an oil spill (a tanker may collide with shallow rocks, or a pipeline may burst). Unfortunately, such spills are all too common (Fig. 7–6). The *Exxon Valdez* disaster off Alaska in 1989, which dumped nearly a quarter million barrels of oil into Prince William Sound, was well publicized, but it was certainly not the largest recent spill. In 1992 alone there were numerous spills, including a tanker that ran aground off the Spanish coast, dumping half a million barrels of crude oil, and a couple of tanker collisions near Indonesia that released 90,000 and 200,000 barrels of oil, respectively. In Russia in the same year, a pipeline break released 18,000 barrels of oil near the town of Uvat in Siberia. In addition, much crude oil is released during normal operations; the oil-carrying tanks of many ships are routinely flooded with seawater to clean them out, and the contaminated water is pumped back into the sea. An estimated 3.3 to 6.6 million tons (3 to 6 million metric tons, or roughly 22 to 44 million barrels) of oil are released into the world's oceans every year.

From 1950 to 1979, world oil production, increased steadily, with only a minor decline around 1975, from 571 million tons (518 million metric tons; there are about 7.33 barrels per metric ton of oil) in 1950 to a record high of 3440 million tons (3122 million metric tons) in 1979. Since then, production has fluctuated; it declined to a post-1979 low of 2886 million tons (2619 million metric tons) in 1983 and then rose slightly to stabilize at about 3200–3275 million tons

(2900–2970 million metric tons) a year. It stood at 3254 million tons (2953 million metric tons) for 1994. The reason for the decline in oil production since 1979 seems to stem from the energy crisis of the 1970s (see Issues in Perspective 7–3) and the growing realization of the environmental damage incurred by oil use. More emphasis is being placed on energy efficiency and the use of alternative energy sources. Some analysts believe

consumption rates, the world's supply of coal could probably last for about two hundred years or more. Of course, this would be considerably shortened if coal consumption increased dramatically, perhaps as a replacement for oil once that resource is exhausted. A major concern over the burning of coal is that, like oil, it emits large quantities of carbon dioxide (coal emits 25% more carbon dioxide than an equivalent amount of oil

FIGURE 7–6
This bird died as a result of the *Braer* oil spill, January 1993, when a tanker grounded off the Shetland Islands, Scotland, spilling an estimated 619,000 barrels (26 million gallons, or 98.4 million liters) of oil. (*Source*: Hodson/ Greenpeace.)

that oil prices and production will continue to be driven by demand well into the future, and that the theoretical maximum level of production will never be reached simply because the demand will not be there. Hopefully, the world will have broken its heavy oil dependence long before supplies are depleted. Still, even with stabilized production, oil supplies nearly 40% of the globe's commercial energy.

Coal

Like oil, coal is a fossil fuel, but in solid rather than liquid form. It is much more abundant than oil, and significant coal deposits are much more evenly distributed throughout the world than are major oil fields (see Table 7–5). Given these factors, some analysts predict that worldwide use of coal will continue to increase in the decades to come (but see the discussion below). At current

and 80% more carbon dioxide than an equivalent amount of natural gas) into the atmosphere, promoting the greenhouse effect. Also, coal burning releases such substances as sulfur dioxide and nitrogen dioxide, major contributors to acid rain. New techniques are being developed to ensure the more complete burning of coal with less pollution. In **fluidized bed combustion**, for example, very small coal particles are burned at very high temperatures in the presence of limestone particles (the limestone helps capture sulfur and other pollutants) while air is blown through them.

At present, coal is used directly in only a handful of major contexts, such as to produce electricity in coal-fired power plants, to heat large plants and buildings, and in the production of iron and steel. In the modern world, coal use on a smaller scale has been generally phased out—few people burn coal directly to heat their homes, for

The U.S. Energy Crisis of the 1970s

After World War II and into the 1960s, energy consumption grew quickly in the United States, and there was a parallel increase in per capita gross domestic product. The use of petroleum in particular expanded rapidly. It formed the raw material for the burgeoning petrochemical industries; oil was a convenient fuel for heating, powering industry, and running electrical generating plants; and, of course, the country's automobile and truck fleet was growing rapidly. The automobile and the open road epitomized the American dream.

Into the 1960s, the U.S. oil market was controlled by a few large firms, and the bulk of America's oil came from domestic sources. Oil was abundant and prices were low. But in the late 1960s and early 1970s, the American demand for oil soared, and foreign imports of oil became more important. Then a crisis hit in late 1973. War had broken out between the Arabs and Israelis, and Arab oil-producing nations embargoed Israel's ally, the United States. Additionally, they reduced their overall output and curtailed shipments to other countries as well. For the first time the OPEC (Organization of Petroleum Exporting Countries) cartel showed its strength; OPEC unilaterally set the terms, and there was not much the rest of the world could do, at least initially.

OPEC was founded in Baghdad, Iraq, in 1960; since its beginning it has been dominated by Arab nations. As of the early 1990s its members included Iran, Iraq, Kuwait, Libya, Saudi Arabia, United Arab Emirates, Qatar, Algeria, Gabon, Nigeria, Indonesia, Ecuador, and Venezuela. As of 1989 OPEC controlled 36% of world oil production. In 1973, however, the members of OPEC accounted for over half of world oil production. With the OPEC cartel flexing its muscles, the price of oil

FIGURE 1

Cars waiting in line to buy gas during the energy crisis of the 1970s. (*Source:* Tony Korody, Sygma.)

skyrocketed. In the late 1960s, the cost of Persian Gulf oil was $1.00 to $1.20 a barrel, in 1974 it was five times that price, and by late 1978 oil was $12 to $13 a barrel. Then, even before the effects of the 1973–1974 oil crisis were over, a secondary crisis hit in 1979. Iran, a major supplier of oil, suffered a political revolution. The Shah of Iran was deposed, the flow of oil from Iran was disrupted, and the price of oil jumped to $32 to $40 a barrel in 1981. These increases had a major disruptive effect on the American lifestyle and way of thinking (■ Fig. 1). Not only did Americans have to pay more for gasoline, but they had to wait in line at the service station, sometimes for hours. Many states imposed gasoline rationing. The price of all energy soared, including electricity rates.

Many electrical generating plants burned oil directly, and the increases in oil prices drove natural gas and coal prices up as well.

For all its intensity, the energy crisis of the 1970s did not last long. By the early 1980s, OPEC had lost much of its clout, as its members did not always honor the OPEC-mandated production quotas. Meanwhile, the United States and other nations began to conserve energy, increase their energy efficiencies, and develop new sources of energy (including nontraditional sources, such as solar power). Electrical generating plants shifted away from oil; in 1977 about 17% of U.S. electricity was generated by oil-burning plants; by 1986 this number had been reduced to 5.5%. Perhaps most importantly, higher oil prices led to increased exploration and the development of new oil supplies not controlled by the OPEC cartel. In the 1980s, oil prices stabilized and then actually fell to about $15 a barrel. Oil was once again cheap and abundant. Whereas the mid-1970s experienced a major oil crisis, the mid-1980s saw a glut of oil.

Nevertheless, the 1970s energy crisis had shaken Americans' complacency. Suddenly, the nation realized how dependent it was upon the massive consumption of inexpensive, high-quality energy and how fragile those energy supplies could be when they originated in large part from an unstable, volatile part of the world (namely, the Middle East). For the first time, people on a large scale (especially people in high government positions) questioned the wisdom of our massive energy consumption and dependence on foreign energy sources. More importantly, people began to think in terms of resource exhaustion. Oil, as well as coal and natural gas, would not last forever. The 1973 oil crisis was brought on artificially

(continued)

by a handful of hostile nations, but someday the oil wells would run dry and there would be nothing anyone could do about it. This would constitute a real crisis.

On a more fundamental level, some people began to ask whether one Western industrial society had the right to appropriate for itself such a disproportionately large share of the world's resources. Americans' profligate consumption of fossil fuels was also causing hitherto unheard of pollution to the land, waters, and air. The health of people, as well as other organisms, was being endangered. Was this right? What about the future generations who would inherit our degraded and depleted planet? On moral and ethical grounds, some philosophers, politicians, and citizens began to seriously question

American energy consumption patterns.

As a result of such thinking, combined with the high cost of oil, the 1970s witnessed a surge of interest in the development of "alternative" energy sources, such as solar power, geothermal power, and wind power. Research and development was encouraged by government programs, funding, and tax incentives. Additionally, there was an emphasis on energy efficiency and conservation, be it in automobile efficiencies, home energy improvements, or increased productivity per energy used in the industrial workplace.

This intensity diminished when oil became cheap and abundant once again. After the Reagan administration took over the reins from the Carter administration in 1981, programs aimed at energy conser-

vation and the development of alternative energy sources were severely curtailed or eliminated. Although the public, in part, began to take energy for granted again, the energy crisis of the 1970s could not be completely forgotten. Some analysts warned that it could happen again, and that the next crisis could be much more severe. A few even predicted a major crisis before the year 2000. It is impossible to know what will happen as the 1990s progress, but already one can detect a resurgence of interest in energy-related issues. After an interlude of a decade or so, there is a renewed interest in increasing energy efficiencies and developing alternative energy technologies that are both sustainable and environmentally friendly (see Chapter 9 for further discussion).

---

instance—because it is bulky, cumbersome to handle and transport on a small scale, and extremely dirty and polluting. To overcome some of these disadvantages and increase the use of coal, various organizations are working on coal gasification and liquefaction techniques that can produce natural gas, alcohol, and oil replacements from solid coal. The main drawback with such technologies is that at the moment they are not economically competitive with natural gas and petroleum products. Methane or gasoline produced from coal can cost over 50% more than the equivalent substances refined from natural gas or petroleum taken from the ground. Furthermore, while transforming coal into liquid and gaseous hydrocarbons may help mitigate pollution and the greenhouse effect, these new products are certainly not pollution-free. At best, such techniques can only serve as short-term, stop-gap measures to fend off the fossil fuel crisis.

Since the middle of this century, global consumption of coal has more than doubled, climbing from 974 million tons (884 million metric tons) of oil equivalent per year in 1950 to 2419

million tons (2195 million metric tons) of oil equivalent in the peak year of 1989. Since 1989 global coal consumption has declined very slightly, coming in at 2295 million tons (2083 million metric tons) of oil equivalent in 1994. The worldwide decline in coal use, it has been suggested, may be a symptom of the global recession that took place in the early 1990s. Analysts are divided when it comes to predicting the future of worldwide coal use. On the one hand, it is an abundant, widely distributed fuel, and many developing countries are dependent on it, especially if they cannot afford oil, natural gas, or other sources of energy. China, with a population of over 1.2 billion, extracts 75% of its energy requirements from coal. India is also a leading user of coal. If the developing world continues to expand its use of coal, worldwide consumption could be driven up.

On the other hand, some analysts predict that worldwide coal use has already reached a plateau. General improvements in energy efficiency, as have been instituted in Russia and other republics of the former Soviet Union, may be eliminating the need for major increases in coal use. Increasingly, governments are instituting and enforcing environmental regulations that discourage the use of coal. When it comes to meeting environmental standards, coal is a poor match for other forms of energy. Additionally, there is a trend toward eliminating the subsidies for coal production and use that historically have been provided by many governments, including Germany and the United Kingdom. Often coal workers lose their jobs as a result, however, and major strikes by miners in recent years (for instance, in England in 1992) have slowed progress toward eliminating coal subsidies. Only time will tell whether worldwide coal use will increase or decrease.

Natural Gas

A fossil fuel that takes a gaseous form, natural gas is currently the third most commonly used fuel. Its use is growing rapidly due to its versatility and relative abundance, as well as to the fact that it burns more cleanly than other fossil fuels (producing less carbon dioxide and other pollutants than coal or oil).

Nevertheless, there is some fear that economies based on natural gas will not be able to last much longer than economies that depend on oil. Based on current consumption rates, the world's known natural gas reserves will be depleted by the middle of the twenty-first century. However, it is now widely believed that natural gas resources are much more abundant than once assumed. In the past natural gas was often found as a by-product of the search for oil, and in some cases the natural gas was simply released or burned off the top of oil pockets. Today natural gas reserves are being discovered in areas not associated with oil deposits, and various research groups have suggested that our lack of understanding of natural gas geology may have led to overly conservative estimates of the extent of natural gas resources. It is now known that whereas oil is primarily limited to relatively shallow deposits, methane (natural gas) can be found at much more extreme depths. At such depths large amounts of natural gas may be highly compressed into small volumes. New exploration and drilling techniques are making it easier to locate and tap such natural gas resources. Natural gas has also been discovered in association with coal seams. Another advantage of natural gas is that deposits are somewhat more evenly distributed around the globe than are major petroleum fields (● Table 7–7). While the majority of proven reserves of oil occur in the Middle East, significant proven reserves of natural gas are found in the former Soviet Union and the Middle East, and smaller reserves in North America, Africa, Latin America, and Western Europe.

Worldwide production (and likewise consumption) of natural gas has grown approximately 12-fold since the middle of the century, from 198 million tons (180 million metric tons) of oil equivalent in 1950 to about 2300 million tons (2100 million metric tons) of oil equivalent a year currently. Some analysts suggest that natural gas use may double over the next two to three decades and then continue to be used at a level of about 4000–4400 million tons (3700–4000 million metric tons) of oil equivalent a year for several decades. Ultimately, some predict, natural gas will be the fossil fuel to usher in the final transition to a solar-

TABLE 7–7 *Proven Natural Gas Reserves, by Country*

COUNTRY	NATURAL GAS RESERVES (Billion Cubic Meters)
Former Soviet Union	52,000
Iran	17,000
Canada	7,578
Argentina	7,154
United Arab Emirates	5,492
Saudi Arabia	5,135
United States	4,930
Qatar	4,621
Algeria	3,250
Iraq	3,115
Venezuela	2,993
Indonesia	2,423
Norway	2,295
Australia	2,170
Mexico	2,060
Malaysia	1,485
Kuwait	1,370
Libya	1,218
India	1,100
China	1,000

[*Note*: 1 billion cubic meters equals approximately 1.308 billion cubic yards.]

(*Source*: C. Flavin, "Building a bridge to sustainable energy," *in* L. R. Brown *et al.*, *State of the World 1992* [New York: W. W. Norton, 1992], p. 40. Reprinted with permission of Worldwatch Institute, Washington, D.C., Copyright 1992.)

hydrogen and alternative energy global economy (see Issues in Perspective 9–1 in Chapter 9).

Can Fossil Fuel Supplies Increase on a Human Timescale?

Of course, the simple answer to this question is no. As we have seen, the geological processes involved in the formation of fossil fuel resources are imperceptibly slow from a human perspective. Yet a superficial reading of certain statistics may suggest that our fossil fuel supplies have actually increased over time. For, example, in 1970 the ratio of oil reserves to production was 31 years, but by 1989 the ratio had increased to 41 years. Even more dramatically, over the same period the ratio of reserves to production for natural gas increased from 38 to 60 years!

Superficially, it may appear that there was more oil and natural gas available in 1990 than in 1970. Of course, this is not the case—there were about 450 billion fewer barrels of oil and 1440 trillion fewer cubic yards (1100 trillion fewer cubic meters) of natural gas in the world (the amount consumed between 1970 and 1990). What changed was that more oil deposits and natural gas deposits were discovered between 1970 and 1990, thus increasing the known reserves of these fossil fuels. Some might argue that the successful history of oil and gas exploration between 1970 and 1990 demonstrates that there are still plenty of deposits to be discovered, but this too is a false argument. There is an absolute amount of fossil fuels still buried in the crust of the Earth. With exploration and discovery, some of this fixed amount is shifted from the category of "undiscovered reserves" to "known reserves." Every time we do this, the amount of undiscovered reserves is decreased. By definition, we can never know precisely the quantity of unknown reserves that remain (for they are "unknown"), but we can estimate their quantity by various means. One way to gauge the extent of undiscovered reserves is by how easy it is to find them—the more abundant the undiscovered reserves are, the easier they are to locate.

In fact, in many parts of the world in the last quarter century, and since about 1940 in the continental United States, it has become progressively more difficult, with progressively more sophisticated instrumentation and deeper drilling rigs in more obscure places, to locate previously undiscovered reserves of oil. This clearly indicates that we are quickly locating the last major fields of undiscovered reserves. It would be unwise to anticipate that the rate of past oil discoveries will continue into the future.

Because natural gas is much cleaner burning than oil and coal, many people advocate using natural gas in place of other fossil fuels. This may sound feasible as the known reserves of natural gas will last for approximately 60 years at constant 1989 consumption rates, which may give us enough time to develop and fully implement energy alternatives that are not based on fossil fuels. But as Meadows, Meadows, and Randers (1992) note, there is an important catch to this happy scenario.

First, currently known natural gas reserves are not going to last 60 years (or 52 years as shown in Table 7–5) if natural gas is increasingly used as a replacement for oil and coal. Rather than remaining at constant early 1990s consumption rates, the use of natural gas will skyrocket. Countering this tendency, however, undiscovered reserves of natural gas will surely be found (there is greater potential for discovering natural gas than oil, since oil exploration has been stressed in the past). Meadows, Meadows, and Randers (1992) generously assume that in the final analysis, enough natural gas will be discovered to quadruple the 1990 known reserves. This would mean that in terms of 1989–1990 annual production and consumption rates, there would be approximately 240 years worth of natural gas—enough to last until 2230 if annual consumption rates remain constant ("constant use" line in ■ Fig. 7–7).

It is totally unrealistic, however, to assume that the use rate of natural gas will remain constant at the 1990 level, especially as the world population

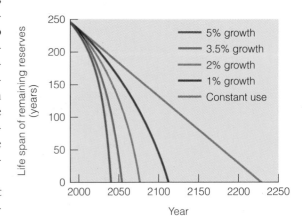

■ **FIGURE 7–7**
Depletion of the world's natural gas reserves assuming different rates of growth in consumption. It is initially assumed that in 1990 there are approximately 240 years worth of natural gas reserves (based on 1990 annual production rates). (*Source:* Data from D. H. Meadows, D. L. Meadows, and J. Randers, *Beyond the Limits* [Post Mills, Vt.: Chelsea Green, 1992], p. 73. Reprinted from *Beyond the Limits* copyright © 1992 by Meadows, Meadows, and Randers. With permission from Chelsea Green Publishing Co., White River Junction, Vermont.)

grows, the less-developed countries continue to develop, and natural gas is used as a cleaner alternative to other fossil fuels. Between 1970 and 1990, the use of natural gas grew at a rate of 3.5% a year. If this rate of increase in consumption continues, then even if the known reserves of natural gas quadruple, they will be exhausted in a mere 64 years, in about 2054 ("3.5% growth" line in Fig. 7–7). In fact, it seems likely that the rate of increase of natural gas consumption will accelerate in the future. If it increases by an average of 5% a year, which seems reasonable, then the quadrupled supply of reserves will be used up in only 50 years. Obviously, we cannot base our long-term energy future on natural gas, simply because it does not exist in sufficient abundance to last through the next century at any reasonably projected rates of further discovery and use.

Why We Must Stop Burning Fossil Fuels

Whether we are in danger of running out of fossil fuels or not, most people who have seriously considered the matter agree that we must greatly curb our use of these fuels. One consideration is the degree to which the United States and many other industrialized societies are dependent on foreign oil (see Issues in Perspective 7–4). Even more importantly, the burning of coal, and to a lesser extent the burning of petroleum products and natural gas, has created environmental havoc on a global scale—the potential for global warming due to the "greenhouse effect," acid rain, air pollution, damage to the land's surface as a result of mining and drilling activities (especially harmful is **strip-mining** for coal), water pollution, and so forth (▬ Fig. 7–8).

The fossil fuels are composed principally of carbon and hydrogen derived from once living organisms. When a fossil fuel is burned, the carbon in the fuel combines with oxygen (O_2) from the air to form carbon dioxide (CO_2), and the hydrogen combines with atmospheric oxygen to form water (H_2O). During these reactions, energy in the form of heat is released, and the released heat also causes the reaction to proceed further.

A high-grade coal is almost pure carbon tainted by small quantities of other elements (such as sulfur and various metals). As the coal is burned, it gives off mostly carbon dioxide, plus small

▬ **FIGURE 7–8**
Environmental impacts of the coal fuel cycle. Similar impacts are caused by the oil and natural gas cycles. (*Source*: C. Hall, C. Cleveland, and R. Kaufman, *Energy and Resource Quality* [Niwot, Colo.: University Press of Colorado, 1986], p. 366; by permission of the publisher.)

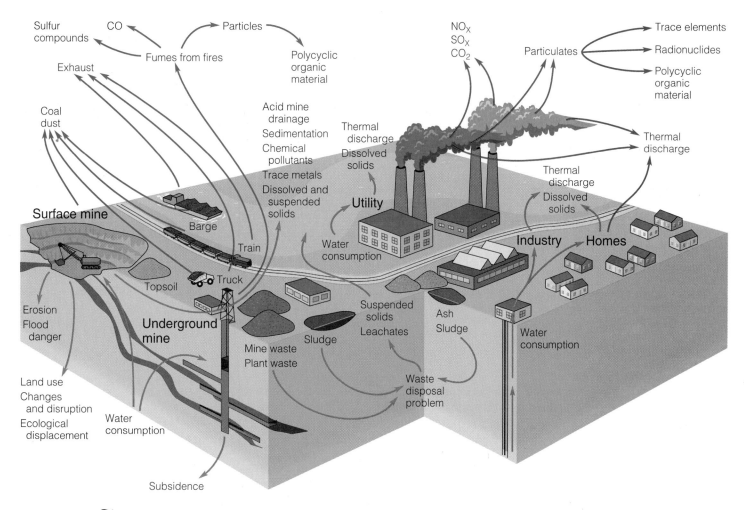

The Hidden Costs of Foreign Oil Dependence

A secure supply of energy is critical for any nation, for without energy the country runs the risk of collapse. When a nation is heavily dependent upon foreign oil (or foreign natural gas, coal, or uranium), it may need to spend vast sums of money, and even enter into armed conflict, to guard its energy supplies. We saw this happen in the Persian Gulf. In January 1991, the United States attacked Iraqi forces that had taken over the country of Kuwait, a small oil-rich nation on the northwestern corner of the Gulf, and threatened to disrupt the free flow of oil. Six weeks later, the Gulf War was over, but beyond the loss of life it cost approximately $40 billion outright and caused considerable environmental damage to the area. Even before the Gulf War broke out, the hidden costs of Gulf oil meant that this supply was far from a bargain. Ehrlich and Ehrlich (1991) have estimated that prior to January 1991 the costs of the routine U.S. military maneuvers that took place in the Gulf to guard the oil added approximately $25 to the real cost of a barrel of oil. Between 1974 and 1989, the price of oil on the world market fluctuated between $12 and $48, so this hidden cost effectively doubled the cost of oil. Of course, this extra $25 per barrel was not added to the price of the oil, but was paid by American taxpayers as part of the country's outlays for defense.

In addition to the cost in lives and money spent to wage the war and then rebuild the damaged infrastructure of Kuwait and Iraq, the war extracted a very high price in terms of environmental dam-

FIGURE 1

A Kuwaiti man observes an oil well that was deliberately set on fire by Iraqi troops.
(*Source*: Reuters/Bettmann.)

age. During the war, Iraq resorted to ecological sabotage. Many Kuwaiti oil wells were deliberately damaged and set on fire (Fig. 1), while oil reservoirs were allowed to leak onto the land and into the water. Millions of barrels of Kuwaiti oil leaked into the Gulf, forming an oil slick tens of miles long that damaged coasts and wildlife. Approximately 700 wells were set on fire, burning about 3 million barrels of

oil a day. Even after the war ended in late February 1991, many of these wells continued to burn—the last one was not capped until November 1991. As they burned, they released millions of tons of smoke, carbon dioxide, carbon monoxide, sulfur dioxide, and other pollutants into the atmosphere. Million of tons of acid rain came down in the Gulf region. During the summer of 1991, the smoke and air pollution caused the temperatures in Kuwait to be 10 to 27°F (5.6 to 15°C) lower than normal. Smoke and acid rain from the burning oil were detected over a thousand miles (over 1600 km) away. Another hundred or so oil wells spilled oil all over the Kuwaiti desert—reportedly, the lakes of oil were 6 feet (2 meters) deep in some areas. Scarce freshwater supplies throughout the region were contaminated.

Though the burning oil wells were dramatic and horrible, in hindsight many experts suggest that the worst long-term damage to Iraq and Kuwait occurred when the vegetation and soils of the fragile desert ecosystems were subjected to massive bombings, trenches dug by bulldozers, and the military maneuvers of soldiers and motorized armored vehicles. As a result, an estimated 25% of the land surface of Kuwait has been damaged. In both countries, wind erosion has increased significantly, causing an increase in sandstorms and an intensification of desertification processes. In an area already heavily dependent upon imports of food, the loss of what little soils there were can only worsen the situation.

amounts of sulfur dioxide and other pollutants. Carbon dioxide is the dominant greenhouse gas. Natural gas, in contrast, contains a large amount of hydrogen (the formula for methane is CH_4); thus, when it is burned, less carbon dioxide is emitted per unit of heat given off. Some of the gas given off by methane takes the form of water vapor, which does not appear to pose any environmental problems. For these reasons, natural gas is considered to burn much more cleanly than coal, yet even natural gas combustion produces significant amounts of carbon dioxide. Furthermore, unburned natural gas, if released into the atmosphere, is itself a powerful greenhouse gas. Chapter 18 discusses the greenhouse gases and their effects in detail.

Fossil fuel procurement is also extremely damaging to the environment. Oil and natural gas prospecting and drilling can involve the construction of access roads, the movement of heavy equipment, the erection of large drilling rigs or platforms (both on land and at sea), and so forth—all of which degrade the natural environment. Oil spills, either at wells or during transportation, have gained notoriety, but perhaps more damaging are

(a)

(b)

FIGURE 7–9
Coal mining is hard work that can be both dangerous to the miners and very damaging to the land. (a) A typical American strip mine. (b) Two Czech coal miners taking a break at the end of their shift. (*Sources*: (a) William W. Knaver II/Visuals Unlimited (b) Gilles Bassignac/Gamma Liaison.)

ing, in which the usable coal is separated from impurities, results in unsightly and dangerous waste banks that can catch fire.

Coal mining is an extremely dangerous and physically demanding profession. Black lung disease plagues many miners, and miners are regularly killed in accidents. The average coal miner dies several years prematurely as compared to the rest of the population at a similar socioeconomic level.

The Bottom Line on Fossil Fuels

The intensive use of fossil fuels facilitated the development of the modern Western industrialized society that dominates much of the world today. Now, however, many people believe that it is time to wean ourselves away from our reliance on fossil fuels. They have served their purpose, but their continued use may be more destructive than constructive.

We have already referred to the environmental degradation and adverse health effects associated with the continued high consumption of fossil fuels; Chapters 17 and 18 provide detailed discussions. Another problem is that in the long term, our fossil fuel resources are finite. Currently

"routine" leaks and emissions of petroleum compounds from wells, pipes, and tankers. Coal mining is extremely damaging to the environment and dangerous to the miners (■ Fig. 7–9). Strip-mining may involve the removal of up to a 100 feet (30 meters) of soil to get to the coal, and in the United States alone, it is estimated that over a million acres (405,000 hectares) have been strip-mined and not yet reclaimed while another 65,000 acres (26,000 hectares) continue to be strip-mined annually. Underground coal mines are little better. They can result in land subsidence, while water seeping into them can form acids (from the sulfur and other compounds that commonly occur in coal) that then leak out and contaminate land, streams, and lakes. Underground coal fires are often virtually impossible to extinguish and may smolder for decades; hundreds of such uncontrolled fires are reported in the United States each year. Coal dust can cause explosions. Coal wash-the world reserve to production ratios for coal, oil, and natural gas are approximately 200–400 years, 45–50 years, and 52–60 years, respectively (the estimate of coal reserves depends on the grade of coal and therefore covers a large range). Of course, some new supplies of fossil fuels will be discovered in the years to come, so the proven reserves will increase further. But the production and consumption of fossil fuels will also change over time. Predicting the future is always difficult, but trying to take all factors into account, some environmental economists predict that realistically, if we continue to use fossil fuels at our current rates, the oil will genuinely run out in about 60 years (in the middle of the twenty-first century), natural gas supplies will be depleted in about 120 years, and the world supply of coal will last another 1500 years. As we have already shown, a major switch to natural gas will deplete these supplies more quickly.

As long as we have coal, it will be technically feasible to maintain our current reliance on fossil fuels. Gaseous and liquid energy sources, which can substitute for natural gas, gasoline, oil, diesel fuel, and so on, can be manufactured from coal through gasefication and liquefaction processes. From this perspective, we can be sure that we have at least a few centuries worth of fossil fuels remaining. There is no current danger of running out of fossil fuels. The immediate concern is the environmental degradation that the continued large-scale use of fossil fuels entails.

But what about the more distant future, say, two thousand years from now? In A.D. 4000, the people of the world will look back at our civilization as an anomaly. We can be sure that their civilization will not be dependent on fossil fuels. The "Age of Fossil Fuels" will have been a short chapter in the history of humanity.

𝓗YDROPOWER

Hydroelectricity is the fourth largest source of commercial energy production and consumption globally, trailing far behind oil, coal, and natural gas. Unlike the fossil fuels, **hydropower** is a renewable resource. The basic principle behind this source of energy is the damming of rivers to create artificial waterfalls ( Fig. 7–10), although natural waterfalls are occasionally used. The falling water is used to turn turbines that drive electrical generators. The great advantage of hydropower is that once the dam is built and the turbines are in operation, it is a relatively cheap and very clean source of electrical energy. An operating hydropower plant produces no waste; it does not spew carbon dioxide or other pollutants into the atmosphere, as do fossil fuel–powered plants, and no toxic, hazardous, or radioactive waste is generated. An operating hydropower plant can be clean, safe, and efficient. For this reason, some people strongly support the construction of more hydropower plants to displace the use of fossil fuels and nuclear power. Nevertheless, the United States is unlikely to build any more large-scale hydroelectric power plants, although they continue to be constructed in other parts of the world.

Despite its advantages, hydropower also has drawbacks. The construction of a major hydro-

FIGURE 7–10
An aerial view of Hoover Dam, a large hydroelectric power plant built on the Colorado River, in Nevada, in 1935. (*Source*: Lowell Georgia/Science Source/Photo Researchers.)

electric power plant is extremely expensive—it is a capital-intensive proposition—and in the process large quantities of fossil fuels (to power machinery) and materials are consumed. Large-scale hydroelectric operations purposefully flood huge tracts of land and seriously disturb natural ecosystems. Forests and other natural habitats are destroyed, along with local villages (often inhabited by indigenous peoples, such as the native peoples of Brazil); farmland is lost, people are displaced, erosion rates are increased, water may become polluted and choked with particulate matter, water temperature and flow are affected downstream (often harming plants and animals), and severe unanticipated flooding can occur.

Currently, China has begun construction of what will be the world's largest hydroelectric dam. It will be 600 feet high (183 meters), damming part of the Yangtze River's Three Gorges area at a cost of an estimated $10 billion. When completed, this project will result in massive flooding of an area 370 miles (600 kilometers) long. Large amounts of farmland will be lost (a problem for any country, see Chapter 13), and approximately 1.1 million people will have to be moved from the flooded area. No one can fully predict what the ecological effects of this dam will be.

Once a hydroelectric plant is built across a river, the mineral and dissolved oxygen contents of the water on both sides of the dam are often affected. Evaporation of water from the relatively still reservoir tends to increase the concentration of salts and minerals in the water, and water leaving the reservoir usually has a higher temperature and lower dissolved oxygen content than it did before the plant was built. These changes can radically effect the flora and fauna that live in the river and along its banks. The dams can also create conditions that favor the spread of disease. The larvae of malaria-carrying mosquitoes, the larval stages of flies that transmit the disease known as river blindness, freshwater snails that are the hosts for the parasites (schistosomes) that cause bilharzia, and other disease vectors can be favored by water changes brought about by artificial dams.

Large dams can also affect coastlines and coastal fisheries by obstructing the passage of nutrients and particulate matter to the sea. The construction of the Egyptian Aswan Dam resulted in the trapping of nutrients that previously flowed into the Mediterranean, resulting in damage to the Mediterranean sardine fishery. Similarly, by trapping sand and silt, dams can cause coastlines to flood. Normally, the new sand and silt would replace material that is eroded from the coastal beaches; when this supply of new material is cut

off by the dam, the beaches continue to erode and the ocean creeps landward. After the Volta Dam was built in West Africa, some 10,000 people on the coast of Togo reportedly lost their homes to the Atlantic Ocean in this manner.

In many ways, giant hydroelectric power plants share the problems of other large power plants, be they coal fueled or nuclear fueled. The setup expenses of a major hydropower plant are enormous. The plant must be carefully maintained and operated. The consequences of a major accident or failure, such as the dam cracking and giving way, could be catastrophic. Also, contrary to popular belief, most large hydropower projects have only a limited life span. The critical water reservoirs behind the dam often fill up with the sand and silt that are not allowed to pass downstream. Such silting can occur very rapidly, especially if the upstream watersheds are deforested and/or subjected to poor agricultural practices that lead to accelerated erosion (see Chapter 13). Once the reservoir is silted up, the usefulness of the hydropower plant is greatly diminished. The deep reservoir is necessary for storing energy during periods of high rainfall and runoff and for regulating production, so that a steady stream of electricity can be produced when needed. Without the reservoir, the plant becomes an intermittent source of electricity at best.

In the United States, traditionally hydropower plants have been very large. The first major hydropower plant was completed at Niagara Falls in 1895, and in the early and mid-twentieth century, numerous large plants were constructed. Hoover Dam, built in 1935, is typical of the dams of this era; it has an electrical energy output capacity of about 1300–1400 megawatts. But many operating hydroelectric plants in the United States are much smaller. At present the country has more than 2000 hydropower facilities of all sizes, with an estimated total capacity of 73,000 megawatts. A recent Federal Energy Regulatory Commission study identified another 5000 sites that have the potential to sustain hydropower facilities. If all of these sites were developed, they would contribute another 74,000 megawatts of capacity. Thus, one can conclude that the United States could double its use of hydropower.

Such statistics can be misleading, however. Some of the best sites for further development of hydropower capacity are found in scenic areas, parks, and wildernesses. Federal, state, and local legislation and regulations (especially the federal 1968 National Wild and Scenic Rivers Act) will hamper or stop the building of hydropower plants on many prime sites. Studies of the remaining sites indicate that most would be un-

EnviroNet
www.jbpub.com/environet

economical to develop given the current relatively inexpensive cost of energy in this country. But the primary hindrance to further development of hydropower seems to be the environmental disruption caused by large dams.

Small-scale hydropower plants may be more compatible with the natural environment. Some small-scale plants do not even use dams. Located on fast streams and rivers, such damless facilities direct water flow directly through the turbines located in the middle of the channel or off to one side. Damless facilities can avoid many of the undesirable environmental impacts associated with dams. Unfortunately, damless plants require a fast rate of water flow and are suitable for only a very small number of sites.

Most types of small-scale hydropower facilities utilize dams, but many take advantage of smaller dams with lower heads (the distance the water drops from the top of the reservoir to the bottom of the dam). It has been repeatedly suggested that many already existing small dams could be fitted with electrical generators. In the United States alone, there are approximately 70,000 dams on rivers and streams, mostly small dams, that are not currently used to generate electricity. These dams are used for such purposes as navigation, flood control, irrigation, and so on. Potentially, it has been argued, many of these dams could be fitted with the equipment to generate electricity, and some proponents of hydroelectric power advocate the further development of this potential resource. But such small-scale hydroelectric facilities can provide power only to people in the immediate vicinity of the plant or dam. Furthermore, such small operations may prove to be relatively unreliable, intermittent energy sources. Also, given the continued presence of cheap fossil fuels in the United States, the costs of converting these dams to energy-producing facilities may be prohibitive.

Another way of increasing the hydropower capacity of the country is to upgrade and refurbish existing hydropower plants to increase their capacities. This generally costs much less per kilowatt of capacity gained than building new plants. An added advantage of refurbishing and upgrading is that additional environmental deterioration can often be minimized. Replacing old turbines with new, more efficient versions, for instance, may place no additional pressure on the environment. Reconstructing and enlarging a dam, however, might. Of course, upgrading can only squeeze so much energy from existing hydroelectric facilities; at best, a 10% increase in overall capacity may be gained.

Globally, the prospects for further hydropower development look more promising than in the United States. Currently, the United States and Canada each contain about 13% of the world's hydroelectric capacity, the former Soviet Union maintains about 10%, Brazil about 9%, and China currently 5% (but this will increase when the Three Gorges Project is completed). The developing world in particular is increasing its hydropower capacity at an incredible rate; in the 1980s, dozens of developing countries doubled, or better, their hydropower capacities. These countries are utilizing smaller facilities as well as huge centralized hydropower plants. Localized, small-scale energy production may be more feasible and compatible with local economies and energy use patterns in some developing countries than it is in many heavily industrialized nations that are wedded to centralized grid systems of power production and transmission. Thus, China, for instance, has more than 86,000 small hydroelectric power plants in operation. There are tens to hundreds of thousands of dams already in existence around the world that are not currently used to produce hydropower. Converting these dams to small-scale hydroelectric power plants may be relatively efficient and inexpensive (not requiring inordinate up-front costs per conversion, even though smaller plants tend to be somewhat more expensive per kilowatt of capacity than large plants) and may also have minimal detrimental impacts on the environment.

Since 1950, worldwide hydroelectric generating capacity has increased from 44,500 megawatts to about 650,000 megawatts. Experts estimate that the current global capacity represents about 25% of the world's theoretical hydroelectric potential, but certainly 100% of the global potential will never be reached due to environmental and social concerns over hydropower. Although energy generated by hydropower will continue to increase globally over the next few decades, it is doubtful if it will ever contribute as much power as oil, coal, or gas currently do.

SUMMARY

Human society is dependent on energy, and through the course of history, humans have utilized ever increasing amounts of energy. Furthermore, in terms of both absolute energy used and per capita energy use, the industrialized countries use much more energy than the developing nations. Commercially, the fossil fuels (oil, coal, and natural gas) dominate energy production and consumption, although other forms of fuels are coming into wider use, particularly for electrical generation—namely, hydroelectric power, nuclear power (discussed in Chapter 8), and various alternative energy sources such as solar power, geothermal power, wind power, and so on (discussed in Chapter 9).

Humans' energy consumption in the future raises several basic concerns. The fossil fuels upon which we currently rely are nonrenewable and may someday be depleted. By what mechanisms will humans obtain energy once our fossil fuel supplies are exhausted? Nuclear power and the alternative energy sources, as well as energy efficiency and conservation measures, may be the key. Many researchers, however, believe that our immediate concern is not running out of fossil fuels per se, but dealing with the environmental degradation caused by the burning of fossil fuels: acid rain and other forms of pollution, increasing levels of carbon dioxide in the atmosphere that may promote global warming, environmental degradation caused by the mining of coal or the drilling for oil, and damage to the environment when mishaps occur—such as an oil spill—during the transportation of fossil fuels. Due to these detrimental environmental effects, we may be forced to curtail our dependence on fossil fuels even before the pressure of depleted supplies is felt. In addition, dependence on foreign oil can leave a nation vulnerable to the manipulations of oil-exporting countries—witness the U.S. "energy crisis" of the 1970s.

In a modern industrialized society, electricity generation and distribution through a grid of power lines is of major importance. Around the world, coal-burning electrical power plants are the most common, followed by hydroelectric power plants, nuclear plants, natural gas–burning plants, and oil-burning plants. Large-scale, centralized, complex, and expensive generating plants connected to consumers through an elaborate system of hardware are a classic example of what energy consultant Amory B. Lovins has termed "hard" energy technologies. Electricity is a high-quality, versatile, concentrated form of energy that has many end-use applications. But in some cases the end-uses of the energy are low-grade applications (such as heating a room in a building). In the future, some predict that "soft" energy technologies, such as passive solar space heating and decentralized electricity generation using alternative energy sources, may progressively replace some current hard energy technologies. Other analysts believe that large-scale hydroelectric power and nuclear energy, both classic hard technologies, will be of increasing importance.

KEY TERMS

alternative energy
anthracite
bituminous coal
blackout
brownout
BTU
calorie
coal
combined-cycle turbine
efficiency
electricity
energy

entropy
fluidized bed combustion
fossil fuel
generator
hard technology
hydropower
joule
lignite
megawatt
natural gas
oil
oil shale
peak load

peat
petajoule
petroleum
power
power plant
quad
soft technology
strip-mine
terawatt
thermodynamics
turbine
watt
work

STUDY QUESTIONS

1. Define the terms *energy* and *work*.
2. What are some of the more common units of energy? How do they relate to one another?
3. Name the basic laws of thermodynamics. Why are they important when considering energy transformations?
4. Discuss the history (trends) of human energy use over the last few centuries.
5. Summarize the current global energy situation. Which countries use the most energy? The least?
6. Speculate on global energy use in the future. Justify your speculations.
7. What is a power plant? How do most power plants operate?
8. Distinguish between "hard" and "soft" energy technologies, citing examples of each.
9. Why is modern industrial society so de-

pendent on fossil fuels? Can we maintain this dependence in the future?

10. What does it mean to say that fossil fuels are a nonrenewable resource?

11. Briefly describe the principles of hydroelectric power generation.

12. What factors contributed to the U.S. energy crisis of the 1970s?

13. What is oil shale?

14. Referring to Tables 7–2 and 7–5, calculate the percentage of the world's commercial energy production generated by the developing countries. What percentage of the world's commercial energy consumption is used by the developing countries? What percentage of the world's proven oil reserves occur in the developing countries?

15. Referring to Tables 7–2 and 7–5, calculate the percentage of the world's commercial energy production generated by the industrialized countries. What percentage of the world's commercial energy consumption is used by the industrialized countries? What percentage of the world's proven oil reserves occur in the industrialized countries?

ESSAY QUESTIONS

1. Describe the origin of each of the major types of fossil fuels: oil, coal, and natural gas.

2. Describe the environmental degradation attributed to the use of fossil fuels.

3. Discuss the potential consequences of a nation being overly dependent on foreign oil supplies.

4. Discuss the pros and cons of each of the major types of fossil fuels: oil, coal, and natural gas.

5. Discuss the pros and cons of hydroelectric power.

SUGGESTED READINGS

Anderson, V. 1993. *Energy efficiency policies.* London and New York: Routledge.

Brower, M. 1992. *Cool energy: Renewable solutions to environmental problems.* Cambridge, Mass.: MIT Press.

Brown, L. R., N. Lenssen, and H. Kane. 1995. *Vital signs 1995.* New York: W. W. Norton.

Cassedy, E. S., and P. Z. Grossman. 1990. *Introduction to energy: Resources, technology, and society.* Cambridge: Cambridge University Press.

Ehrlich, P. R., and A. H. Ehrlich. 1991. *Healing the planet: Strategies for resolving the environmental crisis.* Reading, Mass.: Addison–Wesley.

Flavin, C., and N. Lenssen. 1994. *Power surge: Guide to the coming energy revolution.* New York: W. W. Norton.

Hall, C. A. S., C. J. Cleveland, and R. Kaufmann. 1986 (1992 reprint). *Energy and resource quality: The ecology of the economic process.* Niwot, Colo.: University Press of Colorado.

Hollander, J. M. 1992. *The energy-environment connection.* Washington, D.C.: Island Press.

Meadows, D. H., D. L. Meadows, and J. Randers. 1992. *Beyond the limits: Confronting global collapse, envisioning a sustainable future.* Post Mills, Vt.: Chelsea Green Publishing Company.

World Resources Institute. 1994. *World resources 1994–95.* New York: Oxford University Press.

NUCLEAR ENERGY

P R O L O G U E   *French Nuclear Leadership—Blessing or Curse?*

France is the undisputed leader in nuclear power technology. Three-quarters of French electricity is produced by nuclear power, and France has the second largest nuclear generating capacity in the world (the United States has the largest, but also has four and a half times the population of France). Unlike the United States and many other nuclear countries, France utilizes fast-breeder plutonium reactors, which produce plutonium that can later be used as reactor fuel, and has a well-developed reprocessing program (to separate plutonium from spent reactor fuel).

French nuclear facilities include the Superphenix reactor, the world's largest fast-breeder plutonium reactor, and the Hague plant, the world's largest commercial nuclear reprocessing facility (located near the coast of Normandy). The Hague complex, covering an area of some 7400

PHOTO   *The French Superphenix nuclear reactor.* (*Source:* A. Brucelle/Sygma.)

acres (3000 hectares) and built at a cost of about $11.3 billion, extracts plutonium from spent nuclear fuel; then the plutonium can be mixed with uranium and used to run nuclear power plants. Such reprocessing greatly expands the amount of useful energy that can be derived from the original nuclear fuel. The reason the French have invested so heavily in nuclear power, and particularly plutonium breeder reactors and reprocessing facilities, was summarized succinctly by Jean-Pierre Laurent, assistant director of reprocessing: "We do it [reprocess reactor fuel] because it has a big energy value, and we need our energy independence. France has no oil fields [or at least no large oil fields]. One gram (0.035 ounces) of plutonium equals a [metric] ton [1.102 tons]* of oil. Calculate the oilfields at the Hague, and you have Qatar."

Indeed, the French nuclear program has been remarkably successful. France has achieved a high degree of energy independence and has never experienced a major nuclear accident comparable to Chernobyl in Ukraine or Three Mile Island in the United States. Furthermore, nuclear power generation does not contribute substantially to potential global warming (greenhouse gases are not emitted).

Still, the French nuclear program has many critics. One major concern is nuclear proliferation. Potentially, only 18 pounds (8.2 kg) of high-grade plutonium-239 would be necessary to make a bomb as strong as the one used on Hiroshima during World War II. With the collapse of the Soviet Union, small amounts of plutonium and uranium have been turning up on the black market, primarily in Germany. This black market nuclear material seems to be originating from former Soviet labs and reactors, but critics of the French reprocessing program worry that terrorists might seize bomb-grade plutonium en route from the Hague plant to a nuclear reactor or smuggle plutonium out of the plant despite the tight security precautions.

Another worry is that France is becoming the "atomic garbage can" for nuclear waste from around the world. Not only does spent fuel from French reactors end up at the Hague, but also fuel from 27 foreign utilities, ranging from Japan to Germany. After the useful plutonium is extracted, high-level nuclear waste is left over. According to French law, foreign nuclear waste must be sent back to its country of origin, but some critics question whether this is consistently done at the Hague plant. Plant officials also admit that "authorized" releases of radioactive gases into the air and radioactive liquids into the English Channel occur routinely. The officials contend that the releases are so small as to be harmless, but critics strongly disagree. Independent radiation monitoring groups have detected plutonium on Normandy beaches, radioactive strontium-90 in the water table, and nuclear contamination in a stream adjacent to the reprocessing plant. The detected radioactivity could be from other sources, however, including fallout from past atmospheric nuclear bomb testing, natural sources, or the Chernobyl disaster. A limited 1980s study of the population around the plant found high rates of leukemia and respiratory cancers, but whether these effects are attributable to increased radiation exposure or to other factors, such as abnormally high alcohol consumption, is unclear.

The Hague plant and its surrounding environment in Normandy serve as a microcosm illustrating the issues surrounding nuclear power on a global level. Nuclear facilities are expensive to build and operate, but they can help a country achieve energy independence from fossil fuels. Nuclear power is relatively clean in that greenhouse gases and related pollutants are not released into the atmosphere, yet the potential for radioactive contamination of the environment is the subject of an ongoing debate. Should spent reactor fuel be reprocessed to derive the maximum energy possible from the nuclear materials, or are the risks of nuclear proliferation (nuclear bombs falling into the wrong hands) too great? And ultimately what is to be done with the nuclear waste that is an inevitable part of any nuclear power program? These are issues that cannot be ignored as we enter the twenty-first century.

———

*Unless otherwise noted, *tons* refers to short tons (2000 pounds).

INTRODUCTION

Nuclear power supplies roughly 5% of the world's commercial energy overall, but accounts for a much larger percentage of the electrical generating capacity in certain industrial countries. More than 430 commercial nuclear reactors are currently in operation in some 30 countries, and approximately 40 nuclear plants are under active construction. The United States generates 21% of its electricity from nuclear power while many other countries, including Belgium, France, Lithuania, and Spain, depend on nuclear power for more than 25% of their electricity (● Table 8–1). Japan continues to invest in nuclear power, and India is developing its nuclear capacity. In contrast, Austria is nuclear-free and it, along with the Philippines, does not plan to develop nuclear power. Due to public pressure, Sweden is dismantling its nuclear power plants and should be nuclear-free in the early twenty-first century.

Nuclear power was first developed during World War II by the United States, but initially research focused on military applications such as the use of nuclear technology to build bombs and power submarines. The U.S. Atomic Energy Act of 1954 paved the way for private industry to develop nuclear energy, and by 1983, 80 nuclear power plants were operating in the United States. As nuclear plants proliferated in the 1960s and 1970s, however, the public became increasingly concerned about their safety. It was also discovered that nuclear power was not as inexpensive and efficient as had been predicted (see Table 7–4 in Chapter 7). In fact, in the United States electricity generated by nuclear power plants is currently more expensive than electricity generated by any other major technology. Nuclear-generated electricity can cost two to four times as much as electricity generated at a plant powered by natural gas, coal, or wind. Nuclear power plants are very expensive to build, mining and refining uranium ore is a considerable undertaking, accidents and malfunctions incur significant monetary losses, and the ultimate decommissioning of plants will require considerable sums of money (which could ultimately raise the cost of nuclear power to even higher levels).

Since 1978 there have been no new orders for nuclear power plants in the United States, and about half of the proposed nuclear power plants that had construction permits in 1979 have been canceled. Many other developed countries have overtaken the United States in the research, de-

TABLE 8–1: *Some of the Leading Countries in the Use of Nuclear Power*

COUNTRY	NUMBER OF REACTORS	ELECTRICITY FROM NUCLEAR GENERATORS (% OF TOTAL)	NUCLEAR ENERGY SUPPLIED IN 1993 (BILLIONS OF KILOWATT-HOURS)
Belgium	7	58.9	39.5
Bulgaria	6	36.9	14.0
Canada	22	17.3	88.6
Czech Republic	4	29.2	12.6
Finland	4	32.4	18.8
France	57	77.7	350.2
Germany	21	29.7	145.0
Hungary	4	43.3	13.0
Japan	48	30.9	246.3
Korea, S.	9	40.3	55.4
Lithuania	2	87.2	12.3
Russia	29	12.5	119.2
Slovakia	4	53.6	11.0
Slovenia	1	35.5	3.8
Spain	9	36.0	53.6
Sweden	12	42.0	58.9
Switzerland	5	37.9	22.0
Ukraine	15	32.9	75.2
United Kingdom	35	26.3	79.8
United States	109	21.2	610.3

(*Source:* Data compiled from *The World Almanac and Book of Facts, 1995* [Mahweh, N. J.: Funk and Wagnalls Corporation, 1994].)

velopment, and implementation of nuclear power capability. Still, with more than a hundred operating nuclear power plants, the United States has the largest total monetary investment in nuclear power. Some observers worry that the United States is no longer a leader in advanced peacetime nuclear technology. Others feel that we are still too dependent on nuclear power.

PRINCIPLES OF NUCLEAR POWER

Nuclear energy potentially encompasses two different, but related, types of reactions: fission and fusion. During nuclear **fission**, a radioactive **isotope** (see Chapter 2) of a heavy element, such as a **uranium** or **plutonium atom**, is split into **daughter products**, and simultaneously energy is released. During **fusion**, isotopes of some light element (or elements) are fused together to make a heavier element (for instance, heavy isotopes of hydrogen bonding to form helium); in the process, energy is also released. All

EnviroNet
www.jbpub.com/environet

commercially operating nuclear reactors are run by fission. The Sun generates light and energy through fusion reactions, but on Earth controlled fusion is still only in the developmental stage.

Fission

In fission a **neutron** penetrates the nucleus of a fissionable atom (easily split by neutron penetration, such as uranium-235 $[^{235}_{92}U]$) and causes the nucleus to split into two or more smaller nuclei (these smaller nuclei, although nonfissionable, are highly radioactive). In the process, a tremendous amount of energy is released. The newly formed nuclei are positively charged and repel each other; as a result they travel apart at high speeds and correspondingly high kinetic energies. In addition, if other fissionable atoms are nearby, they may be induced to fission by the extra neutrons released by the first fissioning atom; thus, a **chain reaction** takes place (Fig. 8–1).

As a chain reaction occurs, the nuclei and neutrons traveling at high

● Proton
○ Neutron

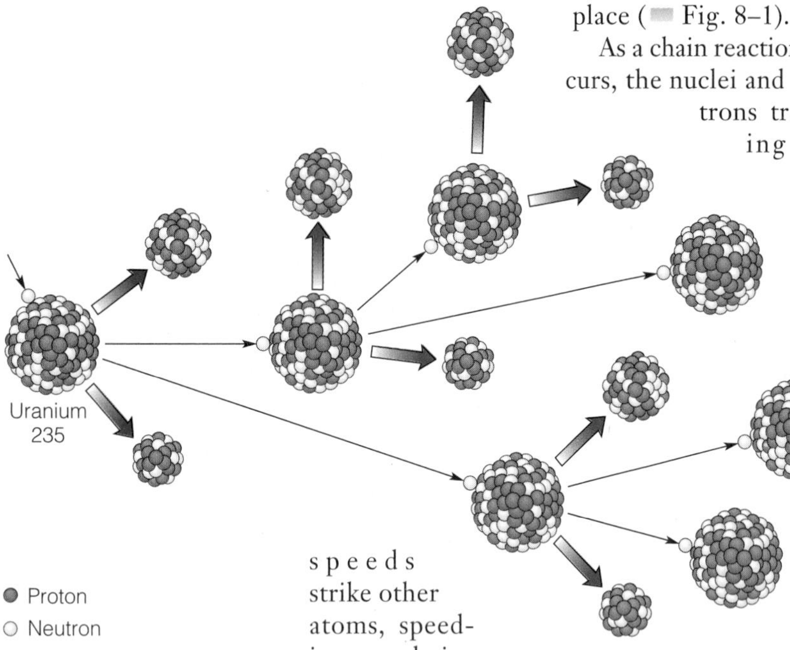

 FIGURE 8–1
Diagram illustrating a nuclear chain reaction.

speeds strike other atoms, speeding up their motions; heat is released, and the temperature increases. A very quick, uncontrolled, and explosively violent chain reaction is the principle behind an atomic bomb. In a nuclear reactor, a chain reaction also takes place, but it is controlled and moderated.

Uranium is a naturally occurring element that has a readily fissionable isotope. The two main isotopes of uranium are nonfissionable uranium-238 (about 99.3% of naturally occurring uranium) and fissionable uranium-235 (about 0.7% of all uranium). To induce a sustained fission reaction, one must increase the probability that excess neutrons from one fission reaction will cause other fissionable atoms to split. This can be done in two major ways: (1) increase the concentration of fissionable material (the method commonly used in atomic bombs, and to a slight extent in some common types of nuclear reactors), or (2) change the characteristics of the neutrons such that they are more likely to be captured by fissionable U-235 than by nonfissionable U-238. The neutrons released by the fissioning of U-235 are called fast neutrons because they initially travel at very high speeds. As it turns out, fast neutrons are readily captured by nonfissionable U-238 due to its internal characteristics. If the speed of the neutrons is curtailed, however, making them slow neutrons, they are more readily captured by fissionable U-235, causing the atom to fission and give off more fast neutrons. So, simply slowing down the speed of the neutrons will cause a higher proportion to be captured by fissionable U-235. A nuclear reactor uses a moderator such as graphite (a form of carbon), beryllium, or water for this purpose. The **moderator** slows the neutrons down without itself absorbing too many neutrons. This process encourages the U-235 to pick up the slow neutrons to produce energy and more fast neutrons.

Modern nuclear power plants use a nuclear reactor, with a sustained but controlled fission chain reaction, to generate tremendous amounts of heat. The heat is then used to boil water, producing steam that powers a turbine that turns a generator and produces electricity. The typical nuclear reactor has a **core** containing the uranium (or other fissionable element, such as plutonium) fuel (Fig. 8–2), the moderator, and control rods of some substance that readily absorbs neutrons, such as cadmium or boron. When the control rods are fully inserted, they absorb enough of the neutrons to halt the nuclear chain reaction. By selectively inserting the control rods, the number, or flux, of neutrons can be regulated and thus the rate of fission and energy release controlled. In some reactors, if the control rods are removed completely and excess heat is not removed quickly from the reactor core, the core may get so hot that it will begin to melt.

Water typically circulates around the core to cool it and is heated in the process. Because the water exposed to the core potentially becomes radioactive, it is recycled and recooled in the primary water loop. The primary water loop, in turn, heats a secondary water loop that produces steam to operate a turbine. The turbine is connected to a generator that produces electricity (Fig. 8–3).

FIGURE 8–2
The interior of the containment structure of the Trojan nuclear power plant, Rainier, Oregon. In the center of the photograph is the reactor core positioned under 35 feet (10.7 meters) of water. (*Source*: Mark Marten, U.S. Department of Energy/Photo Researchers.)

The reactor core and primary water loop are housed within a thick steel tank, or pressure vessel, that is designed to contain all radioactive traces. In most reactors the **reactor vessel** is housed in a containment structure composed of thick steel-reinforced concrete. The containment structure is designed to protect the outside environment from major radioactive contamination if the nuclear reactor should fail.

The principal type of reactor used in the United States is the **light water reactor (LWR)**. Currently, all commercial nuclear power plants in the United States, and about 75% of the nuclear plants worldwide, are LWRs (some U.S. research and military reactors are not LWRs). Light water reactors are named after their moderator, which is ordinary or light water (as opposed to heavy water, which contains an abundance of the hydrogen isotope deuterium). Chernobyl-type reactors use a graphite moderator and have other basic design differences from American-type LWRs (see the discussion later in the chapter).

The fuel used in typical LWRs is uranium that has been slightly **enriched** in fissionable U-235. The fuel has to be so enriched because ordinary water, while slowing the neutrons down, actually captures too many of the neutrons to sustain a chain reaction with uranium composed of its natural isotopic abundances. Typically, an LWR's fuel contains about 3% U-235 and 97% U-238. U-238 is not normally fissionable, but it is a **fer-**

tile isotope that, by absorbing a neutron, can give rise to a fissionable element. As U-235 fissions, it gives off neutrons. Some of these neutrons go into fissioning other U-235 atoms, but others will be absorbed by U-238 atoms. A U-238 atom that

FIGURE 8–3
A schematic diagram of a typical pressurized light water reactor power plant.

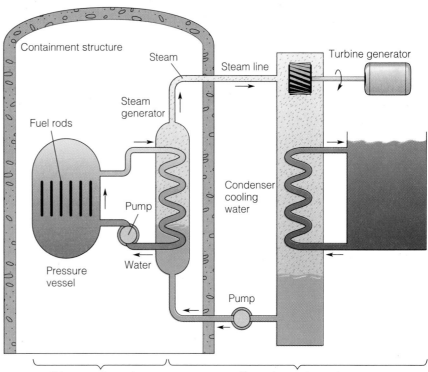

captures a neutron will ultimately be transformed to plutonium-239 ($^{239}_{94}$Pu). Pu-239 is a fissionable isotope, and once formed, it can undergo fission with a release of energy just as U-235 does.

Breeder reactors take advantage of the ability of non-fissionable U-238 to be converted to fissionable Pu-239. With a breeder reactor, the 99.3% of uranium that is nonfissionable can be put to use, thus greatly extending the amount of energy that can be generated from uranium ore deposits. Furthermore **thorium-232** ($^{232}_{90}$Th), an element that is several times more abundant in the Earth's crust than uranium, can be used in a breeder reactor to produce fissionable U-233.

In many ways breeder reactors seem to be a dream come true: they provide abundant energy and produce more fuel as the initial fuel source is used. In 1979 a National Academy of Sciences study estimated that with breeder reactors, the United States could satisfy its electricity requirements for over a hundred thousand years using just domestic uranium supplies. Yet no breeder reactors are operating in the United States. Why?

To recover the fissionable plutonium that is produced in a breeder reactor, the used fuel and uranium/plutonium blanket around the core must be reprocessed. In reprocessing, the fissionable materials are isolated and concentrated to be used as fuel for a nuclear reactor. But this same fissionable material could be used to make an atomic bomb. A terrorist group or hostile country would need to steal only a small amount of weapons-grade, concentrated fissionable material to produce an atomic bomb. In addition, given the high concentrations of fissionable material that could accumulate in a breeder reactor, and the fact that Pu-239 is fissionable by fast neutrons, some people fear that a breeder reactor might even have the potential to explode. In contrast, light water nonbreeder reactors theoretically never have high enough concentrations of fissionable materials to produce an actual atomic explosion, although an uncontrolled chain reaction could result in a meltdown, inducing nonatomic explosions (such as huge quantities of steam breaking containing pipes and vessels, or water being converted to hydrogen and oxygen, which could then explode).

Even if we could ensure that no fissionable material would be lost or stolen from a **reprocessing facility**, reprocessing spent nuclear fuel presents other problems, In particular, it is extremely dangerous and expensive. The spent fuel is highly radioactive and must be dissolved in strong toxic acids to extract the uranium and plutonium. Due to the high levels of radiation involved, much of the reprocessing must be done by remote control. The plants must be meticulously designed to avoid radiation leakage. For these reasons, along with concern over **nuclear proliferation** (the proliferation of atomic bombs), reprocessing is not being actively pursued in the United States. So far the Nuclear Fuel Services plant, which operated in West Valley, New York, from 1966 to 1972 has been the only commercial reprocessing plant in the United States.

Fusion

During fusion, the nuclei of light elements are combined, or fused, together to form a heavier element, releasing a large amount of energy in the process. Extremely high temperatures are necessary to initiate fusion reactions, and on Earth the first artificial fusion reaction was attained in 1954—in the form of a successfully detonated hydrogen bomb. Controlled and sustained fusion reactions are still in the developmental stages and are not yet economically feasible as a source of commercial energy.

Methods currently being developed are based on the fusing of either two deuterium atoms (hydrogen atoms having a neutron as well as a proton in the nucleus), or a deuterium and a tritium atom (a hydrogen atom with two neutrons and a proton in the nucleus), to form a single helium atom plus a neutron. These reactions require temperatures in excess of 72 million degrees F (40 million degrees C). Two basic approaches are being developed to contain controlled fusion reactions: (1) magnetic confinement and (2) high-energy lasers and particle beams.

In magnetic confinement, powerful electromagnets surround the fusion chamber and repel the fusion materials as they approach the walls of the chamber. Various types of magnet confinement reactors have been designed and tested experimentally; the most common and successful design is known as a tokamak. A **tokamak** is a large (the size of a house) machine with a doughnut-shaped vacuum reactor vessel surrounded by magnetic coils.

Fusion reactions can also be initiated by bombarding a fuel pellet, containing deuterium or a deuterium-tritium mixture, with laser or particle beams from all directions. For a split second, the fuel pellet will remain suspended within the reaction chamber and implode with tremendous force and pressure, attaining enormous temperatures. If the pressure and temperature are great enough, fusion will occur. The Case Study describes an attempt to initiate fusion without high temperatures.

Cold Fusion: Faulty Science?

Most work on developing fusion has been predicated on the assumption that extremely high temperatures are necessary to initiate and sustain fusion reactions. Over the years, however, a limited amount of research has considered the possibility of "cold" or "room-temperature" fusion. Obviously, fusion reactions that generated a surplus of energy at low temperatures would be of great use in the development of commercial fusion power sources.

In March 1989, two chemists made headlines when they announced that they had produced fusion at room temperature, generating significantly more energy than the process consumed. Martin Fleischmann (University of Southampton, United Kingdom) and B. Stanley Pons (University of Utah) had carried out the following experiment: They placed two electrodes in a container filled with heavy water (water composed of deuterium and oxygen rather than normal hydrogen and oxygen); the negative electrode was composed of the metal palladium. A current was then run through the water. As a current passes through water, it breaks the water molecules into hydrogen (in this case, the deuterium isotope) and oxygen ions (charged particles). The deuterium (hydrogen) ions are positively charged and are therefore attracted to the negative palladium electrode. According to Fleischmann and Pons, as the deuterium nuclei are attracted to the palladium electrode, they are squeezed together, and some of them fuse to form helium, tritium, and neutrons. In the process of fusion, energy will be emitted—and, according to Fleischmann and Pons, significantly more energy is produced than is applied to the electrodes in the first place.

If the Fleischmann and Pons experiment were to work successfully and consistently, it would provide a major new energy source that could be commercially marketed very readily. Understandably, the announcement of their results caused quite a sensation—and a flurry in other laboratories as researchers tried to duplicate the experiment. Unfortunately, scientists at other laboratories have never been able to fully duplicate Fleischmann and Pons's reported results. Indeed, many researchers could find no evidence of room-temperature fusion when they tried to replicate the experiment. The present consensus of the scientific community is that Fleischmann and Pons were incorrect. They did not produce a surplus of energy through a **cold fusion** reaction; perhaps their initial results were due to faulty equipment or a poorly designed experiment.

Questions

1. What would the implications be if a method of "cold fusion" really were developed?
2. Why do you think Fleischmann and Pons were in such an apparent rush to announce their discovery? Should they have repeated, analyzed, and authenticated their experiment more thoroughly before going to the media? What types of social and peer pressures is any scientist subject to? Can any scientist really be a disinterested and objective observer of nature?
3. Assuming that Fleischmann and Pons did not knowingly and purposefully falsify their data, should they be "punished" for their "mistake"? Given their damaged reputations, do you think either has much of a future in the field of science? How might the situation change if genuine cold fusion technology, based on the so far unsuccessful Fleischmann and Pons techniques, is developed in the future?

In many ways, fusion would be an ideal energy source—especially if deuterium-deuterium fusion reactions can be harnessed. Deuterium makes up only a small percentage of all hydrogen atoms (about 1 out of every 6700 hydrogen atoms), but hydrogen is the most abundant element in the universe. The deuterium contained in 30 gallons (113.5 liters) of seawater, if totally fused, would release as much energy as 10,000 gallons (37,850 liters) of gasoline. Some researchers have estimated that if the deuterium in the top 10 feet (3 m) of water in Earth's oceans were used as a fuel in fusion reactors, it could satisfy the energy needs of all humans for about 50 million years.

Another advantage is that fusion does not produce fissionable materials that could be incorporated into the production of bombs. Fusion also produces much less radiation than fission, although some undesirable radioactivity is associated with fusion reactions. A sustained fusion reaction produces a dangerous number of neutrons. Every time two hydrogen atoms fuse to form a helium atom, a neutron is produced. These neutrons would cause the internal parts of the reactor to become highly radioactive. The neutron bombardment would weaken the fusion reactor over time, as would the intense heat generated by the fusion reaction.

Some people predict that fusion power could solve many of the world's fundamental material problems. The extremely high temperatures generated during the fusion process could be used to vaporize any and all waste materials; wastes would be broken down to their constituent atoms. The atoms could then be sorted out according to weight or other physical properties and reused—the ultimate recycling. Piles of waste—garbage, sewage, refuse—could be vaporized and sorted into "piles" of carbon atoms, oxygen atoms, iron atoms, gold atoms, copper atoms, and so on. The raw atoms could then be used to produce whatever is needed. Furthermore, with a virtually unlimited source of energy, humans could synthesize their own elements by fusing hydrogen nuclei together. We are unlikely to exhaust the supply of hydrogen since it is estimated that over 90% of the atoms in the universe are hydrogen atoms.

𝒯HE NUCLEAR FUEL PRODUCTION PROCESS

Conventional, nonbreeder fission reactors utilize uranium as their primary fuel source. The uranium must be extracted from uranium ore (Fig. 8–4). Most uranium ore contains a relatively small percentage of actual uranium—

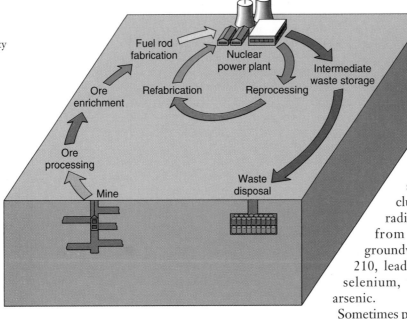

FIGURE 8–4
The fuel cycle for electricity generation using a fission reactor.

typically, only 0.1% uranium metal by weight. Once mined, ore is concentrated during the **milling process**. There the ore is crushed and leached using various chemicals (such as sulfuric acid or sodium carbonate); then the uranium is precipitated from the solution. The result of the milling process is the formation of the substance U_3O_8, referred to as **yellowcake** (due to its color) or natural uranium.

Yellowcake is composed of 85% pure uranium by weight, but the uranium is still in its natural isotopic mixture of 99.3% nonfissionable U-238 and only 0.7% fissionable U-235. To be used in a typical American nuclear reactor, it must be en-

riched in the fissionable U-235 (Fig. 8–5). The enriched uranium is made into fuel pellets, which are placed into fuel rods and used to power a reactor. The remaining depleted uranium (high in nonfissionable U-238, but low in U-235) is a radioactive waste.

Mining and processing uranium can have a major impact on the environment. A typical light water fission reactor with a 1000-megawatt capacity may require more than 155,000 tons (140,000 metric tons) of uranium ore to produce the fuel it consumes in a year. The mining operation to obtain this raw ore may extend over 18 acres (7 hectares) and displace as much as 2.755 million tons (2.5 million metric tons) of rock and earth.

The milling and concentrating process produces wastes in the form of solid tailings and sludge; an estimated 1421 tons of sludge are produced for every ton of yellowcake. The sludge wastes are pumped into settling ponds covering several acres (hectares), where the solids settle to the bottom. The uranium tailings and other mining and milling residues contain both radioactive nuclides and trace amounts of very toxic metals that can easily escape into the general environment. Substances of special concern include radioactive radon-222 (a gas), radium-226 (which is easily leached from residues and can enter the groundwater), thorium-230, polonium-210, lead-210, and toxic metals such as selenium, vanadium, molybdenum, and arsenic.

Sometimes piles of tailings are capped with an impermeable layer, such as concrete or clay, and then covered with soil and "reclaimed." Case studies have demonstrated, however, that the land is far from totally reclaimed—biomass and productivity are greatly diminished relative to what they were prior to mining operations, and plants and animals may continue to take in toxic trace elements and radioactive nuclides. Another, perhaps preferable, method is to minimize the volume of tailings and residues in the first place by using underground leaching techniques. Wells are drilled into the ore, and solutions are pumped down that will dissolve the minerals. The solution can then be brought to the surface through collection wells, and the uranium is removed from the so-

lution. The solution itself can then be pumped back into the ore and used again. Leach mining generates a much smaller volume of tailings, but it may produce significant amounts of sludge waste—these are often allowed to dry and are then buried. A major problem with leaching techniques is that unless care is taken, the underground water in nearby aquifers may become contaminated.

URANIUM RESOURCES

Uranium resources, like fossil-fuels, are a nonrenewable source of energy. Assessing potential uranium resources is very difficult, but clearly some high-grade deposits of uranium ore (as in the western United States) are already being depleted. Like other mineral resources, concentrated uranium deposits are not spread evenly over the globe. Significant concentrations occur in Algeria, Australia, Brazil, Canada, the Central African Republic, Gabon, France, India, Niger, South Africa, Spain, and the United States. Based on current consumption, a world dependent on fission power, and not utilizing breeder reactors, might deplete these high-grade, currently economically minable uranium resources in only a couple of centuries.

Other sources of uranium exist. Seawater, for example, contains uranium, but it is so diffuse, large amounts of energy would be required to extract it. On a more positive note, uranium that would be uneconomical to mine for its own sake is recovered as a by-product during the mining and refining of certain other minerals. By-product uranium has been produced from phosphate plants and from the mining and refining of copper. The end of the Cold War has also raised the possibility that some weapons-grade uranium can be recycled for power plants (see Issues in Perspective 8–1). Some lower-grade deposits of uranium also have the potential to be utilized. An example is the Chattanooga shale, which covers large areas in the east-central United States. Its uranium content is so low, however, that a 1000-megawatt fission reactor would require 30 times more shale to power it than if the uranium were obtained from higher-grade ore.

ADVANTAGES AND DISADVANTAGES OF NUCLEAR POWER

The Safety Record of Nuclear Power

Advocates of nuclear power rightfully claim that, in practice, nuclear power generation has thus far

Bombs to Fuel

A major concern over nuclear power generation in the past has been the fear that nuclear fuel or waste products could be diverted to the production of nuclear bombs. With the recent disintegration of the Soviet Union, the road may lead the other way. Russia is in the process of retiring many nuclear arms, and a big problem is what to do with the uranium enriched in U-235 that formed the basis of many nuclear weapons (Fig. 1). The material could be stored, but that would not eliminate the risk that this genuinely weapons-grade material could fall into the wrong hands.

Another possibility is to dilute it once again with U-238 and use it in nuclear power plants. Apparently, the Russians have more enriched uranium than they need for their own plants in the near future, and as they are strapped for cash, they have offered to sell the concentrated uranium to the United States, France, and Japan for use in power plants. Such sales would ensure that the material would not be recycled back into weapons, but the proposed deals also present potential problems. Not only does shipping enriched uranium out of Russia pose the risk of accidents or theft, but dumping massive amounts of enriched uranium on the open market could cause uranium prices to drop, driving some commercial uranium producers out of business and hurting the uranium enrichment business.

FIGURE 1
Intercontinental nuclear ballistic missiles on parade in Moscow, November 1990.
(*Source:* P. LeSegretain/Sygma.)

The biggest loser might be the U.S. Department of Energy, which in running a federal uranium enrichment business is the world's largest supplier of reactor fuel. Already, the federal government (and thus the taxpayers) has lost billions of dollars on this project, which expanded its processing facilities in the 1980s even as orders for nuclear power plants were being canceled and the demand for nuclear fuel was declining. Furthermore, it may cost an additional $20 billion to clean up contaminated sites associated with the venture. On the positive side, certain companies stand to earn a substantial amount from opening plants that would dilute Russia's weapons-grade uranium and process it into reactor fuel.

proven to be the safest form of large-scale commercial power generation. Nuclear power plants, so far, are much safer (in terms of human lives lost) and less damaging to the environment than fossil fuel–burning power plants, and they are also safer than hydroelectric power plants. Nuclear plants have a solid safety record despite several widely publicized accidents and the fact that minor mishaps occur routinely at nuclear facilities.

Other sources of electricity generation also have many accidents, though they do not seem to attract as much attention from the media and the public as accidents at nuclear power plants. Furthermore, coal-fired power plants kill people on a routine basis—the pollution they give off literally kills innocent members of the public. Additionally, the air pollution, acid rain, and greenhouse gases they release are causing untold property damage (estimated at billions of dollars a year in the United States alone), disrupting ecosystems, and potentially changing the global climate (see Chapters 17 and 18). Hydroelectric power plants, though apparently clean and natural, cause untold environmental havoc by flooding upstream areas and reducing water flow downstream. The disruption they cause to natural water flow can encourage the proliferation of disease-bearing organisms, and a large dam failure could conceivably kill hundreds of thousands of people and cause billions of dollars worth of property damage.

Dr. Bernard L. Cohen, a professor of physics and radiation health at the University of Pittsburgh, has studied the pros and cons of nuclear power for many years. Cohen has attempted to quantify the **risk** to human life that nuclear power plants pose as compared to other types of electric power generation. To do this, he expresses risk as the **loss of life expectancy (LLE)**. The LLE is the average amount that a life will be shortened by the risk under consideration. In his book *The Nuclear Energy Option*, Cohen explains the concept of an LLE this way: "[S]tatistics indicate that an average 40-year-old person will live another 37.3 years, so if that person takes a risk that has a 1% chance of being immediately fatal, it causes an LLE of 0.373 years (0.01 × 37.3)." Notice that the LLE does not mean that taking a particular risk will remove 0.373 years from an individual's life, but that if thousands of people take that risk, a few will die prematurely, and the average life expectancy for those taking the risk will be decreased by 0.373 years. Cohen has calculated the LLE for a number of activities and conditions (Table 8–2).

Coal-fired power plants are the chief competitor of nuclear plants. According to Cohen, air pollution in the United States causes an estimated 100,000 deaths per year (admittedly, most of these are among the weak, sick, and elderly), and the air pollution attributed to coal-burning power plants is responsible for at least 30,000 of these deaths a year. From this he calculates that the average American has an LLE of 30 days (0.082 years) due to coal-burning power plants, and the average coal-burning power plant causes about 70 deaths per year due to the pollution it gives off, or about 3000 deaths over its operating lifetime. In contrast, Cohen has calculated that if all electricity in the United States were generated by nuclear power, the LLE for the average American would be about 0.04 to 1.5 days (the lower LLE is based on Nuclear Regulatory Commission data; the higher LLE is based on information from the antinuclear Union of Concerned Scientists).

TABLE 8–2 *Loss of Life Expectancy (LLE) Due to Various Risks*[a]

ACTIVITY OR RISK	LLE (DAYS)
Living in poverty	3500
Being male (vs. female)	2800
Cigarettes (male)	2300
*Heart disease	2100
Being unmarried	2000
Being black (vs. white)	2000
Socioeconomic status, low	1500
Working as a coal miner	1100
*Cancer	980
30 lb (13.6 kg) overweight	900
Grade school dropout	800
*Suboptimal medical care	550
*Stroke	520
15 lb (6.8 kg) overweight	450
*All accidents	400
Vietnam army service	400
Living in Southeast (SC, MS, GA, LA, AL)	350
Mining construction (accidents only)	320
*Alcohol	230
Motor vehicle accidents	180
*Pneumonia, influenza	130
*Drug abuse	100
*Suicide	95
*Homicide	90
*Air pollution	80
Occupational accidents	74
*AIDS	70
Small car (vs. midsize)	60
Married to smoker	50
*Drowning	40
*Speed limit: 65 vs. 55 miles per hour	40
*Falls	39
Poison + suffocation + asphyxiation	37
*Radon in homes	35
*Fire, burns	27
Coffee: 2 1/2 cups/day	26
Radiation worker, age 18–65	25
*Firearms	11
Birth control pills	5
*All electricity, nuclear (UCS)	1.5
Peanut butter (1 tbs/day)	1.1
*Hurricanes, tornadoes	1
*Airline crashes	1
*Dam failures	1
Living near nuclear plant	0.4
*All electricity, nuclear (NRC)	0.04

[a] Asterisks indicate averages over total U.S. population; others refer to those exposed.
(*Source*: B. L. Cohen, *The Nuclear Energy Option* [New York: Plenum Press, 1990], p. 128. Reprinted through the courtesy of Dr. Bernard L. Cohen and Plenum Press.)

Independent of these estimated LLEs, Cohen suggests that the extraction of uranium ore for use as a fuel source can save lives in the long run by removing a major source of natural radon emissions. It has been estimated that environmental radon exposure currently causes approximately 14,000 fatal lung cancers a year in the United States.

According to Cohen, nuclear power is extremely safe and the hazards of high-level radioactive waste, low-level wastes, and routine emissions of radioactive gases into the environment have been greatly exaggerated in the public's mind. In fact, radioactive substances that naturally occur in coal are emitted into the atmosphere when coal is burned. Even major accidents—such as so-called **meltdowns**—in American-design reactors pose little risk to the public at large (as explained later, a Chernobyl-type accident would not occur in the United States). Averaged over time, we could expect less than five deaths per year from nuclear power plant accidents. Cohen estimates that the average meltdown (more accurately referred to as "core damage" to the reactor) would cause 400 fatalities, mostly from cancers caused by slightly increased exposures to radiation, and a few hundred million dollars worth of off-site damage. From this he concludes that a meltdown would have to occur in the United States every five days to make nuclear power as dangerous to the public as coal burning. From the perspective of monetary damage, a meltdown would have to occur once every other month to match the off-site property damage done by coal-fired power plants.

The actual chances of a meltdown depend on a number of assumptions and on how one defines a "meltdown." In the mid-1970s one study estimated that a meltdown could be expected once every 20,000 years of reactor operation (1000 reactors operating for 20 years would equal 20,000 reactor-years of operation). The Union of Concerned Scientists, in contrast, has estimated that a meltdown might occur once every 2000 reactor-years. In fact, over a period of more than 30 years, and thousands of reactor-years of operation, the worst accident of an American-style reactor was Three Mile Island where part of the fuel melted, but did not escape from the reactor vessel. Among all reactors worldwide, including those that could not be licensed in the United States, the worst disaster was Chernobyl, which, as we explain later, was inadvertently the result of an experiment—it was not simply a matter of the reactor failing.

Drawbacks of Nuclear Power

Two major categories of negative environmental impacts are associated with the use of conventional nuclear fission reactors. The first are the types of impacts that occur with any large power plant that uses a bulky fuel. Enormous amounts of energy, land, and materials must be utilized to build the plant; mining the enormous amounts of uranium ore needed to feed the plant involves substantial energy and potential environmental degradation; and during routine operations, large quantities of water are used for cooling, and disruptive amounts of waste heat are dumped into the environment (such thermal pollution can be extremely damaging to the natural flora and fauna). Eventually, after 30 or 40 years or less, an aging nuclear power plant must be decommissioned; this too requires enormous amounts of energy and materials.

One of the chief advantages of nuclear power is that it does not produce harmful, carbon-based greenhouse gases such as carbon dioxide, nor does it spew particulates, sulfur dioxide, and similar harmful substances into the environment. Looking at the entire process, however, and not just at the actual operation of a nuclear power plant, reveals that greenhouse gases are produced. The building and later decommissioning of nuclear power plants involve the use of energy derived from fossil fuels, as do the mining and processing of uranium ore and the transportation and storage of the uranium fuel and spent fuel. It is sometimes suggested that nuclear power helps to decrease the U.S. dependence on foreign oil, but in fact many processes associated with nuclear power are driven by oil. Furthermore, nuclear power is used almost exclusively to generate electricity, and at most a mere 6% of the oil used in the United States goes toward generating electricity. The real competitor with nuclear power for electricity generation is coal. Coal burning is extremely dirty and is known to be causing severe environmental degradation. Nuclear advocates rightfully point out that the large-scale substitution of nuclear power plants for coal-burning plants would avoid many of the problems inherent in coal-burning technology. However, nuclear power generation contributes its own set of wastes and attendant problems.

The second category of disadvantages of nuclear power is inherent and specific to this technology: the dangers of **radioactivity**. The very basis of nuclear power production involves radioactivity. A typical modern nuclear power plant contains within its walls radiation equivalent to that of a thousand Hiroshima bombs, and this leads to fears that radioactive wastes may inadvertently leak into the environment, accidents may occur (perhaps resulting in a reactor meltdown or explosion), or fissionable isotopes may fall into the wrong hands. Compounding these concerns are a number of widely publicized mishaps, and the fact that there is still no long-term, satisfactory method of disposing of the radioactive wastes generated by nuclear power plants. Many people are concerned that a single "worst-case" nuclear accident could nullify all the potential benefits of nuclear power. A 1982 study by the Sandia National Laboratory in New Mexico predicted that a major accident in the United States might cause 50,000 to 100,000 immediate deaths and up to another 40,000 subsequent deaths due to radiation-induced cancer; monetary damages would amount to at least $100 billion. Even the Chernobyl accident was not a "worst-case" scenario—indeed, some argue it was relatively minor compared to what could happen.

Radiation

We are exposed to various forms of natural radiation constantly and continuously—the Earth's rocks contain radioactive elements and we are bombarded by cosmic rays from outer space—but any threats posed by natural radiation are compounded when we add to the radiation levels artificially.

Radiation can take many different forms. It can consist of particles, such as **alpha particles**, which are essentially energetic helium nuclei; **beta particles**, which are high-speed electrons; or electrically neutral neutrons. Radiation also includes electromagnetic radiation such as the higher-energy, short-wavelength X rays and **gamma rays**. Such radiation is dangerous both because it can kill cells directly and because it causes ionizing effects (therefore it is said to be **ionizing radiation**). As the particles (alpha and beta particles) or rays (gamma or X rays) hit other, electrically neutral atoms, they may cause these atoms to lose electrons and thus gain an electrical charge—or become ionized. In the tissues of an organism, such ionized atoms can cause structural damage to important molecules, produce mutations in the genetic material of the cell (DNA), and induce cancers.

Radioactive atoms, known variously as radioisotopes or **radionuclides**, are unstable atoms that undergo spontaneous disintegration (radioactive decay) and in the process give off radiation. At the temperatures and pressures that humans live under, nothing can stop radioactive decay from occurring. When a radionuclide decays, it gives off particles and/or rays, and this radiation will affect any atoms or molecules it encounters. If the radionuclide happens to be inside a human body, it will damage atoms, molecules, and cells as it disintegrates. Cells that grow and di-

vide rapidly are usually most affected by radiation. Thus, fetuses and children are generally more prone to radiation damage than are adults. In adults, cells in the bone marrow that make red blood cells, cells lining the digestive tract, and cells of the thyroid, stomach, testes, ovaries, lungs, and breasts are particularly sensitive to radiation.

Radiation occurs naturally in many rocks that contain radioactive substances, such as natural uranium, thorium, and potassium-40. Radioactive radon gas is released as uranium decays in rocks and soil. Cosmic rays, high-energy particles that bombard the Earth from outer space, are another major source of natural radiation. As one ascends into the atmosphere, the intensity of cosmic rays increases. Frequent flights in modern jet airplanes at altitudes of tens of thousands of feet (thousands of meters) can result in significant radiation exposure from cosmic rays. It is estimated that 1000 hours of flying time per year result in the absorption of approximately one rem (● Table 8–3) due to cosmic rays. The person staying on the ground will be exposed to only about one-twentieth to one-tenth of this dose of cosmic rays.

An important aspect of radiation, and also of many chemical carcinogens, is that no **"threshold" of exposure** is necessary to potentially produce deleterious effects. In contrast, some poisons (for example, carbon monoxide) will have no deleterious effects on the typical individual unless the exposure reaches a certain "threshold" level. Since a single particle of radiation, or a single molecule of many chemical carcinogens, can cause damage to a single molecule in a single cell, resulting in cancer or some other disease, any level of radiation—no matter how small—is dangerous. Studies have also suggested that a single, larger dose of radiation may in some cases be less harmful in the long run than chronic exposure to much lower levels of radiation over extended periods of time (see Issues in Perspective 8–2, page 211). A 1991 study of employees exposed to low levels of radiation (supposedly acceptable levels) over long periods of time at the U.S. Oak Ridge National Laboratory revealed that leukemia rates were 63% higher among those exposed than among an equivalent nonexposed population. A 1990 study of the children of employees at the Sellafield nuclear reprocessing facility in England demonstrated that these children were seven to eight times more likely to develop leukemia than children whose parent or parents had not been exposed to low-level, but legal, doses of radiation over long periods of time. In contrast, the children of Japanese parents who were exposed to large one-time blasts of radiation during the

- *Curie* A curie (named after Marie and Pierre Curie, the discoverers of radium) is a measure of how radioactive a substance is. One curie (Ci) is the amount of radiation given off by a gram (0.035 ounces) of pure radium-226, equal to approximately 37 billion radioactive disintegrations (particles or rays being ejected) per second. A microcurie (mCi) is a millionth of a curie; a picocurie (pCi) is a trillionth of a curie. A becquerel (Bq) is defined as one decay per second; therefore 1 Ci equals 37 billion Bq.

- *Rad* A rad (derived from "radiation absorbed dose") is a measure of the amount of energy deposited in living tissue by radiation passing through it. A rad is defined as 100 ergs of energy deposited per gram of tissue. An erg is the amount of energy, or work done, by a force of 1 dyne acting through 1 centimeter; a dyne is the force required to accelerate a mass of 1 gram 1 centimeter per second per second.

  A human exposed to over 3000 rads will die within a few hours, first suffering from brain and central nervous system damage. A person exposed to 400 to 3000 rads over a short period of time will die within a few weeks, usually due to hemorrhages and other damage to the digestive system. An exposure of 250 rads will cause half of those exposed to die within two months due to damage to the bone marrow and blood vessels. A hundred rads will severely burn the skin, and a mere 5 rads can cause vomiting and diarrhea.

  A millirad (mrad) is one-thousandth of a rad. The international unit gray (Gy) is equal to 100 rads.

- *Rem* The rem (variously said to be derived from "radiation equivalent man" or "roentgen equivalent man"—Wilhelm Roentgen discovered X rays in 1895) measures the relative biological impact of absorbed radiation. The same number of rads of radiation can have different biological effects, depending on the type of radiation. A rem is a dose of radiation that produces biological effects in a human equivalent to the effects that are produced by exposure to one rad of X rays. A millirem (mrem) is one-thousandth of a rem. A centisievert, another measure of the biological effects of radiation, is equivalent to a rem. The international unit sievert (Sv) is equal to 100 rems.

  Depending upon where they live (elevation is particularly important) and other factors, Americans are typically exposed to between 200 and 360 millirems of ionizing radiation a year. About 80% of this radiation is background radiation, which comes from naturally occurring elements and cosmic rays. The other 20% of exposure is due to human-made radiation or radionuclides, such as remains from nuclear weapons explosions, waste and releases from nuclear power plants, nuclear medicine and medical X rays, and radiation given off by computers, televisions, and other machines.

ture, it would first be taken up by the grass. Next cows eating the grass would concentrate the strontium further in their milk and tissues, and finally very concentrated levels of the material would be found in the humans who drank the cows' milk or ate their flesh. Furthermore, radionuclides are not dispersed throughout the organism that ingests them, but are concentrated in certain tissues or organs. Thus, strontium-90 replaces the calcium atoms in bones and there does its damage, increasing the risk of leukemia and other blood-related diseases. Radionuclides, like other pollutants and toxins in general, also tend to be more damaging to the young and otherwise vulnerable (for instance, the weak or very old).

As they undergo natural fission, radionuclides eventually decay away to such small amounts that they are imperceptible. On a human time scale, however, many persist for very long periods. The half-life (the time required for half the atoms of a sample of a certain radioactive isotope to undergo radioactive decay) may be only a matter of days, or it may be measured in tens of thousands, millions, or billions of years. Radon-222 has a half-life of only about 3.8 days, and iodine-131 has a half-life of about 8 days, but the deadly plutonium-239 has a half-life of 24,000 years while uranium-233 has a half-life of 162,000 years. In rough terms the danger to humans and other organisms from moderate amounts of radionuclides lasts for about 10 times the half-life; after that period, enough has usually decayed away that the remaining quantities are negligible. Accordingly, the troublesome effects of radon-222 or iodine-131 may last only a few months (though this is plenty of time to induce cancers, mutations, disease, and possibly death in exposed organisms), the dangers of many radionuclides with intermediate half-lives of tens of years will last for hundreds of years, and the harmful effects of any plutonium will be with us for at least a quarter million years.

Of course, radiation from nuclear power plants is not a problem if it is not released into the environment. Unfortunately, however, radiation is sometimes inadvertently released, as occurred with the Chernobyl and Three Mile Island accidents.

CHERNOBYL AND THREE MILE ISLAND

The Chernobyl Disaster

In April 1986, a major nuclear reactor blew up, creating the single worst nuclear power plant dis-

bombing of Hiroshima and Nagasaki do not show such high incidences of leukemia.

Nuclear power plants, and the activities associated with them (such as fuel mining, processing, and disposal), invariably release radionuclides into the environment. Even small releases of radionuclides can be very dangerous for a number of reasons. In natural systems, these radioactive elements tend not to disperse, but rather are concentrated by either physical or biological processes. If a radioactive substance is spread evenly over an area, it will become approximately 10 times as concentrated in each step of the food chain. Thus, for example, if radioactive strontium from a nuclear fallout covered a pas-

The Petkau Effect

A substantial body of evidence indicates that extremely low doses of radiation are considerably more damaging to biological organisms than was initially suspected. This evidence is succinctly reviewed by Ralph Graeub in his book *The Petkau Effect: Nuclear Radiation, People and Trees* (1992). Most studies of the deleterious effects of radiation exposure undertaken before about 1960 came to the conclusion that low doses of radiation, up to perhaps a thousand times the annual background level of radiation that most people are exposed to, have little or no adverse health effect.

Beginning in the late 1950s, however, epidemiological studies began to suggest that low doses of artificial radiation, such as from X rays, fallout from atmospheric nuclear bomb testing, and the "normal" release of fission products from nuclear reactors, correlated with rises in childhood leukemia rates, spontaneous miscarriages, underweight births, and infant deaths.

In 1972 Abram Petkau, a scientist at the Canadian Atomic Energy Commission's Whiteshell Nuclear Research Establishment in Manitoba, discovered that cell membranes that could withstand relatively large radiation doses administered in short bursts would rupture when subjected to very low intensity radiation over a long period of time. Experts in the field had not expected this conclusion.

Petkau found that the observed radiation damage to cell membranes was due to other factors than simple disruption of DNA or other large molecules by being hit directly by radiation. The low doses of radiation produced O_2^- "free radicals" from normal O_2 dissolved in the fluid bathing the cell. When a free-radical oxygen molecule diffused to the cell membrane, it would initiate a series of reactions that caused the membrane to dissolve or break. The fluid of the cell would subsequently leak out, and the cell would die. A single free-radical oxygen molecule could destroy an entire cell. At high doses of radiation over short periods of time, many free-radical oxygen molecules

are created, and as they bump into one another, they deactivate each other, becoming regular oxygen. Large doses of radiation in short bursts are "overkill," and estimated radiation damage, or lack of damage, cannot be scaled down from such studies in a linear fashion.

Studies undertaken over the last three decades, combined with the known mechanism of the "**Petkau effect**," lend strong support to the suspicion that very small doses of radiation released by nuclear reactors and as fallout from bomb testing have a serious detrimental long-term effect not only on humanity, but on all living organisms. Such radionuclides find their way into the water and soil, thence into the systems of plants and the higher food chain. Radioactive strontium and iodine, for instance, are particularly insidious in milk—and milk is fed to children, who are the most vulnerable to radiation damage. Not only leukemia and other forms of cancer, infant mortality, and underweight births have been attributed to such low-level radiation, but also the decline of forests and other ecosystems, lowered learning abilities among humans, increased susceptibility to AIDS and other related immune system diseases, increased incidences of criminality (perhaps due to decreased mental capacities), and so on.

A study undertaken at the Ecological Sciences Department of the Battelle Northwest Laboratory, Hanford, Washington, found that rainbow trout exposed to extremely low concentrations (as low as 40 millirads—see Table 8–3) of tritium, a radioactive isotope of hydrogen, during early embryonic development suffered permanent suppression of immune system functions. These studies are extremely important because tritium is a major contributor to the radioactivity of the effluent from current fission power plants and would also most likely be released by any fusion-based reactors of the future.

A 1990 Massachusetts Health Department study found that the incidence of leukemia was four times higher than normally expected in 22 towns located within roughly 20 miles (32 km) of the Pilgrim nu-

clear power plant near Plymouth, Massachusetts. Atmospheric radioactive releases from the power plant were a likely cause of these abnormally high rates of leukemia.

Ronegelap Island, in Micronesia, suffered from fallout of an atomic bomb test on the Marshall Islands. During the 15 years following the test, children on the island consistently developed thyroid diseases and suffered from both mental and physical developmental deficiencies. In fact, radioactive isotopes such as iodine-131 collect in the thyroid, causing damage. Since the thyroid affects brain development, it is not surprising that decreased learning ability and impaired mental functions—even outright mental retardation—can be caused by radionuclides released into the environment. One study has demonstrated a highly significant correlation between declines in SAT (Scholastic Aptitude Test) scores and when and where children were carried in utero, born, and spent their earliest months relative to fallout from atmospheric atomic bomb testing carried out in Nevada during the 1950s and early 1960s. The state of Utah, very close to the Nevada test site and recipient of much radioactive fallout, had the highest decline in SAT scores for the cohorts of students born in 1956 through 1958. During those years, atomic bomb testing was in its heyday, and the recorded radioactive iodine content of cow's milk (a food frequently ingested by young children and pregnant or lactating mothers) was at a peak.

Plants and entire ecosystems are also affected by low levels of artificially released radiation. It has been found that artificial radioactive substances released into the atmosphere promote the formation of sulfur trioxide from sulfur dioxide, which in turn produces dangerously high levels of sulfuric acid, a key ingredient of "acid rain" (see Chapter 17). It is also believed that artificial radiation products can promote the production of dangerous ground level ozone (O_3) from molecular oxygen (O_2) and nitrogen oxides (NO_x) from atmospheric nitrogen (N_2).

aster so far ( Fig. 8–6). The Chernobyl nuclear reactor site, located on the Pripet River about 80 miles (130 km) from Kiev in Ukraine, consisted of four reactors. The Number 4 reactor exploded, releasing an estimated 185 to 250 million curies of radioactivity into the environment (official Soviet estimates initially stated that 50 million curies were released, but it is now known

mer Soviet Union) may result from the effects of Chernobyl over the next several decades. Chernousenko has suggested that perhaps 35 million people have been damaged by the high levels of radiation released from Chernobyl.

When the Chernobyl reactor exploded, a thick cloud of radioactive gases rose about a mile (1.6 km) into the atmosphere. These gases very

FIGURE 8–6
The damaged Chernobyl reactor as it appeared on May 28, 1986. (*Source*: Sovfoto/Eastfoto.)

that these numbers are too low). Within the first few months, according to official reports, 31 people died as a direct result of the explosion and the release of radiation (this includes a dozen firefighters who died of radiation poisoning), but the unofficial reports of mortalities are much higher. Dr. Vladimir Chernousenko, a nuclear physicist who was the scientific supervisor of the emergency damage control team sent into Chernobyl after the accident, has suggested that as many as 5000 to 7000 people may have died as a result of being exposed to radiation during the cleanup operations. The number who will ultimately die prematurely because of the incident could number in the tens of thousands. Immediately following the accident hundreds of people were diagnosed as having radiation sickness, and over 100,000 people living within 18.5 miles (30 km) of Chernobyl had to be evacuated. It has been estimated that as many as 40,000 to 70,000 additional cancer deaths (many of them occurring outside the for-

quickly covered much of the Northern Hemisphere, affecting areas over a thousand miles (over 1600 km) away. In Scandinavia, Germany, and Great Britain, plants and animals were contaminated by radioactivity for years and declared unsafe for human consumption. In Lapland the reindeer were declared unfit for human consumption due to radioactive contamination. In Italy thousands of tons of vegetables were unusable. In Corsica, as a result of eating local contaminated cheeses and other milk products, children were found to have large accumulations of radioactive iodine-131 in their thyroid glands (the gland in the neck that regulates growth). In all, over a hundred million Europeans were subjected to either voluntary or mandatory food restrictions over the next few years.

In Ukraine people in the contaminated areas suffered from numerous sicknesses, their immune systems weakened by the radiation. Trees and animals very close to the reactor simply died, but further away they suffered mutations manifested as deformities and abnormalities. Rates of farm animals born with serious deformities continued to rise throughout the late 1980s ( Fig. 8–7). Despite the dangers, the Soviet government did not ban or destroy large quantities of contaminated meat, milk products, and vegetables grown in regions adversely affected by the accident. Instead, the food reportedly was shipped to other parts of the country and mixed with uncontaminated produce. The former Soviet Union continually suffered from food shortages so the government apparently decided that it would be better not to "waste" even the radioactively contaminated food.

Three years after the Chernobyl accident, the official reports stated that the severely contaminated area around the nuclear power plant was much larger than first estimated. Over an area of approximately 3900 square miles (10,000 km²), contamination was at a level of 15 curies or

dent, and no one knows what the ultimate costs may be. The direct costs are expected to be greater than the Soviet government's total investment in nuclear power before the accident. Crude financial costs include not only the loss of an expensive nuclear reactor and the "cleanup" and evacuation costs, but also medical expenses, lost food production, loss of agricultural land, loss of villages and cities that had to be abandoned, and lost business investments and potential. Damage, and therefore costs, due to the accident will continue to manifest themselves for centuries. But the most pervasive and devastating costs cannot even be calculated monetarily; they manifest themselves socially, psychologically, and physiologically. What are the costs of tens of thousands of cancers that result in suffering and decreased life expectancies? What are the costs of birth defects and chromosomal abnormalities that appear generations later? What will our great-great-grandchildren think of the catastrophe called Chernobyl?

FIGURE 8–7
A colt born in Ukraine after the Chernobyl accident has deformed legs and even extra legs and hooves. (*Source:* Igor Kostin/Sygma.)

higher per square kilometer—a very unsafe level. According to some estimates, a quarter million people still lived in badly contaminated areas. Four years after the accident, 627,000 Soviets were under permanent observation for symptoms and effects of radiation poisoning.

The financial costs of the Chernobyl accident totaled about $13 billion four years after the inci-

The Chernobyl accident was initiated by operator error, but various design defects (such as inadequate control systems and the lack of a containment vessel) made matters worse. The accident occurred during a test of the backup electrical system. The operators were supposed to slow down the reactor so that it would run at a low level during the test, but they found they had

Only the gallant but suicidal work of firefighters and other emergency workers kept the fire from spreading to an adjacent nuclear reactor. Thousands of tons of boron, lead, and other radiation-absorbing materials had to be dropped onto the reactor, but unfortunately much or all of this material may have missed the actual core. Nitrogen was pumped under the reactor vessel to cool it, and finally the damaged reactor was entombed in reinforced concrete to try to contain the remaining radiation (Fig. 8–8). No one is sure how long this tomb will hold; the radiation may begin to destroy it and leak through. Already there are reports that this concrete tomb is riddled with holes, structurally unstable, and could collapse at any time. Approximately 1000 square miles (2600 km²) of land around Chernobyl will remain contaminated with high levels of radioactivity into the indefinite future.

Irrespective of the reasons for the Chernobyl accident, the fact is that a major disaster occurred. Furthermore, over a dozen reactors of the same design type are still operating in Russia, Ukraine, and Lithuania. Despite the early predictions of nuclear advocates that the probability of a major catastrophe was negligible, we now know that catastrophes do occur. Chernobyl was not even the first major nuclear accident.

Three Mile Island and Other Accidents

In March 1979, a nuclear meltdown nearly occurred in the United States. At the Three Mile Island nuclear power plant (Fig. 8–9) near Harrisburg, Pennsylvania, a minor problem developed in the plumbing of TMI Unit 2 with the end result that cooling water drained away from the reactor and the core began to partially melt—the worst commercial nuclear power plant accident in the United States to date. Operator errors, a stuck valve, faulty sensors, and design errors are all partially to blame for what happened at Three Mile Island. Although some radioactive gas was released due to the accident (only one thousandth as much as at Chernobyl), fortunately the containment structure around the reactor held most of the radioactivity in—about 18 billion curies of radioactivity that could have been released had the structure failed (compare this to the mere 185–250 million curies released at Chernobyl). Nuclear advocates have hailed the Three Mile Island accident as "proof" that a more serious accident would not occur in the United States—for the containment structure did hold. Many experts, however, have concluded that luck more than anything else kept the Three Mile

slowed it too much. To speed up the reaction again, they pulled out too many control rods and reduced the amount of water cooling the reactor. The reaction sped up, but quickly went out of control. Intense heat caused an explosion that blew the roof, weighing about 1000 tons (900 metric tons), off the reactor and shot radioactive elements into the atmosphere, and a major fire started. Recent studies indicate that the actual reactor core at Chernobyl underwent a meltdown, burning through a steel and gravel barrier 6 feet (1.8 m) thick; it remained exposed for 10 days, all the while releasing radiation.

Island accident from being worse. Some scientists have calculated that the core, which reached temperatures in the range of 4800 to 5000°F (2650–2750°C) or higher, was just short of becoming hot enough to totally melt down. If emergency measures had not been initiated when they were, given another 20 to 30 minutes, the core might have completely melted through the steel reactor vessel and containment unit, releasing all 18 billion curies of radioactivity.

More than a decade after the accident, the reactor core is still highly radioactive and dangerous despite a billion dollars spent on cleaning up (the final cost is expected to be at least twice that amount). No one knows for certain what the health effects of Three Mile Island are, in large part because no one is certain how much radiation was actually released. A few days after the accident the then-governor of Pennsylvania, Richard Thornburgh, evacuated all young children and pregnant women from within a 5-mile (8 km) radius of Three Mile Island as a safety precaution. Over 150,000 other people within an approximately 15-mile (24 km) radius of the plant voluntarily left the area for several days or more. At the least there is evidence that due to radioactive-induced damage to immune systems, Three Mile Island contributed to the premature deaths of some elderly people in the affected area. Dairy farmers reported that many animals died shortly after the accident, local residents have come down with leukemia and other cancers, and one study suggested that an increase in infant mortality and severe thyroid disorders in babies born after the accident was due to the effects of radiation exposure.

Chernobyl and Three Mile Island are not the only serious nuclear accidents that have occurred since the beginning of the nuclear age. Two often-cited catastrophes took place in 1957. A toxic fire at England's Windscale (now known as Sellafield) nuclear reactor released large quantities of radioactive polonium and iodine-131, contaminating some 530,00 gallons (2 million liters) of local farms' milk; the condemned milk was dumped into local rivers and the Atlantic Ocean. The radiation released is estimated to have caused several hundred cancers and possibly birth defects. The Windscale reactor was used to produce plutonium for nuclear weapons, and a graphite moderator overheated, temperature indicators malfunctioned, and a fire ensued. The incidence of leukemia in the vicinity of Windscale is now 10 times above the national average for England.

In late 1957, an explosion occurred at a Soviet nuclear weapons factory known as Chelyabinsk-40, near the city of Kyshtym in the Ural Mountains; reportedly, hundreds of people died from radioactive contamination, and over 10,000 people were evacuated from the contaminated area. Few of the details of what happened at Chelyabinsk are known; apparently, a tank full of radioactive gases exploded. Soviet officials did not even acknowledge that this accident had occurred until 1988. Currently, the region around the plant is sealed off, and over 30 towns in the area have disappeared—they no longer can be found on maps of the region.

Besides these major accidents, over the past four decades there have been literally tens of thousands of minor accidents and mishaps at nuclear power plants, thousands of emergency shutdowns, and hundreds of thousands of cases where nuclear power plant workers were exposed to higher than permissible levels of radiation. Overall, one can argue that the safety record of the nuclear industry is abysmal. Between 1979 and 1990, the Nuclear Regulatory Commission (NRC) recorded 33,000 mishaps at nuclear power plants in the United States; a thousand of these were considered to be "particularly significant." In the United States, in 1985 alone there were 430 emergency nuclear plant shutdowns, and in 18 of these cases, the core of the reactor was damaged. Among 14 Western countries, 150 serious accidents occurred at nuclear power plants from 1971 to 1984.

FIGURE 8–9
The Three Mile Island nuclear power plant near Harrisburg, Pennsylvania.
(*Source*: F. Edwords/Visuals Unlimited.)

Many of these accidents are clearly attributable to human error, but that does not stop them from happening. A classic case in point is the fire that broke out at the Brown's Ferry nuclear power plant near Decatur, Alabama, in 1975. It was initiated by a maintenance worker using a candle to check for air leaks around electrical cables. A meltdown was just barely averted; several core-cooling systems were destroyed during the fire, but a supplemental pump did go into action and siphoned cooling water to the reactor core. It seems that given human imperfections, nuclear accidents are unavoidable—indeed, at least minor mishaps appear to be par for the industry. In testimony before a committee of the U.S. House of Representatives on 22 May 1986 the then NRC Commissioner James Asseltine stated: "We can expect to see another serious [nuclear] accident in this country during the next 20 years" (quoted in Naar, 1990, p. 153). Galperin (1992, p. 85) states that "some NRC officials still estimate a 45% chance of a Chernobyl-scale accident occurring in the United States by the year 2000; the likelihood that one will happen somewhere in the world before then is even higher."

Could a Chernobyl-Style Accident Happen in the United States?

The Chernobyl accident demonstrated some of the dangers of nuclear power generation: some types of reactors can explode and spread radioactive debris around the globe. The effects of a major nuclear disaster are not limited to the country in which it occurs. Nuclear power advocates, however, have argued that the Chernobyl accident simply points up the flaws in Soviet-style reactors. Indeed, some experts contend that the type of accident that occurred at Chernobyl could not occur in the United States because the design of American-type reactors is very different from the design of reactors built in the former Soviet Union.

The two principal types of reactors in use today are (1) American-type light water reactors, which burn uranium enriched to 3% U-235 and use ordinary water as a moderator, and (2) Soviet-type reactors, which burn either natural or only very slightly enriched uranium, but use a graphite moderator. The Chernobyl accident involved the latter type of reactor.

In American-type reactors, the water moderator circulates around the fuel rods, serving also to cool them. In a Soviet-type graphite reactor, the core is essentially a large block of graphite with holes in it in which the uranium fuel rods are placed. Water also flows around the fuel rods through tubes in these holes, removing heat. But unlike an American-type reactor, where the water actually promotes the fission reaction in its capacity as a moderator, in Soviet-type reactors the water captures some neutrons and thus slows down the chain reaction. The water is said to "poison" the fission reaction.

In an American-type reactor, if the supply of water around the fuel rods is reduced or lost (such as during an accident— perhaps the reactor overheats and water boils off), the chain reaction will slow down because it has lost its moderator. Note, however, that an American-type reactor that has lost its water can still overheat because newly formed fission products will continue to undergo radioactive decay, thus giving off heat. In contrast, if a Soviet-type graphite reactor loses its water, the fission reaction will speed up, and temperatures will rise dramatically. If temperatures rise high enough, the graphite moderator (composed of carbon, as is coal) will catch on fire. A burning graphite moderator, with fuel rods buried inside it, is an excellent way to inject radioactive dust into the atmosphere, which is what happened during the Chernobyl accident. For these reasons, American-type light water reactors are considered more stable and much safer.

Soviet-type graphite reactors offer certain advantages, however. Such reactors can burn either natural uranium or only very slightly enriched uranium, saving the trouble and expense of enriching the natural uranium. They can also be used to produce weapons-grade plutonium. In the reactor U-238 is converted into Pu-239, which can then be used in weapons manufacturing. If the Pu-239 is left in the reactor for too long (longer than about 30 days), a substantial portion may be converted to Pu-240. Pu-240 is not well-suited to bomb production; too high a percentage of Pu-240 in the plutonium results in much less powerful explosions. A typical Soviet-type reactor contains over a thousand separate fuel rods, each enclosed in its own tube in the graphite moderator. The fuel rods can easily be removed and replaced one at a time without shutting down the whole reactor. If the reactor is being used to produce plutonium for bombs, fuel rods can easily be changed on a monthly basis. In contrast, in a typical American-type reactor, all of the fuel is encased within the reactor vessel, and changing the fuel is a major undertaking. The entire reactor must be shut down for about a month while the vessel is opened and the fuel is changed (Fig. 8–10). Typically, an American-type reactor is at least partially refueled every 12 to 18 months, although particular fuel pellets may remain within the vessel for several years. This severely restricts the possibility of using an American-type commercial reactor for the production of weapons-grade fissionable material.

One other important difference between American-type and Soviet-type nuclear reactors is worth noting: Soviet-type reactors, such as the one at Chernobyl, do not include the elaborate containment structures of American-type commercial reactors because containment structures would interfere with the operators' ability to change the fuel regularly. If the fuel cannot be changed regularly, then the reactor cannot be used to produce weapons-grade material.

SAFER NUCLEAR REACTORS

The typical nuclear reactor is very large and complex. In the United States, the average nuclear reactor has about 40,000 valves compared to about 4000 valves for a coal-burning power plant that generates approximately the same amount of electricity. Ten times as many valves means 10 times as many chances for a valve to go bad or be turned the wrong way, perhaps leading to an accident. The complexity of nuclear reactors makes them difficult to build, especially where the designs are not standardized and each reactor is essentially designed and built from scratch. During the building of nuclear reactors, such errors as improper weldings, air bubbles in cement, unstable foundations, and even a reactor vessel that was initially installed backward (fortunately, someone noticed the mistake some months later before the plant was completed) have been documented.

This complexity makes nuclear reactors very expensive to build. Due to this great expense, commercial utilities tend to build large reactors that have the capacity to generate large amounts of energy that can be sold to cover the expense of the reactor and still generate a profit. Thus, commercial nuclear reactors in the United States typically have a capacity of 1000 megawatts or greater. Of course, the larger the reactor, the larger the potential catastrophe if anything malfunctions.

Addressing these sorts of concerns, a new series of nuclear fission reactors are currently being designed. These reactors will probably be smaller and will include such features as passive safety systems, and modular designs.

Passive safety systems will depend on natural forces, such as gravity, to cool and control the reactor, especially in the event that an accident oc-

curs. Rather than relying on pumps and complex mazes of pipes to bring water to an overheating core, a passive design might have cooling water located in storage tanks directly above the reactor vessel. Under normal conditions, the water would not be released, but in an emergency, valves would open, and the water would be dumped directly on the core to cool it. Valves could even be installed that would open automatically if the temperature rose above a certain point. The core itself might be buried in a cavity underground to protect it from such dangers as an airplane crashing into it (perhaps an unlikely event, but potentially disastrous if it should occur). Pilot tests of small experimental reactors incorporating such passive safety systems have met with success.

Building standardized reactors that are made of modular components (series of identical sub-

FIGURE 8–10
A technician carefully inspects fuel rods before they are inserted into a reactor. (*Source:* Science VU—API/Visuals Unlimited.)

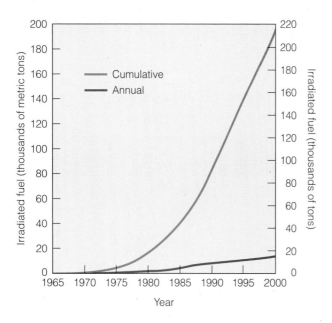

■ **FIGURE 8–11**
World generation of
irradiated fuel from
commercial nuclear power
plants, 1965–2000. (*Source:*
Based on data from L. R. Brown *et
al.*, *State of the World 1992* [New
York: W. W. Norton, 1992], p. 51,
and L. R. Brown, N. Lenssen, and
H. Kane, *Vital Signs 1995* [New
York: W. W. Norton, 1995], p. 89.
Reprinted with permission of
Worldwatch Institute, Washington,
D.C., Copyright 1992.)

units) could reduce the risks of errors occurring during construction. The modules might even be prefabricated in a factory and then brought to the construction site. Assembly procedures could be streamlined, and the risk of potential errors reduced. Standardization and modular construction would also reduce costs, and make it more practical to build smaller nuclear power plants. Such smaller reactors might also run at lower temperatures than the reactors currently in use; lower-temperature reactors would probably mean overall safer reactors. A reactor design currently under development in Great Britain has a planned output of only 320 megawatts.

*D*ISPOSAL OF NUCLEAR WASTES

Although nuclear reactors have been on line since the 1950s, and massive amounts of radioactive wastes have been generated by nuclear reactors and nuclear weapons–manufacturing facilities, no satisfactory plan has been implemented to dispose of these wastes. Nuclear wastes include spent fuel, radioactive products generated in the core of a reactor during operation, contaminated materials and clothing, and radioactive mining wastes and tailings. (Wastes from the use of radioisotopes in medicine, smoke alarms, and the like are also radioactive, but pose a relatively minor problem.) Some of this material is highly radioactive and will remain so for hundreds of thousands or millions of years; other nuclear waste materials are characterized by low, but still very dangerous, levels of radioactivity. It is estimated that worldwide more than 154,000 tons

(140,000 metric tons) of irradiated nuclear fuel and hundreds of thousands of tons of other radioactive wastes have accumulated from commercial nuclear power generation. The amount of irradiated uranium fuel waste has approximately doubled since 1989 and is continuing to accumulate at a fast pace (■ Fig. 8–11). By the end of the century, it could amount to more than 209,000 tons (190,000 metric tons).

This irradiated uranium fuel includes some of the most hazardous types of radioactive wastes. In the United States, irradiated uranium is less than 1% by volume of all radioactive wastes, but accounts for 95% of the radioactivity of radioactive wastes. The typical American commercial reactor discharges about 33 tons (30 metric tons) of irradiated fuel each year. Initially, this fuel is extremely radioactive and hot and decays relatively quickly—but it will continue to emit significant quantities of radiation for thousands of years.

Currently, more than 30 countries are operating nuclear power plants, yet nowhere in the world has a permanent disposal system for high-level nuclear wastes been fully developed, much less put into place. Instead, the spent fuel rods and other high-level wastes are generally stored "temporarily" on-site in pools of water (■ Fig. 8–12). So much high-level, extremely toxic nuclear waste is now stored in this manner that many reactors are running out of temporary storage space. Low-level nuclear wastes, which occur in much larger volume, have generally been placed in steel drums and the like and buried in shallow landfills. In the United States in 1989, for example, 60,000 cubic yards (46,000 m³) of civilian low-level wastes (mostly generated by the nuclear power industry), as well as nearly 100,000 cubic yards (76,000 m³) of weapons-generated low-level waste were disposed of in shallow trenches. At numerous such sites, the radioactive wastes have leached into the ground, contaminating soils and water.

The nuclear industry began and expanded without ever fully tackling the problem of waste disposal. So far, despite years of work, no results have been forthcoming. Part of the difficulty is that nuclear waste disposal involves complex technical, political, and social issues. Given their toxicity, nuclear wastes must be perfectly contained, for even small leaks can have potentially disastrous effects. Furthermore, the wastes must be contained and guarded for tens of thousands to millions of years, a time span that is almost incomprehensible considering that our species has inhabited the planet for only a few tens of thousands to perhaps a hundred thousand years. The nuclear wastes are not simply "worthless" wastes; certain high-level nuclear wastes, such as those containing fissionable uranium or plutonium, are the essential ingredient of nuclear weapons. Therefore, they must be guarded and remain secure so that they do not fall into the wrong hands. Even the transportation of nuclear wastes to a permanent, secure repository is fraught with difficulties. What if an accident happens during transportation and the wastes are released into the environment? What if a hostile group seizes a convoy carrying high-level nuclear wastes? Already some jurisdictions have banned the transportation of nuclear wastes through their territory, making any transportation routes longer, more circuitous, and potentially more dangerous.

Many suggestions for dealing with nuclear wastes have been put forth. Some people have suggested that we get them off the planet completely, perhaps by loading them onto rockets and shooting them into the Sun. The costs of such an undertaking would be almost incalculable given the volume of wastes that must be disposed of. Depending on the rocket engines used, massive amounts of energy would be required, and massive amounts of greenhouse gases would be added to the atmosphere during the process, effectively nullifying one of the primary advantages of nuclear power in the first place. Furthermore, the valuable raw materials that would go into the manufacture of such rockets would be lost forever, putting even more pressure on our dwindling mineral supplies (see Chapter 10). Finally, think of the disastrous consequences if a rocket ship laden with high-level nuclear waste were to explode in the atmosphere.

Schemes to bury nuclear wastes at the bottom of the oceans or inside glaciers in Antarctica have also been proposed. But both the oceans and the ice are very delicate ecosystems, and contamination by nuclear wastes could have extremely damaging effects. The heat given off by radioactive wastes might even begin to melt the relatively unstable Antarctic ice sheets. Furthermore, both the oceans and ice have already been contaminated by nuclear wastes. Nuclear fallout from weapons testing is detectable even in the polar regions. From the 1940s through the 1960s, barrels of radioactive wastes were often dumped directly into the oceans. Now a number of these barrels are leaking and contaminating the seas.

Some persons have suggested that radioactive wastes could be inserted into subduction zones at colliding plate boundaries (see Chapter 2) and thus forced deep into the Earth. This scheme appears to be extremely unrealistic, however. The initial insertion of the radioactive wastes would

FIGURE 8–12
A fuel rod storage pool at a nuclear power plant. (*Source*: Science VU/Visuals Unlimited.)

probably require deep excavation or drilling in a very active geologic terrain. Rates of subduction are so slow (several inches or tens of centimeters a year), that the wastes would take an inordinately long time to be subducted into the Earth. Finally, since subduction zones are very active geologically (ringed by areas of intense earthquake and volcanic activity), the radioactive materials could be spewed back to the surface before they are safely subducted into the lower layers of the Earth's crust.

■ FIGURE 8–13
Interior view of the storage facilities at the Yucca Mountain proposed national nuclear waste repository. (*Source:* Sander/Gamma Liaison.)

Another suggestion is to store radioactive wastes on otherwise deserted islands, at least temporarily until more permanent disposal facilities are established. Again, such a scheme poses grave risks to the biosphere, and the islands would have to be heavily guarded on a permanent basis.

Another idea that is being actively explored by scientists in the United States, France, Japan, and Russia is to convert radioactive wastes to less dangerous, or shorter-lived, isotopes by bombarding the waste with neutrons. Such transmutation of elements would be technically difficult, however, and probably very energy-intensive and expensive.

The suggestion currently favored by many governmental and nongovernmental authorities in the United States and other countries that use nuclear power is to develop disposal facilities buried deep underground in geologically stable regions, perhaps in old mines. The U.S. National Research Council has concluded that geological burial is the "best, safest long-term option" for disposing of high-level radioactive waste (see Issues in Perspective 8–3). The problem is to find an underground formation that is isolated from the general environment (for instance, groundwater cannot be flowing through the site) and is not in an area of geological activity such as earthquakes or volcanic eruptions. One must be able to guarantee that the site will remain stable for tens of thousands to millions of years—a virtual impossibility given the active nature of the Earth's crust (see Chapter 2). Even if a geologically appropriate site is located, social and political considerations can be a problem. When a nuclear waste disposal facility is proposed, local residents tend to give a NIMBY ("not in my back yard") response.

Old salt mines have been proposed as storage facilities, but some mines have water percolating into them that forms a very corrosive brine. This solution will damage the steel drums containing the radioactive wastes and allow the contents to leak out. In 1987 Congress proposed that Yucca Mountain, located about 85 miles (136 km) northwest of Las Vegas, Nevada, on land owned by the Shoshone Native Americans, should become the ultimate national nuclear waste repository (■ Fig. 8–13). From a political perspective, Yucca Mountain has advantages as a nuclear repository site: the population of Nevada is fairly small, which limits potential opposition, and the site is part of the former Nevada Test Site where nuclear weapons were tested, thus setting a precedent for nuclear-related activities in the area. Yet it is unclear if Yucca Mountain is appropriate from a geological perspective. Various U.S. Geological Survey geologists and engineers who have evaluated the site have raised questions about it. Yucca Mountain is surrounded by geological faults and volcanoes. Since 1857 eight major earthquakes have occurred within a 250 mile (400 km) radius of Yucca Mountain. Although none of the volcanoes in the immediate vicinity have erupted in historical times, estimates are that one volcano erupted a mere 5000 years ago. Thus, Yucca Mountain's geological stability for even the next 10,000 or 20,000 years seems questionable.

Another major problem with Yucca Mountain, or virtually any proposed nuclear waste repository on land, is that predicting the climate of the area

Radioactive Waste—An "Unsolved Problem" or a "Trivial Technical Problem"?

Although opponents of nuclear power view the disposal of nuclear waste as a major unsolved problem, proponents of nuclear power such as Dr. Bernard L. Cohen maintain that "radioactive waste disposal is a rather trivial technical problem" (Cohen, 1990, p. 173). Cohen contends that just because the waste produced by nuclear power plants is radioactive, it is not necessarily more dangerous than the greenhouse gases, sulfur dioxide (the principal cause of acid rain), particulates, and even radioactive radon gas spewed into the air by coal-fired power plants. He also suggests a rather simple solution to the radioactive waste problem.

Cohen argues that rather than attempting to dispose of spent reactor fuel directly, we should reprocess it to separate the still usable uranium and plutonium and then dispose of the remaining (and much less bulky) wastes. He points out that without reprocessing, the supply of uranium could run out in less than a hundred years, whereas with reprocessing (and breeder technology) the nuclear fuel supply is virtually inexhaustible. Although the United States does no reprocessing at present due primarily to public opposition spurred by fear of nuclear proliferation, many other countries already operate reprocessing plants.

In outline, Cohen's scenario for high-level waste disposal is that 35 tons (32 metric tons) of spent fuel produced per year by a typical 1000 megawatt power plant would be reprocessed, resulting in a ton and a half (1.36 metric tons) of high-level radioactive wastes. This waste would then be vitrified, that is, turned into glass, using a technology already developed. The total would be about 15 tons (13.6 metric tons) of glass. Once in glass form, the waste would be shipped to a federal repository, such as the proposed Yucca Mountain site, and there buried deep underground. To protect the radioactive waste from coming into contact with

groundwater or the environment in general, the glass would be encased within a stainless steel container that would in turn be enclosed in a corrosion-resistant casing and further protected by several more layers of material before being placed in its underground rock vault. With all of these precautions, advocates of nuclear power feel that there is a minuscule chance that large amounts of radioactivity will be released. As a bottom line, Cohen estimates that we can expect about 0.018 fatalities, spread over millions of years, from the properly stored high-level wastes produced by a single nuclear power plant over the course of a year. Most of these fatalities would be due to eventual release of the waste as the rock is eroded down to the level of the buried waste—but by the time this occurred, most of the radioactivity from the wastes would be gone since the radioactive isotopes constantly decay away.

Cohen and others contend that the real problem with radioactive waste "has been the waste of taxpayers' money spent to protect us from the imagined dangers of nuclear waste" (Cohen, 1990, p. 213). As an example of money wasted, Cohen cites the case of West Valley, New York. West Valley was the site of a commercial fuel-reprocessing plant that operated from 1966 until it was permanently shut down in 1972. After the plant was closed, the operators had to decide what to do with high-level wastes stored in an underground tank.

Although the site was well protected from leakage—the tank was actually one tank inside another tank, surrounded by a concrete vault within a gravel-lined cavity within highly impermeable clay—it was feared that the tank might leak, allowing radioactive wastes to enter the groundwater and eventually Lake Erie, where they might affect tens of thousands of people. Cohen contends that even if the tank had leaked, any radioactivity would have caused little harm by the time it reached the public at large. Still, given the situation, to do

nothing is not a very satisfactory course of action in most people's minds.

One proposal was to pour a cement mixture into the tank, thus converting it into a large block of stable, albeit radioactive, cement. This procedure would have cost an estimated $20 million. There would be very little chance that the barriers to the tank would be breached and the cement then eroded away by groundwater so as to release the radioactivity. However, to be on the safe side, Cohen suggests that a $15 million trust fund could have been set up to pay for monitoring and surveillance of the site forever.

Another option, the one finally selected, was to remove the high-level waste from the tank, convert it to glass, and bury it in a deep underground repository as described previously. This procedure will cost considerably more money—about $1 billion—and is potentially much more dangerous than doing nothing or pouring in cement. In removing the waste, transporting it, converting it to glass, and reburying it, there is always the risk that some will be lost or spilled into the environment. Furthermore, the workers carrying out the procedure will be exposed to levels of radiation that are higher than ordinary background levels of radiation. Indeed, this exposure of the workers alone quite possibly could cause more damage than the waste ever would if it were simply left in its tank at West Valley. In sum, not only is about $965 million more being spent on the West Valley waste than need be, but the risk of detrimental effects due to the waste has actually increased. Although this approach may not seem to make sense, consider it from a local political perspective—local politicians respond to local concerns, and the local folks want the radioactive waste completely removed. Likewise, at a national level, senators and representatives can be persuaded that cleaning up the radioactive mess in this manner is the correct course of action.

for the next ten thousand years or so is impossible. At present, Yucca Mountain is located in a desert, and the water table is very deep below the surface. This is good because any water seeping into the repository could corrode canisters and mobilize radioactive waste. But given the potential for climatic change (see Chapter 18), there are no guarantees that Yucca Mountain will not experience significantly increased levels of precipitation in the future. Rainwater could not only seep into and leach the radioactive waste, resulting in radioactive runoff, but it could also cause the water table to rise and flood the nuclear waste. The net result could be massive leaking of high-level radioactive wastes into the groundwater system.

Military Defense Plant Waste

In addition to the radioactive wastes accumulating at commercial reactors and civilian dumps and repositories, radioactive wastes are also presenting a major problem at military plants and installations. Reportedly, military installations are plagued by unsafe working conditions, and their storage facilities for radioactive waste are inadequate; some have been charged with releasing radioactive substances into the environment. One of the worst in the United States is the Hanford Nuclear Reservation in Washington State. In 1956, 450,000 gallons (1.7 million liters) of high-level radioactive waste were spilled there, and in December 1988, the Department of Energy acknowledged that radioactive wastes leaking from Hanford had contaminated underground water supplies used for drinking and crop irrigation. Radioactive wastes reportedly have entered the Columbia River and then been carried to the Pacific Ocean, contaminating shellfishes hundreds of miles away.

The U.S. Office of Technology Assessment has stated that there is "evidence that air, groundwater, surface water, sediments, and soil, as well as vegetation and wildlife, have been contaminated at most, if not all, of the Department of Energy nuclear weapons sites" (quoted in Lenssen, 1992, p. 52). According to current estimates the U.S. government, and thus ultimately the taxpayers, will have to spend $200 billion to $300 billion over the next 60 years to clean up nuclear weapons facilities and related installations.

The situation in the former Soviet Union is believed to be even worse. When manufacturing nuclear weapons materials, the Soviets typically dumped wastes into the nearest river or lake. The Chelyabinsk-40 weapons facility in the Ural Mountains dumped its wastes into the Techa River, and as early as 1951, Soviet scientists were detecting radioactivity 940 miles (1500 km) away in the Arctic Ocean. The Soviets consequently decided to dump the radioactive wastes into the inland Lake Karachay. As a result, the lake became so radioactive that it is believed that to this day a person who dared to stand on the shore for only an hour would die of radiation poisoning. In 1967 a hot summer dried up the lake, and the wind carried radioactive dust 45 miles (75 km) away, spreading contamination over an area inhabited by 41,000 persons. As in the United States, the cost of cleaning up this nuclear nightmare will be enormous—and even so, it is unlikely that all the land and waters affected will ever be returned to anything close to their natural conditions.

$\mathcal{D}$ ECOMMISSIONING NUCLEAR REACTORS

A nuclear reactor cannot last forever. The high temperatures and radiation bombardment, especially the neutron bombardment of the reactor vessel, cause it to weaken and become brittle over time. If allowed to run for a long enough period of time, eventually the whole plant will become contaminated and weakened by radiation. Pipes may begin to break, instruments may fail, and structural components collapse. The reactor vessel could even rupture. For these reasons, any nuclear power plant, even if it has a flawless record of operation, must eventually be taken out of service—it must be **decommissioned**.

Many researchers consider the appropriate life span of a good nuclear reactor to be in the range of 30 to 40 years. Until recently, nuclear power plants in the United States were only licensed for 40 years, after which they would have to be decommissioned. Since more than 60 nuclear power plants in the country began operating in the 1960s, we are currently approaching a time when many of these plants should begin planning for decommissioning. In June 1991, however, the Nuclear Regulatory Commission approved a plan that allows plants to apply for a renewal of their operating license for up to 20 more years. This ruling may push the costs and problems of massive decommissionings into the future, but many people worry that it may also increase the risks of major accidents as the aging plants continue to operate.

A fully operational large-scale commercial nuclear power plant has never been fully decommissioned in the United States, and scientists are not in complete agreement on what decommissioning will involve or how much it will cost. The spent fuel will have to be removed from the reactor site and eventually stored in some permanent storage facility. As far as the reactor complex itself, several options have been suggested. The plant could simply be closed up, fenced off, and put under guard. Such mothballing is perhaps the cheapest solution in the short run and also allows the plant to be reopened in the future. Or the plant could be further dismantled in the future, after the levels of radiation have died down. In some ways however, mothballing is also the most dangerous option because the radioactivity is still on site; if not guarded carefully, it could be disturbed purposefully or inadvertently, perhaps resulting in radiation leaking into the surrounding environment. A second option is to entomb the plant—seal it off by encasing it in concrete and steel so that nothing, including radioactivity, can get in or out. Entombment is currently being used to deal with the damaged Chernobyl reactor. Finally, a decommissioned power plant could be totally dismantled. All components, structures, and so on would be taken apart or cut up. All materials contaminated with radioactivity, including soil and water, would be removed to a safe facility for the permanent storage of radioactive waste.

Estimated costs to completely decommission and dismantle a nuclear power plant are $3 billion or more. For comparison, building a nuclear plant costs approximately $4 to $9 billion, and takes about 15 years. If the plant runs at full capacity for 40 years, it will generate about $12 billion worth of electricity. In reality, however, typical U.S. power plants operate at only about 60% capacity.

GLOBAL NUCLEAR POWER TODAY AND IN THE FUTURE

Between 1960 and 1990, the world's electrical generating capacity of nuclear power plants increased steadily from 0.8 gigawatts in 1960 to 329 gigawatts in 1990 (Fig. 8–14; see Appendix A for an explanation of gigawatts and related units). Since 1990 the world's nuclear capacity has remained around 326 to 340 gigawatts. This electricity is produced by some 430 commercial nuclear power plants, of which approximately 25%

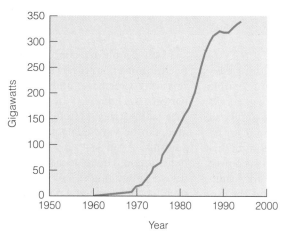

FIGURE 8–14
World electrical generating capacity of nuclear power plants, 1960–1994. (*Source*: L. R. Brown, H. Kane, and D. M. Roodman, Vital Signs 1994 [New York: W. W. Norton, 1994], p. 53, updated based on L. R. Brown, N. Lenssen, and H. Kane, *Vital Signs 1995* [New York: W. W. Norton, 1995], p. 53. Reprinted with permission of Worldwatch Institute, Washington, D.C., Copyright 1994.)

are located in the United States. Some analysts predict that the global nuclear generating capacity may rise slightly above 340–350 gigawatts, but that it will peak before the year 2000 and then subsequently decline slightly before reaching a stable plateau.

Around the world new nuclear reactors are being built while older reactors are being taken off line. As older plants age in North America and Western Europe, many large plants, perhaps several dozen by the beginning of the next century, could be decommissioned without being locally replaced by new nuclear power plants. Instead, coal plants, natural gas plants, and alternative energy sources (see Chapter 9) could pick up the slack in these countries. In Canada and the United States, the active construction of nuclear power plants has come to a virtual halt, as it has in most Western European countries except France. France continues to remain heavily invested in nuclear power, and a few new plants are still under construction there.

Even as nuclear power plays a lesser role in the West, it is increasing in the East. Japan continues to build new nuclear power plants, as does South Korea. India is actively developing its nuclear capacity. Reportedly, China, Taiwan, and possibly Thailand are planning to build new nuclear power plants in the future. Russia and Ukraine have plans for more than 20 nuclear reactors. Thus, if current construction and decommissioning trends continue, by the middle or end of the next century nuclear power could be a predominantly eastern European and Asian phenomenon.

Nuclear power is a way of generating electricity by harnessing the energy within atoms. Nuclear power plants are generally large, expensive, and complex—a classic form of "hard" energy technology (see Chapter 7). Due to the dangers of the radioactivity associated with nuclear power, the concern over the potential for proliferation of nuclear weapons, and the fact that the problem of permanent disposal of nuclear waste has not yet been satisfactorily solved, nuclear power has been and remains extremely controversial. Nuclear power generation contributes very little in the way of greenhouse gases and other nonradioactive pollutants, and utilizing breeder reactors and reprocessing spent nuclear fuel could assure large quantities of energy to power industrial society far into the future. Advocates of nuclear power highlight these advantages.

Many people are opposed to the use of nuclear power, however. Nuclear power is relatively expensive, and many potential dangers are inherent in the technology. The radioactive materials used and generated can be very damaging to living organisms. A nuclear power plant, opponents argue, could be subject to a major disaster that might kill or injure large numbers of people and possibly spread radioactive contaminants over a large area of the globe. In recent decades, two actual nuclear accidents, Chernobyl and Three Mile Island, have drawn much attention. Finally, nuclear power plants generate large amounts of high-level radioactive waste that must be disposed of, and eventually, the nuclear power plant must be decommissioned at substantial expense.

The world's electrical generating capacity using nuclear power plants increased steadily from the 1960s until about 1990, but since then it has remained relatively stable. Currently, some 430 commercial nuclear power plants are in operation (about 25% are located in the United States). Some analysts predict that over the next 20 years, approximately the same number of new nuclear reactors will come on line as older plants go off; thus, the total number of nuclear power plants may remain stable on a global level. However, it appears that the global distribution of nuclear power plants may change. Older plants in North America and Western Europe (with the exception of France) will generally not be replaced by new nuclear power plants; rather natural gas, coal, and alternative energy sources will have to fill the gap. Simultaneously, countries such as Japan, South Korea, China, Taiwan, Thailand, Russia, and Ukraine will be increasing their nuclear capacities. Nuclear power generation will continue to be important for many years to come.

K E Y   T E R M S

alpha particle
atom
beta particle
breeder reactor
chain reaction
cold fusion
core
daughter product
decommission
enrichment
fertile isotope
fission

fusion
gamma ray
ionizing radiation
isotope
light water reactor (LWR)
loss of life expectancy (LLE)
meltdown
milling process
moderator
neutron
nuclear power
nuclear proliferation
Petkau effect

plutonium
radioactivity
radionuclide
reactor vessel
reprocessing facility
risk
thorium
threshold of exposure
tokamak
uranium
yellowcake

S T U D Y   Q U E S T I O N S

1. Describe the current role of nuclear power in the global commercial energy budget.
2. Is nuclear power generation a "hard" or "soft" technology? Why?
3. Explain the principles behind modern nuclear fission power plants.
4. What is fusion? In what context have human-induced fusion reactions taken place on Earth?

5. What is "nuclear proliferation"? Why are some people so concerned about it?
6. Describe the nuclear fuel production process.
7. What are some of the advantages of nuclear power? Some of the disadvantages?
8. How long could nuclear fuel supplies last? Under what conditions? How will the consideration of breeder technology affect your answers to these questions?
9. Explain what is meant by the "Petkau

effect."
10. Discuss the nature of radioactivity.
11. What are some of the radioactive wastes produced by nuclear power plants?
12. What steps are being taken to produce safer nuclear reactors?
13. Given current trends, what might be the role of global nuclear power in the middle of the twenty-first century?
14. Plutonium-239 has a half-life of approximately 24,000 years. If we start with 7

ounces avoirdupois (198.44666 g) of plutonium-239, how much plutonium will remain after 120,000 years? (Express your answer in both ounces and grams.)

15. Radon-222 has a half-life of approximately 3.8 days. If we start with 9 ounces avoirdupois (255.14569 g) of radon-222, how much radon will remain after 19 days? (Express your answer in both ounces and grams.)

ESSAY QUESTIONS

1. Why is nuclear power so controversial? Is this controversy justified or simply the result of some people's ignorance of the technology involved?

2. What is your position on nuclear power? Justify your answer.

3. Why are the topics of nuclear power and nuclear waste disposal in large part military and national security issues?

4. Describe the Chernobyl and Three Mile Island accidents. How did these incidents affect the public's perception of nuclear power?

5. What methods have been suggested to dispose of the high-level and low-level radioactive wastes that result from nuclear power generation?

SUGGESTED READINGS

Brown, L. R., N. Lenssen, and H. Kane. 1995. *Vital signs 1995*. New York: W. W. Norton.

Cassedy, E. S., and P. Z. Grossman. 1990. *Introduction to energy: Resources, technology, and society*. Cambridge: Cambridge University Press.

Cohen, B. L. 1990. *The nuclear energy option: An alternative for the 90s*. New York and London: Plenum Press.

Galperin, A. L. 1992. *Nuclear energy, nuclear waste*. New York and Philadelphia: Chelsea House Publishers.

Graeub, R. 1992. *The Petkau effect: Nuclear radiation, people and trees*. New York: Four Walls Eight Windows.

Hall, C. A. S., C. J. Cleveland, and R. Kaufmann. 1986 (1992 reprint). *Energy and resource quality: The ecology of the economic process*. Niwot, Colo.: University Press of Colorado.

Herman, R. 1990. *Fusion: The search for endless energy*. Cambridge: Cambridge University Press.

Hollander, J. M. 1992. *The energy–environment connection*. Washington, D.C.: Island Press.

Jagger, J. 1991. *The nuclear lion*. New York: Plenum Press.

Lenssen, N. 1992. "Confronting nuclear waste." In L. R. Brown, *et al.*, *State of the world 1992*, pp. 44–65. New York: W. W. Norton.

Medvedev, Z. 1990. *The legacy of Chernobyl*. New York: W. W. Norton.

Naar, J. 1990. *Design for a livable planet: How you can help clean up the environment*. New York: Harper and Row.

Peat, F. D. 1990. *Cold fusion: The making of a scientific controversy*. Chicago: Contemporary Books.

CHAPTER 9

ALTERNATIVE ENERGY SOURCES AND ENERGY CONSERVATION

PROLOGUE   *Off-the-Grid Options*

An estimated two billion people living in rural areas of the South (the developing countries) do not have access to electricity from a centralized grid system of power lines connected to large power plants. The only electricity many of these people know is from small disposable batteries, or perhaps larger automobile batteries, used to power transistor radios, televisions, and other small appliances. They burn fuelwood for cooking and use kerosene lamps for lighting. Extending power grid systems into rural areas is so expensive—

PHOTO   *External view of a gasification plant where biogas is produced from the pulp (bagasse) of the cereal sweet sorghum. This Italian plant is part of a project funded by the Commission of European Communities.* (*Source:* Tommaso Guicciardini/ Science Photo Library/Photo Researchers.)

it costs about $16,000 per mile ($10,000/km)—that many people have little prospect of ever graduating from batteries if they must wait for the grid to come to them.

An alternative approach is to make households and communities independent of a regional or national power grid system. A small household photovoltaic solar system, consisting of solar panels, a storage battery, control box, wiring, and fixtures, can be set up for under $1000 and be sufficient to power several lights, a radio, a television, and some other small appliance (Fig. 9–1). Such systems have many advantages: they are clean and efficient and do not produce any pollution or greenhouse gases; they are long-lasting if properly maintained; and they make the family self-sufficient (costly disposable batteries and kerosene no longer must be purchased from outsiders). A number of countries have launched programs to bring photovoltaic systems to their rural populations. The Dominican Republic, which has some 380,000 rural families, about 20% of whom could afford a small photovoltaic system, has conducted one of the most successful programs. Thousands of such systems have been installed in that country since 1985; the major barrier to further growth is simply financing—many families need short-term loans to fund their electrification. Worldwide hundreds of thousands of photovoltaic systems have been installed in such countries as Colombia, India, Mexico, Sri Lanka, and South Africa.

FIGURE 9–1

This home in rural northern Michigan (near Mancelona) depends on photovoltaic solar panels and the burning of wood to supply most of the energy it needs. (*Source:* John Sohlden/Visuals Unlimited.)

Photovoltaic systems are not the only way to bring electricity to rural off-the-grid areas. In India and China, biogas digesters, essentially vats that use fermentation to convert biological wastes (such as animal dung) into a methane–carbon dioxide mixture, number in the millions. Some biogas digesters are family sized while others are large enough to supply a village. The gas produced can be used directly for cooking or running small engines or used to power generators that produce electricity.

Another approach that has found particular favor in many rural areas of India is to harness wind power to produce electricity. Recent advances in wind turbine technology have made this form of electricity generation much more reliable and less expensive than it once was. Small clusters of wind machines can be located in remote areas to supply electricity to villages that are off the main grid.

Decentralized, off-the-grid, **alternative energy** sources (alternative to fossil fuels, nuclear power, and large-scale hydroelectric plants) such as solar, biogas, and wind power may someday supply electricity to the majority of the world's people. Some advocates of these and related alternative energy sources believe that ultimately they could supply all of the world's electricity needs without utilizing a single fossil fuel–burning or nuclear power plant.

*I*NTRODUCTION

Solar power, geothermal power, wind power, and the burning of biomass (such as wood, dung, urban waste, methane produced from garbage, or alcohol fermented from plants) all provide significant amounts of energy in local settings, although they account for only a small percentage of the global energy budget. These, and even more minor sources of energy (such as ocean thermal power), present alternatives to the **"big five" energy sources** that we have discussed in the last two chapters: coal, oil, natural gas, hydro, and nuclear power.

The alternative forms of energy generation are usually thought of as renewable, sustainable (or at least potentially sustainable), and environmentally benign. As we shall see, however, some potential environmental problems are associated with all of these sources of energy, and geothermal energy in particular is not strictly a renewable or sustainable energy source. Of the big five energy

sources, hydroelectric power is most closely associated with the alternative energy sources. As we saw in Chapter 7, hydroelectric power is potentially renewable and sustainable (although overly large and mismanaged hydroelectric dams can lead to environmental abuse and long-term damage). Many futurists envision smaller-scale hydroelectric power plants playing an increasingly important role in the decades to come.

In the long run, it may be inevitable that hydroelectric power and alternative energy sources will have to make up a greater percentage of the energy produced once nonrenewable fossil fuel supplies are exhausted, especially if public confidence in nuclear power continues to falter. Alternative energy forms, such as electricity generated by wind or solar thermal power, stand to become increasingly popular as they become cost competitive with traditional methods of generating electricity (see Table 7–4 in Chapter 7).

Alternative energy sources have received a big boost in recent years with the rise of **independent power producers (IPPs)**. IPPs construct electricity-generating plants and then sell the electricity to the large utilities. In many cases the IPP plants use alternative energy technologies and are relatively small, innovative, and environmentally friendly. Such independent power generation is supported in the United States by the Public Utility Regulatory Policies Act of 1978, which allows smaller, independent, unregulated power companies to build generating plants that use renewable fuels (such as wind or solar power). But IPPs are not just an American phenomenon; they are appearing around the world and herald a new emphasis on alternative energy sources.

Along with the development of alternative energy sources, increased attention is being paid to energy conservation and efficiency—doing more with less energy. Already great strides are being made in this area, and it is likely to attract greater interest in the future.

$\mathcal{B}$IOMASS

The burning of biomass, especially fuelwood, has served as a major source of energy for most of recorded history. Even today billions of people, perhaps more than half of the world's population, burn wood or other plant or animal products (such as animal waste) as their principal source of energy. Biomass provides as much as 15% of all energy consumed worldwide; in some developing countries, it provides up to 90% of the energy

consumed. In the United States, about 4% of energy demands are supplied by biomass. Most of this is accounted for by the paper and pulp industry, which burns large quantities of wood and paper milling wastes to supply energy for its needs. Other substantial consumers of biomass in the United States include households that burn wood as a primary source of heat (about 5% fall into this category, and another 20% occasionally burn wood in a stove or fireplace), commercial industries and establishments that burn wood as a source of energy (in some cases, simply for space-heating purposes), and **waste-to-energy** facilities that burn municipal solid waste (see Chapter 19). Biomass-derived fuels, such as **ethanol**, currently account for a very small percentage of the U.S. energy budget, although about 8% of the gasoline sold in the United States contains ethanol.

Raw Sources of Biomass Energy

Sources of **biomass energy** can be classified into three major categories: wastes, standing forests, and energy crops. Wastes include such things as wood scraps, unusable parts of trees, pulp residue, paper scraps generated by the wood and paper industry, and municipal solid waste. During lumbering operations in timber forests, many sticks, branches, leaves, stumps, and roots are left over. Potentially, these could be collected and burned for energy (however, they are important sources of nutrients for regrowth). Likewise, agricultural wastes from food crops, such as leaves, stems, stalks, and even surplus or damaged food items, can serve as a source of biomass energy. In the United States, surplus corn is the principal raw material for the ethanol industry. A final large source of biomass energy is the organic material found in municipal solid waste (discussed in Chapter 19).

Natural standing forests afford a vast source of biomass energy, but unless harvested in a low-impact sustainable manner, they are a nonrenewable resource. Furthermore, diverting wood from forests for the purpose of energy use may compete directly with interests in other forest products, such as lumber for building and the furniture industry. Of course, clear-cutting forests for any purpose presents major environmental concerns (see Chapter 12). All too often, timbering results in soil erosion and ecosystem destruction.

Many advocates of increased use of biomass energy envision crops grown specifically for fuel purposes. Fast-growing varieties of trees, as well as grasses and other crops, could be commercially

raised on large monoculture **energy farms**. The biomass would be harvested and the fuel burnt directly or converted into other types of fuels (such as biogas, methanol, or ethanol). Coppicing trees (ones that will regenerate from stumps left in the ground) and perennial grasses may be particularly well-suited to energy farming. The crop could be clear-cut, but no further planting would be necessary because a new crop would grow from the stumps and roots already in the ground.

Such dedicated biomass plantations would require vast amounts of land—land that is fertile and could potentially be used for other purposes such as food crops (see Chapter 13). Indeed, growing crops for energy generally requires more land than any other energy generation technique (Table 9–1).

Biomass Fuels and Technologies

Raw biomass energy sources can be treated in a number of different ways. Wood and other fuels can be burned directly. Biomass can be made into such fuels as methanol and **syngas** by **thermochemical conversion**. Or biomass can be biochemically converted into fuels like ethanol and biogas. In this section, we discuss each of these technologies briefly.

Direct Burning

Biomass can be burned directly for heat, and the heat can fire a modern electrical generating plant. Such direct combustion is certainly the oldest form of biomass energy technology, and it can be sustainable if practiced carefully. Forests can be planted and then managed and harvested to provide fuelwood. A wood-burning electrical power plant currently in use in Vermont is less expensive to operate than a coal-burning plant.

Factories and utilities can also burn various biomass waste products as an energy source (Fig. 9–2). For example, many pulp and paper companies burn wood, pulp, and paper by-products and waste. Peanut shells, rice husks, peach pits, cherry pits, and so forth, and even municipal waste, can all potentially be used to fuel factories or commercial electrical power plants.

Thermochemical Conversion

Heating biomass in an oxygen-deficient or oxygen-free atmosphere transforms the material into generally simpler substances that can themselves be used as fuels. The classic and oldest example of such thermochemical conversion is the production of charcoal from wood. Modern thermochemical

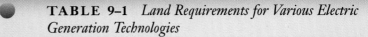

TABLE 9–1 *Land Requirements for Various Electric Generation Technologies*

TECHNOLOGY	LAND REQUIREMENT	
	Square Mile-Years per Exajoule [a]	Square Kilometer–Years per Exajoule [a]
Dedicated biomass plantation	48,250–96,500	125,000–250,000
Large hydro	3204–96,500	8300–250,000
Small hydro	66–6562	170–17,000
Wind[b]	116–6562	300–17,000
Photovoltaic central station	656–1274	1700–3300
Solar thermal trough	270–1158	700–3000
Bituminous coal	259–1274	670–3300
Lignite coal	2586	6700
Natural gas–fired turbine	77–259	200–670

Note that a square mile–year is a square mile used for one year, and a square kilometer–year is a square kilometer used for one year. One exajoule is equal to 1000 petajoules; in 1991 the total world commercial energy consumption was approximately 321.43 exajoules (see Table 7–2 in Chapter 7). Also note that many alternative energy sources, such as wind and solar power, actually require less land than some conventional energy sources, such as coal and hydroelectric power. For instance, large hydroelectric power plants can require the flooding of vast tracts of land, and strip-mining for coal can devour huge land areas (often leaving the land devastated and virtually unusable once the coal has been mined).

[a]End-use energy figure averaged over assumed 30-year life cycles for power plants, mines, and so on.
[b]The lower range for wind includes only land occupied by turbines and service roads, while the higher number includes total area for a project.
(*Source:* Data from L. R. Brown *et al.*, *State of the World 1995* [New York: W.W. Norton, 1995], p. 73. Reprinted with permission of Worldwatch Institute, Washington, D.C., Copyright 1995.)

conversion technologies can produce petroleum and natural gas substitutes from biomass or coal; the two best-known products are syngas and methanol.

Syngas, also known as coal gas or town gas, was invented at the end of the eighteenth century and used in many urban areas in the early nineteenth century for light and heat. Syngas is basically a mixture of hydrogen gas (H_2) and carbon monoxide (CO) that is produced by exposing steam (H_2O) to a heated carbon source (such as coal or a biomass). Syngas has less energy content per volume than natural gas, but can be used in much the same way. Syngas can be burned directly for heat or used to power gas turbines and other equipment. A potential problem is that syngas produced under certain conditions may contain unacceptably high levels of tars, oils, and other compounds that may cause excess pollution and damage equipment.

Syngas or other biomass derivatives can be subjected to liquefaction and, via a series of catalytic

FIGURE 9–2
A 12.5 megawatt electric power plant at Eye, Suffolk, England, that burns a mixture of wood shavings, straw, and chicken droppings from local poultry farms. The ash is used as a fertilizer. (*Source:* James King-Holmes/Science Photo Library/Photo Researchers.)

reactions, converted to a liquid fuel, methanol (also known as methyl alcohol, CH_3OH). Methanol is extremely versatile and, among other uses, can be burned in automobiles. A standard gasoline-powered vehicle needs only relatively minor modifications to burn methanol. Currently, many racing cars use methanol because it delivers a faster acceleration.

In addition, chemical conversion techniques can be used to transform organic material into a wide range of oils, lubricants, and raw materials for the petrochemical industry. For instance, special oilseed crops and microalgae can be chemically converted into diesel fuel. Currently, however, most of these substitutes cannot economically compete with their fossil fuel counterparts.

Biochemical Conversion

Biochemical conversion of biomass into useful fuel involves harnessing microorganisms to carry out the conversion. The oldest form of biochemical conversion utilized by humans is probably simple fermentation of foods (such as grapes, corn, and barley) by microscopic yeast cells to produce ethanol (ethyl alcohol, C_2H_5OH). For hundreds of years, ethanol has been produced on a moderately large scale, for it forms the basis of the alcoholic beverage industry, but it can also be produced specifically as a fuel source.

Automobiles can be built to run directly on ethanol or on any mixture of ethanol and gasoline. In the United States, it is common to find a 1:9 ethanol-gasoline mixture known as gasohol.

In the United States, the source of ethanol is usually surplus corn, but in Brazil sugarcane is grown for the express purpose of converting it into automobile fuels. Brazil produces about 4 billion gallons (15.14 billion liters) of ethanol fuel each year—by comparison, U.S. production is less than a billion gallons (3.8 billion liters) annually—and most new cars there are designed to burn pure ethanol.

Besides ethanol, the other commonly used fuel produced by biochemical conversion is biogas, which is a mixture of methane (natural gas, CH_4) and carbon dioxide (CO_2). Biogas is often referred to simply as "methane"; methane and methane–carbon dioxide mixtures are also known as swamp gas or marsh gas. Biogas is produced when anaerobic bacteria digest organic matter in the absence of oxygen. This process occurs naturally in the deep layers of organic material in the bottoms of swamps or in some landfills. Many landfills now have pipe systems to draw off the biogas; it can be used as a fuel source directly, or the methane can be purified and sold to natural gas distributors. Special reactors (also known as **biogas digesters**) can be used to promote the production of biogas: organic material and microbes are placed in the reactor, basically, a large, sealed container, and the oxygen is removed; then the microbes digest the biomass and produce biogas. When reactors are carefully controlled and monitored, the biogas can consist of up to 95% pure methane. The residue from the reactor can be used as a fertilizer and soil conditioner.

Environmental Advantages and Disadvantages of Biomass Energy

Biomass energy has become an extremely controversial subject among environmentalists, in part because of the diverse sources and technologies that fall into this category. The environmental appeal of biomass energy is that, in theory, fuelwood or other biomass fuel is a renewable energy source; in practice, however, it often is not. To be truly renewable and cause no deleterious environmental impact, every time a tree (or other plant) was cut down and burned, a new tree would have to be planted and assured of surviving. During growth the new tree would theoretically absorb the carbon dioxide given off by the burning of the old tree. In point of fact, however, forests are often harvested for fuelwood in an unsustainable manner, leading to their destruction and ultimately to desertification. Burning forest or agricultural residues, dung, or other animal wastes can deprive the soil of nutrients that should be recycled back to the earth, reducing the soil's fertility and making it much more difficult for the land to support either natural vegetation or human-planted crops. Fuelwood gathering, biomass burning, and their attendant problems are causing an environmental nightmare in many developing countries.

Traditional biomass use, especially in developing countries, is typically very inefficient: from 3 to 10 times more energy may be used than is actually needed to accomplish the task at hand. For example, when food is cooked over an open fire, most of the heat is lost. Using a simple but efficient stove can cut the wood used by one-third to one-half. In some cases, wood use could be cut even further by introducing solar box cookers that can cook food by using the rays of the Sun instead of burning fuelwood or animal waste. As described earlier, biogas digesters can be used to convert manure and other organic wastes to methane for use in cooking, heating, lighting, and other purposes.

In industrial countries, some people are strong advocates of the waste-to-energy approach, essentially burning garbage to generate electricity in specially designed incinerators. The major problem is that this approach discourages reuse and recycling, and the facilities can generate large quantities of air pollutants and hazardous waste.

Energy farms where crops such as fast-growing trees or grasses are raised specifically for use as fuel also have their advocates, but critics argue that these farms will suffer from the same problems as traditional food farms including soil erosion and massive pesticide, herbicide, and fertilizer use. Although soil damage and losses could be reduced by improving management techniques, raising energy crops would create another problem by displacing food crops in a world where there is already a shortage of food in many areas. Nor is raising energy crops on marginal lands that are not currently cultivated for food a solution, for those lands may be very prone to environmental degradation and perhaps should not be planted.

Furthermore, it is unlikely that energy crops, even under the best of circumstances, could ever supply the majority of the energy requirements of a major industrial nation. For instance, even if the entire annual U.S. corn crop were converted to ethanol, it would supply only a fifth of the country's motor-vehicle fuel needs. To make matters worse, in some cases the biomass conversion processes are extremely inefficient. In some instances, converting corn to ethanol actually requires more energy than the energy value of the final ethanol produced, but this inefficiency occurs largely because corn is not really a good energy crop (it is used because there is a surplus left over from food production). Ethanol made from certain fast-growing grasses may contain five times as much energy as was used to grow and process the plants.

A major disadvantage of any biomass burning is that it is a major contributor to air pollution and the greenhouse effect when done unsustainably (that is, when replacements are not planted for all the materials burned). Biomass burning or combustion of biomass-derived fuels can emit carbon monoxide, nitrogen oxides, and particulate matter (such as ash and soot) into the air. The burning of biomass found in municipal solid waste can be extremely dangerous from this perspective, potentially releasing known carcinogens and heavy metals into the environment. Some have suggested that alcohol-based biofuels may release significant quantities of formaldehyde and other aldehydes (known carcinogens) when burned, but some studies indicate that such emissions from biofuels are less than those produced from comparable fossil fuels.

In summary, the long-term role of biomass in the energy mix of modern developed countries is uncertain. Biomass energy, in the form of biofuels like ethanol, may be most important as a transitional measure between our virtually total dependence on fossil fuels and the full-scale introduction of a truly clean and environmentally benign energy system, such as a solar-hydrogen economy (see Issues in Perspective 9–1).

$\mathcal{S}$OLAR ENERGY

Much of the energy we use currently is indirectly **solar energy**. Fossil fuels, wood, and other biomass combustibles are the result of organisms that trapped the Sun's energy into a form that we can conveniently employ. Hydropower and wind power also derive from the Sun, in that the Sun differentially heats the atmosphere, causing the winds, and evaporates water and recycles it as rain,

which lets our rivers flow. Potentially, the Sun provides the Earth with more energy every day than humans would ever be able to use. While humans currently harness energy at a rate of about 13 terawatts (TW), the light and heat of the Sun deliver energy to the Earth's surface at a rate of about 80,000 TW. In just 20 days, the Earth receives energy from the Sun equal to all of the energy stored on Earth as fossil fuels.

Of course, this energy from the Sun is often dilute, diffuse, and **intermittent** (the Sun only shines during the day), but if even a small fraction of this energy were harnessed, it could potentially solve many of our current energy problems. The main obstacle to utilizing solar energy appears to be its dispersed nature. A multimegawatt solar-based power plant comparable in capacity to current power plants might require the use of large tracts of land (see Table 9–1) to set up solar energy collectors of some sort. Furthermore, while sunlight is free, any large power plant is a capital-intensive investment initially (the Case Study discusses other potential drawbacks of solar power). While large centralized solar power plants are feasible in some areas such as desert regions, solar energy also lends itself to small-scale, decentralized, dispersed applications, such as passive and active lighting and heating of buildings, localized small-scale electrical generation, use of individual solar-powered ovens for cooking, solar hot water heaters, and so on. Widespread use of solar power in such situations could entail enormous energy savings.

Direct Use of Solar Energy and Passive Solar Designs

Humans have long been aware that they can harness solar energy directly. For thousands of years, people have understood how to build their homes so that they face the Sun and take maximum advantage of incoming solar energy that can be used to passively heat the living quarters (Fig. 9–3). Similarly, gardeners have long known how to trap the Sun's energy in greenhouses, even simulating relatively tropical conditions in temperate climates. Modern solar technology encompasses two major themes: (1) simply trapping solar heat and light and redirecting it to purposes useful for people, and (2) directly or indirectly converting solar energy into electricity.

Sunlight striking the surface of the Earth at any one spot may be either direct or diffuse, although there is a continuous gradation between the extremes. Direct sunlight has traveled through the atmosphere with very little scattering or diffraction;

FIGURE 9–3
The headquarters of the Rocky Mountain Institute (an energy think tank founded in 1982 by Hunter and Amory Lovins), located in Old Snowmass, Colorado Rockies, relies heavily on solar energy for space and water heating. (*Source:* Jeanette Darnauer/Rocky Mountain Institute.)

$\mathcal{P}$ROBLEMS OF RESOURCE DEPLETION   SECTION 2

The Natural Gas Transition to a Solar-Hydrogen Economy

It is very clear that in the near future the world will have to stop burning fossil fuels at the high rate of the past few decades. Yet the world will continue to require large amounts of energy: the size of the human population continues to grow, and the developing nations rightfully desire to improve the living conditions of their peoples. A post–fossil fuel energy economy will be necessary.

The energy to be used in this post–fossil fuel world has been the subject of much discussion, but two major routes have been advocated: (1) a strong reliance on nuclear power supplemented by a mix of other energy sources, such as hydroelectric, solar, wind, and geothermal, or (2) a strong reliance on solar and other "clean" and renewable energy forms, combined with hydrogen gas as a way to store and transport energy conveniently—a so-called solar-hydrogen economy.

The idea behind a **solar-hydrogen economy** is that it would be based on renewable energy in the form of solar power plants (using photovoltaics or thermal solar technologies) and wind- and water-driven power plants, supplemented by such technologies as geothermal power, tidal power, and combustion of biomass to a limited (and sustainable) extent. The primary form of power generation would be electricity, but it would be produced intermittently when the Sun was shining brightly or the winds were blowing hard. Thus, peak electricity production and peak demand would not necessarily correspond in many areas, creating a problem for electricity is notoriously difficult to store (although new superconducting technology may help to alleviate this problem, as discussed later in Issues in Perspective 9–2). Therefore surplus electricity (not used directly by private consumers or industry) would be used to subject water to electrolysis to form hydrogen gas. Essentially, an electrical current passed through water will break the water (H_2O) into hydrogen (H_2) and oxygen (O_2). The hydrogen can then be stored, and burned when needed to generate electricity or heat, in a manner very similar to natural gas. When hydrogen gas is burned, it releases energy as it recombines with oxygen in the atmosphere to produce water. Burning hydrogen gas is extremely clean (small amounts of nitrogen oxides [NO_X] may form, but hopefully with proper technology this hazard can be minimized). Furthermore, water to form hydrogen gas is extremely abundant, and the water can be recycled as the hydrogen combines with oxygen to form water once again.

Advocates of a solar-hydrogen economy point out that with the proper technology, much of which already exists, hydrogen gas can be used in place of virtually all fossil fuels. Hydrogen could be used to heat buildings, run appliances, power motor vehicles, and fuel airplanes. Alternatively, hydrogen-burning fuel cells where the hydrogen is once again chemically combined with oxygen to produce an electric current could be used to run electrical appliances or motors (Fig. 1). Automobiles powered by electric motors and hydrogen-burning fuel cells could become standard in the next century.

▬ FIGURE 1

A Ballard Fuel Cell Stack, a type of hydrogen fuel cell produced by Ballard Power Systems Inc. of North Vancouver, British Columbia, Canada. (*Source:* Photo courtesy of Ballard Power Systems Inc.)

Hydrogen is bulky, however, relative to the amount of energy to be derived from a cubic unit, and it is dangerously explosive. Still, these drawbacks seem relatively minor. After all, fossil fuels, especially natural gas, can be very dangerous, explosive substances, too. As for the bulk of hydrogen gas, this consideration may be negligible if, as some suggest, many hydrogen-powered vehicles may be up to twice as energy-efficient as their fossil fuel–powered equivalents.

Even strong proponents of a solar-hydrogen economy realize that the world cannot switch instantaneously to this type of energy mixture. They envision a transitional stage in which the world switches first to a relatively abundant and relatively clean fuel—natural gas. Natural gas use and technology are already familiar, and natural gas burns much more cleanly than oil or coal (substituting natural gas in many situations decreases carbon dioxide emissions by 30 to 65% and decreases other air pollutants by 90 to 99%). Natural gas is also relatively abundant. As natural gas technologies and infrastructures are developed and put into place, they will form the basis of the future hydrogen use. Much of the hardware (piping systems, furnaces, engines, and so on) that is used for natural gas can easily be converted to hydrogen use when the time comes.

In summary, the steps to a sustainable solar-hydrogen economy would include the following: substitution of natural gas for other fossil fuels and the development of a natural gas–based technology and infrastructure; the concerted development of solar-powered electrical generating facilities (supplemented by other renewable energy sources) to replace other types of electric power plants; continued research and development in hydrogen production, storage, transportation, and use; and finally the complete substitution of hydrogen for natural gas.

Drawbacks of Solar Power

Despite appearances, solar power is not totally "clean." Cohen (1990) estimates that the production and deployment of solar cell arrays and wind turbines would use about 3% of the fossil fuel that would be burned in a coal-burning power plant to generate approximately the same amount of electricity. Thus, he concludes that solar technology produces approximately 3% as much air pollution as coal burning. This is a drastic improvement, but far from pollution-free.

Various solar technologies also generate toxic waste. Producing solar cells on a large scale requires large quantities of highly poisonous chemicals, such as hydrofluoric acid, boron trifluoride, arsenic, cadmium, tellurium, and selenium compounds (Cohen, 1990, p. 268). Photovoltaic cells and other solar energy systems have a life expectancy of 30 years or so. Thus, large portions of systems must be replaced or refitted every few decades. Doing so will entail manufacturing new systems, generating poisonous wastes and pollution in the process, and disposing of the used components.

Because of the diffuse nature of sunlight, solar systems will have to cover large areas. A major solar-generating facility might cover a circular area 5 miles (8 km) in diameter with photovoltaic cells or mirrors and reflectors to capture sunlight. Many of these systems may be set up in deserts where the ecosystem is extremely fragile; solar power plants and the human activity they entail could be very disruptive to the local biota. Many types of solar systems will also need large amounts of water, a substance already in short supply in desert environments.

Another major problem with using solar technology for electricity generation is that the power source is intermittent. Sunshine is not available at night or on rainy or overcast days; the flux of sunshine also varies seasonally (two or three times more solar energy is received during the summer than in the winter in some areas). Yet we use electricity 24 hours a day throughout the year. One solution to this problem is to collect energy when the Sun is out and put it into storage. But with current technology, the direct storage of electricity is notoriously difficult. Batteries are large, bulky, expensive, and dangerous (they contain many poisonous chemicals). Any battery system that is regularly subjected to charging and discharging degrades and must be replaced periodically.

An alternative is to pump water (using Sun-generated electricity) uphill into a reservoir during the daylight hours and subsequently release the water downhill as needed, using it to drive a generator that produces electricity. Essentially, this is a form of "artificial" hydroelectric power, and all of the problems associated with hydroelectric dams (flooding large areas, disrupting natural water flow, high cost of construction and maintenance, the chance of the dam breaking) are applicable to such a system. Another possibility is to compress gas into tanks and then release it again to drive generators when the Sun is not available. But, as described in Issues in Perspective 9–1, perhaps the most popular concept at the moment is to use electricity to produce hydrogen gas, which is clean burning and easily stored and transported.

Another way to deal with the intermittent availability of solar energy is to supplement solar systems with backup systems for generating electric power. But backup systems need to be able to start and stop on a regular, short-term basis, so they would almost inevitably have to burn fossil fuel. Except on a very small scale, backup systems do not make sense environmentally or economically. Essentially, the whole country would have to be covered with both a solar and a nonsolar electrical grid. A complete complement of fully operating nonsolar (that is, fossil fuel or nuclear) power plants would be needed to supply electricity at night, at considerable cost. A large power plant cannot simply be turned off during the day and turned on at night. Indeed, many people believe that at least in the foreseeable future, solar energy, and not conventional power, will be the backup. Solar energy can serve as a supplement to conventional power sources, especially during the summer when electricity to run air conditioners is in high demand.

If it comes to pass, the large-scale implementation of solar systems will entail a whole new set of environmental concerns. If past experience with other new technologies is any indication, many of the problems associated with solar technologies will not be anticipated—they will manifest themselves only after years of large-scale operation.

Questions

1. In his book *The Nuclear Energy Option: An Alternative for the 90s*, Dr. Bernard L. Cohen outlines a number of potential problems with the large-scale implementation of solar power. If you were discussing solar power with him, how might you respond to some of the issues he raises? Do other forms of electrical generation also produce poisonous chemicals? Are such chemicals harmful if they are *not* released into the environment? What is the realistic life expectancy of various types of conventional (fossil fuel, hydroelectric, and nuclear) power plants? What happens to any power plant once it has exceeded its useful life? How do the land requirements for a solar-based power plant compare to those for various types of conventional plants?

2. How can we attempt to anticipate the new, and as yet possibly unknown, environmental concerns that may be associated with the large-scale implementation of solar power plants in the future?

3. In general, should we fear or embrace new technologies? Or is this not the correct question to ask?

---

generally, direct sunlight is bright and leaves sharp shadows. Direct sunlight can be concentrated with mirrors and lenses to form very energetic, focused beams. Diffuse sunlight has been scattered and diffracted by the atmosphere, clouds, and haze before reaching the surface of Earth. To the naked eye, diffuse sunlight does not appear as bright as direct sunlight, and it leaves soft shadows.

The distinction between direct and diffuse sunlight is important because some technologies require direct sunlight, whereas others can utilize either direct or diffuse sunlight. The appropriate solar technology will depend on the area because the amount of cloud cover and atmospheric turbulence experienced through the course of a year vary from place to place. In the United States, for instance, Albuquerque receives about 70% of its sunlight as direct radiation whereas Boston receives over half of its sunlight in a diffuse form.

The time-honored way to utilize solar energy is through **passive solar design** of houses and other structures—using the inherent characteristics of the building to capture heat and light from the Sun. Such architecture has been practiced for thousands of years, but has to a certain extent been lost, or at least greatly deemphasized, with the coming of the industrial age. With cheap, convenient fossil fuels readily available, architects and builders no longer worried about orienting houses toward the south (in the Northern Hemisphere) to capture the heat and light during the winter months. Likewise windows were no longer required as a primary source of light once electric lights were widely introduced; in many buildings today, electric lights are used for illumination during daylight hours.

With passive solar design, the entire building becomes a solar collector. Passive solar strategies include the installation of large, south-facing windows and few or no north-facing windows. The windows allow incoming sunlight but trap heat. New types of glass with better thermal and light properties continue to be developed, including superinsulated glasses and electrochromic windows that can change their optical properties in response to small electrical currents and either block or admit sunlight as necessary to maintain a comfortable interior temperature. Windows and skylights also provide natural lighting that can displace artificial, energy-burning electrical lighting. Lightpipes, mirrors, and reflecting surfaces can be used to illuminate even the deep recesses of a building during the day.

Modern passive solar design usually stresses well-insulated buildings to keep heat in when it is cold outside and keep the interior cool when it is hot outside. In many cases, "thermal masses" are incorporated into the building to store excess heat and then release it as needed. Traditional thermal masses include stone and brick walls (including interior walls), tile floors, and sod or earth (such as a house built into a hillside or with a sod roof). A thermal mass like an interior brick wall or tile floor will absorb excess heat during the day and then release it during the cooler night, helping to keep the interior of the house at a relatively constant temperature. Future passive solar systems will incorporate new developments in heat storage, such as phase-change materials in walls (described later in the chapter).

By absorbing excess heat, thermal masses, can also cool a structure. Earth (soil) around and under a building can absorb quite a bit of excess heat. For hundreds of years, people have stored perishables in underground cellars where they remained cool during the summer, but did not freeze (if the cellar was dug properly) in the winter. Shade trees situated around a small building can keep it remarkably cool during even the hottest summers. Inside the building, windows and skylights can be adjusted to admit or block solar light and heat, natural ventilation will contribute greatly to efficient cooling, and water can be allowed to evaporate to cool the interior further.

The key to passive solar techniques is to design the building with such considerations in mind from the beginning. Adding passive solar systems to the initial design of a new house often raises the cost of construction by only 3 to 5% (usually less than 10%). Unfortunately, retrofitting an existing building so that it becomes an efficient passive solar system is usually very difficult or impossible, although many buildings can be improved by the installation of new windows, skylights, insulation, or thermal masses. Accordingly, some advocates of passive solar design believe that local building codes and ordinances should be modified to encourage passive solar design in new construction.

A major drawback of passive solar design is that it is not easily applied to larger, more compact buildings, such as large office buildings, skyscrapers, and major apartment complexes. But even in these cases, foresight can lead to the successful implementation of passive solar techniques. Buildings can be oriented relative to the Sun and windows placed appropriately. Interior atriums can reduce the need for artificial lighting and cooling. Natural ventilation can be used; in many large buildings today, the windows cannot be opened, and a mechanical system must pump cool air throughout the building year-round. The bottom line is that even large structures can benefit from passive solar techniques.

Active Solar Techniques

A building's energy consumption can also be reduced by utilizing **active solar techniques**. The basic active solar system uses a **flat-plate col-**

lector. In the simplest case, this device consists of a black metal plate that absorbs heat from the Sun when it is struck by sunlight (either direct or diffuse). The heat is transferred to a liquid (such as water or alcohol) carried in pipes in contact with the metal plate. The heat of the hot liquid can then be used as desired. Water run through the pipes might be heated and used directly as hot water for washing or cooking; the hot liquid might be run through pipes to heat the interior of the building; or the heat could be stored in a thermal reservoir (such as a large tank of hot water) and used as needed.

Active solar collectors are usually placed on the tops of buildings, facing the predominant direction of the Sun in that part of the world. Putting solar collectors on roofs keeps them from taking up space that could be used for other purposes. Some systems collect solar heat during daylight hours and store a portion to heat the building at night or on a rainy day when the Sun is not at full intensity. Large solar collectors can be built to serve a community; for instance, special ponds filled with a combination of salt and water can trap and store solar energy.

The major use of active solar collectors is to produce hot water and secondarily to provide space heating for building interiors. (Nearly 25% of all fossil fuel energy consumed in the United States goes toward space heating and cooling of buildings and heating hot water.) At present, active solar collectors are used extensively in such countries as Australia, Cyprus, Israel, and Japan. In Israel 65% of the homes have solar water heaters, as do 90% of the homes in Cyprus. In the United States, active solar collectors are not used as much as they could be. With low energy prices and the large up-front costs of installing even a simple solar water heater, most Americans are unwilling (or unable) to make the necessary capital investment. Flat-plate collectors are relatively simple to manufacture and install, but their prices will remain high as long as there is little market for them. Some people predict that demand would increase if the systems were less expensive, but until demand actually does increase, manufacturers cannot justify investing in the equipment that will allow mass production and bring prices down. It seems to be a vicious circle that will be broken only by sharp increases in conventional fuel prices or government intervention (such as tax incentives to install solar collectors).

Heat collected by active solar collectors can potentially be used to cool buildings as well as to heat them. To actively cool a building using solar energy, a system similar to that used in a gas-powered refrigerator might be used. Currently, such systems are still in the developmental stage, but they could become widespread in the next century.

Electricity from the Sun

Active **solar thermal technology** (that is, using the Sun to heat substances) is not limited to flat-plate collectors. In areas with a high incidence of direct sunlight, mirrors, reflectors, or lenses can be used to concentrate the Sun's rays to superheat a liquid; then the hot liquid can be used to generate electricity. For example, between 1984 and 1990, LUZ International Limited built nine solar thermal electric power plants in the Mojave Desert and sold electricity to the Southern California Edison Company. (Unfortunately, LUZ went bankrupt in 1991, putting a halt to its plans to build additional solar power plants. The plants it built are now owned by private investors and continue to operate. The major reason that LUZ went bankrupt was a tax structure that requires solar power plants to pay much heavier taxes than conventional power plants.) In the solar thermal trough system used by LUZ, trough-shaped mirrors focus the sunlight on steel pipes encased in glass tubes. The Sun's rays heat a synthetic oil inside the pipes to more than 750°F (400°C). The hot oil is then used to turn liquid water into steam, which drives a turbine connected to an electric generator. Through advanced computer technology, light-sensitive instrumentation, and microprocessors, the mirrors track the Sun throughout the day to maintain the high temperatures necessary to produce the steam.

Other forms of solar thermal technologies include parabolic dish collectors that focus sunlight onto a single point; the heat can then be used to generate electricity. In another method, mirrors focus sunlight on a solar receiver mounted on top of a tower, which may be up to 660 feet (200 m) tall (Fig. 9–4). The sunlight heats fluids, such as molten salts, in the receiver. The fluids can then be used to generate steam and power a turbine connected to an electric generator. A major advantage of such "power towers," as they have been called, is that the hot molten liquid can be used to generate electricity even after the Sun has set. Although initially expensive, solar thermal–generated electricity has become cheaper since the mid-1980s (Fig. 9–5); some analysts believe that the price may fall to only 5 to 6 cents per kilowatt-hour by the year 2000 (see Table 7–4 in Chapter 7).

Sunlight can also be used to generate electricity through **photovoltaics**. Photovoltaics utilize semiconductor technology to generate electricity directly from sunlight. At present, various silicon substances are most commonly used for this purpose. A variation on simple photovoltaic systems, which produce electricity and send it to consumers directly, are photovoltaic systems that use some of the electricity they generate to split water into its component gases, hydrogen and oxygen. The hydrogen can then be used as fuel.

Many photovoltaic cells are used in small consumer products, such as portable calculators, but the real potential lies in the application of photovoltaics to power homes, factories, and other commercial ventures. Photovoltaic systems are convenient because they can operate alone in remote areas with either direct or diffuse sunlight. They are already used for telecommunication and signaling devices, in space applications (such as satellites and manned space missions), and to provide power to small villages that are far from other sources of electricity. In the United States and other developed countries, photovoltaic systems are already being used by some utility companies to supply extra electricity to grids during peak hours. The use of photovoltaics is expected to increase in the coming decades, especially in developing countries.

The main constraint on the use of photovoltaics at present is their cost. Currently, generating electricity using certain photovoltaic systems is about six times as expensive as using fossil fuels (of course, such comparisons are misleading because fossil fuels may not be available in a certain area, fossil fuels cause environmental damage that is not accounted for in their cost, and the cost of photovoltaic systems is primarily a capital expense). Since the mid-1970s, however, the manufacturing cost of photovoltaic cells has been steadily decreasing (▬ Fig. 9–6) while their efficiency at converting sunlight into electricity has been steadily increasing. As the price has dropped, sales of photovoltaic systems have increased sharply from only 0.1 megawatts worldwide in 1971 to nearly 70 megawatts in 1994 (the United States, Japan, and Europe account for about 90% of world photovoltaic sales). As these trends continue, photovoltaic systems will become increasingly competitive, and expectations are that they will play an ever larger role in our global energy budget.

On the negative side, however, historically relatively little funding has been spent on research and development (R & D) in solar power, including photovoltaics. In 1991, the latest year for which accurate figures are available (● Table 9–2), the governments of the industrial nations spent $289 million for R & D on solar power, while spending $989 million on coal R & D and $4.49 billion on nuclear power. If more R & D money could be spent on photovoltaics and other forms of solar power, these energy systems could contribute much more substantially to the global energy budget many decades sooner than will be the case otherwise.

▬ **FIGURE 9–4**
Solar One (at left), a solar thermal facility in the Mojave Desert near Barstow, California. The mirrors focus sunlight on a solar receiver mounted on top of a tower. Solar One was a pilot plant that is currently being retrofitted as the Solar Two project. Solar Two uses an advanced molten salt system (a mixture of sodium and potassium nitrate) instead of a water-steam system. Once the salts are heated to approximately 1050°F (565°C) they can be used to produce steam that drives a turbine connected to an electric generator, or they can be stored and used to produce steam at a later time. (*Source:* Courtesy of Southern California Edison Company.)

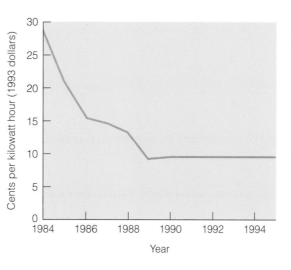

▬ **FIGURE 9–5**
Cost of electricity from new solar thermal plants. (*Source:* Modified from C. Flavin and N. Lenssen, *Power Surge: Guide to the Coming Energy Revolution.* [New York: W. W. Norton, 1994], p. 146. Reprinted with permission of Worldwatch Institute, Washington, D.C., Copyright 1994.)

FIGURE 9–6
(a) World photovoltaic shipments, 1971–1994; (b) average factory prices for photovoltaic modules, 1975–1994. (*Source:* L. R. Brown, H. Kane, and D. M. Roodman, *Vital Signs 1994* [New York: W. W. Norton, 1994], p. 55, updated based on L. R. Brown, N. Lenssen, and H. Kane, *Vital Signs 1995* [New York: W. W. Norton, 1995], p. 57. Reprinted with permission of Worldwatch Institute, Washington, D.C., Copyright 1994.)

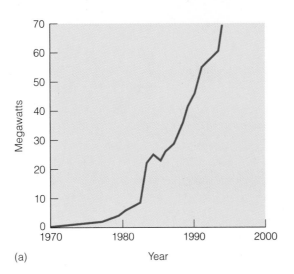

(a)

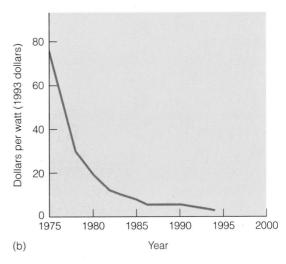

(b)

WIND POWER

Humans have been utilizing **wind power** for thousands of years for such applications as windmills and sailing ships. In the first quarter of the twentieth century, wind-powered irrigation pumps were very common in the United States, but their use gradually declined as inexpensive oil and gas became more readily available.

TABLE 9–2 *Government Research and Development Spending by Twenty-Three Member Countries of the International Energy Agency*

Technology	TOTAL, 1978–1991		1991	
	Amount (Billions of 1991 Dollars)	Share (%)	Amount (Billions of 1991 Dollars)	Share (%)
Nuclear fission	59.8	52	3.6	47
Nuclear fusion	12.2	11	0.9	12
Gas turbines[a]	10.9	9	0.6	8
Other fossil technologies	14.4	13	1.3	17
Photovoltaics	2.7	2	0.2	3
Other renewables	7.1	7	0.4	5
End-use efficiency	6.6	6	0.6	8
Fuel cells	1.0	1	<0.1	1
Total[b]	114.7	100	7.6	100

Note that between 1978 and 1991, 63% of the R & D funds was spent on nuclear research, and another 22% was spent on fossil fuel research. These spending priorities continue to the present day.

[a]Mostly spent by defense ministries for aircraft development, but has commercial applications.
[b]Columns may not add to totals due to rounding.
(*Source:* C. Flavin and N. Lenssen, *Power Surge: Guide to the Coming Energy Revolution* [New York: W. W. Norton, 1994], p. 303. Reprinted with permission of Worldwatch Institute, Washington, D.C., Copyright 1994.)

In the last 20 years, fluctuations in oil prices and the realization that our fossil fuel reserves are limited have helped rekindle interest in wind power. Today wind generates less than 0.1% of the world's electricity, but its use is growing quickly (■ Fig. 9–7). Denmark, Sweden, and the United States are leaders in the large-scale commercial application of wind power. Other countries, including China, Greece, India, and the Netherlands (the traditional user of windmills), are also planning the large-scale use of wind power. **Wind farms**—vast tracts of land covered with wind-powered turbines, some with 300-foot (91 m) blades—currently generate billions of kilowatt-hours of electricity per year at competitive prices (■ Fig. 9–8). Indeed, like the costs of solar thermal and photovoltaic power, the costs of wind-derived electricity have decreased dramatically in the last 10 years (see Table 7–4 in Chapter 7). Conservatively, some researchers estimate that wind power could supply about 12% of the world's electricity needs. Other analysts have optimistically (but perhaps unrealistically) suggested that up to 100% of electricity needs could be met by wind power in some areas, such as Europe.

In the United States, as much as 20% of the demand for electricity could be met if wind power were fully developed. It cannot be developed in some areas because sufficient winds do not blow consistently. In general, the most suitable areas for wind turbines in the United States are along the west coast, along the northeast coast, along ridges in the Appalachian and Rocky Mountains, and in a large area of the Great Plains. Already 1% of California's electricity demands are supplied by wind power, and wind farms with a capacity of 10 to 250 megawatts are being planned in several states including Iowa, Illinois, Minnesota, and Maine. Currently, the

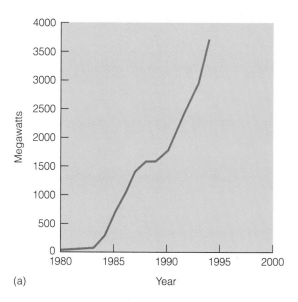

(a)   Year

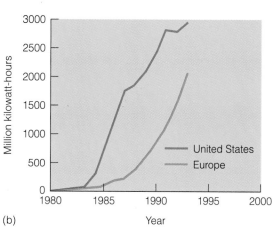

(b)   Year

FIGURE 9–7
(a) World wind energy–generating capacity, 1980–1994; (b) wind energy generation in the United States and Europe, 1980–1993. (*Source:* L. R. Brown, H. Kane, and D. M. Roodman, *Vital Signs 1994* [New York: W. W. Norton, 1994], p. 51, updated based on L. R. Brown, N. Lenssen, and H. Kane, *Vital Signs 1995* [New York: W. W. Norton, 1995], p. 55. Reprinted with permission of Worldwatch Institute, Washington, D.C., Copyright 1994.)

United States has a wind energy-generating capacity of slightly over 1700 megawatts.

Modern wind turbines are relatively simple machines that consist of blades and a rotor connected to an electrical generator, along with a control system, all mounted on top of a tall tower. In intermediate-sized and large wind turbines, a transmission and gears connect the rotor shaft to the generator; in some smaller wind turbines, the rotor is connected to the generator directly. Most wind machines have rotors with two or three blades mounted on the end of a horizontal shaft and look like huge fans or airplane propellers, but a few wind machines have blades that look like the end of an eggbeater mounted on a vertical shaft. Conventional propeller-like wind machines are controlled from the ground so that they face into the wind.

Currently, in the United States, the emphasis has been on intermediate-size machines with capacities of 50 to 500 kilowatts. The machines stand on towers about 100 to 165 feet (30–50 m) tall, and a single wind farm may contain thousands of machines. Such wind farms can feed electricity into the local utility grid.

Small wind machines with capacities of 0.25 to 50 kilowatts are also becoming more popular in the United States and other countries as well. Small wind turbines are well-suited to supplying power in rural locations that are not on a major grid, especially in developing countries. In some cases, small wind turbines can be combined with a photovoltaic system to increase the reliability of the power supply.

Wind power offers many advantages. It is very safe and generally environmentally benign. Wind machines are typically erected along coasts (some can even stand in water offshore) or in mountain passes, where a constant and steady wind supply is assured; these areas are often not in high demand for other purposes. On farms cattle can graze and crops can be planted around wind turbines. In the Great Plains, agricultural farms and wind farms can coexist peacefully on the same land.

Nevertheless, wind power has faced some heated local opposition. Wind farms have been subjected to the NIMBY (not in my back yard) syndrome. Some people complain that wind machines are noisy and say they are ugly and destroy the aesthetic qualities of the landscape. Perhaps the most serious concrete environmental problem with wind machines, however, has been bird deaths. Birds may collide with the blades or be electrocuted if they land on certain parts of the machine. In Altamont Pass in California, where a number of wind machines are located, several dozen rare golden eagles and scores of other large birds of prey have been killed by wind turbines. Researchers are currently trying to devise systems that will solve this problem.

Bird deaths aside, the major practical drawback of wind power currently is the intermittent nature of the energy source. Although prevailing wind patterns for any given location can be determined and predicted overall (as mariners did for centuries), on a seasonal and even daily basis, wind speeds and directions can be subject to rapid and wide fluctuations. Many large utilities are understandably wary of relying too heavily on the unknown "whims" of the wind. Furthermore, on a seasonal and daily basis, the strongest and steadiest winds may not blow during the time of peak demand for electricity. For these reasons, wind power has little chance of becoming a major or dominant source of electrical power

www.jbpub.com/environet

until large-scale electrical storage facilities become readily available.

Despite its drawbacks, wind power capacity continues to expand. In 1980 the global wind energy–generating capacity was a mere 10 megawatts; by 1994 it had grown to 3710 megawatts, and the growth shows no signs of abating. In the United States, wind power received a boost from the passage of the National Energy Policy Act of 1992, which includes a tax credit of 1.5 cents per kilowatt-hour of wind-generated electricity. The European Community has set a goal of installing 8000 megawatts of wind power electric generating capacity by the year 2005, including national goals of 1000 megawatts each for the Netherlands, Germany, and Denmark. The United States and Ukraine are discussing a cooperative venture to build a 500-megawatt wind farm to replace power currently supplied by one of the Chernobyl nuclear reactors. All told, the immediate future of wind power looks very bright.

$\mathcal{G}$EOTHERMAL ENERGY

As discussed in Chapter 2, the interior of the Earth is very hot. This heat, which is primarily generated by radioactive decay within the Earth, reaches the surface by such means as molten rock, erupting volcanoes, and hot geysers and springs. The principle behind geothermal power is to tap and harness this natural heat from the Earth's interior. **Geothermal energy** can either be used directly for such purposes as heating buildings, or it can be used to produce electricity (generally, either by utilizing naturally vented steam directly or by heating water to produce steam to drive a turbine generator). Geothermal energy has already found widespread use in some areas such as California, which produces about 6% of its electricity geothermally (■ Fig. 9–9). In the United States as a whole, geothermal energy constitutes about 0.2% of the primary energy consumed (coming in after the fossil fuels, hydroelectric power, nuclear power, and biomass energy). Many researchers predict that geothermal energy use will continue to expand in the future.

Geothermal power is not practical everywhere; it is most easily utilized along plate margins and at other points where hot magma comes close to the surface. Thus, some of the most likely areas for developing geothermal power lie along the Pacific rim from New Zealand to New Guinea, the Philippines, Japan, the western coast of the United States, Mexico, Central America, and the Pacific coast of South America. Iceland, which lies on the Mid-Atlantic Ridge, already heats some 80% of its houses and many of its other buildings with geothermally heated hot water. Hawaii is also well-suited to the utilization of geothermal power.

There are four basic types of geothermal deposits: **hydrothermal fluid reservoirs** (the only deposits currently used commercially), geopressured brines, magma, and hot dry rock. Hydrothermal reservoirs are basically areas of the crust where hot rock occurs at relatively shallow depths and natural groundwater is heated, sometimes to extremely high temperatures. Such reservoirs may naturally manifest themselves on the surface as hot springs or geysers. The most useful, but also by far the rarest, are the steam-dominated hydrothermal reservoirs. At The Gey-

sers in northern California, over two dozen power plants are fueled by the naturally produced and vented steam. Hot water–dominated hydrothermal deposits can also be used to run electricity-producing power plants; with lower-temperature deposits, the hot water is often used to heat homes and other buildings in the vicinity directly.

Geopressured brines are naturally occurring deposits of hot, salty water (brine) under pressure at depths of 10,000 to 20,000 feet (3000–6000 m). Such brines may contain significant quantities of dissolved gases, including methane. Potentially, these brines could be tapped for their heat content, dissolved gases, and pressure (which could be converted to useful forms of energy). Like fossil fuels, however, once a geopressured brine is exploited, it cannot be expected to renew itself on a human time frame.

Magmas, or hot molten rock, are also a potential source of geothermal energy. Where magmas approach the surface, such as around active or not long dormant volcanoes (for instance, on the Hawaiian Islands), pipes could be inserted into the magma and water circulated through the pipes. The heated water or steam could then be used to drive turbines. Although progress has been made in finding ways to prevent the pipes from melting—the magma is typically at temperatures of 1100 to 2400°F (600–1300°C)—this

FIGURE 9–9
The Geysers is a steam-dominated geothermal field in Sonoma County, California. (*Source:* U.S. Department of Energy.)

power-generating technique is still a long way from commercial application.

The long-term future of geothermal power may lie in the developing field of hot dry rock technology. Although the temperature of the Earth increases with depth virtually everywhere, this geothermal gradient is much more pronounced in some areas, reaching 200°F per mile of depth (70°C/km) in some places. In hot dry rock technology, a hole is drilled some 2 to 6 miles (3–10 km) deep into the subsurface rock, until a sufficiently hot and thick layer of hard, dry rock is found. Once such a layer is located, two wells placed relatively close together are established in the rock. Next the rock between the two wells is fractured. Then cold water is pumped down one well, the hot rock heats the water, and it is withdrawn from the second well for use in generating electricity or for direct heating applications. Successful tests of hot dry rock techniques have been carried out in the United States, Great Britain, and Japan, but no commercial plants based on this principle have yet been constructed.

Geothermal energy production, though often considered relatively clean compared to traditional fossil fuels, is not without environmental hazards. By its nature, it tends to expel excessive quantities of heat into the environment that may cause thermal pollution, killing plants and animals and disrupting natural ecosystems. Some of the hot underground water contains dissolved salts, other minerals, and heavy metals that are toxic pollutants on the surface. Hydrogen sulfide and other dangerous gases may be released from vents. Tons of hydrogen sulfide are released daily at The Geysers, despite the efficient scrubbers used at the plants to minimize air pollution. Furthermore, sludge is produced by the scrubbers and by the condensation of vented steam. Some sludge contains such high concentrations of heavy metals that it must be treated as a hazardous waste. Such waste could potentially be reinjected deep underground, but care must be taken to avoid contaminating freshwater aquifers.

Geothermal operations also require large quantities of water. Geothermal power plants currently in operation use water as a cooling and condensing agent, and hot dry rock techniques will also utilize considerable quantities of water.

In a sense, geothermal energy is an undepletable energy source, at least on a human timescale, because the Earth is not going to cool anytime soon. On a small scale, however, this resource can be depleted—and in some cases, quite rapidly. Naturally circulating hot water flow can be inadvertently diverted over time, thereby dis-rupting easy access to the energy. Hydrothermal fluid reservoirs often contain "fossil water" under pressure that is withdrawn by a power plant faster than it is replenished. The Geysers, for instance, has experienced significant drops in steam pressure due to overproduction since 1987, resulting in a 25% reduction in power output. And ultimately, any hot rocks will cool down if heat is withdrawn from them quickly enough. Like any natural resource, geothermal energy must be managed carefully to maximize its potential.

Globally, the use of geothermal energy has increased dramatically over the last 50 years. Worldwide installed geothermal electrical generating capacity has risen from about 240 megawatts in 1950 to over 10,000 megawatts currently, and it is projected to continue growing at approximately 10% per year for the next decade. Approximately half of this geothermal electrical capacity is found in the United States. Other large users are the Philippines, Mexico, and Italy. Geothermal electricity typically costs 4.5 to 6 cents per kilowatt-hour compared to 5 to 7 cents for fossil fuel–generated electricity. In addition to geothermal electricity, currently over 12,000 megawatts of geothermal energy are used worldwide in such direct applications as space heating, water heating, and manufacturing processes.

OCEAN ENERGY

The oceans are a vast, if sometimes diffuse and seemingly uncontrollable, source of energy. Various ways of exploiting this **ocean energy** are currently being researched. The waves, tides, and currents all have potential as energy sources. In 1995 a small electrical power station was installed off the coast of Scotland that runs on wave energy. The regularity of the tides can be used to drive mechanical systems, and this mechanical power can then be transformed into electricity (■ Fig. 9–10). A **tidal power** station operates by allowing water at the high tide to flow into a reservoir or bay through sluice gates; then the gates are shut, forming a dam. At low tide the water is released through a turbine and used to generate electricity. Ultimately, this energy comes from the Moon, which generates the tides as it orbits the Earth.

A 240-megawatt tidal plant has been operating in France since 1966 and a 20-megawatt facility is currently operating in the Bay of Fundy, Nova Scotia. In most areas, the difference in height between high and low tide is not enough to efficiently drive a turbine, but due to local topographic conditions, the Bay of Fundy is an exception: there the difference between high and low tide can be as much as 53 feet (16 m). Another problem with tidal power is that it is very intermittent; power is generated only after high tides, and the times of the tides change daily. A final potential drawback is that the artificial damming and releasing of water may be extremely disruptive to local marine life.

Another system of extracting usable energy from the oceans, now under development, is known as **ocean thermal energy conversion (OTEC)**. Due to solar heating, the surface waters of the oceans in tropical latitudes are warmer than the waters at depth, setting up a temperature gradient: the temperature differential can be as much as 45°F (25°C). An OTEC plant is a giant heat engine that exploits the temperature differential to run a turbine and generate electricity.

The idea of OTEC was first proposed in the 1880s, and the first experimental OTEC machine was built off the coast of Cuba in 1929, but it consumed more energy pumping seawater than it produced. No commercial OTEC plant has yet been built, although experimental plants have been tested off the coast of Hawaii and in Japan.

The amount of energy stored in the thermal layers of the oceans is immense, but this energy is diffuse and extracting it presents numerous practical problems. Due to the small temperature differentials involved, thermodynamically OTEC units cannot help but be very inefficient. Vast quantities of warm and cold seawater would have to be pumped through the plant, necessitating the use of vast amounts of energy; and large pipes would have to be extended far into the ocean depths. Developing such systems will be expensive, and some experts believe that only a relatively small amount of useful energy can eventually be extracted; other researchers, however, feel that the technical obstacles to OTEC implementation can be overcome.

OTEC advocates have suggested three basic ways that such plants could be built and used: (1) An OTEC plant could be built onshore and seawater piped in, a system best suited to mid-oceanic islands with little continental shelf surrounding them. (2) OTEC plants could be built offshore on platforms similar to those used to support offshore oil and gas drilling operations, but the electricity would have to be transmitted back to shore through extremely long underwater transmission cables. (3) OTEC systems could be built on ships that would cruise the oceans, stopping to generate electricity when they found a good thermal differential. Since transmitting the energy back to land would be difficult, the ships might use the energy directly to produce high-value products onboard, or the electricity generated could be used to split water into hydrogen and oxygen, and the hydrogen stored and then sold in port as a fuel.

Given the current state of funding and lack of serious interest in OTEC technology, we are unlikely to see any commercial OTEC applications before the end of the century. Furthermore, the potential detrimental effects that OTEC use might have on the marine environment have aroused concern. Pumping deep-lying water to the surface will disturb ocean temperature gradients and modify ocean chemistry, and many marine organisms are dependent on very specific temperature and chemical requirements for survival. Nutrients and minerals brought from the depths will potentially encourage the abnormal proliferation of some organisms at the expense of others. On an even

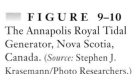

FIGURE 9–10
The Annapolis Royal Tidal Generator, Nova Scotia, Canada. (*Source:* Stephen J. Krasemann/Photo Researchers.)

larger scale, if OTEC technology were applied on a massive global scale, the surface temperatures of the oceans could experience a significant cooling, affecting ocean currents and climatic patterns in unknown ways.

Energy Storage

A major obstacle to the widespread use of many alternative fuels is the problem of **energy storage** and transportation. One of the reasons that the fossil fuels in general, and oil in particular, came to dominate the world energy mix is because of their ease of storage and transportation. Petroleum products pack a high quantity of energy in a small amount of space, and the energy is easily obtainable by combustion. Clean-burning hydrogen gas (see Issues in Perspective 9–1) offers some of the same advantages, but being a bulky and light gas, it is much more difficult to store. Electricity is one of the most versatile energy sources, but it is difficult to store in large quantities. Most electricity is shipped through wires as soon as it is produced and used almost immediately by a consumer.

Of the big five energy sources powering the modern world (oil, coal, natural gas, hydroelectric power, and nuclear power), the only one that actively stores newly transformed energy and then releases it as needed is hydropower. The artificial lake created by the dam at the power plant effectively stores energy when it stores water that was raised to higher elevations by evaporation and subsequent precipitation during the hydrologic cycle. When humans need energy, water is released through the dam to power turbines connected to electrical generators.

Electrical Energy Storage

A standard hydroelectric power plant relies directly on the Sun to cycle water through the hydrologic cycle, but the principle of water being dammed at a higher elevation can be used as a general energy storage system in what is commonly known as **pumped hydroelectric storage (PHS)**. In PHS electricity is used to drive pumps that transfer water from a lower reservoir to a higher one. Electricity can then be regenerated by allowing the water to flow through a turbine on its way back to the lower reservoir. The initial electricity used to pump the water to the higher reservoir might be excess electricity generated during the day by a power plant using solar thermal or photovoltaic technologies; during the

night, electricity could then be generated using the PHS system. PHS is primarily suited to large-scale storage and typically involves reservoirs that are as large as the lakes found behind conventional hydroelectric power plants. Several dozen PHS facilities are in use by electrical utilities in the United States. These systems are used mostly to store energy produced during off-peak hours; extra electricity is then produced during peak hours. Reported efficiencies are in the 70 to 75% range (that is, at least a quarter of the energy is lost during the storage and retrieval process).

PHS systems are expensive to build and suffer from all of the environmental problems associated with large hydroelectric dams. Vast areas of land must be flooded, potentially disrupting wildlife, recreational activities, and ecosystem operation. An ideal site for a PHS facility is a location with two adjacent valleys, one of which is at a substantially higher elevation than the other. An interesting alternative to building PHS systems above ground using natural valleys is to build them partially or wholly underground. Such a project is being pursued near Akron, Ohio, in an old limestone mine. Water will be pumped to an aboveground reservoir, and when energy is needed, the water will fall 2200 feet (670 m) down into the mine; as the water falls, it will turn turbines and generate electricity. Then the water can be pumped out of the mine and back into the reservoir. Building this system will cost an estimated $1.7 billion.

Related to underground PHS is **compressed air energy storage (CAES)**. In this system, electricity is used to pump air under pressure into a storage reservoir. The reservoir must be confined and free of leaks; commonly used reservoirs include underground caverns (especially in salt domes), abandoned mines, abandoned natural gas wells, and partially empty aquifers. The compressed air in the reservoir stores energy. When the energy is needed, the pressurized air is released. Usually, the air does not generate electricity directly, but is passed through a modified gas turbine, greatly increasing its efficiency and energy output. Since some gas is also burned in operating the turbine, however, the system is neither completely pollution-free nor self-contained.

The most common way to store electrical energy is with batteries. The principle of the **battery** was first developed by Alessandro Volta around 1800. All batteries work on basically the same principle. In the battery are substances that act as electron donors or receptors. When a battery is charged, electrical energy (essentially, a stream of electrons) is converted into chemical

EnviroNet
www.jbpub.com/environet

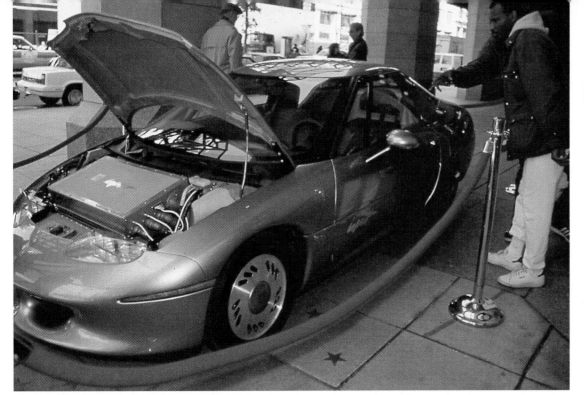

FIGURE 9-11
A battery-powered electric automobile on display in Washington, D.C. (*Source:* P. F. Gero/Sygma.).

energy in the form of molecular bonds. During discharge the chemical process is reversed. Today the most common batteries are of the lead-acid variety, utilizing lead plates and dilute sulfuric acid. Various types of miniature batteries and dry cells are commonly used in electronics equipment.

The problem with current battery technology is that the batteries tend to be heavy and bulky relative to the amount of energy they store. This is not a major problem for small applications, but for larger-scale, longer-term applications, it is a serious limitation. Also, batteries do not last forever; typical lead-acid batteries, for instance, can only be run through 500 to 2000 charge/discharge cycles.

Some futurists anticipate an increasing demand for medium-sized batteries in the future, such as batteries that can be used to power electric cars (Fig. 9-11). Already California has passed laws mandating that 10% of all new cars sold in the state by the year 2003 be zero-emission cars; essentially, this means that 10% of the cars will have to be electric cars. Electric cars in existence today, using conventional battery technology, tend to have driving ranges of only about 70 to 100 miles (112–160 km) before recharging is necessary, and recharging can take three hours. Such a car might be appropriate for short commutes, but would be unsuited to long-distance travel. Also, while an electric car in isolation may give off zero emissions, it must be recharged from some energy source. If it is recharged by electricity produced by photovoltaic cells or a hydroelectric power plant, then it may indeed truly be a zero-emission vehicle. If it is recharged by electricity generated by a coal-burning electrical power plant, however, then it is ultimately still responsible for the emission of greenhouse gases and pollutants, although perhaps considerably less than a standard gasoline-powered car.

Currently, a new generation of lighter batteries that can store more energy per unit weight for longer periods of time is under development. These newer batteries utilize nonconventional combinations of elements as electrodes and electrolytes, such as zinc-bromine, zinc-chlorine, or hydrogen–nickel oxide. The next generation of batteries also promises to be longer lasting than current conventional batteries, but so far they are also much more expensive. Another promising line of research involves high-temperature batteries, such as a sulfur-sodium–based battery that must be maintained at a temperature above 570°F (300°C) in order to operate. Such batteries may be better suited to stationary uses, such as storing excess electricity produced by a power plant during off-peak hours and then releasing it again during peak hours. Conventional lead-acid batteries are already being used in this way. In Chino, California, Southern California Edison operates the largest lead-acid battery storage facility in the world. It has a 10-megawatt discharge capacity, and when fully charged, it can maintain this level of output for four hours.

Somewhat similar to batteries are **fuel cells**. In a typical fuel cell, hydrogen gas (H_2) is passed by

Superconductivity

When an electrical current, a stream of electrons, passes through an ordinary conductor such as a copper or aluminum wire, the electrons transfer some of their energy to the conductor, causing it to heat up. The conductor has a certain resistance to the flow of electrons. This resistance is used to advantage in certain appliances, such as toasters or electric stoves and ovens, where the purpose is to generate heat. But in other situations, it causes energy to be wasted. In fact, a good portion of the electricity generated by the typical commercial power plant never reaches its destination—it is lost during transmission through power lines.

Superconductors are substances that allow electrons to pass through them with virtually no friction or resistance, thus allowing almost 100% energy transmission. The superconductive properties of various substances have been known since 1911 when H. Kamerlingh Onnes of the University of Leiden first discovered **superconductivity** while studying the electrical properties of mercury at very low temperatures. The problem was that super-

conductivity was only observed at extremely low temperatures, so low that they approached absolute zero (approximately –459°F, approximately –273°C, or 0 K). The primary way to obtain such low temperatures was by using costly liquid helium, which has a temperature of about –452°F (–269°C). As long as superconducting phenomena could only be made to occur at such cold temperatures, their practical usefulness was severely limited. For many years, the highest temperature for a superconductor was –418°F (–250°C), obtained in 1973.

A major breakthrough came in 1986 when IBM (Zurich) researchers K. Alex Müller and J. Georg Bednorz and their team developed a new class of high-temperature ceramic-based superconductors. This discovery opened up a whole new field of research in superconductivity and earned Müller and Bednorz a Nobel Prize in Physics in 1987. One of the leaders in this research is C. W. (Paul) Chu at the University of Houston who, in 1987, developed a superconductor that worked at about –300°F (–184°C). This temperature is above the boiling point of liquid ni-

trogen (about –321°F [–196°C]), a much more easily and inexpensively obtained coolant than liquid helium. Since then the temperatures at which superconductivity can be made to take place using sophisticated new ceramic substances have continued to increase (Fig. 1). There are indications that superconductivity could take place at over –100°F (–73°C). The ultimate achievement, of course, would be to induce superconductivity to occur at 75°F (24°C)—room temperature.

High-temperature superconductivity will have all sorts of applications and benefits, including helping to alleviate the global energy crunch. Superconducting motors and generators have much higher energy-conversion efficiencies. Transmission of electrical energy through superconducting power lines will virtually eliminate power loss. Currently, to help reduce the amount of power lost during transmission, electric companies must situate power plants relatively close to the consumers they supply. With superconductor technology, the power plants could be located thousands of miles (thousands of kilometers) away. This is extremely im-

a catalyst that separates the hydrogen atoms into hydrogen ions and electrons. The electrons, carrying energy, can be used to power an electric motor or virtually any other electric device. The hydrogen ions are combined with oxygen (O_2) to form water. Potentially, fuel cells could be used to power electric cars; the cars would carry refillable tanks full of hydrogen and would emit only water.

Another device that can be used to store energy is a simple **flywheel** (perhaps initially put into motion by an electric motor). The flywheel, spinning in a mounted case, in a vacuum at a rate of up to 200,000 revolutions per minute, stores kinetic energy that can be converted to electrical

energy (using a standard electric generator) as needed. Currently under development is a flywheel device that is half the size of a standard clothes washer and could be mass-produced. Such devices might sit in the basement of a building and store energy (solar energy during the day or cheap electricity at night) and then release it on demand. The best flywheel energy storage systems could operate with energy conversion efficiencies of 90% or higher.

Finally, though only in the formative stages currently, **superconducting magnetic energy storage (SMES)** systems may become an important way of storing electrical energy in the future. In these systems, superconducting loops or

FIGURE 1

A scientist at the Argonne National Laboratory, Argonne, Illinois, fills silver tubes with a high-temperature superconducting powder. The powder-filled tubes can then be made into superconducting wire. (*Source:* U.S. Department of Energy.)

portant, especially if such alternative power sources as solar, wind, and geothermal are used on a large scale. Electrical energy could conceivably be generated at solar-powered plants in deserts of the western United States and then transmitted to any part of the country.

As we have seen, a major problem with solar, wind, and other alternative energy sources is that they are intermittent, and large-scale storage of energy for later use has proved difficult. Superconductivity may solve this problem. As the text describes, electrical energy could be stored in superconducting loops where the current would circulate around almost indefinitely without losing energy. Electrical energy would be fed into the coils during times of high electrical productivity (for instance, using solar-driven systems, when the Sun is shining brightly) and released later as needed. Even with conventional fossil fuel and nuclear-powered electrical generating plants, the use of superconducting storage coils would allow the more efficient use of electrical generating capacity. On a much smaller scale, perhaps small superconducting storage coils could replace batteries to

power electrically driven ships, trucks, or possibly even private automobiles.

In the realm of transportation, superconducting technology may revive the railroad industry. A new type of train, known as a "maglev" (magnetic levitation) train, uses superconductors to generate tremendous repulsive magnetic forces that actually levitate the train a few inches (a few centimeters) above its specially designed track or guideway. The train is then powered in lateral motion by a series of magnets along the guideway that, when activated in sequence, pull the train along. A maglev train eliminates the friction and mechanical resistance encountered by regular trains as their wheels roll along the track; such friction increases with speed and wastes a great deal of energy. As a result, maglev trains are much more energy-efficient and can reach much higher speeds than conventional trains. The Japanese National Railways has already built an experimental maglev train that can reach speeds of 400 miles (644 km) per hour.

coils would be used to store electrical energy by simply allowing the current to circulate around a closed loop of nearly zero resistance (for a discussion of superconductivity, see Issues in Perspective 9–2). Current could be drawn off as needed, or added to recharge the loop. Small-scale studies have shown that this technology is technically possible, but it is still very expensive and has yet to be developed into a commercially viable storage option. To have large enough capacities to be economically viable for utility companies, SMES rings may have to be miles (many kilometers) in diameter. Besides occupying large areas of land such devices present other potential environmental problems. Whenever an

electrical charge moves, it sets up a magnetic field. Magnetic fields may pose health threats (see Chapter 17). The large amount of electricity circulating in an SMES coil generates an extremely intense magnetic field. Granted, the intensity of this field drops off rapidly as one moves away from the facility, but even so we do not fully understand the environmental consequences these magnetic fields may have.

Heat Storage

Much energy, especially in temperate and cold climates, is used to provide heat for homes, offices, and other buildings. Heat (thermal) energy can be stored using a number of techniques; the three most common are sensible heat storage, latent heat storage, and thermochemical heat storage.

Sensible Heat Storage

Sensible heat storage is probably the oldest form of thermal energy storage. It simply involves allowing a material substance to heat up and then release its heat again. For instance, a mud or stone wall facing open sunlight will absorb and store heat during the day; at night, when the air temperature cools down, the wall will radiate heat as it cools. Such passive systems of energy storage have been used for centuries, perhaps almost unconsciously. Many materials, including rock, clay, water, and oil, can serve as a medium for sensible heat storage. Modern systems can be extremely complex and may include piping heat-exchanging fluids to and from a sensible heat storage unit, such as a large body of buried clay or crushed rock. Specially designed ponds filled with stratified saline waters are especially well suited to sensible heat storage. The pond is allowed to heat up during the day by incident sunlight, and then heat is drawn off as needed through pipes set in the bottom of the pond.

Traditionally, sensible heat storage has been used in houses and other buildings to moderate fluctuations in external temperatures on a daily basis. But similar principles can be utilized on a much larger scale to store heat on a seasonal basis. Thus, a sensible heat system could store heat from the Sun, gathered by solar collectors during the summer, and release it during the winter. The heat might be stored in an underground pit or cavern filled with clay, rock, or saline water. Pipes would feed heat into the storage facility during the summer and then withdraw the heat during the winter. The main constraint is that such systems require a large storage volume and thus involve a large initial expense. Once developed, they will probably be best suited to serving a large facility or group of buildings tightly clustered together.

Latent Heat Storage

Latent heat storage is based on phase changes in materials. For instance, when an ice cube melts, it absorbs energy. To freeze the water again, energy must be removed. A number of substances, such as certain salts and waxes, change from the liquid to the solid phase near room temperature. Research is being done on incorporating appropriate materials within capsules set into walls of a building. As the substances melted from a solid to a liquid state, the walls would absorb heat; subsequently, as the inside of the building cooled, the substances would release heat by changing back to a solid. The same technique could be applied to phase changes from the liquid to the gaseous state. As a liquid evaporates, it absorbs heat. As it condenses once again, it radiates heat.

Like sensible heat storage, latent heat storage has the potential to be used on both a small and a large scale. Large tanks could hold suitable salts, for instance, that would absorb energy by melting and release it again as they cool. The energy could be siphoned off as the salts cool and perhaps be used to heat a series of buildings or even applied to some industrial process.

Related to the concept of latent heat storage is a method used to cool an increasing number of commercial buildings during hot summers. Ice is made from water at night, during the off-peak hours when electricity is cheapest. During the day, air is cooled by circulating it over the ice as the ice melts; then the cool air is vented throughout the building. This system is much more efficient than traditional air conditioning.

Thermochemical Heat Storage

In **thermochemical heat storage**, reversible chemical reactions are used to store heat energy. One process being developed in Israel is to use solar heat to combine methane (CH_4) and steam (H_2O) to form carbon monoxide (CO) and hydrogen gas (H_2). When the carbon monoxide and hydrogen mixture, known as syngas, is exposed to a catalyst, the constituents recombine to form methane and steam, in the process releasing the stored energy. The methane and steam can then be reused to form more syngas. An advantage of this system is that the syngas can be stored until needed without any loss of energy or transported to wherever energy is needed. This system approaches the proposed system of using hydrogen, produced by the electrolysis of water into H_2 and O_2, to store and transport energy (see Issues in Perspective 9–1).

Methane and steam are not the only pair of substances that produce a reversible chemical reaction that might be used for thermochemical heat storage. Other suggestions for pairs of reactants/products include ammonia/nitrogen and hydrogen, and calcium oxide and water/calcium hydroxide.

ℰNERGY CONSERVATION

Most authorities agree that the simplest and cheapest way of stretching our energy resources and mitigating energy-related problems is through improving **energy conservation** (decreasing the demand for energy) and increasing **energy efficiency** (increasing the usable output per unit of energy). Energy conservation and efficiency go hand-in-hand in that increasing efficiency is often the best way to conserve energy. A simple anecdote can help clarify the relationship of conservation to efficiency. Suppose that a room is illuminated at night using four standard 100-watt incandescent bulbs. One way to conserve energy would be to turn off three of the bulbs. But that strategy would sacrifice illumination. Another way to conserve energy, through increased efficiency, would be to replace the incandescent bulbs with four compact fluorescent lamp (CFL) bulbs. Each CFL bulb draws only 25 watts of electricity yet produces the light equivalent of a 100-watt incandescent bulb. Thus, the energy consumption has been cut from 400 watts to 100 watts without sacrificing quality. But perhaps we should also rethink our standards when considering energy conservation. Perhaps the room is over-lighted with four bulbs so even more energy might be conserved by using only two 25-watt CFL bulbs and turning them off when no one is in the room.

A relatively small investment in energy efficiency can pay off handsomely in the long run. A car that gets better gas mileage may cost slightly more, but the difference in cost will be more than made up by the gas that is saved and the environmental degradation prevented. Likewise, CFL bulbs cost $15 to $20 apiece initially, but over their lifetime they may save $35 to $55 per bulb in electricity costs. On a different scale, one study of Brazil concluded that investing $10 billion in making the country electrically more efficient could save approximately $44 billion in projected electrical needs.

Reductions in energy consumption need not result in a decrease in living standards—in many cases living standards are actually increased. But increasing energy efficiency may ultimately entail a qualitatively different lifestyle, as energy-intensive activities are replaced by more labor-intensive activities. Some analysts predict a **decentralization** of energy supplies and sources, especially as alternative energy sources continue to make inroads in the global energy budget. Residences and business may become partially or wholly energy self-sufficient as they consume less energy and use local energy-generating options such as photovoltaic cells mounted on the roof.

To many people, "energy conservation and efficiency" means more than reducing the energy used per se; it also means reducing the amount of energy obtained from nonrenewable fossil fuel resources. The aim is to reduce the environmental degradation that the big three energy sources (oil, coal, and natural gas) engender, especially the release of atmospheric carbon, which may be responsible for global warming (see Chapter 18). Studies of the **carbon efficiency** of the world economy show that from an economic point of view the world has managed to raise its output per unit of carbon released. In 1950 one pound of carbon was released for every $1.07 worth of world economic output (or a kilogram of carbon for every $2.35); currently, about $1.45 of output is generated for every pound of carbon released ($3.20 per kilogram). This increase in carbon efficiency over the last half-century is the result of many factors working together: improved energy efficiency, spurred on by the oil crisis of the 1970s; increased emphasis on energy sources that produce virtually no carbon (the only carbon emitted is during construction and maintenance), such as solar, wind, hydroelectric, geothermal, and nuclear power; shifting from the use of oil and coal to natural gas (which emits less carbon per unit of energy); and increasing emphasis on communications and various high-tech industries that use relatively little energy per economic contribution versus traditional heavy, energy-intensive industries.

Interestingly, the carbon efficiency of developing countries used to be higher than that of industrialized countries, but in the last few decades, this situation has generally been reversed. Formerly, the developing countries relied primarily on manual labor, but as they have begun to industrialize, many have become very energy-intensive. In many cases, these countries invest in less energy-efficient technologies simply because the up-front costs are lower. In contrast, many of the developed countries have been expanding their economic output while keeping carbon emissions stable. Japan's economic output is about $4.55 per pound ($10.00 per kilogram) of carbon; in contrast, the United States has an economic output of slightly under $1.82 per pound ($4.00 per kilogram) of carbon. Theoretically, there is no limit to how high carbon efficiencies could climb. The exclusive use of virtually carbon-free energy sources would cause the carbon efficiency index to approach infinity.

EnviroNet
www.jbpub.com/environet

Energy Efficiency at a National Level

At a national level, some countries are much more energy-efficient than others. Energy efficiency can be measured in various ways: total energy consumption per year for a particular country; energy consumption per person per year in a particular country (per capita energy consumption); or primary energy consumption per unit of gross national product (that is, how energy-efficient a country is in producing goods and services) (● Table 9–3). For example, the People's Republic of China uses about 36% of the energy used by the United States, even though China has more than four times as many people. The per capita annual consumption of energy in China is less than a tenth of that in the United

TABLE 9–3 *Primary Energy Consumption, Energy Consumption per Million Persons, and Energy Intensity for Selected Countries, Early 1990s*

COUNTRY	PRIMARY ENERGY CONSUMPTION	ENERGY CONSUMPTION PER MILLION PERSONS	GNP/EC	ENERGY INTENSITY
United States	82.19	.33	68,687	14.5
Russia	32.72	.22	15,770	63.4
China	29.22	.025	14,566	68.6
Japan	19.01	.15	174,995	5.7
Germany	14.11	.18	108,712	9.1
Canada	10.97	.41	51,032	19.5
France	9.71	.17	120,185	8.3
United Kingdom	9.68	.17	98,743	10.1
Ukraine	8.75	.17	13,035	76.7
India	8.51	.01	33,450	29.8
Italy	7.00	.12	153,296	6.5
Brazil	6.07	.04	72,932	13.7

Note: Primary energy consumption is in quads per year; energy consumption per million persons is in quads per year per million persons; GNP/EC is gross national product in millions of dollars per quad of primary energy consumed; energy intensity is billions of BTUs consumed per $1 million of gross national product.
(*Source:* Figures calculated from data published in *The World Almanac and Book of Facts 1995* [Mahweh, N.J.: Funk and Wagnalls Corporation, 1994] and *World Resources 1994–95* [New York: Oxford University Press, 1994].)

States. Yet, when we compare China's economic output to that of the United States, we find that China uses more than four times as much energy to produce the same amount of gross national product. In other words, in this respect China is much less energy-efficient than the United States.

The ratio of a country's energy consumption to its economic output is the country's **energy in-** tensity. In general, developing countries have higher energy intensities than the developed countries—that is, they are less energy-efficient even though they may use considerably less energy overall and per capita than the developed countries do. By becoming increasingly energy-efficient, over the last two decades various industrialized nations (such as Japan, France, Italy, Germany, and other western European nations) have been able to decrease their energy intensities while maintaining strong economic growth and high standards of living. Thus, a country can increase its economic output while simultaneously decreasing its relative energy consumption—a concept virtually unimaginable before the 1970s.

Improving Energy Efficiency

Energy efficiency can be improved at every level. Electricity, for instance, tends to be very inefficient. It is estimated that the average American electric power company loses about two and a half times as much energy as it delivers. In each step of the conversion process, a sizable portion of the energy available is lost (remember the laws of thermodynamics in Chapter 7). More energy is lost as electricity is transmitted through power lines. Rather than turning the energy stored in coal into electric power and using it to run heaters that warm a building, it would be more efficient from an energy perspective—it would take much less coal—to heat the same building by burning the coal directly in a stove or furnace within the building.

Much energy could be saved, which is the same as gaining energy, by simply (1) not converting energy from one form to another unnecessarily, (2) increasing the efficiency at which energy is converted from one form to another, (3) not transporting energy unnecessarily, and (4) increasing the efficiency by which energy is transported. Unnecessary energy conversions and transport can be decreased by planning and decentralizing energy reserves and networks. Sometimes several widely scattered, smaller, self-sufficient power plants may be more efficient than one large, centralized plant. Energy conversion and transmission can sometimes be made more efficient by simply readjusting and fine-tuning old equipment. More important in this area, though, is the development of new technologies. Superconductor technology, for instance, may dramatically increase the efficiency of all aspects of electrical energy use.

An old, but newly resurrected, technology, which can sometimes more than double the usable energy produced by a power plant, is **cogeneration**. The basic principle behind cogeneration is that a power plant simultaneously produces several types of energy, such as electricity and heat, that can be used locally. Thus, an electrical power plant may heat water to produce steam; the steam in turn is used to power a turbine, which is connected to a generator that produces electricity. In conventional plants, the spent steam is treated as waste, and its heat content is discarded into the environment, often with deleterious results for the local wildlife. In cogeneration the spent steam or hot water is used for some other purpose, such as to heat buildings. The main disadvantage to cogeneration plants is that the closer they are to where the heat is to be used, the more successful they tend to be; ideally, the power plant should be located right within the community it serves. For this reason, relatively small-scale cogeneration plants appear to have more potential for community acceptance and energy efficiency than large-scale versions.

Heavy and light industry can save much energy and increase energy efficiency in many ways. Tremendous energy savings have been achieved in this sector by using recycled materials. In general, recycling saves energy. Recycling steel, for example, uses only 14% of the energy that it would take to produce a ton of steel from the raw ores, and recycling aluminum saves about 95% of the energy that it would take to produce the same amount of aluminum from the raw ore bauxite.

In the United States, over a third of all energy consumption is used in residential and commercial buildings, primarily for lighting, heating or cooling the interior space, and running small appliances. Energy can be saved by using more efficient heating, cooling, and lighting systems. Many existing buildings can be insulated much better than they are, and new construction materials and techniques enable new buildings to be superinsulated. In a well-designed, well-insulated, and sealed modern building, the interior will retain the heat given off by lights, human bodies, and various appliances; ideally, little additional heat should be needed. During the warm months, the insulation will keep heat out and cool air in the structure. Of course, a superinsulated building should also be well ventilated to prevent the buildup of harmful indoor pollutants. Such buildings should be designed and situated to take maximum advantage of passive solar heating during the cold months and to minimize such effects during the warm months. With such approaches, a home can use 50 to 90% less energy than does the average American house.

In western industrialized countries, such as the United States, the transportation sector consumes about a third of all energy used. Automobiles and other light road vehicles account for about 80% of energy consumption in transportation. Oil is used to fuel about 99% of all transportation needs.

Currently, over 700 million vehicles are on the roads worldwide, and more than 75% of these are cars. Of these cars, slightly over a third are in the United States (although we have only one-twentieth of the world's population), slightly over a third are in Europe, and the remainder are spread over the rest of the globe. The vehicle growth rate is very high, and based on present rates, there may be 800 million vehicles on the roads by the end of the century, and perhaps nearly one and a half billion by about 2030. Given the number of automobiles and other vehicles, it is imperative that something be done to control the amount of fossil fuel energy they consume and the amount of pollution they produce (see Issues in Perspective 9–3).

Encouraging Energy Savings— Voluntary versus Mandatory Measures

How do we encourage energy conservation? Will individuals, companies, and nations do it voluntarily? Or must conservation and efficiency measures be actively encouraged with subsidies and tax incentives and disincentives (for instance, high taxes on gasoline) or even mandated by law? These are difficult questions, and they elicit diverse reactions from various special interest groups. The health of our environment should not be seen as a "special interest," however; it is a necessity that should be everyone's concern.

Perhaps the most effective way to encourage voluntary energy conservation is through education. Sometimes a very practical approach that appeals to the individual's basic instincts can be effective. Improving the insulation in one's home or buying a more fuel-efficient car will not only repay the investment, and then begin to line the consumer's pocketbook, but will be good for the global environment as well. Also, advertising and popular culture can change our perceptions and instincts radically. In the past, wasting energy was a status symbol or considered "sexy"—think of the 1960s generation with their "muscle cars" that guzzled gas and generated tremendous amounts of horsepower for no practical reason. With proper education (starting very early), being energy-efficient will become a mark of status.

Across the United States, electric utilities are adopting strategies that are both good for the en-

Improving the Fuel Economy of Gasoline-Powered Vehicles

Despite continued advances in the development of cars and trucks powered by electricity, natural gas, or biomass fuels, automobiles and light trucks that burn some form of conventional gasoline or diesel are likely to be the mainstay of the private transportation sector for many years to come. Thus, it is imperative that the fuel economy of the vehicle fleet be increased. The more miles per gallon (at an international level, often expressed in terms of liters per 100 kilometers) we can squeeze out of our gasoline, the greater the reduction in environmental deterioration caused by petroleum burning and the longer our fossil fuel supplies will last. We know that we can improve the fuel efficiency of automobiles. The U.S. government first imposed fuel efficiency standards during the oil crisis of the mid-1970s, when the average fuel economy was 18 miles per gallon (13 L/100 km); by 1992 it had risen to a standard of 27.5 miles per gallon (8.5 L/100 km) for new cars sold in the United States. Using existing technologies, prototype automobiles have been built that attain average fuel economies of better than 78 miles per gallon (3.0 L/100 km).

What are some of the technical options that can be utilized to increase fuel efficiency? To begin with, up to 70–80% of the energy in gasoline can be lost due to inefficient engines. Newly developed engines, which burn "leaner" due to delicate electronic oxygen sensors, can increase fuel efficiencies by some 20%. The development of efficient two-stroke engines, as compared to the standard four-stroke engines used in cars today, may help increase engine efficiencies. In addition, work is proceeding on ceramic materials that could be used in the manufacture of engines, particularly advanced diesel engines. The new ceramics can withstand much higher temperatures, thus reducing the need for cooling and decreasing the amount of energy lost.

Besides improvements in engine design, fuel efficiencies can be improved in many other ways. When power is transmitted from the engine to the wheels, some usable energy is lost. Some automobile manufacturers are designing more efficient transmission systems, including continuously variable transmissions that allow the engine to operate at its maximum efficiency even as the driver of the car speeds up or slows down. Another area of promise is the increased streamlining of automobiles and the reduction of excess weight. Well-designed streamlined profiles not only may be aesthetically pleasing, but they reduce aerodynamic drag and increase fuel efficiency. Likewise, excess weight adds to fuel consumption. Increasingly, automobile manufacturers are substituting composite plastics and lightweight metals, such as aluminum and magnesium, for the traditional steel in cars.

Perhaps the most exciting development is the prospect of storing excess energy from the engine and then applying it as needed. Think about driving a car: as you brake, enormous amounts of energy are lost because the engine continues to run, yet serves very little function (it may drive a generator or alternator to power the lights and other accessories). Likewise, when you sit at a red light or in heavy traffic, the idling engine consumes gasoline and wastes energy. Now some auto manufacturers, including Toyota and Volkswagen, are working on energy storage systems that will capture this excess en-

vironment, in that they save energy, and good for business, in that they reduce demand that cannot be readily met by the utility. This new approach is commonly referred to as "demand-side management" (DSM, also known as "negawatts"). DSM aims to improve the efficiency with which electricity is used, rather than stressing the production of ever increasing amounts of electricity. At present, U.S. utilities are investing about $2 billion a year in DSM; it is an investment that is well worthwhile. DSM saves the company both short-term operating expenses and the considerable long-term expenses of building new power plants to increase production.

Much to the surprise of consumers, some utilities have found it cost-effective to actively promote energy savings, sometimes even offering to pay for home improvements. Utilities have helped customers improve the insulation of their homes, distributed high-efficiency compact fluorescent lightbulbs, and promoted the installation of high-efficiency air conditioners and heaters. In the long run, the utility's savings can be split between stockholders and the consumers, who benefit from lower rates than would be the case otherwise.

Energy conservation can be promoted at every governmental level—local, state, and national. A first step is for government to set a positive example by using the most up-to-date energy-efficient technologies. The single largest consumer of energy in the United States is the federal government. The government can help fund the re-

ergy, store it temporarily, and then apply it to the powering of the vehicle when needed. Most of the systems under development consist of a flywheel that is charged with the excess energy coming from the engine. In Volkswagen's system, the engine will actually shut down once the flywheel contains enough stored energy. The car then runs off the power of the flywheel until the energy level drops to a certain point; then the engine starts back up again. In another system, being developed at the University of Wisconsin with the support of Toyota, not only is excess energy from the engine saved and stored, but an advanced transmission system actually captures kinetic energy from the vehicle's wheels when it brakes and stores the energy in a flywheel.

It should be noted, though, that many environmentalists advocate not just increasing the efficiency of automobiles, but eventually eliminating them alto-

FIGURE 1

An example of a "bicycle culture," Nanjing, China.
(*Source:* Jeff Greenberg/Visuals Unlimited.)

gether. More and more emphasis is being placed on efficient public transportation and environmentally friendly modes of transportation, such as walking and bicycling. For the past decade, production and sales of automobiles worldwide have hovered around 35 million a year. Thus, although the automobile fleet continues to

increase, it is not growing as fast as it might. As the environmental degradation caused by automobiles is recognized, conscientious citizens are restricting their auto use, and many cities, especially in Europe and Japan, are placing restrictions on the use and ownership of cars. For instance, Amsterdam is phasing out the use of motor vehicles except for public transportation and delivery purposes.

While automobile production has stabilized at about 35 million per year, bicycles are being produced at a rate of over 100 million per year globally (approximately 111 million bicycles were produced in 1994). This means that environmentally sound bicycles are being added to the transportation fleet much more quickly than automobiles. Indeed, in many parts of the world bicycles greatly outnumber cars. In China, for instance, there are about 250 bikes for every automobile (Fig. 1).

search and development of new products and then be their first consumer. In this way, the government can not only save energy but can help create a market for new, energy-efficient technologies. For instance, if all government vehicles had to meet very stringent fuel-efficiency requirements, automobile manufacturers would have an automatic incentive to build cars to these specifications. Once the cars were under production, they could be marketed to the general public relatively easily.

Governments could simply mandate energy efficiency measures within their jurisdiction, but such heavy-handedness is often unpopular. Through direct funding, the federal government in particular can encourage the research and development

necessary to produce energy-efficient alternatives. Tax breaks and subsidies can be given to industries and individuals that are more energy responsible, and traditional energy consumption can be taxed heavily so that the price consumers pay reflects the real cost of the product. For example, many people contend that gasoline should be much more heavily taxed in the United States. In many European countries and Japan, gasoline costs several times the average price in the United States due to the heavy taxes imposed. These taxes are not just a way to discourage gasoline consumption and raise funds for the government, but reflect and help to cover the real costs of burning a gallon of gasoline. The cost of gasoline in the United States is not fully reflected in the price. The real cost involves much more than the cost of pumping the gas out of the ground and transporting it to the gas station; the real cost also includes such items as road building and maintenance, traffic regulation, health care needed due to traffic injuries, and the environmental degradation caused by burning that gallon of gas and releasing pollutants into the atmosphere. In the United States today, these additional costs, not covered by the price paid at the service station, are covered by government subsidies using money derived from taxes. Furthermore, the gallon of gas that the average American burns to drive less than 30 miles (or one liter to drive less than 12.7 kilometers) costs nature untold numbers of organisms and millions of years to produce.

Wouldn't it be fairer if the direct consumer, the person driving the automobile, paid a larger share of the true cost of a gallon of gas? Some people think so, but others argue that stiff gasoline taxes are regressive—they unfairly tax those who can least afford it because gasoline is a "necessity" (one has to drive to work) and not a luxury. A system could be devised that would exempt or otherwise subsidize low-income persons or impose different rates so that recreational driving would be more costly than driving to work. But

such a system would be complicated and lend itself to cheating and abuse. Many people argue that what we need instead is more mass transportation systems, such as buses and trains.

An alternative is to tax cars according to their fuel efficiencies. If gas guzzler taxes were set high enough to pay for all the environmental damage a gas guzzler causes over its operating life, the average fuel efficiency of new automobiles would almost certainly increase quickly. Another suggestion is to tax the energy content of all fuels (not just gasoline). Also, various "carbon taxes" have been suggested that could be imposed on all fuel sources (see Chapter 20). The basic idea is that a particular fuel, no matter how it is consumed, would be taxed in proportion to the amount of carbon dioxide and other greenhouse gases and pollutants it emits into the atmosphere per unit of energy it produces. Thus, coal produces about twice the amount of greenhouse gases as natural gas does, so coal would be taxed twice as heavily per unit of energy generated. A very clean fuel, like pure hydrogen, might not be taxed at all. The idea is to discourage the burning of some fuels while simultaneously encouraging the use of cleaner fuels that are less damaging to the environment.

SUMMARY

Various alternative energy sources, such as biomass energy, solar energy, wind power, and geothermal energy, can be extremely important locally although they still contribute only a small fraction of the world's energy currently. The use of alternative energy sources is rapidly expanding, however. Solar energy and wind power, in particular, are quickly becoming cost-competitive with traditional means of electricity generation, such as large coal-burning power plants. Furthermore, alternative energy sources are generally more environmentally benign (producing less pollutants or greenhouse gases) than traditional fossil fuel–based energy sources. And unlike typical, large-scale "hard" technologies (see Chapters 7 and 8), alternative energy technologies can often be applied at "appropriate" scales—passive solar heating of a dwelling, a small photovoltaic solar system

to power a single building, a moderate-sized wind farm to supply energy to a couple of villages, or a large solar thermal power plant to feed electricity into an established power grid. Perhaps the most important advantage of most alternative energy sources is that they are based on renewable "fuels" such as free sunlight or wind.

A traditional problem with some forms of alternative energy, such as solar or wind power, is that the sources of energy are intermittent—the wind does not always blow steadily, and the Sun does not shine at night or very brightly on rainy or overcast days. The increased use of such alternative energy sources has necessitated advances in energy storage systems, including electrical energy storage and heat storage. In the future, clean-burning hydrogen fuel may serve as a convenient way of storing and transporting energy (serving many of the

same functions as oil and natural gas do today). Superconductivity applications, thermochemical heat storage, sensible and latent heat storage, as well as other energy storage means, may also become increasingly important in the years to come.

Another way to address society's needs for energy is through increasing energy efficiencies and energy conservation. After all, people do not desire energy per se, but the things that can be accomplished with energy, from cooking a meal, to heating a home, running a television, lighting a house, traveling across a continent, or producing new manufactured goods. Much progress has been made in this area in recent years, and governments in particular can encourage energy savings by instituting policies that reward the wise use of energy and discourage wasteful energy practices.

active solar technique
alternative energy
battery
"big five" energy sources
biochemical conversion
biogas digester
biomass energy
carbon efficiency
cogeneration
compressed air energy storage (CAES)
decentralization
energy conservation
energy efficiency
energy farm

energy intensity
energy storage
ethanol
flat-plate collector
flywheel energy storage system
fuel cell
geothermal energy
hydrothermal fluid reservoir
independent power producer (IPP)
intermittent power source
latent heat storage
ocean energy
ocean thermal energy conversion (OTEC)
passive solar design
photovoltaic

pumped hydroelectric storage (PHS)
sensible heat storage
solar energy
solar-hydrogen economy
solar thermal technology
superconducting magnetic energy
   storage (SMES)
superconductivity
syngas
thermochemical conversion
thermochemical heat storage
tidal power
waste-to-energy
wind farm
wind power

STUDY QUESTIONS

1. Define "alternative energy." How do alternative energy sources differ from traditional energy sources?
2. List some of the important advantages and disadvantages common to many alternative energy sources.
3. Describe the basic concept behind wind power.
4. Describe the various types of biomass fuels and technologies.
5. What is "geothermal energy"? Is geothermal energy a renewable energy source?
6. Describe some of the means currently being used to harness solar energy.
7. What attempts are being made to harness ocean energy?
8. What are the pros and cons of "waste-to-energy" techniques?
9. List some of the major ways of storing electrical energy. Which are already widely used today?
10. What is superconductivity? What potential importance does it have for energy storage and conservation?
11. List three major ways of storing heat energy.
12. Why have some major utility companies recently been promoting energy savings programs rather than simply attempting to sell more electricity to their customers?
13. What role might natural gas play in the transition to a post-fossil fuel economy?
14. Referring to Table 9–1, calculate the amount of land required to generate 33 exajoules of electricity (the approximate amount of electricity generated in the United States annually) using solar thermal trough technology. (Express your answer in both square kilometer–years and square mile–years [one square kilometer equals 0.386 square miles].)
15. Referring to Table 9–1, calculate the amount of land required to generate 33 exajoules of electricity by burning bituminous coal. (Express your answer in both square kilometer–years and square mile–years.)

ESSAY QUESTIONS

1. What is a "solar-hydrogen economy"? Do you think it is feasible or just a pipe dream? Justify your answer.
2. Describe the various ways that energy efficiencies can be improved in industral societies and developing countries.
3. How can local and national governments encourage energy savings?
4. What is the distinction, if any, between energy conservation and energy efficiency?
5. Discuss the concept of "energy intensity." How does energy intensity relate to a nation's overall energy consumption? To a nation's overall economic production? How does energy intensity relate to the per capita energy consumption of a nation's citizens? To the per capita economic production? Some thinkers believe that all nations should strive to decrease their energy intensities, even if this means using more energy overall. What are some of the economic assumptions that underlie such a belief?

Anderson, V. 1993. *Energy efficiency policies*. London and New York: Routledge.

Brower, M. 1992. *Cool energy: Renewable solutions to environmental problems*. Cambridge, Mass.: MIT Press.

Brown, L. N. Lenssen, and H. Kane. 1995. *Vital signs 1995*. New York: W. W. Norton.

Cassedy, E. S., and P. Z. Grossman. 1990. *Introduction to energy: Resources, technology, and society*. Cambridge: Cambridge University Press.

Cohen, B. L. 1990. *The nuclear energy option: An alternative for the 90s*. New York and London: Plenum Press.

Ehrlich, P. R., and A. H. Ehrlich. 1991. *Healing the planet: Strategies for resolving the environmental crisis*. Reading, Mass.: Addison-Wesley.

Flavin, C. 1992. Building a bridge to sustainable energy. In L. R. Brown *et al.*, *State of the world 1992*, pp. 27–45. New York: W. W. Norton.

_____ 1995. Harnessing the Sun and the wind. In L. R. Brown *et al.*, *State of the world 1995*, pp. 58–75. New York: W. W. Norton.

Flavin, C., and N. Lenssen. 1994. *Power surge: Guide to the coming energy revolution*. New York: W. W. Norton.

Franck, I., and D. Brownstone. 1992. *The green encyclopedia*. New York: Prentice-Hall General Reference.

Hall, C. A. S., C. J. Cleveland, and R. Kaufmann. 1986 (1992 reprint). *Energy and resource quality: The ecology of the economic process*. Niwot, Colo.: University Press of Colorado.

Hollander, J. M. 1992. *The energy-environment connection*. Washington, D.C.: Island Press.

INERAL RESOURCES

P R O L O G U E   *Mineral Reserves—No End in Sight?*

*I*n the 1960s and 1970s, some environmentalists predicted that by the end of the century our
    finite supplies of many minerals and metals, such as phosphate rock, copper, and nickel,
would be nearly exhausted and the prices for any remaining reserves would be astronomical. The
predicted crisis has not materialized, however. If anything, many minerals and metals appear to be
more "common" today than they were two decades earlier. For instance, the price of nickel today
is about 65% of its 1975 price, while copper sells for 78% of its 1975 price, and phosphate rock is
only 26% of its 1975 price. The story is similar for virtually every metal and mineral. Yet mineral
and metal resources really are finite, so why are their prices dropping even as the world's popula-

PHOTO   *The Bingham Canyon copper mine in Utah is the single largest human-made excavation in the world.* (*Source:* Courtesy of the Kennecott Corporation.)

tion is surging at an incredible rate? Intuitively, it would seem that demand, and therefore prices, should increase, not decrease.

Many factors affect mineral and metal prices. New deposits may be discovered, and newly developed technologies may make it possible to economically recover minerals and metals from previously known, but low-grade deposits. Recycling (which is cheaper than mining and processing virgin ore) over the past two decades has decreased the need for new sources of minerals and metals, as has the continued substitution of relatively abundant materials for traditional, but scarcer materials (such as the use of glass optical fibers in place of traditional copper wire). Even when certain metals are still utilized, smaller amounts are needed due to increasingly sophisticated engineering, particularly miniaturization of electronic equipment. Given all of these trends, it is unlikely that we will literally run out of metals and minerals in the next few decades.

Even so, the trend of increasing mineral and metal consumption over time cannot be ignored. Demand has actually increased even as prices have dropped. Today the average citizen of an industrialized nation uses 2.3 times as much aluminum and 1.3 times as much copper as the typical citizen did 30 years ago (of course, recycling rates of these metals have also increased over the last 30 years). Likewise, in the developing countries, the consumption of aluminum and copper has increased by factors of 5.3 and 2.8, respectively, during the same period. These increases are especially noteworthy when we consider that more than 2.5 billion people have been added to our planet over the same time period (all of whom consume increased amounts of mineral and metal resources).

Another important consideration is that per capita consumption of minerals and metals is much greater in the industrialized nations than in the developing nations (over 20 times as much aluminum and 16 times as much copper per person in the industrialized world as in the developing world). As the developing world continues to industrialize, the consumption of minerals and metals will probably accelerate. This could have an increasingly detrimental impact on the natural environment (remember the equation, $I = P \times T$ [impact equals population times technology] from Chapter 1). Many researchers contend that our immediate and short-term concerns should not be the eventual depletion of our mineral and metal resources (the effective life of such resources can be expanded many times over by recycling and similar strategies), but rather the environmental destruction caused by continued mineral exploitation. Such thinkers emphasize the development of ever more efficient and environmentally friendly ways of mining, processing, using, and disposing of mineral and metal resources—a strategy that ultimately should benefit everyone.

$\mathcal{I}$NTRODUCTION

Modern technological society is heavily dependent upon mineral resources ( Fig. 10–1), as were many "advanced" civilizations of the past. **Mineral resource** refers not only to **minerals** in a strict sense (such as quartz, diamond, mica, or graphite), but also to material substances composed of minerals or extracted from minerals. Thus, mineral resources include ores, metals, gravel, sand, marble, granite, phosphate rock, and so on, including elements and compounds that can be extracted from earth materials. These are usually inorganic compounds, although some deposits may be concentrated or accumulated by life-forms—limestone, when composed of the calcium carbonate of the shells of sea creatures, is a classic example.

Throughout history different mineral resources have played key roles in the development and progress of civilization. The major periods of prehistory and history are named after minerals: the Stone Age, Bronze Age, and Iron Age. We currently live in the Iron Age, although some suggest that we have already entered the age of silicon, an extremely important metal in the production of semiconductors, the mainstay of our current electronics.

$\mathcal{I}$YPES OF MINERAL RESOURCES

Minerals can be divided into different categories. **Metallic minerals** include iron, aluminum, cop-

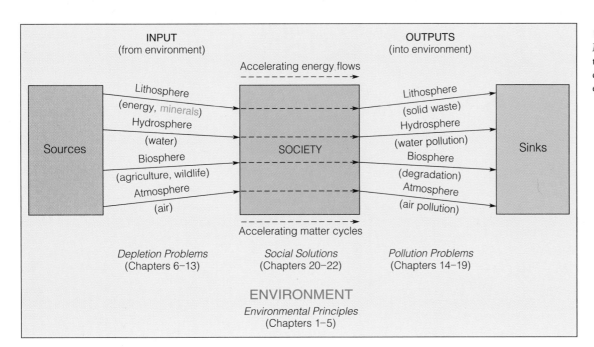

per, zinc, lead, gold, and so on. Metallic minerals are often referred to as **ferrous** (iron and related metals such as chromium, manganese, nickel, and molybdenum, which are commonly alloyed with iron) or **nonferrous** (gold, copper, silver, and so forth). **Nonmetallic minerals**, a second major category, can be divided into two groups: **structural materials**, such as building stone, sand, gravel, and other components of cement and concrete, and **industrial materials**, such as fertilizer components (phosphorus and potassium), salts, sulfur, other nonmetals used in manufacturing, asbestos, abrasive minerals (such as emery, or corundum, and industrial diamonds), and so on. The gemstones and semiprecious minerals that serve no pragmatic function constitute a third category—they are purely of ornamental and aesthetic value. Finally, uranium (see Chapter 8) and the fossil fuels (coal, oil, and natural gas—see Chapter 7) are sometimes regarded as a fourth category of **energy minerals**.

RELATIVE DEMANDS AND VALUES OF MINERAL RESOURCES— AN OVERVIEW

Of all nonrenewable geological resources, including the fossil fuels (▨ Fig. 10–2 and ● Table 10–1, page 261), the greatest demand in terms of total bulk quantity is for basic sand, gravel, crushed stone (road aggregates), and building stone. These are the raw bulk materials used in

constructing roads, bridges, buildings, and so forth. Despite the demand, however, they make up only a small percentage (about 4 to 10% of the total value of nonrenewable mineral materials, including the fossil fuels) of the total value of raw materials consumed each year due to their worldwide abundance. Virtually all of the cost involved with these materials pays for their extraction and shipment—the material itself may be almost "free." No one is concerned that we will run out of sand and gravel in the near future; indeed, it is doubtful that we could ever exhaust the supply of these materials, although certain fine building stones, such as high-grade marble from a particular quarry, may be exhausted and clean sand to fill holes (natural or human-made) may become scarce locally.

In terms of bulk, fossil fuels are the class of nonrenewable, mined resources that are next highest in demand. Due to their increasing scarcity and modern society's dependence on them, the fossil fuels are currently the most valuable sector of our mined materials (fossil fuels account for over 50% of the total value of nonrenewable mineral materials). Fossil fuels are discussed in Chapter 7.

The remaining mineral resources that are significant on a global scale are metals (iron, aluminum, copper, zinc, and so on) plus certain other elements and compounds (such as sulfur, phosphorus, salt, lime, soda ash, and potash). These substances form the basis of discussion for this chapter.

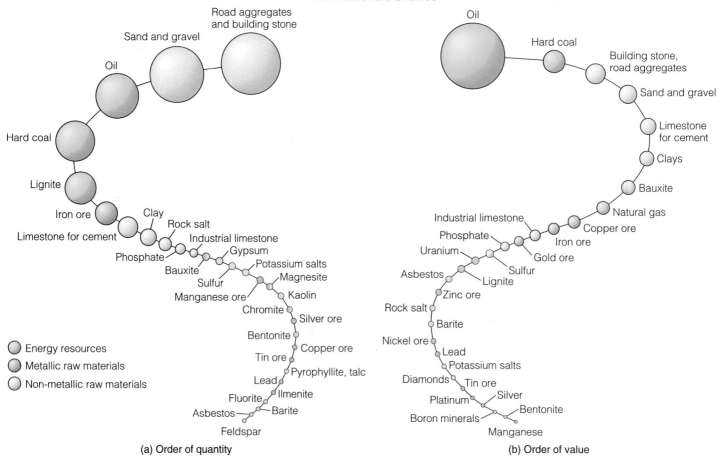

FIGURE 10–2

Raw materials snakes: (a) in order of world production by quantity, and (b) in order of economic value. Note that while the relative ordering of the various materials is accurate, the relative sizes of the circles are merely diagrammatic. (*Source*: A. A. Archer *et al.*, ed., *Man's Dependence on the Earth* [Paris: UNESCO, 1987], p. 68. © UNESCO 1987. Reproduced by permission of UNESCO.)

Figure 10–3 shows per capita consumption of several metal resources in the United States. Worldwide total metal consumption has increased dramatically since World War II, nearly quintupling during that period to more than 2.75 billion tons (2.5 billion metric tons)* annually in the 1990s. Our industrialized economy is built on the consumption of ever larger amounts of materials (Fig. 10–4, page 262). Some of this material goes into constructing infrastructure, such as roads, bridges, and hospitals, or producing other durable objects. A large part of it, however, consists of materials that are quickly discarded as wastes—such as the **tailings** from mining (the residue after the high-grade ore is extracted), inexpensive "disposable" electronic equipment, batteries, and cars (which are typically

discarded after several years). Although some of this material can be recycled (see the later discussion), mineral resources are inherently nonrenewable. Once a particular copper or gold deposit is mined to exhaustion, it is gone forever; it does not "grow" back.

Certain minerals are classified as critical when they are necessary for the production of essential goods. Substitutes for minerals considered critical either have not been found or are rarer than the **critical minerals** themselves. A **strategic mineral** is a critical mineral that a particular country or countries must import from areas that are potentially unstable politically, militarily, or socially. Problems in these areas could result in supplies of a particular mineral being disrupted. Due to the unequal distribution of mineral deposits around the world and the depletion of once-existing deposits, many countries including the United States and Canada have small or non-existent reserves of certain important min-

*Unless otherwise noted, *tons* refers to short tons (2000 pounds).

TABLE 10–1
Estimated World Production of Selected Minerals, 1990

MINERAL	PRODUCTION (THOUSANDS OF METRIC TONS)[a,b]
Metals	
Pig iron	552,000
Aluminum	18,100
Copper	8,920
Manganese	8,600
Zinc	7,300
Chromium	3,784
Lead	3,350
Nickel	949
Tin	216
Molybdenum	114
Titanium	102
Silver	15
Mercury	6
Platinum-group metals	0.3
Gold	0.2
Nonmetals	
Stone	11,000,000
Sand and gravel	9,000,000
Clays	500,000
Salt	191,000
Phosphate rock	166,350
Lime	135,300
Gypsum	99,000
Soda ash	32,000
Potash	28,125

[a]All data exclude recycling.
[b]One metric ton equals approximately 1.102 English tons.
(Source: J. E. Young, "Mining the Earth." In L. R. Brown et al., *State of the World 1992* [New York: W. W. Norton, 1992], p. 102. Reprinted with permission of Worldwatch Institute, Washington, D.C., Copyright 1992.)

ℳINERAL DEPOSITS, ORES, AND RESERVES

Mineral resources are finite and exhaustible, just like fossil fuel resources. Furthermore, these resources are not distributed evenly over the face of the globe. Various types of **mineral deposits**, like fossil fuel deposits, formed only under special geological conditions.

On a global scale a few elements (namely oxygen, silicon, aluminum, iron, calcium, sodium, magnesium, and potassium) are extremely abundant, making up over 99% of the Earth's crust by weight (see Table 4–2 in Chapter 4). But even for these abundant elements, the practically obtainable supply is not inexhaustible. To economically obtain most mineral products, we must locate mineral deposits formed by natural geological processes. But not all mineral deposits are usable. An **ore** deposit is a mineral deposit that can be economically mined at a certain time and place with a certain technology. Depending on supply, demand, and other factors, a mineral deposit that is not considered an ore deposit one year, may be considered an ore deposit the next year (perhaps because the price of the mineral has risen enough to offset extraction costs).

Reserves are identified ore deposits that have yet to be exploited. Reserve estimates for a particular mineral will vary over time, increasing as

FIGURE 10–3 (below) Approximate annual per capita consumption of mineral resources by Americans.

erals (● Table 10–2, page 263), and must depend upon imports for much of their critical and strategic mineral supplies. Certain strategic minerals, such as cobalt, manganese, platinum, and chromium, come primarily from central and southern Africa and countries that formerly made up the Soviet Union. Unless mineral trade is kept open, it is not inconceivable that, in the future, wars could be fought over strategic mineral supplies. As a temporary defense against mineral "blackmail," the U.S. government maintains a National Defense Stockpile of strategic minerals—an emergency stock of certain minerals that is presumably sufficient to meet basic military requirements for at least three years under conventional wartime conditions.

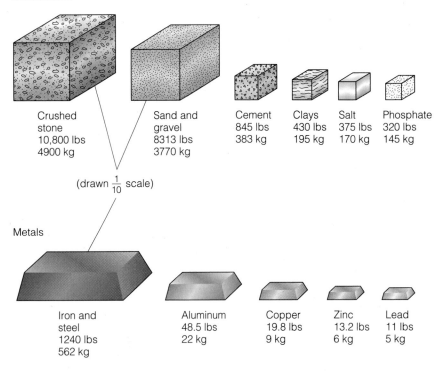

Nonmetallics

Crushed stone 10,800 lbs 4900 kg

Sand and gravel 8313 lbs 3770 kg

(drawn 1/10 scale)

Cement 845 lbs 383 kg

Clays 430 lbs 195 kg

Salt 375 lbs 170 kg

Phosphate 320 lbs 145 kg

Metals

Iron and steel 1240 lbs 562 kg

Aluminum 48.5 lbs 22 kg

Copper 19.8 lbs 9 kg

Zinc 13.2 lbs 6 kg

Lead 11 lbs 5 kg

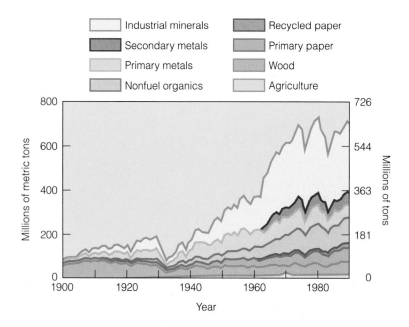

Legend:
- Industrial minerals
- Secondary metals
- Primary metals
- Nonfuel organics
- Recycled paper
- Primary paper
- Wood
- Agriculture

FIGURE 10–4
U.S. material consumption trends, 1900–1989. (*Source: World Resources Institute, World Resources 1994–1995* [New York: Oxford University Press, 1994], p. 15. Reprinted with the permission of World Resources Institute.)

new mineral deposits are located, as improved technology and more efficient methods of extraction decrease the costs of exploiting deposits, or as economic factors drive prices up, causing lower-grade deposits to become ore deposits. Reserve estimates will decrease as known deposits of a particular mineral are exhausted or if market prices fall, making it economically unfeasible to mine lower-grade deposits.

Iron and aluminum illustrate the concept of reserves. Given the abundance of these minerals in the Earth's crust, the supplies seem virtually inexhaustible. According to estimates, given current consumption rates, the iron and aluminum in the Earth's crust could last more than a million years and a hundred million years, respectively—without recycling. But when only proven, economically viable world reserves (in the form of ore deposits) of iron and aluminum are considered, estimates are that at present-day production and consumption rates (again, without recycling) there will be a severe shortage of these metals within a few hundred to a couple of thousand years. Which view is more realistic will be determined by the amount of energy and the kinds of sources that will be available in the future. With unlimited amounts of energy, we could extract virtually unlimited amounts of aluminum from very low-grade, diffuse deposits. But extracting from low-grade ores, even with unlimited energy, will surely cause environmental disruption and degradation on a scale even more massive than that of current mining.

Many substances are much rarer than aluminum or iron. For instance, copper makes up on average only 55 to 63 parts per million (ppm) of the Earth's crust, and tin only 2 ppm. To have a minable ore of most metals, the metal must occur in the rock at a concentration of tens to thousands of times higher than in ordinary rock. Even with unlimited amounts of energy, there is an upper limit to the quantity of minerals that can be produced. In the real world where energy is limited and minerals must be produced from ore deposits, taking world production, consumption, and reserves into account, it has been estimated that our known **virgin supplies of ores** for copper, tin, lead, zinc, and various other metals will be exhausted within a century.

The Formation of Mineral Deposits

Mineral deposits are formed by natural geological processes. Various geological activities concentrate different types of minerals and elements. In searching for new mineral deposits, exploration geologists must have a clear idea what types of minerals they are searching for and the type of setting where the minerals are most likely to be found.

The major geological processes described in Chapter 2 have the capacity to concentrate minerals or elements into potential ore deposits. During the rock cycle, weathering may dissolve or physically remove certain elements and minerals, leaving behind a concentrated residue of the remaining minerals. **Sedimentary processes** can concentrate minerals through precipitation from a solution or by differential settling of grains in moving or still water. Certain minerals may selectively crystallize out of a hot, molten body of rock during the **magmatic processes** that form igneous rocks. During the formation of metamorphic rocks, elements may be mobilized in the rock, resulting in mineral changes and sometimes giving rise to economically useful mineral concentrations. The high temperatures associated with igneous and many metamorphic processes often result in **hydrothermal processes** taking place—hot water dissolves, transports, and subsequently re-precipitates and concentrates elements and minerals in deposits. In this section we will briefly discuss a few of the more important mineral-concentrating processes.

When a body of molten rock—a magma—cools deep below the surface of the Earth, it does not solidify all at once. The high-temperature minerals crystallize out of the magma first. Then, as the magma cools, progressively lower-temperature minerals form crystals. The solid crystals that form are more dense than the liquid magma and settle

TABLE 10-2 *World, U.S., and Canadian Reserves of Various Metals (in Thousands of Metric Tons)[a]*

MINERAL RESOURCE	USES	WORLD RESERVES	U.S. RESERVES	CANADIAN RESERVES	MAJOR PRODUCING COUNTRIES
Bauxite	Ore of aluminum	21,559,000	38,000	0	Australia, Guinea, Jamaica, Brazil
Chromium	Alloys, electroplating	418,900	0	0	South Africa, CIS[b], India, Turkey, Zimbabwe
Copper	Alloys, electric wires	321,000	55,000	12,000	Chile, USA, Canada, CIS
Gold	Jewelry, circuitry in computers, communications equipment, dentistry	42	5	1.8	South Africa, USA, CIS, Australia, Canada
Iron ore	Iron and steel	64,648,000	3,800,000	4,600,000	CIS, Brazil, Australia, China, Canada, Venezuela, Mauritania
Lead	Storage batteries, solder, pipes	70,440	11,000	7,000	CIS, USA, Mexico, Canada, Peru
Manganese	Iron and steel production	812,800	0	0	CIS, South Africa, Gabon, Australia, Brazil, France
Nickel	Stainless steel	48,660	30	8,130	CIS, Canada, New Caledonia, Norway, Dominican Republic
Silver	Jewelry, photography, dentistry	780	190	26.8	Mexico, USA, Peru, CIS, Canada
Tin	Coating on metal, tin cans, alloys, solder	5,930	20	60	China, Brazil, Indonesia, Malaysia
Titanium	Alloys; white pigment in paint, paper, and plastics	288,600	8,100	27,000	Australia, Norway, CIS
Zinc	Iron and steel alloys, rubber products, medicines	143,910	20,000	21,000	Canada, Australia, CIS, China, Peru, Mexico, Spain

[a]One metric ton equals approximately 1.102 English tons.
[b]Commonwealth of Independent States (includes much of the former Soviet Union).

to the bottom. Consequently, a large magma that cools and solidifies undisturbed will develop layering. Specific minerals and suites of minerals will be isolated in separate layers, with the highest-temperature minerals in the bottom layer and the progressively lower-temperature minerals in subsequently higher layers.

The largest known layered igneous intrusion is the Bushveld intrusion of South Africa (■ Fig. 10–5) which is more than 4.4 miles (7 km) thick and covers an area some 300 miles (480 km) long and 150 miles (240 km) wide. Some important elements found in the bottom layers of the Bushveld and similar intrusions include chromium (found in the mineral chromite) and platinum.

Pegmatites are unusual rocks that often form in conjunction with a cooling magma at high pressures. During the cooling and solidification of a magma, many of the elements most commonly found in rocks are solidified out first. The re-

maining magma becomes more highly concentrated in relatively rarer elements, with an unusually high water content. This residual magma finally solidifies as a pegmatite—a rock type characterized by the formation of extremely large crystals. Most pegmatites are composed primarily of the minerals feldspar and quartz, but pegmatites also often contain high concentrations of such elements as beryllium, uranium, boron, and lithium. Beryllium may form the basis of beautiful emeralds, and the boron combined with other elements may form tourmaline. Other significant minerals found in pegmatites include mica, garnet, fluorite, uraninite, and many others. Pegmatites may be mined for such economically important elements as beryllium, columbium, tantalum, bismuth, uranium, thorium, and various rare-earth metals.

Often associated with hot magmas are hydrothermally formed ore deposits. *Hydrothermal*

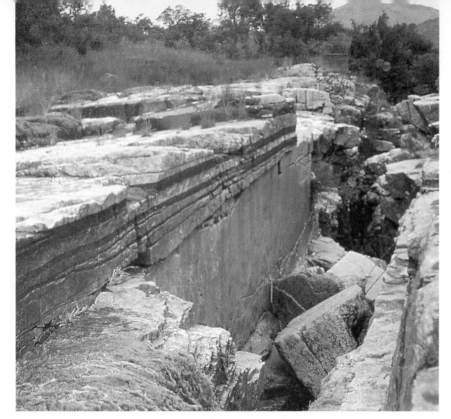

FIGURE 10-5
The Bushveld Complex is a layered igneous intrusion in South Africa that serves as an important source of such metals as chromium and platinum. Seen here are chromitite seams (containing chromite) interlayered with anorthosite and underlain by pyroxenite at Dwars River Bridge (Dwars River Subsuite of the Rustenburg Layered Suite of the Bushveld Complex.) (*Source:* Council for Geoscience, South Africa. Courtesy of Nico Keyser, Geological Survey of South Africa.)

literally means "hot water" (hydro = water, thermal = hot), and this aptly describes how hydrothemal deposits form. Hot water circulates through rock and dissolves various elements, such as the important metals lead, copper, gold, silver, zinc, and others. The hot water solution then migrates through cracks and the natural pores of rocks, coming into contact with different physical and chemical conditions as it cools. Under the correct conditions, certain elements precipitate out of the hydrothermal solution to form a concentrated mineral deposit. When the hot solution is funneled through a crack, fault, or fracture in a rock where precipitation can take place, a very concentrated, high-grade hydrothermal vein deposit may form. In contrast, when the hot solution is flowing through a large volume of porous rock when precipitation occurs, a low-grade disseminated ore deposit may result. Many commercially important copper deposits take this form; the copper is usually associated with significant amounts of zinc, molybdenum, silver, gold, and other metals.

In addition to forming below the surface of the Earth through magmatic and hydrothermal processes, minerals can also be concentrated to form ore deposits on the Earth's surface through sedimentary and weathering processes. As we discussed in Chapter 2, during the rock cycle rocks exposed at the surface are subjected to chemical and physical weathering. Naturally, the more soluble minerals and ions are dissolved away first, and the relatively insoluble materials are left as a

residue. Certain minerals, such as those that are high in iron and aluminum, are relatively insoluble and therefore become concentrated in heavily weathered areas. Bauxite, the principal source of aluminum, commonly forms in this manner in tropical regions. During weathering a rock may also be broken down into grains and clasts, such as the sand on a typical beach. When these sedimentary grains are transported by wind or water, they can become sorted by their relative weights. Gold nuggets or flakes that are mined from a stream are the classic example. The gold nuggets were weathered out of the softer surrounding rock and then washed into streams where the heavy gold settled and accumulated on the bottom of the stream bed. These are known as **placer deposits**.

Rivers may carry minerals to the open oceans and form placer deposits on beaches or on the continental margins. Such metals as gold, platinum, silver, titanium, tungsten, copper, and iron have been found concentrated in this manner on shores and coastlines, as have nonmetallic minerals such as diamonds.

Many sedimentary rocks are formed by precipitation of minerals from an aqueous (watery) medium. When dissolved ions in a body of water become too concentrated, they must be removed by precipitation. A classic example is a shallow, very salty sea—once the salt content increases above a certain point, the salt ions precipitate out to form an **evaporite** deposit. Evaporite deposits can also be formed by the partial or complete evaporation of a landlocked lake. Important evaporite deposit minerals include rock salt, gypsum, borax, sodium sulfate, and sodium carbonate.

Minerals can precipitate out of a water body due to chemical changes other than simple evaporation. Changes in the pH (acidity) of the water may cause certain ions to precipitate. Likewise, the addition of chemicals or ions may cause ions that were previously dissolved in the water to precipitate. About 2.6 billion years ago, such a chemical change occurred, causing massive amounts of iron previously dissolved in the waters of the ancient oceans to precipitate as what are now known as banded-iron formations (Fig. 10–6).

Modern plate tectonic theory (see Chapter 2) provides a theoretical framework that is useful in explaining the large-scale, or global, distribution of major mineral deposits. Mineral deposits tend to be concentrated where plates have converged and one plate is subducted under another plate. The subducted rocks are melted, magma is created and rises to the surface, and concentrated ore deposits may form. Figure 10–7 summarizes the relationship between ore deposits and tectonic processes.

FIGURE 10–6

A typical banded-iron formation. On the early Earth there was no molecular oxygen, and under such conditions iron commonly forms the ion Fe^{2+} which is easily dissolved in water. However, in the presence of free oxygen Fe^{2+} will be stripped of an electron to become Fe^{3+}, an ion that will precipitate from the water, collecting on the surface bottom as a layer of reddish-colored, iron-rich minerals. In the early history of the Earth microscopic photosynthetic organisms evolved, and as they photosynthesized they released free molecular oxygen. By about 2.6 billion years ago enough free oxygen had built up in the atomosphere such that it began to react with the Fe^{2+} ions in sea water, causing them to change to Fe^{3+} ions and precipitate. For the next half billion years or more the iron of the oceans precipitated, forming the banded-iron formations. Once most of the dissolved iron was removed from the oceans, banded-iron formations were no longer formed. Now, some two billion years later about 90% of all the iron ore mined by humans comes from these ancient deposits.

(*Source:* M. Lustbader/Photo Researchers.)

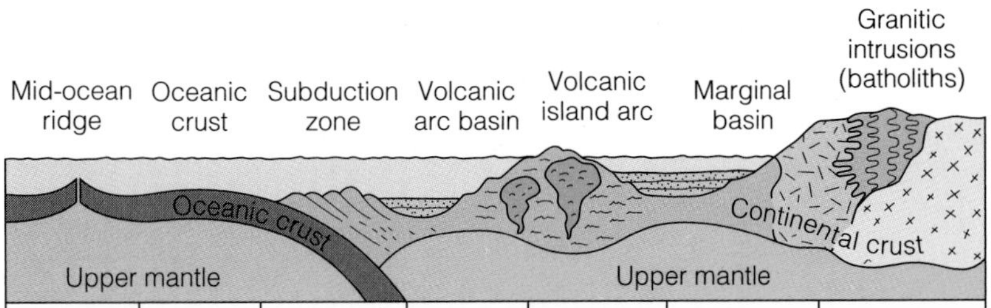

	Mid-ocean ridge	Oceanic crust	Subduction zone	Volcanic arc basin	Volcanic island arc	Marginal basin	Granitic intrusions (batholiths)
Metals	Copper and zinc as metallic oxides and sulfides	Manganese, cobalt, nickel	Chromium	Copper, lead, zinc	Copper, molybdenum, gold, silver, lead, mercury, tin	Copper, zinc, gold, chromium (petroleum)	Copper, tungsten, tin, iron, gold, silver, molybdenum
Deposit type	Volcanogenic massive sulfide	Sea-floor nodules	Chromite in serpentine rock (high-pressure, low-temp., metamorphic)	Stratabound	Porphyry copper; hydrothermal veins	Volcanogenic massive sulfide; evaporites	Contact metamorphic; hydrothermal veins

FIGURE 10–7

Relationships between metallic ore deposits and tectonic processes.

$\mathcal{E}$NVIRONMENTAL DEGRADATION DUE TO MINERAL EXPLOITATION

Mining can be a nasty business; it can be one of the most environmentally damaging activities undertaken by humans (excluding modern warfare). Over 400 years ago, the German mineralogist Georgius Agricola (1490–1555) described the environmental degradation caused in his time by mining in Saxony:

> The fields are devastated by mining operations . . . the woods and groves are cut down, for there is need of an endless amount of wood for timbers, machines, and the smelting of metals. And when the woods and groves are felled, then are exterminated the beasts and birds. . . . Further, when the ores are washed, the water which has been used poisons the brooks and streams, and either destroys the fish or drives them away. (quoted in Young, 1992, pp. 104–5)

The situation has only intensified since Agricola's time. Today, more land is devastated due to the direct effects of mining activities than by any other human activity. Around the globe many millions of acres (millions of hectares) of land have been laid waste, trees destroyed, earth and rock churned up, and billions of tons of air and water pollutants and solid waste in the form of tailings have been generated (Fig. 10–8) (Issues in Perspective 10–1 describes a law that for over a century has encouraged mining, and its attendant environmental devastation, in the United States).

The largest human excavations in the world are open-pit mines. Metal smelters typically produce enormous quantities of air pollution, including sulfur dioxide (causing acid deposition) and many toxic heavy metals—lead, cadmium, and arsenic among them. An estimated 8% of worldwide sulfur emissions into the atmosphere come from smelters. **Dead zones**, in which no vegetation or animal life can survive, cover thousands of acres (thousands of hectares) around many large smelters. The mining industry routinely uses hundreds of tons of mercury, cyanide compounds, and other very toxic substances to remove metals from ores. Acid drainage flows from abandoned mines and tailing piles. Removed overburden (rock and soil removed during mining), tailings, and other wastes pile up in massive amounts. On a global scale, mining operations have become a force as powerful as natural erosional processes. It is estimated that more than 25.3 billion tons (23 billion metric tons) of nonfuel minerals are removed from the Earth annually, and including the overburden, the total amount of material artifi-

FIGURE 10–8
Tailings from an open-pit copper mine, Morenci, Arizona. (*Source:* Carlyn Galati/Visuals Unlimited.)

The General Mining Act of 1872

In the United States, under an 1872 law, certain hard-rock minerals—such as iron, lead, copper, gold, and silver—found on public lands are virtually free to anyone who stakes a claim to them. In many cases prospectors or mining companies can purchase ("patent") the land for about $5 or less per acre ($12 or less per hectare). The law was originally passed to encourage the exploration, development, and settlement of the wild, inhospitable western frontier. A century and a quarter ago, most gold mining was done on a small scale, with picks, shovels, and pans (■ Fig. 1). Today, under the same law, large corporations are using heavy equipment to open huge mines. In some cases they move enormous masses of rock and earth, grind the material up, and wash it with cyanide compounds to extract tiny gold specks. They may leave the site without adequately reclaiming the land, they pay nothing for the gold they extract, and they do not even pay rent on the federal land they occupy.

An estimated $4 billion worth of minerals are removed from U.S. public lands each year. Since 1872, an estimated 3.2 million acres (1.3 million hectares—an area approximately the size of Connecticut) of public lands have been sold at nominal prices, and $230 billion worth of minerals have been virtually given away. And the mining companies have left behind an estimated 70 billion tons (64 billion metric tons) of tailings and 550,000 abandoned mines and open pits. To make matters worse, some of the land that was ostensibly patented for mining purposes has since been sold (at enormous profits) and used to build private homes, luxury resorts, and gambling casinos. In a few cases huge profits have been made almost literally overnight. In one famous case, 17,000 acres (6900 hectares) of oil-shale claims near Rifle, Colorado, were purchased ("patented") under the 1872 General Min-

■ **FIGURE 1**
California gold miners, as depicted in an American wood engraving, 1856. (*Source:* The Granger Collection, New York.)

ing Act for $42,000 and then sold only a month later to Shell Oil for $37 million.

Understandably, a number of individuals and organizations would like to see the 1872 law changed (as we write this, a moratorium has been imposed on further land transfers). Bills have been introduced in Congress that would prohibit the sale of public lands for mining, require mining companies to pay rent plus 12.5% royalties on the metal they mine, and set standards for reclamation of the land once mining operations are completed. This would be similar to the current situation with oil and coal extraction; companies must pay royalties to the federal government for fossil fuels that are extracted from public lands.

The 1872 rules have supporters, however—especially in the mining industry. Owners and management of mining companies, and miners and their families tend

to support the old law and oppose any changes. They argue that the law encourages free enterprise, and that free enterprise is the basis of America's strength. By encouraging people to use their ingenuity to extract the raw materials and turn them into useful products, the law stimulates economic growth and creates jobs. Others argue, however, that the 1872 law reflects an anachronistic way of thinking, based on the notion of abundance and the belief that more material can always be obtained from nature at the virgin frontier. They point out that the law does not recognize the finite nature, the ultimate scarcity, of natural resources. For this reason, they say, the 1872 law, along with many of our political and economic institutions, is based on a false model of nature and must be changed to better correspond with reality.

cially moved by humans in mining each year may be twice the amount of sediment carried annually by all of the world's rivers.

The mineral industry is one of the largest consumers of energy worldwide. Approximately 1% of all the world's energy goes toward aluminum production each year, and over 5% of the world's energy goes toward steelmaking annually. Much of the energy used in the mining industry is acquired from burning fossil fuels, charcoal, or fuel wood (causing all of the problems associated with massive energy use; see Chapters 7 through 9).

Few accurate and current statistics on the overall damage caused by mining are available, although many well-known "environmental disaster areas" (Young, 1992) have resulted from mining and smelting operations (● Table 10–3). In 1980 the U.S. Council on Environmental Quality estimated that 1.41 million acres (571,000 hectares) were mined globally during 1976, of which approximately 926,000 acres (375,000 hectares) were nonfuel mineral mining; most of the remainder was mining for coal.

We can get a glimpse of the magnitude of the total destruction by focusing on the United States. As of 1991, abandoned and operating coal and metal mines covered an estimated 22.24 million acres (9 million hectares) of land; for comparison, 39.5 million acres (16 million hectares) of land in the United States are covered by pavement (roads, parking lots, and so forth). Each year nonfuel mineral mining in the United States produces an estimated 1.1 to 1.43 billion tons (1.0–1.3 billion metric tons) of waste. This is about six to seven times the amount of municipal solid waste produced by the United States annually.

Much of the volume of the waste from mining is overburden—the rock and dirt above the ore deposit that must be removed in order to obtain the ore. Overburden can be relatively safe and may be used in reclaiming land after mining, so it need not pose a major environmental problem. If the overburden is allowed to erode away and thus be dispersed, however, it may have a major negative impact on the environment: once flourishing land loses its topsoil and associated flora, streams become clogged with silt, and wildlife is destroyed.

Generally more hazardous are the tailings. These may leach and produce acids, and the leachate may contain heavy metals or other toxic substances. An estimated 10,000 miles (16,000 km) worth of streams in the western United States have been damaged by leaching and drainage from mines and piles of mining wastes. Smelting and refining metals from minerals also release pollutants into the atmosphere, such as heavy metals (like arsenic and lead) and sulfur oxides.

Mining can contribute directly to deforestation. Charcoal, a necessary fuel in many mining and refining operations, is created by partially burning wood. In Brazil, for example, 123,500 acres (193 square miles, or 50,000 hectares) of forest will be destroyed each year to produce charcoal to fuel the Grande Carajás iron ore mining and smelting project. If a proposed bauxite mine and smelter are also constructed, the devastation will be even worse. In the northwestern portion of the Brazilian Amazon, diamonds, uranium, and gold have been discovered in territory where the Yanomami Indians live. Miners are now invading the area and threatening both the forest and the native populations. The Case Study describes how mining has affected another native population.

Many mineral products have no ready substitutes. Petrochemical products, such as plastic compounds, can be substituted for some mineral uses, but these products have their own environmental drawbacks. The use of metals and other minerals is not in itself generally harmful to the environment; the vast majority of harm is done during the initial mining and processing of the minerals. In the past, the easiest, most convenient way to obtain more mineral products was usually considered to be the mining of more virgin ore. With reuse and recycling of already extracted mineral products, the mining of virgin ore could become a rare event.

The Steps in Copper Production— An Example of Mineral Mining

Mining and final production of any metal involve a number of steps, each of which consumes large amounts of energy and produces various types of wastes and pollutants. As an example of typical metal mining, we can briefly look at the major stages of the copper production process (■ Fig. 10–9, page 271).

Most copper ore is taken from open-pit mines. The overburden (soil and rock) must be removed; then the raw ore is extracted. The amount of material moved at a single mine can be staggering. Currently, the record is held by the Bingham Canyon copper mine in Utah, owned by Kennecott Copper. This open-pit mine, currently over half a mile (800 meters) deep and approximately two and a half miles (4 km) wide, is the single largest human excavation in the world. An estimated 3.6 billion tons (3.3 billion metric tons) of material, equal to seven times the amount of dirt and rock moved in digging the Panama

TABLE 10–3 *Selected Examples of Environmental Impacts of Mineral Extraction and Processing*

LOCATION	OPERATION	ENVIRONMENTAL IMPACTS
Sudbury, Ontario, Canada	Nickel smelting	This is one of the world's best-known environmental "dead zones." Little or no vegetation survives in a 40-square-mile (10,400-hectare) area surrounding the smelter. Acid fallout from the operation destroyed the fish population in lakes within 40 miles (65 km). Conditions improved after completion of the world's tallest smokestack, but there is still significant sulfur dioxide damage downwind of Sudbury.
Pará State, Brazil	Grande Carajás iron ore project	Wood requirements for smelting ore will require cutting 193 square miles (50,000 hectares) of tropical forest annually during the 250-year life of the project.
Amazon basin, Brazil	Gold mining	The region has been invaded by hundreds of thousands of miners digging for gold, clogging rivers with sediment, and releasing some 110 tons (100 metric tons) of mercury into the ecosystem annually.
Ilo-Locumba area, Peru	Copper mining and smelting	Each year, the Ilo smelter emits 660,000 tons (600,000 metric tons) of sulfur compounds, and nearly 52.3 million cubic yards (40 million m^3) of tailings containing lead, zinc, copper, aluminum, and traces of cyanide are dumped into the ocean, poisoning marine life in a 77-square-mile (20,000-hectare) area. Nearly 882,000 tons (800,000 metric tons) of slag are dumped in the sea yearly.
Panguana mine, Bougainville, Papua New Guinea	Copper sulfide ore mining	Before the mine closed in 1989, the operation had dumped 661 million tons (600 million metric tons) of tailings into the Kawerong River. The wastes cover 7 square miles (1800 hectares) in the Kawerong River system, including a 2.7-square-mile (700-hectare) delta. No aquatic life survives in the river. Local anger generated by the destruction was a major cause of a civil war.
Nauru, South Pacific	Phosphate mining	When mining is completed in 1998–2008, 80% of the 8-square-mile (2100-hectare) island will be uninhabitable. The people of Nauru have initiated legal action to control the mining.
Butte, Montana, and the Clark Fork River basin	Gold and silver mining, milling and smelting	Contaminated with high concentrations of copper, cadmium, arsenic, and lead in surface and subsurface waters, this basin is the nation's largest complex of Superfund sites[a]. Covering a land area one–fifth the size of Rhode Island are 125 years' accumulations of mining waste, mill tailings, and smelter slag and flue dust. Contamination is believed to be responsible for the area's unusually high mortality rates from serious disease. EPA estimates $100 million for cleanup.

[a]Superfund is discussed in Chapter 19.

(*Sources*: J. E. Young, "Mining the Earth." In L. R. Brown *et al.*, *State of the World 1992* [New York: W. W. Norton, 1992], p. 106, and B. W. Pipkin, *Geology and the Environment* [St. Paul: West Publishing Co., 1994], p. 375. Reprinted with permission of Worldwatch Institute, Washington, D.C., Copyright 1994.)

Canal, have been removed from this single mine. The overburden taken from a mine may be relatively harmless, if handled properly. If released into the general environment, however, it can cause dust clouds and silt that clogs streams, lakes, and other waterways. If it contains sulfur compounds (which are common in rocks accompanying metal ores), it may react with water to form sulfuric acid, which can damage local soils, waters, and ecosystems.

Once removed from the ground, the ore is transported to a **milling** operation where it is

CASE STUDY

Trading a Mountain for a Hole in the Ground

assive mining has the ability to obliterate natural landmarks. Goldsmith and colleagues tell the story of the obliteration of Mt. Fubilan in New Guinea ( Fig. 1):

For the Ok people of the highlands of central New Guinea, Mt. Fubilan was a sacred mountain, sitting on top of the land of the

dead. In the late 1960s they were persuaded to lease their mountain to a mining company. To the utter astonishment of the Ok, the company began systematically to scoop away the peak of Fubilan. Within the next two decades, the 2,000-m (6,560-foot) peak will have ceased to exist. In order to exploit Mt. Fubilan's reserves of copper and gold, the mining company in-

tends to remove the sacred mountain altogether. When the mine is finally exhausted, all that will be left is a hole in the ground, 1,200 m (3,900 feet) deep.

Questions

1. Is it "right" for the mining company to do what it is doing? On the one hand, everyone seems to benefit—the mining company makes a profit, the Ok profit monetarily from their mountain, and the world can use the minerals derived from Mt. Fubilan. On the other hand, it can be argued that we have a moral and aesthetic obligation to preserve natural wonders such as Mt. Fubilan. The mining company can be viewed as simply exploiting the Ok and their land. What do you think?
2. When the Ok leased the mountain to the mining company, do you believe they realized that it would be entirely destroyed? What responsibility, or moral obligation, does a mining company have to explain all of the "fine print" to people who may not be familiar with legal contracts?
3. Considering that the mountain was sacred to the Ok, what does its destruction say about the mining company's regard for the Ok religion and culture? Should primitive beliefs be allowed to stand in the way of modern technological progress?

(*Source*: E. Goldsmith, N. Hildyard, P. McCully, and P. Bunyard, *Imperiled Planet: Restoring Our Endangered Ecosystems* [Cambridge, Mass.: MIT Press, 1990], p. 201.)

FIGURE 1 Mt. Fubilan in the process of being mined for gold and copper, 1984. (*Source:* Dr. David Hyndman, The University of Queensland.)

---

crushed, ground, and concentrated; this process physically removes rock and impurities containing little copper, so that the resulting material is more concentrated in copper than the original ore. Large volumes of waste tailings are produced during the milling process. Tailings, which typically consist of finely ground and pulverized material, pose more of a threat than the overburden, because they can easily be spread throughout the environment. The finely ground tailings can promote the release of various toxic metals and contaminants, such as arsenic, cadmium, lead, zinc, and unrecovered copper, that

were previously bound up in the solid rock. Such contamination and acid drainage from the significant amounts of sulfur usually found in tailings are not the only threats posed by piles of tailings. During milling and ore concentration, various harmful solvents, such as toluene, are used to extract the copper. Residues of these chemicals may be found in the tailings. At the Bingham Canyon copper mine, piles of tailings cover some 5200 acres (2100 hectares) of land.

During **smelting** the concentrate is first roasted, then run through a smelting furnace at extremely high temperatures to produce the crude copper. As already mentioned, smelting produces enormous amounts of air pollution, including acid rain; and as the toxic heavy metals, acid rain, and other contaminants emitted by a smelter are deposited on the land's surface, dead zones are created around the smelter. In England two thousand years of metal smelting have effectively destroyed the fertility and usefulness of an estimated 990,000 acres (400,000 hectares) of agricultural land.

The crude copper is later remelted and further refined in a refining furnace. The copper may be refined once again using an electrolytic process to remove any remaining impurities, including more valuable metals such as gold and silver that often occur in small quantities with copper in nature. The resulting refined copper metal is then ready for use by industry, government, or direct consumers. Two of the laws that apply to copper and other mineral mining in the United States are examined in Issues in Perspective 10–1 and 10–2.

TRENDS IN MINERAL USE

In global terms, mineral use has tended to increase over time. Before the nineteenth century, human use of minerals was relatively insignificant compared to the abundance of minerals in geological deposits. Since the Industrial Revolution and its associated technological developments and burgeoning population, however, the use of mineral resources has increased at very high rates. Between roughly 1750 and 1900, the world's population doubled, but mineral use increased by a factor of 10. Between 1900 and the present, mineral use increased by 13-fold or more. The use of certain metals has increased even more dramatically. Current annual world production of crude pig iron is approximately 607 million tons (552 million metric tons), 22,000 times the production of three centuries ago. Copper and zinc production have increased by factors of 560 and 7300, respectively, in the last two hundred years. As noted earlier, mineral consumption in the industrialized countries is much higher than in the developing nations. Americans use about 25 times as much nickel per person as do citizens of India and four times as much steel and 23 times as much aluminum as the average Mexican. According to one estimate, the United States consumed more minerals between 1940 and 1976 than did all of humanity up to the year 1940.

Yet since the 1970s, the use of raw materials in the United States and Western Europe has leveled off (see Fig. 10–4) or even declined. One reason for this trend is that Western industrial economies are placing more emphasis on high-technology goods and consumer services that utilize fewer raw materials; in addition, the infrastructure of most industrialized nations is firmly in place— major construction and public works projects are less common than they once were.

Nevertheless, in absolute terms, the demand for minerals is still extremely high, and the developing countries will need ever more minerals as they industrialize. Furthermore within the next few decades, some industrialized countries may need to replace major segments of their aging infrastructures, thus once again sharply increasing the demand for mineral resources. Also, as new

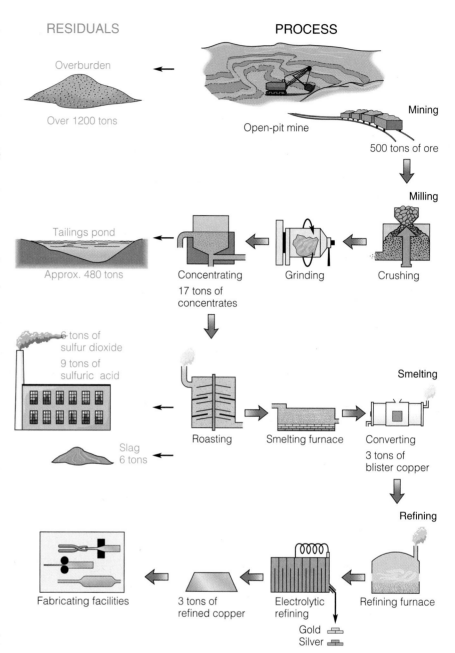

FIGURE 10–9
Principal stages of the copper production process. (Tonnages are only approximate and are based on an ore grade of about 0.6% copper.)

Loopholes for Miners

Congress enacted the Surface Mining Control and Reclamation Act in an attempt to limit the damage done to the landscape and waterways by surface mining for minerals or fossil fuels. The law, which is administered by the Department of the Interior (DOI), calls for land to be restored to something like its original condition after mining has taken place. Under various administrations, however, the DOI has loosened the requirements, and failed to enforce those that were in place.

As originally conceived, the act also had a serious, if unintentional, loophole. Surface mines with an area of two acres (0.8 hectare) or less were exempt from the act. The idea was that a private owner/user could mine on a very small scale with little damage to the environment. However, large companies began to mine their claims and properties in two-acre and smaller sites that were separated from each other by perhaps only a few yards

(meters) of unmined land. Alternatively, they set up small "dummy" companies that would mine two-acre sites. In this way they could keep their mining operations exempt from regulation. In Kentucky in the mid-1980s, half of all coal mined was extracted from mines that were exempt from the Reclamation Act. Congress eventually closed this loophole by eliminating the small-mine exemption in 1987, but by then much environmental damage had already been done.

---

technologies are developed, such as high-speed railway systems, new infrastructure components may have to be built.

The bottom line is that on a global scale, humans are currently depleting their mineral resources very quickly. It is unclear, though, whether mineral **scarcity** will ever reach the point that we actually run out of most minerals. The effects of environmental degradation and attendant pollution caused by mineral extraction and refining may force us to curtail the exploitation of mineral deposits before they are exhausted.

Increasing Mineral Scarcity and Growth in Demand for Minerals

The proven reserves (the identified ore deposits) of some minerals have increased with time as new deposits have been located (Issues in Perspective 10–3 describes mineral deposits that continue to be discovered in polar regions) or changing technological and economic conditions have made the exploitation of low-grade deposits economically feasible. Citing this apparent increase in reserves, some people have suggested that we are in no danger of exhausting most of our mineral supplies. Unfortunately, this argument does not hold up to close scrutiny. As Ophuls and Boyan (1992) have demonstrated, demands for mineral resources are generally increasing exponentially, and even if the known stocks are increased by a

factor of 10 or 100, their life expectancy does not change appreciably—it will simply take a few more generations to deplete the stock.

Ophuls and Boyan (1992) began by examining a hypothetical example. Assume that we have 50,000 tons of a certain mineral in our reserves and that current demand for this mineral is 100 tons per year. Then, if demand does not change, our reserves should last approximately 500 years. But given the expected growth of the global population and the trend toward industrialization of the developing countries demand is virtually certain to increase. This means that the reserves will not last 500 years. But can we estimate how long they will last?

The demand for metals such as tin, zinc, copper, and aluminum grows about 1 to 4% per year (● Table 10–4). If we assume that demand increases by 3.5% per year, then annual demand will double approximately every 20 years (● Table 10–5). After approximately 80 years, the demand for the mineral will be 1600 tons per year, yet because humans have been drawing from the reserve for 80 years, only 5000 tons will remain. This means that the reserves will last only another three years. Thus, when an exponential growth rate in the demand for the mineral is taken into account, the reserves last only about 83 years instead of the 500 years calculated utilizing the current demand rate. In this example, the stock is said to have a **static reserve** of 500 years, but an **exponential reserve** of 83 years.

ISSUES IN PERSPECTIVE 10-3

Mining Threatens the Polar Wilderness

Mining is not limited to inhabited parts of the globe; it is even a potential threat to the polar regions, especially the Antarctic, which has a large variety of minerals including copper, uranium, and platinum. In fact, the Dufeck Massif in the Pensacola Mountains of Antarctica may be one of the richest mineral areas in the world (Fig. 1). The Antarctic also contains abundant fossil fuel deposits; the largest known deposit of coal is located in the Transantarctic Mountain Range, and oil and gas deposits are found offshore. The Arctic also has mineral and fossil fuel deposits, and tens of millions of dollars a year are sometimes spent just on gold prospecting in the far north.

At present, Antarctica is not owned by any nation; instead, it is under the international management of the nations that signed the 1961 Antarctic Treaty. But disagreements have arisen about how much, if any, of the Antarctic's mineral and fossil fuel resources should be exploited. Some countries and organizations believe that the Antarctic should be treated as an international wilderness park to be preserved in pristine condition. Mining would be totally banned. Others believe that with appropriate safeguards and regulation, the area's natural wealth can be exploited without damaging the environment.

FIGURE 1
The mountains of Antarctica contain some of the richest mineral deposits in the world. (*Source:* Sally Wiener Grotta/The Stock Market.)

Mining and drilling in polar regions can be even more hazardous than in other areas. Due to the harsh conditions and the sensitive nature of the delicate ecologies, oil spills and pollution can have an even more profound impact in polar regions than elsewhere. In the ocean surrounding the Antarctic, floating icebergs, many miles (dozens of kilometers) long, are a constant threat—they could cause massive damage if they ran into a ship or an offshore drilling or mining operation. If an offshore oil well were damaged by an iceberg, it might spill millions of barrels of oil into the sea.

Exponential reserves are more realistic—they better reflect how long a known stock or mineral reserve will last in the real world where demand increases over time. Exponential reserves are also generally much shorter than static reserves.

But as we have already observed, reserves and stocks of minerals can also increase over time. Ophuls and Boyan (1992) address this point by readjusting their hypothetical example. Assume once again that beginning demand for the substance is 100 tons per year and that demand grows 3.5% per year, but now assume that the stock of the mineral increases from 50,000 tons to 500,000 tons (that is, it increases by 10 times). As a result, the static reserve will increase from 500 years to 5000 years, but the exponential reserve will only increase from 83 years to 147 years. Under realistic conditions—where demand is continually growing for a certain mineral—increasing the available amount of the mineral by a factor of 10 does not even double the life expectancy of the stock.

TABLE 10–4 *Identified Global Reserves of Selected Important Metals*

METAL	STATIC RESERVE (YEARS)	GROWTH RATE OF DEMAND (%)	DOUBLING TIME (YEARS)	EXPONENTIAL RESERVE (YEARS)
Aluminum	224	4.0	18	99
Copper	41	2.7	26	23
Iron	167	2.4	29	66
Lead	22	1.8	39	11
Nickel	65	3.0	23	36
Tin	21	1.0	70	16
Zinc	21	2.0	35	17

Identified reserves are reserves that are known to exist and are thought to be economically recoverable using current technology. "Static reserve" is an estimate of how long the reserve will last given current consumption rates; "exponential reserve" considers the growth rate of demand in estimating how long the reserve will last.
(*Source*: W. Ophuls, and A. S. Boyan, Jr., *Ecology and the Politics of Scarcity Revisited* [New York: W. H. Freeman, 1992], p. 73. From: *Ecology and the Politics of Scarcity Revisited* by Ophuls and Boyan. Copyright © 1992 by W. H. Freeman and Company. Used with permission.)

Looking at examples of real minerals (Tables 10–4 and ● 10–6), it is clear that the demand is now so great that whether we look at static reserves or exponential reserves, or use a conservative or liberal estimate of remaining mineral stocks, the known supplies of a number of minerals will be exhausted within only a few decades. According to some compilations, the absolute demand for certain metals, such as aluminum, copper, steel, nickel, and zinc, has remained fairly constant since the mid-1970s, but the demand for these substances is so high that the static reserves will be short-lived. Even if the supplies of many minerals suddenly doubled or tripled and demand

TABLE 10–5 *The Effect of Increasing Demand on Mineral Reserves*

TIME		REMAINING STOCK (TONS)	CURRENT DEMAND (TONS PER ANNUM)	STATIC RESERVE (YEARS)
	Start	50,000	100	500
After	20 years	47,000	200	235
After	40 years	41,000	400	103
After	60 years	29,000	800	36
After	80 years	5,000	1600	3

In this example, demand for a hypothetical mineral resource of finite dimensions grows exponentially at 3.5% per year; note that absolute demand doubles every 20 years.
(*Source*: W. Ophuls, and A. S. Boyan, Jr., *Ecology and the Politics of Scarcity Revisited* [New York: W. H. Freeman, 1992], p. 70. From: *Ecology and the Politics of Scarcity Revisited* by Ophuls and Boyan. Copyright © 1992 by W. H. Freeman and Company. Used with permission.)

remained stable rather than increased, the supplies would still be exhausted relatively quickly. Given this impending scarcity of many minerals, and the tremendous environmental damage resulting from mining, some experts believe that we must curtail our demand for minerals significantly, or at least consistently recycle metals and other minerals. In other words, we need to emphasize the "three R's"—reduce, reuse, and recycle (Chapters 6 and 19)—as well as find substitutes for minerals in short supply.

WHAT ACCOUNTS FOR THE PRICES OF MINERALS?

Minerals, including the precious metals, are artificially cheap. Since the middle of this century, the overall trend in the prices (using stable [non-inflated] dollars) of various metals and other minerals, has generally been downward. Prices have tended to decline even though mineral deposits are a nonrenewable resource, mineral consumption has been generally rising worldwide, and the environmental costs of mineral extraction and production are rapidly mounting. Given these factors, common sense might suggest that mineral prices should be increasing rapidly. Why then are they falling?

One reason is that known reserves for many metals and other substances have grown at least as fast as production over the last few decades. Given this record, most experts do not foresee any imminent shortages even when known reserves seem to be sufficient for only a few decades. Consequently, in the near future, the absolute limits to, and relative scarcity of, mineral resources will have little impact on the price of most minerals.

A second reason prices have declined is that the current price of most raw mineral products reflects only the immediate costs of their extraction. In many cases, as when the minerals are on public land obtained from the government, the source of the minerals, the ore body, is virtually free. Nor does the price the consumer pays include **externalities**. Externalities are environmental, social, and other costs that are not included in the prices of products that cause the costs. In this sense, mineral production is heavily subsidized by the public, for the public must ultimately bear the burden of the environmental devastation caused by mineral production. But even more immediately and directly, the mining and mineral industry is heavily subsidized. In the United States and many other countries, mining companies receive major tax exemptions and deductions from their gross income; the lost taxes are equivalent to subsidizing the industry to the tune of billions of dollars. Mining companies are often de facto exempt from many environmental regulations, including laws governing pollution emissions and land reclamation. Low-interest loans, loan guarantees, and direct investments by governments and financial institutions such as the World Bank contribute to maintaining mineral prices at artificially low levels.

Governments have traditionally supported mineral production for several reasons. Mineral production is historically associated with national security concerns—metals are needed to build weapons. Minerals are also important for the economies of many countries. The developed nations tend to think a healthy economy is synonymous with economic growth, and traditionally economic growth has been closely linked to manufacturing and heavy industry, which require large supplies of mineral products. Consequently, governments have tried to ensure that the manufacturing sector received a constant flow of inexpensive raw materials. Historically, opening up virgin mineral deposits was a way to attract people to frontiers that "needed" to be developed, or so politicians felt (see, for example, Issues in Perspective 10–1). For many present-day developing countries, mineral exports are the primary means of earning currency to pay off their international debts. Such nations have an incentive to open, subsidize, and maintain large mining operations, no matter what the environmental costs.

DEALING WITH MINERAL SCARCITY

There are two basic strategies for coping with mineral scarcities: increasing the supply of the substance (by locating new ore deposits or **recycling** old materials), or decreasing the demand for the substance (by finding alternatives or substitutes for the substance or simply eliminating the need for it through technological developments and changes in lifestyle).

Expanding the Resource Base

In the past, humans relieved the demand for more raw minerals by simply going out and discovering new mineral deposits, but the days of finding significant new ore deposits are almost surely over. The major geological provinces on land where deposits are found have for the most part already been heavily explored. The number of

	TABLE 10–6 *Maximum Global Reserves of Selected Important Metals*		
METAL		STATIC RESERVE (YEARS)	EXPONENTIAL RESERVE (YEARS)
Aluminum		2238	160
Copper		66	33
Iron		236	78
Lead		37	18
Nickel		144	56
Tin		21	16
Zinc		42	30

Maximum reserves, as opposed to the identified reserves listed in Table 10–4, include marginally economic and subeconomic mineral deposits (for instance, low-grade mineral ores that are not currently feasible to mine). Exponential reserves are calculated assuming the growth rates listed in Table 10–4. (*Source:* W. Ophuls, and A. S. Boyan, Jr., *Ecology and the Politics of Scarcity Revisited* [New York: W. H. Freeman, 1992], p. 76. From: *Ecology and the Politics of Scarcity Revisited* by Ophuls and Boyan. Copyright © 1992 by W. H. Freeman and Company. Used with permission.)

new discoveries of large and/or high-grade deposits has been declining for several years. The high-grade deposits that remain to be discovered will be smaller, less accessible, and more expensive to exploit. Significant new mineral deposits may be found under the sea, although the technical difficulties and expense of mining in deep water have yet to be worked out (see Issues in Perspective 10–4 on deep-sea manganese nodules). In general, drilling deeper into the crust is not a solution either, for most rich mineral deposits are found in the upper regions of the crust, and the cost of mining rises exponentially as one penetrates extreme depths.

Utilizing progressively lower-grade ores as high-grade deposits are depleted may sound feasible in theory, but in practice it does not work for all minerals. For a few of the geologically common minerals (namely, iron, aluminum, manganese, magnesium, chromium, and titanium), higher-grade ores are rare, but the lower the grade of the ores, the more abundant they are. Of course, as lower grades of ore are worked, the extraction costs increase dramatically, as do the energy requirements, concomitant pollution, and other environmental costs associated with mining, processing, and disposing of huge volumes of rock. As discussed in Chapter 6, the amount of waste produced for every ton of metal extracted rises exponentially, as progressively lower grades of ore are mined. In the United States, for instance, the amount of waste generated by copper mining has increased dramatically as the average grade of copper ore has steadily dropped from

Manganese Nodules on the Sea Floor

$\mathcal{M}$anganese nodules are potato-sized balls or conglomerations composed of concentric layers of metallic oxides around a core nucleus (such as a piece of fish bone, a tooth, or a small rock) much like the layers of an onion (■ Fig. 1). They are found in varying numbers on the floors of all of the world's oceans. These nodules contain 10 to 35% manganese and iron by weight and usually 0.2% to 2.5% copper, nickel, and cobalt, along with trace elements of titanium, aluminum, molybdenum, lead, strontium, and other metals.

Some people believe that large-scale mining of manganese nodules could solve many of our metal scarcity problems. In fact, some suggest, since the nodules are actively accumulating (growing), they could in effect be viewed as a renewable resource. But even if we could economically mine the manganese nodules, we would surely deplete this resource much more quickly than it renewed itself. Once the nodules are mined, they are no longer sitting on the bottom of the ocean with exposed surfaces to collect further accreting metals. In this sense, heavily mining the nodules may be analogous to killing an organism. In addition, we do not know how large-scale removal of the nodules would affect the chemistry and ecosystems of the oceans; we might end up doing irreparable damage to the ocean system.

Aside from such theoretical considerations, most of the nodules are under

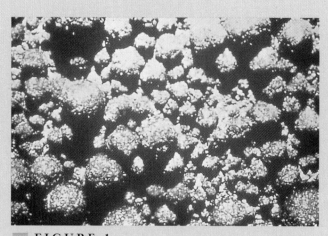

■ **FIGURE 1**

Manganese nodules found on the ocean floor. (*Source:* Dr. Bruce Heezen, Courtesy of Scripps Institution of Oceanography, University of California.)

13,000 to 16,500 feet (4000 to 5000 m) of water and spread over a wide area, so the energy needed to collect them and bring them to the surface could be staggering. But even if sufficient energy were available to make it economically feasible to mine the manganese nodules, acquiring them would still present technological difficulties. Suggestions include sucking them off the ocean floor with a vacuum-type system or perhaps dredging them up with buckets. Any such sea-floor "strip" mining would cause untold damage to the seabed.

If the technical and energy problems can be worked out, one other obstacle still must be faced in mining manganese nodules. The question of who owns them will need to be addressed, as will the issue of whether they should be allocated under an international agreement and mined under international supervision or simply treated as an unclaimed resource to be exploited by whoever can get to them first.

about 2.5% in 1905 to about 0.5% today. The increase in waste simply reflects the fact that more raw rock must be mined, crushed, sorted, and so on in order to extract the metal. As more rock is mined and processed, more energy is consumed, and more of the landscape is devastated. Most of the energy consumed in mining is derived from fossil fuels; thus, mining ever lower grades of mineral ores contributes to the quickening pace of fossil fuel depletion and the resulting pollution generated when the fuel is burned.

Most metals are geologically scarce and are not found in a continuous gradation from high-grade ores to lower-grade deposits. Metals such as copper, tin, and zinc have been geologically concentrated into the high-grade, minable deposits that humans are currently exploiting. Once these deposits are depleted, the next lower grade of "ore" is essentially ordinary rock that may contain only approximately 0.1% to 0.001% of the amount of metals found in the high-grade ores. Enormous amounts of rock "ore" would have to be processed to obtain relatively small amounts of metal. Likewise, some people have argued that an abundant supply of metals is dissolved in seawater, but huge amounts of seawater would have to be processed to extract these metals because their concentrations are so low. For example, to extract a year's supply of zinc for the world, one would have to process approximately 82.7 billion tons (75 billion metric tons, or 7.5×10^{13} kg), of ordinary rock or 1.33×10^{17} (133,000,000 billion) gallons (503,400,000 billion liters) of seawater—assuming that the extraction processes were 100% efficient.

"Mining" ordinary rock or seawater for scarce minerals and elements would not only be energy and cost prohibitive, but it would cause untold environmental devastation on a much larger scale than the considerable damage already caused by the mining of high-grade deposits.

Recycling

As we have seen, in an absolute sense, the stock of any mineral on and within the Earth's crust is finite and can only decrease. Yet, in a fundamental way, we never appreciably decrease the stock of any element on Earth (fissionable elements, such as uranium, used in nuclear processes would be the exception to this rule). As we use materials, the atoms of which they are composed physically still exist; they are simply in altered arrangements. Metals and many other substances can be recycled. In effect, recycling can be viewed as increasing the effective or usable amount of a substance that we have at our disposal. Moreover, recycling often consumes less energy than extracting raw, virgin material.

Recycling has practical limits, however. During the recycling process, the **recovery rate**—how much of the original material can actually be recovered and recycled—is always less than 100%. For instance, if we begin with a ton of aluminum and manufacture a ton of aluminum cans and other products, use these products for a number of years, and then attempt to gather them all up and melt them down into pure metal, we will end up with something less than a ton of aluminum. Normal wear, rust and corrosion, gears grinding against each other, and so on will result in some loss of metal—perhaps microscopic filings—that are unrecoverable. In the very process of recycling and producing new products, there will be some loss. Heating the metal, cutting it, or crushing it will result in less than 100% recovery. A recycling recovery rate of 90% is extremely difficult to achieve for most metals. The only metals for which a higher rate of recovery is normally possible are precious metals, such as gold, that are relatively nonreactive (so they do not corrode) and are used primarily in jewelry or other products not subject to heavy physical wear. In fact, the current recycling efficiency for many common metals is about 30% or less.

As a hypothetical example, assume that we have a recycling rate of about 80%. If we begin with one ton of aluminum, utilize it in products, and subsequently recycle it entirely once a year, then the next year we will have only 0.8 tons of the metal; after two years, we will have only 0.64 tons of the metal; after three years, we will have only 0.512 tons, and so on. If we keep doing this and then sum up all of the metal used from year to year, we will find that, in effect, the one ton of aluminum was stretched into five tons. Turning one ton into five tons through recycling may help, but given increasing demands for metals, it can only slightly delay the inevitable exhaustion of the supply. In a practical sense, recycling alone, without the input of new raw materials, cannot satisfy current demands indefinitely.

Furthermore, even if recycling extends the effective amount of a substance over a number of years, it does not increase the amount of the substance at any one time. Returning to our ton of aluminum, no matter how meticulously we recycle, we can only manufacture a ton's worth of goods from a ton of aluminum at any one time.

Recycling also contributes to pollution, diverts resources such as fresh water, and requires the use of energy. Granted, recycling usually requires much less energy than mining and refining raw ore (producing aluminum from recycled goods uses 90% to 97% less energy than is required to produce the same aluminum from raw ore).

In some cases, recycling used products that were not designed with recycling in mind can be extremely difficult and labor-intensive. For example, the metals used for many manufacturing and industrial purposes must be quite pure—they cannot be contaminated by small amounts of other metals. Thus, one cannot simply take a junk car and "melt it down." The various metals must be carefully separated, and even then large amounts of energy may be required to purify the resulting metal.

It is virtually impossible to recycle some substances in certain uses. Many uses of materials are dissipative—under normal use, they are degraded and dispersed. Examples of such materials include dyes, paints, inks, cleansers, solvents, cosmetics, fertilizers, and pesticides. Metals used in dyes and paints, for instance, cannot be recovered. As the relative need for certain metals (for instance, copper) decreases and demand remains relatively steady, a greater proportion of consumption may well be for dissipative uses. Even when consumption is relatively low, if the uses are dissipative, the metals cannot be recycled—once they are consumed, they are gone for good. Eventually, the supplies of such metals, if subjected to constant consumption without recycling, must run dry.

Substitutability

As the Earth's population continues to grow, recycling may not be enough; we could conceivably reach a point where there is simply not enough copper, for instance, to produce all of the copper piping and wiring demanded. The absolute amount of copper is limited, no matter how carefully we recycle. We can cope with these situations by finding **substitutes**. By manufacturing household pipes from plastics, making wires out of metals other than copper, and utilizing fiber optics in place of wires, we cannot increase the supply of copper, but we can lower the demand, at least relative to what it might have been. Notice, however, that even with substitutes, real demand may still increase as the number of consumers increases. Thus, the demand for copper is increasing by approximately 2.7% per year despite many substitutes.

Certain metals are valued for their physical properties and characteristics, which can sometimes be found in other substances. To use an often cited example, the metal tin is relatively scarce from a global perspective. At current consumption rates, the known reserves of tin will be exhausted in 20 to 30 years. Tin is desirable because it is durable, malleable, and light, but each of these properties can also be found in other substances. Thus, tin cans have been largely replaced by aluminum and steel cans and by glass jars and bottles. Replacements can also be found for many other increasingly scarce metals, such as lead, zinc, and mercury.

Substitution only deals temporarily with the scarcity of one or a few metals (or other substances), however. It is not a solution to the generally increasing demand, and therefore scarcity, of all minerals and other exhaustible resources because ultimately the reserves of the substitutes will themselves become depleted. Some people have suggested that plastics could substitute for vast quantities of metals, for example (and indeed great strides have been made in this direction), but most plastics are derived from petroleum products—which are also nonrenewable, rapidly diminishing resources.

In some cases certain elements or compounds have unique properties, and there is little realistic hope of finding a ready substitute. Platinum and other metals are used as catalysts in industrial processes, mercury is the only metal that is liquid at room temperature, and small but critical amounts of certain elements (such as copper, lead, zinc, mercury, nickel, tin, manganese, chromium, cobalt, and titanium) are absolutely necessary in modern metallurgy. The prospects of developing a totally new system of metallurgical techniques seem remote.

Unfortunately, a few substances that have no ready substitute and cannot be recycled very efficiently also happen to be in very short supply and extremely high demand; they are also critical to life in a direct way. Perhaps the best example of such a substance is phosphorus. Phosphorus is essential to all living organisms: it is used in DNA, in cell membranes, and in the bony tissue of vertebrates, among other things. Without phosphorus, life as we know it could not exist. Not surprisingly, phosphorus is a key component of fertilizer. Phosphorus has no known substitute. It is produced commercially from nonrenewable deposits of phosphate rock, and these deposits are relatively rare and being depleted very quickly. Estimates vary, but assuming current conditions and consumption rates, the practically minable phosphorus supply could be depleted in less than 100 years or, most optimistically, in about 1300 years.

Phosphorus is difficult to recycle because it is used in a diffuse form (for example, spread on the ground as fertilizer), which makes it very difficult to recover. One way of recycling phosphorus would be to crush bones and extract the phosphorus from them, but the recovery rate would probably be fairly low.

Conservation and Durability

Just as the demand for energy can be reduced by conserving energy, so too can we reduce our demand for mineral resources by **conservation**. We can simply use less.

A very simple way to reduce the demand for mineral resources is to produce **durable** goods that are designed to last as long as possible. This can be done by building better quality products to begin with and designing products so that they can be repaired, rebuilt, modified, or refurbished as they grow old—rather than simply discarding and replacing them. In some cases considerable energy and mineral savings can be accomplished simply by reusing goods, rather than discarding them. Food and drink packaging is a classic example. The refillable glass bottle can typically be reused (washed and refilled) dozens of times. Simple reuse, as compared to recycling (which entails breaking down the product and using the raw materials to make a new product), conserves valuable mineral resources and saves energy and money.

Another strategy is to reduce the size of products where possible, a concept sometimes referred to as **dematerialization**. A smaller, lighter car uses a correspondingly smaller amount of mineral resources and may serve the function equally well. Indeed, a smaller car may be more fuel efficient. Miniaturization, as in electronics, can also save substantial amounts of raw materials and energy—and miniaturized electronic components can be faster, more dependable, and more powerful. Take computers, for example: computations that in the 1950s required tons of computer hardware housed in its own building can now be accomplished with a system that fits into a briefcase.

Specific cases of dematerialization must be analyzed carefully; in some cases first impressions can be deceiving. If a smaller, lighter product lasts only 75% as long as the product that is 25% heavier, the heavier, longer-lasting product will in this case use less material over time. Environmentally, it may sometimes be worthwhile to utilize a more durable product, if it lasts significantly longer, rather than a dematerialized product. In other cases a dematerialized product may last even longer than the heavier product.

Another consideration is that while dematerialized products may require substantially less material to produce, due to the complexity of their designs and incorporated materials (such as various sophisticated alloys), they may be virtually impossible to disassemble and recycle once they have come to the end of their useful lives. This is the case with many modern electronic devices, such as transistors, circuit boards, and batteries. In practice, it is not always cost-effective or energy-effective to separate and refine the small quantities of various valuable metals that occur in much electronic equipment (although recently advances have been made in recycling metals from electronic circuit boards and other computer hardware). The metals used in manufacturing a portable television, radio, or calculator may be lost to humanity forever. Such products are often intended to be permanently discarded once their useful life is over; indeed, in many cases they are built in such a manner that they are very difficult or impossible to repair even if they malfunction prematurely.

SUMMARY

Mineral resources, from gravel for building roads to phosphate for use in fertilizers and metals that are the basis of much of industrial technology, are an absolute necessity for modern society. Mineral resources are finite and nonrenewable, and the production and processing of minerals can be extremely damaging to the environment. Intuitively, it might seem that minerals should become increasingly scarce with time, especially as the world's population continues to grow and the demand for minerals expands. Yet the prices of many minerals have actually dropped over the last two decades. This decline can be explained in several different ways. New deposits are constantly being discovered, and new technologies allow the efficient processing of lower-grade ores. Recycling and the substitution of one mineral for another have increased the effective supply of many minerals. Dematerialization—the reduction in the size of products (for instance, smaller and lighter cars)—has decreased the demand for some minerals.

Nevertheless, some analysts predict that we may eventually have to recognize that there are only finite supplies (or at least finite high-grade ores) of certain minerals. Other analysts suggest that we will never face this barrier because we will have to drastically curtail our use of certain minerals well before the supplies are exhausted due to the environmental degradation such use causes. Mining and processing of minerals and metals are often very damaging to land, can be very energy-intensive, and can contribute significantly to water and air pollution problems. Still other analysts believe that continued progress in recycling, substitutability, conservation of material resources, new mineral exploration, and new mining and processing technologies will assure adequate mineral supplies far into the future while also minimizing any negative environmental consequences traditionally associated with mineral usage.

KEY TERMS

conservation
critical mineral
dead zone
dematerialization
durability
energy mineral

evaporite
exponential reserve
externality
ferrous
hydrothermal process
industrial material
infrastructure

magmatic process
metallic mineral
milling
mineral
mineral deposit
mineral reserve
mineral resource

nonferrous
nonmetallic mineral
ore
pegmatite
placer deposit
recovery rate

recycling
scarcity
sedimentary process
smelting
static reserve
strategic mineral

structural material
substitutability
tailings
virgin ore

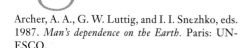

STUDY QUESTIONS

1. What is a mineral resource?
2. List some of the major types of mineral resources. Which are most important in terms of quantity used? Which are most important in terms of economic value?
3. Why are mineral resources said to be nonrenewable?
4. Briefly describe some of the ways in which mineral resources formed.
5. What is an ore deposit?
6. Distinguish between mineral deposits, ores, and reserves.
7. What is the difference between a static reserve and an exponential reserve?

8. Describe the broad historical trends in mineral and metal use.
9. How have mineral scarcity and the demand for more minerals been dealt with in the past?
10. Discuss the advantages and disadvantages of the following strategies to deal with mineral scarcity: recycling, substitutability, conservation, and durability.
11. Why has the mining industry received special treatment from governments, including the U.S. government, in the past?
12. Describe the steps in the mining and processing of a typical metal such as copper.
13. What is "dematerialization"?

14. If a certain ore body of tin contains 0.7% tin by weight, how much ore will have to be mined and processed (assuming complete recovery of all the tin) to produce one metric ton (1000 kilograms, or 2204.623 pounds, or 1.1023 English tons) of tin? (Express your answer in both metric tons and tons.)
15. If a certain ore body of copper contains 0.4% copper by weight, how much ore would have to be mined and processed (assuming complete recovery of all the copper) to produce one metric ton of copper? (Express your answer in both metric tons and tons.)

ESSAY QUESTIONS

1. What types of environmental degradation are associated with mineral usage?
2. Have mineral and metal prices generally increased or decreased over the last couple of decades? What accounts for these trends?
3. Do you believe we will ever run out of mineral resources (will demand for minerals ever outstrip supplies)? Justify your answer.

4. Should Antarctica be mined for minerals? Why or why not?
5. Should the manganese nodules on the sea floor be commercially mined? Justify your answer.

SUGGESTED READINGS

Archer, A. A., G. W. Luttig, and I. I. Snezhko, eds. 1987. *Man's dependence on the Earth*. Paris: UNESCO.

Ausubel, J. H., and H. E. Sladovich, eds. 1989. *Technology and environment*. Washington, D.C.: National Academy Press.

Corson, W. H., ed. 1990. *The global ecology handbook: What you can do about the environmental crisis*. Boston: Beacon Press.

Durning, A. 1992. *How much is enough? The consumer society and the future of the Earth*. New York: W. W. Norton.

Friday, L., and R. Laskey, eds. 1989. *The fragile environment*. Cambridge: Cambridge University Press.

Goldsmith, E., N. Hildyard, P. McCully, and P. Bunyard. 1990. *Imperiled planet: Restoring our endangered ecosystems*. Cambridge, Mass.: MIT Press.

Goudie, A. 1990. *The human impact on the natural environment*, 3rd ed. Cambridge, Mass.: MIT Press.

Lean, G., D. Hinrichsen, and A. Markham. 1990. *WWF Atlas of the environment* [2d ed., 1994]. New York: Prentice Hall.

Meadows, D. H., D. L. Meadows, and J. Randers. 1992. *Beyond the limits: Confronting global collapse, envisioning a sustainable future*. Post Mills, Vt.: Chelsea Green.

Ophuls, W., and A. S. Boyan, Jr. 1992. *Ecology and the politics of scarcity revisited: The unraveling of the American dream*. New York: W. H. Freeman.

Pipkin, B. W. 1994. *Geology and the environment*. St. Paul: West Publishing Company.

Turner, B. L., II, W. C. Clark, R. W. Kates, J. F. Richards, J. T. Mathews, and W. B. Meyer, eds. 1990. *The Earth as transformed by human action*. Cambridge: Cambridge University Press.

World Resources Institute. 1994. *World resources 1994–95*. New York: Oxford University Press.

Young, J. E. 1992. "Mining the Earth." In L. R. Brown *et al.*, *State of the world 1992*, pp. 100–118. New York: W. W. Norton.

WATER RESOURCES

PROLOGUE   *Wally's Garden Hose—Alaskan Water for Thirsty California*

*A*s the most populous U.S. state, California has an abundance of people but a severe shortage of water, especially in southern California. Many solutions have been proposed, such as towing icebergs, redirecting rivers in Oregon, and desalination plants in Mexico. Most of these proposals have not withstood close scrutiny, but one that has received increasing attention lately is an improbable plan to pipe fresh water undersea from Alaska to California.

PHOTO   *Could Alaskan glaciers such as this provide water for California?* (*Source*: Charlie Ott/Photo Researchers.)

This giant aqueduct is often called "Wally's garden hose" because it has been championed by Alaskan governor Walter Hickel for over 20 years. He notes that the Arctic has few people and lots of fresh water, in the form of glaciers and rivers of their meltwaters. At an estimated cost of $150 billion, the 2000-mile (3200 km) long "hose" would deliver one trillion gallons (3.8 trillion L [liters]) of Alaskan water per year to southern California. This is about 10% of the water used there. Engineers rank this proposed scheme with such huge undertakings as the Panama Canal and the tunnel under the English Channel.

Opponents of the plan point out the high environmental and economic costs. Many environmental advocates argue that restraining California's growing thirst is more important, and continuing to supply its water needs only encourages more growth. "California is a thirsty vampire for water, and the vampire is out of control again," said a Sierra Club official. The $150 billion cost would likely be paid largely by the state of California, and most would have to be borrowed. This amount exceeds the total borrowed annually by all state and local governments in the United States combined. But, according to Governor Hickel, the cost to the average Californian would ultimately be as little as the cost of a can of soda per day.

INTRODUCTION

Water is one of the most remarkable materials on Earth. Despite its chemical simplicity, H_2O, its properties make it absolutely essential for all life. The Earth is very rich in water, which covers over 70% of the planet's surface. If this water were evenly distributed, it would cover the entire Earth to a depth of 2 miles (3.2 km). More than 97% of this is salt water, however, and is not usable by land life. About 30% of the world's renewable fresh water supplies are already being used; this is about eight times the yearly flow of the Mississippi River. Even so, enough fresh water is available to support over 20 billion people if it were evenly distributed. Unfortunately, because of variable climatic and geologic conditions, fresh water is not uniformly distributed so that even in a world with fewer than 6 billion people, many areas suffer from severe water shortages.

Such natural shortages are greatly aggravated by mismanagement of local water supplies, especially (1) lack of water conservation and (2) water pollution. Lack of water conservation is most evident in agriculture, which accounts for over 70% of water consumed worldwide and 80% consumed in the United States. For example, farmers in the western United States waste vast amounts of water because they do not pay its true cost. The government heavily subsidizes the water cost, so farmers do not bother to conserve during irrigation where much water evaporates. This wasted water could be used by such water-short urban areas as Los Angeles. Even worse, the farmers often grow water-intensive crops, such as rice, tomatoes, and many fruits, that could easily be grown elsewhere where water is more plentiful.

Mismanagement from water pollution is an especially large problem in developing countries. Indeed, a main cause of human misery in the world is not thirst, which very few people die from, but death and disease from polluted drinking water. Only about half the people in the world have access to safe drinking water.

WATER AND THE HYDROLOGIC CYCLE

Water: A Most Unusual Substance

Water is so common that we often assume it is a typical liquid. But, in fact, nearly all of its chemical and physical properties are unusual when compared to other liquids. These unique properties account for why water is the major component of most cells and living tissue. Some of these properties and the reasons they are so important to the Earth and its life include the following:

- *Density.* Water is the only common liquid that expands when it freezes. This causes ice to float so that it remains on the top of frozen lakes. If water were like most liquids, ice forming on lake tops would sink to the bottom, allowing the lakes to freeze solid each winter, killing fishes, plants, and other familiar life-forms. Also, much of the activity that shapes our evolving landscapes derives from this property: much weathering of rocks occurs when water freezes in the cracks and expands, breaking the rock apart.

- *Boiling point.* If water were similar to most other liquids on Earth, it would boil at normal surface temperatures and thus exist only as a gas. This would render it useless to life, which needs water in the liquid state, such as in the bloodstream.
- *Specific heat.* Specific heat is the amount of energy required to raise the temperature of a substance. The specific heat of water is higher than any commonly known liquid except ammonia. It is five times higher than most common heavy solids. As a result, water takes much longer to heat up than most substances in our environment and also longer to cool down. In short, water temperature fluctuates less than land temperature so that large bodies of water, such as the oceans, serve as moderating influences on climate. Without the northward-moving Gulf Stream, for example, Great Britain would suffer much colder winters.
- *Solvent.* Water is a better solvent than any other common liquid, which means that it dissolves more substances. This property makes water the most effective liquid for transporting dissolved nutrients, as in the bloodstream, and eliminating wastes from living tissue. Indeed, water is crucial for transporting nutrients, such as phosphorus, throughout the biosphere. This dissolving ability also explains why water is the most important agent in eroding the landscape and why tropical areas are much more eroded than deserts. Unfortunately, this ability is also the reason water is so easily polluted and often stays polluted for such a long time.

Most of water's unusual properties are easily explained by the water molecule itself. Most important is that although the H_2O molecule as a whole is electrically neutral, it contains electric charges (▬ Fig. 11–1). These charges are distributed in a "bipolar" manner, meaning that the water molecule has a positive charge at one end and a negative charge at the other end. These charges create a relatively strong attraction between water molecules, which explains why water boils at such high temperatures. Without such bonding, water would boil at $-328°F$ ($-200°C$). Strong electric charges are also important in increasing the chemical reactivity of a substance, which explains why water is such a good solvent.

TABLE 11–1 *Major Dissolved Substances in Seawater*

ION	PARTS PER THOUSAND	PERCENT
Chloride	19	55
Sodium	11	31
Sulfate	3	8
Magnesium	1	3
Calcium	½	1
Potassium	½	1
Total	35	99

The Hydrologic Cycle

While the "blue planet" Earth is rich in water, 97.4% of this water is salt water, which contains about *35 parts per thousand* (equal to 3.5%) dissolved substances (● Table 11–1). Sodium chloride (NaCl), or "table salt," is the most abundant of these substances with sodium and chlorine atoms making up about 86%. Magnesium, calcium, and other atoms in lesser amounts make up the rest. Indeed, salt water in the sea contains dozens of elements, such as gold, in trace amounts. Unfortunately, the vast majority of them occur in such small amounts that they are not economically recoverable because so much energy must be expended to obtain them. Nor is salt water generally usable for drinking, agricultural, or industrial purposes. Drinking water requires dissolved substances of no more than 1 part per thousand. Industry requires even less because salts destroy the machinery.

We must therefore turn to the 2.6% of Earth's water that is fresh water to satisfy most of our needs. About three-fourths of this occurs as ice and is inaccessible (▬ Fig. 11–2). Even worse, 90% of this ice occurs in Antarctica. Only about *0.6%* of Earth's water is fresh water in the readily available liquid state. The vast majority of this occurs as groundwater. Only a very tiny fraction (less than 0.014%) of Earth's water occurs as the fresh water lakes and rivers that we usually associate with water.

All of Earth's waters, whether freshwater or saltwater, are connected through the hydrologic cycle. Recall from Chapter 2 that the hydrologic cycle is the "great pump" that circulates water through the atmosphere, land, and oceans. The circulation is powered by energy from the Sun. This global water

www.jbpub.com/environet

▬ **FIGURE 11–1**
The water molecule, consisting of two hydrogen (H) atoms and one oxygen (O) atom.

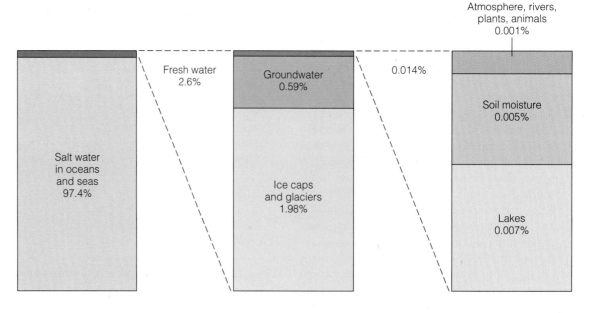

cycle involves two main processes: (1) evapotranspiration and (2) precipitation. **Evapotranspiration** is the transfer of water into the atmosphere (as the gas, water vapor) by evaporation and transpiration. Evaporation occurs from heating of liquid water by the Sun, and transpiration is the release of water vapor by plants. **Precipitation** occurs when water falls to the ground as rain, snow, sleet, or hail. In short, evapotranspiration removes water from the liquid state, and precipitation puts it back.

Let us follow this cycle, by starting with the evaporation of ocean water, which amounts to about 102,000 cubic miles (425,000 km³) of water per year. Most of this precipitates back into the oceans, but about 9600 cubic miles (40,000 km³) falls on land. The cycle is completed when about 9600 cubic miles (40,000 km³) of water return to the oceans as runoff via rivers or groundwater flow. The cycle is therefore in equilibrium

in that the same amount of water taken from the sea by evaporation and precipitated onto the land is returned to the sea by runoff from the land. The most important part of the hydrologic cycle to humans is this 9600 cubic miles (40,000 km³) of runoff because it provides most of our water supply, as discussed below.

How fast does water move through this system? Each year, evapotranspiration removes an amount of water equivalent to a 39-inch (1 m) thick layer around the globe. It takes about 40,000 years to recycle all the water in the oceans. In contrast, the much smaller water reservoir of the atmosphere recycles in 9 to 10 days (depending on seasonal variation). Stream and river water is fully renewed about every two weeks.

WATER DEMAND

In 1993, the United States used about 338 billion gallons (1.3 trillion L) of fresh water per day, or about 1400 gallons (5300 L) per person. This is more than any other nation and more than twice the average usage of water in Europe. Yet humans require only about 1 gallon (3.785 L) of water per day for our biological needs. Why do we use so much? In the United States, 41% of the water is used by agriculture, 38% to cool power generators, and 11% for industrial manufacturing. ● Table 11–2 shows some of examples of how much water is required to produce various agricultural and industrial products. Only about 10% of the water, or 140 gallons (530 L) per day, is directly used by the public. Some of this is for fire hydrants and other municipal uses. ● Table 11–3 shows the

TABLE 11–2 *Water Used to Make Various Agricultural and Industrial Products*

AGRICULTURAL PRODUCTS	GALLONS	LITERS	INDUSTRIAL PRODUCTS	GALLONS	LITERS
Egg, 1	40	151	Refine 1 gallon of crude oil	10	38
Milk, 1 glass	100	380	Sunday paper	280	1060
Flour, 1 pound	75	285	Aluminum, 1 pound	1000	3800
Rice, 1 pound	560	2120	Automobile, 1	100,000	380,000
Beef, 1 pound	800	3030			

(*Source*: Based on U.S. Geological Survey data, 1992.)

daily water use of an average American family of four; each person uses about 61 gallons (230 L).

All of these figures largely reflect the amount of water withdrawn from the water supply. **Withdrawn water** is water that is taken from its source (such as a river, lake, or aquifer), but it may be returned to its source after use. For example, a power plant may withdraw water from a river to cool generators, but return the water to the river when done.

Consumed water is water that is withdrawn but *not returned* to the original source: it is "lost" to the local part of the hydrologic cycle, usually by evaporation. Approximately a quarter of all water withdrawn in the U.S. is consumed, and agriculture accounts for 80% of the water consumed in the United States (Fig. 11–3). California agriculture alone accounts for about one-third of total U.S. water consumption. Of all the water consumed in agriculture, 85% is used for irrigation, which is extremely inefficient, in that on average only about 37% of the source water is actually absorbed by the plants being irrigated. The rest is mostly evaporated from the drainage ditches as the water travels to the crops.

TABLE 11–3 *Daily Water Use for an American Family of Four People*

	GALLONS	LITERS
Toilet flushing	100	380
Showers and baths	80	303
Laundry	35	132
Dishwashing	15	57
Bathroom sink	8	30
Utility sink	5	19
Total	243	921

(*Source*: U.S. Environmental Protection Agency, 1993.)

In summary: *industry is the greatest withdrawer of water, but agriculture is the greatest consumer.* Industry (including power plants) withdraws more water, but it returns a vastly higher proportion than agriculture does. Unfortunately, this returned water is not always clean and must be treated. Thus, even water that is not technically "consumed" is often rendered unusable for other purposes such as drinking.

Since 1950, total world water withdrawal has more than tripled (Fig. 11–4). Per capita withdrawal has more than doubled in that time. Because water conservation has led to a relative slowing of demand growth in industrialized countries in recent years, the rapid growth of global demand is caused mainly by increasing withdrawal in developing nations. Developing countries are using more water for the same basic reasons that their use of all resources is increasing: (1) increasing population growth (more people) and (2) increasing per capita demand (more water per person). Per capita demand rises with industrialization because water is needed to produce water-

FIGURE 11–4
Estimated annual world water use, projected until the year 2000. Agriculture is the largest user by far. (*Source*: Adapted from *State of the World 1993*, edited by Lester R. Brown, *et al.*, with the permission of W. W. Norton & Company, Inc. Copyright © 1993 by Worldwatch Institute.)

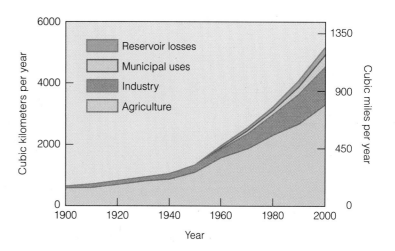

intensive consumer items (see Tables 11–2 and 11–3).

As in the United States, agriculture is the main user of water worldwide, accounting for about 73%. Industry uses about 21% and domestic use is about 6%. Use varies from country to country, however. Agriculture is the greatest withdrawer in many countries, even in such industrialized nations as Italy and Australia. In a few countries, such as Indonesia, household withdrawal outweighs agricultural or industrial use.

$\mathcal{W}$ATER SUPPLY

Water shortages occur when supply does not meet demands. For now at least, such shortages are mainly regional problems that occur because the hydrologic cycle distributes water very unevenly.

Regional Water Shortages: Inequalities in the Hydrologic Cycle

Figure 11–5 illustrates the inequalities in the hydrologic cycle. **Surplus areas** receive more precipitation than is needed by well-established vegetation, including crops. In contrast, **deficit areas** receive less precipitation than is needed by well-established vegetation.

Figure 11–5 exhibits two main patterns:

1. Severe deficit areas are deserts found mainly in Australia, the western United States, and especially Africa and the Middle East. These correspond strongly to rainfall patterns: most deserts tend to occur at about 30° north and south latitude.
2. Major surplus areas are especially prominent in South America, Asia, and eastern North America. About two-thirds of stream flow in the United States is east of the Mississippi River. Most of the one-third found west of the Mississippi is confined to the Northwest.

Perhaps the most surprising aspect of these patterns is that so much of Africa is water deficit–ridden. Although we often think of Africa as a continent rich in lush, tropical forests, this is true of only the central part. North Africa and the Middle East, for instance, withdraw a huge fraction of available water.

A Global Water Shortage?

Regional and local water shortages have always existed because of the inequalities of the hydrologic cycle. Even small bands of hunters and gatherers long ago experienced droughts and other serious shortages. The mysterious Anasazi "cliff-dwellers" of the American Southwest, for example, are thought to have abandoned their

FIGURE 11–5
Regions of water surplus (green) and deficiency (brown) in the world. Deficit areas receive less precipitation than is needed by well-established vegetation; surplus areas receive more. (*Source*: M. Falkenmark, "Water and Mankind," *Ambio 6* [1977]: 5. Reprinted with permission of *Ambio*.)

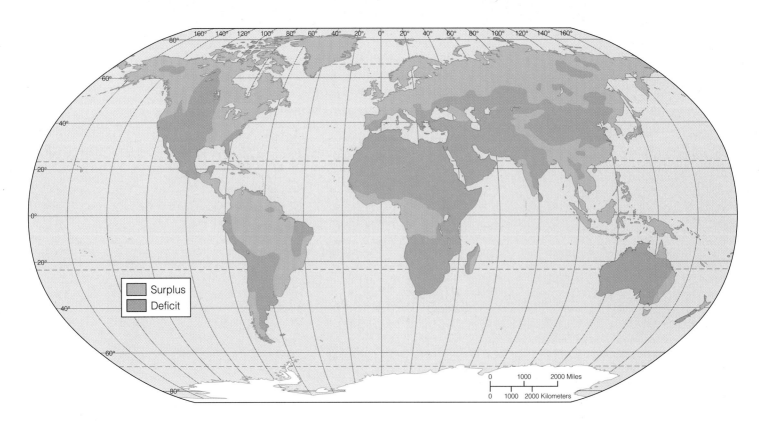

dwellings because of a long-term drought hundreds of years ago (Fig. 11–6). With the rapid growth in population and industrialization (and consequent per capita water use), increasing demand has, of course, increased the extent of regional and local shortages.

Does this mean that countries with surplus water from the hydrologic cycle will not suffer water shortages? Not necessarily! A global view indicates that the entire hydrologic cycle is nearing the limits of use. If this occurs, even surplus areas will experience shortages. Recall that the hydrologic cycle annually creates about 9600 cubic miles, or 40,000 cubic kilometers, of freshwater runoff from the land to the sea. It is estimated that about 9000 cubic kilometers of this runoff are accessible in the form of a stable, predictable supply, such as rivers, that can be captured by dams, canals, and other methods (Fig. 11–7). Because it is supplied annually by the Sun (evapotranspiration), this accessible runoff could potentially be used year after year without ever depleting other freshwater resources on land such as ancient groundwater. In regional and local terms, surplus areas are those that receive a lavish supply of this accessible runoff—so lavish, in fact, that much runs back into the sea because there is no need to retain it. The other, inaccessible 31,000 cubic kilometers are lost as flood runoff or flow into the sea in uninhabited areas. Although most of the fresh water transported over land occurs as flood runoff, it is not accessible because it is too unpredictable and too dispersed to be economically captured.

Currently, humans use about half of the 9000 cubic kilometers (see Fig. 11–4), but the projections in Figure 11–7 suggest that by the year 2000, we will be nearing the limits of the accessible water. Figure 11–5 shows some of the key areas where water shortages are now becoming apparent. The demands made by consumption and pollution will come close to exhausting the accessible runoff, and even this will be accessible only if an extensive dam-building program is undertaken in underdeveloped surplus areas such as much of South America. Another striking aspect of the global projections in Figure 11–7 is the amount of accessible water that will be rendered unusable by pollution. Direct consumption accounts for only about half of the water used; pollution accounts for the other half. Issues in Perspective 11–1 describes some of the difficulties people in developing countries face in obtaining safe drinking water due to pollution and other problems.

The messages of such global projections are not all bad. By pointing out the limits to present trends, projections tell us where corrections can

FIGURE 11–6

Native Americans, often called "cliff dwellers," lived in these cliffs in the southwestern United States before a drought apparently forced them to leave. (*Source*: John Gerlach/Visuals Unlimited.)

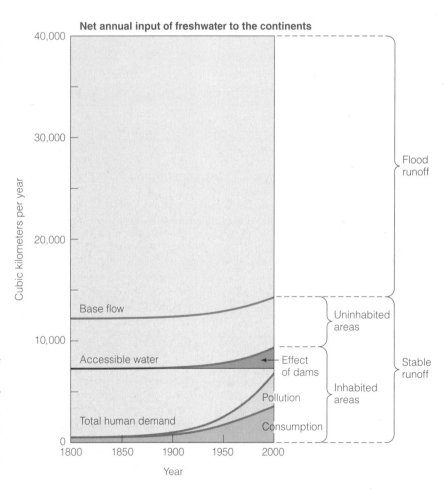

FIGURE 11–7

Of the total input of freshwater to the continents, only about 9000 cubic kilometers will be accessible in inhabited areas by the year 2000. This will barely exceed the total amount of water that will be used by humans either through direct consumption or by rendering it unusable through pollution. Note: $4.1655 km^3$ equals approximately 1 $mile^3$. (*Source*: D. H. Meadows, D. L. Meadows, and J. Randers, *Beyond the Limits* [Post Mills, Vt.: Chelsea Green, 1992], p. 55. Reprinted from *Beyond the Limits*. Copyright © 1992 by Meadows, Meadows, and Randers. With permission from Chelsea Green Publishing Company, White River Junction, Vermont.)

The Global Safe Drinking Water Crisis

Alexandria, Egypt, known as the "Paris of the Middle East," still has the appearance of a lovely city—but only when viewed from afar. The turquoise waters of the Mediterranean Sea that were once pristine are now brown and smelly and often transmit diseases to those who dare swim in them. The spray that a car sends up when it travels through residential neighborhoods near the coast is not rainfall or water from leaking mains; it is wastewater from the multi-family dwellings that are provided with water but not with a sewer line. Residents walk on boards to get to their homes and neighborhood shops, and children play in the sewage-filled pools outside their homes.

The impact on public health is apparent in the city's infant mortality rate, which is in the 100-per-1000 live births range. In more developed countries, the infant mortality rate is 10-per-1000 live births. Egyptians suffer the highest rates of water-borne diseases in the Middle East, and Alexandrians have the highest rates in all of Egypt. The reason for such high rates is poor sanitation, especially the absence of an adequate sewer system.

Many of the cities in developing countries do not have an adequate supply of safe drinking water. Limited water resources, inadequate facilities for treating and distributing water, and the absence of proper sewerage all contribute to the shortage ( Fig. 1). Despite efforts over the last half-century by industrialized countries and international agencies, the situation in these cities is actually worsening.

The poor in developing countries have long been perceived as being unable to pay for household water service. In reality, however, because the urban poor of these countries are generally not provided with public water service, they have to buy water, often of questionable quality, from private, unregulated vendors. Buying small amounts of water from vendors is more expensive by far than obtaining water from municipal sources.

FIGURE 1
A "floating market" in Thailand illustrates the demands placed on water in urbanized areas of developing nations. (*Source*: George Chan/Photo Researchers.)

A study of the water-vending system in Onitsha, Nigeria, found that these private vendors were responsible for more than 95% of water sales to the city's residents. The poor were annually paying water vendors twice the operational and maintenance costs and 70% of the annual capital costs of the new municipal water system. The new municipal water system in Onitsha was planned without any participation from the city's residents. As a result, they were unsure of its reliability and quality and were reluctant to connect to the system. Instead, they continued to pay high prices for a much inferior service.

Visitors to these cities may see an impressive skyline with modern hotels, offices, and apartment buildings. What they do not see is the absence of physical infrastructure, such as sewers and water lines, to serve these buildings. In cities where the public water supply is inadequate and developers sink wells, which lower the water table, land subsidence often results, and, in coastal areas, saltwater intrusion ultimately fouls the wells. The absence of sewerage is even more serious. The wastewater is discharged with little if any treatment into drainage channels and urban streams so that the surficial groundwater and the soil become badly contaminated. In Bangkok, for example, household wastewater is discharged into the klongs, or canals. Pipes containing water destined for homes run through the klongs, and when the water pressure in the pipes is low, wastewater in the klongs seeps into the pipes.

The lack of basic water and sanitation services leads to a number of problems. For example, although water-borne diseases are completely manageable in the industrialized world, they extract a heavy toll in the less developing countries. Also, many hours each day are spent fetching water—time that might be put to more socially and economically productive uses.

The problem is worsening. By 2000, people living in cities will constitute about 50, 40, and 85% of the populations of Asia, Africa, and Latin America, respectively. Moreover, the number of cities with more than 1 million inhabitants will have increased to more than five times the number in 1950. In addition, 18 out of a total of 22 "giant cities" (urban areas with more than 10 million inhabitants) will be in developing countries by 2000, compared to only 1 out of a total of 4 such cities in 1960.

Lack of technology or funds cannot alone explain the failure of some developing countries to provide an adequate water supply and sanitation services. Even in cases where funds are available and the required technology involves only well-established practices, projects have not been sustained. As this suggests, solving the water supply problems of these countries will not be a simple matter and will require more fundamental changes than merely providing funding.

be made. For example, as we will see later in this chapter, the 9000 cubic kilometers accessible to us can be used much more effectively. Conservation and water pollution controls alone can reduce per capita consumption and pollution, respectively, slowing the demand curve in Figure 11–7.

Types of Water Resources

Surplus areas are rich in water resources. These resources are usually categorized as either (1) surface waters or (2) groundwater. Deficit areas also usually have these two types of water resources, although, of course, in shorter supply. Thus, even the arid areas of the western United States have a few major rivers, such as the Colorado River, and groundwater supplies. Because precipitation is lower in those areas, however, these resources are replenished much more slowly when used.

Surface Waters

Humans have traditionally used surface waters where possible because they are more accessible than groundwater. Surface waters include both (1) flowing waters, such as streams and rivers, and (2) basinal waters, such as ponds and lakes.

About 20% of the precipitation that falls on land flows over the surface, first as sheet wash, then as riverlets, and then as streams. The streams (often called "tributaries") eventually merge together into a large river. As the running water flows from the riverlets through the rivers, it carves out progressively larger channels, creating a tree-like pattern (Fig. 11–8). The region drained by such a network is called a **drainage basin**. The drainage basin of the Mississippi River covers much of the upper Midwest, for example. **Discharge**, the volume of water carried in a channel, increases with the size of the channel. Thus, the larger streams in a drainage basin carry larger quantities of water.

Stream and river valleys, from the Nile to the Mississippi, have always been among the most heavily populated areas. The reasons are many: (1) soil on the floodplain is rich with nutrients deposited when the river overflows; (2) the water provides a ready means of transportation and shipping; (3) moving water carries wastes away more readily than lakes and other standing supplies of water; and (4) the river provides a source of clean drinking water. These various uses often conflict, however, and the conflicts have intensified as growing numbers of humans have placed ever more pressures on stream and river resources. Rivers used for extensive waste disposal, for example, are not useful for drinking water or

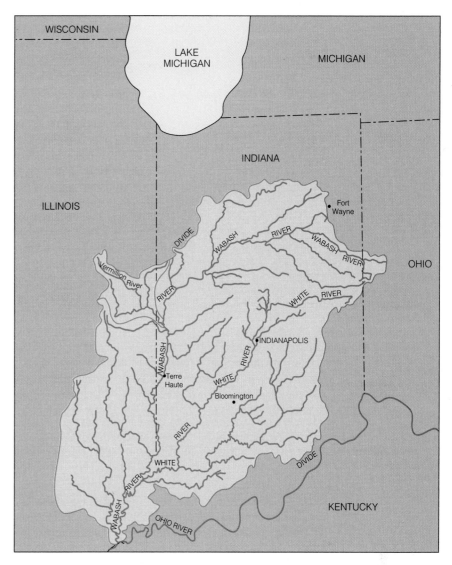

even recreational activities. In 1969, such large amounts of industrial waste were dumped into the Cuyahoga River near Cleveland, Ohio, that the river caught on fire. Such incidents led to the passage of the U.S. Clean Water Act and other legislation in the early 1970s which has succeeded in keeping flowing waters available for many uses (Chapter 16).

Basinal fresh waters, such as ponds and lakes, are more readily polluted than flowing waters. Ponds and lakes form where water accumulates in basins (local depressions) in the land. Wastes are not carried away, but tend to accumulate in the basin. The water supply in even very large basins such as the Aral Sea can be depleted if enough demands are made on it (Issues in Perspective 11–2).

Groundwater

Recall that the vast majority of accessible fresh water occurs as groundwater (Fig. 11-2). Indeed, groundwater supplies the drinking water for

FIGURE 11–8
Drainage basin of the Wabash River showing tree-like pattern of tributaries that drain into larger channels.

The Shrinking Aral Sea

Signs of irrigation overstepping ecological limits are evident among the world's rivers, lakes, and streams. By far the most dramatic is the shrinking Aral Sea in central Asia (Fig. 1). Fully 95% of the former Soviet Union's cotton harvest was grown in this region, as well as a third of the country's fruits, a quarter of its vegetables, and 40% of its rice.

Because of the dry climate, 90% of the croplands in the area must be irrigated. As production expanded during the 1960s and 1970s, increasing amounts of water were diverted from the region's two major rivers, the Amu Dar'ya and Syr Dar'ya—the only sources of replenishment for the Aral Sea other than the meager rainfall. By 1980, flows in these rivers' lower stretches had been reduced to a trickle, and the sea had contracted markedly.

The Aral's surface area has shrunk by more than 40% since 1960, volume has dropped by two-thirds, and salinity levels have risen threefold. All native fish species have disappeared, devastating the region's fishing industry. Winds pick up salt from the dry seabed and annually dump 43 million tons (39 million metric tons) of it on surrounding cropland, damaging harvests. If no corrective measures are taken, the Aral—once the world's fourth largest freshwater lake—could be reduced to a main body in the south with a salinity well above the ocean's and several small brine lakes in the north.

Saving the Aral, even in its diminished form, became a high priority in the former Soviet Union. A long-standing plan to divert water from north-flowing Siberian rivers southwest into central Asia was shelved because of concerns over the scheme's environmental effects and its exorbitant cost—estimated at between $70 billion and $156 billion at the mid-October 1989 exchange rate.

Planners hoped that curtailing agricultural water use in the Aral basin would be sufficient to preserve the sea. In September 1988, the Communist Party Central Committee laid out a strategy aimed at raising average flows into the sea threefold over average levels during the 1980s by the year 2005, largely by making irrigation systems more efficient. But by 1996, this plan had not been implemented.

(a)

(b)

FIGURE 1

Location (a) and 1985 space shuttle view (b) of the Aral Sea. (*Source for (b)*: NASA.)

about half the United States population and will likely provide much more in the future. **Ground-water** is a general term referring to water beneath the Earth's surface. It occurs because about 10% of the water falling as precipitation ultimately enters the ground, infiltrating down through the soil and rock (Figure 11–9). As the water is pulled downward by gravity, it fills the rock pores, called voids, until it is stopped by a layer of impermeable rock. As the infiltrating water "backs up," it forms the **zone of saturation**, which consists of voids that are fully saturated with water (Fig. 11–9). Above this is the **zone of aeration**, which consists of voids that may be moist but are not saturated. The **water table** is the boundary between the zones of saturation and aeration. The rock that contains the zone of saturation is known as an **aquifer** (*aqua* = water; *fero* = containing). An aquifer must be a relatively permeable rock, such as sandstone, gravel, fractured limestone, or fractured granite.

Impermeable rocks that obstruct water flow are called **aquicludes**. Shales and other clay-related rocks are common aquicludes. Aquicludes can separate the zone of saturation into one or more aquifers, often called **confined aquifers** (Fig. 11–10). These confined aquifers are supplied with water from one or more **recharge areas**, from which rainfall infiltrates into them (Fig. 11–10). If the aquifer is sufficiently confined by aquicludes so that pressure is built up from the recharge, an **artesian well** can result. The pressure causes the water to flow freely, without the pumping (or the

bucket wells of western movies) required by most aquifers. Waste-well injection into deep confined aquifers was once a common method of waste disposal because it was erroneously thought that wastes would not leak into the higher aquifers that often provide drinking water. But aquicludes often have fissures or other openings that allow water to move between aquifers; "confined" aquifers are rarely completely confined. Waste-well injection has consequently been banned in many areas.

In areas of high rainfall, the water table tends to be near the surface. This is especially true in low-lying places such as Florida, which is near sea level.

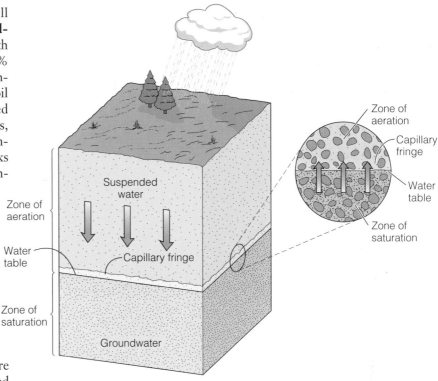

FIGURE 11–9
Rainfall infiltrates the soil, moving downward to form the zone of saturation. The top of this zone is the water table.

FIGURE 11–10
Water from a recharge area flows into sandstone aquifers enclosed by aquicludes.

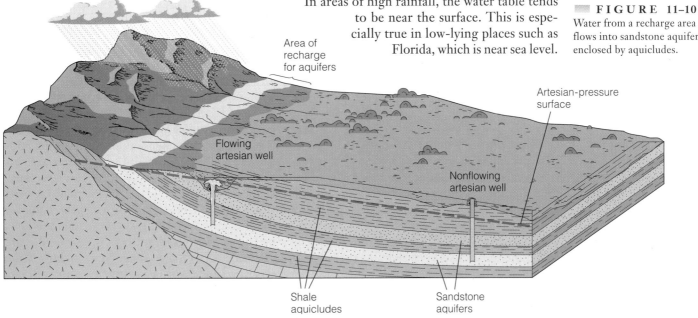

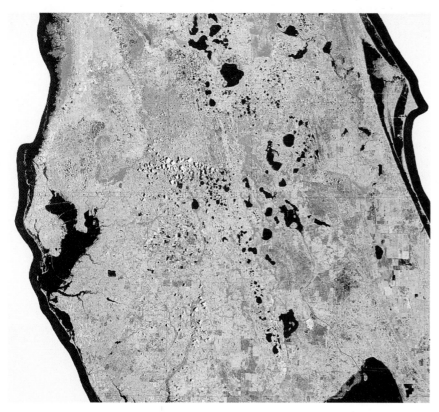

FIGURE 11-11
Florida's many lakes are caused by a combination of high rainfall and low-lying areas, including some created by sinkholes. This satellite image of central Florida shows hundreds of lakes and thousands of sinkholes. The area is underlain by limestone. (*Source*: U.S. Geological Survey.)

In such areas, lakes and rivers are especially abundant because they occur where the land surface dips below the water table (Fig. 11–11). Where the ocean is nearby, groundwater closest to the ocean will be composed of salt water. The saltwater groundwater will migrate inland if humans withdraw too much water, as we will see shortly.

Groundwater Problems Nearly all areas of the Earth have groundwater supplies. Despite this wealth of water, two groups of problems have arisen that reduce groundwater's utility:

- Discharge problems
    1. Groundwater pollution
- Withdrawal problems
    2. Depletion
    3. Land subsidence
    4. Salt water intrusion

Discharge problems arise from the discharge of toxins, metals, organics, and many other materials into the groundwater supply. Groundwater pollution is discussed in detail in Chapter 16. Note here, however, that groundwater pollution is generally considered to be the greatest water pollution problem of the future. Until a few years ago, most research and legislation generally neglected groundwater pollution, concentrating instead on surface waters. However, groundwater's slow movement (an average of about 50 feet

or 15.2 m per year) causes pollutants to stay in the water for long periods of time. Thus, seepage from surface wastes, well-injected wastes, septic tanks, and many other sources of pollution have created many long-term groundwater problems that will take much time and money to clean up.

Withdrawal problems arise from the removal of groundwater from aquifers. Depletion occurs when groundwater is withdrawn faster than the aquifer can be recharged. Aquifers can be depleted even in areas of very high rainfall because human-made pumps remove groundwater at a much greater rate than the aquifers recharge. Recharge water must infiltrate through the sediment and rock, which usually takes years. Geologists estimate that the average aquifer takes at least 200 years to fully recharge. In such cases, groundwater becomes a nonrenewable resource that is "mined," in terms of a human lifetime. Much of central and south Florida, for example, is already suffering severe groundwater shortages despite its very high rainfall. Depletion is often greatly aggravated by paving over recharge areas, preventing water from infiltrating. Another problem is the destruction of swamps and other wetlands. These are major recharge areas because they retain water for long periods, purifying the water and allowing it to infiltrate the aquifer. For this reason, wetlands are often called the "kidneys" of the hydrologic cycle. When wetlands are paved over or filled in, the aquifer's recharge ability is reduced. The United States has already lost about *half* its wetlands to urban and agricultural development.

Recharge time is longest in areas with lower rainfall. Deserts and other water-deficit areas tend to have aquifers at great depth so that deep wells must be drilled to reach them. This groundwater is often called "fossil" water because it was deposited thousands of years ago, when the climate was wetter in the area. As a result of the water's age, its quality is often poor, such as being highly saline. Even more importantly, when water is withdrawn in such arid areas, it often takes thousands of years to recharge. When high demand occurs in areas of low rainfall such as southern California with its dense population or the midwestern United States with its intensive agriculture, groundwater supply problems are especially acute (Fig. 11–12). The great Ogallala aquifer of the Great Plains provides the water for the "breadbasket" of the world. Yet this aquifer is perhaps half depleted, with recharge rates that are vastly slower in today's drier climate: most of the Ogallala aquifer formed many thousands of years ago during the wetter Ice Age climate (Issues in Perspective 11–3).

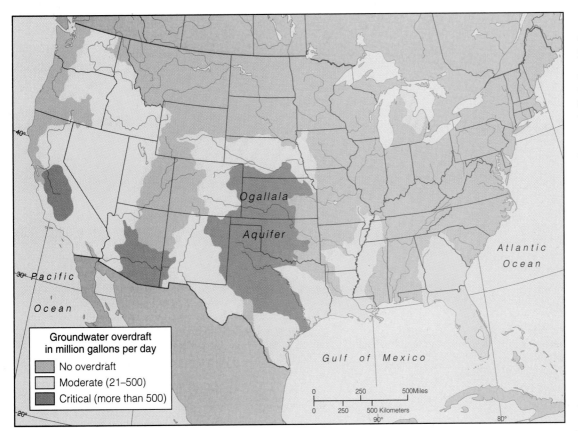

FIGURE 11–12
Areas of groundwater overdraft where groundwater is being pumped out faster than it recharges. Note the Ogallala (or "High Plains") aquifer overdraft in the central United States. Note: 1 gallon equals approximately 3.785 liters. (*Source:* U.S. Geological Survey.)

The rate of groundwater depletion can be estimated by the rate that the water table falls in an area. The global extent of groundwater depletion is apparent in this small sampling of global rates:

WATER TABLE FALL RATE

Tucson, Arizona	7 feet (2.1 m) per year
Beijing, China	3 feet (0.91 m) per year
Manila, Philippines	30 feet (9.1 m) per year
Tamil Nadu, India	90 feet (27.4 m) per year

The second withdrawal problem, land subsidence, is more localized than depletion. Nevertheless, subsidence is very costly to those who live in areas where it occurs. Land subsidence means that the land "sinks," causing buildings, roads, and other surficial structures to sink with it. Subsidence occurs where depletion of groundwater causes the water table to fall. At first, this lowering is localized around the well, where water table drawdown forms a **cone of depression** (Figure 11–13, page 295). As more wells are drilled to draw water from the aquifer, the entire water table will lower. In many cases, a lower water table does not lead to significant land subsidence. This is very fortunate because water tables have been lowered in most parts of the United States and many areas of the world from rapid withdrawal, as we just have seen. In some cases, however, the grains of sediment composing the aquifer have very large voids or are otherwise supported by the water pressure of the groundwater. Removal of that water causes the voids to close up as the sediment or rock grains crowd closer together. This loss of rock volume underground causes the overlying land to subside.

Subsidence tends to be especially bad in urbanized areas (high withdrawal) with aquifers of sediment that are highly saturated with water. A notable example is Mexico City, which will soon be the largest city in the world. It was built on an ancient lake bed so that massive groundwater withdrawal has caused the ground to sink by many feet. Some buildings must now be entered by the second floor. Houston, Texas; Venice, Italy; and other coastal cities are suffering significant subsidence. Efforts have been made to reverse subsidence by pumping water back into the aquifer. Aside from the high cost, however, the ability of the aquifer to hold water is often permanently reduced because the void space, once diminished, cannot be re-created.

Sinkholes are a special type of land subsidence caused by water withdrawal. These are depressions in the ground that occur when the thin layer of rock overlying a previously existing un-

The Ogallala Aquifer

The Ogallala (or "High Plains") aquifer underlies most of Nebraska and sizable portions of Colorado, Kansas, and the Texas and Oklahoma panhandles (Fig. 1). This area is one of the largest and most important agricultural regions in the United States. It accounts for about 25% of U.S. feed-grain exports and 40% of wheat, flour, and cotton exports. More than 14 million acres (5.7 million hectares) of land are irrigated with water pumped from the Ogallala. Yields on irrigated land may be triple the yields on similar land cultivated by dry farming (no irrigation).

The Ogallala's water was, for the most part, stored during the retreat of the Pleistocene continental ice sheets (the last Ice Age). Present recharge is insufficient over most of the region (see Fig. 1). Each year, farmers draw from the Ogallala more water than the entire flow of the Colorado River. In 1930, the average thickness of the saturated zone of the Ogallala aquifer was nearly 66 ft (20 m); currently, it is less than 10 ft (3 m), with the water table dropping by amounts ranging from 6 inches (15 cm) to 3.3 ft (1 m) per year. Overall, it is believed that the Ogallala will be effectively depleted within four decades. In areas of especially rapid drawdown, it could be locally drained in less than a decade.

Reversion to dry farming, where possible at all, will greatly diminish yields.

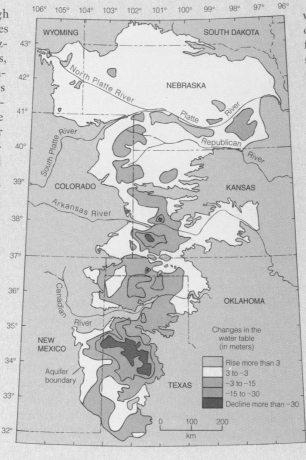

FIGURE 1

The Ogallala aquifer.

Less vigorous vegetation may lead to a partial return to pre-irrigation, Dust Bowl–type conditions. Alternative local sources of municipal water are not at all apparent in many places. Planners in Texas and Oklahoma have advanced ambitious water-transport schemes as solutions. Texas is considering alternatives that would involve transferring water now draining into the Mississippi River from northeastern Texas across the state to the panhandle. Oklahoma's Comprehensive Water Plan would draw on the Red River and Arkansas River basins. Such schemes would cost billions of dollars, perhaps tens of billions, and could take a decade or longer to complete. Before the projects are completed, however, acute water shortages can be expected in the areas of most urgent need. Even if and when the transport networks are finished, the cost of the water may be 10 times what farmers in the region can comfortably afford to pay if their products are to remain fully competitive in the marketplace. There seem to be no easy solutions. Perhaps because of this, progress toward any solution has been slow. Meanwhile, the draining of the Ogallala aquifer continues unabated.

It is noteworthy that in the short term farmers have little incentive to exercise restraint, due in large part to federal policies. Price supports encourage the growing of crops like cotton that require irrigation in the southern part of the region. The government shares the cost of soil-conservation programs and provides for crop-disaster payments, thus giving compensation for the natural consequences of water depletion. And, in fact, federal tax policy provides for groundwater depletion allowances (tax breaks) for High Plains farmers using pumped groundwater, with larger breaks for heavier groundwater use.

derground cavern collapses into the cavern (Fig. 11–14). Sinkholes are especially common in areas underlain by limestone, such as much of the southeastern United States and the Yucatán of Mexico. This limestone is often dissolved by groundwater to form underground caverns. Water pressure from the groundwater helps support the overlying land surface, so a drop in the water table from heavy withdrawal removes that support, causing the ground to collapse.

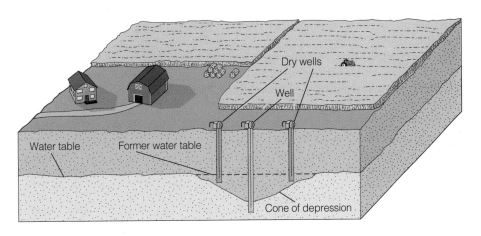

The third withdrawal problem is saltwater intrusion. Normally, the groundwater underlying coastal regions has an upper layer of fresh water, underlain by salt water. This layering occurs because rain, falling as fresh water, is less dense than salt water; it therefore tends to form a lens, floating above the salt water. This is also why oceanic islands are habitable by humans: islands the size of several acres or more have their own underground fresh water supply from the rains. Unfortunately, rapid pumping of either coastal or island fresh groundwaters can cause the underlying salt water to migrate upward, "intruding" into the fresh water. This degrades the quality of the fresh water for drinking, agriculture, and other uses. Saltwater intrusion is a significant problem in many coastal cities. Sections of the Gulf Coast and some parts of California are especially affected. Globally, such cities as Manila in the Philippines and Lima, Peru, have major problems with it.

These four groundwater problems are not exclusive: some areas are plagued by all four. For example, some urban areas of the Gulf Coast, such as Tampa, Florida, have problems with groundwater pollution, depletion, land subsidence (and sinkholes), and saltwater intrusion.

This section discusses five ways that water resources can be extended. The first three are familiar as methods of reducing the input of any resource (Chapter 6): increased efficiency, recycling, and substitution. In the case of water, recycling refers to recycling wastewater. One of the many ways of substituting other liquids for fresh water is substituting plentiful seawater for naturally occurring fresh water by using desalination. The last two methods of extending water supplies are dams and canals, which do not reduce total demand. They shift water supplies from one region to another where they are needed more, extending water supplies locally but reducing them elsewhere.

Increased Efficiency

A major theme in environmental science is that input reduction is the best all-around solution to most environmental problems. The reduction of resource inputs by conservation not only prolongs the time that the resource will last, but reduces the pollution and other disturbances generated when the resource is extracted and used. Water resources provide many opportunities for conservation because they have been used so waste-

$\mathcal{I}$NCREASING OUR WATER RESOURCES

Although much of the United States and many other parts of the world are facing critical shortages of water, these shortages are not insurmountable. Indeed, the main reason most shortages exist is simply that, until recently, water resources were taken for granted. On the positive side this means that water resources can often be extended with relatively little sacrifice, simply by cutting the "fat" from past wasteful uses.

fully and inefficiently in the past. Water-rich areas have had no incentive to conserve.

Agriculture in particular and industry account for the large majority of water withdrawn and consumed in nearly all modern societies, so more efficient use in these areas is especially important. This will involve both technical and social changes. A classic example of technical change is **microirrigation** (sometimes called "drip" irrigation) whereby water is transported to crops via pipes instead of open ditches that promote evaporation. The water is then dripped onto the plants from tiny holes in the pipes installed on or below the soil. This increases the water that reaches the plant from 37% to as high as 95%. By saving nearly 300%, vast amounts of water are conserved. This method has been very effective in water-poor countries such as Israel where it is used on nearly half the irrigated land (Table 11–4). Only 3% of U.S. irrigation is by microirrigation, largely because of its expense. The initial cost is about $1500 to $3000 per 2.5 acres (about 1 hectare), so it is used mainly on highly valued fruit and vegetable crops. But the use of microirrigation is rapidly growing in the United States, especially in the West where incorporation of the true environmental costs of food production is raising prices (discussed below). Similarly, industrial engineers have found it relatively easy to design production technologies that use much less water to produce everything from newspapers to aluminum. Recycling the same water during production is but one example of a design change. While such technical changes may temporarily increase costs, they often ultimately lower costs compared to what would be paid for a steadily decreasing water supply.

Conserving water often requires social changes in addition to technical change. The average person can usually do much to conserve water. Far from being painful, these changes require little personal sacrifice and may even save money. Simply shaving with a basin instead of running water reduces water used by 2000% (Fig. 11–15). Installing low-flush toilets and taking shorter showers are especially important because flushing and showers are, by far, the two greatest personal uses of water (Table 11–3). Changes in diet can reduce agricultural water loss. Much more water is required to raise domestic animals for food than to produce the same amount of food as crops; in general, we use fewer resources when eating "lower on the food chain" (Chapter 13). Home lawns and gardens often use much water so switching to plants with low water needs and other landscaping changes can save water.

TABLE 11–4 *Use of Micro-irrigation, Leading Countries and the World, 1991*

COUNTRY	AREA UNDER MICRO-IRRIGATION AS A PERCENTAGE OF TOTAL IRRIGATED LAND
United States	3.0
Spain	4.8
Australia	7.8
Israel	48.7
South Africa	9.0
Egypt	2.6
Mexico	1.2
France	4.8
Thailand	1.0
Colombia	5.7
Cyprus	71.4
Portugal	3.7
Italy	0.7
Brazil	0.7
China	<0.1
India	<0.1
Jordan	21.1
Taiwan	2.4
Morocco	0.8
Chile	0.7
World	0.7

(*Source:* Adapted from *State of the World 1993*, edited by Lester R. Brown *et al.*, with the permission of W. W. Norton & Company, Inc. Copyright © 1993 by Worldwatch Institute.)

Xeriscaping (pronounced "zeriscaping") is landscaping designed to save water. It includes drought-tolerant plants and many other changes such as weed control, watering times, and height of mower settings.

Desalination

Since 97.4% of Earth's water is salt water, removal of dissolved salts, called desalination, would obviously create a huge supply of fresh water. Unfortunately, desalination is expensive, even with the latest, most efficient technology. It is therefore economical only where other sources of water are even more expensive or are not available. Over 50% of the world's desalination capacity is located in the Persian Gulf region, where about 2 billion gallons (7.8 billion L) are produced per day. Worldwide, nearly 7500 desalination plants produced about 3.4 billion gallons (12.9 billion L) per day in 1993. Growing numbers of cities are turning to desalination because they have exhausted other sources. For example, Santa Barbara, California, spent about $37 million in 1994 to build a facility that produces fresh water at four to six times the cost of the city's present supplies. Those supplies are being depleted so rapidly, however, that the city anticipates much higher future prices and considers the plant a worthwhile investment. Key West, Florida, has used desalination for years; other plants in Florida will soon raise state production from 50 million gallons (190 million L) per day to 250 million gallons (950 million L).

The main reason for the high cost of desalination is the cost of energy. Recall that on average seawater has about 35 parts per thousand of dissolved solids, which must be reduced to less than 1 part per thousand for drinking and industrial uses. About 200 pounds (91 kg) of salt are produced for every 1,000 gallons (3800 L) processed. As a desalination plant often processes many millions of gallons per day, millions of pounds of salt must be removed daily. Disposing of all this salt is another major cost of desalination. Landfill costs are rising fast, and the concentrated salt cannot be dumped into the ocean without damage to ecosystems. Some economic uses, such as de-iceing roads, have been found for this salt, but without costly treatment, it is generally not clean enough for many purposes. In some cases, costs of desalination may be reduced by producing water that is still too salty for drinking and industry, but is nevertheless useful for such purposes as watering salt-tolerant plants. For example, the largest plant in the United States, in Yuma, Arizona, purifies 72 million gallons (273 million L) of irrigation water per day.

The membrane and the distillation desalination methods have proven to be the most effective in minimizing energy costs. The **membrane method** (also called the filter and reverse-osmosis method) removes dissolved ions by passing the liquid through a membrane at high pressure. This method is generally cheaper and faster than distillation. A large municipal plant can process several billion gallons per day. The membrane method is generally unable to desalinate normal salt water on a large scale because it rapidly clogs the tiny pores. The method has proved highly effective for areas that can desalinate brackish (moderately salty) water including brackish groundwater. Many cities near the ocean therefore pump brackish water from underground when using this method. An example is Santa

WATER SAVINGS GUIDE

CONSERVATIVE USE WILL SAVE WATER		NORMAL USE WILL WASTE WATER
Wet down, soap-up, rinse off 4 gallons	SHOWER	Regular shower 25 gallons
May we suggest a shower?	TUB BATH	Full tub 36 gallons
Minimize flushing Each use consumes 5–7 gallons	TOILET	Frequent flushing is very wasteful
Fill basin 1 gallon	WASHING HANDS	Tap running 2 gallons
Fill basin 1 gallon	SHAVING	Tap running 20 gallons
Wet brush Rinse briefly ½ gallon	BRUSHING TEETH	Tap running 10 gallons
Take only as much as you require	ICE	Unused ice goes down the drain
Please report immediately	LEAKS	A small drip wastes 25 gallons a day
Turn off light, TV, heaters, and air conditioning when not in room	ENERGY	Wasting energy also wastes water

THANK YOU FOR USING THIS COLUMN . . . . AND **NOT** THIS ONE

■ FIGURE 11–15
Ways to conserve water. Note: 1 gallon equals approximately 3.785 liters. (*Source:* Reprinted by permission of the San Francisco Convention & Visitors Bureau.)

Catalina Island off the coast of southern California (■ Fig. 11–16a).

The second desalination method, **distillation**, relies on heat: when salt water evaporates, the dissolved solids are left behind. Such a device can be designed in many ways, but the most common is the **multistage flash distillation (MSF)** method. This pipes cold seawater through a series of coils in chambers that become progressively hotter; the heated seawater is then routed back, underneath the coils (Fig. 11–16b). Fresh water condenses on the outside of the coils from the boiling seawater at the bottom. This method is over six times more efficient than simply heating a single chamber. Even so, MSF is about twice as costly as the membrane method because of the energy costs of heating the water. However, the higher cost and slower rate are more than offset where fully saline waters must be processed. Furthermore, the higher costs are often partially offset by locating MSF plants alongside electric power plants and using the heat they produce as a byproduct. Solar energy is used for desalination on a small scale, but sunlight is too dilute to make this method practical at large scales: even under

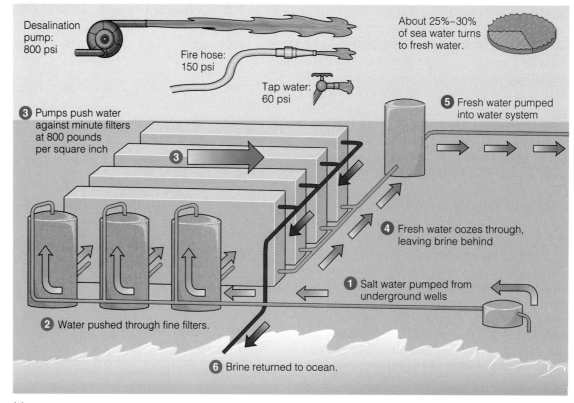

(a)

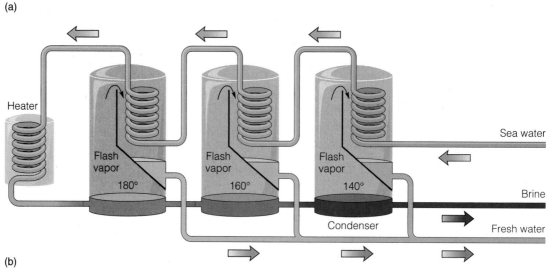

(b)

ideal conditions, only about 0.2 gallons per square foot (8.12 L per m³) can be collected per day. Many square miles of land would be required to rival the output of an average MSF plant.

Wastewater Reclamation

Most of us do not like the idea of drinking waste-water, especially reclaimed sewage. Nevertheless, wastewater can be safe to drink if it is properly treated. Chapter 16 discusses that wastewater treatment in detail. Here we will simply note that most municipalities treat their wastewater and then release it into nearby rivers, lakes, or oceans. People downstream or elsewhere often drink and use this water. Many natural processes such as dilution help reduce pollutant levels, even if the water has traveled only a few miles, but constant testing is needed to guarantee safety.

Recently, many cities have begun to consider reusing their own wastewater directly. This so-called **closed loop reclamation** involves treating the wastewater to the level needed before direct reuse. For drinking water, this means using advanced—and very expensive—treatment to render the water safe. Even if this is done, the water must be stored in tanks or ponds for a few days before it is safe to drink. A number of cities, especially in arid parts of South Africa, have successfully produced drinking water in this way. Denver, Colorado, has a well-known plant. However, it is often much more economical to use closed loop reclamation to produce water for non-drinking purposes and save natural sources for drinking. **Gray water** is untreated or partially treated wastewater that is used for watering golf courses and lawns instead of using cleaner water of drinkable quality.

Despite our emotional reactions to wastewater, it is generally much cheaper to treat wastewater than to desalinate seawater, especially if we only need to produce gray water or some other type of partially treated water. For instance, in 1991, it cost $4 to produce 1000 gallons (3800 L) of drinking water from desalination. In contrast, reclaiming moderately polluted water cost only about 50 cents per 1000 gallons (3800 L), and this was for drinkable reclaimed water. Some experts suggest that the city of the future will have closed loop reclamation engineered into the natural environment through the "3 R's": return, repurify, and reuse. In this system, treated wastewater is returned to irrigate crops; the water is renovated (purified) by percolation as groundwater and is then reusable as drinking water.

Dams and Reservoirs

All of the ways of extending water resources discussed so far have a major advantage: they use water more efficiently and produce more for society in general. In contrast, dams and reservoirs, and canals, simply redistribute water from water-surplus areas with low populations to water-deficit areas with high populations. This results in no net gain, and often a net loss, for society in general because water is lost during storage and transport by evaporation, soil infiltration, and other processes. Nevertheless, redistribution is often the most economical way to meet society's water needs and can have minimal environmental impact if properly designed.

Dams are structures that obstruct river or stream flow to make lakes (Fig. 11–17). By keeping water from flowing downstream, dams allow people upstream to have preferential use. There are more than 36,000 major dams in the world (and hundreds of thousands of smaller dams). Dams are built for one or more of three reasons: (1) provide better control of water flow to minimize flood damage, (2) create a

reservoir, the lake, that can serve as a water source for nearby populations, and (3) provide hydroelectric power. Even well-designed dams have some environmental impacts. These include the following:

1. *Sediment accumulation.* Occurs in the lake as sediment is trapped by the dam. Unless the sediment is removed, the reservoir will fill up in a few decades to a few hundred years.
2. *Scouring downstream.* Occurs because the water that escapes the dam has little sediment. Such "sediment-starved" stream flow will scour out the river bottom on the other side of the dam.
3. *Water loss.* Occurs from evaporation of water from the lake. The scale of this loss is vast: in Texas, about three times as much water is lost from evaporation of reservoirs as is used by industry and cities. Attempts to reduce the loss by spreading a "skin" of chemicals have not proven effective.

FIGURE 11–17
A flood control dam in the Tennessee Valley also produces electricity. (*Source:* John D. Cunningham/Visuals Unlimited.)

4. *Salination.* Occurs because evaporation of water leaves dissolved minerals behind, causing the lake to become progressively saltier.
5. *Dam breaks.* Occasionally occur from heavy rainfalls, leading to disastrous flooding downriver.
6. *Biological disturbances.* Occurs because dams can disturb both land and aquatic life. One of the most obvious effects is when dams block migration patterns of fishes, such as spawning salmon in the northwestern United States. Fish ladders built to allow migration around the dam are often ineffective. A second cause of biological disturbance is loss of both land and aquatic habitats. Land habitats can be flooded upstream; downstream aquatic habitats can suffer from decreased water flow. One of the most infamous examples is the Aswan Dam on the Nile River, which led to massive disease outbreaks and loss of crop production along the Nile, among many other biological impacts.

One often-proposed solution to the many environmental and social problems caused by dams is to make more use of natural methods of flood control, such as wetlands and local geological conditions. This suggestion runs counter to the traditional policy, often used by the U.S. Army Corps of Engineers, which is to alter natural conditions with dams, channelization, and other means, according to economic and engineering criteria, without much consideration to environmental impacts. This alternative has received renewed attention since the great flood of 1993 in the Mississippi River system. Many environmental groups noted that dam breaks and many kinds of damage will occur again unless more consideration is given to conforming to natural conditions instead of trying to alter them.

Canals

Canals, or aqueducts, are artificial channels built to transfer water over long distances. As urban areas grow, they often exceed local water supplies, and canals become necessary for further growth. For example, New York City has imported water for over 100 years, moving to sources progressively farther away, such as upstate New York. Many long canals are even more important for large cities in dry areas. In California, two-thirds of the water runoff is north of San Francisco while two-thirds of the water use is south of San Francisco. Since the early 1900s, the growth of cities in southern California, especially Los Angeles, has led to the construction of many canals to import water from the north and from the Colorado River. Population growth in southern California has continued to increase in recent years, causing ever greater water demands. This has led to increasing legal and social confrontations as people in other areas, especially farmers, object to the diversion of their water to urban areas. Such disputes illustrate the disadvantage of redistribution. There is no net gain for society, whereas conservation, desalination, and wastewater recycling result in greater amounts of available water. Cities such as Santa Barbara and San Diego are turning to all of these solutions and moving away from water importation.

In Florida, a vast artificial system containing 1400 miles (2250 km) of canals has drained away much of the water feeding the Everglades for use in urban centers and especially agriculture (Fig. 11–18). Whereas canals have led to shortages and disputes over water rights in California, those in Florida illustrate another potential hazard of canals: habitat destruction and pollution (see Issues in Perspective 11–4). The Everglades ecosystem is one of the largest and most unique wetland habitats in North America. But it is drying up and becoming polluted as water is diverted away by canals. At the same time, straightening or **channelization** of the Kissimmee River is causing more pollution to flow into the Everglades. This pollution not only causes species extinction but affects water quality because the Everglades serves as a major recharge area for water supplies in South Florida.

The ultimate example of water importation is the North American Water Pipeline Association (NAWPA), which has been proposed to transport meltwaters of northern Canada to the western and midwestern United States (Fig. 11–19, page 304). In the east, this would involve diverting water into the Great Lakes, from which water is easily redistributed south using the huge Mississippi River system. In the west, waters from the Yukon and Mackenzie Rivers would flood the Rocky Mountain Trench, converting it to a huge canal carrying water into the arid western United States. This project would take decades to implement and has been rejected as both uneconomical and environmentally harmful. Many studies have shown massive environmental impacts ranging from regional climate change to the introduction of many exotic species of fishes and other life into the Great Lakes and the lakes of the western United States. Such introductions often cause ex-

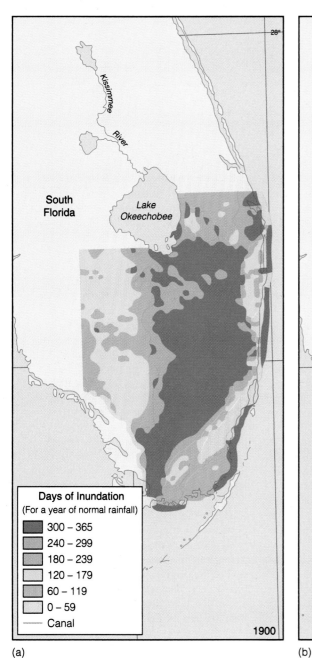

(a)

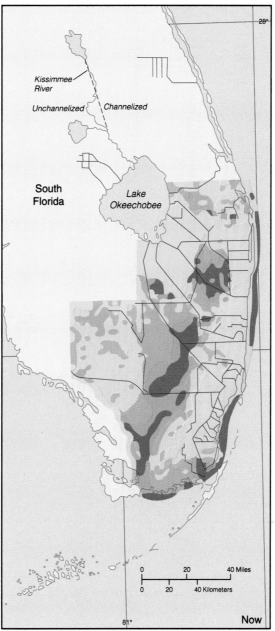

(b)

Days of Inundation
(For a year of normal rainfall)

- 300 – 365
- 240 – 299
- 180 – 239
- 120 – 179
- 60 – 119
- 0 – 59
- Canal

FIGURE 11–18
Computer models of the Everglades drainage system show that the number of days that the land is inundated (covered by water) has been greatly reduced since 1900 (a). (b) Canals now drain rainwater away before the land can be saturated for long periods, especially the "permanent" wetlands shown in deep blue. (*Source*: Modified from South Florida Water Management District data.)

tinctions of native forms (Chapter 12). They would be especially damaging to the western lakes which have been largely isolated since the last Ice Age.

Despite such economic and environmental costs, there will probably be increasing social pressures for water importation. Such pressures will grow not only because of increasing population growth in California and other parts of the West, but also because of agricultural needs. Recall that agriculture is the greatest consumer of water, and the West and Midwest are vast dry agricultural areas. Added pressure to import will

come from the depletion of the Ogallala aquifer underlying the Midwest early in the twenty-first century (see Issues in Perspective 11–3).

SOCIAL SOLUTIONS TO WATER SCARCITY

We have discussed many ways that society can extend water supplies, from conservation to redistribution by canals. Like all technical solutions to environmental problems, however, these solutions

Saving the Everglades

Between 1962 and 1971, a canal was "channelized" through the Kissimmee River as part of a flood-control project for central Florida. As a result, flow was diverted from 103 miles (166 km) of meandering river channel and a floodplain 1 to 2 miles (1.6 to 3.2 km) wide, through a canal 30 feet (9 m) deep, 250 to 450 feet (76–137 m) wide, and 56 miles (90 km) long. Six dam-like structures were built along the canal to maintain stable water levels in five terraced impoundments.

Channelizing destroyed or degraded most of the fish and wildlife habitat once provided by the river and its floodplain wetlands. Although remnants of the former river channel remain on either side of the canal, the flowing river ecosystem has been replaced by a series of relatively stagnant reservoirs and a central deep canal. The channelizing of the Kissimmee also affected the Everglades National Park because wetlands along the meandering river no longer filter pollutants. The short deep channel allows pollution to flow directly down the Kissimmee drainage system. The Everglades is a vast sheet of fresh water that nourishes all of South Florida, supplying drinking water for four million Floridians. Drainage, urban development,

and polluted runoff of fertilizer and pesticides from cane and dairy acreage, caused by the channelizing of the Kissimmee River, have shrunk the glades to half their original 4000 square miles (10,360 km²).

Years of ditching, diking, and draining to control coastline flooding and make land suitable for farming have had devastating effects on wildlife and the water supply. Nesting birds are down by 90%—from 900,000 in 1931 to 90,000 today. The park's last two breeding female panthers died of mercury-related symptoms in 1991. And native plants are being displaced by a 100,000-acre (40,500-hectare) infestation of thirsty melaleuca trees. Their seeds were once sown from airplanes in an attempt to dry up the marsh for development. A 1990 drought, the worst in three decades, has further drained the fragile ecosystem. Evaporation from the Everglades' wetlands sets off a chain reaction that produces much of South Florida's rainfall. Just a few inches of variation in the water level can mean life or death for Everglades plants and animals.

The fate of another environmental treasure may be tied to the Everglades: Florida's living coral reef. Some scientists think parts of this 200-mile (322 km) long reef—a marine nursery unique on the

continent—are dying. The reef is so fragile that natural diseases, changes in sea level, and human pollution, as well as water-management practices in the Everglades, can affect its future.

Saving the Everglades is not a short-term project. It must be perpetual. Most of what has been lost is gone forever. South Florida's population explosion steadily threatens what's left. A settlement has been reached that orders state officials and sugarcane growers to start an 11-year cleanup of agricultural runoff that is believed to be among the culprits killing the Everglades. The plan calls for creating a 35,000-acre (14,175-hectare) pollution filtering marsh in the Everglades Agricultural Area by 1997 (■ Fig. 1). It will act as a buffer between farm fields and water conservation areas such as the Loxahatchee National Wildlife Refuge and Everglades National Park, removing most of the harmful phosphorus from the water.

Restoring the Kissimmee River also plays an important role in saving the Everglades. Studies by the South Florida Water Management District show that restoration of the original ecosystem is possible. Conversely, those studies showed that if no action is taken, degradation of the remaining natural flora and fauna will con-

have important social aspects. For instance, conservation is strongly influenced by economics, such as the price of water. Similarly, laws governing water use, especially in the western United States, have enormous influence on where dams and canals can be built.

Economics of Water Use

When a resource is cheap, it will be wasted. Only when the resource is costly do consumers have an incentive to conserve or reduce resource input by more efficient use, recycling, or substitution

(■ Figure 11–20, page 305). In the case of water resources, wastewater reclamation is an example of recycling. Substitution could include switching to desalinated salt water instead of depleting groundwater or using liquids besides water.

The low cost of water in the United States has offered little incentive to conserve. Most water supply systems charge only a fraction of the total cost of obtaining, storing, treating, and delivering water. The average family pays less than 1 percent of its income for water. As a result, many states and local areas are increasing water prices to provide more incentive to reduce water

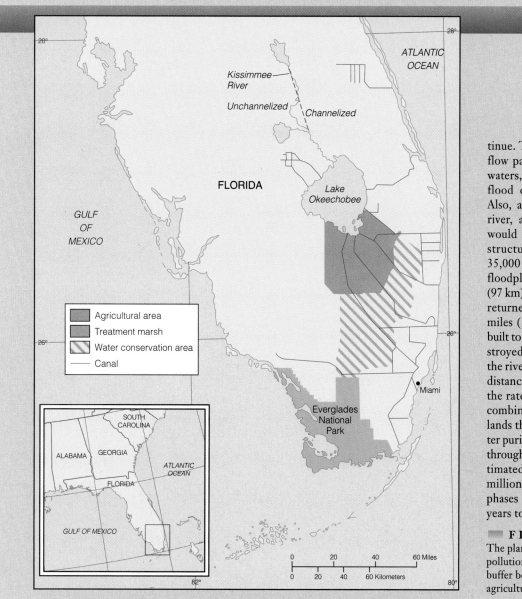

tinue. The plan is to restore more natural flow patterns to the river from its headwaters, which are currently regulated for flood control and water conservation. Also, along the channelized part of the river, about 29 miles (47 km) of canal would be backfilled and accompanying structures removed. Under this plan, 35,000 acres (14,175 hectares) of original floodplain wetlands and almost 60 miles (97 km) of original river channel would be returned to natural conditions. Some 11 miles (18 km) of river channel would be built to replace river channel physically destroyed by canal construction. Restoring the river to its original state lengthens the distance it has to travel, as well as slowing the rate at which the water moves. This, combined with the replanting of the wetlands that were destroyed, allows for better purification of the water as it percolates through the original river channel. The estimated cost of the project exceeds $500 million. The project would be done in phases and would likely require 10 to 15 years to complete.

■ FIGURE 1
The plan to save the Everglades calls for pollution-filtering marshes to serve as a buffer between the Everglades and the agricultural area to the north.

use: for each 1 percent increase in cost, water use in homes initially decreases by about half a percent. As costs rise, cities find it economical to monitor water supplies more closely, reducing waste. New York City is among those cities now installing universal water metering, a meter for each household.

Stop Subsidizing Water for Agriculture

As the largest consumer of water, agriculture is an especially important target for conservation. California is a good example. Farmers use 85% of California's water, much of it for the irrigation of water-intensive crops. Because of California's agricultural history, farmers not only have "first rights" to water, but pay far less (often less than 10% of the price to urban users) because their water is subsidized by the government. In the early 1990s urban areas began to rebel against this practice and urged their state legislators to reduce subsidies to farmers. As expected, this has led to less water use by farmers. One response has been to grow high-priced crops such as certain fruits, nuts, and vegetables instead of water-intensive crops such as rice. A similar situation oc-

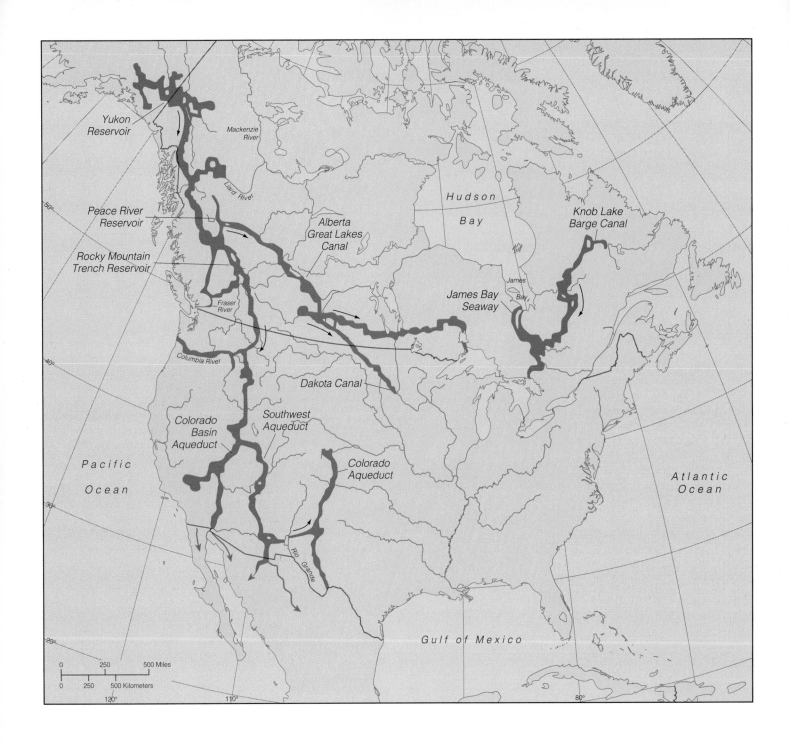

Labels on map:
Yukon Reservoir
Mackenzie River
Peace River Reservoir
Liard River
Rocky Mountain Trench Reservoir
Fraser River
Alberta Great Lakes Canal
Hudson Bay
Knob Lake Barge Canal
James Bay
James Bay Seaway
Columbia River
Dakota Canal
Colorado Basin Aqueduct
Southwest Aqueduct
Colorado Aqueduct
Rio Grande
Pacific Ocean
Atlantic Ocean
Gulf of Mexico
0 250 500 Miles
0 250 500 Kilometers

FIGURE 11–19
Proposed major river diversions in North America. (*Source*: From R. Bocking in M. C. Healey and R. R. Wallace, eds., *Canadian Bulletin of Fisheries and Aquatic Sciences* 215 [1987]: 106. Reproduced with permission of the Minister of Supply and Services, Canada, 1995.)

curs in many other parts of the western and southwestern United States where federal taxes have historically funded projects to supply cheap water to farmers. Society as a whole does not necessarily suffer from refusal to subsidize cheap water because water-intensive crops can still be grown in other parts of the nation where water is more common, such as the eastern United States. They can also be imported from other countries, or perhaps most desirably, the higher costs will promote water conservation techniques, such as

microirrigation, which are now rarely used in the United States (Table 11–4).

Taxing Water Use in Industry and Households

Although water for industry and household use is less heavily subsidized, it is still very cheap. As a result, state and local governments have found that increasing the price of water via taxes or other means can greatly reduce the amount of

ℙROBLEMS OF RESOURCE DEPLETION   SECTION 2

water used. Often these taxes are levied as **efflu-ent charges**, which is the cost of disposing of industrial wastewater. This illustrates again how input management not only conserves resources but reduces pollution. For example, water withdrawals by U.S. manufacturing industries in the year 2000 are expected to be 62% less than in 1977 because of increased taxes on wastewater disposal. Similarly, increased prices on domestic water encourage people to conserve using low-flush toilets, shorter showers, and other means. In some countries, higher prices also encourage domestic water recycling and reclamation. Japan and Singapore, for example, have long used reclaimed wastewater in flush toilets.

Increasing the cost of a resource to its true or "environ-mental" cost will discourage both rapid depletion and pollution that occurs when a resource is very cheap (Chapters 1, 6, 20). The improved efficiency of resource use often reduces not only overall environmental costs, but also economic costs to society. Industrial recycling of water is a good example (see Issues in Perspective 11–5). Cities can also gain from this. Beijing, China, has recently invested in more modern plumbing, leakage reduction, and recycling of water. This will save billions of gallons of water per year, at a much lower dollar cost than the water development project originally planned to import water from farther away.

Legal Control of Water Use

As one of the most important components of living things, water probably has more laws governing its use than any other resource. In the United States, a hierarchy of laws extends from the federal to the local level; as with all resources, federal law takes precedence where there is conflict between levels. Most direct regulation is found at the state level, however, for reasons that date back to homesteading and the use of the land when it was originally settled. This also explains why legal control of water is best developed for surface water, which has been intensively used through the years. In contrast, the rapidly grow-

ing use and pollution of underground waters have led to a confusion of legal activity in recent years. These difficulties are magnified because groundwater is much more difficult to monitor than surface water and moves so slowly that depletion and pollution often take years to detect and remedy (Chapter 16).

Surface Waters

Laws regulating surface waters can be divided into two basic types: riparian law and appropriation law. **Riparian law** dictates that the owner of land

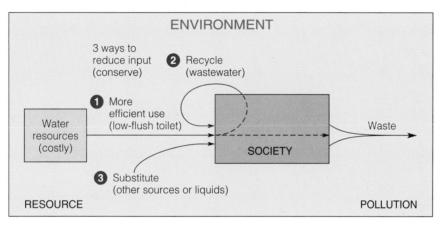

has the right to withdraw water that is adjacent to the land, such as from a river or lake. (*Riparian* means "bank," as in riverbank, in Latin.) A key provision is that the water must be returned in a relatively unpolluted condition, so that owners of adjacent land, such as downstream, do not have their water rights violated. Riparian law is a common-law idea, meaning that it evolved through practical use, as opposed to being dictated from theory or administrative decree.

Riparian law is practiced mainly east of the Mississippi River. It worked well in those states, where water is relatively plentiful and areas were settled gradually. In contrast, all the western states have at least some degree of appropriation law. **Appropriation law** dictates that owners of land may be denied the right to withdraw water if a more beneficial use is found. In short, government, usually the state, can "appropriate" the water. The reason for this type of law in the western United States is obvious: water has often been scarce so it had to be closely managed. Water from the Colorado River, for instance, is tightly regulated by state and federal agencies (Fig. 11–21, page 307). Under riparian law someone could, in theory,

FIGURE 11–20
Three ways to conserve water (reduce water input to society), with examples: more efficient use, recycling, and substitution. If water resources become more costly to the water users, they will have an incentive to use these three methods of conservation. Conservation also tends to reduce water pollution because less wastewater is produced and water flow into natural waters is reduced.

Industrial Recycling of Water

Making the products we use in everyday life requires huge amounts of water. Producing just 2.2 pounds (1 kg) of paper can take as much as 1,540 pounds (700 kg) of water.

Although industry accounts for much of the world's water use, in contrast to agriculture, only a small fraction of industrial water is actually consumed. Most of it is used for cooling, processing, and other activities that may heat or pollute water, but do not consume it.

So far, the main motivation for industrial water recycling has come from pollution control laws. Most of the world's wealthiest countries now require industries to meet specific water quality standards before releasing wastewater to the environment. As it turns out, the most effective and economical way to comply with these requirements is often to treat and recycle water, thereby discharging less. Pollution control laws have not only helped clean up rivers, lakes, and streams, they have promoted conservation and more efficient water use.

Japan, the United States, and the former West Germany are among the countries that have achieved striking gains in industrial water productivity. Three industries—chemicals, iron and steel, and pulp and paper manufacturing—account for 60% of Japan's industrial water use, and each has boosted its water recycling rate markedly since the early 1970s. Industrial output, meanwhile, has been climbing steadily. As a result, in 1989, Japanese industries produced $77 worth of output from every 35 cubic feet (1 m³) of water, compared with $21 in 1965. In just over two decades, the nation more than tripled its industrial water productivity.

Similarly, U.S. industry's total water use has fallen 36% since 1950, while industrial output has risen by almost 400%. And in the former West Germany, total industrial water use today is at the same level as in 1975, while industrial output has risen 44%. State-of-the-art paper manufacturing plants there now use only 15.4 pounds (7 kg) of water to produce 2.2 pounds (1 kg) of paper, 1% as much as older factories elsewhere.

Although these gains are impressive, achievements by individual companies facing water supply constraints show clearly that further large cuts are possible. For instance, a detailed look at 15 companies in San Jose, California, including several computer makers, a food processor, and a metal finisher, found that by adopting a diverse set of conservation measures they collectively reduced their annual water use by enough to supply about 9200 San Jose households. Water savings ranged from 27 to 90%, and in most cases the payback period was less than 12 months (● Table 1).

One positive outcome of California's drought is that this state, which has an economy larger than all but seven countries, may now be the world's leader in industrial water recycling. Manufacturers of all kinds—aircraft, chemicals, computers, and oil refineries—have boosted their water efficiency dramatically in a matter of years. A survey of 640 manufacturing plants in 12 California counties documented a 19% reduction in water use during a drought between 1985 and 1989. These savings, which derived from such measures as recycling cooling and process water, reducing flow rates, and fixing leaks, came on top of impressive conservation gains made during the previous 15 years in response to increasingly strict environmental standards.

Unfortunately, few developing countries are yet giving industries the incentives they need to adopt more efficient water practices. Most neither charge appropriately for water and wastewater services nor enforce pollution control regulations adequately.

Given the proper incentives, industries of many types have shown they can cut their water needs 40 to 90% with available technologies and practices, while at the same time protecting water from pollution. Closing the industrial water and wastewater cycle is not only technically possible, it increasingly makes good economic and environmental sense.

TABLE 1 *San Jose, California: Industrial Water Conservation and Cost-Effectiveness, Selected Companies*

COMPANY	WATER USE				WATER SAVINGS (%)	PAYBACK PERIOD ON INVESTMENT (MONTHS)
	BEFORE CONSERVATION		AFTER CONSERVATION			
	(millions of cubic feet per year)	(thousands of cubic meters per year)	(millions of cubic feet per year)	(thousands of cubic meters per year)		
IBM	14.8	420	1.48	42	90	3.6
California PaperBoard Company	87.3	2473	24.3	689	72	2.4
Hewlett-Packard	3	87	1.48	42	52	3.6

(*Source:* Worldwatch Institute, based on City of San Jose, Brown and Caldwell Consultants, and California Department of Water Resources, *Case Studies of Industrial Water Conservation in the San Jose Area* [Sacramento: California Department of Water Resources, 1990].)

own all rights to water in a river running through their land and restrict access by other people.

The greater state control of water under appropriation law makes it better suited for implementing environmentally optimum management. For example, if a study shows that an industry is being exceptionally wasteful, the state can threaten to appropriate the water if the industry does not take conservation measures. In contrast, under riparian law, if the industry owns the land along the river, the state may have to file suit and undergo expensive, prolonged litigation to make the industry change its ways.

Even where the state can appropriate water to carry out environmentally optimal solutions, complex legal battles often ensue. In areas with insufficient water, different parties usually claim rights to the same water. These disputes frequently involve parties wanting to use water for environmental reasons, such as for wildlife, versus parties who want to use the water for agriculture, industry, or domestic purposes.

Groundwater

Until recently, groundwater was virtually unregulated. Owners of land above the water were considered to have rights to the water, much as in riparian law. Even today, people in many rural areas are generally free to drill holes and withdraw water. In areas with rapid groundwater recharge or low population, this practice created few problems. Now, however, the rapidly falling water tables of many areas have required much stricter laws on drilling and withdrawal. Most of these are local, municipal ordinances that prohibit withdrawal inside city or county limits without a permit. Similarly, many cities regulate water usage, such as prohibiting lawn sprinkling during the afternoon when evaporation is high. Groundwater depletion is easier to regulate than groundwater pollution (discussed in Chapter 16). There is increasing pressure on the U.S. Congress to enact a single coherent set of laws regulating groundwater depletion and pollution to replace the piecemeal regulation now occurring under many local and federal statutes.

Which Are Better: Economic or Legal Solutions?

Whether economic or legal solutions are better depends on the type of water resource problem.

FIGURE 11–21
The Colorado River is one of the few large sources of water in the southwestern United States. The Colorado is seen here winding through the desert near Moab, Utah. (*Source*: Aaron A. Strong/Gamma Liaison.)

Most economists agree that market conditions provide the optimal allocation of resources when many parties want access to them. For example, in California, where many farmers and city dwellers want access to water, one effective solution is to make all parties pay a price for the water that incorporates the environmental costs. This could include taxing water, removing subsidies, or otherwise raising the costs to all parties (see Issues in Perspective 11–6). Such an economic so-

Water and the Marketplace

Farmers use a huge proportion of the water in the western United States to produce a shrinking share of output and jobs. In California, farmers account for 75% of the state's annual water consumption, but they produce only about 10% of its $700 billion gross product. Much of what western farmers grow is important for the feeding of America. But a lot, like cotton, isn't. Congressional estimates of the annual cost of subsidizing water for crops range up to about $1.5 billion. Some California farmers get water for as little as $2 for 326,000 gallons (1.2 million L). Los Angeles water users pay about $545, while San Franciscans pay $300 for that amount of water. Apart from the dollar toll, critics contend that the practice is hastening the day when the 17 western states will face an ultimate problem: not enough water, too many people.

The overtaxed Colorado River can no longer be relied on as a source of much needed water. As California's chronic water shortages reach a crisis point, a solution may finally be at hand: the state is considering instituting the nation's first large-scale market for water. Such a market would allow farmers with excess supply to sell it to thirsty cities and businesses or even to other farmers. If the market for water works as planned, California could solve its problems without having to build huge new dams or reservoirs.

There's increasing evidence that markets for water could work. It is estimated that by diverting just 7% of the water farmers now use, cities would have adequate supplies for the next 20 years.

The new market still has to overcome formidable political and practical obstacles before becoming reality. For one thing, some observers fear that cities such as Los Angeles could bid up the cost of water high enough to price farmers, small towns, and environmental needs out of the market. It could also take years to rebuild the crumbling levees of the Sacramento River delta, which would have to carry most of the water being bought by cities at both ends of the state. And if farmers sell too much water and stop growing crops, rural communities could disappear as support businesses close.

The idea of allowing water to be bought and sold has developed political support among many environmentalists. Even with frequent flooding in California, the drought is continuing. And California suffers from human-made problems as well: many farmers have incentives to use more water than they really need. For example, some farmers have exclusive rights to buy reservoir water for as little as 2¢ per 1000 gallons (3800 L) through the Central Valley Project. That supply can be cut back only in a severe drought—and even then, many farmers can pump groundwater to make up for the loss. By contrast, cities pay up to 50 times as much because their water comes mostly from the newer, more expensive State Water Project. And conservation is discouraged because farmers can lose their water allotment if they don't use it all. That means consumers must skimp on showers, and businesses must cut back, while farmers plant water-intensive crops such as alfalfa and cotton.

Proponents say almost everyone would benefit from a water market. Farmers who sold water would have to fallow land or pump groundwater, but they'd be paid by cities for that water—at least as much as they'd get from growing crops. Otherwise, they wouldn't sell. Moreover, while they might have to pay higher prices for Central Valley Project water, their remaining supplies would be more certain. Cities could assure supplies without building new projects, and even the environment might gain because large-scale new construction might not be needed. During shortages, rising prices would encourage local water districts to build reservoirs to catch the higher-value water. And farmers might put extra money earned from water sales into conservation equipment that would free up more water. The result could be more stable water supplies.

lution not only tends to distribute costs more equitably, but it is often the only practical way of regulating water use: regulating a resource that is being used by many parties is often very costly because of the equipment and personnel needed to monitor use.

Legal solutions are therefore often most applicable where only a few parties use the resource, making monitoring possible. Also, legal regulation is often preferable where a resource is in very short supply, so that waste is minimized through stricter control than a market approach allows.

SUMMARY

Water, an essential substance for life, has many unusual properties. Its density, boiling point, specific heat, and solvency are affected by the structure of the water molecule, which is bipolar. Although there is an abundance of water on this planet, 97.4% of it is salt water and not generally usable. Only about 0.6% of the total water volume on Earth is fresh water in the liquid state, and this is mainly groundwater.

The hydrologic cycle acts as a pump, cycling water through evapotranspiration and precipitation. Water takes 40,000 years to recycle through this system in the oceans whereas streams are renewed every two weeks. The United States has the highest demand for water in the world, using 1400 gallons (5300 L) per person per day in 1993. The majority of this water is used for agriculture and industry. Although industry withdraws the most water, agriculture consumes the most because of evaporation.

Demand for water is growing worldwide, especially in developing countries. Per capita demand increases with industrialization as well as population growth.

Even though all readily available fresh water is not being used, many people suffer from chronic water shortages due to the inequality of water distribution. Deficit areas include desert areas, generally found at 30° north and south latitude; surplus areas include South America, Asia, and eastern North America. Local water inequalities present a similar problem on a smaller scale. Even areas of surplus are not safe from water shortages if pollution and rapid withdrawal occur.

There are two types of water resources: surface waters and groundwater. Surface waters include streams, rivers, and lakes. Lakes, given their stationary nature, are more susceptible to pollution than streams and rivers. Groundwater is contained within aquifers under the surface and is marked by the water table, the boundary between the zone of saturation and the zone of aeration. Two main problems have arisen with groundwater that make it difficult to use effectively: discharge and withdrawal problems. Discharge problems include groundwater pollution by toxins, metals, and organics that enter the water

supply. These pollutants may take a long time to be removed due to the slow movement of groundwater. Withdrawal problems include depletion, land subsidence, and saltwater intrusions.

Our water resources can be extended in several ways. The best ways involve conservation, or input reduction, which also reduces pollution. Examples include increased efficiency of use, such as microirrigation, and recycling of industrial and city wastewater. Desalination often uses the membrane method or a distillation method. Canals and dams and reservoirs are also means of extending water resources. However, they have many environmental impacts, including, sediment accumulation, scouring downstream, water loss, salination, dam breaks, and biological disturbances. Stopping water subsidies for agriculture and taxing water use will provide incentives to reduce water consumption. Laws have been developed for surface waters, including riparian and appropriation laws used primarily in the eastern and western United States, respectively.

KEY TERMS

appropriation law
aquicludes
aquifer
artesian well
channelization
closed loop reclamation
cone of depression
confined aquifers
consumed water
dams

deficit areas
discharge
distillation
drainage basin
effluent charges
evapotranspiration
gray water
groundwater
membrane method
microirrigation
multistage flash distillation (MSF)

precipitation
recharge areas
riparian law
sinkholes
surplus areas
water table
withdrawn water
xeriscaping
zone of aeration
zone of saturation

STUDY QUESTIONS

1. How does the structure of the water molecule explain water's unusual properties?
2. What percentage of the Earth's water is readily available in the liquid state as groundwater? As surface water?
3. Why is agriculture a greater consumer of water than industry? How can microirrigation reduce this consumption?
4. What are the major deficit areas of the world?
5. Name and define the two types of laws regulating water resources in the United States. Where are they used?
6. Why have streams and river valleys usually been among the most populated areas?
7. What are three withdrawal problems associated with groundwater? How does wetland destruction promote withdrawal

and pollution problems in groundwater? What percentage of U.S. wetlands have been lost?
8. Why are most well-injections not a good method of waste disposal?
9. Which four household activities in the American family use the most water (list in decreasing order)? How many gallons of water does the average person in the Unites States use per day? How much

more is this than biological needs?

10. Why are dams and reservoirs less efficient and more harmful than other ways of extending water resources?

11. The global water cycle involves what two main processes? Define these two processes. How much water returns to the oceans as runoff?

12. Define: aquiclude, aquifer, cone of depression, and water table.

13. What happens when the cost of a water resource is increased? Name some ways to do this.

14. Using Figure 11–4, what was the estimated world water use in 1960? In 1990? (Put your answers in units of cubic kilometers per year.) Using a ruler, estimate the percentage of total world water use that will be used by industry in the year 2000.

15. Suppose a river carries 10 cubic miles of water into the ocean over 10 years. Convert this amount of water to cubic kilometers, given that 1 cubic mile = 4.1655 cubic km.

ESSAY QUESTIONS

1. Why is water an unusual substance? List and explain its properties.

2. Why do billions of people suffer from water shortages if we are not using all readily available fresh water?

3. Discuss three basic ways of reducing water inputs to society. Explain each and give examples. (Hint: one way is increased efficiency of use.)

4. Discuss the economics of water use, focusing on ways to pay the "true cost" of water. Why is the "true cost" often underpaid? Give examples.

5. What are the two main desalination methods? Explain how they function.

SUGGESTED READINGS

Clarke, R. 1993. *Water: The international crisis.* Cambridge, Mass.: MIT Press.

Feldman, D. 1991. *Water resources management: In search of an environmental ethic.* Baltimore: Johns Hopkins University Press.

Gleick, P. 1993. *Water in crisis: A guide to the world's fresh water resources.* New York: Oxford University Press.

Hillel, D. 1994. *Rivers of Eden: The struggle for water and the quest for peace in the Middle East.* New York: Oxford University Press.

Hundley, N. 1992. *The great thirst: Californians and water.* Berkeley, Calif.: University of California Press.

Ingram, C. 1991. *The drinking water book.* Berkeley, Calif.: Ten Speed Press.

Nalman, R., ed. 1992. *Watershed management: Balancing sustainability and environmental change.* New York: Springer-Verlag.

Pearce, F. 1992. *The dammed: Rivers, dams, and the coming world water crisis.* London: Bodley Head.

Postel, S. 1992. *Last oasis: Facing water scarcity.* New York: W. W. Norton.

Reisner, M. 1990. *Overtapped oasis: Reform or revolution for western water.* Washington, D.C.: Island Press.

World Resources Institute. 1994 and each year. *Information please environmental almanac,* "Water Supplies" chapter. New York: Houghton Mifflin.

CONSERVING BIOLOGICAL RESOURCES

OUTLINE

PHOTO   *African elephants are making a comeback in some areas.* (*Source:* Don W. Fawcett/Visuals Unlimited.)

In the contiguous United States, the bald eagle has rebounded from 400 nesting pairs in the 1960s to over 3000 pairs today. A flock of 20 whooping cranes has grown to 200. Bison have gone from just under 1100 to over 20,000. Even more important are success stories in tropical countries, which are the cradle for most of the world's biological diversity. But in these countries, which are beset by overpopulation and poverty, merely passing laws prohibiting killing does not work as well as it has in the United States. The most successful strategies in the tropics have fought extinction by removing economic incentives to kill species. An example is elephant survival.

Once home to millions of elephants, Africa had fewer than 700,000 by the late 1980s and was projected to have fewer than 25,000 by the early twenty-first century. Richard Leakey, son of the famed anthropologist and director of Kenya's Wildlife Services, had seen poachers reduce Kenya's elephant population by 70% in 10 years, killing them at the rate of three per day.

Leakey took action. Game wardens were issued new vehicles, automatic weapons, and surveillance aircraft, with orders to shoot poachers on sight. Within weeks, elephant killing dropped dramatically, from three per day to one per month. More importantly for the elephants' long-term survival, Leakey joined with many other conservationists in calling for a global ban on sales of ivory. In 1989, over 80 member nations of the Convention on International Trade in Endangered Species (CITES) agreed to this ban. It has been enormously successful. Before the ban, ivory in Africa sold for about $100 per pound. By 1990, the price had plummeted 20-fold to $5 per pound, and the elephant decline had slowed by 80%. Many bans had been instituted before, but the key difference here was the widespread resolve by people in many industrialized nations to stop buying ivory billiard balls, carved ivory, and other items. By removing the economic incentive to kill elephants, potential buyers of ivory did much more to stop the killing than armies of game wardens could accomplish.

But what of the poachers? Leakey realized that the local poverty would be magnified without the income formerly provided from ivory. He therefore turned to the growing market for "ecotourism," where tourists visit rainforests and go on safaris. By providing employment as hotel workers, guides, and many other local jobs, ecotourism provides incentives to maintain the pristine natural environment. More than half a million tourists come to Kenya each year to see the elephants, spending nearly $500 million. At that price, each live elephant is worth about $20,000, or about 10 times its value as a dead donor of tusks. Furthermore, live elephants are a renewable resource, providing income for millennia.

Leakey was ousted from his job in a controversial disagreement with Kenyan authorities in 1994, but his successor, David Western, is building on Leakey's work. By sharing tourist dollars with farmers and ranchers owning lands surrounding game preserves, he is promoting "community" or "grassroots" management of wildlife. Encouraging local inhabitants to preserve the natural habitat around game preserves, instead of converting it to crops and ranching, is a growing trend in developing nations.

INTRODUCTION

EnviroNet
www.jbpub.com/environet

Society depends on biological resources in many ways: agriculture and wilderness recreation are just two examples (Fig. 12–1). In this chapter we focus on the current rapid loss of natural biological resources, often called the "extinction crisis." We examine why biological diversity is being lost, why it is worth saving, and how to go about saving it. Few people truly want to see species become extinct, and the effort to slow the loss of perhaps thousands of species each year is gaining national and international support. One indication is the very rapid growth of **conservation biology**, a new subdiscipline of biology that draws from genetics, ecology, and many other fields to find practical ways of saving species.

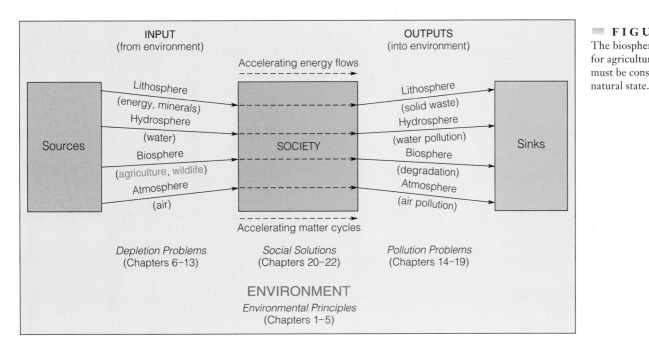

FIGURE 12-1
The biosphere can be utilized for agriculture, but some of it must be conserved in its natural state.

WHAT IS BIODIVERSITY?

Biological diversity, or **biodiversity**, has many definitions, but they all involve the variety of living things in a given area. The U.S. Office of Technology Assessment, for instance, defines biodiversity as "the variety and variability among living organisms and the ecological complexes in which they occur."

One reason for the lack of a precise definition is that life is hierarchical. For example, genes occur in cells, cells occur in organisms, and organisms occur in ecosystems (Chapter 3). At what level do we measure the diversity of life in an area? The number of genes? Organisms? Ecosystems? All can be used.

Measuring Biodiversity

Although one can measure biodiversity by counting the variety of genes or ecosystems in an area, the most common method is to count species. Species diversity, or **species richness**, is the number of species that occur in an area. Using species richness is largely a matter of convenience: It is easier to tabulate the number of species in an area than to count genes or ecosystems. Fortunately, species diversity is generally a good indicator of genetic and ecosystem diversity as well. Nevertheless, even species richness omits important information about biodiversity such as the abundance of each species.

Biodiversity can be measured at all geographic scales, from local to regional to global. Figure 12-2a illustrates low diversity at both the local and regional scales. Regions with low diversity often have fewer species at the local level as well. As Figure 12-2b shows, regions with high diversity tend to be composed of local biological communities with high diversity. The tropics, for instance, tend to have very high species richness at both the local and regional level, compared to areas of similar size in temperate zones.

Global Biodiversity: How Many Species?

No one knows how many species live on Earth. **Taxonomists**, the biologists who classify and describe organisms, have described about 1.8 million species. Of these, 56% are insects, and 14% are plants; vertebrates such as birds, mammals,

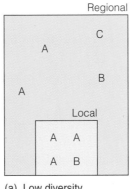

(a) Low diversity

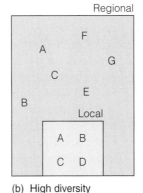

(b) High diversity

FIGURE 12-2
Letters (A, B, C, and so on) represent species living in an area: (a) low diversity at both the local and regional scales; (b) high diversity at both scales.

and fishes are just 3%. Only about 15% of described species occur in the oceans.

But these 1.8 million species are a highly biased sample and may not reflect the true species richness of the biosphere. For one thing, vertebrates are much more widely studied and therefore much better known than nonvertebrates: only one or two new species of birds are described each year whereas hundreds of new invertebrates are found. A recent study reported over 4000 bacteria species in a single gram of Norwegian soil. Most of these species were previously unknown.

Another problem is that most biologists have been concentrated in North America and Europe, but most species live in the tropics (Chapter 3). The areas with most species are thus the least known! Similarly, most biologists study life on land, but the oceans cover 70% of the Earth and contain unknown numbers of species. Hence, the described species likely considerably underestimate invertebrates and species that exist in the tropics and the oceans.

How Estimates are Made

Describing all species on Earth could take centuries, so biologists have devised a number of ways to develop immediate biodiversity estimates from limited information. The following are just three examples of the many methods of estimating global diversity from small samples:

1. *Rainforest insect samples.* Terry Erwin of the Smithsonian Institution has become well known for his studies of the very diverse tropical insect communities. Since most species are insects, and most insects are tropical, these studies are important for global estimates. Erwin (and others) use insecticides to kill and collect all the insects on the canopy (upper branches) of a tropical tree (Fig. 12–3). In Panama, for example, 1200 beetle species were found on the canopy of a single tree. Since about 40% of all insects are beetles, we can estimate that perhaps 3000 insect species occur there. But only about two-thirds of the species occur on the canopy (the rest occur on roots, bark, and other places). The total number of insects on this *one tree* is thus estimated at 4500 species! Since many of these insects occur only on one tree species, and since there are about 50,000 species of tropical trees, it seems that many tropical insect species must exist. Erwin estimates the insect species on Earth at more than 30 million.

2. *Ecological ratios.* Another method is to use well-studied groups to predict the diversity of less-studied groups that are associated with them. In Europe, for example, there are about six fungus species for each plant species. Plant species have been relatively well described, and it is estimated that 270,000 plant species exist worldwide. Thus, there may be as many as 1.6 million fungus species if the 6:1 ratio is applicable throughout the world. Only 69,000 fungus species have been described.

3. *Species-area curves.* The **species-area curve** has been very influential since the 1960s. Whenever the number of species is counted in a gradually enlarged area of sampling, the result is a curve as in Figure 12–4. The number of species rises rapidly at first, but it slows as the area of sampling increases because the same species are encountered again and again. Repeated surveys in the tropics and temperate areas have shown that small areas of rainforest contain many more species, often over 100 times more species, than areas of temperature forest. By using the known shape of the species-area

FIGURE 12–3
Tropical trees are often the home of hundreds of insect species. These trees are in Costa Rica. (*Source:* Gary Braasch/Tony Stone Images.)

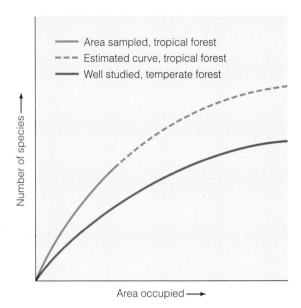

Number of species ⟶

Area occupied ⟶

FIGURE 12–4

A species-area curve plots the number of species found in increasingly larger areas. The temperate forests are well studied compared to tropical forests. Only small areas have been examined in most tropical forests so many species diversity estimates for large areas are derived from extrapolated projections as indicated by the dashed line.

curve, one can predict how many more species will be found in larger unsampled areas of tropical and temperate regions.

Biodiversity Today: A Rare Wealth in Time

All methods of estimating global biodiversity involve a certain amount of extrapolation, so understandably there is still wide disagreement over how many species exist. Estimates range from as low as 5 million species to as high as 100 million. Biologists generally agree, though, that fewer species live in the ocean than on land. Estimates for the ocean range from 1 million to 10 million species. But despite having fewer species, the oceans have more "fundamental" biodiversity: 32 phyla are found in the oceans compared to just 12 phyla on land. A phylum, such as echinoderms or mollusks, is a much more distinct taxonomic unit of biodiversity than a species (Chapter 3).

Whatever the exact number of species today, the fossil record indicates that we live in a special time of Earth history. Detailed compilations of fossil data show that the number of families in the oceans has generally increased through time (Fig. 12–5). Evolution has produced new families that have added to overall biodiversity. Estimates based on species produce similar results.

We apparently live at a time when global biodiversity is near its all-time peak.

BIODIVERSITY LOSS

Extinction is the death of a group. In most cases, people mean species extinction when they refer to extinction, but other kinds occur. Local extinction, or **extirpation**, means that a species has died out in a local area. Grizzly bears, for example, once inhabited Colorado and many other areas of the western United States. They were hunted into local extinction in most areas, but persist in Canada and a few parts of their original U.S. range. **Ecological extinction** means that a species has become so rare that it has essentially no role or impact on its ecosystem. Many of these species are called the "living dead" because their rarity dooms them to eventual total extinction in the wild. The Florida panther, which has a population size between 30 and 50 individuals, cannot possibly survive without much help because of inbreeding and other problems of small populations discussed below (Fig. 12–6). Tigers, rhinos, and many other animals suffer similar problems and will likely survive only if drastic action is taken soon. Even then, such species may survive only in zoos and parks outside their original habitat.

All these different kinds of extinction have one key aspect in common: they all cause biodiversity loss. The loss of a species, or especially a higher group such as a family, is an irreversible loss of a unique pool of genes and individuals that evolution took millions of years to produce. However, extirpations (local extinctions) and ecological extinctions also result in **biological impoverishment**, or the loss of variety in the biosphere

EnviroNet
www.jbpub.com/environet

FIGURE 12–5

The number of families in the ocean has generally increased until the present. Five mass extinctions have temporarily lowered biodiversity. Will a sixth mass extinction occur in the near future? (*Source:* Modified from Raup and Sepkoski (1982), University of Chicago, Department of Geophysical Sciences.)

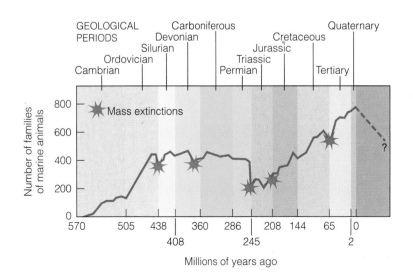

Millions of years ago

FIGURE 12–6

colder temperatures killed off many tropical species. The last mass extinction, which included the disappearance of the dinosaurs, occurred about 65 million years ago and may have been caused by a large meteorite impact.

Despite widespread interest in past catastrophic mass extinctions, careful analysis of the fossil record shows that over 90% of all extinct species died out during "normal" background times. In his popular book, *Extinction: Bad Genes or Bad Luck?*, David Raup points out that the average extinction rate throughout Earth history was probably just a few species per year. Common estimates are that between 2 and 10 species per year died out from "natural causes" such as volcanic eruptions, floods, and violent weather changes on the local level.

Current Biodiversity Loss: The Sixth Mass Extinction?

The European Age of Expansion in the fifteenth and sixteenth centuries initiated a wave of extinction that has continued to accelerate. ● Table 12–1 shows the number of recorded species extinctions since the year 1600. The table shows that 2.1% of mammal species and 1.3% of bird species on Earth have gone extinct in the last four centuries. While these numbers may not seem especially alarming, they almost certainly underestimate the true nature of the "extinction crisis" for a number of reasons:

1. The extinction rate of birds and mammals has been increasing rapidly. Between 1600 and 1700, the extinction rate was only about one species per 10 years. Between 1850 and 1950, the rate was one species *every year*. Preliminary evidence indicates that the extinction rate has increased yet again since 1950.
2. Some species of birds and mammals became extinct before they were described. So the true extinction rate is probably higher than is recorded in Table 12–1.
3. Species are not officially "recorded" as extinct until they have not been seen for 50 years. This lag also means that the true extinction rate of birds and mammals is probably higher than in Table 12–1.
4. Many species of birds and mammals have so few individuals remaining alive that the species is doomed to extinction. These "living dead" are not yet recorded as extinct, but will be in the near future.

Birds and mammals are among the best described groups, so the extinction rates for the oth-

even where species have not yet gone extinct. Even though members of an extirpated species may be alive elsewhere, their local extinction reduces the variety of life in that area. Also, with a local extinction, some of the total genetic variation of the species usually is lost. Similarly, ecologically extinct species often lose much of their genetic and individual variation so that the overall diversity of life on Earth is diminished by their extreme rarity.

Biological impoverishment by local or ecological extinction is much more common than species extinction. But because local and ecological extinctions are rarely reported, this kind of impoverishment goes unnoticed by most of the media and the public. This is one reason why the "extinction crisis" may be more urgent than is commonly perceived.

Biodiversity Losses before Humans

Extinction is the ultimate fate of all species. The fossil record indicates that, since life began over 3.5 billion years ago, over 95% of all species that existed are now extinct. Figure 12–5 shows that some of these past extinctions occurred during **mass extinctions**. These were catastrophic events that killed over 60% of all species on Earth. Most of the five past mass extinctions were caused by climatic disruption of habitat, especially global cooling. This caused sea level changes, and the

TABLE 12–1 *Recorded Extinctions, 1600 to the Present*

Numerous additional species have presumably gone extinct without being recorded by scientists.

	MAINLAND	ISLAND	OCEAN	TOTAL	APPROXIMATE NUMBER OF SPECIES	PERCENTAGE OF GROUP EXTINCT SINCE 1600
Mammals	30	51	2	83	4,000	2.1
Birds	21	92	0	113	9,000	1.3
Reptiles	1	20	0	21	6,300	0.3
Amphibians	2	0	0	2	4,200	0.05
Fishes	22	1	0	23	19,100	0.1
Invertebrates	49	48	1	98	1,000,000+	0.01
Flowering plants	245	139	0	384	250,000	0.2

(*Source:* R. B. Primack, *Essentials of Conservation Biology* [Sunderland, Mass.: Sinauer, 1993], p. 81. Reprinted by permission of Sinauer Associates, Inc.)

ers are likely to be underestimated even more significantly. Table 12–1, for example, lists a tiny extinction rate of 0.01% for invertebrates, but as we noted earlier, the vast majority of invertebrates have yet to be described. Many experts estimate that, in reality, dozens of insect species go extinct each day.

To solve such problems, other methods are used to estimate the rate of species extinction. Many of these use species-area curves to predict the effects of habitat destruction. Figure 12–7 shows that a loss of 50% of habitat area can result in about 10% of the species in the area becoming extinct. A 90% habitat loss eliminates 50% of the species.

Table 12–2, page 318, shows a variety of extinction rate estimates based on the species-area curve and other methods. As these indicate, between 1 and 11% of all species on Earth are lost each decade. The average estimate is around 5% per decade, which translates into an extinction rate of at least 50 species per day. This is much higher than the recorded rates of Table 12–1 because many extinctions have gone unrecorded. This is many hundreds of times higher than the "normal" average extinction rate of about 2–10 species extinctions per year, as estimated from the fossil record. Such currently high rates lead many, perhaps most, biologists to predict that as many as half the world's species could be extinct sometime in the twenty-first century.

Causes of Extinction

Extinction is caused by environmental change. Species can adapt to environmental change if it is not too rapid (Chapter 3), but the changes caused by human population growth and technology have been too massive and too rapid to allow many species to adapt.

For convenience, we can categorize all environmental changes that cause extinction into two basic categories: (1) changes in the physical environment and (2) changes in the biological environment (Table 12–3, page 318). Biological changes occur in three ways: introducing species, overhunting, and removing species (= secondary extinctions).

It is usually extremely difficult to identify which of the four causes in Table 12–3 was involved in a particular extinction. In most cases, species extinction occurs from *more than one cause*. For instance, all four causes have led to the decline of the Florida panther. Loss of habitat from development, overhunting, dozens of introduced species, and loss of prey species have combined to reduce the panther population drastically in the last 200 years.

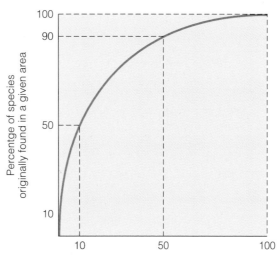

FIGURE 12–7
Preserving 50% of total habitat area often leaves about 90% of the original species remaining alive. Preserving only 10% of the area leaves about 50% of the species. (*Source:* R. B. Primack, *Essentials of Conservation Biology* [Sunderland, Mass.: Sinauer, 1993], p. 89. Reprinted by permission of Sinauer Associates, Inc.)

TABLE 12–2 Estimated Rates of Extinction

ESTIMATE	GLOBAL LOSS PER DECADE (%)	METHOD OF ESTIMATION
One million species between 1975 and 2000	4	Extrapolation of past exponentially increasing trend
15–20% of species between 1980 and 2000	8–11	Estimated species-area curve; forest loss based on U.S. government projections
12% of plant species in Western Hemisphere tropics 15% of bird species in Amazon basin	—	Species-area curve
2000 plant species per year in tropics and subtropics	8	Loss of half the species in area likely to be deforested by 2015
25% of species between 1985 and 2015	9	As above
At least 7% of plant species	7	Half of species lost over next decade in 10 "hot spots" covering 3.5% of forest area
0.2–0.3% per year	2–3	Half of rainforest species assumed lost in tropical rainforests to be local endemics and becoming extinct with forest loss
5–15% forest species by 2020	2–5	Species-area curve
2–8% loss between 1990 and 2015	1–5	Species-area curve; range includes current rate of forest loss and 50% increase

(*Source:* W. V. Reid, "How Many Species Will There Be?" in T. C. Whitmore and J. A. Sayer, eds., *Tropical Deforestation and Species Extinction* [London: Chapman & Hall, 1992]. Reprinted by permission of Chapman & Hall.)

This combination of causes is reflected in ▬ Figure 12–8, which shows the recorded causes of bird, mammal, and other historical extinctions. One reason why most are recorded as "unknown" is that a number of causes interact in complex ways. Where the cause of extinction could be reasonably well documented, introduced species was most common, followed by habitat disruption and overhunting. There was apparently no example where species removal (secondary extinc-

tion) led to extinction by itself, although it was involved in many of the "unknown" causes.

Keeping in mind that extinction-causing environmental changes often occur together, we now discuss each of these four causes of extinction. We will try to focus on examples where one cause has clearly played a major role.

Habitat Disruption

Habitat disruption refers to disturbance of the physical environment in which a species lives. Such disturbances can range from minor to drastic. Minor disturbances, such as mild chemical changes from air pollution, tend to affect only the most susceptible species.

In contrast, extreme physical changes in habitat can eliminate many species from the area. Deforestation of tropical rainforest by burning and other agricultural practices is one of the most publicized examples of massive habitat disruption. ▬ Figure 12–9 shows the projected loss of this critical habitat if current trends continue. Recall that the tropics contain many more species than other areas (Chapter 3). By some estimates, rainforests contain over 50% of the world's species

TABLE 12–3 Four Ways That Humans Cause Population Decline and Species Extinction

	EXAMPLES
Change physical environment:	
1. Habitat disruption	Drain swamp, toxic pollution
Change biological environment:	
2. Introduce new species	New predator
3. Overhunting	Big-game hunting
4. Secondary extinctions	Loss of food species

Causes of extinction

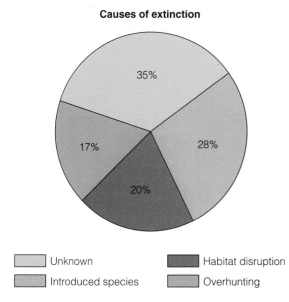

- Unknown
- Introduced species
- Habitat disruption
- Overhunting

FIGURE 12–8

Recorded causes of known mammal, bird, reptile, and fish species extinctions since 1600. Total sample = 405 species extinctions. (*Source:* Data from R. B. Primack, *Essentials of Conservation Biology* [Sunderland, Mass.: Sinauer, 1993], p. 117.)

even though they cover only 7% of the Earth. As of 1995, about one-half of the rainforest had been deforested. Recalling the species-area curve of Figure 12–7, some experts note that this 50% rainforest loss could mean perhaps a 10% rainforest species loss so far. But the curve also shows that continued habitat loss will soon result in a rapid decrease in species number.

Habitat disruption is usually a "piecemeal" process, with the habitat being broken into progressively smaller and more isolated fragments. Such **habitat fragmentation** has occurred in nearly all places where modern agriculture and urban society have moved in.

Habitat fragmentation is especially disruptive for two reasons. For one thing, remaining areas of habitat become separated and form "islands" of refuge in a "sea" of hostile environment. If the islands are too far apart, members of a species may not be able to reach other members in order to reproduce. The species could die out if all the isolated islands of habitat are so small that no island can maintain a self-sustaining population.

Secondly, habitat fragmentation leads to **edge effects** (Fig. 12–10). Housecats, dogs, wind and temperature changes, and many other disturbances from the surrounding area can penetrate along the edges of the preserved area, resulting in loss of habitat. Edge effects may be very dramatic. For instance, roads that occupy only 2% of a certain area may actually disrupt about 50% of the habitat! Habitat fragmentation is one of the main causes of decline in global and North American songbird populations (see Issues in Perspective 12–1).

Habitat disruption is not limited to land. Water pollution, dams, and other activities have a huge impact on fishes, clams, and other species in lakes and rivers because such species are confined in limited areas. Even the oceans are suffering widespread disruptions as raw sewage,

FIGURE 12–9

Past decline of tropical rainforests and projected decline by year 2000 if current deforestation rates continue.

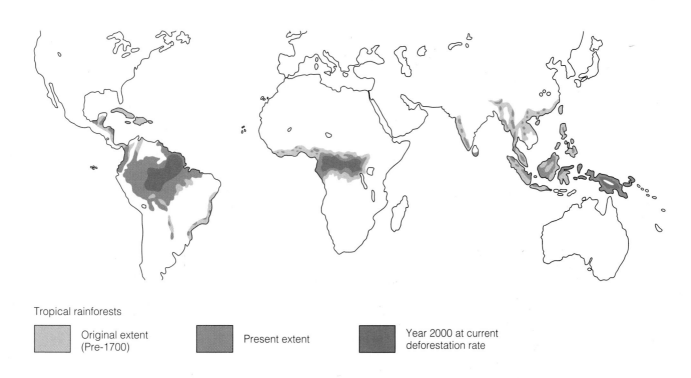

Tropical rainforests

- Original extent (Pre-1700)
- Present extent
- Year 2000 at current deforestation rate

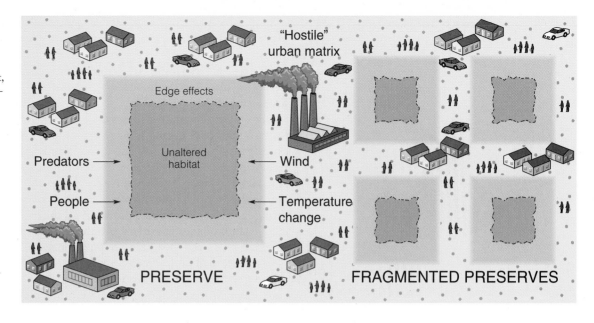

FIGURE 12–10
Even though the fragmented preserves on the right may seem similar in total area to the single preserve on the left, the amount of unaltered habitat is greatly reduced from edge effects.

FIGURE 12–11
Critical and threatened coral reefs of the world. (*Source:* Adapted from P. Weber, "Reviving Coral Reefs," in L. Brown *et al.*, eds., *State of the World 1993* [New York: W. W. Norton, 1993].)

toxic chemicals, sediments, and other pollutants are poured into them. Extinctions and ecological damage in the oceans are difficult to monitor, but a recent study of coral reefs found signs of extensive damage. Reefs are good biodiversity indicators because they support a great variety of species. Many reefs are in critical condition, meaning that they could be lost in 10–20 years (Fig. 12–11). An estimated 5–10% of the world's reefs are already "dead." At current rates, another 60% could be lost in the next 20–40 years. The major cause of death is sedimentation from logging, farming, mining, construction, and other coastal activities. The suspended sediment blocks sunlight, smothers the reefs, and has many other harmful effects.

Introduced Species

In many parts of the world, populations of new, so-called **exotic**, or nonnative, **species** have been introduced, sometimes with devastating effects. More than 1500 species of nonnative insects, including fire ants, gypsy moths, Japanese beetles, and "killer bees," have become established in the United States since 1860. Many other kinds of organisms have also been introduced. Well-known U.S. examples include kudzu, walking catfish, and English starlings. Unfortunately, once an exotic species becomes established, it is virtually impossible to remove.

The economic toll of exotic species is astonishing. The U.S. Office of Technology Assess-

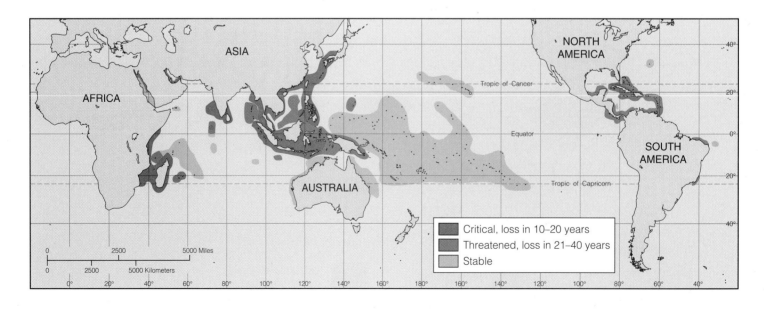

$\mathscr{P}$ROBLEMS OF RESOURCE DEPLETION   SECTION 2

The "Miner's Canary": Decline of Songbirds

In the 1980s, amateur birdwatchers began to notice a pronounced decline in the abundance of many different songbird species in North America. A number of statistical studies have confirmed the birdwatchers' observations. Table 1 shows the results of a study comparing bird sightings in the 1940s and in the 1980s in the Washington, D.C., area.

The loss of songbirds is alarming in many ways. One reason is the obvious reduction in quality of life to people who enjoy their beauty and singing. But more alarming to some is that songbirds are sensitive to many environmental changes. They are like the "miner's canary": these birds were kept in mines because they were more sensitive than people to bad air. A sick or dying bird was a warning.

Nor are songbirds declining only in North America. In 1994, the Worldwatch Institute reported that two-thirds of the songbird species of the world were experiencing a decline in abundance.

What is causing such declines? As usual, all the causes of extinction probably play at least some role: loss of food species and introduction of predators are clearly involved with some songbird losses. But John Terborgh of Duke University and many other bird experts have suggested that habitat loss and fragmentation are key factors in the decline. Indeed, songbirds are hit with a "one-two" punch of habitat loss. Many migrate from North America to the tropics, and they are losing habitat in both places. Species that spend winters in the tropics are declining faster than those that do not. One reason is that tropical deforestation is removing their wintering sites.

TABLE 1 *Sightings of Songbird Species in Rock Creek Park, District of Columbia*

Species	MEAN NUMBER OF PAIRS SIGHTED		Percentage Change
	In 1940s	In 1980s	
Migrants			
Red-eyed vireo	41.5	5.8	−86.0
Ovenbird	38.8	3.3	−91.5
Acadian flycatcher	21.5	0.1	−99.5
Wood thrush	16.3	3.9	−76.1
Yellow-throated vireo	6.0	0.0	−100.0
Hooded warbler	5.0	0.0	−100.0
Scarlet tanager	7.3	3.5	−52.1
Black-and-white warbler	3.0	0.0	−100.0
Nonmigrants			
Carolina chickadee	5.0	4.3	−14.0
Tufted titmouse	5.0	4.5	−10.0
Downy woodpecker	3.5	3.0	−14.3
White-breasted nuthatch	3.5	3.1	−11.4

(*Source:* Reprinted by permission of the National Audubon Society.)

But even songbirds that stay in North America all the time are declining. Here the reason is apparently habitat disruption in North America, especially from forest fragmentation. Investigations since the early 1980s have shown that fragmented forests can greatly hinder songbird reproduction because of edge effects. Nest predators, such as raccoons, opossums, and housecats, take a much greater toll where forest fragmentation produces edges that allow easier access to nests. Nests that are deep in the forest and thus less exposed are less preyed upon.

Furthermore, cowbirds destroy more eggs through nest parasitism when the forest is fragmented. Cowbirds lay eggs in songbird nests, and the songbirds raise cowbird chicks instead of their own. Cowbirds prefer disturbed farmland, so loss of forests promotes the spread of cowbirds and opens up songbird habitat to access by these nest parasites.

ment estimated that over $100 billion in damage would be caused by nonnative species during the 1990s. About 17% of the more than 1500 insect species introduced into North America are pests requiring the use of pesticides for control. Unfortunately, many introductions have been purposely done. The English starling, perhaps the most common bird in the United States today, was introduced in a Shakespearean play in the early 1900s (Chapter 3). Game animals have

Invasion of the Zebra Mussels

An oceangoing ship teems with alien life. The organisms come aboard when the ship takes on ballast water from the harbor. A ship will "ballast up" for several reasons. One is stability: a lightly loaded vessel may ride too high, and is thus more liable to capsize. Another reason is propulsion: the propeller of an underloaded ship may rise half out of the water. To avoid these problems, a ship may distribute ballast water through a network of tanks inside the hull.

In 1986 or late 1985, a ship leaving a freshwater European port for North America began to take on ballast. As it did, several members of the harbor's population came aboard along with the water. Alas for North America, one of them was a hardy Asian bivalve named *Dreissena polymorpha*, the zebra mussel, which over a 150-year period had spread from the region of the Caspian Sea into much of Europe, plugging water pipes (◼ Fig. 1) and clamping onto the hulls of boats. The unknown ship that carried the zebra mussel across the Atlantic was headed for the St. Lawrence Seaway. Past Quebec City it sailed, past Montreal, past Toronto, and on through Lake Erie. When the ship finally reached its destination and flushed its ballast somewhere above Detroit, a founding population of zebra mussels tumbled into Lake St. Clair—and a new continent.

Biologists are hastening to quantify

◼ **FIGURE 1**
Zebra mussels clog pipes, causing billions of dollars in damage. This view shows a pipe cut in half to show how the mussels attach. (*Source:* Peter Yates/Science Photo Library/Photo Researchers.)

the effects of this "invasion," as the introduction of any new species is called, but already the costs have been staggering. Propelled by relentless fertility and a talent for spreading themselves abroad, zebra mussels are clogging the intakes of power stations and water treatment plants; coloniz-

ing navigation buoys in such numbers that they drag them under; fouling fishing nets, marine engines, and hulls of boats; and displacing spawning grounds that are the mainstay of a commercial and sports fishery valued in the billions. In North America, the zebra mussel seems to have

been introduced for hunting or fishing (striped bass in Tennessee), and predators to reduce pests (mongoose in Hawaii). The kudzu plant now overgrows and smothers many acres of land in the southeastern United States at a yearly cost exceeding $1 billion. Yet in the 1930s the federal government paid farmers to plant it to control soil erosion.

Although purposeful introductions have been sharply curtailed, accidental introductions continue to increase, as international trade and travel

expand. The very destructive zebra mussel is an example of a species that "hitchhiked" from one nation to another (Issues in Perspective 12–2). Studies show that the large majority of "hitchhikers" and new species fail to become established, but because so many introductions occur, some of them eventually succeed. Humans promote this both by providing transportation for nonnative species and by disturbing native ecosystems. By upsetting natural interactions, we make it easier for new species to become established.

found a very hospitable environment. They have already swept down the length of Lake Erie and penetrated Lake Ontario.

The zebra mussel is a tiny but troublesome mollusk. It is no more than half an inch (1.27 cm) long and comes in a handsome shell marked by alternating bands of light and dark. In addition to the tongue-like "feet" that mussels use to push themselves along the bottom, zebra mussels, alone among freshwater mussels, possess thread that allows the mussel to attach itself to hard surfaces like rocks or steel or other mussels. And unlike native mussel larvae, which disperse themselves by hitching rides on fish, zebra mussel larvae are veligers, meaning that each possesses cilia, tiny hairlike fibers that enable it to suspend itself in water. Zebra mussel larvae in a current can spread with remarkable swiftness.

There seems to be no doubt that the zebra mussel will colonize much of this vast continent. They can survive almost anywhere in a range that covers about two-thirds of the United States and the southern part of Canada. In terms of temperature, only Canada's cold northern lakes and the warmer waters of the American South will not sustain them. Their reproductive rates are amazing. A female zebra mussel can produce 40,000 eggs a year, and the male a like amount of sperm. Even if only a small percentage of these eggs are fertilized and advance to maturity, the rate of proliferation will be impressive. For example, on Hen Island Reef in Lake Erie, the density was 2900 zebra mussels to the square yard (3500 to the square meter) on the first reading; five months later, the count was 19,230 per square yard (23,000 per square meter).

The zebra mussel also threatens native fishes with its insatiable appetite for phytoplankton, the microscopic green plants at the very bottom of the aquatic food chain. Because many fishes feed on the zooplankton that eat phytoplankton, tinkering with phytoplankton is tinkering with one of nature's building blocks. If the mussels deplete the phytoplankton, the population of zooplankton could crash with disastrous consequences for certain fishes, for the fishes that prey on those fishes, and for the ducks that eat them and the people who catch them. In this way the zebra mussel, in what amounts to a nanosecond of evolutionary time, could alter the ecosystem of the entire Great Lakes and, ultimately, most of the United States.

Nothing will stop the zebra mussel's spread. But can it be held in check? One possibility is to force incoming ships to discharge freshwater ballast at sea and replace it with saltwater ballast. Another is ozonation, an environmentally benign oxidant that chews away at the soft parts of the organism. Ozonation could be helpful to power and water treatment plants that are trying to prevent zebra mussels from clogging their intakes, but it is extremely expensive, costing an estimated $9 billion per plant. Even then, ozonation can only alleviate specific problems here and there; it cannot do anything to halt the overall proliferation of the zebra mussel.

A fish called the drum, a bottom feeder, does seem to like the mussel, but unfortunately this benefits only the lowly drum itself. Apparently, it is not an extremely tasty fish. At one site in Lake Erie, a diving duck has begun to prey on the zebra mussels. Unfortunately, Europeans have found that only overwintering waterfowl have an effect on mussel control.

And the mussels' next stop? The Mississippi. As it is, there is no conceivable way of preventing their spread. Even if 99% of the boats leaving the Great Lakes scraped their hulls, one boat with mature mussels could be catastrophic. The Mississippi River will be a good environment for them. Spreading through the waterways that lace the continent, the mussels' progeny will drift by the hundreds of thousands on the rich warm currents. Carried on boats and the feet of water birds, the invaders will make their way up streams and over land. Thus, a tiny but troublesome mollusk, accidentally introduced into a North American lake a few years ago, may soon infest most of the continent.

Exotic species are especially important as a cause of extinction on islands. Because of their isolation, native island species are often poorly adapted to cope with new species. As a result, new species not only have an easier time becoming established on islands but also have a more devastating impact on native island species than on continental species. Predators and competitors have driven many native prey and competitor species to extinction. Others survive only in carefully protected preserves.

An example are ground birds that evolved on many islands, such as New Zealand and Hawaii, in the absence of large predators. The introduction of domestic cats and dogs alone has driven dozens of island ground bird species to extinction or near extinction (Fig. 12–12). The introduction of the brown tree snake to Guam has effectively eliminated 11 of 18 native bird species on the island. In some areas of Guam, over *5000 snakes* per square mile (over 1900 per km²) have been counted!

■ FIGURE 12–12
The New Zealand kakapo once numbered in the hundreds of thousands. But this flightless bird was no match for dogs, cats, and other introduced species. The forty or so remaining birds survive on two outer islands, which are carefully protected sanctuaries. (*Source:* Science VU/ Visuals Unlimited.)

Although large continents suffer relatively fewer species extinctions from introduced species, they certainly experience major impacts. The kudzu plant has driven out many local plant populations where it grows. Freshwater lakes and rivers are especially susceptible to destructive invasions, perhaps because they are confined environments, leaving native organisms nowhere to go. Exotic aquatic plants such as hyacinth and hydrilla now cover vast areas of many of Florida's lakes, choking out other plants and blocking sunlight. No less than 50 of the 133 fish species sampled in a recent California study were found to be introduced. Many extinctions have occurred from such introductions so that native fishes, clams, and other freshwater groups are among the groups most strongly affected by exotics (recall Issues in Perspective 12–2). A 1993 study by the American Fisheries Society reported that 72% of the nearly 300 species of freshwater clams in North America were either extinct or in decline.

The most dramatic devastation by an introduced fish is in East Africa in Lake Victoria where a single species, the Nile perch, has already exterminated over 35 species of native fishes in just a few years. If it continues as expected, several hundred more native fish species will become extinct in Lake Victoria from the perch, setting a record for the greatest number of extinctions from a single introduction.

Land species on continents can also become extinct from introductions. The decline of the Florida panther has been accelerated by many invading species. Indeed, South Florida is often said to have more exotics than any other part of the United States. The Florida Department of Natural Resources has estimated that 20% of the 1650 plant species and 23% of the 44 mammal species in South Florida are established nonnatives. In part, this is because South Florida is an "island" of tropical environment isolated on the Florida peninsula from the rest of Latin America.

Overhunting

Overhunting, or "overkill," is species decline caused by excessive shooting, trapping, or poisoning of organisms. Usually, this is done for sport or economic reasons. It is very difficult for humans to cause the extinction of "pest" species, such as roaches or mice, this way because they are so abundant and reproduce so rapidly.

Overhunting has been very effective in eliminating many other kinds of plants and animals, however, especially organisms that were initially rare and/or reproduce slowly. Recall from Chapter 3 that most species are rare in nature so many can be eliminated this way. This is especially true of most large animals and plants, which tend to have much lower abundances and slower reproduction than small organisms.

Unfortunately, large animals are also the species most often killed for sport or economic motives. Economic motives include killing to protect domesticated animals from predators or to sell parts of the animal itself. Elephant ivory, leopard skins, rhino horns, and tropical bird feathers are but a few examples.

This preference for killing large animals, combined with their low abundance and reproductive rate, means that overhunting has caused drastic reductions in large species throughout the world. This process may have begun with prehistoric humans causing extinctions of the woolly mammoth, saber-tooth cats, and other large animals. As killing technology has improved, so has the effectiveness of overhunting. A classic example is the North American bison, which declined from many millions of individuals to under 1100 in just a few decades (■ Fig. 12–13). Today virtually all large species are in decline, including both planteaters, such as elephants, rhinos, and pandas, and meateaters, such as large cats and dog relatives. Nor are ocean-dwellers spared, for most whale species are also in decline.

Secondary Extinctions

Secondary extinctions occur when the extinction of one group causes the extinction of another. Often this involves the loss of a food species. For example, the familiar panda bear of China subsists largely on a diet of bamboo. As the bamboo is being destroyed, the panda may become extinct from that cause alone. Other examples are more subtle, reflecting the complex and unpredictable interactions among organisms that make the effects of human disturbances so difficult to predict. The well-known extinction of the dodo bird, for instance, has caused the *Calveria* tree to become unable to reproduce. When the dodo ate the seeds of the tree, it digested the outer seed covering, allowing the seeds to grow (■ Fig. 12–14).

Minimum Viable Populations

Extinction can occur even if the population is not reduced directly to zero. Even if many individu-

FIGURE 12–13
Slaughter of Buffalo (bison) *on
the Kansas Pacific Railroad*,
from *Plains of the Great West*
(1877) by Richard Irving
Dodge, 1877. (*Source:* Courtesy
of the John Hay Library, Brown
University.)

als survive the disturbances, the population may never recover if it becomes too small. The species will fall into an **extinction vortex**.

There are two basic causes for this extinction vortex. One is that small populations may have breeding problems. Too few females may be left, or if the population is too dispersed, individuals may not be able to locate each other to mate. Even if there are enough mates and they can find each other, genetic inbreeding is a major problem in small populations. This leads to birth defects and many other malformities. For example, many males in the remaining population of only 30–50 Florida panthers suffer from testicular and other malformities.

Aside from breeding, the second cause of the extinction vortex is that small populations are much more easily wiped out by random environmental fluctuations, such as an abnormally harsh winter, that would not significantly affect larger groups. The chance of being wiped out increases exponentially with decreasing population size.

The smallest population size needed to stay above the extinction vortex is often called the **minimum viable population (MVP)**. If a population falls below this size, it is said to be no longer "viable," and long-term breeding problems and environmental fluctuations will eventually finish the population off. This is what we meant earlier by the

"living dead," when habitat fragmentation leaves too few individuals in each isolated fragment.

In the past, calculations of MVP have been oversimplified. Some ecologists initially suggested, for instance, that an MVP of perhaps 500 individuals would permit almost any species to survive for many years. But most ecologists now acknowledge that there is no such "magic" number for MVP that applies to all species. Organisms vary widely in their ability to rebound from low numbers. Organisms that breed and grow rapidly,

FIGURE 12–14
The now-extinct dodo bird
was crucial to the reproduction of the *Calveria* tree.
(*Source:* The Granger Collection,
New York.)

for example, will often recover from lower population sizes than slow-growing organisms and therefore often have lower MVPs. In general, most "population viability analyses," which seek to estimate how long a certain population will persist, indicate that at least a *few thousand* individuals must remain alive to ensure long-term survival of most species. In this case, "long-term" survival means more than a few decades.

Community and Ecosystem Degradation

A growing criticism is that conservationists have focused too much on "species chauvinism." While much money has been devoted to saving a few highly publicized species, entire ecosystems are rapidly being degraded or even disappearing. As a result, there is increasing interest in saving endangered ecosystems as well as endangered species.

We saw in Chapter 3 that a community consists of all populations of species that inhabit an area. An ecosystem is a community plus its physical environment. A community or ecosystem becomes extinct when the populations composing it die out. For example, a forest fire or bulldozer may completely destroy large areas of a certain forest community so that it becomes extinct.

Community Degradation

Communities and ecosystems are more likely to be degraded by human activity than completely destroyed, however. By "degraded" we mean that some species within the community or ecosystem suffer major decreases in abundance. A classic type of disturbance is pollution of a community's water, soil, or air. A basic effect of disturbance is **ecosystem simplification**, meaning that the number of species in the ecosystem declines. In addition, some of the remaining species become "superabundant." These are the species that thrive in the polluted environment, such as certain sewage-eating bacteria or "trash" fishes such as garfishes that have adapted to low-oxygen waters.

Besides simplifying structure, a disturbance can also disrupt the "function" of communities (and ecosystems) by altering the flow of matter and energy through them. The flow of excess nutrients into the ecosystem can cause eutrophication and other disruptions often involving rapid population growth and decay. Conversely, slash and burn agriculture and other disturbances will often lead to "leaky" ecosystems, with excess nutrient flow out of the system (Chapter 3).

Indicators of Ecosystem "Health"

Some species in a community or ecosystem are more susceptible to disturbances than others. These are often called **indicator species** because they indicate the "health" of an ecosystem. A decline in the abundance of indicator species is evidence that the entire ecosystem may soon decline (see Issues in Perspective 12–1). For example, some trees, such as the Fraser firs in the Smoky Mountain National Park, are more sensitive to air pollution than others and will be affected by it first.

Are Diverse Communities More Easily Disturbed?

Until the early 1970s, many ecologists believed that the more species a community had, the more difficult it was to disturb. Although there is still much ongoing research and debate, mathematical models and field data show that the relationship between diversity, or number of species, and stability, or ease of disturbance, in a community is much more complicated than ecologists formerly believed.

Most ecologists now agree that stability is lowest in communities with very low diversity. In monoculture, for example, only one plant, such as corn, is grown for many acres. Such simple communities are easily disturbed, such as by an invading pest that can wipe out much of the community if the corn plants are susceptible. In communities that have more plant species and therefore support more kinds of animals, too, it is very unlikely that all the plant species will be susceptible to a single pest. Thus, increasing diversity leads to redundancy: if a species is lost, such as a food species, other species will still exist to support at least part of the community.

However, after a certain point, increasing diversity may make a community easier to disturb. Increasing diversity means that more species are interacting, creating more complex food webs (Chapter 3). Many mathematical models show that such complex webs can become very sensitive because minor changes can "cascade" through the community. For example, many species can become dependent on certain **keystone species** for food, reproduction, or some other basic need. If the keystone species are removed, many parts of the community can be drastically affected. This seems to be especially true of some highly diverse tropical communities. Because they have been undisturbed for so long, they have built up highly intricate interactions that are easily disturbed.

STOPPING EXTINCTIONS

Why worry about extinctions? Some people argue that humans have little need of wildlife. They view elephants, exotic tropical insects or plants, and the like as curiosities that have no immediate value and are little concerned at the prospect of their loss. To others, this is an absurd attitude. They take the opposite view and want to preserve all nature for its own sake. They see humans as the intruders and insist that all extinctions must be stopped as soon as possible. Between these two extremes are many practical realities.

Reasons to Stop Extinctions: The Many Values of Biodiversity

People who worry least about extinction tend to place only direct values on biodiversity. Recall from Chapter 6 that direct values are based on the immediate economic gain made when a resource is destructively harvested. Examples include whaling, logging, and illegal trade in endangered species.

Illegal trade is an especially good example because the entire value of an organism is reduced to the price it brings, either dead or alive, in the marketplace. The World Wildlife Fund estimates that illegal trade in wild animals globally produces $2 to $3 billion per year. ● Table 12–4 shows some of the organisms, or their parts, that are highly prized by buyers. Rhino horns are used as aphrodisiacs, daggers, and other adornments. Many other species, such as the imperial Amazon macaw and mountain gorilla, are popular pets or attractions.

But such direct short-term valuation of an organism omits many other potential values, called "indirect values" in Chapter 6. When these are ignored, the "true" value of a species is underestimated. ▬ Figure 12–15 summarizes six indirect values for biological resources; we call them the "6 e's" to make them easier to remember. These are the same as the "5 e's" of Chapter 6, but with the additional "e" of evolutionary value that biological resources have.

Indirect Values: The "Six E's"

An ethical reason to save species is that humans have no right to destroy other species to the point that they are gone forever. According to this view, animals have intrinsic rights of their own, outside extrinsic human needs. This includes the right to live a life that is relatively free from pain.

TABLE 12–4 *Typical Species Prices (1990 Rates)*

INTERNATIONAL SPECIES	PRICE ($U.S.)	NORTH AMERICAN SPECIES	PRICE ($U.S.)
Olive python	1,500	Bald eagle	2,500
Rhinoceros horn	12,500/pound	Golden eagle	200
Tiger skin (Siberian)	3,500	Gila monster	200
Tiger meat	130/pound	Peregrine falcon	10,000
Cockatoo	2,000	Grizzly bear	5,000
Leopard	8,500	Grizzly bear claw necklace	2,500
Snow leopard	14,000	Polar bear	6,000
Elephant tusk	250/pound	Black bear paw pad	150
Walrus tusk	50/pound	Reindeer antlers	35/pound
Mountain gorilla	150,000	Mountain lion	500
Giant panda	3,700	Mountain goat	3,500
Ocelot	40,000/coat	Saguaro cactus	15,000
Imperial Amazon macaw	30,000		

(*Source:* U.S. Fish and Wildlife Service.)

The esthetic (aesthetic) and emotional reasons to save species are that biological diversity makes life more enjoyable and enriching. Given the mental and physical rejuvenation many of us experience after a long hike or other outdoor recreation, this argument alone would seem to have much validity. Certainly, such recreation would be less rejuvenating if we had only the same few species to experience all the time.

Indirect economic values include the many nondestructive ways that humans can use species. "Ecotourism" and sustainable harvesting of exotic foods, medicines, and many other materials are two examples discussed later as practical social incentives for providing jobs while preserving species. When measured over many years, such sustainable economic benefits of biodiversity are generally greater than the short-term economic gain from selling an organism for its skin, horns, or other values.

www.jbpub.com/environet

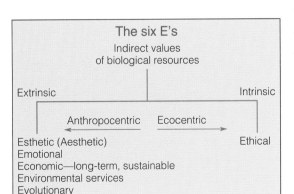

The six E's
Indirect values
of biological resources

Extrinsic — Intrinsic

Anthropocentric ← → Ecocentric

Esthetic (Aesthetic)
Emotional
Economic—long-term, sustainable
Environmental services
Evolutionary
Ethical

▬ **FIGURE 12–15**
The "6 e's" represent potential indirect values of wild biological resources.

Environmental services refer to the value of biodiversity in providing us with many of life's essentials. Ecosystems are environmental support systems that provide us with things that we now take for granted: oxygen to breathe (from plants), drinkable water (purified by microbial activity), and many other natural chemical cycles that occur via ecosystem functions. If we remove too many species from an ecosystem, ecosystem function will be impaired. If we lose too many species in too many ecosystems, environmental services of the entire biosphere could be impaired.

The last indirect value of Figure 12–15 is the evolutionary value of species. This is the value of today's species to future generations. Rather

than being constant entities, species often change to adapt to new environmental conditions. But the *raw material of evolution is variation.* As biodiversity disappears, the biosphere will become less able to adapt to change because fewer species will be alive. An impoverished biosphere today means an impoverished biosphere for future generations.

A practical example of the loss of evolutionary value is food production by humans. Today only about 30 plant species provide 95% of the world's nutrition. Just four of these, wheat, corn, rice, and potatoes, provide most of the world's food, and all four have been subjected to centuries of inbreeding. Do we want our diet to be so bland and monotonous forever? Botanists estimate that at least 75,000 edible plant species exist, many su-

perior in flavor and nutrition to those commonly eaten in the United States (Fig. 12–16).

The ability of species to adapt to change also has other important implications for our future food supply. Low diversity makes organisms more susceptible to extinction. Inbreeding of most crop species makes them notoriously susceptible to diseases and insects. By interbreeding wild species with closely related cultivated forms, resistance to disease and general hardiness can often be improved, and genetic engineering now allows us to combine useful traits from species that cannot interbreed naturally (Chapter 13).

It is thus economically advantageous to maximize diversity both by growing a variety of crops and by having as many different crop species at our disposal as possible. Yet if current rates of extinction continue, some 25,000 plant species will die out by the year 2000 before we have a chance to study them. Some biologists have proposed that "gene banks" be set up as a reservoir to save seeds, spores, sperm, and other genetic materials for species that cannot be saved in the wild (Chapter 13). Currently, seed banks contain only a small fraction of most plant varieties, and many wild species have yet to be collected and described.

We have focused on plants, but similar arguments can be made for domesticated animal species. Breeding cattle with buffalo ("beefalo") to improve the stamina of cattle breeds and their resistance to predation is one of many examples where wild genes have been useful. Similarly, many wild animal species are themselves potentially tasty and healthy food sources, even without being interbred with existing food species (Issues in Perspective 12–3).

Which Species to Save?

Extinction rates are now so high that many species will inevitably go extinct. Others may survive with adequate attention, but the cost of saving all of them far exceeds the limited monetary and human resources available for saving species. Thus, painful decisions will have to be made concerning which species we want to save the most.

Conservation biologists often use the concept of **species triage** to refer to the difficult process of selecting which species to try to save from extinction. *Triage* is a medical term used in emer-

Emu-burgers, Anyone?

A good example of the unexplored food potential of many exotic species is the growing popularity of the emu. Emus are large, ostrich-like running birds native to Australia. In 1994, more than one million emus were being raised in the United States by some 7500 breeders. Why raise emus? One reason is the increasing popularity of the meat. Ground emu meat has only 30% of the fat of a hamburger and is often said to have a beefy taste. About 5% of Australians eat emu meat regularly. The U.S. Department of Agriculture has approved emu meat imports from Australia and is soon expected to approve the sale of U.S.-raised emu meat in supermarkets.

Aside from its lower food fat content, the emu offers other advantages. It is very efficient in converting plant food to meat: A cow needs up to 10 pounds (4.5 kg) of feed to gain 1 pound (0.45 kg). In contrast, an emu can gain 4 pounds (1.8 kg) on the same amount of feed. Emus, in other words, are about four times more efficient than cattle in converting plants to animal protein. Furthermore, many parts of the emu can be sold. Its lint-free feathers are sought for cleaning computer parts, the skin can be tanned, and each adult contains a gallon (3.785 liters) of oil that is used for ointments and lotions.

Like most new items, emu-burgers are still expensive because they are relatively rare. But if emu ranching continues to grow, along with demand for emu products, the American Emu Association predicts that emus could become very common animals in the United States. On the other hand, many groups, such as those concerned with environmental exploitation and animal rights, denounce the domestication of another wild species to be bred as a "product" for human consumption.

---

gency rooms: some patients will probably die, and some will probably live, so most attention should be focused on those in the middle who may live or die. And so it is with species. "Weedy" species such as squirrels and deer are in no danger of extinction while other species are among the "living dead," with so few individuals left that they will likely go extinct. Many experts therefore argue that conservation efforts should be directed at those species that are at risk and can still be saved. Unfortunately, the number of species at risk far outweighs the social resources currently allotted to preserving them.

Which Species Are at Risk?

Species are not equally likely to become extinct. For many reasons, some species are more able than others to survive environmental change. A well-known example of a very resilient group are cockroaches, which have existed for over 300 million years and will probably be alive for millions more. ● Table 12–5 identifies nine characteristics that make some species more susceptible to extinction than others. Island species are sensitive to the introduction of new species because they have been isolated for a long time. Indeed, most of the bird and mammal extinctions until now have been of island-dwelling species. Species with limited habitats become extinct easily because they have so little habitat, human activity can quickly eliminate it. For instance, one species of tropical insect will often be adapted to only one part on one kind of local plant. When the plant is eradicated, so is that insect species, along with others that are adapted to other parts of the plant.

Species with large territories die off quickly because they need lots of area to support them. This has been shown repeatedly when apparently "large" game reserves are set up and wide-ranging species (such as large predators) still die out. When a single individual needs many square miles to forage, it takes a very large reserve to preserve enough individuals to maintain the species. Many species are naturally rare, even without human disturbance; such species are obviously prone to extinction because they have few individuals to begin with. Low reproductive rates make it difficult for a species to rebound from habitat disturbance, hunting, or other causes of population declines. Economic and sporting value cause species to be sought by hunters. Predators are generally high on the food pyramid so they are relatively less abundant than many other organisms. Sensitivity to pollution is another trait leading to extinction. Finally, some species may

TABLE 12–5 *Characteristics of Extinction Susceptibility*

CHARACTERISTICS	REASON CHARACTERISTICS TEND TO CAUSE EXTINCTION	EXAMPLES
1. Island species	Unable to compete with introduced species.	More than half of the native plant species in Hawaii
2. Species with limited habitats or breeding areas	Some species are found in only a few ecosystems.	Woodland caribou, Everglade crocodile, red-cockaded woodpecker
3. Species that require large territories to survive	Widespread habitat destruction.	California condor, blue whale, Bengal tiger, Florida panther
4. Species with low reproductive rates	Many species evolved low reproductive rates because predation was low.	Blue whale, California condor, polar bear, rhinoceros, Florida manatee
5. Rare species	Few individuals to replenish population.	Tropical insects, rhinoceros
6. Species that are economically valuable or hunted for sport	Hunting pressures by humans.	Snow leopard, blue whale, elephant, rhinoceros, tiger
7. Predators	Often killed to reduce predation of domestic stock.	Grizzly bear, timber wolf, Bengal tiger
8. Species that are susceptible to pollution	Some species are more susceptible than others to industrial pollution.	Bald eagle (susceptible to certain pesticides), pelicans
9. Species with inadaptive behaviors	Behaviors promote death in human environments.	Manatees swimming toward motorboats

show behaviors that promote extinction. Some birds fly into windshields. Recent data on the Florida manatee indicates that it tends to swim toward motorboats for some reason. Boat injuries are the leading cause of death.

These nine traits can *co-occur*: many species have more than one of the traits and are thus much more likely to become extinct. For example, large animals tend to be rarer, require larger territories, and also have lower reproductive rates than small animals. If the large animal is also a predator and is hunted for sport, then it has at least five of the traits that promote extinction. Similarly, the Florida manatee not only swims toward boats but has low reproductive rates.

Are All Species Equally Important?

So many species are at risk that they cannot all be saved from extinction. In 1994, more than 50% of all crayfishes and freshwater clams (mussels) in the United States were at risk (Fig. 12–17). At least 30% of plant, amphibian, and fish species were at risk, and over 15% of mammal species.

With so many species at risk, triage decisions cannot be made on the basis of risk alone. Con-

servation biologists therefore often ask whether one species is "more important" than another. Ethically, perhaps one could argue that all species are equal; an insect may have as much right to live as a panther.

But in other ways, in particular, in ecological and evolutionary importance, all species are not equal. Ecological importance reflects the role a species plays in its ecological community. Keystone species play large roles because they affect so many other species. Large predators, for example, often control the population dynamics of many herbivores. When the predators, such as wolves, are removed, the herbivore population may increase rapidly, overgrazing plants and causing massive ecological disruption. Similarly, certain plants are crucial food for many animal species in some ecosystems. Extinction of keystone species will often have cascading effects on many species, even causing "secondary" extinctions. Many therefore argue that saving keystone species should be a priority.

Evolutionary importance varies among species because all species do not have the same potential for contributing to future biodiversity. **Unique species** are not closely related to any

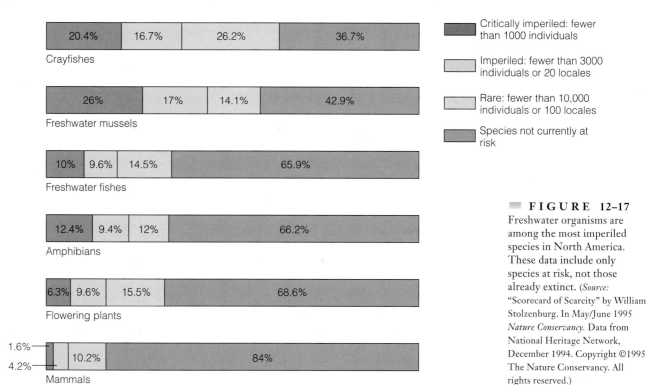

20.4%	16.7%	26.2%	36.7%

Crayfishes

26%	17%	14.1%	42.9%

Freshwater mussels

10%	9.6%	14.5%	65.9%

Freshwater fishes

12.4%	9.4%	12%	66.2%

Amphibians

6.3%	9.6%	15.5%	68.6%

Flowering plants

1.6%
4.2%

10.2%		84%

Mammals

- **Critically imperiled:** fewer than 1000 individuals
- **Imperiled:** fewer than 3000 individuals or 20 locales
- **Rare:** fewer than 10,000 individuals or 100 locales
- **Species not currently at risk**

FIGURE 12–17
Freshwater organisms are among the most imperiled species in North America. These data include only species at risk, not those already extinct. (*Source:* "Scorecard of Scarcity" by William Stolzenburg. In May/June 1995 *Nature Conservancy.* Data from National Heritage Network, December 1994. Copyright ©1995 The Nature Conservancy. All rights reserved.)

other living species (Fig. 12–18). Unique species represent unusual gene pools, with many genes and traits not found in other species. The loss of a unique species often represents a much greater loss of genetic and evolutionary potential than the loss of a species with many living close relatives. Pandas, for example, are a very unique species of bear. Unlike most bears, which eat many kinds of food, the panda is specialized for eating bamboo. The panda is a result of very un-

likely evolutionary events that are unlikely to recur, and the Earth may never again see anything similar to it.

Rather than concentrating on species of ecological and evolutionary importance, to the regret of some biologists, conservation efforts have often focused on high-profile **charismatic species** that attract public support. The Florida panther and the bald eagle are examples of charismatic species. Focusing on such species is not necessarily bad because they are sometimes ecologically and evolutionarily important. Furthermore, because they are usually large animals and often predators, large areas must be set aside for them. These large preserves often contain the habitat of many other species in danger of extinction. For this reason, large charismatic species such as the Florida panther are also called **umbrella species.** Many other species are also protected under the "umbrella" set aside to preserve the panther.

How to Save Species

Because extinction is caused by change in a species's environment, such as habitat disruption or introduced species, the best way to save any species is to preserve its natural environment. This task is actually quite complex and involves two key steps: (1) selecting and designing preserves on the basis of ecological principles and

FIGURE 12–18
Unique species have no living closely related species.

(2) using legal and economic principles to establish and maintain the preserves. The first step is largely scientific, the second largely social.

Selecting Preserves

Creating a preserve involves more than just setting aside a section of land or water. Preservation of habitats containing many nonnative species or abundant native species often does little to maximize global biodiversity. Instead, preserves should be selected that save native species that are rare and in danger of extinction.

Historically, natural habitat preservation has usually arisen from the desire to preserve (1) unique or scenic landscapes or (2) popular charismatic species. The first national park, for example, was Yellowstone National Park created in 1872 for its scenic beauty. Many of the first game preserves were in Europe to preserve disappearing large game animals. One of the earliest was established in Poland in 1564 to attempt to preserve wild cattle.

But as many native species become rare at increasing rates, it is clear that simply preserving a few unique habitats or habitats of a few charismatic species will not suffice. If the goal is to save many threatened species, a more comprehensive approach is needed. A common approach has been to use popular charismatic species as um-

brella species to preserve large areas, but this approach has its limitations. Many rare species are narrowly distributed in areas that are not currently occupied by umbrella species.

Consequently, another approach that is increasing in popularity is to identify **hot spots**. Hot spots are areas of exceptionally high species richness, especially concentrations of localized rare species that occur nowhere else. Hot spots are generally areas of great geographic diversity that have promoted lots of evolutionary change.

Figure 12–19 shows a number of global hot spots for plant species. Ecologist Norman Myers has estimated that these cover just 0.5% of the Earth's land surface but contain the only habitat of about 20% of the Earth's plant species. Similar analyses of birds indicate that about one-fourth of the world's bird species are confined to just 2% of the Earth's land surface. Hot spots for birds do not necessarily occur in the same areas as plant hot spots. In the United States a number of hot spots, for various groups, have been identified (Table 2–6).

Unfortunately, the use of hot spots and similar scientific methods of identifying preserves is a very recent development. Most preserves in the United States and the world have been, and continue to be, selected on the basis of *other criteria*: scenic beauty, popular species, or practical and political considerations. Such methods do not

FIGURE 12–19
Global hot spots for plant biodiversity. (*Source:* G. K. Meffe and C. R. Carroll, *Principles of Conservation Biology* [Sunderland, Mass.: Sinauer, 1994], p. 123. Reprinted by permission of Sinauer Associates, Inc.)

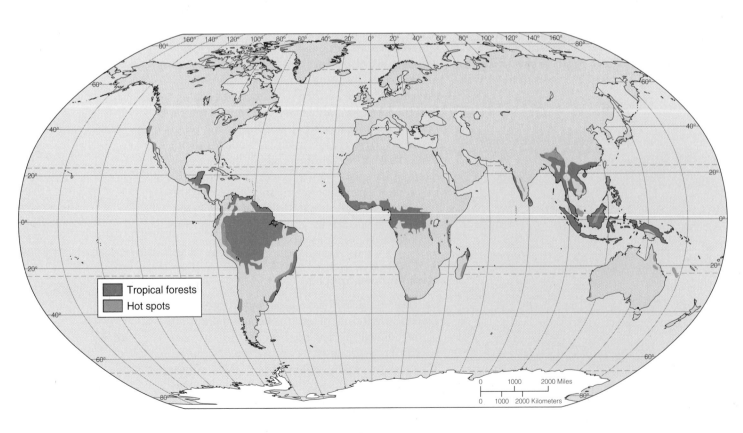

Tropical forests
Hot spots

maximize the amount of native biodiversity preserved. In fact, many hot spots in the United States and the world are already nearly destroyed. By many estimates, all of the plant hot spots in Figure 12–19 will be gone within 30 years.

Designing Preserves

After a location is selected, the design of the preserve is critical. Species preservation is maximized by three key characteristics: size, shape, and connectivity. Larger size increases the number of species contained in the preserve. Rounder shape minimizes "edge effects" because the perimeter (edge) is smaller relative to the area inside than with other shapes. Connectivity is the opposite of fragmentation. Increasing the connections (corridors) between potential fragments allows members of the same species to immigrate and interbreed.

Buffer zones are another important preserve characteristic (Fig. 12–20). Buffer zones are areas of moderately utilized land that provide a transition into the unmodified natural habitat in the core preserve where no human disturbance is allowed. For example, campgrounds and limited cattle grazing may be permitted in the outermost buffer zone, with hiking in the innermost buffer zone. Buffer zones are a major departure from traditional preserves that were viewed as "islands" of natural habitat in a hostile "matrix" of agricultural or urban landscape.

Buffer zones are very important for both psychological and practical reasons. Sharp boundaries, as were used around traditional preserves, tend to promote the idea that nature should be

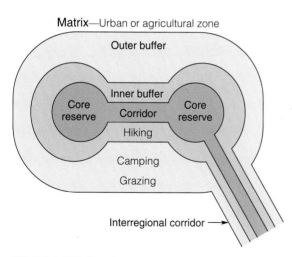

FIGURE 12–20

Buffer zones can be used to support economic activities around a core of natural habitat. (*Source:* Modified from R. Noss and A. Cooperrider, *Saving Nature's Legacy* [Washington, D.C.: Island Press, 1994], p. 148.)

TABLE 12–6 *Hot Spots of Species Richness in the Continental United States*

	AREAS OF GREATEST SPECIES RICHNESS
Vascular plants	California, followed by Texas, Arizona, Oregon, and Florida (in that order)
Trees	Southeastern Coastal Plain and Piedmont, northern Florida
Mollusks	Tennessee River system (Tennessee, Alabama) and Coosa River system (Alabama)
Butterflies	Western Great Plains and Central Rocky Mountains (Colorado)
Fishes	Cumberland Plateau in the Tennessee and Cumberland River drainages
Amphibians	Southern Appalachians and Piedmont
Reptiles	Gulf Coastal Plain (eastern Texas)
Birds (breeding)	Sierra Nevada, southeastern Arizona–southwestern New Mexico
Mammals	Sierra Nevada and, secondarily, southern Cascades and desert Southwest

(*Source:* Granted with permission from *Saving Nature's Legacy* by Reed F. Noss and Allen Y. Cooperrider. Copyright © 1994 by Defenders of Wildlife. Published by Island Press, Washington, D.C. and Covelo, California.)

"fenced in" and humans "fenced out"; such boundaries suggest that humans are separate from nature rather than being part of nature. On a practical level, conservation biologists have found that inhabitants of areas surrounding preserves must derive some benefits from the preserve. Many preserves have been established in developing nations only to have the endangered species poached unto extinction because local inhabitants needed food or money. The elephant poaching discussed in the Prologue is an example. Buffer zones integrate some of the area surrounding the preserve into the local economy without harming the core preserve. By permitting moderate recreational, forestry, farming, and other activities, buffer zones provide jobs and income with no ill effects on species in the core preserve. Indeed, endangered species in the core preserve occasionally wander into the buffer zones, providing thrills for tourists, income for inhabitants, and larger forage area for the endangered species.

Species Preservation in the United States

Unfortunately, preservation of natural habitat in the United States has only begun to utilize these principles. In many cases, the remaining natural habitats are small, irregularly shaped, and fragmented and unconnected and have few or no planned buffer zones.

Figure 12–21 shows the natural habitat managed by the federal government. The National Park System includes 50 major parks and many smaller recreation areas. The National Forest System includes 156 forests. The National Wildlife Refuge System consists of 503 refuges. These national systems include a huge amount of land—about 42% of the United States is for public use. But as the figure shows, the land in these three systems is often small, fragmented, irregularly shaped, and unbuffered. This is especially true in the midwestern and eastern United States.

Furthermore, most of this land is *not protected* natural habitat. Less than half the land in each system is set aside as protected, designated wilderness area. In the National Forest System, the largest system by far in the lower 48 states, only 15% is wilderness.

Where it is not designated wilderness, much of the land in all three systems is managed by the **multiple-use principle**. This allows many uses at the same time, such as logging, mining, grazing, farming, oil exploration, hunting, and fishing. Many of these uses conflict with species preservation because they can lead to significant habitat disruption. This problem is especially common in the National Forest System where taxpayers have subsidized road building, cheap logging, and other activities.

Solution: Preserve Networks

The small, fragmented nature of many preserved areas has contributed to a steady decline in biodiversity in the United States. Large species that need large areas have especially suffered. For example, Yellowstone National Park contains only about 100 grizzly bears (Fig. 12–22). This is far too few to form a sustainable minimum viable population, and the bears are showing signs of inbreeding and population decline.

Many conservation biologists suggest that the solution is to (1) expand the size of existing preserves, (2) create buffer zones, and (3) create habitat corridors that connect the preserves. Such "preserve networks" would allow habitat preservation in the United States to have the desirable characteristics of preserve design discussed above. Many of the pro-

FIGURE 12–21
Three major systems of public lands that contain some natural habitat. (*Source:* Data from U.S. Geological Survey.)

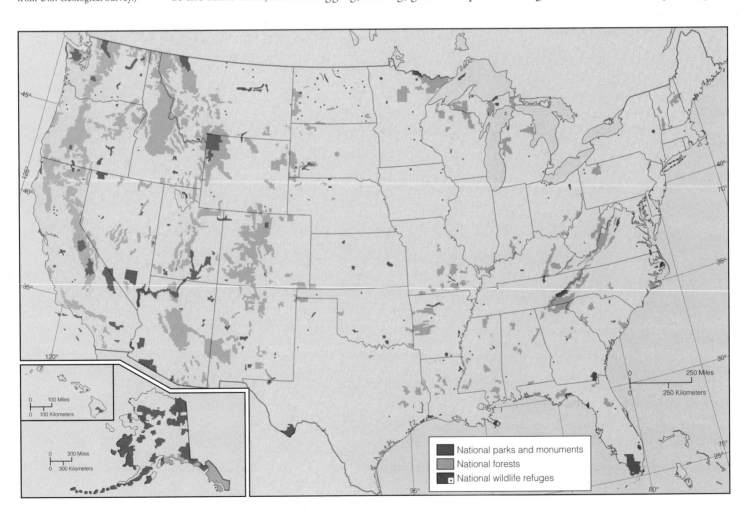

National parks and monuments
National forests
National wildlife refuges

PROBLEMS OF RESOURCE DEPLETION   SECTION 2

FIGURE 12–22
Yellowstone National Park, like many parks, is far too small to sustain viable populations of large mammals such as grizzly bears for many years. (*Source:* Joe McDonald/ Visuals Unlimited.)

posals for extensive networks have been criticized as unrealistic; one plan, for example, includes much of Florida (■ Fig. 12–23). But most wildlife experts agree that corridors, buffers, and other network concepts will eventually be necessary if many of the wide-ranging species are to survive.

One goal of the National Biological Survey (NBS) is to survey and assess where species occur, and provide information needed to develop such networks.

Protection by Buying Land

One of the most successful ways to set aside protected land has simply been to buy it. The Nature Conservancy is an outstanding example of a group that has made a huge impact by doing this. Founded in 1951, the Nature Conservancy had a membership of over 700,000 in 1993. By using a large fund of donations (over $150 million), the Conservancy has created the largest system of private natural areas and wildlife sanctuaries in the world. It includes more than 6.9 million acres (2.8 million hectares) in the United States and almost three times that much outside the United States. By focusing on buying species-rich threatened habitats, buffer zones, and corridors, the Conservancy has greatly enhanced the survival chances of many species in the United States.

Protection by Better Forest Management

Only about 22% of the commercial forest area in the United States is in national forests. Much of the remainder is owned by private companies that grow trees for commercial logging. Many rare species occur in these private forests, and many more could exist there if current forestry practices were discontinued. ● Table 12–7, page 337, describes the impact of many forestry techniques that emphasize maximum wood production over biodiversity and ecological function.

An important result of the emphasis on wood production is the loss of old-growth, or "virgin," forests. More than 95% of such forests have been cut down in the lower 48 states. Old-growth forest takes many decades to grow because it is a late-successional, climax stage in forest growth (Chapter 3). Old-growth timber is generally denser, higher-quality wood. Old-growth forests are also rich in species not found in early-growth forests.

Because timber takes so long to grow, timber companies tend to raise only early successional trees, such as certain pine species, that grow quickly. These can be cut down in a few years and replanted to start the cycle anew. This practice may maximize wood production, but it reduces overall biodiversity in U.S. forests.

Protection by the Law

Most species at risk of extinction occur on privately owned land rather than federal land. Early laws to protect such species focused on the trade and sale of their skins and other products, but in recent decades, the statute that has been most widely used to protect species and their habitats is the **Endangered Species Act** of 1973. This act directs the U.S. Fish and Wildlife Service to maintain a list of species that are endangered or

FIGURE 12-23

(a) In the image, urban development along Florida's Atlantic coast, from West Palm Beach to Miami, is easily seen. The Everglades are depicted in green tones with scattered red spots of subtropical forest. The dark blue areas to the west of the Everglades are cypress swamps, and the red region along the southwest coast is composed of dense mangroves. (b) A proposed plan to connect existing natural habitats in Florida by using buffer zones, especially along rivers. Such plans become more urgent as urban development continues— as seen in the false-color image from the Landsat 5 satellite in (a). (*Sources:* (a) Terranova International/Science Source/Photo Researchers. (b) R.F. Noss, "Protecting Natural Areas in Fragmented Landscapes," *Natural Areas Journal* 7 [1987]: 2–13.)

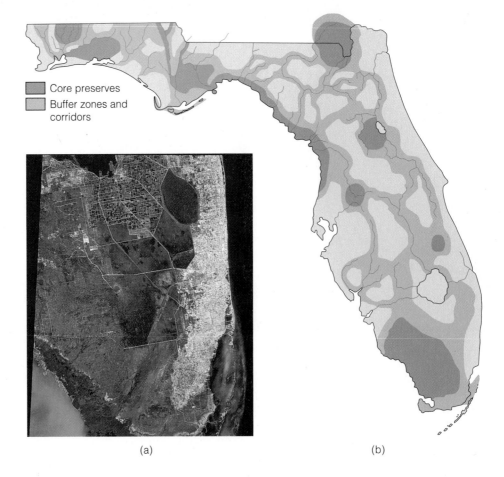

Core preserves

Buffer zones and corridors

(a)

(b)

threatened. Endangered species are in immediate danger of extinction. Threatened species are likely to be endangered soon. The Service is also directed to produce a recovery plan for each listed species and protect its designated "critical habitat" needed for survival.

The Endangered Species Act is very controversial, and Congress has often debated whether the act should be reauthorized in its present form. Many people want to weaken or even eliminate the act while many others want to strengthen it. Opponents claim the act has cost billions of dollars and violates the Fifth Amendment's ban on taking property without compensation by preventing property owners from developing their land when it contains habitat of an endangered species.

Opponents also point out that the act has been relatively ineffective. The number of listed species has grown much more rapidly than the number of delisted species—40 species listed each year on average compared to 1 species delisted (Fig. 12–24, page 338). Delisted species include both species that are no longer endangered or threatened, such as the brown pelican, and species that have gone extinct, so even some of the delistings indicate failures, not success.

Overall, only about 10% of listed species were classified as "improving" in 1993 by the Fish and Wildlife Service. All the rest were only stabilized or declining. Furthermore, hundreds, perhaps thousands, of candidate species that are already rare are waiting to be listed.

Supporters of the act argue that it has not worked well because it is too weak, not too strong, and that far too little money has been spent on enforcement (about $70 million in 1995). State and federal agencies combined spend about $200 million per year to protect endangered species; this is less than 4% of the money spent annually on U.S. lawn care and less than a dollar per person. Furthermore, most of this money is spent on just a few species. In 1991, just 7 species out of the more than 600 listed received over half the money. The top three species were all popular charismatic species: the bald eagle ($24 million), the Florida scrub jay ($20 million), and the Florida manatee ($15 million). Meanwhile many species at the bottom of the list received a tiny fraction of the budget. Only $100 was spent on the protection of each of three mint species, for example.

Supporters of the act also note that the listing process takes so long that many species are too

TABLE 12-7 *Common Forestry Practices and Their Effects on Biodiversity*

FORESTRY PRACTICE	PURPOSE	EFFECT ON BIODIVERSITY
Planting of exotics (nonnative species) or genetically "improved" tree species	Improved yield of commercial tree species	Replacement of native species
Pesticide spraying	Protection of forest tree species of commercial value	Reduction in vast numbers of non-target insect species; secondary effects on nontarget organisms; major disruption of ecosystem
Clear-cutting/reforestation	Maximum utilization of existing tree biomass/maximum speed of new forest growth	Artificial cycle of disturbance; loss of species richness; loss of structural and functional diversity
Clear-cutting/even-aged management	"Efficient" regulation of the forest; maximum profit from growing trees	Shortened successional cycle; loss of forest structural diversity
Slash-burning	Site preparation for new forest; esthetics ("neatening up" the forest)	Major loss of structure, biomass, and nutrients from forest ecosystem
Tree thinning	Increased growth of commercial tree species	Reduced structural diversity in forest
Brush removal/herbicide spraying	Removal of species believed to be delaying reestablishment of commercial tree species	Truncated succession with loss of important successional processes; loss of species richness
The Bottom Line		
Maximum production of commercial sawtimber and pulpwood	Maximum forest output; maximum profit	Reduced structural and species diversity of forest; deterioration of forest ecosystem

(*Source:* Granted with permission from *Saving Nature's Legacy* by Reed F. Noss and Allen Y. Cooperrider. Copyright © 1994 by Defenders of Wildlife. Published by Island Press, Washington, D.C. and Covelo, California.)

close to extinction to be saved when they are finally listed. A 1993 study found that the average population size at the time of listing was only 119 for plant species and 1000 for animal species, far below the numbers thought to be necessary to assure long-term survival.

The Endangered Species Act has also been opposed in the courts. Landowners, logging companies, and other organizations have brought suit against the government, claiming that the act violates the right to private property. In 1994, a federal appeals court held that the act protects species, not habitat, a ruling that would have significantly weakened the act. But in June 1995, the U.S. Supreme Court overturned the appeals court, stating that habitat alteration can lead to species extinction and that Congress intended the law to halt species extinction "whatever the cost." While supporters of the act welcomed the decision, opponents saw it as one more reason why Congress should change the act itself.

A potential solution may be to protect entire ecosystems before species are on the verge of extinction, instead of focusing on "one species at a time" and waiting until it is in imminent danger. Both critics and opponents of the act are expressing interest in this approach (see the Case Study, page 339).

Species Preservation Around the World

Overall, 5.9% of the world's total land area (excluding Antarctica) is protected, far below the 10% goal established by the World Conservation Union. Only North and Central America currently exceed this goal, with 11.7% of the land area protected. Europe and Oceania are close with 9.3% and 9.9%, respectively, but in the countries that made up the former Soviet Union, only 1.1% of the land is protected. South America, Asia, and Africa protect 6.4%, 4.4%, and 4.6% of their land, respectively.

Furthermore, even these percentages are overstated in that many of the designated "protected" areas, especially in developing nations, are poorly regulated and enforced. Also, most of these pro-

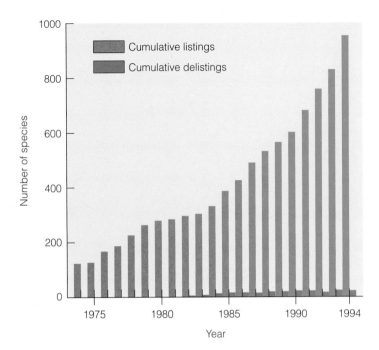

FIGURE 12–24

The number of species being listed as endangered species is growing much faster than the number being delisted. (*Source:* Data from U.S. Fish and Wildlife Service, 1995.)

tected areas are too small to support species of large animals for a long time. Less than 2% of the world's protected areas include at least 2.5 million acres (1 million hectares), which is estimated to be the minimum area needed to sustain minimum viable populations of a few thousand individuals of large mammal species for many years.

Laws Protecting Endangered Species

In addition to preserves for endangered species, international laws make it illegal to trade, transport, and sell products made from such species. In 1975, 81 countries signed the **Convention on International Trade in Endangered Species (CITES)**, which outlaws trade in endangered species products. By 1993, 119 nations had signed the treaty, which prohibits trade in 675 species. Though CITES has helped reduce illegal trade in some areas, illegal wildlife trade continues to proliferate (Fig. 12–25). Unfortunately, thousands of animals die each year, especially tropical birds, in the process of being smuggled into the United States and other nations that are the main markets for illegal wildlife. Stricter laws passed by the U.S. Congress in 1993, outlawing possession of such wildlife, attempt to discourage this trade.

Sustainable Uses of Biodiversity

Conservation biologists agree that governmental decrees alone will not solve the extinction crisis. Establishing preserves and prohibiting trade in endangered species will not work as long as people, especially local inhabitants, are poor and must rely on destructive uses of biodiversity to stay alive.

Instead, sustainable uses of biodiversity must be developed and encouraged. Sustainable uses provide incentives to save species while also respecting the right of all people to support their families and have a decent quality of life. This is sometimes called the **bottom-up approach** to biodiversity conservation because it permits local citizens to play a role in planning and establishing preserves. In contrast, with the top-down approach, national and regional governments simply establish preserves regardless of the needs of local citizens. Buffer zones surrounding preserves are an example of the application of the principle of sustainable use.

Other sustainable uses extend into the core preserve itself. **Ecotourism**, which the Ecotourism Society defines as "responsible travel to natural areas that conserves the environment and sustains the well-being of the local people," is an example. For instance, tourists might be allowed to visit natural habitats to view endangered species such as orangutans (see Issues in Perspective 12–4). Ecotourism has enormous po-

FIGURE 12–25

Trade in illegal wildlife continues to grow globally. Here we see an ocelot pelt being sold in Panama. (*Source:* A. Kerstitch/ Visuals Unlimited.)

Are Habitat Conservation Plans the Answer?
The California Gnatcatcher Example

In 1982, Congress passed an amendment to the Endangered Species Act that was intended to meet some of the main criticisms of the original act. Opponents had charged that the act (1) interfered with economic growth, (2) emphasized saving species rather than whole ecosystems, and (3) waited until a species was on the verge of extinction before protecting it. The amendment created a new approach designed to make the act more flexible, reduce economic costs, and protect many species before they are near extinction.

The new approach is called a habitat conservation plan (HCP). Under an HCP, some of the habitat of an endangered species can be destroyed (called an "incidental take") as long as a plan is drawn up to reduce future losses. An HCP usually evolves as a compromise from discussions among landowners, developers, environmental groups, local governments, and the U.S. Fish and Wildlife Service, which eventually must approve the HCP. Ideally an HCP will protect all current or potentially endangered species in an area, while simultaneously permitting human use of nearby lands as deemed necessary by social consent.

By 1994, 7 HCPs had been approved and another 60 were under discussion from California to Key Largo, Florida. Each HCP is unique and some are more successful than others. California has the most HCPs to have been approved. The first was at San Bruno Mountain south of San Francisco, which emerged as a compromise between housing developers and environmentalists

FIGURE 1

The California gnatcatcher has generated national controversy. (*Source:* Anthony Mercieca/Photo Researchers.)

wanting to save the mission blue butterfly. In fact, this conflict at San Bruno led to the legislation creating the HCP concept.

A good example of the complexities an HCP can encounter involved the coastal sage scrub habitat of southern California. This habitat includes some of the nation's most expensive real estate in prime locations around Los Angeles, San Diego, and nearby areas. But it is also home to a rare songbird called the California gnatcatcher (■ Fig. 1). Only 2600 pairs remain, with 70–90% of the habitat already destroyed. In 1993, after three years of discussion among developers, environmentalists, and government officials, Interior Secretary Bruce Babbitt announced that the gnatcatcher would be listed as "threatened" instead of "endangered" as proposed by the U.S. Fish and Wildlife Service. The less urgent "threatened" status allows officials to work out the details of an HCP that may permit development on some of the remaining scrub habitat. But the HCP will also call for establishing up to 12 reserves that will benefit as many as 40 other coastal sage scrub species that are also in jeopardy from this disappearing habitat.

Questions

1. Many environmentalists strongly dislike the HCP concept because they believe it is "giving away" species and habitat to development. Can you think of a better way to resolve habitat versus development conflicts? Explain.

2. Since "extinction is forever," why would anyone ever approve of the HCP concept? How could development ever be justified over the irreversible loss of species? Explain.

3. Would you approve of an HCP that permitted one species to go extinct, but allowed 5 other species to survive? If it allowed 10 others to survive? Twenty others? Explain your reasoning.

---

tential because the travel industry is the second largest industry in the world. (Agriculture is the largest.) In 1994, tourism generated over $195 billion and employed 127 million people worldwide (equal to about half the U.S. population). If properly done, ecotourism can reduce local poverty, conserve nature, and educate the public about both biological and cultural diversity.

Another sustainable use of native biodiversity in a core preserve is **sustainable harvesting**. Sometimes called "extractive forestry," sustainable harvesting includes the harvesting of nuts, fruits, and many other products that can be extracted from an ecosystem without harming it. Specific examples include collecting Brazil nuts and tapping rubber trees in the rainforest for sale to industrialized nations. ● Table 12–8 lists just a few of the many commercial and industrial products now derived from tropical rainforests. Animals such as parrots can also be sustainably harvested, in theory, although most pet bird groups recommend buying captive-bred birds.

Ecotourism: Much Promise, but Some Limitations

One of the fastest-growing ways of providing people with economic incentives to conserve biodiversity is ecotourism (█ Fig. 1). This huge worldwide industry could have a substantial impact on slowing the destruction of biodiversity and reducing population growth. If ecotourism can become sufficiently widespread in the developing world, it can help reduce poverty, thereby helping reduce population growth, while simultaneously promoting conservation of biological resources.

To many people, ecotourism simply means "nature" tours. But it is much more than that. Veteran tour guide Arthur Frommer has written (in *Travel Holiday*) that "real ecotourism utilizes the travel facilities created by the native population. It avoids international hotel chains in favor of properties owned and managed by locals. Adherents dine not on steaks and wine flown in from abroad, but on regional dishes, supporting the community's economy. Finally, ecotourism respects not only the local environment, but the native culture of an area." Furthermore, to be done correctly, ecotourism must not harm the local ecosystems in any significant way.

Examples of this fast-growing industry abound throughout the world. This growth is driven by widespread environmental concern combined with the fact that ecotours can be an enjoyable escape from the routine of industrialized society. Travel agencies arrange ecotours that range from a few days in an air-conditioned boat cruising the Amazon to weeks of hiking in the Himalaya Mountains in Nepal. Many of these tours do accomplish at least some of the goals of ecotours. In Nepal, for example, the Annapurna Conservation Area Project (ACAP) relies heavily on entry fees and other money provided by hikers in the Himalayas. Every year, vast tracts of forest in these mountains are cleared for fuel and other needs by Nepal's growing population. The ACAP is attempting to create a large forest preserve and funds local hiking guides and other jobs that conserve the resources.

Another example is the Orangutan Rehabilitation Centre in Bukit Lawang, Indonesia. This project rehabilitates orangutans illegally held in captivity or displaced by deforestation and returns them to natural habitats. Because of the great international interest in this disappearing primate species, the Indonesian government is promoting the Centre as a destination where tourists can view orangs in their habitat. Consequently, it has become one of the most popular ecotours in Southeast Asia and is bringing in much revenue to help support the Centre.

While ecotourism can help preserve natural habitat and promote a sustainable economy, it has limitations. One is that many natural areas are not suitable for ecotourism. Many ecosystems are simply not appealing enough to the general public to provide a large pool of visitors. Aesthetic sites, such as coral reefs, rainforests, and pristine mountain hikes are popular, as are areas with charismatic species, such as elephants or grizzly bears. But many ecosystems lack the spectacular scenery or unique creatures necessary to draw sufficient visitors. In all likelihood, large portions of deserts, swamps, tundra, and many other areas cannot be preserved via ecotourism. Indeed, some experts suggest that only a few isolated, relatively unique ecosystems can be completely supported by ecotours.

Even where ecotourism is feasible, practical problems arise. Money generated by ecotours does not always contribute to the local economy, especially in poor developing nations. Some fees from the Orangutan Rehabilitation Centre, for example, have gone to government officials in Jakarta. Also, in many cases, native species and ecosystems have been harmed by crowds of people and all the activity. Motorized "tundra buggies" that take crowds to see Hudson Bay polar bears have been criticized as seriously disturbing the bears. Similarily, the Manuel Antonio National Park in the heart of the Costa Rican rainforest now gets 1000 visitors per day and 300 once-wild monkeys have become garbage feeders. Even native cultural diversity can be damaged. Some boat tours along the Amazon now stop and trade with native Indians who previously had little contact with civilization. This has often caused cultural disruption.

FIGURE 1

"Ecotourists" on a ride in India to view a few remaining rhinos. (*Source:* Joe McDonald/Visuals Unlimited.)

Sustainably harvested products can also be used for health care at home. Most of the primary health care in many developing countries is provided by traditional healers using native plant remedies. The World Health Organization estimates that nearly 3 billion people use wild-harvested medicines, with an annual value of up to $15 billion.

Studies often show that the long-term value of a rainforest is greater when sustainably harvested for medicines, rubber, foods, and other products than when it is logged, burned for grazing cattle, or otherwise destructively exploited for short-term profits. The long-term value from sustainable harvesting is even greater if the preserve can also be used for ecotourism. The total revenue for Amboseli National Park in Africa, for example, has been estimated at about 40 times the revenue that would be produced from farming the same land. Each lion was estimated as worth $27,000 in tourist revenue, over twice its value either dead or alive in the illegal wildlife market.

Potential Uses of Biodiversity

Many of the most important uses of biodiversity have not been discovered. Indeed, the economic potential of the vast genetic diversity of the rainforest and many other areas has barely been explored. These potential uses provide another cogent economic incentive to save species before they go extinct.

Many of these potential uses are chemical, especially drug related. An estimated 25% of all U.S. prescription drugs contain compounds derived from plants. With so many undescribed plants, many potentially useful medicines will be lost if they are allowed to become extinct. For instance, the rare Pacific yew was found to be useful in fighting cancer (Fig. 12–26). This potential has led to a new field, called **chemical prospecting**, where biologists and chemists are rapidly compiling a huge database of the chemical potential of various species. One of the most effective types of chemical prospecting uses the knowledge of native healers, or shamans, about the medicinal properties of local plants. But chemical prospecting is not limited to rainforest species or even land species. Many marine organisms have yielded chemical compounds now widely used as medicines, foods, and other products.

Although chemical prospecting has been very successful in finding potential uses for biodiversity, many local inhabitants still do not benefit from it. Typically, drug and agricultural companies and other businesses that profit from

TABLE 12–8 *Commercial and Industrial Products Derived from Tropical Rainforests*

PRODUCT	VALUE OF IMPORTS BY REGION (MILLIONS OF U.S. DOLLARS)	MARKET SHARE OF RAINFOREST PRODUCTS (%)	REGION RECEIVING IMPORTS
Commercial products			
Fruit and vegetable juices	4,000	100	World
Cut flowers	2,500	100	World
Food additives	750	100	United States, European Community
Spices	439	Small	United States
Nuts	216	100	World
Food colorings	140	10	World
Vitamins	67	Small	United States
Fiber	54	100	United States
Industrial products			
Fuel	60,000	<1	United States
Pesticides	16,000	1	World
Natural rubber	666	100	United States
Tannins	170	Large	United States
Construction material	12	1	United States
Natural waxes	9.3	100	United States

(*Source:* T. Carr, H. Pedersen, and S. Ramaswamy, "Rain Forest Entrepreneurs," *Environment*, September 1993. Reprinted with permission of the Helen Dwight Reid Educational Foundation. Published by Heldref Publications, 1319 Eighteenth St. N.W., Washington, D.C. 20036–1802. Copyright © 1993.)

the genetic diversity of developing nations are owned and operated by citizens in industrialized nations in the Northern Hemisphere. This inability of the developing nations to profit from their own biodiversity was a major issue at the 1992 Earth Summit in Rio de Janeiro (Chapter 22). After heated debate, 158 nations signed the **Convention on Biological Diversity (CBD)**, which acknowledged that developing nations deserve a greater share of the profits generated from genetic resources by agriculture and genetic technology. In essence, this means that genetic resources are similar to intellectual property rights that can be patented, with profits returning to local populations where the genetic information originated. Such **genetic patent rights** would allow native people who conserve their biodiversity to receive some of the enormous profits often derived from pharmaceuticals, agriculture, and other uses of their genetic resources.

Unfortunately, the commitments made by the signers of the CBD are largely nonbinding and often vaguely worded, leading some to suggest that the document is worthless. Others point out that at least the convention brought biodiversity

FIGURE 12–26
The Pacific yew tree has contributed greatly to curing certain types of cancer. (*Source:* Tom and Pat Leeson/Photo Researchers.)

tive research program with collaborative agreements with the pharmaceutical industry. For example, in 1992 under an innovative agreement with Merck & Company, INBio was paid $1 million to do chemical prospecting and provide Merck with well-identified and documented plant and insect samples for use in Merck's drug discovery program. Costa Rican citizens not only benefit from services and technology supplied to the University of Costa Rica, but 10% of the $1 million goes to the Costa Rican National Park Fund.

Protecting Marine Species

Although the extinction of land species has attracted more attention than the extinction of species living in water, aquatic species, in both freshwater and marine environments, are also being decimated by widespread human disturbances. Protection of aquatic species has also lagged behind that of land species for many reasons. One is that people cannot see the extent to which biodiversity loss is occurring there. In addition, in some ways, aquatic species are more difficult to protect. Large bodies of water, especially oceans, are classic "commons" that are not clearly owned by any one nation. Consequently, regulating protected areas can be difficult. Pollution discharge in one area, for example, may travel hundreds of miles in an ocean current.

Nevertheless, there is growing interest in protecting these crucial marine habitats, especially nearshore bays and reefs that are being overvisited by tourists and contaminated by water pollution. Governments are establishing **marine protected areas**, which are areas of ocean that are set aside as preserves for marine life. In theory, fishing, construction, tourism, pollution and other human disturbances are closely regulated and restricted in these areas, but the restrictions are often difficult to enforce, especially in poor developing nations with relatively few resources.

In the United States, marine protected areas are included in the National Marine Sanctuary program. This program was created in 1972, a full century after Yellowstone was dedicated as the first national park, illustrating how marine protection has lagged behind. Since 1972, 12 sanctuaries have been established under the jurisdiction of the National Oceanic and Atmospheric Association. One of the largest is the 220-mile-long (354 km long) Florida Keys sanctuary where fishing and coral collecting are restricted because of widespread ecosystem disruption by humans (Fig. 12–27).

to global attention and will serve as a focal point for further discussion.

Fortunately, governments and private industry are beginning to help local citizens in developing nations to receive some of the profits derived from their biodiversity. Shaman Pharmaceuticals, Inc. (SPI) is a well-known example of "green entrepreneurship" by individuals in private industry. SPI relies on local shamans for leads on potentially useful drugs: it then markets the products by entering into agreements with pharmaceutical companies. The company has funneled many of its profits back to the local populations where the plants are found, providing health care, sustainable economic development, and land conservation.

Probably the best-known example of government-sponsored efforts to bring biodiversity profits to native populations is Costa Rica's INBio, the National Institute of Biodiversity, which combines a very ac-

(a)

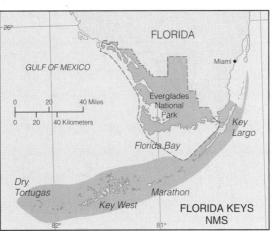

(b)

Many marine biologists argue that many more such sanctuaries desperately need to be established, especially throughout the Caribbean where poor nations have allowed massive destruction of coral reefs and other crucial marine habitats. Buffer zones, ecotourism, sustainable harvesting, and many other economic incentives, if properly applied, can be used to promote marine preserves just as effectively as with forest and other land preserves.

Breeding in Captivity and Reintroductions

So far our focus has been on preservation of natural habitat because it is the best way to save species. Breeding in captivity and restoring species back into the wild are almost always much more expensive and less effective than preserving habitat and saving species in the wild. Animals tend to be unhappy outside their natural state, especially in older zoos where conditions are poor (■ Fig. 12–28). Even under the best of conditions, animals often do not readily breed, as in the well-known pandas. Furthermore, there are far too few zoos in the world to sustain sufficient populations of all the world's endangered species, even if only endangered large charismatic mammal species were considered. Yet the reality is that habitat continues to be destroyed at alarming rates in many areas so that captive breeding is a necessity to save many species. As conditions become very desperate, as with the now-extinct dusky seaside sparrow, genetic material (sperm and egg) is being frozen for future use as a "gene bank".

One use of captive breeding is for the animals and plants to proliferate and attain sufficient population size for some to be released back into the wild. A **reintroduction** is the release of plants and animals back into habitat that they formerly occupied. The American bison ("buffalo"), for example, became extinct throughout most of the West, but is now being reintroduced in many areas. The controversial reintroduction of wolves into some parks and other areas in the United States is another example. Another approach is that of **introduction** of species into new areas they did not formerly occupy. Many African savanna species, such as lions, antelope, and rhinos, have been successfully introduced onto game preserves in Florida and Texas, for instance.

Another use of captive breeding is to raise plants and animals for sale. Emu-breeding (Issues in Perspective 12–3) is but one example of many exotic species becoming popular in U.S. breeding farms. Other examples include tropical fishes and birds. Some people oppose breeding exotic species for pets and foods for a variety of reasons

including animal rights and because it creates markets for captive animals. But supporters point out that such breeding helps reduce the market for the illegal wildlife trade by satisfying the demand for exotic animals and plants without taking them from their native habitat.

$\mathcal{P}$UBLIC LANDS

The largest landowner in the United States is the federal government. A glance at Figure 12–21 shows that vast tracts of land are federally owned, especially in the western states. The government owns more than 45% of California, Nevada, Utah, Idaho, Wyoming, Arizona, and Alaska. Nor does this figure include the large amount of public land owned by state and local governments.

The management of public lands has been a matter of controversy since they began to be established more than a century ago. On one side have been "preservationists" who argue that public natural resources should be preserved as much as possible as pristine wilderness. On the other side have been "conservationists" who argue that public resources should be open to mining, logging, grazing, and other human uses. This controversy peaked in the early 1900s when it was essentially won by those seeking access to the resources; hence, the conservationist philosophy and the "multiple-use" principle discussed earlier have dominated much public land use (Chapters 1, 6, and 22). Many historians note that this philosophy was probably inevitable given the rich resources, sparse population, and rapidly growing industrial economy of the United States.

An End to Subsidized Abuse of Public Land?

In recent years, support for more preservationist policies toward public land use has been growing. The multiple-use approach has historically been used to justify very high levels of resource extraction, which have often resulted in widespread and highly visible environmental damage to public lands. In the western United States, many areas of public land where mineral deposits once existed are now scarred by active and abandoned mines. Each year, most of these mines produce tons of toxic acid and heavy metal drainage that contaminates the soil and water. Similarly, overgrazing of public lands by privately owned cattle damages native vegetation, destroys wildlife habitats, and encourages widespread growth of nonnative "weeds." Logging on public lands is a major reason why the remnants of ancient old-growth forests are rapidly dwindling.

Much of this destructive resource extraction has been accelerated by subsidies from federal tax money. Mining, grazing, logging, and other activities have been conducted at very cheap prices, far below market cost, because taxpayers pay much of the cost. The 1872 Mining Law, which allows miners to lease public land for about $5 or less per acre (0.4 hectare), is a good example (Chapter 10). Grazing is much cheaper on public land than on nearby private land. The World Resources Institute estimates that these subsidies cost more than $1 billion per year in public funds spent and taxes not collected from land users. Although public resistance to this subsidized damage is growing, the opponents of subsidies have had difficulty achieving political change. The Clinton administration and some members of Congress have attempted to reduce these subsidized activities, but their efforts have generally been defeated by intense lobbying and the opposition of senators and representatives from the western states. One of the leading lobbyists has been the "Wise Use Movement," which consists of a variety of individuals and organizations that seek to maximize private utilization of public lands (Chapter 22).

National Parks: Overcrowded and Underfunded

The first major national park in the United States was Yellowstone National Park, established in 1872. As more parks were established, usually through acts of Congress, it became apparent that an organization was needed to manage them. Accordingly, the U.S. National Park Service was founded in 1916. In 1995, the National Park System covered 80 million acres (32 million hectares) and included 368 sites ranging from major parks such as Yellowstone to urban recreation areas, battlefields, trails, rivers, prehistoric ruins, and homes of presidents. Often areas in the park system are designated as "national rivers," "national monuments," "national lakeshores," and so on to specify their significance. California has 23 parks, the most of any state. The idea of national parks has been very successful. The spread of such parks worldwide has led some observers to comment that national parks are one of America's great exports. More than 100 nations now contain over 1200 national parks.

But in recent years the National Park System has increasingly suffered from a number of problems. One is overcrowding ( Fig. 12–29). The National Park Service reports that the number of annual visitors to the national parks has risen dramatically from 22 million in 1946 to 133 million in 1966 and 265 million in 1994. A staggering 360 million people, more than the U.S. population, are expected to visit the parks in the year 2000. Attendance is increasing faster than the U.S. population and thus reflects the public's growing interest in the national parks.

People who want to camp or rent cabins at the more popular parks, such as Yellowstone, Yosemite, and Great Smoky Mountain, generally must make advance reservations. In 1994, for example, 8.7 million people visited Great Smoky Mountain National Park. The parks often turn away hundreds of potential visitors for lack of space. Traffic jams, air pollution from cars, and crime have become problems. In 1993, more than 16,000 "resources violations," such as poaching and theft of Native American and Civil War relics, occurred.

The Funding Problem

Funding to maintain the national parks has not kept pace with the increasing attendance. The 1995 National Park Service budget of $1.5 billion forced the service to delay maintenance, reduce staff and programs, and allow environmental problems to continue. The service had a $4.5 billion backlog of high-priority construction projects, $2 billion of unfunded land acquisitions, and $800 million worth of unfunded repairs. Lack of maintenance leads to problems ranging from rusting cannons at Gettysburg to complaints of raw sewage at Mammoth Cave in Kentucky and Sequoia National Park. Roads in many parks have gone unrepaired. The Grand Canyon alone needs an estimated $350 million worth of road, sewer, and other repairs. Park rangers suffer, too. Over 50% of their housing units have problems such as rotting floors, faulty wiring, or insect infestation.

One reason for the underfunding has been the recent effort to reduce federal government spending. But a number of observers, including some prominent park officials, argue that part of the problem is that Congress has purchased new national parks at the expense of the parks already in existence. Between 1975 and 1995, Congress established 83 new parks. Due to the growing interest in preserving the environment, establishing parks is very popular with the voters, so money for purchasing land has been relatively easy to obtain. In contrast, funding for sewage treatment, road repairs, and other maintenance needs has less popular appeal.

Two possible solutions to the funding problem have attracted considerable support: (1) making the parks more self-sufficient by relying on visitor fees and other private sources, and (2) removing some of the less popular or less unique parks from the park system. Advocates of increased self-sufficiency point out that park visitors spend more than $10 billion annually, but much of this money does not go toward park maintenance. Instead, a large amount goes to private businesses. In 1993, for instance, concession stand operators in the parks took in $657 million, but paid less than $19 million in franchise fees, or less than 3% of their sales income, to the park service. Therefore, there is growing

▬ **FIGURE 12–29**
Bumper-to-bumper traffic is a common sight in the more popular national parks. This scene shows a traffic jam and bison in Yellowstone National Park, Wyoming. (*Source:* Jeff Foott/Bruce Coleman Inc.)

public and political pressure to raise the franchise fees as a way of increasing park income. Raising entrance or activity fees is another possibility. The National Park Service spends about $900 million per year on visitor services but collects only about $100 million in entrance and activity fees.

Removing some existing parks from the National Park System is another option. Many critics point out that numerous sites attract few visitors but are costly to maintain. The Yukon-Charley Rivers National Preserve in Alaska, for instance, has an annual budget of more than $500,000 but receives less than 1000 visitors per year. Critics argue that such wilderness can be preserved at less cost either by allowing private conservation groups to purchase it, or by managing it outside the National Park System. Some groups are also interested in conducting mining or logging activities in parks in Alaska and the western United States that have few visitors. Congress is considering selling dozens of smaller urban parks, battlefields, and monuments to local governments or private groups. San Francisco's Golden Gate National Recreation Area and Cleveland's Cuyahoga Valley National Park are examples. Removal of parks from the park system is not new; Congress has "de-authorized" 24 parks since 1916.

Recreation or Preservation? The Dilemma

Some critics do not agree that the solution to the overcrowding problem is increased funding for more facilities and staff. Instead, they argue that the number of visitors should be reduced altogether. They contend that too many visitors will despoil the natural beauty and contribute to the extinction of endangered species in the parks.

At the heart of the debate is whether the main purpose of national parks is to serve human needs or to preserve natural areas. The multiple-use philosophy that has dominated since the early 1900s has tended to emphasize human uses. But public interest in preserving natural areas is increasing as visitors to many of the major parks encounter huge crowds, traffic jams, commercialism, air pollution, and other unpleasant aspects of urban life.

As a result, public support for reducing the size of crowds in national parks and perhaps limiting public access is growing. One solution has been to designate some lands in the park system as "wilderness areas." Under the **Wilderness Act of 1964**, a designated wilderness area is federal land that is to be managed to retain its "primeval character," with "no commercial enterprise and no

permanent road and no motorized vehicles." The amount of land set aside as designated wilderness has increased greatly since 1970:

- 1970—10.4 million acres (4.2 million hectares).
- 1980—79.7 million acres (32.3 million hectares).
- 1993—95.4 million acres (38.6 million hectares).

These figures include land in the National Forest and Wildlife Refuge Systems, as well as in the National Park System.

Interest in preservation has also led to two other trends: (1) increasing the size of parks by acquiring adjacent land through purchases or donations and (2) restoring parks to a more natural condition. We saw the importance of expanding park size when we examined the role of buffer zones and corridors among preserves. Donations often come from conservation groups. In 1995, for example, a local conservation group purchased a few hundred acres of important black bear habitat and donated it to the Great Smoky Mountain National Park (▬ Fig. 12–30).

Park restoration efforts include allowing some forested areas to return to the old-growth con-

▬ FIGURE 12–30
The recent donation of critical black bear habitat to the Great Smoky Mountain National Park is a good example of how private citizens can enhance the preservation of public lands. (*Source:* William J. Weber/Visuals Unlimited.)

dition and reintroducing native species that were exterminated by humans, such as the recent reintroduction of wolves into the Great Smoky Mountain and Yellowstone National Parks. This project also illustrates the conflict that can arise from the multiple use of public land. Many environmentalists welcome the return of the wolf while farmers and others argue that the wolves pose a threat to humans and livestock.

National Forests

The United States contains about 737 million acres (298 million hectares) of forests. About two-thirds of this land is classified as commercial timberland, meaning it is available for timber production. Only about 15% of this commercial timberland is owned by companies directly involved in producing forest or paper products. Instead, the timberland occurs on federal, state, and other public land. Most of the federal forests are in the National Forest System and are managed by the U.S. Forest Service (see Fig. 12–21). Indeed, nearly half of the large commercially valuable timber trees in the United States are found on Forest Service land. This includes the last virgin stands of old-growth forests in the continental United States, which are found in the national forests of the Pacific Northwest.

Utilization or Preservation?
The Dilemma (Again)

The dilemmas that arise from multiple use of public land are especially common in national forest management because the National Forest System was originally designed to allow considerable utilization of natural resources. While national parks were mainly designed for recreation and to protect wildlife, water, and all natural resources, national forests were designed not only to provide these resources but *also* to provide U.S. citizens with access to the land for livestock grazing and the extraction of wood and mineral resources. This difference is evident in the fact that the National Park Service and the Fish and Wildlife Agencies are in the Department of the Interior while the Forest Service is in the Department of Agriculture. As a result, national forest management has historically been less inclined

toward preservation. Because the National Forest System is so large, this philosophy helps explain the lack of wilderness preservation in the United States.

Clear-cutting strips the land bare of trees, promoting erosion and water pollution and devastating habitat. This photograph was taken in Willamette National Forest, Oregon. (*Source:* Peter K. Ziminski/Visuals Unlimited.)

But with the growing public interest in environmental preservation, the traditional methods of forest management have come to be criticized as unnecessarily destructive to wildlife and their habitat. As we saw in Table 12–7, these methods include planting nonnative species and pesticide spraying. Of special note is the controversial practice of **clear-cutting**, also called "even-aged" management (Fig. 12–31). In this tree-harvesting system, an entire stand of trees is completely removed, and the site is prepared for planting a new "crop" of trees. Clear-cuts are unattractive, as the land is stripped bare of trees, and can contribute greatly to increased sedimentation and erosion, which not only deplete the soil but often pollute local streams. Very large clear-cuts are no longer practiced in the United States. But even patchworks of clear-cuts can be harmful and unattractive, especially since they often require large road networks to be built into the forest and roads promote "edge effects" as noted earlier.

An alternative to clear-cutting is **selective cutting**, also called "uneven-aged" management. In this method, only certain trees in the stand are cut down, so the land is not stripped bare. Selective cutting is generally more expensive than clear-

www.jbpub.com/environet

cutting, however, and is not without its own environmental problems. Roads must often still be built, and selective cutting usually alters normal forest development because shade-intolerant trees such as most pines and the Douglas fir cannot grow. Nevertheless, the "New Forestry" is a movement to incorporate biodiversity preservation into forest management, and selective cutting is preferred over clear-cutting. Replanting and careful restoration of harvested forest are promoted. Indeed, the forest products industry is the largest planter of new trees in the country; one-third more wood is grown each year in the United States than is harvested or lost to fire, insects, or disease.

Subsidized Abuse? The Tongass National Forest Example

We noted earlier that taxpayer dollars are often used to subsidize rapid, and often harmful, depletion of natural resources. In the case of national forests, the Forest Service each year loses money on timber sales in most of its forests. If the cost of roads built by the government for the logging companies is included, the Forest Service shows a net loss of millions of dollars, according to data from the Wilderness Society and other environmental groups. Such groups therefore argue that the emphasis on tree production is outmoded at a time when forests often contain endangered species and shrinking, rare ecosystems. These shrinking forest ecosytems are not limited to the northern spotted owl and the old-growth forests of the Pacific Northwest, but include many other areas containing dozens of endangered aquatic species (such as freshwater clams) and birds (such as the red-cockaded woodpecker of the southeastern United States).

The public lands of Alaska are especially important because they contain the largest natural areas remaining in the United States and also the largest amount of untapped resources. As a result, the stakes are high for both developers and environmentalists, and so is the controversy. The Tongass National Forest, for example, in southeastern Alaska contains the last intact stretch of America's only temperate rainforest, which once extended down the Pacific Coast to California (Figure 12–32). Currently, timber companies are pushing hard for the right to log the heart of the Tongass Forest and have won considerable support in Congress. Alaskans living near the forest point out that although past logging restrictions have cost jobs, they have also improved tourism and commercial fishing, which were harmed by the clear-cutting operations. A similar controversy is brewing over the Arctic Na-

FIGURE 12–32
The Tongass National Forest of southern Alaska contains the last large area of America's temperate rainforest. This summer view of the Tongass shows the fireweed in bloom; Mendenhall Glacier can be seen in the distance. (*Source:* Jeff Greenberg/Visuals Unlimited.)

*P*ROBLEMS OF RESOURCE DEPLETION   SECTION 2

tional Wildlife Refuge, the largest wildlife preserve in the United States, where oil companies want to drill. Critics point out that the damage to wildlife, especially caribou, from the roads and development could be enormous. And according to geological estimates, there may be little oil in that area anyway. Whatever happens in the Tongass and Arctic Refuge, it seems likely that the debate over preservation versus extraction of Alaska's wealth will persist for many years to come, demonstrating the controversies inherent in the multiple-use concept.

SUMMARY

Conservation biology is the rapidly growing new field that seeks to preserve biodiversity. Biodiversity has many definitions, but basically refers to the variety of living things. Biodiversity can be measured in many ways, but species richness or species diversity is one of the most practical and common measures.

No one is sure how many species now exist on Earth. About 1.8 million species have been described, but some groups are much better studied than others. Estimates of the total number of species on Earth range from 5 million to 100 million species. The oceans may have fewer species, but do have more phyla. We live at a time in Earth history when total species diversity is near an all-time peak, although rapid extinctions are changing this.

Extinction is the death of a group. Local extinction, or extirpation, removes a species from part of its range. With ecological extinction, a species is so rare that it has no significant role in its ecosystem. Biological impoverishment by local and ecological extinction is very common today. Five mass extinctions have occurred in the geologic past. Most were caused by climatic changes. The average extinction rate before humans has been estimated at 2–10 species extinctions per year.

Many biologists think that the "sixth mass extinction" will occur in the next few decades. An average estimate is that 50 species per day are becoming extinct. Extinction has four basic causes: habitat disruption, introduced species, overhunting, and secondary extinctions. Most species extinctions involve two or more of these causes acting in combination. Extinction can occur even if the population size is not reduced directly to zero. If the population size is too small, the species will fall into an extinction vortex caused by inbreeding and other processes that inevitably lead to extinction. The minimum viable population (MVP) is the smallest population size

needed to stay above the extinction vortex. In many species, the MVP is at least a few thousand individuals.

Biological communities can also go extinct and be degraded, as occurs in ecosystem simplification. The health of an ecosystem can be inferred from indicator species. Diverse communities may, or may not, be more easily disturbed.

Biodiversity has many potential values, represented by the "6 e's": ethical, esthetic, emotional, economic, environmental services, and evolutionary values. People vary in how much they ascribe to these values, but they can all be used to justify stopping extinctions. Because so many species are at risk of extinction, species triage is a common practice. This involves determining which species are most at risk, and which of those are most important for ecological and evolutionary reasons.

The best way to save species is to preserve natural habitats. Selecting preserves on the basis of diversity "hot spots" and other scientific criteria is much better than using scenic beauty or charismatic species. Four key characteristics of a well-designed preserve are large size, round shape, high connectivity, and buffer zones. Species preservation in the United States often lacks these, partly because of multiple-use demands placed on many public lands. One solution is to construct preserve "networks" by buying land, better forest management, and legal protection. A major source of legal protection in the United States is the Endangered Species Act. This act is highly controversial, being criticized by some as too strong and by others as too weak.

Species preservation outside the United States varies greatly among nations. But, as in the United States, most preserves are too small to sustain large species. A major law protecting endangered species globally is CITES, which outlaws trade in endangered species. Laws alone are not enough to save species globally. Sustainable uses of

biodiversity must be promoted to provide jobs and incentives to save species, especially in developing nations. Examples include the use of preserve buffer zones for grazing and recreation and the use of the core preserve itself for ecotourism and sustainable harvesting. Potential uses of biodiversity, such as medicines and agriculture, also provide strong economic incentives to preserve it. Establishing genetic patent rights will permit local inhabitants to share in the profits from their biodiversity.

The importance of protecting marine species is becoming widely recognized in the establishment of marine protected areas, such as the National Marine Sanctuary program in the United States. Captive breeding is a much less efficient way of stopping extinction, but is a valuable last resort, especially if captive species can be reintroduced or introduced back into the wild.

Public lands comprise a vast area of the United States, especially in the West and in Alaska. For over a hundred years, a controversy has ensued between "preservationists" who wish to preserve natural ecosystems and "conservationists" who want these public resources to be open to mining, logging, and other uses. In general, the multiple-use philosophy of the conservationists has been the dominant approach. But growing public interest in environmental preservation has led to increasing pressure to reduce "cheap" exploitation of public lands through logging, mining, and grazing that are subsidized by taxpayer dollars. The National Park System was established to preserve national treasures of many kinds. The system is currently burdened by overcrowded parks and lack of money for maintenance and staff. Suggested solutions include making the parks more financially self-sufficient by collecting fees and removing some parks from the system. Some argue that park preservation should be improved by designating more wilderness areas to limit access, increasing park sizes, and restoring wolves and other native species. The National Forest System differs from the park system in that its mission includes providing public access to natural resources. The Forest Service is required to provide opportunities for mining and logging companies, a mission that often conflicts with preservation of endangered native species. The "New Forestry" attempts to produce trees with minimal harm to natural ecosystems. But the often conflicting demands of multiple use, such as preservation versus exploitation, suggest that controversy over public land use will continue indefinitely. The debate over public land in Alaska, such as the Tongass National Forest, is a good example.

*K*EY TERMS

biodiversity
biological impoverishment
bottom-up approach
buffer zones
charismatic species
chemical prospecting
clear-cutting
conservation biology
Convention on Biological Diversity (CBD)
Convention on International Trade in Endangered Species (CITES)
ecological extinction
ecosystem simplification

ecotourism
edge effects
Endangered Species Act
exotic species
extinction
extinction vortex
extirpation
genetic patent rights
habitat fragmentation
hot spots
indicator species
introduction
keystone species
marine protected areas

mass extinctions
minimum viable population (MVP)
multiple-use principle
National Marine Sanctuary
reintroduction
selective cutting
species-area curve
species richness
species triage
sustainable harvesting
taxonomists
umbrella species
unique species
Wilderness Act of 1964

*S*TUDY QUESTIONS

1. Is species richness at local scales related to species richness at regional scales? Explain and give an example.
2. What is the "bottom-up" approach? How are buffer zones, ecotourism, and sustainable harvesting related to this?
3. What is a species-area curve? What does it predict if 90% of a habitat is destroyed?
4. What is biological impoverishment? What causes it?
5. How many mass extinctions have occurred before now? What was the average extinction rate before humans? How much higher is the rate now?
6. Name and describe two key reasons why habitat fragmentation is one of the most destructive ways of disrupting habitat.
7. Name the four main causes of extinction.

Which are biological? Do most extinctions involve just one cause?
8. What is an extinction vortex? What are two basic causes of an extinction vortex? What is the minimum viable population?
9. Where are exotic species an especially important cause of extinction? Why? Give examples.
10. Are diverse communities more easily disturbed? Explain.
11. Are all species equally important? Give two major examples. Where do unique species fit in?
12. How are genetic patent rights important in promoting biodiversity conservation? Give specific examples. What is chemical prospecting?
13. What is a hot spot? How can hot spots be

used in selecting the location of preserves?
14. What are two widely suggested solutions to the national park funding problem?
15. Compare and contrast selective cutting and clear-cutting.
16. If you estimate that 50 species per day are going extinct, how many species will be extinct in a year? In 100 years? What percentage of all species will be extinct in 100 years, if there are 10 million species on Earth?
17. If you estimate that 100 species per day are going extinct, how many species will be extinct in a year? In 100 years? What percentage of all species will be extinct in 100 years, if there are 10 million species on Earth?

*E*SSAY QUESTIONS

1. Why is biodiversity important? Discuss some of its many values, and indicate the ones you favor the most.
2. What are the characteristics of a well-designed preserve? How are they related to "edge effects" and minimum viable population sizes?
3. What is "ecotourism"? Discuss its advantages and disadvantages in saving species.
4. Are marine species being threatened? By what? Discuss possible solutions.
5. Discuss the pros and cons of the U.S. Endangered Species Act. Is it a failure? A success? How should it be improved?
6. Discuss the problems of the U.S. Forest Service and those of the National Park Service. What differences and similarities do you see in the problems of the two agencies?

Baker, R. 1993. *Environmental management in the tropics*. Boca Raton, Fla.: CRC Press.

Berger, J. J. 1990. *Environmental restoration*. Washington D.C.: Island Press.

Fiedler, P. L. and S. Jain, eds. 1992. *Conservation biology*. New York: Chapman & Hall.

Frome, M. 1992. *Regreening the national parks*. Tucson: University of Arizona Press.

Jacobs, L. 1992. *Waste of the West: Public lands ranching*. Tucson: Lynn Jacobs.

Jordan, C. F. 1995. *Conservation*. New York: Wiley.

Jordan, W. R., M. Gilpin, and J. Aber. 1987. *Restoration ecology*. Cambridge: Cambridge University Press.

Meffe, G. K., and C. R. Carroll. 1994. *Principles of conservation biology*. Sunderland, Mass.: Sinauer.

Norton, B. G., ed. 1986. *The preservation of species*. Princeton: Princeton University Press.

Noss, R., and A. Cooperrider. 1994. *Saving nature's legacy*. Washington, D.C.: Island Press.

O'Toole, R. 1987. *Reforming the forest service*. Covelo, Calif.: Island Press.

Primack, R. B. 1993. *Essentials of conservation biology*. Sunderland, Mass.: Sinauer.

Terborgh, J. 1992. *Diversity and the tropical rain forest*. New York: W. H. Freeman.

Tobin, R. J. 1990. *The expendable future: U.S. politics and the protection of biodiversity*. Durham, N.C.: Duke University Press.

Wilson, E. O. 1992, *The diversity of life*. Cambridge, Mass.: Harvard University Press.

FEEDING THE WORLD

PROLOGUE *Making a Small Dent in World Hunger*

With nearly a billion chronically undernourished people in the world today, world hunger is a real problem. Most of the hungry live in the South (in the developing countries), and without assistance, they have little hope of improving their situation. But assistance does not always need to mean massive inputs of relief supplies or monetary funds; assistance can take the form of a small-scale, low-budget, one-to-one exchange of information and, in some cases, seeds. An example of a small nonprofit organization that takes this approach, and makes a difference, is the Educational Concerns for Hunger Organization ("Echo" for short).

With only five full-time paid employees, a half dozen interns, and an annual operating budget of $300,000, Echo serves indigenous and peasant farmers, as well as urban gardeners, in over a hundred developing countries. Echo has an experimental 12.5-acre (5-hectare) farm

PHOTO   *Grain delivered by a relief agency, Burundi, March 1995.* (Source: Liz Gilbert, Sygma.)

near North Fort Myers, Florida, where scientists experiment with new planting techniques and seed varieties. Echo also maintains a seed bank containing nearly two hundred edible species, and about 450 varieties, of plants—many of which are little known tropical forms. Echo acts as a clearinghouse, receiving farming tips and agricultural information from around the world. Echo distributes this information, along with sample seeds when appropriate, through its newsletter *Development Notes* free of charge to qualified volunteers and community leaders working with farmers and gardeners in the developing world.

Echo's goal is a modest one. It is not trying to solve all of the world's hunger problems, but to help people and communities grow their own food and thereby reduce hunger and increase the quality of life locally.

Certainly, organizations like Echo make a difference to thousands of communities. But ultimately, some researchers believe, they will not be able to address the massive amount of hunger that may plague the world if the planet's population continues to grow at present rates (see Chapter 5). But Echo and like-minded organizations are doing more than simply feeding "poor" people with a free handout. They are helping to educate people (and in some cases particularly the women who tend the fields) so that they can become self-sufficient in a sustainable, environmentally friendly manner. With such education and newfound self-respect may come the frame of mind that is open to more "responsible" family planning (see the discussion in Chapter 5 of how education and improvement in the status and self-sufficiency of women correlate with decreased birth rates). At any rate, the important work that small organizations like Echo are accomplishing is not diminished just because there is still more work to be done—there are still many mouths to be fed.

INTRODUCTION

We are part of the global biosphere, and as such we are ultimately dependent upon other living organisms for virtually all aspects of our lives. Many of the ways we depend on other organisms are obvious. Trees shade us; green plants and other photosynthetic organisms produce the oxygen (O_2) that we breathe and absorb carbon dioxide; worms and microorganisms prepare the soil for us and recycle necessary nutrients; insects pollinate our crops. We do not fully understand all of the complex interrelationships among bacterial and other microorganismal, plant, fungus, and animal species that make up the biosphere, and we have no way of knowing what roles certain seemingly insignificant species perform now or will play in the future.

Modern industry and medical technology are dependent on animals and plants for a plethora of important drugs and other substances. All of our fossil fuels were formed by organisms over millions of years (see Chapter 7), as were many commercially important rock and ore deposits (such as limestone and phosphate deposits; see Chapter 10). Biological resources provide a large percentage of the raw materials that we utilize (such as wood, natural rubber, and leather).

But perhaps most importantly, we are totally dependent on other organisms as a source of nutrition (Fig. 13–1). We raise plants and animals to eat; we harvest wild plants and animals as food

(for example, fishes). In the present chapter, we focus on this most fundamental use of biological resources by humans. Since the majority of the world's food needs are met today by the cultivation of crops, we include a discussion of the soil resources that form the basis of **agriculture**.

FOOD AS A BIOLOGICAL RESOURCE

All of the food that humankind depends on is derived from other organisms. Although we eat many different types of plants and animals, actually only a very small number of species provide the vast majority of our foodstuffs. Only 20 different species of plants supply 80% of the world's food supply, and just three kinds of plants constitute 65% of the food supply—namely rice, wheat, and maize (corn). Global **grain** production currently stands at about 1.87 billion tons* (1.7 billion metric tons) per year. Likewise, animal protein (meat production) is dominated by only a few terrestrial species: poultry, sheep and goats, pigs, and cattle. Globally, about 198 million tons

---

*Unless otherwise noted, *tons* refers to "short" tons (2000 pounds).

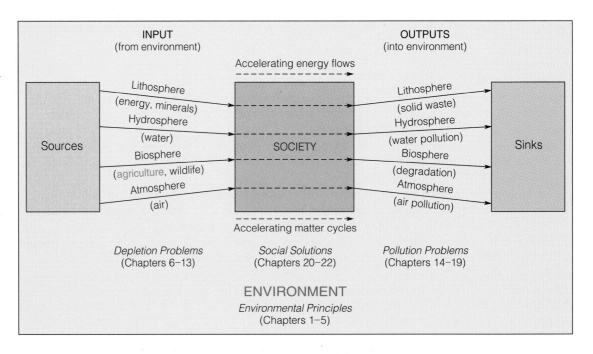

EnviroNet
www.jbpub.com/environet

(180 million metric tons) of such animal meats are harvested each year. Also extremely important, at approximately 110 million tons (100 million metric tons) per year globally, is the fish and aquatic organism catch.

Hunger

Terms such as **hunger** and malnutrition can be hard to define, though their meaning can be painfully obvious when one sees a starving human. To maintain good health, a person must have adequate nutrition—proper amounts of protein and various vitamins and minerals—and an adequate supply of kilocalories as an energy source (in popular usage, kilocalories are often referred to simply as "calories," but a kilocalorie or Calorie is actually equal to 1000 calories; see Issues in Perspective 7–1 in Chapter 7). The amount of kilocalories and nutrients individuals require also depends on their age, sex, and other characteristics. Statistics of global hunger are often based on the number of kilocalories available or ingested per person per day. According to the United Nations, the recommended daily intake per person is 2350 kilocalories. The U.S. National Research Council recommends a kilocaloric intake of 2700 and 2000 for the average adult male and the average adult female, respectively.

From a simple kilocaloric point of view, many people do not consume enough to live and work actively. According to one recent study, in nearly four dozen countries the average daily kilocaloric intake was less than required for people to carry out productive work. Most of these nations are in sub-Saharan Africa and Asia. As an example, in Ghana the average intake is only about 73% of the needed kilocalories; as a result, 31% of the children aged two to five years experience stunted growth, among other problems. In India an estimated 37% of the population are unable to buy enough food to sustain themselves normally.

Studies have demonstrated that in many countries malnutrition is correlated with high death rates, particularly among children. Children suffering from malnutrition are characterized by stunted growth, reduced mental functions and learning capacities, and lowered general activity levels. Damage caused by severe malnutrition may be irreversible. One study found that increasing the per capita consumption of food from slightly under 2000 kilocalories to 2700–3200 kilocalories was associated with an approximately 50% decrease in the death rate (Fig. 13–2).

Besides an adequate intake of kilocalories, a healthy person requires proper amounts of vitamins and minerals. Vitamin and mineral deficiencies can cause many symptoms: for instance, general poor health; blindness (vitamin A deficiencies cause blindness in up to 500,000 preschool children annually); mental retardation; learning disabilities; decreased work capacity; decreased resistance to illnesses, diseases, and infections; and premature death. About a billion people, primarily in developing countries, currently suffer from vitamin and mineral deficiencies while another billion are at risk.

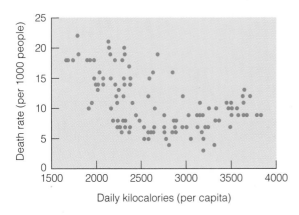

FIGURE 13–2

The relationship between the daily energy supply per capita in 1989 and the crude death rate per 1000 people in 1990 for 119 countries. Note that both too little and too much food, as measured using kilocalories, results in an increased death rate. (*Source:* From H. R. Pullian and N. M. Haddad, "Human Population Growth and the Carrying Capacity Concept." In *Bulletin of the Ecological Society of America* [September 1994], p. 150.)

Feeding the World Today

Currently, at least 800 million people do not eat enough every day for a normal, healthy life, at least 500 million people are chronically hungry, about 24 million of the 140 to 150 million infants born annually are underweight, and more than 200 million children are seriously undernourished. Approximately 13 million people die each year due to hunger (about 35,000 a day), and many more people are weakened by hunger and therefore succumb to other factors (such as disease) more easily. Even in the United States it is estimated that some 30 million people (almost half of them children) are suffering from chronic malnutrition. Why are so many people in need of food, especially when some countries have grain surpluses? In part, the large inequities in food distribution are related to political and social problems; all too often, food is withheld as a weapon (Fig. 13–3), especially in internal struggles in developing nations. But political considerations are only part of the problem.

In fact, perfect management of the world's current food production might just barely feed the global population, but this would be only a temporary measure, for soon the global population will outrun current food supplies. Based on the peak grain harvests of the mid-1980s (since then per capita grain production has generally declined; see the discussion later in the chapter), researchers have calculated the percentage of the world's population that could be fed using various diet models. In the United

States, the typical citizen consumes about 30% of his or her kilocalories from animal products, such as meat and cheese—a notoriously inefficient way of deriving energy from foodstuffs (see Issues in Perspective 13–1). If the entire world followed the American dietary example, less than half of the present global population could be fed. Typical Latin Americans consume about 10% of their kilocalories from animal sources. Using the Latin American diet as a model, about 4 billion people could be fed based on the record harvests of the mid-1980s. Only with everyone maintaining a strictly vegetarian diet, and assuming perfect food distribution systems (which is unrealistic given current political and transportation problems), could the current population of 5.8 billion be fed. If we could considerably decrease the waste factor (for example, up to 40% of all food typically spoils or is eaten by insects, rats, or other pests, and much food is thrown away as "leftovers," made into food for nonessential house pets, and so forth), perhaps 8 billion people worldwide could be fed a subsistence diet.

But such measures would be of little consequence to the billions of extra mouths that will need to be fed by the end of the twenty-first century—especially if the world's population reaches

FIGURE 13–3

Canadian soldiers with United Nations aid trucks carrying food are stopped by Bosnian Serb forces near Srebrenica, Bosnia-Herzegovina, April 1993. (*Source:* Art Zamur/Gamma Liaison.)

Eating Animal Products

One result of the Green Revolution is that meat and dairy production and consumption have steadily grown since the middle of the twentieth century (Fig. 1). Increased grain yields have made it economically feasible to feed livestock grains, such as maize and barley. The animals are raised on specialized farms in a factory-like setting (Fig. 2).

Traditionally, meat, eggs, and dairy products made up at least a small percentage of the human diet, as they still do in such countries as Egypt and India (in India dairy products are eaten, but generally not meat), but today this aspect of the diet has been greatly overemphasized in some countries, especially the United States. The average person in the United States consumes about 247 pounds (112 kg) of meat per year, in Italy about 170 pounds (77 kilograms), in Japan about 90.5 pounds (41 kg), in Egypt about 31 pounds (14 kg), and in India only about 4.5 pounds (2 kg). To satisfy current world demands for animal products, there are an estimated 4 billion sheep, goats, cattle, pigs, horses, buffalo, and camels, along with an estimated 11 billion domesticated fowl, on the planet.

The drawbacks of such intensive consumption of livestock are readily apparent. Herds of cattle and other animals are causing increased deforestation, desertification, and other forms of ecological damage. Some areas of tropical forest, for instance, are cut, burned, and then seeded

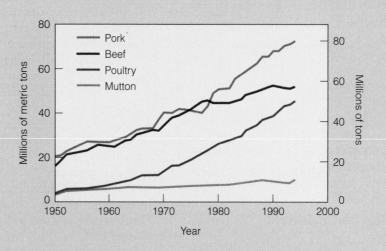

FIGURE 1

World meat production by type, 1950–1994. (*Source:* Based on data found in L. R. Brown, N. Lenssen, and H. Kane, *Vital Signs 1995* [New York: W. W. Norton, 1995], p. 31. Reprinted with permission of Worldwatch Institute, Washington, D.C., Copyright 1994.)

with grass to create pastureland for cattle ranchers. Much of the resulting inexpensive beef is then shipped to countries such as the United States that have a high per capita consumption of red meat. Often this consumption takes the form of low-priced hamburgers sold at fast-food restaurants. Some fast-food chains have advertised that they do not use rainforest beef in their hamburgers; certainly, this is commendable action on their part. Yet even if they avoid rainforest cattle, such fast-food chains still encourage beef consumption, which creates a greater demand for beef, which raises the price of beef and ulti-

mately encourages the destruction of tropical forests in order to raise cattle—even if those cattle do not go directly into the production of a particular restaurant's food. Perhaps a more environmentally friendly approach for the restaurants would be to encourage fast-food vegetarian meals (as some are already beginning to do).

Using rainforest land for pasture quickly destroys the fertility of the soils—especially since the grasses planted as cattle forage are not native to the area and thus do not last. Collectively, cattle also emit large quantities of the greenhouse gas methane into the atmosphere. Ammonia and other sub-

8 to 10 billion. There seem to be few options for dealing with this situation. One possibility is to increase global food production dramatically and ensure that the food is equitably distributed. But whether major gains in global food production will be possible is a point of heated debate. Some analysts argue that innovative agricultural techniques, combined with advances in biotechnology (see p. 371 and Issues in Perspective 13–3), will allow us to significantly increase food production. Other researchers believe that global food production has already peaked (see the following discussion) and that even maintaining current levels will be difficult. With few realistic prospects for significant increases in world agricultural output, some analysts argue that the only way out of the predicament is to control world population growth (see Chapter 5).

of millions of people are starving, approximately 38% of the planet's grain goes to feed livestock. In the United States, 67% of domestic grain consumption goes to feed livestock, compared with 57% in the European Community nations and the former Soviet Union, about 33% in the Middle East, and only 3% in India.

The situation is exacerbated by the energy-intensive nature of livestock production in the United States and other developed countries. The industry is heavily dependent on energy, fertilizers, herbicides, and pesticides to raise the feed grain and so forth. For instance, the production of 2.2 pounds (1 kg) of pork in the United States requires 15.2 pounds (6.9 kg) of grain and the burning of about 30,000 kilocalories of fossil fuel (about a gallon, or almost four liters, of gasoline). Eggs are among the most efficiently produced animal food, requiring only 5.7 pounds (2.6 kg) of grain and 10,000 kilocalories of energy per 2.2 pounds (1 kg) of eggs, but even this is vastly less efficient than eating the grain directly.

What's the bottom line? If we have any hopes of feeding the entire world adequately, then perhaps we should start eating lower on the food chain. Try eating more plant products directly—grains, vegetables, and fruits. It will benefit your personal health and will also be better for the planet and global population as a whole.

FIGURE 2
A turkey farm, Salinas, California. (*Source:* Tom Nebbia/The Stock Market.)

stances in livestock manure are potent pollutants. High levels of meat consumption are not even healthy for humans—diets that include a high percentage of meat increase the risks of certain forms of cancer, stroke, and heart disease.

As basic ecological principles tell us (see Chapter 3), a diet that relies heavily on meat requires greater resources and more energy than a more vegetarian diet. Producing food for humans by feeding plants (such as grains) to animals is much less efficient than simply feeding humans the plants directly. It can take up to 16 pounds of feed to produce a pound of beef (or 16 kg of feed to produce 1 kg of beef), 7 pounds of feed to produce a pound of pork, and 3 pounds of feed to produce a pound of chicken or eggs. Globally, many more people can be fed on a vegetarian diet than on a diet that includes a high percentage of animal products. Even though hundreds

Food for the Future

If the world population continues to grow, we will need more food in the future. World food production could be increased through two basic, but certainly not mutually exclusive, strategies: increase the amount of land under cultivation, or increase the yield per unit of land under cultivation. Meadows, Meadows, and Randers (1992) have noted that today roughly 3.7 billion acres (1.5 billion hectares) of land worldwide are under some form of cultivation—an average of 0.64 acres (0.26 hectares) per person. According to various theoretical estimates, there are between 4.9 and 9.9 billion acres (between 2 and 4 billion hectares) of **cultivable land** on Earth (much of the variation in the estimates is due to the use of different criteria for defining "cultivable land"—how fer-

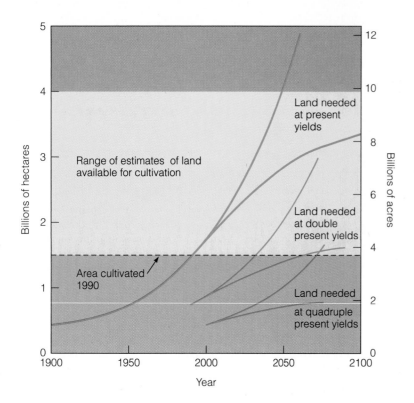

The chart shows "Billions of hectares" on the left y-axis (0 to 5) and "Billions of acres" on the right y-axis (0 to 12), with "Year" on the x-axis (1900 to 2100). Labels include "Range of estimates of land available for cultivation," "Area cultivated 1990," "Land needed at present yields," "Land needed at double present yields," and "Land needed at quadruple present yields."

FIGURE 13–4

Possible land futures. The pairs of lines show the amount of land needed to maintain present per capita food production if the world population continues to grow exponentially at current rates (upper line of each pair) or if the world population grows according to early 1990s World Bank forecasts (lower line of each pair). The heavy solid pair of lines shows land requirements at present crop yields; the two lighter pairs of lines show land requirements at double and quadruple present crop yields. The yellow shaded area is the range of estimates of land that could possibly be cultivated for food; note that much of this land is currently covered with forests. (*Source:* D. H. Meadows, D. L. Meadows, and J. Randers, *Beyond the Limits* [Post Mills, Vt.: Chelsea Green, 1992], p. 51. Reprinted from *Beyond the Limits* copyright© by Meadows, Meadows, and Randers. With permission from Chelsea Green Publishing Co., White River Junction, Vermont.)

tile the soil must be, how much water must be available, and so on).

Meadows, Meadows, and Randers (1992) have outlined several scenarios involving various combinations of land cultivation and yields on a global scale (summarized in ▦ Fig. 13–4). If the population continues to increase at its current exponential rate and present average yields continue, then before the year 2050 all of the theoretical 9.9 billion acres (4 billion hectares) of cultivable land will have to be put into production, and by the end of the twenty-first century, the population will quickly outstrip its food supply. This scenario assumes, unrealistically, that the present high crop yields of prime land can be maintained, even on marginally arable land. It also assumes that no cultivable land is lost during the next century, which is also unrealistic because, as a later section explains, the absolute amount of cultivable land on Earth is declining due to various factors.

The picture improves if world population grows according to the somewhat optimistic forecasts of the World Bank, which predicts a decline in the population growth rate worldwide. Even so, to sustain the world's population, at current yields the amount of land under cultivation will have to be doubled by the middle of the next century—an unrealistic prospect.

Things look even better if we assume that with technological innovations, crop yields can be doubled. Given this assumption, if the population

continues to grow at the present rate, land under cultivation will not need to reach the 7.4 billion–acre (3 billion–hectare) mark until about 2075. If the population increases according to World Bank projections, we can sustain the Earth's population through the twenty-first century with under 4.9 billion acres (2 billion hectares) of cultivated land. If we assume that the yields can be quadrupled (a very unrealistic assumption, given present knowledge) on all cultivated land, then the land currently under production will be sufficient until the second half of the twenty-first century if the population continues to grow at its current rate. Note, however, that because of the nature of exponential growth, in the twenty-second century more than 9.9 billion acres (4 billion hectares) of cultivable land will be needed, even if yields are quadrupled. If World Bank forecasts for population growth hold, then quadrupling yields will allow us to feed the world for as long as those high yields can be maintained without increasing the amount of land under cultivation. But such high yields would almost certainly be temporary (and unsustainable); once yields declined, the world situation would revert to one of the scenarios previously discussed (see Fig. 13–4).

Some optimistic studies have concluded that if we really wanted to, we could grow enough food to support a global population of 50 billion people. Such conclusions, however, are based on totally unrealistic assumptions. For one thing, they assume that all potentially arable land would be cultivated, including land occupied by forests and land that is of marginal fertility or is so arid that massive irrigation would be necessary. The human population would have to live in areas, such as the polar regions, where agriculture is totally impossible, while the potentially arable land beneath our current cities and towns would be put under the plow. Furthermore, these studies assume the yields on all this land would either match, or with technoagricultural advances, surpass those that have been attained under ideal conditions on the most fertile land in the past. Such super high yields are only a pipe dream at present. Finally, these projections ignore the detrimental and nonsustainable aspects of modern agriculture (discussed in a later section) and the consequences (climatic and otherwise) of destroying the world's remaining forests. The question of where the massive quantities of energy, **fertilizers**, **pesticides**, **herbicides**, and freshwater necessary for modern, intensive, high-yield agriculture will come from is not addressed, nor are the attendant problems of pollution caused by chemical use, topsoil loss and exhaustion, soil salinization, and waterlogging addressed. To suggest that we could feed close to 50 billion people is irresponsible—indeed, it is a lie.

A more conservative estimate is that we could potentially feed about 8 billion people, but even this estimate assumes better yields than occur today in many agricultural areas. Although some increase in yields may be possible (the best farmers in Iowa, for instance, can produce four times the world's average corn yield per acre), in recent years global yields have shown signs of leveling off, and we cannot necesarily count on further large increases in the future.

Furthermore, even with better yields, there would not be much room for growing nonfood products, such as rubber trees, wood trees, flowers, or plants to turn into fuel. In addition, the 8 billion estimate does not take into account the inevitable losses in arable land. Such an estimate also assumes perfect distribution of foodstuffs, which is politically unrealistic, and assumes that the majority of people will give up meat and eat basically a grain diet. Finally, we should note that such estimates assume "average" weather conditions. But given the fluctuations in weather, some "below average" years and the resulting shortfalls in agricultural production would seem to be inevitable.

Taking all these factors into account, some experts insist that we are just about at the limit of the number of people we can realistically expect to feed. And they note that even now, with 15% of the world's population underfed, we do not do a very good job of feeding a mere 5.8 billion. Still, it must be pointed out that this is a very controversial area of research. New crop varieties continue to be developed, and new methods of farming and more efficient equipment have yet to be used around the world. Even if crop yields have leveled off in the last few years, that does not necessarily mean they will remain at these levels for all time. They may begin to increase once again as successful new cultivation techniques spread around the world.

Agricultural Food Production and Supplies

Grain (rice, wheat, maize, sorghum, barley, oats, rye, millet, and so on) forms the backbone of the world's food supply, and thus global annual grain production takes on an extreme importance. Since 1950 total world grain production, as well as per capita grain production, has soared—in large part due to the **"Green Revolution"** discussed later (■ Fig. 13–5). The historical per

capita peak was reached in 1984 when 763 pounds (346 kg) of grain per person were produced; the absolute peak production was reached in 1990 when 1962 million tons (1780 million metric tons) of grain were produced worldwide, but because of population increases only 741 pounds (336 kg) of grain were produced per person. In 1992 the world produced 1957 million tons (1776 million metric tons) of grain, or 697 pounds (316 kg) a person (or about 91% of the peak per capita production in 1984). In 1993, however, absolute grain production dropped to 1870 million tons (1697 million metric tons), and per capita production was only 673 pounds (305 kg)—88.2% of the peak in 1984. In 1994 grain production was up to 1925 million tons (1747 million metric tons), or 686 pounds (311 kg) per person.

The data on world grain harvests in 1992 and 1993 tell an important story. Globally, 1992 was a fairly good year for grain production, although re-

■ **FIGURE 13–5**
(a) World grain production, 1950–1994; and (b) world grain production per person, 1950–1994. (*Source:* Based on data found in L. R. Brown, H. Kane, and D. M. Roodman, *Vital Signs 1994* [New York: W. W. Norton, 1994] and L. R. Brown, N. Lenssen, and H. Kane, *Vital Signs 1995* [New York: W. W. Norton, 1995]. Reprinted with permission of Worldwatch Institute, Washington, D.C., Copyright 1994.)

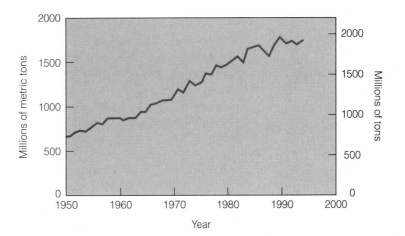

(a)

(b)

gional variations were evident; favorable weather produced an exceptional harvest in the United States, for example, while parts of Africa suffered extreme drought. Due to political unrest, civil wars, lack of transportation routes, and other logistic problems, it was impossible to import adequate supplies of food into such countries as Somalia and the Sudan with the result that tens of thousands of people in these areas died of starvation. Even adequate supplies of food on a global basis will not ensure that everyone is adequately fed.

Conditions were very different in 1993 and demonstrate how weather patterns influence global food supplies. The drop in the 1993 harvest was due primarily to one factor—too much rain and the resultant flooding of cornfields in the United States (see Issues in Perspective 2–3 in Chapter 2). The four largest grain producers in the world are the United States, China, India, and the area of the former Soviet Union. The United States normally produces about 40% of the world's corn, but when U.S. corn production dropped by nearly one-third in 1993, the effects were felt around the globe. Compounding the situation, 1993 also saw a very slight drop (about 2%) in rice production due to abnormally cool and rainy weather in northeastern Asia. More "normal" conditions in 1994 allowed world grain production to increase slightly.

Not all grain grown is used for human consumption. Since 1960, 34 to 41% of the world's grain supply each year has been used to feed livestock and poultry. To raise livestock and poultry on grains, farmers must routinely include a protein supplement in the animals' diet. The most important such supplement is the protein-rich soybean, which is also a valuable source of oil and protein for humans. Thus, the global annual soybean crop, though relatively small in terms of absolute tonnage, is extremely important. Yet over the past decade soybean production has been stagnant, remaining at about 41.9 to 52.0 pounds (19–23.6 kg) per person annually (prior to 1994, world per capita soybean production never rose above 46.3 pounds [21 kg], but exceptional weather produced a 1994 bumper harvest in the U.S. that raised average global production to 52.0 pounds [23.6 kg]). Because the soybean does not respond well to typical intensive farming techniques, making it difficult to increase yields per unit of land, the primary way to increase soybean production is to expand the land area devoted to growing soybeans. But around the world good agricultural land is in scarce supply, so world soybean production may remain stagnant. The United States accounts for over half of global soybean production (only the U.S. corn harvest is more valuable in terms of dollars it brings in) while Brazil, Argentina, and China together produce almost 40% of the global soybean crop.

As Issues in Perspective 13–1 pointed out, it is far more efficient to consume grains and other plants directly rather than feeding them to animals and then consuming the animals. As the world population continues to increase and per capita grain production remains stable or declines, it may become necessary to allocate less grain to animals if we want to ensure that all humans are fed adequately.

Not all grain produced in a given year is consumed in that year. An important statistic is the amount of **carryover grain stocks** from one year to the next (Fig. 13–6). As of the beginning of the 1995 harvest year, there were 328 million tons (298 million metric tons) of carryover grain stocks worldwide, 62 days use worth of grain (the

FIGURE 13–6
(a) World grain carryover stocks, 1963–1995; and (b) world grain carryover stocks as days of consumption, 1963–1995. (*Source:* Based on data found in L. R. Brown, H. Kane, and D. M. Roodman, *Vital Signs 1994* [New York: W. W. Norton, 1994] and L. R. Brown, N. Lenssen, and H. Kane, *Vital Signs 1995* [New York: W. W. Norton, 1995]. Reprinted with permission of Worldwatch Institute, Washington, D.C., Copyright 1994.)

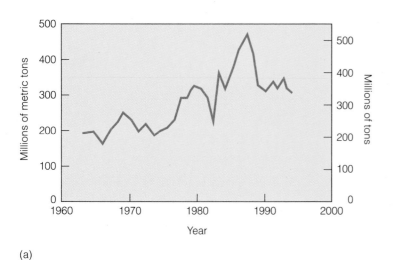

(a)

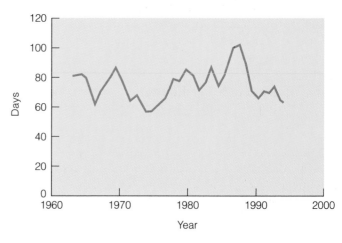

(b)

world uses about 5.3 million tons [4.8 million metric tons] of grain a day). This current carryover stock is disturbingly low; the record high was in 1987 with 104 days worth of carryover stock, and the low was in 1973 with only 56 days of carryover stock. The size of the world's grain carryover stock is often used as an indicator of global food security. When the stocks drop below about 60 days worth, as they did in the early 1970s, grain prices usually begin to fluctuate widely with step increases. In such cases, it becomes even more difficult for the poor to obtain adequate food.

Some observers point out that, historically, there has always been grain to buy—as expressed in stockpiles of grain around the world. They contend that the primary reason hunger exists in the world today is because poor nations cannot afford to buy food. The best way to ensure that all people are adequately fed, some researchers maintain, is to expand food production in temperate regions (such as the United States) where advanced agricultural technologies and transportation systems are already in place. Furthermore, there must be a global free trade policy for food. A worldwide free market system for food would discourage inefficient, often government-subsidized, food production in marginal areas. For instance, in India overpumping of groundwater supplies using free government-provided electricity has resulted in lowered water tables, salinization, and waterlogged soils. Indonesia, in the name of "self-sufficiency," has cleared 1.5 million acres (607,000 hectares) of tropical rainforest to grow soybeans for use as chicken feed. The problem is that the cost of Indonesian soybeans is higher than the price for soybeans on the world market. Likewise, India produces milk at a cost above world market prices. According to some analysts, if free market policies were in place, it would be economically unproductive to graze animals or cultivate crops on marginal, environmentally sensitive lands. In their view, free trade/free market policies would encourage the most economical, environmentally friendly, and efficient production of food such that globally the maximum number of people could be fed.

Even those who espouse a "free market solution" to world hunger must acknowledge that the problems of debt, particularly on the part of developing countries, trade imbalances, and restrictions on free market policies are complex and not easily solved. Politically, it would be very difficult to have a genuine global free market system for food products. Furthermore, even if free trade/free market policies could accomplish the equitable distribution of food around the world,

there must be enough food to go around. At present, the food supply does appear to be adequate, but as we have already discussed, if the global population continues to grow, it is far from certain that there will be enough food to feed everyone in the future.

Land, Fertilizers, and Water Devoted to Agricultural Production

An enormous amount of land is devoted to agricultural use (and not all agriculture is devoted to food production: see the Case Study). Globally, approximately 8 billion acres (3.3 billion hectares) of land are used for grazing animals, about 1.7 billion acres (700 million hectares) are devoted to grains, and 568–593 million acres (230–240 million hectares) are artificially irrigated to grow crops.

Taking a closer look at one of the more important agricultural resource statistics, worldwide grain area harvested, we find that it has increased less than 20% since 1950: 1465 million acres (593 million hectares) in 1950 versus approximately 1717 million acres (695 million hectares) today. The high was reached in 1981 with 1816 million acres (735 million hectares). Over the last five years, the amount of land devoted to grain has been relatively stagnant. Every year new land is put under cultivation as forests are cut and dry areas are irrigated, but other land is removed from cultivation due to such factors as soil exhaustion, degradation, and the building of residences and shopping malls. At present there is a rough balance between land newly put under cultivation each year and land removed from cultivation. But some observers fear that by the next century the cropland area may begin to diminish.

More importantly, though, due to global population growth the amount of grain area harvested per person has steadily declined from 0.57 acres (0.23 hectares) in 1950 to the present 0.32 acres (0.13 hectares). But despite this steady decrease in per capita area devoted to grain, as we have already noted, per capita world grain production has risen dramatically since 1950. Grain production per person rose from 545 pounds (247 kg) in 1950 to 686 pounds (311 kg) in 1994 even though almost twice as much land was devoted to grain harvesting per person in 1950. Increases in yields from an average of 0.47 tons per acre (1.06 metric tons per hectare) in 1950 to 1.16 tons per acre (2.60 metric tons per hectare) in 1994 were behind this rise in production. It was accomplished through intensive, often mechanized, farming techniques using specially bred varieties of crops and massive doses of artificial fertilizers, pesti-

Should the Choice of Clothing Be an Environmental Issue?

Although we tend to associate agricultural commodities with food items, there is still a large market for nonfood agricultural products. Many of the nonfood agricultural products that the average consumer encounters on a daily basis are found in clothing and cloth products. Especially important in this regard are cotton, wool, linen, leather, furs, and silk.

Often it is very difficult for the environmentally conscientious consumer to know what types of clothing to buy. Perhaps the ultimate in "natural materials," fur, has come under fierce criticism (Fig. 1). Animal rights advocates have been very successful in persuading the public to abandon the use of natural furs, and many public figures—from royalty to movie stars—have given up their furs. Most animal rights activists argue that slaughtering animals, particularly wild animals, is cruel and violates the animals' inherent rights. The fur industry counters that about 75% of U.S. domestic furs are farm-raised minks. The minks, it is claimed, are raised humanely and killed painlessly. Furthermore, a mink farm can be an ecologically sound, sustainable operation that causes little pollution and uses few petroleum-based resources. And a pure mink coat is totally biodegradable once its useful life is over. In many respects one could argue that mink fur products are much more environmentally friendly than products made out of synthetic fibers produced from

nonrenewable petroleum resources. Synthetic fiber production not only depletes a valuable and limited resource, but also generates massive amounts of pollution—pollution that degrades the natural habitats of animals in the wild, thereby impinging on their "rights." Nevertheless, popular opinion seems to be with the antifur movement—of course, it probably helps that furs tend to be an expensive luxury item that can be easily avoided.

But if furs are to be avoided, what about leather in shoes, belts, jackets, and other products? Is leather, the skin of animals, any less noxious from an animal rights point of view? And for that matter, what about eating meat? Is it rational to avoid furs, yet wear leather and eat hamburgers—especially when the leather and beef may actually cause much more environmental degradation than raising minks on farms?

Leaving the heated controversy over the use of animal products, what about plant products such as cotton? Many people think of cotton as an all-natural organic fiber that must be much more environmentally friendly than synthetic petroleum-based alternatives such as rayon, dacron, and nylon. The cotton industry's advertisements have certainly played on such sentiments. Theoretically at least, cotton can be raised in a sustainable manner using environmentally benign techniques, and once the cotton clothing or other product has exceeded its useful life expectancy, it

can be allowed to decompose, perhaps in a compost pile, and ultimately be reincorporated into the soil. The cycle of petroleum-based clothes, in contrast, is inherently nonsustainable. They are produced from nonrenewable resources using massive amounts of energy as well as producing large quantities of pollutants, and the synthetic materials are not biodegradable and thus cannot ultimately be recycled.

Unfortunately, making the environmentally correct choice between synthetics and natural fibers like cotton is not easy. The cotton industry has been blamed for releasing massive amounts of pollutants into the environment. Indeed, the cotton industry is the third-largest user of pesticides worldwide. Massive amounts of chemicals are used not only in growing the crop, but also in processing, cleaning, and dyeing the cotton to produce cloth. Cotton fields have been blamed for continuing soil deterioration and loss. As actually practiced, cotton growing is often unsustainable. In many areas, it has been argued, farmers grow cotton as a cash crop instead of raising foodstuffs. As the world population continues to increase, there is more and more concern over agricultural lands being devoted to nonfood products of any type, including cotton and tobacco.

Both natural and synthetic fabrics present other problems as well. Many modern fabrics, including some "natural" silks and linens, must be dry-cleaned—a process that utilizes

cides, herbicides, and in some cases artificial irrigation (the "Green Revolution" is discussed further later). A clear indicator of this trend is global fertilizer use during the last half of the twentieth century.

In 1950, 15.4 million tons (14 million metric tons) of fertilizer, or 12.1 pounds (5.5 kg) per person, were used worldwide. The annual use of fertilizer rose steadily to an all-time high of 161 million tons (146 million metric tons), or 61.7 pounds (28 kilograms) per person, in 1989. Over the last few years, global fertilizer use has dropped slightly: 133 million tons (121 million metric tons), or 47.6 pounds (21.6 kilograms) per person,

were used in 1994. This recent decline has been attributed primarily to declines in fertilizer use in the former Soviet Union and Eastern Europe following the removal of government fertilizer subsidies. Additionally, some farmers are using fertilizer more efficiently (with standard methods, much fertilizer never reaches the intended plants: instead it runs off the land and pollutes ground and surface waters). Farmers are also finding that most crops have reached their peak response to fertilizer dosages. In many areas using more fertilizer does little or nothing to further increase crop yields. For most of the period since World War II, crop production could be increased by

toxic solvents, some of which contribute to atmospheric ozone depletion.

Thus, the environmentally concerned consumer faces a quandary when buying products made of cloth and related materials. There seem to be no widely available options that are undoubtedly the "right" choice from a whole Earth perspective. Clothing manufactured from organically grown cotton is not readily available, for instance, in contrast to organically grown food, which can be easily obtained in most areas or grown at home. Some environmentalists support the wearing of wool, contending that the wool industry tends to use fewer harmful chemicals than most of the rest of the clothing industry. But overgrazing, including by sheep, is a major cause of soil degradation.

At present, the most practical advice to the environmentally conscientious consumer is to simply use common sense and avoid excess. Clothing should not be purchased unnecessarily. Many middle- and upper-class Americans have far more clothing than they ever use on a regular basis. Faddish clothing that quickly goes out of style and is not worn again should be avoided. Choose strong, practical, durable clothing that can be worn for a long time, and use it until it is genuinely worn out. Then, instead of discarding it in the garbage—an effort should be made to reuse the fabric (perhaps to make other articles, such as rugs) or recycle the fiber; alternately, the clothing may be sold or given away. Likewise, environmentally aware consumers can purchase most or all of their clothing used, from thrift shops and the like, and save a substantial amount of money as well as helping the Earth. Good quality children's clothing in particular can often be purchased second hand because young children tend to outgrow their clothing before they wear it out. Finally, only clothing that can be washed using conventional and safe means should be purchased. Clothes that need to be dry-cleaned should be avoided.

■ **FIGURE 1**
Protesting the use of furs in New York City.
(*Source*: Ted Whittenkraus/Visuals Unlimited.)

Questions

1. What is your opinion on wearing furs, using leather products, and eating meat? Do you perhaps avoid furs but still consume meat (as many people do)? Explain and justify your opinions.

2. Discuss the pros and cons of cotton clothing versus clothing made from synthetic fibers. Pragmatically, can the average American easily avoid cotton clothing?

3. Given the number of starving people in the world, do you think that some fields currently used to grow nonfood agricultural products should be devoted to food crops instead? Is the solution to world hunger to be found in growing more food? Or is it a problem of global food distribution? Or must other factors (such as population increases discussed in Chapter 5) be considered?

adding more fertilizer despite the diminishing per capita land area devoted to crops. However, this era seems now to have ended—substantial crop increases no longer are easily obtained by simply adding more fertilizer.

In many regions, **irrigation** is essential to grow crops that would not otherwise survive. Interestingly, since about 1961 the global irrigated land area has grown at about the same rate as the world's population. Thus, in 1961 there were 343 million acres (139 million hectares) of irrigated land worldwide, or about 0.111 acres (0.045 hectares) per person, and today there are about 580–593 million acres (235–240 million hectares) of irrigated land, or about 0.101 acres (0.041 hectares) per person. Unfortunately, as is discussed further below, much irrigated land is watered unsustainably. Some analysts predict that the growth in irrigated land cannot continue for very long into the future. As with the amount of land devoted to grain harvests generally, we will see a per capita decline in irrigated land area by the year 2000.

The Effects of Agriculture

Most agriculture alters and manipulates natural ecosystems, transforming them into artificial ecosystems that are inherently unstable and can only survive with constant human attention. Maximum food production is the only goal.

The Pioneer Stage and Its Effects In nature, during the process of **ecological succession** (see Chapter 3), a clear patch of land will be colonized by successive groups of plants and animals. The first settlers will generally be smaller, fast-growing, pioneer plants. Then larger, slower-growing, and longer-lasting plants will progressively replace the original colonists. The final stage of succession is the **climax community**, which in most terrestrial areas consists of mature forest composed of large trees interspersed with younger trees and other plants and animals.

In clearing land for agricultural use, farmers essentially begin the cycle of succession anew. But the farmer does not allow succession to follow its natural course and reach a climax stage. Instead, the land is artificially maintained at the **pioneer stage**; furthermore, the pioneer plants that are allowed to grow on the land are carefully picked, maintained, and managed. Corn (maize), wheat, or rice may be planted as the pioneer plant; other weeds are eliminated (many major food crops are essentially cultivated weeds). When the crop has matured, it is harvested; the next season the land is cleared, and the system begins again. Most agricultural systems emphasize the pioneer stage of succession because this is when an ecosystem is most productive (although not most efficient in energy use). In this stage, virtually all the energy and nutrients utilized by the plants go into growth. In contrast, in the climax stage much of the energy and most of the nutrients go into maintaining the system; the only new growth that occurs replaces plants that die.

But the long-term arrestment of ecosystems at the pioneer stage leads to major problems. Pioneer ecosystems are inherently unstable, and this instability is exacerbated by the human habit of planting only one variety of plant per field at a time (**monoculture**). In a mature, climax ecosystem, the complex relationships and interactions between many species of plants and animals promote long-term stability. In the climax community, there are natural checks and balances on predator-prey relations (including insect attacks on vulnerable plants), disease, population explosions of particular species, and so on. Climax communities are also less susceptible to the ravages of climatic fluctuations such as droughts or floods. In the artificial environment of a crop field, pests, disease, and the vagaries of climate must be mitigated to a greater extent by human intervention. Pests might be controlled by applying poisonous chemicals to a field. Watering or irrigation may compensate for a lack of rain.

Pioneer stages also extract a heavy toll of nutrients from the soil without replenishing them. Replenishment occurs naturally during later stages of ecological succession, but when humans harvest and remove their pioneer crops, the nutrients are lost from the land and must be restored by artificial fertilization. In contrast, the climax community is characterized by complementary, even symbiotic relationships between organisms. The nutrients extracted by one organism are eventually passed on to and restored by another organism. The cycle of growth, death, decay, and regrowth—all on the same parcel of land—ensures continued recycling of raw materials.

The characteristics of pioneer communities that make modern monoculture farming so productive and successful on a short-term basis cause continued environmental degradation in the long term. Rapid nutrient uptake (absorption) without recycling destroys the soil's fertility. Lack of a balanced vegetation, or no vegetation at all between harvesting and the next planting season, to hold the soil in place and absorb moisture can lead to massive erosion of valuable topsoil, flash floods, dust storms, and droughts. Monocultures are notoriously susceptible to attack by disease and pests uncontrolled by natural predators or other mitigating agents.

The Effects of Irrigation In areas where irrigation is necessary, a whole new set of problems is encountered, in particular, **salinization** and **waterlogging**. All soils contain various mineral salts. Under natural conditions, in areas that are characterized by relatively high rainfall and good drainage, these salts are washed out of the soil and travel, through water flow, to the sea. This is why the sea is salty—it is the final resting place where salts from the land surface accumulate. In contrast, arid regions tend to have higher natural concentrations of salts in the soil and in any groundwater or standing bodies of water simply because there is not a constant flow of water to remove the salt. Irrigating arid land dissolves the salts in the soil, and as the water evaporates, the salts are drawn toward the surface. Many artificially irrigated lands are poorly drained, and as a result, the salts simply remain in the upper levels of the soil rather than being flushed out and carried to the sea. Furthermore, the poorly drained land and soils themselves can become waterlogged, and the water table can rise over time, as the groundwater and soils become progressively saltier. Accumulated mineral salts are toxic to most plant life, and as land becomes increasingly salinized, it may reach a point where it can no longer support most crops or other plants (Fig. 13–7).

Traditional Methods of Coping with Agriculture's Effects

A traditional and time-honored way of circumventing the problems inherent in agriculture is to occupy the land for a year or two, often utilizing slash and burn or swidden tech-

tate crops and the pasturing of livestock from field to field and season to season. With proper rotation, nutrients that were utilized by one crop can be restored by the next crop. For instance, periodically planting a field with legumes (members of the pea and bean family) will restore nitrogen to the soil since these plants' roots attract soil bacteria that have the ability to remove nitrogen from the air and produce nitrogen compounds upon which other forms of life are dependent. Crop ro-

FIGURE 13–7
Salt-affect agricultural land near Katanning, Western Australia. (*Source:* Bill Bachman/Photo Researchers.)

niques, and then move on. In this way the natural ecological cycle of succession can occur once again; the land is allowed to regenerate and replenish itself. This method is feasible as long as the human population in any one area is relatively small, and they are willing to pick up and move on a regular basis.

A variation on this theme is to maintain a permanent place of residence, but utilize alternating fields in different years. In late ancient and medieval Europe, many farmers used a "two-field system" in which only half of their land was planted with crops in any particular year; the other half lay fallow. Native wild plants would colonize the fallow land, and farm animals were allowed to graze there; their manure helped to restore fertility to the soil. Fallow fields could also serve as a home for wildlife, such as birds, that could help keep insects and other pests in check. Each year the crops would be planted on the previous year's fallow land. A related method is to ro-

tation also tends to decrease the threat of pests and disease. If the same crop is planted in the same field year after year, a colony of a harmful pest or disease agent (be it a rodent, insect, fungus, or other life-form) can take up permanent residence in or near the field. Such a colony has less chance of establishing itself if crops are rotated from year to year.

Another traditional way to avoid the problems inherent in some agricultural practices is to promote diversity (see Issues in Perspective 13–2). This can take many forms and is not unrelated to the concept of crop rotation. In many traditional, aboriginal agricultures, numerous varieties of many different crops are planted each season; the aboriginals of Amazonia, for instance, used at least 70 varieties of manioc (a group of tropical plants with edible roots, also known as cassava or tapioca). In some cases many different types of plants are cultivated within a small area, even planted together in the same space—mimicking some of the characteristics of a climax community. In Central America the farmers have traditionally interplanted maize (corn), beans, and squash. The three crops benefit one another, and the system leads to greater long-term productivity and sustainability than planting a single crop at a time. The more varied diet such interplanting promotes is also nutritionally preferable for humans. In addition, using a variety of crops is a form of insurance—one does not put all of one's eggs in a single basket. Different crops and varieties have different tolerances for adverse pest, soil, disease, and climatic conditions. Even if unexpected rains or droughts occur or an abnormal fungus or insect plague strikes, it is less likely to destroy the entire harvest if a variety of plants have been cultivated.

Modern Agriculture's "Solutions": Fertilizers, Pesticides, and Herbicides

"Modern" agricultural techniques of the late nineteenth and twentieth centuries have avoided many of the traditional methods used to cope with the inherent weaknesses in artificial agriculture. This has resulted in the "quick fix" of bumper crops, but has been at the expense of the land, nonrenewable mineral and energy resources, and long-term sustainability.

Much modern agriculture is synonymous with the circumvention of biological agents in the restoration of depleted soil fertility; crop diversity, crop rotation, and even manure use are abandoned. Instead, minerals and chemicals are mined, processed, and applied directly to croplands in the form of fertilizers; simultaneously, irrigation efforts are intensified. Sometimes this has been referred to as "force-feeding" the land.

The main nutrients applied to the soil are phosphorus, potassium, and nitrogen. Phosphorus and potassium are mined from mineral deposits; as mentioned in Chapter 10, phosphorus in particular is in short supply. Nitrogen was initially supplied from manure or from bird droppings known as "guano." Some isolated islands contain huge mountains of bird droppings, and these were mined for the nitrogen content. Now, however, artificial nitrogen-bearing fertilizers can be manufactured synthetically using the abundant nitrogen of the atmosphere.

The heavy use of fertilizers was accompanied by an increasing emphasis on monoculture (planting huge fields with a single variety of a single crop). Monoculture allows the farmer to tailor the fertilizers to the specific needs of the particular crop and increases efficiency in mechanical harvesting and processing of the crop. But monoculture brought with it increasing problems from pests and diseases that found a happy point of attack in the huge, ecologically unstable fields. This meant that such pests and diseases needed to be controlled. The preferred way to control them was through the use of more chemicals—synthetic pesticides and herbicides that could be designed to kill everything except the crop being cultivated. In the United States, pesticide use in agriculture rose from about 340 million pounds (154 million kg) per year in 1965 to a peak of about 890 million pounds (404 million kg) in the early 1980s. Since then U.S. pesticide consumption has dropped slightly; it is currently 750–800 million pounds (340–363 million kg) per year.

But such techniques led to obvious problems. Despite the massive addition of fertilizers, the soils slowly became exhausted. While the major nutrients extracted by the plants were being temporarily restored, many trace elements necessary for the ultimate sustainability of agriculture were not—examples of such trace elements include zinc, iron, boron, copper, molybdenum, and manganese. Furthermore, good healthy soil is more than just a handful of dry minerals and fertilizers. It is full of organic debris, humus, and living organisms including worms, beneficial insects, fungi, and bacteria. These organisms help mix and aerate the nutrients. The texture, structure, and quality of the soil are necessary for the roots of plants to take hold and the soil to retain water—which helps minimize both droughts and waterlogging of the earth below. Dumping massive amounts of toxic substances (in the form of pesticides and herbicides) literally kills the soil. Dead soil loses its structure and no longer functions properly. Given the massive amounts of poisons regularly used in some modern agriculture and the length of time they last before breaking down into less harmful substances, the soil can be irrevocably destroyed. (Many of these pesticides are extremely hazardous to their human creators as well as being harmful to the soil. Walking through some cropfields can be dangerous to one's health due to all the toxic chemicals used on the plants.) An unstable, dead soil may quickly erode away, perhaps further spreading the noxious chemicals that killed it.

The Green Revolution

Shortly after the end of World War II, modern, chemically based agriculture began to be used on a large scale in the industrialized countries. In the 1960s the Food and Agriculture Organization of the United Nations began a massive program to increase world food production, especially in the de-

Seed Banks

Around the world as forests are cleared and organisms are assaulted by humans, species are going extinct. This results in a loss of natural biodiversity, and as each species has its own genetic material—its own germ plasm—the ultimate result is a loss of genes. Sometimes this destruction of species and their contained germ plasm is referred to as "genetic erosion." Using traditional breeding methods or modern biotechnology, plant breeders and researchers can manipulate the germ plasm of species to develop new breeds and varieties of plants and animals, including the common domesticated crops that the vast majority of humans depend on. But the plant and animal breeders must have the raw material—the raw genes—to use in their manipulations. Genetic erosion is a very serious problem since once the species or variety and its genes are gone, they are lost forever.

As the many traditional varieties of crops give way to a handful of super-productive strains introduced as part of the Green Revolution, older varieties run the risk of going extinct. For example, in India traditionally 30,000 varieties of rice were grown, but now three-quarters of the rice production on the subcontinent is based on fewer than 10 varieties. Likewise, Sri Lankan farmers traditionally grew approximately 2000 varieties of rice; now they concentrate on only five major varieties. Similarly, about 22,000 varieties of wheat are known, but only a very small number of them make up the majority of wheat production. Current estimates are that by the middle of the twenty-first century at least 25% of all plant species will be extinct.

Of course, the best ways to stem genetic erosion are to preserve the natural habitats where wild species and varieties live and to encourage the growing of traditional crops as opposed to large, modern monocultures. A second, less desirable way—but necessary given the present situation of continued environmental destruction—is to preserve as large a sample of the natural biodiversity as possible in parks, preserves, zoos, botanical gardens, and seed banks. Such techniques tend to be more successful for seed-bearing plants than for animals—many animals will not breed in captivity and thus cannot be maintained for any substantial length of time. Also, most animal species are insects that do not lend themselves to the setting of a traditional zoo or park. For plants, however, large seed banks have been established throughout the world. Though modern techniques allow some seeds to be stored for

FIGURE 1
Agricultural Research Service technician Jim Bruce prepares to retrieve a seed sample from USDA's National Seed Storage Laboratory, Fort Collins, Colorado. (*Source:* Photo courtesy of ARS, USDA.)

decades, even in seed banks the seeds cannot be stored indefinitely and still remain viable (alive); periodically, they must be grown and new, fresh seeds produced.

One of the largest seed banks is the U.S. Department of Agriculture's National Seed Storage Laboratory at Colorado State University, Fort Collins, Colorado, where 228,000 seed samples are stored (Fig. 1). The gene bank of the International Rice Research Institute in Los Banos, the Philippines, has a collection of some 86,000 varieties of rice. The International Potato Center in Peru preserves thousands of types of potatoes. The Royal Botanical Gardens at Kew, England, is amassing a collection of thousands of seeds from threatened arid, semi-arid, and tropical regions. Around the world hundreds of institutions, groups, and private individuals are preserving the genetic heritage of the plant world. This heritage is invaluable for breeding new crops that can resist new pests and other onslaughts.

In the past epidemics have destroyed substantial portions of crops, with devastating results for the peoples who depended on them. The classical Mayans may have overspecialized on just a few varieties of maize (corn) that were then destroyed around 900 A.D. by a virus—resulting in the collapse of Mayan civilization. The Irish potato famine of 1845, which caused nearly a million human deaths by starvation, began when a fungus was introduced from Mexico. Another fungus, the corn leaf blight, destroyed half the corn crop in states from Florida to Texas in 1970. With access to the variety of germ plasm stored in seed and gene banks, plant breeders have a chance to stave off such disasters by developing new, resistant strains of the affected crops. Growing many different varieties of crops lessens the impact of epidemics.

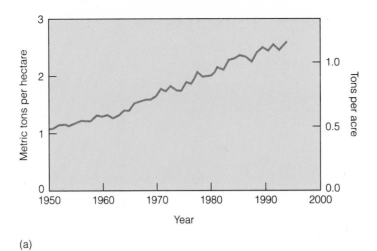

(a)

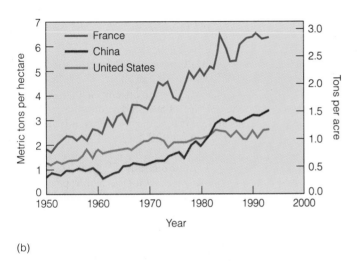

(b)

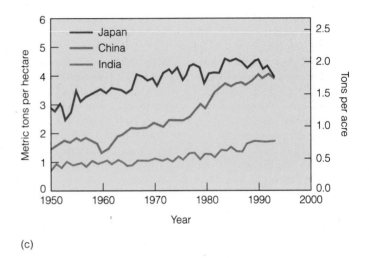

(c)

■ **FIGURE 13–8**
(a) World grain yields, 1950–1994; (b) wheat yields in the United States, France, and China, 1950–1993; and (c) rice yields in Japan, China, and India, 1950–1993. These spectacular increases in yields were a result of the Green Revolution. (*Source:* Based on data found in L. R. Brown, H. Kane, and D. M. Roodman, *Vital Signs 1994* [New York: W. W. Norton, 1994] and L. R. Brown, N. Lenssen, and H. Kane, *Vital Signs 1995* [New York: W. W. Norton, 1995]. Reprinted with permission of Worldwatch Institute, Washington, D.C., Copyright 1994.)

veloping countries. This effort was based on the use of modern agricultural techniques applied to high-yielding, western-designed crops. The resulting food production gains of the 1950s through 1980s (■ Fig. 13–8) are often termed the Green Revolution.

The immediate, short-term gains of the Green Revolution were truly impressive. For instance, according to one estimate, between 1950 and 1985 world grain production rose from approximately 661 million tons (600 million metric tons) per year to over 1984 million tons (1800 million metric tons) per year, with an average annual growth rate of 2.7%. This growth rate in grain production was slightly greater than the rate of human population growth across the planet, with the net result that per capita grain production rose (see Fig. 13–5). By other estimates, cereal grain harvests increased by more than two and a half times, between 1950 and 1984, while world population slightly more than doubled; therefore, the per capita production of cereals increased slightly over this 35-year period.

Given the increase in the Earth's population from just slightly over 3 billion in 1960 to the present 5.8 billion, the Green Revolution may have staved off immediate starvation for billions, but this has come at a price. For reasons discussed in the last section, the massive application of "modern" agricultural techniques has resulted in numerous problems, and it is unclear whether current food production levels will be maintainable for much longer. The mid-1980s saw record harvests, but these quickly vanished as droughts in certain countries during 1987 and 1988 cut into world grain stocks, bringing them to their lowest levels in many years (see Fig. 13–6). Even with better weather in 1989, the world grain harvest came in an estimated 19.8 million tons (18 million metric tons) below the projected consumption of 1857 million tons (1685 million metric tons), thus cutting into stocks further.

More telling, perhaps, is that the average annual rates of global food production expansion have been steadily declining since the 1960s. Between 1966 and 1976, global food production increased at an average rate of 3.5% a year, but between 1980 and 1990, it averaged only 2.2% a year. In other words, the Green Revolution was giving fewer and fewer results. If this decline continues, very shortly the annual increases in food production will fall below the rate of population growth (about 1.7%). We must expect such a decline, for the Green Revolution techniques are on the whole based on unsustainable agricultural practices.

In many areas **soil fertility** is declining rapidly as nutrients are extracted from the soil, but not returned in kind. Massive irrigation, even in countries where forms of irrigation have been successfully carried out for millennia, is causing waterlogging and salinization at unprecedented rates. In arid and semiarid regions, this often leads to **desertification** (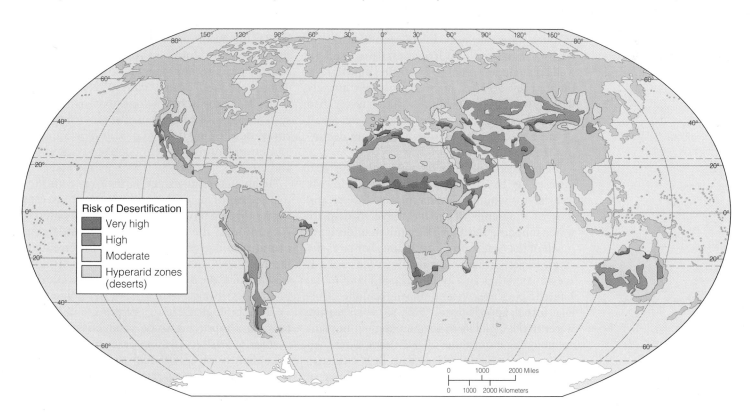 Fig. 13–9), the spread of desertlike conditions due to human exploitation and misuse of the land. In China over 2.2 million acres (900,000 hectares) of agricultural land have had to be abandoned since 1980 due to problems with salinization and waterlogging. Similarly, 7.2 million acres (2.9 million hectares) were removed from use in the Soviet Union between 1971 and 1985, and in India the newly irrigated land that is put into production each year is counterbalanced by damaged land that must be removed from production. In Egypt irrigation has been a necessity since ancient times, yet traditionally the fields were not used continuously—

the fields were allowed to lie fallow, and thus the accumulating salts could be naturally washed out and the land rejuvenated. Since about 1960 intensive modern irrigation has caused salinization of about a third of Egypt's cultivated land, and an estimated 90% is suffering from the effects of waterlogging.

Just as serious as nutrient depletion, salinization, and waterlogging are the effects of toxics (in the form of pesticides and herbicides) and soil erosion. Pollution from herbicides and pesticides is a global problem: it destroys not only the living organisms in the soil, but other wildlife and vegetation as well, and is directly harmful to the human population. Denuded soils quickly erode, and topsoil loss is a serious global problem (discussed further below). A study in Tanzania found that land with natural vegetation cover suffered virtually no topsoil loss and absorbed almost all the rainfall, compared to land that was either artificially cultivated or left bare. It has been estimated that currently about 28.7 billion tons (26 billion metric tons) of topsoil are lost worldwide due to erosion every year. It can take up to 1000 years to form a layer of soil 0.4 inch (1 centimeter) thick, yet it can be lost in just a few years due to poor agricultural management. At current rates of erosion, some researchers estimate that the once fertile land of the U.S. corn belt could be nearly depleted of topsoil before the middle of the twenty-first century.

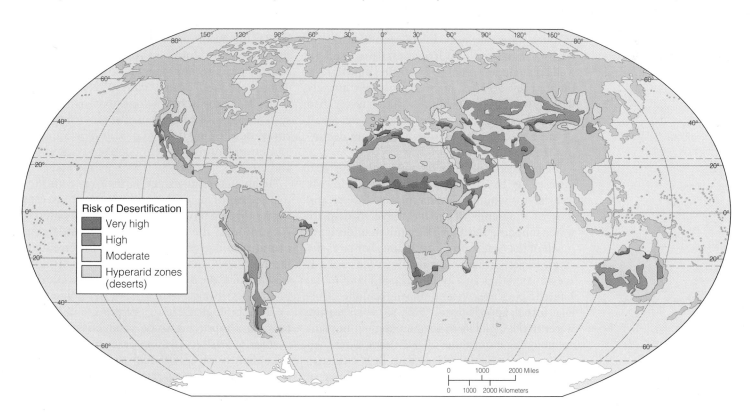

FIGURE 13–9
Deserts and areas at risk of desertification. (*Source:* Based on United Nations data.)

The Green Revolution has also been held responsible for the contamination and depletion of groundwater supplies in many parts of the world. Agrochemicals—artificial fertilizers, pesticides, herbicides, nitrates (derived from fertilizers), and other chemicals (many of which are highly toxic and carcinogenic)—applied in abundance to fields have penetrated down and polluted groundwater supplies. An estimated 50 million people in the United States are potentially exposed to pesticide-contaminated groundwater used for drinking. Contaminated groundwater is often virtually impossible to clean up. Underground aquifers are cool, dark, and well protected; they are characterized by poor water circulation, contain little in the way of life-forms, and thus form an ideal place for contaminants to be stored and remain stable (and toxic) for centuries or millennia. Deep in the aquifer there are no natural mechanisms to break down or neutralize contaminating toxics, so they remain indefinitely. Many authorities feel that in most cases a badly contaminated groundwater supply must simply be dismissed as a future source of fresh water.

The Green Revolution has also greatly stressed the supplies of fresh water. Many of the miracle crops of the Green Revolution were hybrid varieties that, though they may have been more productive, required much more water than traditional varieties of wheat and rice. In addition, in some areas crops for export were introduced that required even greater amounts of water—a case in point is sugarcane, which can require 10 times as much water as wheat. Furthermore, arid land was put under artificial irrigation using modern wells that tapped deep underground aquifers. In the past few decades, many areas have routinely withdrawn water from aquifers much faster than the aquifers are recharged by rain. The net result of these practices is that water tables are declining around the world.

In many parts of India, the water table has been lowered by 16–32 feet (5–10 meters) below its natural (pre–human intervention) levels, and tens of thousands of villages have inadequate water supplies. The Ogallala aquifer, underlying much of the American Great Plains, contains the single largest groundwater supply in the world. It is estimated that 20% of all irrigated land in the United States uses water pumped from the Ogallala. It took approximately 500,000 years for the water in the Ogallala to accumulate, but humans are pumping it out about 10,000 times faster than it is currently being replenished. Best estimates are that the Ogallala will be totally depleted of water in 25 to 50 years.

Beyond the Green Revolution—Integrated Pest Management and Biological Control

The acme of the Green Revolution, with its heavy dependence on synthetic chemical compounds—fertilizers, pesticides, and herbicides—and its use of water-consuming, genetically identical monocultures grown in factory-style intensity with the help of heavy equipment powered by fossil fuels, has now passed. The gains of the Green Revolution were impressive, but they were achieved unsustainably. The down side of the Green Revolution has been environmental damage to an extent previously unknown in recorded history.

Fortunately, "new" (in fact, based on traditional practices), ecologically sound, and sustainable methods of growing food are being used by an increasing number of farmers around the world. New methods of "no-till" planting, where only a narrow slit is cut through the sod and crop residues in order to plant the new crop, can help protect the soil from erosion and degradation. Drip irrigation techniques can drastically reduce water usage and losses and help avoid such problems as soil salinization and waterlogging. Also popular are the concepts of **Integrated Pest Management (IPM)**, the use of **biological controls**, and **organic farming** (see Chapter 15 for further discussion of these topics).

The basic philosophy behind IPM and biological control is that the farmer does not try to totally eliminate pests, as was often the idea behind using massive amounts of poisons as part of the Green Revolution, but simply attempts to control pests so that they do not cause serious damage. IPM advocates "natural" controls, such as the use of the pests' biological predators. IPM systems also use cultural practices, such as **crop rotation**, allowing fields to lie fallow periodically, and interplanting, to help control various pests and weeds.

To an increasing extent, farmers are returning to the use of natural fertilizers—such as crop wastes that are plowed back into the soil or left to rot on top of the soil, natural compost, animal manures, and even human wastes. In some areas farmers have taken up true organic farming, which avoids the use of any synthetic chemicals—be they fertilizers, pesticides, or herbicides.

IPM, biological control of pests, and organic farming are proving to be productive and economically feasible. In some cases the yields have been slightly lower (although sometimes they are higher), but since the farmers did not have to purchase chemicals, their costs were lower and their profits the same or higher as they would have been using more conventional methods. In fact, one study of nine crops in 15 U.S. states found that the farmers using IPM systems had a collective profit of $579 million more than their projected earnings using other methods. Thus, these new techniques are economically viable—they will not drive farmers out of business, nor cause a dramatic drop in food production. Most importantly, however, they do not deteriorate the land and general environment to the extent that the techniques of the Green Revolution did. In fact, at their best, organic farming and IPM, combined with very limited use of synthetic chemicals, appear to be sustainable—a claim the Green Revolution could never approach.

Biotechnology and Transgenic Crops

The Green Revolution was based on many new "miracle" strains of crops that grew faster and produced higher yields. Many hope that we can continue to increase food production through **biotechnology** and **bioengineering**—the artificial use and manipulation of organisms toward human ends, including genetic manipulations that can in effect produce new types of organisms (see Issues in Perspective 13–3). Genetically transformed crops (**transgenic** varieties) are already a reality. By the year 2000, 50 or more genetically engineered fruits, vegetables, and other products are expected to be available to the American consumer.

In 1994 the Flavr Savr tomato, developed by Calgene, Inc., of Davis, California, became the first genetically engineered whole food product to hit the markets. Essentially, the Flavr Savr has been designed so that an altered gene blocks production of a certain enzyme that controls ripening and softening. Normally, tomatoes are harvested before they are ripe, shipped, and then artificially ripened (such as by using ethylene gas) once they reach their destination. Flavor is lost with such procedures, though, and an estimated 30% of the tomato crop is still destroyed by rotting or damaged during shipping. The Flavr Savr can be left on the vine longer, so it ripens naturally and develops a better flavor, resists spoiling during the shipping process, and has a longer shelf life once it arrives at a supermarket or home. Many other fruits and vegetables are plagued by the same ripening and spoilage problems, and could potentially benefit from similar genetic engineering. Already work is being actively pursued with bananas (notorious for their short shelf lives and difficulty in shipping).

Genetic engineering can also change the taste or other properties of plants by modifying their sugar and starch content. Peas, corn, tomatoes, and other crops can be made sweeter, or the starch content of potatoes can be raised, making them more suitable for potato chips.

In the long run, genetic engineering's most important contribution may be to increase the resistance of crops to insect and disease vectors. The common bacterium *Bacillus thuringiensis* (commonly abbreviated as BT) naturally produces a substance that is toxic to certain types of pest caterpillars. For several decades, BT and its derivatives have been used as a natural pesticide on crops with good results; it is relatively nontoxic to birds, mammals, and various nonpest insects. Through biotechnology, the BT bacterial genes can be implanted into the crops themselves so that they produce the toxin. Such a transgenic organism is in effect mostly plant but also part bacterium. Already corn, potato, and cotton versions have been developed; assuming they are approved by the U.S. government, they should come into common use within the next decade. Spiders and other creatures also produce toxins that kill insect pests. Work is proceeding on inserting the appropriate spider genes, for instance, into suitable crops. Plants that resist viral, bacterial, and fungal diseases are also being designed by implanting genes from various viruses, bacteria, plants, and animals into crop plants.

Clearly, transgenic crops will require reduced loads of standard pesticides and will have an advantage in resisting diseases. However, researchers point out that genetically engineered crops must be utilized carefully. Many insects and diseases can evolve very rapidly. If too much reliance is placed on one or a few types of transgenic crops, natural pest populations may rapidly evolve immunities to the toxins given off by the crops. Already there are reports of insects that can tolerate fairly high levels of BT toxins. This situation is analogous to cases where insect populations evolve the ability to withstand the assaults of standard insecticides. To prevent immunities from developing in the pest insects or disease vectors, IPM (integrated pest management) techniques can be used in conjunction with transgenic crops. For example, different types of transgenic and standard crops might be combined in the same field. The unaltered, nonresistant stands of plants would act as a feeding and breeding ground for insects that are not immune to the toxins engineered into the transgenic crops. Thus, the more damaging individuals—those carrying nat-

EnviroNet
www.jbpub.com/environet

Bioengineering

In recent years scientists have been making many advances in biotechnology. Using recombinant DNA techniques, which employ special enzymes to cut and splice sections of DNA, specific genes or gene fragments can be removed from one species, modified or tailored as necessary, and inserted into another species. Genes need not even come from closely related species; animal genes can be inserted into plants.

Sometimes a technique known as a "gene gun" is used: DNA-coated particles are injected into a plant cell. The plant cell may then incorporate the DNA into its own system, and using the techniques of tissue culture, a complete plant can be grown from the single cell. Through continued tissue culture, multiple copies of a bioengineered plant can be produced. Once the plants reach a certain size, they can be transferred to a field and grown like any regular crop. Currently, clonal propagation and tissue culture techniques are commonly used to produce such plants as bananas and potatoes.

Tissue culture techniques also allow scientists to produce plants that are absolutely disease-free. If cultivated using traditional methods, such as tuber propagation or the production of seeds, a diseased plant may pass the disease pathogen (virus or microorganism) on to its offspring. With tissue culture, a diseased strain can be restored to health. Cell and embryo cloning techniques can also be applied to animals, such as cattle. Eggs can be artificially inseminated in the laboratory, genetically engineered, and finally implanted in surrogate mothers for final development into viable organisms.

Advanced tissue culture techniques may even eliminate the need to raise the entire adult organism. In a laboratory setting, plant tissue cultures many be induced to produce only that part of the plant that humans desire, such as the fruit or the oils, without "wasting" energy on the production of leaves, stems, and roots. Such techniques are already used to produce some flavorings and drugs, and similar methods have been applied to yeast and other microorganisms to produce special chemicals.

Advanced bioengineering techniques will surely account for many exciting innovations in the near future. Yet bioengineering is not without controversy. Concerns have been expressed that transgenic organisms might "escape" into nature and do untold damage to natural ecological systems. Past experience with natural organisms introduced by humans into new settings has demonstrated the potential for havoc. Yet many bioengineered organisms, such as specially designed bacteria, can grow only under very special conditions, and promoters doubt that they would ever survive in the "wild." Around the globe over a thousand field tests of bioengineered plants have been conducted, and no accidents or ill effects have occurred.

Some consumers fear that the ingestion of transgenic foods might be inherently harmful to human health. After undertaking extensive studies, specifically of the genetically engineered Flavr Savr tomato, the U.S. Food and Drug Administration (FDA) has concluded that transgenic foods are as safe as unaltered foods. Indeed, some transgenic foods may be even safer than "natural" edible foods that contain low lev-

ural immunities—would never be allowed to dominate the population. By not overusing the resistant strains of crops, their effectiveness will be maintained.

Efforts are underway to genetically alter plant crops so that they will have increased tolerances to stresses such as drought, cold, heat, or high soil salinities. So far, however, less progress has been made in this area than in developing insect- and disease-resistant strains. Stress-tolerant crops could be a real boon in developing countries that have only marginally arable lands, suffer from soil salinization, or lack adequate irrigation systems. Some observers worry, however, that in the long run stress-tolerant crops could cause more harm than good by encouraging the continued cultivation of marginal, fragile, or already damaged lands until they are completely destroyed.

From a human dietary perspective, an extremely important potential of genetic engineering is to improve the nutritional content of familiar foods. People whose staple is rice often suffer from vitamin A deficiency; thus, researchers are working to engineer a rice variety that will contain substantial quantities of vitamin A. Likewise, levels of various proteins might be increased both in crops that are eaten directly by humans and in those used as feed for farm animals.

Genetic engineering is also being used to meet the specialized needs of consumers in industrial countries. Coffee with a lower caffeine content is being developed. Rapeseed (oilseed, canola) varieties are being developed that will

els of toxins. The FDA has ruled that transgenic foods merit special testing only if they contain increased levels of toxins, allergens, or substances not normally found in roughly equivalent foods.

Another area of concern is who should own, pay for, and be allowed to use newly bioengineered organisms. Should an individual or company that engineers a new organism be allowed to patent that organism just as any other invention can be patented? In the United States, all new life-forms, other than humans, are subject to being patented. The patent holder can then charge potential users of the life-form. Advocates of the patent system argue that developing a new strain of crop or bacterium can be very costly and that the investor deserves an equitable return on the money and energy spent in the endeavor. On the other hand, allowing patents on new life-forms dampens the free exchange of scientific knowledge, often to the disadvantage of developing countries, which could most benefit from bioengineering advances but can least afford to pay patent fees. For these reasons,

many developing countries in particular have refused to acknowledge or respect patent claims on life-forms.

Some developing countries are especially bitter about the prospect of paying patent fees for the use of transgenic life-forms when the new organisms have been engineered from the genes of natural species that come from their forests. The tropical regions of the world (which are mostly in developing countries) are vast genetic repositories, and scientists, pharmaceutical company representatives, and others have traditionally felt free to remove plants and animals without compensating the local government. The genetic material so harvested then forms the basis for bioengineered, patented life-forms and their derivatives (such as medicines), which may produce huge profits for the investors and may even be offered back to the host country for a price. Understandably, the governments of the developing nations are demanding just compensation for the use of their natural genetic resources. The Convention on Biodiversity, signed by over 150 countries at the 1992

Earth Summit, calls, in general terms, for just such compensation, but the specific details of what particular genetic material is worth can be difficult to work out.

Yet resolutions to these problems are being found. Nonprofit organizations are developing transgenic crops and other organisms that will be made available for use by developing countries free of charge. International aid agencies are pumping money and expertise into biotechnology research to benefit underdeveloped nations. National governments of some developing nations are pursuing their own biotechnology research programs. And even large for-profit companies are forming partnerships with developing countries. Perhaps the best example is the alliance between Merck, a giant pharmaceutical company, and the Costa Rican National Biodiversity Institute. Merck not only paid outright for the right to prospect for drugs in the country's forests, but it agreed to help train native Costa Ricans in drug research and will pay royalties to Costa Rica on any products that it develops from the venture.

produce specialized oils for use as lubricants, in cosmetics, for soaps, and in cooking. A mustard family plant has been designed to produce the biodegradable plastic known as polyhydroxybutyrate (PHB), which is similar to polypropylene (derived from petroleum). One concern over this kind of research is that currently many specialty oils, waxes, and rubbers are derived from tropical forests and are among the major exports of the developing countries. Successful development of "oil crops" could restrict the market for these goods. At the same time, however, by growing "plastic crops," the developing countries could produce their own plastics without relying on oil or petrochemical facilities. Additionally, biodegradable plastics could alleviate many of the disposal problems associated with traditional nonbiodegradable plastics (see Chapter 19).

Nonagricultural Food Sources

It is sometimes suggested that we could feed extra billions by harvesting the natural, renewable biological resources that grow wild on land and in the seas. Humans have been hunting wildlife and collecting naturally growing edible plants for millennia, but the reserves of such sources are virtually depleted. Certainly, traditional hunting and gathering on land is not a viable option for feeding anything but an infinitesimally small proportion of the current global population.

The ocean, however, is often viewed in a different light. Using modern techniques, tens of millions of tons of fish and other seafood are harvested from the sea each year. The oceans are so vast, couldn't we make a dent in our food shortages (especially protein shortages, for fish is high in protein) by drawing more from this resource?

Many people have a mistaken impression of the magnitude and abundance of life in the seas. They may be familiar with the productive shallow-water coastal and reefal areas, which are unrepresentative of the vast majority of the oceans. Most of the open ocean is a "biological desert" that is very sparsely populated by life-forms. Only certain areas where nutrients upwell and collect near the surface are highly productive. Unfortunately, we are already closely approaching, and have perhaps now surpassed, the maximum sustainable yield of fishing from the oceans: estimated at approximately 88 to 110 million tons (80 to 100 million metric tons) of fish a year. Fishing on the open oceans has often been done on a massive scale utilizing driftnets. These huge nylon nets—some are up to 30 miles (50 kg) long and 40 feet (12 m) deep—indiscriminately catch everything in their path—squid, fishes, dolphins, seals, sea turtles, and even water birds. The oceans are literally mined; fishes and other organisms are removed

much more quickly than they can replenish themselves. Many animals in addition to the desired fishes are caught inadvertently; these carcasses are simply thrown overboard as waste. Fortunately, there has been mounting international pressure to limit the use of driftnets. Since 1992 the United Nations has imposed an international moratorium on the use of driftnets over 1.55 miles (2.5 kg) long. But even if driftnets are totally banned, some fishing fleets will continue to utilize them illegally on the high seas. Furthermore, many broken pieces of nets or damaged and abandoned nets ("ghost nets") are floating unattended through the oceans. These ghost nets continue to catch and kill sea organisms indiscriminately.

Already certain species of ocean organisms have been overexploited by humans, perhaps to the point of **commercial extinction**—that is, it is no longer economically viable to harvest them. Populations that have dropped to such low levels may never fully recover; indeed, they may become extinct. Classic examples of such overexploitation include the Peruvian anchovy fishery, the Alaskan king crab fishery, and the exploitation of whales. The Peruvian anchovy industry more than tripled its catch from 1960 to 1970, peaking at about 14.3 million tons (13 million metric tons) in 1970. By 1973 it had collapsed to less than 2.2 million tons (2 million metric tons), possibly due to both overexploitation and adverse climatic conditions. It has never recovered the levels of peak production. The Alaskan king crab story presents a similar scenario: peak production in 1980 was 93,000 tons (84,000 metric tons), but this dropped to 7700 tons (7000 metric tons) in 1985 and has not fully recovered since. Whales have been hunted to commercial extinction over several centuries, beginning on a large scale in the 1700s and early 1800s and continuing into the present century. First, one species of whale and then another has been hunted to commercial extinction; whalers simply switched from species to species as each became depleted. The right whale, the sperm whale, the humpback whale, the giant blue whale, the fin whale, and the sei and minke whales have all been heavily hunted and are now greatly reduced in population sizes—in some cases their current populations are only a few percent of what they were before humans intervened.

Taking a global perspective, until only about a decade ago world fish catches were increasing virtually every year. In 1950 the world catch (including freshwater catches and fish farming) totaled 24 million tons (22 million metric tons), or 18.96 pounds (8.6 kg) of seafood per person (■ Fig. 13–10). In

FIGURE 13–10
(a) World fish catches, 1950–1994; and (b) world fish catch per person, 1950–1994. (*Source: Based on data found in L. R. Brown, H. Kane, and D. M. Roodman, Vital Signs 1994* [New York: W. W. Norton, 1994] and L. R. Brown, N. Lenssen, and H. Kane, *Vital Signs 1995* [New York: W. W. Norton, 1995]. Reprinted with permission of Worldwatch Institute, Washington, D.C., Copyright 1994.)

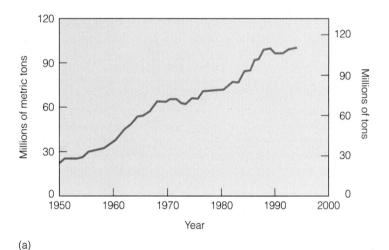

(a)

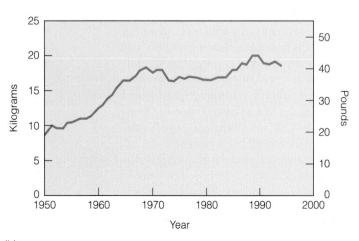

(b)

1989, a record year, the catch was 110 million tons (100 million metric tons), and the per capita catch was 42.3 pounds (19.2 kg)—the record year in terms of fish per capita was actually 1988 at 42.8 pounds (19.4 kg). Since 1989 the annual catch has generally been somewhat over 100 million tons (in the high 90s million metric tons), and with the increasing world population, by 1994 the per capita catch had fallen to 39.7 pounds (18.0 kg) despite a record catch of 111 million tons (101 million metric tons). Even though the worldwide fish harvest has apparently stabilized, locally fish catches have fluctuated dramatically. The total marine catch has been stagnant for several years at about 92 to 93 million tons (about 84 million metric tons) annually; the remainder of the catch consists of the freshwater catch and fish farming. Some authorities worry that with continued high levels of fishing, the supply might undergo a major global collapse. Accordingly, some governments are limiting fish catches; they reason that it is better to protect fish stocks now (even if it means a loss of jobs in the short term) to ensure continued fishing in the future. The European Community, for instance, is reducing its fishing fleet by about one-fifth, and Iceland is severely restricting its cod catch.

In addition to mining our oceans, we are polluting them at a tremendous rate. Some seafood species are being killed off altogether, and others contain such high levels of toxic chemicals that they are unfit to eat. Many coastal cities continue to dump their raw or inadequately treated sewage and waste directly into the oceans. Every year European countries dump a variety of pollutants into the North Sea including approximately 50,000 tons (46,000 metric tons) of phosphorus, 120 tons (110 metric tons) of mercury, and 24,000 tons (21,800 metric tons) of lead. This pollution is destroying the wildlife. In 1988, 10,000 seals died in the North Sea, apparently from a viral infection that they could not fight off because the pollutants in the water had weakened their immune systems. Beluga whales inhabiting the St. Lawrence River contain such high levels of heavy metals, PCBs, and other pollutants in their flesh that their corpses are classified as toxic waste when they die.

The surfaces of the oceans are manifesting the symptoms of the "pollution disease." Around the world, surface algal blooms, sometimes called the "red tide," are appearing with increasing frequency. Currently, about two dozen red tides occur each year in Hong Kong's harbor, where they were unknown before the mid-1970s. In a red tide, tiny algae that live as phytoplankton in the upper layers of the oceans proliferate out of control. Apparently, sewage, fertilizer runoff, and other pollutants that are released into the water are fit nutrients for the algae, which grow uncontrollably on the surface of the water. As the algae grow, they deplete the oxygen in the water that is necessary for the survival of other organisms. Shellfishes, crabs, shrimp, a variety of fishes, and numerous other organisms can literally be suffocated under the red tide ( Fig. 13–11). An algal bloom off the coast of Norway reportedly killed more than 1.34 million pounds (609,000 kg) of salmon and trout. If poisoned shellfish are eaten by other organisms, including humans, they can cause food poisoning in the consumers.

Perhaps even more pernicious than overfishing and pollution are the effects that global warming and the destruction of the ozone layer may have on marine life. Abnormally warm ocean temperatures appear to be killing reefs, and in 1988 when ozone levels reportedly declined 15% due to the ozone hole over Antarctica, phyto-

FIGURE 13–11
Red tide seen along a coastline.
(*Source:* S. Berry/Visuals Unlimited.)

plankton levels also decreased by 15–20%. Phytoplankton are the small, photosynthetic organisms that inhabit the top layer of the oceans; they form the basis of the oceanic food chain and also help the oceans to absorb carbon dioxide (the prime greenhouse gas). If increasing global heating and destruction of the ozone layer adversely affect the phytoplankton, this will obviously have a detrimental effect on the entire ocean ecosystem. Some researchers have even suggested that life in the oceans may collapse. As phytoplankton die, the oceans will take up less carbon dioxide, which will lead to increased global warming, which in turn will accelerate the destruction of the ocean ecosystem. Ironically, both too much phytoplankton (producing red tide) and too few phytoplankton (destroying the base of the marine food chain) are extremely detrimental to oceanic ecosystems.

What about the possibility of increased "fish farming" through **aquaculture** (used to refer to aquatic organism farming in general, or freshwater seafood farming in particular) or **mariculture** (saltwater seafood farming)? Organisms such as salmon, shrimp, and edible seaweed are already being raised under controlled conditions

in many countries. Aquaculture systems can be extremely productive and efficient at producing animal protein—generally more efficient than terrestrial farms (see Issues in Perspective 13–4). The drawbacks of aquaculture are that it is very labor-intensive, it can involve very intricate management of delicate ecosystems, and it is not suited to all locations. One must have adequate water of the right purity, salinity, and so forth, and temperatures need to be maintained within close tolerances. The start-up and maintenance costs of aquaculture can be relatively high. Some of the best locations for aquaculture are coastal areas that are being destroyed by pollution and development. For these sorts of reasons, many experts have little hope that aquaculture will ever significantly relieve the world's hunger.

THE SOIL OF THE EARTH

Soil is one of our most precious commodities: it is vital for the health and well-being not only of human civilization, but of most terrestrial ecosystems. Without soil we could not grow food, our single most important activity.

Yet we are quickly squandering our natural inheritance of soils. Various estimates suggest that we are losing soil to **erosion** at a rate of 27.5 to 82.6 billion tons (25–75 billion metric tons) a year globally. The annual loss of topsoil from agricultural lands averages about 7.6 tons per acre (17 metric tons per hectare) in the United States and Europe and as much as 13.4 to 17.8 tons per acre (30–40 metric tons per hectare) in parts of Asia, Africa, and South America. In contrast, erosion rates in undisturbed natural forests are on the order of 0.0018 to 0.022 tons per acre (0.004 to 0.05 metric tons per hectare) per year. It has been estimated that soil erosion costs the United States some $44 billion a year in direct damage to agricultural lands and indirect damage to infrastructures, waterways, and health (Fig. 13–12). Globally, the direct and indirect costs of soil erosion may be close to $400 billion a year.

As soils are depleted on prime agricultural lands, crop yields decrease. For every inch (2.54 cm) of topsoil lost, average corn and wheat yields drop by about 6%. Generally, at least 6 inches (15 cm) of topsoil are needed to grow crops. Once the layer of topsoil has become too thin, the land is no longer useful for agricultural production.

We can sustain some soil loss, for soil is continually produced on the surface of the Earth. The generation and maintenance of soils are functions that are performed for "free" by healthy natural ecosystems. Under the best of conditions, however, soil formation is a very slow process. Some scientists have estimated that soil is forming in the United States at an average rate of only about an inch (about 2.5 cm) per century, which is equivalent to about 1.65 tons per acre (3.7 metric tons per hectare) per year; other researchers suggest

Aquaculture and Mariculture

As catches from natural fisheries have stabilized or even decreased, production from fish farms has doubled in the last 10 years. At present, about 15.3 million tons (13.9 million metric tons) of seafood protein are produced by aquaculture and mariculture annually. China is the leader in fish farming, producing almost half of the world's output. The next largest producer is India, which farms more than 1.1 million tons (1 million metric tons) of seafood a year, and Japan is a close runner up.

Fish farms produce not only fishes, such as flounder, salmon, tilapia, and catfishes, but also oysters, clams, shrimp, prawns, and many other aquatic organisms (Fig. 1). About two-thirds of fish farming activities take place along inland rivers and in lakes, ponds, and artificial tanks, while the remainder are located along the coasts, in bays, and sometimes even in the open ocean.

An important reason for the steady expansion of aquaculture and mariculture is that fishes and other aquatic organisms are typically very efficient at turning feed from plants into animal meat. Fishes are cold-blooded so they do not burn excess calories to keep warm. The water they live in helps support their body weight, so they expend less energy than comparable terrestrial animals. As a result, only two pounds (or less) of feed is typically required to produce a pound of fish, far less than is needed to produce an equivalent amount of beef or pork (see Issues in Perspective 13–1).

There are numerous drawbacks to fish farming, however. Aquatic farming naturally requires tremendous quantities of clean water, a substance in increasingly short supply (see Chapter 11). Of course, the water is not consumed in the same way that water is when crop plants are irrigated, but fouling of the water environment can be a real problem. Excess organic wastes may pollute the water to the extent that all aquatic organisms suffer; for instance, excess wastes may induce algae blooms, resulting in oxygen depletion and suffocation of fishes, mollusks, and crustaceans.

Like any animal farmers, fish farmers must generally purchase grain products to feed their stock. Specialized and expensive equipment may be necessary, especially if the stock is being raised in artificial tanks, ponds, or holding areas. Hormones, antibodies, vaccines, and other medical supplies may be required. The dense populations of fish that are typical of modern fish farms are extremely vulnerable to infectious diseases. Inbreeding, resulting in genetically weakened strains, can also be a problem, particularly if cultivated organisms escape and interbreed with a wild population.

But perhaps the biggest problem with fish farming is the space it requires. The best settings for fish farms are along coasts, rivers, and lakes. But these same areas are considered prime waterfront property, and land values are often very high. Furthermore, in some areas coastal mangrove forests and other wetland areas have been cleared in order to build fish farms. But these coastal wetlands are the breeding grounds for wild fishes, so clearing such areas often causes natural (wild) fish populations to decline.

Still, fish farming continues to expand, and with good reason. It is one of the most efficient means of turning plant products into animal meat. And with proper management, fish farming can have a very low impact on the environment. As the population increases in future years, we can expect that more and more of the animal protein in our diet will come from the cultivated aquatic realm.

FIGURE 1

A Chinese aquaculture facility located next to residential apartments.
(*Source:* Sylvan Wittwer/Visuals Unlimited.)

that the average rate may be closer to 0.45 tons per acre (1 metric ton per hectare) per year. Around the world some studies suggest that average rates of topsoil formation may be as little as an inch (2.5 cm) in 500 or a 1000 years. The inescapable conclusion is that we are losing our soils more quickly than they are forming. At present, modern civilization is living off—and eroding into—the capital of the past (the soils accumulated over many thousands of years), rather than using the soils in a sustainable manner. We need to learn to live off income; that is, to deplete the soils no faster than they are forming under natural conditions.

What Is Soil?

Soil is a combination of weathered, disintegrated, decomposed rocks and minerals (technically known as regolith) plus the decayed remains of plants and animals (organic matter or humus), small living animals, plants, fungi, bacteria, other microscopic organisms, water, and air (good soil has commercial value:—see Issues in Perspective 13–5). Typical soil is about 50% mineral and organic matter by volume and about 50% water and air. There are literally thousands of different types of soils around the world, but they all serve the same vital functions in the ecosystems in which they are found. Soils hold nutrients and water in place so that the surface fauna and flora can grow and thrive. Without healthy, porous soils, most rainwater quickly runs off the surface of the land instead of soaking in. Soils supply the vital nutrients, such as usable nitrogen, phosphorus, sulfur, carbon, hydrogen, oxygen, and various trace elements and important compounds, to the plants that grow in the soil. As organisms die and are decomposed in the top layer of the soil, the nutrients are recycled back to the above-ground organisms.

Healthy soil is alive, a complex ecosystem unto itself. Without its living components, soil lacks its characteristic properties—texture, fertility, and the ability to dispose of wastes and recycle nutrients. An amazing number of organisms can live in a handful of soil. Larger animals that live in soils include earthworms, mites (relatives of spiders and ticks), millipedes, and insects. Under a square yard (0.84 m²) of pasture in Denmark, researchers found 40,000 small earthworms and related organisms, almost 10 million roundworms, and more than 40,000 mites and insects. This is not even taking truly microscopic organisms into account. An ounce (28.35 g) of good forest soil can contain well over 28 million bacteria, about 3 million yeast cells, and 1.4 million individual fungi organisms. An ounce of good agricultural soil can contain over 70 billion bacteria, 11 million fungi, 1.4 million algae organisms, and 850,000 protozoa.

A typical well-developed soil is not a homogeneous mass. It consists of layers or **soil horizons** that are approximately parallel to the surface of the Earth. The horizons have different biological, physical, and chemical attributes, such as the amount of living and dead organisms and organic matter they contain, water and air content, texture, structure, color, and mineral content. In any particular part of the world, the soil horizons develop to a characteristic degree based on the underlying bedrock, under the influence of the climate, flora, and fauna over time. In some places many horizons develop, whereas elsewhere only one or two horizons are distinguishable. From top to bottom, a typical soil profile (a vertical section through the soil at a particular locality) may exhibit the following basic soil horizons: the uppermost organic matter and humus (heavily decomposed organic matter), the **topsoil** (a mixture of mineral matter and humus, alive with microscopic and macroscopic organisms), the subsoil (composed mainly of minerals), a layer of partially disintegrated rock, and the underlying bedrock.

Global Assessment of Soil Degradation

For many years, the amount and degree of **soil degradation**, leading to land degradation, has been a topic of extreme controversy. For several decades, certain environmentalists have enumerated cases of **deforestation**, overgrazing, desertification, and clear destruction of once fertile lands. At the same time, other experts pointed out that crop yields and livestock production have increased significantly since World War II and concluded that land degradation is not a major global problem. This dispute was essentially unresolvable without a global database on soil degradation.

A major study entitled the Global Assessment of Soil Degradation (GLASOD) was sponsored by the United Nations Environment Programme and coordinated by the International Soil Reference and Information Centre in the Netherlands. GLASOD is actually a part of a larger study that is undertaking a very precise assessment of world soils and terrains, but that study will not be completed before the first decade of the twenty-first century. Given the importance of soil degradation, however, the preliminary GLASOD study was recently released.

Topsoil as a "Crop"

In the United States, topsoil has become a commodity that is openly bought and sold. Currently, in New England topsoil ranges in price from about $8 to $22 a cubic yard (0.765 m³) or more, depending on the quality of the soil and the location. This has lead to abuses by developers, landscapers, and others. Increasingly, developers are purchasing former farmland to build houses and other structures. In many cases, before starting construction, they remove most of the topsoil and sell it (Fig. 1), leaving unsuspecting homeowners wondering why

developed land sells for in most areas. Of course, once the topsoil has been removed and sold, the potential uses of the land are severely limited. It can no longer be used for agricultural purposes, and it is less desirable for certain building purposes. Left abandoned, the land will only deteriorate further.

Much of the topsoil goes to landfills where it is needed to cover the layers of garbage and eventually to cap the landfill once it is closed (see Chapter 19). Another portion of it goes for commercial landscaping. There is also a large demand for

FIGURE 1
During construction, such as for this new shopping mall, valuable topsoil may be removed and sold. (*Source:* W. A. Banaszewski/Visuals Unlimited.)

the soils in their yards are so thin.

Recently, however, some developers have discovered that it can be profitable to buy land solely for the purpose of removing and selling the topsoil, without even necessarily building on it afterward. In parts of New England, the rich topsoil is 10 feet (3 m) thick or more. An acre with topsoil 9 feet (2.74 m) thick will yield 14,520 cubic yards (11,108 m³) of topsoil; at the modest price of $10 a cubic yard, the topsoil could potentially be sold for $145,200—considerably more than un-

clean soil at hazardous waste cleanup sites. As part of many hazardous waste cleanups, contaminated soil must be removed and disposed of, leaving a need for fresh soil. Thus, a leaking oil tank in a residential area may contribute directly to the destruction of fertile agricultural land.

Some action has been taken to stop the wholesale removal of topsoils. A few local communities have passed laws against the practice, but even in places where it is illegal, topsoil sales continue to flourish. Another approach is for governments and

private organizations to buy or otherwise acquire land, or at least the development rights to land, in order to preserve it. In Massachusetts the state's Agricultural Restriction Program purchases the development rights to agricultural lands, usually for about 50 to 80% of the value of the land, and then allows farmers to continue to use the land for agricultural purposes. Unfortunately, the program does not have enough money to purchase rights to all the land that it would like to protect. There is a long waiting list of farmers eager to sell their development rights. In a related program, the Massachusetts Department of Environmental Management purchases farmland outright in order to protect it. But again funds always seem to be short; as of this writing, only about 10,000 acres (4000 hectares) had been purchased through this program.

An increasingly popular way to protect former farmlands, wooded areas, wetlands, and other open space from encroaching development is through private local landtrusts. The typical landtrust is a nonprofit charitable organization set up to hold and preserve land and development rights to land for the good of the local community. Landtrusts may acquire land through purchases or donations (since the gift is to a charitable organization, the donor often receives an immediate, tangible benefit in the form of a tax deduction). Even when landowners do not want to sell or donate their land outright, they may be interested in selling or donating deed restrictions to a landtrust. Thousands of landtrusts across the country, and around the world, can make a big difference in preserving our valuable soils, lands, and natural biotic resources. Grassroots landtrusts epitomize the old environmentalist saying: "Think globally, act locally."

The Rock Fences and Walls of New England— Symptoms of Environmental Destruction?

Recently, researchers such as geologist Robert M. Thorson at the University of Connecticut have developed a new theory on the rocks forming the stone fences and walls that are so common in New England (Fig. 1). Hitherto, it was generally assumed that the rocks were the rubble left after the retreat of the glaciers from the last ice age, and that the farmers had to clear the rocks away before they could till the fields. Thorson suggests the scenario is not quite so simple.

When Europeans first settled in New England, the land was covered with forests, but within a couple of centuries, three-quarters of the forests were removed. In the more densely populated areas, the land was stripped clear well before the American Revolution. Once cleared, much of the land was converted to farms, and thus the farmers had to clear the fields of rocks. But, Thorson has suggested, the very act of clearing the land of forest cover created much of the excess rock debris in the first place. Deforestation reduced the natural insulation of the soil and surface of the land, and freeze-thaw cycles freed subsurface stones and rock fragments, causing them to work up to the surface. During the winter, water in the soil and in cracks in rocks freezes and expands, breaking and lifting the rocks in the process. Once a rock is raised, sand, silt, and other small debris fall under it so that the rock never

FIGURE 1
This colonial stone fence in Attleboro, Massachusetts, is typical of the stone fences and walls found throughout the fields and forests of New England. (*Source:* Robert Thayer/Projections.)

drops completely to its lower level again. With repeated freezing and thawing, the rock works its way up through the soil column. The farmers found that their fields seemed to be growing rocks on a regular basis and that they periodically had to clear the rocks away. To dispose of the rocks, they simply dumped them along the edges of the fields, forming what would later be

considered the quaint New England stone fences and walls.

According to this interpretation, New England's stone fences record the progressive deforestation, soil degradation, and general environmental deterioration of the New England countryside at the hands of European settlers.

GLASOD, unlike many earlier studies, only looked at soil/land degradation that has occurred due to human intervention since World War II, specifically, from 1945 to 1990 (see Issues in Perspective 13–6 for an earlier example of land degradation). Hundreds of soil scientists measured the degree, area, and causes of land degradation since 1945, and the results were compiled by continental regions and globally (Table 13–1). The findings were alarming.

Globally, more than 4.85 billion acres (1.96 billion hectares), or 17% of the vegetated land surface of Earth, have been degraded by humans to some extent in less than half a century. Over 3 billion acres (1.2 billion hectares) were classified as suffering from moderate, severe, or extreme degradation. In the GLASOD classification system, light soil degradation applies to areas where only part of the topsoil has been lost, only shallow rills appear in the soil's surface, or only slight

TABLE 13–1 *Human-Induced Soil Degradation, 1945–1990*

REGION	TOTAL DEGRADED AREA (MILLION ACRES)	TOTAL DEGRADED AREA (MILLION HECTARES)	DEGRADED AREA AS A PERCENTAGE OF VEGETATED LAND
World			
Total degraded area	4854.0	1964.4	17.0
Moderate, severe, and extreme	3003.3	1215.4	10.5
Light	1850.8	749.0	6.5
Europe			
Total degraded area	540.9	218.9	23.1
Moderate, severe, and extreme	391.2	158.3	16.7
Light	149.7	60.6	6.4
Africa			
Total degraded area	1221.2	494.2	22.1
Moderate, severe, and extreme	792.2	320.6	14.4
Light	429.0	173.6	7.8
Asia			
Total degraded area	1845.8	747.0	19.8
Moderate, severe, and extreme	1118.1	452.5	12.0
Light	727.7	294.5	7.8
Oceania			
Total degraded area	254.3	102.9	13.1
Moderate, severe, and extreme	15.3	6.2	0.8
Light	238.7	96.6	12.3
North America			
Total degraded area	236.0	95.5	5.3
Moderate, severe, and extreme	194.5	78.7	4.4
Light	41.5	16.8	0.9
Central America and Mexico			
Total degraded area	155.2	62.8	24.8
Moderate, severe, and extreme	150.5	60.9	24.1
Light	4.7	1.9	0.7
South America			
Total degraded area	601.4	243.4	14.0
Moderate, severe, and extreme	342.2	138.5	8.0
Light	259.0	104.8	6.0

Note: Totals may not add because of rounding.
(*Source:* Data from World Resources Institute, *World Resources 1992–93* [New York: Oxford University Press, 1992], p. 112. From *World Resources 1992–93*. Copyright © 1992 by The World Resources Institute. Reprinted by permission of Oxford University Press, Inc.)

salinization has occurred; on rangelands, it means that 70% or so of the land is still covered by the native perennial plants. Lightly degraded soils may be restored through sound farming and conservation practices that can be carried out by the average farmer or landowner.

Moderately degraded soil is characterized by substantial topsoil loss, gullying, and erosion due to wind and water. Rangelands maintain 30 to 70% of their native vegetation cover, but the soil that remains is poor in nutrients, marked by a decrease in the ability of microorganisms to de-

compose and recycle organic matter. The land may also suffer from moderate salinization and/or compaction (such as from overgrazing by cattle on pastureland or from the use of heavy machinery on farmland). Compacted soil does not allow proper air circulation, water retention, or root penetration. According to the GLASOD study, moderately degraded soil can generally be restored to its former quality only through national-scale programs with sufficient funding to provide technical expertise. Major undertakings, such as cutting ditches to drain waterlogged soils or creating contouring, may be necessary to restore these soils. Worldwide 2.25 billion acres (910 million hectares) have suffered moderate degradation due to humans since 1945.

Severely degraded soil shows all of the characteristics of moderate degradation, but in much more pronounced form. Erosion has progressed to a much greater degree. In applicable areas, less than 30% of the native vegetation remains. Severely degraded soil is poor in nutrients, to the point that crop growth is badly hindered—if crops will grow at all. Severely degraded land can be restored only with great effort and expense; in most situations it is simply abandoned. Between 1945 and 1990, 740 million acres (300 million hectares) were severely degraded by humans.

Extreme degradation is documented in areas where soils have been either completely removed due to erosion or are so badly damaged that nothing can be realistically done on a human timescale to restore them. Extreme degradation has been caused by massive overgrazing, deforestation, or overirrigation. Since World War II approximately 22 million acres (9 million hectares) of land have been reduced to the level of extreme degradation.

In terms of land area, Asia and Africa have experienced the most soil degradation (Table 13–1), but in terms of percentage of vegetated land, the biggest problems are in Central America and Mexico, followed closely by Europe, Africa, and Asia. North America records the smallest percentage of degraded soils, although the total area of 5.3% showing some degradation (with 4.4% suffering from moderate to extreme degradation) is still considerable. Oceania is also in relatively good shape compared to the world average, especially since the vast majority of its degraded land is only lightly degraded.

The GLASOD study also documented the types and causes of soil degradation. Globally, the most common type of soil degradation is water erosion (56% of all soil degradation), which results in topsoil loss, as well as the formation of gullies, rills, and other topographic damage. Wind erosion (at 28%) occurs on all continents, but is particularly significant in arid and semiarid climates, where it may remove topsoil or bury it under sand and form hollows and dunes. Wind erosion usually occurs when the native vegetation is removed. Degradation by wind erosion leads to full-scale desertification.

Also extremely significant on a worldwide scale are chemical degradation (12%) and physical degradation (4%) of soils. In these forms of degradation, the soil remains in place on the land, but it is badly damaged. Chemical degradation includes salinization from improper irrigation techniques; overuse of pesticides, fertilizers, or other chemicals on soils; acidification due to airborne or other pollutants contaminating the soil; and damage from chemical spills or industrial accidents. Physical degradation includes compaction by heavy machinery and some types of waterlogging.

On a worldwide basis, livestock overgrazing, deforestation, and agricultural activities account for over 90% of the soil degradation since 1945. Overgrazing is responsible for 35% of land degradation, deforestation for 30%, and agricultural activities for 28%. Of course, these percentages vary greatly by continent. In Oceania (including Australia) and Africa, 80% and 49%, respectively, of land degradation are due to overgrazing, whereas in North America 66% is due to agricultural activities. Globally, overexploitation of land (stripping it of natural vegetation for use as fuelwood, but not including commericial and large-scale deforestation) and industrialization (essentially, industrial waste products that damage the soil) account for only about 7% of land degradation.

Unfortunately, damage from soil and land degradation is still occurring. As ▬ Figure 13–13 shows, every inhabited continent has areas that are at serious risk.

The U.S. Midwest and Great Plains, the breadbasket area, have experienced various degrees of soil degradation. The Soil Conservation Service has determined that approximately a quarter of all U.S cropland is eroding away faster than is sustainable. Central America is suffering from extreme soil degradation and is an area of serious concern for the future. Most of this damage is a result of deforestation and overgrazing, but improper agricultural practices are also an important factor. In South America, areas of intensive deforestation are particularly in danger of continued soil degradation, as is the mountainous region on the west coast.

Europe, particularly the middle and eastern portions, is suffering from extreme soil degradation that is predicted to continue into the future. Much of this is due to pollutants, including industrial and urban wastes and pesticides that have damaged the soil. Asia is also suffering from severe and continuing soil degradation, especially in India, China, and Southeast Asia. Asian soil degradation is caused primarily by deforestation, agriculture, and overgrazing. Africa suffers from

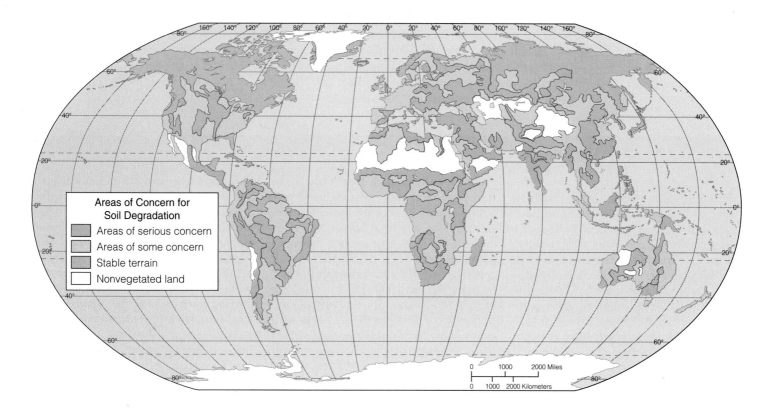

FIGURE 13–13
Areas of concern for soil
degradation. (*Source:* World
Resources Institute, *World
Resources 1992–93* [New York:
Oxford University Press, 1992],
p. 117. From *World Resources
1992–93*. Copyright © 1992 by
The World Resources Institute.
Reprinted by permission of Oxford
University Press, Inc.)

continued soil degradation and desertification, especially along the north coast, in the sub-Saharan Sahel region, and in South Africa. Overgrazing, wind erosion, and poor agricultural practices are to blame for much of Africa's problems. Compared to the rest of the world, Australia is an area of only moderate soil degradation. Most of Australia's problems with soil deterioration result from overgrazing.

Stopping Soil Degradation

As the world population continues to increase, stabilization and restoration of soil resources will become increasingly important. Since World War II agricultural yields have increased greatly, but crop yields would have been even higher with healthier soils. Unfortunately, for decades modern agricultural technologies have masked the soil deterioration by increasing yields even as the soil has become degraded. But if unsustainable agricultural practices continue, the soil will become so degraded that despite our fertilizers, pesticides, and high-yield crop varieties, we will still not be able to produce a good harvest. Once the soil is dead or eroded away, the land becomes barren.

Techniques, such as no-till sowing of crops, drip irrigation, crop rotation, and leaving land fallow, can mitigate or prevent soil degradation, but farmers often do not practice them for simple economic reasons. Farmers often find that it does not make short-term economic sense to invest very heavily (if at all) in soil conservation, preservation, or restoration efforts. Of course, in emphasizing the maximization of short-term profits, the farmer is destroying the capital upon which the business depends, but in a fertile area, the soil may take half a century to become severely degraded—longer than the individual farmer may stay in business. Classically, the next generation would move on to new land, but the world is now running out of new land to place under the plow.

Aside from economic considerations, even if an isolated farmer desires to practice soil conservation techniques, often this is impossible because the action required to stop soil degradation may go beyond the scale of a single farm. As we have discussed, many factors are causing soils to degrade around the world. Soil conservation measures, such as watershed management and river and catchment basin maintenance, may be required on a regional or national level. Such projects can only be implemented by governmental authorities on a local, national, or even international level. An isolated farmer may be virtually helpless if the government does not support and implement sound conservation policies.

Ultimately, it seems that the problem of global soil degradation can only be solved through a variety of actions addressing a multitude of causes on every level from the individual to the international community. The long-term needs of society, which essentially means sustainability in practical terms, must take precedence over all other concerns, be they personal short-term economic gains, debt payment on the part of a poor government, or political jockeying in the international arena. Without healthy soil, civilization as we know it cannot survive.

SUMMARY

With 5.8 billion people on the Earth to feed, and 800 million or more without enough to eat, food production and distribution are major concerns. All of the food we eat is derived from other organisms, and globally only a very small number of species provide the majority of our foodstuffs—an estimated 65% of the food supply consists of rice, wheat, and maize (corn). Animal protein is dominated by poultry, mutton, pork, beef, and fish and aquatic organisms harvested from the oceans.

The Green Revolution after World War II allowed food supplies to increase rapidly—in some cases faster than the human population of the globe. In recent years, however, absolute global grain production has stagnated, and world grain production per person has actually dropped. Likewise the world fish catch, an important source of protein, has apparently plateaued. At present, there is theoretically enough food available to feed all of the people on Earth, but distribution systems are not always adequate to get the food where it is needed. Poor countries may not have enough money to purchase food, while the citizens of rich countries may suffer from diseases induced by eating too rich a diet. The whole subject of food production, distribution, and the future global food supply is fraught with controversy. Some researchers believe that the growing human population will outstrip the food supply, while other researchers firmly believe that continued improvements in agricultural techniques and crop varieties will lead to further substantial increases in global food production. Biotechnology, in particular, may help alleviate the current strain on the food supply.

Ultimately, to ensure the continued nourishment of the human population into the indefinite future, food must be produced and harvested in a sustainable manner. This means taking care of our oceans and our soils. Action is being taken to protect the fisheries by limiting ocean fishing and restricting the pollution of the oceans. Around the world agricultural soils are being degraded at phenomenal rates; in some cases, short-term gains in food production have come at the expense of the long-term health of the soil. Fortunately, the problem of soil degradation is finally being acknowledged in many areas, and programs are underway, or being planned, to correct the situation and restore our soils. Still, the subject of soil degradation will be a serious concern in many parts of the world for decades to come. But if properly maintained, soil is a renewable resource, and thus there is hope that it can be utilized in a sustainable manner.

KEY TERMS

agriculture
aquaculture
bioengineering
biological control
biotechnology
carryover grain stocks
climax community
commercial extinction
crop rotation
cultivable land
deforestation

desertification
ecological succession
erosion
fertilizer
grain
Green Revolution
herbicide
hunger
Integrated Pest Management (IPM)
irrigation
mariculture
monoculture

organic farming
pesticide
pioneer stage of succession
salinization
soil
soil degradation
soil fertility
soil horizon
topsoil
transgenic crops
waterlogging

STUDY QUESTIONS

1. Is there currently enough food to feed everyone on Earth?
2. How do diets differ around the world?
3. What three plant species supply most of the world's food?
4. What was the Green Revolution?
5. Why do some people avoid eating meat?
6. Do you believe that the world could adequately feed a population of 10 billion?

Justify your answer.
7. What is the major nonagricultural food source? Is it being used sustainably?
8. How might biotechnology and bioengineering help us deal with increasing food

scarcity?

9. How does Integrated Pest Management attempt to control crop pests?
10. Discuss the types and extent of soil degradation that are occurring globally.
11. Why are soil and potential soil degradation such important issues?
12. What is being done to help stop global soil degradation?
13. Given that the world population contin-ues to grow, more food will be needed in the future. What are two basic strategies that can be pursued to increase world food production?
14. Currently, about 3.7 billion acres (1.5 billion hectares) of land worldwide are under cultivation. Assuming that currently just enough food is produced to feed everyone on Earth, if the world population increases from 5.8 billion to 8 billion, and yields per unit area of land remain constant, then approximately how much more land will need to be cultivated to feed everyone?
15. Using the same assumptions as in Question 14, how much more land will need to be cultivated if the world population increases from 5.8 billion to 10 billion?

ESSAY QUESTIONS

1. Describe the present global food situation. Is everyone fed adequately?
2. What are the high and low estimates of the number of people that could be fed in the future? What types of assumptions are these estimates based on?
3. Describe the effects of modern intensive agriculture.
4. In your opinion, should the choice of clothing be an environmental issue? Justify your answer.
5. Discuss the advantages and disadvantages of aquaculture and mariculture.

SUGGESTED READINGS

Allen, T. F. H., and T. W. Hoekstra. 1992. *Toward a unified ecology* (Complexity in Ecological Systems Series). New York: Columbia University Press.

Brown, L. R., N. Lenssen, and H. Kane. 1995. *Vital signs 1995: The trends that are shaping our future.* New York: W. W. Norton.

Colchester, M., and L. Lohmann, eds. 1993. *The struggle for land and the fate of the forests.* London: The World Rainforest Movement/The Ecologist/Zed Books.

Corson, W. H., ed. 1990. *The gobal ecology handbook: What you can do about the environmental crisis.* Boston: Beacon Press.

Cutter, S. L., H. L. Renwick, and W. H. Renwick. 1991. *Exploitation, conservation, preservation,* 2d ed. New York: John Wiley.

Ehrlich, P. R., and A. H. Ehrlich. 1991. *Healing the planet: Strategies for resolving the environmental crisis.* Reading, Mass.: Addison-Wesley.

Goodland, R. 1990. *Race to save the tropics: Ecology and economics for a sustainable future.* Washington, D.C.: Island Press.

Hillel, D. J. 1991. *Out of the Earth: Civilization and the life of the soil.* New York: Free Press.

Meadows, D. H., D. L. Meadows, and J. Randers. 1992. *Beyond the limits: Confronting global collapse, en-visioning a sustainable future.* Post Mills, Vt.: Chelsea Green Publishing Company.

Meyers, N. 1992. *The primary source: Tropical forests and our future.* New York: W. W. Norton.

Wilson, E. O. 1992. *The diversity of life.* Cambridge, Mass.: Belknap, Harvard University Press.

Woodwell, G. W., ed. 1990. *The Earth in transition: Patterns and processes of biotic impoverishment.* Cambridge: Cambridge University Press.

World Resources Institute. 1994. *World resources 1994–95.* New York: Oxford Unversity Press.

PROBLEMS OF ENVIRONMENTAL DEGRADATION

Pollution and waste are symptoms, not causes, of the environmental crisis.

PAUL HAWKEN, businessman and environmentalist

The economy is like a huge digestive tract, with a flow of inputs and outputs. Sustainable economies will mimic more efficient, not bigger, digestive tracts.

HERMAN DALY, environmental economist

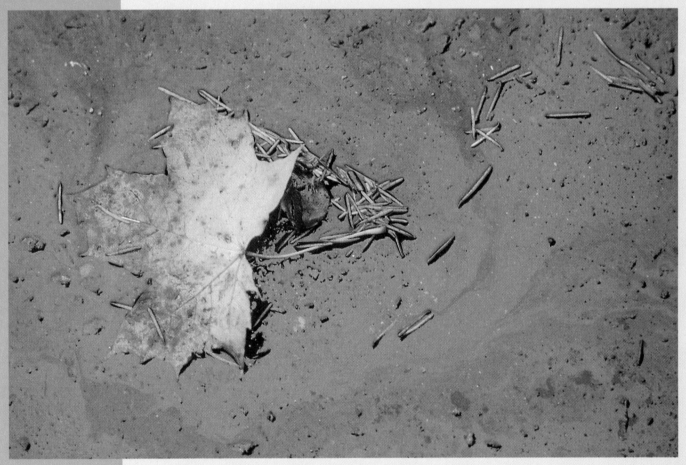

PHOTO   *Spilled oil creates a rainbow of colors in a pond.* (*Source:* Randy Duchaine/The Stock Market.)

PRINCIPLES OF POLLUTION CONTROL

P R O L O G U E   *Industrial Ecology—3M and the 3P's*

In 1975, Joseph Ling was head of the 3M (Minnesota Mining and Manufacturing, also known as MMM) company's environmental department. He developed a program for reducing pollution that has become a standard for hundreds of companies and is taught in engineering and business schools all over the world. Ling called the program Pollution Prevention Pays (3P). Its goal was to design pollution out of the manufacturing process. By reformulating products, redesigning equipment, and recovering and recycling waste, the 3P program not only reduced pollution, but also saved money by making production more efficient. Between 1975 and 1994, 3M saved $750 million in production costs while reducing air pollution by 120,000 tons (109,000 metric tons)*, wastewater by 1 billion gallons (3.8

---

*Unless otherwise noted, *tons* refers to short tons (2000 pounds).

PHOTO *3M helped pioneer industrial technologies that improve efficiency and reduce pollution. Shown here is 3M scientist Diwa Ratnam who helped develop a soap pad made from recycled plastic soda bottles and containing biodegradable soap.*(*Source:* Courtesy 3M Company.)

billion L [liters]), and solid waste by 410,000 tons (372,000 metric tons). The 3P program has given rise to a new approach to environmental engineering that can be called "industrial hygiene": its goal is to design industrial methods that curtail waste. 3M's experience illustrates, once again, that input (source) reduction by increasing efficiency can be the best solution to many environmental problems. This approach conserves resources and reduces pollution while the increased efficiency can reduce operating costs. Businesses and the economy perform better while improving the environment. Industrial hygiene has been so effective and widespread that the amount of hazardous and toxic waste produced by industry decreased far faster than most forecasters, including the Environmental Protection Agency (EPA), had predicted. By the early 1990s, some toxic treatment and disposal companies were going out of business for lack of waste to treat. This was quite a surprise to many, who had predicted that industrial waste treatment would be a booming business for decades to come.

In 1989, Robert Frosch and Nicholas Gallopoulos coined a term that may describe the "next step" after industrial hygiene. They published an article in *Scientific American* called "Strategies for Manufacturing" that discussed "industrial ecology." Instead of just designing processes that minimize waste, industrial ecology seeks to design processes that use any remaining waste as the raw materials for other production processes. This is an exciting glimpse at a truly sustainable economy. The basic philosophy of industrial ecology is simple but profound: For whatever you produce, (1) take as little as possible from the environment, and (2) use as much as you can of what you take. Thus, where the term *industrial ecology* once seemed an oxymoron, or contradiction in terms, it may represent a first step toward a holistic society where nature and economics are unified instead of in conflict.

INTRODUCTION

Up to this point, the book has focused on environmental problems caused by resource depletion, or excess inputs to society. We now turn to the second major category of environmental problems, those caused by too many outputs by society (Fig. 14–1).

WHAT IS POLLUTION?

Pollution generally refers to excess outputs by society into the environment. In this case, *excess* means something produced in amounts high enough to be harmful to us, other life, or valued objects such as cars and buildings. Anything can be harmful if it is concentrated enough, so all matter and energy can cause pollution if locally produced in sufficient amounts. Because pollution is such a widespread environmental problem, many aspects of it deserve special consideration:

- *Pollution as matter cycling and energy flow.* In Chapter 4 we saw that all of the environment, including land, sea, air, and life, ultimately consists of matter cycles and energy flows. Pollution represents *local concentrations* in the matter cycle or energy flow. The rapid burning of fossil fuels, for instance, releases tons of carbon into the atmosphere that was stored underground as coal and petroleum. Similarly, con-

centrations of energy can be a form of pollution. Heat pollution is a serious form of air and water pollution. Astronomers speak of "light pollution" from nearby cities that disrupts their view of the stars.

Matter and energy are in constant motion (cycling and flowing, respectively), so their concentrations in the environment are eventually dispersed. As is often said, "dilution is the solution to pollution." Conversely, pollution damage increases as the environment's ability to absorb or "dilute" the pollutant is exceeded. For example, a large river has a much greater **absorptive ability** than a standing pond not only because (1) the river has a greater water volume but also because (2) the moving water disperses the pollutant more quickly.

- *Pollution as an accelerated natural process.* We associate pollution with belching factories, but many natural processes have been causing pollution for billions of years. For example, volcanoes release gases that are harmful to life, affect global climate, and cause acid rain. Many organisms produce highly toxic chemicals.

Humans, however, cause pollution at a much greater rate than nature for two reasons, related to both the quantity and the quality of our waste:

FIGURE 14–1
Pollution problems result
from accelerating flows of
matter and energy through society that overwhelm a sink's
ability to absorb the
throughput. Increased population and traditional
("nongreen") resource-
intensive technologies have
accelerated throughput.

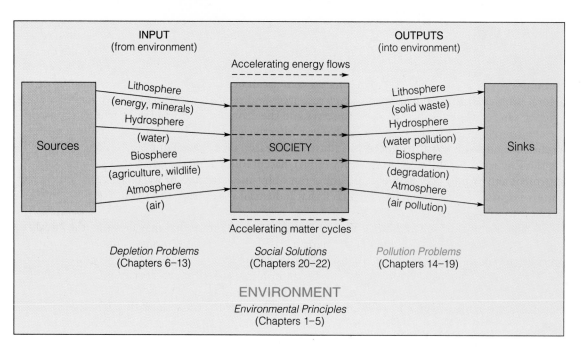

1. The quantity of waste produced is vast. For example, the 6.5 billion tons (5.9 billion metric tons) of carbon we release annually from combustion, especially the burning of fossil fuels, far exceeds what would be released from forest fires and other natural combustion sources (Chapter 18). The average American accounts for more than 1 ton (0.9 metric ton) of waste per day when industrial, agricultural, household, and transportation activities are included.

2. The quality of our waste accelerates pollution because it includes so many new substances. Though often not more harmful than natural materials, these substances are not easily decomposed by natural processes and are therefore more persistent. This quality aspect of waste began in 1856 when the first human-made industrial chemical was created, an artificial dye. In 1895, the first bladder cancer associated with artificial dyes was reported. Between 1957 and 1990, the American Chemical Society recorded 10 million new chemicals. Now the society registers new chemicals at the rate of *70 per hour*. Most are synthetic organic chemicals (SOCs) that contain carbon because the carbon atom bonds easily with atoms of other elements and other carbon atoms to form many types of molecules. Only about 500 of the chemicals invented each year ever reach a wide market. Still, more than 70,000 chemicals are in everyday use worldwide, and the United States alone produces over 100 million tons (91 million metric tons) of SOCs each year. Yet less than 1 percent of the chemicals on the market have ever been completely evaluated as potential health or ecological hazards. Most have been subjected to very little, if any, testing.

- *Pollution as a stepwise process.* A main reason that humans produce so much waste is that large concentrations of matter and energy are produced as by-products ("waste") during each step of many human activities (■ Fig. 14–2). Because "everything must go somewhere" as either energy flowing or matter cycling, this waste often ends up polluting water, air, or land. Increasingly, engineers are using **Life Cycle Analysis (LCA)** to pinpoint steps that can be either eliminated or made more efficient. Both measures reduce waste generation. LCA analyzes the entire "life cycle" of a product (such as an appliance), from mining of raw materials to its eventual disposal by the consumer, and measures how much energy and matter are used at each step.

Sometimes called "cradle to grave" analysis, LCA is most widely practiced in Germany where laws require that cars and many appliances be recycled. For example, all of the various parts in a car or appliance have their own manufacturing steps. To recycle the entire car or appliance, the life cycle of each part must be studied. In Germany, the parts are labeled (with computer barcodes) when

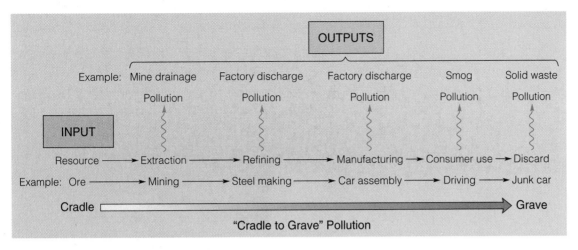

they are assembled to make it easier to dismantle and recycle them when the car or appliance is discarded.

- *Pollution = population × technology*. Recall from Chapter 1 that environmental impact (I) equals population (P) × technology (T). In this case, the amount of pollution produced by society depends on two basic factors, the number of people (P) and the amount of waste produced per person, mainly determined by technology (T):

Population × waste per capita = total pollution

Total pollution therefore increases as populations grow and as waste per capita (per person) grows. In the past, waste per capita has been strongly correlated with the rapid growth of resource-intensive ("nongreen") industry and technology (Chapter 1). Source reduction through increased efficiency, such as the 3P's in the Prologue, reduces waste per capita. "Green" technologies emphasize source reduction as a main goal. The need for reduction is especially great in the United States, which has among the world's highest per capita air, water, and land pollution. Recall that each U.S. citizen accounts for more than 2000 pounds (907 kg) of waste per day when transportation, agricultural, industrial, and household wastes are included. As a result, with 5% of the world's population, the United States produces perhaps 50% of the world's solid waste and 20 to 35% of most other pollutants.

- *Sources and sinks*. Four major pollutant sources may be identified: industry, households, agriculture, and transportation. Thus, pollutants are often classified as industrial pollution, household pollution, and so on. We can also identify three main sinks, or destinations in the environment where these pollutants go: water, air, and land (Fig. 14–1). In other words, all three "spheres" of the physical environment serve as destinations for at least some types of pollutants. Pollutants can therefore also be classified by sink, as air, water, and land pollution. ● Table 14–1 summarizes the four sources and their sinks. Industry and agriculture are the sources that pollute the most sinks. The chemical industry is particularly notorious for its production of very hazardous pollutants.

History of Pollution

Natural pollution is as old as the Earth. Ancient volcanoes, for instance, spewed vast amounts of gases into the atmosphere. Many of these gases affected global climate, causing at least some of the mass extinctions that devastated the biosphere in the past. Nor are humans the only animals that pollute. Huge herds of grazing animals have been known to pollute rivers with urine and feces; droppings from large flocks of birds can contaminate the local environment near nesting areas.

Early humans also polluted the environment. The remains of the first "landfills" are among the most common finds in caves and other sites of fos-

TABLE 14–1 *Major Sources and Sinks of Pollutants*

x = major direct contributor to that sink.

	SINK		
SOURCES	Air	Water	Land
Industry	x	x	x
Households		x	x
Agriculture	x	x	x
Transportation	x		

FIGURE 14–3
A shell mound in Georgia
where prehistoric Native
Americans discarded shellfish
remains and other wastes.
(*Source*: John D. Cunningham/
Visuals Unlimited.)

sil humans. Often these contain the bones of hundreds of fossil animals (Fig. 14–3). The first written records indicate that Egyptians, Greeks, and other early civilizations sometimes had to cope with polluted drinking water. As cities grew and population density increased, so did pollution. Roman laws prohibited dumping in certain areas. One of the earliest references to air pollution dates from 1307 when air pollution in London was so bad that King Edward I banned coal burning. Modern wastewater treatment and the flush toilet did not become common until the 1920s in Europe and the United States. Until that time, pollution of lakes, rivers, and groundwaters from human waste posed enormous threats to drinking water quality. Not until 1912 was the first federal law enacted to set standards for drinking water in the United States.

While pollution has always occurred, the scale and rate of pollution in the last few decades are vastly greater than in the past. In the 1990s, large human populations and fossil fuel–driven technologies are daily producing huge volumes of many different kinds of pollutants on regional and even global scales. These pollute all parts of the environment, from land to water to air to living things.

Pollutant Properties

Persistence is how long a pollutant stays in the environment in unmodified form. When a pollutant is released into the environment, physical, chemical, and biological processes can cause it to decompose. Pollutants with high persistence take a long time to decompose and are obviously the most environmentally damaging. Persistence time ranges from a few seconds for very nonpersistent pollutants to many thousands of years for highly persistent ones.

Bacteria and other organisms often biodegrade natural pollutants, such as fertilizers, but evolution has not provided many organisms that can digest synthetic materials. Consequently, human-made, synthetic substances that are not found in nature tend to be the most persistent pollutants. Many petroleum-based products, such as plastics, can last many decades or even centuries. Such synthetic materials are sometimes called **stock pollutants** because the environment has no capacity to absorb them, so they accumulate rapidly. A possible solution is the new science of bioengineering, whereby humans transfer genes between organisms. Such methods have produced bacteria that are able to digest oil and other persistent and stock pollutants.

Residence time is the time it takes for a pollutant to move through the environment. Pollutants with very low persistence do not have residence times because they do not exist long enough to cycle. For very persistent pollutants, however, residence time is very important because nature can get rid of them only by physically moving them out of a system. For example, mercury is highly toxic, but it cannot be decomposed because it is an element. In the oceans, mercury has a residence time of about 80,000 years before it is buried in the bottom sediment or otherwise cycles out of the seawater.

Residence time has enormous implications for global pollution of the oceans and atmosphere because persistent pollutants do much more damage if they have very long residence times. Perhaps the most important example is the destruction of the ozone layer in the upper atmosphere and global warming caused by chlorofluorocarbons (CFCs) and similar reactive chemicals (Chapter 18). Many CFC compounds have a long residence time, often lasting 60 to 110 years in the atmosphere. During its long lifetime, each CFC molecule destroys about 100,000 ozone molecules and contributes to long-term global warming. As a solution, chemists are developing compounds called hydrofluorocarbons (HFCs) and hydrochlorofluorocarbons (HCFCs) that have much shorter residence times in the atmosphere (Fig. 14–4).

Persistence and residence time specify how long a pollutant is able to do harm. Of equal importance are the harmful properties themselves. A very powerful poison can do much more harm in a few days than a mild pollutant that lasts many decades. Federal environmental laws define **hazardous waste** as having any or all of the following four properties:

- Physically destructive:

  1. **Ignitable** materials are easily ignited and burn rapidly. Examples: gasoline, paints, solvents.
  2. **Corrosive** materials include liquids that are highly acidic or very alkaline. Examples: drain and oven cleaners, chlorine.
  3. **Reactive** materials are very active chemicals that easily cause explosions and/or re-

lease harmful fumes. Examples: chlorine, ammonia, gasoline.

- Biologically destructive:

  4. **Toxic** materials are harmful or fatal when consumed by organisms in relatively small amounts. Examples: pesticides, many manufactured chemicals.

Notice that hazardous waste is a more general term than toxic waste. Although most people use the terms interchangeably, toxic waste is more properly considered as a subset of hazardous waste.

In summary, six properties of materials help define them as pollutants: high persistence, long residence time, easily ignited, corrosivity, reactivity, and toxicity. Wastes with at least one of these properties are likely to be pollutants. Especially damaging wastes, such as some hazardous chemical wastes, may have up to all six properties.

CONTROLLING POLLUTION

We often associate environmental deterioration with smokestacks and pipes pouring out toxic substances. Unfortunately, controlling pollution involves far more than just passing laws that require factories to stop toxic emissions. Realistic efforts to control pollution must consider the many complexities involved.

Myths of Pollution Control

We begin by examining some of the misconceptions about pollution and how it can be con-

FIGURE 14–4
Global-warming and ozone depletion potential for different compounds of CFCs, HCFCs, and HFCs. These are all compared to the commonly used CFC-11, shown as the circle labeled "CFC-11." Circle size is proportional to the atmospheric lifetime for that compound. CFCs have much longer lifetimes and much greater global-warming and ozone depletion potential. (*Source:* Masters, G., *Introduction to Environmental Engineering and Science.* Copyright © 1991, p. 418. Reprinted by permission of Prentice Hall, Upper Saddle River, NJ.)

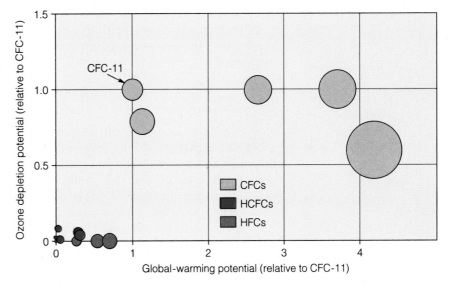

trolled. These myths are widely held and often lead to costly political and economic decisions.

Myth of Purity in Nature

We often hear phrases such as "pristine waters" that imply a certain purity in natural places untouched by humans. In reality, virtually nothing is "pure" in nature. A single drop of water contains about 500 trillion molecules. Even before humans existed, no drop of rain or river water would have contained 500 trillion molecules of only H_2O. Millions or, more likely, billions would have been molecules of various dissolved gases, organic solids, mineral solids, and many other natural "pollutants." Similarly, the "pure" country air we breathe contains a huge number of gases and particles (Chapter 17). Furthermore, even highly polluted water or air usually contains only tiny concentrations, far less than 1%. This is why pollution is measured in parts per million or even billion. Even raw sewage entering treatment facilities is usually at least 99.9% water.

Myth of Zero Pollution

Although eliminating all pollution sounds ideal, zero pollution is an unrealistic goal for four reasons. First, modern society cannot exist without producing pollutants. Everything must go somewhere, so human activities will inevitably produce waste matter and energy. Second, as we will see, the costs of removing all pollutants from any given activity increase exponentially after a given point, making total purity economically impossible in nearly all cases. Third, the benefits of pollutant removal decrease exponentially after a point, making total purity unnecessary. Fourth, not even nature is totally pure. Even if zero pollution were economically feasible, should we necessarily seek an environmental standard higher than nature?

Myth of Zero Risk

Most of us have many misconceptions about risk, including that of a risk-free existence. In reality, every activity, from eating peanut butter to taking a walk, involves some risk. In all activities, including control of pollution, we can therefore at best seek to minimize, not eliminate, the many risks we face. Unfortunately, our efforts to minimize risk are greatly hindered by our inaccurate perceptions of risk (Chapter 15).

Deciding How Much Control: Being Realistic

The pollution myths have had a strong influence on policy, leading to some unrealistic and costly decisions. Pollution control in the 1970s and early 1980s emphasized "rights-based" and "technology-based" approaches. Rights-based control assumes that all individuals, even the most pollutant-sensitive, have a right to be exposed to the least pollution that society can provide. For example, the Clean Air Act of 1970 set pollutant concentrations at levels low enough to protect even the most sensitive citizens. Technology-based control sets pollutant levels according to technological ability; technology-based laws often specify that companies reduce pollution by using the "best available technology." In the past, rights- and technology-based approaches have been very successful in improving many aspects of air and water quality. But many people have argued that they tend to be too stringent and costly because they strive for zero pollution and zero risk, which are unattainable ideals. Determining pollution control based only on the most sensitive individuals or the best technology is a very narrow approach that can lead to overprotection for most of society at an unnecessarily high cost, according to critics.

Rise of the Benefit-Cost Approach

Concerns about a declining U.S. economy have led to increasing interest in lowering the costs of pollution control in recent years. As ▬ Figure 14–5 shows, the portion of U.S. businesses' total expenditures that goes for pollution control has been climbing since the early 1980s; the 1992 per-

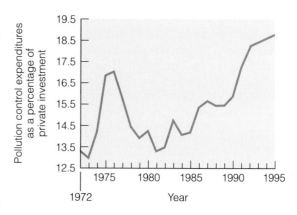

▬ **FIGURE 14–5**

The cost of pollution control has risen from about 13% of business investment in 1972 to more than 18%. (*Source:* U.S. Commerce Department.)

Can Pollution Be Solved by Economic Growth?

Some critics of pollution control argue that the cost of controls greatly outweighs the benefits. They point out that the money spent on pollution control by U.S. businesses—more than $1.2 trillion from 1972 through 1991 or about 15% of all the money spent on fixed investments in that period—is spent on "nonproductive" environmental equipment. The late Edward Denison of the Brookings Institute was well known for his research into why U.S. productivity growth has declined since the 1970s. He concluded that a major factor was environmental regulation, which reduced productivity growth by 0.25 percentage point per year. Although this may seem small, it adds up to a loss of $700 billion of productivity between 1972 and 1991. Another study by Michael Hazilla and Raymond Kopp found that the Clean Air and Clean Water Acts lowered the 1990 GNP by 6% and increased prices by 6% as well. Finally, a 1993 study by the National Bureau of Economic Research showed that environmental regulations lower productivity by three to four times the direct cost of compliance, causing between 3% to 8% loss of productivity in most major industries.

Environmentalists counter by pointing out that although pollution regulations do lead to less growth for some industries, other industries experience higher growth. Oil and chemical industries may suffer, but pollution control industries prosper. A more general point made by environmentalists is that economic growth (such as GNP) is illusory as currently measured because it does not incorporate environmental damages. Instead, it simply adds up the money accumulated so that cleaning up oil spills, for example, is added to the GNP. Similarly, productivity growth of a mining company does not incorporate the environmental costs of acidic waters, cratered landscapes, and other degradations from mining. Thus, a more accurate measure of economic growth, one that included environmental benefits and costs, would lead to different conclusions about pollution controls. A mining company that showed lost productivity from pollution controls might show no loss, or even a gain, in productivity if environmental benefits were included in measures of productivity. Productivity, in other words, should consist of more than just the number of televisions or "widgets" produced; profits should include environmental quality gains. Environmentalists also note that air pollution controls have yielded some gains in productivity that the critics omit: cleaner air and a healthier environment promote more productive workers.

Society must make a fundamental choice between these positions because they envision a drastically different future for pollution control. Critics of past regulations believe that the answer to pollution is *less* control. They point to studies, such as a 1994 study by Gene Grossman and Alan Krueger, that show that environmental deterioration occurs in developing nations but continued economic growth leads to an improved environment (beginning at about $8,000 per capita income). Thus, they think that, by lowering productivity, past pollution controls in the United States have actually decreased environmental quality. On the other hand, environmentalists argue that the improved environment with increasing income occurs only because stricter environmental laws are passed. Increased wealth means that society can afford greater regulation. Environmental advocates also argue that a more accurate definition of productivity, one that included environmental costs and benefits, would show that past pollution controls have improved not just the environment, but productivity as well. They argue that *more* control is needed. Not surprisingly, some people are in the "middle ground" of this debate. Economist Paul Portney published a study that incorporated environmental costs and benefits. It showed that earlier environmental legislation, such as the Clean Air Act of 1970, was a "good buy," in that total environmental and economic benefits exceeded the total costs. In contrast, the 1990 amendments to the Clean Air Act were not a good buy, according to Dr. Portney, because the costs exceed the health and environmental benefits.

Questions

1. Do you think that all environmental legislation, even for very expensive laws, is a "good buy"?
2. Do you think that a nation should regulate pollution, even if the regulations slow economic productivity? Should other species, such as wildlife, be considered when estimating the impact of pollution? What about the impact on "lower" life-forms, such as worms and insects?
3. Finally, should productivity and economic measurements incorporate environmental costs and benefits? What are some problems that might occur with measuring these?

---

centage of 18.5% represented $102 billion, which was more than 2% of the gross national product (GNP). Some critics argue that much, or all, of these costs were a needless drain on the U.S. economy (see the Case Study).

Others argue that the money spent on pollution control has yielded many benefits to human health and the environment. Nonetheless, the trend toward increasing costs, combined with general economic problems, has encouraged a search for less costly approaches. Recall from Chapter 1 that the environmentalism of the 1960s and 1970s has gradually been replaced by a sustainability movement, beginning in the early 1980s. One of the traits of the sustainability movement is its focus on addressing fundamental economic changes, as opposed to the legal mechanisms often emphasized by environmen-

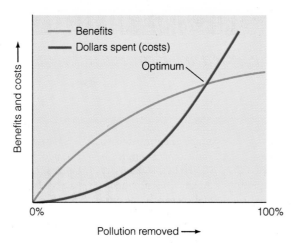

talism (Chapter 1). In the case of pollution control, this has meant replacing the rights- and technology-based approaches with a benefit-cost approach (often called a "utility-based" approach).

Benefit-cost analyses (BCA) address the benefit-cost ratio (Chapter 6). With pollution control, this means finding the greatest relative health and environmental benefits for the least amount of economic cost. As ■ Fig. 14–6 shows, the cost of pollution control increases slowly at first so that the initial reduction in pollution is relatively cheap. But after a certain point, cost increases rapidly as increasingly refined equipment and more energy must be applied to extract the more problematic pollutants, such as finer particles or less soluble gases.

Fortunately, society usually does not have to pay the very high costs of further removal because the detrimental effects of pollution tend to follow a curve that is the inverse of the cost curve. As

pollution is initially removed, rapid benefits accrue, but the "law of diminishing returns" sets in as pollution removal continues, and continued health benefits are much less. The point where the cost and benefit curves intersect can be considered the point where benefit:cost (ratio = 1) is optimized, denoting maximum relative benefit for the cost incurred. Ratios greater than 1 indicate that additional controls could result in a net overall gain to society. Ratios less than 1 indicate "overcontrol," where controls are costing society more than the benefits it receives.

In real situations, the exact shapes of the cost and benefit curves vary, depending on the nature of the pollution. For example, studies show that in the extremely polluted countries of Eastern Europe, particulate matter air pollution behaves roughly as we have just shown. Rapid improvements are gained for relatively little or no cost, until a point is reached, at about 40%, where costs skyrocket (■ Fig. 14–7a). Sulfur dioxide air pollution shows a much different behavior. Costs begin to skyrocket a little sooner, around 30%, but more important, there is virtually no significant benefit from control (■ Fig. 14–7b). It seems that the East Europeans should place higher priority on reduction of particulates than on sulfur dioxide emissions.

While benefit-cost studies are extremely useful in social decisions about pollution control, they are not without problems. Benefit-cost results may be very misleading, or even worthless, if some benefits or costs are omitted or inaccurately estimated. This is very likely when dealing with environmental problems because it is very difficult to estimate the value of many environ-

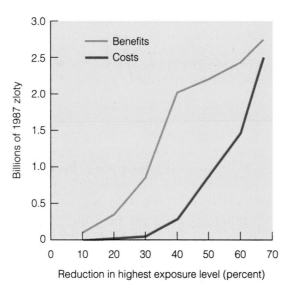

(a) Particulate matter

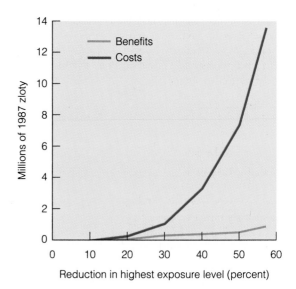

(b) Sulfur dioxide

𝒫ROBLEMS OF ENVIRONMENTAL DEGRADATION   SECTION 3

mental resources. Recall from Chapters 1 and 6, for instance, that society has historically tended to underestimate the true environmental costs of most activities. For example, we can measure the health costs of particulate matter relatively easily using medical data. But we should also include the aesthetic damage done to wilderness areas if plants are killed. What is the value of your favorite fishing lake? How much would you pay to keep it from being polluted? Such environmental benefits of pollution control are not only difficult to place a dollar value on, but people value them differently. To some people, a wilderness area has less value than a shopping mall (Fig. 14–8). Others place no value on the mall.

Input versus Output Controls

Recall from Chapters 1 and 6 that the flow of matter and energy through society can be reduced in two basic ways, input reduction or output management (Fig. 14–9). Input reduction is usually the most desirable way to reduce pollution because it also slows resource depletion and usually saves money, such as by increasing efficiency and reusing/recycling materials.

In contrast, output management deals with the flow of matter and energy only after society is finished with it, when it becomes waste. This rarely promotes resource conservation. It also is generally very expensive compared to input reduction. Wastewater treatment facilities and scrubbers that trap particles and gases in smokestacks are examples of pollution control through output management (Fig. 14–9). Whereas input reduction saves money by increased efficiency and reuse/recycling, output management increases costs even

 FIGURE 14–8
Which do you value more—the shopping mall or the wilderness? Or do you value them the same? Determining how much people value something is extremely difficult, yet it is essential if natural resources are to be conserved and managed. (*Sources:* (left): Dean DeChambeau; (below): Rob Visser/ Greenpeace.)

This "valuation problem" is one of the most fundamental obstacles to solving pollution and other environmental problems (Chapters 1, 6, and 20). A partial solution that economists often use is called the **Contingent Valuation Method (CVM)**; it attempts to "objectively" measure the dollar value of changes in environmental quality, often by using questionnaires and other surveys that ask people what they would pay for various environmental improvements. One survey, for example, found that U.S. citizens would be willing to pay $1.30 to $2.50 per household for air pollution controls on a power plant that was reducing air quality in the scenic Grand Canyon. CVM has been used for more than 20 years and has considerably improved our understanding about environmental values, such as how much people are willing to pay to remove pollutants. Even so, many hurdles remain because personal and social values are inherently subjective, change often, and are difficult to measure.

further because the pollution must be "cleaned up" after it is produced. In the case of pollution control, these added costs include (1) cost of the pollution control equipment, or **abatement devices**, which are relatively expensive, and (2) cost of waste disposal.

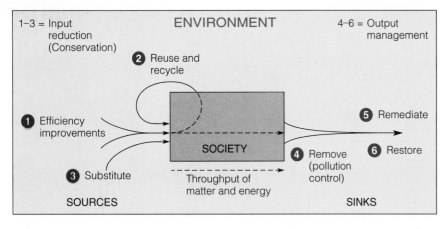

FIGURE 14–9
Input reduction, or conservation, can be accomplished in three ways. Green technologies are used to achieve efficiency improvements, reuse/recycling, and substitution.

An average coal-burning electricity generating plant, for example, produces many tons of toxic ash, sulfur, and other waste that is extremely expensive to remove and dispose of in landfills or incinerators. This demonstrates why input reduction has much higher benefit-cost ratios than output management. If we do not produce the waste to begin with, such as by using low-sulfur coal, there is no need to pay for equipment to eliminate sulfur or pay for its disposal.

Besides pollution control, Figure 14–9 also shows two other kinds of output management, remediation and restoration of the polluted environment. **Remediation** seeks to counteract some of the effects of pollution after it has been released into the environment. For example, lakes polluted with acid rain are sometimes treated with lime to neutralize the acid. Consider how expensive this is compared to stopping acid rain by burning low-sulfur coal or even trapping the sulfur before it is released. Remediation of toxic waste dumps has proven so expensive that the amount of Superfund money originally estimated by Congress is much too small (Chapter 19). A rapidly growing type of remediation that promises to lower costs in some cases is bioremediation, which uses microbes to digest pollutants in groundwater, oil in oil spills, and many other substances.

Restoration, discussed in Chapter 6, is more ambitious than remediation. Rather than just counteracting some of the effects of pollution in the environment, restoration seeks to restore the environment to its former state. Restoration of the Kissimmee River and Everglades in Florida and restoration of the tall-grass prairie in the Midwest are examples. As Figure 14–10 shows, restoration is, not surprisingly, the most expensive of the three output management methods. The eventual cost of partly restoring the Everglades was recently estimated at $2 billion. Furthermore, complete restoration is almost never

accomplished in any project. Once the environment is harmed, it is nearly impossible to fully return it to its former state.

Despite the high costs, pollution reduction attempts have traditionally emphasized output management. Most of the state and federal laws passed during the 1970s and early 1980s, such as the Clean Air and Water Acts and the Superfund Act, mandated pollution controls and pollution cleanup. But as noted above, the early 1980s saw increasing interest in reducing costs, such as by the use of benefit-cost analyses. Such analyses repeatedly indicate that pollution can be reduced much more cheaply by greater application of input reduction methods. As Figure 14–11 shows, enhancing output control with increased efficiency, reuse/recycling, or other input reduction methods can result in more pollution removed for less money. Growing numbers of businesses are recognizing this (see Issues in Perspective 14–1, page 400).

Implementing Pollution Controls

Implementing pollution controls is often the most difficult step because it usually entails an initial monetary cost and/or change in behavior. Even though society as a whole may decide that the benefits of controlling a certain pollutant may outweigh the costs, the average citizen is often reluctant to pay the added costs and sacrifices necessary to bring this about. Even the cheapest forms of pollution control, such as increased energy efficiency, require an initial cost, perhaps such as buying a new, smaller car, that only yields benefits after payment.

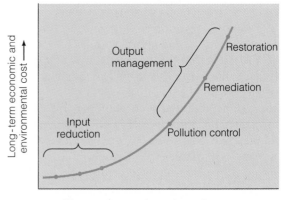

FIGURE 14–10
Input reduction of throughput entails much lower long-term economic and environmental costs than output management does. Restoration and remediation are especially costly forms of output management of throughput.

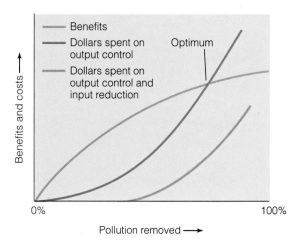

FIGURE 14–11
Using input reduction (such as more efficient machines or recycling) in addition to the traditional output pollution abatements can remove more pollution at even lower costs.

1. *Persuasion.* Ask people to change polluting behaviors.
2. *Regulation.* Pass laws requiring less pollution.
3. *Incentive.* Reward behavior that reduces pollution.

Persuasion can be an effective way of changing people's behavior, especially if it is accompanied by education. People are much more likely to change if they have information about the harmful consequences of their actions. An example would be an advertisement urging people not to pour household chemicals into the sewer system. Persuasion is also relatively inexpensive compared to regulation and incentive methods. But because it has no means of enforcement, persuasion alone is rarely sufficient. By itself, it is generally the least effective of the three methods, but it can be used to supplement the others.

Social scientists tell us that there are three basic ways to promote change in human activities such as those that pollute:

Legal Aspects of Pollution Control

● Table 14–2 lists the major federal laws regulating pollution in the United States. Most of

TABLE 14–2 *Some Federal Laws Regulating Chemicals in the United States*

YEAR FIRST ENACTED	LAW	REGULATORY AGENCY	REGULATED PRODUCTS	REGULATORY MODEL[a]
1938	Food, Drug and Cosmetics Act	FDA	Foods, drugs, and cosmetics, medical devices, veterinary drugs	Risk (food, cosmetics) Balancing (drugs, medical devices)
1947	Federal Insecticide, Fungicide, and Rodenticide Act	EPA	Pesticides	Balancing
1960	Federal Hazardous Substances Act	CPSC[b]	Household products	Risk
1970	Occupational Safety and Health Act	OSHA	Workplace chemicals	Technical feasibility
1970	Clean Air Act	EPA	Air pollutants	Risk (stationary) sources). Technical feasibility (moving vehicles)
1972	Clean Water Act	EPA	Water pollutants	Technical feasibility
1974	Safe Drinking Water Act	EPA	Drinking water contaminants	Technical feasibility
1976	Toxic Substances Control Act	EPA	Industrial chemicals not covered elsewhere	Balancing
1980	Superfund Amendments and Reauthorization	EPA	Contaminants at waste sites	Risk/technical feasibility

[a]"Risk" means the agency considers only risk information when reaching decisions. "Balancing" means that both risks and benefits are considered. "Technical feasibility" means that the law requires the agency to consider not only risks, but also the availability of technology to control risk. Some laws invoke more than one model.
[b]CPSC: Consumer Product Safety Commission.
(*Source:* From Table 8, p. 203, of Joseph V. Rodricks, *Calculated Risks* [New York: Cambridge University Press, 1992]. Reprinted with the permission of Cambridge University Press.)

An Ounce of Prevention—
Redesigning Chemical Manufacturing

The 3P program (Pollution Prevention Pays) described in the Prologue is another example of the old adage, "an ounce of prevention is worth a pound of cure." Doctors know this, too; it is much cheaper to prevent sickness than to treat it. Similarly, it is much cheaper, to the economy and the environment, to produce less waste than to clean it up. The U.S. chemical industry produces more toxic and hazardous pollution than any other source: 638 billion pounds (289 billion kg) of waste per year. The industry must spend $4.4 billion to treat and dispose of all this waste. Chemical engineers, who design the industrial chemical processes, can therefore have an enormous role in reducing pollution by changing the production process.

There are two basic ways to redesign manufacturing processes to produce less waste. One is to recycle and reuse chemicals. In 1993, Sandoz Pharmaceutical gambled $2.1 million on research to develop a recyclable alternative to a solvent used in making its second best–selling drug. The gamble paid off in a big way. Instead of producing 20 pounds of hazardous waste per pound of drug, the new recyclable method produced just 1.7 pounds of waste per pound of drug. By saving $772,000 per year in disposal and other costs, the research gamble will pay for itself many times over in years to come.

A second method of reducing waste is to substitute a less harmful chemical in the production process. American industries, for instance, spray 400 million gallons (1.5 billion L) of paints on products every year. These paints release huge amounts of toxic gases, especially volatile organic compounds (VOCs), a major smog component. Incredibly, more VOC emissions result from painting a car than from the car's engine exhaust during its lifetime! Union Carbide has developed an alternative that eliminates up to 80% of the VOCs from spray paint. Instead of using toxic solvents to dissolve the paint solids, they are dissolved into liquified carbon dioxide under very high pressure. When pumped through a sprayer nozzle, the carbon dioxide depressurizes like a shaken soda, spraying the paint in a fine mist of even-sized particles. Liquified carbon dioxide has similar applications in making plexiglas and other plastics.

While these examples are inspiring, chemical engineers have barely begun to redesign the thousands of chemical manufacturing processes. If done on a large scale, such redesigning could drastically reduce the pollution produced by industry.

---

these laws are discussed in the appropriate chapters that follow, but some key generalizations should be noted here. First, these laws can be subdivided into two basic categories, those using the input approach and those using the output approach. The input approach is used in laws that control the production of toxic chemicals, such as FIFRA (Federal Insecticide, Fungicide, and Rodenticide Act) and TSCA (Toxic Substances Control Act). These laws try to restrict the creation of materials that can become pollutants. Other laws use the output approach, trying to reduce pollution after it has been produced. Examples include the Clean Air and Clean Water Acts, which limit pollution discharges from factories and other places, and the Superfund Amendments, which mandate pollution cleanup. Also note that the laws are administered by different agencies (although the EPA administers most of them), and use different regulatory models.

Regulation by laws is most useful where polluters are few in number and the pollution can be easily monitored. For example, hazardous waste disposal and large factories are relatively easy to oversee. It is also important where the pollution is very dangerous and must be tightly controlled; again this includes toxic and hazardous waste.

Economic Aspects of Pollution Control

The United States has seen a rapid increase in regulatory laws at the local, state, and federal levels. Many businesses and citizens complain that there are too many laws and that they are too complicated, with environmental lawyers and administrators being the main benefactors. Furthermore, laws are not very effective at controlling activities that involve many people acting independently. Thus, it is extremely difficult and costly to regulate pollution where there are many polluters, such as people littering or disposing of used oil. In such circumstances, *incentive* methods are often better.

Rather than using force and other legal threats, incentive methods provide economic rewards for nonpolluting activities. This controls pollution at much lower costs because society does not have to pay for many law enforcement officials to police the many individual polluters. Instead, individuals carry out nonpolluting activities on their own because they are monetarily rewarded for doing so. Two common examples are (1) deposits paid when potential waste is purchased and (2) "pay as you throw" schemes that make the polluter pay for waste discarded (Chapters 1 and 6).

Requiring deposits for such items as aluminum cans will greatly increase the rate of return for can recycling. Generally, the larger the deposit, the higher the rate of return. The use of deposits has been so successful with cans that it is being increasingly applied to other waste items. For example, discarded car engine oil is a hazard to water supplies in many areas. Initial studies show that requiring a deposit when new oil is purchased, and reimbursing the buyer when the waste oil is returned, can drastically reduce oil waste. "Pay as you throw" schemes are also becoming common, especially with solid waste disposal. Both industry and households are being charged for the amount of waste that is picked up by waste disposal companies. Where this system is not practiced, people have no incentive to reduce waste because, for example, curbside garbage pickup costs the same no matter how much is discarded (Fig. 14–12). The same "pay as you throw" principle can apply to any kind of pollution. For example, **effluent taxes** are charged on the basis of how much pollution (effluent) is discharged from a pipe or smokestack.

In summary, regulatory means of pollution control are most effective where polluters are relatively few in number and can be readily monitored. Incentive means are better for pollution from many sources and generally are less costly than regulation. Persuasion is a generally weak but cheap form of social implementation that can supplement the other two.

The 1990 amendments to the Clean Air Act illustrate how a combination of legal and economic methods may be effective where there are intermediate numbers of polluters. These amendments instituted the sale of air pollution permits that industries can buy and sell among themselves. As Chapter 17 explains, this can decrease the overall air pollution in an area at lower economic cost in general by providing incentives to reduce air pollution by the cheapest method. Older factories often find it cheaper to keep polluting and buy the permits from newer factories. The newer factories often find it more profitable to sell the permits and greatly reduce their pollution levels. The

overall result is that air pollution is reduced as much as if all factories partially reduced pollution, but at a much lower cost to society.

Implementing Input Reduction

Notice that our discussion of implementing pollution controls has focused on output methods. This is because society, especially in the United States, still tends to focus on output methods. One reason why change has been so slow is that input reduction, such as burning less fuel or cleaner fuel or producing less waste by precycling, generally requires a larger-scale effort. Instead of the local "Band-Aid" reduction of waste at the end of a pipe or smokestack, input reduction begins earlier in the flow of material through society and therefore usually affects more activities and many more companies and people (Fig. 14–9).

 FIGURE 14–12
When people are charged for the amount of garbage they throw away, they tend to reduce the amount of garbage discarded. (*Source:* Jeff Greenberg/Visuals Unlimited).

Nevertheless, input reduction is becoming more widespread, especially where economic incentives are important. Recall that a major way to promote input reduction is to make currently cheap resources more expensive to reflect their true environmental cost (Chapters 1 and 6). Resource taxes, such as those on fossil fuels, encourage the burning of less fuel. This not only conserves fuel, but produces less air pollution. Similarly, user fees on timber lands raise the price of paper from trees and encourage people to use less paper and to recycle paper.

International and National Aspects

Pollution in both ex-communist countries and developing nations illustrates the economic principles just discussed. Ex-communist countries are generally the most polluted in the world largely because the old communist governments encouraged pollution by subsidizing fossil fuels. This kept prices very low so people had no incentive to conserve. Recent studies by the new governments show that raising energy prices to Western European levels will decrease air pollution by more than 50%. This again demonstrates the effectiveness of input reduction.

Developing countries illustrate input management of pollution in another way, that of in-

vestment in "clean" (green) technologies. Such technologies emphasize hydropower and other renewable resources for electricity generation. Clean technologies not only decrease pollution as those countries industrialize, but according to studies by the World Bank, the overall cost of these technologies is lower than the cost of current technologies due to improved efficiency and less fuel use.

National Pollution

As a leading industrialized country, the United States is the world's leading polluter in many respects. For instance, the United States produces about 20% of the world's greenhouse gas emissions. Nevertheless, water and air pollution in the United States has improved considerably since the early 1970s due to more stringent efforts at all levels of society. Solid waste pollution has lagged behind, but is beginning to improve in the 1990s as landfill space disappears and regulation of toxic waste becomes much more stringent.

An annual overview of toxic pollution in the United States is provided by the **Toxics Release Inventory (TRI)**. The Emergency Planning and Community Right-to-Know Act of 1986 requires industries to report to the EPA the amounts of their toxic releases. The EPA uses these reports to

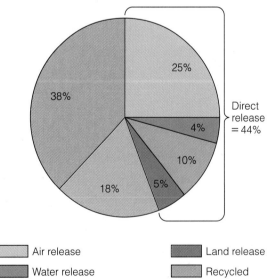

Toxic Releases: Where They Go

Air release	Land release
Water release	Recycled
Underground injection	Treated and disposed of

■ FIGURE 14–13

Most toxic releases reported in the 1992 TRI were either recycled or treated and disposed of. But 44% of toxics were released directly into the environment, mainly into the air. (*Source:* Environmental Protection Agency.)

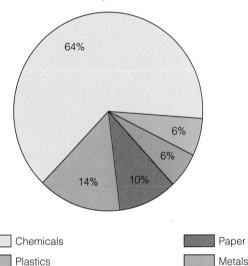

Toxic Releases: Top Five U.S. Industries

Chemicals	Paper
Plastics	Metals
Transportation equipment	

Total release = 2,389 million pounds (1,083 million kilograms)

■ FIGURE 14–14

Nearly two-thirds of the toxic releases reported in the 1992 TRI were from the chemical industry. (*Source:* Environmental Protection Agency.)

A Right to Know

Until the early 1990s, residents of Northfield, Minnesota, never suspected that Sheldahl, Inc., a maker of flexible electronic circuits for automobiles and computers, was a major polluter of their neighborhood. The clean, high-tech plant produced no telltale smoke or odors. But, in reality, Sheldahl, the town's largest employer, was polluting the air with nearly 400 tons (363 metric tons) a year of methylene chloride, a widely used solvent classified as a "probable human carcinogen" although its emission into the air is un-regulated. Once the people of Northfield became aware of the situation, to avoid controversy, Sheldahl immediately volunteered to reduce the emissions by 90% by 1993.

The citizens of Northfield learned about the emissions as a result of a U.S. government database called the Toxics Release Inventory. The report gives communities access to information on polluters in their neighborhoods. The information is made available under the Emergency Planning and Community Right-to-Know Act, adopted in 1986 after the Bhopal disaster in India. The annual reports on industry's toxic emissions have had a significant impact. Dozens of Fortune 500 companies, such as Dow Chemical and DuPont Co., have voluntarily reduced their emissions (see Table 14–3).

The Emergency Planning and Community Right-to-Know Act empowers citizens to act against polluters in their community. The public increasingly measures companies by their emissions numbers and what they are doing about those emissions.

---

produce the TRI. More than 300 toxic substances must be reported. Nevertheless, environmental groups have criticized the TRI for not including all kinds of toxics, and in 1994 EPA administrator Carol Browner requested that the number of reported substances be doubled. Another criticism has been that some polluters are not required to report. Coal-burning power plants and sewage plants are not required to file reports, for instance.

Despite these shortcomings, the TRI data have proved very useful in tracking the flow of toxics in the United States. For example, the 1992 TRI data show that most toxics were recycled or treated (■ Fig. 14–13, page 402). Direct releases (44%) were mostly into the air or as underground injections. Ammonia, hydrochloric acid, and methanol were the chemicals most often released. The TRI data also make it possible to identify the industries that produce the most toxics; historically, the chemical industry has been by far the biggest producer (■ Fig. 14–14, page 402). Variations in state toxic pollution controls are also apparent in the TRI data. The top five states in terms of toxics released in 1992 were Louisiana, Texas, Tennessee, Ohio, and Indiana. By far the most was released in Louisiana and Texas, which have led the TRI list many years. A major reason for this is that southern states have traditionally been poor, have few labor unions,

and have imposed less stringent pollution controls as a way of attracting industry.

On the local level, many environmental and community groups have used TRI data to place pressure on area industries to reduce pollution. Such efforts can be very effective. Issues in Perspective 14–2 describes how one community was able to persuade a major polluter to reduce its toxic emissions, and ● Table 14–3 shows that direct releases into all parts of the environment have declined significantly due at least in part to such community efforts and the publicity generated by the release of the TRI data.

TABLE 14–3 *Direct Releases of Toxic Substances between 1988 and 1992*

	PERCENTAGE CHANGE 1988–1992
Total releases	−35%
Air releases	−32%
Water releases	−12%
Underground injection	−46%
Land releases	−34%

(*Source:* Environmental Protection Agency, 1995.)

SUMMARY

Pollution refers to excess concentrations of substances in the environment that are harmful to us and may be the cause of widespread environmental problems. Humans are causing accelerated pollution rates because of the quantity of waste we produce and the substances within our waste. During each step of many human activities, large concentrations of matter and energy are produced as by-products or waste. Engineers use Life Cycle Analysis (LCA) to eliminate steps or create greater efficiency in many processes. The amount of pollution produced by a society depends on the number of people and the amount of waste they produce. The United States has among the world's highest per capita air, water, and land pollution.

Four major pollutant sources exist: industry, agriculture, households, and transportation. Pollutants from these sources end up in three sinks: water, land, and the air. Natural pollution of these sinks has always occurred from many sources such as volcanoes, animals, and early humans. The growth of population and industrial technology, however, has rapidly accelerated pollution.

Persistence and residence time are two pollutant properties that are significant to the environment. Persistence is the amount of time a pollutant stays in the environment in an unmodified form, and residence time is the length of time needed for a pollutant to move through the environment. These properties indicate the amount of time a pollutant will cause harm to the environment. Federal environmental laws categorize hazardous waste as ignitable, corrosive, reactive, or toxic.

Three myths are associated with the control of pollution. The myth of the purity of nature ignores the fact that nothing in nature is truly "pure." The myth of zero pollution sets up an unrealistic goal of entirely eliminating pollution. The myth of zero risk ignores the fact that we may at best only minimize risk and that this effort is hindered by public misconceptions of risk.

Using a benefit-cost approach, the greatest health and environmental benefits for the least amount of cost are sought. Although costs are usually initially low, they increase rapidly as more energy and increasingly refined equipment are needed to control finer pollutants. Generally, society does not have to pay the continued high costs, however, because the effects of pollution follow an inverse curve relative to the cost curve. Because of the questionable value of a benefit-cost approach, economists have developed the Contingent Valuation Method as an attempt to "objectively" measure the dollar value changes in environmental quality.

Output management may be achieved through pollution control as well as remediation and restoration. Because of the difficulty in implementing pollution control, persuasion, regulation, or economic incentives are often necessary. Laws on pollution control, such as the Clean Air and Clean Water Acts, are based either on the input approach or the output approach. Economic incentives for pollution control include such methods as effluent taxes. Ex-communist countries are among the highest polluters in the world. One reason is their subsidizing of fossil fuels. The United States, a leading industrialized country, is also among the highest polluters. One reason is that resources such as fossil fuels are still relatively inexpensive so there is little incentive to conserve. The Toxics Release Inventory (TRI) provides an annual overview of toxic pollution. Public pressure based on these data has led to a substantial reduction in many toxic releases.

KEY TERMS

abatement devices
absorptive ability
Contingent Valuation Method (CVM)
corrosive
effluent taxes

hazardous waste
ignitable
Life Cycle Analysis (LCA)
persistence
pollution
reactive

remediation
residence time
stock pollutants
toxic
Toxics Release Inventory (TRI)

STUDY QUESTIONS

1. What is Life Cycle Analysis (LCA)? How does it reduce waste generation? What is another name for LCA?
2. What are the four major sources of pollutants?
3. What is a possible solution to the problem of stock pollutants?
4. What is the importance of residence time for global pollution?
5. What percentage of U.S. GNP is spent on pollution control each year?
6. Why is nothing in nature truly pure?
7. What are some problems associated with benefit-cost studies? What does a benefit-cost ratio over 1 indicate?
8. How does output management increase pollution control costs compared to input management?
9. Benefit-cost solutions to pollution control represent a utility-based approach that differs from two approaches used in the past. Identify these earlier approaches. What method uses questionnaires to try to "objectively" estimate the dollar value of changes in environmental quality?
10. Name the three basic ways to promote change in human activities, such as reducing pollution.
11. According to the TRI, into which part of the environment do most toxics that are directly released go? According to the TRI, which industry is the major source of most toxic releases?
12. Define effluent taxes, remediation, Life Cycle Analysis, and pollution.
13. Why do ex-communist nations often have so much pollution? How can clean (green) technology decrease overall eco-

nomic costs?

14. According to the TRI, total reported pollutant releases for all U.S. industries in 1992, were 3182 million pounds. If the top five industries released 2389 million pounds (Fig. 14–14), what percentage of the total did the top five release? How many kilograms is this (1 kg = 2.205 lb)?

15. According to the TRI, total reported pollutant releases for all U.S. industries in 1992, were 3182 million pounds. This amount is a 35% reduction compared to total releases in 1988. How much was released in 1988? How many kilograms is this (1 kg = 2.205 lb)?

ESSAY QUESTIONS

1. Pollution has always occurred in the environment. Name several early or ancient examples of pollution, both human and nonhuman.

2. What are the two subdivisions of hazardous waste as defined by federal environmental laws? Summarize their definitions and give examples of each characteristic.

3. Explain the three common myths of pollution control.

4. How have the pollution control myths influenced public policy? Give examples.

5. What are the main arguments concerning the costs of pollution control?

SUGGESTED READINGS

Allan, R. 1992. *Waste not, want not.* London: Earthscan.

Commoner, B. 1990. *Making peace with the planet.* New York: Pantheon.

Corson, W. H., ed. 1990. *The global ecology handbook: What you can do about the environmental crisis.* Boston: Beacon Press.

Earth Works Group. 1990. *The recycler's handbook: Simple things you can do.* Berkeley, Calif.: Earth Works Press.

Eblen, R., and W. Eblen, eds. 1994. *The encyclopedia of the environment.* New York: Houghton Mifflin.

Ehrlich, P. R., and A. H. Ehrlich. 1991. *Healing the planet.* Reading, Mass.: Addison-Wesley.

Gourlay, K. A. 1992. *World of waste: Dilemmas of industrial development.* Atlantic Heights, N.J.: Zed Books.

Kharbanda, O. P., and E. Stallworthy. 1990. *Waste management: Toward a sustainable society.* New York: Auburn House.

Meadows, D. H., D. L. Meadows, and J. Randers. 1992. *Beyond the limits.* Post Mills, VT.: Chelsea Green.

Theodore, L., and Y. McGuinn. 1992. *Pollution prevention.* New York: Van Nostrand Reinhold.

Wolf, N., and E. Feldman. 1990. *Plastics: America's packaging dilemma.* Washington, D.C.: Island Press.

World Resources Institute. 1994 and yearly. *The information please environmental almanac.* New York: Houghton Mifflin.

Young, J. E. 1991. *Discarding the throwaway society.* Washington, D.C.: Worldwatch Institute.

*T*OXICOLOGY, PESTICIDES, AND RISK

PROLOGUE   *To Save Mickey Mouse Sculptures, Disney Wishes upon a Bug*

*T*he Australian eugenia tree is prized by many gardeners for its lush leaves and, especially, its ability to be sculpted into hedges and shrubs. Gardeners at Disneyland sculpted figures of Mickey Mouse, Pluto, and other cartoon characters from eugenia, much to the delight of visitors. Eugenia hedges also form an important landscape element within the park and serve as a visual screen around the park. But sometime in the late 1980s, trouble arrived for the eugenia tree, possibly as a stowaway in a tourist's suitcase or in the hold of a jetliner. The eugenia psyllid is an aphidlike Australian insect with larvae that voraciously devour eugenia tree leaves, making them blister and causing discoloration. They also stunt tree growth. Although millions of dollars were spent on chemical pesticides, the psyllid bug spread throughout California until every eugenia tree in the state was infested. In 1991, Disney officials called on Professor Donald Dahlsten (University of California, Berkeley) for help.

PHOTO   *Eugenia hedges at Disneyland, such as the one seen here behind Dumbo, were spared damage by the use of biological pest control.*

Dahlsten is an expert in biological pest control, which uses natural enemies, instead of chemicals, to reduce pest populations. Dahlsten, along with Dr. Donald M. Kent (an ecologist with Walt Disney Imagineering), decided to take a visit to the rainforest home of the eugenia tree to try and find what kept the psyllid bug under control in its native habitat. Clues were evident in the dead psyllid larvae, which were all penetrated by holes. Further work showed that the predator was a tiny wasp, just half the size of the psyllid larvae; the wasp punched the holes to kill the larvae and to deposit its eggs. Upon receiving permission from Australian authorities, some of the wasps were transported to the United States in tiny capsules. In the United States, the wasps underwent six months of quarantine and testing in the laboratory to see if they might ravage other insects or plants. Fortunately, the wasps seem to specialize in psyllid bugs. In July 1992, more than 100 wasps were released at Disneyland. A year later, the psyllid population was reduced by 90%, and the eugenia trees showed a definite improvement. A few more years will be needed to be sure that this is a success story. Sometimes pest populations rebound or the introduced predators start devouring other species. But, so far, the experiment has worked well, so well that the wasps have been released to control the psyllid bugs elsewhere, including at the San Diego Zoo.

$\mathcal{I}$ NTRODUCTION

In this chapter, we examine the effects of especially harmful pollutants, those that are poisonous or toxic in relatively small amounts. These pollutants are of great environmental importance because they can affect humans and all other living things, including entire ecosystems. Usually, harmful pollutants are chemical byproducts of industrial processes such as dioxin. Increased efficiency and reuse/recycling can reduce such byproducts. In other cases, the toxic material is purposely produced, as with pesticides. In the past few years, pesticides produced in the United States have become more deadly. Even though the quantity of pesticides produced is lower, they are generally more harmful. Another area of concern is that exposure to harmful chemicals of all kinds is on the rise. As more are produced worldwide, large-scale accidents and spills have been increasing.

An estimated 2% of the thousands of new chemicals available each year are sufficiently harmful to be considered toxic.

Brief History and Future of Toxicology

Ancient alchemists and mystics were the earliest known practitioners of toxicology. They determined the harmful effects of natural products such as herbs, berries, and even minerals. Ancient Greek and Roman writings described the effects of hemlock (the poisonous herbs, not the trees) and snake venoms (■ Fig. 15–1). By the Middle Ages, people were apparently using toxicological knowledge for political gain by using poison to eliminate their enemies.

■ **FIGURE 15–1**
The Athenian philosopher Socrates (circa 470–399 B.C.) drank hemlock after being condemned to death (depicted here in the 1787 painting by Jacques Louis David, *The Death of Socrates*). (*Source*: The Granger Collection, New York.)

$\mathcal{I}$ OXICOLOGY: THE SCIENCE OF POISONS

Toxicology studies the effects of chemicals that are harmful or fatal when consumed by organisms in relatively small amounts. A conventional pollutant may be deadly in parts per million whereas a toxic pollutant can be deadly in parts per trillion or even less. Toxic pollutants include not only pesticides, which are purposely made to be toxic to certain target organisms, but thousands of other chemicals that have toxicity as a side-effect. Recall (Chapter 14) that more than 70 new chemicals are registered every hour and more than 70,000 chemicals are in everyday use worldwide.

Paracelsus, a Swiss physician of the early sixteenth century, is often called the "father of modern toxicology." Many of his theories have withstood the test of time and are still valid. He recognized, for example, that controlled experimentation is needed to accurately identify the toxicity of materials. He also discovered that a single chemical can cause a toxic response. By the late nineteenth century, toxicology was growing rapidly, especially the study of manufactured chemicals. Since the first human-made industrial chemical was produced in 1856 (Chapter 14), the exponential growth of chemical innovation and production has overwhelmed attempts to perform thorough toxicological studies on all manufactured substances. There are essentially no toxicological data on about 75% of the 70,000 chemicals in everyday use, and less than 2% of these chemicals have been completely evaluated, especially for long-term effects on health. Fortunately, the large majority of chemicals do not prove to be extremely harmful when evaluation is finally carried out.

Future Directions in Toxicology

Recent advances in toxicology have led to new subdisciplines that have greatly improved its effectiveness, and will therefore aid in developing less toxic substances. Four of the most promising subdisciplines are briefly described here.

Molecular toxicology examines the interaction of toxic chemicals with cellular enzymes. By identifying the molecular mechanism by which toxic chemicals harm cells, we can predict the toxicity of new chemicals simply by knowing what their chemical structure is. This holds great promise for reducing the need for animal testing, discussed below, which now relies on "trial and error" to predict toxicity of new chemicals, with little or no insight into the chemical mechanisms that cause the harm.

Immunotoxicology examines how chemicals affect the immune system. Many toxic substances, called "immunotoxicants," have subtle long-term effects on the body's ability to defend itself against diseases, but the complexity of the immune system made it very difficult to study these effects. Now newly developed tests enable researchers to identify immunotoxicants with some confidence.

Behavioral toxicology studies chemicals that can cause disorders of behavior or learning. Traditional toxicology studied only damage to physical tissues; behavioral toxicology has identified many chemicals that can affect behavior or learning but cause no observable tissue damage.

Ecotoxicology is the study of how chemicals affect entire ecosystems. This field has enormous potential because some chemicals have no effect on some species, but can greatly affect others. Furthermore, the long-term impacts of such differential effects are very complex, as they affect predator-prey interactions, population growth, and many other ecological dynamics. Examples involving food web concentration of chemicals are discussed later.

Effects of Toxic Substances

Toxicologists trace the path of a toxic substance through the body in five steps identified by the acronym **ADMSE:** absorption, distribution, metabolism, storage, and excretion. Absorption of toxic substances can occur in three ways: ingestion with food or drink, inhalation, or skin contact (Fig. 15–2). The body rarely absorbs 100% of any substance that enters it. For example, about 50% of the lead in food is absorbed— and much less if the lead is in a chemically nonreactive form. After toxic substances enter, they can be distributed via the blood to cells where they are metabolized (Fig. 15–2). Metabolism

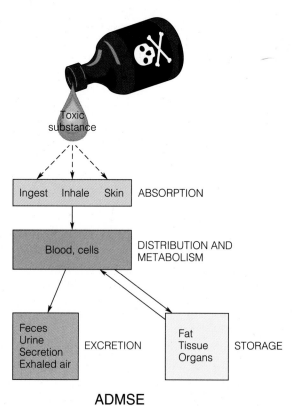

ADMSE

 FIGURE 15–2
ADMSE traces the path of toxic substances through the body: absorption, distribution, metabolism, storage, and excretion.

refers to the body's biochemical response to the toxic substance. Sometimes metabolism can detoxify the poison, rendering it less harmful in the body. In other cases, the opposite occurs, and harmless substances are made harmful.

At this point, sufficient amounts of a deadly poison can cause organ damage. **Acute toxicity** occurs when toxic substances are harmful shortly after exposure. Several organs are especially susceptible to short-term damage by toxic substances. As major filters of blood, the liver and kidneys are vulnerable because toxic substances are carried by the bloodstream. Also, as filters, the liver and kidneys readily accumulate the toxic substance. Examples of toxic substances that have commonly led to liver damage include carbon tetrachloride, DDT, heavy metals such as iron, and overdoses of drugs such as acetaminophen. Lungs and the bloodstream are highly vulnerable to gaseous toxic substances. Many toxic substances destroy fragile lung tissue, and the bloodstream can be affected by gases such as carbon monoxide that destroy the blood's ability to carry oxygen.

If the toxic substance does not cause immediate death through acute toxicity, it can subsequently either be excreted or stored (Fig. 15–2). Storage can lead to long-term effects called **chronic toxicity**. Even very low doses can have effects, if exposure occurs for a long time. Chronic toxic substances are by far the most difficult for society to cope with because their effects are subtle and long-ranging, making it very difficult to determine their impact on humans and other living things. Two important examples of chronic toxic substances are carcinogens and teratogens.

A **carcinogen** is a cancer-producing substance. Cancer is the uncontrolled multiplication of cells, often forming tumors and spreading throughout the body. Cancer causes about 22% of U.S. deaths annually. There are many kinds of cancers, some of which can be inherited. In many cases, however, environmental factors, such as diet and chemicals in the workplace, can contribute to or directly cause cancer. Tobacco and diet are the two most important environmental factors, accounting for perhaps two-thirds of avoidable (not inherited) cancer deaths (● Table 15–1). Notice that these, like most causes of cancer deaths, are largely related to our personal lifestyle choices. Pollution and food additives, cancer causes often associated with environmental problems, are a very small percentage. Such estimates are very approximate because it is obviously impossible to do con-

trolled experiments with humans. Nevertheless, similar results from many rigorous statistical studies lead most cancer experts to consider these figures valid as rough estimates of noninherited cancer causes.

Two types of chronic toxicity can cause birth defects. A **mutagen** is a substance that causes genetic mutations in sperm or egg cells. A **teratogen** is a substance that affects fetal development, such as when the mother drinks alcohol or has other harmful chemicals in her body. Teratogens are common because development is a very complex sequence of cellular and biochemical interactions and is therefore easily disturbed. A general rule of thumb is that sensitivity to chemicals decreases with age, at least until old age is reached. Very young embryos are most sensitive to chemicals because cell multiplication, organ formation, and many other delicate growth processes are occurring (▬ Fig. 15–3). This is why pregnant women are discouraged from smoking, drinking alcohol, and taking drugs. Once organs have formed, development can still be disturbed in many ways, but these tend to be less drastic than organ malformities, limb losses, and other defects of early development. In all organisms, younger individuals exhibit greater environmental sensitivity than adults. For example, the symptoms of lead poisoning including nerve damage and learning disabilities are more severe in children than in adults because their nervous system is still developing. When a natural ecosystem such as a stream is polluted, the first organisms to die are usually larvae and other kinds of juveniles.

TABLE 15–1 *Estimated Causes of Cancer Deaths*

FACTOR	PERCENTAGE OF TOTAL CANCER DEATHS
Tobacco	30
Alcohol	3
Diet	35
Reproductive and sexual behavior	7
Occupation	4
Food additives	<1
Pollution	2
Industrial products	<1
Sunlight, ultraviolet light, other radiation	3
Medicines, medical procedures	1
Infections or inherited factors	13
TOTAL	100

(*Source:* Data from R. Doll and R. Peto, "Avoidable Risks of Cancer in the U.S.," *Journal of the National Cancer Institute 66* [1981]: 1191–1308.)

FIGURE 15-3
Infant development occurs over three periods: pre-embryonic, embryonic, and fetal. Each bar indicates when an organ system develops. The yellow portions indicate periods most sensitive to agents that can cause major birth defects.

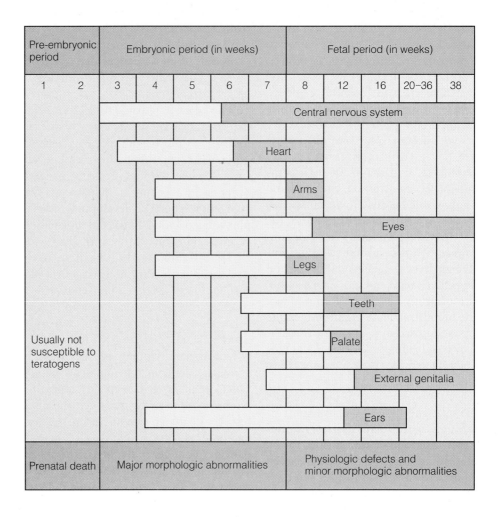

Toxic Risk Assessment

One of the most important changes in environmental policy in the 1980s was the incorporation of risk measurements into environmental decision making. This was based on the realization that everything involves costs (including risk) and that the benefits of substances must be weighed against the risks to humans and other organisms (Chapter 14). During the 1990s interest in risk has grown even more.

For this policy to work, we must have some way to measure the risks. One way is through the use of **epidemiological statistics**, which examine correlations between environmental factors and the health of humans and other organisms. The strong relationship between smoking cigarettes and developing lung cancer, for instance, is statistically highly significant. But this approach has two disadvantages. First, such statistical correlations examine harm "after the fact," so that much damage has already occurred by the time we determine that a chemical was harmful. Second, the best evidence in science is usually based on controlled experiments, where certain variables are held constant. Information on toxicity therefore often requires the direct testing of a chemical's effect on organisms under controlled conditions. Of course, humans are not usually tested directly, so animals ranging from bacteria to primates are used (Fig. 15–4). But animal testing raises the issue of animal rights (see Issues in Perspective 15–1).

Toxic risk assessment in the United States is a four-step process:

1. *Toxic identification.* Determines if a chemical is toxic, usually by testing microbes.
2. *Dose-response assessment.* Determines the strength of toxicity, often by testing mice.
3. *Exposure assessment.* Determines how often humans are exposed to the chemical.
4. *Risk characterization.* Considers the scientific data from steps 1–3 along with societal values to reach a final decision.

The first two steps use animals; dose-response assessment may test "higher animals," including dogs or monkeys.

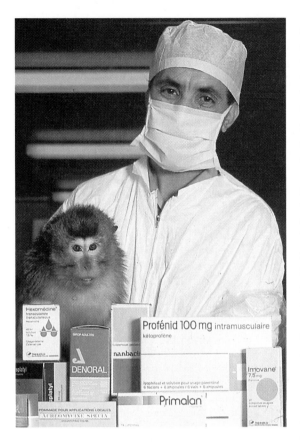

Toxic Identification

In the initial step of toxic identification, researchers seek evidence if a certain substance is toxic. Given the number of new chemicals developed each year, it is impossible to thoroughly test each chemical for toxicity. Instead, government agencies and manufacturers use hierarchical sequences of tests, called **bioassays**, to test each chemical. A relatively short, inexpensive initial test is administered to search for any possible indications of harmful effects. If harmful effects are indicated, then progressively more thorough tests are carried out until statistical analysis shows that the chemical is harmful (or not) with a high degree of certainty

An example is the test sequence for cancer, which begins with a short-term test to see if the chemical may cause mutations. The most widely used mutagenicity test, called the Ames test, subjects special strains of bacteria to the chemical. These bacteria are specially bred to be incapable of normal reproduction by cell division. If the bacteria begin to multiply and form visible colonies after the test chemical has been applied, it is likely to be mutagenic because only bacteria that have mutated back to a form capable of normal cell division can reproduce. As some mutagens can cause cancer, a series of more thorough tests for carcinogenesis is begun. These involve longer-term tests (several months), using mice and rats, to see if tumors develop in specific organs. If these tests also show signs of carcinogenic properties, the chemical is subjected to an even lengthier and more costly set of tests, the chronic carcinogenesis bioassay. This involves hundreds or thousands of animals over a period of several years.

These procedures for identifying toxic substances have two basic problems: (1) they do not test humans directly, and (2) they cannot detect very small risks. With animal tests, we can never be totally certain that a chemical is safe for humans. The complex biochemistry of even closely related species often differs in subtle ways, called **intrinsic factors**, so that a chemical that has no effect on one species may have acute or long-term effects on another. The inability to detect very small risk arises because even the long-term testing of thousands of animals cannot generate statistically certain evidence on chemicals that have slight effects.

Dose-response Assessment

If a chemical shows evidence of toxicity in the bioassays, the next step is to measure the strength of toxicity. **Biotoxins** and **supertoxins** can cause death in very tiny amounts; less than a drop can kill an adult human. Conversely, the chemical may be slightly toxic, with only very large doses being harmful. Toxic strength is essential to know because the benefits may outweigh the harm if the substance has nontoxic uses, such as aspirin, and is toxic only in amounts much greater than normally encountered. Any substance can cause harm in sufficient amounts, even vitamins and other nutrients that we require in moderation (Fig. 15–5).

Dose-response assessment is based on the application of various doses of the test toxic sub-

FIGURE 15–4

Animals are used to test the effects of substances on humans. Seen at left with the researcher is a rhesus monkey. (*Source:* Yves Forestier/Sygma.)

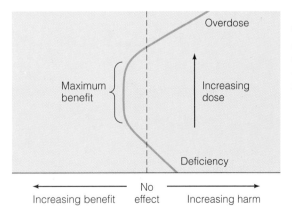

FIGURE 15–5

Too little or too much of even healthful substances can be harmful by causing a deficiency or an overdose, respectively.

Should We Use Animals to Test Products? Which Animals?

Many people question whether animals should be used to test products. Animal activist groups, such as People for the Ethical Treatment of Animals (PETA) and the Animal Liberation Front (ALF), oppose animal experimentation. While some argue that no animals should be used for experimentation, others oppose the use of only certain kinds of animals (such as monkeys and apes). Others agree that animal experimentation is needed, but call for more humane treatment: the amount of pain inflicted, which is often ignored, should be considered.

While most animal rights advocates take a nonviolent approach, others have acted violently. The National Association for Biomedical Research documented 107 attacks on institutions conducting animal research between 1981 and 1994. The monetary damage from these attacks was estimated at more than $7.7 million, which does not include the loss of scientific data that could have saved human lives or even animal lives in the case of data used for veterinary medicine.

Perhaps the most desirable solution to the animal-testing controversy is to find ways of testing products that provide the same toxicological information but do not use "higher" animals (such as mammals) or

at least do not inflict pain or kill them. Fortunately, several new methods are becoming available, although none is fully satisfactory for all purposes. These methods include computer models, "in vitro" tests of cell cultures, and use of microbes and invertebrates. Computer models based on previously gathered data can be very powerful predictors if properly utilized. Knowing the biochemical pathways of how one substance is metabolized, for instance, can allow us to predict how a similar substance will affect an organism. Unfortunately, computer models are always limited by the quality of the data and the accuracy of the assumptions made. Just one inaccurate assumption out of hundreds can nullify the model and produce invalid results. Consequently, many toxicologists are skeptical that models will ever replace high-quality data gathered under controlled laboratory conditions. In vitro tests of cells or tissues can avoid animal pain or death where the cells can be grown in the lab. But such tests are very incomplete compared to whole-animal data because they provide little information on how organ systems in the animal will interact if exposed to the chemical.

Fewer objections are raised to the use of microorganisms and invertebrates such as shellfishes or insects, but chemical testing on them is often criticized for two rea-

sons. One is scientific: the less closely related a species is to humans, the less similar to humans are its biological responses to chemicals. Hence, vertebrates, especially monkeys and apes, provide the closest analogs to humans. In contrast, the genes, biochemistry, and physiology of microbes and invertebrates are often so different from our own, that the data produced are useless for human toxicology. The other problem is ethical: can we say that a mammal, for example, deserves more humane treatment than, say, a shellfish? If so, is this just because we are mammals? Or is it because mammals are "smarter" or feel more pain? And where do we draw the line? Is it valid to subject some mammals, such as mice, to pain, but not others, such as monkeys?

These questions cut to the very heart of the animal-testing issue, and there are, as we often find in environmental issues, no simple answers. Perhaps a "techno-solution" can eventually be found, such as the use of very complex computer models or cloning of cell tissues that will provide precise toxicological information. But until that time, animal testing seems certain to remain controversial as the debate over the needs of humans versus the rights of animals continues.

---

stance to a number of organisms, usually animals, to see what the response is: no harm, impairment, or death. The statistics generated are then used to make probabilistic statements on the chemical's effect on humans. Lethal dose curves, which examine the dose needed to cause death in the test organism, are among the most common types of statistics. The usual pattern in any population of organisms is a bell-shaped curve. Some individuals are much more sensitive to the toxic substance than others, some are more tolerant, and most are intermediate (Fig. 15–6). The midpoint represents the dose that kills 50% of the

population, called **LD-50** meaning Lethal Dose 50%. LD-50 has become the standard reference for summarizing the toxicity of substances.

Most LD-50 studies attempt to measure acute toxicity by using relatively high doses to produce death in a few days. It is also very important to see if a chemical will cause harm over a long period of time. We are exposed to many chemicals daily in small amounts. Long-term testing for chronic toxicity is generally much more expensive than tests for acute toxicity, however. Toxicologists therefore try to derive as much information as they can from short-term testing. This is possi-

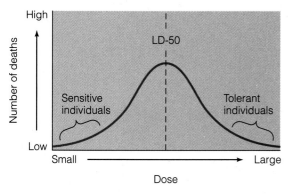

FIGURE 15-6

Sensitive individuals die at small doses, but a few tolerant individuals can sustain large doses. Most of the population dies at doses around LD-50, which is the dose where 50% of the population has died.

ble because, as ▬ Figure 15–7 shows, chemicals that are acutely very toxic (low LD-50) also tend to be chronically very toxic. Those chemicals that cause immediate harm in low doses can also cause long-term harm in lower doses than most chemicals. All the chemicals plotted cause chronic death and do so at lower doses than they cause acute death. Note that predictions of chronic toxicity with this method are far from perfect. Some of the points fall well below the regression line; all of these represent chemicals whose chronic toxicity is greater (requiring much smaller doses to cause chronic death) than would be predicted by the tests for acute toxicity. In some cases, such as the circled data point, the chronic toxicity may be much greater (requiring extremely small doses to cause chronic death) than predicted.

LD-50 estimates suffer from the same two problems as toxic identification: they use non-human data and cannot detect very small effects that accumulate over a long time. The problem of small effects is most pronounced with cancer-causing substances. For noncarcinogenic substances, it is usually assumed that there is a **toxic threshold** below which no harm is done. For carcinogens, it is often conservatively assumed that exposure to *any amount* will create some increased chance of cancer in a population, so there is no threshold. For example, a study of mice may indicate that only 100 cancers may be produced in a population of one million mice over the next few years. Even though the calculated risk is very small (0.01%), it may be considered serious enough to make a chemical product unmarketable. Under this assumption, all of the chemicals in Figure 15–7 would be considered too harmful to produce, if they caused cancer. This is because, at some dose, all of those shown are chronically toxic.

More problems arise when we extend dose-response findings to human toxicity. Species differences, or intrinsic factors, complicate dose-response experiments for the same reason that they affect toxic identification. The difference in sensitivities of organisms to the same toxic substance is quite striking, even among the same kinds of animals. In general, more closely related species tend to have more similar sensitivities because they share more biochemical and physiological traits. But in many cases, one species, such as one strain of lab mouse, is greatly affected by a chemical while a closely related species is not. Obviously, then extending findings from mice to humans is not necessarily valid because of our intrinsic biological differences.

Another obstacle to extending animal results to humans are differences in body sizes, often called "scaling factors." For example, **dosage** is generally measured as the amount of a substance administered to the organism divided by the body weight of the organism. When LD-50 data on mice are applied to humans, the data must therefore be adjusted for body weight differences between mice and humans, as shown in ● Table 15–2.

In the past, tragic deaths and human suffering have occurred when such species and scaling differences were not adequately taken into account. Products were released onto the market for human consumption because animal testing seemed to indicate that they were safe. Probably, the best-known example is thalidomide, which was released in Europe in 1962 as a tranquilizer for pregnant women. Tests with seven different nonhuman species indicated that the drug was

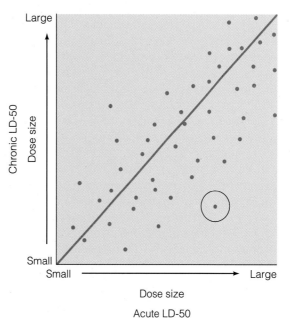

FIGURE 15–7

These hypothetical data illustrate the approximate correlation between a chemical's acute LD-50 and its chronic LD-50. The circled point shows that the correlation is only approximate, however: this chemical produces acute effects at relatively high doses, but can cause chronic, long-term effects at unusually low doses. The pattern in this figure is commonly found in toxicological studies of many kinds of chemicals.

TABLE 15–2 *Approximate Comparison of LD-50 Values with Lethal Doses for Human Adults*

ORAL LD-50 FOR ANY ANIMAL (MG/KG)	PROBABLE LETHAL ORAL DOSES FOR HUMAN ADULT
Less than 5	A few drops
5 to 50	A "pinch" to 1 teaspoon
50 to 500	1 teaspoon to 2 tablespoons
500 to 5000	1 ounce to 1 pint (1 pound)
5000 to 15,000	1 pint to 1 quart (2 pounds)

safe for humans, but it turned out to cause severe birth defects. Tragically, more than 10,000 deformed babies were born as a direct result of thalidomide. Dozens of similar examples have occurred, although the outcomes were usually less drastic. To cite just two examples, bendectin to control nausea in pregnant women was found to cause birth defects; oraflex to control arthritis pain was found to cause kidney damage. Clearly, data gained from animal testing must be applied to humans with very great caution. Initial tests using human volunteers, often people who are seriously ill and may benefit from the medication, are important in preventing the widespread release of a potentially harmful product. Even these are inadequate when the number of human subjects in the sample is too small.

Exposure Assessment

While much public attention is given to identifying and measuring the toxicity of chemicals, the amount of exposure is equally important. Even very toxic substances can do no harm if we are not exposed to them in sufficient amounts. The first step in exposure assessment is to determine possible pathways by which toxic chemicals may reach humans. The three most important pathways are inhalation (air transport), eating (food transport), and drinking (water transport). Pathways can involve many steps, and many substances have a number of different, often complex pathways.

In addition to mobility, the persistence of a substance is also important. Persistence refers to whether the substance remains intact long enough to be transported long distances. In the case of exposure by food, a crucial property is the tendency toward bioconcentration. **Bioconcentration** (sometimes called bioaccumulation or biomagnification) is the tendency of a substance to accumulate in living tissue; it involves two steps. First, an organism takes in a substance, but does not excrete or metabolize it. Then, a predator eats that organism and in the process ingests the substance already accumulated by its prey (■ Fig. 15–8). This second step is common in fishes, shellfishes, carnivores such as eagles and cats, and other organisms that prey on smaller organisms so that the chemical is concentrated by passage through the food pyramid (Chapter 3). Mollusks, such as scallops, are exceptionally prone to bioconcentration because they feed by filtering millions of tiny plankton from the water.

Bioconcentration depends not only on the organisms present when pollution occurs, but also on the properties of the substance. The **bioconcentration factor (BCF)** measures the tendency for concentration by a given substance. For example:

$$DDT \text{ concentration in a fish} = DDT \text{ concentration in water} \times BCF$$

$$540 \text{ mg/kg} = 0.01 \text{ mg/L} \times 54,000 \text{ L/kg}$$

The fish has about 540 milligrams of DDT per kilogram of fish. The higher the BCF, the greater the tendency for the substance to be bioconcentrated. Two common groups of chemicals are especially notable for their high BCFs: chlorinated hydrocarbons and heavy metals. Chlorinated hydrocarbons are synthetic organic (carbon-containing) compounds that have many uses in our society including plastics, electrical insulation, and some pesticides. Examples include PCBs, used as electrical insulation, and the insecticides aldrin,

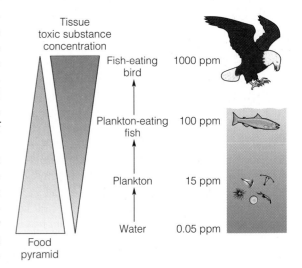

FIGURE 15–8

Organisms occurring higher on the food pyramid tend to have increasingly greater concentrations of toxic substances in their tissue. (Note: ppm=parts per million.)

chlordane, and DDT. Two properties of chlorinated hydrocarbons make them especially likely to become bioconcentrated: their high persistence and their high fat solubility. This combination explains why molecules of DDT are found in unexpected places, including polar bear and penguin fat because atmospheric dust has carried the DDT molecules to polar regions (▬ Fig. 15–9).

Recently, a relatively unstudied impact of toxic pollutants on wildlife and humans has been arousing concern. Often called **environmental hormones**, these pollutants send false signals to the complex hormonal systems that regulate reproduction, immunity, behavior, and growth. The result can be infertility, behavioral and growth abnormalities, and low resistance to disease. Some ecologists suspect that hundreds of chemical products may have caused population declines in many species of birds, fishes, and other wildlife, but the effects are usually so subtle and complex that they are difficult to prove.

Heavy metals, the second large group susceptible to bioconcentration, include such elements as lead, mercury, zinc, copper, and cadmium, among others. In trace amounts, many of these actually ensure proper functioning of enzymes by binding with them, but when we ingest too much of these required elements such as zinc, or the wrong kind, such as mercury, this tendency to bind with enzymes can impair their function. Because enzymes in the central nervous system are especially sensitive, heavy metal poisoning often causes insanity, mental impairment, paralysis, and other forms of painful nerve damage that can ultimately cause death. Birth defects can occur because DNA in genes can be affected, and kidney damage is common. This protein-binding capacity also promotes bioconcentration because the metallic atoms become attached to proteins instead of being excreted. The metals accumulate in the body over time, causing progressive damage, as well as accumulating up the food chain to become more concentrated in the larger predators.

The classic example is "Minamata disease," which occurred in Minamata, Japan, in the mid-1950s when mercury waste was dumped into the bay where villagers fished. Mercury concentrated in fish tissue resulted in 50 deaths and permanent illness in at least 150 others. The Minamata tragedy led to increased awareness of heavy metal pollution and improved measures of control. But past pollution is a lingering problem because heavy metals tend to bind to clay and other particles in sediment. This concentrates the metals so that factory discharges that occurred many decades ago will continue to pollute local waters until they are cleaned up at great expense. Usually, the sediment must be excavated and reburied elsewhere. Because of past and present pollution, heavy metal content is continually monitored in the tissues of food organisms. You have probably heard of periodic reports of canned tuna with a high mercury content.

A final key aspect of exposure assessment is that we can be exposed to many chemicals simultaneously. Consequently, we need to understand how substances can affect us when they interact with one another. There are three basic kinds of interactions: antagonistic, additive, and synergistic (▬ Fig. 15–10).

▬ **FIGURE 15–9**
Even polar bears living far from large human populations have fatty tissues containing DDT and other bioconcentrated pollutants. Seen here is a polar bear at Churchill, Manitoba, Canada. (*Source:* Joe McDonald, Visuals Unlimited.)

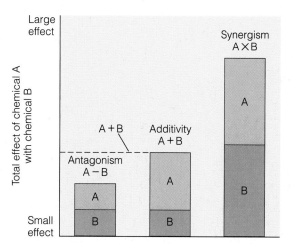

▬ **FIGURE 15–10**
Three kinds of chemical interactions: antagonism (B cancels or subtracts from A), additivity (A and B have additive effects), and synergism (A and B multiply each other's effects).

Antagonism occurs when substances work against each other and cancel each other's effects. For example, deadly snake venoms, such as nerve toxin, can be neutralized by chemical antidotes that destroy the toxic molecules. **Additivity** occurs when the toxic effects are added together. If chemical A harms the liver and chemical B harms the kidneys, then exposure to both will harm the liver and kidneys. **Synergism** occurs when the toxic effects are *multiplied* through interaction, making this the most dangerous type of interaction of all. For example, smoking cigarettes increases your chance of getting lung cancer, as does inhaling radon gas. But a smoker who is exposed to radon gas has a much higher chance of developing lung cancer than one would predict by adding the chances of getting cancer from smoking and radon gas. Tobacco ash particles in the lungs serve as attachment areas for radioactive radon particles, greatly enhancing the chance of getting lung cancer.

Risk Characterization

The fourth step of toxic risk assessment is risk characterization, which combines scientific data from the first three steps with societal values to reach a decision about what to do with a new chemical. Is it too dangerous to be marketed? Do the risks outweigh the benefits? Because human emotions, economics, and many other social

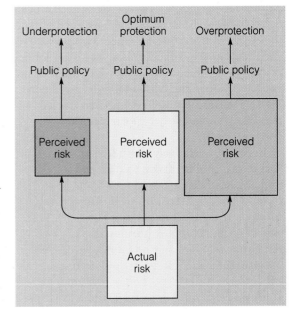

FIGURE 15–11

Misperception of actual risk can result in over- or underprotection. Both are unnecessarily costly to society.

variables are involved, this is often the most complex step of all.

Risk refers to any potential danger. The first three steps of toxic assessment provide data on the risk of newly invented chemicals. Unfortunately, even when data are available, our perception of risk is often distorted and does not accurately reflect the actual risk. Consequently, our efforts to try to guard ourselves against perceived risks can lead to under- or overprotection (Fig. 15–11). The average American is much more likely to die from eating peanut butter than from being struck by lightning (Table 15–3), yet most of us worry much more about lightning (at least when we are caught in a storm, and indeed the risk of being killed by lightning may then be much higher than shown in Table 15–3).

There are two basic reasons for such misperceptions of risk. One is that our emotions play a large role in how we interpret facts. As Figure 15–12 shows, the most "dreaded" (highly perceived) risks are hazards that are neither observable nor controllable, such as radioactive waste. Observable and controllable hazards, such as motorcycles, are perceived as less risky than nuclear power, even though statistically the risk is much higher.

The second reason for risk misperception is the way we receive information about environmental hazards. Nearly all the news media tend to focus on dramatic spectacles, such as oil spills, rather than long-term problems because the media have

TABLE 15–3 *Annual Risk Calculated as Number of Deaths per 100,000 People in the United States*

ACTIVITY/EXPOSURE	ANNUAL RISK (DEATHS PER 100,000 PERSONS AT RISK)
Motorcycling	2000
All causes, all ages	1000
Smoking (all causes)	300
Smoking (cancer)	120
Fire fighting	80
Hang gliding	80
Coal mining	63
Farming	36
Motor vehicles	24
Rodeo performer	3
Fires	2.8
Chlorinated drinking water (chemical by-products)	0.8
4 tbs peanut butter/day (aflatoxin)	0.8
3 oz charcoal broiled steak/day	0.5
Floods	0.06
Lightning	0.05
Hit by meteorite	0.000 006

(*Source:* P. Slovic, *Risk Analysis* 6 [New York: Plenum, 1986]: 405–15. Reprinted with permission of Plenum Publishing Corporation.)

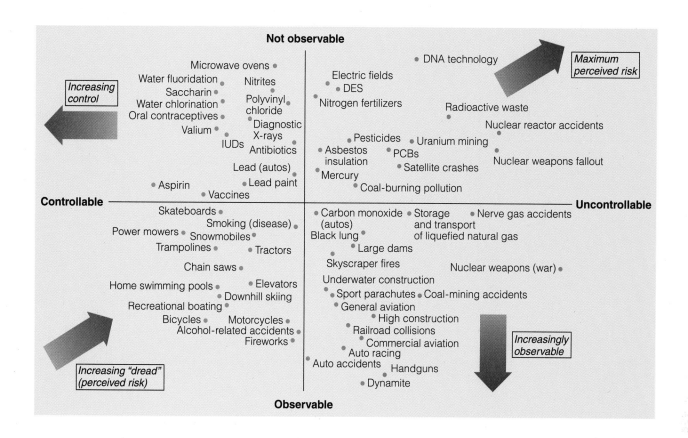

FIGURE 15–12 (caption at right)

found that people tend to be more interesed in dramatic events. While spectacles such as oil spills represent short-term local risks, the most dangerous risks to society as a whole are often more long term in nature, such as global warming and species extinctions. In the case of oil, the large majority of oil pollution of the oceans comes from land runoff, ship bilge discharges, and other sources besides oil spills (Chapter 16). This problem is aggravated by the media's policy of presenting both "sides" of an issue. When "experts" disagree over the dangers of environmental hazards, such as global warming, the public becomes confused and tends to discount the hazards.

Public misperception of risk results in wasteful and inefficient spending of money on environmental problems. As we saw in Chapter 1 (Fig. 1–4), much more money is spent on problems of lower overall risk such as sewage and hazardous wastes than on high-risk problems such as global warming and indoor radon. Some have proposed that such spending inefficiencies could be avoided by using benefit-cost analyses that incorporate accurate risk information. In practice, this has proven very difficult, however, largely because so many of the benefits and costs, including risk, are very difficult to measure (Chapters 6, 14, and 20). The statistical risks of death in Table 15–3, for example, omit many other crucial considerations

needed for a complete benefit-cost analysis. What about the risks of nonlethal injuries, which are omitted from simple "death count" tabulations? Or, the risks to wildlife and ecosystems? Or the social groups that will suffer the highest risk, and obtain the least benefit, from a proposed activity? This last consideration is crucial because risks, costs, and benefits are almost never equally distributed. As a result of such complexities, society has spent enormous resources in legal, political, and public debates over the costs and benefits of many substances (see Issues in Perspective 15–2).

PESTICIDES: POLLUTANTS MADE TO KILL

A **pesticide** is a chemical manufactured to kill organisms that humans consider to be undesirable. Specific kinds of pesticides refer to the targeted pests: insecticides, herbicides, rodenticides, and fungicides. Herbicides are the most commonly used, followed by insecticides. More than 100,000 chemicals are recorded as potential pesticides.

More than 1.1 billion pounds (500 million kg) of pesticides are applied each year in the United States at a cost exceeding $4 billion. It is estimated that this saves $64 billion in crops. Household pest

www.jbpub.com/environet

To Worry or Not to Worry?
Chlorine, Dioxin, and PCBs

An excellent example of the complexity of the benefit-cost decisions facing society today is the intense debate over chlorine and its derived chemical compounds. Chlorine is a very reactive element. It can combine with many other elements to produce thousands of substances including: plastics, pesticides, cosmetics, antifreeze, drugs, paints, and solvents. Furthermore, these compounds are often very stable because the chemical bonding with chlorine is so strong. Chlorine-related industries employ 1.4 million people in the United States and Canada.

But the same properties that make chlorine so useful also make it dangerous. Chlorine compounds are often toxic, even in small amounts. Furthermore, their high stability allows them to persist for a long time in the environment and often bioaccumulate in living tissue. CFCs are chlorine-based chemicals that pose a threat to the ozone layer because they persist for many decades in the atmosphere. An especially controversial group of chemicals are the "organochlorines," which are formed from chlorine and carbon. Many are considered to be potentially toxic and they are extremely common. *Half* of the 362 synthetic chemicals found in a recent survey of the water, sediment, and aquatic organisms of the Great Lakes were organochlorines.

Two of the best known organochlorines are dioxin and PCBs. Dioxin is a family of over 75 related compounds, some of which are extremely toxic to laboratory animals in very small amounts. Dioxin has long been suspected to be a potent human carcinogen, but it is difficult to prove with laboratory animals. An opportunity to directly test its effects arose in 1976, when an industrial accident spewed large amounts of dioxin into the air in Seveso, Italy. Studies of local citizens still living in the area 15 years later showed exceptionally high rates of liver and other cancers. People who moved away just after the accident showed no such effects, indicating the importance of long-term exposure.

Dioxin also appears to have many other harmful effects in addition to cancer. In 1992 the U.S. Environmental Protection Agency released a major study showing that even small amounts of dioxin significantly affect the immune, reproductive, and nervous systems. For example, lowered sperm counts, birth defects, and lowered disease resistance may occur. This study provoked so much debate that a $4 million reassessment study was done, with contributions from more than 100 scientists from universities, governments, and private labs around the world. The reassessment confirmed many previous results and provided insight into how dioxin harms humans: it disrupts cell and tissue growth and function by binding to cellular proteins. The reassessment was unsuccessful in specifying just how much dioxin exposure is needed to harm humans. But most data indicate that humans are in the middle range of sensitivity; some organisms are much more sensitive than humans to dioxin's effects, others less so. Continued research was called for and will no doubt occur for years to come.

eradication (mainly mice, termites, and other insects) is a $5 billion a year industry. Worldwide, more than $20 billion per year is spent on pesticides. Chemical pesticides have many disadvantages, however, ranging from harming people and ecosystems to evolved immunity of pests. About 45,000 accidental pesticide poisonings occur in the United States each year, resulting in about 50 deaths per year. However, many more people may die of cancer caused by pesticide exposure. A National Academy of Science study estimated that 20,000 people per year get cancer because of pesticides; even if only 10% of these die, the death rate would be 2,000 per year.

Furthermore, because pests can develop immunities to pesticides and new pests are introduced by human transport, increasing use of new pesticides, has not reduced the number of pests. Farmers still lose about one-third of their crops to pests, just as they did 50 years ago before advanced pesticides were invented (Fig. 15–13, page 420). Therefore, the current trend in the United States and some other parts of the world is toward nonchemical controls, such as using natural enemies (see the Prologue). In undisturbed ecosystems, natural enemies control pest populations 5 to 10 times more effectively than chemical pesticides, with little or no harm to other organisms.

Three Stages of Pesticide Evolution

Inorganic Pesticides

The first stage of pesticide use began more than 4500 years ago when the Sumerians used sulfur to kill insects. Other inorganic chemical pesticides

Although complete understanding of dioxin's impacts remains elusive, we have a fairly good understanding of how humans are exposed to dioxin and, thus, how to reduce exposure. While dioxin does occur in nature, such as from volcanoes and forest fires, most of it is a product of modern industry. Even though just 30 pounds (13.6 kg) of dioxin are released each year in the United States, it is so pervasive that everyone has been exposed. Most exposure comes from eating meats and dairy products from animals that have eaten plants contaminated by dioxin emissions. What kind of industries emit dioxins? *Waste combustion*, especially medical and city waste, accounts for about 95% of all dioxin emissions. This is one reason why many communities oppose waste incinerators. Other sources of dioxin are the chemical manufacture of chlorine compounds, such as pesticides, and pulp and paper mills. Bleaching paper with chlorine is an especially important source. In response to growing pressure, many paper companies are switching away from chlo-

rine to other substances such as chlorine dioxide, which produces less dioxin. Oxygen compounds, such as ozone, that produce no dioxins can also be used but are more costly.

Another well-known organochlorine group are PCBs (polychlorinated biphenyls). These were once common in electrical insulation, paints, and many other industrial products. Their properties and effects on humans are similar in many ways to those of dioxin. In fact, combustion of PCBs will produce dioxin. Manufacture of PCBs in the United States ceased in 1978. They have been slowly disappearing since then, but are still common because of their persistence. Industrial waste sites and other old dump sites often have high concentrations of PCBs; they are one of the main challenges of hazardous waste cleanups.

In response to the problem of chlorine compounds, Greenpeace and other groups have recently campaigned to ban all use of chlorine by industry. The evidence of potential harm to humans and other life can

be used to support such a ban. But society also has to consider the overall benefits and costs. The costs of banning chlorine in industry are very high; according to some estimates, a switch to other compounds would cost consumers more than $91 billion. Chlorine-based materials compose over half the pharmaceuticals on the market, for instance. Similarly, cleanup of dioxin and PCBs is exacting a huge cost right now. As much as $100 billion may ultimately be spent in the United States to remove PCBs from the environment. Is it worth it? Many people argue that while no one can deny that some harm is done by such compounds, the huge monetary costs to society will greatly outweigh the health and ecological benefits of removing these compounds. Once again, we see the problem of measuring true environmental costs. It is difficult to make monetary decisions when we cannot measure such things as just how many human lives are lost and how many ecosystems are seriously harmed by these chemicals.

include copper, arsenic, and lead. These substances were used in many parts of the world until the early 1900s, but are now generally banned as pesticides because of their high persistence and, especially, their non-specific toxicity. They can readily harm or kill nearly all forms of life, including humans.

Synthetic Organic Pesticides

The second stage, synthetic organic pesticides, revolutionized pest control when they were invented around the time of World War II. Initially, they were heralded as a "cure-all" that would result in the total elimination of pest species, but this has decidedly not been the case. Organic pesticides have caused a growing number of environmental and health problems and have steadily

declined in effectiveness as pest species have become immune to them.

There are three basic kinds of synthetic organic pesticides (● Table 15–4). **Chlorinated hydrocarbons** include chlordane, DDT, and other familiar pesticides. These are nerve toxins that cause paralysis, convulsions, and death. They are broad-spectrum toxins, attacking any organisms with central nervous systems. While these are the cheapest groups of pesticides, they also cause the most long-term harm to biological communities because they are easily bioconcentrated in the food pyramid. Chlorinated hydrocarbons are "organochlorines," which often have high persistence and tend to be concentrated in tissue (see Issues in Perspective 15–2). DDT in particular has one of the highest fat solubilities ever measured, and the body tissue of organisms often be-

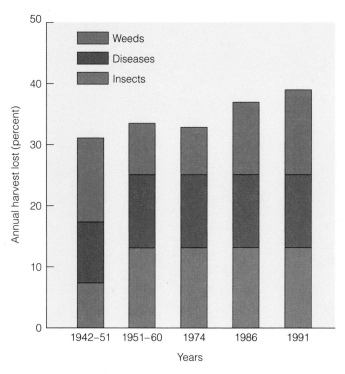

FIGURE 15–13

The amount of the annual harvest lost to pests (weeds, diseases, insects) in the United States has changed little since 1942 despite vast increases in chemical pesticide use. (*Source:* Based on data compiled by David Pimentel, Cornell University. Data used with the permission of David Pimentel.)

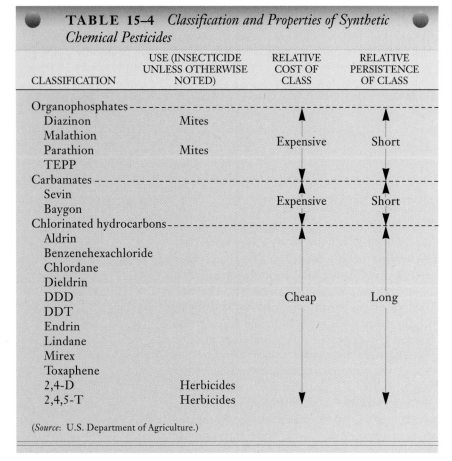

TABLE 15–4 *Classification and Properties of Synthetic Chemical Pesticides*

CLASSIFICATION	USE (INSECTICIDE UNLESS OTHERWISE NOTED)	RELATIVE COST OF CLASS	RELATIVE PERSISTENCE OF CLASS
Organophosphates			
Diazinon	Mites		
Malathion			
Parathion	Mites	Expensive	Short
TEPP			
Carbamates			
Sevin			
Baygon		Expensive	Short
Chlorinated hydrocarbons			
Aldrin			
Benzenehexachloride			
Chlordane			
Dieldrin			
DDD			
DDT		Cheap	Long
Endrin			
Lindane			
Mirex			
Toxaphene			
2,4-D	Herbicides		
2,4,5-T	Herbicides		

(*Source*: U.S. Department of Agriculture.)

comes concentrated to over 1000 times the surrounding levels. For this reason, DDT and most of the other chlorinated hydrocarbons in Table 15–4 have been banned in the United States. As a result, the concentration of such persistent pesticides in human tissue has steadily decreased in recent years.

The other two groups of organic pesticides, **organophosphates** and especially **carbamates**, are less persistent, lasting only a matter of days, weeks, or months in the environment compared to decades for chlorinated hydrocarbons. However, these two groups are also more expensive and much more toxic to humans. An adult human would have to ingest more than a pound (0.45 kg) of DDT in one sitting to cause death, but much smaller amounts of organophosphates or carbamates, which are rapidly absorbed by human skin, lungs, and the digestive tract. Like chlorinated hydrocarbons, organophosphates and carbamates attack the nervous system of the pest, but in a different manner. They attack an enzyme that controls nerve impulses, setting off a stream of uncontrolled impulses that cause the organism to twitch violently before death from organ failure. Common examples of organophosphates are malathion and parathion; sevin is a common carbamate (Table 15–4).

Biochemicals: Bacterial Toxins and Synthetic Hormones

The third and most recent stage of pesticides is the commercial production of chemicals that are ordinarily found in nature and can be used to control pests. Such naturally occurring biochemicals have the advantage of being very nonpersistent. Unlike many artificial chemicals, biochemicals are readily degraded into nontoxic forms by microbial digestion and other natural processes.

Bacterial toxins are pesticides that are made by such bacteria as *Bacillus thuringiensis*. These are toxic to a number of insect pests, such as Japanese beetles. Synthetic hormones are biochemicals that mimic hormones of pests, especially insects. Two basic types are especially important. One type interferes with growth regulating hormones. For example, insects must periodically shed, or molt, their hard outer skeleton in order to grow (Fig. 15–14). Synthetic growth hormones inhibit the hormones that control molting. Being unable to shed their outer skeleton, the juvenile insects die. **Pheromones** are the second type of synthetic hormone; these are the biochemical scents used by males or females to attract the opposite sex. Artificial pheromones are used to attract individuals to traps where they are killed. Pheromones are so powerful that only a drop can attract hundreds of individuals from many miles away.

Synthetic hormones have two major advantages over the nonpersistent synthetic organic pesticides. First, they are generally more specific and more likely to affect only the target species. For example, mammals and birds are generally unaffected by insect hormones. Second, only small doses are needed because they have such a powerful effect on the target species.

Problems with Chemical Pesticides

In 1962, Rachel Carson published *Silent Spring*, the first book that warned against the ecological and health effects of widespread pesticide use. Since then, many studies have confirmed much of what she said. Specifically, three main problems have emerged that severely limit the long-term utility of pesticides: nontarget toxicity, secondary pest outbreaks, and increasing immunity. These problems are especially severe with synthetic organic pesticides, which continue to be widely used because biochemical pesticides are not yet available for many pests. Also, biochemical pesticides are often less effective. Trapping pests by

attractants is not only much more labor-intensive but it generally reduces the pest population less than a potent poison would. A heavy poison dose will kill more than 90% of the pest individuals, whereas dozens of traps will kill only a few percent. Nor are the biochemical pesticides completely free of any of the following problems.

Nontarget Toxicity

The widely used organic pesticides can have devastating effects on nontarget species. Just one of countless illustrations occurred in 1958 when massive doses of the chlorinated hydrocarbon dieldrin were applied on Illinois farmland to eradicate the Japanese beetle. Cattle and sheep were poisoned, 90% of local cats died, 12 species of wild mammals and 19 species of birds were decimated, with robins, starlings, pheasants, and other birds virtually eliminated. Even synthetic hormones can affect nontarget species. For instance, synthetic growth hormones can affect nonpest insects because many insects have hormones that are biochemically similar. Nontarget

FIGURE 15–14
Biochemicals that prevent insects from molting or shedding their outer skeleton are effective at reducing reproduction in a certain insect species without harming other species. Seen here is a cicada emerging from its nymphal case. (*Source*: Roy David Farris/Visuals Unlimited.)

toxicity is enhanced in the more persistent and fat-soluble organic pesticides such as chlorinated hydrocarbons. This often results in increased toxicity in organisms high on the food pyramid from bioconcentration. Pesticides come in many different forms, such as dusts and sprays, which can be carried great distances by air and water. Over 7200 miles (11,585 km) of U.S. rivers and 2.5 million acres (1 million hectares) of lakes have restricted or banned fishing, largely due to pesticide contamination. In 1987, the EPA listed pesticide pollution as the third greatest threat to natural ecosystems.

Non-target toxicity is also directly hazardous to humans. Pesticides cause an estimated 10,000 deaths and 1 million injuries each year worldwide. These occur from a variety of toxic effects, ranging from immediate to long-term tissue accumulation. Immediate effects are most likely from exposure to the highly toxic organophosphates and carbamates. Temporary symptoms include nausea, blurred vision, and convulsions. Permanent symptoms from exposure to higher concentrations include damage to major organs (heart, lungs, and especially liver and kidneys) and brain and other nervous system damage. Chlorinated hydrocarbons tend to cause chronic toxicity leading to cancer, birth defects, and mutations. An example is Agent Orange, a chlorinated hydrocarbon herbicide used in Vietnam to defoliate forests. Now believed to cause cancer and birth defects, it has been banned in the United States since 1985. In 1987, the EPA ranked pesticides as the third leading environmental cancer risk.

How much pesticide do we ingest in our food? As 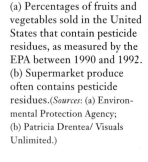 Figure 15–15a shows, a majority of the tested fruits and vegetables eaten in the United States contain pesticide residues. One special cause of concern is that many of these residues include pesticides banned in the United States, such as DDT and many other chlorinated hydrocarbons. Despite the ban on use in the United States, they continue to be manufactured here and shipped to developing countries where they are widely used because of their low cost. U.S. citizens continue to be exposed to these pesticides because much of the produce grown in these developing countries is imported by the United States in what is sometimes called a "circle of poison." Most of the residues on supermarket produce occur in such low concentrations that many experts are not concerned. Nevertheless, efforts to regulate pesticide use can fail (discussed later), and increasing numbers of consumers are willing to pay more for foods grown organically without pesticides.

Secondary Pest Outbreaks

Recall from Chapter 3 that populations are constrained by biological interactions such as predation and competition. When a pesticide strongly reduces key predators or competitors, the species they had kept in check often experience a population "explosion." Cotton pests in Central America are a prime example. In 1950, synthetic organic pesticides were applied to reduce the boll weevil, resulting in much greater crop yields. By 1955, however, a number of secondary pests that were less affected by the pesticide, such as the cotton aphid and cotton bollworm, began to reduce crop yields again. These pests had been limited by competition from the boll weevil. The typical response to such sec-

■ **FIGURE 15–15**
(a) Percentages of fruits and vegetables sold in the United States that contain pesticide residues, as measured by the EPA between 1990 and 1992. (b) Supermarket produce often contains pesticide residues.(*Sources*: (a) Environmental Protection Agency; (b) Patricia Drentea/ Visuals Unlimited.)

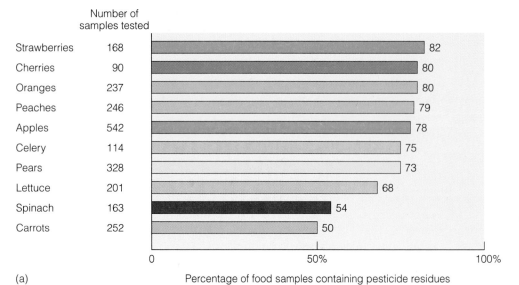

Number of samples tested

Food	Number of samples tested	Percentage
Strawberries	168	82
Cherries	90	80
Oranges	237	80
Peaches	246	79
Apples	542	78
Celery	114	75
Pears	328	73
Lettuce	201	68
Spinach	163	54
Carrots	252	50

0   50%   100%

(a)   Percentage of food samples containing pesticide residues

(b)

ondary pest outbreaks is to apply a different kind of pesticide. By the 1960s, farmers were combating eight pest species instead of the original two with an average of 28 applications of various pesticides per year.

Evolved Immunity

In many ways, evolved immunity is the most serious problem of all because it demands the constant development of new pesticides, each with its own potential for environmental impacts. Individuals in a species vary in their tolerance for toxic substances. Therefore, when we apply pesticides, the surviving individuals will be those with a higher tolerance. These survivors will tend to pass this tolerance on to their offspring, so the population will become progressively enriched in individuals tolerant to the toxic substance. In short, the pest population will become adapted to the pesticide through natural selection (Chapter 3).

Pests become immune to pesticides with striking speed. In the last few decades, insects, plant diseases (such as fungi), and weeds have shown an exponential increase in the number of pesticide-resistant species (Fig. 15–16). Even about 10 species of rodents are immune to some brands of rat poison. Perhaps the most impressive pest in this regard is the common housefly, which has become immune to almost every pesticide invented so far, even a synthetic growth hormone designed for it. The rate of adaptation is so high largely because pests are generally fast-growing organisms that reproduce often and are adapted to a wide range of conditions. In fact, these "weedy" traits are why they are pests to begin with. Their fast growth ensures that tolerant traits are passed on to offspring quickly, so that evolution occurs quickly. Their broad adaptations ensure that at least a few tolerant individuals will likely occur somewhere in the population. The result is what is often called the **pesticide treadmill**: to keep up with the rapid pace of evolving pesticide immunity, new pesticides must constantly be developed.

Reducing Chemical Pesticide Use

The problems with chemical pesticides have caused a recent shift in agriculture toward Integrated Pest Management (IPM), which seeks to reduce the use of chemical pesticides by relying on other methods of pest control, such as natural predators and breeding pest-resistant crops (Chapter 13). IPM is becoming increasingly common in the United States and many parts of the world. A 1991 poll of U.S. farmers showed that more than half were seeking to reduce pesticide use. As Figure 15–17 shows, U.S. pesticide use has leveled off and begun to decrease since the late 1970s (part of this decrease can be attributed to more lethal pesticides, so that less is needed).

IPM is yet another example of the efficiency of source reduction. Reducing the amount of pollutant produced is much easier than trying to control pollutant dispersal or cleaning up the pollution after it is released into the environment (Chapter 14). Less than 1% of sprayed pesticides actually reaches pests. The rest is carried off by

EnviroNet
www.jbpub.com/environet

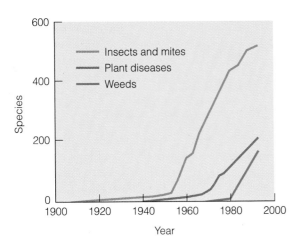

FIGURE 15–16
Pesticide-resistant species have increased exponentially since 1908. (*Source: Reprinted From Vital Signs 1994* by Lester R. Brown *et al.* with permission of Worldwatch Institute, Washington, D.C., Copyright © 1994.)

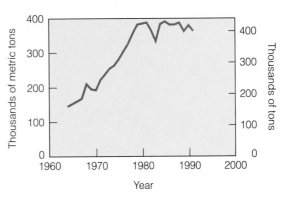

FIGURE 15–17
Pesticide use in the United States has leveled off since the late 1970s. Note that these data record only the weight of active ingredients, which are but a fraction of formulated pesticides. (*Source: Reprinted From Vital Signs 1994* by Lester R. Brown *et al.* with permission of Worldwatch Institute, Washington, D.C., Copyright © 1994.)

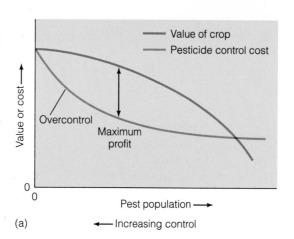

(a)

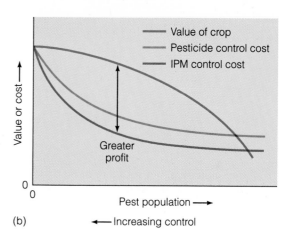

(b)

water and other transport methods to pollute groundwater, soil, and other parts of the environment. Source reduction—in this case, spraying less pesticide—is the best way to reduce such pollution.

Besides reducing pesticide pollution, IPM is beneficial in other ways. It is often cheaper than chemical pesticides. ■ Figure 15–18a shows that the farmer's greatest profit is obtained at an intermediate level of pest control. Initially, pest control is relatively cheap. But if one seeks to reduce pest populations to near zero, the familiar "law of diminishing returns" sets in, and costs skyrocket as ever greater amounts of pesticides must be applied. This is "overcontrol." Figure 15–18b shows that where IPM decreases costs of control, a greater profit can be realized. In this way farmers have reduced their use of pesticides by up to 90% without increasing the price of food to the consumer. Furthermore, the gain is much greater if environmental benefits are included in the economic calculations. A 1991 study by David Pimentel and other researchers at Cornell University found that nearly $1 billion is spent in the United States annually to counter the environmental and health damage from pesticides. Considerably more damage is simply not recorded or reported.

Furthermore, the use of non-chemical methods actually improves the efficiency of chemical pesticides when they must be used. Immunity to chemicals develops much more slowly when the pests are exposed to the chemicals less often. Most experts predict that these benefits will cause IPM to be increasingly used in the United States and worldwide. Indeed, the main obstacles now are a shortage of teachers trained in IPM and a lack of funds to finance the education of farmers in IPM.

Pesticide reduction through IPM is often associated with farms and agriculture, but cities and households are significant contributors to pesticide pollution. U.S. suburban lawns use more chemical pesticide per acre than U.S. cropland. Similarly, golf courses pour tons of pesticides, fertilizer, and other pollutants into local waterways. Should homeowners and golf courses reduce pesticide pollution by substituting more natural plants for lawns (see the Case Study)?

ℒEGAL ASPECTS OF TOXIC SUBSTANCE AND PESTICIDE CONTROL

Three major federal statutes are of special importance to toxic substance input reduction because they limit the actual production of toxic substances. In contrast, most other federal laws limit the release and environmental exposure of toxic substances after they are produced. (For a list of federal statutes regulating toxic substances, see Table 14–2 in Chapter 14.)

The **Toxic Substances Control Act (TSCA)** was designed to regulate toxic substances not covered under other laws. Its basic goals are to require industry to produce data on environmental effects of chemicals and to prevent harm to humans and the environment, while not creating unnecessary barriers to technology. These objectives exemplify the ambiguity inherent in many regulations because the protection of humans and the environment often conflicts with the promotion of technology. What is an "unnecessary" barrier, for example?

The centerpiece of the TSCA is the "premanufacturing notice," which requires the chemical industry to notify the EPA 90 days before a new chemical is to be manufactured for sale. This notice must contain information on the chemical identity, molecular structure, and test data ob-

Should We Rethink Lawns and Golf Courses?

awns and golf courses are excellent examples of how small-scale activities that we take for granted can accumulate to cause widespread environmental harm. Both lawns and golf courses have become traditions in the United States and other developed countries, ironically, because of our desire to enjoy nature (Fig. 1). Yet, as so often happens, traditional activities can become environmentally damaging if they are carried out on a huge scale by many individuals.

If all the lawns in the United States were assembled together, they would cover an area of 25 million acres (10 million hectares), which is equivalent to the combined area of Vermont, New Hampshire, Massachusetts, Connecticut, Rhode Island, and Delaware. This makes lawn grass the largest single crop in the United States, in terms of area. We care so much for our lawns that we spend $25 billion on the lawn care industry each year.

Many psychologists believe that lawns, and our care for them, are a way to feel close to nature. The smell and images of greenery are pleasant to many of us. Unfortunately, this particular way of staying close to nature is actually very "unenvironmental." Suburban lawns account for much of household water use, which is a serious problem in water-poor areas such as the southwestern United States and southern California. Furthermore, lawns average more than *three times* more pesticides per acre than an equivalent area of cropland. U.S. lawns absorb more synthetic fertilizers than the entire nation of India applies to all its food crops. Finally, mowing the lawn for an hour with a power mower can produce as much air pollution as driving a car for 50 miles (80 km).

What can we do? F. Herbert Bormann edited a book called *Redesigning the American Lawn: A Search for Environmental Harmony*

(1993). This book's answer is that if we wish to enjoy nature, we should stop trying so hard to cultivate the grasses and other plants that are not native to our backyards. The huge investment in water, pesticides, fertilizer, and mowing in the typical suburban lawn is only needed because we attempt to grow nonnative plants. Instead, it is suggested that we step

FIGURE 1
Golf courses use more pesticides and fertilizers, and cause more water pollution, per acre than most farms. (*Source*: Dean DeChambeau.)

back and let some of the native plants, such as crabgrass, chickweed, and many others, become established. We call such plants "weeds," but they are really just native plants that recur because they are better suited to the environment. Bormann and his Yale colleagues suggest that a totally environmental "Freedom Lawn" would consist entirely of native plants, would require less care and still provide the same feeling, if not more, of being close to nature.

On a per acre basis, golf courses are even more harmful than lawns. Golf courses use nearly *seven times* as much pesticide per acre as cropland, twice as much as the average for lawns. A single golf course can cover 200 acres (81 hectares) and usually requires even more fertilizer per acre than a lawn. The United States already has more than 14,600 golf

courses occupying an area larger than the state of Delaware, and furthermore, the rate of new golf course construction is increasing. From 1991 to 1994, more than 350 new courses were built or older courses expanded each year. This is twice the rate of the mid-1980s.

All these pesticides have had visible effects. In New York alone, 25 cases of bird kills related to golf course pesticides have been reported since 1971; in some cases hundreds of birds died. Human health effects could be very serious. A 1993 study by the University of Iowa Medical School examined data on the cause of death of 618 golf course superintendents between 1970 and 1992. It showed that the superintendents had exceptionally high frequencies of cancers of the lung, brain, intestine, prostate, and some lymphomas. These are often related to pesticides, and the study recommended more restricted use of pesticides and better protective clothing for golf course workers.

What can be done? As with lawns, there are more "environmentally friendly" ways to design golf courses. An example often cited is the 220-acre (89-hectare) Spanish Bay course in northern California. It is built on a former landfill and is designed to limit pesticide use where possible.

Questions

1. Do you think lawns and golf courses should be redesigned? Perhaps you are like many Sierra Club members: one in every six members is a regular golf player. Some are not concerned, and others have had to rethink their hobby.

2. What about lawns? If you owned a home, would you have a traditional yard and mow the lawn on weekends?

3. What are some alternatives to grass lawns? How would you redesign golf courses to be less environmentally harmful?

tained from the toxic identification, dose-response assessment, and risk characterization procedures discussed earlier. The EPA uses this (and other) information to decide whether the chemical can be produced, should be banned, or requires further testing. The TSCA has caused hundreds of chemicals to be withdrawn that would otherwise have been sold.

Unfortunately, more than 60,000 chemicals were already in use in 1976 when the TSCA was enacted. This was far too many to test, so nearly all of these chemicals were simply "grandfathered in:" They continue to be sold without any testing. But these pre-1976 chemicals make up more than 99.9% of the 6 trillion pounds (2.7 trillion kg) of chemical products made in the United States each year.

The **Federal Insecticide, Fungicide, and Rodenticide Act (FIFRA)** requires anyone wishing to manufacture a pesticide to register that product with the EPA. By 1990, more than 24,000 pesticides had been registered. As with other toxic substances under the TSCA, the EPA may ban the pesticide, permit manufacture (sometimes under limited use), or require further testing if it is deemed to present an "unreasonable risk" to humans and the environment. But, again, the agency's mandate is ambiguous: What is an "unreasonable" risk? The importance of ensuring the safety of pesticides before they are used is clear when (1) less than 1% of all fruits and vegetables are inspected by the Food and Drug Administration, (2) some pesticides are not tested for, and (3) tests take an average of 28 days, so that the produce is often sold before the tests are completed. Unfortunately, because about 25% of U.S. produce is imported from countries that use EPA-banned pesticides, we are still exposed.

Even if manufacture and use in the United States are permitted, each pesticide must be reregistered every five years and may be banned if information has emerged that it is exceptionally harmful. Recall that DDT and many other chlorinated hydrocarbons were taken off the market in the United States. A major problem with FIFRA is that pesticide manufacturers are not required to list "inert" chemicals when they label the pesticide for consumers. Such "inert" chemicals often constitute more than 80% of the pesticide and are sometimes very harmful in their own right. But the manufacturers insist that they must withhold this information to prevent competitors from discovering their formulas. A national telephone network, 800-858-PEST, has

EnviroNet
www.jbpub.com/environet

been established to obtain pesticide information.

The oldest statute regulating production of toxic substances is the Food, Drug and Cosmetics Act, which authorizes the Food and Drug Administration (FDA) to test products to see if they are safe to market for human use. The FDA is often criticized for being overcautious and taking too long to test medical products that could save lives. On the other hand, the agency has a very difficult job because a highly toxic product could take many lives.

The most controversial provision of the Food, Drug and Cosmetics Act is the **Delaney Clause**, which was passed in 1958 during the Eisenhower administration's "war on cancer." This clause explicitly prohibits even minuscule amounts of pesticides and other chemicals in processed foods if the chemicals are found to harm lab animals. Critics of the clause, especially in the agricultural and chemical industries, argue that the costs far outweigh the benefits. They maintain that evidence indicates that such minuscule amounts of chemicals do little, if any, harm and that regulating such tiny amounts has cost society many billions of dollars each year. As a result, there has been considerable interest in repealing the Delaney Clause. In 1995, the EPA used the clause to add 34 more chemicals to the list of substances that are prohibited from being found, even in trace amounts, in processed foods. Because these 34 include parathion, captan, and other cheap, common farm chemicals, this move caused an outcry among makers and users of the chemicals and stimulated even more congressional discussion of repealing the clause.

Toxic Torts

The complexities of regulating toxic chemicals are enormous. Errors will inevitably be made in a large economy (see Issues in Perspective 15–3). When errors happen, the next line of protection—one that is increasingly being used—is the so-called **toxic tort**, a lawsuit by individuals against manufacturers for harm that has occurred. This area of law is very chaotic and varies from state to state because torts are governed by state law. Basically, the harmed individual(s) must prove that the company was negligent in not providing adequate warning or in marketing a product that was unnecessarily dangerous.

For example, one can sue a chemical manufacturer for negligence if it produces toxic chemicals that cause harm to unknowing consumers. As we have noted, in practice, it is very difficult to

Breakfast Cereal and Pesticides: An Example of Regulatory Problems

In July 1994, U.S. consumers learned that millions of boxes of breakfast cereal containing an unauthorized pesticide had been sold for more than a year before the pesticide was found by government regulatory agencies. Inspectors from the FDA and the EPA reported that at least 11 kinds of oat cereals were tainted by the pesticide chlorpyrifos-ethyl, which was sprayed on the oats during storage. "There is no question that the public has been eating adulterated cereals for at least a year," said one FDA official. "Apparently this went on for 13 months, and the company did not know it. . . . That's very disturbing. This could have been a more serious pesticide."

Upon receiving the report, the cereal manufacturer immediately tested the cereal with its own toxicologists and verified the government's findings. Fifty million boxes of unsold cereal were quarantined, although some speculated that this cereal would be sold to nations that did not ban this pesticide, with the EPA notifying the buyers of the contamination.

Was anyone seriously harmed? No one really knows. The cereal manufacturer released statements saying that the tainted cereal was no danger to public health. But government officials were more cautious. The EPA began to evaluate toxicity and exposure data in order to estimate the risk to people who consumed the cereal.

Who was to blame? The main culprit in this case was apparently an independent contractor who knowingly sprayed the oats with cheaper, potentially more harmful chemicals. He then billed the cereal manufacturer for the more expensive, safer chemicals that he should have been using. But some would also argue that the cereal manufacturer should have monitored its supplies more closely and that the government agencies should have done more routine inspections.

Who pays for such errors? Aside from potential health effects on consumers, the cereal company lost millions of dollars on lost shipments and bad publicity. The independent contractor who committed the crime is under investigation.

Regulatory problems such as this are unavoidable in a huge, complex economy. Furthermore, nearly all experts agree that many similar cases, on a smaller scale, probably go unreported. But episodes such as this do have the beneficial impact of increasing public and political awareness, and stimulating regulators to improve their methods.

---

prove that a certain chemical causes cancer or other chronic illness. Nevertheless, many individuals have won millions of dollars in compensatory damages (for medical bills and other expenses to recover their original quality of life) and, less often, punitive damages, which are awarded to punish the company. An important environmental benefit of toxic torts is that chemical companies are now taking special care to police the toxic properties of the chemicals they market. Even if a toxic chemical gets by the EPA review process, the companies know that they are liable to lawsuits if negligence or exceptional toxicity can be shown.

Toxic torts can also be brought where a product is contaminated through the manufacturer's negligence. People who unknowingly consumed the contaminated breakfast cereal described in Issues in Perspective 15–3 could sue the cereal manufacturer, but they would need to show that they were harmed by the consumption.

Industrial Accidents

Accidental releases of industrial chemicals into the environment form a special class of toxic torts because of their huge potential for catastrophic ecological and human harm. This was made evident in the "Bhopal disaster" in India in December 1984 when approximately 16.5 tons (15 metric tons) of deadly pesticide gas were accidentally released (■ Fig. 15–19). The gas covered more than 30 square miles (77 km^2) and exposed up to 600,000 people. Local inhabitants estimate that at least 7000 people died immediately, but much suffering continues. Recent medical reports indicate that at least 50,000 people suffer a variety of serious ailments and perhaps one person dies every two days from the effects. Union Carbide, which owned the pesticide plant, was held legally responsible for the accident and paid various types of compensations to some individuals. Such cases are often the subject of "class-action" lawsuits,

FIGURE 15–19
Victims of the Union Carbide Bhopal disaster, December 1984. (*Source*: Baldev/Sygma.)

where a single group, like the citizens of Bhopal, sues the party responsible for the accident. But by 1995, many thousands of sick Bhopal citizens were complaining that they had received nothing.

Despite the warning of Bhopal, the potential for similar catastrophes is growing as chemical industries expand in developing nations, and industrial accidents are statistically increasing. In the eight years following Bhopal, there were 106 major accidents, compared to just 74 in the eight years before. Nor is the United States exempt. In 1995 the National Environment Law Center concluded that about 10 billion pounds (4.5 billion kg) of extremely hazardous chemicals are stored in the United States. Between 1980 and 1990, 15 incidents of industrial accidental gas releases that exceeded Bhopal in quantity and toxicity occurred in the United States.

SUMMARY

Toxicology studies how chemicals harm living organisms. Four important subdisciplines include molecular toxicology, immunotoxicology, behavioral toxicology, and ecotoxicology. The toxic pathway through the body is traced by "ADMSE": absorption, distribution, metabolism, storage, and excretion. Toxic effects may be acute, causing immediate harm, or chronic, involving longterm harm. Examples of chronic toxic substances are carcinogens and teratogens.

Toxic risk assessment in the United States involves four steps. Identification uses bioassays to determine if a chemical is toxic. Dose-response assessment determines the strength of toxicity, such as measured by LD-50. Many problems arise in such testing because of differences between humans and animals and the inability to detect very small effects. The third step is exposure assessment, which examines the pathways by which toxic substances can reach humans, including bio-

concentration of chlorinated hydrocarbons and heavy metals. The fourth step is risk characterization, which combines dose-response and exposure assessment data with societal values to decide if the benefits of a chemical outweigh the costs (risks). This step is often very controversial because risk is difficult to measure in most cases and risks are usually unequally distributed among social groups. Benefit-cost analyses are therefore rarely simple to carry out in practice despite the widespread desire to apply them.

Pesticides have evolved through three stages: inorganic, synthetic organic, and biochemical. Three major problems with all chemical pesticides are nontarget toxicity, secondary pest outbreaks, and evolved immunity leading to the "pesticide treadmill." Such problems have led to increasing interest in Integrated Pest Management which minimizes pesticide use by relying on natural enemies, pest-resistant crops, and other alternatives.

Among the most important laws regulating toxic chemicals in the United States are the Toxic Substances Control Act, the Federal Insecticide, Fungicide, and Rodenticide Act, and the Food, Drug and Cosmetics Act. This last act includes the Delaney Clause, which is one of the most controversial of all environmental regulations because it sets very low limits on the amount of pesticide and other chemical residues that are allowed in processed food. Only a tiny fraction of the more than 70,000 chemicals produced and sold have been fully tested for toxicity. Thousands more chemicals are being produced yearly. As the regulation of toxic chemicals becomes more complex, lawsuits by individuals against chemical producers, called "toxic torts," are increasingly common. Despite such tragedies as the "Bhopal disaster" of 1984, industrial accidents involving large chemical releases are increasingly common in the United States and globally.

KEY TERMS

acute toxicity
additivity
ADMSE
antagonism
behavioral toxicology

bioassays
bioconcentration
bioconcentration factor (BCF)
biotoxins
carbamates
carcinogen

chlorinated hydrocarbons
chronic toxicity
Delaney Clause
dosage
ecotoxicology
environmental hormones

epidemiological statistics
Federal Insecticide, Fungicide, and
    Rodenticide Act (FIFRA)
heavy metals
immunotoxicology
intrinsic factors
LD-50

molecular toxicology
mutagen
organophosphates
pesticide
pesticide treadmill
pheromones
risk

supertoxins
synergism
teratogen
toxicology
Toxic Substances Control Act (TSCA)
toxic threshold
toxic tort

STUDY QUESTIONS

1. What is toxicology? Who was the "father of modern toxicology"?
2. What are epidemiological statistics? What are the disadvantages of using them? Why are they used at all?
3. What is ADMSE?
4. What are chronic toxic substances? Give examples and define the terms.
5. Name three kinds of synthetic organic pesticides. Which kind has the longest persistence and is easily bioconcentrated? Give two examples.
6. What is bioconcentration? What kinds of substances tend to bioconcentrate? Give examples.

7. What is an "environmental hormone"? How can these hormones harm organisms?
8. Define risk. How does perceived risk vary from actual risk? Why do people sometimes perceive risk inaccurately?
9. Name and describe the three basic kinds of chemical interactions among substances in the environment.
10. What causes secondary pest outbreaks?
11. What causes evolved immunity?
12. Why are Americans still exposed to pesticides banned in the United States? What percentage of fruits and vegetables are inspected by the FDA?
13. What does the Toxic Substances Control Act require industry to do? What is the

"centerpiece" of the act? What happened to the chemicals already being produced before the act was enacted in 1976?
14. It is estimated that pesticides cause up to 1 million injuries to humans each year. What percentage of the human population is this, if there are 5.8 billion people?
15. Less than 1% of sprayed chemical pesticides usually reach pests. If someone sprayed 1 million gallons (3.785 million liters) on a field, how many gallons (and liters) would reach the pests assuming that 1% of the spray did. (Recall 1 gallon = 3.785 L.)

ESSAY QUESTIONS

1. Why is estimating risk so complicated? How does this increase the difficulty of benefit-cost analyses?
2. What problems are associated with using animals to predict the effect of chemicals

on humans?
3. List and discuss the three stages of pesticide evolution. What are the advantages of biochemicals?
4. List and discuss the problems associated with chemical pesticides.

5. Why are toxic torts becoming more common? How do the public and the environment benefit from them? Are there any disadvantages to these torts? To society? To the economy? If so, discuss them.

SUGGESTED READINGS

Beeby, A. 1994. *Applying ecology*. New York: Chapman & Hall.

Briggs, S. 1992. *Basic guide to pesticides*. Washington D.C.: Tayler & Francis.

Cooke, R. 1992. *Experts in uncertainty: Subjective probability and expert opinion*. Oxford: Oxford University Press.

Crone, H. 1986. *Chemicals in society*. Cambridge: Cambridge University Press.

Dawes, R. 1988. *Rational choice in an uncertain world*. New York: Harcourt Brace Jovanovich.

Francis, B. 1994. *Toxic substances in the environment*. New York: Wiley.

Freedman, B. 1994. *Environmental ecology*. New York: Academic Press.

Harte, J. *et al.* 1992. *Toxics A to Z: A guide to everyday pollution hazards*. Berkeley: University of California Press.

Hynes, P. 1989. *The recurring silent spring*. New

York: Pergamon Press.

Moriarity, F. 1988. *Ecotoxicology*. London: Academic Press

Paustenbach, D., ed. 1989. *The risk assessment of environmental and human health hazards*. New York: Wiley.

Rodricks, J. 1992. *Calculated risks*. Cambridge: Cambridge University Press.

Shrader-Frechette, K. 1991. *Risk and rationality*. Berkeley: University of California Press.

W ATER POLLUTION

P R O L O G U E   *Reborn Boise River Shows Benefits of the Clean Water Act*

rench fur trappers named the Boise River for its pristine forests (boisee means "wooded"). But the city of Boise, Idaho, began to use the Boise River for waste disposal, and by the early 1900s the river was a floating dump. By 1962, untreated wastes from slaughterhouses, sawmills, other industries, and households had produced a river that was clogged with rotting carcasses, grease, raw sewage, and even rusting automobiles. Dozens of similar examples of "urban rivers" being used for city wastes could be found, including the Charles River in Boston and the American River in Sacramento.

   Such blatant environmental degradations helped fuel the environmental activism of the 1960s and a flurry of landmark environmental laws during the 1970s. One of the most successful has been the Clean Water Act of 1972. This act provided federal funding for

PHOTO   *Floating down the restored Boise River, Idaho.* (*Source: David R. Frazier Photolibrary.*)

wastewater treatment and spurred many other improvements in "end-of-pipe" waste removal that have drastically improved water quality in urban rivers and many other surface waters in the United States.

The payoff has been increased economic activity as well as a cleaner environment. In Boise, for example, thousands of people now swim and canoe in the river, and the annual Boise River Festival draws about half a million people and adds $20 million to the local economy. With the return of ducks, bald eagles, trout, and forests, the river is so appealing that companies try to locate their headquarters near it and riverside housing is at a premium. "The cleanup of the river certainly had the impact of being a stimulus to the economy of our community," says the Boise Chamber of Commerce president. The Boise River also illustrates the importance of local action. State and local money provided many "matching funds" for wastewater treatment and other improvements. Local government passed laws banning certain polluting activities and established the "Greenbelt" along the river bank. Local citizens built shelters for ducks and other nesting animals. Boy Scouts put chicken wire around newly planted trees to keep beavers from chewing them to pieces. The main problem now may be to keep people from loving the Boise River too much. Because of its beauty, a lot of people want to enjoy it, increasing public demand for access including real estate development. "Our big problem now," says a retired wildlife official, "is to keep the cotton-picking developers out of it."

NTRODUCTION

We saw in Chapter 11 that water is an excellent solvent, meaning that it readily dissolves substances. As a result, humans have long dumped their wastes into natural waters because the waste was quickly diluted and dispersed. Such natural processes of purification are effective as long as human population density is relatively low compared to the amount of water available. But the rapid increase in human populations has so overwhelmed the natural purification processes that pollution of both fresh and oceanic waters has become a global crisis.

Polluted water is rendered unusable for its intended purpose. Even if water is unfit for human drinking, it is not polluted if that water is normally used for watering a golf course and is still safe for that purpose. Unfortunately, many of the pollutants that find their way into the waters of the environment are often extremely toxic and render the water unusable for any purpose: humans cannot drink it, farmers cannot water crops with it, and it is too corrosive or otherwise harmful to machinery for industrial use. **Contaminated water** is rendered unusable for drinking. Disease organisms, heavy metals, and many other toxic substances causing death or illness can contaminate water. Potable water is water that is safe to drink.

Damages and Suffering

Water pollution is highly costly both in the effects it has on the health of humans, other organisms, and ecosystems and in the economic damage it in-

flicts on industries including agriculture. The effects on human health are greatest in developing nations that do not yet have widespread modernized wastewater treatment. The World Health Organization estimates that about one-third of the world's people have inadequate sanitation. ( Fig. 16–1) This leads to deadly outbreaks of cholera, typhoid, hepatitis, and many other diseases. Estimates vary on the exact number of deaths caused by water pollution, but they range from 2 million to 25 million deaths per year worldwide. Most of these are infants, often suffering from intestinal diseases.

Modernized societies have a much lower incidence of waterborne diseases. In the United States, improvements in sanitation beginning around 1850 have led to a steady decline in waterborne disease. By 1920, outbreaks of cholera and typhoid were rare. But problems still occur. The Centers for Disease Control estimate that almost a million cases of unreported waterborne illness occur each year in the United States and that waterborne illness causes 900 deaths. In 1993, for example, a breakdown of the Milwaukee water supply system caused about 403,000 people to become ill and contributed to the deaths of at least 9 people.

Aside from its effects on human health, water pollution in the United States causes widespread damage to aquatic ecosystems such as rivers, lakes, wetlands, and coastal marine areas. A 1992 survey by the Environmental Protection Agency (EPA) found that more than 17,000, or about 10%, of the nation's streams, rivers, and bays are

www.jbpub.com/environet

FIGURE 16–1
Inadequate sanitation is a major cause of disease for at least one-third of the world's people. Seen here is an open sewer and slum housing, Belize City, Belize. (*Source*: David S. Addison/Visuals Unlimited.)

significantly polluted. Furthermore, about one-quarter of the nation's usable groundwater is contaminated. Groundwater is the only source of drinking water for about half of the U.S. population. The EPA estimates that total economic damages from water pollution in the United States exceed $20 billion per year.

Future of U.S. Water Pollution Control

The Clean Water Act of 1972 was reauthorized in 1995, as it is every five years or so. The main purpose of the reauthorizations is to rectify de-

ficiencies in the laws that have become apparent over time. The Clean Water Act, along with the Safe Drinking Water Act of 1974, has already played an enormous role in improving water quality, and these laws and their modifications will largely determine how water pollution is controlled in coming years.

One of the most widely discussed deficiencies of water pollution control in the United States, and nearly all industrialized nations, is the emphasis on "end-of-pipe" methods. The EPA estimates that about $575 billion was spent on water pollution control between 1972 and 1994. Nearly all of this was used for "end-of-pipe" methods, with $75 billion spent on building and upgrading urban sewage treatment plants. The remaining $500 billion was spent by taxpayers and private industries on treating industrial and other wastes not directly associated with city sewer systems.

While the end-of-pipe approach has been successful in reducing localized sources of water pollution (often called "point" sources because the pollution is discharged at a single point), many problems such as pollution of native ecosystems and groundwaters arise from nonlocalized or nonpoint sources, such as runoff from farm fields and urban areas that contains pesticides, oils, and other pollutants. In 1994, for example, the EPA estimated that runoff from agricultural lands accounted for 72% of the pollution in "impaired" rivers. A major focus of future water pollution control has therefore been on reducing runoff and other nonlocalized sources. This is much more difficult, but it can be accomplished through input reduction such as using less pesticide, fertilizer, and many other substances that end up in our waters. Thus, instead of concentrating on output reduction by end-of-pipe methods, it is often much more effective to stop pollution at the source (Chapters 1, 6, 14). Input controls are cheaper than end-of-pipe methods, so this approach will also address the problem of rising costs of water pollution control.

Other key problems the United States must address include (1) the obsolescence and age of many urban wastewater treatment plants (many were built in the 1970s); (2) increasing concern over toxic chemicals, such as chlorine-related compounds (resulting from the use of chlorine to disinfect water) and many newly invented chemicals; (3) the lack of an integrated network of water testing facilities to provide comprehensive data on water quality; and (4) pollution of waters that have been largely neglected until recently. While cleanup efforts have focused on lakes and rivers, groundwater, marine waters, and wetlands have continued to suffer increasing pollution and need immediate protection.

WATER PURIFICATION IN NATURE

The water cycle (discussed in Chapter 11), driven largely by the energy of the Sun, purifies water in many ways. Rain, streams, lakes, and groundwaters therefore tend to be relatively clean of dissolved matter and are usually drinkable in the natural state. Water is purified in nature through a number of processes (Fig. 16–2). For convenience, these can be grouped into two basic categories: physical and chemical processes.

- *Physical Processes.* The four physical processes involve forces such as gravity. These processes are important in removing the larger particles and debris and thus often account for the removal of the bulk of the material in water.
  1. **Dilution** is the reduction in concentration of a pollutant when it is discharged into water. Dilution increases as one moves away from the point of pollutant discharge (Fig. 16–2). Not surprisingly, the faster the water moves, the more effective the dilu-

tion is because more water flows past the point of discharge in a given period of time (Fig. 16–3). Indeed, fast-moving streams can remove the waste of up to about five times more people than slow-moving streams.
  2. **Sedimentation** is the settling out of suspended particles (Fig. 16–2). Sedimentation

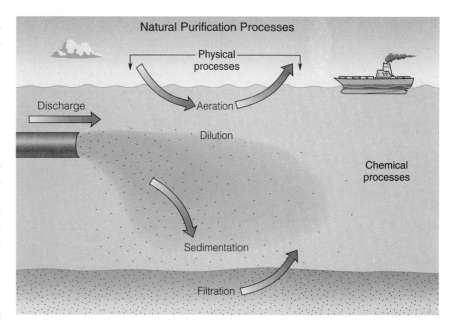

FIGURE 16–2
Five natural purification processes—chemical processes and four physical ones.

FIGURE 16–3
Fast-moving waters such as rivers or streams dilute waste faster than standing waters. This waste pipe in Merseyside, England, is emitting chemically polluted water. (*Source*: David Woodfall/Tony Stone Images.)

varies with particle size and water velocity, occurring most readily with larger particles and in slow-moving waters. Very fine particles (such as clay) can stay suspended for long periods and travel great distances.

3. **Filtration** is the percolation of water through sand and other settled sediment to remove suspended particles (Fig. 16–2). Even very fine particles can be filtered out if the water percolates through fine sediment.

4. **Aeration** is the release of gaseous impurities into the atmosphere (Fig. 16–2). Water, like all liquids, contains many substances in the form of dissolved gases. Aeration is greatly accelerated when more water is exposed to the air as where the water trickles over rocks in shallow streams. It is also more effective in warm and fast-moving waters.

■ *Chemical Processes.* Natural waters contain many dissolved minerals and gases that chemically interact in complex ways. Most of these reactions are biochemical, involving enzymes and many other chemicals produced by organisms, especially microbes. Humans have put these microbes to work as major degraders of waste in sewage treatment plants. A number of inorganic (nonbiological) chemical reactions are also important in purifying water. Many elements, such as iron and phosphorus, may react with one another to form molecules that are insoluble in water. Upon reaction, the molecules will therefore precipitate out and settle on the bottom.

POLLUTION: OVERWHELMING NATURAL PURIFICATION

As human populations and per capita use of water have both increased, the quantity of wastes released into natural waters has increased exponentially, overwhelming natural processes for removing wastes from the waters in many areas. In addition to this massive increase in quantity, the quality of the waste has become increasingly toxic in recent decades. The rapid growth of the chemical and other industries has created a huge outpouring of thousands of new chemicals every year in the United States alone (Chapter 15). Moreover, these chemicals are often highly resistant to degradation and persist in the water for some time. The result has been increasingly severe water pollution affecting increasingly larger bodies of water. Entire ocean basins such as the Mediterranean Sea are now becoming significantly polluted.

Water pollution can be classified by (1) its composition (what it is), (2) its source (where it originates), and (3) its fate (where it goes).

The next sections examine these three categories in that order.

Composition and Properties of Water Pollutants

The U.S. Public Health Service classifies water pollutants into eight general categories by composition, as shown in ● Table 16–1. In reading about these pollutants, recall from earlier chapters that such pollutants often interact synergistically to become exceptionally toxic and may also undergo bioaccumulation in living tissue. Influx of two weak toxic substances into a lake, for example, may lead to a massive fish kill when their joint effects are combined.

Oxygen-Demanding Wastes

Oxygen-demanding wastes include materials produced by plants and animals, such as body wastes in sewage and unused body parts from food preparation. That something as "natural" as body waste is a highly destructive pollutant is a good illustration of how anything is harmful in too great a quantity (Chapter 15). In this case, low levels of plant and animal matter provide food for the microbes in natural waters that live by decomposing such matter. Too much plant and animal waste, however, leads to a rapid increase in the rate of

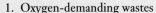

TABLE 16–1 *Classes of Water Pollutants, with Some Examples*

1. Oxygen-demanding wastes	Plant and animal material
2. Infectious agents	Bacteria and viruses
3. Plant nutrients	Fertilizers, such as nitrates and phosphates
4. Organic chemicals	Pesticides, such as DDT, detergent molecules
5. Inorganic chemicals	Acids from coal mine drainage, inorganic chemicals such as iron from steel plants
6. Sediment from land erosion	Clay silt on stream bed, which may reduce or even destroy life-forms living at the solid-liquid interface
7. Radioactive substances	Waste products from mining and processing of radioactive material, radioactive isotopes after use
8. Heat from industry	Cooling water used in steam generation of electricity

(*Source:* U.S. Public Health Service.)

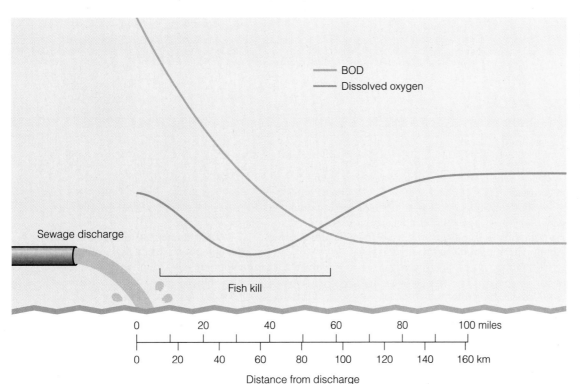

FIGURE 16–4
Biological oxygen demand
(BOD) decreases away from
sewage discharge point. Fish
kills can occur for many miles
downstream from lack of
oxygen.

—— BOD
—— Dissolved oxygen

Sewage discharge

Fish kill

| 0 | 20 | 40 | 60 | 80 | 100 miles |

| 0 | 20 | 40 | 60 | 80 | 100 | 120 | 140 | 160 km |

Distance from discharge

decomposition. Because decomposition requires oxygen, the **biological oxygen demand (BOD)**, defined as the amount of oxygen used by organisms in a particular stream, lake, or other body of water to carry out decomposition, also increases. As ▬ Figure 16–4 shows, the rise in BOD from decomposition depletes the oxygen available in the water for other organisms, such as fishes, causing them to die. Unfortunately for fishermen, game fish such as trout tend to be less tolerant of low oxygen content than other fishes.

Infectious Agents

Four major kinds of disease-causing agents are involved in water pollution: bacteria, viruses, protozoa, and parasitic worms. These are usually found in association with oxygen-demanding wastes in sewage and other waters carrying plant, animal, and especially human wastes. Before modern sewage treatment plants, outbreaks of cholera, typhoid fever, and diphtheria were major causes of human death, and as noted above, they still are in areas with poor sanitation. Modern sewage treatment plants can easily remove most of these pathogens simply by adding chlorine, which is highly toxic to many life-forms. However, some pathogens, including the protozoan *Giardia* and a number of kinds of hepatitis viruses, are resistant to chlorine. These are often associ-

ated with human feces and can cause diarrhea, cramps, and other illnesses if wastewater treatment plants are ineffective. The illness of over 400,000 people in Milwaukee in 1993 was caused by a combination of factors, including a contaminated water supply, poor water treatment, and an especially resistant parasite called *Cryptosporidium* (see Issues in Perspective 16–1).

Plant Nutrients

Plant nutrients are another example of how too much of a "good thing" can be a major pollutant. Plants in aquatic ecosystems (such as algae) are adapted to a fairly narrow set of environmental conditions, including the chemical nutrients in the water. Ecologists have found that there is generally one nutrient, called the "limiting nutrient," that limits plant growth (Chapter 4). If large amounts of this limiting nutrient suddenly become available, plant populations will increase rapidly. The result is sometimes called an "algal bloom," which appears as a green "scum" on the water (▬ Fig. 16–5, page 437). As the plants die, microbial decomposition will increase the BOD, and the animal life will suffocate, as discussed above. This process of abundant plant growth is called **eutrophication** (Greek *eu* = good, *trophikos* = food, so "good food" is a rough translation).

EnviroNet
www.jbpub.com/environet

The Milwaukee Incident

In 1993, a series of events culminated in a major outbreak of a waterborne illness, commonly known as "traveler's diarrhea," among the residents of Milwaukee, Wisconsin. The culprit was the small parasitic organism named *Cryptosporidium*, which assembles along the inner membrane of the intestines. More than 50% of the 800,000 individuals served by the city's water system (approximately 403,000) were infected by this organism. The symptoms varied in severity and generally lasted two weeks. Individuals with compromised immune systems, including those suffering from AIDS or cancer, and the elderly suffered the most. Nine deaths resulted from the outbreak. One death was directly connected to *Cryptosporidium* contamination while eight other deaths of infected individuals were indirectly linked to the parasite.

The source of the outbreak was identified within several days, and Milwaukee's mayor, John O. Norquist, recommended that all users of city water boil their water prior to drinking or washing food. Though

the contamination was remedied eight days later, questions remained. How did the drinking water become contaminated with this infectious agent? And why did the municipal water treatment facilities fail to remove this organism?

Upon investigation, it was found that the *Cryptosporidium* most likely came from either (1) infected cattle on farms upstream, whose runoff flowed into the Milwaukee River and from it into Lake Michigan, the source of the city's water, or (2) Milwaukee's own sewage system discharge, which also flowed into Lake Michigan just a few miles from the city's source water intake.

In either case, the water treatment facilities should have been able to eliminate the problem. In fact, one facility was functioning adequately, but the second facility, which processed the greater volume of infected water, was not. In an effort to correct an earlier problem with the quality of its water, this facility was using polyaluminum chloride to lower the corrosiveness of the water, but this measure inadver-

tently decreased the effectiveness of the sand filters used to eliminate *Cryptosporidium* as well as other solids from the treated water.

Though incidents of drinking water contamination affecting large numbers of people are not common in the United States, the Milwaukee incident was not the first case. Between 1984 and 1992, three major outbreaks occurred. *Cryptosporidium* infestation hit Braun Station, Texas, in 1984, and in 1987 thousands of residents of Carrollton, Georgia, were affected. Medford, Oregon, also experienced a similar outbreak in 1992.

What should be learned from these events? They reveal the imperative need to address and deal with nonlocalized sources of contamination of our water supply. They also illustrate the delicate balance of water treatment processes. The complex intricacies of these processes should not be altered randomly or haphazardly. Instead, thorough evaluations must be performed to determine any possible ramifications from system changes.

In freshwater lakes, rivers, and streams, the limiting nutrient is usually phosphorus. In many marine waters, it tends to be nitrogen. Fertilizers and human sewage are rich in both phosphorus and nitrogen so pollution of fresh or salt waters by either of these causes eutrophication. Eutrophication (and BOD increase in general) is usually greatest in standing bodies of water, where water circulation is slow.

Organic Chemicals

Some organic (carbon-containing) chemicals are natural, such as petroleum or coal; these can be toxic to many species. But many other organic chemicals are human-made. Most of the many thousands of chemicals invented each year are organic because of carbon's unique bonding abili-

ties. As a result, thousands of synthetic organic chemicals (SOCs) are now used in industry, agriculture, and other activities. Synthetic organic chemicals are among the most abundant and most toxic pollutants. They also tend to bioconcentrate (Chapter 15). Among the most common organic pollutants are organochlorines, including some pesticides.

In 1994, a study (by the Environmental Working Group) reported that the drinking water of some 14 million Americans contains traces of pesticides. Most of these people live in the midwestern states where herbicides used to control weeds in crops are washed into the water supply. Indeed, 67 kinds of pesticides were found in midwestern drinking water supplies between 1987 and 1994. These, and similar findings, have spurred the U.S. Congress and many states to propose stronger laws regulating drinking water supplies, but many environmental groups consider these proposed laws to be too weak.

Inorganic Chemicals

The inorganic chemicals, which are not carbon based, form a broad group. Two of the most destructive water pollutants in this category are metals and acids. Metals are naturally occurring elements such as arsenic, zinc, lead, and mercury. In high concentrations, metals often have a very toxic effect on living organisms because metal atoms will chemically bind to protein molecules such as enzymes, interfering with their functioning. Chapter 15 described the well-known example of mercury poisoning near Minamata, Japan, where the residents ate fish from the waters into which a local industry was discharging mercury. A more common metal that can cause health damage is lead. It is often carried in tap water in homes with old plumbing. Like mercury, lead attacks the nervous system (see Issues In Perspective 16–2).

A second major type of inorganic pollution is the release of acids into natural waters. This can occur through "acid rain" (Chapter 17) or from discharge of acidic waters including drainage of coal and metal mines. Aquatic organisms, such as different kinds of fishes vary greatly in their tolerance to acidity.

Sediment Pollution

Sediment from erosion is the sixth major type of pollution (Table 16–1). We do not often think of sediment as pollution, but human activities can cause thousands of times more sediment to be introduced into natural waters than would otherwise occur. This sediment has many detrimental effects to human use, causing the water to be murky and aesthetically unappealing. In economic terms, it fills in channels and reservoirs and damages power-generating equipment. It is also very detrimental to aquatic organisms. For example, sediment can impair gills and other organs of fishes and shellfishes and reduce the amount of sunlight available to underwater plants, thereby slowing down production at the base of the food pyramid. Many coral reefs in the Florida Keys, the Caribbean, and other parts of the world, for instance, are being destroyed by dredging operations that stir up large amounts of sediment and kill the tiny coral animals.

Radioactivity

Radioactive substances are often discharged into natural waters by nuclear power plants. Radioactivity has many detrimental effects on living organisms, ranging from nearly immediate death to cancer, mutations, and sterility. The radioactivity of the substances released by power plants

■ **FIGURE 16–5**
The discharge of nutrients into natural waters can lead to the rapid growth of algae and other plants. (*Source:* Doug Sokell/Visuals Unlimited.)

is generally considered to be so limited as to be harmless, but this practice is still controversial (Chapter 8).

Thermal Pollution

Heat as a water pollutant often comes from hot industrial waters, such as those discharged by power-generating plants. These heated waters can seriously disturb aquatic ecosystems. Fishes have

Lead: The Insidious Contaminant

In 1992, the Environmental Protection Agency conducted a series of tests on water systems nationwide. The agency was looking for lead contamination. What it found was alarming.

Excessive lead levels were detected in 819 water systems, which serve nearly 12% (30 million individuals) of the U.S. population. Though not every home serviced by those systems had high lead levels, the overall results illustrated that lead contamination of drinking water is a serious problem. Historically, government and public concern over lead toxicity led to laws requiring the removal of lead-based paints and leaded gasoline from the U.S. marketplace.

The concern over high lead levels is justified by the serious effects of lead poisoning. In adults, it can result in peripheral neuritis, or the loss of neural control over the muscles of the extremities. In children, chronic exposure results in brain malformation and dysfunction, which can be manifested as behavioral disturbances, mental retardation, or even death. Even low levels of lead can produce insidious toxicity as the lead accumulates in bone tissue only to be released later as an endogenous toxin. Therefore, a child may continue to suffer from lead poisoning long after the source of the lead contamination is eliminated.

While the EPA maximum safe level for lead is 15 parts per billion (ppb), Charleston, South Carolina's water system tested at 165 ppb. This system alone services more than 50,000 people. Excessively high levels were detected at Grosse Pointe Park, Michigan (324 ppb), and Goose Creek, South Carolina (257 ppb); the highest levels were found at the U.S. Marine Corps' Camp Lejeune in North Carolina (4843 ppb).

Typically, the difference between lead and other contaminants is that lead leaches into drinking water *after* source water has been treated at a water treatment facility.

So unlike other contaminants, it cannot be removed or filtered out at the plant. Instead, it leaches out of lead plumbing, lead-containing alloys used in brass fixtures, and lead-based solder used to join copper pipes. Homes built prior to 1930 often have lead plumbing and therefore a high potential for lead contamination of their drinking water. Even recently built homes may be at risk if the water is soft and corrosive, enabling it to leach lead out of fittings and solder. Additionally, public waters with high corrosive levels have the ability to dissolve lead from anywhere in the delivery system. Older cities, particularly in the eastern and midwestern United States, which have used lead in their water systems, pose a potential public health hazard.

Households concerned about lead can have their drinking water tested by a qualified laboratory to determine the presence and degree of lead contamination. Then, corrective measures can be taken to reduce lead exposure.

---

distinct temperature tolerances for spawning, egg development, and growth. By changing the water temperature, certain organisms may be eliminated and others may prosper. In many cases, a temperature change of only a few degrees can completely exclude a species from breeding in the area. As with low-oxygen waters and acidity, game fishes tend to be more sensitive to temperature changes than most other fishes. Plants, plankton, and shellfishes are also highly sensitive to temperature changes. For example, green algae grow best between 86 and 95°F (30–35°C) while blue-green algae grow best between 95 and 104°F (35–40°C). As blue-green algae are a poorer food source than green algae, an increase in the water temperature and the resulting shift from green to blue-green algae will have a big impact on animals higher on the food web. Heated water is not always bad, however. The endangered manatees of Florida often crowd into the warm discharge waters of power plants during cold winter periods.

In addition to exceeding the temperature tolerances of organisms, heated water affects the oxygen supply. Warmer water is able to hold less oxygen than cooler water. As ▬ Figure 16–6 shows, the ability to dissolve oxygen ("solubility") decreases exponentially with increasing temperature. Even if some organisms are not directly affected by increases in temperature, they may be affected indirectly because they cannot tolerate the lower oxygen content of the water.

Sources of Water Pollutants

Virtually all human activities produce some kind of environmental disturbance that can contaminate surrounding waters with the eight pollutants just discussed. Eating (body wastes), gardening (pesticide and sediment runoff), and many other

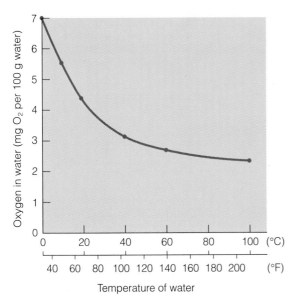

FIGURE 16-6

The ability of water to retain dissolved oxygen decreases rapidly with increasing water temperature. (*Source*: Data from *McGraw-Hill Encyclopedia of Science and Technology 1992.*)

activities create by-products that can find their way into the water cycle. For convenience we can assign the large majority of the sources for the eight pollutant groups to three broad categories of waste: (1) industrial, (2) agricultural, and (3) domestic wastes.

Agricultural sources of water pollution tend to be nonpoint sources, which discharge pollutants from many locations, such as pesticide runoff from crops (Fig. 16–7). Industrial and domestic wastes are often point sources, which discharge pollutants at easily identified single locations, such as discharge pipes.

Industrial Wastes

Wastes from industry serve as major sources for all eight types of water pollutants. Many major industries contribute significantly to water pollution, but some of the most important are the (1) manufacturing, (2) power-generating, (3) mining and construction, and (4) food processing industries.

Manufacturing industries contribute many of the most highly toxic pollutants, such as organic chemicals and heavy metals. In many cases, both the product, such as paint or pesticides, and the by-products from the manufacturing process are highly toxic to many organisms, including humans. A key problem with such toxic wastes is not just the many kinds produced, but the sheer volume of each kind. Many billions of pounds of waste are produced each year, especially by the chemical in-

dustry, which is the largest producer of toxic and hazardous waste by far (Chapter 15).

Power-generating industries are the major contributors of heat and radioactivity. Nearly all power plants, whatever the fuel, are major sources of thermal (heat) pollution. Radioactivity from nuclear power plants can pollute waters in a variety of ways, including discharge of mildly radioactive wastewater and groundwater pollution by buried radioactive waste.

The mining and construction industries are major contributors of sediment and acid drainage. Sediment pollution occurs because both industries can denude the land of vegetation. As Figure 16–8 shows, construction in particular results in a drastic rise in the rate of land erosion and transportation of sediment into streams. Acid drainage is mainly a product of mining coal and metallic ore minerals. Because acid drainage occurs only in regions where mining is important, this environmental problem is often overlooked. Yet more than 12,000 miles (19,300 km) of streams in the United States have been seriously affected by acid drainage from mining operations.

Food processing industries include slaughterhouses, canning factories, and many other plants that produce large amounts of animal and plant parts that become oxygen-demanding wastes in nearby waters. These are also sources of waterborne diseases.

Agricultural Wastes

Agricultural wastes are generated by the cultivation of crops and animals. Globally, agriculture is

FIGURE 16–7

Pesticides are a major source of pollution of surface waters and groundwater. (*Source*: Rick Ashley/Visuals Unlimited.)

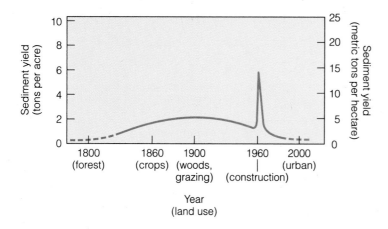

FIGURE 16–8
Agriculture causes some
increase in erosion, but
construction causes a drastic
increase in drainage of
sediment into streams.
(*Source*: From Sheldon Judson,
"Erosion of the Land," *American
Scientist 56* [1968]: 366. Reprinted
with permission of *American
Scientist*.)

the leading source of sediment pollution, from plowing and other activities that remove plant cover and disturb the soil. Agriculture is also a major contributor of organic chemicals, especially pesticides.

The other three major agricultural pollutants have biological aspects. Oxygen-demanding wastes are largely body wastes produced by livestock. Livestock produce five times as much waste per pound as humans and are therefore the major cause of this type of pollution. Infectious agents are nearly always found in body wastes so livestock are also major producers of this type of pollutant. Agriculture is the major source of plant nutrient pollution through runoff carrying fertilizers applied to crops.

Domestic Wastes

Domestic wastes are those produced by households. Most domestic waste is from sewage or septic tank leakage that ends up in natural waters. Many cities still dump untreated or barely treated sewage directly into rivers, lakes, or coastal waters. The bulk of domestic waste pollution therefore consists of body wastes and other oxygen-demanding wastes. In addition, domestic sources may be a major contributor of infectious agents and plant nutrients. Infectious agents are a common hazard of all human waste. Plant nutrients occur in the form of nitrogen and phosphorus. These come not only from human waste, but also from fertilizers used extensively in household lawns and gardens.

Fate of Pollutants

Ultimately, most pollutants find their way into natural waters. This is inevitable given the dissolving power of water and its tendency to flow toward rivers and basins. The natural waters

that ultimately absorb the pollutants can be divided between fresh water and marine water. The fresh waters, in turn, can be either surface water (rivers and streams, or lakes) or groundwater.

Freshwater: Rivers and Streams

Rivers and streams drain water that falls on upland areas. Recall that moving water dilutes and decomposes pollutants more rapidly than standing water. But then why are more than 10% of U.S. rivers and streams significantly polluted? A main reason is that all three major sources of pollution—industry, agriculture, and domestic (cities)—are concentrated along rivers. Industries and cities have historically been located along rivers because the rivers provide transportation and have historically been a convenient place to discharge wastes. The very fact that fast-moving waters carry off wastes and purify themselves more readily, has encouraged people to pollute them in ever-greater amounts. Agricultural activities have likewise tended to be concentrated near rivers. River floodplains are exceptionally fertile due to the many nutrients that are deposited in the soil when the river overflows.

One of the unique aspects of river pollution, as compared to other types of water pollution, is that "everyone is downstream from someone else." If a city or factory discharges waste, it is sure to find its way into someone's drinking water downstream (Fig. 16–9). This is not so bad if the next water user is far enough downstream that the natural purification processes have time to act. But many types of pollution are discharged into rivers, and the purification processes remove them at varying speeds. Some heavy metals, for example, are removed relatively quickly because suspended clay and organic particles have a slight electric charge and adsorb ("attach") the metal atoms. When the clay or organic particles settle out of the water, they take the metal atoms with them. But pollutants that are very persistent in the water can actually accumulate downstream, causing great hazards for those living at the "end of the line." For instance, New Orleans draws much of its water from the Mississippi River, just before it empties into the Gulf of Mexico (Fig. 16–10). The city has had many problems with water quality because some of the hundreds of industrial chemicals in the water are often detected in amounts high enough to be harmful. Many residents and visitors drink only bottled water.

The Clean Water Act of 1972, along with other environmental laws such as those regulating pesticide use, has led to a substantial im-

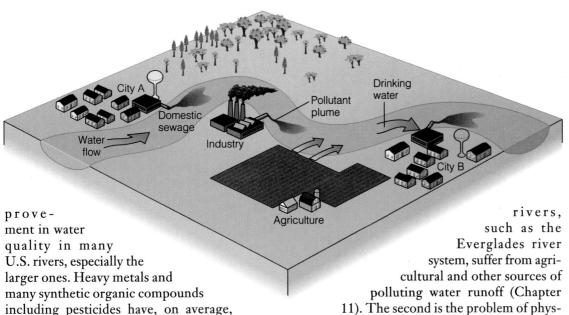

FIGURE 16–9
One city's wastewater is another city's drinking water because "everyone is downstream from someone else."

prove-
ment in water
quality in many
U.S. rivers, especially the
larger ones. Heavy metals and
many synthetic organic compounds
including pesticides have, on average,
substantially decreased since the early 1970s.

Despite these improvements, many U.S. rivers remain in serious trouble, and some are declining rapidly. American Rivers, an organization based in Washington, D.C., periodically releases reports on the status of U.S. rivers. ● Table 16–2 shows the 1993 list of the 10 most endangered rivers. The reasons for their decline illustrate two key causes of current and future problems in U.S. rivers. One is nonpoint pollution. Some of the rivers, such as the Everglades river system, suffer from agricultural and other sources of polluting water runoff (Chapter 11). The second is the problem of physical alteration of rivers. Alterations can take four forms, often called the "four horsemen" of river destruction: dams, diversion of water (canals), channel alteration, and land development. These alter flow patterns, increase sediment pollution, and alter water temperature, among many other changes that reduce water quality and destroy aquatic ecosystems (Chapter 11). While many of the problems of point source pollution have been addressed, rivers (and streams) in many areas

FIGURE 16–10
The Mississippi River contains many kinds of pollutants by the time it reaches the "end of the line" at New Orleans. (*Source*: Fred E. Hossler/Visuals Unlimited.)

TABLE 16–2 *Endangered Rivers of 1993: Location and Reasons for Endangerment*

1. Rio Grande (U.S. and Mexico) and Rio Conchos (Mexico) river system; water pollution, irrigation diversions.

2. Columbia and Snake river system, including the Yakima River (northwestern United States and western Canada); hydroelectric dams, habitat destruction, and water diversions.

3. Everglades (Florida); agricultural pollution and water diversions.

4. Anacostia River (District of Columbia); rainwater runoff, urban trash, and chemicals.

5. Virgin River (Utah, Arizona, and Nevada); dams, water projects.

6. Rogue and Illinois river system (Oregon); water withdrawal, mining, timber harvest.

7. Penobscot River (Maine); dam and power plant.

8. Clavey River (California); proposed hydropower dams.

9. Alsek and Tatshenshini River system (Alaska and British Columbia); proposed open-pit copper mine.

10. Platte River (Nebraska); development water, diversions, dams.

(*Source:* American Rivers 1993 List.)

will continue to decline until nonpoint pollution and physical alteration of rivers are addressed.

Fresh Water: Lakes

Lakes are subjected to many of the same pollutants as rivers. But lakes are more easily polluted than rivers for at least three reasons. First, lake waters circulate much more slowly. Deep waters in many lakes are circulated only during seasonal temperature changes. Second, lakes are often "dead ends," being basins into which water flows. Pollutants therefore accumulate in lakes, having nowhere else to go. Third, lakes often contain less water than rivers, especially if you consider the amount of water that flows through a river over time. Smaller lakes, of course, are polluted even faster than larger ones.

Lake Erie is a classic example of lake pollution. Because of its very large size, Lake Erie (like the other Great Lakes) was thought to be extremely resistant to pollution. However, the close proximity of many large industries and cities, eventually began to overwhelm the lake's natural purification systems. By the late 1960s, sewer systems serving over nine million people were emptying into the lake on the U.S. side alone. Tons of industrial waste from steel mills, paper mills, auto plants, and many others were added daily. By the early 1970s, the lake was declared "dying, if not dead" by many experts, based on the fact that game fishes and many other organisms were absent from large parts of the lake and increasingly rare in the remainder. Much of the problem was due to widespread eutrophication, with rampant algal growth and decay causing oxygen to be depleted in the lake. A major contributing factor was that even though Lake Erie is nearly 300 miles (483 km) long, it is very shallow, with an average depth of less than 65 feet (20 m). Recently, the lake seems to be making a partial recovery, thanks to concerted action taken since the early 1970s. Pollution from industry and sewers has been greatly reduced by water treatment before discharge (Fig. 16–11). Game fishes have begun to reappear in areas where they had disappeared, oxygen levels are up, and there are many other hopeful signs that water pollution problems are being corrected. But, unfortunately, many of these gains are being offset by increasingly severe biological damage from dozens of introduced species, especially the zebra mussel (Chapter 12).

FIGURE 16–11
Lake Erie may cover a large area, but it is relatively shallow and was readily polluted by surrounding cities and industries. Seen here is a view from Perry's Monument, Put-in-Bay, South Bass Island, Lake Erie, Ottawa Co., Ohio. (*Source:* David M. Dennis/Tom Stack & Associates.)

Most fresh water is groundwater (Chapter 11). As human populations increase and industrialize, demand for this resource is rising. Unfortunately, there has been an accompanying rapid increase in pollution of groundwater. Recall that about half of the U.S. population relies on groundwater as their only source of drinking water, yet about one-fourth of the usable U.S. groundwater is already contaminated. Careers in groundwater analysis and management, such as "hydrogeology," are among the fastest-growing fields in many countries.

A main reason why groundwater is so easy to pollute is that it moves so slowly. The water must migrate through pores in the aquifer rock. Groundwater flow rates vary, but the average is only a few inches (several centimeters) per day. Compare this to a river where water usually moves many hundreds or thousands of feet (up to thousands of meters) per day. We have already seen (Chapter 11) how this slow movement causes water shortages due to the long times required to recharge aquifers. The slow movement also leads to pollution for the same reasons that lakes are more easily polluted than rivers: natural purification processes such as aeration and dilution are slowed. Once pollution occurs, groundwater tends to stay polluted for a long time, often for decades. Some aquifers will take many centuries to become purified if only natural processes are relied upon.

Table 16–3 lists nine major sources of groundwater pollution. Only one of these is intentional: deep-well injection, which involves pumping waste into a deep aquifer. Ideally, this aquifer is separated from higher "drinking water" aquifers by an impermeable barrier such as a shale layer. However, the barrier may be fractured, permitting leakage upward. The eight major sources of unintentional groundwater pollution in the table can be subdivided into three basic categories. One of these is saltwater pollution from overpumping the aquifer, as discussed in Chapter 11.

The other two categories are easily distinguished: surficial percolation and underground leakage. Some examples are shown in Figure 16–12. The four surficial sources involve downward percolation of rainwater that has percolated through landfills, waste disposal ponds (such as where industries put toxic chemicals), spills, and various agriculture and land-use products, including fertilizers, animal waste, and salt sprinkled on roads to melt ice. The three underground sources include leakage from septic tanks, buried wastes, and underground storage (such as gasoline

and fuel oil tanks). Septic tank pollutants are primarily oxygen-demanding wastes, while buried wastes tend to be highly toxic chemical by-products of industry.

Petroleum product leakage from underground fuel tanks is one of the most common types of groundwater pollution. The EPA has estimated that more than 50% of such tanks leak before they are removed. As Figure 16–13 shows, volatile organic compounds and petroleum products, both mainly from leaking petroleum storage tanks, rank third and fourth among groundwater pollutants in the United States. Nitrates (fertilizers) and pesticides rank first and second, respectively, illustrating that nonpoint sources are also a problem for groundwater; both enter the aquifer mainly as runoff from farms and other cultivated areas.

Much progress has recently been made in reducing many sources of groundwater pollution.

TABLE 16–3 *Major Sources of Groundwater Pollution*	
UNINTENTIONAL	INTENTIONAL
Surficial percolation:	1. Deep-well injection
1. Landfills	
2. Waste disposal ponds	
3. Spills	
4. Agriculture and land use	
Undergound leakage:	
5. Septic tanks	
6. Buried wastes	
7. Underground storage tanks	
Overpumping:	
8. Saltwater intrusion	

Disposal of waste by deep-well injection has been greatly curtailed in most areas by strict regulations. Reduction of solid waste through recycling and other means has slowed the use of landfills. Even where landfills are being used, they are often designed with linings and other barriers that reduce percolation into the groundwater (Chapter 19). Federal legislation passed in the early 1990s requires many gas station owners to replace their older underground tanks with new tanks designed to minimize leakage. Some of the most dangerous sources are the more than 77,000 toxic waste disposal sites in the United States such as disposal ponds, buried wastes, and some landfills. An estimated 82 billion gallons (310 billion L) of

FIGURE 16–12
(a) Leaking septic tanks can soon pollute local groundwater. (b) Nearly all landfills eventually form leachate that diffuses into the groundwater.

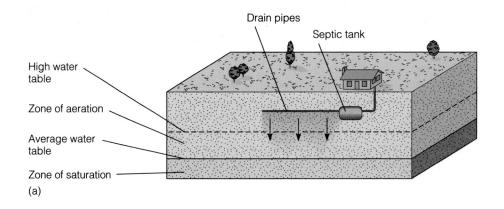

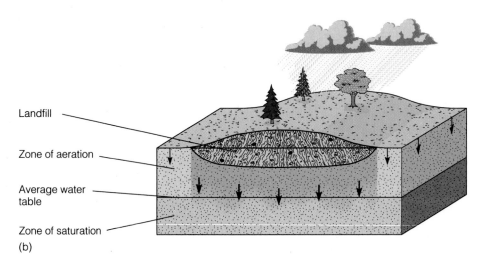

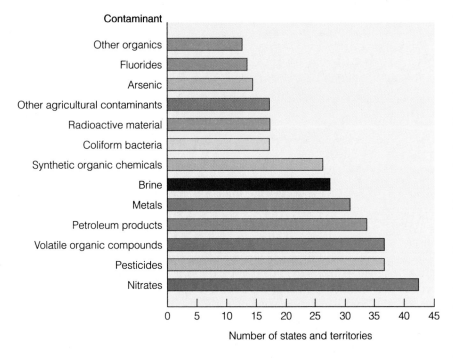

FIGURE 16–13

Major contaminants of U.S. groundwater: Nitrates (from fertilizer) and pesticides are mainly from agriculture. Volatile organic compounds (VOCs) and petroleum products come from oil and chemical storage tanks underground. The rest come largely from hazardous waste sites and leaking sewage and septic tanks. (*Source:* Environmental Protection Agency, 1990.)

water percolate through these sites each day. Like polluted rivers and lakes, nonpoint sources will remain a major challenge for years to come.

Marine Waters: Chemicals and Sediments

In 1990, a group of scientists appointed by the United Nations issued a major report that concluded that the oceans have contamination and litter that can be observed from the poles to the tropics, from the beaches to the deep sea. But this pollution is not evenly distributed; most coastal areas are polluted, but the open oceans are relatively unpolluted. One reason for this distribution is that most ocean pollution comes from land-based activities. As Figure 16–14 shows, runoff (44%) and atmospheric pollution (33%—mainly from factories and other land-based sources) comprise 77% of marine pollution.

The disproportionate pollution of coastal waters is unfortunate for both ecological and economic reasons. Recall from Chapter 3 that coastal waters contain some of our most productive ecosystems. Because of rich nutrient runoff from land, nearshore estuaries are the "nurseries" of vast numbers of young organisms. Furthermore,

Activities That Pollute the Oceans

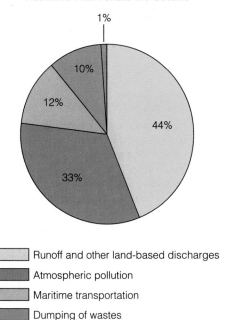

Runoff and other land-based discharges
Atmospheric pollution
Maritime transportation
Dumping of wastes
Offshore oil production

FIGURE 16–14
Runoff from land is the largest source of ocean pollution, followed by atmospheric (air) pollution. (*Source: The State of the Marine Environment*, Reports and Studies No. 39 [New York: United Nations, 1990], p. 88.)

Sources of Marine Oil Pollution

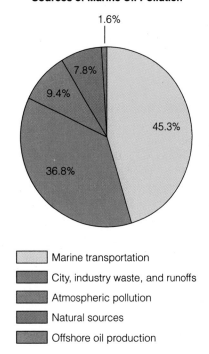

Marine transportation
City, industry waste, and runoffs
Atmospheric pollution
Natural sources
Offshore oil production

FIGURE 16–15
Marine transportation and land-based runoffs are the main sources of ocean oil pollution. Note that percentage values do not add up to 100% due to rounding. (*Source:* Data from 1994 *Information Please Environmental Almanac*, p. 320.)

young organisms, such as larvae, are the most sensitive to pollution. The widespread destruction caused when estuaries and coastlines are developed aggravates this problem. The economic consequences are also significant. More than 99% of the global catch of marine fish comes from within 200 miles (322 km) of shore; much of the decline in the worldwide fishing industry (Chapter 13) is attributable to loss of coastal habitat.

Agricultural runoff is the main source for sediment, plant nutrients, and pathogens. Industry is the main source for synthetic organic chemicals, such as toxic chemical waste. Domestic (city) waste is the main source of oxygen-demanding waste, especially through discharge of sewage. Unfortunately, city sewage is often not treated before being discharged into the ocean. To save money, most coastal municipalities of the world simply discharge raw waste directly into the sea. For example, about 85% of the sewage discharge from cities in the Mediterranean is untreated. Long pipes are often used to transport the waste a few miles out to sea, so local impacts of the waste were thought to be negligible. However, the rapid growth of coastal populations has begun to overwhelm the purifying abilities of many local marine waters, and currents often bring polluted

waters back to shore. More than 2500 beach closings occurred in the United States in 1992, most of them for this reason. Most of these closings occurred in just three states: New York, Florida, and California each had more than 600 closings. The problem is even greater in less-developed countries where sewage is rarely treated anywhere.

Marine Waters: Oil and Litter

Oil spills probably receive more attention in the media than all the other ocean pollutants combined. Most oil pollution, however, does not come from spills. As ▬ Figure 16–15 shows, about 46% comes from two land-based sources: atmospheric pollution (9.4%), and city, industry waste, and runoff (36.8%). Marine transportation provides another 45%, but less than one-third of this is from oil spills. Most comes from routine ship operations. For example, tankers often discharge oily bilge and ballast water at sea. On average, about a ton of oil is discharged for every thousand tons of oil transported by sea. The result is the continuous presence of oil slicks concentrated along shipping lanes used by oil tankers. Motorboats are also a major source of oil pollution (see the Case Study).

Are Motorboats More Harmful Than Oil Spills?

Recall from Chapter 15 that we often inaccurately perceive risk, leading to many misconceptions about environmental problems. As a result, we worry about, and spend money on, relatively minor problems while largely ignoring serious environmental challenges. An example is the public perception of oil spills compared to the water pollution caused by motorboats.

Large oil spills, such as the 1989 *Exxon Valdez* spill in Alaska, quickly become a focus of widespread public interest. Such spills can be devastating to the local marine life. The 35,000 tons (31,760 metric tons) of oil spilled into Prince William Sound killed between 300,000 and 645,000 birds plus thousands of fish. Over 300 otters were stricken although most survived. The fishing industry lost many millions of dollars, and Exxon spent about $3 billion on the cleanup effort. But the *Valdez* spill was actually much smaller than a number of other tanker spills that have occurred since World War II, and the amount of oil involved was less than one-fortieth of that purposely spilled into the Persian Gulf by Iraq during the Gulf War. In-

deed, oil spills are a relatively small source of overall oil pollution in the sea.

Yet the average person associates oil pollution with such large spills and is usually unaware of the much greater oil pollution caused by the millions of motorized pleasure boats in the world (Fig. 1). The United States alone has nearly 10 million such boats. Worldwide, these boats emit about 520,000 tons (472,000 metric tons) of oil and oil products into the atmosphere. Another 260,000 tons (236,000 metric tons) is leaked into the water, equivalent to more than seven times the amount spilled by the *Exxon Valdez*.

Why do motorboats leak so much oil? The problem is not just that there are so many—more than 20 million worldwide. According to Andre Mele, author of the book *Polluting for Pleasure*, there are two additional reasons why they cause so much water pollution. First, boat engines are inefficient. A small outboard motor gets a mere 2 to 4 miles per gallon (0.85 to 1.7 km per liter) compared to 20

miles per gallon (8.5 km per liter) for the average automobile. Second, many boat motors are two-stroke motors that run on a mix of oil and gasoline. These are more than eight times more polluting than standard (4-stroke) engines because 25% of their fuel is emitted half-burned through the exhaust system into the water.

The widespread motorboat pollution is a good example of how the cumulative small actions of many individuals can cause harm on a large scale. For decades, motorboat engines were subject to virtually no environmental regulations. What harm could come from small motors? Fortunately, as the scope of the problem has become evident, the EPA has proposed rulings that require major reductions in emissions for all new outboard motors sold, beginning in 1998. This measure has been criticized, however, for waiting too long and for not providing incentives to remove the numerous old motors that will continue in use for many years.

Questions

1. In Chapter 15, we discussed how observable and controllable activities are perceived as being less risky and harmful even when they may be more harmful. Does this apply to the perception that motorboats are less harmful to the environment than oil spills?
2. Has reading this reduced your desire to buy a motorboat? Can you think of any alternatives to buying one?
3. Exxon eventually paid $18.3 million to rescue and treat 357 otters after the *Valdez* spill. There are more than 10,000 otters in the area, and most of these were not threatened. Do you think the $18.3 million was well spent? Why or why not?

 FIGURE 1
Motorboats are a significant source of pollution.
(*Source*: Bill Bachmann/Photo Researchers.)

Despite their relatively modest contribution to overall oil pollution, oil spills can cause massive devastation to the local environments where they occur. This is why they receive so much media coverage. What happens to local environments when oil spills occur? Table 16–4 provides a

general outline of the physical and biological events. Long-term events, that continue for many years, include tar balls washing up on local beaches and scarcity of marine life. In some cases, species that are highly sensitive to oil have never returned. Long-term economic effects in-

TABLE 16–4 *Physical and Biological Events after an Oil Spill*

PHYSICAL EVENTS

Within hours:

1. Oil spreads on top of the water and "lighter" (more volatile) oil molecules on the water's surface evaporate.

Within days:

2. Heavier oil droplets sink to the bottom sediment.

Within weeks:

3. "Tar balls" wash up on shore as the heaviest oil droplets coalesce.

BIOLOGICAL EVENTS

Within hours:

1. Fishes, shellfishes, and plankton die from suffocation and metabolic poisoning.

Within days:

2. Birds and sea mammals die from freezing (oil destroys the tiny air pockets that make feathers and hair good insulators). Oil ingested during cleaning is toxic.

clean up of 157 miles (253 km) of Texas coastline was typical of many U.S. coastlines: it collected 307 tons (279 metric tons) of litter. The litter collected in a typical beach cleanup is about two-thirds (64%) plastic; most of this is plastic cigarette filters, followed by pieces of plastic. Metal, glass, and paper make up most of the remainder. Plastic is not just a problem for popular beaches. Plastic's durability, combined with its ability to float, allows plastic litter to travel very long distances. Recent surveys of remote locations, thousands of miles from large landmasses, have found increasing amounts of plastic debris.

Besides the obvious ugliness of marine litter, it is harmful to marine life. It is estimated that up to 2 million seabirds and 100,000 marine mammals die each year from eating or being entangled in plastics. The extent of this problem is evident from a study on Midway Island in the Pacific, which found that 90% of the albatross chicks had plastic in their digestive tracts. A random global sampling found that 25% of the world's seabirds have such undigested plastic particles. Sea turtles and marine mammals (such as porpoises and seals) often die from eating plastic, especially bags that they apparently mistake for jellyfish. In addition, birds, turtles, and mammals are killed when discarded plastic bands, such as six-pack

clude a decline in tourism and fishing. Fishing losses occur not only from death and a decline in breeding but also because the fishes and shellfishes that survive may contain high concentrations of oil in their tissue, often for many years.

Marine litter is one of the most rapidly increasing kinds of water pollution. Such litter includes materials of many kinds, usually discarded from boats. In the past, it was common practice to dump trash at sea; municipalities used boats to routinely dump tons of garbage. They assumed that the sea is so vast that the garbage would effectively "disappear." But the rapid growth of human populations and material goods worldwide has begun to overwhelm the ocean's ability to absorb and decompose the solid waste. More than 6.6 million tons (6 million metric tons) of shipboard litter alone are tossed into the sea each year.* This great volume is made worse by the widespread use of plastics, which are extremely durable, often taking many decades to decompose. The impact of plastic is evident in the litter cleared from the beaches each year (Fig. 16–16). A brief three-hour

 FIGURE 16–16
Tons of litter accumulate each year on an average beach. This photograph is of the beach at Oranjestad, Aruba. (*Source*: Richard L. Carlton/ Visuals Unlimited.)

---

*Unless otherwise noted, *tons* refers to short tons (2000 pounds).

rings, encircle their bodies and strangle them as they grow. Discarded fishing nets have also become a major cause of death, entangling and strangling the animals.

$\mathcal{S}$ LOWING POLLUTION: REDUCTION, TREATMENT, AND REMEDIATION

In Chapter 14, we discussed various ways of slowing pollution. Most of these are currently used to slow water pollution, including (1) source reduction of waste, (2) treating wastewaters before they are discharged into natural waters, and (3) remediating (cleaning up) natural waters after they have been polluted. These are listed in order of generally increasing cost. It is usually much more costly to clean up a polluted lake than to produce less pollutant at the source. At present, most of society's efforts are directed at the second method, treating polluted wastewaters, so most of our discussion will focus on that.

Source Reduction: Efficiency, Recycling, and Substitution

Source (input) reduction reduces pollution by producing less waste (Chapters 1, 6, and 14). Reducing the use of water-polluting materials is the least costly way of slowing pollution because it saves the cost of treating polluted discharge waters or cleaning up polluted natural waters. Furthermore, it is the only effective way of slowing pollution from the many nonpoint sources, such as agricultural runoff.

Efficiency

One way of reducing the introduction of polluting materials into natural waters is improved efficiency, or using less of a polluting product. An example is oil. Between 1974 and 1986, the total number of oil spills worldwide decreased from 1450 to 118 per year. While much of this decrease was from better transportation methods (such as improved oil containment), some of the decrease was from oil conservation. Following the OPEC embargo in the early 1970s, world exports decreased about 25% between 1977 and 1986 as higher oil prices led to increased energy efficiency. In other cases, concerns over the water-polluting effects of materials have led to improved efficiency. This is one reason for reduced growth of pesticide use in the United States (Chapter 15). Soil conservation efforts are yet another example

(Chapter 13). These not only promote sustainable agriculture, but also reduce sediment pollution into nearby waters; pollution from fertilizer is often reduced as well because natural soil fertility is retained.

Recycling

Recycling plastics, chemicals, and many other materials helps to reduce litter and nearly all types of water pollution because less waste is produced. Recycling of city and industrial wastewater, as in "closed loop reclamation," is a rapidly growing method of reducing water pollution while also extending water supplies, as discussed in Chapter 11.

Substitution

Another method of source reduction is the substitution of other materials for water-polluting materials in manufactured products. A classic example is the reduction of the amount of phosphate in detergents. As the limiting plant nutrient in many aquatic ecosystems, phosphate pollution is a main cause of eutrophication. Until the early 1980s, a typical detergent contained about 9% phosphorus by weight, and more than 500 million pounds (227 million kg) of phosphorus were being dumped into U.S. wastewaters yearly. The use of phosphate substitutes by manufacturers has significantly reduced phosphate pollution from domestic and industrial wastewaters. Other examples are biodegradable packaging (instead of plastic) and pesticides that decompose before they reach natural waters.

Treating Wastewater

Until recently, most efforts at pollution control have neglected the generally more effective and less costly methods of source (input) reduction just discussed. Instead, pollution control has emphasized output controls (Chapters 1, 6, and 14). For water pollution, this has meant an emphasis on wastewater treatment by industry, cities, and households.

Wastewater Treatment

The overwhelming importance of proper wastewater treatment is illustrated by those countries that lack it. As noted early in this chapter, inadequate water sanitation accounts for much of the world's sickness and death. Even early civilizations realized that the human waste that accumulated under crowded conditions led to rapid disease transmission. The first known sewer system was

FIGURE 16–17
The main sewer of ancient
Rome, the "Cloaca Maxima,"
as seen in an 18th-century en-
graving by Piranesi. (*Source:*
The Bettmann Archive.)

built in Mesopotamia more than 5000 years ago.
It was made of clay pipes that were used to carry
wastes away from the cities. Some major Roman
sewers are still used today (Fig. 16–17). The
flush toilet was invented in the late 1800s, removing the need to carry the waste to the sewer canals
in buckets. Carts that picked up and carried the
buckets were called "honeywagons," a term still
used to refer to garbage trucks in many regions.

Although the early sewer systems greatly relieved the health problems of local urban populations, they increasingly damaged the health of the
local aquatic ecosystems and contaminated drinking water "downstream" because they dumped the
raw sewage directly into rivers or lakes. Therefore,
scientists began to develop ways of treating the
wastewater; by the 1920s, modern treatment had
come into widespread use in North America and
Europe.

Treatment today is often carried out by municipal treatment ("sewage") plants, which serve
as the endpoint for waters carried by city sewer
systems. These sewer waters often carry both domestic and industrial wastes. The composition of

these highly polluted sewer waters varies from city
to city, depending largely on what industries are
allowed to dump waste into the sewer system and
how much they are required to treat it before discharge into the sewers. But even the most highly
polluted wastewaters are usually more than 99.9%
water. Once the polluted sewer water reaches the
municipal plant, its treatment is generally divided
into three basic stages: primary, secondary, and advanced (or tertiary). Each stage is progressively
more expensive, and only areas with special needs
or problems use advanced treatment.

Primary and Secondary Treatment

Primary treatment uses physical processes, especially screening and settling, to remove materials. A typical primary treatment sequence,
shown in Figure 16–18, has three basic steps:
(1) A bar screen removes branches, garbage, and
other large objects. (2) The grit chamber holds
the wastewater for a few minutes while the sand
and other coarse sediments settle out. (3) The primary settling tank holds the wastewater for about

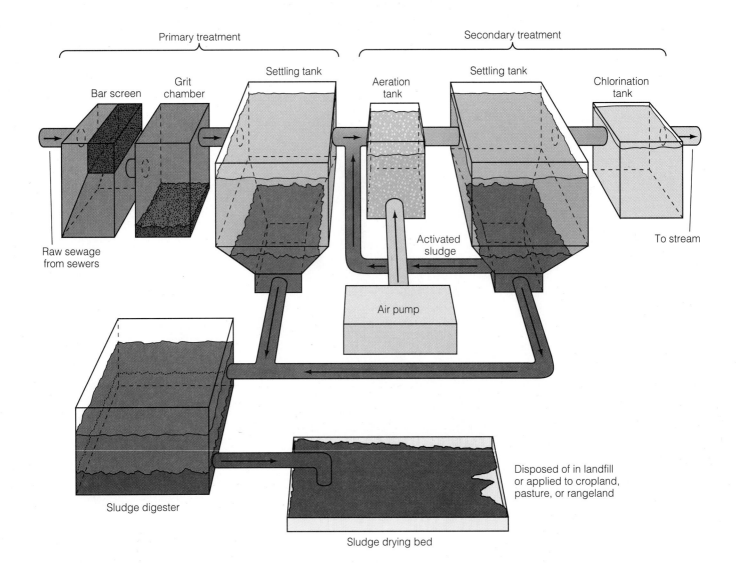

Primary treatment — Secondary treatment

Bar screen | Grit chamber | Settling tank | Aeration tank | Settling tank | Chlorination tank

Raw sewage from sewers

Activated sludge

Air pump

To stream

Sludge digester

Disposed of in landfill or applied to cropland, pasture, or rangeland

Sludge drying bed

FIGURE 16–18
Conventional wastewater treatment plants utilize a two-step process of primary and secondary treatment. Note the disposal of sludge.

two to three hours, allowing finer sediments and organic solids to settle out (or float, where they are skimmed off). These settled sediments and solids, called sludge, contain large numbers of bacteria, fungi, protozoa, and algae. These are piped into a sludge digester that uses bacteria to decompose the sludge. After removal of water in the sludge drying bed, the digested sludge is usually taken to a landfill. As landfills become full (Chapter 19), alternatives for sludge disposal are being explored, such as incineration and use as a soil conditioner. Unfortunately, sludge usually has high concentrations of toxic synthetic organic chemicals, heavy metals, and pathogens that require costly treatment before the nutrient-rich sludge can be used for crops. The toxic chemicals and metals also cause problems when the sludge is incinerated.

Primary treatment typically removes about 60% of the suspended solids and 35% of the oxygen-demanding waste, or BOD. As recently as the early 1970s, this is all the treatment received

by the sewage of about one-fourth of the U.S. population. Primary treatment alone is inadequate to prevent many long-term health and ecological problems, however, so secondary treatment has been required by U.S. law since 1977. When it follows primary treatment, **secondary treatment** uses biological (microbial) processes to remove up to 90% of both the suspended solids and BOD.

As Figure 16–18 shows, in secondary treatment the water discharged from primary treatment is subjected to three basic steps: (1) An aeration tank mixes oxygen, wastewater, and bacteria together. The bacteria digest the sewage. (2) A secondary settling tank allows the many fine organic particles in the digested wastewater to form more sludge, which is then piped back to the sludge digester. (3) A chlorination tank, which adds chlorine to the water, is the last treatment. Chlorine is a highly reactive chemical and is very effective for killing disease-causing organisms, although it produces potentially toxic chemicals (discussed later) that have become very controversial.

𝒫ROBLEMS OF ENVIRONMENTAL DEGRADATION   SECTION 3

Advanced (Tertiary) Treatment

Despite its effectiveness in removing BOD and suspended solids, secondary treatment is relatively ineffective in removing (1) plant nutrients, (2) toxic chemicals (especially synthetic organics and metals), and (3) some pathogens. Secondary treatment may be adequate if treated water is discharged into natural waters where natural purification eventually eliminates these pollutants before drinking. However, some situations require advanced treatment to remove some of these beforehand. As much as 50% of the nitrogen and 70% of the phosphorus often remain in the wastewater after secondary treatment. Therefore, treatment plants that discharge the treated waters into such sensitive ecosystems as Lake Tahoe use advanced treatment to remove the nutrients.

Dozens of kinds of advanced treatment are available. They use a wide variety of methods, from physical processes such as microfiltration, heating, electricity, and evaporation, to chemical processes such as oxidation and precipitation. An example of a physical process is carbon adsorption, which is commonly used to remove synthetic organic molecules, such as PCBs or pesticides. The wastewater goes through filters of fine carbon particles. The carbon is so finely ground that a single handful has the surface area of an acre, allowing the organic molecules to adsorb ("attach") to the carbon. An example of a common chemical process is chemical precipitation, which is often used to remove metals. Lowering the acidity of the wastewater, for instance, can cause metals to precipitate out of the water into a solid mass that can be easily removed. Advanced treatment is often used as a part of closed loop wastewater reclamation, discussed in Chapter 11.

Septic Tanks

In areas without a sewer system (mostly rural areas), individual homes use septic tanks. A **septic tank** which is usually made of watertight concrete and often has a capacity of about 1000 gallons (3785 L), is buried underground to receive household sewage. Waste from the house (such as from the flush toilets) undergoes settling in the tank for several days, and sludge forms at the bottom. The more liquid part of the flow passes across the top of the tank into the absorption field where the polluted water diffuses outward into the soil (Fig. 16–19). The waste is decomposed by bacteria in the tank and by soil bacteria in the absorption field.

Soils with finer sediment (such as clay or silt) are most suitable for septic tanks because they slow down the rate of diffusion, giving bacteria more time to work. They also provide more surface area for bacteria. In fact, septic tanks should not be built on land with coarse sediment (such as gravel) or underlain by fractured rocks (such as limestone) because the rapidly moving wastewater will pollute the groundwater. On the other hand, if the soil is too fine or the water table is high, the septic tank will back up because outward diffusion in the absorption field is impeded. After about three years, the sludge must be pumped out of even properly working septic tanks. The absorption field usually becomes saturated in a decade or so, causing persistent problems of backing up. This is why septic tanks are generally unacceptable for houses on lots of less than half an acre (one-fifth hectare) of land; the absorption field becomes saturated in just a few years.

Remediation: Cleaning Up Polluted Waters

Although cleaning up polluted waters is much more expensive than reducing pollutant input or treating waters before discharge, it is sometimes the only option. Groundwater can be treated with

FIGURE 16–19
Septic tanks permit sewage to settle and then disperse into an absorption field of soil where bacteria digest it.

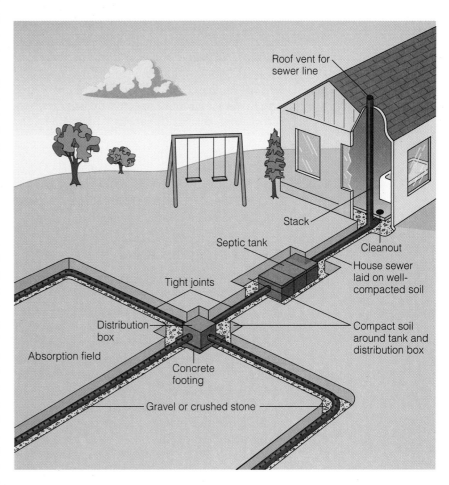

microbes to decompose organic pollutants. This is accomplished either by (1) injecting "seed" microbes into the polluted groundwater or (2) injecting nutrients and oxygen into the groundwater to stimulate growth in microbes already there. This is often used to treat groundwater contaminated with gasoline. Groundwater can also be pumped to the surface, treated, and pumped back underground.

Polluted surface waters (lakes, rivers, oceanic) can be dredged to remove contaminated sediment. Lake acidity caused by acid rain can be treated with chemicals. Chemical bases such as lime are disseminated in the lake to neutralize acidity.

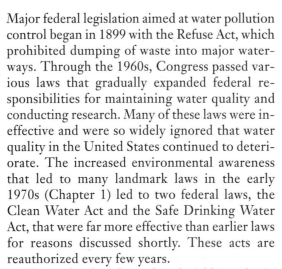

LEGAL AND SOCIAL SOLUTIONS

Major federal legislation aimed at water pollution control began in 1899 with the Refuse Act, which prohibited dumping of waste into major waterways. Through the 1960s, Congress passed various laws that gradually expanded federal responsibilities for maintaining water quality and conducting research. Many of these laws were ineffective and were so widely ignored that water quality in the United States continued to deteriorate. The increased environmental awareness that led to many landmark laws in the early 1970s (Chapter 1) led to two federal laws, the Clean Water Act and the Safe Drinking Water Act, that were far more effective than earlier laws for reasons discussed shortly. These acts are reauthorized every few years.

Many other laws have also played key roles in improving water quality. These include the Coastal Zone Management Act, Federal Insecticide, Fungicide, and Rodenticide Act, Toxic Substances Control Act, and the Ocean Dumping Ban Act.

Cleaner Rivers and Lakes

The **Clean Water Act (CWA)** of 1972, along with its 1977 and 1987 amendments, has been very successful in its goal of improving the water quality of lakes and rivers. The act (1) provided for enforcement by the EPA with stiff penalties, (2) created a system for identifying new point sources, (3) established water quality standards for discharged wastewaters, (4) set pretreatment standards for industrial wastes prior to discharge, and (5) provided federal funding to build wastewater treatment plants.

While all five provisions have been important to the CWA's success, the funding for treatment plants and enforcement by the EPA have been es-

pecially crucial. Before the act was passed, many local communities could not afford wastewater treatment and often dumped highly toxic material into local waters despite local and federal laws against it. Through federal subsidies, the CWA provided up to 75% of the cost of building treatment plants. As a result, many thousands of sewage treatment plants were constructed in the 1970s; more than 10,000 plants have been built since 1981 (▬ Fig. 16–20). In addition, the EPA was authorized to (1) establish specific water quality criteria (pollutant concentrations) that had to be met, (2) monitor surface waters to ensure compliance, and (3) punish violators. By 1993, the EPA had established limits for about 130 priority pollutants that were being monitored.

Cleaner Drinking Water

The Clean Water Act focused on improving water quality of rivers and lakes by reducing pollution in wastewater discharge. The **Safe Drinking Water Act (SDWA)** of 1974 was explicitly aimed at improving drinking water. It set more rigorous standards that applied to over 60,000 public water supply systems with 25 or more customers.

Public Water Supplies

About 10% of the water used in the United States is distributed by the public water systems as the "tap water" found in all major U.S. cities and towns. This water is usually withdrawn from local groundwaters, rivers, or lakes and is often stored in reservoirs that allow sediment to settle out and other pollutants to decompose through natural processes. Before distribution to public taps, the water is sometimes treated, especially if it is from a river or lake. A variety of treatments are used including (1) coagulation to cause suspended particles (including most bacteria) to settle out, (2) filtration by clay or sand filters to remove remaining suspended particles and chemicals, and (3) disinfection, usually by chlorine.

These methods are very effective in removing most pollutants, and tap water is generally safe. Nevertheless, the increasing age of treatment facilities, the growing number of chemical pollutants, the potential dangers of chlorine compounds, and other problems have caused many citizens to opt for other sources of drinking water besides tap water, as we discuss later.

Safe Drinking Water Act

Like the Clean Water Act, the Safe Drinking Water Act authorized the EPA to monitor drink-

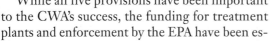

FIGURE 16–20
Until recently, construction of conventional wastewater treatment plants has been heavily subsidized with government funds. Seen here is the Hill Canyon Wastewater Treatment Plant in Thousand Oaks, California. (*Source:* Dean DeChambeau.)

ing water supplied by the public systems and other drinking water sources. Since 1974, standards have been added for more contaminants as they become progressively more common. For instance, a 1988 study listed over 2100 contaminants found in U.S. drinking water since the SDWA was passed in 1974. In 1986 a series of strengthening amendments were added to the SDWA. These amendments (1) required the EPA to speed up the creation of standards for 85 new contaminants, (2) increased civil and criminal penalties for violations of all standards, and (3) required the use of lead-free solder in plumbing pipes. Before 1986, water pipe solder often contained about 50% lead, which has led to widespread lead contamination of tap water in many homes (see Issues in Perspective 16–2).

The drinking water standards required by the SDWA fall into two categories. **Primary standards** specify contaminant levels based on health-related criteria. **Secondary standards** are based on nonhealth criteria. These improve the quality of water in aesthetic and other ways. For example, taste, color, odor, and corrosivity have secondary standards. Because secondary standards do not directly relate to life-threatening characteristics, they are generally not legally enforced.

They represent guidelines that water systems try to follow when possible. Another familiar secondary standard is **hardness** which is the amount of calcium, magnesium, and other ions in the water. "Hard water," which has high amounts of these ions, causes two annoying problems for water users. One is that these ions react with soap to produce gummy deposits, such as a "bathtub ring." These deposits makes all cleaning, from dishes to baths to laundry, more difficult. In addition, when hard water is heated, it forms rock-like "scales" (mineral deposits) that can clog pipes. Adding water softeners to hard water removes the ions and can reduce these problems.

Primary standards are actively enforced because human lives are directly affected. Contaminants that are covered by primary standards are classed into four basic categories: inorganic chemicals, organic chemicals, radioactive matter, and microbes (pathogens). Note that these are also four of the eight main classes of water pollutants discussed above. The remaining four—heat, sediment, oxygen-demanding wastes, and plant nutrients—are harmful to ecosystems, but are usually not toxic to humans in small amounts and are therefore omitted from drinking water standards.

TABLE 16–5 *Maximum Contaminant Levels (MCLs) For Certain Inorganic Chemicals*

CONTAMINANT	PRINCIPAL HEALTH EFFECTS	MAXIMUM CONTAMINANT LEVELS (mg/L)
Arsenic	Dermal and nervous system toxicity effects	0.05
Barium	Circulatory system effects	1.0
Cadmium	Kidney effects	0.010
Chromium	Liver/kidney effects	0.05
Fluoride	Skeletal damage	1.8
Lead	Central and peripheral nervous system damage; kidney effects; highly toxic to infants and pregnant women	0.05
Mercury	Central nervous system disorders; kidney effects	0.002
Nitrate and nitrite	Methemoglobinemia (blue-baby syndrome)	10.0
Selenium	Gastrointestinal effects	0.01
Silver	Skin discoloration (argyria)	0.05

(*Source:* Environmental Protection Agency, 1990.)

● Table 16–5 shows **maximum contaminant levels (MCLs)** for some inorganic chemicals. MCLs are the highest concentration allowed by the EPA; water with concentrations exceeding this level is considered harmful to at least some people if consumed over a lifetime. The EPA has similar listings of MCLs for organic chemicals, radioactive matter, and microbes. Examples of common organic chemicals with MCLs are pesticides, petrochemicals, and chlorine by-products, discussed below. The most common radioactive contaminant is dissolved radon gas, which enters groundwater from surrounding rocks. Radon is colorless, tasteless, and odorless, and it is potentially very dangerous where it occurs (Chapter 17).

Microbial contaminants, the fourth category, include disease-causing microorganisms, mainly certain bacteria and viruses. Because running separate standard tests for each of the many species of disease-causing microbes would be too expensive, a simple test for one kind of microbe, coliform bacteria, is carried out. **Coliform bacteria**, especially *Escherichia coli*,

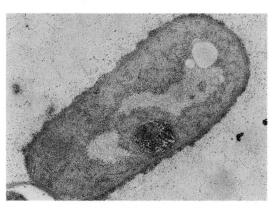

FIGURE 16–21
E. coli are extremely common symbiotic organisms in the human intestine. (*Source*: Ralph Slepecky/Visuals Unlimited.)

live in the human intestine in huge numbers, where they aid digestion and perform other functions essential for our health (● Fig. 16–21). Because they have a short life span, large numbers of dead coliform bacteria occur in human feces, about 1.4 billion individuals per ounce (50 million per gram) of feces.

The abundance of coliform bacteria in water is thus an excellent indication of how much human feces has recently entered the water. As human feces are the main source of disease-causing microbes in humans, the abundance of coliform bacteria also provides an estimate of how abundant disease-causing microbes are. Raw sewage contains about 1 virus for every 92,000 coliform bacteria. Similar ratios have been calculated for disease-causing bacteria, worms, and other pathogens. Fortunately, most of these disease-causing organisms have a much lower survival rate than coliform bacteria outside the human body.

Although the EPA has oversight authority, each individual state is largely responsible for monitoring and enforcing the standards on a day-to-day basis. As a result, the effectiveness with which water quality is maintained varies considerably from state to state. Water quality in Maine, Massachusetts, and New Jersey often ranks highest in yearly lists produced by environmental groups. Maine devotes a large part of its drinking water budget to training water system operators and reportedly allows no community to deviate significantly from the SDWA.

Point-of-Use Treatment, Bottled Water, and Alternative Sources

For many reasons, increasing numbers of U.S. citizens are concerned about their drinking water. Annual polls by the Gallup Organization regularly show that about two-thirds of adult Americans have a "great deal" of concern about their drinking water. This has led to a rapid increase in the use of (1) point-of-use treatment, (2) bottled water, and (3) alternative sources such as drilling home wells.

Point-of-use treatment refers to a variety of home treatment devices that alter water quality as it enters the home. Three of the most common are listed in ● Table 16–6: carbon filters, distillation, and re-

TABLE 16–6 *Treatment Methods and Alternative Water Sources: Advantages, Disadvantages, and Costs*

TREATMENT METHOD/ ALTERNATIVE SOURCE	CONTAMINANTS REMOVED/ADVANTAGES	DISADVANTAGES	ESTIMATED COST
Carbon filter	Removes halogentated and some other organics, radon, and residual chlorine.	Bacteria held in carbon may wash into water.	Countertop—under $50 and up. Undersink—$300 and up plus maintenance costs. Whole house—under $1200.
Distillation	Removes heavy organics, inorganics, metals, and microbiological contaminants.	Not effective on volatile organics compounds, trihalomethanes, and radon. May corrode pipes.	$200–$2000 plus maintenance costs.
Reverse osmosis	Best method of removing inorganics, also reduces the level of many organics and metals.	Wastes water—75% to 90% of water is lost in straining process.	$90–$700 and maintenance costs.
Bottled water	Natural spring water from an isolated source could be water of good quality.		$10–$15 per week depending on the size of the household.
Drilling a new well	Possible location of an uncontaminated nearby source.		Averages $10–$15 per foot plus casing and pump costs nationwide, but can range anywhere from $5 to $50 per foot depending on the area.

verse osmosis. The advantages and costs vary, depending on the area, and the quality of the device. Countertop carbon filters are the most common. Not listed in the table are water softeners, which are home treatment devices that replace the calcium and magnesium atoms that make water "hard" with sodium. As ▬ Figure 16–22 shows, hard water is particularly common in the midwestern states. Limestone and other alkaline rocks are major contributors to hardness in surface and ground waters.

The use of bottled water (Table 16–6) in the United States more than doubled between 1984 and 1993. By 1993, Americans were spending more than $2 billion per year for over 2 billion gallons (7.6 billion L) of bottled water. Is it worth it? Some people buy bottled water for improved taste, smell, or color compared to their tap water. But others buy it in the belief that it is healthier than tap water. This is not always true. Of the 700 or so brands on the market, about 80% are not completely natural, and between 25% and 35% of the bottled water companies use public water supplies. The discovery of cancer-causing benzene in bottled Perrier in 1990 alerted many consumers to this problem.

A main reason for this poor quality is that the bottled water industry has been poorly regulated. To help address this, in 1993 the Food and Drug Administration (FDA) proposed stricter rules for labeling bottled water as artesian, distilled, spring, mineral, and purified, for example. However, the many bottlers selling in only one state are regulated by state authorities, not the FDA, so consumers should be aware that many states are much less strict than others. One recommendation is to have your bottled water tested to see if it is consistently high quality. Easier, perhaps, is to see if the bottler belongs to the International Bottled Water Association (IBWA), which encourages members to undergo water testing by independent labs. Consumers can also write the IBWA (113 N. Henry St., Alexandria, VA 22314) for information about a bottling company.

Another possibility is to find an alternative source of water by drilling a new well. Costs of drilling vary considerably depending on how deep clean groundwater is to be found, the type of rocks to be drilled through, and other variables. In some regions, groundwater is extremely high quality and requires no treatment at all for safe tasteful drinking. But because of possible unseen contamination, such water should routinely be tested by professional laboratories. About 15% of Americans rely on private wells or springs.

FIGURE 16–22
Average hardness of
groundwaters for each state.
(*Source:* U.S. Geological Survey.)

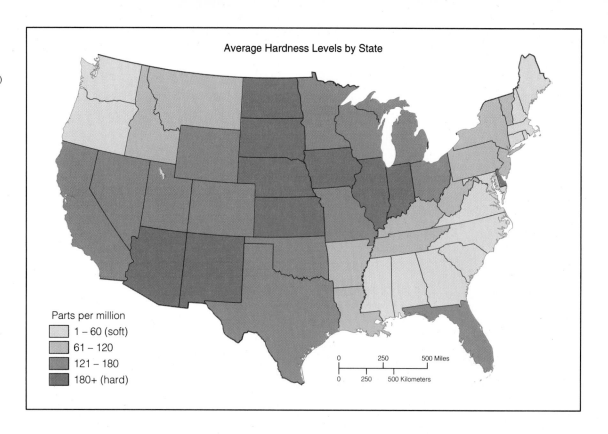

Future Problems

The reauthorization of the Clean Water Act was due in 1993, but was postponed until 1995 due to debate in the U.S. Congress. The Safe Drinking Water Act will also be up for reauthorization soon. Recall that more than $575 billion was spent on water pollution control between 1972 and 1994. A 1993 congressional study estimated that the 1986 Safe Drinking Water Act amendments would increase SDWA compliance costs from $230 million to $1.4 billion per year, a sixfold increase. While many people believe most of this money is well spent, a major topic of debate during reauthorization is how to address the deficiencies in the acts while also curbing the rising costs of water pollution control.

Nonpoint Pollution

In the past, water pollution control has tended to focus on reducing pollution in discharged city and industrial point sources, but as we have seen, nonpoint sources, such as agricultural runoff, are also a huge source of pollution. Obviously, nonpoint pollution is much harder to control because it does not have a single source. Nevertheless, progress is being made. The 1987 amendment to the Clean Water Act required states to identify the major sources of nonpoint pollution and draft a plan to rectify the problems.

The states' responses have varied, but many have been very slow to act; since compliance is largely voluntary, the requirement is often ignored. A 1990 survey of Chesapeake Bay found that only one-fourth of construction sites near the bay had erosion controls such as settling ponds, despite state laws enacted in the 1970s that require such controls (Fig. 16–23). City and county governments often take matters into their own hands, passing zoning ordinances that prohibit agricultural and other activities that increase runoff. Similar laws requiring water-permeable pavement, revegetation of land, sediment ponds to collect runoff, and many other, often costly, means of reducing runoff will be needed in many areas before a significant reduction of nonpoint pollution will be seen. As noted above, various forms of input reduction are often the cheapest way of slowing nonpoint pollution.

Aging Treatment Plants

The incident at Milwaukee (see Issues in Perspective 16–1) was a reminder of what can happen when wastewater treatment plants do not function effectively. Yet, in 1993, the EPA found that more than two-thirds of the nation's wastewater treatment plants had serious lapses in water quality standards. A serious problem is that so much testing is performed by state authorities on a voluntary basis. The EPA, for example, recommends, but does not require, that each water system be closely inspected every three years. In 1993, however, 45 states did not perform sanitary surveys according to EPA specifications.

The cost of upgrading all the nation's facilities to consistently meet the EPA standards has been estimated at $83.5 billion, or more than 12 times the EPA's annual budget. This need to upgrade, unfortunately, comes at a time when governments at all levels are tightening budgets. An important option may be the growing interest in "green technologies" of all kinds (Chapters 1 and 20). Most current wastewater treatment plant technology has not changed significantly since the 1920s and many new designs are available that are cheaper and may yield higher environmental benefits, too (see Issues in Perspective 16–3).

Pollution of Groundwater, Wetlands, and Marine Waters

Until recently, most antipollution efforts were focused on lakes and rivers. Less effort was made to avoid groundwater, wetland, and marine waters contamination. We are no longer able to adopt this attitude. For instance, there are about 5 million underground storage tanks in the United States, mostly storing petroleum products. Perhaps 1 million are leaking into the groundwater. This contamination is especially bad because groundwater takes so long to accumulate and is so costly to clean up. Because groundwater supplies water for about half the U.S. population, we are now realizing the magnitude of the problem.

Most legal protection of groundwater has been at the state and local level. But this has led to much variation in standards across the country, and states often lack the resources to adequately enforce the standards. As a result, there is growing pressure on Congress to pass a groundwater pollution act, similar in scope and strength to the Clean Water Act. In the meantime, federal protection of groundwater is expanding through (1) provisions added to existing hazardous waste laws to address groundwater contamination from hazardous waste sources and (2) provisions added to the Clean Water Act and Safe Drinking Water Act to protect groundwater and increase the testing of groundwater for contaminants.

Interest in protecting wetlands and marine waters has also been increasing. The 1985 "swampbuster provision" of the Farm Bill threatened farmers with loss of federal funding if they grew crops on converted wetlands. The 1990 version of the Farm Bill established a wetlands reserve program of 1 million acres (405,000 hectares). Many other laws protecting wildlife, such as the Endangered Species

Act (Chapter 12), and groundwaters also protect wetlands because wetlands are critical to many endangered species and serve as recharge areas for groundwaters (Chapter 11). Flood control also includes building wetlands to absorb runoff. Protection of marine waters is expanding under the Ocean Dumping Ban Act of 1988 and many other local, state, and federal laws, including a number of international agreements (see Appendix D). These are all very difficult to enforce, however, because the ocean has so many sources of pollution (air, streams, boats) and is a "commons" surrounded by so many nations.

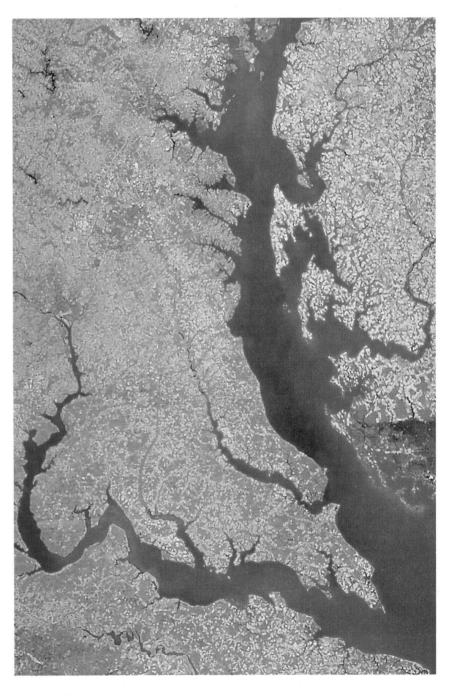

FIGURE 16–23
Chesapeake Bay has suffered major declines of aquatic life due to runoff from cities and agriculture. In this satellite image the cities of Baltimore (upper left) and Washington, D.C. (middle left), can be seen. (*Source*: USGS/TSADO/ Tom Stack & Associates.)

Wetland Sewage Treatment: Cleaner Water, Cheaper, and Prettier

Sewage treatment in the United States has not changed much since the early 1900s. The methods of primary and secondary treatment described in the text have been very successful in improving water quality. But the costs of these traditional methods of treatment are rising due to increasingly strict water quality standards and the gradual removal of huge state and federal subsidies for building municipal treatment facilities. As a result, the public is finally beginning to listen to a small but growing group of wastewater engineers who have said, since the early 1970s, that there are cleaner, cheaper, and even more aesthetic ways to treat wastewater. Most of these utilize natural biological filtering processes found in wetlands, often called the "kidneys" of the water cycle. Cultivating natural systems is cheaper because organisms are already adapted for filtration, and also because many useful marketable by-products are produced such as natural gas (methane), biomass fuel, and even flowers. Aesthetically, many people prefer to view a wetland, even an "engineered" wetland, instead of a chemical treatment plant.

One of the most successful pilot programs is at Cornell University. Designed by Professor William Jewell, this program uses a treatment system that has two basic phases (■ Fig. 1). The first phase passes the wastewater through a series of sand "beds" that contain anaerobic (non-oxgyen-using) bacteria. The bacteria live on the surface of the sand grains and digest much of the sewage while the sand itself acts as a filter for large particles of waste. During the second phase, the wastewater passes into the "wetland" area itself, which is a greenhouse containing plants. A greenhouse is only necessary in cooler climates to permit year-round operation where cold winters would otherwise stop or slow plant growth. The first plants encountered are cattails and other hardy plants, but grasses, trees, and ornamental flowering plants can be planted in the later stages of the greenhouse flow where the wastewater is cleaner (see Fig. 1). The plant roots absorb toxic substances and promote organic decay. Using a variety of plants promotes year-round efficiency because different plants are more active during different seasons and times of day.

This design has been tested with up to 10,000 gallons (37,850 L) per day of sewage from Ithaca, New York, for 52 months. The researchers found that a system such as the one in Figure 1 would require only about 2.3 acres (0.95 hectares) to treat the sewage of 10,000 people. Not only is this less land than a conventional treatment plant would require, but the treated water exceeded the quality of water after secondary treatment at a conventional plant. A larger wetland area produces even higher quality water and can provide tertiary (advanced) treatment at a much lower cost. The test indicated that 9.4 acres (3.8 hectares) could convert the wastewater of 10,000 people into sparkling, clear water of much higher quality than conventional plants release into local rivers. Even larger wetland designs could provide essentially pure water, free of nearly all pollutants, including heavy metals, pesticides, nitrogen and phosphorus, and other troublesome contaminants that are very difficult and costly to remove with conventional advanced treatments.

The apparent monetary savings are also impressive. Estimates based on the Cornell pilot program indicate that the cost of building and operating such a wetland system is perhaps half that, or even less, of a conventional wastewater treatment facility. By replacing high-tech machines with natural purifying ecosystems, the cost of construction is lower. By replacing fossil fuel energy for pumps with sunlight for photosynthesis, the cost of operation is lower. And these costs are reduced even further if energy savings from biomass and natural gas production are incorporated, or if roses and other plants are grown and marketed.

If such cheaper, more efficient sewage treatment methods are available, why

New Toxic Substances

Recall that the U. S. chemical industry produces thousands of new chemical compounds each year, so it is inevitable that some will find their way into water supplies, especially groundwaters. In recent years, problems with toxic pollutants, such as synthetic organics, often the most dangerous of these new chemical compounds, have been increasing. As a result, one of the 1986 amendments to the Safe Drinking Water Act requires the EPA to name 25 new pollutants for possible regulation every three years. New pollutants are most often associated with hazardous waste. A recent survey of over 8000 industrial waste disposal sites found that more than 30% were in permeable rocks over usable water aquifers.

The potentially toxic by-products of using chlorine to disinfect drinking water have recently become the subject of major debate. Chlorine can react with organic material (for example, tiny bits

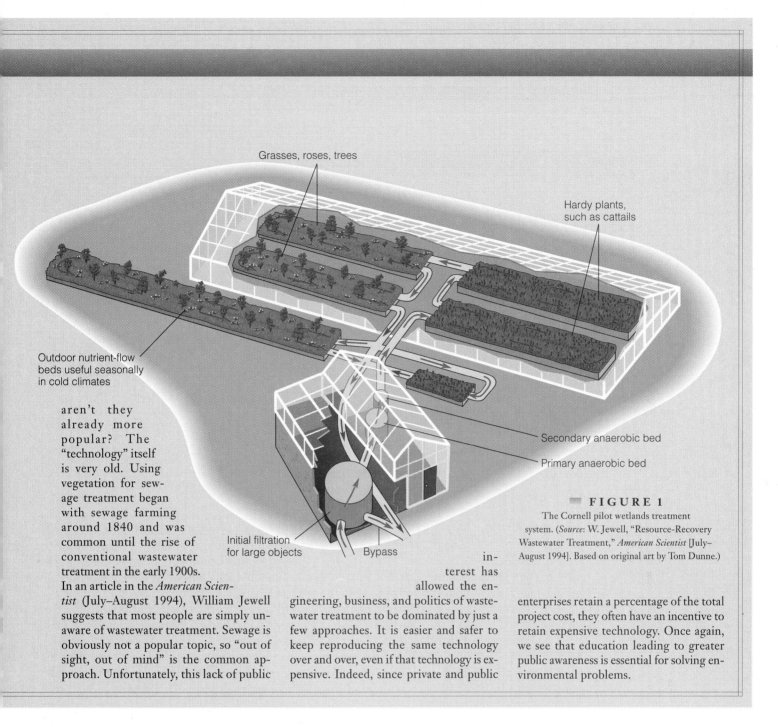

Grasses, roses, trees

Hardy plants,
such as cattails

Outdoor nutrient-flow
beds useful seasonally
in cold climates

Secondary anaerobic bed

Primary anaerobic bed

Initial filtration
for large objects

Bypass

■ FIGURE 1

The Cornell pilot wetlands treatment
system. (*Source*: W. Jewell, "Resource-Recovery
Wastewater Treatment," *American Scientist* [July–
August 1994]. Based on original art by Tom Dunne.)

aren't they already more popular? The "technology" itself is very old. Using vegetation for sewage treatment began with sewage farming around 1840 and was common until the rise of conventional wastewater treatment in the early 1900s. In an article in the *American Scientist* (July–August 1994), William Jewell suggests that most people are simply unaware of wastewater treatment. Sewage is obviously not a popular topic, so "out of sight, out of mind" is the common approach. Unfortunately, this lack of public interest has allowed the engineering, business, and politics of wastewater treatment to be dominated by just a few approaches. It is easier and safer to keep reproducing the same technology over and over, even if that technology is expensive. Indeed, since private and public enterprises retain a percentage of the total project cost, they often have an incentive to retain expensive technology. Once again, we see that education leading to greater public awareness is essential for solving environmental problems.

of plant debris) in the water to produce harmful chemicals such as chlorinated hydrocarbons (Chapter 15). **Ozonation**, which uses the reactive chemical ozone to disinfect the water, is a growing alternative. Ozone produces no harmful residues but is more expensive to use than chlorine.

National Water Testing Network

The United States has never had an integrated network of testing stations for consistently measuring water quality of rivers, lakes, and ocean water. Two networks do exist, one run by the U.S. Geological Survey and the other by the National Stream Quality Accounting Network. But these two networks generally monitor only rivers and streams. Furthermore, while they measure sediments, some minerals, nutrients, and coliform bacteria, they do not measure many toxic and ecological indicators that most water quality experts believe are important to know.

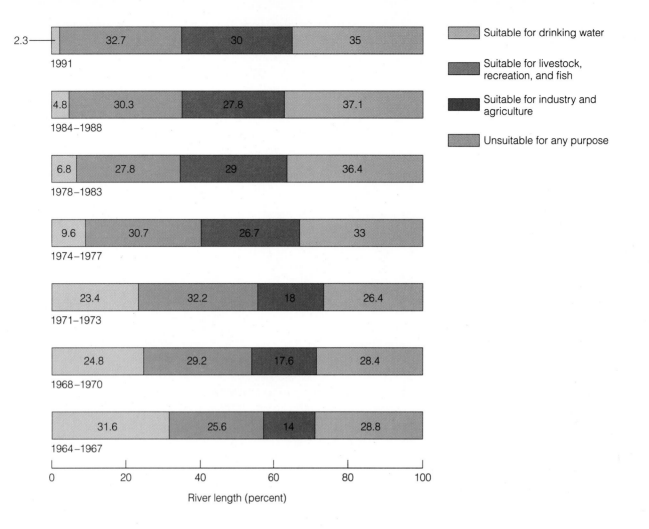

Suitable for drinking water

Suitable for livestock, recreation, and fish

Suitable for industry and agriculture

Unsuitable for any purpose

FIGURE 16–24
The water quality of Poland's rivers has declined drastically over the last few decades, especially the water suitable for drinking. (*Source*: From J. Oleksyn and P. Reich, "Pollution, Habitat Destruction and Biodiversity in Poland," *Conservation Biology 8* [December 1994]: 948. Reprinted by permission of the Society for Conservation Biology and Blackwell Science, Inc.)

Clean Water outside the United States

Recall that poor water quality is a major cause of death in many developing nations. Providing modern water treatment is a primary goal of many development programs of the World Bank, the United Nations, and many other organizations. India, for example, has begun a $200 million project to clean up the 1500-mile-long (2400 km) Ganges River, which provides water for one-third of India's massive population. However, this will scarcely dent the tons of sewage, industrial waste, pesticides, and other pollutants that flow into the Ganges daily.

Water quality is also very poor in many countries in Eastern Europe and in the territory of the former Soviet Union. The Baltic Sea is deteriorating rapidly. Dioxin concentrations are so high that once-popular Baltic cod liver is no longer edible; many fish have large tumors. The main reason is that surrounding cities have no or only primitive wastewater treatment. The sediment in St. Petersburg's harbor has a thousand times the normal concentration of many toxic metals such as lead and cadmium. The Finnish Baltic Marine Environmental Commission estimates the cost of cleaning up the Baltic at $1 billion per year for 20 years. Each year Russia's 2300-mile-long (3700 km) Volga River receives billions of tons of sewage and industrial waste, including toxic waste from more than 3000 factories. Currently, 70% of the fish in the Volga contain mercury. Much of this pollution ends up in the Caspian Sea, which is also rapidly becoming polluted. A growing environmental movement, called Save the Volga, has appeared. But, as in other ex-communist countries, lack of money seriously impedes cleanup efforts.

Poland is sometimes called the most polluted nation in the world because of its high level of industrialization combined with very poor pollution controls. ▪ Figure 16–24 shows how drastically river quality has deteriorated. Today only about 3% of Poland's river water is suitable for drinking, compared to more than 30% in the 1960s. About two-thirds of the total river length is unsuitable as fish habitats.

Polluted water, which is water rendered unusable for its intended purpose, causes damages and suffering to human health, other organisms, and ecosystems as well as economic effects. The Clean Water Act of 1972 has made significant improvements in water quality in the United States. Nevertheless, many deficiencies of water pollution control must still be addressed, including "end-of-pipe" methods, nonlocalized sources of pollution, and rising costs. A major challenge for future water pollution control will be the initiation of modern wastewater treatment in developing nations.

Water is purified in nature by the water cycle through either physical or chemical processes. Physical processes remove the bulk of material in water. These processes include dilution, the reduction in concentration of a pollutant discharged into water; sedimentation, the settling out of suspended particles; filtration, the percolation of water through sediment to remove suspended particles; and aeration, the release of gaseous impurities into the atmosphere. Chemical processes are biochemical reactions, involving enzymes and other chemicals, or inorganic chemical reactions.

Water pollution can be classified in three ways: (1) by composition (2) by source, and (3) by its fate. Pollutants are classified into eight general categories based on their composition. Oxygen-demanding wastes lead to a rapid increase in the rate of decomposition, increasing the biological oxygen demand (BOD). Disease-causing microbes, including bacteria, viruses, protozoa, and parasitic worms, are often associated with oxygen-demanding wastes. Plant nutrients, when found in increased concentrations, may lead to eutrophication if the nutrient is a limiting nutrient. Organic chemicals are often not readily broken down in the environment and lead to water pollution. Minerals and inorganic chemicals, including metals and acids, are highly destructive water pollutants. Sediment from erosion may also cause pollution by clogging gills and reducing the available sunlight. Radioactive substances discharged into water have detrimental effects on the ecosystem, causing death, mutations, and sterility. Additionally, heat is a water pollutant: increasing temperatures may exceed temperature tolerances of organisms as well as reducing the amount of dissolved oxygen in the water.

The sources of water pollutants are either agricultural, which tend to be nonpoint sources, industrial, or domestic wastes. Industrial wastes are a major source of all eight general types of water pollutants. Manufacturing industries contribute organic chemicals and heavy metals. Both products and by-products of this process are often highly toxic. Power-generating industries pollute water through heat and radioactivity. Mining and construction industries produce large amounts of sediment pollution and acid drainage. Agricultural wastes, generated by the cultivation of crops and animals, is a leading source of sediment pollution as well as oxygen-demanding wastes and infectious agents from livestock waste and plant nutrients. Domestic wastes, produced by households, come mainly from sewage and septic tank leakage. Oxygen-demanding wastes, plant nutrients, and infectious agents are all forms of pollutants produced by domestic waste.

Natural waters—both fresh water, including surface waters and groundwater, and marine water—ultimately absorb pollutants. River water, because it is moving, has the ability to dilute and decompose polluted water faster than standing water. More than 10% of U.S. rivers and streams are significantly polluted, however, due to the cities, agriculture, and industries that have built up along them. The current and future problems of U.S. rivers have two main causes: nonpoint pollution and physical alteration, including dams, diversion of waters, channel alteration, and land development. Lakes, plagued by similar pollutants, are more easily polluted than rivers due to slow circulation, accumulation of pollutants, and the lower volume of water. Groundwater is the most easily polluted of all fresh water because it moves very slowly. Groundwater pollution is divided into three categories: saltwater pollution from overpumping of aquifers, surficial percolation, and underground seepage. Marine water pollution causes many ecologic and economic problems, because coastal waters comprise a rich ecosystem. City sewage is often untreated before being dumped into ocean waters. Additionally, oil and litter cause significant water pollution. Although most oil pollution does not come from spills, spills do cause massive devastation to local environments. Marine litter is also a rapidly increasing water pollution problem,

overwhelming the ocean's ability to decompose and absorb solid waste.

Source reduction can be achieved through conservation, recycling, and substitution. Source reduction produces less waste while conservation uses less of polluting products. Recycling results in a lower production of wastes, and substitution allows for fewer water-polluting materials to be used in manufactured products.

Wastewater treatment is brought about by primary and secondary treatment. Primary treatment involves physical processes, screening, and settling to remove materials. Although primary treatment removes 60% of suspended solids and 35% of oxygen-demanding wastes, this is inadequate to ensure long-term health and ecological protection. Therefore, secondary treatment is required, using biological microbial processes. Even secondary treatment, however, is ineffective in removing plant nutrients, toxic chemicals, and some pathogens. Thus, advanced (tertiary) treatment is necessary.

Cleaning up polluted waters, although expensive, is often the only option. The Clean Water Act was effective in improving water quality of groundwater, rivers, and lakes by reducing pollution in wastewater discharge. The Safe Drinking Water Act of 1974 was likewise instrumental in improving drinking water quality. There are two categories of drinking water standards: primary standards, which specify contaminant levels based on health criteria, and secondary standards, based on nonhealth criteria such as water hardness.

Point-of-use treatment involves several home treatment devices that improve the quality of water as it enters the home. These include carbon filters, reverse osmosis, and distillation. Bottled water, though often thought to be healthier than tap water, is not necessarily so due to poor regulation of the industry.

Future problems in water pollution control include nonpoint pollution, which is difficult to regulate, and aging treatment plants. Additionally, groundwater, wetland, and marine pollution will require increased legal protection. New toxic substances introduced by the chemical industry also need to be addressed. Outside the United States, poor water quality is a main cause of death in many developing countries, including the countries of Eastern Europe and the former Soviet Union, and must be improved.

aeration
biological oxygen demand (BOD)
Clean Water Act (CWA)
coliform bacteria
contaminated water
dilution

eutrophication
filtration
hardness
maximum contaminant levels (MCLs)
ozonation
polluted water
primary standards

primary treatment
Safe Drinking Water Act (SDWA)
secondary standards
secondary treatment
sedimentation
septic tank

STUDY QUESTIONS

1. What are three methods of treatment before water is distributed to public taps?
2. What percentage of U.S. streams, rivers, and bays are significantly polluted? How much of the sewage dumped into the Mediterranean Sea is untreated?
3. The Safe Drinking Water Act of 1974 specifies maximum contaminant levels for what four classes of health-threatening water pollutants?
4. Name some of the main deficiencies of water pollution control in the United States.
5. What is the effect of oxygen-demanding wastes as water pollutants?

6. What are the four main types of disease-causing microbes?
7. What is the effect of high concentrations of heavy metals in living organisms?
8. Give examples of how sediment from erosion can be a pollutant.
9. What are two harmful effects of increased temperatures on aquatic organisms?
10. What are two reasons that cities historically have been built along rivers?
11. Give three reasons that lakes are more easily polluted than rivers.
12. What distinguishes a primary from a secondary standard? What is "hard" water and what problems does it cause?

13. Describe the use of microbes such as bacteria to treat polluted groundwater.
14. If a beach cleanup gathered 307 tons (278.6 metric tons) of litter along 157 miles (253 km) of Texas coastline, how much litter per mile was this? How much litter per km? How many tons of plastic were collected if 64% of the total was plastic?
15. If a beach cleanup gathered 600 tons (544.5 metric tons) of litter along 200 miles (322 km) of Florida coastline, how much litter per mile was this? How much litter per km? How many tons of plastic were collected if 64% of the total was plastic?

ESSAY QUESTIONS

1. List and discuss the major future water pollution problems that need to be addressed in the United States. Include suggestions that you would like to see carried out as solutions.
2. What are the major sources of water pollution? Specify the water pollutants produced by each activity, such as agriculture.
3. Discuss why ocean pollution is a growing concern. Include types of ocean pollution and their sources, and suggest potential solutions.
4. Why is groundwater so easily polluted? How is polluted groundwater cleaned up? Discuss problems with the legal regulation of groundwater pollution in the United States, and suggest solutions.
5. Describe the process of wastewater treatment. Include discussion of advanced methods.

SUGGESTED READINGS

Gray, N. F. 1992. *Biology of wastewater treatment.* New York: Oxford University Press.

Hammer, D., ed. 1989. *Constructed wetlands for wastewater treatment.* Chelsea, Mich.: Lewis Publishers.

Horton, T. and W. Eichbaum. 1991. *Turning the tide: Saving the Chesapeake Bay.* Washington, D.C.: Island Press.

Ingram, C. 1991. *The drinking water book.* Berkeley, Calif.: Ten Speed Press.

Marx, W. 1991. *The frail ocean: A blueprint for change in the 1990's and beyond.* San Francisco: Sierra Club Books.

Mason, C. 1991. *Biology of freshwater pollution.* New York: Wiley.

Patrick, R., et al. 1992. *Surface water quality: Have the laws been successful?* Princeton, N.J.: Princeton University Press.

Sierra Club Defense Fund. 1989. *The poisoned well: New strategies for groundwater protection.* Washington, D.C.: Island Press.

Steward, J. C. 1990. *Drinking water hazards.* Hiram, Ohio: Envirographics.

Thorne-Miller, B., and J. Catena. 1991. *The living ocean: Understanding and protecting marine biodiversity.* Washington, D.C.: Island Press.

Van der Leeden, F., et al. 1990. *The water encyclopedia.* Chelsea, Mich.: Lewis Publishers.

Weber, P. 1994. "Safeguarding oceans." In L. R. Brown et al., *State of the World 1994*, pp. 41–60. New York: W. W. Norton.

AIR POLLUTION: LOCAL AND REGIONAL

PROLOGUE   *I Want My MTBE?*

ir pollution in U.S. cities has generally been declining since the early 1970s when key federal pollution laws were passed. The Clean Air Act Amendments of 1990 were aimed at cleaning up the remaining problems, especially smog and other urban pollution from motor vehicles.

On Sunday, November 1, 1992, U.S. drivers first felt the effects of the 1990 amendments. In 39 major metropolitan areas with unhealthy levels of carbon monoxide, only new, cleaner gasoline could be sold as of that date. This new gasoline is regular gasoline blended with liquid compounds called "oxygenates." These compounds add oxygen to the fuel so that it produces more carbon

PHOTO   *Strict legislation has significantly reduced air pollution in many cities, including New York City (seen here on a clear evening). (Source:* Jeff Greenberg/Visuals Unlimited.)

dioxide (CO_2) and less carbon monoxide (CO) when it is burned. The two most commonly used oxygenates are ethanol, made from corn fermentation, and MTBE (methyl tertiary butyl ether), a petrochemical made from methanol.

Have oxygenated fuels worked? In nearly every major city where they are used, the levels of toxic carbon monoxide have dropped significantly and sometimes drastically. Furthermore, smog levels have also declined significantly in cities where oxygenate-blended fuels are burned. Smog is a hazy, acrid form of air pollution that is largely caused by unburned hydrocarbons released from cars. The added oxygen in the fuel reduces the amount of unburned hydrocarbons.

Nor has the cost been very high. The oil industry estimates that blending with oxygenates increases the cost of a gallon of gasoline by only 3 to 5 cents at the pump. Furthermore, oxygenated gasoline is only required in the winter. Cold engines burn fuel less completely, releasing more carbon monoxide and unburned hydrocarbons, so only cold-weather drivers need pay the extra cost.

$\mathcal{I}$NTRODUCTION

EnviroNet
www.jbpub.com/environet

Air pollution is one of the most widespread environmental problems because it occurs at many scales: indoor, local urban and regional, and global (Fig. 17–1). Regional and global air pollution are especially difficult to control because polluters are often very distant from those damaged by their emissions.

Each year outdoor air pollution causes an estimated $16 billion in direct damage in the United States, including crop and livestock damage, cleaning costs to clothes, and weathering of statues and buildings. Many billions of dollars more are lost due to increased health care expenses. In 1990, the Environmental Protection Agency (EPA) reported that over half the U.S. population still lived in cities polluted by too much smog and ozone despite major reductions

since 1970. Indoor air pollution is an even greater hazard. Radon and especially cigarette smoke cost many billions of dollars more. In terms of overall impact, global air pollution is perhaps the greatest single environmental challenge humans will face in the next few hundred years. Climate changes caused by pollution could lead to massive alterations of agriculture, large-scale migration of humans and other organisms, flooding of the world's coastal cities, and many other changes.

In this chapter, we discuss local and regional air pollution and indoor pollution. Global air pollution, including ozone depletion and climate change, are discussed in the next chapter. We will see that local and regional air pollution are largely a problem of cities and industrialization: large concentrations of people and machines

 FIGURE 17–1
Global air pollution occurs when so much pollution, such as carbon dioxide, is released into the atmosphere, that global changes occur. These are covered in Chapter 18. Urban and regional air pollution are more local; pollutants travel less distance and stay in the air for shorter time periods. Acid rain, smog, and other examples are discussed in this chapter. (*Source:* Modified from F. Mackenzie and J. Mackenzie, 1995, *Our Changing Planet* [Englewood Cliffs, N.J.: Prentice-Hall, 1995], p. 237.)

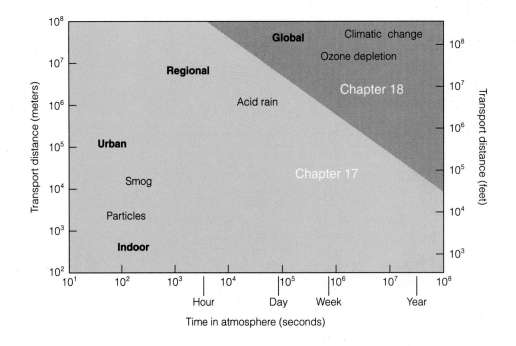

produce large inputs into the atmosphere, especially by combustion of the fossil fuels that we now use to run civilization. Alternative fuels, such as solar energy, would therefore alleviate much air pollution. In contrast, global air pollution is less restricted to cities. The burning of tropical forests is an example.

ATMOSPHERE: THE AIR WE BREATHE

"Pure" air is a myth. The air we breathe varies, depending on where we live. For one thing, it depends on the altitude. The atmosphere is a gaseous envelope held to Earth by gravity (Chapter 2). As you go higher, the gravitational force decreases and the atmosphere becomes less dense. Even at the same altitude, however, there are many minor variations in the local composition of the air. Today these local variations are often due to human-caused pollution, but even before humans, volcanoes, dust storms, and many natural processes released materials into the local atmosphere.

Some components of air vary less than others. The so-called nonvariable gases are found in about the same proportions everywhere. These gases comprise more than 99% of the atmosphere (● Table 17–1). Nitrogen (about 78%) and oxygen (about 21%) make up the large majority of these and of the air in general. The variable gases and particulates are the components that vary locally. The most abundant of these are water vapor, carbon dioxide, and ozone. Many other gases, such as methane and helium, are found in trace amounts. Variable gases and particulates can vary widely. For instance, air in the tropics can have up to 5% water vapor while cold, dry air can have less 0.1% water vapor.

Pollutants, both natural and human-made, can be viewed as variable gases and particulates that occur in sufficient amounts to be harmful. You may wonder how something that is present in trace amounts can be harmful. In the case of buildings, lakes, or other physical entities, the damage accumulates over long periods. For example, long-term exposure to acid rain will cause limestone statues to weather. Global climate change can occur from the addition of just a few parts per million of pollutants, accumulating over centuries. In the case of humans, physical harm can occur quickly as well as over long periods. The average adult inhales about *30 pounds (13.6 kg) of air per day*. We use only about one-fifth of this: the 21% that is oxygen is dissolved in our blood and carried to body cells to drive our metabolism. But because we inhale so much, toxic gases, such as carbon monoxide, can become dissolved in our bloodstream, or particulate matter can become trapped in the lungs and respiratory canals.

LOCAL AND REGIONAL AIR POLLUTION

Until recently, local and regional pollution have received more attention than global or indoor pollution. The United States and most Western industrialized nations have significantly reduced most types of local and regional air pollution since 1970, when strict amendments to the Clean Air Act were passed. This has been achieved by reducing the small group of so-called **criteria pollutants**, which are the source of most local and regional air pollution.

The five basic criteria pollutants are particulates, sulfur oxides, nitrogen oxides, volatile organic compounds, and carbon monoxide. As Figure 17–2 shows, they have two main

TABLE 17–1 *Composition of the Atmosphere*		
NAME	SYMBOL	PERCENTAGE BY VOLUME*
Nonvariable gases		
Nitrogen	N_2	78.08
Oxygen	O_2	20.95
Argon	Ar	0.93
Neon	Ne	0.002
Others		0.001
Variable gases and particulates		
Water vapor	H_2O	0.1 to 4.0
Carbon dioxide	CO_2	0.035
Ozone	O_3	0.000006
Other gases		Trace
Particulates		Normally trace

*Percentages, except for water vapor, are for dry air.

sources: (1) burning of fossil fuels by motor vehicles and stationary sources such as power plants and (2) industrial processes other than fossil fuel combustion. We will discuss each of these five criteria pollutants in turn, but first we should note some key patterns in the United States:

1. All pollutants except nitrogen oxides have decreased significantly since 1970 due to increased pollution controls.

FIGURE 17–2

(a) U.S. emissions of primary air pollutants on a per weight basis; (b) primary sources for those pollutants. (*Source*: Data from U.S. Environmental Protection Agency.)

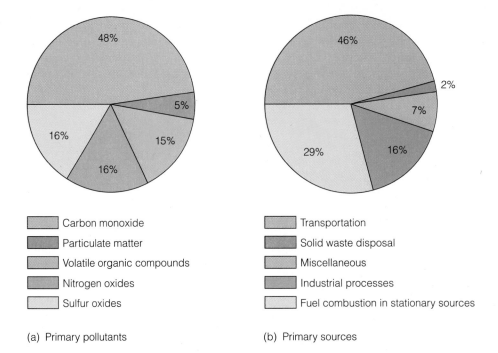

Carbon monoxide

Particulate matter

Volatile organic compounds

Nitrogen oxides

Sulfur oxides

(a) Primary pollutants

Transportation

Solid waste disposal

Miscellaneous

Industrial processes

Fuel combustion in stationary sources

(b) Primary sources

2. Transportation is the largest source of carbon monoxide, volatile organic compounds, and nitrogen oxides. This category includes motorboats, mowers, and small motors, which, until recently have been largely unregulated by air pollution controls.
3. Stationary fuel combustion (mostly coal-burning power plants) is the largest source of sulfur oxides, which cause acid rain.
4. Industrial processes besides fuel burning are the largest source of particulates.

Take special note that fossil fuel burning is the main cause of four of the five criteria pollutants and even plays a large role in the fifth pollutant, particulates. This is one reason why many environmentalists advocate switching to alternative fuels, such as solar or wind (Chapter 9). These energy sources are not only renewable, but would greatly reduce many air pollution problems.

Particulates

Particulates are any particles of dispersed matter, solid or liquid, that are larger than individual molecules. This category is very complex because particulate matter varies widely in composition and size. ● Table 17–2 lists various terms often used to describe particulates. Soot which arises from incomplete fuel combustion in cars and especially coal-burning factories, is generally the most common particulate in urban areas. It comprises at least 50% of the particulate air pollution in most cities of the world. Soot is especially common in developing countries, where air pollution is poorly controlled. If you have visited large cities in developing countries, you know that white clothes can quickly become dirty from the accumulation of dark particles. Particulates also scatter light, reducing visibility (■ Fig. 17–3).

Aside from their effects on clothes, machinery, buildings, and visibility, particulates are the single most damaging air pollutant to lungs. Larger particles are usually trapped in the hairs and lining of the nose and throat and then coughed or sneezed out. Small particulates however, can penetrate deep into the smaller canals and pockets of the respiratory system where they cannot be easily coughed up or otherwise removed. Accumulation of sufficient amounts of these fine particles will cause impaired breathing from blockage and irritation. Examples include "black lung" of coal miners, asbestos fibrosis, and urban emphysema. Many statistical studies show that in-

● **TABLE 17–2** *Common Types of Particulate Matter*

	DESCRIPTION
Aerosols	Any tiny solid or liquid particle
Dusts	Solid particles from grinding or crushing
Fumes	Solid particles occurring when vapors condense
Mist, fog	Liquid particles
Smoke, soot, ash	Solid particles, mostly carbon, from combustion
Smog	Any air pollutant; originally meant smoke plus fog

creases in particulate concentration in the atmosphere are correlated with increased visits to hospitals for respiratory problems, cardiac disorders, bronchitis, and many other illnesses associated with breathing.

An additional problem is that toxic chemicals may become attached to the surface ("adsorbed") of soot particles. These chemicals, such as the toxic metals cadmium or nickel, can be ab-

(a)

sorbed by the blood and cause heavy metal poisoning, usually affecting the nervous system (Chapter 15). Organic chemicals, such as those used in pesticides or manufacturing, are also often adsorbed to soot; these can cause cancer. Because particulate inhalation is cumulative, as are the toxic effects of adsorbed chemicals, the effects are usually most pronounced in the elderly. The EPA estimates that particulates cause up to 50,000 premature deaths each year (about 2% of total deaths) in the United States and Canada.

Despite these effects, particulates are generally not as detrimental to the environment as most other forms of air pollution. For one thing, particulate pollution caused by humans is actually small compared to pollution from natural sources. More than 90% of the particulates in the air come from salt spray, dust storms, and especially volcanoes; humans introduce less than 10%. Second, unlike gaseous air pollutants, particulates settle out of the air in a few days by gravity and rain. They thus tend to be local problems. Third, particulates are among the easiest and cheapest air pollutants to remove at the source.

Reducing Particulate Pollution

As with all pollutants, input reduction is always the cheapest and most effective method. In the case of particulates, this means burning coal that has a low ash content. However, even low-ash coal produces tons of emissions. These are usually removed from the air flow after combustion. Particulates are generally removed from the air flow in a stepwise fashion. Large particles are removed first by a so-called cyclone collector (▬ Fig. 17–4a). This spins the emissions in a vortex, causing the heavier particles to collide with the sides and slide down into a collecting bin at the bottom. This step typically removes more than 90% of the largest particles and is relatively cheap and maintenance-free.

▬ **FIGURE 17–3**
Los Angeles, California, (a) on a clear day and (b) when particulates and other pollutants greatly reduce visibility. (*Sources:* (a) Mark E. Gibson/Visuals Unlimited; (b) Frank Hanna/Visuals Unlimited.)

(b)

Next, the smaller particles are removed by using either electrostatic precipitators or baghouses. **Electrostatic precipitators** take advantage of the small electric charge that most particles carry. A high voltage is created between metal walls, causing the particles to collect on the walls where they are washed or shaken off into a bin. These are very efficient, removing up to 99.9% of small particles. **Baghouses** are a series

FIGURE 17-4

(a) A typical cyclone collector for particulates. (b) A typical baghouse filter for particulate pollution. (*Source*: U.S. Department of Health, Education, and Welfare.)

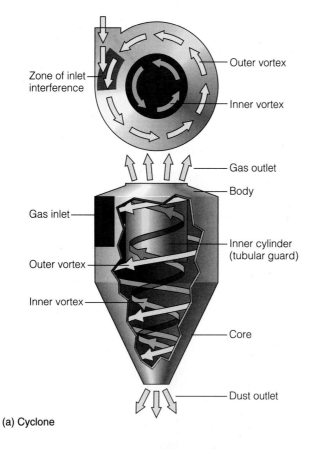

Zone of inlet interference

Outer vortex

Inner vortex

Gas outlet

Body

Gas inlet

Inner cylinder (tubular guard)

Outer vortex

Inner vortex

Core

Dust outlet

(a) Cyclone

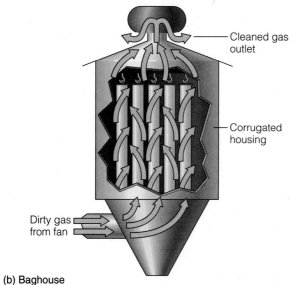

Cleaned gas outlet

Corrugated housing

Dirty gas from fan

(b) Baghouse

of fabric bags that act as filters (Fig. 17–4b). In efficiency and cost, they are similar to precipitators. Despite certain disadvantages, such as fire and explosion potential, baghouse filters are used almost as frequently as precipitators.

Trends in Particulate Pollution

Particulate emissions in the United States have decreased dramatically in the last few decades,

from about 19.8 million tons (18 million metric tons)* in 1970 to about 5.5 million tons (5 million metric tons) in 1994 (Fig. 17–5). Much of this reduction is due to the Clean Air Act Amendments of 1970, which, among other things, required the use of control devices to limit coal particle emissions.

Particulate air pollution has also decreased over the last few decades in nearly all of the other wealthier nations. In contrast, the formerly communist countries of Europe and the developing nations continue to have high levels of particulate pollution largely because they lack the money to invest in controls. Historically, as per capita income increases, particulate emissions decrease because nations have more money to invest in pollution controls.

Sulfur Oxides

Sulfur oxides are produced when fossil fuels that contain sulfur are burned. This oxidizes the sulfur to form SO_x compounds, such as SO_3 or, most commonly, SO_2. Coal generally contains much more sulfur than the other fossil fuels. Consequently, more than 70% of SO_x air pollution in the United States is generated by coal-burning electric power plants.

In terms of overall damage to humans and the environment, SO_x may be the most serious local and regional air pollutant. Sulfur dioxide, or SO_2, is a gas that is toxic to living things. Plants are especially sensitive, exhibiting stunted growth, discoloration, and reduced crop yields. Plant damage has been recorded over 50 miles (80 km) downwind of large sources. Effects on humans range from irritation of mucous linings in the eyes and lungs to death from respiratory and heart failure. Death can occur in just 30 seconds at concentrations as low as 3 parts per million.

SO_2 is also the main cause of **acid rain** (also known as acid precipitation), which is rainfall that is more acidic than normal. Acidity is measured on the **pH scale**, where 7 is neutral and 1 is very acidic (Fig. 17–6). This is a logarithmic scale so a decrease of 1 in pH indicates a 10-fold increase in acidity. Even unpolluted rainfall is slightly acidic, with an average pH of about 5.6, because water combines with naturally occurring carbon dioxide in the air to form the mild carbonic acid. When sulfur oxides are added to the air, water combines to form the much stronger sulfuric acid, causing acid rain. Technically, it be-

---

*Unless otherwise noted, *tons* refers to short tons (2000 pounds).

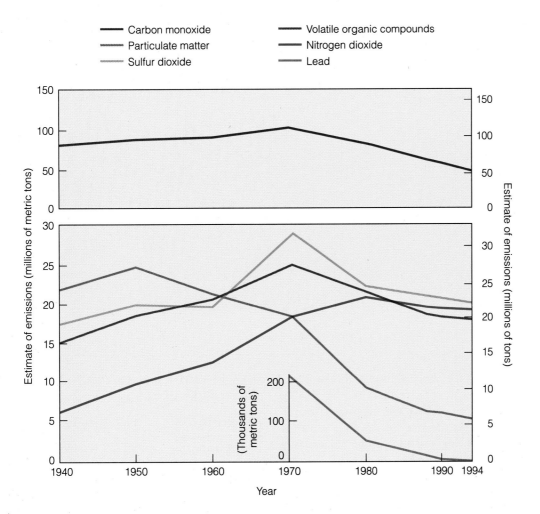

Carbon monoxide · Volatile organic compounds
Particulate matter · Nitrogen dioxide
Sulfur dioxide · Lead

Estimate of emissions (millions of metric tons)

(Thousands of metric tons)

Year

FIGURE 17–5
U.S. emissions of six pollutants from 1940 to 1994. (*Source*: Data from U.S. Environmental Protection Agency.)

comes "acid rain" when its pH is below 5.0. In extremely industrialized urban areas, local "acid fogs" can be produced; likewise, in colder regions "acid snow" may form. For instance, the Los Angeles basin has recorded fogs with a pH of 1.7, below lemon juice.

Such extremely high acidity usually occurs in confined areas near the sulfur oxide sources. More often, the sulfur oxides disperse downwind, often traveling three or four days and many hundreds of miles before falling as acid rain. Dry acid deposition can occur when relatively dry sulfate-containing particles, or sulfuric acid salts, settle out of the air. When combined with moisture, these particles may form a very strong acid. This problem is aggravated by the tall smokestacks built by many coal-burning power plants to prevent local particulate pollution by ejecting emissions high into the atmosphere. As a result, acid rain tends to be concentrated in areas downwind from the large industrial and urban centers that produce the pollution. In North America, acid rain is concentrated in the Great Lakes region, New England, and southern Canada, where the pH is often below 4.5 (Fig. 17–7). These areas are downwind of industrialized areas around the

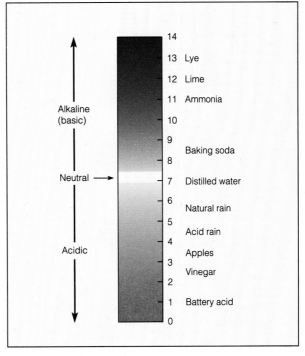

EnviroNet
www.jbpub.com/environet

FIGURE 17–6
On the pH scale, 7 is neutral. Values above 7 are increasingly alkaline, and values under 7 are increasingly acidic.

FIGURE 17–7
Average pH values of rain and
snow in the United States and
Canada. Areas within a con-
tour line have pH values at or
below that shown on the line.

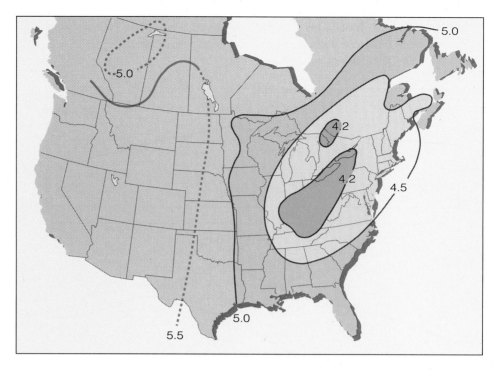

southern Great Lakes such as Cleveland and
Pittsburgh. In Europe, acid rain tends to be
concentrated in northern Germany and Scandinavia, which are downwind of the industrial,
urban areas of England and southern Germany.

Acid rain and acid deposition damage both the
physical and biological environment. Physical
damage includes paint discoloration, corrosion of
metals, and dissolution of marble, mortar, and
other building materials that contain lime, which
reacts with acid. This has caused many buildings
and statues to become pitted and eroded. In the
United States alone, acid rain causes tens of billions of dollars yearly in equipment repairs and
replacement costs. Archaeologists calculate that
acid rain has caused more damage to the marble
buildings of ancient Greece in the last 25 years
than in the entire preceding 2400 years. Whenever possible, the most valuable historic monuments, such as statues and parts of temples on the
Acropolis in Greece, are being moved into museums, and plastic replicas are left in their place.
Biological damage from acid rain is most visible
in forests and lakes. Coniferous trees, such as
pines, are especially sensitive to changes in soil
acidity. Symptoms include yellowing and loss of
needles (Fig. 17–8). Many of the coniferous
forests in New England, Canada, and northern
Europe have begun to show these symptoms,
some drastically. For example, it is estimated that
more than half of western Germany's forests are
deteriorating from acid rain.

Lakes suffer biological damage as their waters
become more acidic. Generally speaking, lake

ecologists have found that larger organisms are
more sensitive to acidity:

- Game fishes   most sensitive
- Invertebrates
- Rough fishes
- Algae
- Microbes   least sensitive

There is much variation within this pattern,
however. Invertebrates such as insects and snails
vary widely, but many suffer damage below pH 6.
Fishes have a lower average pH tolerance because
so-called rough fishes, such as garfishes, can tolerate pH values even below 4. However, many
game fishes, especially trout, are affected at pH
values as high as 6. Larvae and eggs are usually the
most sensitive in all organisms.

Most of the water that fills a lake is runoff that
has percolated through the surrounding rocks and
soil. In many cases, these rocks and soils are more
alkaline than the rain and therefore neutralize
some of the rain's acidity. For example, where
lakes are surrounded by limestone and other
sedimentary rocks that are extremely alkaline,
even highly acid rain is often readily neutralized.
Unfortunately, New England, eastern Canada,
and northern Europe have surface rocks and
soils formed from igneous and other crystalline
rocks that are much lower in alkaline chemicals.
This is a major reason why acid rain affects lakes
so strongly in these areas. For example, about
10% of the lakes in the Adirondack Mountains are
too acidic to support game fishes. An estimated
80% of the lakes in the southern half of Norway,

either no longer support fishes or have nearly reached that level of acidity.

Reducing Sulfur Oxides

As with all pollutants, the most effective and cheapest way of reducing sulfur oxides is through input reduction. In this case, this means reducing the amount of sulfur in coal, which produces the vast majority of sulfur oxide problems. The sulfur content of power plant coal typically ranges from 0.2% to 5.5% (by weight). By switching to low-sulfur coal, sulfur emissions can be reduced from 30% to 90%, depending on the original and the new sulfur contents. Unfortunately, about 85% of U.S. low-sulfur coal reserves are in the western United States, while two-thirds of coal consumption is in the east. Coal's large bulk makes it expensive to transport, so the cost of shipping low-sulfur coal is a major deterrent to its use, given the many tons burned per day by each plant. A growing alternative is to clean high-sulfur coal using a variety of methods. For example, sulfur often occurs in heavy minerals such as pyrite (FeS_2) that readily settle out when the coal is washed in water. Coal cleaning is relatively cheap because it reduces other costs by increasing coal-burning efficiency and reducing waste.

Another option is to use scrubbers. **Scrubbers** are devices that cleanse emissions, usually with water, before they are released into the air. Finely pulverized limestone, mixed with water, is sprayed into the emissions. The gaseous sulfur mixes with the calcium carbonate to form a "sludge" of calcium sulfate (gypsum). Scrubbers can remove about 90% of SO_2 from the emissions, but using them is costly. One problem is the high cost of installation: a scrubber adds 10–20% to the total cost of a new power plant. Operation costs are also high, adding about 1–2 cents per kilowatt-hour of electricity produced. The problem here is that scrubbers often corrode and clog, reducing plant efficiency. Finally, and perhaps most important, is the high cost of removing the highly toxic and acidic gypsum sludge that is produced in vast amounts. For example, a large 1000-megawatt plant burning 3% sulfur coal produces enough sludge each year to cover a square mile (2.59 km²) of land to a depth of over one foot (0.31 m). The cost of disposing of this material is rising rapidly as landfills and other disposal sites fill up. Attempts have been made to use the gypsum in construction, but it is not generally economical compared to gypsum from other sources. Yet another problem with scrubbers in arid areas

is that they use up to 1000 gallons (3785 L) of water per minute in large plants.

Trends in Sulfur Oxide Pollution

Thanks to the Clean Air Act Amendments of 1970, emissions have decreased from about 30.8 million tons (28 million metric tons) in 1970 to about 22 million tons (20 million metric tons) (Fig. 17–5). Much of this reduction was achieved from the use of the control methods described above in industry and stationary combustion sources such as power plants. World Bank data

■ **FIGURE 17–8**
Acid rain damage in the Green Mountains, Vermont. (*Source:* D. Like/Visuals Unlimited.)

show that sulfur oxide pollution is most common in countries of intermediate wealth. Poor countries do not yet have the industrial and electrical capacity to burn large amounts of coal while the wealthiest countries can afford pollution reduction.

Nitrogen Oxides and Volatile Organic Compounds

Nitrogen oxides and volatile organic compounds (VOCs) are discussed together because they are major causes of smog and other photochemical pollutants in urban areas. Nitrogen oxides are usually referred to as NO_x because they are composed of many different oxides, especially NO and NO_2. VOCs include a wide variety of hydrocarbon molecules. A **photochemical pollutant** is produced when sunlight initiates chemical reactions among NO_x, VOCs, and other components of air. These reactions are very complex and can produce many different kinds of photochemical pollutants. Nevertheless, we can summarize the basic photochemical reaction as:

Volatile organics + NO_x + sunlight → photochemicals

These photochemicals create a variety of environmental problems. Direct effects on humans and animals include irritation of eyes, lungs, and other mucous membranes. Plants may suffer stunted growth and death. Photochemicals are examples of **secondary pollutants**, meaning that they are produced by reactions among other air pollutants. **Primary pollutants** are those that are directly emitted, such as SO_x by coal-burning plants.

Smog originally meant air pollution that was a mixture of smoke and fog, but it now refers to the brown haze of photochemical pollutants in urban areas that irritates membranes and reduces visibility (see Issues in Perspective 17–1). **Ozone**, or O_3, is the most abundant photochemical pollutant in smog. Oxygen is very reactive, so the O_3 molecule is particularly destructive, leading to much of the lung irritation in humans and plant damage. Indeed, ozone alone is thought to be responsible for about 90% of all air pollution damage to crops, with a total loss of perhaps 6–7% of U.S. agricultural productivity. This reactivity also leads to damage of the physical environment. Long-term exposure to ozone causes rubber products to crack, for example. Ozone occurs naturally in air in small concentrations and is even crucial for protecting the Earth from solar radiation at very high altitudes (Chapter 18). In highly urbanized areas, however, where concentrations of ozone can be over 10 times higher than the natural near-surface level, its reactive properties are harmful.

In addition to their role in smog, nitrogen oxides contribute significantly to acid rain. While sulfuric acid from SO_x contributes about two-thirds, nitric acid, formed from NO_x and water, contributes about one-third of the acid in acid rain.

Sources of Photochemical Pollutants

NO_x and VOCs are largely produced by fuel combustion. NO_x comes mainly from fossil fuel burning in transportation and power generation; VOCs come from transportation and industry. NO_x is formed when nitrogen in the air and in fuel combines with oxygen during combustion. VOCs are largely gasoline and other fossil fuel (hydrocarbon) molecules that are not completely burned during combustion.

Because so much NO_x and VOC pollution is associated with transportation, urban smog varies considerably with traffic patterns. ▬ Figure 17–9, page 474, shows how morning "rush hour" traffic in Los Angeles causes a peak of nitrogen oxides in the early morning. Photochemical reactions on these oxides and VOCs take about two hours to produce the ozone peak in late morning.

Reducing Photochemical Pollution

Recall that NO_x is formed from nitrogen in air and in the fuel during combustion. Therefore a major method of reducing NO_x has been to alter the combustion process. Because coal-fired power plants emit about 25% of the NO_x pollution in the United States, emphasis has been placed on designing new technologies that control or reduce NO_x production during coal combustion. The so-called low excess air process restricts the amount of air allowed into the combustion chamber. This oxygen-starved environment reduces the oxidation of nitrogen during combustion so that nitrogen in the fuel is released as the harmless N_2 gas. NO_x emissions from coal combustion can be reduced up to 50% by this method.

Reducing NO_x and VOCs from vehicle emissions by changing the combustion process has proved much more difficult than reducing power plant emissions. The problem is that NO_x emissions are *maximized* under the same combustion conditions that *minimize* VOCs and most other pollutants.

This has been a continuing problem for vehicle manufacturers, who are required by law to meet certain emission standards (discussed later). The primary solution has been the de-

Clean Air in Los Angeles

Smog is a major problem in the Los Angeles area. It irritates the eyes and nose, restricts the activities of athletes and people who have breathing disorders, and injures the lungs of both young and old. Southern California's air quality is the worst in the United States. Air pollution in the region reaches unhealthful levels on half the days each year, and it violates four of the six federal standards for healthful air—those for ozone, fine particulates, carbon monoxide, and nitrogen dioxide. In 1991 the South Coast Air Basin exceeded one or more federal health standards on 184 days.

Nevertheless, air quality has improved dramatically since the 1970s. From 1955 to 1992, the peak level of ozone—one of the best indicators of air pollution—declined from 680 parts per billion to 300 parts per billion. The California Air Resources Board recently documented that population exposure to unhealthful ozone levels was halved between 1984 and 1994. Furthermore, the smog levels measured each year from 1992 through 1994 were the lowest on record.

All these improvements were achieved at a time when human activity in the Los Angeles area was increasing at a rapid rate. Since the 1950s, the population has almost tripled, from 4.8 million to 14 million; the number of motor vehicles on the road has more than quadrupled, from 2.3 million to

10.6 million; and the city has become one of the most prosperous in the world.

The hazy days are caused in part by a natural weather phenomenon known as an inversion layer (discussed in the text). Such inversions often form off the coast of Los Angeles as the Pacific Ocean cools the atmosphere just above it. After ocean breezes blow the air mass inland, the layer of cool air may slip underneath a layer of warmer air. The inversion layer traps air pollutants in the cool air near the ground where people live and breathe. The mountains that surround the region compound the problem by preventing the pollutants from dispersing.

Natural materials, such as dust, pollen, fibers, and salt, are important components of haze. But industries and motor vehicles contribute to the problem by adding carbon particles, metallic dust, oil droplets, and water vapor. Automobiles, factories, and other sources also release such raw pollutants as hydrocarbons, water vapor, carbon monoxide, and heavy metals. When these chemicals are exposed to intense sunlight, they react to yield a vast number of secondary pollutants.

Over the years, regulations were gradually developed that concentrated on reducing the major sources of air pollution: particles from trash incineration, emissions from industry, and pollutants from motor vehicles. Now the EPA is preparing standards for airplanes, trains, and ships

that travel through the region. Local governments are trying to reduce traffic by improving the transportation infrastructure and expanding mass transit.

A three-stage plan to attack the pollution has been proposed. The first stage, dubbed Tier I, includes 135 measures that can be accomplished using existing technologies and will be adopted by 1996. The measures limit and reduce pollutants from such sources as electric utilities, motor vehicles, small businesses, and even backyard barbecues. Power plants are installing low-polluting burners and catalysts to reduce nitrogen oxide emissions. Pollution from backyard barbecues will diminish as households use reformulated charcoal lighter fluid and other products for lighting grills. Automotive emissions will decrease because of more stringent tailpipe standards as well as programs encouraging carpools and use of public transportation.

The second stage, or Tier II, will take the region into the twenty-first century. These measures rely on technologies that have just entered the commercial market. The list includes a new house paint that does not release hydrocarbons. Another initiative involves encouraging more widespread use of automobile engines that run on methanol, natural gas, or other alternative fuels. The third stage, Tier III, requires technologies that have not been fully developed but are likely to be available in the next decade or so.

velopment and installation of emission control devices that remove pollutant gases after fuel combustion occurs. These are discussed in the next section. However, a final source of VOC pollution should be mentioned: up to 20% of an auto's emissions can come from evaporation of gasoline from the gas tank and carburetor. This source has been reduced through increasing use of vapor recovery systems in the tank and carburetor that capture and recycle the fumes through the engine.

Also, gas stations are increasingly using vapor recovery nozzles at the pumps.

Trends in VOC and NO_x Pollution

Growing use of vapor recovery systems, emission controls, and other methods has led to a general decline in VOC pollution since about 1970 (Fig. 17–5). Most of this decline has resulted from reduced transportation (vehicle) emissions.

FIGURE 17-9

(a) Rush hour traffic is a familiar sight to nearly all city-dwellers. Such traffic peaks are the main source of many health and other air pollution woes. Seen here is traffic in Calabasas, California, just northwest of Los Angeles. (b) Typical concentrations of NO_x and ozone in Los Angeles over the course of a day. Morning traffic causes a late-morning peak of ozone. (*Sources*: (a) Dean DeChambeau; (b) U.S. Department of Health, Education, and Welfare.)

(a)

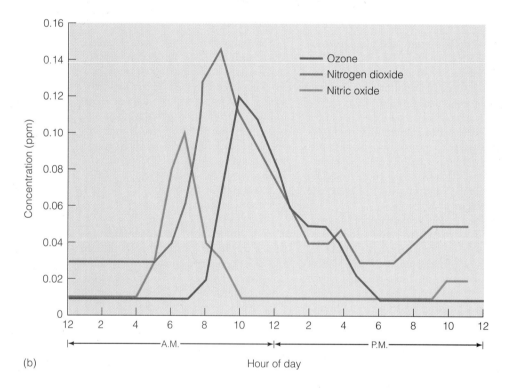

(b)

In contrast, NO_x is the only major air pollutant that has not shown a significant decline due to the engine design difficulties described above (Fig. 17–5). Even so, emission controls and other methods have made some strides in reducing NO_x emissions per car. However, nearly all of this gain has been offset by the increasing number of cars being used, both in the United States and worldwide. Thus, total NO_x emissions in the United States have stayed about the same.

Carbon Monoxide

Carbon monoxide (CO) is a deadly gas in high concentrations, killing more than 230 people every year in the United States. Its deadly effects are all the more dangerous because it is so difficult to detect: it is colorless, odorless, and tasteless. Carbon monoxide has little effect on plants or materials, but in humans and animals it interferes with the ability of the red blood cells to carry oxygen to the organs: the CO molecule attaches to the blood cells more readily than oxygen molecules. Because the brain requires a very large amount of oxygen, dizziness, headaches, and mental impairment are among the first symptoms.

Concentrations as low as 50 ppm will cause headaches and other effects over the course of a few hours. All effects are felt sooner if you are active; the body's cells are depleting oxygen faster and are in greater need of it. This is one reason why jogging during rush hour traffic is often discouraged. Fortunately, the effects of CO are usually reversible, except for extreme exposure. As usual with air pollution, the very young, elderly, and people with certain lung and heart ailments are most at risk.

Sources of Carbon Monoxide Pollution

CO is produced by incomplete combustion, when fossil fuels, wood, tobacco, and other organic materials burn under less than ideal conditions. As a result, the carbon is not fully oxidized to CO_2. For example, an engine with a poor air supply or low burning temperature will produce more CO than an engine that has a better air supply or burns at a higher temperature. Thus, the same high temperatures that cause nitrogen to form NO_x will minimize CO.

About 70% of carbon monoxide emissions in the United States are from transportation, mainly vehicle exhausts. Similarly, cars and trucks are the main source in nearly all cities of the world. The rest comes primarily from fuel combustion at power plants and industry and solid waste combustion. It is ironic that so much attention is given to these sources while many cigarette smokers deliberately produce much higher levels: directly inhaled cigarette smoke contains more than 400 ppm CO, compared to only 5–100 ppm in urban air from very congested, stalled traffic. Even "second-hand" cigarette smoke can raise indoor CO to 20–30 ppm.

Reducing Carbon Monoxide Pollution

Control of CO is closely related to control of NO_x and VOCs. Vehicle emissions are a major contributor of all three. There are three basic ways to reduce vehicle emissions: precombustion, postcombustion, or changing the combustion process. As you can see from Figure 17–5, these methods have been successful in reducing CO emissions (and also VOCs) since 1970 despite a large increase in the number of vehicles driven.

Most automobile manufacturers have traditionally favored postcombustion control because it is easiest and most economical. Postcombustion control devices remove the pollutants from the exhaust gas before it is released into the air. Examples include thermal reactors, which are "afterburners," and exhaust recirculators, which divert the exhaust back into the engine. Both of these reduce emissions by further oxidizing the CO and VOCs, and are thus less useful for reducing NO_x for the reasons noted above. Furthermore, they significantly reduce fuel economy and performance.

For these and other reasons, the auto industry's preferred postcombustion control is the catalytic converter. A "catalyst" is a substance that facilitates and speeds up a chemical reaction. A **catalytic converter** is a device that carries out a number of chemical reactions that convert pollutants to less harmful substances. Because CO, NO_x, and VOCs each have different chemistries, these reactions are quite complex. CO and VOCs must be oxidized to remove them whereas further burning (oxidation) will only make NO_x pollution worse. The solution has been to make "two-stage" catalytic converters. In the first stage, NO_x is converted to harmless nitrogen gas (N_2) by removing oxygen. The second stage acts on CO and VOCs in the opposite way—by oxidizing CO to CO_2 and VOCs to CO_2 and H_2O. Both stages use finely ground particles of platinum as the catalyst.

Changing the combustion process is another way to control emissions. There are many alternatives to the internal combustion engine, and some of these produce fewer emissions. Diesel engines are currently the most popular alternative, although electric motors may be the engine of the future. Diesel engines inject fuel directly into the cylinder. By omitting the need for spark plug ignition, diesels are not only more fuel-efficient, but have very low emissions of CO and VOCs. But on the negative side, diesel combustion in the cylinder produces high temperatures that create high levels of NO_x pollution. Furthermore, high levels of unburned carbon, or "soot," are emitted. Such particulates can be mutagenic and carcinogenic. The NO_x and soot problems can be reduced by exhaust recirculation and filters but have created maintenance problems. Overall, diesels are declining in popularity.

Other alternative engines that have been marketed include the stratified charge engine, gas turbines, and the rotary engine. For economic and other reasons, they have not become popular with consumers so car companies have tended to meet air quality laws (see below) with internal combustion engines linked to catalytic converters. Instead, the car of the future may be the electric car, which runs on a battery (see Fig. 9–11 in Chapter 9). By eliminating combustion in the car, electric cars can nearly eliminate CO, VOC, and NO_x emissions in dense urban traffic. By mandating zero emissions, California law will effectively require 2% of cars sold in 1998 and 10% by 2003 to be electric cars. Note that the net environmental impact of electric cars is largely determined by how the electricity to run them is generated. If a coal-fired plant is used, the net impact could be more of many pollutants, since coal is not only a very "dirty" fuel, but much usable energy is lost in converting coal to electricity. Urban smog and CO pollution would be reduced, but concentrated air pollution would be *shifted* to the local area around the power plant. On the other hand, electricity generated by direct solar, wind, or other cleaner fuels would greatly reduce net air pollution everywhere.

Control of CO, NO_x, and VOC emissions by precombustion methods is also growing. Examples include "reformulating" gasoline before it is burned and using alternative fuels such as methanol, ethanol, compressed natural gas, propane, or hydrogen. All have various advantages and disadvantages. Perhaps the most promising method of reformulating gasoline is **oxygenation**, which blends oxygen-rich liquids into it. By adding oxygen, CO is converted to CO_2 and VOCs are oxidized better. Oxygenation has proved so effective in Denver and other tests that the EPA began requiring wintertime oxygenated gasoline sales in 39 cities in 1992. (Winter is when CO is often worst.) The new gasoline raised fuel prices 3–10 cents per gallon and reduced fuel efficiency by 2–3%. As a result, there has been considerable resistance to this new fuel.

Perhaps the most commonly discussed alternative fuel of the future is **methanol**, which can be produced from natural gas, coal, or biomass. Most commercial methods now use natural gas. Methanol has a much higher octane rating than gasoline, allowing it to burn more completely and reducing CO and VOCs; it also burns at lower temperatures, reducing NO_x. Ozone is reduced by half. But methanol also has disadvantages including higher emissions of formaldehyde; it is also an eye irritant and a possible carcinogen. A practical difficulty is its low volatility, which makes it difficult to start engines on a cold morning. Most important is its low energy content, which is about half that of gasoline; this means gas tanks would have to be twice as large to give cars the same mileage range. A solution is to use a mixture of 85% methanol and 15% gasoline, which eliminates the cold-start problem and improves mileage. Carmakers are introducing "flexible fuel" cars that can run on gasoline or a mix with methanol. In addition to reducing local and regional air pollution, methanol reduces global emissions of CO_2, but only if it is made from natural gas. If methanol is made from coal, CO_2 emissions more than *double*.

Lead

Lead, like other metals, can accumulate in the body and is especially destructive to the nervous system. Lead poisoning can cause brain damage leading to learning disabilities, seizures, and death at high concentrations. Children and pregnant women are most at risk. In 1977, the EPA estimated that 600,000 children in the United States had blood levels of lead that were near, or exceeded, those high enough to cause behavioral changes. Airborne lead occurs mainly as particles that do not travel far from the source. About one-sixth of inhaled lead contributes to poisoning: one-third of all inhaled lead particles become trapped in the lungs, and about half of those are eventually absorbed by the bloodstream.

Fortunately, human exposure to airborne lead has decreased more than 95% since 1970 (Fig. 17–5). The main reason was the gradual elimination of leaded gasoline. Instead of lead additives to reduce "knocking" in the engine, other anti-knock additives are now used. However, lead ingestion from water in lead-contaminated pipes and from lead-based paint continues to be a major health threat to children, especially in urban areas. Pipes and paint are now required to be relatively lead-free so the threat occurs mainly in older homes.

International Trends

In contrast to the United States where most types of local and regional air pollution are declining, the worldwide total of the five criteria pollutants has generally been increasing. A main reason for these international trends is the increasing industrialization of developing nations and their use of fossil fuel technology. As coal-burning power plants, motor vehicles, and industries become more common in places like China, inevitably ever-greater amounts of air pollution are released. The Worldwatch Institute predicts that the number of cars in the world will double, to one billion, by the year 2030.

There are many ways to reduce these trends. Most involve promoting industrialization that reduces or even eliminates fossil fuel use, which is the main source of most air pollution. Mass transportation can have a major impact by reducing the use of cars (see Issues in Perspective 17–2). The average American annually produces nearly 12 tons (11 metric tons) of carbon dioxide, for example, compared to just 2.5 tons (2.3 metric tons) for the average Japanese, largely because of the very low use of mass transit in the United States. Reformulated gasoline and more fuel-efficient technology will also help. Ultimately, however, the most effective way to reduce fossil fuel pollution is the use of alternative fuels: electric cars, hydrogen fuels, wind power, and many others discussed in Chapter 9. As noted in Chapter 1, the widespread use of such green technologies in developing nations and their adoption in developed nations, can simultaneously improve the environment and the economy.

Weather and Air Pollution

Local weather conditions can strongly influence the impact of air pollution. Temperature is especially important. For instance, cars release more air pollution when they are first started on cold winter mornings than in the summer. Because incomplete combustion causes much air pollution, a cold engine does not burn fuel as efficiently and releases greater amounts of CO and other pollutants. You may have noticed that car exhaust smells different on cold winter mornings.

The most important local weather phenomenon that affects air pollution is **thermal inversion**. This occurs when a layer of warm air overlies cooler air, "inverting" the usual condition in which air becomes cooler as altitude increases (Fig. 17–10). The layer of warm air, which can be several yards to several miles thick, acts as a trap for rising air pollution. Such inversions can last up to several days, but are most common at night. Low-lying valleys, such as the Los Angeles area, are most prone to inversions because it is easier for warm air to become trapped. Before air pollution controls were common, inversions could be quite disastrous in urban industrial areas. The most severe urban inversion episode in history occurred from December 5 to December 10, 1952, in London and caused 4000 deaths. Air pollution controls have reduced the frequency of such disasters, but urban air quality is still generally at its worst during periods of thermal inversions.

In addition to weather affecting air pollution, the reverse can occur: air pollution can affect weather. For example, industrialized urban areas tend to experience more rain and snow than surrounding areas due to the pollution they produce. Cities release great amounts of thermal pollution. The concentrated burning of fossil fuels and other energy sources, along with the concrete and metal that retain the Sun's energy, turns cities into "heat islands." Rising hot moist air causes rain when it cools, and this effect is enhanced by the high amounts of particulate air pollution from cities. Particulates, such as soot, form tiny nuclei on which the cooling moisture can condense into droplets. Besides affecting local weather conditions, air pollution can affect global climate. This obviously has a much greater potential effect, as we see in the next chapter.

$\mathcal{S}$ OCIAL SOLUTIONS

We have discussed many technological ways of reducing air pollution. Since most air pollution originates as fossil fuel combustion, these solutions have focused on those fuels. We have seen

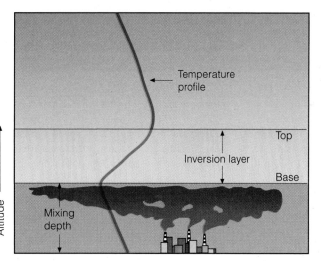

FIGURE 17–10
The warm inversion layer prevents pollutants from rising into the air above it.

three ways to control combustion: (1) precombustion, such as higher fuel efficiency or cleaning coal before use; (2) postcombustion, such as scrubbers; and (3) changing the combustion process, such as in electric cars. We have also discussed how input reduction by using less fossil fuel, especially by using alternative energy technology, is often the most effective solution. Technological reductions will not become widespread, however, unless people have some incentive to use them. In the United States, legal and economic incentives have been used most often.

Mass Transportation

The automobile once promised a dazzling world of speed, freedom, and convenience that would magically convey people wherever they wished to go. Given these alluring qualities, it is not surprising that people around the world enthusiastically embraced the dream of car ownership. But societies that have built their transport systems around the automobile are now waking up to a much harsher reality. The problems created by overreliance on the car are outweighing its benefits.

These problems are numerous and widespread. Traffic congestion and air pollution plague all major cities, and oil dependence makes economies vulnerable. Metropolises with streets designed for cars instead of people are increasingly unlivable. In developing countries, automobiles serve only a small elite and leave the vast majority with inadequate transport.

Automobiles are also a major source of carbon dioxide, the greenhouse gas responsible for over half of the global warming problem. Passenger cars account for more than 13% of the total carbon dioxide emitted from fossil fuels worldwide, or more than 700 million tons (635 million

metric tons) of carbon annually. This figure is projected to increase by up to 75% by the year 2010.

Improving automobile technology can never completely solve these troubles. Enhanced fuel efficiency and pollution control are at least partly offset by the sheer amount of additional driving, as some 35 million new cars roll off the assembly lines each year. Even in the United States, where emission controls are most effective, air pollution is worsening in some cities. And no matter how clean or fuel-efficient automobiles become, they still cause traffic jams. Automobile dominance creates a set of problems so relentless that societies in coming decades will have no choice but to seek transport alternatives.

A new, more rational approach to transportation is needed—one that puts the automobile in its rightful place as one among many options for travel. Buses and trains are more appropriate than private cars as the centerpieces of transportation systems, particularly in the world's most congested cities. At reasonable occupancy rates, public transport uses space and energy many times more efficiently than cars and creates much less pollution.

Public transport comprises many different types of vehicles, but most commonly the term refers to buses and trains (■ Fig. 1). The concept of public transportation also includes organized car and van pools. For U.S. commuters in areas with inadequate bus and train service, this is the only "public" transport option.

Public transport modes vary in fuel use, emissions, and the space they require, but, in carrying reasonable numbers of passengers, they all outperform one-occupant private cars. Energy requirements vary according to the size and design of the vehicle and how many people are on board, but buses and trains require far less fuel per passenger for each mile of travel. The emissions savings from public transport are even more dramatic. Since rapid rail and light rail have electric engines, pollution is measured not from the tailpipe, but at the power plant (which is usually located outside the city, where air quality problems are less acute). Diesel buses, especially in developing countries, are heavy polluters, though the number of cars required to carry an equivalent number of passengers would create more pollution. But the technology exists to control exhaust. In Athens,

Legal Solutions

Legal incentives have been the main reason for the decline in many of the local and regional air pollutants since about 1970. Federal legislation actually began with the Air Pollution Control Act of 1955. This act mainly provided funds for research, but its enactment was a key event because it initiated federal participation in air pollution control. Until 1955, air pollution was considered a local problem and was therefore treated by a hodgepodge of local and state laws that varied widely. The **Clean Air Act** of 1963 was the first of a series of acts and amendments

that exerted increasing federal pressure on air polluters. Not until the Clean Air Act Amendments of 1970, however, were widespread legal standards established that were actually enforced. These standards included the National Ambient Air Quality Standards (NAAQS) and New Source Performance Standards (NSPS). The NAAQS established standards of allowable *concentrations* in surrounding air, whereas the NSPS established standards of allowable emissions, or *rates* at which polluters could emit. The newly established Environmental Protection Agency (EPA) was charged with the task of enforcing these standards.

some buses are fitted with traps to prevent particles from being emitted into the air. Buses can also run on less polluting fuels such as propane (used in parts of Europe) and natural gas (used in Brazil and China). In the Netherlands, test buses that run on natural gas are estimated to emit 90% less nitrogen oxides and 25% less carbon monoxide than diesel engines.

In addition to reducing fuel consumption and pollution, public transportation saves valuable city space. Buses and trains carry more people in each vehicle, and if assigned their own rights-of-way, they can safely run at much higher speeds; in other words, they not only take up less space but occupy it for a shorter time. Thus, comparing ideal conditions for each mode, an underground metro can carry 70,000 passengers past a certain point in a single lane in one hour, surface rapid rail can carry up to 50,000 people, and a trolley or a bus on a separate bus lane, more than 30,000. By contrast, a lane of private cars with four occupants each can move only about 8000 people an hour.

The cost of providing transport is, understandably, the overriding factor in government's decision making. But many public officials fail to make a full accounting. A fair comparison must include a calculation of the full costs of all systems, including their environmental impacts and social consequences, and a consideration of which approach can move more people. With public transport's lower impacts, higher capacities, and greater affordability for the general public, governments could get more for their money.

Similarly, drivers would find public transport more attractive if they kept the full costs in mind. Few U.S. drivers realize that, when the costs are factored in—including fuel, maintenance, insurance, depreciation, and finance charges — they pay $34 per 100 miles (161 km) of driving, or about $1700 an-nually just to commute to work. By contrast, the average public transport fare is $14 per 100 miles (161 km). In highly car-dependent cities, a viable public transport option for commuting could save some households from having to purchase a second or third vehicle.

FIGURE 1
A BART (Bay Area Rapid Transit) station in Oakland, California. (*Source:* L. Linkhart/Visuals Unlimited.)

Air Quality Standards

In applying NAAQS, the EPA established air quality standards for six major pollutants: CO, NO_2, O_3, SO_2, PM-10 (particulate matter), and lead. These are easily measured, occur in significant amounts, and are health threats. They indicate the general "health" of the air. If one or more of these are present in large amounts, then we can infer that other, associated air pollutants are also common. Allowable concentrations in California are often lower, illustrating how federal law may allow states to set stricter standards for air quality and many other environmental regulations.

If you live in a city, you have probably heard of the **Pollutant Standards Index (PSI)**. This index, shown in ● Table 17–3, ranges from 0 (best air quality) to over 400 (worst air quality). The PSI is based on the six major NAAQS pollutants: A value of 100 indicates that at least one of the pollutants has exceeded its air quality standard. In general, the pollutant with the highest concentration determines the overall PSI at any given time. A PSI level of 200 translates into a First Stage Alert, meaning that the elderly and those with respiratory illnesses are advised to stay indoors. At 300, or Second Stage Alert, all people are advised to stay indoors.

TABLE 17–3 *The Pollutant Standards Index*

PSI VALUE	DESCRIPTION	GENERAL HEALTH EFFECTS	PSI EPISODE LEVEL	CAUTIONARY STATEMENTS
0–50	Good	None		
51–100	Moderate	None		
101–199	Unhealthful	Mild aggravation of symptoms in susceptible persons, with irritation symptoms in the healthy population.		Persons with existing heart or respiratory ailments should reduce physical exertion and outdoor activity.
200–299	Very unhealthful	Significant aggravation of symptoms and decreased exercise tolerance in persons with heart or lung disease, with widespread symptoms in the healthy population.	Stage 1 Health advisory alert	Elderly and persons with existing heart or lung disease should stay indoors and reduce physical activity.
300–399	Hazardous	Premature onset of certain diseases in addition to significant aggravation of symptoms and decreased exercise tolerance in healthy persons.	Stage 2 Health advisory warning	Elderly and persons with existing heart or lung disease should stay indoors and avoid physical exertion. General population should avoid outdoor activity.
400–500	Hazardous	Premature death of ill and elderly. Healthy people will experience adverse symptoms that affect their normal activity.	Stage 3 Emergency	All persons should remain indoors, keeping windows and doors closed. All persons should minimize physical exertion and avoid traffic.

(*Source:* U.S. Environmental Protection Agency.)

In 1991, 86 million U.S. citizens (over one-fourth of the population) lived in cities that exceeded at least one air quality standard during the year. Not surprisingly, the PSI varies widely among U.S. cities. One way of comparing the air quality in different cities is to record the number of days per year that the PSI exceeds 100, called "unhealthy" air pollution days. ▪ Figure 17–11 shows that the Los Angeles area has far more unhealthful days than the rest of the United States. Generally speaking, one or more of these three main factors cause most of the unhealthy air in cities: geographic conditions such as valleys that impede circulation, large amounts of automobile traffic, and certain large industrial plants.

Emission Standards

The EPA sets New Source Performance Standards (NSPS) to limit air emissions by certain industries. The affected industries include fossil fuel power plants, incinerators, nitric acid plants, petroleum refineries, sewage treatment plants, and ore smelters. The standards are called "New Source" because they are directed at facilities that are to be constructed, not those that existed before the standards were set. This reflects the economic reality that it is usually much cheaper to design a new plant to produce lower emissions than to modify an existing plant that uses older technology. Of course, this begs the question of what to do with older facilities. By 1977, for instance, only about one-third of the air quality control regions in the United States were meeting the set standards. This deficiency in the 1970 Clean Air Amendments led to the 1977 Clean Air Amendments, which attempted to deal with these so-called nonattainment regions.

Perhaps the most successful policy to result from these amendments were **emission offsets**: to receive a construction permit, a major new pollution source in a nonattainment area must first find ways to reduce emissions from existing sources. Emission offsets have been very efficient in economic terms because they use the free market to find optimal solutions. For example, some-

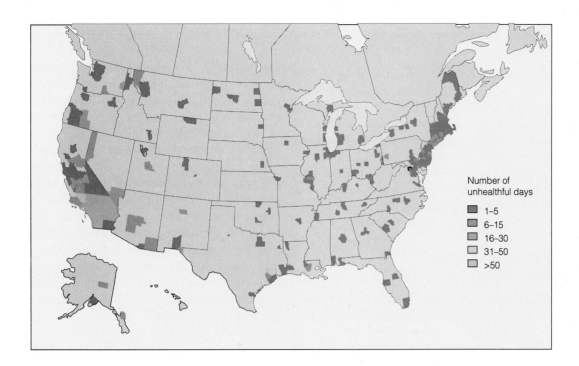

FIGURE 17-11
The number of unhealthful days across the United States when the PSI value of an NAAQS pollutant exceeded 100 during 1990. (*Source*: Data from the Environmental Protection Agency.)

Number of
unhealthful days

- 1–5
- 6–15
- 16–30
- 31–50
- >50

one seeking a construction license may install emission controls on a heavy polluter, even if someone else owns it. Alternatively, the license seeker may buy out the old plant and shut it down.

Clean Air Act Amendments of 1990

In 1990, the U.S. Congress passed a new set of Clean Air Act Amendments (CAAA). These toughened air pollution controls for the first time since 1977. Some of the amendments' major provisions are listed in ● Table 17–4. These provisions focus on three types of local and regional air pollution that were considered inadequately addressed in earlier amendments:

1. *Smog* is a focus of provisions 1–6 as listed in Table 17–4. They were needed because nearly a hundred major cities had not complied with existing regulations. The new amendments required lower tailpipe emissions of NO_x and VOCs by 1994 and even apply to small industrial sources of smog-producing chemicals, such as bakeries. Carmakers are required to redesign pollution controls and encouraged to build electric and other so-called zero- or low-emission cars. Fuel manufacturers are required to produce methanol and the other "reformulated" gasolines described earlier. The EPA estimated the total cost of complying with these six provisions at up to $12 billion yearly.
2. *Acid rain* is a focus of provisions 7–9. Their goal is to reduce SO_2 emissions from coal-burning power plants by half (10 million tons or 9 million metric tons per year) by the year 2000.
3. *Airborne toxics* (air pollutants that are dangerous in small amounts such as airborne mercury, arsenic, and many carcinogens) are a focus of provision 10. In 1988, more than 2.7 billion pounds (1.2 billion kg) of toxic air pollutants were released in the United States. Only seven

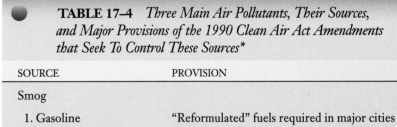

TABLE 17–4 *Three Main Air Pollutants, Their Sources, and Major Provisions of the 1990 Clean Air Act Amendments that Seek To Control These Sources**

SOURCE	PROVISION
Smog	
1. Gasoline	"Reformulated" fuels required in major cities
2. Tailpipe emissions	Reduce NO_x and VOC emissions by about half
3. Tailpipe emissions	Emission controls must last 100,000 miles
4. Tailpipe emissions	Low-emission vehicles to be developed
5. Gas stations	Vapors must be captured during refueling
6. Cities	Reduce smog until federal standards are met
Acid Rain	
7. Power-plants	Reduce nitrogen emissions by one-third
8. Power-plants	Reduce sulfur emissions by one-half
9. Power-plants	Can exchange "pollution credits"
Airborne toxics	
10. Businesses	Reduce toxic air pollutants by 90%

*These provisions are required by federal law, unless they are repealed by later congressional actions.

such pollutants were regulated until 1990; the new amendments regulate 189 kinds of toxics.

These amendments have been very controversial. They will be costly to many businesses, local governments, and citizens. Car prices, fuel prices, local taxes, and business operating costs are increasing as the provisions are phased in. They even fine some employers who have too many employees who drive to work alone instead of car pooling or taking mass transit. As a result, the amendments have encountered considerable resistance from the public and local and state governments.

Regulating the Unregulated: Clunkers, Mowers, and Boats

An easy, cheap way to significantly reduce smog is to regulate two types of gasoline-burning machinery that have previously escaped air pollution controls: (1) "clunker" motor vehicles and (2) mowers, boats, and many other small engines.

"Clunkers" are generally considered to be older cars and trucks, often over ten years old, that are in poor condition. In extreme cases, if not properly tuned, they can emit the same amount of air pollution as about *80 new cars*. Because most clunkers were made when pollution controls were less strict, even a well-tuned clunker usually emits 5–15 times more pollution than a new car. Thus, while the 45 million clunkers dating from 1981 or earlier compose only about 25% of the vehicles on U.S. roads (Fig. 17–12), they produce over *half the vehicle smog*. As a result, nonattainment areas, which are cities that have more

smog than allowed under the 1990 amendments, may require all vehicles in the area to be inspected. If they do not reduce smog, the 83 nonattainment areas will lose hundreds of millions of dollars of federal highway funds. If a clunker fails inspection by producing too much pollution, the owner may either "junk" the clunker or have it repaired or modified to produce lower emissions. Many benefit-cost studies show that repairing clunkers is the cheapest of all options to lower emissions, at least in the short term. In addition, nearly a dozen states already have, or are considering, programs that pay drivers to have their vehicles crushed at a scrap yard. Removing clunkers permanently from the streets, replacing them with mass transportation or modern, low-pollution or zero-emissions vehicles, is favored by many environmentalists.

Another group of unregulated polluters are the wide variety of machines, besides cars and trucks, that use gasoline-powered engines. These include the 89 million lawn mowers, chain saws, leaf blowers, and other lawn and garden equipment that produce 6 million tons (5.4 million metric tons), or 5% of U.S. air pollution (Fig. 17–13).

 FIGURE 17–13
Small internal combustion engines, such as the engine that powers this leaf blower, are a major source of air pollution because they are so numerous. (*Source:* Joe Polillio/Gamma Liaison.)

 FIGURE 17–12
One-quarter of the vehicles on U.S. roads as of July 1993 were made before 1982. (*Source*: Based on data from Ward's Automotive Reports.)

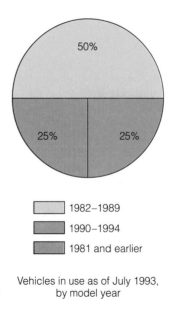

50%

25%   25%

☐ 1982–1989
■ 1990–1994
■ 1981 and earlier

Vehicles in use as of July 1993, by model year

Some of these emit more air pollution per hour of operation than cars (● Table 17–5). One hour with a leaf blower is equal to driving a car 100 miles (161 km). Even greater pollution is produced by other unregulated equipment with larger engines. Using an outboard motorboat for an hour is equal to driving 800 miles (1287 km).

Lawn, farm, and boat engines have been largely unregulated because they were considered insignificant compared to large motor vehicles. But these have become so numerous that they are having a very significant cumulative impact on air quality. Much of the proposed regulation of lawn, farm, and boat engines is similar to earlier regulations that improved car emissions. These regulations will not affect machinery already produced, but they set emission standards that will require manufacturers to use less-polluting engines on new machines. The current EPA proposal for lawn machinery is to require production of reduced-emission equipment in late 1996. The expected cost, according to the EPA, is about an extra $5 per mower, chain saw, or other lawn or garden machine. At this cost, significant reductions in VOCs and carbon monoxide can be achieved through relatively minor design changes. If further reductions are deemed necessary, the EPA may set more stringent limits that require catalytic converters, fuel injection, or other major technological design changes.

Economic Solutions

The atmosphere is a classic example of an environmental "commons." It is a shared resource that people will exploit or pollute as long as they are free to do so: polluters gain many benefits while paying few of the costs of damage to the commons (Chapter 1). Legal restrictions are one method of reducing pollution of a commons. Another method is to make polluters pay more of the true costs of damage to the commons. This can be done in many ways, such as taxation, fees, and other government charges on emissions or amount of fuel burned.

Many economists favor economic solutions because they impose costs on pollution and then allow the market to find a cost-effective way of paying those costs (Chapter 20). We have already discussed how emission offsets do this. The 1990 Clean Air Act Amendments also created a free-market trading system for emission offsets (see Table 17–4). Congress identified 110 utilities and assigned each a number of SO_2 allowances based

● **TABLE 17–5** *Air Pollution Output for Common Machines in an Hour's Use (Compared to Pollution from a Passenger Car)*

MACHINE	POLLUTION EQUIVALENT IN CAR MILES	(KM)
Riding mower	20	(32)
Garden tiller	30	(48)
Garden tractor	30	(48)
Shredder	30	(48)
Generator set	40	(64)
Lawn mower	50	(80)
String trimmer	70	(113)
Leaf blower	100	(161)
Chain saw	200	(322)
Outboard motor	800	(1287)
Forklift	250	(402)
Agricultural tractor	500	(805)
Construction crane	600	(965)
Farm combine	850	(1368)
Crawler tractor	900	(1448)

(*Source:* U.S. Environmental Protection Agency. Office of Mobile Sources, 1993.)

on its history of fuel use. Each allowance represents 1 ton (0.91 metric ton) of sulfur; plants can buy, sell, or trade these allowances. A plant might thus pay for more efficient emission controls and sell its allowances to a plant that would rather buy the "right to pollute." The idea of a "right to pollute" may seem unattractive, but this method will keep the net regional air pollution below any predetermined limit in an efficient way. The first use of the 1990 CAAA allowances occurred in May 1992 when the Tennessee Valley Authority bought the pollution rights to 10,000 tons (9100 metric tons) of SO_2 emissions from Wisconsin Power and Light. California recently passed laws that mandate an even more comprehensive emissions trading scheme, covering 2700 of the state's largest polluters. A 1992 study by California utilities estimated that this new market-based scheme would save Californians an estimated $429 million over current methods of controlling air pollution.

In contrast to emission offsets, which make polluters pay for their outputs, are gasoline, coal, BTU, and other "green" taxes that make polluters pay for the amount of polluting fuel burned (Chapters 1 and 20). These "input reduction" solutions are the most efficient means of all because they not only reduce pollution but also conserve resources. A polluter who has to pay higher prices for fuel will use it more efficiently and use less.

INDOOR AIR POLLUTION

Indoor air pollution as an environmental problem has been receiving increasing attention in recent years. Indeed, indoor air pollution is usually a *greater direct threat* to human health than outdoor air pollution. In 1990, the EPA ranked indoor air pollution as the most important environmental cause of cancers. The cost of health problems from indoor air pollution in the United States is estimated in the tens of billions of dollars. Although there are many kinds of indoor air pollutants, just two, radon and smoking, cause the vast majority of harm.

lives indoors, including time spent in offices on the job. **Sick building syndrome** is a popular medical term that refers to chronic ailments such as headaches, nausea, allergic reactions, and other symptoms that are caused by indoor air pollutants where we work or live.

Sources and Types of Indoor Pollutants

There are many sources of indoor air pollution (Figure 17–14). These sources can be divided into three categories: underground diffusion, combustion, and chemical emissions. In nearly all cases, the harmful effects of indoor pollution can be greatly reduced by increasing ventilation in a building. If properly done, this will not significantly reduce the heating (energy) efficiency of many buildings.

Radon: Death by Diffusion

Radon gas, which is the most harmful indoor pollutant when found in high concentrations, generally enters the home through underground diffusion. Radon is a radioactive decay product of uranium; it is most concentrated in houses built on soil and/or rocks that are rich in naturally occurring uranium minerals and their products.

According to the EPA, radon and related radioactive gases cause an estimated 5,000–20,000 deaths per year in the United States. These deaths occur mainly from lung cancer that is caused by inhaled radioactive particles that become lodged in the lungs. Radon testing of homes is now very common, but efforts to establish the true danger of radon have led to considerable controversy. Most U.S. homes are built on soils that emit relatively harmless amounts of radon, and proving the cause of lung disease is often very difficult (see Issues in Perspective 17–3).

Where underground diffusion of radon is found to be a danger, there are a number of relatively simple and inexpensive ways to greatly reduce indoor concentrations. The precise methods depend on the type of building construction, but the large majority involve increasing ventilation air flow through the building. Increasing air flow through basements, crawl spaces, and other lower parts of buildings is especially effective. For example, large window fans can be used to blow air through basement windows. Another common method is to insert pipes into the basement floor. The pipes draw the radon from the soil and transport it outside where the other end of the pipe exits.

FIGURE 17–14
Sources of indoor air pollution in the home. (*Source:* U.S. Environmental Protection Agency.)

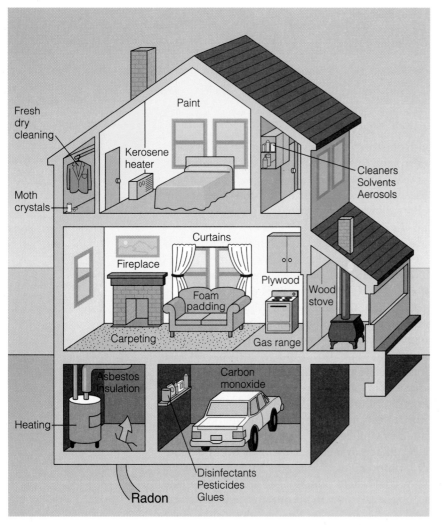

Indoor air pollution is such a threat to human health for two main reasons. First, the indoor environment tends to concentrate pollutants. Some toxic and cancer-causing pollutants can reach air concentrations that are 100 times greater than outside air. Second, on average, people in industrialized societies spend more than 80% of their

The Radon Controversy

Some scientists hotly contest the need for widespread concern about radon and expensive remediation efforts to combat it. The disagreement arises because assessing the radon hazard is very difficult at this time. To assess the degree of risk clearly, scientists must be able to attribute to the hazard the specific fatalities that result from it within a large population. The case for radon is especially troublesome because (1) radon produces lethal consequences only after many years of exposure and has only recently become recognized as a hazard and (2) lung cancer, the terminal disease produced by radon, is produced by many other lung irritants as well, especially passive inhalation of smoke. To use the mortality rate for lung cancers directly, scientists need to be able to distinguish the lung cancers that are caused specifically by radon. At this time, sufficient data are not available to directly assess the radon risk.

Evidence that low concentrations of radon in homes may pose significant risk comes from two indirect observations. The main indication of potential danger comes from known populations of miners exposed to radon in uranium mines. These workers, particularly those who smoke, do have a significantly increased frequency of lung cancer. At these levels of exposure, radon clearly poses a risk for smokers.

In contrast, recent demographic studies that have tried to relate average life span over an area to regional concentrations of geological background radiation have failed to find any link between radiation levels and expected longevity. In fact, North Dakota, which has high background radiation and some very high radon levels (Fig. 1), is the state with the greatest longevity.

box continued on next page

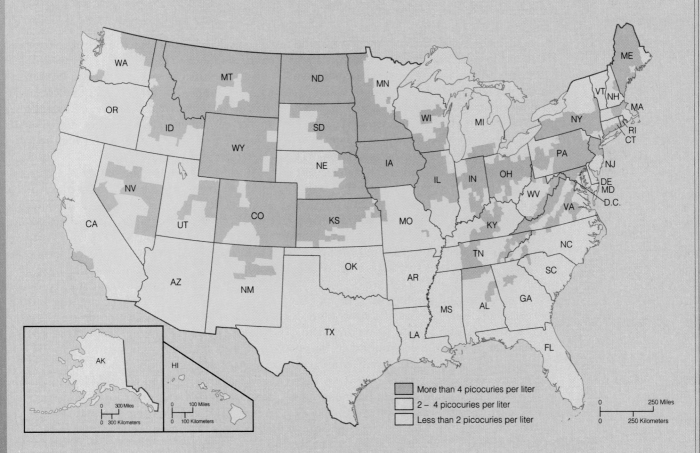

Legend:
More than 4 picocuries per liter
2 – 4 picocuries per liter
Less than 2 picocuries per liter

FIGURE 1

Average indoor radon levels in the United States. (A picocurie is a measure of radioactivity.) (*Source:* U.S. Environmental Protection Agency.)

Problems arise when such indirect evidence becomes the basis for policy. First, the miners who received high doses of radiation from both radon gas and mineral dust are not representative of people who receive only low doses of radon gas at home. Radon concentrations such as those found in uranium mines are rare occurrences, and using an exception like this to develop policy for the general public may lead to unwise mandates and needless terror. In contrast, the regional background radiation studies do not directly address the indoor radon concentrated in specific homes for specific individuals; thus, these regional studies may lead to an interpretation that induces false security.

Combustion: Especially Smoking

Stoves, fireplaces, and heaters are common appliances that emit air pollution from combustion (Fig. 17–14). Recall that carbon monoxide is a poison caused by incomplete combustion; it can cause headaches and even be lethal in closed areas where stoves or heaters are not functioning properly. Certain cancer-causing chemicals, such as hydrocarbons, are also released by combustion. These problems are relatively minor where appliances are functioning efficiently and the building is well ventilated. In developing countries, however, inefficient equipment and poorly designed housing often result in harmful levels of indoor air pollution from heating and cooking. Particulate air pollution from ash particles of wood or coal burned in the home is a major problem. A study by the World Health Organization estimated that indoor particulate levels were more than 20 times higher than considered safe in many developing countries where wood is burned in the home.

The most harmful combustion source of indoor air pollution is tobacco smoke ( Fig. 17–15). Many medical studies have found that smoking causes at least half a million deaths per year in the United States, especially from heart disease and cancer. Furthermore, a 1993 report issued by the EPA concludes that nonsmokers are also affected: "second-hand smoke" causes an estimated 3000 deaths per year in the United States. In addition to carcinogens, tobacco smoke contains carbon monoxide, particulates, and other harmful substances. Finally, smoking can enhance the deadly effects of radon. Smoke particles trapped in the lungs act as attachment sites

EnviroNet
www.jbpub.com/environet

for radioactive radon particles, increasing the chances for lung cancer. This is a classic, if deadly, example of a synergism where two effects enhance one another (Chapter 15).

Chemical Emissions: Source of Many Pollutants

Chemical emissions can come from dozens of sources indoors (Fig. 17–14). Many of these chemical emissions are carcinogenic but only in concentrations that are generally much higher than occur in the large majority of homes. They do, however, often cause headaches, dizziness, and nausea, especially in people with a high sensitivity to certain chemicals.

Mothballs, bleach, shoe polish, cleaning solvents, air fresheners, and many other chemical products emit gases that can be toxic if sufficiently concentrated by poor circulation. Many materials release carcinogenic fumes, such as benzene and formaldehyde. Benzene is emitted by plastics, synthetic fibers, and cleaners; formaldehyde is emitted from foam insulation and wood products such as particle board, plywood, and some glues. Asbestos has received much notoriety as a cause of lung cancer and the lung ailment asbestosis. Once used for fireproofing, insulation, tile, and cement, this fibrous material is now being removed at great expense from old buildings. The need for much of this great cost is hotly debated, in part because only some types of asbestos are harmful (see the Case Study).

Who Pays for Clean Office Air?

In 1994, the Occupational Safety and Health Administration (OSHA) proposed the first regula-

FIGURE 17-15
Cigarette smoke is one of the most hazardous indoor air pollutants. (*Source:* Gilles Bassignac/Gamma Liaison.)

tions governing indoor air quality. The goal is to reduce the frequency of "sick building syndrome" at the workplace. But the proposal has set off a heated debate over the need for the costly changes, estimated at $8 billion for the first year alone, and who should pay for them. Building owners complain that they should not have to pay for expensive ventilation systems or smoking lounges. The workers who smoke and use perfumes and the business tenants that install carpets with toxic chemicals should pay the bill, according to the building owners. The owners also argue that manufacturers of such products, from carpets to cigarettes, should contribute. In contrast, the workers, business tenants, and manufacturers all note that poorly ventilated buildings can greatly enhance the threats of indoor air pollution. This cost, they say, belongs to the building owners.

NOISE POLLUTION

Noise is often defined simply as "unwanted sound." Usually, it is unwanted because the sound is either too loud for comfort or is an annoying mixture of sounds that distract us, such as a distant conversation. However, noise is partly subjective and depends on one's state of mind and hearing sensitivity: many studies show that sounds that harm or annoy some people do not bother others. This subjective aspect is important because it adds to the difficulty of formulating policies to control noise. Some people are not as concerned about certain noises as others and are

unwilling to pay for controls. For example, spending money for airport noise reduction is often controversial.

Noise is a kind of air pollution because it is usually transmitted to our ears through the air that surrounds us. Indeed, when we hear any kind of sound, noise or otherwise, our eardrums are perceiving vibrations being transmitted to us by colliding air molecules. Air molecules thus transmit sound waves in much the same way that water molecules transmit ocean waves. Whereas a large storm at sea provides the energy that sets the water waves in motion, a large explosion, machinery, or some other source provides the energy that sends the sound waves toward you.

Measuring Noise

Loudness increases with intensity, meaning the amount of energy carried by sound waves. Loudness is measured using the **decibel (dB) scale**. ("Deci" refers to the units of 10 used, and "bel" refers to Alexander Graham Bell who was a teacher of the deaf as well as the inventor of the telephone.) The scale is exponential in that each unit of 10 increase in sound level (dB) is a 10-fold increase in sound intensity, or energy (● Table 17–6, page 490). The scale ranges from 0 to over 180, where 10 is the sound made by a leaf rustling and 180 is a rocket engine. Most daily noises in a busy building or city street average around 50–60 dB; in a quiet room, they are about 30–40 dB. Hearing damage begins around 70 dB for long exposure to a sound such as a loud vacuum cleaner. Outside

EnviroNet
www.jbpub.com/environet

Is Asbestos a Classic Example of "Environmental Hypochondria"?

Despite the enormous scope and variety of environmental issues, very few of them have generated as much intense controversy as asbestos (Fig. 1). A major reason for the debate is that the obviously high economic costs of dealing with asbestos, up to $100 billion in the United States, do not clearly yield benefits that are worth the cost. Indeed, critics argue that most types of asbestos pose a much smaller hazard than many daily activities like walking across a street. They argue that asbestos is a classic example of "environmental hypochondria": an illusory environmental hazard produced by anxiety.

"Asbestos" was a term originally used mainly by geologists to refer to fibrous minerals found in certain metamorphic rocks. Because many of these fibers are heat-resistant, asbestos became widely used, especially during the 1950s and early 1960s, for "fireproofing" in building materials. Mines, shipyards, schools, houses, offices, and many structures used asbestos to reduce the chance of fire. But by the early 1970s there was significant scientific evidence that breathing asbestos was harmful. The main problem is that some kinds of asbestos are very crumbly and readily disperse into the air. When inhaled, the needlelike asbestos fibers cannot be broken down in the lungs so they remain as a constant irritant. In these cases, the body's reaction to this irritation over 10–40 years can produce stiffening of lung tissue called "asbesto-

FIGURE 1

A worker wearing a protective suit and mask unloading sacks of asbestos for burial in a landfill. (*Source*: Adam Hart-Davis/Science Source/Photo Researchers.)

sis." This makes breathing difficult and can lead to lung cancer.

The result has been many lawsuits against makers of asbestos products costing many billions of dollars in legal fees and bankrupting companies. Billions more dollars have been spent removing asbestos from buildings. The costs are especially burdensome for the many public school districts that must remove asbestos from schools because they often have limited funds. Indeed, the National School Boards Association testified to Congress in 1995 that $10 billion had so far been spent to remove asbestos from public schools. Some estimates are that the total public school bill for asbestos removal could reach $30 billion. Total costs of asbestos removal in the United States, excluding the enormous legal fees, are estimated at up to $100 billion— approximately twice the cost of the Gulf War and more than one-third the entire annual U.S. military budget.

Is this money well spent? Not according to a growing number of critics. In 1995, *U.S. News & World Report* stated that there is "now a broad consensus among scientists and physicians that asbestos in public buildings is not much of a threat to health" (February 20, p. 61). Recent government reports, including a 1995 study by the U.S. Office of Technology Assessment, say much the same thing. A 1990 EPA report (the "Green Book") states that asbestos removal is

often *not* a building owner's best course of action.

A main reason for this rethinking of the asbestos threat is that more detailed research indicates that most of the asbestos in buildings is not the very dangerous variety. There are many kinds of asbestos, including two very different mineral groups. Most of the proof for toxicity centers around the "amphibole" type of asbestos. For example, one study showed that of 33 factory workers who breathed large doses of this type of asbestos in 1953, 19 workers had died of asbestos-related illness by 1990.

But about 95% of the asbestos used commercially is not of this variety. Instead, it belongs to a second mineral group, the "chrysotile" type of asbestos, which evidently is nowhere near as toxic. It is very difficult to gather toxicity data because no one can measure exactly how much exposure each worker received, but the only clear proof that chrysotile asbestos is harmful is when it is breathed in industrial settings with exceptionally high levels for long periods of time. The result is that many voluntary risks that people want to engage in are apparently much more harmful than this commonly used asbestos. The Harvard University Energy and Environmental Policy Center estimates that cigarette smoking or walking across the street are more than 200 times more dangerous than asbestos in school buildings. A person is three times more likely to be struck by lightning than to be harmed by asbestos in school buildings.

Questions

1. We saw in Chapter 15 that people perceive more risk in an activity when they have little control over it. Does this explain why asbestos may be perceived as being riskier than it really is? Explain.
2. We also saw in Chapter 15 that people perceive more risk when they cannot observe the threat. Is the asbestos threat observable? Explain.
3. List and discuss some other environmental problems that might be criticized as examples of "environmental hypochondria."

noises at this level result in widespread complaints by citizens. At about 130 dB, irreversible hearing loss can occur almost instantaneously.

Health Damage from Noise

The most obvious health damage from loud noises is hearing loss. This occurs from physical damage to the fragile mechanisms in the ear. The damage can occur very rapidly from very loud noises or slowly from long-term exposure to moderately loud noises (Table 17–6). Noise can also lead to a variety of ailments that arise from stress and anxiety induced by loud or distracting noises. Such stress-related ailments can be psychological, such as emotional trauma, or physical, such as headaches, nausea, and high blood pressure. Many studies have shown that such stress-related effects reduce productivity in the workplace.

Control of Noise

Noise can be reduced in three ways: (1) at the source, (2) as it travels to the person, (3) by protecting the person. Reduction at the source is often the easiest and most cost-effective means, reflecting the old engineer's adage that "noise means inefficiency." This is because noise is often caused by vibrations, friction, and other signs that equipment is not functioning efficiently. The solution is to design machinery that minimizes vibrations and friction, such as reducing the number of moving parts. Similarly, the machinery needs to be well maintained, lubricated, and so on. If equipment still produces loud noises after these steps are taken, as often occurs with industrial machines, the other two methods must be used.

Reduction of noise as it travels through the air to the person is achieved by sound-absorbing or **acoustical materials**. Examples include tiles and baffles made of wool or many kinds of synthetic materials that do not transmit sound vibrations efficiently. Car mufflers and jet engine noise deflectors are examples of devices made to reduce noise after it has left the engine source.

The third method of noise reduction, protecting the person, usually uses earplugs or earmuffs. These are made of materials that absorb sound waves before they reach the eardrum—not cotton, which provides little protection when inserted in the ear. Earplugs, and especially earmuffs, can greatly reduce noise up to 50 dB. Their efficiency depends heavily on an "acoustical seal," meaning that they must be inserted tightly, with as little exchange of air into the ear as possible.

$\mathcal{E}$ LECTROMAGNETIC FIELDS

The flow of electricity through wires produces an electromagnetic field (EMF) that can extend through the air for many feet (Fig. 17–16). Concern over the health effects of such fields, in particular, the possibility that they may cause cancer, has been growing since the late 1960s. Numerous studies have often yielded conflicting results, however, so the threat is controversial. Extensive studies carried out in the late 1980s by the Electric Power Research Institute and the Congressional Office of Technology Assessment concluded that health effects of electromagnetic fields could neither be proved nor ruled out.

FIGURE 17–16
Power transmission lines produce enormous electromagnetic fields as electricity flows through them. (*Source:* John D. Cunningham/Visuals Unlimited.)

By 1993, U.S. utility companies had spent over $1 billion on such studies, with no conclusive evidence of harm yet shown. These, and similar high costs for other controversial threats such as radon and asbestos are a main reason that the 1995 Congress showed strong interest in benefit-cost analyses. Such analyses try to determine true risks objectively and to estimate appropriate benefits for money spent on them (Chapters 6 and 15). But many environmentalists note that benefit-cost analyses are often flawed because of the difficulty of measuring benefits and risks accurately. They argue that unforeseen harm could result if spending on EMF and other potential threats is reduced too soon.

Statistical studies, which test for a correlation between cancer and people exposed to high EMF, usually show a weak correlation or none at all. This indicates that EMF "bioeffects" depend on

TABLE 17–6 *Sound Levels on the Decibel (dB) Scale, with Examples and Effects*

Sound Intensity Factor	Sound Level (dB)	Sound Sources	EFFECTS		
			Perceived Loudness	Damage to Hearing	Community Reaction to Outdoor Noise
1,000,000,000,000,000,000	180	Rocket Engine			
100,000,000,000,000,000	170				
10,000,000,000,000,000	160				
1,000,000,000,000,000	150	Jet plane at takeoff	Painful	Traumatic injury	
100,000,000,000,000	140			Injurious range; irreversible damage	
10,000,000,000,000	130	Maximum recorded rock music			
1,000,000,000,000	120	Thunderclap / Textile loom / Auto horn, 3.3 ft (1 m) away	Uncomfortably loud		
100,000,000,000	110	Riveter / Jet flyover at 985 ft (300 m)			
10,000,000,000	100	Newspaper press		Danger zone; progressive loss of hearing	
1,000,000,000	90	Motorcycle, 26 ft (8 m) away / Food blender	Very loud		Vigorous action
100,000,000	80	Diesel truck, 50 mph (80 km/hour), 50 ft (15 m) away / Garbage disposal		Damage begins after long exposure	Threats
10,000,000	70	Vacuum cleaner	Moderately loud		Widespread complaints
1,000,000	60	Ordinary conversation / Air-conditioning unit, 20 ft (6 m) away			Occasional complaints
100,000	50	Light traffic noise, 100 ft (30 m) away			
10,000	40	Average living room / Bedroom	Quiet		No action
1000	30	Library / Soft whisper			
100	20	Broadcasting studio	Very quiet		
10	10	Rustling leaf			
1	0	Threshold of hearing	Barely audible		

many variables. Biological studies, which directly examine the effects of EMF on living cells and tissues in the laboratory, produce similar results. In some cases, biochemical regulation of cell multiplication does seem to be affected, possibly from changes in the flow of electrically charged calcium ions through cell membranes. But the dose-response relationship is clearly very complex and is affected by many variables: (1) frequency and wavelength of the EMF, (2) duration of exposure, (3) kind of cells exposed and type of organisms, (4) and even orientation of the EMF with the Earth's electromagnetic field. Considering that individuals of nearly all species vary in their susceptibility to environmental stresses, it will likely be very difficult to precisely determine EMF effects, if any.

One of the most interesting and useful findings so far is that fields generated by toasters, electric blankets, and other indoor electrical equipment may be a greater threat than the high-voltage transmission lines that receive so much publicity. We spend much more time in close proximity to these indoor appliances, and they can sometimes generate a surprisingly strong electromagnetic field.

SUMMARY

Air pollution, occurring at many scales, poses a significant hazard. Varying in composition depending on location, air is never pure. Nonvariable gases in the air are approximately 99% of the atmosphere and mainly consist of nitrogen and oxygen. Variable gases and particulate concentrations vary widely. When particulates and variable gases occur in harmful quantities, they are termed pollutants.

Reduction of criteria pollutants by most industrialized nations has resulted in decreased local and regional air pollution. The five criteria pollutants are particulates, sulfur oxides, nitrogen oxides, volatile organic compounds, and carbon monoxide. These arise mainly from two sources: burning of fossil fuels by motor vehicles and stationary sources, and industrial processes.

Particulates affect clothes, machinery, buildings, and visibility but are most damaging to the lungs. In general, however, they are not as damaging as other forms of air pollution. As with other pollutants, input reduction is the cheapest and most effective means of reducing particulate pollution. Large particles are removed through a cyclone collector, and small particles are removed through electrostatic precipitators and baghouses.

Sulfur oxides, produced when fossil fuels containing sulfur are burned, are perhaps the most serious local and regional air pollutant. The main cause of acid rain, sulfur oxides cause both physical and biological damage. Discoloration, corrosion of metals, and dissolution of many building materials by acid rain have been extremely costly. Biological damage is most commonly seen in forests and lakes. Lakes in New England and eastern Canada are particularly affected by acid rain because surface rocks are mainly igneous with low alkalinity. Reductions in the amount of sulfur oxides can be brought about by using low-sulfur coal, scrubbers, or coal cleaning.

Nitrogen oxides and volatile organic compounds are major causes of smog and other photochemical pollutants. Two important photochemical pollutants are smog and ozone. Photochemicals can be reduced by altering the combustion process.

Carbon monoxide, affecting mainly humans and animals, inhibits the ability of red blood cells to carry oxygen to the organs. Duration of exposure and the concentration of carbon monoxide determine the amount of damage. Produced by incomplete combustion, carbon monoxide results mainly from transportation and can be reduced through precombustion, postcombustion, and changing the combustion process. Catalytic converters are the main postcombustion method of the auto industry.

Although local and regional air pollution has been declining in the United States, the global total of criteria pollutants has been increasing. The most effective way to reduce fossil fuel pollution is through alternative fuels. Air pollution is strongly affected by varying weather conditions, especially temperature. Thermal inversion, the most important local weather phenomenon to affect air pollution, creates a trap of warm air for rising air pollution. Air pollution can affect local weather conditions, as well as cause global climate changes.

Technological reductions will not become widespread without incentives. In the United States these have taken the form of legal and economic incentives. The Clean Air Act established standards for allowable concentrations in surrounding air and allowable emissions of pollutants. With the creation of the EPA, two levels of allowable concentrations were determined, primary and secondary. The Clean Air Act Amendments of 1990 brought about stricter air pollution controls, focusing on smog, acid rain, and airborne toxic substances. Among the easiest and cheapest ways to reduce smog, however, is to regulate gasoline-burning machines that do not fall within current air pollution controls. These include clunker motor vehicles, mowers, motorboats, and other small engines. In addition to legal controls, economic solutions would force polluters to pay the true costs of damage to the environmental "commons."

Indoor air pollutants cause a greater direct threat to human health than outdoor air pollution because of the concentration of pollutants in the indoor environment and the amount of time spent indoors in an industrialized society. Sources of air pollution are underground diffusion, combustion, and chemical emissions. Radon gas, carried by underground diffusion, is a harmful indoor pollutant when found in high concentrations. The most harmful combustion source of indoor air pollution is tobacco smoke, which causes heart disease and cancer, as well as leading to the problem of second-hand smoke. Chemical emissions are produced from a variety of sources, including mothballs, bleach, and cleaning solvents.

Noise, a different type of air pollutant, is measured on the decibel scale. Health damage resulting from excessive noise includes hearing loss and stress-related ailments. Electromagnetic fields, produced by the flow of electricity through wires, are a source of controversy as to whether they cause adverse health affects.

KEY TERMS

acid rain
acoustical materials
alkaline
baghouses
catalytic converter
Clean Air Act
criteria pollutants
decibel (dB) scale

electrostatic precipitators
emission offsets
methanol
noise
oxygenation
ozone
particulates
photochemical pollutant
pH scale

Pollutant Standards Index (PSI)
primary pollutants
scrubbers
secondary pollutants
sick building syndrome
smog
thermal inversion

STUDY QUESTIONS

1. What are variable gases?
2. What are particulates? List the terms used to describe them. Why are they the most damaging pollutant to lungs?
3. Name the five basic criteria pollutants. What are the two main sources of these pollutants?
4. Where does most acid rain occur in North America? Why does this pattern exist?
5. What does 1 on the pH scale mean? What is the average pH of rainfall? Which fishes are most sensitive to acid waters?

6. What is a photochemical reaction? How does smog form?
7. What is oxygenation? Why is it used?
8. What has been the international trend of pollution by the five criteria pollutants? Why has this trend occurred?
9. What does a value of 100 on the Pollutant Standards Index mean? What percentage of vehicles on U.S. roads are "clunkers"?
10. What did the NAAQS and the NSPS establish? Why are the 1990 Clean Air Act Amendments so controversial?
11. Why is the atmosphere a classic "commons"? Name some economic ways to make polluters pay the true costs of damaging the commons.

12. Why is indoor air pollution a generally greater direct threat to human life than smog and many other forms of air pollution?
13. What are the three main categories of sources of indoor air pollution? How can the harmful effects of these sources be reduced?
14. On the decibel scale, how much greater is the sound intensity (energy) in a noise of 50 dB compared to a noise of 10 dB?
15. On the decibel scale, how much greater is the sound intensity (energy) in a noise of 60 dB compared to a noise of 40 dB?

ESSAY QUESTIONS

1. What are the key patterns related to criteria pollutants in the United States?
2. Describe the methods by which sulfur oxides can be reduced.

3. What are some of the unregulated air pollutors? How many of these are there? Why have they been unregulated?
4. What is noise? Why can it be considered an air pollutant? Discuss ways that noise can be reduced.
5. What was the focus of the 1990 Clean Air Act Amendments? Explain each point and the goals set by the amendments.

SUGGESTED READINGS

Brookins, D. 1990. *The indoor radon controversy*. New York: Columbia University Press.

Bryner, G. 1992. *Blue skies, green politics: The Clean Air Act Amendments of 1990*. Washington, D.C.: Congressional Quarterly Press.

Burns, W. 1973. *Noise and man*. Philadelphia: Lippincott.

Coffel, S., and K. Feiden. 1991. *Indoor pollution*. New York: Random House.

Eagleman, J. R. 1991. *Air pollution meteorology*. Lenexa, Kan.: Trimedia Publishing Co.

Elsom, D. 1992. *Atmospheric pollution*. New York: Blackwell.

Flagan, C. 1988. *Fundamentals of air pollution engineering*. Englewood Cliffs, N.J.: Prentice-Hall.

Hesketh, H. E. 1991. *Air pollution control: Traditional and hazardous pollutants*. Lancaster, Penn.: Technomic Publishing Co.

MacKenzie, J., and M. El-Ashry. 1990. *Air pollution's toll on forests and crops*. New Haven: Yale University Press.

MacKenzie, J., et al. 1992. *The going rate: What it really costs to drive*. Washington, D.C.: World Resources Institute.

Makower, J. 1992. *The green commuter*. Washington, D.C.: National Press.

Mason, B. J. 1992. *Acid rain: Its causes and its effects on inland waters*. New York: Oxford University Press.

Regens, J., and R. Rycroft. 1988. *The acid rain controversy*. Pittsburgh: University of Pittsburgh Press.

Renner, M. 1988. *Rethinking the role of the automobile*. Washington, D.C.: Worldwatch Institute.

GLOBAL AIR POLLUTION: DESTRUCTION OF THE OZONE LAYER AND GLOBAL WARMING

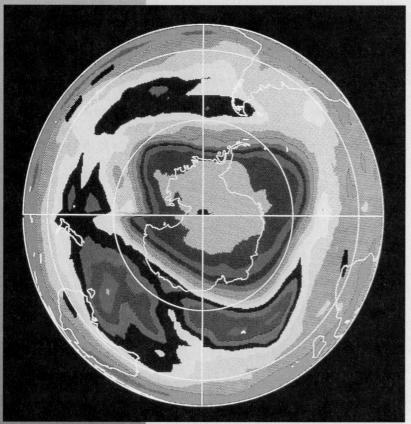

PROLOGUE *Japan's Proposed Technological Fix for the Greenhouse Problem*

he Japanese Ministry of International Trade and Industry, in conjunction with private industry and a number of researchers from universities and scientific organizations, created the Research Institute of Innovative Technology for the Earth (RITE) in 1990 to develop cutting-edge environmental technologies that will be needed in the twenty-first century. The ministry initially provided $80 million in seed money, and within half a year another $45 million was donated by Japanese industry. Now RITE spends some $28 million a year to develop innovative environmental technologies. RITE projects have significant international participation, including scientists from the United States, the United Kingdom, Canada, Australia, Italy, and the Netherlands.

PHOTO   *Nimbus–7 satellite map of atmospheric ozone concentrations in the southern hemisphere, September 28, 1992. The oval-shaped mauve and pink area is the ozone hole over Antarctica. (Source: NASA/Science Source/Photo Researchers.)*

Currently, RITE is sponsoring seven major research projects: (1) developing biodegradable plastics, (2) improving bioreactors that can synthesize chemicals and fuels, (3) using bacteria to produce hydrogen (the hydrogen will be used as a fuel), (4) recycling scrap steel, (5) developing ozone-safe chlorofluorocarbon substitutes, (6) harnessing microorganisms to remove carbon dioxide from industrial exhaust gases, and (7) developing selectively permeable membranes to filter carbon dioxide out of industrial gases.

Thus, three out of seven RITE projects are concerned with global atmospheric changes—stratospheric ozone depletion and potential global warming due to the accumulation of greenhouse gases, particularly carbon dioxide, in the atmosphere. The two carbon dioxide projects are particularly novel and currently claim half of RITE's operating budget.

In one project, RITE researchers collect naturally occurring photosynthetic algae from lakes and hot springs and then use bioengineering techniques to modify the organisms so as to maximize their ability to remove carbon dioxide from the atmosphere. The algae are confined in special apparatuses where they "feed" on industrial waste gases. Biochemists are exploring ways to turn the compounds produced by the algae into fuels, foodstuffs, and other useful products.

In the other carbon dioxide project, scientists are developing and refining selectively permeable membranes that can literally filter carbon dioxide out of industrial smokestacks and exhaust systems —but the research does not end there. By adding hydrogen to the carbon dioxide in the presence of a metal catalyst, methanol or a similar fuel can be synthesized. Ultimately, the filter and the catalyst might be used in conjunction in a closed loop: the methanol would be burned, and waste carbon dioxide would be captured and used to produce more fuel. If these projects succeed, not only might the global environment benefit, but the Japanese investment could reap handsome monetary profits.

 NTRODUCTION

Some environmental problems, by their very nature, are global in scope. Perhaps the two most immediate global environmental threats that we face are climatic change due to the artificial introduction of large amounts of greenhouse gases into the atmosphere and abnormally high incidences of ultraviolet radiation on the surface of Earth due to the destruction of the ozone layer. These problems are interrelated: both are caused by the introduction of large quantities of human-produced gases into the atmosphere, and in many cases the same gases are implicated in both problems. Chlorofluorocarbons (CFCs), for instance, are not only a major culprit in the destruction of the ozone layer, but are also an extremely effective greenhouse gas.

The story of the human assault on the ozone layer now appears to be drawing to a close (although the story is not quite over yet—ozone-depleting compounds will continue to be detectable in the atmosphere for years to come). The problem was discovered about 1974, and by 1990 all the major governmental authorities of the world had agreed on a solution. For the first time in history, political leaders, scientists, corporations, and consumers worked together to find an international solution to a global problem that potentially threatened all life on the planet. The "ozone story" sets a precedent as the world tackles even more complex environmental issues.

We now know that nations can work together if they must. Perhaps the next major global problem that will be systematically and successfully addressed is global warming caused by the accumulation of greenhouse gases.

In this chapter, we first tell the ozone story. Then we address the issue of global warming.

O ZONE DEPLETION

Ozone in Nature

Ozone (O_3) is an important natural component of the **stratosphere** (see Fig. 2–11 in Chapter 2; ozone is also an important pollutant at ground level, see Chapter 17). Ozone occurs in scant amounts between about 6 and 31 miles (10 and 50 km) above sea level and is most strongly concentrated at an altitude of 12 to 16 miles (20–25 km)—the **ozone layer**. Ozone is formed in the stratosphere ( Fig. 18–1) when high-energy **ultraviolet (UV) radiation** splits normal oxygen molecules (O_2) into atomic oxygen (O). The atomic oxygen may then combine with a standard diatomic oxygen molecule (O_2) to form triatomic ozone (O_3). Under natural conditions, ozone is not only formed in the atmosphere, but it is also removed by various reactions. An ozone molecule can absorb UV radiation and split into O_2 and O.

High-energy UV radiation | Oxygen molecule | → | 2 Oxygen atoms | Oxygen atom | + | Oxygen molecule | ⇄ UV radiation | Ozone molecule

The atomic oxygen can then either recombine with an O_2 molecule to form ozone once again, combine with another atomic oxygen to form diatomic oxygen, or combine with some other substance in the stratosphere. In nature, excluding human interference, a dynamic equilibrium exists between ozone production and ozone destruction, such that the stratosphere always contains a small amount of ozone. The amount of stratospheric ozone is so small that if it were all brought down to sea level, it would form a blanket over the surface of Earth only 0.118 inch (3 mm) thick.

Nevertheless, this stratospheric ozone is essential to the preservation of current forms of life on the Earth's surface. The ozone layer acts as a shield that absorbs biologically dangerous UV-B radiation (Fig. 18–2). (Ultraviolet radiation is commonly divided into two bands: UV-A has wavelengths of 320 to 400 nm [nm = nanometers; 1 nm = 10^{-9} m, or one billionth of a meter or approximately 3.937×10^{-8} inch], and the higher-energy UV-B has wavelengths less than 320 nm [sometimes the very shortest wavelength UV, approximately in the range of 200–280 nm, is labeled "UV-C" as in Fig. 18–2].) When an ozone molecule is hit by UV-B wavelengths, it absorbs the radiant energy and photodissociates into O_2 and O while giving off heat. This keeps the UV-B radiation from reaching Earth's surface and also causes a temperature inversion in the stratosphere that helps to maintain relatively stable climatic conditions on and near the ground.

Human Assaults on the Ozone Layer

The stratospheric ozone layer has remained in a dynamic equilibrium for much of geological time, but by the early 1970s scientists had discovered evidence suggesting a decline in the ozone concentration due to human interference. In particular, humans had been injecting enormous quantities of ozone-destroying substances into the atmosphere, especially a class of chemicals known as **chlorofluorocarbons** (CFCs, see Issues in Perspective 18–1). By the mid-1970s, the possible destruction of the ozone layer by artificial chemicals had become a topic of heated controversy. Large chemical companies and many manufacturers downplayed or denied the possibility, while many environmentally oriented citizens called for immediate, even if economically

expensive, action to save the ozone layer. The controversy abated somewhat in the late 1970s after some action was taken to protect the ozone layer (for instance, in 1978 the United States banned the use of CFCs as **aerosol spray** propellants), but it erupted again in the 1980s when an ozone hole was detected over Antarctica.

Historical Background

The ozone layer's modern troubles began innocuously enough in 1928 when chemists discovered a new class of chemicals that could replace sulfur dioxide and ammonia as the basic fluids in refrigerators. This new class of chemicals, which was produced by Du Pont under the trade name of "Freon," became known more generally as the chlorofluorocarbons (CFCs). CFCs were considered a triumph of modern chemistry; they were safe, nonflammable, stable, unreactive chemicals that proved ideal for many purposes. They were put to use in car air conditioners as

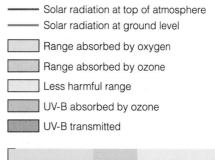

— Solar radiation at top of atmosphere
— Solar radiation at ground level
Range absorbed by oxygen
Range absorbed by ozone
Less harmful range
UV-B absorbed by ozone
UV-B transmitted

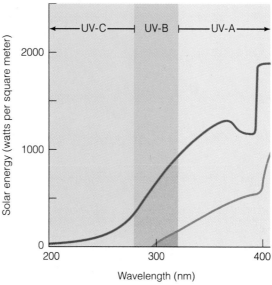

FIGURE 18–1

Schematic representation of the formation of stratospheric ozone. Ozone forms when a free oxygen atom, released by the splitting of an oxygen molecule by cosmic radiation, combines chemically with another oxygen molecule.

FIGURE 18–2

Absorption of ultraviolet light by the atmosphere. (Note that wavelength is in nanometers; one nanometer equals one-billionth of a meter.) (*Source*: D. H. Meadows, D. L. Meadows, and J. Randers, *Beyond the Limits* [Post Mills, Vt.: Chelsea Green, 1992], p. 146. Reprinted from *Beyond the Limits* copyright © 1992 by Meadows, Meadows, and Randers, with permission from Chelsea Green Publishing Co., White River Junction, Vermont.)

CFCs and Other Ozone-Destroying Substances

The substances commonly referred to as CFCs, or chlorofluorocarbons, are artificially produced compounds composed primarily of carbon, fluorine, and chlorine (● Table 1). Two main types of CFCs have received considerable attention as agents of ozone destruction (Fig. 1). CFC-11, otherwise known as trichlorofluoromethane, has the chemical formula $CFCl_3$. CFC-12, or dichlorodifluoromethane, has the composition CF_2Cl_2. Other terms used for these substances include CFMs (for chlorofluoromethanes), Freon (a Du Pont company trade name), and fully halogenated CFCs (meaning that they do not contain any hydrogen atoms). Other commonly used CFCs include CFC-113 (CCl_3CF_3), a commonly used solvent, and CFC-114 and CFC-115. CFCs are extremely stable, inert, non-water-soluble molecules that are quite immune to chemical reaction.

Closely related to the CFCs are the HCFCs, or hydrochlorofluorocarbons. HCFCs contain hydrogen as well as fluorine, chlorine, and carbon. As HCFCs are less stable in the atmosphere than CFCs, they break down more quickly and are less likely to reach the stratosphere and cause damage to the ozone layer. Because HCFCs typically have only 2 to 5% of the ozone-destroying potential of the typical CFCs, they are frequently recommended as a replacement for standard CFCs. Another relative advantage of HCFCs is that scientists have discovered methanotrophic bacteria (bacteria that live on methane) that can degrade HCFCs into simpler substances and thus prevent the HCFCs from accumulating to the same extent as the more stable CFCs. Some of these bacteria appear to be the same forms that are commonly found in soils. These HCFC-digesting bacteria might form the basis of a new waste-processing technology that could safely and efficiently dispose of unwanted HCFCs.

TABLE 1 *Uses, Production Rates, and Residence Times of the Important Ozone-Depleting Chemicals*

COMPOUND NAME	CHEMICAL FORMULA	OZONE DEPLETION POTENTIAL	USES	1985 WORLD PRODUCTION TONS	1985 WORLD PRODUCTION METRIC TONS	RESIDENCE TIME IN ATMOSPHERE (YEARS)
CFC-11	$CFCl_3$	1.0	Refrigeration, aerosol, foam	328,400	298,000	65–75
CFC-12	CF_2Cl_2	0.9–1.9	Refrigeration, aerosol, foam, sterilization, food freezing, heat detectors, warning devices, cosmetics, pressurized blowers	482,700	438,000	100–140
CFC-113	CCl_3CF_3	0.8–0.9	Solvent, cosmetics	152,600	138,500	100–134
CFC-114	$CClF_2CClF_2$	0.7–1.0	Refrigeration			300
CFC-115	$CClF_2CF_3$	0.4–0.6	Refrigeration, whipped topping stabilizer			500
Halon 1301	$CBrF_3$	10.0–13.2	Fire fighting	2,870	2,600	110
Halon 1211	$CClBrF_2$	2.2–3.0	Fire fighting	2,870	2,600	15
HCFC-22	$CHClF_2$	0.05	Refrigeration, aerosol, foam, fire fighting	89,500	81,200	16–20
Methyl chloroform	CH_3CCl_3	0.15	Solvent	550,500	499,500	5.5–10
Carbon tetrachloride	CCl_4	1.2	Solvent	78,500	71,200	50–69

(*Source:* D. H. Meadows, D. L. Meadows, and J. Randers, *Beyond the Limits* [Post Mills, VT.: Chelsea Green, 1992], p. 143. Reprinted from *Beyond the Limits* copyright © 1992 by Meadows, Meadows, and Randers, with permission from Chelsea Green Publishing Co., White River Junction, Vermont.)

Also chemically similar to the CFCs and HCFCs are the HFCs, or hydrofluorocarbons. These substances do not contain chlorine and therefore do not promote ozone layer destruction. Whenever possible, HFCs should be substituted for the more dangerous (to the ozone layer) CFCs and HCFCs. Unfortunately, the various CFCs, HCFCs, and HFCs all have different specific properties, and substitutions are not always easy or even possible.

Other substances that attack stratospheric ozone include the halons, a class of fluorocarbons that contain bromine atoms. The halons release their bromine atoms, which then destroy stratospheric ozone. Halons have been commonly used in fire extinguishers. Methyl chloroform, methyl bromide, and carbon tetrachloride are some other important and widely used chemicals that have ozone layer–destroying properties.

NATURAL CAUSES

A number of naturally occurring substances also have the ability to destroy stratospheric ozone. Most important of these are the hydrogen oxides (HO_x) derived from water vapor, methane (CH_4), hydrogen gas (H_2), and nitrogen oxides (NO_x). The nitrogen oxides, which are very effective destroyers of stratospheric ozone, not only occur naturally but are being supplemented by anthropogenic sources. In particular, nitrogen-containing fertilizers release N_2O into the air; the N_2O can diffuse into the stratosphere and form nitric acid (NO), which has the ability to react with and destroy ozone molecules. However, there is evidence that in the presence of methane and chlorine (perhaps released from a CFC), NO_2 will form from NO; additionally, solar radiation can break the NO_2 into NO and O. The atomic oxygen (O) can combine with O_2 to form ozone (O_3). Nitrogen compounds will also bind with chlorine atoms,

preventing the chlorine from destroying the ozone. Thus, under certain circumstances nitrogen compounds may actually enhance the ozone layer rather than deteriorate it. Similarly, it has been suggested that stratospheric methane may benefit the ozone layer by helping to remove chlorine atoms.

FIGURE 1
Prior to being banned, CFC-11 and CFC-12 were commonly used as aerosol spray propellants. (*Source*: Sinclair Stammers/Science Source/Photo Researchers.)

There are some suggestions that naturally occurring chlorine oxides, such as chlorine monoxide (ClO), may promote the deterioration of stratospheric ozone. During major volcanic eruptions, significant amounts of chlorine may be injected into the stratosphere, but this has never been conclusively demonstrated to be a significant agent of global stratospheric ozone destruction. More troubling, however, is the recent discovery that tiny particulate matter in the stratosphere, known as stratospheric aerosols, may help pro-

mote ozone destruction by providing convenient surface areas where the ozone-destroying reactions can readily take place. In 1982 the eruption of the El Chichón volcano in Mexico launched 6.6 to 7.7 million tons (6 or 7 million metric tons) of sulfate aerosols into the stratosphere, which may have caused ozone levels in the Northern Hemisphere to temporarily drop by as much as 10%. In June 1991 Mt. Pinatubo in the Philippines erupted, injecting an estimated 22 million tons (20 million metric tons) of sulfate aerosols into the stratosphere. Some atmospheric scientists believe that this could further exacerbate the ozone depletion problem for several years to come. Additionally, sulfate aerosols released during the burning of fossil fuels are accumulating in the stratosphere.

well as in refrigerators. They were used as a non-toxic propellant for aerosol cans and as a blowing agent in producing styrofoam and other plastics. They had insulating properties and could also be used as solvents and cleaning agents in the electronics industry. Ironically, the chemical stability that makes CFCs so ideal for use on the Earth's surface is the very characteristic that allows them to reach the stratospheric ozone layer. Since CFCs do not appreciably react on the Earth's surface, they are free to float up into the stratosphere. But under stratospheric conditions, the CFCs readily break down and become a powerful catalyst of ozone destruction.

Applications of CFCs multiplied after their initial discovery, and after World War II the market for these substances expanded rapidly. The global production rates of Freon 11 (= CFC-11, $CFCl_3$) and Freon 12 (= CFC-12, CF_2Cl_2), trade names for two of the most common CFCs, rose from less than 55,000 tons (50,000 metric tons) a year in 1950 to 800,000 tons (725,000 metric tons) in 1976.* An estimated 90% of these chemicals was released directly into the atmosphere during, or immediately after, their use; the remaining 10% was generally released once the equipment in which the chemicals were used (such as a refrigerator) was discarded. Since their invention, approximately 22 million tons (20 million metric tons) of CFCs have been released into the atmosphere. By the early 1970s, CFCs constituted an $8 billion per year industry in the United States alone.

In 1973–1974, however, two chemists at the University of California at Irvine, Mario Molina and Sherwood Rowland, discovered the effect that CFCs accumulating in the stratosphere have on the ozone layer. Molina and Rowland found that CFCs are almost inert in the **troposphere** (the atmospheric layer underlying the stratosphere and covering the immediate surface of Earth; see Chapter 2). CFCs are not even washed out by rain since they are not soluble in water, and so they drift on air currents up into the stratosphere. In the stratosphere, ultraviolet radiation breaks down the CFC molecules, releasing atomic **chlorine**. A free chlorine atom reacts with an ozone molecule, removing one oxygen atom and thus converting the O_3 into O_2. The chlorine monoxide molecule (ClO) is not stable, however; it readily reacts with a free oxygen atom to form a molecule of diatomic oxygen (O_2) and a free chlorine atom once again. Thus, once released from the

CFC, the single chlorine atom acts as a catalyst that can destroy thousands (perhaps 10,000 to 100,000) of ozone molecules. Eventually, the chlorine atom will be washed out of the atmosphere by precipitation.

According to Molina and Rowland's calculations, ozone depletion due to CFCs threatened the very existence of life on our planet. They and other environmentally oriented people quickly lobbied for a ban on CFCs. But the large chemical companies and a few scientists argued that the theory of CFC-induced ozone depletion was speculative and did not justify controlling CFC releases. Part of the problem was that initially there was little empirical evidence to support the Molina-Rowland calculations, due largely to the difficulty of measuring ozone concentrations in the stratosphere. Furthermore, this was not the first time that concerns about ozone depletion had been raised; earlier some researchers had worried about the effects of nuclear bomb detonations on the ozone layer (see also Issues in Perspective 18–2). Still, as news of possible ozone depletion hit the streets, the public responded. By the first half of 1975, the use of CFC-based aerosol spray cans had dropped by 25%, and by 1978 the United States had effectively banned CFCs as an aerosol propellant. Yet CFCs continued to play a major role in other industries, both in North America and around the world.

Despite confirmation by other scientists, including a committee of the U.S. National Academy of Sciences, that the threat to the ozone layer was real, little more action was taken for several years. Then in 1983–1985 a discovery was made that stunned many previously unconcerned observers: based on 30 years of measurements, the British Antarctic Survey found that each spring a hole developed in the ozone layer over the South Pole (see Issues in Perspective 18–3); the hole closed again later in the year. Could this be a result of CFCs released into the atmosphere? NASA's *Nimbus*-7 satellite confirmed the depletion in the ozone layer; curiously, satellites had not detected this ozone hole previously because the computers had been programmed to disregard as errors any data that recorded such low ozone values. Scientific expeditions were quickly mounted to confirm or refute the reality of the Antarctic ozone hole and to try to determine its cause if real. The upshot was that the spring hole was real (the loss of ozone was about 50% in general, but rose as high as 100% in some spots) and that it was caused by chlorine carried up to the stratosphere in CFC molecules. Molina and Rowland had been correct all along.

---

*Unless otherwise noted, *tons* refers to short tons (2000 pounds).

SSTs, U.S. Space Shuttles, and Stratospheric Ozone

The ozone layer is endangered not only by CFCs and other anthropogenic substances originating from the Earth's surface, but also by aircraft, missiles, and space vehicles flying high in the atmosphere. In the early 1970s, when a new generation of aircraft, the supersonic transports (SSTs), was being developed and tested, some analysts predicted that within 30 to 50 years hundreds, or perhaps even thousands, of SSTs would be in operation. SSTs produce oxides of nitrogen in their exhausts, and it was suggested that the wastes of hundreds of SSTs could contribute significantly to a thinning of the ozone layer. This notion caused quite a stir at the time and may have contributed to the demise of the once bright SST industry—although economic factors were probably the primary force involved. At any rate, only a handful of SSTs are currently in operation worldwide (Fig. 1).

Many rockets and missiles, especially those that burn solid rocket fuel, have the

FIGURE 1

Air France's "Concorde" (an SST) at the Anchorage International Airport. (*Source*: Steve McCutcheon/Visuals Unlimited.)

potential to inflict damage on the ozone layer. The U.S. space shuttle in particular releases approximately 265 tons (240 metric tons) of hydrochloric acid into the atmosphere per launch. The chlorine atoms thus released attack and destroy stratospheric ozone. Although the estimates are disputed, according to some calculations, if 10 shuttles burning solid-rocket-fuel boosters are launched each year (approximately the present rate of shuttle missions), these shuttles alone could cause a 10% depletion in the ozone layer by the year 2010.

International action was soon taken. In 1985 representatives of nearly two dozen nations met to consider what should be done to protect the ozone layer. The result was a series of conferences and meetings that culminated in September 1987 with the **Montreal Protocol**. At a meeting hosted by the Canadian government in Montreal, representatives from 24 industrialized countries agreed to freeze CFC production (at 1986 levels) and then gradually decrease CFC and halon (see Issues in Perspective 18–1) production to 50% of 1986 levels by the year 1999. Very quickly, however, it became clear that the protocol did not go far enough. Evidence of a thinning of the ozone layer over the Northern Hemisphere and continued enlargement of the Antarctic ozone hole indicated that more drastic measures were needed. Furthermore, the Montreal Protocol did not cover many ozone-destroying chemicals,

such as methyl chloroform and carbon tetrachloride. And not until March of 1988 did Du Pont officially acknowledge the damage CFCs were causing to the ozone layer and agree to cease CFC production once substitutes were found.

In 1989 the U.S. Congress imposed a stiff excise tax on all ozone-depleting chemicals sold, produced, or imported into the United States. The idea was to discourage the use of CFCs and other ozone-damaging chemicals and to encourage the search for safer substitutes. Yet such a tax could have little effect globally.

By the late 1980s and early 1990s, stratospheric ozone loss was well documented. The largest losses still occur over Antarctica (see Issues in Perspective 18–3). In the Arctic ozone losses have amounted to about a 10% reduction so far. Significant losses have also been recorded over the mid-latitudes both north and south of the equa-

The Ozone Hole over Antarctica

Since the late 1950s the British Antarctic Survey, based at Halley Bay, has collected data on ozone levels over the continent. The researchers have found that the ozone levels undergo an apparently natural seasonal fluctuation, thinning during the southern spring. During the 1980s, however, the survey team observed that this thinning was getting progressively worse each spring (hitting a low during the middle of October) and persisting progressively longer (this trend of thinning ozone has continued into the 1990s, reaching record lows in recent years). The immediate reaction was to suggest that CFCs, which were increasing at a rate of about 5% a year in the atmosphere above the Antarctic, were responsible for the persistence and extent of the ozone hole. While a few scientists questioned the causal link between CFCs and the dilation of the Antarctic ozone hole, most concluded that CFCs were implicated. The "smoking gun," considered by many people to be definitive proof of the link between ozone depletion and chlorine monoxide concentration (derived primarily from CFCs), was found in September 1987. A research airplane flew from South America into the Antarctic ozone hole, gathering data on chlorine and ozone concentrations. As chlorine concentrations rose, ozone concentrations dropped; the curves mirror each other almost perfectly (Fig. 1).

Independent of the potential role of CFCs, exactly why an Antarctic ozone hole forms during the southern spring and then closes up again is not well understood. It may relate to progressive cloud formation and subsequent dissipation during the various seasons of the year. High-elevation stratospheric clouds (which form only under very cold conditions) containing ice particles may enhance ozone de-

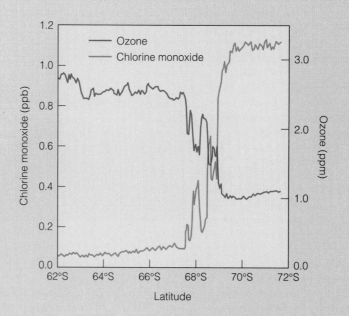

FIGURE 1

On September 16, 1987, a NASA research plane flew from Punta Arenas, Chile (53° south latitude), to 72°S, measuring chlorine monoxide and ozone concentrations. As this graph shows, when the plane entered the ozone hole at about 68°S, the chlorine monoxide concentration shot up while the ozone concentration plummeted. (Note: ppb is parts per billion and ppm is parts per million.) (*Source*: D. H. Meadows, D. L. Meadows, and J. Randers, *Beyond the Limits* [Post Mills, Vt.: Chelsea Green, 1992], p. 152. Reprinted from *Beyond the Limits* copyright © 1992 by Meadows, Meadows, and Randers, with permission from Chelsea Green Publishing Co., White River Junction, Vermont.)

pletion by providing surfaces on which ozone-destroying reactions can occur. The ozone loss at the southern pole may also be a result of global atmospheric circulation patterns, particularly the southern circumpolar vortex that exists as a tight, self-contained southern wind system during the southern winter. It has been suggested that during the Antarctic winter, when it is continuously dark, chlorine forms relatively stable ClOOCl molecules that accumulate within the circumpolar vortex. In spring when light returns, the ClOOCl molecules release their chlorine

atoms, which then catalyze the destruction of ozone, thus accounting for the development of the ozone hole each spring. As summer comes, the circumpolar vortex is dissipated, the ozone-depleted air is dispersed, and ozone levels build up again.

A much smaller and less stable ozone thinning has developed in recent years over the Arctic. In the Northern Hemisphere, the circumpolar vortex is less intense and not as well defined; this may account in large part for the smaller, less-developed Arctic ozone thinning.

tor. Ozone losses of 3 to 10% or more have been recorded over parts of Australia, New Zealand, South Africa, and South America. According to recent data collected by the *Nimbus*-7 satellite, some of the largest decreases in ozone have occurred over the Northern Hemisphere, including North America, Europe, and large portions of Asia, where ozone values have fallen below "normal" (pre–early 1970s) values by as much as 13–14%. Lesser ozone losses have also been documented over the tropics. Averaged over the planet as a whole, it appears that from 1979 to 1991 Earth lost 3% of its stratospheric ozone.

Hopefully, the beginning of the end of the ozone crisis came in June 1990 when 93 countries meeting in London agreed to end the production of CFCs, most halons, and carbon tetrachloride by the year 2000 (with the exception of certain developing countries, which had until 2010 to stop CFC production). Further, methyl chloroform production is to end by the year 2005. An international fund of more than $200 million was also established to assist the developing countries in switching to CFC substitutes, which are often more expensive than the CFCs they replace. One of the main stumbling blocks to controlling worldwide CFC production has been that most of the CFCs have been dumped into the atmosphere by the rich, industrialized countries. Thus, the rich of the world created the problem, but then expect everyone (rich and poor alike) to help in solving it. Meanwhile the developing countries, including China and India with their immense populations, desire the same refrigerators, air conditioners, electronics, and convenience items that have become so common in the West. Only if the developed world contributes to the developing world can global cooperation be anticipated (see Chapter 22).

Given the urgency of the ozone crisis, many of the Montreal Protocol nations met again in Copenhagen in 1992. At this meeting the London amendments were revised, and the proposed phaseout date for all CFCs was moved up to January 1, 1996 (with a 10-year grace period for the developing countries), and a target of 75% reduction by 1994 was set.

The Current Situation

It may appear that the ozone story has come to a happy closure; however, despite the 1990 and 1992 agreements, the story is not over yet. Even with the complete phaseout of CFCs and other chlorine-bearing chemicals, stratospheric chlorine concentrations are expected to remain high well into the twenty-first century as already released CFC molecules rise from the troposphere into the stratosphere (once released, a CFC molecule can take 15 years to make its way up from the Earth's surface to the stratospheric ozone layer). Furthermore, despite the Montreal Protocol and its amendments, as of the early 1990s some developing countries had actually increased their use of CFCs (most CFCs still originate from the industrialized world, however). Realizing the urgency of the situation, some countries have moved up the phaseout schedules; for instance, the 12 members of the European Union promised to stop producing CFCs by the end of 1994.

Even with the accelerated phaseout, the problem will persist. Some of the more common CFCs have life expectancies of between 75 and 110 years, and the chlorine catalyst in the stratosphere can also be quite long-lived. The estimated background level of chlorine in the atmosphere, derived from natural sources such as volcanoes, is about 0.6 ppb (parts per billion). Currently, due to human releases of chlorine-bearing chemicals like CFCs, the concentration of chlorine is about 3.5 ppb, and this number is increasing at a rate of about 5% a year. Assuming that CFC production is phased out by the year 1996 (or 2006 in the case of some developing countries), atmospheric chlorine concentrations are still expected to reach 4.1 ppb by the end of the twentieth century.

Scientists estimate that the ozone layer will continue to be depleted until at least 2050, resulting in ozone losses of as high as 10 to 30% over the northern latitudes where most of the world's population resides. During the latter half of the next century, the ozone may start to build up again, but measurable amounts of CFCs will continue to reside in the atmosphere well into the twenty-fourth century. Thus, even if the 1990 and 1992 agreements are upheld by all nations (perhaps an overly optimistic assumption), the Earth will be subjected to an increasingly thin ozone layer for decades to come.

Effects of Increased Ultraviolet Radiation Reaching the Earth's Surface

Why have people been so concerned about the depletion of the ozone layer? Is a little bit more exposure to ultraviolet radiation really all that bad? A small amount of UV radiation is necessary for the well-being of humans and other organisms. UV radiation promotes the synthesis of Vitamin D in humans and, in small amounts, acts as a germicide to control populations of microorganisms. Yet an increased incidence of UV-B radiation at the Earth's surface can have numerous adverse effects on the health and well-being of humans and other organisms and can also cause the degradation of nonliving materials. For every 1% decrease in the ozone layer, the intensity of UV-B radiation on the Earth's surface increases by 2%.

The most widely publicized problems associated with increasing amounts of UV-B are the projected increases in skin cancer and cataracts among humans. DNA (the genetic material found in all living organisms) is extremely sensitive to, and can be damaged by, UV-B radiation. A solid body of evidence indicates that skin cancer in humans can be caused by UV-induced damage to DNA. The United Nations Environment Programme has estimated that the extra UV-B exposure due to a 10% loss of global ozone could result in a 26% increase in the incidence of nonmelanoma skin cancers. A rise in malignant **melanoma** skin cancers, which are much more dangerous than nonmelanoma cancers, would also be expected. The U.S. Environmental Protection Agency (EPA) has estimated that continued depletion of the ozone layer could cause an additional 800,000 cancer deaths in the United States over the next century.

Some researchers have downplayed the increased risks of skin cancer by pointing out that the incidence of skin cancer among the general population increases as one moves from higher latitudes toward the equator; presumably, this phenomenon is independent of any loss of ozone in the stratosphere (perhaps in warmer areas more people spend more time in the Sun). The National Academy of Sciences, in a 1975 study, found that in the United States the doubling distance for skin cancer was about 600 miles (965 km) south. From this, one can extrapolate that the risk of skin cancer increases about 1% for every six miles (9.65 km) closer to the equator one lives. Thus, a 26% increase in skin cancer, resulting from a 10% loss in ozone, would be the same as if everyone simply moved about 156 miles (250 km) closer to the equator (of course, an impossibility for those already living along the equator). Such reasoning seeks to trivialize the effects of ozone depletion. It does not consider the effects of ozone depletion and increased UV-B radiation exposure on delicately balanced ecosystems, and it is also of little comfort to people who contract cancer due to increased UV-B exposure.

Increased exposures to UV-B have also been linked to increased incidences of **cataracts** (where the lens of the eye becomes opaque), damage to corneas, and retinal disease in humans. It has been estimated that a 10% decrease in the ozone layer could cause more than 1.5 million new cases of cataracts each year. Evidence also suggests that excess dosages of ultraviolet light can suppress the human immune system, allowing the spread of infectious diseases. Furthermore, it has been hypothesized that ultraviolet light may help activate the AIDS virus.

Ultimately, the widespread ecosystem damage caused by increased dosages of UV–B may be more important than its immediate effects on humans. Abnormally high levels of UV radiation inhibit photosynthesis, metabolism, and growth in a number of plants, including food crops such as soybeans, potatoes, sugar beets, beans, tomatoes, lettuce, wheat, sorghum, and peas. The UV-B radiation can destroy cells and also cause mutations. Many tree species are particularly sensitive to UV levels, and increasing amounts of UV may result in a major decline in forest productivity. Insect activity is disrupted by elevated levels of UV radiation, and, of course, the other organisms in a typical terrestrial ecosystem depend on the insects.

Many of the plants and animals in freshwater and marine ecosystems are extremely sensitive to UV levels, especially since UV-B can penetrate several yards (several meters) of water. Phytoplankton (plants and algae that form the bases of many food chains) and fish larvae may be especially susceptible. Reportedly in 1988, when the ozone levels over Antarctica declined by 15% overall, surface phytoplankton levels also decreased by 15–20%. Experimental evidence demonstrates that elevated levels of UV-B radiation will damage fish, shrimp, and crab larvae (and certainly many other species that have not yet been tested).

UV-B exposure can also damage nonliving material objects. For instance, UV exposure will cause or accelerate the breakdown and degradation of various types of paints and plastics, such as polyvinyl chloride (PVC), an important construction material that is used for vinyl siding, garden hoses, and other products that are regularly exposed to sunlight. Such material damage could cost billions of dollars per year.

Although extremely poorly understood at present, major fluctuations in the ozone layer could have significant climatological effects on the Earth's surface. The stratospheric ozone naturally absorbs UV radiation and reemits it as infrared energy (essentially heat) into the troposphere; this contributes to the Earth's energy budget. At present the absorption of UV radiation warms the stratosphere, creating a temperature inversion at the boundary between the troposphere and the stratosphere. Some scientists suggest that a decline in the ozone layer could cause a cooling of the stratosphere, which in turn might cause a cooling of the troposphere and ultimately a slight cooling of the Earth's surface (even though more UV radiation would directly reach the ground). Such a cooling effect could be very small, however. According to one calculation, a 20% reduction in ozone concentrations in the stratosphere would cause only a 0.45°F (0.25°C) decline in surface temperatures. But before jumping to the conclusion that ozone loss will have one good effect—countering global warming due to the greenhouse effect—one must consider that many of the chemicals that are contributing to stratospheric ozone declines are also potent greenhouse gases. The increased greenhouse effects of CFCs and other ozone-destroying gases may more than offset any surface cooling that would otherwise have been brought about by destruction of the ozone layer.

Changes in the concentrations of ozone at different levels in the atmosphere could also affect the temperature gradient of the atmosphere, which in turn could affect atmospheric circulation patterns and climatic patterns on the Earth's surface in unpredicted, but potentially adverse, ways. The relative temperature differences among the various layers of the atmosphere are extremely important in determining convective processes that produce clouds and precipitation patterns. Interfering with this system by depleting the ozone layer could possibly have disastrous effects.

Controlling CFC Releases and Finding Substitutes

Even if the virtual worldwide ban on CFC production after about 2006 is successful, massive amounts of CFCs and other ozone-destroying chemicals will still be in existence. Methyl bromide, which is not a CFC but is an ozone depleter, is currently banned in the United States, but it may continue to be used elsewhere into the twenty-first century. Older refrigerator and air conditioning units containing ozone-depleting substances will still be used for years to come. The CFCs are not dangerous unless they are released into the atmosphere, however. Therefore the equipment should be properly maintained so that the CFCs do not leak into the environment, and if the equipment is drained or junked, the CFCs must be fully recovered and recycled or disposed of properly. In the past, all too often the liquid CFC from an automobile air conditioner was

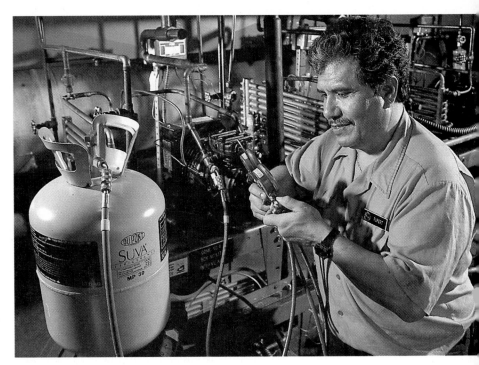

simply poured onto the ground and left to evaporate. When CFCs are used as solvents in cleaning electronic circuit boards or in dry cleaning clothing, the CFC vapors should be recovered so the CFCs can be recycled rather than allowed to evaporate into the atmosphere.

Much research is currently being carried out to develop ozone-safe substitutes for the common CFCs and halons (■ Fig. 18–3). In some cases, HCFCs (hydrochlorofluorocarbons) and HFCs (hydrofluorocarbons) can be substituted directly for the more dangerous CFCs. More often, however, refrigerators and other equipment must be specially designed or retrofitted to handle the substitutes. Some extreme innovative methods are being developed to replace CFCs in refrigeration units, such as the emerging field of thermoacoustics—the use of sound to cool substances. Already a prototype thermoacoustic refrigeration system has been built by Steven Garrett of the Naval Postgraduate School. In the manufacture of foam and styrofoam, chemicals other than CFCs can be used as the foaming agents, although one of them, dimethylene chloride, is a suspected carcinogen and another substitute, pentane, is flammable. Perhaps a better alternative is to use cardboard and paper rather than styrofoam products.

Some CFC uses are almost completely unnecessary. As of the early 1990s, it was estimated that CFC use as an aerosol propellant was still the biggest source of CFC emissions worldwide (even though the United States has banned this

FIGURE 18–3
Installing CFC-free coolant in a large refrigeration unit, Dallas, Texas. (*Source:* Ed Lallo/ Gamma Liaison.)

use since 1978). In some cases, hydrocarbons can be substituted as the propellant, or pump dispensers can be used instead. In other cases, the aerosol product is not essential at all; for example, aerosol underarm deodorants have no known advantage over other types of underarm deodorants. Some electronics and manufacturing companies have been able to redesign their manufacturing processes so that they either do not use CFCs at all or use them in much smaller quantities. For example, Intel, a large electronics company, simply changed the solders and fluxes it used, eliminating the need for cleaning with CFC solvents.

Until CFCs are no longer a part of our society, individual consumers can do many things to help save the ozone layer. Avoid, whenever possible, any product that entails the release of CFCs into the atmosphere during its manufacture, use, or disposal. For example, choose washable clothing rather than outfits that must be dry cleaned. Avoid styrofoam convenience items like plates and coffee cups. Whenever possible, substitute paper or cardboard for styrofoam. One can make do with a car that lacks a CFC-based air conditioner. If you do have a CFC-based car air conditioner, make sure that it is properly maintained (so that it does not leak) and that any mechanic who services it drains the coolant into a proper storage unit and recycles the coolant. When a refrigerator or air conditioner unit is discarded, investigate the possibility of having the refrigerant/coolant recycled. Never buy foam rubber furniture or mattresses that have been manufactured using CFCs (of course, it may be difficult to determine if CFCs were used in the manufacturing process); likewise, when shopping for insulation, avoid CFC-blown foams and look for fiberglass or cellulose insulation instead. Fortunately, as CFCs are phased out worldwide, the average consumer may no longer have to worry about purchasing CFC-utilizing products because they will no longer exist.

Tropospheric Pollution and UV-B

Despite the efforts to control stratospheric ozone depletion, the amount of UV-B radiation reaching the Earth's surface may well continue to increase in the near future as we address the problem of tropospheric air pollution. Some researchers suggest that the increases in UV-B reaching the surface have not been as great as some models of ozone loss have predicted because near-surface atmospheric pollution is actually blocking much of the incoming UV-B radiation.

Sulfate aerosols from power plants produce a haze that reflects and scatters sunlight, decreasing the amount of UV radiation that reaches the surface by up to 18%. The eruption of Mt. Pinatubo (1991), which cast millions of tons (millions of metric tons) of volcanic aerosol particles into the atmosphere, also increased UV scattering in the short run while simultaneously promoting the further depletion of the ozone layer.

Lower atmospheric ozone is a major pollutant that contributes heavily to photochemical smog (see Chapter 17). Still, ozone in the troposphere continues to absorb UV radiation. As industries and automobiles pump pollutants into the lower atmosphere, they inadvertently help protect the surface from UV radiation. As tropospheric air pollution is cleaned up, through tougher emissions standards in particular, the effects of the thinning of the ozone layer may manifest themselves more widely and intensely than has been the case so far.

$\mathcal{G}$ LOBAL WARMING

The Greenhouse Effect

The basic idea behind the **greenhouse effect** is as follows. Short-wavelength, high-energy, solar **radiation** shines from the Sun onto the Earth. Some of this incoming solar radiation is reflected by the atmosphere back into space, some passes though the atmosphere and is absorbed as it heats the air, and about half reaches the Earth's surface. The surface heats up and in the process gives off longer-wavelength, lower-energy (**infrared**, or **heat**), radiation. This infrared radiation passes up into the atmosphere, but instead of being radiated 100% back into space, much of it is absorbed by the atmosphere and reradiated to the surface. This phenomenon occurs because many trace gases (the **greenhouse gases**) in the atmosphere are relatively transparent to the higher-energy sunlight, but trap or reflect the lower-energy infrared radiation. Thus, the greenhouse gases act as a one-way filter, letting energy in the form of sunlight in but not allowing the infrared heat to escape at the same rate. This process is crudely analogous to the way glass in a greenhouse allows sunlight to shine in, but stops much of the longer-wavelength heat from escaping. Even on a cold winter day, the inside of a greenhouse can become quite warm if the Sun is shining.

Likewise, the Earth's surface would be a frozen mass if it were not for the natural greenhouse effect of the atmosphere. Without this phenomenon, average global temperatures might be on the order of 1.4°F (−17°C). Note, however, that with current levels of greenhouse gases, some infrared heat does continue to escape. In recent Earth history, a relative steady-state balance has been achieved that maintains the average global surface temperature at about 59°F (15°C). If no heat escaped, the surface would continue to heat up to unbearable temperatures. The perceived problem is that, due to inadvertent human intervention, greenhouse gases are accumulating very quickly in the atmosphere, and some predict this will lead to catastrophic global warming.

Greenhouse Gases

The best-known greenhouse gas (● Table 18–1) is **carbon dioxide** (CO_2). Carbon dioxide is breathed out or otherwise given off by living organisms (including plants) as they undergo aerobic respiration, and is taken in by green plants during photosynthesis. A small amount of carbon dioxide in the atmosphere is an absolute necessity for life on Earth; without it the planet would be too cold to support living organisms, and plants would lack an essential raw ingredient. But an excess of carbon dioxide will cause the Earth's surface to heat up abnormally.

Clearly, we humans are very quickly adding to the amount of carbon dioxide in the atmosphere (▬ Fig. 18–4). In 1850 the average annual concentration of carbon dioxide was about 250 ppm (parts per million); this increased to 316 ppm by 1959, and by 1995 it had grown to nearly 360

TABLE 18–1 *Greenhouse Gases: Sources and Estimated Relative Contributions to Global Warming*

Note that the estimates of relative greenhouse gas contributions involve significant uncertainties.

GAS	MAJOR SOURCES	PERCENTAGE CONTRIBUTION
Carbon dioxide	Fossil fuels, deforestation	50
Chlorofluoro-carbons, other halocarbons	Refrigeration, solvents, insulation, foams, aerosol propellants, other industrial and commercial uses	20
Methane	Rice paddies, swamps, bogs, cattle and other livestock, termites, fossil fuels, wood burning, landfills	16
Tropospheric ozone	Fossil fuels	8
Nitrogen oxides	Fossil fuels, fertilizers, soils, burning of wood and crop residues	6

(*Source*: Based primarily on estimates made by World Resources Institute; reprinted with permission from World Resources Institute.)

ppm. The CO_2 content of the atmosphere continues to increase.

The primary way we are increasing the CO_2 content of the atmosphere is through the burning of fossil fuels (▬ Fig. 18–5): coal, oil, and gas. For millions of years, the carbon in these fuels has been out of atmospheric circulation, buried deep under the surface of the Earth. But suddenly, over a period of just two centuries (and especially during the last few decades), we have released mas-

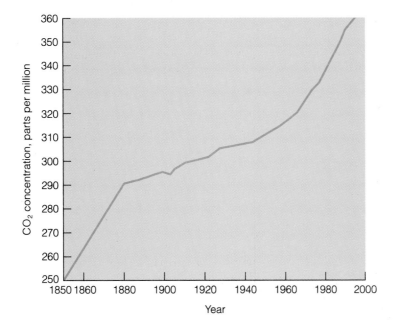

▬ **FIGURE 18–4**
Average annual atmospheric concentrations of carbon dioxide, 1850–1995.

FIGURE 18-5

World carbon emissions from fossil fuel burning,1950–1994. (*Source*: L. R. Brown, H. Kane, and D. M. Roodman, *Vital Signs 1994* [New York: W. W. Norton, 1994], p. 69, with updates from L. R. Brown, N. Lenssen, and H. Kane, *Vital Signs 1995* [New York: W. W. Norton, 1995], p. 67. Reprinted with permission of Worldwatch Institute, copyright © 1994.)

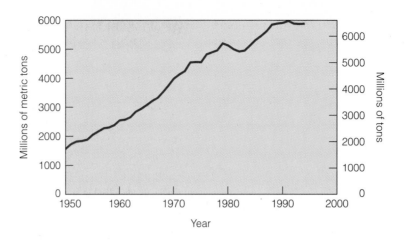

TABLE 18-2 *Greenhouse Index Ranking and Percentage Share of Global Emissions, 1991*

Note that Iraq is ranked 11th, rather than 50th as it was in 1989, primarily due to the oil well fires set in Kuwait by Iraq during the Gulf War.

RANK	COUNTRY	PERCENT	RANK	COUNTRY	PERCENT
1.	United States	19.14	26.	Czechoslovakia	0.70
2.	Former Soviet Union	13.63	27.	Malaysia	0.61
3.	China	9.92	28.	Colombia	0.61
4.	Japan	5.05	29.	Netherlands	0.59
5.	Brazil	4.33	30.	Philippines	0.59
6.	Germany	3.75	31.	Myanmar	0.55
7.	India	3.68	32.	Argentina	0.54
8.	United Kingdom	2.37	33.	Turkey	0.53
9.	Indonesia	1.89	34.	Romania	0.52
10.	Italy	1.72	35.	Bulgaria	0.51
11.	Iraq	1.71	36.	Bolivia	0.48
12.	France	1.63	37.	Pakistan	0.46
13.	Canada	1.62	38.	Belgium	0.40
14.	Mexico	1.43	39.	Peru	0.39
15.	Poland	1.16	40.	Yugoslavia	0.36
16.	Australia	1.13	41.	Nigeria	0.35
17.	South Africa	1.12	42.	Egypt	0.34
18.	Spain	1.01	43.	Vietnam	0.32
19.	Venezuela	1.01	44.	Greece	0.31
20.	Republic of Korea	0.98	45.	Ecuador	0.30
21.	Zaire	0.93	46.	Bangladesh	0.29
22.	Thailand	0.88	47.	Hungary	0.26
23.	Korea, Democratic People's Republic	0.84	48.	Austria	0.25
24.	Islamic Rep. of Iran	0.82	49.	Denmark	0.24
25.	Saudi Arabia	0.78	50.	Algeria	0.23

Note: Data for Germany include both the former Federal Republic of Germany and the former German Democratic Republic. Data for Czechoslovakia include both the Czech Republic and Slovakia. Data for Yugoslavia include Bosnia and Herzegovina, Croatia, Slovenia, and Yugoslavia (Serbia, Montenegro, and Kosovo).
(*Source*: World Resources Institute, *World Resources 1994–95* [New York: Oxford University Press, 1994], p. 201. Reprinted with permission from World Resources Institute.)

sive amounts of this fossilized carbon back into the atmosphere. In 1994, for instance, an estimated 6.5 billion tons (5.9 billion metric tons) of carbon were released worldwide by the combustion of fossil fuels—slightly over 1.1 tons (1 metric ton) of carbon per person on Earth. Each ton of pure carbon released forms approximately 3.66 tons of CO_2, so approximately 23.8 billion tons (21.6 billion metric tons) of CO_2 were released into the atmosphere simply by the burning of fossil fuels in 1994—or over 46 trillion pounds (21 trillion kg) of CO_2. Given that a pound of CO_2 occupies about 8.75 cubic feet at room temperature at sea level, 46 trillion pounds of CO_2 are equivalent to more than 400 trillion cubic feet (37 trillion m³) of CO_2 (of course, the actual volume of CO_2 depends on temperature and pressure conditions in various parts of the atmosphere).

Carbon emissions due to the burning of fossil fuels are produced disproportionately by the people of the industrialized countries (Table 18–2; Fig. 18–6). Indeed, the wealthiest 25% of the world's population burn nearly 70% of all fossil fuels. The United States is the biggest single contributor, producing nearly 20% of the world's CO_2 emissions (primarily from burning fossil fuels) while containing less than 5% of the world's population.

An additional 1.1 to 2.2 billion tons (1–2 billion metric tons) of carbon (4–8 billion tons [3.6–7.3 billion metric tons] of CO_2) are emitted into the atmosphere each year due to deforestation. Like the fossil fuels, which were once living organisms, the extant forests hold vast stores of carbon. When the trees and other plants die and are either burned or allowed to decay, this carbon is converted to CO_2. Furthermore, trees serve the vital function of removing CO_2 from the atmo-

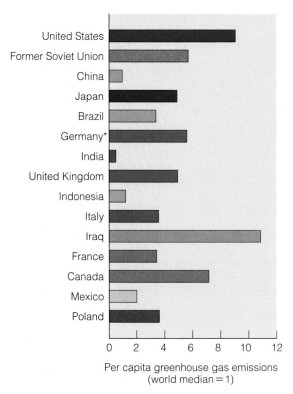

*Data for Germany include both the former Federal Republic of Germany and the former German Democratic Republic.

FIGURE 18–6

Per capita greenhouse gas emissions of the 15 countries with the highest total emissions in 1991. Note that per capita greenhouse gas emissions were abnormally high for Iraq due to the oil well fires set in Kuwait by Iraq during the Gulf War. (*Source*: World Resources Institute, *World Resources 1994–95* [New York: Oxford University Press, 1994], p. 203. Reprinted with permission from World Resources Institute.)

sphere as they grow. Unless deforested areas are quickly replanted, not only is CO_2 emitted directly into the atmosphere, but a vital mechanism for removing excess CO_2 from the atmosphere is destroyed.

Although not yet considered a serious threat, there is another aspect of excess CO_2 production: the oxygen portion of CO_2 comes from the atmosphere, and we (along with all living aerobic creatures) need this oxygen to breathe. For every ton of carbon burned, 2.66 tons of oxygen are taken from the atmosphere. Since the atmosphere is composed of about 20.9% oxygen, the supply may seem virtually unlimited. Yet measurements indicate that the oxygen content of the atmosphere is currently decreasing at a rate of about 13 ppm annually. Oxygen is being lost from the atmosphere, and as more plants are destroyed, it is not being replaced as fast as it once was. The most serious immediate concern is

that falling oxygen levels may adversely affect oxygen concentrations in the oceans and other standing bodies of water. Slight decreases in oxygen concentrations could have severely disruptive effects on many marine organisms.

Although carbon dioxide is blamed for 50 to 70% of the current abnormal global warming, (depending on the authority consulted and how "global warming" is calculated), it is not the only major greenhouse gas (◼ Fig. 18–7). The other major culprits are chlorofluorocarbons (CFCs), **methane** (natural gas, CH_4), tropospheric ozone, and **nitrogen oxides** (NO_x).

The chlorofluorocarbons that promote global warming are the same CFCs that are destroying stratospheric ozone. Indeed, they are up to thousands of times more efficient at absorbing heat and promoting global warming than CO_2. At present, CFCs account for 15 to 25% of the human contribution to global warming. This number would have been even higher if steps had not been taken to reduce the CFCs released into the atmosphere. Thus, there are two good reasons to reduce our reliance on CFCs: to save the ozone layer and to reduce global warming.

Methane accounts for an estimated 15 to 20% of current global warming. Currently, methane does not occur in anywhere near the concentrations of CO_2 in the atmosphere, but it is up to 30 times more effective than CO_2 in trapping heat.

Like CO_2, methane, is a naturally occurring gas that has been present on the Earth's surface since its formation. Methane is produced by bacteria in swamps and other areas as organic matter is decomposed. Termites give off methane as they break down wood, and many animals produce large amounts of methane in their digestive tracts. Ruminants such as cows in particular release enormous quantities of methane into the atmosphere. These natural sources of methane have been intensified by human habits. We raise billions of cows and other livestock, which serve as natural methane factories. Unfortunately, virtually all of this methane is lost to the atmosphere, although some have suggested that we should try to capture it and burn it as a fuel. Rice farming is another major source of methane—in typical rice paddies, large quantities of organic matter rot under a shallow layer of water to produce methane.

The increased use of fossil fuels has also added significant quantities of "fossil" methane to the atmosphere. During coal mining, underground stored reserves of methane are often inadvertently released into the atmosphere. Likewise, methane

FIGURE 18-7

Global greenhouse gas atmospheric concentrations over the last 200 years: (a) carbon dioxide, (b) methane, (c) nitrogen oxides, and (d) CFC-11. (*Source*: D. H. Meadows, D. L. Meadows, and J. Randers, *Beyond the Limits* [Post Mills, Vt.: Chelsea Green, 1992], p. 94. Reprinted from *Beyond the Limits* copyright © 1992 by Meadows, Meaadows, and Randers, with permission from Chelsea Green Publishing Co., White River Junction, Vermont.)

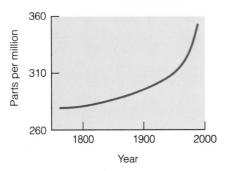

(a) Carbon dioxide

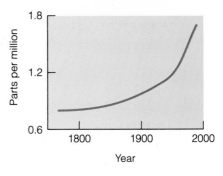

(b) Methane

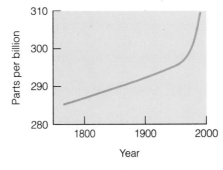

(c) Nitrogen oxides

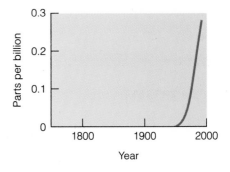

(d) CFC-11

occurs above oil in many oil wells. Although this methane is now generally seen as a valuable resource, in the past (and in some cases to this day) it was considered not worth bothering with and simply released into the air. The current increased use of methane as the fossil fuel of choice (it burns cleaner than coal or gasoline) also opens up the possibility that more stored reserves of methane will make their way into the atmosphere, escaping from leaking tanks or pipelines. As much as 15% of all methane released annually into the atmosphere may be leaking from poorly designed and maintained natural gas lines in Eastern Europe and the former Soviet Union.

Another aspect of natural methane could have extremely serious repercussions. An estimated 14% of all the organic carbon of the world is buried (mostly as partially degraded vegetation) and frozen in the permafrost of the tundra. With increased global warming, which many scientists predict will affect the poles to a greater extent than the Earth as a whole, vast tracts of tundra could begin to melt. Bacteria would then decompose the organic matter, releasing prodigious amounts of methane into the atmosphere. The added methane would accelerate global warming, which in turn would accelerate the production of more methane—setting off what some fear could be a runaway cycle of increased warming and methane production. Some people even fear that

if global temperatures rise high enough, much organic matter found in the soil of temperate regions (where the ground is not frozen) may also be converted to methane or CO_2.

A similar effect may occur in the oceans. The oceans, in particular the cold regions, hold huge stores of organic matter, containing more carbon than all the coal reserves on land. About 42,000 billion tons (36,000 billion metric tons) of carbon are stored in the oceans, compared to about 4400 billion tons (4000 billion metric tons) in fossil fuels. As the oceans slowly warm up, this organic carbon could also decompose, forming methane that will bubble to the surface.

Compared to CO_2, CFCs, and methane, nitrogen oxides (NO_x) and tropospheric ozone are relatively minor greenhouse gases, together accounting for perhaps 10 to 15% of global warming. Nitrogen oxides and tropospheric ozone are important air pollutants in other contexts, contributing to petrochemical fog and acid rain (see Chapter 17); thus, it is important from several standpoints that emissions of these substances be decreased. Nitrogen oxides are formed when chemical fertilizers break down, when coal is burned in power plants, and in general when any fuel is burned at high temperatures (nitrogen and oxygen, the primary components of our atmosphere, combine at high temperatures to form nitrogen oxides). Large quantities of nitrogen oxides are also apparently released during the production of certain synthetic substances, such as nylon stockings and pantyhose.

Other gases also contribute to global warming. Water vapor (H_2O) is a potentially important factor, but virtually nothing can be done to control the amount of water vapor in the atmosphere. The Sun naturally heats the surfaces of the oceans and lakes, and plants naturally transpire, all of which inject large quantities of water vapor into the atmosphere. Of course, this water vapor collects and precipitates out again as rain or snow.

Is Earth Really Warming Up?

Many researchers would respond to this question with a definitive "yes." Fairly accurate records of global temperatures have been kept since 1880, and they show a fairly steady increase in temperature from about 1880 to 1940. From 1940 to the mid-1960s, temperatures underwent a slight cooling and stabilization, but since the 1960s, there has been a dramatic (though somewhat erratic from year to year) increase (Fig. 18–8). Record highs have been reached in the last decade, with the global temperature rising to 59.846°F (15.47°C) in 1990—marking an increase of about 0.9°F (0.5°C) over the course of two decades. In 1991 the overall global temperature dropped to 59.738°F (15.41°C) (though it was still extremely high—in fact, one of the highest temperatures on record), and by 1992 it had dropped to 59.234°F (15.13°C). But this drop in 1991–1992 has been attributed to the 1991 eruption of **Mt. Pinatubo**

in the Philippines—the smoke and ash spewed into the atmosphere had a temporary cooling effect. However, the effects of Mt. Pinatubo have now dissipated, and the general warming trend should pick back up with full speed in the late 1990s. In 1993 the overall global temperature rose to 59.360°F (15.20°C); by 1994 is had risen to 59.576°F (15.32°C).

The eruption of Mt. Pinatubo and its effect on global temperatures raise an interesting point. The cooling effect of atmospheric pollutants, such as soot and acid particles, may be masking much of the global greenhouse warming. The eruption of Mt. Pinatubo shot a fine mist of sulfuric acid and sulfate aerosols into the atmosphere; this material reflects sunlight back into space and so cools the Earth. Scientists predicted that the net effect of the Mt. Pinatubo eruption would be a 0.9°F (0.5°C) relative cooling of the Earth's surface for several years after the eruption. If correct, this means that average global surface temperatures would have risen by about 0.9°F (0.5°C) more during the early 1990s if Mt. Pinatubo had not exploded.

Soot, acid particles, and other aerosols are also injected into the atmosphere through human activities—burning fossil fuels, clearing forests, smelting metals, and so forth. For a long time, many climatologists were a bit puzzled when their theoretical models of the effects of increasing concentrations of greenhouse gases predicted much greater temperature increases than have been actually observed. Only recently has it been widely recognized just how powerful the cooling effect of many anthropogenic airborne pollutants

FIGURE 18–8
Global average temperatures, 1880–1994. (*Source*: Data from B. W. Pipkin, *Geology and the Environment* [St. Paul: West Publishing Company, 1994], p. 326, and L. R. Brown, N. Lenssen, and H. Kane, *Vital Signs 1995* [New York: W. W. Norton, 1995], p. 65. Reprinted with permission of Worldwatch Institute.)

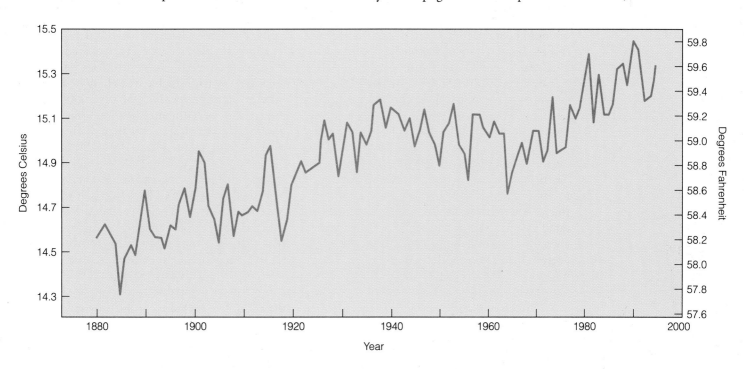

can be. These atmospheric particles not only reflect sunlight back into space, but they form the nuclei of water droplets, promoting the formation of clouds that reflect still more sunlight. According to some recent calculations, atmospheric pollution and particulate matter may be counteracting, or masking, much of the effect of atmospheric greenhouse gases. As progress is made toward reducing global air pollution, greenhouse warming may greatly accelerate.

Other evidence for global warming exists besides direct measurements of atmospheric temperatures. Satellite data of ocean-surface temperatures indicate that the oceans have been warming at a rate of about 0.18°F (0.1°C) per year since the early 1980s. Another way to measure temperature changes over time is by using geophysical borehole data. Heat diffuses from the Earth's surface into the soil and rocks, so by plotting a profile of temperatures at increasing depths it is possible to reconstruct broad temperature trends at the surface. Borehole temperature profiles taken at localities ranging from Alaska to Africa confirm that there has been a distinct warming trend in recent decades.

The retreat of nonpolar glaciers provides another line of evidence for global warming over the last few decades. According to data compiled by the United Nations Environment Programme's World Glacier Inventory, most nonpolar glaciers and ice masses (particularly in Asia, Africa, and South America) have been retreating since the turn of the century; in some cases, they have been experiencing particularly rapid melting and decreases in snow cover over the last 30 years. Many glaciologists believe that tropical glaciers (found on high mountain tops) may be especially sensitive to slight increases in global temperature.

A rise in global temperature from 58.802°F (14.89°C) in 1971 to 59.846°F (15.47°C) in 1990 may not seem very dramatic, but from a broader perspective, it is very rapid indeed. Over the last few million years, the Earth has experienced wide fluctuations in surface temperatures. During the "**Ice Ages**," major portions of Europe and North America were covered with sheets of ice up to thousands of yards (thousands of meters) thick. The end of the last Ice Age came very rapidly by natural standards, yet this warming occurred at a rate of approximately 1.8°F (1°C) every 500 or 600 years. The current global warming rate is about 1.8°F (1°C) every 40 years. Based on present trends, (admittedly taken over a very short timeframe), the surface of the globe is heating up at a rate more than 10 times faster than it ever has during human history or prehistory.

How Much Will Earth Warm Up?

If we keep dumping greenhouse gases into the atmosphere, unquestionably the surface of Earth will warm up. About this there is no doubt—all one has to do is analyze the surface temperatures of Venus and Mars, which are determined in large part by the carbon dioxide in these planets' atmospheres. The real question is how much the surface temperatures on Earth at different locations will be affected by the equivalent of, say, a doubling of CO_2 over preindustrial levels. This topic has been the subject of much debate and speculation, but slowly a consensus seems to be emerging. Many different researchers have come to the conclusion that a doubling of CO_2 levels in the atmosphere will lead to an average global warming of 2.3 to 8.1°F (1.3 to 4.5°C) above the 59°F (15°C) average global surface temperature over the last 10,000 years. It is important to remember that these numbers refer to average global temperature changes; in many specific areas, the increases could be much greater, especially during the winter (● Table 18–3). In 1990 a group of about two hundred scientists working under the auspices of the United Nations **Intergovernmental Panel on Climate Change (IPCC)** concluded that, given the present situation of increasing greenhouse gas emissions into the atmosphere, there is at least a 50% chance that an average global increase in temperature of 3 to 10°F (1.6 to 5.5°C) will take place by about 2050. Their most likely estimate was a 5°F (2.8°C) rise by 2050.

In 1992 the IPCC updated its initial projections, taking the latest scientific data, models, and analyses into account. It concluded that due to ozone depletion and airborne particulate pollution, both of which tend to have a cooling influence on some regions of the globe, global greenhouse warming may be somewhat less pronounced in the short term than at first anticipated. Consequently, the 1992 IPCC revised projections of immediate (over the next hundred years) global warming and sea level rise (caused by global warming, as discussed below) are approximately 20 to 30% lower than the 1990 projections. Still, the updated analysis suggests that a rise in global mean temperature of 4.5°F (2.5°C) and a rise in global sea levels of 19 inches (48 cm) can be expected between 1990 and 2100. This projected warming rate is about five times the rate seen during the previous century, and a 19-inch rise in sea levels could have a significant impact on coastal areas.

TABLE 18–3 *Projected Temperature Changes at Selected Locations in the Northern Hemisphere Following a Doubling of Atmospheric CO_2*

	MEAN TEMPERATURES °F (°C)					
	Winter (Present)	Winter (CO_2 Doubled)	Increase	Summer (Present)	Summer (CO_2 Doubled)	Increase
Calgary, Alberta: 51°N	17.06 (−8.3)	20.66 (−6.3)	3.6 (2)	58.82 (14.9)	62.42 (16.9)	3.6 (2)
Toronto, Ontario: 43°N	26.06 (−3.3)	31.46 (−0.3)	5.4 (3)	69.26 (20.7)	74.66 (23.7)	5.4 (3)
Angmagssalik, Greenland: 65°N	20.66 (−6.3)	35.06 (1.7)	14.4 (8)	44.06 (6.7)	45.86 (7.7)	1.8 (1)
Anchorage, Alaska: 61°N	13.64 (−10.2)	29.84 (−1.2)	16.2 (9)	56.3 (13.5)	63.5 (17.5)	7.2 (4)
San Francisco, California: 37°N	49.1 (9.5)	52.7 (11.5)	3.6 (2)	59.9 (15.5)	65.3 (18.5)	5.4 (3)
Chicago, Illinois: 41°N	27.86 (−2.3)	33.26 (0.7)	5.4 (3)	72.86 (22.7)	78.26 (25.7)	5.4 (3)
Reykyavik, Iceland: 64°N	31.64 (−0.2)	49.64 (9.8)	18 (10)	50.9 (10.5)	54.5 (12.5)	3.6 (2)
Edinburgh, Scotland: 56°N	39.2 (4.0)	53.6 (12.0)	14.4 (8)	57.2 (14.0)	64.4 (18.0)	7.2 (4)
Paris, France: 48°N	38.12 (3.4)	47.12 (8.4)	9 (5)	64.4 (18.0)	68 (20.0)	3.6 (2)
Oslo, Norway: 59°N	25.34 (−3.7)	41.54 (5.3)	16.2 (9)	60.8 (16.0)	68 (20.0)	7.2 (4)
St. Petersburg, Russia: 59°N	19.94 (−6.7)	37.94 (3.3)	18 (10)	62.06 (16.7)	67.46 (19.7)	5.4 (3)
Vladivostok, Russia: 43°N	11.66 (−11.3)	22.46 (−5.3)	10.8 (6)	64.94 (18.3)	68.54 (20.3)	3.6 (2)
Beijing, China: 39°N	26.06 (−3.3)	35.06 (1.7)	9 (5)	77.54 (25.3)	79.34 (26.3)	1.8 (1)

(*Source:* D. D. Kemp, *Global Environmental Issues: A Climatological Approach* [London: Routledge, 1990], p. 153. Reprinted with permission from Routledge.)

Questioning Global Warming

Although they are in the minority, numerous scientists question the concept of global warming both in theory and in practice.

Ice Ages Over the last few million years, the Earth's surface temperature has undergone natural fluctuations, expressed as the Ice Ages (▬ Figs. 18–9, page 512 and 18–10, page 513). Even in historical times, there have been warmer and colder periods, such as the warmer "Medieval Little Optimum" around A.D. 900–1100. At this time Earth's surface was warm enough that ice melted back in the North Atlantic Ocean and the Norsemen colonized Greenland. A couple of hundred years later, the "**Little Ice Age**" set in and the surface became noticeably colder; the colonies in Greenland failed and mountain glaciers advanced. Only in the last few hundred years has Earth begun to warm up again. No one really understands the causes of preindustrial temperature fluctuations (perhaps they are correlated with sunspot activity or other natural phenomena such as slight variations in the tilt and direction of Earth's axis and the shape of its orbit), but they certainly had nothing to do with industrially produced greenhouse gases.

Over the course of billions of years, there has been a general decline in atmospheric CO_2 con-

FIGURE 18–9
Changes in atmospheric CO$_2$
and air temperature for the
last 160,000 years, determined
from air bubbles in the
Vostok, Antarctica, ice core.

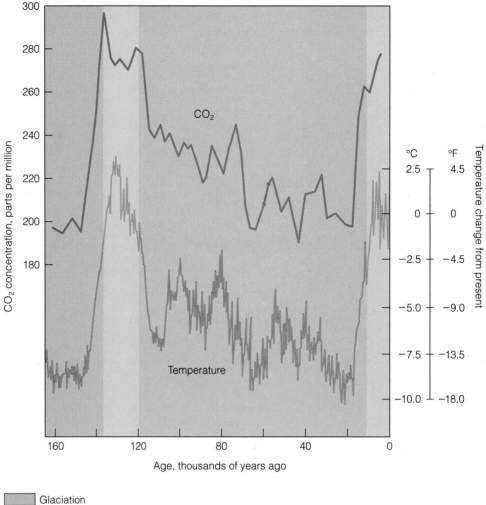

centrations. During the Mesozoic Era (the "time of the dinosaurs," about 245 to 65 million years ago), average global temperatures may have been 9°F (5°C) or more warmer than at present, and CO$_2$ concentrations may have been 5 to 10 times higher. In contrast, CO$_2$ concentrations may have been only 200 ppm about 40,000 years ago during the last great glaciation. Since then they rose naturally to the preindustrial levels of about 250 ppm. Despite the recent rise in CO$_2$ concentrations, a few researchers suggest that the natural long-term decline of atmospheric CO$_2$ concentrations over tens of millions of years, if not reversed, could eventually spell the end of life on our planet in the distant future.

The Pleistocene Ice Ages of the last few million years occurred in cycles of approximately 100,000 to 120,000 years, with each ice age lasting about 100,000 years followed by an approximately 10,000 to 20,000-year interglacial period. The last ice age ended just over 10,000 years ago,

so if the pattern continues, we could soon enter another ice age. Indeed, some scientists (though a minority) strongly believe that we are on the verge of entering the next ice age.

These scientists do not deny that atmospheric CO$_2$ levels are on the rise; in fact, they believe this is evidence in support of their hypothesis. According to the theories of John D. Hamaker and Larry Ephron, during a glacial period the soils of the Earth are fertilized by ground-up mineral matter. At the beginning of an interglacial period, plant life thrives, and as a result, CO$_2$ levels in the atmosphere are relatively low. But toward the end of an interglacial epoch, trees and other plants die off as the mineral nutrients in the soil are exhausted. As forests in particular recede, less CO$_2$ is removed from the air and atmospheric concentrations increase. The immediate result of the increased CO$_2$ levels is greenhouse warming.

But what about the ice age? Ice age proponents believe that most of the warming will occur in

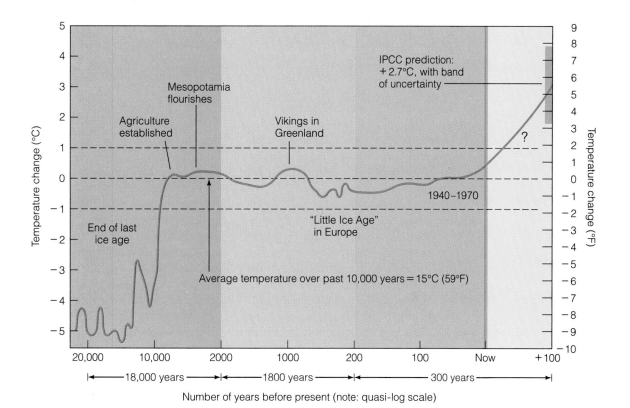

Number of years before present (note: quasi-log scale)

tropical and temperate regions, while the high latitudes will remain cold (or perhaps become even colder: note that many scientists disagree with this analysis and believe that the higher latitudes will warm up relative to the lower latitudes). According to certain ice age proponents, greenhouse warming will reinforce the temperature differences between the tropics and the poles. With increased warming, large quantities of water will evaporate from the low latitudes and move toward the higher latitudes where it will precipitate out as rain and snow. Increased cloud cover, along with increased snow and ice cover, in polar and temperate latitudes will reflect sunlight and eventually cause a cooling trend to set in. Once the cooling begins in earnest, glaciers will grow on land and slowly spread into progressively lower latitudes. Another ice age will be upon us.

What do the proponents of this ice age theory suggest that we do about the situation? Since greenhouse warming will initially trigger the next ice age, many advocate the same measures as do those concerned about global warming—decrease the consumption of fossil fuels, limit the amounts of greenhouse gases that are spewed into the atmosphere, and so on. But some ice age proponents go much further. They advocate spreading minerals (in the form of ground rock) over forest floors all over the world so as to revitalize tree growth. They also advocate planting billions

and billions of new trees to promote CO_2 removal from the atmosphere.

Imprecise Data Some researchers question the whole notion of global warming, not because they believe that another ice age is imminent, but because they see no clear trend in global temperature changes or they question the whole theory of global warming per se. They point to such data as the slight cooling and stabilization of mean global temperatures during the 1940s to 1960s as indicative of a lack of the predicted global warming. They point out that many of the global warming data are imprecise and that we have a mere century's worth of accurate data. With such data it is very difficult to separate the signal from the noise, especially since daily temperatures can fluctuate by tens of degrees and seasonal temperatures can fluctuate much more widely, while the global warming trend that is being sought is only on the order of 0.9°F (0.5°C) over several decades. Local temperature readings during the past century may also be skewed, depending on where they were taken; large urban areas have progressively become "heat islands," so that temperature readings taken in cities may not reflect real Earth surface conditions. One study found what appears to be a relative rise in the night temperatures throughout the United States since about 1930 without a rise in daytime temperatures: such data

FIGURE 18-10
Variations in average global temperature over the past 20,000 years. Also shown is the IPCC's prediction for the next century. (*Source*: A. J. McMichael, *Planetary Overload* [Cambridge: Cambridge University Press, 1993], p. 84. © Cambridge University Press. Reprinted with the permission of Cambridge University Press.)

have been used to argue both for and against the seriousness of possible global warming. Rises in nighttime temperatures without an initial rise in daytime temperatures could be expected to occur as greenhouse gases build up, for they would let sunlight in during the day, but not let heat (infrared radiation) escape back into space at night. Those who downplay the significance of global warming suggest that even if this phenomenon of nighttime temperature rises is real, in and of itself it is probably relatively benign.

Some researchers also argue that even if global warming is occurring, its initial effects might be absorbed by the oceans as they heat up, so atmospheric global warming might be delayed for years, decades, or possibly even centuries. Even if this hypothesis is correct (and data to test it do not exist at present), global ocean warming could potentially have effects just as devastating as global atmospheric warming (especially given the role that oceans play in determining climatic conditions on the surface).

Another aspect of the oceans is that they store a tremendous amount of carbon. The oceans appear to have the capacity to continue to absorb and store much more carbon, but they can do so only at a certain maximum rate. At present, we have far exceeded the capacity of the oceans to absorb our excess CO_2 as fast as we emit it. The oceans now absorb approximately half of the excess CO_2 emitted by humans; the remainder collects in the atmosphere. Nevertheless, without the oceans, CO_2 would collect even faster in the atmosphere than it does currently.

General Circulation Models Among the primary research tools of climatologists are **general circulation models (GCMs)** of the atmosphere. Using GCMs some research groups have predicted that a doubling of the atmosphere's CO_2 levels (or the effective greenhouse equivalent of CO_2, such as smaller amounts of CFCs and methane) from about 300 ppm to 600 ppm will raise the average surface air temperature by about 7.2°F (4°C). Proponents of global warming have placed much emphasis on these predictions, but skeptics have pointed out the limitations of the current generation of GCMs.

GCMs are complex mathematical models that, with the help of supercomputers, simulate the Earth's climatic patterns. In typical GCMs the Earth's surface is conceptually covered with a number of huge boxes (each perhaps a few hundred miles [several hundred kilometers] long on a side, and a few miles [several kilometers] high) laid next to each other and stacked one atop another to a height of several tens of miles (tens of kilometers). Each model uses hundreds of thousands of such boxes. For each box a set of initial conditions is specified, such as air temperature and pressure; H_2O, CO_2, and other gas concentrations; and wind speed and direction. The model also includes expected inflows and outflows from one box to another and from/to the Earth's surface (e.g., CO_2, dust, and other substances spewed into the atmosphere, water evaporated from the oceans, rain and snow precipitated out) and outer space (e.g., incoming solar radiation); equations are used to calculate how matter and energy flow in, through, and out of each box. Once the mathematical model is devised and the initial data are inserted, the model is allowed to run reiteratively, generating predictions as to future climatic conditions on different parts of the Earth's surface.

The actual workings of the atmosphere are so complex, and so many variables and uncertainties are involved, that even the best GCMs are extremely crude in comparison. As a model is run for longer periods of time (to make predictions farther into the future), any errors inherent in the system will accumulate and multiply. Current GCMs are incapable of perfectly predicting present or, retrospectively (also known as retrodiction), past climates with any great accuracy. Critics conclude that predictions of future climatic conditions made by these GCMs are not to be believed. Some adherents of GCM methodology contend that the purpose of these models is not so much to precisely prognosticate the future, but to simply improve our understanding of the atmospheric phenomena being simulated. Even if we must take the actual predictions of the GCMs with a large grain of salt, they can help us make rational choices when it comes to human endeavors that affect the atmosphere and climate.

The use of GCMs is not the only way to model predicted global warming due to the greenhouse effect. Based on the greenhouse effects experienced on Venus and Mars, taking into account the atmospheric CO_2 pressures on these planets and their distances from the Sun, it has been predicted that increasing the effective CO_2 content of Earth's atmosphere to about 600 ppm will cause an average surface warming of only about 0.72°F (0.4°C), or about one-tenth of that predicted by many GCMs. Of course, this prediction is, in turn, disputed by many GCM theorists.

The Consensus View Despite the questions raised concerning the reality of global warming, it should be firmly emphasized here that the vast

TABLE 18–4 *Global Climate Change: The Scientific Consensus on Various Climate Change Issues*

The scientific consensus on global climate change is represented by the findings of the Intergovernmental Panel on Climate Change (IPCC), which brings together several hundred of the world's leading atmospheric scientists under the auspices of the World Meteorological Organization and the United Nations Environment Programme. What is that consensus in practical terms? Jerry Mahlman, director of the Geophysical Fluid Dynamics Laboratory of the U.S. National Oceanic and Atmospheric Administration, has attempted to answer that question by restating IPCC consensus in the following terms: *virtually certain* (nearly unanimous agreement among scientists and no credible alternative view), *very probable* (roughly a 9 out of 10 chance of occurring), *probable* (roughly a 2 out of 3 chance of occurring), and *uncertain* (hypothesized effect for which evidence is lacking).

ISSUE	STATEMENT	CONSENSUS
Basic characteristics	Fundamental physics of the greenhouse effect	Virtually certain
	Added greenhouse gases add heat	Virtually certain
	Greenhouse gases increasing because of human activity	Virtually certain
	Significant reduction of uncertainty will require a decade or more	Virtually certain
	Full recovery will require many centuries	Virtually certain
Projected effects by mid-21st century	Large stratospheric cooling	Virtually certain
	Global mean surface precipitation increase	Very probable
	Reduction of sea ice	Very probable
	Arctic winter surface warming	Very probable
	Rise in global sea level	Very probable
	Local details of climate change	Uncertain
	Tropical storm increases	Uncertain
	Details of next 25 years	Uncertain

(*Source:* World Resources Institute, *World Resources 1994–95* [New York: Oxford University Press, 1994], p. 205. Reprinted with permission from World Resources Institute.)

majority of scientists who have studied the problem are convinced that global warming is real and will change the distribution of resources across the Earth (Table 18–4). There is no doubt that the concentrations of greenhouse gases in our atmosphere are increasing dramatically due to human activities. It is known that these greenhouse gases trap heat that will increase the temperature of the Earth's surface. It is also known that as the Earth heats up, the warming will be unequally distributed, with higher latitudes generally warming up more relative to the lower latitudes; the least change will occur in the equatorial regions. If the rise in temperature is great enough, sea level will surely rise due to thermal expansion of the oceans and possibly the melting of ice. As Dr. James E. Hansen, director of NASA's Goddard Institute for Space Studies, stated in June 1988 at a U.S. Senate hearing, "The greenhouse effect has been detected and is changing our climate now."

What is unclear to many scientists is exactly what effects global warming will have. Exactly how much will the surface of Earth warm? How high will sea levels rise as glaciers melt and the oceans expand? What effect will global warming have on climatic patterns, including wind directions, rainfall patterns, and ocean currents? Has global warming actually begun, or is it still too early to detect it relative to the "background noise" of daily and seasonal temperature fluctuations? These questions may be partially to completely answered in the next half century, as we begin to directly observe more and more of the effects of global warming.

Sometimes experts appear to be at odds with each other on important questions, such as global warming, when in fact they actually agree more than they disagree. Paul and Anne Ehrlich cite an example in their book *Healing the Planet* (1991). In 1990 the statistician Andrew Solow stated that in his estimation the probability of significant climatic warming during the next century was "low" whereas the climatologist Stephen Schneider (National Center for Atmospheric Research) considered it "uncomfortably high." As it turned out, both men considered the probability of significant global warming to be at least 50%. As a statistician who considered results to be significant only if random events could be discounted 95% of the time, Solow considered a probability of only 50% to be low. For Schneider, the atmospheric scientist, a 50% chance was extremely high. Most people would consider even odds of 1 in 4 that major global warming could occur in the near future to be reason enough to take action to mitigate the greenhouse effect. Even if doubts remain about the probability, magnitude, and exact consequences of global warming in the future, it could be foolish to sit back and pursue "business as usual."

Consequences of Global Warming

Sometimes it is suggested that a little bit of global greenhouse warming might not be such a bad thing, especially for people who live in regions visited by harsh winters (see also the Case Study). But, in fact, global warming will not cause overall weather patterns to become consistently warmer and more equitable—indeed, just the opposite may occur in certain regions. As Earth heats up, climatic patterns will shift, and in some places local weather conditions will become much more violent. Cold air currents may be displaced such that, ironically, regions that are currently relatively warm may experience cold snaps and abnormal winter storms. Abnormal frosts that destroyed much of the Florida tomato crop in December 1989 and record low temperatures experienced in Chicago during January 1985 have been attributed to global warming. Due to shifting air currents caused by increased heating of the Earth's surface, cold air masses were displaced from the Arctic.

Climate and Weather

Atmospheric circulation, which ultimately causes what we see as weather (in the short term) and climate (in the longer term), is caused by the differential heating of air masses on the Earth's surface (see Chapter 2). Although establishing the exact effects global warming will have on these patterns is extremely difficult, some educated predictions can be ventured. As more heat is retained in the system, more air will move across the Earth's surface producing winds, clashing warm and cold fronts, and generally more violent weather conditions. Hurricanes, tornadoes, and other dangerous storms will increase in intensity. Some researchers attribute the record number of extremely damaging storms in the last decade to global warming.

Global warming will also dramatically change overall climatic patterns. With increased warming, evaporation from the oceans and other large water masses may increase, which will lead to higher levels of precipitation. But the increased precipitation will not necessarily occur where it falls now—with the changing air currents, the areas of rainfall will be displaced. The American Midwest, often referred to as the "breadbasket" of America (and the world), may experience such intense droughts that it will become a desert. The rain that would have fallen in this area may well be pushed north into Canada. Rainfall may also shift from one season to another; some agricul-

tural regions may receive more rain on average than at present, but the bulk of it will come during the winter months when it is of little use for crops. Changing rainfall patterns, coupled with the generally more violent weather, will cause increasing incidences of flash floods. Ironically, some areas will experience droughts and floods simultaneously; during the height of a drought, a violent cloudburst will cause rivers to swell and flood, but it will not replenish reservoirs, which require gentle, protracted rains in order to recharge.

Due to changing atmospheric circulation patterns, increased heat, and altered rainfall patterns, large portions of temperate regions could experience major declines in soil moisture. The agricultural productivity of these areas could decline, resulting in severe food shortages. An increase of only 3.6°F (2°C) might cause a decline in grain yields of up to 17% in North America and Europe. Unfortunately, the global food situation is already precarious (see Chapter 13); any disruptions due to greenhouse warming will not be easily rectified. Some crops will have a hard time growing under even slightly warmer conditions. Many fruit trees and berries need to be subjected to chilling before they will produce fruit.

It is sometimes naively suggested that global warming will simply push many major agricultural belts in the Northern Hemisphere further north; prime cropland will simply be redistributed. To a certain extent, this may be true. Alaska, Finland, and Denmark, for instance, may experience major increases in crop production. In contrast, the classic breadbaskets of central North America, Europe, the former Soviet Union, and portions of China will become much less productive. But one must remember that established farmers in the central United States are not likely to pack their bags and move north into Canada as global warming sets in. Furthermore, many nonclimatic factors must be considered. Even if warmer weather conditions might theoretically favor the cultivation of the northern Canadian prairies and boreal forests, the soils in these areas are not suitable for growing most food crops.

Another consideration is that global warming will not take place all at once. New climatic zones will not simply replace the old. Decades to centuries of very violent, wandering weather patterns may occur before the climate readjusts to a more or less stable equilibrium. Severe storms and unexpected cold snaps or heat spells are very damaging to any agricultural enterprise. The loss of food production could be one of the most serious immediate consequences of global warming.

The Benefits of CO₂

Some researchers argue that increasing the concentration of carbon dioxide in the atmosphere will have benefits that will far outweigh any deleterious "greenhouse effects." As is well known, CO_2 is an essential raw ingredient on which all photosynthetic green plants rely. There is evidence that throughout much of Earth's history the atmospheric carbon dioxide content was higher than it has been during humankind's existence; thus, many plants may have evolved to grow optimally in somewhat higher concentrations of CO_2. Experiments have shown that doubling the CO_2 content of the air (for instance, from 330 ppm to 660 ppm CO_2) will raise the productivity of many plants by about a third on average. That is, the plants produce more organic matter more efficiently. Yet some authorities contend that even if the rate of photosynthesis for many plants increases in the presence of elevated levels of CO_2, not all of the cultivated crops that humans currently depend upon may respond in this way.

Rising CO_2 concentrations also lead to a decrease in the transpiration (water loss by evaporation from the leaves) rate in many plants. Experiments have demonstrated that on average the amount of water lost by plants in this manner is decreased by one-third if CO_2 content is doubled from 330 to 660 ppm. Overall, this means many plants become much more efficient producers of organic matter as CO_2 concentrations increase; they produce more with less loss of water. Due to these benefits, many commercial nurseries routinely use a CO_2-enriched environment to grow plants (Fig. 1).

But even if increased concentrations of atmospheric CO_2 accelerate plant growth (although there is currently no unambiguous evidence that the increase in CO_2 in the atmosphere so far has produced this result), the ultimate outcome may not be beneficial from a human perspective. Weeds may proliferate more rapidly at the expense of other types of plants. Insects and other pests that feed on plants may also increase in numbers. Some studies demonstrate that certain insects

FIGURE 1

Many modern nurseries routinely use a CO_2-enriched environment to grow plants, such as this chrysanthemum crop. (*Source*: Holt Studios International (Nigel Cattlin)/Photo Researchers.)

feed more rapidly on plants in a high CO_2 environment. Apparently, the fast-growing plant leaves contain lower concentrations of essential nutrients (particularly nitrogen), so the insects must eat more in the same period of time. Other insects are incapable of using this strategy (perhaps they already feed as quickly as they can), and so are not as healthy under elevated CO_2 conditions. It might just be that the latter group of insects are necessary com-

ponents of the local ecosystem, perhaps the pollinators that ensure plant reproduction.

Human crops may also grow faster when subjected to higher concentrations of CO_2, but the growth may be concentrated in parts of the plant that are not consumed or used otherwise. Thus, the rapid growth may yield little net gain for humans.

More critical than any potential increase in plant production are the disruptions that will certainly occur due to increasing surface temperatures on Earth. Insect-plant relations will be assaulted. In higher-latitude temperate regions, the freezing conditions of the annual winter season are extremely important for containing the populations of insects that feed on human crops and other plants. If global warming occurs to the extent that it prevents or mitigates freezes and frosts in certain regions, insect pest populations will proliferate. Of course, the increases in violent storms and abnormal weather patterns that are expected due to global warming will not benefit plant production either, nor will encroaching oceans due to rising sea levels along currently productive coastal areas. These latter disruptions, which might actually decrease the overall net growth of many types of plants, are simply a function of global warming per se, whether this global warming is caused by CO_2 or other greenhouse gases (which do nothing to enhance the growth of plants).

Questions

1. Can the results of greenhouse experiments necessarily be extrapolated up to the scale of the entire Earth?
2. Even if increased concentrations of CO_2 may accelerate the growth of some types of plants, is this always beneficial? What types of unforeseen consequences might result from increased atmospheric concentrations of CO_2?
3. In your opinion, do the predicted "benefits" of increased atmospheric CO_2 concentrations justify—as some people argue—not taking action to counter the buildup of CO_2 in the atmosphere?

Not only will atmospheric circulation patterns change with global warming, but the paths of ocean currents will also be modified. Currently, for instance, cold water sinks in the Arctic Ocean and then travels southward along the bottom of the seas toward the equator. In the tropics the water is warmed and then moves north once again as a surface current, forming what can be thought of as a giant convection cell. With global warming the northern polar regions may heat up enough to disrupt the convection cell; adequate quantities of cold water will no longer sink to the bottom to drive the surface currents back to the pole. The Gulf Stream in particular may slow down, stop flowing, or even change its direction. This could dramatically change local weather and climate patterns. England's weather, for instance, is heavily influenced by the warm waters of the Gulf Stream passing by its shores. If global warming disrupts the Gulf Stream, British winters may become much colder and harsher. Also, disrupting deep-water currents may affect the circulation of nutrients in the oceans, exacting a heavy toll on extremely delicate ocean ecosystems.

Sea Levels

One of the most discussed effects of global warming is the predicted **rise in sea levels**. One study by the EPA predicted that sea levels could rise seven feet (2.2 m) by the year 2100, although some more recent studies, based on IPCC data, predict only a 19-inch (48 cm) rise by that time. But any significant rise in sea level, even a mere 19 inches,

could have devastating effects on the human population and global ecosystems. Approximately one-third of all people live within 37 miles (60 km) of the sea, often at elevations close to sea level, so a rise in sea level would affect them directly, driving them to higher ground. On the east coast of America, such cities as Boston, New York, and Washington, D.C. (to name just a few) would be prone to flooding. Of course, productive agricultural areas would be destroyed as well, fresh water supplies would be contaminated with sea water, coastal wetlands would be wiped out, and further climatic changes would take place. The IPCC estimated that a mere 3-foot (1 m) rise in global sea levels (a distinct possibility within the next few centuries given current trends in global warming) would flood almost 250,000 miles (402,250 km) of coastlines around the world.

Global warming can promote rises in sea level through several mechanisms. It is often suggested that increases in mean global temperature will cause mountain glaciers and polar ice caps to melt (■ Fig. 18–11). As the ice melts, the water will eventually empty into the oceans, raising their level. The gravest concern is that the Antarctic ice cap, which is two miles (3.2 km) thick in places and contains an estimated 80% of all the ice in the world, may undergo significant melting. If the entire Antarctic ice cap were to melt, the mean average sea level would be raised by almost 300 feet (90 m). (In fact, the average level of the oceans is about 200 feet (60 m) higher today than at the end of the last ice age about 10,000 years ago— much of this rise is attributed to the melting of great continental glaciers.) Realistically, though, not many scientists believe that the Antarctic ice cap will melt significantly or very quickly. This ice cap has lasted for about 10 million years, withstanding many warm and cold

■ **FIGURE 18–11**
The Antarctic home of these emperor penguins may be threatened by global warming. (*Source*: Kjell B. Sandved/Visuals Unlimited.)

spells. If it did begin to melt on a large scale, the melting would probably take place very slowly; the core of the ice cap is extremely cold (much colder than ice in many Northern Hemisphere glaciers, for instance) and ice forms a very good insulator. Even with extreme global warming, melting all of Antarctica's ice would take many thousands of years.

Of course, only a very small percentage of Antarctica's ice needs to melt to raise sea level by a few feet, causing global devastation. In recent decades ice shelves have been calving and breaking up, apparently due to warmer temperatures. The breakup and melting of floating ice shelves and icebergs has only a minor effect on global sea levels per se (since the ice is already in the water). But when Antarctic coastal shelf ice melts and breaks away, land-based ice creeps or slides down into the sea, replacing the ice that broke away; consequently, more water is added to the oceans, and the sea levels rise.

Global warming could also cause a rise in sea levels through thermal expansion of water. Liquid water expands and contracts slightly with changes in temperature. Given the tremendous volume of water in the world's oceans, even a slight expansion of the water due to global warming will cause a measurable rise in sea level.

When we speak of changes in sea level, we usually refer to global averages—but to the people or other organisms living near the shore the height that the sea reaches during exceptional high tides or major storms may be even more important. On a local or regional scale global warming will contribute to this aspect of "sea level" also. Increasingly violent storms such as typhoons and hurricanes, accompanied by high winds and changes in barometric pressure, will drive water high onto land. Changes in atmospheric pressure can actually pull the water up, locally raising sea level. Such storm surges will only increase as global warming continues.

Climate Zones and Biodiversity

In another major effect of greenhouse warming, the climatic zones on the Earth's surface will tend to shift from the equator toward the poles. The effects will be devastating for many ecosystems, but forests will be especially hard hit. As climatic zones migrate away from the equator, trees will find themselves living in environments for which they are not adapted. Very small changes in average temperatures could spell death for large tracts of forest. The decline of red spruce populations in the eastern United States since 1800 has been attributed to global warming. One analysis suggests that if the effective concentration of CO_2 in the atmosphere doubles, the ranges of such trees as the eastern hemlock, yellow birch, beech, and sugar maple would have to migrate 300 to 600 miles (480–965 km) north. If the warming occurs rapidly, as is expected, many of the trees will simply die.

Biodiversity, already under assault due to humankind (see Chapter 12), could be further reduced by rapid global warming. Many species of plants and animals require very narrow ranges of temperature and moisture. As greenhouse warming modifies their habitats, they will not be able to adapt or migrate quickly enough, and so will succumb. Species that live on mountaintops or in the high-latitude Arctic and Antarctic regions will have nowhere to relocate. Other animals that could possibly migrate to higher latitudes will be impeded by human barriers (such as roads, farms, and urban areas). Mangrove swamps and other coastal wetlands will be flooded by rising sea levels. Some wildlife will find themselves trapped in artificial wildlife preserves that were originally designed to protect them. Already global warming may be exacting its toll on some relatively immobile species. In Canada long-term studies have documented decreased amounts of ice and longer ice-free seasons on some lakes, and this is affecting the relative populations of various aquatic species. In the Caribbean, corals have been dying; some biologists believe this is due to rising sea temperatures.

General Strategies for Dealing with Global Warming

There are three basic attitudes toward, and ways of dealing with, the potential of massive global warming: (1) The Waiting Strategy holds that since all the data are not yet in, we should wait before taking substantive measures to combat global warming (perhaps the predictions are simply wrong). (2) The Worst Case Scenario Strategy says we should assume that the most pessimistic predictions are valid and act accordingly. (3) The Compromise Strategy says we should follow a path that is environmentally safe and promotes the general well-being of the planet, whether global warming turns out to be a valid phenomenon or not.

Each of these strategies has proponents and opponents. The Reagan and Bush administrations strongly espoused the Waiting Strategy. Their position was that the reality and magnitude of global warming, and its causes, had not yet been

definitively "proven" scientifically, and without such proof, taking serious steps to reduce CO_2 emissions would be premature and inappropriate. National policies, it was argued, must be based only on hard facts. Any actions that would significantly reduce emissions of greenhouse gases would impose a heavy financial burden on the country; enormous amounts of money would be spent, economic output could decrease, and jobs might be lost. Such pain might be for naught if the predicted global warming turned out to be either false or grossly overestimated.

The problem with the Waiting Strategy is that if global warming is real, dealing with the eventual problems (both economic and otherwise) will be more painful and costly than taking measures at an earlier stage. This line of thinking leads some people to argue that even though all the data are not yet in, we should not take the chance that the more pessimistic scenarios will turn out to be true. Those advocating the Worst Case Scenario Strategy believe that as a form of insurance, we should do everything we can to prevent potential global warming. Thus, we should significantly decrease the burning of fossil fuels, halt deforestation, reduce cattle production, reforest areas that have been clear-cut, and so on. If all the appropriate actions are taken, and extreme global warming never occurs, we may never know whether human actions prevented a disaster or whether the predictions were simply incorrect. However, taking no action at all would be taking an unacceptable risk.

The Compromise Strategy, sometimes referred to as the "no regrets strategy" or the "tie-in strategy," takes a middle-of-the-road approach. Its advocates argue that we should develop policies and take actions that will help prevent the worst of global warming while benefiting the environment and society otherwise. For instance, increasing conservation and raising energy efficiencies, curbing the use of fossil fuels, and placing more reliance on renewable energy sources will benefit humankind in the long run whether global warming is real or not. Independent of the greenhouse effect, acid rain and general air pollution will be reduced, decreased coal mining and oil drilling will help preserve the landscape, and reduced dependence on oil in particular will lessen dependence on foreign energy supplies. The main problem with the Compromise Strategy is that if the most dire predictions turn out to be true, the moderate response may be inadequate—too little, too late.

So far, most governments have pursued a weak compromise strategy and taken relatively little ac-

tion. As a result of the 1992 Earth Summit sponsored by the United Nations in Rio de Janeiro, Brazil, over 160 countries signed the United Nations **Framework Convention on Climate Change**. Although the convention establishes no legal obligations or specific target dates, it requires signing countries to use their best efforts to control emissions of greenhouse gases. The convention suggests that emissions of greenhouse gases be stabilized at 1990 levels by the year 2000. By the beginning of 1994, enough nations had ratified the convention to make it a legal document. According to its provisions, certain nations must now produce a national action plan (NAP) explaining the policies they are following to reduce greenhouse emissions and projecting the levels of emissions they intend to allow in the future. The NAPs will then be submitted to a Conference of Parties (established by the convention) for review. The hope is that the participants will then be able to establish specific, legally binding emissions levels.

According to many scientists, the Climate Convention does not go nearly far enough; for instance, the IPCC has estimated that greenhouse gas emissions must be reduced to 60% of 1990 levels just to stabilize the climate. Nevertheless, many commentators view the 1992 convention as an important first step. In 1995 delegates of the countries that ratified the 1992 Rio agreement met in Berlin and agreed to negotiate a new set of targets for reduced emissions of greenhouse gases within the next few years.

Measures to Combat Global Warming

If global warming is real and the worst effects take place, in crude economic terms the devastation that could result around the world will cost tens of trillions of dollars in the long run. One study estimated that an effective doubling of greenhouse gases would lead to economic losses of $58 billion a year for the United States; the largest single loss would be $18 billion a year in agriculture; other losses would come from increased electricity use for air conditioning, urban air pollution, storm damage, reduced water supplies, rising sea levels, reduced lumber yields of forests, increased illness and death due to heat stress, and so forth. A 1990 U.S. government report estimated that instituting the necessary measures to control emissions of greenhouse gases might cost $1 trillion over the next century. However, this is only about $10 billion a year. In 1990 the United States imported over $50 billion worth of imported oil, so cutting our oil imports by 20%

would not only cover the projected costs of greenhouse gas abatement measures, but would also reduce our dependence on foreign oil.

The main ways to control the greenhouse effect are to cut down on emissions of CO_2 and CFCs into the atmosphere and to restore or provide additional sinks for CO_2. Interestingly, virtually all measures that curb greenhouse gas emissions have additional benefits as well. Thus, reducing emissions of CFCs and related gases will help protect the ozone layer as well as helping to mitigate the greenhouse effect.

CO_2 emissions can be readily controlled by increasing energy efficiency and decreasing global dependence on fossil fuels (see Chapter 7). Of course, decreasing our use of fossil fuels offers other benefits as well including reducing air pollution and acid rain, protecting the landscape, and extending the time that our finite supplies of these fuels will last. Alternative, nonpolluting, cleaner energy sources, such as solar and wind technologies, need to be further developed and implemented (see Chapter 9). Nuclear power may also play a much larger role in the future since this form of energy emits very little in the way of greenhouse gases. As Chapter 8 explained, however, there are other drawbacks to increasing our dependence on nuclear power.

One way to discourage the burning of fossil fuels is to impose a **"carbon tax"** on their consumption. A carbon tax is levied in proportion to the amount of carbon emitted during combustion of a particular fossil fuel; accordingly, coal would generally be taxed at a higher rate than natural gas. Such a tax would encourage more efficient energy use and the development of non-carbon-emitting energy technologies; it would also bring the price of burning fossil fuels more in line with the environmental costs they entail (see Chapter 20). The amount of money that could be raised with carbon taxes is truly staggering: in 1990 the Congressional Budget Office estimated that a tax of $28 per ton (0.907 metric ton) of carbon content in fossil fuels would raise over $30 billion a year. Although not strictly a carbon tax, every penny added to the federal taxes on a gallon (3.785 L) of gasoline contributes about $1 billion annually in revenue to the U.S. government.

An argument often heard against carbon taxes is that they are regressive. That is, relatively poorer people pay a much higher proportion of their income for energy than do richer people; therefore, any carbon tax will extract a relatively higher proportion of the income of the poor than of the rich (even if the rich pay a higher amount of carbon tax in absolute terms). A solution might be to couple a stiff carbon tax with lower Social Security and income taxes for the poor.

Another suggestion is to institute a standardized system of emissions permits, on both a national and a global level, that would allow a company or organization to emit a certain amount of CO_2 and other pollutants into the atmosphere. These permits could be sold or traded, so a firm that did not emit its allotted amount of pollutants could sell the "right" to emit the pollutants to another firm. Such a system has been used to control air pollution in California for a number of years and was established at a national level by the 1990 Clean Air Amendments.

Besides the burning of fossil fuels, another important source of greenhouse gases is the CO_2 released during deforestation (Fig. 18–12). A "simple" solution to this problem is to stop cut-

FIGURE 18-12
Deforestation can be clearly seen in this Landsat satellite image of part of the Amazon Basin, Brazil. The original natural forest is dark green; the pale greens, yellows, and browns mark leveled forest. (*Source*: Geospace/Science Source/Photo Researchers.)

ting and burning forests, but, of course, real life is not so simple. Deforestation occurs because people or governments find it to be economically profitable. Nevertheless, saving the Earth's forests will not only help abate the greenhouse effect, but will contribute to the preservation of biodiversity, help protect soils, ameliorate climatic extremes, and serve many other useful and necessary functions (see Chapter 12).

In addition to reducing emissions of greenhouse gases, we can develop sinks that will absorb CO_2. Perhaps the easiest way to do this is to plant trees. Trees, like all photosynthetic plants, convert gaseous CO_2 into a solid form such as cellulose (essentially wood fiber) where it is stored until the tree is burned or allowed to decompose. Planting billions and billions of trees will not only help reduce CO_2 levels in the atmosphere but will restore many of our devastated forests, add scenic beauty, help stabilize eroding soils, provide habitats for wildlife, and help ameliorate climatic extremes. A couple of well-placed shade trees can help keep a house cool in the summer, thus significantly cutting down on the amount of energy needed to air-condition or otherwise cool the house.

The greenhouse effect and stratospheric ozone depletion are both global problems that require global solutions. The ozone problem is now being addressed, and around the world solutions are being implemented. Perhaps this has set a precedent for global cooperation in the face of a potential global disaster. In many respects, greenhouse warming is a much more difficult problem to tackle, however, because greenhouse gases come from many diverse sources and the evidence for global warming is less clear-cut than that for ozone depletion. Consequently, there is less scientific and political consensus concerning the severity of the threat of global warming or how best to address the issue. Still, in the case of greenhouse emissions, every contribution toward the ultimate solution counts. And, as we have seen, the beauty of almost all actions that can be taken to fight global warming is that they offer numerous other benefits in their own right. They are classic examples of "win-win" strategies where everyone stands to benefit.

S UMMARY

Two potential global environmental problems may pose imminent threats to the health and well-being of humans and indeed all of life on Earth: abnormally high incidences of ultraviolet radiation on the Earth's surface due to the depletion of stratospheric ozone, and climatic change (global warming) due to the artificial introduction of large amounts of greenhouse gases into the atmosphere. The two problems are interrelated—both are caused by human-produced gases released into the atmosphere, and in some cases the same gases are implicated in both problems. They differ however, in that there is a general scientific and political consensus concerning the deterioration of the ozone layer, whereas potential global warming remains subject to controversy.

Stratospheric ozone, O_3, naturally absorbs UV radiation (particularly UV-B), thus shielding the Earth's surface from large amounts of UV. Increased UV radiation exposure can result in many deleterious effects, including increases in skin cancer and cataracts among humans, the inhibition of photosynthetic processes in certain plants, the disruption of insect activity, and decreases in the productivity of ocean ecosystems. Disruptions of the ozone layer could also cause the stratosphere to cool, potentially affecting climatic patterns on Earth.

The problem of stratospheric ozone depletion, due in large part to the release of chlorofluorocarbons (CFCs) into the atmosphere, was first discovered in the 1970s, and by the late 1980s and early 1990s, an international solution had been reached. The 1987 Montreal Protocol called for a gradual decrease in global CFC production, but as continued data confirmed the severity of the problem, the timetable for CFC phaseouts was twice moved up: the most recent revision in 1992 calls for all CFCs to be phased out by January 1, 1996 (with a 10-year grace period for developing countries). Even with this action, the CFCs already released into the atmosphere may continue to damage the ozone layer for some years to come. Nevertheless, the global cooperation exhibited in addressing the ozone depletion problem is reassuring and may be a model for other environmental issues.

Many trace atmospheric gases, such as carbon dioxide, methane, water vapor, and CFCs (CFCs do not occur naturally, but are solely human-made), are relatively transparent to sunlight but trap or reflect longer-wave infrared radiation (heat). Thus, the greenhouse gases act as a one-way filter, allowing energy in the form of sunlight to enter the lower atmosphere and strike the Earth's surface, but stopping much of the longer-wavelength heat from escaping. This results in the heating of the Earth's surface and lower atmosphere—the greenhouse effect. Without a natural greenhouse effect, the surface of Earth would be a frozen mass, but too much greenhouse effect could also cause abnormal global warming.

Since the Industrial Revolution, and especially since the beginning of the twentieth century, humans have been releasing increasing quantities of greenhouse gases into the atmosphere. The levels of greenhouse gases in the atmosphere, particularly carbon dioxide, have been rising dramatically (about 250 parts per million CO_2 in 1850 to about 360 ppm CO_2 currently) due, in large measure, to the burning of fossil fuels (coal, oil, and natural gas). Many climatologists are concerned that the increasing levels of greenhouse gases will cause a pattern of global warming. Some researchers contend that this predicted global warming trend has already begun: record highs in global mean temperature have been reached in the late 1980s and 1990s, ocean-surface temperatures seem to have increased over the last decade or more, and nonpolar glaciers have generally been retreating since the last century. Furthermore, certain computer models predict that increased greenhouse gases in the atmosphere will invariably lead to global warming. Still, a minority of scientists remain skeptical, questioning both the accuracy and interpretations of the raw data and the climatological models used to predict global warming.

If global warming is real, and mean world temperatures increase by even a couple of degrees, the consequences could be severe. Atmospheric circulation patterns and climatic zones could be displaced, generally more violent weather conditions might prevail in some areas, and natural vegetation and agricultural patterns could be severely disrupted. Rainfall may be displaced geographically and temporally (from one season to another). Droughts may occur in areas that currently support major crop production. Due to the thermal expansion of the oceans and the melting of glacial ice, sea levels may also rise, perhaps on the order of 19 inches (0.5 m) to over 6.5 feet (2 m), flooding low-lying coastal areas around the world.

At the 1992 Earth Summit held in Rio de Janeiro; more than 160 countries signed the United Nations Framework Convention on Climate Change, promising to use their best efforts to reduce greenhouse emissions—with a goal of stabilizing greenhouse emissions at 1990 levels by the year 2000. But according to many scientists, such as the United Nations Intergovernmental Panel on Climate Change (IPCC), the Climate Convention's measures are not strong enough. The IPCC has estimated that a 60% reduction in greenhouse gas emissions below 1990 levels will be required merely to stabilize the climate. Still, many commentators view the 1992 convention as an important first step toward establishing more specific and binding treaties regulating greenhouse gas emissions.

KEY TERMS

aerosol spray
carbon dioxide
carbon emissions
carbon tax
cataracts
chlorine
chlorofluorocarbon (CFC)
Framework Convention on
  Climate Change
General Circulation Model (GCM)

greenhouse effect
greenhouse gas
heat
ice age
infrared radiation
Intergovernmental Panel on Climate
  Change (IPCC)
Little Ice Age
melanoma
methane
Montreal Protocol

Mount Pinatubo
Nimbus-7
nitrogen oxides
ozone
ozone layer
radiation
sea level rise
stratosphere
troposphere
ultraviolet radiation (UV)

STUDY QUESTIONS

1. Briefly list some of the technological ways in which the Japanese hope to solve the problems of stratospheric ozone deterioration and global greenhouse warming.

2. What is the history of ozone layer deterioration? When was the problem first discovered? How long did it take for the world community to be convinced action should be taken?

3. What are CFCs?

4. Why were CFCs invented? What applications did they have?

5. How do CFCs damage the ozone layer?

6. What is the importance of the ozone layer? What effects will significant thinning of the ozone layer have?

7. Besides CFCs, what other substances can harm the ozone layer?

8. Discuss how tropospheric air pollution may be masking the effects of a decreased ozone layer.

9. What are some of the major greenhouse gases?

10. Describe how the greenhouse effect promotes global warming.

11. Which countries are currently the biggest contributors to potential global warming?

12. How fast have greenhouse gases been accumulating in the atmosphere during this century? Based on the work and projections of various climatologists, how much might the Earth heat up? Would the heating be evenly distributed over the Earth's surface?

13. List some of the potential consequences of significant global warming.

14. Given that the concentration of CO_2 in the atmosphere increased from 316 ppm (parts per million) in 1959 to 357 ppm in 1994, what percentage increase occurred over this period?

15. Given that the concentration of CO_2 in the atmosphere increased from 250 ppm (parts per million) in 1850 to 357 ppm in 1994, what percentage increase occurred over this period?

1. How do the problems of ozone destruction and global warming differ from one another? In what ways are they similar?

2. Describe how humans will be able to manage without CFCs and other ozone-destroying chemicals in the twenty-first century.

3. Discuss the Montreal Protocol and its subsequent amendments.

4. What is the nature of the controversy surrounding potential global warming? Is the evidence for substantial global warming convincing to you? Why or why not?

5. What can, is being, and should (in your opinion) be done to combat global warming? How serious do you think the problem really is? (Be sure to fully justify your answer.)

SUGGESTED READINGS

Brown, L. R., ed. 1991. *The World Watch reader on global environmental issues*. New York: W. W. Norton.

Brown, L. R., N. Lenssen, and H. Kane. 1995. *Vital signs 1995: The trends that are shaping our future*. New York: W. W. Norton.

Cagin, S., and P. Dray. 1993. *Between Earth and sky: How CFCs changed our world and endangered the ozone layer*. New York: Pantheon Books.

Easterbrook, G. 1995. *A moment on the Earth: The coming age of environmental optimism*. New York: Viking.

Ehrlich, P. R., and A. H. Ehrlich. 1991. *Healing the planet: Strategies for resolving the environmental crisis*. Reading, Mass.: Addison-Wesley.

Fisher, D. E. 1990. *Fire and ice: The greenhouse effect, ozone depletion and nuclear winter*. New York: Harper & Row.

Goudie, A. 1990. *The human impact on the natural environment*, 3d ed. Cambridge, Mass.: MIT Press.

Gribbin, J. 1990. *Hothouse Earth: The greenhouse effect and Gaia*. New York: Grove Weidenfeld.

Hollander, J. M. 1992. *The energy-environment connection*. Washington, D.C.: Island Press.

Karplus, W. J. 1992. *The heavens are falling*. New York: Plenum Press.

Kemp, D. D. 1990. *Global environmental issues: A climatological approach*. London and New York: Routledge.

Lehr, J. 1992. *Rational readings on environmental concerns*. New York: Van Nostrand Reinhold.

Levenson, T. 1989. *Ice time: Climate, science, and life on Earth*. New York: Harper & Row.

Mannion, A. M. 1991. *Global environmental change: A natural and cultural history*. New York: John Wiley.

Oppenheimer, M., and R. H. Boyle. 1990. *Dead heat: The race against the greenhouse effect*. New York: Basic Books.

Rifkin, J., with T. Howard. 1989. *Entropy: Into the greenhouse world*, rev. ed. New York: Bantam Books.

Sitarz, D., ed. 1993. *Agenda 21: The Earth Summit strategy to save our planet*. Boulder, Colo.: Earthpress.

Turner, B. L., II, W. C. Clark, R. W. Kates, J. F. Richards, J. T. Mathews, and W. B. Meyer, eds. 1990. *The Earth as transformed by human action*. Cambridge: Cambridge University Press.

World Resources Institute. 1994. *World Resources 1994–95*. New York: Oxford University Press.

CHAPTER *19*

MUNICIPAL SOLID WASTE AND HAZARDOUS WASTE

PROLOGUE   *Recycling in East Hampton*

The town of East Hampton on Long Island, New York, needed to design a new trash disposal system, but the citizens were not sure how to go about it. They decided to ask the advice of the Center for Biology of Natural Systems (CBNS, Queens College, New York), directed by the well-known environmentalist Barry Commoner. CBNS designed a recycling program for the town and then implemented the system among one hundred households for 10 weeks as a test of its feasibility. Each household was given a set of four containers and instructions on how to sort its trash into garbage and yard clippings to be composted, paper, cans and bottles, and other trash. The participating households delivered their separated garbage to a tent next to the landfill (East Hampton residents were already responsible for carting their trash to the dump). There the

PHOTO   *Curbside recycling in the Washington, D.C., area. (Source: Robert Visser/Greenpeace.)*

recyclable materials were sorted further: different types of paper sorted out, cans and other metals separated from glass, and so on. The food and yard waste, along with sludge from the town's sewage treatment plant, was composted.

At the end of the 10-week test CBNS found that more than 80% of the total trash brought in was recyclable using the methods employed. The compost was tested for toxic metals and other substances and found to be suitable for use by gardeners and other people in need of fresh compost. The paper, cans, and glass were transported to a materials recovery facility in Groton, Connecticut, where they were further sorted and then marketed. Part of the nonrecyclable trash consisted of plastics that with developing technology might also be recyclable in the near future: thus, the recovery rate could potentially be raised even higher.

Based on the test, CBNS next designed a full-scale recycling system for the entire town. Such a system reduces the amount of trash that must finally be disposed of in a landfill by about the same amount as incineration—typically, an incinerator burns about 70% by weight of the trash and leaves about 30% as an ash residue to be disposed of by other means. More importantly, the trash residue left after implementation of an intensive recycling program is generally much less hazardous than the toxic ash that remains after incineration. And, of course, with recycling, the 70% reduction in waste is accomplished by placing serviceable raw materials back into the manufacturing loop. Furthermore, using recycled materials to produce new bottles, cans, or newspaper results in a significant savings in energy. In contrast, with incineration these precious raw materials of the "urban ore" go up in smoke or are reduced to potentially hazardous ash, causing potential health problems for those who live in the plant's vicinity. The only thing that is recoverable is some heat that can be used to generate electricity.

CBNS estimated that operating an intensive recycling program would cost East Hampton about 35% less than building and operating an incinerator. All in all, recycling seemed to make sense for East Hampton, and in April 1989 the Town Board adopted the intensive recycling program for trash disposal.

𝒥 NTRODUCTION

The amount of waste generated each year is staggering. No one really knows how much waste humans generate, but much of it originates from the developed countries (poverty tends to generate less waste). Just as the United States is a leader in energy consumption and pollution, this country also produces the most waste per capita. Estimates of the amount of solid waste generated by the United States range from 6 to 10 billion tons (5.4–9 billion metric tons)* a year (depending on how "solid waste" is defined and how the estimates are calculated). Using the former figure, this amounts to about 24 tons (21.8 metric tons) of waste a year for every American or slightly more than 130 pounds (59 kg) of waste a day. Now the average person does not literally throw away 130 pounds of trash each day. Most waste in the United States comes from mining, agricultural, and industrial operations; but ultimately these operations exist to feed and provide for the necessities and desires of the consuming public. The trash that individuals put out for the garbage collector, the **municipal solid waste** (old

newspapers, packaging materials, empty bottles, and so forth), makes up only a bit more than 3% of America's waste ( Fig. 19–1), but this still

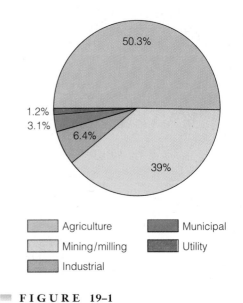

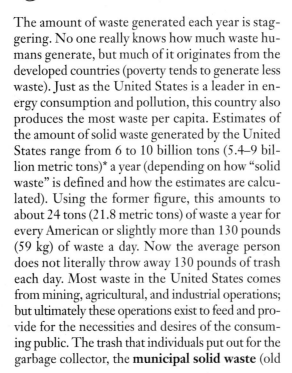

- Agriculture
- Mining/milling
- Industrial
- Municipal
- Utility

FIGURE 19–1

A breakdown, by percentage, of the approximately 6 to 10 billion tons (5.4–9 billion metric tons) of solid waste generated annually in the United States. (*Source:* Environmental Protection Agency.)

---

* Unless otherwise noted, *tons* refers to short tons (2000 pounds).

www.jbpub.com/environet

amounts to nearly 200 million tons (181.5 million metric tons) per year. The average American directly disposes of a little over four pounds (1.8 kg) of trash and garbage each day, significantly more than just a few decades ago (● Table 19–1) and also more than is generated per person in various other countries (▬ Fig. 19–2).

𝒟 EFINING WASTE

Although the words **trash**, **garbage**, **rubbish**, and **refuse**—are often used as synonyms in casual discussions, each has a different and specific technical meaning. *Trash* refers to things like old paper, newspaper, boxes, cans, containers, and so on—generally, objects that are "dry" and nonedible. *Garbage* refers to "wet" discarded matter, such as old food remains, yard waste like grass clippings, dead animals, leftovers from meat packing operations and butcher shops (such as the viscera of slaughtered animals), and so on. Generally, garbage is edible and was often kept separate from trash in the past so that it could be fed to pigs. Today some types of garbage are useful for composting. *Refuse* technically refers to both trash and garbage, while *rubbish* includes not only refuse but also construction and demolition debris, such as old boards, bricks, cinderblocks, beams, tar paper, shingles, and so on. Ultimately, all of these sorts of rubbish are finding their way into our modern landfills.

Here we should point out that no matter what we want to call it or how we wish to define it, waste is a characteristically human concept. Generally, waste per se is not found in nature (although "pollution" may occur naturally in some instances, as when a volcano releases gases that promote acid rain). In a typical ecosystem, there is no waste—the "waste" of one organism is the necessary raw material that another organism depends upon (see Chapter 3). Only humans typically discard waste that cannot be readily recycled and reused by other parts of the biosphere.

Solid Waste

Solid waste, broadly defined, includes a number of items that are not generally thought of as "solid." Certainly, household garbage, trash, refuse, and rubbish are all solid waste, but so too are solids, various semisolids, liquids, and even gases that result from mining, agricultural, commercial, and industrial activities. Often substances such as liquids and gases are confined in solid containers and disposed of with more conventional solid wastes. Sewage, effluent, and

TABLE 19–1 *U.S. per Capita Garbage Output, 1960, 1980, 1995, and 2000 (Projection), in Pounds Per Day*

Note that one pound equals 2.205 kilograms.

WASTE MATERIAL	1960	1980	1995	2000
Total nonfood and nonyard wastes:	1.65	2.57	3.18	3.38
Paper and paperboard	0.91	1.32	1.80	1.96
Glass	0.20	0.36	0.23	0.21
Metals	0.32	0.35	0.34	0.35
Plastics	0.01	0.19	0.40	0.43
Rubber and leather	0.06	0.10	0.10	0.11
Textiles	0.05	0.06	0.09	0.09
Wood	0.09	0.12	0.16	0.17
Other	0.01	0.07	0.06	0.06
Other wastes:				
Food wastes	0.37	0.32	0.28	0.27
Yard wastes	0.61	0.66	0.69	0.70
Miscellaneous organic wastes	0.03	0.06	0.06	0.06
Total waste	2.66	3.61	4.21	4.41

(*Source:* Environmental Protection Agency.)

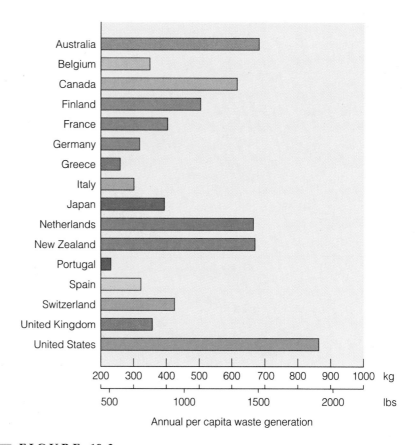

▬ **FIGURE 19–2**

Annual municipal waste generated per person in selected developed nations (note that the data in this figure are for comparative purposes only; due to differences in methods of estimating and accounting, the annual waste generated per person in the United States as shown here does not precisely agree with the data given in Table 19–1).
(*Source:* Data compiled from World Resources Institute, *World Resources 1992–93* [New York: Oxford University Press, 1992], p. 319.)

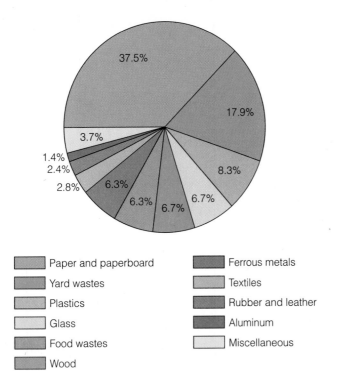

Paper and paperboard	Ferrous metals
Yard wastes	Textiles
Plastics	Rubber and leather
Glass	Aluminum
Food wastes	Miscellaneous
Wood	

FIGURE 19–3
The typical composition of municipal solid waste in the United States according to the weight of various types of materials. Note that due to various rounding, categorization, and estimation factors, the percentages shown here may not agree precisely with those in Table 19–1. (*Source:* Environmental Protection Agency.)

wastewater from commercial enterprises, organizations, and private homes are not solid waste, but once wastewater is treated and various residues are removed from the water to form sludge, the sludge is usually treated as a form of solid waste. Solid waste may be divided into two broad categories depending on its origination: municipal solid waste (produced by various institutions, businesses, and private homes) and industrial solid waste. Another useful distinction is between **hazardous waste** (see page 549) and nonhazardous waste.

It is interesting to look at the composition of typical American municipal solid waste (Fig. 19–3). The largest single component, whether measured by weight or by volume, is paper and paperboard products; other significant components include yard waste (which can easily be composted), plastics (about 8.3% by weight, but almost 20% by volume), metals, glass, and food scraps. The Case Study examines one of the more controversial components of solid waste.

ALTERNATIVE PARADIGMS FOR WASTE MANAGEMENT

For most of human history, wastes were usually disposed of by a "dilute and disperse" strategy. Early gathering and hunting cultures simply left their trash where it fell, and moved on. In the Preindustrial and early Industrial Age, settlements,

communities, and factories were often located near waterways. Streams and rivers not only supplied fresh water from upstream, but also provided a convenient way to get rid of wastes. Waste materials were dumped into the river and washed away. As the water flowed downstream, the wastes and pollutants became less concentrated and were also naturally filtered out or absorbed by organisms and sediments. Wastes were often simply dumped into the seemingly infinite reservoirs of the atmosphere and the oceans. Most rivers eventually run to the sea, and coastal cities could dump raw sewage and waste directly into the ocean. Tall smokestacks could inject waste, in the form of gases and fine particulate matter (smoke), into the skies.

At the beginning of the Industrial Age, two hundred years ago, many philosophers and social thinkers could not conceive of a time when, on a global scale, we would begin to run out of clean air and fresh water—but this is in fact just what is happening (as we examined in Chapters 16–18). Today the pollution of industrial humanity is found throughout the globe, even in the most remote and isolated areas. It has become clear that the dilute and disperse approach to waste management is no longer valid as a general paradigm. The capacities of Earth's natural ecosystems and reservoirs (sinks) for absorbing human-produced wastes are being reached and surpassed. In many cases the natural systems have been so overloaded that not only are they incapable of dealing with all the human-produced waste hurled into them, but they are actually damaged by the excess waste with the result that they can no longer function effectively and efficiently.

Humans have produced innumerable new types of waste that nature was never equipped to deal with, such as new elements (for instance, plutonium and other artificially produced elements and isotopes), synthetic compounds (CFCs, assorted types of plastics, synthetic pesticides, fertilizers, and so forth), and extremely concentrated quantities of substances that are found in nature only in very dilute form, such as heavy metals given off by factory operations. Even under the best of conditions, with certain types of waste, the dilute and disperse strategy will do only that—dilute and disperse—since natural systems lack the capability to absorb and nullify these wastes. Long-lived radioactive isotopes or synthetic compounds simply accumulate throughout the globe.

By the early twentieth century, it was clear that the dilute and disperse strategy had reached its practical limits, and a new concept was introduced—"concentrate and contain." Concentration

The Controversy over Disposable Diapers

In many people's minds, disposable diapers have come to symbolize the garbage crisis. No one can help being aware of them: an estimated 16 billion disposable diapers are added to America's solid waste each year, and disposable diapers are available in over 80 countries around the world. Some of these diapers end up littering our streets, parks, beaches, and sidewalks. But ultimately most end up being incinerated or put into long-term storage in a sanitary landfill. An estimated 85% to 90% of all American babies wear disposable diapers.

People often simply assume that using cloth diapers is the environmentally correct thing to do, and that the contribution of disposable diapers to municipal solid waste must be enormous. But the case for or against disposable diapers is far from clear-cut. Just how big a problem are they?

The best studies done to date, undertaken by the Garbage Project based at the University of Arizona, have found that disposable diapers on average constitute no more than 1.4% (the range was from 0.53% to 1.82%) of the volume of the contents of the typical landfill. This is a significant percentage for a single type of product—although it hardly compares with certain other types of wastes, like newspapers, that are filling up landfills much faster. Even if the actual bulk of disposable diapers being deposited into landfills is not as great as some people had previously estimated, don't the pathogenic microorganisms introduced into a landfill by the feces in the diapers pose a potential public health threat? The Garbage Project's studies indicate that this idea too is based on misconceptions. It turns out that the number

of pathogenic microorganisms in a landfill is not significantly increased by the addition of used disposable diapers. In fact, detailed studies demonstrated that any living microorganisms found in soiled diapers quickly die under the harsh, toxic conditions in the interior of a sanitary landfill.

What about the costs and benefits of cloth versus disposable diapers in terms of energy use, raw material use, and pollution produced? At first thought, many environmentally oriented consumers simply assume that cloth diapers are the lesser of two evils. Cloth diapers are washed and reused 50 or a 100 times or more before being discarded, whereas large quantities of energy go into making each disposable diaper out of plastic and wood pulp. However, various studies comparing the actual raw materials and energy use, along with the attendant pollution, per baby change for cloth versus disposable diapers have arrived at mixed results—there seems to be no clear consensus that one type of diaper is more environmentally benign. The problems with disposable diapers are relatively clear-cut: they use raw resources and fill our landfills or must be incinerated, adding to pollution. Disposable diaper advocates, however, point out that cloth diapers are also environmentally damaging. Cotton must be grown to manufacture the diapers, and large applications of pesticides, representing large amounts of energy and harmful pollution as the excess pesticides enter the ecosystem, are used on most commercial cotton fields. Many cotton fields are also artificially irrigated. Laundering the reusable cotton diapers requires enormous amounts of energy and water and adds a filthy component

to the sewage system that must then be treated. Some studies (admittedly undertaken by proponents of disposable diapers) have concluded that the energy costs, and pollution produced, per cloth diaper use are greater than the energy used to produce, and waste generated by, a single disposable diaper. All things considered, the only clear-cut difference between disposable diapers and reusable diapers from the point of view of the average consumer is that disposable diapers are much more expensive (up to three times as expensive per change) but much more convenient. Due to their convenience, some day-care centers require the use of disposable diapers. Statistics show that when it comes to changing a baby's diaper, most Americans choose convenience most of the time, even if it costs ten or twenty cents more each time.

Questions

1. Do you believe many members of the general public hold misconceptions concerning disposable versus cloth diapers? Can this diaper controversy be legitimately treated as a microcosm of larger environmental issues?

2. Taking everything into account, which do you think are more environmentally benign, cloth or disposable diapers? Should the cloth versus disposable diaper debate be made an "environmental issue" or are there more important issues to worry about?

3. When it comes right down to it, what is the first consideration that most people take into account when deciding what type of diapers to use? How does this attitude reflect many people's views concerning larger environmental issues?

of waste has been utilized to a certain extent for many millennia. North American natives concentrated oyster shells in huge middens, and the ancient cities of the Old World developed large urban trash heaps (which are now much sought after by archaeologists). In many cases concentration was only the first step toward ultimate dispersal. Trash might be collected and brought to a dump to be burned, and the ashes then thrown into a river or harbor. The relatively modern con-

cept of concentration and containment is to collect waste and then permanently isolate it from the rest of the environment. Sanitary landfills and hazardous and radioactive waste disposal sites are tangible expressions of the concentration and containment strategy of waste management. Often the dilute and disperse and concentrate and contain strategies are used in tandem, as in some incinerator operations. Rubbish may be burned in an incinerator, dispersing into the atmosphere a good percentage of its original volume (60% or more), but the remaining bottom ash and collected fly ash constitute a highly concentrated, and often toxic, waste product that must be isolated from the environment, usually by being permanently contained in a specially designed **landfill**. (Bottom ash collects in the bottom of the incinerator, and fly ash is removed from the smoke in the incinerator's chimney.)

There are numerous problems with the concentrate and contain strategy, especially as it is applied to modern industrial wastes. Many modern wastes are synthetic or artificial in nature and are extremely hazardous, especially in concentrated form. Therefore they must be contained securely for very long periods of time, essentially forever. Yet we have learned from experience that perfect containment is very difficult to achieve; even the best-designed landfills may leak, containers can break, accidents and natural disasters happen, and there is always the risk that toxic substances in containment will be purposefully released, for instance, by a terrorist group. Besides these practical problems, containment is also subject to deeper criticisms. Is it fair and right for one generation to use resources for its own advantage and then remove them forever from use at the expense of all future generations? It can be strongly argued that ethically we should not be depriving future people of valuable material resources by converting those materials into hazardous or toxic waste that must be taken out of circulation permanently.

As a result of such considerations, a third strategy toward waste management has been promoted, variously referred to as "resource recovery," "industrial ecosystems," "sustainable waste management," and most optimistically "resource management." The basic philosophy underlying this strategy is that there should be no such thing as material waste, although the energy powering the system may produce waste heat. Under sustainable waste management, unnecessary waste (that is, unnecessary use of materials and energy) is first reduced at the source. Once materials (goods) are used for the designated purpose, all remains are reused or recycled. At the moment, however, we are a long way from achieving this goal. Even if the best reuse and recycling programs currently available were put into place globally, human-produced waste would still exist. A major change in the technology of manufacturing will be necessary if we are to eliminate most or all waste. But in the future, there may be no such thing as waste—only potential resources. Even our twentieth-century dumps and landfills may be viewed as raw resources (antique "urban ore") by the planners of the twenty-fifth century. Until that day comes, however, we will have to continue to address the question of waste management.

Traditional Means of Waste Management

In the twentieth century, humans have dealt with solid wastes in three basic ways: (1) by burning the waste, thus essentially injecting much of it, converted to gases and smoke, into the atmosphere; (2) by storing wastes, including the leftover ash from burning, in dumps, impoundments, and most recently sanitary landfills; and (3) by injecting or burying wastes in rock cavities deep underground (a method proposed for the disposal of industrial and conventional toxic or hazardous waste, as described below, and also for radioactive waste—see Chapter 8). Each of these waste disposal methodologies has its proponents and its critics. In the next few sections, we will consider each briefly.

Incineration

In the industrial technique of **incineration** (Fig. 19–4), trash and garbage are burned in a large furnace at high temperatures to get rid of as much of the refuse as possible. Of course, burning trash is a time-honored procedure, but use of large incinerators dates back only to the late nineteenth century.

During their first 50 years of existence, incinerators were in and out of fashion. Many early incinerators were relatively inefficient, caused massive pollution, and left large quantities of ash and other nonburnables. But by World War II, some seven hundred new and improved incinerators were operating throughout the United States, on

FIGURE 19–4
A trash incineration plant, Detroit, Michigan. (*Source:* John Sohlden/Visuals Unlimited.)

FIGURE 19–5
The interior of the RESCO (Refuse Energy System Company) refuse-to-energy plant in Bridgeport, Connecticut. The crane is transporting waste from the refuse pit to feed the high-temperature furnace. (*Source:* Hank Morgan/Science Source/Photo Researchers.)

both a large and a small scale. Some apartment buildings even had small incinerators to burn the residents' trash. Nevertheless, incinerators continued to cause problems. Aesthetically, incinerators were an offensive intrusion on the skyline, and people who lived near them complained of the odors and said the smoke and gases caused respiratory problems. As early as the 1950s, many incinerators were shut down. The increasing environmental awareness of the late 1960s and early 1970s continued to erode people's confidence in, and tolerance of, incinerators. The Air Quality Act of 1967 and the Clean Air Act Amendments of 1970 established new emission standards that many existing incinerators did not meet; most operators simply closed their incinerators rather than adding costly emission control devices.

But shutting down the incinerators meant that the trash and garbage had to be disposed of some other way. The preferred alternative was sanitary landfills. But by the late 1970s and early 1980s, many cities and municipalities were finding that their landfills were running out of space, and there were fewer and fewer sites available, at least politically. An apparent solution to this predicament was presented by a new breed of incinerators known as resource recovery plants.

The basic idea behind **resource recovery facilities** (or "plants") was that trash and garbage would be burned and the heat generated could be recovered and applied to some useful end, such as generating electricity. Resource recovery facili-

ties, also commonly referred to as waste-to-energy facilities, currently take two basic forms: refuse-derived fuel facilities (RDFs) and mass-burn incinerators. In an RDF, the solid waste is fed into the plant on a conveyer belt. Then, through a series of mechanical operations such as pulverization, shredding, sieving, density separation, and magnetic separation, the waste is sorted into various components—paper, wood, and other combustibles; iron, steel, and other magnetic metals; aluminum; glass; and so on. In this manner recyclable materials can be recovered from the waste, while the shredded combustibles can either be burned on-site to generate electricity or formed into a fuel (often in the form of pellets) that can be sold to conventional coal-fired plants to be burned in place of coal. RDFs are often expensive to operate due to the complicated machinery involved, and also due to the fact that there are often large fluctuations in the markets for the recyclable materials and fuel produced by such a plant. Furthermore, the refuse-derived fuel can not always be sold easily because it may not be of consistent quality.

Mass-burn incinerators take a more direct approach to the waste (□ Fig. 19–5). The unsorted trash and garbage are simply fed into a furnace that burns the refuse at very high temperatures (around 1800 to 2000°F, or 980 to 1100°C). The heat from the burning refuse is used to produce steam that drives a turbine to generate electricity. Whatever is not burned in the incinerator is removed and simply disposed of (for instance, in a landfill).

Problems with Incineration Incinerators not only burn trash, reducing it to ash and gases, they give off—indeed manufacture—huge amounts of toxic pollution. As an example, an early 1990s state-of-the-art incinerator that meets all regulatory requirements burning 2250 tons (2042 metric tons) of refuse a day would emit 5 tons (4.5 metric tons) of lead and 17 tons (15.4 metric tons) of mercury per year, as well as 580 pounds (263 kg) of cadmium, 580 pounds (263 kg) of nickel, 2248 tons (2040 metric tons) of nitrogen oxides, 853 tons (774 metric tons) of sulfur dioxide, 777 tons (705 metric tons) of hydrogen chloride, 87 tons (79 metric tons) of sulfuric acid, 18 tons (16 metric tons) of fluorides, and 98 tons (89 metric tons) of small dust particles. Perhaps most dangerous of all, incinerators produce and expel dioxin.

Dioxin (actually not a single substance as the term is commonly used, but a group of over two hundred related compounds) is considered by

be formed when organic wastes containing chlorine are burned. Plastic containers, paper, and other trash typically found in municipal solid wastes can often give rise to dioxin when burned in incinerators.

Not until the late 1970s was it even realized that dioxin production from incinerators might be a problem. At first, many experts believed that any dioxin in trash would be destroyed by the high temperatures of incineration. In fact, this was essentially true: dioxin is destroyed in the furnace of the incinerator, but dioxin is then synthesized from the chemicals present in the cooler parts of the incinerator beyond the furnace and rises up the smokestack.

Modern incinerators are equipped with all sorts of mechanisms to capture the dioxins, heavy metals, and other toxic substances that would otherwise spew out of their stacks. The gases are subjected to various scrubbers, electrostatic precipitators, and fabric filters that catch the fly ash and toxic components of the gases. Even in the best cases, however, a commercial incinerator that meets all regulations can release substantial quantities of dangerous substances through its stacks. Furthermore, after incineration a substantial bulk of both bottom ash and fly ash remains to be disposed of—usually in a landfill or the equivalent. Some bottom ash may contain toxic levels of contaminants, but in other cases it may be safely deposited in an ordinary landfill or even used to make building materials such as cinder blocks. The fly ash, which contains the dioxin, heavy metals, and other toxic substances that were removed before the gases left the stacks, is typically much more hazardous than the bottom ash.

This hazardous material must be carefully isolated from the environment. In some cases it is chemically stabilized and hardened to a rocklike consistency before being deposited in a specially designed landfill. Unfortunately, abuses have occurred, to everyone's detriment. Incinerator ash containing toxic substances has been improperly dumped in older landfills from which the toxics escaped into the general environment. And in 1986–1988, the cargo ship *Khian Sea* (Fig. 19–6) made news when it sailed the seas, searching for a place to dump its cargo of 16,000 tons (14,500 metric tons) of incinerator ash from Philadelphia, a city

FIGURE 19–6
The cargo ship *Khian Sea*, loaded with incinerator ash from Philadelphia, is approached by a boat carrying members of the American Bureau of Shipping (a private inspection service) as it lies at anchor off Big Stone Beach, Delaware. (*Source:* AP/Wide World Photos.)

some experts to be one of the most toxic chemicals ever manufactured by humans. Exposure to dioxin can cause skin eruptions (which resemble acne), headaches, dizziness, digestive disorders, birth defects, and various forms of cancer. Dioxin was an unintended contaminant of the defoliant Agent Orange that was used during the Vietnam War. It is formed as a by-product in the production of some herbicides, certain bleached papers, and other products. Dioxin can form inadvertently in many situations. In particular, dioxin can

with two mass-burn incinerators but no landfills. After being barred from every port it tried to enter, the ship eventually sailed into Singapore empty—no explanation of the fate of its cargo was forthcoming.

Due to the regulations involved, incineration of waste is generally the most costly form of waste disposal, costing much more per ton of waste than landfilling (landfilling generally costs between $60 and $270 per ton whereas land-based incineration costs range from about $400 to $550 per ton). At present, the construction of a typical mass-burn incinerator that can dispose of 2000 tons (1815 metric tons) of garbage a day will cost about $250 million. Assuming a rate of garbage production of 4 pounds (1.8 kg) per person per day, such an incinerator would service about a million people. To avoid many of the regulations that are applied to land-based incinerators, large amounts of material (especially waste liquids such as oils and solvents) are regularly burned on ship-based incinerators in the open oceans (ocean-based incineration can cost half the price of land-based incineration). This may cut costs by skirting some regulations that do not apply, or cannot be enforced, on the high seas, but, of course, the hazardous materials spewed out by ship-based incinerators still enter the biosphere.

Dumps and Landfills

One of the most ancient, and most common, ways of disposing of solid waste is to simply pile it up in a convenient but out-of-the-way place. Accordingly, most cities, towns, and other populated areas have generally had open **dumps** on their outskirts (Fig. 19–7). There trash and garbage would simply be left to sit or to be picked through by garbage pickers and sifters. In other cases liquid or semiliquid wastes were contained in artificial or natural lakes or impoundments. But open dumps and impoundments tend to be associated with many problems, especially as they grow larger. Aesthetically, they can be smelly and unsightly. They can present serious health hazards, serving as breeding grounds for disease vectors and attracting pests. Dumps can significantly contribute to local air pollution, especially if the trash is periodically ignited and allowed to burn—

as is done at some open dumps to reduce the volume of waste. Chemicals can also leak from an impoundment or leach from a dump, perhaps as it is rained upon, and the resulting runoff can seriously pollute the local surface and ground water.

Despite the problems associated with open dumps, they remain an extremely common form

of solid waste disposal, especially in developing countries. But even in the United States, open dumps are not hard to come by. A few of these dumps are officially sanctioned, but most open dumps in this country are relatively small and illegal—essentially, accumulations of rubbish in relatively deserted areas. The percentage of solid waste that actually ends up in American open dumps is quite small (Issues in Perspective 19–1 describes a type of solid waste that often ends up in large open piles).

Replacing the ancient dumps have been modern techniques of solid waste disposal, such as incineration and the lineal descendant of the open dump, the modern **sanitary landfill**. In the simplest sense, a modern sanitary landfill is essentially a closed dump (Fig. 19–8, page 536). The solid and semisolid wastes are confined to a specific area, usually a giant hole in the ground; after being compacted, they are covered over daily with a layer of soil. Thus, the hole in the ground is filled ("landfill"), and the waste is isolated from the general environment by the periodic dirt covering, making the whole complex relatively "sanitary" as compared to open dumps.

Tires

Tires—car tires, bus tires, truck tires, tractor tires—though only about 1% of the American municipal solid waste stream by weight, pose a major disposal problem (Fig. 1). More than two billion used tires are stockpiled in America today, many of them in large, unsightly outdoor heaps. Every year Americans add an estimated 200 million additional car tires and another 40 million truck, bus, and tractor tires to these piles. Many communities no longer allow tires to be discarded with other rubbish; tires are classified as "special waste," and disposing of them may cost $2 or more apiece. The problem is that tires contain pockets of air and are not easily flattened completely, so they tend to "float" up to the tops of landfills. In floating to the top, they can disrupt and destabilize the other components of the landfill, causing serious damage. They can even float up and break the clay caps that have been placed over landfills. At some older landfills that once accepted tires, the tires that have surfaced must periodically be skimmed off.

Piles of tires are not just eyesores, but contribute to other environmental and health problems. The tires can catch on fire, producing billows of noxious black smoke and fumes. The tire pile is mostly air, which promotes the fire, and the rubber in the tires burns at very high temperatures. As they burn, tires give off dangerous oily liquids. Putting water on the fire in an attempt to extinguish it can cause these liquids to spread, causing more environmental damage. Extinguishing the fire can be extremely difficult. Some tire fires have burned out of control for months.

Piles of tires also provide a breeding ground for rats, mosquitoes, and other disease-spreading pests. Water can collect in tires, providing the perfect incubation site for mosquitoes. Rats and other rodents make their homes in tire piles, especially if the piles are located near a garbage dump (as is often the case) that provides a ready source of food.

Unfortunately, few practical uses have been devised for used tires. Perhaps the most obvious way to cut down on the number of tires entering the waste stream is to make them last longer. Some brands and

FIGURE 1
A typical tire dump. (*Source:* R Calentine/Visuals Unlimited.)

The earliest recorded predecessors of sanitary landfills date to the early 1900s in the United States and to the 1920s in Britain. By the 1930s, sanitary landfills were catching on throughout the United States. In 1945 around 100 American cities had sanitary landfills; by 1960 approximately 1400 cities had adopted this method of solid waste disposal. Today about 70–75% of U.S. municipal solid waste is disposed of in landfills.

Through their 90 years of existence, the philosophy and design of sanitary landfills have undergone major evolutionary shifts. From the beginning, the central idea was that once a landfill was completely filled, it could be covered over with a final layer of clay and dirt, and the "reclaimed" land devoted to some other purpose. This is the concept of sequential land use: what was "wasted" land in the past, perhaps a natural

types of tires last significantly longer than other types, and the life of a used tire can be extended by retreading. Due to their initial expense, many bus and truck tires are commonly retreaded, but most individuals prefer to buy new tires for their passenger cars since new tires tend to cost little more than retreads. But even doubling, tripling, or quadrupling the life span of the average tire will not solve the tire disposal problem. With so many cars on the road, tens of millions of tires will continue to be added to America's waste stream each year.

Reclaiming and recycling the rubber from tires is difficult and expensive. The various synthetic rubber, glass, and steel layers in radial tires make reclamation all the more difficult and generally impractical. Whether whole or cut up, tires have only limited uses. Some playground equipment is composed largely of used tires (Fig. 2); tires are used on boat docks and piers as bumpers; sandals, floor mats, and other products can be made from cut-up tires; and rubber chips produced from chopped-up tires can replace traditional mulch in gardens. Tires, weighted with concrete, have been used to start artificial reefs on coastlines (although

FIGURE 2
This playground and park utilized 3000 recycled tires.
(*Source:* Mitsuhiro Wada/Gamma Liaison.)

not always with satisfactory results); likewise, tires have been used as a primary building material for breakwaters and erosion barriers on beaches. There has been some experimental use of tires packed with cement as a structural material inside the walls of buildings. A promising large-scale secondary use for tires is in "asphalt rubber." Simply put, tires are ground up and mixed with asphalt to produce a material, asphalt rubber, that can be used to surface, repair, and restore roads. Reportedly, several million tires have been used in asphalt rubber in both the United States (especially on federal highways) and Europe. Most secondary uses of tires, however, are rather limited (for instance, only so many playgrounds or breakwaters are needed) and do not solve the problem of what to do with the billions of stockpiled tires and the hundreds of millions more discarded annually.

Tires are sometimes incinerated or burned as fuel in specially designed power plants; a plant that runs off nothing but tires is located in Modesto, California, next to a tire pile that should keep it supplied with fuel for at least a decade. Tires can also be burned with other materials in more conventional power-generating incinerators or as a source of heat and energy for industrial operations such as paper production. Critics of tire burning are concerned about the toxic air pollution and ash that it may produce. In many areas tire burning has not found favor with the public.

swamp or gully, becomes a place to deposit waste, and once the land has been completely filled, the reclaimed land can serve as the site for homes, a park, a factory, or any of numerous other uses. But over the decades, there has been a dramatic shift in thinking as to what land is suitable for landfills. In the early decades of landfill development, the most suitable and desirable locations were thought to be in swamps, marshes, and other low-lying wetlands. Wetlands were viewed as classic "waste land" that served no useful purpose: they were too wet to build on or grow crops, and were believed to breed only disease, insects, and other pests. By filling the wetlands with garbage interbedded with layers of soil, the land could be raised in elevation and made dry and usable. Of course, we now understand the importance of wetlands in the overall global scheme; far from

filling them in, efforts are underway to preserve remaining wetlands. To make matters worse, building sanitary landfills upon wetlands certainly does not isolate the waste from the rest of the environment; in fact, the opposite is true. The natural wetlands provide an easy conduit for liquids, including extremely hazardous and toxic substances, to drain from the landfill and enter surface and ground waters. Thus, a swamp or other wetland is just about the worst possible place to site a sanitary landfill.

cases a preexisting hole such as an abandoned coal or copper mine can be used, but usually not because the surrounding rock will be too permeable. Once the hole (which may be 50 feet [15 m] deep) is excavated, the next step is to line the sides of the cavity with thick layers of dense clay, a thick, sealed plastic liner, and sand and gravel. Many older sanitary landfills are not lined or have inadequate linings, but newer landfills are invariably lined. The liner serves as a barrier to the uncontrolled migration of the leachate out of the sanitary landfill. In the newest landfills, the leachate is not allowed to collect in pools at the bottom of the landfill; if it did, the pool would eventually overflow the sides of the landfill. Instead, pipes and drains in the bottom of the landfill collect the leachate so that it can be removed.

Most landfills now try to stay as dry as possible, so the leachate is removed, collected, and treated. The leachate may be treated like sewage, either being treated at a special plant on site at the landfill or sent to the local municipal sewage facility. Typically, the water is separated from the leachate, purified, and then released into a local river or the ocean. The remaining solid sludge may be

■ FIGURE 19–8
A sanitary landfill in the process of being covered over and replanted, perhaps to be used as a park in the future. (*Source:* Bernd Wittich/Visuals Unlimited.)

Today landfills are sited in areas where contamination of surface and ground waters will not occur. Some of the best sites for sanitary landfills are in arid regions with little rainfall to produce leachates from the landfill. **Leachate** is formed as water percolates through the refuse, either from the top, such as from rain falling on the landfill, or laterally due to groundwater flow intercepting the landfill. Leachate is essentially an aqueous solution containing any chemicals and particles that can be dissolved, leached, or removed from the trash, including in some instances live disease-producing microorganisms. Leachate can be an extremely hazardous and concentrated brew of substances.

Modern sanitary landfills are usually begun by digging a huge hole at a suitable site. In some

dumped into the landfill once again, or it may be burned and then the ashes placed in the landfill. In some cases the sludge can be used as a fertilizer, or it may be safely dumped into the ocean. In other cases the leachate and sludge contain enough toxic substances that they are considered to be a hazardous waste and therefore must be disposed of in a suitable hazardous waste facility.

Besides leachate, sanitary landfills produce **methane gas** as certain organic components in the landfill are decomposed by bacteria. This methane must be removed from the landfill on a regular basis, or it could accumulate and form a hazard if it ignited. In some cases pipes perforated with holes are inserted into wells drilled down into the landfill; the gas can then be collected from these pipes. Or a lattice of perforated pipes may be included within the landfill as the refuse is accumulating. At some landfills the methane is simply burned or released directly into the atmosphere (of course, contributing to the greenhouse effect—see Chapter 18), but at other facilities the methane is collected, purified, and then sold as fuel.

Once a sanitary landfill is full, it is capped with a thick layer of compacted clay and soil. It can then be seeded, landscaped, and developed to serve any number of purposes. Parks, golf courses, and similar facilities are ideally suited for areas underlain by old landfills, but even houses or industrial buildings can be situated on these sites. The materials in the landfill may continue to compact for a number of years after closing, however, causing subsurface subsidence—thus, it is unwise to build major structures on a fresh landfill. Moreover, methane gas will continue to form in the landfill for many years, as may leachate. The methane must continue to be removed long after the landfill has been closed. Likewise, the former landfill and the area adjacent to it should be closely monitored to ensure that no pollutants begin to escape.

About 70–75% of U.S. municipal solid waste is currently disposed of in landfills; the rest is about equally split between recycling and incineration. Yet, over the past two decades, many landfills have closed down, and it is increasingly difficult to open new landfills (due both to their expense and to the NIMBY [Not-In-My-Back-Yard] syndrome). In 1978 there were about 20,000 operating landfills in the United States; by 1988 the number had dropped to about 8000, and in the early 1990s, it was less than 6000. During the same period, however, the average size of landfills has increased. For example, Pennsylvania had 72 landfills in 1989, and the projected remaining life of its landfills was five years. Two years later, Pennsylvania had only 44 landfills, but their estimated remaining life was 15 years.

New EPA regulations are increasing the pressure on the nation's landfill capacity. The requirements include stricter guidelines for landfill liners, leachate collection systems, and groundwater and methane monitoring. This will increase the cost of opening and operating a landfill to an estimated average of $125 million and may force many older landfills that cannot economically be upgraded to meet the new requirements to close down. As of the mid-1990s, the estimated average remaining life expectancy of an American landfill was about 14 years.

Some researchers contend that the whole question of landfills running out of capacity is a political issue rather than a scientific problem for the United States. They argue that the only reason it is harder to site new landfills is the NIMBY syndrome—people do not like the thought of "disgusting" landfills in their communities. One economist has estimated that all of America's projected solid waste for the next 500 years could be easily fit within a single landfill 20 miles (32 km) on each side and 100 yards (91.5 m) deep. This would certainly be a huge landfill, but it would represent only a small dot on a map of the continental United States. Another researcher has suggested that the ideal location for such a national landfill (or landfills) would be in the thick shales that cover most of western South Dakota.

Deep-Well Injection

Various types of industrial or hazardous wastes are sometimes disposed of by injecting them into deep wells drilled into the crust of the Earth. The basic idea is to pump wastes into rocks that are situated well below all freshwater aquifers, so as to avoid contaminating any groundwater supplies. A typical well might be hundreds to several thousands of yards (or meters) deep. For decades the oil industry has used **deep-well injection** to dispose of liquid wastes, such as salty brines, that are often pumped out of the ground in association with oil production—the brines are simply injected back into the rock. But using deep-well injection to get rid of other types of wastes is associated with many potential problems and as a result is opposed by many environmentalists.

Natural earthquakes may divert groundwater flow and allow previously isolated injected waste to contaminate other bodies of groundwater. This could ultimately lead to the spread of the waste and contamination of drinking water. Furthermore, the increased fluid pressure that results from injecting liquid waste deep underground may actually initiate earthquakes. Apparently, the increased fluid pressure allows rocks to move or slide along preexisting joints and fractures. Earthquakes caused by the injection of wastes into deep wells have been reported in Colorado, Texas, Utah, and California. In another case the chemical wastes that had been pumped down a well blew back up and spewed into Lake Erie. Despite such accidents, proponents of deep-well injection point out that taken as a group, most operations have no such problems.

Another concern over deep-well injection is that what constitutes a "deep well" at present may not seem so deep in the future. As we deplete the readily available freshwater aquifers, we need to drill deeper and deeper for usable water. In the future we may need to drill as deep or deeper than the injected waste, but in the process the injected waste may contaminate our efforts. Also, not all wastes should be injected into all rocks. Certain wastes may react adversely with some types of rocks or with the natural pore fluids that already occur in the particular rock.

In areas where deep-well injection of waste is used, once the waste is injected into the rocks and the well plugged, the job is not over. The injection field must be permanently monitored to ensure that the waste does not migrate out of the confining rocks into which it was injected, perhaps through the natural pores of the rock or along natural or artificial cracks, holes, or fractures. After many years, even a properly sealed well may begin to leak.

Garbage as a Source of Revenue for Poorer Communities

Some communities have found that an easy way to attract money and jobs is to take the garbage from other areas. A classic recent example is Kimball County, Nebraska, which allowed a hazardous-waste incinerator to be built in its jurisdiction because this represented a $60 million investment in the financially depressed region. Likewise, New York City's treated sludge is

shipped to a 128,000–acre (51,800–hectare) ranch in Hudspeth County, Texas, which has created 35 badly needed jobs for local residents.

On a global scale, waste is shipped from richer to poorer nations ( Fig. 19–9). In many cases hazardous wastes in particular are shipped from industrialized nations, where tight regulations make the materials expensive to dispose of, to developing nations with looser regulations or lax enforcement of existing regulations. Such overseas shipments are hard to monitor, especially since the material may not be properly identified as hazardous waste. Millions of tons of hazardous waste are being shipped from the United States and Western Europe to Africa, Latin America, and Eastern Europe every year. Sometimes host countries are happy to take the trash; before German unification, East Germany willingly accepted wastes from West Germany and Denmark for a fee. In other instances the disposal is totally surreptitious. In 1988, for instance, the Nigerian government discovered that hazardous wastes from Italy were being dumped in a Nigerian port. To stem the illegal movement of waste, the United Nations Environment Programme oversaw the development of a treaty, adopted by many nations in 1989, to regulate the international movement of hazardous wastes.

Although such waste exchange arrangements can be mutually advantageous, as already pointed out,

■ FIGURE 19–9
Containers of Australian computer waste being impounded by Filipino authorities in Manila. (*Source:* Warford/Greenpeace.)

critics argue that the short-term economic gains are more than offset by the long-term costs and hazards of accepting other people's waste. Ultimately, the waste may pollute and otherwise degrade the environment, causing a self-perpetuating cycle of decreasing property values and the movement of wealth from the area. In the case of a typical landfill or incinerator/landfill operation, eventually the space will be filled, and where will the accepting community be then? When the waste no longer flows in, neither will money and jobs; the community may be left with a pile of garbage that still needs to be monitored.

Dealing with Rubbish and Other Waste in the Near Future

Many nations, experts, and organizations (including the U.S. Environmental Protection Agency) agree on a common approach, at least in principle, to the problem of waste management. Often known as the "waste management hierarchy," this approach involves a list of options ordered from the most desirable to the least desirable along the following lines:

1. **Source reduction**. Reduce the generation of waste in the first place.
2. **Reuse** of products. For instance, washing and reusing beverage containers directly.
3. Recovery and **recycling**. Using "waste" as the raw materials of industrial processes, such as collecting old aluminum cans, melting them down, and using the recovered aluminum to manufacture new products.
4. Waste treatment and incineration. This may include recovering energy as the trash is burned.
5. Storage and disposal. The residual ash and solids of incineration or other waste treatment must ultimately go somewhere. In some cases the material can be used to manufacture items, such as cinder blocks from certain types of incineration ash; as a last resort, it may be permanently disposed of, the ultimate resting place usually being a landfill.

Certainly, the most immediate, and ultimately most beneficial, solution to the solid waste problem is source reduction—utilizing less raw material in the first place. Source reduction can be accomplished in many different ways, including the use of alternative raw materials (such as substituting lighter and stronger aluminum for other materials in some goods), altering the product being produced, and changing manufacturing procedures. Ultimately, source reduction can be accomplished by simply consuming less. Many waste management experts suggest that the best way for the average citizen to help solve the waste management problem is to simply not purchase or use unnecessary goods. But source reduction alone can never solve all our waste problems. Humans require a minimum number of material products to survive, so appropriate source reduction must be combined with other objectives farther down on the waste management hierarchy.

Reuse is next on most people's lists of ways to deal with the garbage crisis. In some ways reuse is really just a form of source reduction. Instead of making 50 soft-drink bottles, use one bottle 50 times. Yet, reuse has not captured the popular imagination to the same degree as recycling.

Lately, recycling has become increasingly popular, and most people view this as a positive development (recycling is discussed in more detail later in the chapter). But some environmentalists argue that as a solution to the refuse problem, recycling is deceptive and misleading and perhaps even contributes to the problem by diverting energy and resources that could be used for more beneficial endeavors—namely, actual waste reduction and reuse of goods. Richard Gilbert, who was a member of the Canadian Federal Task Force on Packaging, expressed this view when he stated in an interview: "Recycling is just a sophisticated twist in the throwaway society. It's number three on anybody's waste-management list. It's deceiving us. It's saying you can still continue to consume as much as before, you just have to throw the stuff into your garbage can in a slightly different way. And it's not hitting at the real issue—our obscene level of consumption. Recycling is just reinforcing the throwaway society" (quoted in Gordon and Suzuki, 1991, p. 189).

Instead, it is argued, we should change our basic consumption habits. We can use and reuse while consuming at a lower rate. For instance, virtually all food-carrying containers could be manufactured so as to be reusable—from the bottles that your beverages come in, to the containers for your cereal (although they may have to be manufactured from something other than cardboard). Reusing, if properly organized, should be no more inconvenient than a recycling or ordinary garbage collection program. Massive reuse would save energy and resources.

Waste treatment, such as incineration, and permanent disposal in landfills are on the bottom of many people's waste management hierarchy. Due to the air pollution and other dangers inherent in some forms of incineration, some environmentalists contend that landfilling and other forms of permanent storage should be placed before incineration in the hierarchy.

In contrast, many proponents of the "waste-to-energy" industry argue that incineration should be much higher on the hierarchy than it already is. Waste-to-energy incineration plants are touted as a form of "recycling"—heat from burning trash is converted to usable energy. Other people suggest that the whole notion of a "waste management hierarchy" is counterproductive. They argue that individual communities should be allowed to pursue an "integrated approach" to waste management, choosing the technologies that best suit local needs. A strong argument against this line of thinking is that waste management is no longer simply a local problem. The world must soon begin addressing this issue in concert if we are not to be overwhelmed by trash and pollution on the land, in our waters, and in the world's atmosphere.

Waste Disposal and Recycling in the United States

According to recent EPA statistics, in the United States as a whole approximately 73% of all municipal solid waste (by weight) is disposed of in landfills, about 14% is incinerated, and the remaining 13% is recycled (however, it is predicted that within the next few years the percentage of municipal waste that is recycled will increase dramatically). When broken down by states, the figures can vary widely from the national averages. For example, Connecticut has a very high incineration rate—some 62%. The state of Washington is a leader in recycling, with an estimated recycling rate of 28%. Given the environmental concerns over landfills and incineration, recycling is steadily increasing in popularity. More and

EnviroNet
www.jbpub.com/environet

more municipalities are mandating certain levels of recycling. For instance, California, Hawaii, Iowa, Massachusetts, New Mexico, and Oregon have set goals to recycle 50% of all municipal waste by the beginning of the twenty-first century. Besides reducing the waste stream, using recycled secondary materials reduces our energy use, water use, mining wastes, and air and water pollution (● Table 19–2).

In the United States, four prominent categories of materials are commonly recycled: glass, metals (especially aluminum, steel, and iron), paper, and plastics. But not all recycling is equal. In just these four categories, we have both **closed-loop** (or nearly closed-loop) recycling, represented by the glasses and metals (these substances can be recycled completely and indefinitely), and various types of **open-loop** recycling with paper and to an even greater extent with plastics (these substances can only be recycled to a limited extent). As cases in point, we will take a brief look at the current status of recycling efforts for these four categories of materials.

Glass

In many ways pure glass is the ideal substance to recycle for it is virtually 100% recyclable. Glass bottles and jars can be melted down to make new glass bottles and jars, and this process can be repeated over and over again in a virtually endless cycle without damaging the raw constituents of the glass—primarily silica-based sand (quartz) and a few other ingredients. Thus, under ideal conditions glass recycling can form a closed-loop system: only energy needs to be added to make new glass products from old. Recycling glass, as compared to producing new glass from virgin materials, entails enormous energy savings, decreases the amount of mining that needs to be carried out, and significantly reduces the amount of air and water pollution generated.

In the United States today, approximately 25 to 35% of all glass produced is manufactured from recycled glass. Around 5 billion glass jars and bottles are recycled every year. Despite these impressive statistics, more could be done. Glass still makes up nearly 7% of U.S. municipal solid waste by weight, and a good percentage of this could easily be recycled. Not all glass products can be easily and directly recycled, however. Objects that contain glass and other substances (for instance, metals), such as lightbulbs, television tubes, and mirrors, are difficult to recycle.

Even when glass cannot be recycled directly back into similar glass products, it can be used for construction materials, such as fiberglass (although this usually requires stringent limits on the chemical composition of the glass). Crushed glass has also been used as a substitute for crushed stone in asphalt used in paving roads and other surfaces (sometimes known as "glasphalt").

Recently the market for recyclable glass has been very strong—between May 1993 and July 1995 the average price paid by glass processors for recyclable clear glass containers increased by 78%. This bodes well for the immediate future of glass recycling.

Metals

Many metals offer the same recycling advantages as glass. Pure metals can be melted and reused over and over again without damage to their substance. For instance, precious metals such as gold and silver, as used in jewelry or tableware, have been recycled in this manner for thousands of years.

In the United States, steel is the most commonly recycled material—more steel is recycled every year than all other materials combined. Over 100 billion pounds (45 billion kg) of steel are recycled in the United States annually, including more than 3.5 billion steel cans; overall, an estimated two-thirds of all steel products are recycled. Steel is relatively easy to separate out for recycling, because it is magnetic, and producing new steel from scrap steel instead of virgin ore entails tremendous savings in energy and mining expenses, as well as considerable reductions in the pollution produced.

Aluminum is also easily and widely recycled. Beverage cans are the best-known example, but aluminum foil, pie plates and other disposable containers, and even parts of cars and appliances can be recycled. Producing aluminum from ore (bauxite) is a very energy-intensive process, so recycling can result in energy savings of up to 90% or more (and also reduces pollution given off during manufacturing by comparable amounts; see Table 19–2). Aluminum cans, trays, and other products are easily identifiable and 100% recyclable, forming the ideal closed-loop system. Currently, about 68% of all aluminum cans and aluminum foil in the United States are recycled. Certainly, this is admirable, but there is little reason why we cannot recycle better than 90%.

Many other metals are also recycled in the United States, although mostly by specialized scrap metal dealers. Some of the more common metals include copper (from copper pipes, wiring, and other products), lead (especially from automobile batteries), zinc, nickel, titanium, and chromium. An emerging industry is the recycling

and processing of old computers, including the circuit boards and chips, for valuable metals such as copper, nickel, cobalt, silver, gold, palladium, and platinum. Still, U.S. municipal solid waste is composed of nearly 8% metals by weight.

Paper

About 38% of America's municipal solid waste is composed of paper and paperboard products. Americans are profligate users of paper, using up to 600 pounds (272 kg) of paper a year per person. For comparison, annual per capita paper use in parts of the former Soviet Union is 25 pounds (11.3 kg), and in China it is only 2 pounds (0.9 kg) —of course, not everyone can get a daily newspaper in China. Of the paper Americans use, 11% is used in books and other relatively durable and permanent objects, and only about 33 to 38% (depending on how the estimate is arrived at) is recycled. Many countries have much higher rates of paper recycling (● Table 19–3). The remainder of the paper ends up as waste. Over 50 million tons (45 million metric tons) of paper products are sent to U.S. landfills each year.

Still, paper, especially cardboard and other corrugated material, is one of the more commonly recycled products in the United States. Indeed, about half of all corrugated paper materials are recycled. Many businesses that depend heavily on cardboard boxes for shipping and packing goods have been recycling the used cardboard for years,

TABLE 19–3 *Wastepaper Use Rates, Selected Countries, 1992*

COUNTRY	SHARE[a] (PERCENT)
Taiwan	98
Denmark	97
Mexico	81
Thailand	80
South Korea	70
Netherlands	70
Japan	53
Germany	52
United Kingdom	60
United States	33
Canada	17
Sweden	14

[a]Amount of wastepaper used in production divided by total amount of paper and paperboard produced.
(*Source:* L. R. Brown, H. Kane, and D. M. Roodman, *Vital Signs 1994* [New York, W. W. Norton, 1994], p. 120. Reprinted with permission of Worldwatch Institute, Washington, D.C., Copyright 1994.)

so networks for recycling cardboard are well established.

Printing and writing paper, computer paper, glossy paper, and newsprint are all recycled to various degrees in different parts of the country. Currently, between 30 and 40% of all U.S. newspapers are recycled. Yet newspapers are still one of the largest components of landfills.

Recycling paper is not exactly comparable to recycling materials such as glass or metals, for paper recycling is ultimately not a closed-loop system. Paper cannot be used over and over endlessly, for the fibers eventually degrade and become unusable for most purposes (see Issues in Perspective 19–2). Realistically, many paper fibers can be recycled no more than six to eight times. To offset this effect, virgin material is often mixed with recycled fibers such that even "recycled" paper may contain a significant percentage of virgin fiber. When purchasing "recycled" paper, it is extremely important to distinguish between "preconsumer" and "postconsumer" recycled content. Preconsumer waste is primarily waste produced during the manufacturing of the paper, such as scraps from cutting sheets of paper; paper companies have traditionally reused this preconsumer waste. Postconsumer content is made from other paper that was actually used for some purpose by the public and then returned to be recycled.

The paper recycling business has historically been a roller coaster. Sometimes old newspapers can be sold for a profit, but at other times a hauler must be paid to take bundled newspapers away. In the late 1980s and early 1990s, some warehouses were full of paper waiting to be recycled. Well-meaning legislators had passed laws requiring the collection of paper for recycling without requiring the use of recycled paper, which would have developed a market for the product. Now, however, the federal government as well as many state governments require all paper used in government offices to have a recycled component. In the past, due to the public's distrust of recycled paper, paper companies were often unwilling to produce it. Today, however, the public is generally more accepting of paper containing recycled content. Indeed, domestically and globally there is a continuing strong demand for paper and paper products, and recycled paper is helping to fill the need. During the five years from 1990 to 1994 over 85 paper mills that could recycle paper products were built in the U.S. In the early 1990s, old newspaper was of negligible value, but as of mid-1995 recyclable newspaper averaged around $60 to $70 a ton (0.91 metric ton) and in some areas of the country prices reached $160 a ton. Likewise, recyclable white ledger paper that sold for about $40 a ton in 1993 was averaging $110 a ton in mid-1995. Old newspapers and scrap paper have become such a valuable commodity across the country that theft of papers from curbside recycling bins has become a significant problem.

Using scrap paper to manufacture other paper is not the only way that paper can be recycled. For instance, recycled paper is already used to manufacture construction materials, such as wallboard, roofing paper, padding, and insulation. Some farmers successfully use shredded newspaper in place of straw for bedding material for animals. Although not exactly recycling in the traditional sense, paper can be either burned directly as fuel or converted into fuel pellets.

Plastics

Plastics are the bane of environmentalists. Though plastics make up only about 8% of U.S. municipal solid waste by weight, by volume they compose about one-fifth of our waste stream. The United States consumes about 14 billion pounds (6.3 billion kg) of plastics each year, but only about 1% of this is recycled. Most plastics are synthetic compounds composed of polymers containing hydrogen, carbon, and oxygen (usually manufactured from petroleum and its derivatives). Typical plastics in use today are not biodegradable or otherwise readily broken down in nature (see Issues in Perspective 19–3); thus, they not only clog our landfills, but produce unsightly litter across the landscape. When burned or incinerated, otherwise inert, and thus nontoxic, plastics can give off many toxic substances, including carcinogens such as dioxin.

The large-scale recycling of plastics faces many practical obstacles. For one, the many different types of plastic, which look very similar, must be sorted according to specific plastic resins. Some common products, such as squeeze bottles for food, are composed of several layers of different types of plastics, making it very difficult to separate them for recycling. Furthermore, even under the best conditions, most plastics cannot be recycled back to their original use. Common plastics can only be recycled in an open-loop system. Unlike a glass bottle, a plastic soda bottle cannot simply be melted down and made into another plastic soda bottle. Not only does the quality of the plastic diminish, but the temperatures at which plastics are melted and remolded are not always high enough to sanitize the plastic for use as

Paper versus Plastic

Which is less damaging to the environment, paper or plastic? Which fills up our landfills? Which should you use over the other? Many people instinctively answer that paper is less degrading to the environment—after all, paper is made from natural plant fibers, is biodegradable, and is recyclable. In contrast, most plastic is manufactured using scarce petrochemicals, is not always easily or economically recyclable, and, once manufactured, may last virtually indefinitely. Virtually no common plastic products are truly biodegradable (see Issues in Perspective 19–3).

Yet in the United States, paper and cardboard make up over a third of all municipal waste by weight (Luxembourg at 17% has the lowest rate for a developed country on record), whereas plastic accounts for about 8% (among developed countries, plastic makes up between 3% [New Zealand and Portugal] and 13% [Switzerland] of municipal waste). Even though paper and wood products may theoretically be biodegradable, in most landfills they do not biodegrade; conditions within a landfill are generally not amenable to microorganismal growth. Thus, for the environmentally aware consumer, the choice between disposable plastic and paper products is not always clear-cut. Here we will review some of the pluses and minuses of using paper versus plastic.

Tremendous numbers of trees are chopped down every year to be pulped and turned into paper products. Yet, as everyone knows, paper is "recyclable," so why do we have to cut down many new trees at all? Why can't we just recycle a larger proportion of the massive amounts of paper that end up either deposited in landfills or burned in incinerators? A major hurdle to paper recycling is that the paper fibers are modified as they are used and reused. To be recycled, discarded paper must be deinked and converted to pulp before it can be manufactured into new paper. In the process of pulping, the paper fibers are broken. Therefore paper made from recycled fibers will be composed of shorter fibers than the original paper, resulting in a lower-quality paper of inferior strength. As paper is recycled over and over again, the fibers become progressively shorter, and the paper's quality and strength diminish. Thus, the value of paper made from progressively recycled fibers and its potential uses drop off sharply. At some point the fibers become too short to produce serviceable paper for most purposes. For instance, newsprint or other paper that is too weak cannot be run through typical high-speed presses without tearing or other problems. Thus, even under ideal conditions, paper fibers cannot be recycled indefinitely, and a percentage of virgin wood pulp must be injected from time to time. Barry Commoner, in his book *Making Peace with the Planet* (1992), reports that for this reason the *Los Angeles Times* is printed on paper containing about 80% recycled material and 20% virgin fibers. Yet newsprint made of 80% recycled fiber is certainly preferable to newsprint made of 100% virgin fiber. Also, there are many important uses for very low-quality, short-fiber paper—such as the ever useful toilet tissue.

Of course, not only can paper be recycled, but many paper products can actually be reused. Paper bags, cardboard boxes, even paper from photocopy machines can be reused. Grocery bags, for instance, typically need not be discarded after one use. Manila envelopes and boxes can often be used to package and send things through the mail several times. Many times photocopies are on one side only; why not photocopy on both sides of the paper (this not only saves paper, but saves space as well) or use the backs of old one-sided photocopies as notepaper? Rather than being insulted that someone writes to you on the back of "scrap paper," feel proud that the writer is environmentally conscientious enough to reuse the paper.

Compared to paper, plastics generally have fewer uses—and accordingly make up a lesser volume of our solid waste. But many of the common uses of plastic are identical to some of the uses of paper. Both plastics and paper are used heavily in packaging, indeed often in tandem (for instance, the plastic bottle with a paper label, the cardboard box or drink container that is plastic lined, the cardboard backing to an otherwise plastic container). Plastic bags can be used over and over again, often more times than a comparable paper bag. But once the plastic bag is torn or broken, it must be discarded—plastic cannot yet be recycled as easily as paper. Over the years, plastic bags, containers, and other items have become lighter and less bulky while retaining their strength—so once they end up in the landfill, they occupy even less room. On the other hand, when plastics (and paper in some cases) are burned in an incinerator, they may give off many toxic substances, including the deadly dioxins (see the text). Recently, much research has been devoted to developing reuse and recycling options for standard plastics, and truly biodegradable plastics may play a significant role in the future (see Issues in Perspective 19–3).

Biodegradable Plastics

The development of fully **biodegradable plastics** is still in the early stages. One problem is that the term *biodegradable* has been used in various senses. Deterioration or the simple loss of physical integrity and breakdown of plastic over time is not necessarily biodegradation. Likewise, photodegradation—the breakdown of plastics when exposed over a period of time to light—is not synonymous with biodegradation. Photodegradation has been suggested as a solution to the problem of plastic litter on our streets and beaches, but photodegradation is of virtually no value when a plastic is buried in a dump or landfill protected from light.

Some corporations have marketed "degradable" plastics, such as plastic garbage bags, but critics have charged that such products are actually misleading and may cause more damage than traditional nondegradable products. In many cases these plastics simply deteriorate into smaller pieces, but the plastic itself remains—albeit in small particles. These small particles, though not obvious to the naked eye and thus a solution to the aesthetic problem of "litter," may become widely dispersed in the environment, carrying any dangerous chemical ingredients with them. Furthermore, these microscopic particles are much harder to pick up and actually remove from the environment than macroscopic plastic bags and other debris.

True biodegradation involves the biochemical transformation of compounds by microorganisms. Researchers distinguish between primary and ultimate biodegradation. Primary biodegradation is the initial biochemical transformation of the plastic into smaller, shorter segments of material. The products of this initial stage may be dangerous or toxic. Thus, undergoing only partial (primary) biodegradation, which results in the release of toxic chemicals, may be less desirable environmentally than undergoing no biodegradation at all. During ultimate biodegradation, the intermediate products resulting from primary biodegradation are broken down into simple substances such as carbon dioxide, water, and methane. As a general rule, if a plastic undergoes full biodegradation, the bulk of the ultimate end products (CO_2, H_2O, CH_4) will be relatively benign environmentally (of course, carbon dioxide and methane will contribute to the greenhouse effect).

Approaches to making biodegradable plastics include introducing "weak" points so that the plastics can be more easily broken down, synthesizing plastics from natural molecules produced by plants or microorganisms (such as cellulose or starch), and producing plastics that are composites of traditional artificial substances and organismally produced molecules.

Encouraging work is proceeding on the development of cellulose-based materials. At Argonne National Laboratory in Argonne, Illinois, work on producing biodegradable plastics from potato starch and other plant products is nearing the stage of commercial testing. The basic idea is to convert starch found in food processing waste into lactic acid via fermentation. The lactic acid can then be synthesized into polylactic acid (chains of lactic acid) to be used to produce environmentally safe, biodegradable plastics. In addition to a variety of potential uses such as bags for yard waste that can be composted along with the clippings, a novel application for these plastics would be in the production of time-released pesticides and fertilizers. Pesticides and fertilizers could potentially be encased in degradable plastic before being spread over fields. As the plastic slowly broke down, the pesticide or fertilizer would be released. Such a system might greatly improve the efficiency of fertilizer and pesticide use, decreasing the amount that needs to be applied to a given area.

Perhaps the most encouraging work to date has been done on developing plastics made from bacterial polyesters. Some types of soil bacteria produce a class of compounds commonly known as PHAs (poly/betahydroxalkanoates) and PHB (polyhydroxybutyrate), which can be used to produce fully biodegradable plastic. These bacteria can be grown under controlled laboratory conditions to produce large amounts of these polymers. In Europe such bacterially produced plastic has been used to manufacture biodegradable shampoo bottles. Recently, researchers from Michigan State University and James Madison University (Virginia) were able to successfully insert the bacterial genes for production of PHB into a test plant. A concern with this approach, however, is that using arable land for plastic-bearing plants instead of food crops will exacerbate the problem of feeding the world.

Furthermore, even truly biodegradable plastics will not necessarily end our plastic waste worries because most landfills do little to promote the activity of microorganisms. Thus, if biodegradable plastics come into widespread use, special composting facilities may have to be established to promote their degradation.

a food or beverage container. In order to recycle plastics, secondary uses must generally be found for them.

To make it easier to identify different types of plastics for potential recycling, many plastic manufacturers have adopted a voluntary coding system that appears on containers, bags, and other products. This code takes the form of a number within a recycling triangle and generally an acronym below the triangle (● Table 19–4). Of the categories of plastic listed in Table 19–4, only PETE and HDPE are currently recycled to any appreciable extent, however. Still, the amount of plastic that is recycled continues to increase, and demand for good recyclable plastic is strong. The price paid for recyclable clear plastic containers increased by 40% in just two years, from June 1993 to June 1995.

Despite the small but significant progress that has been made in recycling plastics, it should be emphasized that recycling plastics once is quantitatively and qualitatively different from the reuse of paper fibers half a dozen times (after which the fibers can theoretically be composted, as described below) or the virtually endless recycling without degradation of some types of glass and metal. Eventually, second-generation plastic products, such as lawn furniture made from recycled milk jugs, must be disposed of. Furthermore, today's typical plastics are manufactured from scarce fossil fuel resources in an energy-intensive fashion, often producing significant amounts of pollution as a by-product. For these reasons many environmentally concerned citizens continue to look askance at plastics.

Composting

Many experts agree that **composting** is generally underutilized in the United States (■ Fig. 19–10). About 25% of our solid municipal waste, by weight, consists of yard wastes and food wastes, which are easily composted to make fertile humus or topsoil. It is ironic that such organics are often either buried in landfills, where they are permanently removed from the ecosystem and generally do not biodegrade to any considerable extent due to insufficient oxygen and/or moisture, or incinerated, when they could be used to produce natural fertilizer or topsoil—substances that are sorely need for our agricultural lands (see Chapter 13). Furthermore, if not contaminated with heavy metals or other toxic substances, sewage sludge (consisting, in large part, of dead bacteria—sewage sludge is *not* the same as raw sewage) can be composted to make a nat-

ural fertilizer. In addition, the paper, wood, leather, textiles, and other biodegradable substances that make up about 40 to 50% of our municipal waste stream could also be composted. Composting these latter substances may not pro-

TABLE 19–4 *Coding System for Plastics*

Polyethylene terephthalate (also known as PET)— this is a transparent plastic (although it may be colored) commonly used to make two-liter soda bottles and other containers such as peanut butter jars. PETE is used in approximately 25% of all plastic bottles. It can be recycled into such items as strapping (for packaging), fiberfill for winter clothing, carpets, surfboards, sailboat hulls, and the like.

High-density polyethylene—this plastic is commonly used to manufacture plastic milk jugs, bleach and detergent bottles, motor-oil bottles, plastic bags, and other containers. HDPE is used in more than 50% of all plastic bottles. It can be recycled into trash cans, detergent bottles, drainage pipes, base cups for soda bottles, and other similar items.

Vinyl or polyvinyl chloride (also known as PVC)—this is used in the manufacture of vinyl siding, plastic pipes and hoses, shower curtains, and so forth; it is also used to make some cooking-oil and shampoo bottles, as well as bottles for some household chemicals. It can be recycled into fencing, house siding, handrails, pipes, and similar items.

Low-density polyethylene—a plastic commonly used to make cellophane wrap, it is also used to manufacture bread bags, trash bags, and other types of containers. It can be recycled into grocery and garbage bags.

Polypropylene—a lightweight plastic commonly used in packaging some foods (for instance, some margarine and yogurt containers) and for certain types of lids and caps. It can be recycled into car-battery cases, bird feeders, and water pails.

Polystyrene—this is the substance that is commonly known as "styrofoam," used to make coffee cups, plastic peanuts for packing, egg cartons, meat trays, plastic utensils, videocassettes, and so forth. It has been recycled into tape dispensers and reusable cafeteria trays.

Other: Plastic resins other than the six basic categories listed above, as well as objects produced from several different types of plastics mixed together. Mixtures of plastics can sometimes be recycled into "plastic lumber" and used to manufacture benches, lawn furniture, picnic tables, marine pilings, and other types of outdoor equipment.

duce high-grade humus or topsoil, but it will provide a low-grade compost that could be used for nonagricultural purposes such as landfill cover, strip-mine reclamation, reforestation projects, or clean fill in areas along roads or construction sites. A fully implemented program of reuse, recycling, and composting, combined with separation and

Depending on the quality, compost has numerous uses. High-quality compost can be used to help replace lost topsoil on farms. The amounts of compost that could be used for this purpose are enormous; it takes an estimated 65 tons (59 metric tons) of compost to add just an inch (2.54 cm) of topsoil to an acre (0.4 hectare) of land. But then the potential for producing good compost is also large. Composting the organic wastes of a community of one million people could produce an estimated 600 tons (544.5 metric tons) of compost daily. Compost is also widely used in the nursery and landscaping industries, it is necessary for many types of land reclamation projects, and, of course, sanitary landfills need compost or soil between the trash layers and as a cap on top once the landfill is closed.

FIGURE 19–10
A community compost center.
(*Source*: Bernd Wittich/Visuals Unlimited.)

www.jbpub.com/environet

removal of hazardous waste for special disposal, would leave very little material to be placed in a landfill. Under such a system, landfills would be receptacles primarily for synthetic, nonrecyclable, and nonbiodegradable substances such as certain types of plastics and synthetic textiles.

Composting has occurred in nature for hundreds of millions of years. It is a free service provided by the microorganisms of the soil. When leaves and other organic material fall to the ground in a natural ecosystem, they are "eaten" by microscopic decomposers that attack the organic matter and break it down into smaller molecules, which can then be recycled in the ecosystem. This is the natural process by which humus and soil form.

Virtually anyone can facilitate composting; it can be carried out on a small or large scale, in a low-tech or high-tech fashion. Many individuals and families have compost piles or bins in their backyards. Grass clippings and other yard refuse, perhaps along with kitchen scraps, animal manure, and some dirt, are piled together. As long as the pile is properly aerated (it helps to stir the compost or turn it over occasionally) and has sufficient moisture (in temperate climates, the rain provides all the moisture needed), the microorganisms will do their job. The organic matter will decompose to form good compost. During the composting process, the aerobic microorganisms generate heat (the interiors of backyard compost piles can reach temperatures of up to 160°F [70°C]) that naturally kills many pathogenic bacteria and weeds, thus "sterilizing" the resultant compost. In large-scale commercial or community composting operations, care must be taken that the compost does not overheat, killing the very microorganisms that promote the composting process.

Recycling—Closing the Loop

Millions of Americans carefully sort their trash, then dutifully deliver the various categories of recyclables to a recycling center, or place the separated trash outside for curbside recyclable collection. Certainly, recycling will help address the solid waste problem in the United States, but sorting trash and taking it to a recycling center is only the first step. The materials must actually be recycled. Unbeknownst to many citizen recyclers, not all the material that is collected for recycling is actually recycled. The problem is not that the material could not potentially be recycled, but that markets for recyclables do not always exist.

While communities and the general public have been extremely eager to sort and collect recyclables, the capacity for processing recyclable materials has not always expanded accordingly. For instance, in the early 1990s, the market for used paper was so poor, millions of tons of it were accumulating in warehouses. Fortunately, as discussed above, this situation is now vastly improved. Similarly, mountains of plastic bottles and sorted glass sometimes await recycling. In September 1992, the company Waste Management of Seattle, Inc., had a reported 6000 tons (5445 metric tons) of glass for which it could not find a ready market. In other cases segregated paper and other trash intended for recycling have been incinerated or landfilled because there was no market for the material and storing it was uneconomical. However, it does look like the market for recyclables is now, in the late 1990s, gaining strength and momentum. If this trend continues, such problems will be a thing of the past.

Still, such situations have presented a dilemma for some recycling advocates who have had to decide whether to tell the public that their "recycling" efforts were for naught. Some leaders of the recycling movement have been known to practice deception, believing that it is important to encourage the recycling habit, even when the material is not recycled. They hoped that if the beginning of the recycling loop—sorting and collection—remained intact, the remainder of the loop—processing plants and markets—would eventually develop. Based on the current strength of the recyclable market, early indications are that this strategy has worked.

Strengthening the Market for Recyclables

Various ways of strengthening the market for recyclables have been suggested, not all of which have proved equally effective. Some local governments have mandated the collection of sorted recyclable materials, but collecting cannot lead to recycling if there are no markets for recyclables. In some instances, such short-sighted laws have actually driven trash collectors into bankruptcy when they were forced to spend extra time and money picking up recyclables but could not sell them.

Indeed, there is a popular misconception that the collection, sorting, and selling of recyclable trash should be a profit-earning venture for a community or at worst a break even situation. In fact, recycling may be costly, at least until markets develop (see Issues in Perspective 19-4 for another example of how recycling can be costly). But, even if markets must be "artificially" created through tax incentives and other means, recycling can still pay off if the ultimate cost is less than or equal to the cost of waste disposal otherwise. Indeed, disposal of waste by any means is expensive. According to the EPA, the United States spends more than $30 billion on waste disposal annually, and that figure is rising by about 17% a year. By the year 2000, we could be spending $75 billion a year on waste disposal.

If we are to increase the rate of recycling, both increased research and development and economic incentives will be needed. Although reuse and recycling have been carried out on a limited scale for ages, recycling of twenty-first century goods on a twenty-first century scale will require new technology. New ways to sort, clean, and reuse materials will certainly be welcome. Perhaps even more importantly, technical innovations may allow products manufactured from recycled materials to be of equal or better quality than products produced from virgin materials. To close the recycling loop, products manufactured from recycled materials must be purchased by consumers. This means that the recycled goods must be competitive on the open market, from both a quality and a cost perspective. At present, some products manufactured from virgin materials cost less than they would were it not for various tax breaks and subsidies that apply to the virgin materials; instead, tax incentives and subsidies could favor products manufactured from recycled materials. Local, state, and national governments can give an economic boost to recycling efforts by mandating the use of certain minimum levels of recycled materials in various new products, thus creating a ready market for recycled materials.

Industrial Ecosystems

Natural ecosystems do not produce any material waste; the "waste" of one organism is the lifeblood of other organisms. Likewise, an **industrial ecosystem** does not produce any waste; the effluents of one industrial process form the raw materials for another industrial process. Already some companies are finding that they can sell their effluents for a profit, whereas previously they had to pay to dispose of the same effluents as "waste." "One steel-processing company reprocesses the sulfuric acid used in its mills and reuses the acid to make ferrous sulfate compounds that it sells to magnetic tape manufacturers" (Kumar and Murck 1992, p. 191). A key component to the success of industrial ecosystems is communication. The company with a particular effluent must be able to locate the potential users of the material. Accordingly, information networks are being established in many countries (for example, France, Germany, and Belgium) and in various regions of the United States to put potential consumers of effluents in touch with the appropriate producers.

If the industrial ecosystem is to properly mimic natural ecosystems, virtually all materials must be reused/recycled. This means that not just manufacturing effluents but goods discarded by society at large must reenter the system as raw materials.

Due to the human penchant for treating symptoms rather than root problems, however, in some instances we are backsliding from the ideals of the industrial ecosystem. Take the typical automobile as an example: it is probably much more difficult to recycle all of the components found in a car today than it was in the 1920s. A modern automobile is manufactured from numerous different alloys of metal, including iron, steel, aluminum, nickel, lead, and copper, various polymers

Paying Extra to Recycle

Many recycling proponents argue that recycling and incineration are not compatible and should not be used in conjunction with each other; pragmatically, there is no such thing as an "integrated approach" to waste management that utilizes both incinerators, even if they are waste-to-energy facilities, and recycling. Large, expensive incinerators need to consume enormous amounts of materials to operate efficiently and economically. But in many cases, the materials that the incinerator consumes are the same materials that could be recycled. Some communities have signed contracts with incinerator operators only to find that they cannot meet their trash quotas if they institute recycling programs. In some cases communities have found themselves paying hefty penalties for not supplying an incinerator with enough trash.

An example of such a situation occurred in Massachusetts. An incinerator run by Wheelabrator Technologies in North Andover collects garbage from 23 Massachusetts communities that helped to underwrite the construction of the plant. The Wheelabrator plant burns garbage and uses the heat to produce energy; it has a capacity of 1500 tons (1360 metric tons) a day. To stay financially solvent, the incinerator charges tipping fees and sells the electricity it produces. When the plant opened in 1985, the communities agreed to a 20-year contract for the incinerator to take their garbage. Buried within the contract, however, was a clause specifying that the communities would pay a penalty if they failed to deliver as much trash to the incinerator as was anticipated. Apparently, at the time no one thought that a deficit of trash would be a problem.

But seven years later things had changed. Communities such as Andover were reducing the amount of garbage they had to send to the incinerator. In part this was blamed on the recession that occurred during these years—people were not purchasing as much and disposing of as much garbage as they did formerly. But many communities were also promoting recycling as a way to reduce their garbage output and help Massachusetts reach its goal of recycling 46% of the state's trash by the year 2000. Many communities made great strides in reducing the amount of garbage to be incinerated, but now they found they were penalized for not producing enough trash.

Reportedly, various communities were forced to pay Wheelabrator up to $300,000 a year. Don Marquis, the town manager of Arlington, Massachusetts, was quoted as saying: "In essence we have to pay for recycling twice. We pay to recycle, and we pay because we're not taking our trash to the North Andover incinerator" (quoted in the *Boston Globe*, January 17, 1993, p. 36). Understandably, such situations do not encourage recycling among the general public. Money that could be spent on curbside pickup for recyclables and recycling centers is instead paid in penalties to an incinerator.

What is the solution to such predicaments? Some suggest that this "problem" is not a problem at all. The communities involved should simply pay the penalties and wait for the economy to improve. With an improved economy, it is argued, consumption and waste production will surely increase, and there will be enough trash to satisfy both the recycling interests and the incinerators. Such an attitude essentially views more trash, rather than less, as positive. Another solution is to ban the type of penalty clause that led to the communities' difficulties. In 1987 Massachusetts enacted a law that does not allow penalty clauses in incinerator contracts if trash output is reduced by recycling. But the law does not apply to contracts signed before 1987, some of which are for periods of 20 or 25 years. Another suggestion is that the state or federal government should pay the penalties; this simply spreads the penalties over a larger taxpayer base without solving the real problem. Finally, some promoters of incinerators believe these facilities will receive a larger share of the nation's garbage as new regulations force more existing landfills to close and make it harder and more expensive for new landfills to open.

of plastic, rubber, cardboard, and so forth. The typical car has a very short life span and produces enormous amounts of waste during its operation (it not only spews pollution into the atmosphere, but runs through tires that typically end up in landfills—see Issues in Perspective 19–1). Eventually, the car is junked, and although many of its materials could be recycled, the sad truth is that often they are not. It requires a lot of time and effort to strip a car and separate its components for reuse or recycling. Furthermore, because of impurities, goods manufactured from the recycled materials may be inferior to goods manufactured from virgin materials.

As increasing numbers of vehicles have been put into service, they have produced increasing levels of pollution. A typical response to this problem has been to design ever more sophisticated cars that produce less pollution; that is, the symptom—pollution from car exhausts—is attacked. A much simpler, though surely less popular, alternative would be to attack the root problem—namely, too many cars.

In the 1970s, catalytic converters began to be widely used on the exhaust systems of automobiles to reduce various pollutants in the exhaust before it enters the atmosphere. But catalytic converters also have drawbacks; while helping to solve one environmental problem, they exacerbated another. Standard catalytic converters rely on the use of scarce platinum group metals. Before the extensive use of catalytic converters, platinum group metals were typically recycled at efficiencies of 85% or higher due to their rarity and value. Early catalytic converters were not designed with recycling in mind, so their introduction substantially reduced the rate of recycling among platinum group metals, deviating from the ideal of the industrial ecosystem. Fortunately, systems are now being developed to remove catalytic converters from old cars and recover the platinum group metals. Likewise, the metals from discarded computers and other electronic equipment are increasingly being recycled.

HAZARDOUS WASTE

The Comprehensive Environmental Response, Compensation, and Liability Act (CERCLA), the federal statute passed in 1980 that established Superfund (see page 552), defines a hazardous substance as "any substance that, when released into the environment, may present substantial danger to public health, welfare, or the environment." CERCLA goes on to define extremely hazardous substances as substances that "could cause serious, irreversible health effects from a single exposure." Hazardous waste is essentially waste composed of such hazardous substances. Hazardous waste can originate from the home (such as household cleaners or pesticides), local or national government operations, agricultural use, industry, or other sources (● Table 19–5). Hazardous waste often includes substances that are chemically reactive, corrosive, flammable, explosive, or toxic to living organisms (toxic materials are harmful or fatal when consumed by organisms in relatively small amounts).

EnviroNet
www.jbpub.com/environet

TABLE 19–5 *Health Effects of Selected Hazardous Substances*

CHEMICAL	SOURCE	HEALTH EFFECTS
Pesticides		
DDT	Insecticides	Cancer; damages liver, embryo, bird eggs
BHC	Insecticides	Cancer, embryo damage
Petrochemicals		
Benzene	Solvents, pharmaceuticals, and detergent production	Headaches, nausea, loss of muscle coordination, leukemia, linked to damage of bone marrow
Vinyl chloride	Plastics production	Lung and liver cancer, depresses central nervous system, suspected embryotoxin
Other organic chemicals		
Dioxin	Herbicides, waste incineration	Cancer, birth defects, skin disease
PCBs	Electronics, hydraulic fluid, fluorescent lights	Skin damage, possible gastrointestinal damage, possibly cancer causing
Heavy metals		
Lead	Paint, gasoline	Neurotoxic; causes headaches, irritability, mental impairment in children; damages brain, liver, and kidneys
Cadmium	Zinc processing, batteries, fertilizer processing	Cancer in animals, damage to liver and kidneys

(*Source*: Based primarily on data compiled by World Resources Institute and published in *World Resources 1987* [New York: Basic Books, 1987]. Reprinted with permission from World Resources Institute.)

There are three main categories of hazardous waste: organic compounds, inorganic compounds and elements, and radioactive waste. Organic compounds are carbon-based substances that also contain a substantial percentage of hydrogen and oxygen. Some organic compounds are naturally formed molecules, some are derived from once-living material such as petroleum and other fossil fuels, and some are totally artificial substances synthesized in the laboratory. Many fertilizers, pesticides, organic dyes, plastics, and other substances are organic compounds. Theoretically, at least, organic compounds should be degradable into simple, nontoxic substances such as carbon dioxide and water (plus some residue). In reality, however, many are not easily decomposed in nature and persist for extremely long periods of time. Sometimes incineration can be applied successfully to break down and detoxify hazardous organic compounds; another approach is to use microbes that can chemically attack and degrade some such substances. Bacteria have been used with success to help clean up oil spills.

Inorganic hazardous compounds have little or no carbon, but they commonly contain heavy metals such as lead, mercury, cadmium, copper, arsenic, iron, aluminum, manganese, chromium, beryllium, nickel, selenium, zinc, silver, and others. Some heavy metals are necessary to life in small, or trace, amounts, but all are toxic to organisms in larger doses. All of these elements occur naturally in the environment, usually in low concentrations, and are cycled through the Earth's chemical and biological systems. The problem is that modern industry has mined and released much higher concentrations of heavy metals than the natural geochemical and biological systems are capable of readily handling. Therefore, once released into the environment, these substances tend to slowly accumulate, often to toxic levels. Once dispersed in the general environment, like all hazardous substances, they are very difficult to remove. In order to dispose of toxic inorganic compounds safely they are sometimes combined with various chemicals that transform the material into a stable, cementlike block that can be buried or otherwise disposed of. The idea is that the solid block will resist leaching and thus not allow the inorganic compounds to escape into the environment. However, the best way to deal with such inorganic compounds is to not allow them to mingle with the general environment at all. Rather than being discarded, waste substances containing heavy metals should be recycled whenever possible.

Radioactive waste is the third generally recognized category of hazardous waste. We have already discussed radioactivity and certain types of radioactive waste in Chapter 8. Besides nuclear power plants, radioactive waste is generated by nuclear weapons manufacturing facilities, medical facilities (radioactive equipment and treatments), some research labs, and many common commercial, industrial, and home functions (for instance, the radioactive elements of home smoke detectors). High-level radioactive waste, from nuclear power plants and weapons facilities, is disposed of according to special regulations and handling procedures. But much low-level radioactive waste is considered to be below regulatory concern, and no special precautions are taken in disposing of it. In some cases radioactive material has been incinerated along with other rubbish or been disposed of in municipal dumps and landfills.

Hazardous waste is a major problem due both to its inherent dangers and to the amount that continues to be produced each year. No one really knows how much hazardous waste is produced in the world every year, but the United States alone produces more than 286.5 million tons (260 million metric tons) annually. World production must be at least twice this amount. Much of this waste comes from the chemical, paper, and petroleum industries.

The best way to control the influx of hazardous substances into the waste stream is simply to reduce the amounts used in the first place and then reuse and recycle such substances whenever possible rather than disposing of them. Many manufacturing processes use or generate hazardous substances. In some cases the amounts of these substances can be reduced by making the processes more efficient. Better information networks would enable hazardous material generated by one manufacturer to be passed on to another company that could use it (see the earlier discussion of industrial ecosystems). Sometimes biodegradable and environmentally benign substances can be substituted for artificial, synthetic, or less environmentally friendly chemical substances; an example would be using natural, biologically based fertilizers, pesticides, and herbicides in place of synthetic chemicals. Even around the house, the average consumer can buy less toxic, more environmentally friendly paints, sprays, cleansers, and other chemicals.

Hazardous waste disposal is now recognized as a special problem that requires special techniques and solutions. All too often in the past, however, hazardous wastes were disposed of improperly with little concern for long-term consequences, even though their disposal was technically legal at the time. What are now recognized as hazardous substances were often thrown away along with ordinary wastes. Now we are haunted by hazardous waste dump sites across the nation, and indeed around the world. One of the first to come to the attention of the nation was Love Canal.

Love Canal

Love Canal ( Fig. 19–11), in the town of Niagara Falls, New York, was excavated in the 1890s as part of a failed development project. From 1947 to 1953, Hooker Chemical and Plastics Corporation used the canal as a disposal site. An estimated 21,900 tons (19,873 metric tons) of chemical wastes were deposited in the abandoned canal, mostly contained in 55-gallon (208-liter) steel drums. Numerous hazardous wastes, including powerful carcinogens, were buried in the canal—substances such as dioxin, benzene, chloroform, and dichlorethylene. In 1953 the canal was closed and covered with a clay surface.

Hooker Corporation sold the canal and adjacent land to the Board of Education of Niagara Falls for only $1.00, but with the warning that the canal had been filled with chemical waste and the provision that Hooker Corporation would not be held liable for any injury, death, damage, or other loss of life or property due to this waste. Despite these warnings, the Board of Education located an elementary school directly on top of the filled-in canal. Furthermore, the board sold land to developers who built several hundred houses there, federally subsidized apartments were built in the area, and even a housing project for retired persons was erected in the vicinity.

As early as the mid-1960s, the residents of the Love Canal area began to complain to city officials about noxious chemical fumes. By the early 1970s, some residents noticed that strange liquids were seeping into their basements, but not until 1975–1977 did Love Canal become known nationwide. During these years the area received relatively heavy rainfalls and snowfalls, and this increased surface water set off a number of major problems. Increasing quantities of hazardous

chemicals seeped into basements and sewers, and pools of chemically contaminated water appeared at ground level. Vegetation died, animals and humans developed illnesses and sores, and reportedly the rubber on bicycle tires and the bottoms of tennis shoes began disintegrating. In places the land surface collapsed and the 55-gallon steel drums appeared. In one yard a swimming pool popped out of its foundation and floated in a small lake of chemicals. As conditions got worse, there were increased reports of illnesses, as well as allegations of miscarriages and birth defects due to the chemicals buried in Love Canal.

By August 1978, the situation had deteriorated to the point where the New York State Department of Health declared a health emergency for the area. New York State purchased over two hundred homes close to the canal and relocated the

residents. President Jimmy Carter declared a state of emergency for the area, and in 1980 over seven hundred additional families were told to leave the vicinity. In the end numerous houses, apartments, and the school had to be abandoned; approximately two hundred homes were actually destroyed.

Relocation of families and cleanup of the Love Canal site cost an estimated $275 million, and this does not include the indirect costs of psychological trauma among the residents, as well as their potentially continuing health problems. The actual cleanup during the 1980s required that

FIGURE 19–11
An evacuated home in the Love Canal community, Niagara Falls, New York. (*Source:* Lisa Bunin/Greenpeace.)

some buildings be demolished, soils and sediments contaminated with toxic substances be removed and treated, and wastes migrating through the groundwater be contained and removed. By the early 1990s, the EPA judged the Love Canal area to be fully restored, and a community is once more occupying the area.

Love Canal demonstrates how a little bit of care and foresight at one of many points might have either averted or mitigated the damage. Steel drums filled with dangerous chemicals will inevitably corrode, disintegrate, and leak. When the drums were deposited during the 1940s and 1950s, Hooker Corporation might have anticipated the consequences, at least in part. The company might have undertaken a study, for instance, to determine approximately how long it would take for the drums to leak, how the chemicals would enter the groundwater, the paths the contamination would take, and what areas would be affected to what degree. Of course, such a study would have cost a significant amount of money, and the outcome of the study would most likely have been negative (that is, suggesting limitations to the disposal of the chemicals). Furthermore, Hooker was under no legal obligations to undertake such a study at the time of the waste disposal.

Later in the process, the Niagara Falls Board of Education might have heeded Hooker's warning that chemical wastes had been disposed of in Love Canal. Still later, when residents of the area first began complaining about noxious fumes in the 1960s and then reported the seepage of strange chemicals into their basements, the city of Niagara Falls might have immediately responded by thoroughly evaluating the problem and formulating a way to control the situation. Such studies would have been costly. But the bottom line is that early studies at any stage would have ultimately proven extremely cost-effective. Potentially hundreds of millions of dollars in property damage and cleanup costs, not to mention the health hazards, could have been avoided by timely analysis and predictions of the potential future problems. Once things got out of hand and the Love Canal disaster occurred, the state of New York and the federal government picked up much of the tab. In hindsight, the state and federal government would have saved enormous expenses if they had funded thorough analyses of Love Canal and its potential hazards early on.

Superfund

After the chemical contamination of Love Canal was exposed, the United States realized that something had to be done about hazardous waste sites. In 1980 Congress passed the Comprehensive Environmental Response, Compensation, and Liability Act (CERCLA), authorizing the Environmental Protection Agency (EPA) to recommend which hazardous waste sites should be given the highest priority in cleanup efforts. Accordingly, in that year the EPA set out to identify all hazardous waste sites in the United States, determine what dangers to health and well-being each posed, and what measures would be required to clean each site up. The agency compiled a National Priorities List (NPL) of high-priority sites that merited action. The cleanup and related operations were to be funded by taxes on the chemical and petroleum industries, as well as assessments on various corporate polluters. Initially, $1.6 billion was allocated to a Hazardous Substance Response Fund, commonly referred to as "**Superfund**," to be used for cleanup activities.

Unfortunately, despite the best of intentions, Superfund has been plagued by problems. Amid allegations of mismanagement and misappropriation of funds, some critics have charged that Superfund is actually a Superscandal. By the early 1990s, according to the Office of Technology Assessment (OTA), more than 31,500 hazardous waste sites had been identified, 1200 of which were NPL sites. Yet, after spending some $11.1 billion contributed by federal agencies and private industry (the $11.1 billion excludes administrative costs), less than a hundred high-priority sites had been cleaned up. No one really knows how much it will cost to clean up all of the hazardous waste sites identified by the EPA. According to one estimate, the average cleanup cost for a single site ranges from $21 million to $30 million; on that basis, the NPL sites could cost $37 billion to clean up. Some analysts have estimated that the cost of cleaning up all hazardous waste nationwide could range from $750 billion to $1 trillion and require more than 50 years of sustained effort.

Many critics of Superfund are particularly irritated that much of the money does not go to on-the-ground cleanup efforts or for research into new methods of detoxifying hazardous sites and building safer waste disposal areas. Rather, enormous amounts of money are spent on legal fees as various businesses and government agencies engage in litigation over who should pay for the cleanup of a particular site. Approximately $200 billion of the estimated $1 trillion cost will be used to cover legal fees. A Rand Corporation study found that between 1986 and 1989, $1.2 billion of the money spent by Superfund went to lawyers, while only about $0.1 billion was spent

on actual cleanup. Under present Superfund arrangements, the biggest polluters bear the largest financial burden for cleanup, so lengthy court battles ensue over who contributed the most waste to each site.

To solve some of these problems, new regulations and "no-fault" programs have been proposed. Under no-fault policies, all companies would be required to help finance cleanup efforts, whether they were directly involved in creating the problem in the first place or not. Of course, many "clean" companies and organizations regard such policies as inherently unfair—why should they help pay for damage caused by other companies? Or should the federal government simply pick up the entire tab, which means that the public will ultimately pay for the cleanups? There are no easy answers as to how to fund the enormous cleanup costs that we face in the future.

The necessity and effectiveness of Superfund cleanup operations have also been questioned. Some researchers suggest that the health risks of many hazardous waste sites have been overstated, and in some cases, cleanup efforts may disturb toxic materials and create more of a hazard than if the site were simply left alone. Various EPA studies have suggested that problems such as indoor pollution and outdoor air pollution (see Chapters 14, 15, and 17) pose a greater health risk than hazardous waste—the logical conclusion being that limited resources might better be expended on cleaning up these other environmental problems rather than focusing on hazardous waste sites.

The United States is not the only country that faces huge price tags to clean up its hazardous waste problems; similar situations exist around the globe. The small country of the Netherlands will have to spend at least $1.5 billion to clean up its hazardous waste sites. The former West Germany needed an estimated $10 billion to clean up its own hazardous waste sites; now with the unification of East and West Germany, the price will sharply increase. Some of the worst toxic dump sites and environmental hazards are in Eastern Europe and the countries of the former Soviet Union. Developing nations are also plagued by toxic dumps and rampant pollution; in many cases, the dumping of hazardous waste is inadequately regulated. In Mexico City, for instance, wastewater contaminated with heavy metals and toxic organic chemicals is discharged into the municipal sewer system. From there, with very little treatment, it is transported to agricultural areas for use in irrigation, with the result that toxic substances have been found in vegetables and other crops. Likewise, in China some 441 million tons (400 million metric tons) of industrial wastes and mining tailings are annually dumped on the outskirts of cities or into lakes, streams, and rivers with devastating results—148,260 acres (60,000 hectares) of land in China may be covered with hazardous material.

The Bhopal Disaster

One of the most infamous industrial chemical disasters occurred at the Union Carbide pesticide-producing plant located in **Bhopal**, India, on December 3, 1984. Apparently, a faulty valve allowed water to leak into a tank containing approximately 16.5 tons (15 metric tons) of liquid methyl isocyanate, an extremely toxic substance. The water and methyl isocyanate reacted chemically, producing high temperatures and pressures that vaporized the liquid; ultimately, the material escaped as a deadly cloud above the city of 800,000 people. Unfortunately, there were no emergency plans or procedures in place, and no one really knew how to deal with the situation. The results were devastating—several thousand people died immediately, and over the next few years thousands more (estimates run as high as 10,000) died as a result of methyl isocyanate poisoning. In addition to the deaths, an estimated 50,000 to perhaps 500,000 were injured to some degree as a result of the disaster.

The Bhopal disaster should not have occurred. A number of safety devices at the Union Carbide plant were not operational at the time of the disaster; indeed, some had been turned off for months. As a result of the disaster, billions of dollars in damage claims were brought against Union Carbide, and murder charges were filed against top managers of the Bhopal plant: the suits and criminal charges have still not been settled.

The Bhopal disaster suddenly made people aware of the inherent dangers of many industrial processes, especially if plans are not in place to deal with extraordinary disaster. In the United States, the Bhopal incident caused Americans to look with increasing suspicion at the chemical industry and helped inspire Congress to pass the Emergency Planning and Community Right-to-Know Act, which established the important **Toxics Release Inventory**.

Toxics Release Inventory

In October 1986, Congress passed the Emergency Planning and Community Right-to-Know Act as Title III of the Superfund Amendments and

Reauthorization Act. Under this law larger companies and organizations must report their production, use, and release of more than 300 potentially hazardous chemicals listed by the EPA. Based on this information, the EPA produces an annual report, known as the Toxics Release Inventory (TRI). With the release of the 1987 TRI, for the first time Americans could get an overall picture of how much toxic material the country's industries were emitting. Based on the material gathered for the TRI, in 1992 (the latest year for which figures are currently available) 3.2 billion pounds (1.45 billion kg) of over 300 EPA-listed toxic chemicals were released or disposed of by U.S. industry. Five major industries (chemicals, primary metals, paper, plastics, and transportation equipment) accounted for 2.389 billion pounds (1.083 billion kg) of these wastes (see Figures 14–13 and 14–14 in Chapter 14 for other examples of TRI data).

Over the past decade, the TRIs have had some very positive benefits. They have enabled citizens and communities, armed with data, to put pressure on companies to cut emissions of hazardous substances (see Issues in Perspective 14–2 in Chapter 14). Likewise, people in high-level management positions were themselves appalled by the amounts of toxic chemicals their own factories were releasing. Many industries are now taking voluntary actions to reduce the amount of toxic material released into the environment. For example, over 700 major companies joined a voluntary EPA program in which they promised to attempt to reduce their emissions of 17 major toxic chemicals by one-half by the mid-1990s. The Chemical Manufacturing Association has reported that collectively its members reduced their releases of chemicals listed on the TRI by about a third between 1987 and 1990.

Despite the good that the TRI has done, it has not gone without criticism. Many different types of businesses, especially smaller businesses such as dry cleaners and photographic processors, are not required to submit information to the EPA. Furthermore, the list of toxic chemicals compiled by the EPA, is not complete. Perhaps most critically, the TRI is merely a compilation of certain toxic chemicals released directly by large facilities (companies are required to report releases of 25,000 pounds [11,338 kg] or more for each listed chemical). It does not include small releases by individuals, small businesses, municipalities, and other organizations; yet these can add up. Also, many hazardous and toxic chemicals are incorporated into end products (paints, stains, coolants, and so forth) that are used by a consumer, but

eventually released into the environment—again, these are not accounted for in the TRI. The U.S. General Accounting Office estimated in 1991 that the then current laws might allow as much as 95% of the total chemical emissions in the United States to go unreported. While certainly an important step toward accounting for our chemical waste, the TRI may represent merely the proverbial "tip of the iceberg."

New Technologies for Dealing with Hazardous Waste

Engineers and scientists have long grappled with the problem of what to do with hazardous wastes. Common solutions have involved isolating such wastes from the environment in a permanent waste disposal site, such as a landfill or deep in the ground through deep-well injection. A relatively new approach is to treat hazardous and toxic wastes so as to eliminate or reduce their harmful properties. For decades this was attempted by simply burning the waste, but in many cases burning at temperatures that are not sufficiently high actually compounds the problem by creating and releasing molecules that are more harmful than the initial substance (for example, dioxin and heavy metals may be released during standard incineration, as discussed earlier).

In recent years several laboratories have concentrated on developing more efficient ways to destroy and neutralize toxic chemicals. Westinghouse Electric Company is working on a "plasma torch" that can reportedly generate temperatures up to 10,000°F (5500°C). The torch would be trained on toxic organic chemicals, such as PCBs (see Issues in Perspective 19–5), and break them down into relatively simple and harmless gases. The Westinghouse plasma torch is small enough so that it can be mounted on the back of a truck and brought to hazardous waste dump sites. In this way extra transportation of hazardous waste can be avoided, lessening the chance that an accident might happen on the way to a disposal facility. A potential drawback of plasma torch technology is that it may consume large amounts of energy to destroy a significant amount of hazardous waste.

The Solar Energy Research Institute in Colorado and Sandia National Laboratory in New Mexico, both U.S. government organizations, are researching ways to destroy toxic chemicals using solar energy. One method resembles in principle some solar energy collectors described in Chapter 9. Water contaminated with toxic organic chemicals is mixed with catalysts and then pumped through tubes

PCBs

Some modern wastes, especially synthetic chemical wastes, are extremely persistent and widespread. In the far future our descendants will more than likely be able to readily identify traces of these twentieth-century compounds; they will form clear "chemical fossils" marking our existence. PCBs are a case in point. They have diffused around the world and are now found in virtually all humans and many other living creatures, as well as in soil, water, and ice samples.

The PCBs, or polychlorinated biphenyls, are a group of synthetic organic compounds that are not found in nature. For many years they were put to numerous uses, such as in insulation, lubricants, hydraulic fluids, paints, dyes, fluorescent lights, and fluids used in electrical transformers and capacitors. Then it was found that PCBs appear to be highly toxic: they were implicated in damage to the skin and liver, they appear to cause reproductive problems and increase the incidence of birth defects, and they may be carcinogenic and are possibly associated with hypertension and heart disease. In large amounts they can induce such immediate effects as nausea, vomiting, and diarrhea. Some authorities have contended that many of the adverse effects attributed to PCBs may actually be due to trace amounts of highly toxic dioxins and polychlorinated dibenzofurans (PCDFs) commonly associated with PCBs, but even if this is the case, it makes little difference to the sufferers of such toxic poisoning. If PCBs are heated or burned at certain temperatures, such as in an inadvertent fire or perhaps in a dump or incinerator where they are burned purposefully at relatively low temperatures, dioxin and PCDFs will be produced and given off.

Due to their toxicity, PCBs were banned from most uses in the United States and the European Community in 1976. Nevertheless, large concentrations of PCBs persist in dump sites and older electrical equipment, for example. In the developing world, especially Latin America, PCBs continue to be used; in some areas their use is even increasing rather than decreasing.

PCBs are very persistent, widely diffused, and difficult to isolate and destroy. In the 1980s the EPA estimated that virtually 100% of the American population had detectable traces of PCBs in their bodies. Likewise, PCBs are found in fishes, birds, and other wildlife. The good news, however, is that the ban on PCBs in the United States is showing positive results. Decreases in the concentration of PCBs found in samples of human and animal tissue over the past 25 years have been documented. The bad news is that the levels of numerous other potentially dangerous chemicals in the environment are on the rise.

There have been several major PCB spills and contaminations. In Japan fish have been accidentally contaminated with PCB-laden oil during processing, resulting in stomach and liver cancer, among other effects, when the fish were consumed by humans. In June 1979, transformer fluid containing PCBs leaked into 1.9 million pounds (0.86 million kg) of animal feed that was subsequently distributed to farms in Minnesota, Montana, Idaho, Washington, and North Dakota. Levels of PCBs up to 50 times those allowed by law collected in chickens who ate the feed, as well as in their eggs. Bakeries and other food processing plants that used the contaminated eggs and chickens had to dispose of their products, and approximately 400,000 chickens and more than a million eggs were destroyed. In 1981 an explosion took place in an office building in Binghamton, New York. An electrical transformer cracked, and PCBs leaked into the fire that had started. Ash containing PCBs, PCDFs, and dioxins permeated the building, and the entire area had to be sealed off. The cost of completely decontaminating the building was on the order of $19 million.

One of the worst cases of intentional PCB dumping occurred along the Hudson River. For about three decades, ending in 1977, two General Electric power plants released thousands of pounds of PCBs into the river. The PCBs sank to the bottom and slowly moved downstream, spreading noxious pollution along their way. Due to the PCBs entering the fish population, New York State had to ban commercial fishing of striped bass in the Hudson River and published warnings against eating about a dozen other species of fishes from the river. General Electric paid a $3 million fine to the state and stopped dumping the PCBs. But the fine was merely a token amount relative to the cost of the environmental damage that General Electric caused. To clean up the mess, up to 40 miles (64 km) of riverbed may have to be dredged to remove the PCBs, and the material removed may have to be landfilled as hazardous waste; this process would cost hundreds of millions of dollars. As an alternative, General Electric has suggested utilizing bioremediation—bacteria would be used to digest and break down the PCBs and other dangerous compounds—as a possible way to deal with the problem. No one is sure how successful such a procedure would be, however. So far the contamination still persists in the Hudson River, and only moderate cleanup efforts have actually begun.

while the Sun's light is focused on the mixture. The ultraviolet light of the Sun has the ability to break down and destroy up to 90% or more of the contaminants. In another method the Sun's light is focused on a special vessel containing toxic organic chemicals. The solar energy can raise the temperature inside the vessel to very high levels, converting the more complex chemicals into simple substances such as carbon monoxide and hydrogen gas. It has even been suggested that these products could then be used as a fuel; either the CO and H_2 can be used to form methanol, or the hydrogen gas can be burned directly. In a related process magnified sunlight focused on a container full of dioxin broke down 99.999% of the dioxin into simpler, relatively harmless substances.

Bioremediation

Bioremediation, or biotreatment, is the use of bacteria and other small organisms (such as single-celled and multicellular microbes and fungi) to clean up or reduce unwanted concentrations of certain substances. Essentially, the microorganisms eat or digest unwanted chemicals, transforming them into simpler, less harmful, or useful forms. Certain bacteria, for instance, will attack oil and related organic substances, converting the material into primarily water and carbon dioxide.

The biological action of microorganisms has been a necessary part of nature ever since life originated nearly four billion years ago. Microorganisms convert kitchen waste into compost, and bacteria have been used commercially for years to treat sewage and even to concentrate metals such as copper and nickel from low-grade ores. Recently, microorganisms have been finding much wider applications, especially in oil spills, at toxic and hazardous waste sites, and as biological "scrubbers" to remove dangerous pollutants from factory emissions before they leave the facility. Certain strains of bacteria and fungi can digest even extremely dangerous chemicals, such as DDT (the insecticide), TNT (the explosive), PCBs, dioxins, tolulene, naphthalene, xylene, carbon tetrachloride, toxic nitrates, asphalt products, creosote (a wood preservative), and many other substances. If a bacterium cannot be found in nature to perform a certain job, researchers may be able to genetically engineer one in the laboratory. Of course, the substances produced as organisms digest dangerous compounds may also be extremely dangerous. For example, DDT may be degraded to an even more toxic substance than the original pesticide. One must be careful in applying bioremediation techniques in specific cases.

After the *Exxon Valdez* oil spill of March 1989 ( Fig. 19–12), simple bioremediation techniques were used on a very small scale with quite encouraging results. Liquid farm fertilizers were sprayed on a portion of an oily beach, and after approximately two weeks, the oil on the beach was significantly reduced, compared to a test area that had been left untreated. No microorganisms per se had been added to the beach—essential nutrients had simply been spread to encourage the growth of already present bacteria that would digest the oil. The success of this simple experiment has had wide ramifications for the prospects of bioremediation. Prior to this time, the EPA generally did not sanction the use of microorganisms for cleaning up oil spills or hazardous waste sites. Since the initial success of the *Exxon Valdez* experiment, bioremediation has been put to work cleaning up hundreds of sites overseen by the EPA.

Today dozens of companies are developing and marketing biotreatment products—everything from bacteria and nutrients to help clean out a home septic system, to mixtures that are specifically designed to deal with gasoline spills and other hazardous materials. Bioremediation tends to be cheaper than traditional treatment methods such as incineration of contaminated soil, and it has the distinct advantage that it can often be applied on site. For example, imagine that some toxic substance, such as a petroleum product, has leaked into the ground. Instead of digging up hundreds of tons of contaminated soil and transporting it to an incinerator, large augers can drill into the soil and mix in bacteria and nutrients. The bacteria then attack the substance, breaking it down into harmless chemicals. Such techniques have already been used to treat soil contaminated with creosote at a lumber-treatment plant and at a 40-acre (16-hectare) site near Los Angeles where the soil had been contaminated with marine fuel.

Biotreatment is also finding many useful applications to avoid releasing pollutants into the environment in the first place. Microbes are of particular use in treating volatile organic compounds (VOCs) that are often released as gaseous fumes from factories and small businesses, such as dry cleaners, print shops, auto body shops, and even bakeries. In one technique the fumes are passed through layers of well-humidified and aerated peat moss and compost that contain bacteria. The gases are caught on wet films covering the compost and peat moss and can then be broken

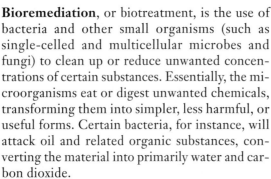

EnviroNet
www.jbpub.com/environet

down into harmless gases (mostly water and carbon dioxide) by the bacteria. This is a relatively low-tech, inexpensive, but very effective method of substantially reducing the release of harmful VOCs. Bacteria simply do the work of chemical degradation for free. Such systems are already finding wide use in the Netherlands and Germany.

Bioremediation currently is most commonly used to break down various hazardous organic compounds (substances made up primarily of car-

uranium compounds into an insoluble form that is easily removed from contaminated water; there are hopes that similar techniques can be used with other radioactive substances.

Some concerns have been expressed over the large-scale use of bioremediation methods. It is fine when the organisms do what we want them to do, but what if populations escape and start attacking substances that we do not want broken down? Will wild populations of asphalt-eating

and tar-eating bacteria suddenly attack our roads? Will treated wood, which was meant to last, become the foodstuff of roving packs of microbes? What damage might genetically engineered bacteria cause if they escape the laboratory or enclosed waste sites where they are put to work? Advocates of biotreatment techniques point out that most of the bacteria put to work already exist as naturally occurring populations. These populations are relatively small and stable and must be coaxed into attacking specific substances on a large scale by providing extra nutrients (or manipulating other factors, such as the temperature,

FIGURE 19–12
A cleanup crew works on the beach of Smith Island shortly after the Exxon Valdez oil spill of March 1989. (*Source:* Reuters/Bettmann.)

bon, hydrogen, and oxygen) into simpler, non-toxic substances. In some cases several different organisms may be needed to complete the job. But biotreatment is finding even wider applications. Organisms cannot destroy heavy metals or radioactive substances, but in some instances they can concentrate them or put them into a less mobile form so that they are easier to deal with. Fungi have been used to convert water-soluble selenium salts to a gaseous form as part of a program to clean a contaminated reservoir. Scientists at the U.S. Geological Survey have discovered species of bacteria that can convert water-soluble

pH, or oxygen conditions). As mentioned already, the bioremediation experiment performed in the wake of the *Exxon Valdez* oil spill consisted of nothing more than supplying essential nutrients to spur on the already existing bacteria population. Once the job is completed, the bacteria population dies back to normal levels. As for genetically engineered bacteria, such organisms could be specially designed so that they will live only under very controlled conditions. Therefore, if they should escape, they would not be able to survive.

Interestingly, certain waste sites have been purposefully designed so that biological activity will not occur; here, of course, we refer to the modern, dry sanitary landfill. Many natural bacteria that exist in the backyard compost pile need a warm, wet, well-aerated environment to thrive—exactly what is avoided in many modern, lined, dry, covered landfills. As a result, the trash and garbage in landfills just sit there and do not appreciably decompose.

SUMMARY

Staggering amounts of solid and hazardous waste are generated both in the United States and worldwide every year. In the United States, on the order of 6 to 10 billion tons (5.4–9 billion metric tons) of solid waste and about 286.5 million tons (260 million metric tons) of hazardous waste are produced annually. Such waste comes from various mining, agricultural, and industrial operations, as well as from the municipal waste stream. Dealing with this waste is a major business and a major concern of some environmentalists.

Several alternative paradigms have been applied to waste management: the dilute and disperse strategy (for example, burning trash or releasing wastes into rivers), the concentrate and contain strategy (for example, isolating waste in a sanitary landfill), and resource recovery (for example, reusing and recycling). All of these strategies continue to be used to some degree through such techniques as incineration, waste-to-energy facilities, landfilling, deep-well injection, and modern recycling programs. There are major drawbacks to some forms of incineration (greenhouse gases and noxious fumes may be released into the air, and hazardous waste in the form of the remaining ash may be produced), landfilling (landfills may leak leachate, valuable materials that could be recycled are removed from circulation, sites for new landfills may be in short supply in some areas), and deep-well injection (pumping wastes into the ground may contaminate groundwater supplies and initiate earthquakes).

Most waste management experts today view source reduction—reducing the amount of waste in the first place—along with reuse of products and recycling of ma-terials, as the most desirable option for dealing with the waste stream. However, source reduction is not always easy, practical, or feasible. Reuse and recycling may be difficult if the proper networks and markets are not in place. Still, there has been a major effort in the United States (and around the world) to increase the level of recycling. In particular, large amounts of glass, metals, paper, and plastics are recycled. Recycling not only reduces the amount of waste that must be disposed of, but generally saves energy as well (it takes more energy to refine metal or produce glass from virgin materials than from recycled materials). Organic garbage, such as yard and food wastes, sewage sludge, much paper waste, and some new biodegradable plastics, can be composted. Compost has many uses, from replacing topsoil on farms to use in land reclamation projects and in the landscaping and nursery industries.

Hazardous waste, which includes substances that are chemically reactive, corrosive, flammable, explosive, or toxic to living organisms, has proliferated with the development of modern industrial society. The disaster in the Love Canal area of the town of Niagara Falls, New York, brought the problems of hazardous waste disposal sites to national attention in the 1970s. In 1980 the U.S. Federal Comprehensive Environmental Response, Compensation, and Liability Act was passed, establishing "Superfund" to address the cleaning up of hazardous waste sites and spills. As a result, thousands of hazardous waste sites have been identified in the United States, and billions of dollars have been spent on the problem. However, Superfund has been plagued by problems. Relatively few hazardous waste sites have actually been cleaned up, and enormous amounts of money have been spent on legal fees rather than on cleanup efforts or necessary research. A major concern is often determining who is to blame for a particular hazardous waste site and thus who is to be responsible for the cleanup. The necessity and effectiveness of many Superfund cleanup operations have also been questioned. Some researchers suggest that the health risks of many hazardous waste sites have been overstated, and in some cases cleanup of a site may disturb toxic materials, creating more of a hazard than if the site had been simply left alone. Many countries other than the United States are also plagued by numerous hazardous waste sites.

The Bhopal incident (December 1984) is one of the most infamous industrial chemical disasters. A deadly cloud of methyl isocyanate released by accident from the Union Carbide pesticide-producing plant killed several thousand people and may have injured up to 500,000. As a result of concern engendered by the Bhopal tragedy, the U.S. Congress passed the Emergency Planning and Community Right-to-Know Act (1986), which called for the development of emergency procedures for responding to the accidental release of hazardous substances, the reporting of hazardous chemical inventories held by industries and other organizations, and the reporting of toxic chemical releases. This act has helped the industries, government, and the American public get a handle on just how extensive the hazardous waste problem is, thus allowing it to be addressed more accurately and effectively.

Much current research concerns how to deal more effectively with hazardous wastes. Progress is being made in developing new ways to isolate and store hazardous wastes and treat such wastes using high temperatures (including through solar techniques) so as to break them down into less harmful products. A particularly promising and innovative approach may be the use of bioremediation techniques, which put microorganisms to work to detoxify, clean up, and reduce unwanted concentrations of hazardous wastes. Essentially, the microorganisms eat or digest unwanted chemicals, transforming them into simpler, less harmful, or useful chemicals.

KEY TERMS

Bhopal
biodegradable plastic
bioremediation
closed-loop recycling
compost
deep-well injection
dioxin
dump
garbage

hazardous waste
incineration
industrial ecosystem
landfill
leachate
Love Canal
methane gas
municipal solid waste
open-loop recycling
recycling

refuse
resource recovery facility
reuse
rubbish
sanitary landfill
solid waste
source reduction
Superfund
Toxics Release Inventory
trash

STUDY QUESTIONS

1. How did East Hampton deal with its need for a new trash disposal system?
2. Define solid waste and its subcategories. Define hazardous waste. What different types of hazardous waste are there?
3. How can garbage be a source of revenue for some communities? What are the positive and negative aspects of such an enterprise?
4. Describe the "waste management hierarchy." Is there universal agreement on this hierarchy?
5. Why do some environmentalists object to too heavy an emphasis on recycling?

6. How do glass, metal, paper, and plastic recycling differ from one another?
7. How are most municipal wastes disposed of in the United States? How much is recycled?
8. What are the prospects of having a significant proportion of our plastics be biodegradable in the future?
9. Briefly describe the process and benefits of composting.
10. Comment on the controversies surrounding the paper versus plastics debate, and the disposable versus cloth diapers debate.
11. Briefly describe the concept of an industrial ecosystem.

12. What is Superfund? What has it accomplished? Why has it been controversial?
13. What is the Toxics Release Inventory? What purpose does it serve?
14. Based on the data presented in Table 19–1, the per capita daily garbage output of the average American increased by what percentage from 1960 to 1980?
15. Based on the data presented in Table 19–1, the per capita daily garbage output of the average American is predicted to increase by what percentage from 1980 to 2000?

ESSAY QUESTIONS

1. Describe the extent of the solid and hazardous waste problem in the United States and around the world. How serious are these problems compared to other environmental issues discussed in this book?
2. Discuss the alternative paradigms that have historically been used for waste management. What are the pros and cons of each? Which are still in common use?
3. Discuss both the benefits and drawbacks of the following techniques of waste disposal: incineration, resource recovery facilities, dumps and landfills, and deep-well injection. What are some of the new technologies that are being developed to deal with hazardous waste?
4. Describe the advantages and disadvantages of source reduction, reuse, and recycling. What can and should be done to encourage recycling?
5. Describe the Love Canal and Bhopal incidents. What practical effects, especially legislatively, did they have?

SUGGESTED READINGS

Alexander, J. H. 1993. *In defense of garbage*. New York: Praeger.

Bridgewater, A., and K. Lidgren. 1981. *Household waste management in Europe: Economics and techniques*. New York: Van Nostrand Reinhold.

Carless, J. 1992. *Taking out the trash*. Washington, D.C.: Island Press.

Church, T. W., and R. T. Nakamura. 1993. *Cleaning up the mess: Implementation strategies in Superfund*. Washington, D.C.: Brookings Institution.

Commoner, B. 1992. *Making peace with the planet*. New York: The New Press.

Crampton, N. 1989. *Complete trash: The best way to get rid of practically everything around the house*. New York: M. Evans & Company.

Dadd, D. L. (in collaboration with S. Lett and J. Collins). 1990. *Nontoxic, natural, and earthwise: How to protect yourself and your family from harmful products and live in harmony with the Earth.* Los Angeles: Jeremy P. Tucker.

Denison, R. A., and J. Ruston, eds. 1990. *Recycling and incineration: Evaluating the choices.* Washington, D.C.: Island Press.

Durning, A. 1992. *How much is enough? The consumer society and the future of the Earth.* New York: W. W. Norton.

Easterbrook, G. 1995. *A moment on the Earth: The coming age of environmental optimism.* New York: Viking.

Erickson, J. 1992. *World out of balance: Our polluted planet.* Blue Ridge Summit, Penn.: TAB Books.

Famighetti, R. ed. 1994. *The world almanac and book of facts 1995.* Mahwah, N.J.: Funk & Wagnalls Corporation.

Gordon, A., and D. Suzuki. 1991. *It's a matter of survival.* Cambridge, Mass.: Harvard University Press.

Harte, J., C. Holdren, R. Schneider, and C. Shirley. 1991. *Toxics A to Z: A guide to everyday pollution hazards.* Berkeley: University of California Press.

Kumar, R., and B. Murck. 1992. *On common ground.* New York: John Wiley.

Lynch, K. 1990. *Wasting away.* San Francisco: Sierra Club Books.

Rathje, W., and C. Murphy. 1992. *Rubbish! The archaeology of garbage.* New York: Harper Collins.

Setterberg, F., and L. Shavelson. 1993. *Toxic nation: The fight to save our communities from chemical contamination.* New York: John Wiley & Sons.

World Resources Institute. 1994. *World resources 1994-95.* New York: Oxford University Press.

OCIAL SOLUTIONS

A culture of permanence will not come quickly. We can expect no instant revolutions in social values. All we can realistically hope for is painfully slow progress . . . punctuated by rapid advances. When most people see a large automobile and think first of the air pollution it causes rather than the social status it conveys, environmental ethics will have arrived.

ALAN DURNING, *How Much Is Enough?* (1992)

PHOTO   *A road-building and colonization project in the Brazilian Amazon, funded by a loan from the World Bank, resulted in the destruction of millions of acres of forest. In the future loans will more often promote conservation and environmentally friendly, sustainable development. (Source: Loren McIntyre.)*

ENVIRONMENTAL ECONOMICS

PROLOGUE   *Redefining Progress—A Small but Determined Group*

*H*istorians have recorded many cases where societies have severely damaged other cultures or the natural environment in the "name of progress." Most economists, for example, have traditionally used the GNP, or Gross National Product, which measures output of goods and services, as an indicator of economic growth. An increase in GNP was desirable, and a nation was considered to be making economic progress when its GNP rose. But growing numbers of economists (and many others) are questioning whether a rising GNP actually represents progress. They point out that the GNP measures only monetary benefits, not the quality of life, because it ignores many of the environmental and social costs that occur with many economic activities. This approach encourages environmental damage because people can make products (and money) while ignoring the environmental costs.

Until recently, these criticisms of GNP had little impact on the "real world" of business and government accounting. But alternative, more realistic ways of measuring economic progress are increasingly being used due, in part, to the efforts of organizations such as Redefining Progress, a small but determined research and advocacy group in San Francisco. As an alternative to the GNP, the group is promoting the use of the Genuine Progress Indicator (GPI), which incorporates many costs that the GNP ignores including resource

PHOTO   *Progress as depicted in an 1868 Currier and Ives illustration: "Across the Continent: Westward the Course of Empire Takes Its Way" by the artist Frances F. Palmer. (Source: "Across the Continent: Westward the Course of the Empire Takes Its Way."* Artist: Frances F. Palmer; Publisher: Currier & Ives, 1868; Museum of the City of New York, 56.300.107. The Harry T. Peters Collection.)

depletion and pollution damages. Ultimately, the group hopes the U.S. government, the World Bank, and many other institutions will adopt the GPI. The group's executive director has noted that the power to define what constitutes progress is tremendously important. "It amounts to a statement about the very purpose and values of our nation. Those who cling to the GNP as a measure of progress implicitly deny the value of the social, moral, and natural capital that has made our country strong." Redefining Progress is working with a wide range of groups and individuals to build political momentum and broad-based community support for the GPI.

$\mathcal{I}$ NTRODUCTION

Economics is often defined as the study of scarcity and how we cope with it. Economics is thus concerned with environmental issues in two basic ways. The most obvious is resource scarcity. In the resource section of the book, we saw how humans are depleting a variety of resources, or inputs to society. Economics is also concerned with outputs, or pollution. Thus, it addresses fresh air, clean water, and other basic needs when they become scarce from pollution and other forms of environmental degradation. Economic realities are an inevitable part of solving all environmental problems, so we have discussed them throughout this book. In this chapter, we provide an overview that covers many basic principles of economics and the environment.

$\mathcal{E}$ CONOMICS VERSUS ENVIRONMENTAL SCIENCE?

Economics and environmental science are frequently depicted as natural enemies. Indeed, economists and environmental scientists are often critical of each other. A main reason for the conflict is that the two disciplines have fundamentally different ways of looking at the world, especially in three areas (Table 20–1):

- *Time span of outlook.* Environmental science has historically been concerned with species interactions, natural cycles, and other aspects of nature that reflect the long-term impact of resource depletion and pollution on the biosphere. Such a long-term view is useful when considering such problems as global warming or radioactive waste whose impacts last hundreds to millions of years. In contrast, economics is a social science that deals with human time scales and focuses on short-term problems, such as unemployment and taxes, that are measured in yearly or even monthly terms.
- *Priorities.* Traditional economists have mainly been concerned with society, especially how so-

ciety produces, distributes, and consumes goods and services. They tend to view nature as a resource to be used for these purposes. Environmental scientists have tended to place higher priority on preserving the natural environment than producing more goods and services.

- *Social solutions.* Economists are social scientists and know that incentives are often the most effective way to regulate human behavior. Environmental scientists have tended to emphasize persuasion and laws such as the Endangered Species Act as solutions to environmental problems.

The popular news media tend to reinforce the idea that economics and environmental science are fundamentally opposed by presenting such stories as "development versus wildlife preserves" or "tuna versus dolphins." One of the best-known examples is the spotted owl controversy, which was widely discussed in terms of "jobs [logging the forest] versus environment [preserving the forest habitat of the spotted owl]."

EnviroNet
www.jbpub.com/environet

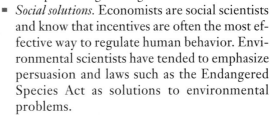

TABLE 20–1 *Three Areas Where Economics and Environmental Science Differ*

	TIME SPAN	PRIORITIES	SOCIAL SOLUTIONS
Economics	Short term	Society	Incentives
Environmental science	Long term	Environment	Laws, persuasion

In a limited sense, these apparent conflicts are real. A logger who loses his job to an endangered species would certainly see a conflict. In a broader sense, however, the conflict between economics and the environment is really a false dichotomy. A **false dichotomy** is when a complex question becomes polarized into an "either-or" issue. The dichotomy of "jobs or environment" is false because usually the ultimate choice is really jobs *and* environmental preservation. For instance, if the "jobs" view prevails and the old growth forest is harvested, many loggers will still

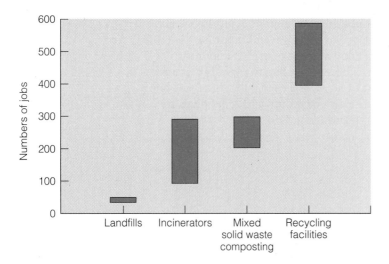

FIGURE 20–1

The number of jobs created for each 1.1 million tons (million metric tons) of waste processed in New York City. A range is shown for the different processes because some facilities (such as different incinerators or different recycling facilities) are more efficient than others. Recycling creates the most jobs, even when the variation is included. (*Source:* Reprinted from Worldwatch Paper #104, "Jobs in a Sustainable Economy," by Michael Renner with permission of Worldwatch Institute, Washington, D.C., copyright © 1991.)

be out of a job in a few years as the remaining forest disappears. On a larger scale, in many countries where the tropical rainforests have been destroyed, the local inhabitants have lost their way of life and live in abject poverty. The same could be said for fishermen in overfished fishing grounds such as offshore New England, farmers who have exhausted the soils in Africa or Haiti, and countless other examples.

These examples show that controlled use of resources often provides more employment in the long term. Fishermen, loggers, farmers, and many others can only remain employed if their resource base is not depleted. In other cases, the loss of environmentally damaging occupations will usually be more than compensated by new occupations that promote environmental preservation. We have discussed many examples throughout this book where activities that help preserve the environment usually create more jobs than they eliminate. Many of these new jobs are in pollution cleanup. Since the early 1970s, the U.S. environmental cleanup business, including pollution control and toxic waste remediation, has grown 20% per year, according to Michael Silverstein, author of *The Environmental Economic Revolution*. This growth has created two million new jobs in 65,000 new firms with annual sales of more than $130 billion per year in the early 1990s.

Even more jobs are created by "indirect" environmental activities such as increased efficiency, recycling, renewable resource use, and other forms of "input reduction" discussed below. For example, the Worldwatch Institute reports that to produce 1000 gigawatt-hours of electricity, the following numbers of workers are needed:

- Unsustainable fuels:
  - Nuclear plant—100 workers
  - Coal-fired plant—116 workers
- Sustainable fuels:
  - Solar thermal plant—248 workers
  - Wind farm—542 workers

In another example, data from the New York City Department of Sanitation show that recycling produces at least 10 times more jobs per 1.1 million tons (1 million metric tons)* of waste than landfills (Fig. 20–1). Environmental laws, increased business interest in efficiency, and increasing public demand for thousands of "green" consumer items such as organic foods and recycled clothing, will likely cause further growth in environmental jobs.

Environmentally "friendly" activities produce so many jobs because they are labor-intensive. They rely on people instead of large amounts of energy and machinery. In contrast, many highly polluting, resource-depleting industries are just the opposite, using much energy and few people. As Table 20–2 shows, five manufacturing industries—oil refining and coal products, chemicals, primary metals, paper, and food products—account for over 80% of both energy use and toxics release. Yet they account for only 22% of total employment. The discrepancy is particularly great for the chemical industry, which produces about 58% of the toxic releases and uses 21% of the energy, while accounting for just 5.5% of the total manufacturing jobs.

Despite the greater job-generating capacity of many environmentally related activities, some older industries promote the belief that environmental preservation causes job losses. Companies threaten to close or relocate (often to another country) if they are forced to comply with environmental laws. This is sometimes called "greenmail," or job blackmail. But such industries are often inefficient, rely on depleted resources, or have declining employment from increased automation or international competition (Fig. 20–2). In fact, a 1994 report published by Eban Goodstein of the Economic Policy Institute showed that only 0.1% of job layoffs were from environmental regulations.

---

*Unless otherwise noted, *tons* refers to short tons (2000 pounds).

Environmental Economics: Blending the Dichotomy

The increasing integration of jobs and environmental preservation has led to the development of a new discipline, called **environmental economics**. (This discipline and its subdisciplines are also sometimes called ecological or green economics.) Environmental economics studies society and the natural environment as a single system. It treats both the short-term need for jobs and the long-term need to protect the environment as goals. Similarly, producing goods and services and protecting the environment have equal priority.

Traditional economics focused on the production and consumption of goods in society as if they were isolated from the environment. Economics largely ignored the environmental costs of extracting source materials from the natural environment, such as the costs of depletion to future generations. Similarly, economic theory largely ignored the environment as a sink for waste and pollution. Basic economic texts still often describe the air, water, and other environmental resources as "free goods." In contrast, environmental economics incorporates environmental considerations into its theory and practice. The environmental costs and benefits of mining, pollution,

TABLE 20–2 *Energy Use, Pollution, and Employment by Economic Activity, United States*

INDUSTRY	EMPLOYMENT	ENERGY USE	TOXICS RELEASE
	(Percent of all Manufacturing)		
Refining and coal products	0.8	31.2	3.7
Chemicals	5.5	21.2	58.4
Primary metal	4.0	14.0	12.5
Paper	3.6	11.5	13.6
Food products	8.4	4.8	1.4
Stone, clay, and glass	3.1	4.7	0.5
Lumber and wood products	3.9	2.0	0.2
Transportation equipment	10.6	1.7	1.6
Fabricated metal	7.4	1.7	1.5
Nonelectrical machinery	10.7	1.4	0.4
Electrical machinery	10.7	1.1	1.4
Printing and publishing	8.0	0.6	0.3
Other manufacturing	23.3	4.1	4.2
ALL MANUFACTURING	100.0	100.0	100.0

(*Source*: Reprinted from Worldwatch Paper #104, "Jobs in a Sustainable Economy," by Michael Renner with permission of Worldwatch Institute, Washington, D.C., copyright © 1991.)

and other production activities are included in economic calculations. A reason for this different approach is that when traditional economics arose, human populations and technological im-

FIGURE 20–2
Older, obsolete industries sometimes blame environmental regulations for closing them down or causing layoffs. But such regulations actually cause only a tiny fraction of total job losses. Seen here is an abandoned limestone mill in Bainbridge, Pennsylvania. (*Source*: Jeffrey Howe/Visuals Unlimited.)

FIGURE 20–3

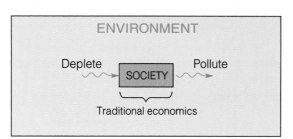

(a) Small population and little technology: Society has low impact on environment

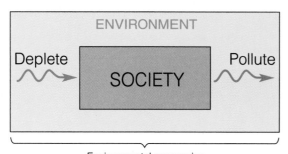

Environmental economics

(b) Larger population and increased technology: Society has great impact on environment

pacts were much smaller than now (Fig. 20–3). Society has greatly increased in size, while the environment has remained finite. The human impacts are now so great that they can no longer be ignored.

What Is Sustainable Growth?

Traditional economics is based on the principle that economic growth is extremely desirable. This view arose because economic growth, by increasing the quantity and quality of goods and services, has led to a general improvement in the human condition. As long as human populations and the technological capacity to consume and produce were relatively low, environmental costs of growth were not of much concern. Environmental economics agrees that economic growth can be desirable, such as where people are poor, but argues that the goal should be growth that can

be sustained for a long time, not growth "at any cost." **Sustainable growth** both preserves the environment and permits a nation's economy to increase in size, creating jobs and improving the human condition.

Sustainable growth differs from unsustainable growth in four basic ways (Table 20–3):

1. *Resource use.* As we have seen, traditional economics was based in part on the idea of "infinite" resources. Accordingly, unsustainable growth maximizes resource use and thus the rate of resource depletion. Economist Kenneth Boulding has called this approach **cowboy economics** because it views the environment as a source of endless space and riches like the Old West. In contrast, sustainable growth recognizes that resources are finite and that the rate of resource depletion must be slowed if we are to have growth in the long term. Accordingly, sustainable growth emphasizes minimizing resource use by reducing inputs to society through increased efficiency, reuse/recycling, and substitution of renewable resources (Fig. 20–4).
2. *Pollution control.* Reducing inputs not only reduces the rate of resource depletion, but also reduces the pollution associated with mining, processing, manufacturing, using, and disposing of goods. In contrast, unsustainable growth, with its emphasis on maximizing input, concentrates on output management, that is, controlling pollution after the resource is used. Consequently, unsustainable growth relies on abatement devices, such as wastewater treatment and smokestack scrubbers, that are much more expensive than reducing the waste stream on the input side.
3. *Resource fate.* Sustainable growth emphasizes reuse and recycling of matter instead of discarding matter in the one-way flow that is characteristic of the unsustainable **throwaway society**. Reuse and recycling not only reduce pollution from solid waste but reduce depletion of virgin resources.
4. *Resource type.* Sustainable growth substitutes renewable resources where possible. For example, paper containers are preferable to plastic made from petroleum. Future generations will be able to manufacture more paper from trees, but the petroleum from which plastic is made will likely be gone well within the next century. Also, renewable resources tend to be biological in origin and therefore often more biodegradable. Renewable energy is preferred over nonrenewable forms.

TABLE 20–3 *Unsustainable Growth versus Sustainable Growth*

	UNSUSTAINABLE	SUSTAINABLE
Resource use	Inefficient	Efficient
Pollution control	Output reduction	Input reduction
Resource fate	Matter discarded	Matter recycled
Resource type	Nonrenewable	Renewable

Efficiency improvements, reuse/recycling, and substitution, the hallmarks of sustainable growth (Fig. 20–4), are among the major kinds of "green technologies" that will provide many jobs in the future. Unfortunately, the United States may be falling behind in developing these critical technologies (see Issues in Perspective 20–1). Note that green technologies tend to reduce, rather than increase, the flow of goods through society. The improvement in living standards that occurs with sustainable growth comes mainly from increasing the *quality* of items produced, not the quantity. The well-known environmental economist Herman Daly has compared the economy to a digestive tract. A sustainable economy does not increase the size of the tract, but it does improve the digestion process. Thus, the change is qualitative, not quantitative.

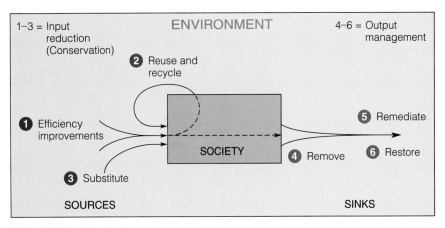

▬ FIGURE 20–4

Sustainable growth emphasizes input reduction of throughput (matter and energy) through efficiency improvements, reuse/recycling, and substitution. Unsustainable growth has little concern for input reduction and focuses on output management to address pollution problems.

Measuring Sustainable Growth

As the Prologue described, the traditional economic measurement of Gross National Product (GNP) is not very satisfactory because GNP does not subtract environmental costs that may occur when wealth is created. For example, when trees are cut and sold for timber, they add to the GNP. In counting only immediate, short-term dollars, however, GNP ignores the greater net wealth that might have been created if the forest were managed to produce goods over a long period of time. Nigeria, for example, was once a major exporter of timber, but it overcut most of its forest resources and now imports many more forest products than it exports.

Four other examples also illustrate how misleading GNP can be:

1. The *Exxon Valdez* oil spill in March 1989 actually caused U.S. GNP to rise because much of the $2.2 billion spent on labor and equipment for cleanup was added to income.
2. The tens of billions of dollars spent on health care for illnesses caused by air pollution in the United States generally add to GNP.
3. The timber and increased agricultural production obtained through rainforest destruction add to the GNP of those countries even though the destruction leads to the widespread extinction of many tropical species. The permanently lost genetic variations in those species might have produced lifesaving drugs, foods, and many other economic benefits that would have been much greater than the immediate income from the timber and agriculture.
4. Poverty, disease, and human misery increased globally during the 1980s and early 1990s even though the Gross World Product (GWP—the global equivalent of GNP) actually rose by 42% between 1980 and 1994. By 1994, the GWP was $20.1 trillion (calculated in 1987 dollars).

Examples such as these have caused some economists to seek indicators of economic well-being that account for environmental costs (see the Prologue). One of the best-known alternatives to the GNP is the **Index of Sustainable Economic Welfare (ISEW)**, developed by the economists Herman Daly and John Cobb. The ISEW helps us measure sustainable growth that creates income and jobs without exacting a high environmental cost. It includes several environmental measures such as depletion of nonrenewable resources, loss of farmland from erosion and urbanization, wetlands loss, damage from air and water pollution, and even estimates of long-term damage from global warming and ozone depletion. Because it includes so many variables, the ISEW is much more difficult to compute than GNP, especially for developing nations where environmental monitoring is poor. Enough U.S. data are available, however, and when the U.S. ISEW is computed, it presents a very different picture of the nation's well-being than GNP does: instead of steadily increasing, ISEW has remained static or declined slightly since the late 1960s (▬ Fig. 20–5, page 569). It seems likely that once data are available for other countries, their ISEWs will show even greater declines in many cases. Developing countries with high populations and rapid environmental destruction are especially likely to show declines.

Green Gold: Is America Losing the Environmental Technology Race?

In their 1994 book, *Green Gold*, Curtis Moore and Alan Miller argue that the United States is falling behind Germany and Japan in the rapidly growing field of environmental technology. Such technology reduces the human impact on the natural environment by reducing resource depletion through increased efficiency, reducing pollution, improving recycling, and similar means. Demand for environmental technologies is growing so rapidly that they represent "green gold" for the companies that design and produce them.

Moore and Miller point out that Germany and Japan have invested much more in this industry than the United States has and are consequently becoming dominant in many areas. Ironically, the basic research for many, if not most, of these "green" technologies was carried out in the United States, especially in the 1970s. But while the 1980s saw increasing interest in environmental protection in Germany and Japan, the opposite was happening in the United States. As environmental policies and legislation became less stringent, the incentive to develop and improve environmental technologies declined in the United States.

A good example is the "homes-from-pollution" process, which removes sulfur gas from the smokestacks of coal-burning electric power plants and mixes it with other materials to produce wallboard, mortar, gypsum, and other construction materials. Since sulfur is the main cause of acid rain, this serves the dual purpose of reducing pollution and producing useful products. But although the process originated in the United States and was first installed in 1973 at the Cholla I power plant in Arizona, the technology was not perfected, widely used, and marketed until after its export to Germany in 1980. Now German companies are exporting this technology all over the world for a sizable profit.

The Germans had a real incentive to develop this technology. German pollution laws are the strictest in the world, so sulfur emissions must be very low. Also, the sulfur collected from smokestacks cannot be deposited in landfills due to strict restrictions on solid waste. As a result, Germany had a strong need for the homes-from-pollution technology. In contrast, the United States enacted "tall stack" laws that allowed power plants to build very high smokestacks that ejected the sulfur high into the air. Thus, U.S. plants had no need for the homes-from-pollution technology.

Similarly, solar cells (photovoltaics) were originally developed for the U.S. space program in the 1950s. But during the 1980s, federal funding for solar cells dropped from $150 million to zero, and the United States became increasingly dependent on cheap foreign oil. Now Japan leads the world in producing solar cells. The same is true for hydrogen fuel-cell technology, high-efficiency lightbulbs, and many other environmental technologies that were invented in the United States but are now mainly produced by Germany and Japan.

Unfortunately, and perhaps tragically according to some economists, many political and business leaders in the United States continue to adhere to the view that the environment can be protected only at the expense of the economy. In reality, the opposite is true: Environmental protection benefits the economy. As Takefumi Fukumizu, representative of Japan's Ministry of International Trade and Industry, has said, there is "an inescapable economic necessity to improve energy efficiency and environmental technologies, which . . . would reduce costs and create a profitable world market." This market is indeed hugely profitable; by some estimates, environmental technologies could generate over a trillion dollars per year in sales. Will the United States continue to invent environmental technologies and then permit other nations to develop, market, and reap the main benefits of this large, growing market?

ECONOMICS OF SUSTAINABLE GROWTH

Two basic economic systems have been used in the modern world, and neither has fostered sustainable growth. In **command economies**, the government tells individuals what to produce and sets prices for those products. The collapse of the Soviet Union demonstrated the major problem with command economies: the system develops widespread inefficiencies because product costs, being artificially set, do not reflect real costs. These massive inefficiencies are also why more environmental damage has occurred in the countries of the former Soviet Union and other command economies than in countries with the other type of economy. These **market economies**, as they are called, are based on the "invisible hand," first discussed by Adam Smith over two hundred years ago. In a pure market economy, production and costs are determined

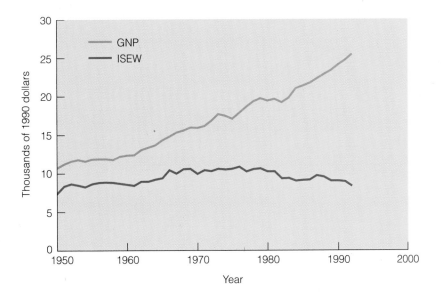

FIGURE 20–5
Per capita GNP and ISEW for the United States. (*Source:* Reprinted from *Saving the Planet: How to Shape an Environmentally Sustainable Global Economy* by Lester R. Brown, Christopher Flavin, and Sandra Postel, with the permission of W. W. Norton & Company, Inc. Copyright © 1991 by Worldwatch Institute.)

by competition among individuals. Smith argued that self-interested individuals promote optimum allocation of resources in society, as if driven by an invisible hand. This system is more efficient than command economies because the laws of supply and demand set prices that generally reflect real costs to society.

Externalities: Market Failures and the Environment

Despite their general efficiency in allocating resources, market economies are not perfect. Economists have long noted that "market failures" occur where society is not always benefited by the individual pursuit of self-interest. For example, until the enactment of laws regulating child employment, children were used as a cheap source of labor in the "sweatshops" of the late 1800s (Fig. 20–6). Child labor exacted a toll on society in the form of the psychological and physical injury to the children's development that was not included in the price of the cheap clothing or other products they made. Economists call such market failures **externalities**: some costs of production are not included in (are "external" to) the price of the product. With externalities, society as a whole pays a cost that should be paid by the producer and consumer of the product. Externalities are a major reason why no "pure" market economy exists. Regulations and other forms of intervention that we will discuss shortly are necessary. Thus, almost all real economies in the world are "mixed" economies, which combine varying degrees of market and command traits. In the United States, the market economy traits are generally more prominent than in Western European countries although both have mixed economies.

Pollution, resource depletion, and the many other ways that humans degrade their environment are environmental externalities, which society is forced to pay because they are not paid by the industry or other activity that produces the degradation. But how can markets generate such damaging externalities? Markets are generally efficient because they are based on individuals making rational decisions to maximize benefits and minimize costs. In theory, then, markets should act to reduce environmental degradation before the environmental costs exceed the benefits of production. The problem is that markets only work if the commodity is privately owned.

FIGURE 20–6
During the Industrial Revolution, children often worked long hours in U.S. and European factories. Child labor continues to be used in many developing nations today. (*Source*: J.P. Laffont/ Sygma.)

In Chapter 1, we examined Garrett Hardin's 1968 essay on "The Tragedy of the Commons." Resources that are public goods, or "commons," will eventually become depleted or polluted if the free market is left unchecked. Unlike a privately owned good, no one person or organization has a vested interest in taking care of public goods. If individuals are left to pursue their own interests, they will destroy the commons, rendering it useless to everyone including themselves. This behavior is actually quite logical: because no one owns the commons, someone else will deplete or pollute the resource if you do not.

Tragedy of the Commons: Depletion and Pollution

Depletion of a public resource is stimulated by the economic law of supply and demand: the price of goods increases as their supply diminishes. Thus, the scarcer the resource, the more expensive it will become. For example, the OPEC embargo of the early 1970s caused petroleum prices to skyrocket. A key implication for public goods is that as the resource becomes scarcer, there will be increasing pressure to exploit the resource even more. *Scarcity promotes even greater scarcity* because rising prices reward people who exploit what resource remains. Among the many examples that could be cited are the overexploitation of fishing grounds in many parts of today's oceans, overexploitation of game animals such as rhinos, soil exhaustion and erosion from overuse, and depletion of the highest-grade ore deposits in the United States.

Unsustainable growth is also characterized by pollution of the environmental commons for the same reason: because no one has a vested interest in the commonly held property, people will freely pollute it. Thus, air pollution occurs because the atmosphere is a commonly held good that no one owns. The same is true for water pollution, for virtually no one owns an entire lake, much less an entire river, or ocean. Litter is usually worst in public parks, along highways, and so on.

Solution: Internalizing Environmental Externalities

The solution to environmental externalities is to "internalize" the environmental costs by forcing the depleters and polluters to pay for the damage incurred to public environmental property. In the case of depletion of a commons, the greater price that accompanies scarcity must be counteracted. One way to do this is to impose a **severance tax**, which is levied on minerals as they are extracted. Many states levy severance taxes on coal that is mined. To offset the high price of scarce supplies, such a tax ideally would increase as the resource became depleted. Miners, drillers, loggers, fishermen, and other resource harvesters would then be discouraged from harvesting further. For renewable resources such as fishes or lobster, the tax would decrease once the supply (populations) had rebounded. For miners and other harvesters of nonrenewable resources, the tax would stay high, encouraging the industry to invest in finding alternative resources to use, conservation, and recycling. Similar taxes and other methods discussed below could be used in the case of pollution of a commons to force polluters to pay the costs of pollution.

What's the Environment Worth? Cost Problems

A major obstacle to internalizing, or paying for, environmental costs has always been determining what those costs are. Four main costs influence and thus complicate the calculation of overall environmental costs of an activity: (1) intangible costs, (2) hidden costs, (3) future costs, and (4) unequally distributed costs.

Intangible costs include destruction of scenery and other subjective costs that are very difficult to measure because people place different values on them. To some people, a view of wilderness landscape has no value; to others, it is priceless. **Hidden costs** are environmental degradations that we are unaware of; for example, the full effects of pesticides and other pollutants with chronic toxicity may not be evident for many years. **Future costs** are costs that are passed on to future generations. In theory, most environmental damage, especially to nonrenewable resources, includes at least some future costs. Some impacts, however, may have only future costs: they have no discernible cost now, but the cost will arise in the future. For example, most plants now going extinct have not been studied for their food and medicinal potential. A plant species that might go unnoticed now could be the best way to fight a disease that arises in the future. A major problem with all three of these costs is that society tends to ignore them. Intangible costs are not "real" costs to people who place little value on the environment. Hidden costs are not visible. Future costs are ignored by present generations who "discount the future" (Chapter 1) because it is uncertain.

The problem with the last category—**unequally distributed costs**—is not ignorance but that environmental costs are almost never distributed evenly throughout society. Poorer people tend to pay relatively more of many envi-

FIGURE 20–7

Poor families in many nations tend to bear a greater share of the burden of environmental problems. This lower-income family lives near a waste site in Huntington Park south of Los Angeles. (*Source*: Michael Newman/PhotoEdit.)

ronmental costs (Fig. 20–7). The factory that has to pay higher costs for pollution control simply passes that cost on to the consumer by raising the price of its product. Whether the product is a car, tires, food, or clothing, the poorer person feels the impact of the higher cost more strongly. Similarly, poorer people tend to be the ones who become unemployed when a factory is closed because it pollutes too much or because the costs of controlling pollution are too high for it to operate profitably. Unequal distribution of cost creates much of the environmental controversy you hear about in the news media. For instance, the spotted owl controversy is largely caused because loggers in the area must bear much more of the cost (their jobs) of preserving the owl's habitat than, say, fire fighters living in Oklahoma. The same is true when nuclear power plants are shut down, factories are closed, and many other activities are slowed for environmental reasons.

Pay Up! Persuasion, Regulation, Motivation

One can attempt to overcome these problems and determine "true environmental costs." The Con-

tingent Valuation Method (CVM) discussed in Chapter 14 uses surveys and other techniques to find out how much people are willing to pay to visit national parks. This helps measure the "intangible cost" if a park is degraded. But the science of making such measurements is just beginning, and estimates are often controversial. For example, the economist Paul Portney released a study in 1992 showing that the benefits of the Clean Air Act of 1970 exceeded the monetary costs. But he concluded this was not true of the Clear Air Act Amendments of 1990 where the total costs of up to $36 billion by the year 2005 would not be balanced by the benefits, which ranged up to $25 billion. Other economists, however, have questioned his results, which involve dozens of estimates about "true environmental costs," including effects of air pollution on human health and ecosystems.

Despite such problems, attempts at estimating environmental costs must be made because society can no longer afford to ignore them. Using such cost estimates, industrial societies have begun to discourage depletion and pollution by requiring resource depleters, and especially polluters, to pay costs of environmental degradation. As we will see, the current payments are generally far below the level needed for a sustainable global economy, but social pressures are growing to attain that goal. Polls regularly show that the majority of U.S. citizens are willing to pay extra for a cleaner environment

Society can extract payment for formerly free environmental externalities in three basic ways: persuasion, government regulation, and economic motivation or incentives (Table 20–4). As Chapter 14 explained, persuasion usually only influences a few people. It is particularly ineffective for industrial activities since cheaters are rewarded by having lower costs and will soon drive conscientious industries that pay more en-

TABLE 20–4 *Methods of Promoting Payment for Externalities*

	EFFECTIVENESS	COST OF IMPLEMENTING	BEST SUITED FOR
Persuasion	Least	Lowest	As a supplement to other means
Regulation	Moderate	Highest	Situations with a few major violators
Economic motivation	Most	Moderate	Situations with many violators

vironmental costs out of business. Persuasion's low cost, however, makes it a useful supplement in conjunction with regulation and/or economic incentives.

Government regulation restricts depletion and pollution by passing laws. Regulation is deceptively appealing. It is the most direct way to prevent environmentally damaging activities: ban plastic, require pollution controls, fine people for littering, close polluting factories, and so on (Fig. 20–8). Many economists, however, including prominent environmental economists such as Lester Brown, agree that regulation is often more inefficient and more costly than using economic incentives. One reason is the high cost of enforcing regulations where many people are involved. Costs of enforcement are increased further because people often try to evade the laws. Thus, enforcement entails costs of monitoring plus costs of catching lawbreakers, prosecuting them, and, sometimes, keeping them in jail. For example, imagine the costs of trying to enforce a law requiring people to take public transportation to work once a week. In contrast, an economic incentive such as higher gasoline prices will encourage smaller cars, fuel economy, car pooling, and use of public transportation. Similarly, more people may recycle items if they are paid for doing so than if a law is passed requiring them to recycle.

Another criticism of regulations is that they tend to be relatively inflexible. For example, a law that requires all factories to meet the same rigid air quality standards for emissions does not take into account the age of the factories or what they produce. Such laws can lead to high prices for the consumer and force factories to close. The 1990 Clean Air Act Amendments, which allow trading and buying of pollution "permits," achieve the same level of control at less social cost by recognizing that some factories can eliminate many

 FIGURE 20–8
Laws against environmental damage are easy to make but sometimes difficult and costly to enforce. This photograph of illegal dumping was taken in Alaska. (*Source*: Ken Graham/Greenpeace.)

emissions very cheaply while others cannot (Chapter 17). Factories that would otherwise have to close can stay open and save jobs while other, newer or different factories can cut emissions to a greater degree.

Despite the drawbacks, regulation has been successfully used during the last few decades by many industrial nations, especially the United States (Chapters 1 and 22). Regulation is most useful where there are few violators and each violator can do great harm to the environment. Nuclear waste disposal fits both of these criteria and is thus probably best controlled by regulation. Manufacturing CFCs, hunting whales, and trade in endangered species are other examples of easily regulated activities. The great improvement in air and water quality in the United States has largely been due to the Clean Air Act, Safe Drinking Water Act, and other laws passed in the early 1970s that set uniform standards. In recent years, however, rising costs of regulation, changing economic conditions, increasing emphasis on input reduction, and many other factors have led to increasing interest in economic incentives as a way of sustaining the environment.

Economic Incentives to Sustain the Environment

By rewarding individuals monetarily, economic incentives help meet many goals effectively. Incentives are less expensive than regulation because they save on enforcement costs and are more flexible: producers and consumers decide how to pay for the change to meet the goal. As each chooses the least costly way to achieve the goal, society as a whole has lower indirect costs. Environmental economists most often promote two basic types of economic incentives: government incentives and privatization.

Government incentives include taxes, subsidies, licenses, fees, vouchers, and many other ways that local, state, and national government can reward or discourage behaviors. In Chapter 1, we noted that these government incentives are often called "green fees." The government incentives most often suggested are various types of taxes, or "green taxes." For example, sulfur dioxide emissions can be discouraged directly by taxing emissions or indirectly by taxing high-sulfur coal, electricity consumption, or electricity generation (Fig. 20–9). Such taxes are advocated by many economists as a relatively simple way to improve the functioning of the market to reflect an activity's "true environmental cost," meaning the cost of externalities. Green taxes can do this by (1) serving as an incentive to slow depletion and pollution and (2) raising money that can go toward paying other environmental costs.

Green taxes are often an effective incentive because they promote all the major aspects of a sustainable economy: less depletion, recycling and use of renewable resources, and less pollution at the source. For example, a carbon tax on fossil fuels promotes conservation, encourages alternative energy research, and reduces greenhouse gas pollution (Chapters 1, 6, and 18). Similar taxes can be levied on water, to promote conservation and desalination; on metals, to promote conservation and recycling; and so on. Raising the price encourages people to stop "discounting the future," conserve resources, and slow pollution and solid waste disposal, as well as save money. Green taxes, also raise money for environmental uses. Many billions of dollars could be raised by taxing polluting substances and scarce resources, especially from a carbon tax on fossil fuels.

Many estimates often suggest that the overall burden of green taxes need not be great. The United States already has among the lowest taxes of all industrialized countries and imposes relatively few green taxes compared to Western Europe. More importantly, green taxes need *not* add new taxes; instead taxes can be shifted from one activity to another. Income taxes, for instance, could be reduced by the revenue generated by the green taxes. Taxes tend to discourage the activity being taxed. Instead of discouraging work, as income taxes do, green taxes discourage depletion and pollution.

The burden of green taxes could also be reduced by stopping subsidies on environmentally damaging activities. Many nations have a "reverse green tax": instead of discouraging environmental damage with taxes, they actually encourage damage with government subsidies (payments). Examples in the United States include the following:

1. Subsidized mining of virgin ore deposits, which discourages recycling of metals (Chapter 10).
2. Subsidized irrigation water for farmers, as in California (Chapter 11).
3. Subsidized grazing of animals on government land. In 1993, a rancher could graze cattle on federal land for less than one-fourth the cost of nearby private lands (Chapter 12).
4. Subsidized logging in government-owned forests (Chapter 12).

Many other countries also subsidize resource use and encourage rapid depletion. Until recently, Brazil promoted logging of rainforests by building roads, making direct payments to timber companies, and many other subsidies. According to the World Bank, many agricultural countries subsidize pesticides, up to 89% of the cost.

Such subsidies decrease costs below market price, resulting in massive waste and pollution. For example, the World Bank estimated that a staggering 6000 million tons (5445 million metric tons) of carbon pollution could have been eliminated between 1991 and 2000 if developing countries and the former Soviet countries had stopped subsidizing fossil fuels. Most such consumption subsidies are artifacts of outdated economic policies and protectionist trade policies. For instance, the United States once wanted to encourage mining of ores to provide a growing manufacturing economy with cheap raw materials. Environmental economics argues, however, that these subsidies do not promote sustainable economies. By lowering costs well below the "true" cost, they discourage conservation, recycling, and pollution reduction (Chapter 1).

The second basic economic incentive is **privatization**, in which environmental resources become the property of individuals. By transferring resources from the commons to individuals or companies that have a vested interest in them, the basic cause of the "tragedy of the commons" is removed. Examples include commercial forests that raise trees for timber, commercial parks

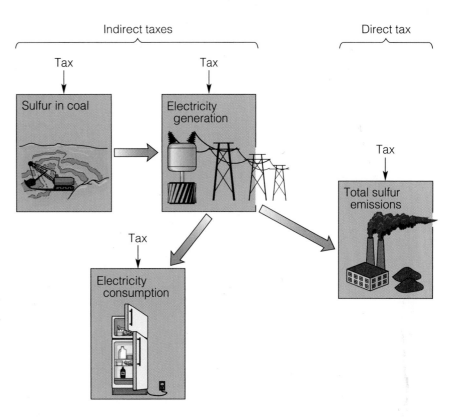

FIGURE 20–9
"Green taxes" can be indirect, such as a tax on sulfur in coal or on electricity generation or consumption, or direct, such as a tax on sulfur emitted.

that raise endangered species, and individual ownership of water rights in the western United States.

Despite some success with privatization, many environmental economists believe that it is often less useful than green taxes (and other green fees) in solving environmental problems. One problem is that many environmental commons cannot practically be privatized. For instance, how can you "own" a part of the atmosphere? Similarly, it is impractical to have ownership of the oceans or rivers that travel through land owned by many people. Another problem is that even where private ownership is practical, there is no guarantee that market prices will always reflect true environmental costs. For example, private ownership of oil and ore deposits will still lead to depletion of those resources unless society implements regulations, taxes, or some other mechanisms that prevent market failure.

Summary: The Low Cost of Sustainability

Many environmental economists believe that the transition to a sustainable economy can be made with surprisingly little sacrifice, if it is begun soon. They say the transition can be paid for by the savings that will be realized when currently wasted resources are used more efficiently. Three types of change will help to pay for currently existing externalities:

1. Cost-free changes to eliminate policies that cause environmental damage.
2. Investments that are economically and environmentally profitable.
3. Changes that cost money but are environmentally profitable.

The first two types of changes require no economic sacrifices. First, we can simply stop subsidies and other government policies that actively promote environmental damage, such as subsidized mining and rainforest destruction. Second, public and private investments in water supplies, conservation, and other activities will not only pay for themselves but will make a monetary profit. We saw, for example, that many investments in energy efficiency not only reduce fossil fuel pollution and conserve resources, but also increase net profits by reducing waste (Chapter 9). In some cases, private investments in businesses that develop such green technology can benefit both the environment and the investor. "Green investing" is a type of socially responsible investing that has become increasingly popular as an alternative to investments made on the basis of profits alone (see the Case Study). Ending current taxpayer subsidies that promote unsustainable businesses, such as the fossil fuel and nuclear industries, would encourage green investing by giving sustainable industries a level playing field. Businesses would have a greater incentive, for example, to develop more fuel-efficient cars and alternative fuels.

Only the third group of changes require actual monetary sacrifice. Examples would be green taxes on smokestack emissions and landfill wastes, which would raise the cost of products and garbage removal. However, even these measures have no net cost when the benefits of a cleaner environment are included in the calculation.

The basic effect of these changes would be to restructure the economy and rechannel industry and jobs into producing goods and services that the environment can sustain for many centuries. To repeat a key point, this change will not lead to unemployment, but will shift employment to sustainable jobs. For example, as internal combustion engines become less important, employment making solar batteries will increase. And, as noted above, such sustainable activities tend to provide more jobs than unsustainable ones. Of course, the transition to sustainability will not always be easy, but economic transitions have historically required social adaptations (Fig. 20–10). The difficulties can be minimized if the transition is gradually carried out. A phase-in period of 5 to 10 years is often suggested.

Unfortunately, the current transition to sustainability is too gradual for most who are concerned for the environment. In the United States, there has been very little support for green taxes. In 1990, Congress approved a 4 cent per gallon (3.785 liters) gasoline tax, but this is a small fraction of the tax required to significantly discourage auto use, lead to more efficient cars, and reduce emissions. Studies show that current prices

FIGURE 20–10
Economic transitions often involve the demise of some careers, forcing people to adjust by seeking new careers. The village blacksmith, as depicted in this late 18th century American engraving, is now a thing of the past. (*Source*: The Granger Collection, New York.)

Would You Be a Green Investor?

EnviroNet
www.jbpub.com/environet

Economists often say that "people vote with their dollar," especially in a market economy. This means that our spending reflects what we truly value. A good example is the growing popularity of "socially responsible investing," also known as SRI to investment brokers.

Socially responsible investing refers to financial investments that are based on more than merely the desire to maximize your profit return. You tell your investment broker, for instance, that you want to avoid investing in certain companies because you disapprove of some of their activities and do not want to support them. Popular examples are "socially screened" mutual funds that seek to invest only in companies that have a clean record on the environment or other social issues. The first socially screened fund was the Pax World Fund, created in 1970 to avoid investing in suppliers to the Vietnam War.

In the early 1990s, the number of socially responsible investors grew dramatically. According to the Investor Responsibility Research Center (IRRC), which promotes SRI by supplying subscribers with information about corporate behavior on social issues, the number of socially screened mutual funds grew at four times the rate of traditional funds. Total assets of these funds are well over $9 billion.

The specific social issues promoted vary among the mutual funds. Some funds consider a wide range of issues. While these issues usually include the environment, they also include a company's hiring practices on women and minorities and its record on animal testing. Investment in tobacco and alcohol companies may also be avoided. But some funds are strictly environmental; in fact, a 1993 survey of money managers concluded that the issue that concerned most investors is the environment. Green Century Capital Management and Merrill Lynch's

Ecological Trust are examples of funds that focus on a company's environmental record.

But, as always, one must be wary of the "greenwashing" problem. Recall from Chapter 1 that "greenwashing" refers to false environmental claims that are sometimes made by companies to use the popularity of environmental issues to attract consumers or, in this case, investors. A number of waste management companies, for instance are known as "environmental sector" stocks because they are in the pollution control and trash collection business. Some brokers have therefore included them as desirable "green" investments. But many of these companies have been fined millions of dollars for flagrant environmental violations such as illegal dumping and disposal of waste. Most environmental funds avoid them, preferring instead to invest in companies with no environmental violations, especially if the company actively promotes sustainability by making recycled products, helping rebuild wetlands on its property, and so on.

Another point to consider is how important profitability is to you. Some money managers caution investors that environmental (and all SRI) funds and stocks may, on average, produce lower rates of return. This is not always true; the Parnassus Fund is often cited as a consistently high-performing investment. But brokers often note that because SRI funds are constrained in where they can invest, they may not be as productive.

On the other hand, many investors are willing to risk lower profits because they are concerned about how a company makes its money. Does this potential sacrifice have any effect? Does SRI work? Although SRI is still relatively new, it already appears to be having a significant effect. One sign of this is the rapid growth of organizations like the IRRC that provide subscribers with information about a company's record on social is-

sues. Perhaps even more significant is that the major pension funds, the real titans of investment, are beginning to consider SRI. With the vast amounts of money they have at their disposal, these funds can strongly influence a company by threatening to withdraw their investments. In 1990, the world's largest pension fund, the teachers' and professors' retirement fund with assets of over $100 billion, began allowing members to put money into socially screened accounts. These members often send "resolutions" to companies requesting that they adhere to specific environmental principles. As one official noted, "companies who receive a resolution from a public pension fund take it very seriously."

So, does the investment future look "green"? It is already becoming standard practice before company mergers and buyouts to do an "environmental analysis" on a company's environmental record. According to a veteran Wall Street broker, "the companies that are . . . getting themselves into cleaner businesses are the ones that look good for the future. We are in between a long period when it paid to be dirty and when it will be seen as profitable to be clean."

Questions

1. If you had $10,000 to invest right now, would you be a "green" investor? Why or why not? Which companies would you specifically prefer to invest in?
2. If you had $10,000 to invest right now, would socially responsible investing (of any kind) be an option for you? Why or why not? Which companies would you specifically prefer to invest in?
3. Some critics have called SRI a mere ploy to gain money from "bleeding hearts." Is this unjustified cynicism? Do they have a valid point?

---

must be doubled or tripled to significantly shift consumption patterns. In the case of gasoline, a tax of at least $1 per gallon will be required. Such a tax would put U.S. gasoline costs at about the level of those in Western Europe and Japan,

where the high costs have greatly improved conservation and efficiency. The speed and power of green taxes to improve the environment were demonstrated in 1989 when a high tax on leaded gasoline went into effect in the United Kingdom.

Just one year later, in 1990, the use of unleaded gasoline had climbed from 4% to 30%.

POVERTY AND THE GLOBAL ENVIRONMENT

Global environmental problems are tightly interwoven with poor economic conditions. Poor nations find themselves in a vicious cycle. Poverty often correlates with overpopulation, which then leads to ecological decline as greater numbers of people overuse resources and pollute. As natural resources dwindle and are degraded, poverty increases, often leading to more population growth. Many nations, even those as different as Poland and Haiti, illustrate how economic problems are closely related to environmental problems.

In 1996, more than 1.3 billion of the world's 5.8 billion people live in abject poverty, with incomes less than a dollar per day. Billions more have standards of living well below that of U.S. and Canadian citizens. Increasing the standard of living in these countries involves far more than simply "developing" their economies by transferring current technologies to make their agricultural economies more industrial. Most current technologies use far more resources than the world could afford if everyone used them. The wealthiest 25% of the world's population now consume about 75% of the world's resources. The environmental economist Herman Daly has estimated that for all developing nations to attain the income levels of the leading industrial nations such as Japan and the United States, the consumption of the Earth's resources would have to increase by a factor of 36, or *3600%*, if current technologies are used to industrialize. For example, many geologists estimate that the world's entire oil supply would be gone in just a few years if all countries used as much per person as the United States. In addition to consuming more resources, the technologies used by the wealthiest nations also produce much more solid waste, greenhouse gases, and other pollution per person. (Fig. 20–11).

The solution, as noted earlier, is to lift developing nations out of poverty by transferring sustainable, or green, technologies that produce sustainable growth (also recall Chapter 1). Issues in Perspective 20–2 discusses a specific example.

Origins of Global Poverty

Economic theories of the 1940s through 1970s generally maintained that the poverty of the developing (then called Third World) countries was a temporary stage. Their agricultural economies, which produced little wealth, were largely a product of nineteenth-century colonial policies that had made little effort to modernize the native societies. Supposedly, trade with richer nations and some monetary aid would in time provide the technology and other necessities for the poor economies to reach **economic takeoff**. This was the point where poor countries could produce enough wealth to financially support themselves, export manufactured goods, and eventually attain the living standards of the United States, Canada, Europe, and other industrialized (First World) countries. As early as 1948, President Harry Truman, in his inaugural address, urged not only the rebuilding of Europe with the Marshall Plan, but the development of the world's poor countries. President John F. Kennedy declared the 1960s to be the "decade of development" and pledged 1% of the U.S. GNP toward this goal.

Unfortunately, economic takeoff has not occurred in most poor countries. Instead of becoming richer, poor nations have become poorer

FIGURE 20–11
(a) Municipal waste and (b) carbon dioxide are just two of many pollutants that increase rapidly with increasing wealth. (*Source:* Excerpted from *World Development Report 1992*. Copyright © 1992 by The International Bank for Reconstruction and Development/The World Bank. Reprinted by permission of Oxford University Press, Inc.)

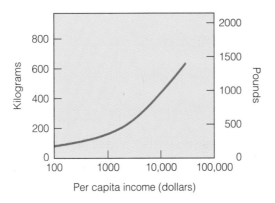

(a) Municipal wastes per capita

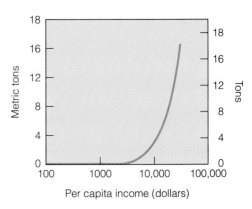

(b) Carbon dioxide emissions per capita

Cookstoves in Poor Nations:
Small Is Beautiful (and Sustainable)

In his classic 1973 book, *Small Is Beautiful*, E. F. Schumacher argued eloquently for the importance of "appropriate technology." These are sustainable technologies that are affordable and can be produced and maintained locally. Such technologies not only have less environmental impact than traditional industrial technologies, but they promote sustainable economic growth and increase the standard of living in poor nations.

The immense power of such small-scale local technologies occurs from the cumulative effects when many people use them. Thus, as often happens, large-scale change is a product of seemingly mundane trivial changes multiplied many times. One of the most dramatic examples is the cookstove. Half of the world's population, mainly in developing nations, prepare food and heat their homes with fires that burn dung, wood, or other combustible materials.

While seemingly rather harmless, these cookstoves are major causes of massive environmental destruction. Many thousands of acres of forests and other ecosystems are denuded and degraded as people seek firewood and other biomass fuels. Besides the obvious harm to the ecosystem, deforestation and plant denudation are a major cause of soil erosion. Human health suffers too. Smoke from indoor fires often exceeds 20 times the limit of ash and other pollutant levels recommended by the World Health Organization.

Traditional cookstoves can be improved in a number of ways. The most basic is to increase the heating efficiency. Traditional open fires with a pot above are only about 10% efficient; 90% of the heat goes into the air and is wasted. Traditional metal stoves are not much better. Lining the stove with ceramic, brick, or clay increases the heating efficiency to at least 20% and often as much as 40%.

FIGURE 1

A solar oven, being used in Kenya, that cooks food in a glass-covered box. (*Source*: Daniel M. Kammen, Princeton University.)

Increasing efficiency to just 20% can reduce the amount of firewood (ecological damage) and smoke (human health damage) by half, a good example of how powerful such a simple change can be. Using less firewood or other fuel also saves money. In Kenya, switching to more efficient cookstoves typically saves about $65 per year, as much as one-fifth the annual income of many families. Since the cost of such lined cookstoves is usually less than $5, this is a good investment. China has over 120 million insulated cookstoves due to a government program promoting them. Millions of similar stoves are becoming popular throughout Asia and Africa, thanks to dozens of government and private programs.

A second, usually better, type of improvement is the solar cookstove or oven (Fig. 1). When the Sun shines, the food cooks in a glass-covered box that traps the heat. The walls and floor of the box are lined with reflective metal or foil. On a sunny day, meat stews and rice dishes can be fully cooked in two to five hours. No biomass fuel is used, and no unhealthy smoke is produced.

The solar cookstove is still relatively new and is not yet as widely used as insulated biomass cookstoves. Cost is a factor too since the solar cookstove, at $20–40 apiece, is considerably more expensive. But mass production of solar cookstoves, often by local craftspeople, is expected to greatly reduce prices, just as it has with the insulated biomass cookstoves over the last few years. Considering that solar energy greatly reduces the need to buy firewood or other fuels, and thus saves even more money, they should become quite popular.

The experience with cookstove improvements has been educational in many ways. Early efforts to introduce the new technologies were unsuccessful because many social factors, such as community needs and customs, were not considered. In many areas, people will adopt newer cookstoves only when community groups are allowed to modify the designs and local artisans become stove makers. Improved cookstoves thus not only reduce harm to the environment, they also produce jobs for the community.

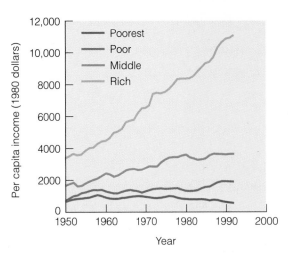

relative to the richer nations (▥ Fig. 20–12). In 1950, the average income in the rich nations was about 7 times as much as the average income in the poorest nations. By the early 1990s, the differential had risen to almost 20.

Why haven't the poorer countries experienced economic takeoff? Economists disagree on the answer, but a number of factors seem important. First, much of the money acquired by developing nations has been badly mismanaged. Instead of investing in roads, education, and other necessities for building a prosperous economy, they have often spent the money on military equipment to help keep dictators and elite social classes in power. Recent trends toward democracy in Africa, Asia, and Latin America may alleviate this problem. A second, and more important, reason is that the world is much more competitive than when the United States and other developed countries were industrializing. It is very difficult for less developed countries to make products that can compete with advanced technologies.

As a result, poorer countries must sell whatever products they can, which usually means their natural resources. Often these are nonrenewable: oil, high-grade ores, native species being driven toward extinction, and so on. Rather than investing in equipment and other capital that will create more wealth, these countries are spending their resources in ways that will not provide them with long-term sustainable growth. We saw in Chapter 1 that the loss of these irreplaceable natural resources is accelerating because they are "cheap." The price paid for these resources, mainly by consumers in the industrialized nations, does not reflect their true environmental costs. The value of such resources to future generations, to local peoples, and to local ecosystems is "discounted" (and often totally omitted) by the consumers who buy them.

Eliminating Global Poverty

The growing disparity between poor and rich countries has led to concern that a new "economic" war between North and South will replace the now-defunct military Cold War between East and West. As ▥ Figure 20–13 shows, most of the wealthier nations are in the higher latitudes, mainly in the Northern Hemisphere (an exception is Australia). Poor countries are found to the south, around the equator and in most of the Southern Hemisphere. These poor tropical nations share many common interests, as is readily apparent at the United Nations, where poor countries often form voting blocs on international issues. One solution to this growing poor-rich division is political: national governments must meet and reach agreements on international issues that affect them all. International meetings on economic and military issues have been held for years, but not until 1992 did international environmental issues came to the fore. In that year, the **Earth Summit** in Rio de Janeiro, which was attended by 178 nations, addressed global concerns such as global warming, biodiversity, and deforestation (Chapter 22). Although the summit was a great success in demonstrating global concern for these issues, and some important agreements were signed, many participants fear that many of the agreements will be ineffective because they either lack means of enforcement or take steps that are too little or too late to rectify major environmental problems (Chapter 22).

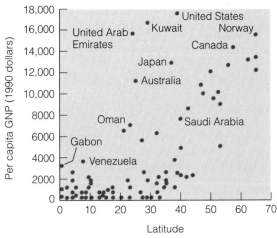

FIGURE 20–13
Tropical nations, located near the equator at 0° latitude, often have significantly lower per capita GNPs. (*Source:* Reprinted with permission from M. Huston, "Biological Diversity, Soils, and Economics," *Science* [1993]: 1679. Copyright © 1993 American Association for the Advancement of Science. Also appears in M. Huston, *Biological Diversity* [New York: Cambridge University Press, 1994].)

Economic Aid

We noted earlier that economic aid has not led to economic takeoff because of mismanagement and the competitive global economy, among other factors. For these and other reasons, many wealthier countries have reduced their aid to poor countries in recent years. Most industrialized countries have never come close to giving the 1% GNP pledged in the early 1960s. The United States has given among the lowest proportionate aid levels of any nation. In 1994, the United States donated about $10 billion or 0.17% of GNP to foreign aid. Norway and the Netherlands ranked among the highest in the world, donating about 1% of their GNPs. Furthermore, much U.S. aid has always gone to just a few nations, such as Israel and Egypt, for military reasons.

The lack of donated money has meant that poor countries have had to borrow from richer countries, causing a so-called **Third World debt crisis**, also called a "debt bomb" (Chapter 1). By the early 1990s, the debt of the developing nations ("Third World") had reached $1.3 trillion, amounting to nearly half of those countries' collective GNP. Because the interest on this debt is higher than the foreign aid provided by rich countries, since 1982 there has been a net flow of money from the poor nations to the rich nations; in 1994, the net flow was more than $50 billion.

As a first step in resolving this debt crisis, the United Nations estimates that the environmental and developmental programs proposed at the Earth Summit would require rich countries to contribute at least 0.7% of their GNP as aid to the poor countries. This sum is relatively small compared to the amount spent on the military, which is being reduced in most rich nations with the end of the Cold War (■ Fig. 20–14).

Besides direct payments, the rich nations can provide many other types of economic aid to ease the debt crisis. One is cancellation of debt. By 1993, the United States, Germany, Canada, and Great Britain had canceled ("written off") over $5 billion in loans to African nations, largely for humanitarian reasons. However, this is a tiny fraction compared to the $1.3 trillion owed by the poor countries. The Worldwatch Institute estimates that about 60% of this debt, or about $780 billion, will have to be canceled, if the poor countries are to save enough money (instead of making loan payments) to begin sustainable development. The sum does not seem so great when compared to the Gulf War's cost of about $40 billion, which was raised in a few months, and especially when the benefits of saving the global environment are compared to the benefits of fighting a brief war for an unsustainable resource (oil). Even so, outright cancellation of such a large debt is very unpopular among the taxpayers of richer nations.

To make the cancellation more appealing, some observers have suggested that the debt be traded for something valuable. Among the most notable trades are the "debt-for-nature-swaps" suggested by the biologist Thomas Lovejoy. With these, a conservation organization pays about 15–30% of the debt to the lender, and the rest of the debt is canceled. In exchange, the poor country carries out specified environmental programs. In Chapter 12, for instance, we saw that land was set aside for preservation of tropical forests. Other examples include Costa Rica, where the Dutch government in 1989 swapped $33 million in debt for $10 million worth of programs in reforestation, water resource management, and soil conservation. Similarly, in 1991 the United States announced a plan to allow Poland to cancel 10% of its debt if the money was spent instead on toxic clean–up and other badly needed environmental restoration.

Nevertheless, debt cancellation, debt "swaps," and even direct donations of money are largely Band–Aid, short-term solutions. The fundamental problem is that the developing nations are not being paid the true costs for their resources, when such values as environmental uses are considered (Chapter 1). If the value of reducing global warming, conserving rare species and rare genes for agriculture and pharmaceuticals, and preserving uses for future generations were

FIGURE 20–14
Military spending dwarfs the money spent for development aid. The disparity is greatest in the United States, which annually spends about 5% of its GNP on military needs and far less than 0.5% on development. OECD average refers to the Organization of Economic Cooperation and Development nations. (*Source: U.S. News and World Report,* June 15, 1992, p. 13; data from United Nations. Copyright © June 15, 1992, U.S. News & World Report.)

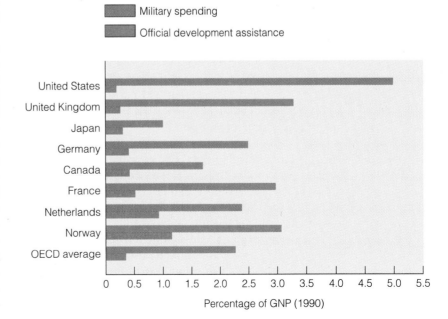

Military spending
Official development assistance

Percentage of GNP (1990)

included in the payments, money would flow into these poor nations. Such a flow is *not aid*; it is simply the proper payment for the true value of their resources.

Developing a Sustainable Economy

Most environmental economists agree that a sustainable world economy can still be built, but only if major steps are taken within the next two

the early 1980s, the World Bank and similar institutions came under intense criticism for disregarding the environmental impacts of their loans. They funded dam building and irrigation projects that destroyed huge tracts of land and polluted rivers; massive construction and deforestation projects were funded in many countries (Fig. 20–15). This criticism led to the creation of an Environment Department in the bank that investigates the environmental impacts of funded

FIGURE 20–15 Financing the building of dams in developing nations was once a very common, and very ecologically destructive, practice of the World Bank. Persistent pressures by many environmental groups have helped reduce, but not eliminate, such financing of unnecessary environmental damage. Shown here is the Itaipu Dam, a Brazilian hydroelectric project. (*Source:* Andrew Davis/ Greenpeace.)

decades. These steps can be summarized as follows: (1) increase the flow of money into developing countries, reversing the present flow away from them; (2) channel the money flow into activities that not only produce wealth but are sustainable; and (3) establish some social order that promotes fair distribution of that wealth or access to it.

Many experts believe that these steps can be most effectively carried out if a central global financial institution oversees the money flow. For instance, if richer nations were to contribute 0.7% of their GNP as discussed above, the money would be given to this central institution, which would then distribute it. A possible candidate is the World Bank, which is already the largest international lender in the world. In 1992, the bank and regional development banks loaned more than $33 billion. Despite the many advantages of having a single, central institution, political differences among countries probably render it impractical. Also, there is no guarantee that the money would be distributed in the best way. In

projects. However, this department has been widely criticized as being too small (54 people of the more than 4000 employed by the bank) and ineffective; environmentally damaging loans still occur.

Sustainable Economic Takeoff

Once enough money is made available to developing countries through a mixture of loans and gifts, most economists believe that further funding will be added from two new sources: private investment and economic growth. Private investment from richer countries will occur as the poorer countries develop stable, growing economies. This economic growth will itself produce profits that can be reinvested and help pay off debts.

● Table 20–5 outlines the estimated costs and long-term benefits of many environmental programs that can be undertaken in developing countries, as calculated by the World Bank in

TABLE 20–5 *Estimated Costs and Long-Term Benefits of Selected Environmental Programs*

PROGRAM	BILLIONS OF DOLLARS A YEAR	AS A PERCENTAGE OF GDP IN 2000	AS A PERCENTAGE OF GDP GROWTH, 1990–2000	LONG TERM BENEFITS
Increased investment in water and sanitation	10.0	0.2	0.5	Over 2 billion more people provided with service. Major labor savings and health benefits. Child mortality reduced by more than 3 million a year.
Controlling particular matter (PM) emissions from coal-fired power stations	2.0	0.04	0.1 ⎫	PM emissions virtually eliminated. Large reductions in respiratory illnesses and acid deposition.
Reducing acid deposition from new coal-fired stations	5.0	0.1	0.25 ⎭	
Changing to unleaded fuels; controls on the main pollutants from vehicles	10.0	0.2	0.5	Elimination of pollution from lead; more than 90% reductions in other pollutants.
Reducing emissions, effluents, and waste from industry	10.0–15.0	0.2–0.3	0.5–0.7	Appreciable reductions in levels of ambient pollution despite rapid industrial growth. Low-waste processes often a source of cost savings for industry.
Soil conservation and reforestation, including extension and training	15.0–20.0	0.3–0.4	0.7–1.0 ⎫	Improvements in yields and productivity of agriculture and forests. Lower pressures on natural forests. All areas eventually brought under sustainable forms of cultivation.
Additional resources for agricultural and forestry research, in relation to projected levels, and for resource surveys	5.0	0.1	0.2 ⎭	
Family planning (incremental costs of an expanded program)	7.0	0.1	0.3	Long-term world population stabilizes at 10 billion instead of 12.5 billion.
Increasing primary and secondary education for girls	2.5	0.05	0.1	Primary education for girls extended to 25 million more girls, and secondary education to 21 million more.

(*Source: World Development Report 1992* [New York: World Bank, 1992], p. 174.)

1992. The costs are estimated as a percentage of the GDP (Gross Domestic Product) of developing countries in the year 2000. GDP is the amount of wealth produced within a country, as opposed to GNP, which includes exports and wealth produced from outside the country. The key point is that the cost of all these environmental programs is only a small fraction of the wealth produced by a healthy, growing economy. The total estimated cost of the programs listed in the table is about $75 billion, or only about 1.4% of the combined GDPs of developing countries in the year 2000. Of course, Table 20–5 is not comprehensive, but the World Bank estimates that even if rainforest protection, pollution cleanup, alternative energy development, and other comprehensive items were included, the cost by the year 2000 would still not exceed 3% of the GDP of the developing countries. These estimates are obviously very approximate, but they provide an essential view of the true economic costs of a global, sustainable society. They show that such a society is a *realistic*, attainable goal.

SUMMARY

Although not traditionally associated with environmentalism, economics is concerned with environmental issues in two basic ways: resource scarcity and output, otherwise known as pollution. Often a superficial dichotomy is drawn between economics and environmental science because they have fundamentally different perspectives on the time spans of their outlooks, their priorities, and the social solutions they recommend. But this is a false dichotomy, as demonstrated by the newly developing field of environmental economics. Environmental economics blends the short-term need for jobs and the long-term need to protect the environment.

Environmental economics recognizes the need for sustainable growth, which uses minimal resources, controls pollution by input control, and relies on renewable resources. Thus, sustainable growth allows for increasing quantity and especially quality of goods and services, yet protects the environment. Although the GNP has long been used as an indicator of a country's well-being, it is a misleading figure. The GNP does not subtract the environmental costs incurred when wealth is created. A well-known alternative is the Index of Sustainable Economic Welfare, which includes several environmental measures.

There are two basic types of economic systems. In a command economy, such as the former Soviet Union, the government determines what is produced and sets prices. In a market economy, which is based on the "invisible hand," price competition among businesses determines costs. Market failures occur in a market economy when society is not benefited by this individual pursuit of self-interest. These market failures, known as externalities, do not include all costs of production in the price of a product.

When dealing with the environment, externalities include resource depletion and pollution. Because the environment is held in common by all, the "tragedy of the commons," as suggested by Garrett Hardin, may occur. As public goods become scarcer, there is increasing pressure to exploit the remaining resources, creating even greater scarcity and leading to more depletion and pollution.

The solution to environmental externalities is to internalize the cost by forcing depleters and polluters to pay for the "true" environmental costs. Environmental costs are determined and complicated by intangible costs, hidden costs, future costs, and unequal distributions of cost. Society can extract payment for environmental externalities by persuasion, government regulation, and economic motivation, including green taxes and privatization.

The solution to global poverty and many global environment problems is sustainable development. The developing countries have not experienced economic takeoff for various reasons including their mismanagement of money and the competitive world in which they are becoming industrialized. The developing nations' debt crisis may be at least partly resolved by direct economic aid and cancellation of debts. Environmental economists believe that a sustainable world economy may be built by increasing the flow of money to developing nations and channeling money into wealth-producing, sustainable activities within a social structure that fairly distributes the wealth.

KEY TERMS

command economies
cowboy economics
Earth Summit
economics
economic takeoff
environmental economics

externalities
false dichotomy
future costs
hidden costs
Index of Sustainable Economic Welfare (ISEW)
intangible costs

market economies
privatization
severance tax
sustainable growth
Third World Debt Crisis
throwaway society
unequally distributed costs

STUDY QUESTIONS

1. What are two ways in which economics is concerned with environmental issues? Name three ways that the economic approach differs from that of environmental science.
2. What is a "false dichotomy"? Why is the issue of "jobs versus environment" a false dichotomy?
3. Why do environmentally "friendly" activities produce so many jobs? What is "greenmail"?
4. Define environmental economics, sustainable growth, and cowboy economics.
5. How does traditional economics measure the total output of goods and services of a country? What environmental measures does the ISEW include?
6. What are the two basic economic systems of the modern world? Which is more efficient? Why?
7. What are externalities? What is the tragedy of the commons?
8. Why does scarcity promote even greater scarcity? Give an example.
9. What is a severance tax? What is its purpose?
10. List and define the four main costs that complicate the calculation of the overall environmental costs of an activity.
11. What are three basic ways that society can extract payment for a formerly free environmental externality? Define them. Which is least effective?
12. What is "economic takeoff"? What are some factors that explain why it has not occurred in many poor nations?
13. In what year did the net flow of money begin to flow from poor to rich nations? What is the fundamental problem causing this net flow in the wrong direction? Give examples.
14. The 1994 report by the Economic Policy Institute concluded that only 0.1% of job layoffs occurred from environmental regulations. The same report concluded that a change in business ownership caused about 3.5% of layoffs. For each job lost from environmental regulations, how many jobs were lost from a change in business ownership?
15. The 1994 report by the Economic Policy Institute concluded that only 0.1% of job layoffs occurred from environmental regulations. The same report concluded that falling product demand caused about 21% of layoffs. For each job lost from environmental regulations, how many jobs were lost from falling demand?

ESSAY QUESTIONS

1. Why is there a false dichotomy between economics and environmental science?
2. What is the basis of traditional economics, and how does it differ from environmental economics? How did traditional economics arise?
3. What are the four main costs influencing the calculation of the overall environmental costs of an activity? What problems are associated with each?
4. Explain the concept of green taxes. Provide examples and explain the advantages and disadvantages of their use.
5. Why hasn't economic takeoff occurred in most poor countries?

SUGGESTED READINGS

Anderson, T., and D. Leal. 1990. *Free market environmentalism*. San Francisco: Pacific Research Institute for Public Policy.

Anderson, V. 1991. *Alternative economic indicators*. New York: Routledge.

Berle, G. 1991. *The green entrepreneur*. New York: McGraw-Hill.

Brown, L., *et al*. 1991. *Saving the planet: How to shape an environmentally sustainable global economy*. New York: W. W. Norton.

Cairncross, F. 1992. *Costing the Earth*. Boston: Harvard Business School.

Constanza, R., ed. 1992. *Ecological economics: The science and management of sustainability*. New York: Columbia University Press.

Daly, H., 1991. *Steady-state economics*. Covelo, Calif.: Island Press.

Daly, H., and K. Townsend, ed. 1993. *Valuing the Earth: Economics, ecology, ethics*. Cambridge, Mass.: MIT Press.

Dorfman, R., and N. Dorfman. 1993. *Economics of the environment: Selected readings*. New York: W. W. Norton.

Kahn, J. 1995. *The economic approach to environmental and natural resources*. Orlando, Fla.: Harcourt Brace.

Moore, C., and A. Miller, 1994. *Green gold*. Boston: Beacon Press.

Pearce, D., *et al*. 1990. *Sustainable development*. London: Edward Elgar.

Repetto, R., *et al*. 1992. *Green fees*. Washington, D.C.: World Resources Institute.

Silverstein, M. 1993. *The environmental economic revolution*. New York: St. Martin's Press.

Turner, R. K., *et al*. 1993. *Environmental economics: An elementary introduction*. Baltimore: Johns Hopkins University Press.

ENVIRONMENTAL ETHICS

PROLOGUE *Animal Rights or Freedom of Religious Expression?*

S anteria is an Afro-Cuban religion that has been practiced for centuries; among the rituals Santerians perform is animal sacrifice. In 1987 the Santerian Church of Lukumi Babaya Aye purchased land in Hialeah, Florida, to build a church and practice its religion. This upset many citizens of Hialeah, and ordinances were passed outlawing animal sacrifice in the city. The Santerians contested the laws, contending that their right to freedom of religious expression had been violated. Eventually, the argument was carried all the way to the U.S. Supreme Court, which in June 1993 unanimously struck down the city ordinances as unconstitutional.

Writing on behalf of the Court, Justice Anthony Kennedy said that laws that burden religious practices are permissible if they are "neutral and of general applicability" and thus do not discriminate against one particular kind of religion. In the case of the Hialeah ban,

PHOTO   *Residents of Hialeah, Florida, protest against animal sacrifice as practiced by Santerians. (Source: Tony Savino/Sygma.)*

however, Justice Kennedy wrote, "The ordinances' texts and operation demonstrate that they are not neutral, but have as their object the suppression of Santeria's central element, animal sacrifice. . . . Our review confirms that the laws in question were enacted by officials who did not understand, failed to perceive or chose to ignore the fact that their official actions violated the nation's essential commitment to religious freedom."

Animal rights groups, including the Humane Society of the United States and the Massachusetts Society for the Prevention of Cruelty to Animals, questioned the Supreme Court's ruling. What about the rights of the animals? Do they have the right to a life free of unnecessary cruelty and killing as part of a human religious practice? Certainly, the Supreme Court would not have ruled in favor of the Santerians if they practiced human sacrifice. From a moral and ethical point of view, what is the difference between human life and nonhuman animal life? Are animals (and by extension, the entire natural world) here simply for human use and pleasure? Or do animals (and perhaps even whole ecosystems) have the right to exist and follow their own pursuits and interests independent of human interference? Do nonhuman organisms have moral status? These types of questions can become very important when considering some environmental issues. If animals have inherent rights and moral status, then we need to think twice not only about using them in religious practices, but also about destroying their habitats purely for human gain. Is it acceptable to destroy a virgin forest to build a cathedral or a shopping mall? If animals have no rights, then perhaps we need not be constrained in dealing with them.

The Supreme Court ruling on the Hialeah ordinances has another potential implication besides the animal rights issue. Some religions, such as those practiced by certain Native American groups, regard specific areas of land (such as a mountain and its ecosystem, a forest, or a prairie) as sacred and important to their religion. Is it permissible for a mining company to destroy a sacred mountain to obtain the mineral resources it may contain? Or does such an action illegally deny the people who hold the mountain sacred the right to practice their religion unencumbered? If the Santerians have a right to practice their animal sacrifice, why shouldn't our hypothetical "mountainists" be guaranteed protection of their mountain? Or do the economic interests of Western industrialists who want to mine the mountain override any religious interests that an indigenous people may have in preserving it? On what ethical basis should we address such an issue? As we shall see in this chapter, certain "deep ecologists" would argue that the mountain and its ecosystem have an inherent right to exist that is completely independent of any human interests.

INTRODUCTION

Practical, or applied, environmental science often involves decision making. We may be faced with difficult choices that force us to weigh options and balance interests. Is harvesting an old-growth forest justified if it may mean the elimination of an ecosystem? Do human concerns (jobs, lumber for building homes) outweigh the concerns of the animals and plants that live in the forest? Is humankind (*Homo sapiens*) more important than other natural creatures? Should we build a nuclear power plant that can readily supply the electricity desired by a community even though the nuclear waste products will impose a major burden on future generations? Do the immediate interests of living persons (who need electricity now) count for more than the interests of unborn generations (who will have to monitor, and perhaps be contaminated by, their ancestors' wastes)? When a factory dumps so much waste in a river that all the organisms in the river die, do their deaths matter if no people are interested in the organisms anyway? Is pollution only "bad" if it interferes with human interests and concerns? Or do the interests and concerns of other organisms, or even species and ecosystems, carry weight? Is nature here only to serve humans? Or do we have an obligation to respect and protect the natural world for its own sake? Do animals, plants, and perhaps even rivers, ecosystems, and biomes have "rights"?

Such concerns are in the realm of **ethics**. Scientific analysis may be able to determine, or predict, the consequences of a particular action (such as continuing to dump ozone-destroying CFCs into the atmosphere—see Chapter 18), but science alone cannot answer the question of what course of action we ought to take (continue to manufacture CFCs, or ban them even if this produces hardships for many humans). Questions of what ought to be done can only be answered

EnviroNet
www.jbpub.com/environet

based on some set of **values**. Ethics is the philosophical study of **moral** values; it involves distinguishing good from bad, right from wrong, and developing and justifying sets of moral principles, duties, and obligations. In the simplest sense, environmental ethics is the application of ethical study to environmental concerns. A key aspect of environmental ethics is developing and justifying a theory of the moral relations between humans, non-human species, and the natural environment (including nonliving entities).

Environmental ethics can be viewed as an integral part of a more comprehensive environmental philosophy: a description and understanding of exactly how the Earth (world, universe) works and the position of humans within that world. Ultimately, a sound environmental ethic and environmental philosophy must be grounded in a clear understanding of science, but they involve much more than simple science for they guide human thought and actions. The importance of environmental ethics and philosophy cannot be understated: these issues affect every one of us on a daily basis. Every human decision made with respect to environmental issues is made in the context of some environmental philosophy, whether that philosophy is well thought out and explicit or vague and unarticulated (perhaps not even consciously acknowledged by the decisionmaker). Given the importance of environmental ethics, it is well worth our time to briefly explore this subject in the context of an environmental science text.

ETHICS

If ethics is concerned with right and wrong, good and bad, then where do these moral values come from? Do they exist independently of humans?

FIGURE 21–1

God overseeing the creation of the world, as depicted in an illumination from an English Psalter, circa 1215. (*Source:* The Granger Collection, New York.)

Moral realists believe that moral values are objective and real, and that humans can discover these values through study and reasoning (logic), conscience, intuition, or revelation. Many mainstream Western religions take this stance, defining good in terms of an objectively real God and God's teachings or divine revelations (Fig. 21–1). Secular forms of realism in ethics also exist, such as the concept that the universe is inherently orderly (it is understandable and makes sense), and that by study and rational thinking we can discover the proper ethical/moral position of humans in the world.

Some people view all moral values as simply human creations that have no objective validity outside the context of a particular society, culture, or way of thinking. Such a **moral antirealist** position maintains that humans (either collectively or individually) do not discover values, but rather create them, either consciously and deliberately or perhaps more often unconsciously. The antirealists do not necessarily deny the importance of moral values: however moral values are arrived at, they are extremely important in that they underlie human decisions and actions. Indeed, one might believe that most moral values are human creations—cultural artifacts—yet still attempt to discover objective moral values.

Sometimes the antirealist stance is equated with the cynical ethical **relativist view**. Relativists say that ethical controversies are "all a matter of opinion," and that there is no objective or rational way to determine right or wrong, good or bad. According to this way of thinking, ethics and morals are "simply" a function of, or relative to, an individual's feelings, religion, culture, and so on. If no code of ethics is universally true, then we might as well dispense with the pursuit of ethics altogether. Ultimately, any code of morals is simply an arbitrary, silly game that can never be proven to be true.

Such a relativist attitude is usually an excuse for not engaging in careful, critical thinking. Whether one adopts a realist or antirealist view of morals and ethical concerns, certain decisions and actions (as opposed to other decisions and actions) can be supported with sound reasons. A decision or action that is supported by substantial evidence (such as rational reasons within the context of a coherent and logical ethical/environmental philosophy) might certainly be judged more favorably than an arbitrary decision made in an ethical vacuum without thinking through all the ramifications of the decision. We may never be able to "prove" that a certain decision or judgment is the "universally best" and only allowable decision, but we can certainly subscribe to standards of ethical reasoning and thought that will produce, on the whole, more satisfactory decisions and actions than the "nonanalysis" of the true relativist.

We should also note that one of the prime pieces of evidence that some ethical relativists use to support their position is the "fact" that many people, cultures, and societies disagree about ethical issues. (Relativists often ignore the "fact" that most human cultures share many moral precepts against behaviors such as murdering innocent people, stealing, cheating friends, and so forth.) Some cultures find infanticide permissible or even morally obligatory in certain contexts (such as when additional children impose an undue hardship on the already existing members of the society), whereas other religions or cultures consider contraception (much less abortion or infanticide) to be morally wrong. Such disagreements do not "prove" that there are no better or worse answers to ethical questions, any more than the fact that many societies have traditionally believed that the Sun orbits the Earth, while modern science teaches that the Earth orbits the Sun, "proves" that we can never objectively solve this problem of celestial mechanics. Disagreement *per se* has no bearing on whether or not a better or worse (more or less rational or objective) answer to a question or ethical issue can be proposed. Furthermore, the best answers to questions are not necessarily the answers that the majority of people have espoused in the past. In the end, the ethical or moral relativist position typically tends to be taken by those with agendas other than the rational and critical thinking through of ethical concerns. The ethical relativist position can serve as a convenient way of justifying doing exactly what one wants to do anyway, regardless of the environmental outcome: I will build the factory (at a tidy profit), even though it will destroy a major estuary system, for in the end who can judge which is more important, the factory and the jobs it creates and the money it earns, or the survival of an ecosystem that is relatively "unused" (by humans)?

Ethics is a large, complex, and controversial field of study. It affects everyone, for we all must constantly make ethical decisions, yet many people avoid confronting ethics head-on. This is unfortunate, since ethics involves some of our most fundamental assumptions and ways of thinking—our moral value system. Ethics can be liberating in that it can show us alternative ways of thinking about issues (Issues in Perspective 21–1 describes some environmental issues and the ethical questions they raise). One goal of ethics is simply to catalog and describe the various ethical approaches—the different ethical principles and moral values—that are (or have been, or could be) held by people; this is often known as **descriptive ethics**. Descriptive ethics does not necessarily pass judgment on whether one ethical system is better or worse than another (although different systems may be critically compared); the main point is to document the range of ethical systems that are feasible. This chapter is primarily concerned with descriptive ethics—it reviews various ethical positions that have been taken relative to the environment. By reviewing these systems, one may be better able to understand, refine, or even formulate one's own ethical system and philosophy.

Normative ethics goes beyond the simply descriptive. Drawing upon a certain ethical system or philosophy, it renders ethical opinions and judgments of actions and prescribes appropriate (ethical) behavior (sometimes normative ethics is called prescriptive ethics, as opposed to descriptive ethics). Normative ethics tells us what we should and should not do—what is right and wrong, good and bad—within the context of a certain ethical system. Normative ethics is probably what comes to mind when most people think of ethics.

Finally, we can consider **philosophical ethics**, which involves thinking about ethical controversies and underlying values, principles, or rules at an abstract level. Philosophical ethics analyzes and evaluates the underlying bases of normative judgments within and among ethical systems and places these judgments and systems within a larger philosophical context. In turn, from theories, generalizations, and systems developed during the study of philosophical ethics, normative judgments and actions can be derived and cogently defended.

Environmental Racism, Environmental Equity, Environmental Justice

Since the early 1980s, a number of studies have demonstrated that minority groups (such as African Americans and Hispanics) and people of lower socioeconomic status are affected disproportionately by environmental hazards and risks (▮ Fig. 1). Is this fair, right, just, or ethical?

Factories that emit hazardous substances are more often than not located in minority and lower-income neighborhoods (such as documented in a 1993 study of Los Angeles). Nationwide studies have demonstrated that facilities for treating or incinerating hazardous waste are on average located in communities with twice the minority population of communities without such facilities (24% minority members compared to 12% for communities lacking such facilities). A 1992 study of the enforcement of environmental laws by the U.S. Environmental Protection Agency (EPA) found that the fines levied on environmental violators were, on average, five times higher when the violations occurred in predominantly white communities than when they occurred in minority communities. Likewise, the EPA was generally quicker to deal with hazardous waste sites in predominantly white communities. At all economic levels, black children suffer from

higher blood lead levels than white children. An estimated 300,000 farm workers suffer from pesticide poisoning each year, and 80% of all farm workers are minority members (the largest number being Hispanics). In the American Southwest, Navajo land has been contaminated by uranium mining. But then some tribes want the economic benefits that ensue from mining or waste disposal on their lands. And one could argue that minority and low-income persons may be attracted by the generally lower real estate prices found near some factories and dumps.

The concept of **environmental racism** can trace its modern origins to 1979 when the residents of a predominantly African-American community in Houston, Texas, unsuccessfully tried to stop a new solid waste facility from being located in their neighborhood. The term *environmental racism* was first used in 1982 in connection with an attempt by a black community in Warren County, North Carolina, to stop PCB (polychlorinated biphenyl) contaminated soil from other parts of the state from being deposited in a local landfill. The community took the issue to court, and large demonstrations were held that resulted in the arrest of some 500 protesters. Ultimately, the court ruled against

the black community, but the case raised awareness about environmental racism and related issues and resulted in the development of a nationwide network of minority environmental activists.

One of the leaders in Warren County was the Reverend Benjamin J. Chavis, Jr., who later became the executive director of the National Association for the Advancement of Colored People (NAACP). Chavis has stated that: "Environmental racism is racial discrimination in environmental policy making and the unequal enforcement of environmental laws and regulations. It is the deliberate targeting of people of color communities for toxic waste facilities and the official sanctioning of a life-threatening presence of poisons and pollutants in people of color communities. It is also manifested in the history of excluding people of color from the leadership of the environmental movement."

Despite the clear evidence that environmental racism, as defined by Reverend Chavis, exists, addressing the issue can be complex. As more than one court decision has pointed out, just because a company that emits hazardous waste has a history of siting its facilities in minority neighborhoods, this does not prove that the company is intentionally discriminatory—

MAJOR TRADITIONS IN WESTERN ETHICAL THOUGHT

Whereas environmental ethics—the ethical relationship between humans and the natural environment—has attracted concerted attention only in the last few decades, ethics as a whole has been an important part of Western philosophical thought for thousands of years. Most readers of this book probably come from a Western Judeo-Christian background or at least live in a society heavily influenced by Western and Judeo-Christian values; therefore, it is important to review some of

the main ethical traditions in Western philosophy and see how they have been applied to environmental issues.

Judeo-Christian Environmental Ethics

Western attitudes, and therefore ethics, toward the environment have been heavily influenced by the teachings of the Judeo-Christian religions. The book of Genesis states:

> And God said, Let us make man in our image, after our likeness: and let them have dominion over the fish of the sea, and over the fowl of the air, and over the cattle, and over all the earth, and over every

FIGURE 1

Toxic waste and race: An unnatural association. A 1994 report by the Center for Policy Alternatives in Washington, D.C., found that people of color—defined by the report as the total population less non-Hispanic whites—are currently 47% more likely than are whites to live near a commercial toxic waste facility. (*Source:* From "Toxic Waste and Race: An Unnatural Association," by Johnny Johnson, *Scientific American*, December 1994, p. 26. Copyright © 1994 by Scientific American, Inc. All rights reserved.)

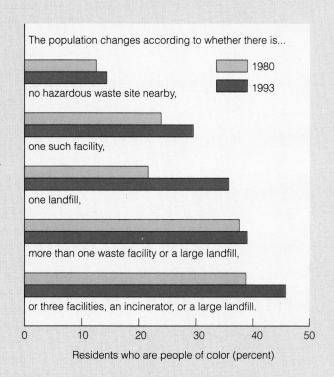

The population changes according to whether there is...

☐ 1980
■ 1993

no hazardous waste site nearby,

one such facility,

one landfill,

more than one waste facility or a large landfill,

or three facilities, an incinerator, or a large landfill.

Residents who are people of color (percent)

deliberately targeting people of color. Property values may be lower in the minority neighborhoods. Higher-income, and predominantly white, neighborhoods have more money and political clout to op-pose objectionable facilities. Essentially, then, the present system can be seen as fostering environmental racism; if so, perhaps the root problem—the system—must be changed. Many activists advocate empow-ering minority and underclass peoples by giving them a greater say in the decision-making processes. We should also note that historically the environmental movement arose, at least in part, from the desire of the wealthier classes to preserve part of the "wilderness" for their own pleasure and to protect the quality of their own lives. Therefore, it is not surprising that historically whites of the higher economic classes have been leaders of the environmental movement. Currently, there is a push for more minority members to take active leadership roles in environmental groups throughout the nation and the world.

The EPA now officially acknowledges that environmental racism is an issue that needs to be addressed. The agency has espoused **environmental equity** for all U.S. citizens as a necessary guiding principle for future decisions. But some environmentalists fear that environmental equity will simply mean spreading environmental risks equally among all people; they say more is needed. **Environmental justice**, as described by Reverend Chavis, aims not only to correct the injustices of environmental racism but also to reduce the environmental risks for all people. The ultimate goal is to have a cleaner, healthier, more livable planet that everyone can enjoy.

creeping thing that creepeth upon the earth. So God created man in his *own* image, in the image of God created he him; male and female created he them. And God blessed them, and God said unto them, Be fruitful, and multiply, and replenish the earth, and subdue it: and have dominion over the fish of the sea, and over the fowl of the air, and over every living thing that moveth upon the earth. (Gen. 1:26–28, King James Version)

Based on this passage, generations of theologians and laypeople have concluded that humanity is special, having been created in the "image" of God, and separate from the rest of nature. Humans were destined to rule over the rest of the world and use it for their benefit. Additionally, God enjoined humans to increase their population and spread across the Earth. Another general theme throughout the Bible is that the world (at least after the fall of Adam and Eve) is a sinful place. Earth is merely a temporary dwelling for humans, who should be concerned primarily with the spiritual afterlife (of course, the earthly life is important in obtaining "heaven" in the afterlife).

Many environmental thinkers have suggested that such Judeo-Christian beliefs have contributed to recent environmental degradation by humans. The Judeo-Christian values just outlined are either relatively indifferent or even openly hostile to en-

FIGURE 21–2
St. Francis of Assisi preaching to the birds; Pradella panel painted by Giotto (circa 1266–1337). (*Source*: The Granger Collection, New York.)

vironmental concerns. Humans and their concerns are more important than the natural environment. God created nature simply to serve and benefit humankind. At the extreme, for many fundamentalist Christians in particular, environmental issues are simply irrelevant because the end of the world (the apocalypse) is expected very soon. Why bother trying to conserve resources or preserve the environment if the end of the world (as foretold in the book of Revelation) is imminent? In the 1980s, James Watt, then the U.S. Secretary of the Interior and a conservative Christian, was quoted as having said, "I don't know how many future generations we can count on before the Lord [i.e., Jesus Christ] returns." Given that Watt reduced pollution controls on industry and encouraged the development of public lands, some inferred that due to his religious beliefs (as well as his economic views) Watt was relatively indifferent to the future of the environment.

Other members of the Judeo-Christian tradition have espoused a different attitude, that of

stewardship. According to this view, God created nature, and humans have a duty to protect and preserve it—be stewards or keepers of nature—on God's behalf. To abuse or misuse nature is to slight God and God's works. The concept of Christian stewardship has gained prominence recently among many Christian denominations, but its roots can be traced back to at least the time of St. Francis of Assisi (1181/2–1226), who espoused an early form of Christian stewardship (Fig. 21–2). Francis specifically viewed all animals as integral parts of God's creation that had a right to exist independent of any purpose they might serve for humans. For Francis the natural world reflected the grace and nature of God. At the time, however, such views were generally ignored or condemned.

The Teleological Tradition

The ancient Greek philosopher Aristotle (384–322 B.C.) developed a concept of science and ethics that is sometimes referred to as the **teleological tradition**. According to Aristotle, every being and every object in nature (as well as among human artifacts) has a purpose, function, end, final cause, or utility in the overall natural design and order of the world and universe. For instance, the function (telos) of a mammal's lungs is to aid in breathing (inhaling fresh oxygenated air and exhaling stale, used air). The function of a chair is to provide a place for a person to sit and rest. A thing is good when it fulfills its natural function.

Aristotle also distinguished between living and nonliving things. Living organisms have a psyche, spirit, or soul, and all living things are distinguished by their characteristic activities, such as growth (seen in plants, animals, and humans), sensation (found in animals and humans), and thinking (a characteristic of humans). According to Aristotle all living things have natural activities and functions, and it is good when they fulfill these natural functions.

In the Middle Ages, some Christian theologians, such as Thomas Aquinas (1225–1274), adopted and refined Aristotle's teleological tradition. The functioning of all natural objects, including all living organisms, was part of God's plan and purpose. Nature was created by God and reveals God's plans and purpose; nature, as a reflection of God, is good. In the eighteenth and nineteenth centuries, these concepts were refined even further. William Paley (1743–1805) and other natural theologians saw God's handiwork in all of nature. Their "argument from design" asserted that the perfection and complexity of the natural world, especially as seen in intricate and "perfectly adapted" organisms, prove that the world in all its glory must have been created by an intelligent Designer (that is, God). The classic analogy used by natural theologians is that of a watch and a watchmaker. Small pieces of metal cannot assemble themselves naturally into a functioning watch, so if we find a watch in a field, we know that a human (and perhaps specifically, a watchmaker) must have preceded us there and dropped the watch. The watch itself must have been made by human activity—it shows clear evidence of design, plan, and purpose. In nature we find that even the simplest organisms are much more complex than a mechanical watch, so organisms too must be the result of a Designer.

In 1859 this simple teleological way of thinking was, for all practical purposes, destroyed with the advent of modern evolutionary theory. In that year Charles Darwin (1809–1882;  Fig. 21–3) published *On the Origin of Species by Means of Natural Selection, or the Preservation of Favored Races in the Struggle for Life*; this book clearly demonstrated that organisms are actually not as perfectly adapted as they might initially seem to be, and that the adaptations and functions of the organisms can be explained by the workings of natural processes independent of a divine Creator.

Today, a modified teleological tradition continues to hold some influence among many environmentalists. Some ecologists and environmentalists consider the organisms composing a natural ecosystem to be in harmonious, well-functioning relationships with one another (even if the ecosystem and the contained species are the result of natural evolutionary processes). Each organism or species is considered to have its own distinctive role and function, each contributes to the overall system in its own way, and each has an inherent good. In this view, undisturbed nature may be considered good, whereas undue human interference with natural systems is considered wrong.

Utilitarianism

One of the most influential ethical traditions in the modern West is **utilitarianism**, perhaps best developed in the works of the nineteenth-century philosophers Jeremy Bentham and John Stuart Mill. The basic principle of utilitarianism is that the overall good should be maximized, often expressed in the phrase "the greatest good for the greatest number." Decisions or actions are ethical insofar as they maximize good. Utilitarianism's emphasis on maximizing good for the greatest number is often closely linked with the concept of democracy and has been extremely influential in economics and public policy decisions (including decisions that impact the environment).

A major concern of utilitarianism is to distinguish what is "good." In this context good has been variously considered to be either pleasure (or at least the absence of pain) or the satisfaction of desires or preferences. Another major concern, particularly in an environmental context, is whose pleasures and pains, satisfaction or thwarting of desires, are to be considered. Another way of expressing this is to pose the question: Who deserves **moral status**? A slaveowner in ancient Rome might have said that the pleasure or desires of slaves did not count because the slaves were simply property and did not have moral status. Today, all philosophers would certainly agree that any and all competent human beings have moral status. But what about other sentient beings, such as dogs, cats, zebras, hippos, and other animals? Most people today agree that such animals feel pleasure and have desires, but are those pleasures or desires morally significant? Do the pleasures and desires of humans always outweigh those of other animals? Given a certain action, such as building a hydroelectric dam that will provide a community with much-needed electricity but at the same time flood the home of many wild animals, how do we judge and balance the good or bad effects on peo-

FIGURE 21–3 Charles Robert Darwin (at left); oil painting over a photograph. (*Source:* The Granger Collection, New York.)

ple versus those on other living creatures? One answer, adopted by some utilitarians, is to consider only the pleasures and desires of humans. This answer is not very satisfactory to many environmentalists, however; they suggest that moral status should be extended to nonhuman organisms and, in some cases, even to rivers, mountains, and ecosystems (see the discussion later).

Even if we consider human beings to be the only entities that deserve moral status, another question can be raised: Which humans? Do we consider only living humans? Or do we need to take unborn generations into account? Should we maximize good (ensure human pleasure and ful-

fill human desires) among living people by depleting the Earth's scarce resources, or should we take a long-term view and concern ourselves with future generations? Classical nineteenth-century utilitarianism focused primarily on the short-term maximization of the good among living people, but at that time humans did not have the same power to affect the future that we do today. Now we have the ability to precipitate global changes (such as global warming, depletion of the ozone layer, large-scale reduction of biodiversity, production of radioactive wastes, pollution of the land and oceans with hazardous and toxic chemicals, and so forth) that could affect generations far into the future (■ Fig. 21–4). How do we weigh the pleasures and desires of these future generations against the pleasures and desires of living people?

Regardless of who is given moral status, in practice utilitarianism often faces the problem of trying to measure and quantify the good produced by various actions. Since good usually cannot be quantified directly, substitutes that can be measured and quantified are used as an indirect measure of good. Such substitutes might include life expectancy among a population (the idea being that a longer average life is inherently good, independent of any measure of the quality of life) or average annual income (on the assumption that the more money people have, the happier they probably are, although the validity of this assertion is uncertain). In many cases an economic analysis may substitute for analysis of the good versus bad produced by a certain action. With regard to environmental questions, this can immediately lead to complications. Given a proposal to build a new coal-burning power plant in a virgin mountain valley, we can probably easily estimate the cost of building and operating the plant and the value of the electricity it will produce, but how do we put a dollar amount on the losses incurred during the building and operation of the plant? How do we measure the value of the scenic view that will be lost? How do we measure the value of the trees and lakes destroyed by acid precipitation produced by the power plant? What dollar figure do we put on the expected slightly shortened life expectancy of people living in the vicinity of the plant? Questions like this can plague utilitarians when they attempt to apply their ethical system to real-life cases. All too often certain factors that cannot be readily quantified are simply not taken into consideration.

Still, a human-centered (humanistic) utilitarianism remains central to much Western thinking. Benefit-cost analyses often implicitly assume utilitarianism. In this mode of thinking, human good is given primary or exclusive consideration when decisions are made: whatever action on balance produces more good than bad, more pleasure than pain, for humans is the ethically correct decision. Thus, from a human-centered utilitarian position, pollution is not bad or morally objectionable per se, except insofar as it thwarts human desires or causes pain and suffering to humans. Indeed, a certain level of pollution might be considered morally appropriate if it contributes or is necessary to obtain other human goods, such as material objects or economic productiveness.

Duties and Rights

Another very influential tradition in Western ethics has been **deontology** (from the Greek word *deon*, obligation or duty), or the study of moral obligations and duties. The classical proponent of such views was the German philosopher Immanuel Kant (1724–1804). Kant viewed humans as free and rational beings who can choose their actions and are therefore responsible for those actions. But, according to the Kantian view, humans can only be held responsible for the consequences of their actions that they can anticipate or control. If we build a hydroelectric dam for all the right reasons (it will provide electricity and jobs and supply water for irrigation), but once it is built discover major negative consequences that could not be previously anticipated (organisms living in the artificial lake behind the dam spread disease), we cannot be held morally accountable for these negative consequences. This, of course, is not to say that we should not attempt to correct the situation even after the dam has been built.

Deontologists stress rationality in determining ethical actions and moral obligations. Kant sought to elucidate ethical principles that would be rational and acceptable to all persons at all times. According to Kant, the fundamental **duty** of all humans, which he called the "categorical imperative," is to act in ways that are acceptable to all rational beings. Among other things, this means treating all humans as rational, autonomous beings who have their own purposes and goals. We should not treat other humans as mere objects or only as a means to our ends. If all humans act according to these ideas, this will establish the fundamental ethical **rights** of all humans. No one will treat anyone else as a mere object; each person will have the right to be treated as an autonomous, free, thinking being who is in pursuit of her or his own goals. Kant and the deontologists stress respect, equality, and freedom among competent, rational human beings who fulfill their duties to one another.

The Kantian tradition has been extremely influential over the last 250 years. Kantian influences are readily apparent in the concepts of inalienable rights, civil liberties, and democratic institutions where free and rational persons respect one another and participate in government on an equal basis. From an environmental perspective, however, the deontological tradition can be viewed as extremely **anthropocentric** (human-centered). Taking an extreme Kantian view, only free and rational beings (namely, competent adult humans) have rights. Nonhuman organisms—and the environment at large—may be viewed as simply a means to human ends.

John Locke and Property Rights

Not exactly an ethical tradition, but a theory that has greatly affected Western environmental thinking, is the notion of **property rights**—particularly, the theory of private property rights. The English theorist John Locke (1632–1704) developed a detailed theory of private property that forms the basis of much thinking on the subject even today. According to Locke, in an original state of nature, land (used here in a general sense to include bodies of water) and its resources are unowned, but every person (human being) owns his or her body and the labor produced by that body. When a person mixes her or his labor (which is privately owned) with the unowned land or resources, then that person comes to own the

land or the resources derived from it. Thus, by mixing the owned labor of the body with the unowned material objects of nature, the objects of nature come to be owned by the owner of the labor. The classic example of the Lockean concept of the acquisition of property is the settler who goes into the wilderness, clears the land, builds a house and plants crops, and thereby becomes a property owner (Fig. 21–5). Of course, this scenario tends to ignore any indigenous people

FIGURE 21–5
Nineteenth-century settlers could become property owners by mixing their labor with unowned land or other resources. (*Source*: Historic VU/ Visuals Unlimited.)

who may have occupied the land previously, and it accords property rights only to humans and ignores the fauna and flora that occupy the land.

Even within a Lockean framework, however, property owners' control over their property may not be so complete that they can do anything they want with it. The reason is that the rights of other property owners (and people in general, whether or not they own property) may restrict the rights of a particular property owner. One does not necessarily have the right to store or dispose of toxic waste on one's own private property if doing so may injure other persons. The toxic waste may leak into the groundwater and migrate to other people's land, or the simple fact of having a toxic waste dump in the neighborhood may lower surrounding property values.

Ultimately, some people question the entire notion of private property, at least in its more extreme Western forms. Many non-Western cultures have a much more vague concept of property. Many nomadic peoples, for instance, do not recognize the concept of private ownership of land and its resources.

ENVIRONMENTAL ETHICS AND ENVIRONMENTAL PHILOSOPHIES

Traditionally, most Western ethical theories and philosophies have focused primarily or exclusively on the relationships among human beings. In the twentieth century, however, a number of ethical systems have been formulated that emphasize the environment and the relationship of human beings to other living organisms and the environment at large. Here we will briefly review some of these newer philosophies.

Biocentric Ethics

As opposed to anthropocentric ethics, **biocentric** (life-centered) ethics views all living things as having inherent worth. Living organisms are good in their own right and deserve the consideration and respect of humans—not because the organisms necessarily have rights per se, but because humans have the duty to treat other forms of life reasonably and with good intentions (Issues in Perspective 21-2, page 596, discusses some of the related issues raised by animal rights). From a practical point of view, this does not mean that living organisms cannot be killed, but many biocentrists avoid the taking of life whenever possible. When life is taken, it should be done consciously with the killer acknowledging responsibility.

In many ways, biocentrism is not so much a set of ethical rules or principles as an attitude toward all living organisms: a "worldview." An early biocentrist was Albert Schweitzer (1875–1965) who summarized his views with the phrase "Ehrfurcht vor dem Leben" (commonly translated as "reverence for life"). The views of Schweitzer and like-minded individuals harken back to ancient Greek philosophers, including Plato (ca. 427–347 B.C.) and Aristotle, who stressed virtue and moral character rather than rules or principles of conduct.

Ecocentric Ethics

Going beyond biocentric ethics, some thinkers have developed various forms of **ecocentric** (ecological-centered) ethics. According to such views (and they are quite diverse on the specifics), not only do humans and other living organisms merit moral consideration, but so do nonliving natural objects and relationships, such as rivers, forests, entire species, ecosystems, biomes, and natural processes like biogeochemical cycles and weather systems. Ecocentric ethical approaches are holistic, considering the whole (such as an ecosystem composed of various species and their relationships to each other and nonliving objects) to have an inherent value and therefore deserving of moral consideration independent of human-imposed values.

One of the most important figures in the development of modern ecocentric environmental ethics was Aldo Leopold (1887–1948; ▪ Fig. 21–6), author of many works including *A Sand County Almanac* (1949). Leopold's most important contribution may have been his development of what he called a "land ethic." Leopold was a professional forest manager who was involved in the campaign to exterminate undesirable predators ("varmints"), such as wolves, mountain lions, coyotes, bobcats, foxes, skunks, and so forth, that preyed on both domestic and wild animals useful to humans. But over the years of his involvement in such activities, Leopold came to a deep understanding and appreciation for ecology and the natural world, and he developed a new environmental philosophy and ethic.

Leopold came to view the "inanimate world"—ecosystems, and ultimately the Earth itself—as a type of "living organism." Killing predators in particular (as Leopold had done in earlier years) was wrong not because of the harm and pain it inflicted on the individual animals, but because it damaged the ecosystem as a whole. In Leopold's view the ecosystem itself has inherent moral value, and humans should develop a love for the land and its inhabitants; this love is expressed through our stewardship of the land. At the core of Leopold's concept of a land ethic is the idea that modern humans have a duty to care for the land and its inhabitants (the ecosystem) because, given the impact of human technology, the ecosystem can no longer care for itself.

The idea that ecosystems could have moral standing is a radical concept in the context of Western ethical thinking. As we saw in our review of major ethical traditions, much of Western morality has been based on the dual concepts of humanism and individualism. Initially, only humans—and sometimes more specifically only living humans—were the subject of moral consideration. Although many people even today still regard only living humans as worthy of moral status, some ethical systems would now include future generations, sentient (feeling) nonhuman organisms, and even all organisms. Likewise, only individuals (whether human individuals or animal individuals) have traditionally been viewed as the objects of moral consideration. Leopold's land ethic is neither humanistic nor individualistic. Moral value is not limited to humans or even to other individual organisms; entire species (collections of individuals) and ecosystems (numerous individuals from many different species, and the nonbiotic objects they interact with) are granted moral status. Thus, land (including the organisms that live on and in it) itself has value and moral status.

According to Leopold, people must "quit thinking about decent land-use as solely an economic problem. Examine each question in terms of what is ethically and esthetically right, as well as what is economically expedient. A thing is right when it tends to preserve the integrity, stability, and beauty of the biotic community. It is wrong when it tends otherwise."

Some critics of Leopold's land ethic (as well as critics of ecocentric ethics in general) have charged that if the land ethic were taken literally, it could lead to environmental fascism (ecofascism) or even genocide of the human species. The

reasoning here is that the natural biological ecosystems would be best served by the elimination of human populations—thus leading to human genocide. Or, viewed another way, the land ethic requires that the individual human be subordinated to the good of the land—thus leading to a form of fascism. Although ecofascists may exist, Leopold was clearly not a member of this camp. Leopold regarded his land ethic as an addition to the humanistic, anthropocentric, individualistic ethical point of view. According to Leopold's way of thinking, it was necessary, but not sufficient, to take the needs and desires of individual people and other organisms into account when considering ethical issues; in addition, one must also look at the bigger picture and adopt a holistic approach.

Leopold's views do not exclude human beings from acting as predators or even raising livestock, as long as their actions do not unduly disrupt the integrity of natural ecosystems. But determining what degree of disruption of natural systems by humans is permissible in specific cases and under what conditions is difficult. In specific situations, Leopold's land ethic does not always provide ready answers as to what actions should be taken. A more profound question is why we should value ecosystems and the like in and of themselves. Perhaps we value them simply because they are useful to humans, but this answer shifts us back to an anthropocentric point of view. Or are individual ecosystems important because they contribute to the well-being and stability of the Earth as a whole? But what does this matter, except in the anthropocentric sense that we want a healthy Earth for humans to live on? Leopold never provided a full and systematically rigorous justification for his land ethic. Indeed, some critics have accused him of falling into an ancient philosophical trap known as the "naturalistic fallacy."

The naturalistic fallacy is the incorrect idea or belief that what "is" is necessarily what "ought" to be. As Plato pointed out in his *Republic*, statements of fact do not necessarily translate into positive value judgments. Just because a certain

Animal Rights

Do animals have rights? Do animals have moral status? Or do only humans have moral status and rights? For that matter, should all humans have rights? After all, less than 150 years ago, some people in some parts of the United States still kept human slaves, and less than 80 years ago, American women were not allowed to vote (■ Fig. 1). Today there is certainly agreement that all human beings have moral status and certain basic rights, but what about non-human animals?

Western thought has had a long tradition of treating all nonhuman animals and plants as objects. Classical Kantian ethics treated animals and plants as merely a means for humans to achieve their goals and ends. The influential philosopher René Descartes (1596–1650) treated animals and plants as simply thoughtless machines that might respond to stimuli, but did not possess feelings or consciousness; thus, they did not rightfully deserve moral status. One could legitimately hunt, kill, eat, pen, or even "torture" animals (of course, by Cartesian standards it would not really be torture since animals have no feelings) with no moral qualms.

In recent times, an increasing number of people have begun to wonder if animals, particularly the "higher" animals such as domesticated mammals and pets, should have moral status—that is, inherent rights. In practical terms, this issue is often linked to the question of whether various types of animals can experience pleasure and pain and to what degree they experience these sensations. A related issue is how much animals understand, how (if at all) they per-

ceive the past, and how much they can anticipate the future. In other words, how sentient are animals? These questions can be addressed scientifically and clearly demonstrate the interplay between scientific information and ethical theories.

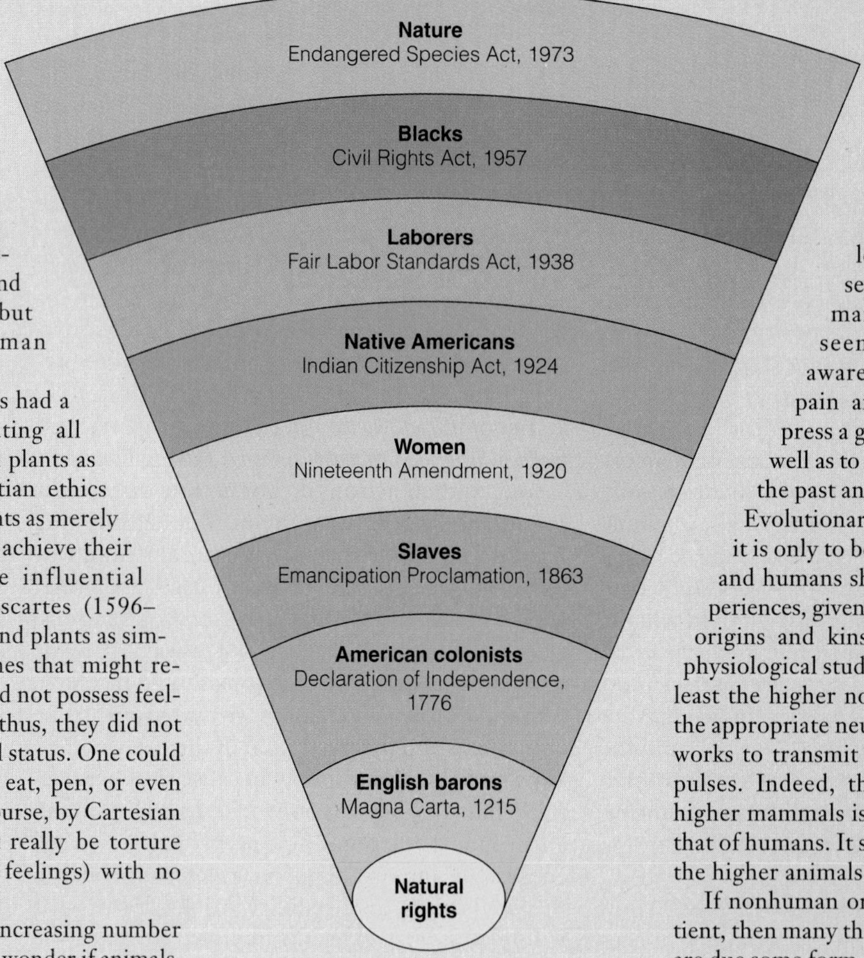

People who are in intimate contact with animals on a regular basis, such as with dog or cat companions, have long intuitively realized that at least some animals are sentient beings. Higher mammals, for instance, seem to possess a keen awareness of pleasure and pain and can sense and express a gauntlet of emotions, as well as to some degree remember the past and anticipate the future. Evolutionary theory indicates that it is only to be expected that animals and humans should share similar experiences, given our collective common origins and kinships. Anatomical and physiological studies demonstrate that at least the higher nonhuman animals have the appropriate neural structures and networks to transmit pleasure and pain impulses. Indeed, the neural anatomy of higher mammals is remarkably similar to that of humans. It seems clear that at least the higher animals are fully sentient.

If nonhuman organisms are fully sentient, then many theorists reason that they are due some form of moral consideration. In response to this idea, a strong animal rights movement has developed over the past few decades. Animal rights activists object to the use of live animals in testing new drugs and cosmetics: the animals suf-

Nature
Endangered Species Act, 1973

Blacks
Civil Rights Act, 1957

Laborers
Fair Labor Standards Act, 1938

Native Americans
Indian Citizenship Act, 1924

Women
Nineteenth Amendment, 1920

Slaves
Emancipation Proclamation, 1863

American colonists
Declaration of Independence, 1776

English barons
Magna Carta, 1215

Natural rights

■ **FIGURE 1**

The expanding concept of rights. (*Source*: R. F. Nash, *The Rights of Nature* [Madison: University of Wisconsin Press, 1989], p. 7. Reprinted by permission of The University of Wisconsin Press.)

fer pain and death simply for the benefit of humans. They may object to hunting animals, wearing furs and leather, exploiting animals on farms for food, locking up animals in cages or zoological parks, or even keeping animals as pets where the animal takes a position subservient to a human "master." In a larger context, animal rights activists argue that what is good for humans might not be good for animals, and human interests and concerns should not always outweigh animal interests. The benefit to humans of developing a piece of pristine forest may not be sufficient to offset the suffering of the animals that currently live in the forest.

Animal rights theorists view their ideas as part of the historical development of morality (▇ Figs. 1 and 2). Just as humans (and in particular human males) have learned to successively extend moral consideration beyond the confines of gender (acknowledging the moral status of women) and the local tribe, nation, and race, so humans must learn to extend moral consideration beyond the confines of our own species to other sentient organisms. Although some people may think it absurd to give moral consideration to animals, animal rightists point out that at one time some white American males thought it absurd to disrupt the basic economy of the southern United States simply to relieve the alleged suffering of a few black slaves. It is just as unjustifiable for members of one particular species (humans, *Homo sapiens*) to regard the feelings and concerns of other organisms as of less moral significance as it is for one race of humans to dismiss another race as of less moral significance.

Some practical criticisms of the typical animal rights stance have been advanced. If an animal rights theorist stresses the

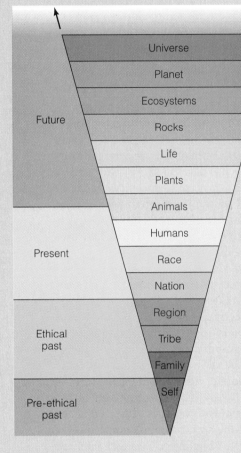

FIGURE 2

The evolution of ethics. (*Source*: R. F. Nash, *The Rights of Nature* [Madison: University of Wisconsin Press, 1989], p. 5. Reprinted by permission of The University of Wisconsin Press.)

concept of sentience as the basis for moral standing, where do we draw the line? Certainly, cats, dogs, rhinos, zebras, and hippos are sentient and therefore bear moral consideration by this criterion. But what about snakes, frogs, lobsters, shrimp,

clams, and bacteria? And what is the ultimate basis for sentience as a criterion for moral standing in the first place? Do animals have a degree of moral standing only insofar as they resemble humans in their abilities to feel pleasure and pain and perhaps to process cognitive information? Do life-forms that differ significantly from humans receive no moral credit? What about vegetable rights? After all, plants are living organisms too, so should not plants also be accorded some degree of moral consideration?

Some theorists also ask whether all sentient animals should be accorded equal moral status. For instance, is a stray domestic cat just as important from a moral point of view as a member of a rare, endangered species of rhino? If we had to choose between saving two hundred stray cats or a dozen rhinos, should we assume that each individual has the same moral status and therefore on utilitarian grounds maximize the good by saving the two hundred cats while letting the dozen rhinos (which might be the last members of their species) expire? To many people, such reasoning seems intuitively wrong—the rare rhinos should be saved first (although in actuality many humans expend much time, energy, and money supporting animal shelters for stray domestic cats and dogs even as many rare and endangered species go extinct in the wild). Yet what justification would we have for favoring rhinos over stray cats? Do rhinos bear a higher moral status than stray cats, or would we save the rhinos simply so that we humans would have the pleasure of knowing that the rhinos exist as a species?

nation is ruled by a dictator does not mean that dictatorial rule is ethically correct or good for that nation. Likewise, just because natural ecosystems exist does not mean that they are to be preferred over other possibilities. On the other hand, what "is" may be what "ought" to be. A powerful argument, based in part on the teleological tradition, can be marshaled to justify the concept that nature and natural activities and relationships (as in a well-functioning and stable ecosystem) are inherently good. Here we see the antagonisms of various Western ethical traditions reflected in the debate over Leopold's land ethic.

Deep Ecology

Related to Leopold's land ethic, but in many ways even broader and more diverse is **deep ecology**. This movement, which encompasses a diverse group of loosely related environmental philosophies and ethics, has developed over the last few decades. The term *deep ecology* was first coined in the early 1970s by the Norwegian philosopher and mountaineer Arne Naess. Naess drew a distinction between "shallow ecology," which focuses on fighting pollution, managing resources, and protecting the health and welfare of humans (especially in the developed countries), and deep ecology, which takes a holistic and nonanthropocentric perspective, rejecting the human versus environment dichotomy. Although similar to Leopold's thinking in many respects, deep ecologists tend to be even more extreme in their nonanthropocentric views. Some deep ecologists are radically egalitarian, completely abandoning any humanistic vestiges. They consider humans at best one species among equal species and believe even "inanimate" objects such as rivers and mountains have intrinsic value, purpose, and moral rights.

To some extent, the deep ecology movement transcends the secular and espouses the spiritual and religious in its understanding of, and ethic toward, the environment. The origins of such concepts can be traced back to the earliest beginnings of civilization and beyond. A common tradition in many cultures is the return of humans to nature to seek inspiration and divine revelation in the majesty of the wilderness. Old Testament prophets sought God in the wilderness, and holy men the world over have taken to the solitude of the mountains or deserts. European romantics of the eighteenth and nineteenth centuries sought the sublimity of nature, and the New England transcendentalists, such as Ralph Waldo Emerson (1803–1882) and Henry David Thoreau (1817–1862), sought a deeper understanding of reality by escaping to the wilderness of nature.

John Muir (1838–1914), founder of the Sierra Club and one of the great early preservationists, regarded nature as sacred. In 1864 Muir had a religious experience that changed his life and possibly the course of environmentalism. While wandering through the Canadian woods in the Great Lakes area, Muir came across two buds of a rare orchid species on the bank of a stream. Muir later stated that "I felt as if I were in the presence of superior beings who loved me and beckoned me to come. I sat down beside them and wept for joy." Muir recognized the supreme beauty of the flowers and the fact that they existed without any reference to humans—no human might ever have seen them if he had not stumbled upon them. Yet the orchids, Muir believed, had value and purpose nevertheless. This experience caused him to question the human-centered assumptions upon which he had been raised, and from this arose his sense that everything in nature has a right to exist and follow its own path. Muir effectively became a deep ecologist.

Deep ecology involves a major shift in mindset and worldview away from the perspective that has dominated Western thought for centuries. Many deep ecologists reject the notion of the self or individual as an isolated entity; instead, they believe that the self is continuous with the world at large and that ultimately self is indistinguishable from other. Since the self is part of the world, ecology and a proper ethical attitude toward the environment at large are a matter of self-respect. Some commentators feel that such deep ecological notions are more akin to the philosophy and religion of Buddhism than to most mainstream Western traditions.

Social Ecology

Social ecology, which was developed to a great extent by Murray Bookchin, attempts to identify social factors that are the underlying causes of current environmental crises. Social ecologists note that Western societies in particular have a number of formal and informal social and political institutions based on hierarchy, stratification, and domination. Examples include class structure, racism, sexism, capitalism, private ownership of property, centralization of government, certain forms of religion, and bureaucracies, as well as more nebulous psychological, intellectual, and emotional manipulation and coercion. Based on such institutions and social practices, some humans dominate and control other humans and material goods; similarly, humans' relationships with nonhuman organisms, nature, and the environment in general are also characterized by oppression and domination. Just as some humans dominate and exploit other humans in society, so too do humans exploit the environment in nature. This exploitation of the environment by humans has led to the current environmental crisis (Issues in Perspective 21–3 describes the steps some radical environmentalists have taken to deal with the crisis).

As a first step toward solving these problems, Bookchin and some other social ecologists argue that all humans must become free from oppression and domination by other humans. All humans must be able to reach their own potential as independent, conscious, thinking beings free of external control. In a practical environmental context, many social ecologists advocate the scaling back, decentralization, and diversification of governmental institutions and authorities. Some social ecologists envision a world composed of small, local communities that are sustainable and self-sufficient and fit harmoniously into the natural environment. Such communities, if operated sustainably, would not deplete resources and would not dump excess pollution into the surrounding countryside. All decision-making authority would reside within the community; decisions should be made by the local people who will be affected by the consequences. Sustainable agriculture on a small scale would be an appropriate means of subsistence for such communities, and low-impact (and perhaps relatively low-tech) technologies would be used that do not harm the environment. So-called appropriate technologies would be favored over the centralized technologies that have become an integral part of much of twentieth-century Western civilization. For instance, electricity might be generated using solar panels on individual homes instead of by a large, centralized coal-burning or nuclear power plant.

Ecofeminism

Ecofeminism is an approach to the current environmental crisis that has arisen out of the more general thinking of the modern feminist movement. Like social ecology, ecofeminism analyzes societal and cultural traits that may have led to the degradation of our environment, but ecofeminism is more specific in that it identifies the oppression of women by a traditional patriarchal society as a major form of social domina-

tion that has precipitated other forms of exploitation and domination, including exploitation of the environment.

According to ecofeminists, the patriarchal (male-dominated) societies that have dominated civilization for many millennia are characterized by strong hierarchical social organizations, occupational specialization, commerce, and militarism. Violence toward both women and nature is considered a structural feature of patriarchal social organization. Nature is often characterized as a female or virgin woman that is "subdued," "tamed," "conquered," "wedded to man," "made a slave to man," or even "raped." In contrast, matriarchal (female-dominated) cultures tend to subsist on sustainable agricultural methods; are relatively unspecialized, democratic, and peaceful; and generally do not cause drastic disturbances in the environment. Nature may be viewed as the "mother" of the people, and all good is provided by Mother Nature.

Theoretical support for ecofeminist ethics is provided by the work of Carol Gilligan. Gilligan contends that men and women typically have very different types of self-conceptions and therefore approach moral questions in different ways. Men typically (Gilligan realizes that there are many exceptions to the generalities she presents) view themselves as isolated egos and define themselves through individual actions and achievements. Women, in contrast, typically define themselves through relationships with other people and their surroundings, particularly relationships involving nurturance and care; thus, women tend not to see themselves as isolated egos. Male individualism manifests itself in a morality conceived in terms of rights and rules, whereas women conceive of morality in terms of relationships and accommodations. Thus, male-dominated ethics is often based on the rights of individuals, which can easily lead to the exploitation and degradation of the environment, whereas female-dominated ethics stresses the need to create healthy, sustainable relationships, which promote the maintenance of the natural environment.

NON-WESTERN PERSPECTIVES ON ENVIRONMENTAL ETHICS

Most readers of this book probably come from a Western industrial background and thus are most familiar with Western ethical philosophies. Many Western environmentalists and ethical theorists, though, have found inspiration in non-Western

Civil Disobedience and Ecoterrorism

The environmental crises that we face today are severe. Working within the established legal, economic, and political system can be frustratingly slow, especially when an environmental activist believes that strong action should already have been taken. Sometimes the established social institutions seem to fail. Furthermore, some environmentalists (such as some deep ecologists, social ecologists, and ecofeminists) believe the very social institutions and cultural framework of society are the cause of many of today's environmental problems. What is to be done? Many radical environmentalists have turned to extralegal, or even downright illegal, tactics.

The tradition of civil disobedience, where a person or group actively protests or fights policies by openingly choosing to disobey a law that they believe is immoral or unjust, has a long history going back at least to Socrates (470?–399 B.C.). In this century both Mahatma Gandhi and civil rights activist Martin Luther King, Jr., are prime examples of leaders who used nonviolence and civil disobedience. Among environmental groups, Greenpeace is well known for its acts of civil disobedience. Greenpeace members have used such tactics as chaining themselves across the entrances to power plants, climbing trees that are to be logged, sailing their ships into restricted waters where nuclear tests are to take place, climbing smokestacks to hang antipollution banners, and blocking and ramming whaling and fishing vessels. Such acts may not only have immediate results, such as at least temporarily stopping a nuclear bomb test, but more importantly they generate publicity and focus public attention on environmental concerns. Many feel that acts of nonviolent civil disobedience may be

■ FIGURE 1
The Sea Shepherd Conservation Society vessel *Sea Shepherd II* ramming a Japanese driftnetter in protest of illegal driftnetting activities. (*Source*: Courtesy of Sea Shepherd Conservation Society, 3107A Washington Blvd., Marina del Rey, CA.)

morally justified as long as no one is hurt, no serious physical damage is incurred, and the perpetrators of the acts publicly accept responsibility and concomitant punishment for their acts.

What if even civil disobedience is not enough? Can illegal acts of sabotage and violence against people and property in the name of an environmental cause be morally justified? Some radical environmentalists feel they can be. They believe that conditions have deteriorated so far, and the stakes are so high, that an actual war may have to be waged to save the environment. Certain members of the radical groups Earth First! (the name is always followed by an exclamation mark) and the Sea Shepherd Conservation Society (■ Fig. 1), for instance, have sometimes encouraged "ecosabotage," "ecotage," or "**ecoterrorism**." Committing sabotage against property that is environmentally detrimental, such as whaling ships, lumber mills, power plants, or bulldozers and other heavy machinery, is sometimes referred to as "monkeywrenching" (after

the title of an environmental novel by Edward Abbey, *The Monkey Wrench Gang*).

Radical environmentalists have secretly dismantled or destroyed logging, digging, and fishing equipment. Their tactics include pouring sand or sugar into the gas tanks of vehicles and cutting pipes, wires, or linkages to equipment engines. Some groups have cut power lines, pulled up survey stakes, sunk whaling boats, destroyed whale processing facilities, and perhaps most notoriously "spiked" trees. Spiking trees involves driving large metal nails or spikes into the trunks of trees to discourage logging. When a saw hits a spike, it can be badly damaged. In fact, when a typical modern chain saw or other power machinery in a lumber mill hits a spike, the results can be extremely serious. Saw blades may snap and go flying with tremendous force, perhaps badly injuring or even killing the logger or lumber mill worker.

Are such violent ecoterrorist acts morally justifiable? Under peacetime conditions, murder is never justified, but during wartime a nation may charge its armies with killing (which, one can argue, differs from murdering) the enemy. And if the conflict is considered a just war, the general populace may even feel good about this killing and treat the soldiers who did the most killing as heroes when they return home. In wartime it may be morally defensible to use tactics that should not be tolerated under peacetime conditions. Radical environmentalists contend that they too are involved in a war, perhaps the most important war ever fought: the war to save the planet.

perspectives. As we have already noted, the spirituality associated with some aspects of the deep ecology movement may be akin to some aspects of traditional Buddhism. Thus, some deep ecologists hold that the self (of a human or another being) is not an isolated ego, but is continuous with the world at large; ultimately, one may reach enlightenment, which includes the dissolution of the illusory ego.

Fritz Schumacher, an economist who enjoys wide influence among environmentalists (his most famous work is the 1973 book *Small Is Beautiful*, originally entitled "Economics as if People Mattered"), drew heavily upon his firsthand experiences with a Buddhist society in Burma (Fig. 21–7). Schumacher pointed out that unlike the West, Budhist society is characterized by

to life could be much more environmentally benign than many Western industrial approaches.

The Hindu political and spiritual leader Mahatma (a title meaning "great soul") Mohandas Gandhi (1869–1948) of India has had a strong influence on some sectors of the Western environmental movement. Gandhi advocated strict nonviolence toward, and love for, all living things. He believed that we must disassociate ourselves from selfish interests and desires, and live as simply as possible. Gandhi was a strict vegetarian; he ate mostly fruit and nuts so that not even living plants would be harmed by his need for food. Gandhi advocated economic stability and self-reliance; he opposed Western-style large-scale industrialization. He pointed out that if India, with its huge population, exploited the world in the same man-

 FIGURE 21–7
Buddhist monks at the Inle Lake Monastery, Burma, March 1986. (*Source*: A. Tannenbaum/ Sygma.)

simplicity, nonviolence, and the absence of a craving for material wealth. Whereas modern Western economists tend to measure a society's standard of living by the amount of goods it consumes annually (a utilitarian approach that equates consumption with pleasure and good), a Buddhist sees this measurement as irrational. To a traditional Buddhist, consumption is merely a means to an end (namely, human well-being), not an end in itself. The Buddhist way is to maximize the end (human well-being in this case) with a minimum of consumption. It is easy to see how such an approach

ner that England did in his time, the Earth would be environmentally devastated. Clearly, the way of life that Gandhi advocated, if put into wide practice, would help alleviate many of the pressing environmental problems that we currently face.

The culture of China also contrasts strikingly with much of current Western thinking. Whereas over the last three centuries the West has emphasized the rights of individual humans, China has been influenced by a long tradition of Confucianism (going back nearly 2500 years) that is

Global Population and Ethical Considerations

With approximately 5.8 billion people on Earth, virtually every major environmental problem is exacerbated by overpopulation. Many environmental activists regard overpopulation as the root cause of the current global environmental crisis, yet in many circles discussion of population control is taboo. Out of religious or ethical considerations, many people object to any control on human reproduction. To have children is a fundamental desire of many persons. Some have suggested that the family is the fundamental and natural unit of society, and that it is a fundamental human right for the family itself to make all choices and decisions about family size, that is, how many children a couple chooses to have. Those who advocate population control have been accused of racism, because they tend to be wealthy whites from the industrialized nations urging the use of birth control in nonwhite developing nations. Abortion, which is often used where contraception fails, is viewed as murder of the unborn in some quarters.

Out of equally strong ethical convictions, many people regard population control as a primary duty. Given the current state of affairs, limiting human population is the only way that the globe can be saved. Neglecting population control in the developing countries results in increased poverty, starvation, and death among the already poor peoples of the world, and increasing the wealthy population of the developed world places further burdens on the already over-stressed global environmental support system. In the end, if the global population continues to grow, we may all be doomed. The "right" of a couple to have as many children as they please when they please ends when this "right" affects the "rights" of other humans (and possibly nonhuman organisms also) to live in a healthy, safe, functioning environment.

Taking a somewhat utilitarian view, we might wish to maximize the "good" in the world. If we focus only on human good, then we might maximize the total amount of human good by increasing the number of people in the world. As long as a human life, on average, contains more good than bad,

then the more people there are, the more good there is. According to this way of thinking, population control will only be called for when adding more lives begins to bring more bad into the world than good. But how do we determine when this point is reached? Who can judge for the world as a whole? Even in a region plagued by starvation and disease, not everyone will necessarily agree that on average another human life will create more bad than good. And in an affluent region, not everyone will necessarily agree that an additional human life will bring more good than bad.

Even within this framework, other considerations must be taken into account. What are the future implications of increasing (or decreasing) the human population now? Perhaps increasing the human population will increase the amount of human good in this generation, but bring about untold misery in the long run. Do we factor potential future generations into our analysis?

Maximizing the total human good in the world may not even be an appropriate strategy. If we maximize the total human good by increasing the population to the point where adding more people will start to decrease the total amount of good, then we will end up with many people whose lives are only marginally good. This consideration has led some people to argue that instead of maximizing the total human good in the world, we should maximize the average amount of good per human life. Essentially, this approach emphasizes quality over quantity. By this way of thinking, a small population where individual lives are characterized by a great deal of "good" (however good is defined) would be preferable to a larger population where the average human life contains even slightly less good. In extreme cases, one could even contend that it is ultimately better to allow an overly large population to reduce its size by such natural (if somewhat cruel) means as starvation and disease so that those who survive can have a higher average amount of good in their lives. The alternative might be to barely maintain, perhaps through relief efforts, those on the brink of starvation—but

such actions can result in a general lowering of the average amount of good per individual. Certainly, many people find it morally more acceptable to control population growth by the use of birth control so that more lives are not conceived in the first place. Actual population reductions will come about as people die of old age.

Those who espouse the maximization of the average human good generally believe the present world needs a strong policy of population reduction. In both the developed and the developing nations, most people would probably be better off, on average, if there were fewer people around. Fewer people would mean more resources per person and less poverty, starvation, and crowding throughout the world.

So far in this discussion, we have focused only on human good. But what about the rights, interests, and therefore the good of the nonhuman organisms, species, and ecosystems with whom we humans share the planet? If we take these other creatures into account, as the ecocentrists (such as the deep ecologists) insist we must, then clearly the humans already inhabiting the globe are having detrimental effects on other life-forms and the Earth as a whole (as is discussed at length elsewhere in this book). From the ecocentric perspective, it is clear that drastic reductions in the human population are needed.

Questions

1. Do you believe that each person has a fundamental human right to decide how many children to have? Or do people have a fundamental duty to control their own breeding? Justify your answer.

2. Do you think that it is appropriate to attempt to maximize the "good" in the world? If so, what exactly is "good" and how should it be maximized? If you don't believe that the "good" should be maximized, explain why not.

3. Do nonhuman species have "rights" or "interests"? Justify your answer. If they do have rights and interests, how do those rights and interests affect the issue of global human population?

characterized by a holistic philosophy. In China the individual is seen primarily as a component of society as a whole, and the interests of the individual are properly subordinated to those of the society. Extrapolating such ideas to a broader environmental context, not only should the interests and desires of an individual human be subordinate to his or her society, but human society should be seen as simply a component of the larger whole—the biosphere and ecosphere. Mere human interests should be subordinated to the interests of the Earth and life as a whole. Unfortunately, however, this traditional view has not prevented twentieth-century China from having a severe and detrimental impact on the environment.

A number of North American environmentalists have also drawn inspiration from the ethics and religions of the natives of the New World. At the time of initial European contact in the late fifteenth through seventeenth centuries, people had already been living and thriving on the American continents for perhaps as long as 40,000 years. Native American tribes inhabited virtually all of the Americas; the land was hardly the "uninhabited wilderness" that many Europeans believed it to be. While the Native Americans certainly left their mark on the land, and their cultures were not always sustainable (witness the sudden collapse of the Mayan civilization in Mesoamerica shortly after A.D. 800 possibly due to overcultivation of fragile soils), many diverse Native American beliefs have come to be viewed as environmentally compatible and useful in addressing our current environmental problems.

Many Native American tribes viewed the land and its living inhabitants as sacred. The land was the free domain of all living creatures; the Western notion of land ownership or private posses-sion was alien to most Native Americans. Many of the indigenous Americans felt a oneness with nature and often regarded plants and animals as relatives, not mere resources. Human destiny and well-being were thought to be intimately linked to the destiny and well-being of other organisms. These cultures sought to maintain natural balances, and their sympathy and identification with other living beings certainly helped to prevent much excessive exploitation of the environment.

THE IMPORTANCE OF ENVIRONMENTAL ETHICS

In this chapter we have presented a very brief survey of some of the more important and influential ethical theories and philosophies that bear on environmental issues. Without exception, all competent, rational, adult human beings act on the basis of some ethical theory. The ethical theory that underlies the actions of a particular individual may have been consciously developed, systematically analyzed, and rationally justified. Or, perhaps more frequently, the ethical basis of an individual's actions may be somewhat incoherent, vague, and unarticulated. An individual may adopt differing ethical stances in different situations or at different times in her or his life. The purpose of this chapter is not to espouse one ethical theory over another, but to present a sampling of a range of ethical approaches. As we have seen throughout this book, ethical issues are closely linked to the differing attitudes that people hold when evaluating environmental issues. When faced with an environmental decision to make, one should always take ethical considerations, as well as scientific facts, into account (see the Case Study on page 602 for an example).

EnviroNet
www.jbpub.com/environet

SUMMARY

Although scientific analysis may be able to predict or determine the consequences of a particular action (such as destroying the rainforests), science alone cannot indicate the course of action humans should take. Questions of what ought to be done are answered on the basis of some set of values. Ethics is the philosophical study of moral values; environmental ethics is the application of ethical studies to environmental concerns. A key topic of environmental ethics is the development and justification of a theory of the moral relations among humans, nonhuman species, and the natural environment. Environmental ethics can be viewed as an integral part of a more comprehensive environmental philosophy: a description and understanding of how the world works and the position of humans within the world.

Judeo-Christian views have had a major influence on Western ethical thought, but interpretations of this tradition can differ. On the one hand, humankind may be viewed as destined to rule over, and benefit from, the rest of the world, but on the other hand, humans may be regarded as the stewards of the world, who are responsible for caring for it. Aristotle's teleological tradition, which holds that every being and every object has a purpose, function, end, or final cause, has also exerted a strong influence on ethical thinking. During the Middle Ages, all living creatures were often viewed as part of God's plan. In a modern context, the organisms of a natural ecosystem may be seen as forming a harmonious, well-functioning whole.

Utilitarianism, espousing the concept that overall "good" should be maximized, exerts a powerful influence on the thinking of many people. Utilitarianism is often an underlying assumption of benefit-cost analyses. Various concepts of duties, rights, and obligations have also played a crucial role in environmental ethical thinking. A major question in recent years has been, Who has rights? Just living humans, or living and future humans, or animals as well, or also plants and entire ecosystems? The concept of property rights also enters into this controversy: Who owns what, and what can or should a property owner do with his or her property?

Out of such ethical and philosophical considerations, a number of environmental philosophies have arisen, including biocentric (life-centered) philosophies, eco-centric (ecological-centered) philosophies, and the deep ecology movement (which takes a holistic and nonanthropocentric perspective, while rejecting the classic humans versus the environment dichotomy). Other philosophical approaches include those of social ecology (which attempts to identify social factors that underlie the current environmental crises) and ecofeminism (which holds that the oppression of women in a traditional patriarchal society may induce other forms of exploitation and domination, including exploitation of the environment).

Non-Western perspectives on environmental ethics are also important to consider. Some forms of traditional Buddhism, for instance, hold that the self is not an isolated ego. This view leads to a different type of economy (arguably more environmentally friendly) that is characterized by relative simplicity, nonviolence, and the absence of a craving for material wealth.

Consumption is a means to an end, not an end in itself. The Hindu Mahatma Mohandas Gandhi advocated a strict nonviolence toward and love for all living things, as well as economic stability and self-reliance (as opposed to Western-style large-scale industrialization). Chinese Confucianism is characterized by a holistic philosophy where the interests of the individual are subordinated to those of society; extrapolating such ideas to a broader environmental context, human society and interests should be subordinated to the interests of life and the Earth as a whole. Many Native American tribes viewed the land and its living inhabitants as sacred. Many felt a oneness with nature and had no concept of land ownership or private possession. Human destiny and well-being were viewed as intimately linked to the destiny and well-being of other organisms, helping to prevent overly excessive exploitation of the environment.

KEY TERMS

animal rights
anthropocentric
biocentric
deep ecology
deontology
descriptive ethics
duty
ecocentric
ecofeminism

ecoterrorism
environmental equity
environmental justice
environmental racism
ethics
morals
moral antirealism
moral realism
moral status
normative ethics

philosophical ethics
property rights
relativistic view
rights
social ecology
teleological tradition
utilitarianism
values

STUDY QUESTIONS

1. Define ethics and environmental ethics.
2. Why is environmental ethics important to the study of environmental science?
3. Distinguish between descriptive ethics, normative ethics, and philosophical ethics.

Briefly describe the following major traditions in Western ethical thought:

4. Judeo-Christian views.

5. Teleological tradition.
6. Utilitarianism.
7. Duties and rights.
8. How has each of the traditions listed in Questions 4 through 7 influenced thinking about the environment?
9. What is the relationship between classic utilitarianism and modern benefit-cost analyses?
10. What are the rights of a property owner?

What are, or should be, the limits to those rights?

Briefly discuss the origins, assertions, and bases of the following environmental philosophies:

11. Biocentric ethics.
12. Ecocentric ethics.
13. Deep ecology.
14. Social ecology.
15. Ecofeminism.

ESSAY QUESTIONS

1. What is an environmental philosophy? What is your environmental philosophy? How did you arrive at it?
2. Describe the main approaches that have been taken toward ethics. Be sure to include the following in your discussion: moral realism, moral antirealism, and relativistic attitudes.
3. Why is ethics sometimes so controversial?
4. What entities or beings, in your opinion, have rights—and to what degree? What entities have moral status? Be sure to justify your answer.
5. Describe a sampling of non-Western perspectives on environmental ethics. How can these new or different perspectives benefit and enrich Westerners?

SUGGESTED READINGS

The following list is certainly not all-inclusive; more titles can be found in the bibliographies of the books that follow. Particularly noteworthy for the wide range of important papers they reprint are the books edited by Dobson (1991), VanDeVeer and Pierce (1986), and List (1993).

Adams, C., ed. 1993. *Ecofeminism and the sacred.* New York: Continuum.

Daly, H. E., and K. N. Townsend, ed. 1993. *Valuing the Earth: Economics, ecology, ethics.* Cambridge, Mass.: MIT Press.

DesJardins, J. R. 1993. *Environmental ethics: An introduction to environmental philosophy.* Belmont, Calif.: Wadsworth.

Devall, B., and G. Sessions. 1985. *Deep ecology: Living as if nature mattered.* Salt Lake City: Peregrine Smith Books.

Dobson, A., ed. 1991. *The green reader.* San Francisco: Mercury House.

Dowie, M. 1995. *Losing ground: American environmentalism at the close of the twentieth century.* Cambridge, Mass.: MIT Press.

Easterbrook, G. 1995. *A moment on the Earth: The coming age of environmental optimism.* New York: Viking.

Goldsmith, E. 1993. *The way: An ecological worldview.* Boston: Shambhala.

Hargrove, E. C. 1989. *Foundations of environmental ethics.* Englewood Cliffs, N.J.: Prentice-Hall.

Leopold, A. 1949. *A Sand County almanac.* New York: Oxford University Press.

Lewis, M. W. 1992. *Green delusions: An environmentalist critique of radical environmentalism.* Durham, N.C.: Duke University Press.

List, P. C., ed. 1993. *Radical environmentalism: Philosophy and tactics.* Belmont, Calif: Wadsworth.

Merchant, C. 1992. *Radical ecology: The search for a livable world.* New York: Routledge.

Nash, R. F. 1989. *The rights of nature: A history of environmental ethics.* Madison: University of Wisconsin Press.

———1990. *American environmentalism: Readings in conservation history,* 3d ed. New York: McGraw-Hill.

Rockefeller, S. C., and J. C. Elder. 1992. *Spirit and nature: Why the environment is a religious issue, an interfaith dialogue.* Boston: Beacon Press.

Rolston, H., III. 1989. *Philosophy gone wild: Environmental ethics.* Buffalo: Prometheus Books.

Sagoff, M. 1988. *The economy of the Earth: Philosophy, law, and the environment.* Cambridge: Cambridge University Press.

Scarce, R. 1990. *Eco-warriors: Understanding the radical environmental movement.* Chicago: Noble Press.

Schumacher, E. F. 1973. *Small is beautiful: Economics as if people mattered.* New York: Harper and Row.

Seager, J. 1993. *Earth follies: Coming to feminist terms with the global environmental crisis.* New York: Routledge.

Shabecoff, P. 1993. *A fierce green fire: The American environmental movement.* New York: Hill & Wang.

VanDeVeer, D., and C. Pierce, eds. 1986. *People, penguins, and plastic trees: Basic issues in environmental ethics.* Belmont, Calif.: Wadsworth.

Young, J. 1990. *Sustaining the Earth.* Cambridge, Mass.: Harvard University Press.

Zimmerman, M. E., gen. ed. 1993. *Environmental philosophy: From animal rights to radical ecology.* Englewood Cliffs, N.J.: Prentice-Hall.

CHAPTER 22

HISTORICAL, SOCIAL, AND LEGAL ASPECTS OF THE CURRENT ENVIRONMENTAL CRISIS

PROLOGUE   *The Green Movement*

he **Green movement** is a political and social movement that has arisen out of more traditional environmentalism in the latter half of the twentieth century. Much of its
philosophical underpinnings lie in the deep ecology, social ecology, and ecofeminist analyses
of our environmental plight (see Chapter 21). The Greens offer a radical new philosophy and
ideology (indeed, a new paradigm) for carrying out business in the economic, social, and
political realms—one that differs dramatically from traditional Western "business as usual."

PHOTO   *Celebrating Earth Day in New York City, April 22, 1990. (Source: A. Tannenbaum/Sygma.)*

Greens are interested in specific issues, such as saving an endangered species, protecting an old-growth forest, or shutting down a nuclear power plant, but they go beyond the particular to pursue the underlying reasons for such problems. Greens believe that we must address the root causes of current environmental degradation, not just its symptoms. The Greens maintain that all the various isolated environmental problems that society now faces stem from the current Westernized political and economic system. Not only does this system foster and promote environmental damage, but according to some Greens, exploitation and degradation of the environment are necessary components of the system. If we are to solve the global environmental crisis, we must make a revolutionary break and establish new, Earth-amenable social institutions. This will certainly necessitate a fundamental change in philosophy, values, and lifestyle for many people.

What kind of world do the Greens envision? A diversity of opinions can be found in the Green camp, and many refuse to predict exactly what the future will be like (for who can predict the future?). But certainly it will be based on sustainability and a more frugal approach to material goods than the profligacy of modern Western society. Reuse and recycling will be the norm. Production and authority may be decentralized, possibly spread throughout a series of semi-autonomous, somewhat self-sufficient city-states linked in loose confederations. Diffuse sources of power, such as small solar devices that deliver energy locally, will be in favor. "Appropriate" (also known as "intermediate") small-scale technologies will replace large-scale centralized technologies. Large factories that serve an entire nation or the world may give way to local cottage industries. Farming and food production will be localized, feeding primarily the inhabitants of the immediate area. Energy patterns will change. The energy-intensive manufacturing and food production processes that have dominated Western societies since the middle of the twentieth century will disappear. Human labor will have dignity and worth once again, and society will return to dependence on labor-intensive processes in manufacturing and raising foodstuffs.

True global sustainability will mean increased equity among the peoples and cultures of the world and will assure an intergenerational equity as well. It will be necessary to stabilize, and even reduce, the size of the global population. Decentralization of the means of production and political-economic authority will put an end to the twentieth-century trend toward global homogenization, in which most countries have strived to develop along Western lines. Many Greens expect to see a resurgence in cultural diversity. A wide variety of lifestyles will be found within and among societies.

Thus far, the Green movement is most prominent in Europe. Germany and the United Kingdom in particular have strong, active Green political parties. In the United States, the environmental movement is generally still dominated by narrowly focused special interest groups (for instance, the local community group fighting to keep the incinerator or nuclear power plant out of their neighborhood) and by groups that firmly believe that the environmental problems we face can be solved by working within the present political and social institutions. Such staunch environmental, but non-Green (with a capital "G") groups include the Sierra Club, the Audubon Society, Friends of the Earth, and the Wilderness Society, among others.

INTRODUCTION

The current environmental "crisis" did not "just happen." The situation we find ourselves in is the result of definite historical trends and human actions. Although we may not have intended to bring about global environmental changes, humans are clearly responsible for much of the massive environmental degradation that has occurred. The depletion of the stratospheric ozone layer by artificial CFCs, to cite just one example, cannot be attributed to natural causes.

Humans are social creatures, and a human society's most characteristic attributes are its **social institutions**—its familial, political, educational, religious, and economic systems. The social institutions of any society reflect and express its underlying beliefs and values. Some critics argue that the values, beliefs, and institutions of modern, technologically oriented Western society (as it originated in Western Europe and thence spread to America and the rest of the world) are directly responsible for fomenting the environmental degradation that we currently face. More optimistically, it has been suggested that even though Western society may have brought on the current global environmental crisis, it also contains the necessary technology and institutions to

address that crisis. Other observers, such as the Greens, disagree; they believe that the world's environmental problems will be resolved only by a radical remodeling of Western values and social institutions.

In this chapter we briefly explore social, legal, and historical aspects of the current environmental crisis. As the focus of this book is environmental *science* and not environmental *studies*, we do not deal with these issues in as much depth as we have dealt with some of the more scientific aspects. Nevertheless, science cannot be divorced from society. Science does not exist in a vacuum, and of all the sciences, environmental science is perhaps the most intimately bound up with social, political, and historical factors.

Here we focus primarily on Western social institutions and values, particularly as manifested in the United States, for several reasons: (1) As we have already noted, many critics blame the current global environmental degradation on Western values and social institutions. (2) In many regards these Western values and institutions find their fullest expression in the United States. (3) Much of the world is apparently striving to emulate the United States in many respects, such as in industrial development and material affluence. (4) Because the United States arguably leads the world in pollution emissions, resource exploitation, energy use, and general environmental degradation, it can provide a particularly valuable case history. (5) The environmental history of the United States is in some ways more accessible than that of other major countries, at least since the time of European contact. Since European explorers first reached the "virgin" continent about five centuries ago (of course, the Native Americans had already modified the "natural" environment to some extent), there has been a fairly continuous recorded history of the environmental changes that have occurred. In comparison, major human-induced environmental changes have been taking place in Europe, Africa, and Asia since before recorded history (although great strides have been made toward reconstructing the environmental history of Europe and, indeed the whole world).

AN HISTORICAL PERSPECTIVE ON AMERICAN ENVIRONMENTALISM

When Europeans first colonized America, it was certainly not an "uninhabited wilderness." The Americas had been inhabited for tens of thousands of years by peoples who had crossed over the Bering Strait from Asia at the end of the last ice age. These indigenous peoples (■ Fig. 22–1), whom the Europeans called "Indians" (and are now commonly referred to as "Native Americans"), had spread throughout the two continents. North America may have had on the order of 5 million human inhabitants at the time of European contact.

It is a myth that the native North Americans did not modify the environment, for they certainly did. They cleared fields, planted crops, hunted game, built dwellings, and so on, but they did not modify the natural environment in the same way that the European settlers did. On the whole the North American natives appear to have lived in a relatively sustainable manner for thousands of years. In part, this may have been due to their small populations and relatively simple material culture, but their complex belief systems also fostered sustainable living. In general, Native Americans did not believe in the ownership of land and nature. They viewed themselves more as a part of nature than apart from nature.

The earliest European colonists certainly viewed nature and human society as a dichotomy. Humans were separate and above nature, not a part of it. The Europeans felt a need to subdue, tame, and exploit the "uninhabited wilderness" of North America for humankind's benefit. This **frontier mentality** of the earliest colonists continued to exert a major influence on American development for the next four hundred years. The limitless natural resources of the vast continent were ripe for the taking. In the 1600s, the English colonies in New England survived in large part by shipping lumber, beaver skins, and other natural resources back to Europe in exchange for manufactured goods. As forests and animal populations in coastal areas were decimated, the Europeans simply moved farther inland.

The forests in particular were seen not just as a resource to be exploited, but as a nuisance to be eliminated: they were dark and sheltered savages and wild beasts. Accordingly, the forests were cleared to make agricultural fields and gardens. The once wild land was cultivated, as most of the land of Europe had been for many centuries (or even millennia). This frontier mentality was reinforced by the then dominant interpretation of Judeo-Christian theology, which saw the world and nature as having been created by God for humankind (see Chapter 21).

This approach of exploiting the land and its natural resources and then moving on dominated American environmental thinking for about 250 years (ca. 1620s through the 1870s) as the coun-

FIGURE 22-1
The English navigator
Bartholomew Gosnold (died
1607) trading with the Native
Americans, possibly in the
area of Buzzards Bay, Cape
Cod, Massachusetts (colored
line engraving, 1634). (*Source:*
The Granger Collection, New
York.)

try continued to expand westward. Wildlife, like the American bison (see Issues in Perspective 22-1), was decimated in many areas, forests were destroyed, and soils eroded as they were put under the plow. The U.S. government encouraged the expansion of the frontier by transferring government-owned land and natural resources to private hands. The Homestead Act of 1862 gave each qualified settler in the Great Plains area and elsewhere 160 acres (64.75 hectares) free of charge. Likewise, the Railroad Acts of the 1850s and 1860s gave away large tracts of land to railroad companies to encourage them to build railroad lines that could move people and goods across the country. Vestiges of the frontier mentality remain an integral part of the American psyche to this day.

The First Century of American Environmentalism

But even as the West was being "won," certain thinkers were questioning the rampant exploitation of natural resources. The New England **transcendentalists**, such as Ralph Waldo Emerson (1803–1882) and Henry David Thoreau (1817–1862), decried the human destruction of the environment. Thoreau mourned the decline and loss of numerous species from his native eastern Massachusetts, such as bear, moose, deer, porcupines, wolves, and beavers, as well as the great reduction in the size and diversity of the forests. To gain a better appreciation for nature, he built a cabin in the woods on Walden Pond near Concord, Massachusetts. From his two years living alone there came *Walden, or Life in the Woods* (1854). *Walden* has become an American classic, inspiring generations of naturalists, ecologists, and environmentalists.

In 1864 George Perkins Marsh published an exhaustive study entitled *Man and Nature; or Physical Geography as Modified by Human Action.* Marsh had grown up in Vermont, but traveled widely. His compilation documented how human intervention had resulted in the destruction of forests, soils, and waters and greatly modified flora and fauna. Marsh's work, using clear scientific evidence and case studies, challenged the no-

The North American Bison

The story of the near-extinction of the North American bison (also known as the American buffalo) is a sad tale of the exploitation and wanton destruction of the members of a species. Only a few centuries ago, some 12 to 20 million, or more, bison (*Bison bison*) roamed through North America. Two subspecies inhabited the continent. The more numerous plains bison lived mainly east of the Sierra Nevada and inhabited most of what is now the United States except the Great Lakes area, New England, and parts of the southeast coast. The plains bison extended north into Manitoba, Saskatchewan, and eastern Alberta (Canada). The woodland, wood, or mountain bison (of the same species, but generally considered a distinct subspecies) inhabited the Rocky Mountain region from Colorado to Alberta and even further north.

Europeans and their descendants were not the only people to hunt the bison en masse. Certain Native American tribes survived almost exclusively by hunting the bison, often utilizing the entire carcass for everything from food to fuel to shelter and tools. Indeed, this reliance on the bison became a prime incentive for the white man to decimate the bison herds in the nineteenth century. It was often said that every dead buffalo (bison) meant a dead Indian (of course, this was a bit of an exaggeration).

At any rate, buffalo hunting was certainly not confined to those of European extraction. At one site in southeastern Colorado, dating from about 6500 B.C., Paleo-Indians drove a herd of close to two hundred bison to their death over the edge of a gorge. In historical times, the North American Indians sometimes hunted down buffalo in huge numbers, aided by the horse and firearms, which they adopted from the Europeans. As late as the autumn of 1883, when the buffalo was virtually extinct, Sitting Bull and his comrades took about two months to decimate a herd of about ten thousand in North Dakota. Nevertheless, despite these abuses, the major blame for the near-extinction of the bison must be placed on the heads of the white men.

As the continent was civilized, the buffalo quickly declined. By about 1800 buffalo were extinct east of the Mississippi River, yet they remained extremely abundant elsewhere in North America as late as the 1860s. On the plains, herds of bison 5 miles (8 km) in breadth and some 50 miles (80 km) long, could be seen, with the animals so closely spaced that "the whole country was covered with what appeared to be a monstrous moving brown blanket" (letter from Col. C. Goodnight in the early 1860s).

The introduction of the railroad made it easy for professional hunters to reach the herds and for bison products to be shipped back East. In the late 1860s, the first transcontinental railway divided the plains buffalo into a southern herd and a northern herd. As professional hunters were joined by amateurs, hundreds of thousands, then millions of bison were slaughtered. So many carcasses were left to rot on the plains that settlers complained of the stench. By 1875, so few members of the southern herd were left that both Kansas and Colorado passed laws attempting to protect the buffalo. Still, 100,000 more buffalo were killed during the winter of 1877–1878. A few hundred survivors made their way to Texas, but by 1889 they too had been shot—and thus ended the southern herd.

Between 1881 and 1883, the northern herd came under massive attack by both whites and Indians. By 1884, the northern herd was virtually wiped out in the United States, and by 1885 the wood or forest buffalo of Canada was almost extinct in the wild.

Why were the buffalo hunted so heavily? Some hunters were after the meat, for which there was a considerable market. Others wanted the hides, which could be made into good leather. And fur traders sought "buffalo robes" to be used as overcoats and wraps. Buffalo fat could be used in the manufacture of soap and candles, and buffalo horns were used in hat racks.

Many buffalo were killed for pure sport, which, it was claimed, could become highly addictive. Expeditions were arranged where interested parties could test their shooting skill, and have a bit of adventure, by slaughtering wild buffalo from a railway car.

tion of an inexhaustible Earth. Marsh did not argue against humankind's intervention in, and transformation of, nature. But he did suggest it must be done with knowledge and foresight, if irreparable damage and negative consequences were to be avoided. His work laid the groundwork for the late nineteenth-century conservation and preservation movements.

Two figures dominate American environmentalism in the late nineteenth and early twentieth centuries: Gifford Pinchot (1865–1946) and John Muir (1838–1914) (Fig. 22–2, page 612). While both supported environmentalism, they took very different approaches to the problem. Pinchot, though born in Connecticut, was professionally trained in Europe as a forester and believed in using the latest scientific knowledge to manage the land. His aim was to produce the maximum sustained yield in forestry. Taking a utilitarian approach, Pinchot basically thought that the forests

Even after the buffalo were gone, the ground in many areas was literally covered with their bones (Fig. 1). Homesteaders collected the bones and burned them as fuel. These bones had many other uses as well. They were shipped back East by the trainload where they were ground up for fertilizer and used in sugar refining (to neutralize acids). The hooves and horns were used in the manufacture of glue. Well into the twentieth century, buffalo bones were being shipped to the East for commercial use.

The demise of the North American buffalo occurred in a flash, and only after the fact did the Canadian and U. S. governments intercede to try to halt the destruction. Canada passed legislation to protect the buffalo in 1885, but the U. S. government waited until 1899. By the 1890s, only two groups of bison remained in North America: a mixed lot of plains and forest and wood buffalo in Canada,

and a small herd of plains buffalo in Yellowstone Park. At the close of the nineteenth century, William T. Hornaday, director of the New York Zoological Park, made a census of all known living North American buffalo and found just under 1100. In 1905 Hornaday founded the American Bison Society, with the primary goal of saving the American buffalo from extinction.

The American Bison Society, with support from President Theodore Roosevelt and others, quickly established reservations for the bison, where they were provided with shelter and fodder as necessary. Results were achieved quickly: in 1910 there were over 2100 bison in North America, and by the 1930s there were over 20,000. Today ranchers keep herds throughout the continental United States, and there are sizable herds in government reservations such as Yellowstone Park and the Wood Buffalo Park in Alberta, Canada.

A sad footnote to the otherwise happy resurrection of the North American buffalo is that the wood or forest bison no longer exists as a distinct subspecies. The last remaining herd of pure forest bison inhabited the Wood Buffalo Park, but unfortunately in the 1920s plains bison were introduced to the same park. Naturally, the two subspecies mixed and hybridized, and the rarer forest bison ceased to exist as a pure-breed form.

FIGURE 1
Piles of North American bison (buffalo) bones could be found throughout the West in the late nineteenth century. (*Source*: Science VU/Visuals Unlimited.)

and other natural resources should be managed so as to obtain the most benefit for the greatest number of people. As such, he was an advocate of **conservationism**. From 1898 to 1910, Pinchot was chief forester for the U.S. Division of Forestry (reestablished as the U.S. Forest Service in 1905, with Pinchot at the helm), so he was well able to implement his philosophy.

Muir was born in Scotland, but came to America as a child. Largely on his own, he explored

much of the U.S. and Canadian wilderness, becoming an accomplished naturalist. He also visited Asia, North Africa, Australia, and New Zealand, writing about his travels for newspapers and magazines. Through his experiences Muir came to believe that nature has an inherent value and right to exist in and of itself independent of any value it may have for humankind (see Chapter 21). Thus, Muir took a strict **preservationist** position. He had a particular interest in the

Sierra Nevada Mountains of western North America and founded the environmentalist group the Sierra Club in 1892. Muir advocated the creation of national parks that would be protected from any type of human intervention. In partic-

FIGURE 22–2
Gifford Pinchot (right) and John Muir (far right). (*Sources:* (right) The Granger Collection, New York; (far right) The Bettmann Archive.)

ular, he was instrumental in convincing the government to establish Yosemite National Park in 1890 (■ Fig. 22–3).

Although strong allies in the general environmental movement, Muir and Pinchot clashed over many philosophical and practical issues. Their greatest battle was over the damming of the Hetch Hetchy Valley (adjacent to Yosemite Valley) through which the Tuolumne River flows. This valley was of great scenic beauty, and Muir, with his preservationist stance, advocated preserving and protecting it. Pinchot, taking the more utilitarian approach of the classic conservationist, supported damming the river to develop a supply of fresh water for the San Francisco region. After protracted debate, Pinchot's views won, and in 1913 the Hetch Hetchy Valley was dammed. Some have speculated that this defeat contributed to Muir's death the following year. But Muir's reputation and message have only been enhanced

with time. The Sierra Club remains one of the foremost environmental groups in America today. Meanwhile modern environmentalists continue to debate the merits of conservationism versus preservationism.

In the late nineteenth and early twentieth centuries the most widely held environmental stance was **progressive conservationism**. Influenced by Pinchot and like-minded individuals, the federal government took an increasingly active role in protecting forests and other natural resources for the public. In 1872 Yellowstone National Park was established, and in 1891 the Forest Reserve Act permitted the president to establish forest reserves (which later became national forests). The 1890 U.S. census declared that there was no longer a definable American frontier, conceptually closing an era in American environmental history.

Theodore Roosevelt (1858–1919), who served as president from 1901 to 1909, contributed greatly to the environmental cause. Roosevelt loved the outdoors and was an established naturalist and conservationist in his own right. Pinchot served as a key adviser to Roosevelt, and under his administration large tracts of land were added to the national forests. Roosevelt also protected the Grand Canyon and other areas that would later become national parks, and he sponsored a White House Conference of Governors to discuss conservation issues. In 1908 the National Conservation Commission was charged with making an inventory of the country's natural resources.

During the depression, the federal government instituted massive programs aimed at both creating employment and restoring the environment. The Civilian Conservation Corps put otherwise unemployed citizens to work planting trees, developing and maintaining park and recreation areas, restoring waterways, building flood control devices (such as levees and dams), controlling soil

The Great Depression of the late 1920s and 1930s and the administration of Franklin D. Roosevelt (1882–1945; president 1933–1945) affected attitudes toward natural resource management and conservation. The economic depression of this time can be attributed, at least in part, to the exhaustion and degradation of the land in parts of the United States. In the Appalachian region of the Southeast, for instance, the forests had been decimated and farming had exhausted the soil, causing widespread erosion and flooding. In the Midwest and Great Plains, the once fertile soils had been overcultivated, and severe soil erosion set in. With just a few dry years, the "Dust Bowl" was created. Wind storms stripped the land of the soil, creating huge dust clouds and causing havoc for the population and the ecosystem (Fig. 22–4).

erosion, and protecting wildlife. During this period, the Tennessee Valley Authority was established to address economic and resource management issues in the depressed Tennessee Valley. As part of this program, forests were replanted and dams (for hydroelectric power and flood control) were built. Likewise, dams were constructed in many arid regions of the western United States. One of the most famous is Hoover Dam on the Colorado River (near the Nevada-Arizona border); built in 1935, it created the water reservoir known as Lake Mead. Dam construction promoted agriculture and provided hydroelectric energy to fuel industry. Thus, these government programs were viewed as not only conserving natural resources, but promoting economic growth as well.

Other developments included the founding of the Soil Erosion Service (later renamed the Soil

FIGURE 22–3
Valley of the Yosemite (1864), an oil painting by the German-American landscape painter Albert Bierstadt (1830–1902). (*Source:* Albert Bierstadt, *Valley of the Yosemite* (1864). Gift of Mrs. Maxim Karolik for the M. and M. Karolik Collection of American Paintings, 1815–1865. Courtesy of the Museum of Fine Arts, Boston.)

FIGURE 22–4
Dust clouds envelop Lamar, Colorado, during the great drought of 1934. (*Source:* The Granger Collection, New York.)

Conservation Service) in 1933 and the creation of the Agricultural Adjustment Administration (later to become the Agricultural Stabilization and Conservation Service). Researchers studied the causes and prevention of soil erosion and shared their findings with farmers. In addition, the government began to pay some farmers to reduce their crop production, thereby helping to stabilize prices and reduce soil erosion. To reduce soil erosion caused by overgrazing, some limits were placed on the grazing of animals on federal lands.

The onset of World War II (America's direct involvement on the battlefield lasted from 1941 to 1945) saw conservation and resource management issues take a backseat to other concerns. The war forced the United States to mobilize; industrial and technological efforts concentrated on military production and winning the war. The experience of this war generally reinforced the American public's belief in social progress through economic growth and technological achievements. The development of the atomic bomb, for instance, led to the "atoms for peace" program and the construction of commercial nuclear power plants that would presumably generate clean and inexpensive energy for all. Science and technology could finally make the American Dream come true.

Environmentalism since World War II

Unfortunately, the technological advances of World War II and the immediate postwar period had the potential to unleash devastating effects on the environment. Production methods, using newly developed technologies, shifted from labor-intensive processes to energy-intensive processes that consumed enormous quantities of energy, often in the form of fossil fuels. Synthetic chemicals increasingly substituted for "natural" resources. This was the age of plastics and the automobile. Individualism, perhaps best expressed in the American ideal of at least one car per family and the freedom to drive on the open road, led inevitably to an unprecedented per capita consumption of natural resources. The Green Revolution, which fed the burgeoning population, was based on energy-intensive, as well as fertilizer-, herbicide-, and pesticide-intensive, "factory farming." Economic growth reached unprecedented levels.

But all was not perfect. With the new technologies and consumption habits came new environmental concerns. Greater and greater levels of toxic chemicals and other dangerous wastes were generated and, in many cases, released into the environment. Nuclear power, in some people's opinions, was a catastrophe waiting to happen. Conservationists began to suggest that we were quickly depleting our resources and degrading the quality of our air, water, and land. Concern over the quality of life, not just the quantity of material goods, became the focus of much environmentalism in the 1960s and 1970s.

In 1963 Rachel Carson's book *Silent Spring* described the adverse effects of pesticides and warned of the environmental disaster that might befall us if we continued to pollute. Carson's book made a strong impact, and some historians consider its publication the beginning of the modern era of American environmentalism. The 1960s and early 1970s were a time of change in American society. The civil rights movement was challenging long-accepted forms of discrimination. The hippie counterculture was questioning traditional values, and as U.S. involvement in the Vietnam War escalated, more and more people were protesting the establishment. Many of the initial environmental concerns were people oriented: we needed to protect the quality of the air, water, and land and preserve wildlife and wilderness for the benefit of humans. With the *Apollo* missions to the Moon (culminating with the first human landing on the Moon in 1969), photographs of the Earth taken from outer space were widely circulated. The concept of "Spaceship Earth" gained wide currency: we are all on one tiny planet drifting through space; Earth is all we have, so we had better take care of it.

The 1960s and 1970s also witnessed the passing of a number of federal laws that still form the basis for environmental protection in the United States (see Appendix C). In 1970 the Environmental Protection Agency (EPA) was established, and on April 22, 1970, much of the country enthusiastically celebrated the first "Earth Day." In many ways this was a time of idealism. Even as people finally acknowledged the existence of environmental problems, they assumed the problems could be solved.

By the mid-1970s, however, public concern with the environment had declined. Oil shortages were occurring (though artificially created by the OPEC cartel), and the country faced economic recession. All too often, it seems, when the public has to choose between the economy and the environment, the economy wins. By the late 1970s and early 1980s, an active backlash against environmentalism was under way. Many of the dire predictions made by environmentalists in the 1960s did not seem to have come true. The Reagan administration (1981–1989) valued economic growth over environmental protection and long-term responsible resource management. Then,

too, the 1980s was the decade of the "yuppies"—the young urban professionals who often seemed to care more about making money than anything else.

Nevertheless, environmentalism was not completely dead in the late 1970s and 1980s. Love Canal came to the public's attention in 1978 and led to the Superfund legislation with its efforts to clean up toxic and hazardous wastes. The Three Mile Island nuclear power plant accident in Pennsylvania occurred in 1979, effectively putting a damper on the further development of nuclear power in the United States. Then the Chernobyl nuclear power plant disaster in Russia in 1986 confirmed some people's worst fears. Even as the Reagan administration downplayed environmental issues, environmental groups such as the Sierra Club counted hundreds of thousands of new members. The radical environmental organization Earth First! was organized in 1980 and quickly grew in membership. By the end of the decade, the United States had joined other nations in signing the Montreal Protocol to save the ozone layer (1987), and the 1989 oil spill in Prince William Sound, Alaska, helped bring environmental issues to the forefront of the public's attention once again. The 1990–91 Gulf War led many people to once more reassess the wisdom of America's heavy reliance on foreign oil. Record heat waves and unexpected severe storms at the end of the decade caused many to take the notion of global warming seriously. And the global population continued to increase with no end in sight even as per capita food production declined. All in all, by the end of the 1980s environmental issues were coming once again to center stage. Earth Day 1990 received more attention than any Earth Day since the first in 1970. The end of the Cold War, the breakup of the former Soviet Union, and the reunification of East and West Germany now allow (indeed, require) us to focus attention on cleaning up the world and developing societies that can survive into the twenty-first century and beyond.

In 1993 a Democratic administration took the reins from the Republican Reagan-Bush team that had held the White House for twelve years. President Bill Clinton expressed concern and interest in environmental issues, but perhaps more significantly Vice President Al Gore, author of the widely read book *Earth in the Balance: Ecology and the Human Spirit* (1992), is an avowed environmentalist. Before joining the Clinton ticket, Gore had launched a presidential campaign based in part on an explicit pro-environmental platform.

The Wise Use Movement

One manifestation of the recent backlash against environmentalism has been the development of the **Wise Use movement**. This loose collection of about 500 mostly conservative and/or business-affiliated organizations originated at a 1988 conference held in Reno, Nevada, organized by the Center for the Defense of Free Enterprise (CDFE). At the conference, CDFE leader Ron Arnold coined the term "Wise Use," explaining that "it taps a psychological need for symbolic ambiguity."

The avowed goal of the Wise Use movement is to eliminate or nullify most environmentally based laws and regulations. Wise Users see such laws as generally overly expensive and disruptive of free enterprise, they argue that the laws lead to the destruction of jobs by putting the good of the environment before that of people. One of the Wise Use leaders, Chuck Cushman, has stated that environmentalists are "just followers of a new paganism that worships trees and sacrifices people."

The Wise Users espouse laissez-faire economic theory and believe that landowners should be allowed to use their land as they see fit, regardless of any negative environmental repercussions. Wise Users have fought against the designation of natural areas as national landmarks and opposed the expansion of parks; they favor the economic development (some would say exploitation) of national forests, wetlands, and other environmentally sensitive areas.

The Wise Use movement has been heavily influenced by the 1987 book *Takings* by Richard Epstein, a University of Chicago professor. A clause of the Fifth Amendment of the U.S. Constitution states that ". . . nor shall private property be taken for public use, without just compensation." Wise Users, who advocate a very broad interpretation of this clause, argue that any owner of private property should be compensated by the government for any income that might be lost by governmental actions. Thus, for example, an environmental regulation that prohibits building on a certain piece of land could be viewed as "taking" a "property right" because it decreases the land's value—therefore the owner should be compensated for the loss. Similarly, laws that prevent an individual or company from polluting on its own land (perhaps by burning rubbish or dumping wastes into a stream) would also constitute a "taking" by the government for which the landowner should be compensated.

Takings bills have been introduced into the U.S. Congress and dozens of state legislatures, although as yet most have been defeated. But Wise Use lobbying efforts have been intensifying and have helped to delay renewal of the Endangered Species Act, reauthorization of the Clean Water Act and Safe Drinking Water Act, and passage of bills to reform the Mining Law of 1872. They have also helped to prevent the EPA from attaining cabinet status and to weaken legislation to establish a national biological survey of native plants, animals, and ecosystems.

Despite the Wise Use movement's success in at least stalling environmental legislation, the legal and philosophical basis of takings is tenuous. Many government actions also increase property values, such as installing roads and sewers, zoning regulations, and environmental regulations that keep a private individual's property from being fouled by pollution. If landowners should be compensated for loss of property value incurred by certain governmental actions, should they also be forced to pay whenever governmental actions maintain or increase their property's value? Wetlands protection, for instance, can prevent the flooding of nearby buildings and assure a continued supply of clean drinking water, among other benefits. Individual property owners who feel they are being treated unfairly already

---

In America today (1996), however, a strong backlash against the environmental movement is arising once again (see Issues in Perspective 22–2). The November 1994 election brought a majority of Republicans, many of whom are generally unsympathetic to environmental concerns, into Congress. In Washington and in state houses across the country, environmental legislation has been stalled, and environmental lobbying groups are losing their political clout. Recent polls show that while the public is still generally interested in environmental issues, the economy, crime, health, and welfare are more immediate concerns. Many of the older, established environmental groups are facing budget shortfalls (as generous contributions have become less frequent) and declining memberships. Greenpeace has lost a million members since its high of 2.5 million in 1990, and its revenues are down by a third. Likewise, the Wilderness Society has seen a 30% drop in membership since 1990, forcing it to close offices and lay off employees. The Sierra Club is facing its worst financial situation in 20 years, and its looming multimillion-dollar deficit is forcing it

have appropriate channels (such as the court system) for filing a grievance. Furthermore, most legal historians argue that the Fifth Amendment clause refers only to situations where the government actually takes property from individuals, such as to build a road. In the nineteenth century the U.S. Supreme Court ruled that "[A]ll property in this country is held under implied obligation that the owner's use of it shall not be injurious to the community." In other words, landowners must not use their land in such a manner as would harm or be a nuisance to other people.

Many Wise Use leaders and takings advocates play on the sympathies of small, individual landowners. They can garner support from those sympathetic to the "little person" just trying to scrape by while fighting the big, bad, governmental bureaucracy. But, in fact, much of the Wise Use/takings agenda would most benefit large landowners (and less than 5% of U.S. landowners control nearly three-quarters of the privately owned land). Environmental regulations that the Wise Users would abolish help protect average citizens and their property. Pollution control laws are just one example: allowing a large private company to dispose of wastes in whatever manner it sees fit could result in severe damage to neighboring property values, not to mention the negative ramifications for the entire community at large.

Another alarming trend among anti-environmentalists, including some Wise Users, is their use of intimidation tactics. In some cases, they simply harass environmentally minded citizens, such as by name calling or by hanging environmentalists in effigy. In other cases, they work through the legal system with the tactic known as SLAPP (strategic lawsuits against public participation).

Such lawsuits have been brought against environmentally oriented citizens for writing letters to public officials or even private individuals, circulating petitions, participating in public hearings, and so on. The filers are usually large businesses or organizations that sue over such issues as alleged defamation or interference with business. Those being sued may have a legal right to voice their opinion under the First Amendment, but then SLAPP suits are not really meant to be won in court. Their goal is simply to intimidate, and they are often very successful. Ordinary people may be quite unnerved at receiving a letter announcing they are being sued for perhaps $1 million. Often the person being sued cannot afford the legal fees and lost time needed to fight the battle in court and will be forced to settle out of court, a usual condition being that they not speak out on the issue again. Approximately 90% of SLAPPs that make it to court are thrown out by judges.

SLAPPs are usually brought against individuals who can be successfully intimidated; rarely are they brought against large organizations that can fight back. Thus, one way for environmentally concerned individuals to avoid being SLAPPed is to become associated with large environmental organizations.

One should also stay calm, make sure your facts are correct, and never give your opponent a legitimate basis for bringing a SLAPP. If SLAPPed, it may pay to fight back. In some cases when SLAPPs have gone to court, not only did the business bringing the suit lose, but the citizen being sued won significant monetary damages. In one well-publicized case, an environmentalist who was initially SLAPPed filed a countersuit and ultimately was awarded $86.5 million in damages (although she negotiated to end the legal proceedings for an undisclosed sum). Finally, on both state and national levels, legislation has been either proposed or passed that would block or quickly dismiss most SLAPP suits.

to lay off employees. A *USA Today* poll found that the 10 largest environmental groups in America collectively lost 6.5% of their membership between 1990 and 1994.

Part of the problem with the largest environmental groups and agencies may be that they have actually grown into massive bureaucracies—and in the process lost the trust of many grassroots environmentalists. The Sierra Club, for instance, has a $40 million annual budget, including a Washington lobby group, a $6 million book business, and a $3 million worldwide ecotourism operation. Environmental agencies in the state and federal governments have become notorious for their regulations, bureaucratic hoops, and red tape. Washington pollster Celinda Lake noted that "Today, if you ask a typical American to name a bureaucrat, he'll point to someone in some environmental agency."

But even as larger, established environmental organizations are declining, many newer, smaller, local and grassroots organizations are springing up, often in response to environmental threats in their own communities. Grassroot organizing seems to be the wave of the environmental future. Estimates are that some 6000 grassroots environmental organizations are active in the United States. On college campuses, interest in the environment is on the upswing; environmental studies programs are expanding and evolving. Environmental awareness has become part of the worldview of the generation that is now entering adulthood. And their concern is not just with local recycling programs or nuclear power plants; instead, they are focusing on the broader issues that must be faced in the next century—the acheivement of long-term sustainability and the fundamental changes in society that this may entail.

ARE WESTERN SOCIETAL VALUES TO BE BLAMED FOR THE CURRENT ENVIRONMENTAL CRISIS?

Every human society has social institutions—based ultimately on fundamental beliefs, behaviors, and cultural norms—that govern the interactions of the vast majority of its people with each other and with the surrounding physical and biological environment. The most basic social institutions of a society are those governing (1) family organization and relationships, which provide most importantly for the raising of children; (2) economic concerns, which provide for the production and distribution of material goods and services; (3) political concerns, which provide for the distribution of power and prestige and the protection of members of society from each other and from external enemies; (4) educational concerns, which provide for the transmission of knowledge and the cultural heritage from one person and generation to another; and (5) religious concerns, which provide for the establishment of a moral and ethical code and an explanation of the meaning and purpose of human life within the society.

Fundamental values and norms, and therefore the social institutions through which these values and norms are expressed, may vary from one society to another. The social institutions of any particular society constrain the manner in which members of the society interact with each other and their environment. For instance, a particular society may value the concept of private ownership and the right of landowners to do anything they please with their land. A landowner who clear-cuts a large forest and replaces it with an open dump may cause severe problems for the other members of the society as leachate from the dump flows onto their property. Yet the norms and social institutions of the society may limit the ability of the other members to stop the landowner from pursuing such activities. The situation may effectively be unresolvable until the social institutions are modified, perhaps by incorporating the concept that private landowners can do whatever they want on their land as long as it does not affect anyone else detrimentally. Many thinkers contend that social institutions (and the underlying norms and values) must change and evolve over time as a human society expands and develops technologically.

Western Values and Social Institutions

According to many observers, the dominant social institutions in the modern world are those that incorporate the values, norms, beliefs, and ideologies found in Western European and American society. Around the world indigenous cultures are going extinct, only to be replaced by the homogenizing Western culture. The whole world seems to be industrializing and adopting Western technology, and simultaneously adopting Western values, beliefs, and social institutions. Here we use Western beliefs and social institutions in a broad sense to include the entire spectrum from classic capitalism (with its emphasis on private property and private ownership of the means of production)—to various forms of socialism and communism (which de-emphasize private property and stress varying degrees of public property and government intervention in the means of production and the distribution of goods and services). Non-Western beliefs and social institutions include those represented by traditional Hindu, Buddhist, and Confucian societies (to give a few major examples) and those found among many indigenous peoples such as the Native Americans or Australian aborigines prior to European contact.

Classic Western institutions (whether capitalist, socialist, or communist) are based on the concept of increasing rates of economic growth, increasing development, increasing the provision of material goods and services, and increasing the standard of living for everyone. In simple terms, these institutions rely on the "pie" increasing in size so that everyone's slice of the pie gets larger. In an ideal capitalist system, for instance, the rich and elite may get richer, but the poor don't get poorer. As the pie gets bigger, even the small slices that the lower classes receive will, in absolute terms, get bigger. As long as the pie continues to grow, everyone makes material progress over time, and general standards of living rise. But it appears we will soon reach, or perhaps have already reached, the absolute limits to the size of the pie. It can be argued that we can no longer continue to expand—to pursue business as usual, because the physical environment will not support continued human expansion. The strategy that worked so successfully for hundreds of years, as long as there was a relative abundance of untapped natural resources, must now be modified.

Some critics contend that the current environmental crisis can ultimately be traced to a few fundamental beliefs that dominate Western culture (for further discussion from an ethical point of view, see Chapter 21):

1. Western society and culture are dominated by an anthropocentric and humanistic worldview. Humankind is dominant over nature, humans are superior to all other living things, and human interests come before those of other species or inanimate objects. There is a dichotomy between nature and human society. Humans must conquer, tame, and subdue nature.
2. Western culture emphasizes the individual human and often promotes individual achievements, even to the detriment of the collective good. An individual who exploits a natural resource, such as an oil field, for his or her own gain and profit is regarded as an industrious, ingenious person to be admired even though his or her actions may cause damage to society in the long run.
3. Western beliefs are dominated by materialism, the idea that the production and consumption of material goods are necessary for a good life. To satisfy this materialistic urge, Western society must draw on the physical environment.
4. According to traditional Western thinking, the natural world is virtually unlimited, containing a wide variety of free (except for the human labor needed to procure them) and inexhaustible resources. In this view, not only can we take from the natural world with impunity, but we can dump our wastes back into nature. As a sink to absorb wastes, the atmosphere, rivers, oceans, and even the surface of the land itself are, for all practical purposes, infinite. Nature is the ultimate provider of resources and the ultimate sink for wastes.
5. Western society and culture are based on a growth ethic. Progress is measured in terms of growth; bigger and more are better. People who produce and consume large quantities of goods are better off. Social institutions depend on an expanding economy. Sustainable living, which does not involve continually exploiting new resources and new frontiers, is antithetical to this basic Western worldview.
6. Western society and cultural institutions emphasize technological and scientific knowledge and achievements over other types of knowledge, such as moral or aesthetic knowledge and achievements. This is not to say that the arts are not valued in the West, for they certainly are, but technology that can be used to manipulate the physical environment to achieve the material goals of society is even more im-

portant. Indeed, Western society seems almost to have a blind faith that technology can solve all problems and achieve all goals. We sometimes hear comments such as "If we can put a man on the Moon, we should be able to eliminate greed and social strife." The fallacy here is that putting a person on the Moon is a relatively straightforward technological problem (▨ Fig. 22–5). Eliminating greed or social strife, however, is a complex sociocultural problem that is not directly amenable to technological solution, although, of course, technology may contribute to the solution by providing an adequate supply of food and material goods for everyone.

▨ **FIGURE 22–5**
Edwin E. Aldrin, Jr., stands on the Moon in a photograph taken by Neil A. Armstrong, July 1969. (*Source:* NASA.)

Some critics maintain that Western economic and political institutions in particular promote beliefs that lead to abuse of the environment. For instance, in capitalistic systems private property owners make the decisions about the means of production of goods and services. These property owners attempt to maximize their own profits while often ignoring or discounting the damage that might ensue to the general environment that is shared with the rest of the population. Even in socialist and communist systems, where economic decisions about the means of production and the modes of distribution of goods and services are made by the government, the traditional emphasis is on increasing economic growth and supplying ever more goods and services to the populace. In practice, environmental considerations take a back seat to sociopolitical concerns. The net result is that in traditional Western systems the environmental costs of goods and services are not factored into the price of a product. The market fails to take account of "externalities," the social and environmental costs of goods and services that are not reflected in the price that consumers pay. For instance, the $1.50 that a consumer may pay for a gallon of gasoline primarily reflects the cost of pumping, refining, and transporting the petroleum; it does not reflect the cost of the health and environmental damage that burning the gallon of gasoline will cause, nor does it necessarily reflect the government expenses of protecting and securing the supply of oil—think of the wars that have been fought over oil supplies. In the case of gasoline, even exploration, refining, and marketing are partially subsidized by the U.S. government.

Political decisions in traditional Western systems often promote the economic system that leads to environmental abuse. In capitalistic systems, business groups and business-funded lobbyists are extremely influential, and such groups typically wish to keep to a minimum legislation that protects the environment at the expense of business, such as legislation that would factor externalities into the cost of products. Lobbyists claim such legislation will reduce profits—reduce economic growth (upon which the entire system is based)—causing unemployment and social disruption. In socialist and communist systems, much the same line of thinking takes place except that the government and business are one and the same. Indeed, repressive communist systems may result in even greater damage to the environment than capitalistic systems; in communist systems, any dissenters who might speak on behalf of the environment may be crushed so that the state can successfully conceal environmental degradation from the populace and the world at large.

Alternatively, one can argue that the fundamental beliefs and social institutions of Western society are not the source of environmental problems, but rather may be our only hope for a solution. In this view, the concept of special Western guilt for global environmental destruction is a myth. Primordial innocence never existed; neither did the noble savage who lived in true harmony with nature. Aboriginal peoples in such areas as Madagascar, Hawaii, and New Zealand caused numerous species to go extinct and generally wrought ecological devastation on their lands. For thousands of years, the Chinese have been involved in the wholesale extermination of many wildlife species, including elephants, tigers, and rhinoceroses (Fig. 22–6), and have contributed to many other environmental problems as Issues in Perspective 22–3 describes. Indigenous, traditional East Asian pharmacology advocated the use of preparations made from rhinoceros horn or tiger penis as remedies for all sorts of afflictions—Western medical science is much more effective and less damaging to the environment. Only

FIGURE 22–6
Traditional Chinese medicines often include ingredients derived from rare species. (*Source:* Will and Deni McIntyre/ Photo Researchers.)

Environmental Problems in China

Although Americans and Europeans often think of massive pollution and environmental degradation as being primarily a Western problem, this is far from the truth. Pollution and associated environmental deterioration are found around the globe, a particularly egregious example being China (Fig. 1).

China, with a population of over 1.2 billion, is industrializing rapidly and is experiencing the environmental destruction that such development often brings. Throughout the country, the water, air, and land are suffering from massive pollution. Acid rain causes over $3 billion worth of damage to forests, crops, and buildings each year; sometimes the acid rain is carried into neighboring countries such as Japan and Korea. China is the world's third largest contributor of greenhouse gases that are promoting global warming (after the United States and the countries of the former Soviet Union).

Many of China's air pollution problems are due to the massive burning of sulfur-containing coal. China is the world's largest consumer of coal and burns over 1.1 billion tons (1 billion metric tons)* a year; coal fills 75% of China's energy requirements. In many parts of northern China, coal is burned directly to heat buildings. In some cities thick acidic fog and smog hang in the air, at times making it impossible to see more than 10 to 13 feet

*Unless otherwise noted, *tons* refers to short tons (2000 pounds).

(3–4 m) ahead. In many Chinese cities, air pollution is in excess of World Health Organization minimum standards by a factor of five or six, meaning the air quality is seven or eight times as bad as in New York City. To guard against the coal dust in the air, many Chinese wear surgical masks when they go outside (particu-

FIGURE 1

A haze of pollution hangs over this street in Beijing, China. Notice that one woman is wearing a surgical mask to help guard against inhaling coal dust and other particulates. (*Source:* Forrest Anderson/Gamma Liaison.)

larly in the winter when more coal is burned for heating). The leading cause of death in China is lung disease.

China also suffers from major water pollution. Factories dump tens of billions of tons of industrial wastes into streams and rivers, and an estimated 85% of all Chinese cities are finding that clean water is in short supply. Outside the cities, estimates are that only one in seven Chinese has access to safe drinking water.

Chinese officials acknowledge the environmental problems of their country, but economic development remains their top priority. Currently, China spends only about 0.8% of its gross national product on environmental projects, but the World Bank has estimated that China should be spending 1.5% of its GNP just to control current environmental deterioration. Throughout China local officials charged with protecting the environment must generally raise money through taxes and fines. In many areas businesses are allowed to pollute as long as they pay a tax, and when outright fines are imposed on polluters, they are usually very small. The official Chinese position remains that economic progress will not be sacrificed for the sake of environmental preservation.

through Western technology and human ingenuity, promoted by Western concepts of individualism, resource expansion, and development, can we ever satisfy the needs and cravings of all the world's population—or so some thinkers argue.

According to one school of thought, there are no resource limits as long as we do not limit human creativity to develop and exploit new resources. In the nineteenth century, for example, some pessimists believed that modern civilization would eventually run out of high-quality energy sources as coal and other fossil fuels were depleted. But in the twentieth century, Western technology has learned to harness the hitherto unimagined energy contained within the atom. We now have hundreds of fission nuclear power plants in operation around the world, and the development of fusion as a controllable energy source is just a matter of time. Likewise, aluminum was once an unknown metal. For several decades after it was first discovered (around 1825), it was extremely rare and costly. Now aluminum is very common and is put to the most mundane uses, such as packaging food and beverages. To cite just one more example, the Green Revolution after World War II allowed increased harvests that would have been unthinkable just 50 years earlier. Even the physical limits of Earth, according to extreme advocates of this point of view, represent no absolute limits. We have already proved that we are capable of space travel, and the universe is unimaginably large. Similarly, Europe may have seemed very small and crowded in 1450, but a century later Europeans were colonizing an entire New World (North and South America) that was unimagined by the pessimists of the mid-fifteenth century.

It is not our purpose here to decide whether Western values and social institutions are the cause of, or the solution to, the current environmental crisis. Indeed, some persons have argued that there is no environmental crisis. Ultimately, it may be that Westernization was both the cause of, and the solution to, the global environmental crisis of the late twentieth century. Only time will tell.

Sustainable Development/ Sustainable Growth

Classically, it has been argued that a strong correlation exists between economic development and growth and environmental degradation. As humans increase their rates of growth and expand their production of goods and services, more and more resources are depleted, more wastes are spewed into the environment, and the environment suffers. But does economic growth have to lead to environmental degradation? Perhaps not. Many environmentalists believe that we must adopt a new paradigm—a new way of thinking and acting, a new ideology—that has been labeled **sustainable development** or "sustainable growth." Sustainable development focuses on making social, economic, and political progress to satisfy global human needs, desires, aspirations, and potential without damaging the environment. In this context *development* does not refer to old notions of simply increasing industrial output and increasing consumption of goods and services. Rather, "[d]evelopment involves a progressive transformation of economy and society" (World Commission on Environment and Development 1987). Sustainable development emphasizes equity in managing the world's resources—equity among different peoples and nations of the world, and equity between one generation and another. We must not leave a degraded environment to the future simply in order to live a certain lifestyle in the present. One country should not disproportionately use global resources or cause irrevocable environmental degradation that affects other peoples or the entire Earth. The key word is sustainability, meaning to prolong indefinitely into the future the ability of Earth to support and provide for not only humans, but for all life on the planet.

Solving the Environmental Crisis by Refocusing Western Political-Economic Structures

As we have already discussed, one of the major failings of traditional Western economics is the failure to include the environmental consequences of goods and services in their market prices. The environmental costs are externalized and not paid directly by the producer or the consumer; instead, the price is absorbed by the populace as a whole. For too long, companies and individuals have been allowed to freely exploit raw resources and dump their wastes back into the commons (such as a factory dumping waste into a public river or the global atmosphere). This allows a few to profit at the expense of the majority. By fostering economic growth, the traditional Western political-economic structure actually encourages resource depletion and pollution, at least as long as there continue to be resources to deplete and some place to dump the resultant wastes. Economic growth and the increasing profits and employment it brings have been the traditional goal of both Western business and Western governmental/political institutions. But this goal is very short-sighted, for it discounts long-term environmental degradation due to present practices.

In the United States, an environmentally conscientious company may often feel trapped. If it practices business as usual, externalizing envi-

ronmental costs of production, then damage to the environment results. But if the company internalizes the environmental costs, perhaps by using a more expensive manufacturing system that eliminates harmful emissions, then the product will cost more; since the public will generally purchase the cheaper product, the company will not be able to compete and may eventually go bankrupt. Likewise, the politician who is perceived as putting the environment before jobs (although this is often a false dichotomy) may soon be voted out of office.

But this analysis is too simplistic. In at least some cases, the public does not automatically purchase the cheapest product or always vote for the politician who will lower taxes and increase income. Education has already gone a long way toward changing public perceptions and actions. The fact that a product is environmentally sound can be used to help market it even if the product does cost a bit more than its competitors. Along these lines, two classic success stories are The Body Shop and Ben & Jerry's. The Body Shop is an international outlet chain that specializes in hair and skin products. Anita Roddick, who founded the chain in the United Kingdom, has managed to combine her environmental concerns with corporate success (to the tune of hundreds of millions of dollars in sales each year through some 600 shops in 18 countries). The Body Shop purchases its raw materials from indigenous peoples, uses refillable bottles, and does not allow the use of animals in testing its products. It also supports environmentally sustainable development and human rights. The Vermont-based ice cream company known as Ben & Jerry's, with sales of some $90 million a year, plays an active role in environmental affairs. Ben Cohen sees to it that 7.5% of the company's profits are used to fund environmental and social projects, and the company actively lobbies on behalf of environmental issues. The Body Shop, Ben & Jerry's, and like-minded corporations have all attracted a loyal stream of customers; environmentally oriented consumers can feel good about buying such products. Likewise throughout the world "green" politicians are gaining influence and power.

Playing on the environmental sympathies of the public, however, can carry some businesses only so far—governments must also become involved. Environmentally progressive businesspersons may favor government intervention that allows for the internalization of externalities across an industry. That way different businesses and corporations can compete fairly while also re-

ducing or eliminating the environmental damage they cause. Government intervention can take the form of regulations that protect the environment. Government subsidies that promote the exploitation of virgin resources can be eliminated. Government-imposed limitations on corporate liability for environmental damage could be eliminated; likewise, government-subsidized insurance programs that cover environmental hazards and damages could be curtailed. Why, for instance, do we need the Price-Anderson Act of 1957, which limits the liability of the nuclear industry in case of an accident, other than to promote the development of nuclear power? Laws can be (and are) passed that set limits on permissible amounts of pollution that can be spewed into the environment. Certain types of toxic or hazardous materials can be banned. Particular resources, such as a forest or wilderness area, can be preserved through government intervention. Government can also help internalize environmental costs by instituting stiff "green" taxes on waste emissions, resource depletion, energy use (such as carbon taxes or taxes on nuclear energy production to reduce the accumulation of radioactive wastes), and so on. Such environmental taxes can go a long way toward correcting the market by internalizing the indirect costs of products.

The government could also actively subsidize environmentally compatible technologies and activities. For instance, it could give tax breaks to companies that install appropriate technologies (such as solar heating systems or pollution-reducing equipment) or pay bonuses for devising more efficient means of production.

Some analysts argue that we should also create markets for the "right" or "privilege" to pollute (as was done to a certain extent with the 1990 Clean Air Act Amendments). For instance, the government could sell permits that allow the holder to dump wastes, up to a certain level, into a particular river or the air. The sum total of the pollution permitted would not be more than can be safely and sustainably handled by the environment. Pollution permits could be bought, sold, and traded on the open market. A manufacturer that wanted to discharge pollutants into a river would have to pay for the appropriate permits and thus would be forced to internalize the cost of the pollution. A competing manufacturer might be able to produce the same product by a different (perhaps more expensive), nonpolluting technology and therefore would save the expense of purchasing pollution permits. Concerned citizens, environmental organizations, or even the government might buy and hold pollution permits in order to curb waste emissions. Savvy investors might put their money into pollution permits just as today they invest in real estate.

A conceptual problem with pollution permits concerns who has the right to establish and sell them in the first place. Perhaps a global governmental authority would be needed since some types of pollution are global in nature. But should the "privilege" to pollute be legitimized and privatized in such a manner? On the face of it, one can argue that such a system will increase inequity between peoples—those who hold pollution permits will be a rung above those who do not. Those who are allowed to pollute can cause damage and injury to those who cannot, while the latter have no way to reciprocate. As the global population expands (and every indication is that it will continue to grow for many years), pollution will inevitably increase, and those holding the limited number of pollution permits will gain in power and wealth at the expense of everyone else. Thus, pollution permits may be at odds with the concept of sustainable development and the goal of global equity among all peoples. Alternatively, we could simply insist that individuals and corporations not pollute and instead carry on their businesses in a sustainable manner that does not threaten the environment or human health.

In the United States and many other countries, corporations can be forced to internalize external costs to a certain extent through the court system. An individual or community that is hurt or damaged by a company's negligence or illegal acts can file a lawsuit against the corporation. The courts may force the company to comply with existing regulations, change its activities, or pay a large

monetary settlement. In this manner the company is made to internalize certain factors that were previously mere externalities. For example, a company may be compelled to take responsibility for the injuries that ensue when it dumps toxic waste into a river. Using the judiciary system in this way leads to numerous problems, however. On a practical level, considerable knowledge and a substantial initial outlay of money are generally needed to attack a large corporation that can afford to hire good lawyers. In most areas the court systems are already crowded, and a case may take years to come to trial or arbitration. In many situations, such as damage due to air pollution, it may be difficult or impossible to identify the particular corporation that is directly responsible for the damage in order to take it to court. Lawsuits are perhaps most effective when used by individuals or small groups of victims to remedy damages that can be clearly attributed to the actions of a single or possibly a few corporations.

Political solutions to environmental problems are becoming increasingly prominent as more and more citizens are becoming environmentally aware. Citizens can form environmental interest groups that lobby the government at all levels, or an individual can write directly to governmental officials about environmental concerns. Citizens can support (with donations, time, and votes) candidates who are pro-environment. Individuals and groups can also influence public opinion and governmental decisions through the educational system and the media. Sitting on a local school committee or writing letters to the local newspaper can be very effective.

Beyond working within the confines of the current political system by voting, lobbying, testifying before committees, and so forth, one can also engage in political action outside the established route. Some environmentalists contend that because the established political system encourages the continued degradation of the environment, we have a moral obligation to challenge the legitimacy of the current system and the status quo. Increasingly, some people are calling for an environmental revolution that will radically change our values and the way we do business. Grassroots movements of concerned individuals on a local, national, and ultimately international level may be necessary to challenge and overturn the status quo. Tactics that can be used include marches, boycotts, protests, and mass meetings demanding change (Fig. 22–7). If nothing else, such activities can focus awareness and concern, forcing politicians to make what were once peripheral issues central concerns. Just as the U.S. civil rights movement used such tactics with great success, so too might the current environmental movement.

 NVIRONMENTAL LAW

Law and the Environment— A General Overview

Over the past century, and especially over the last 50 years, society has turned increasingly to legal avenues to protect the environment. As we shall see in the remainder of this chapter, a number of laws dealing with environmental issues have been enacted on the local, national, and international levels. Yet there are many gaps in these laws, for this field is still developing. Initially, the prime motivating force behind most environmental legislation was to protect human safety and welfare, but now certain aspects of the environment (for instance, endangered organisms) are coming to be viewed as having legal standing and legal rights (see also Chapter 21). Increasingly, environmental advocates and their attorneys are defending the environment from assault and injury by human beings.

In the broadest sense, the field of **environmental law** encompasses all of the laws, statutes, regulations, agreements, treaties, declarations, resolutions, and the like that have bearing on environmental issues. Environmental laws range in scale from local community ordinances prohibiting litter on the streets to international treaties regulating trade in endangered species or the release of stratospheric ozone–destroying substances. Many authorities divide environmental **legal instruments** (laws, treaties, regulations, conventions, and so on) into two categories: **hard laws**, which are legally binding and mandatory, and **soft laws**, which are not legally binding, but act more as a guide to policy. This distinction is particularly useful in analyzing international treaties, conventions, and agreements. Many international legal instruments are not binding on the signing nations, but tremendous moral and public pressure may be brought to ensure that the signatories more or less conform to the agreement. In contrast, hard laws force the parties to comply or else. But or else what? Enforcing hard laws at the international level may be difficult. Countries wishing to see an environmentally friendly treaty honored may impose trade or other sanctions against an offender, but to this date, nations rarely go to war over environmental protection per se, although certainly countries have gone to war over the control of scarce natural resources. Many international environmental treaties are initiated by, or fall under the aegis of, the United Nations (UN), but the UN has only limited powers of enforcement.

The legal and philosophical basis for environmental laws can be approached from several different directions. In a narrow sense, one can argue that pollution is a nuisance or negligent behavior that detracts from others' property and personal rights. Thus, pollution in particular and environmental degradation in general, can be viewed as **common law torts** (wrongs) that are within the jurisdiction of the law. More broadly, one can contend that fundamental human rights include the right to a safe, healthy environment. Any government should use its authority and power to promote the general welfare of its citizens and subjects, and this includes enacting laws that address environmental concerns. Using the U.S. legal system as an example, some scholars have argued that the Ninth Amendment to the U.S. Constitution (which reads "The enumeration in the Constitution, of certain rights, shall not be construed to deny or disparage others retained by the people.") can be interpreted as guaranteeing the people's right to a healthy, clean, and safe environment. Nowhere in the Constitution are environmental issues mentioned explicitly (of course, such topics were perhaps not a major concern in the late eighteenth century), but one can argue that the right to a healthy and healthful environment is so fundamental that it did not need to be explicitly enumerated in the Constitution.

In the broadest context, one can justify environmental legislation as simply protecting the fundamental rights of not only humans, but all organisms and even inanimate objects and Earth itself (for further discussion, see Chapter 21). Human-mandated environmental laws are necessary only to the degree that humans fail to be considerate of the larger nature of which they are necessarily a part. If people did not exploit and abuse the environment, there would be no need for environmental legislation.

International Environmental Law

At the international level, a number of environmental treaties, conventions, agreements, and protocols (approximately 170 at last count) have been established. These legal instruments are binding and enforceable to varying degrees, and all are dependent on independent and autonomous governments becoming signatories and

FIGURE 22–8
Delegates meet during the
"Earth Summit" held in Rio
de Janeiro, June 1992. (*Source:*
Allan Tannenbaum/Sygma.)

pledging their support. Unfortunately, many "global" treaties and agreements have received less than global support, and even when technically binding on participating countries, they are very difficult to enforce. Nevertheless, the latter half of the twentieth century has witnessed great strides in international cooperation to protect and preserve the environment. Conventions and agreements have been established providing for, among other things, the protection of areas of outstanding natural or cultural value; restrictions on trade in endangered species; protection of migratory species; a legal framework for the use of the oceans and their resources, including which areas fall under national jurisdictions; and the prevention of marine pollution (Appendix D describes these and other international legal instruments in more detail).

Some of the most important soft legal instruments of recent years emerged from the United Nations Conference on Environment and Development (UNCED, popularly known as the "Earth Summit"), which was held in Rio de Janeiro in June 1992 (Fig. 22–8). It is generally considered to be the largest summit ever held on any topic—delegates from more than 175 countries, including more than 100 heads of state, attended. This conference can be viewed as the final ending of the Cold War, marking a new

beginning where money that would once have been spent on military expenditures can now be funneled into environmental protection and sustainable global development. As a result of the Earth Summit, a number of soft treaties and declarations were formulated. Environmentalists hope these will lay the groundwork for future hard agreements.

- *Climate Treaty (United Nations Framework Convention on Climate Change).* This treaty, formulated at the Rio Conference, establishes broad principles and outlines the potential moral and legal obligations of nations to curb the release of greenhouse gases that could cause global warming. It suggests stabilizing greenhouse gas emissions at 1990 levels by the year 2000. Overall, the treaty is very weak and effectively nonbinding, but it sets a precedent and lays the groundwork for further international discussions on the topic. Signatories are required to conduct national inventories of greenhouse gas emissions and subsequently submit plans for controlling these emissions. Future discussions could result in harder, more binding agreements.
- *Biodiversity Treaty (United Nations Convention on Biological Diversity).* This treaty is aimed at promoting the preservation and careful manage-

ment (including sustainable use) of biological diversity and begins to address the issue of genetic engineering using genes found in rare species. It imposes no binding legal obligations on the signing nations, however, and it does not totally clarify the relationship between nations that exploit the genes of species and the nations that are the repositories of the species bearing the genes. For instance, if a representative of a developed country (such as a scientist employed by a large pharmaceutical corporation) finds that a gene of a newly discovered indigenous species in a developing country has great medicinal, and therefore economic, value, who shares in the fruits of this discovery? Does the developing nation have a right to profit from the discovery? It is generally hoped that the preliminary Biodiversity Treaty formulated at the Earth Summit in 1992 will lay the groundwork for hard agreements addressing these types of issues.

- *Forest Agreement (Statement of Agreement on Forest Principles).* Environmentalists hoped that the Earth Summit would provide a forum to develop an international treaty aimed at protecting the world's remaining forests. However, the developing nations (especially India and Malaysia) generally took the stance that forests within their boundaries were subject only to their authority and thus could not be the subject of an international agreement. Part of the problem is that the developed nations (the North) long ago cut down much of their forest areas en route to achieving their wealthy, developed status. The developing nations (the South) demand the right to follow a similar path in promoting their own internal development. Essentially, the countries of the South do not want to remain in relative poverty while protecting their forests for, as they see it, the relative benefit of the North. The final general statement on world forests produced by the Earth Summit contained few new ideas and accomplished little in the way of promoting the preservation of the Earth's forests.
- *Rio Declaration.* This statement, which came out of the Earth Summit, was signed by many nations, generally committing participants to pursue sustainable development and work to rid the world of poverty. The statement declares that developed countries have a special responsibility to help in global restoration efforts since they have the financial resources to afford such efforts, and historically, the developed countries have been the largest contrib-

utors to global environmental degradation. The Rio Declaration, like other Earth Summit documents, is nonbinding but it does carry some moral and political obligations.

- *Agenda 21.* This 800-page document from the Earth Summit contains recommendations as to how countries can pursue sustainable development and protect the environment. It covers such topics as decentralization of decision making relative to the management of local natural resources, land reform to increase the land rights of rural and indigenous peoples, ways to improve the status and participation of women in the context of sustainable development, and the development and adoption of taxes and other economic incentives that promote sustainability with the concomitant removal of subsidies that are at odds with the preservation of natural resources. The UN established the new Commission on Sustainable Development to report on progress made toward the goals and recommendations outlined in *Agenda 21.*

The negotiation of international environmental treaties and other legal instruments, such as those just outlined, is an important step. Nevertheless, it is generally extremely difficult to monitor and enforce international treaties. Indeed, some critics argue that many of the approximately 170 environmental treaties currently in existence are virtually meaningless because they are not enforced.

Many treaties require signatory countries to self-report on their progress in fulfilling the requirements of the treaty, but this self-monitoring is generally not sufficient. Usually, only a minority of nations submit the required reports, and even then the data may be incomplete (Fig. 22–9).

FIGURE 22–9
Self-reporting by individual countries about their progress in adhering to environmental treaties is not a sufficient monitoring tactic since many nations fail to file the required reports. (*Source:* Figure based on an illustration by Johnny Johnson in "Making Environmental Treaties Work," by H. F. French, *Scientific American,* December 1994, p. 96. Copyright © 1994 by Scientific American, Inc. All rights reserved.)

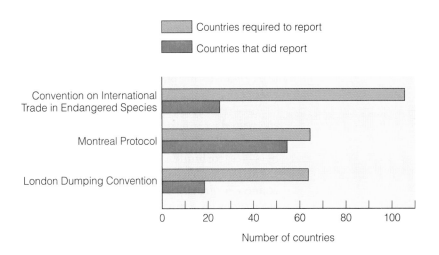

Some treaties, such as the Montreal Protocol, include voting mechanisms that allow a majority of participating nations to vote stricter measures into effect after the fact; these measures then become binding on all original signatories. Thus, unanimous consent is not required to modify the agreement (some argue that consensus may actually be reached more quickly because dissenting countries know they may be outvoted). Still, once the agreement is in place, ensuring that all participating countries live up to it can be difficult.

Short of military action, which very few people would advocate, peer pressure, moral persuasion, and public embarrassment have been found to be surprisingly effective in forcing nations to comply with the provisions of environmental treaties. For most nations and their leaders, "public face," or how the nation and its government is viewed by the world community, is very important. To maintain or improve their image, governments may comply with environmental treaties rather than risk being publicly embarrassed. In recent years, nongovernmental organizations (NGOs), such as citizens' groups, business organizations, and environmental coalitions, have been extremely helpful in forcing compliance of international environmental treaties. NGOs are often quite willing to gather and publicize incriminating information on nations that are unwilling to live up to the letter, or even spirit, of an environmental treaty. Acknowledging the value and contributions of NGOs, the UN and its affiliated agencies have been encouraging the increased involvement of NGOs not just in monitoring environmental treaties, but also in helping to initiate and formulate them.

Money and trade can also be useful in implementing and enforcing international environmental agreements. Understandably, many developing nations are much more willing to implement a treaty if they receive financial assistance (see Issues in Perspective 22–4). Thus, under the 1990 amendments to the Montreal Protocol, a fund containing several hundred million dollars was established to help developing countries finance the phaseout of ozone-depleting chemicals.

Another way to force compliance with environmental treaties is by trade incentives and disincentives. For instance, Montreal Protocol members are forbidden to purchase CFCs from countries that have not signed the convention. A country or group of countries can impose trade embargoes on nations that do not fulfill the requirements of an environmental treaty. Some environmentalists fear, however, that international trade agreements may interfere with the use of trade sanctions to force nations to behave in an environmentally sound manner. Depending on the interpretation, certain provisions of the General Agreement on Tariffs and Trade (GATT), which sets the basic rules for global trade, may make it illegal to restrict trade based on certain environmental concerns (see Issues in Perspective 22–4).

Environmental Law and Regulation in the United States

In the United States, the national government is composed of three branches: the legislative, the executive, and the judicial. The **legislative branch** makes the basic laws and also allocates funds; the federal legislative body is the Congress, composed of the House of Representatives and the Senate. The **executive branch**, consisting of the president, vice president, and the president's appointees, is charged with administering and enforcing the laws of the country. The **judicial branch**, or the court system (at the highest level, the U.S. Supreme Court), interprets the laws of the land, including the U.S. Constitution, and renders judgments in trials and disputes. Each state has a somewhat similar government. At the local level, a city may have a mayor (the executive) and a city council (the legislative branch).

At all levels, all three branches of government have a role to play in environmental issues. Legislatures may pass laws that protect, or harm, the environment—or at least regulate human affairs that affect the environment. The actual influence that a particular law has depends on how it is administered and enforced. Issues in Perspective 22–5, page 631, describes how laws are sometimes used in a manner contrary to what was intended. Finally, disputes over the implementation of laws are often decided in the courts. In some cases the judiciary may define and clarify what may originally have been a fairly vague law.

Extremely important on a national level are the **regulatory agencies** that deal with environmental concerns. Once a law is enacted by Congress, it is typically administered by a regulatory agency in the executive branch of government. From an environmental perspective, some of the more important national regulatory agencies are the Environmental Protection Agency, the Department of Energy, the Department of the Interior, the Department of Agriculture, and the Bureau of Land Management. The effectiveness of a particular law often depends on the agency administering it. Furthermore, the regulatory

Development Assistance, World Trade, and Sustainable Development

Today, global environmental issues are inexorably associated with the broader issues of the relationships between the North and the South—the industrialized nations and the developing nations—as well as the movement to liberalize world trade. Furthermore, the concept of sustainable development includes the notion of equity between different peoples and nations of the world, so it is only fair that the developed countries help the developing countries address environmental issues of global impact.

Clearly, unilateral action by a single nation will do little to correct global environmental problems that are collectively caused by many countries. For instance, curbs on greenhouse or CFC emissions by a single country will not solve the global problem of atmospheric deterioration. In addition, we now realize that environmental deterioration and the depletion of resources, particularly in developing countries, often promote cycles of poverty that lead to further environmental deterioration. The North is increasingly pressuring the South to end environmental deterioration and protect its remaining natural resources (such as tropical rainforests) for the good of the planet as a whole, yet the North has not set a very good example of resource conservation in the past. Furthermore, many developing countries are heavily in debt to developed countries and must exploit their natural resources to service that debt.

Many developing countries receive financial assistance from industrialized countries in the form of forgiveness of debts, developmental assistance, investment by private organizations, and grants from both governments and nongovernmental organizations. In 1991 (the latest year for which accurate figures are available), approximately $131 billion in such assistance passed from developed to de-

veloping nations. Of course, much of this money does not go directly toward promoting environmental causes. The 1992 Earth Summit calculated that implementing the activities proposed by the conference in developing countries would cost more than $600 billion annually. This would require substantial assistance from the industrialized nations. Currently, the most important source of assistance is the almost $57 billion a year coming from the Development Assistance Countries (DACs) (Fig. 1).

To fund the proposed programs, the Earth Summit recommended that the DACs raise their assistance from the current average of 0.33% of GNP (Gross National Product) to an average of 0.7% of GNP. At present, only Norway, Denmark, Sweden, the Netherlands, and Finland have reached this goal, while France is not far behind. Although the United States is the single largest contributor in absolute terms (more than $11 billion in 1991), it is among the lowest in terms of percentage of GNP (about 0.2% in 1991, including forgiveness of nonofficial development assistance debt).

Since development assistance funds will likely be inadequate to implement the proposed projects, some have suggested that a system of environmental taxation be established. Taxes could be levied on fossil fuel consumption, global income, international trade in particular natural resources, use of the oceans and other global commons, energy-wasting consumer items, pollutant emissions, defense spending and arms trading, and so forth. Of course, establishing a global authority that could levy these taxes and equitably distribute the revenues would be very difficult, especially since the taxes would impinge on the authority of sovereign nations. Another suggestion is that the "peace dividend" resulting from the reduction in military spending since the

end of the Cold War (more than $100 billion a year) could be used to support sustainable development. Of course, most countries that have a peace dividend also have plenty of domestic programs that require funding.

Trade protections imposed by industrialized countries in particular have sometimes made it difficult for the developing countries to expand their exports, thus making it more difficult to pay their debts. Inability to service their debts can then promote further environmental deterioration.

International trade agreements, such as the General Agreement on Tariffs and Trade (GATT) and the North American Free Trade Agreement (NAFTA), can also have direct environmental ramifications. Major issues include whether free trade in goods and products will also entail free trade in pollutants or environmentally destructive practices. A country that requires recyclable, and thus more expensive, packaging places an added burden on foreign manufacturers who do not have to comply with the same requirements at home. The result can be trade disputes and international discord. GATT acknowledges that individual nations may enact environmental, health, and safety laws as long as they are "necessary" and are the "least trade restrictive" way of dealing with the issue, but defining "necessary" in this context can be difficult. NAFTA has similar provisions, including the requirement that such national laws be based on "scientific principles" and "risk assessment." But as some commentators have noted, many U.S. environmental laws are based more on political compromise than science and thus may not meet the standards of NAFTA or other international trade agreements.

As a graphic example of how trade agreements and environmental concerns
continued on the next page

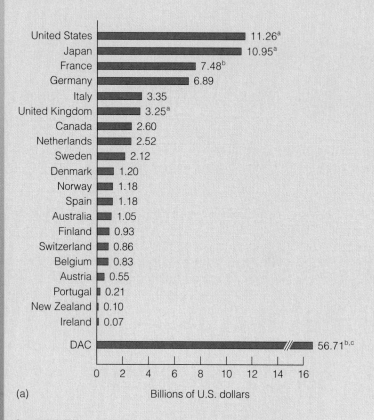
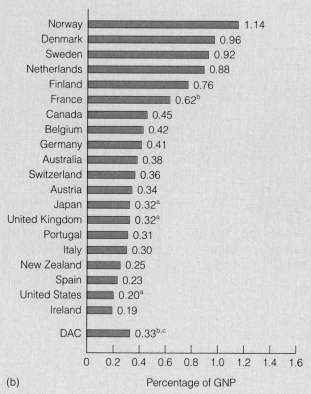

(a) Billions of U.S. dollars

(b) Percentage of GNP

ᵃ Includes forgiveness of nonofficial development assistance debt.
ᵇ Includes overseas territories but excludes overseas departments.
ᶜ Excludes forgiveness of nonofficial development assistance debt.

FIGURE 1

Net official assistance from Development Assistance Countries (DACs) in 1991. (a) In billions of U.S. dollars; (b) as a percentage of Gross National Product (GNP). (*Source:* World Resources Institute, *World* *Resources 1994–95* [New York: Oxford University Press, 1994], p. 227. Used with the permission of World Resources Institute.)

can clash, in 1991 a GATT panel of judges ruled that the United States had violated then current GATT agreements. The problem was that the U.S. Marine Mammal Protection Act banned the import of tuna caught using the types of nets that kill dolphins. Mexico was the challenging nation in this case, and the United States and Mexico privately settled the issue. Nevertheless the ruling is still unnerving to environmentalists.

Some observers have argued that lax environmental laws can be viewed as a government subsidy that makes it less expensive to produce certain goods in certain countries. Therefore, they suggest nations with stricter environmental standards should be allowed to place duties on cheaper goods made under lax environmental regulations to bring their price up to what they would cost without government subsidies. Understandably, however, countries with less stringent environmental requirements resist the inclusion of such provisions in international environmental treaties.

Environmental Laws Used to Fight Environmentalism

For decades environmentalists have fought hard to get strict environmental legislation on the books. The purpose, of course, is to protect the environment and end pollution and other destructive practices. Recently, however, certain businesses and other organizations have been fighting tough environmental regulations with the laws that were intended to keep environmental abusers in check. In 1992, for instance, when Congress passed legislation to curb certain damaging pesticide and irrigation practices that had been used for years, Westlands Water District, a California irrigation agency, filed suit to block implementation of the new legislation until an environmental impact study could be undertaken. Even if the study ultimately upholds the need for the new legislation, the farmers are allowed to carry on business as usual while the study is being carried out (which could take many years).

In many instances, anti-environmental groups can exploit the elaborate procedures mandated by many environmental laws—detailed reviews, assessments, and impact statements may be required, and strict deadlines may have to be met. As long as there are delays, and the process is tied up in lawsuits, logging companies, mining companies, or other businesses can continue to operate as usual. In some cases, delays can ultimately mean court defeats for environmentalists. A good case in point is the Bruneau hot spring snail, a tiny gastropod that lives in hot springs of the desert country of Owyhee County, Idaho. In the middle 1980s, scientists discovered that the hot springs were drying up due at least in part to heavy water pumping for irrigation by farmers and cattle ranchers. Subsequently, the Fish and Wildlife Service proposed classifying the snail as an endangered species which would almost certainly have resulted in restrictions on irrigation pumping in its habitat.

Before the snail could be listed as endangered, however, a number of farmers and ranchers complained to Idaho's representatives in Congress, who in turn complained to the Fish and Wildlife Service. The upshot was that plans to protect the snail were delayed until a group of environmentalists finally sued to have the snail listed as endangered. But then the Idaho Farm Bureau and a local cattleman's association sued in turn, arguing that the government had violated the Endangered Species Act's requirement that a final decision on a proposed species's listing as endangered be made within 18 months of the initial proposal for listing. The environmentalists contended that things had moved so slowly because the cattle and farming interests had delayed the process, but a federal judge recently ruled in favor of the farmers and cattle ranchers, and the snail's federal protection was lifted.

---

agencies often have considerable latitude in interpreting and implementing a law. For instance, Congress may pass a law requiring certain industries to maintain emissions of specific pollutants at acceptable levels; the appropriate regulatory agency must then determine exactly what constitutes "acceptable" levels. The influence that regulatory agencies can have was demonstrated during the Reagan administration. The Reagan era was marked by the weakening and dismantling of much of the federal bureaucracy charged with administering environmental laws. As a result, between 1981 and 1988, enforcement of laws governing pollution and hazardous waste was extremely lax, and many government-owned natural resources were made available to individuals and companies for private profit. For instance, the Reagan administration increased the leasing of

continental shelf areas and national forests for oil and mineral exploration, exploitation, and timbering. These actions were not simply the result of negligence when it came to environmental concerns, but were pursued as an integral part of the administration's pro-business, free-market approach to government and economic affairs.

Regulatory agencies are subject to the influences of political opinion and professional lobbyists. As the agencies set standards and guidelines for the enforcement of environmental laws, they often expend considerable energy gathering information and conducting studies. Advisory committees may make recommendations, and interested parties may testify at public and private hearings. The levels set for "acceptable" emissions of pollutants, for instance, may be the result of negotiation

EnviroNet
www.jbpub.com/environet

and compromise among different interests. Ultimately, the existence of any regulatory agency is dependent upon the legislature, for it supplies the agency's funds. If members of Congress perceive strong public opposition to the policies of a certain agency, they may simply cut the agency's funding.

Decision-Making in the Public Arena

EnviroNet
www.jbpub.com/environet

As administrators implement environmental laws by developing specific rules, regulations, and guidelines, many decisions must be made at many different levels (see the Case Study for some criticisms of U.S. environmental regulations and decision making). All decisions must include some political, social, and ethical values; there is no such thing as a politically neutral decision, although certainly some decisions come closer than others. Many "rational" decisions are based on evidence and "proof." At a fundamental level, the standards of proof that are accepted can vary greatly depending on a particular person's outlook and inclinations. For instance, given the question of whether a certain chemical in small concentrations is harmful to human or environmental health, an identical study can be interpreted in more than one way. The chemical's manufacturer may presume the chemical to be harmless until "proven" otherwise, so a scientific study that simply suggests (perhaps based on a weak statistical correlation) that the chemical has ill effects will be rejected. On the other hand, an environmentalist or health advocate may, in the name of safety, presume the chemical is dangerous if there is any evidence, no matter how weak, to that effect. Thus, both the manufacturer and the environmentalist will use the same study to bolster their arguments. In this case the disagreement boils down to the use of different standards of proof for the chemical's harmfulness or harmlessness. How stringent a standard of proof should be is not a scientific question, but a political, moral, and philosophical question. In such a case, there is no neutral middle ground. Accepting a middle-of-the-road standard of proof for our hypothetical chemical is not a neutral decision, but a decision that essentially weighs environmental and health issues equally with the economic concerns of the manufacturer and thus arrives at a practical compromise between the two camps.

In making policy decisions concerning environmental affairs, three basic techniques are commonly relied upon: (1) soliciting the best pro-fessional judgments of experts in the relevant field or fields, (2) basing new policies on the precedents of previous ones (sometimes known as **boot-strapping**), and (3) the use of **benefit-cost analyses** (also referred to as risk-benefit analyses). These techniques are not mutually exclusive; in practice they are often used in conjunction with one another. Here we briefly discuss each of these techniques.

Judgments of Experts

Relying on the judgments of experts would seem to make good sense, for who is more knowledgeable in a particular field than a trained expert? But such a strategy quickly runs into problems. Equally competent and well-credentialed experts within even a narrowly circumscribed field may disagree. On the other hand, if the professionals agree, it may simply be because they have all been subjected to similar training and backgrounds and therefore carry similar underlying assumptions and biases—they represent a single point of view, but not necessarily the only point of view. And for any given situation, which experts should be consulted? If a decision has to be made as to whether, how, and to what extent to log an old-growth forest, who should be consulted? Professional foresters, zoologists, logging company executives, professional employees of environmental organizations, economists, and others might all be considered relevant experts, but could have very different views on the situation. Ultimately, the relevant knowledge that professionals can offer should be taken into consideration, but as we have already pointed out, the ultimate decision-making process must include more than simply objective knowledge. A decision can only be reached by combining the knowledge and judgments of the experts with political, social, and ethical values.

Precedents

In many situations, new or revised policies and decisions are based on the precedents set by older decisions and policies. Previously established standards are applied to new situations. As an example, in attempting to establish health standards for the use of a new synthetic chemical, one might allow risks to the health of the public and the environment that are similar to the risks posed by other chemicals that are already in use. This method of decision making and policy setting puts great emphasis on the status quo; essentially, the

U.S Environmental Policy—Misguided or Enlightened?

In recent years, U.S. environmental policy has come under heavy criticism from certain sectors. Critics charge that all too often environmental policy has been guided by what the public perceives as risks, rather than by responsible scientific analysis. As a result, billions of dollars have been wasted fighting environmental "problems" that actually pose little risk while more important issues and hazards receive relatively little funding.

The toxic waste program, including Superfund and related programs (see Chapter 19), is generally cited as one of the most wasteful programs. More than $10 billion a year is spent to clean up hazardous and toxic waste sites, often at a cost of more than $10 million an acre ($25 million a hectare), but whether the money is well spent is questionable. In many cases the toxic sites are made "pristine," yet they continue to be surrounded by other hazardous sites. Some have cogently argued that the most practical and economical way to deal with many hazardous and toxic waste sites is simply to stabilize them (so that they do not spread chemicals and other dangerous substances) and then fence them off from the public. Spending millions of dollars to clean up such sites to the point where children can eat the dirt with impunity does not make sense, but often this is what is done: sites are cleaned to the point that the dirt is safe to eat. Then the site is left unused.

Another example of a misguided policy, critics contend, was the removal of asbestos from schools and other public buildings at a cost of $15 to $20 billion. After the fact, an EPA study concluded that removing the asbestos, which releases tiny asbestos fibers into the air, is often more dangerous than simply leaving it in place. Now the official recommendation is to leave asbestos alone unless it is crumbling or otherwise damaged.

Yet while large amounts of money have been spent on asbestos removal and cleaning up hazardous and toxic waste sites, relatively little has been done to address other problems that may be far more serious. Thousands of lakes across the country are contaminated by mercury, which poisons wildlife and potentially causes nervous disorders and other problems in humans. In 1990, during the debates over the Clean Air Act, it was proposed in Congress that limits on mercury emissions should be imposed on coal-burning electrical power plants. The limits were not instituted, however, because Congress felt that the utilities were already being required to spend considerable sums of money on limiting acid rain-promoting emissions.

Another example of a pressing environmental issue that is not being adequately addressed is lead contamination. Several federal studies have concluded that exposure to lead (such as lead paint, lead-laden dust, and lead in the air, though use of unleaded gasolines has significantly decreased the latter problem) is one of the gravest environmental threats to children. Lead poisoning can lead to hyperactivity, learning disabilities, and reduced intelligence. Despite the severity of the problem, only about $250 million is spent on addressing lead exposure each year, compared to the billions spent on cleaning up toxic waste sites.

The sweeping, complex, and strict environmental laws of the United States cost an estimated $150 billion a year (about $100 billion from industry and the rest from local, state, and federal government, though ultimately it is the citizens who pay), yet in some cases it is unclear what we get for the money. Critics contend that much of the money is wasted. In Tucson, Arizona, where many of the waterways are dry much of the year, millions of dollars must be spent to monitor potential pollutants in nonexistent water in dry streambeds. In other cases the EPA has set such low limits (measured in parts per billion) for admissible levels of contamination in water and soil that they can only be detected by the most sensitive and sophisticated equip-ment. To maintain EPA standards, enormous sums of money may have to be spent. And in many contexts "experts" not associated with the EPA have contended that such trace contamination, though not permissible under EPA regulations, may be harmless.

Yet any issue usually has at least two sides. The general trend of U.S. environmental policy over the last few decades still has many supporters. Daniel F. Becker, director of the Global Warming and Energy Program at the Sierra Club, has suggested that the view that U.S. environmental policy has been fundamentally misguided is "an effort to legitimize pollution. . . . There are powerful forces who have an economic stake in de-emphasizing environmental damage." Or as David D. Doniger, a senior lawyer with the Natural Resources Defense Council, has argued: "We don't need a new paradigm [for U.S. environmental policy]. For 35 years, the policy of the Government has been that when there is uncertainty about a threat it is better to be safe than sorry. When you are operating at the limits of what science knows, the big mistake would be to underestimate the real danger and leave people unprotected."

Questions

1. What are some examples of wasteful environmental programs that have been sponsored, funded, or promoted by the U.S. government? Are they wasteful only in hindsight? Might critics of such programs have a "hidden" agenda?

2. Should the government spend money to protect the public from possible, but not certain, environmental threats? How about probable, but still not certain, environmental threats?

3. Do you think the general paradigm for U.S. government environmental policy needs to be changed? Why or why not? To what extent should the government be involved in environmental issues?

decision maker assumes that the current standard is the best until trouble ensues. Then the policy or standard is revised just enough to solve the immediate problem.

This mode of policy making is sometimes referred to as "bootstrapping" (after the old adage of pulling oneself up by one's bootstraps, that is, without anyone else's help) because present policies and decisions are the result of the slow accumulation and refinement of past policies and decisions. This method of policy making is also referred to as "**muddling along**" or following the political path of least resistance. Since the decision makers are tied to precedent, they have little opportunity to make major policy revisions or consider new types of data and radical alternatives to current policies. Such muddling along tends to promote business as usual and can be an effective way of dealing with slight variations on old themes. It may fail completely, however, when novel and unprecedented situations arise. For instance, scientific and technological innovations such as bioengineered organisms, new medical techniques, or sophisticated electronic wizardry may initially fall outside the boundaries of the issues addressed by established policies. New policies, not just refinements of the old, may be needed.

Benefit-Cost Analysis

Another popular approach to decision making and policy formulation is benefit-cost (or risk-benefit) analysis. The task of a benefit-cost analysis is to establish what potential decisions could be made and then determine for each the costs, or risks, versus the benefits. For any particular decision, there may be a statistical probability of good or bad effects, and these probabilities must be taken into account. Benefit-cost analyses usually quantify in one way or another the benefits and costs of each potential decision, and the rational course to pursue is considered to be the decision that bears the least cost but most benefit. Benefits and costs are often quantified in monetary terms, but other measures can also be used such as human lives lost or saved, infant mortality rates, loss of productive work time at a factory, and so on. Classic Western benefit-cost analysis is often closely associated with utilitarianism (see Chapter 21) and its efforts to maximize "the greatest good for the greatest number." Of course, it is often difficult, if not impossible, to simultaneously maximize two different variables.

Benefit-cost analyses often have a broad appeal because, at least superficially, they use numbers and appear to be scientific and rigorous. Naively, people may believe that such analyses can lead to purely rational, objective decisions and policies. This is not to deny the importance of benefit-cost analysis, which can lead to refined and critical thinking about a problem. But, as we have already stressed, no decision can be made in a political, social, or ethical vacuum. Unfortunately, benefit-cost analyses may contain built-in, and perhaps unacknowledged, political, social, and ethical variables that become incorporated into the ultimate decision.

Benefit-cost analyses often consider very different types of entities and need to equate them in order to quantify them. For instance, in designing a new car, an automobile manufacturer may do a benefit-cost analysis. The more the company must spend to make a better car, the higher the price it has to charge for the car. All other things being equal, higher-priced cars tend to sell more slowly, but better-quality cars tend to sell more quickly. A benefit-cost analysis could help the manufacturer optimize profits by determining how well a car should be built; the benefits of better sales are weighed against the costs of building the better car, and the increase in sales of cheaper cars against the decline in sales if the car is more expensive. But what if the more expensive, but less profitable, car is safer and better for the environment? The typical capitalistic business perspective does not take such considerations into account as long as they do not affect the bottom line—the company's profit. From an ethical perspective, however, such considerations might be more important than the bottom line.

But if the car manufacturer is forced to internalize the costs/risks the cars pose to human health and the environment, these considerations will enter the analysis. Assume, for instance, that if the car crashes, passengers are likely to die because the car was poorly designed and inexpensively built. The manufacturer is sued and has to pay, on average, $1 million per life lost in such accidents. In terms of the manufacturer's benefit-cost analysis, a human life is now worth $1 million. Assume further that such a death occurs in 1 in every 100,000 cars, and the manufacturer would have to pay $100 per car to avoid the problem that leads to the deaths. A simple benefit-cost analysis indicates the manufacturer is much better off paying $1 million to the family of a dead victim once in every 100,000 cars than paying $10 million ($100 × 100,000) to make 100,000 cars safer. Of course, this overly simplistic analysis ignores such issues as the loss in sales that might ensue from bad publicity. Many people, however, would find the decision to build a cheaper car at a greater profit, even though an occasional life is lost, to be morally reprehensible. This example shows one of the major limitations of benefit-cost analysis: all factors must be quantified in terms of a common unit (in this case, dollars).

Many benefit-cost analyses do not take all considerations into account or at least do not weight them equally. Typically, considerations that directly affect the decision or policy maker are given the most weight. Returning to our hypothetical car manufacturer, perhaps a more expensive car that yields less profit produces less pollution and waste and therefore is also considerably less costly (that is, less damaging) to the global environment. This will be of no direct concern to the car manufacturer who is only trying to maximize profits, as long as the company does not need to pay the costs of environmental damage caused by the cheaper, and therefore more profitable, cars. A strong governmental authority charged with regulating the automobile industry, however, may factor environmental costs into its benefit-cost analysis when determining what policies and regulations to set for the industry. But even if we take environmental damages into account, how do we place a dollar figure on them so they can be incorporated into our quantitative analysis? What is the value of a forest undamaged by acid rain? Is the value simply the value of the lumber that resides in the trees, or is it something more? How much is it worth, in dollars, to have a city free of photochemical smog? Do we simply add the medical costs of pollution-induced diseases and the costs of pollution-induced damage to buildings and other structures? Or is there a value in having a clean, healthy environment beyond the immediate expenses avoided by not living in a polluted environment? What is the value of a scenic vista, a wildlife preserve, or a healthy forest with no immediate utilitarian use?

These examples are only a few of the issues that can be very difficult to factor into a benefit-cost analysis. Another criticism is that very often benefit-cost analyses consider only a subset of contemporary humans (in our hypothetical ex-

ample, perhaps only the owners of the automobile manufacturing company). But it can be cogently argued that the environment belongs not just to living humans, but to future generations and to nonhuman beings as well (see also Chapter 21). In a benefit-cost analysis of, say, open-pit coal mining or a major hydroelectric power dam, to what extent should the benefits and costs for nonhuman organisms and future generations be taken into account?

These criticisms of benefit-cost analyses do not mean that this technique is without legitimate uses. Such analyses can often be extremely useful, even if they are not used as the sole criterion for arriving at a decision. Especially when opposing groups apply independent benefit-cost analyses to the same problem, these techniques can help clarify differences in underlying assumptions and values that lead to disagreements. Perhaps the greatest benefit of the technique is that when used correctly, it can promote thoughtful, rational, critical thinking on important issues.

Ethical Considerations

Another way to arrive at decisions and establish policy is to formulate opinions solely on the basis of an underlying, well-thought-out philosophy and ethics (see Chapter 21). This means making decisions and establishing policies on the basis of what is considered to be inherently right and good, not by simply balancing immediate, or even long-term, costs and benefits. Of course, not everyone agrees on what is ultimately "right" and "good" or shares the same values, and some persons consider making decisions on the basis of a benefit-cost analysis to be inherently "right." Others think decisions based on ethical considerations are nonrational and simply political or ideological. But, as we have tried to show, any particular benefit-cost analysis is inherently value-laden simply by virtue of the way it is formulated and the potential alternatives, costs, and benefits it incorporates. As long as humans must make decisions, there will be room for discussion and argument as to which paths should be followed.

SUMMARY

Human social institutions reflect the underlying beliefs and values of a society and in large measure can also help to determine or constrain the actions of the society.

Some critics argue that the values, beliefs, and institutions of modern, technologically oriented Western society are in large part directly responsible for a large portion of the environmental degradation that we

currently face. Others point out that non-Western societies have also caused massive environmental deterioration and that the concept of a "noble savage" living in perfect harmony with the natural environment is largely a myth. Furthermore, it may only be through Western technology and social, legal, and political institutions that we may be able to successfully address the current environmental crisis.

When Europeans first colonized the Americas, they did not enter an uninhabited wilderness; yet, even after tens of thousands of years, the Native Americans generally had not modified the natural environment as intensely as the Europeans did in only a few centuries. The earliest European settlers viewed nature and human society as a dichotomy and had a frontier mentality of exploiting and subduing nature for humankind's benefit. This early attitude has continued to exert a strong influence on American thinking. By the nineteenth century, however, certain thinkers were questioning the rampant exploitation of natural resources. In the late nineteenth and early twentieth centuries, American environmentalism was dominated by the somewhat conflicting views of the conservationist Gifford Pinchot and the preservationist John Muir. While both supported environmentalism, these two men and their followers advocated different approaches to the issue. Pinchot, adopting a utilitarian point of view, believed in managing forests and natural resources so as to obtain the greatest benefit for the greatest number of people. Muir believed that nature has inherent value and a right to exist in and of itself independent of any value it may have for humans.

During the twentieth century, the U.S. government has, at various times, instituted massive programs aimed at preserving and restoring the environment, including the development of park and recreation systems, restoration of waterways, flood control, and protection of wildlife. The 1960s and 1970s witnessed the passing of a number of federal statutes that still form the legal basis of environmental protection in the United States. Despite temporary swings in public interest in the environment, concern about such issues remains strong.

At an international level, environmental legal instruments (laws, treaties, regulations, conventions, and so on) fall into two general categories: hard laws, which are legally binding and mandatory, and soft laws, which are not legally binding, but act more as a guide to policy. Unfortunately, it is generally difficult to monitor and enforce global environmental laws. At an international level, peer pressure and public embarrassment (how the world community views a nation), along with moral persuasion, have been found to be surprisingly effective in convincing nations to comply with environmental regulations. Trade sanctions, incentives, and disincentives have also been used on occasion to persuade recalcitrant countries to comply; however, global trade agreements may restrict the legal ability to use trade sanctions in defense of environmental concerns.

Increasingly, people are realizing that simple laws, whether on a local, national, or international level, ultimately will not be sufficient to solve the environmental degradation that the world faces. Many environmentalists believe that a new paradigm—a concept known as "sustainable development"—is needed. Sustainable development focuses on simultaneously making social, economic, and political progress to satisfy global human needs, desires, aspirations, and potential without damaging the environment. Sustainable development emphasizes equity in managing the world's resources—equity among different peoples and nations of the world, and equity between one generation and another. We must not leave future generations with a degraded world simply because we wish to enjoy a certain lifestyle in the present. One country should not disproportionately use global resources or cause irrevocable environmental degradation that affects other peoples or the entire Earth. The key word is "sustainability," to prolong indefinitely into the future the Earth's ability to support and provide not only for humans, but for all life on the planet.

$\mathcal{K}$EY TERMS

benefit-cost analysis
bootstrapping
common law
conservationism
environmental law
executive branch
frontier mentality

Green movement
hard laws
judicial branch
legal instrument
legislative branch
muddling along
preservationism
progressive conservationism

regulatory agency
social institution
soft laws
sustainable development
tort
transcendentalist
Wise Use movement

$\mathcal{S}$TUDY QUESTIONS

1. What is the Green movement, and what does it hope to accomplish?
2. What is the Wise Use movement, and what does it hope to accomplish?
3. List some of the basic social institutions of Western society. Are they to be blamed for the current environmental crisis?
4. How might it be argued that Western social institutions and technology are the key to solving our environmental problems?
5. Compare and contrast the approaches of conservationists and preservationists to environmental issues.
6. Describe the environmental stance that was known as progressive conservationism.
7. How did the Great Depression and World War II affect environmental attitudes in the United States?
8. What are the philosophical and historical bases for environmental laws?
9. Distinguish between hard and soft laws.
10. What was accomplished at the 1992 Earth Summit?
11. Why is it difficult to enforce international environmental laws? How can compliance be encouraged?

12. Explain how environmental laws and regulations are arrived at and instituted in the United States. Who makes the laws? Who makes the regulations? Who enforces them?

13. List the various ways that environmental decisions, especially public policy decisions, may be arrived at.

14. What are the pros and cons of benefit-cost analyses? Why is this method of decision making often strongly favored as well as sometimes strongly criticized?

15. Why has U.S. environmental policy been criticized in recent years?

ESSAY QUESTIONS

1. Give a brief historical overview of American environmentalism. What are the major chapters or periods in this history? What was accomplished in each?

2. Discuss the historical trends in federal legislation and interest in and public sympathy toward environmental issues. What is the mood of the country relative to these matters today?

3. Do you think Western societal values are to blame for the current environmental crisis? Justify your answer.

4. Describe and discuss the concept of sustainable development. Do you believe we should be striving toward this goal? If your answer is yes, how might it be accomplished? If your answer is no, what alternatives do you propose?

5. Describe some of the major international environmental laws, treaties, conventions, declarations, and protocols that are currently on the books.

SUGGESTED READINGS

Bormann, F. H., and S. R. Kellert, eds. 1991. *Ecology, economics, ethics: The broken circle*. New Haven: Yale University Press.

Brown, L. R. 1992. "Launching the environmental revolution," In *State of the World 1992*, ed. L. R. Brown *et al.*, pp. 174–190. New York: W. W. Norton.

Buchholz, R. A. 1993. *Principles of environmental management: The greening of business*. Englewood Cliffs, N.J.: Prentice-Hall.

Caldwell, L. K. 1990. *Between two worlds*. Cambridge: Cambridge University Press.

Cronon, W. 1983. *Changes in the land: Indians, colonists, and the ecology of New England*. New York: Hill & Wang.

Cutter, S. L., H. L. Renwick, and W. H. Renwick. 1991. *Exploitation, conservation, preservation*, 2d ed. New York: John Wiley.

Deal, C. 1993. *The Greenpeace guide to anti-environmental organizations*. Berkeley, Calif.: Odonian Press.

Dobson, A., ed. 1991. *The green reader*. San Francisco: Mercury House.

Dooge, J. C. I., *et al.*, ed. 1992. *An agenda of science for environment and development into the 21st century*. Cambridge: Cambridge University Press.

Easterbrook, G. 1995. *A moment on the Earth: The coming age of environmental optimism*. New York: Viking.

Franck, I., and D. Brownstone. 1992. *The green encyclopedia*. New York: Prentice-Hall General Reference.

Gore, A. 1992. *Earth in the balance: Ecology and the human spirit*. Boston: Houghton Mifflin.

Hardin, G. 1993. *Living within limits: Ecology, economics, and population taboos*. New York: Oxford University Press.

Harte, J., C. Holdren, R. Schneider, and C. Shirley. 1991. *Toxics A to Z: A guide to everyday pollution hazards*. Berkeley: University of California Press.

Kubasek, N. K., and G. S. Silverman. 1994. *Environmental law*. Englewood Cliffs, N. J.: Prentice-Hall.

Kumar, R., and B. Murck. 1992. *On common ground*. New York: John Wiley.

Moeller, D. W. 1992. *Environmental health*. Cambridge, Mass.: Harvard University Press.

Nash, R. F. 1990. *American environmentalism: Readings in conservation history*, 3d ed. New York: McGraw-Hill.

Norton, B. G. 1991. *Toward unity among environmentalists*. New York: Oxford University Press.

Ophuls, W., and A. S. Boyan, Jr. 1992. *Ecology and the politics of scarcity revisited: The unraveling of the American dream*. New York: W. H. Freeman.

Petulla, J. M. 1988. *American environmental history*, 2d ed. Columbus, Ohio: Merrill Publishing Company.

Ponting, C. 1992. *A green history of the world*. New York: St. Martin's Press.

Rifkin, J., and C. G. Rifkin. 1992. *Voting green: Your complete environmental guide to making political choices in the 1990s*. New York: Doubleday.

Shabecoff, P. 1993. *A fierce green fire: The American environmental movement*. New York: Hill & Wang.

Turner, B. L., II, W. C. Clark, R. W. Kates, J. F. Richards, J. T. Mathews, and W. B. Meyer, eds. 1990. *The Earth as transformed by human action*. Cambridge: Cambridge University Press.

World Commission on Environment and Development (G. H. Brundtland, chairman). 1987. *Our common future*. New York: Oxford University Press.

World Resources Institute. 1994. *World Resources 1994–95*. New York: Oxford University Press.

Worster, D. 1993. *The wealth of nature: Environmental history and the ecological imagination*. New York: Oxford University Press.

Young, J. 1990. *Sustaining the Earth*. Cambridge, Mass.: Harvard University Press.

EnviroNet
www.jbpub.com/environet

ENVIRONMENTAL LITERACY

Experts can explain anything in the objective world to us, yet we understand our own lives less and less. . . . We live in the postmodern world, where everything is possible and almost nothing is certain. Something is being born . . . one age is succeeding another.

VACLAV HAVEL, playwright, human rights campaigner, and president of the Czech Republic

Our global society and the global environment continue to change at a quickening pace. We are, indeed, entering a new age. One aspect of the coming age will be an increased environmental awareness among all peoples. Humankind can no longer be insensitive to environmental issues—for if we do not take concerted action to address environmental problems, they will quickly overwhelm us. Environmental issues are no longer a "special interest," but are taking center stage in the political, economic, and social arenas. Every citizen of the planet must have a working knowledge of environmental issues; everyone must be environmentally literate.

In the past environmental science has often been considered a negative discipline that held out little hope for the future. Through-

PHOTO *People watching a solar-powered television in the Republic of Niger.* (*Source:* John Chiasson/Gamma Liaison.)

out this book we have tried to demonstrate the various ways that environmental science can, and indeed must, become the "science of reality." This means that environmentalists must do more than criticize the status quo. It requires that we move beyond simply reacting to problems and relying on emotional persuasion and abstract formulations. We must proactively seek long-term solutions that are practical, sustainable, and realistic—solutions grounded in factual knowledge. Doing so will not always be easy, for in some cases it will require more than simple technological fixes: the very fabric and mind-set of modern society may have to be modified. This can only come about through increasing environmental literacy.

In his 1992 book entitled *Ecological Literacy*, the philosopher David Orr discusses the importance of moving beyond heated dialogues toward cooperation in building a sustainable society for all living things. This means that we should approach environmental problems by first becoming environmentally literate—by taking the time to learn the basic facts. Without this step, political, social, and personal biases will determine the outcome of environmental problem solving, often to the long-term detriment of both the environment and society. Admittedly, environmental literacy is not easy in today's "information age," which immerses all of us in a sea of facts. Sorting out the relevant from the irrelevant, the important from the trivial, can be extremely difficult. But this is what textbooks are for—to provide a distillation and overview of the fundamentals. Here we have attempted to provide a foundation upon which you, the reader of this book, can build as you learn more about environmental issues.

But we hope you will not be satisfied to simply learn about environmental issues. Become actively involved! You should never think that you, as an environmentally literate individual, cannot make a difference. You can have an impact—through the way you think, the way you vote, and the way you live your life. Nearly all so-called global environmental problems are aggregations of local problems. Global warming, species extinctions, ozone depletion, and certainly many regional problems result from the nearly countless actions of numerous individuals. Since the problems arise from individuals, the solutions must also arise at that level. Global change will occur; the global society of the future will not be the society we know today. The question is, how will society change? Will the change be environmentally sustainable? The collective actions of all of us will determine the future. When global society consists entirely of people who care enough about the environment and future generations to act accordingly, we will finally be able to solve our environmental problems. The very notion of global environmental problems will become an historical relic. We look forward to a society that is at peace with the environment.

Common Measures of Energy and Power

- *Joule (J)*. The basic unit of energy, heat, or work as measured using the metric system; equal to a force of one newton times one meter. From a macroscopic human perspective, this is a very small amount of energy. The burning tip of a wooden match gives off an estimated 1000 joules of energy.
- *Calorie (cal)*. A basic unit of heat energy in the metric system. A calorie is the quantity of energy that will warm one gram of water one degree Celsius. One calorie equals 4.184 joules.
- *Kilocalorie (kcal or Cal)*. 1000 calories or 4184 joules.
- *British thermal unit (BTU)* The basic unit of energy in the English system. The energy that, when converted to heat, will raise the temperature of one pound of water one degree Fahrenheit. One BTU is equal to 0.252 kcalories.
- *Quad (Q)*. One quadrillion (10^{15} or 1,000,000,000,000,000) BTUs of energy. One quad is equivalent to the amount of energy contained in approximately 171–172 million barrels of oil, 36 million metric tons of coal, or a trillion cubic feet of natural gas.
- *Petajoule (PJ)*. One quadrillion joules. There are approximately 1054 petajoules to a quad. One petajoule is approximately equivalent to the energy contained in 163,400 "U.N. standard" barrels of oil (see *barrel*) or 34,140 "U.N. standard" metric tons of coal (see *metric ton*).
- *Terajoule (TJ)*. 10^{12} joules. One thousand terajoules is equal to one petajoule.
- *Exajoule (EJ)*. 10^{18} joules. An exajoule is equal to 1000 petajoules or 1 million terajoules.
- *Barrel*. A measure of volume of petroleum oil, containing about 42 gallons or about 159 liters. Depending on the quality of the particular oil, a typical barrel of petroleum may produce between about 5 and 6 million BTUs of energy when completely burned (see *quad* and *petajoule*).
- *Cubic feet (cu. ft)*. A measure of volume that is used to measure natural gas. A cubic foot of dry natural gas can produce approximately 1031 BTUs of energy.
- *Metric ton*. 1000 kilograms (2204.6 pounds or 1.1 English "short" tons). This unit is commonly used to measure amounts of coal (see *quad* and *petajoule*). A standard metric ton of coal may produce 27–28 million BTUs when completely burned, but the energy produced by an actual ton of coal will vary considerably depending on its grade and quality. Oil is also often measured in terms of metric tons. Depending on the type of oil, the exact number of barrels per metric ton will vary, but it is generally about 7.33 barrels of oil per metric ton.
- *Therm*. A measure of natural gas, equal to 100,000 BTUs. A therm of gas is equivalent to approximately 97 cubic feet of natural gas.
- *Watt*. A measure of power, energy consumption, or conversion. It is commonly used in connection with electricity. One watt is equal to one joule of work or energy per second. A 100-watt lightbulb consumes 100 joules of energy per second, or 360,000 joules per hour.
- *Kilowatt (kW)*. Energy conversion at the rate of 1000 watts (1000 joules per second).
- *Megawatt (MW)*. Energy conversion of 1000 kilowatts (1 million joules per second), or 1 million watts. Many conventional nuclear power plants have generating capacities of 1000 megawatts or more; that is, they can produce 1000 million (1 billion) joules of energy per second (enough energy to power 10 million 100-watt lightbulbs).
- *Gigawatt (GW)*. Energy conversion of 1 million (1,000,000) kilowatts.
- *Terawatt (TW)*. Energy conversion of 1 billion (1,000,000,000) kilowatts.
- *Horsepower (hp)*. A somewhat obsolete (except for cars and mechanical engines in some countries) term for power that is approximately equivalent to 750 watts or three-quarters of a kilowatt.
- *Kilowatt-hour (kWh)*. A measure of energy based on the concept of the kilowatt; the energy converted or consumed during an hour if the energy is being converted or consumed continuously at the rate of 1 kilowatt. A kilowatt-hour equals 3.6 million joules, 860.4 kcalories, and 3413 BTUs.
- *Kilowatt-year (kW-yr)*. The energy converted or consumed during a year if the energy is being converted or consumed continuously at the rate of 1 kilowatt. A kilowatt-year is approximately equivalent to the amount of energy given off when 1050 kilograms (approximately one metric ton) of coal are burned. If people consume 1 kilowatt-year of energy per year (1 kW-yr/yr), their average rate of energy consumption is 1 kilowatt.
- *Megawatt-year (MW-yr)*. The energy converted or consumed during a year at the rate of 1 megawatt. A megawatt-year equals 3.156 × 10^{13} joules, 7.542 × 10^9 kcalories, and 2.993 × 10^{10} BTUs.

- *Terawatt-year (TW-yr).* The energy converted or consumed during a year at the rate of 1 terawatt. A terawatt-year is approximately equivalent to the energy given off by burning a billion metric tons of coal. The world as a whole consumed approximately 10 terawatt-years worth of energy in the single year 1980; thus, for 1980 we can express the total world energy consumption rate as approximately 10 TW (10 TW-yr/yr equals 10 terawatts). One terawatt-year is equal to approximately 31.6×10^{18} joules, 31,600 petajoules, or 31.6 million terajoules.

English/Metric Conversion Table

This table is meant as a handy reference guide to some of the basic English and metric units involving length, mass (weight), area, volume, and temperature. It is not intended to be comprehensive. For common measures of energy and power, see Appendix A.

Conversion values (from English to metric, or vice versa) are rounded unless designated as exact equivalents.

ENGLISH TO METRIC

	English	Metric
Length:	1 inch (in)	2.54 centimeters (cm) (exactly)
	1 foot (ft)	30.48 cm (exactly)
		0.3048 meters (m) (exactly)
	1 yard (yd)	91.44 cm (exactly)
		0.9144 m (exactly)
	1 mile (5280 ft)	1609.34 m (exactly)
		1.60934 kilometers (km) (exactly)
Mass (weight):	1 ounce, avoirdupois	23.3495 grams (gr)
	1 pound (lb), avoirdupois	453.59237 gr (exactly)
		0.45359237 kilograms (kg) (exactly)
	1 ton, net or short (2000 lb)	907.18474 kg
		0.90718474 metric ton
Area:	1 square inch (in^2)	6.4516 cm^2 (exactly)
	1 square foot (ft^2)	0.092903 m^2 (exactly)
	1 square yard (yd^2)	0.836127 m^2
	1 acre (43,560 ft^2)	4046.856 m^2
		0.4046856 hectares (ha)
	1 square mile	258.9975 ha
		2.589975 km^2
Volume:	1 cubic inch (in^3)	16.38706 cm^3
	1 cubic foot (ft^3)	0.028317 m^3
	1 cubic yard (yd^3)	0.764555 m^3
	1 gallon (U.S.)	3.785 liters (L)
	1 liquid quart (U.S.)	0.946 L
	1 liquid ounce (U.S.)	29.573 milliliters (ml)

Temperature: 1 degree Fahrenheit equals 5/9 (.555555) degree Celsius (centigrade). To convert a temperature in degrees Fahrenheit to the equivalent temperature in Celsius, subtract 32 and divide by 1.8:
degrees C = (degrees F − 32)/1.8

METRIC TO ENGLISH

	Metric	English
Length:	1 centimeter (cm)	0.393701 in
	1 meter (m)	39.3701 in
		3.28084 ft
		1.09361 yd
	1 kilometer (km)	3280.84 ft
		0.62137 mile

METRIC TO ENGLISH

Metric	English
Mass (weight): 1 gram (gr)	0.042827 ounce, avoirdupois
1 kilogram (kg)	2.204623 lb
1 metric ton	1.10231 short tons
Area: 1 cm^2	0.155 in^2
1 m^2	10.7639 ft^2
	1.19599 yd^2
1 hectare	2.47105 acres
1 km^2	247.105 acres
	0.3861 mile^2
Volume: 1 cm^3	0.06102 in^3
1 m^3	35.3145 ft^3
	1.3079 yd^3
1 liter (L)	1.057 quarts
	0.2642 gallon (U.S.)
1 milliliter (ml)	0.0338 liquid ounce (U.S.)

Temperature: 1 degree Celsius (centigrade) equals 9/5 (1.8 exactly) degrees Fahrenheit. To convert a temperature in degrees Celsius to the equivalent temperature in Farhrenheit, multiply by 1.8 and then add 32:

degrees F = (degrees C $\times$ 1.8) + 32

SELECTED MAJOR PIECES OF U.S. ENVIRONMENTAL LEGISLATION

This appendix briefly lists, in chronological order, some of the *major* pieces of U.S. federal environmental legislation since the middle of the nineteenth century. This list is not meant to be comprehensive or all-inclusive; in particular, it does not include many minor acts, amendments, reauthorizations, expirations, and repeals of acts. A review of this list will provide an overview of the development of U.S. governmental concerns about the environment at a national level.

- *Railroad Acts of the 1850s and 1860s.* Large tracts of land granted to railroad companies to encourage the building of railroad lines across the country.
- *Homestead Act of 1862.* Qualified settlers in the Great Plains area and elsewhere would receive 160 acres (64.75 hectares) free of charge.
- *Mining Act of 1872.* Prospectors and mining companies can stake claims and purchase ("patent") public lands for very small fees. The act was passed to encourage the exploration and development of the western frontier.
- *Timber Culture Act of 1873.* Gave 160 acres (64.75 hectares) of western lands away to anyone who would plant trees on 40 of the acres (16.2 hectares).
- *Forest Reserve Act of 1891.* The president can establish forest reserves, later to be national forests, on public lands.
- *Forest Management Act of 1897.* Clarified the concept of forest reserves—uses of the forest include preservation, watershed protection, and timber growing—and authorized sales of timber.
- *River and Harbor Act of 1899.* Established the legal basis for banning the pollution of navigable waterways.
- *Lacey Act of 1900.* Interstate shipment of game killed in violation of state laws is a federal offense.
- *Reclamation (Newlands) Act of 1902.* Establishes the Bureau of Reclamation in the Department of the Interior.
- *Antiquities Act of 1906.* Areas of scientific and/or historic interest on federal lands can be reserved as national monuments.
- *Weeks Act of 1911.* Purchases of forested land at the headwaters of navigable streams to be included in the National Forest System—This allowed the founding of national forests in the East.
- *Public Health Service Act of 1912.* Authorized investigations of water pollution related to disease and public health.
- *National Park Service Act of 1916.* Established the National Park Service.
- *Migratory Bird Treaty Act of 1918.* Imposed restrictions on the hunting of migratory birds.
- *Mineral Leasing Act of 1920.* Regulation of mining on federal lands.
- *Federal Water Power Act of 1920.* Authorized Federal Power Commission to issue licenses for hydropower.
- *Oil Pollution Act of 1924.* Prohibited oil discharges in coastal waters.
- *Clarke-McNary Act of 1924.* Extended federal ability to buy lands for National Forest System; encouraged cooperation among federal, state, and private sectors in forest management.
- *McSweeney-McNary Act of 1928.* Authorized federal forestry research program.
- *Taylor Grazing Act of 1934.* Gave the Secretary of the Interior power to create grazing districts, issue grazing permits, and collect grazing fees on public domain lands.
- *Soil Conservation Act of 1935.* Established the Soil Conservation Service in the Department of Agriculture; erosion control measures addressed.
- *Omnibus Flood Control Act of 1936.* Established national flood prevention policy.
- *Federal Aid in Wildlife Restoration (Pittman-Robertson) Act of 1937.* Federal funds for wildlife protection made available to states.

- *Federal Food, Drug, and Cosmetic Act of 1938.* Quality protection of consumer foods, drugs, and cosmetics.
- *Public Health Services Act of 1944.* Regulated biological products.
- *Federal Insecticide, Fungicide, and Rodenticide Act of 1947.* Protection of farmers and others from dangerous and ineffective pesticides. Amended in the 1970s.
- *Atomic Energy Act of 1946.* Primarily concerned with the development of better weapons.
- *Federal Water Pollution Control Law of 1948.* Regulation of waste disposal.
- *Dangerous Cargo Act of 1952.* Regulation of the shipment of toxic substances.
- *Atomic Energy Act of 1954.* Development of nuclear power generation; regulation of radioactive materials.
- *Water Pollution Control Act of 1956.* Federal grants for water treatment plants.
- *Price-Anderson Act of 1957.* Limited the liability of both the owner of a nuclear power plant and the government to a fraction of the potential claims in case of a major accident.
- *Poultry Products Inspection Act of 1957.* Regulation of poultry food and feed, and color additives and pesticide residues in poultry.
- *Multiple Use and Sustained Yield Act of 1960.* Definition of purpose of national forests includes nonmaterial benefits.
- *Federal Hazardous Substances Act of 1960.* Requirements for labeling consumer products containing hazardous substances.
- *Clean Air Act of 1963.* Federal hearings on air quality.
- *Wilderness Act of 1964.* National Wilderness Preservation System established.
- *Federal Water Pollution Control Act (Clean Water Act) of 1964.* Restoration and maintenance of the country's waters. Amendments added in 1972 and 1977; programs reauthorized in 1986.
- *Land and Water Conservation Fund Act of 1965.* Money made available for local, state, and federal acquisition of open space and park land.
- *Solid Waste Disposal Act of 1965.* Established minimum federal guidelines for solid waste disposal.
- *National Historic Preservation Act of 1966.* Preservation of historic localities.
- *Endangered Species Act of 1966.* Federal government involved in rare species and habitat protection.
- *Animal Welfare Act of 1966.* Provided for humane transport and care of cats, dogs, and certain other animals.

- *Federal Meat Inspection Act of 1967.* Regulation of animal food and feed, and color additives and pesticide residues in meat.
- *National Wild and Scenic Rivers Act of 1968.* Identification of areas of scenic beauty for recreation and preservation.
- *National Trails System Act of 1968.* A complement to the National Wild and Scenic Rivers Act of 1968.
- *Clean Air Act of 1970.* Protection and enhancement of the quality of the nation's air resources. Amendments added in 1977 and 1990.
- *National Environmental Policy Act of 1969/1970.* Signed January 1, 1970. Established policies to prevent damage to the environment and to promote the health and welfare of humans; environmental impact statements required for large construction projects regulated, undertaken, or funded by the federal government. The act set up the Council on Environmental Quality as an independent agency in the White House. The Environmental Protection Agency (EPA) was also established by presidential order in 1970.
- *Resource Recovery Act of 1970.* Amendment to the Solid Waste Disposal Act of 1965; federal guidelines for waste disposal extended; waste minimization, recycling encouraged.
- *Egg Products Inspection Act of 1970.* Regulation of poultry food and feed, and color additives and pesticide residues in eggs.
- *Occupational Safety and Health Act of 1970.* Promotion of safe working conditions for all people.
- *Poison Prevention Act of 1970.* Special packaging of certain household substances required to protect children from injury by poisoning.
- *Alaska Native Claims Settlement Act of 1971.* Federal government can nominate lands of national interest for permanent protection.
- *Federal Environmental Pesticide Control Act of 1972.* Registration of pesticides using data from tests; registration not permitted if there is an unreasonable adverse risk to the environment.
- *Ocean Dumping Act of 1972; Marine Protection, Research, and Sanctuaries Act of 1972; Coastal Zone Management Act of 1972; Ports and Waterways Safety Act of 1972.* These acts help protect and regulate the oceans, coastal areas, and waterways.
- *Marine Mammal Protection Act of 1972.* For the protection, conservation, and encouragement of international research on marine mammals; established the Marine Mammal Commission.
- *Consumer Product Safety Act of 1972.* Protection

of consumers from hazardous products that pose an unreasonable risk of injury or illness.

- *Endangered Species Act of 1973.* Federal involvement in protecting endangered species extended.
- *Lead-Based Paint Poisoning Prevention Act of 1973.* Regulation of lead paint in toys, cooking and eating utensils, and other items.
- *Safe Drinking Water Act of 1974.* Ensures minimum standards and regulates contaminants in public water supplies.
- *Hazardous Materials Transportation Act of 1974.* Protection against risks involved in the transportation of hazardous materials.
- *Energy Policy and Conservation Act of 1975.* Energy conservation and efficiency measures promoted.
- *Toxic Substances Control Act of 1976.* Regulation of toxic substances exclusive of radioactive materials, pesticides, drugs, food additives, alcohol, and tobacco, which are regulated under other laws.
- *Federal Land Policy and Management Act of 1976.* Multiple-use concept of public lands under the control of the Bureau of Land Management.
- *Resource Conservation and Recovery Act of 1976.* "Cradle to grave" tracking system established as a way to attempt to control the disposal of hazardous waste; states encouraged to develop comprehensive solid waste management plans that may include waste minimization, resource recovery such as recycling, and conservation; government agencies directed or encouraged to buy products with a recycled content.
- *Noise Control Act of 1976.* Protection against noise levels that pose a jeopardy to health or human welfare.
- *Surface Mining Control and Reclamation Act of 1977.* Regulates surface mining and encourages reclamation of mined land.
- *Federal Mine Safety and Health Act of 1977.* Safety standards in mines.
- *National Energy Act of 1977.* Coal burning emphasized because coal was abundant in the United States, even though it is "dirty."
- *Uranium Mill Tailings Act of 1978.* Control of hazards from tailings sites.
- *Hazardous Liquid Pipeline Safety Act of 1979.* Regulation of pipeline transportation of hazardous liquids.

- *Comprehensive Environmental Response, Compensation, and Liability Act (Superfund) of 1980.* An act to clean up hazardous waste sites and spills; Superfund established for this purpose.
- *Alaska National Interest Lands Conservation Act of 1980.* Protected 104 million acres (42 million hectares).
- *Fish and Wildlife Conservation Act of 1980.* Nongame species protected.
- *Low-Level Radioactive Waste Policy Act of 1980.* Regulation of disposal of wastes that are contaminated with low levels of radioactivity.
- *Asbestos School Hazard Abatement Act of 1984.* Helps to defray the costs of dealing with asbestos in schools.
- *Superfund Amendments and Reauthorization Act (SARA) of 1986.* New cleanup standards for hazardous waste sites established, permanent cleanup emphasized, regulations of underground storage tanks.
- *Asbestos Hazard Emergency Response Act of 1986.* Strengthens EPA regulations concerning asbestos.
- *Emergency Planning and Community Right-to-Know Act of 1986.* Requires annual Toxics Release Inventory by major industries.
- *Clean Air Act Amendments of 1990.* Includes requirements to control the emission of sulfur dioxide and nitrogen oxides, which cause acid rain, as well as addressing the topics of urban smog, automobile emissions, toxic air pollution, and depletion of the ozone layer; selling and trading of air pollution credits/allowances established.
- *National Environmental Education Act of 1990.* Established a nonprofit national environmental education and training foundation and authorized the funding of educational programs especially for elementary and secondary school children.
- *Surface Transportation Act of 1991.* $151 billion transportation bill that encourages use of mass transit but gives states flexibility in how to spend federal transportation money.
- *Federal Michigan Scenic Rivers Act of 1992.* Protected 1000 miles (1600 km) of rivers in Michigan from development.

SELECTED PIECES OF INTERNATIONAL ENVIRONMENTAL LEGISLATION

This appendix provides a brief overview of the most important international conventions and agreements that form the basis of current international environmental law.

- *Convention Concerning the Protection of the World Cultural and Natural Heritage.* This international agreement was signed in Paris in 1972 for the purpose of preserving areas of cultural or natural "outstanding universal value" for posterity. Criteria for designating an area a World Natural Heritage Site include the presence of aesthetically outstanding or scientifically important features or areas that are home to threatened or endangered species of plants or animals. A World Heritage Committee decides on the areas to be listed under the convention. The nations signing the agreement promise to protect and preserve designated areas in their territory and also to honor and protect listed areas in other countries. Presumably, for instance, areas listed under the agreement would be sacrosanct even in time of war between adversaries that had signed the convention. The agreement also established a World Heritage Fund, with contributions from various countries, to assist in identifying and conserving important areas (especially in developing countries). Over 90 World National Heritage Sites have been designated in approximately 40 countries. Sites in the United States include Yellowstone National Park, Everglades National Park, Grand Canyon National Park, Redwood National Park, Great Smoky Mountains National Park, and Yosemite National Park. Thus, the United States has a legal obligation to preserve these areas not only for its own citizens, but also for the international community.
- *Convention on International Trade in Endangered Species of Wild Fauna and Flora (CITES).* CITES is an international agreement, dating back to 1973 (it first went into force in 1975 and has been amended several times since), that controls and monitors the international trade in endangered or threatened species of plants and animals (either whole organisms, parts of organisms, or products derived from the organisms). Under the convention, international imports and exports of various endangered, threatened, or potentially threatened species are tightly controlled and limited (in some cases, no trade in certain species is permitted). Countries abiding by CITES annually file reports on animal and plant imports and exports with the CITES organization, and CITES includes a scientific staff that works with governments to help them assess the status of various wild species with an eye to potential threats posed by trade in that species or products produced from it. Over a hundred nations participate in, and abide by the regulations of, CITES. Many experts consider CITES to be the most successful international agreement that has yet been produced for the preservation of wildlife.
- *Convention on Long-Range Transboundary Air Pollution (LRTAP).* LRTAP is an agreement that was initially adopted by various countries, mostly from Europe and North America, in 1979; it went into effect in 1983. Its primary purpose is to combat acid rain and other forms of international air pollution through mutual cooperation, exchange of information, research, and development of cleaner technologies.
- *Convention on the Conservation of Migratory Species of Wild Animals (Bonn Convention) or Migratory Species Convention.* This convention was formulated in Bonn, Germany, in 1979 and came into force in 1983. Its purpose is to protect endangered and threatened migratory species of animals, such as birds, that regularly cross national boundaries. Unfortunately, the effectiveness of the Migratory Species Convention is limited due to the small number of participating countries (less than three dozen).

- *Convention on the Law of the Sea (or Law of the Sea Convention, LOSC).* This is a United Nations (UN) treaty that was adopted in 1982 after decades of work, and the actual mandates of the convention do not go into force until various dates in the 1990s. Basically, this convention provides a legal framework for all international agreements and disputes regarding the oceans and seas, including the use of the oceans and their resources for all purposes, such as navigation, laying cables and pipelines, constructing artificial islands, dumping wastes, fishing, mining the oceans' floors for minerals, and the scientific study of the oceans. It defines what areas along the coasts fall under national jurisdiction, such as the continental shelves and various islands near the mainland, versus what areas come under international jurisdiction. This convention recognizes Exclusive Economic Zones (EEZs), which are areas extending from a nation's coast, usually about 200 nautical miles (230 standard miles, or 370.4 km) out, in which the nation claims sovereign territorial rights to exploit, preserve, and manage the natural resources of the local ocean area. The LOSC sets a general framework for defining rights and duties relative to the oceans, even within the EEZs in some cases, and ways to preserve the marine environment. Some observers have referred to the LOSC as a "constitution for the oceans." Unfortunately, the LOSC has not yet come into full force because it has not been ratified by the required number of nations worldwide.
- *Convention on the Prevention of Marine Pollution by Dumping of Waste and Other Matter (London Dumping Convention, LDC).* This agreement was adopted in London in 1972 and became effective in 1975. Its purpose is to control pollution of the oceans by the deliberate dumping of wastes (other than the disposal of wastes that is part of the normal operation of ships and aircrafts over the seas). Substances are classified according to the hazard they present to the oceans. Certain substances are absolutely prohibited from being dumped at sea; they include high-level radioactive wastes, substances containing certain heavy metals, various classes of toxic and hazardous wastes, certain types of synthetic organic compounds, and so forth. The convention allows other substances, such as certain pesticide by-products and organic waste compounds, to be dumped by permit. Other clauses cover monitoring and research on waste disposal in the oceans, promotion of marine antipollution techniques, and methods of handling mining debris resulting from the mining of the seabed. The most notable disagreements among the nations participating in the LDC revolve around the topics of whether, and how much, incineration at sea should be allowed and whether any radioactive wastes (low-level or high-level) should be dumped at sea.
- *Convention on Wetlands of International Importance, Especially as Waterfowl Habitat (Ramsar Convention or Wetlands Convention).* This international agreement was adopted in Ramsar, Iran, in 1971 and went into force in 1975. Its basic purpose, as its title implies, is to preserve wetlands around the world, especially those that are important to migratory waterfowl. Under this convention, more than 500 areas have been designated as wetlands of international importance to be preserved. In the United States, for instance, the Everglades, Chesapeake Bay, and the Okefenokee (the well-known swamp in Georgia and Florida) have been so designated. While of obvious importance in protecting wetlands, the Ramsar Convention has come under some criticism from environmentalists for not providing clear guidelines for the selection, management, and preservation of wetlands.
- *Montreal Protocol on Substances That Deplete the Ozone Layer.* This international agreement was formulated in Montreal, Canada, in 1987 to phase out the production and release of CFCs and other substances that destroy the stratospheric ozone layer. In 1990 the Montreal Protocol was amended to speed up the phaseout. At this time a fund was also established to help finance the phaseout of ozone-depleting chemicals in developing countries. The Montreal Protocol and its subsequent amendments have been hailed by some as the best example to date of true international cooperation in addressing an environmental problem and taking definite action to correct the situation (see Chapter 18 for a fuller discussion of the efforts to save the ozone layer).

In addition to these relatively "hard" international agreements, there have also been a number of "soft" international legal instruments. Among the more historic and important documents in this category are the following:

- *Declaration of the Conference on the Human Environment (Stockholm Declaration).* This document resulted from the 1972 United Nations Conference on the Human Environment held in Stockholm. A nonbinding document, it has served as a guide to national and international efforts to protect the environment.

- *World Conservation Strategy.* In 1980 the International Union for Conservation of Nature and Natural Resources, in conjunction with the UN Environment Programme, the World Wildlife Fund, the Food and Agriculture Organization of the UN, and the United Nations Educational, Scientific, and Cultural Organization, published the report *World Conservation Strategy: Living Resource Conservation for Sustainable Development.* This influential document stressed human responsibility for actions that affect the environment and proposed three main resource conservation goals that humans should strive for: (1) maintenance of basic ecological processes and life-support systems, (2) preservation of genetic diversity among the world's organisms, and (3) the sustainable use of species and ecosystems. These goals were adopted by many nations and laid the groundwork for further developments along these lines.

- *World Charter for Nature.* This is a nonbinding international declaration of conservation principles adopted by the UN General Assembly in 1982.

- *Man and the Biosphere Program (MAB).* This international UN Program, established in 1970, is devoted to improving the relationship of humans to the natural environment. It includes scientific research, preservation, and training activities. A major focus of the program is biosphere reserves, protected areas that are set aside for the purpose of pursuing MAB's goal. A typical biosphere reserve consists of a core area composed of a natural ecosystem. Surrounding the core area is a buffer zone used for research and education; further from the core is a transition area that may contain human settlements and be used for recreational or other purposes. Several hundred biosphere reserves have been established in more than 70 different countries.

- *Brundtland Report.* In 1987 the World Commission on Environment and Development, chaired by Gro Harlem Brundtland of Norway, published its report entitled *Our Common Future* (which takes the form of an approximately 400-page book). This report was endorsed by the UN General Assembly and has been called one of the most important recent documents on the future of the world. It calls for a revival of economic growth, particularly in the developing countries, but such growth must take the form of sustainable development. It also calls for the equitable distribution of benefits around the world, such that the basic needs and aspirations of all peoples are fulfilled, the conservation of natural resources, progress toward the goal of a sustainable population level, the reorientation of technology to be environmentally friendly, and the combining of environmental and economic issues in decision making. The World Commission on Environment and Development was established by the UN in 1983 to report specifically on the topics covered in *Our Common Future;* with publication of the report, the commission ceased to exist. In 1988, however, the Centre for Our Common Future (headquartered in Geneva) was established to promote the goals articulated in *Our Common Future.*

SELECTED ENVIRONMENTAL ORGANIZATIONS

This appendix contains the names, addresses, and phone and fax numbers (where available) of selected organizations and United States government agencies that are concerned with various aspects of environmental issues. The nongovernmental organizations are listed first, followed by a list of governmental organizations. These listings are certainly not complete or comprehensive—there are literally thousands of organizations, large and small, concerned with various environmental issues—but they are representative. By contacting and networking with these and other organizations, you can learn more about environmental issues. Better yet, you will become involved!

Nongovernmental Organizations

Advocates for Youth
(formerly Center for Population Options)
1025 Vermont Avenue NW, Suite 200
Washington, DC 20005
Phone: 202-347-5700
Fax: 202-347-2263

Advocates for Youth works to increase the opportunities for and abilities of youth to make healthy decisions about sexuality. Since 1980, Advocates for Youth has provided information, education and advocacy to youth-serving agencies and professionals, policy makers and the media. [Quoted from the AFY mission statement.]

Air and Waste Management Association
One Gateway Center, 3rd Floor
Pittsburgh, PA 15222
Phone: 412-232-3444
Fax: 412-232-3450

Founded in 1907, the goal of the A&WMA is to work toward a cleaner environment. It does this by providing a neutral forum where all viewpoints (technical, scientific, economic, social, political, and public health) concerning environmental management issues, focussing on air, waste, and pollution prevention, receive equal consideration.

American Association for World Health
1129 20th Street NW, Suite 400
Washington, DC 20036
Phone: 202-466-5883
Fax: 202-466-5896

An organization that concentrates on health issues.

American Forestry Association
1516 P Street NW
Washington, DC 20005
Phone: 202-667-3300
Fax: 202-667-7751

An organization concerned with the conservation of soil and forests, and also air and water pollution issues.

American Lung Association
1740 Broadway
New York, NY 10019-4374
Phone: 800-LUNG-USA
Fax: 212-265-5642

The mission of the American Lung Association is to prevent lung disease and promote lung health. In this context, the ALA is concerned with the health effects of indoor and outdoor air pollution.

American Rivers, Inc.
801 Pennsylvania Avenue SE, Suite 400
Washington, DC 20036
Phone: 202-547-6900
Fax: 202-543-6142

A leading American river conservation organization, AR sponsors programs promoting the protection of America's most magnificent remaining wild rivers; the reform of hydropower policies, the protection and restoration of endangered fisheries, aquatic habitats, and natural floodplains; the reform of policies that "dewater" the rivers and streams of the American West; the clean-up of rivers and the protection of safe drinking water supplies; and the restoration of neglected rivers in metropolitan areas.

Bread for the World
1100 Wayne Avenue, Suite 1000
Silver Spring, MD 20910
Phone: 301-608-2400
Fax: 301-608-2401

Bread for the World is a Christian citizens movement that lobbies our nation's decision makers on policy issues related to hunger and poverty worldwide. The Bread for the World Institute does education and research related to hunger, including issues such as agriculture and food supply, debt, trade, economics, foreign aid, employment, sustainable development, and domestic hunger and poverty. [Description provided by BFTW.]

Center for Clean Air Policy
(formerly Center for Acid Rain and Clean Air Policy Analysis)
444 N. Capitol Street, Suite 602
Washington, DC 20001
Phone: 202-624-7709
Fax: 202-508-3829

The CCAP was established in 1985 by a group of governors to develop and promote innovative policy approaches to major state, federal, and international environmental and energy problems. The Center's work is guided by the belief that sound energy and environmental policy solutions serve both economic and environmental interests.

Center for Marine Conservation
(formerly Center for Environmental Education)
1725 DeSales Street NW, Suite 500
Washington, DC 20036
Phone: 202-429-5609
Fax: 202-872-0619

The Center for Marine Conservation, an education and advocacy group, is fighting to eliminate such problems as: overexploitation of fishes and other marine wildlife, physical alteration of marine ecosystems, and pollution in all forms.

Center for Science in the Public Interest
1875 Connecticut Avenue NW, Suite 300
Washington, DC 20009
Phone: 202-332-9110
Fax: 202-265-4954

An organization concerned with sustainable agriculture, food, nutrition, and alcohol; publishers of the *Nutrition Action Health Letter.*

Chesapeake Bay Foundation
162 Prince George Street
Annapolis, MD 21401
Phone: 410-268-8816
Fax: 410-268-6687

A nonprofit conservation organization working to save the Chesapeake Bay through programs in environmental education, environmental defense and promotion of wise environmental stewardship, and land conservation.

Citizens Clearinghouse for Hazardous Waste
P.O. Box 6806
Falls Church, VA 22040-6806
Phone: 703-237-2249
Fax: 703-237-7449

CCHW works "with grassroots community groups on a broad range of environmental issues, including toxic waste, solid waste, air pollution, incinerators, medical waste, radioactive waste, pesticides, sewage and industrial pollution." CCHW has "also begun to work with communities exploring environmentally sound economic development." [Quotations from a CCHW flyer.]

Clean Water Action
76 Summer Street
Boston, MA 02110
Phone: 617-423-4661
Fax: 617-423-4870

A group that works to affect change at the local, state, and national levels. As of 1995, CWA was focussing on the following types of issues: safe and affordable drinking water, mobilizing the "green" vote to elect "green" candidates, reduction of mercury and other heavy metals in waters, battery recycling, reductions in radioactive waste, creating sustainable jobs, and increasing energy conservation and the use of renewable energy sources.

Common Cause
2030 M Street NW
Washington, DC 20036
Phone: 202-833-1200
Fax: 202-659-3716

Common Cause is a nonpartisan citizens' lobbying group founded in 1970. It is "a leading force in the battle for honest and accountable government at the national, state, and local level." [Quoted from a Common Cause brochure.] CC priorities include: enactment of legislation to fundamentally reform congressional campaigns, upholding standards of ethics and making government officials accountable for their actions, and pressing for adherence to basic principles of civil and equal rights for all citizens.

Community Transportation Association of America
725 15th Street NW, Suite 900
Washington, DC 20005
Phone: 800-527-8279
Fax: [Not provided]

An organization that supplies technical assistance for specialized and rural transportation projects.

CONCERN, Inc.
1794 Columbia Road NW
Washington, DC 20009
Phone: 202-328-8160
Fax: 202-387-3378

CONCERN's mission is to broaden public participation in the protection of the environment. The goal is to promote environmental literacy and action by supplying citizens with the information they need to be effective advocates in their communities for policies and programs that improve environmental quality and public health. CONCERN is a non-profit environmental organization, founded in 1970 and based in Washington, DC. CONCERN's programs are funded by foundations, individual supporters and the sales of its publications. [Adapted from CONCERN's mission statement.]

Conservation International
1015 18th Street NW, Suite 1000
Washington, DC 20036
Phone: 202-429-5660; 1-800-406-2306
Fax: 202-887-5188

Conservation International (CI) is a field-based, non-profit membership organization working to preserve biological diversity and the ecological processes that sustain life on Earth. CI operates under the premise that because environmental degradation is motivated by economics, the solutions must also be economically-based. CI's solutions work because they save the natural world and better the lives of people throughout the developing world. [Description supplied by CI.]

Consumer Federation of America
1424 16th Street NW
Washington, DC 20036
Phone: 202-387-6121
Fax: [Not provided]

This is an advocacy group, composed of numerous individual consumer-related organizations, that deals with a number of issues, such as related to indoor air pollution and energy.

Critical Mass Energy Project
215 Pennsylvania Avenue SE
Washington, DC 20003
Phone: 202-546-4996
Fax: [Not provided]
(See Public Citizen)

Defenders of Wildlife
1101 14th Street NW, #1400
Washington, DC 20005-5601
Phone: 202-682-9400
Fax: 202-682-1331

A group that works to protect and enhance wildlife and their associated habitats.

Ducks Unlimited, Inc.
One Waterfowl Way
Memphis, TN 38120
Phone: 901-758-3825
Fax: [Not provided]

The mission of Ducks Unlimited is to fulfill the annual life cycle of North American waterfowl by protecting, enhancing, restoring and managing important wetlands and associated uplands. [Quoted from the DU mission statement.]

Earth First!
P.O. Box 5176
Missoula, MT 59806
Phone: 415-788-3666
Fax: [Not provided]

A movement that supports the preservation of wilderness and the intrinsic value of the Earth. Earth First! members often believe that it is essentially futile to work within "the system" (established governments and organizations) and therefore have been alleged to use extra-legal means (such as environmental sabotage) to further their goals.

Earth Island Institute
300 Broadway, Suite 28
San Francisco, CA 94133-3312
Phone: 415-788-3666
Fax: 415-788-7324

The Earth Island Institute is a network of innovative activists dedicated to the Earth and its diverse communities. EII projects focus on specific environmental threats and offer creative, effective solutions. EII publishes *Earth Island Journal*. [Adapted from an EII brochure.]

Earthwatch Expeditions, Inc.
680 Mount Auburn Street
P.O. Box 403
Watertown, MA 02272
Phone: 617-926-8200
Fax: 617-926-8532

Earthwatch, an international nonprofit organization founded in 1972, offers the public unique opportunities to work side-by-side with noted scientists on one-to-three week field research projects worldwide. These cultural and environmental research expeditions represent over twenty disciplines, and range from building solar ovens in Kenya to saving endangered sea turtles in the Caribbean. No special skills are necessary; all training is done in the field. Earthwatch expedition participants support the research and cover food and lodging with tax-deductible contributions ranging from $595 to $2,400. Airfare is additional. To date, over 40,000 people have worked on Earthwatch scientific research expeditions across the U.S. and around the world. [Description supplied by Earthwatch.]

Environmental Action Foundation
6930 Carroll Avenue, Suite 600
Takoma Park, MD 20912
Phone: 301-891-1100
Fax: 301-891-2218

Environmental Action Foundation is a non-profit national membership organization with an enduring mission to bring our society into greater harmony with ecological and social justice imperatives. Toward this end, EAF develops campaigns and projects that help a broad array of grassroots activists more effectively shape the communities where they live and work. [Description provided by EAF.]

Environmental Defense Fund, Inc.
257 Park Avenue S., 16th Floor
New York, NY 10010
Phone: 212-505-2100
Fax: 212-505-2375

An organization that works to develop economically viable solutions to environmental problems.

Environmental Law Institute
1616 P Street NW
Washington, DC 20036
Phone: 202-328-5150
Fax: 202-328-5002

An independent research and education center, the Environmental Law Institute advances environmental protection by improving law, policy, and management. ELI researches pressing problems, educates professionals and citizens about the nature of these issues, and convenes all sectors in forging effective solutions. [Description provided by ELI.]

Freedom from Hunger
1644 DaVinci Court
P.O. Box 2000
Davis, CA 95617
Phone: 916-758-6200
Fax: 916-758-6241

An organization devoted to the development of programs aimed at the elimination of hunger around the world. Freedom from Hunger develops innovative programs for eliminating chronic hunger by providing resources and information that empowers families and communities to help themselves. To help the rural hungry in developing countries make choices that will move them beyond hunger, FFH supports programs that provide very poor women with cash credit through poverty lending for income-generating activities that are linked to participatory adult education. These Credit with Education programs, in turn, result in overall improvement in health and nutrition, birth spacing, food production and storage, and better management of small businesses. FFH provides technical and financial support to local organizations to help them develop and expand Credit with Education programs which are currently operating in Bolivia, Burkina Faso, Ghana, Honduras, Mali, Thailand, Togo, and Uganda. [Description provided by FFH.]

Friends of the Earth
1025 Vermont Avenue NW, 3rd Floor
Washington, DC 20005
Phone: 202-783-7400
Fax: 202-783-0444

Friends of the Earth is committed to global advocacy on behalf of the planet. FOE is distinguished by its international approach to global problems, such as ozone depletion, drinking water contamination and disposal of hazardous wastes, and its forthright advocacy work on Capitol Hill on behalf of its members and grassroots citizens' groups nationwide. [Description adapted from a statement by FOE.]

The Green Center
(formerly the New Alchemy Institute)
237 Hatchville Road
East Falmouth, MA 02536
Phone: 508-564-6301
Fax: None

The Green Center, Inc., on Cape Cod is a non-profit educational institute with the following primary goals: creation of ecologically derived forms of energy, agriculture, aquaculture, housing, and landscapes. The ultimate goal is to live in harmony with nature.

Greenpeace USA
1436 U Street NW
Washington, DC 20009
Phone: 202-462-1177
Fax: 202-462-4507

An international activist organization concerned with such issues as disarmament, pollution, hazardous wastes, and protection of the oceans.

Habitat for Humanity International
121 Habitat Street
Americus, GA 31709
Phone: 912-924-6935; 1-800-HABITAT
Fax: 912-924-6541

Habitat for Humanity International (HFHI) is a nonprofit, ecumenical Christian housing ministry. HFHI seeks to eliminate poverty housing and homelessness from the world, and to make decent shelter a matter of conscience and action. Habitat invites people from all walks of life to work together in partnership to help build houses with families in need. [Description quoted from an HFHI fact sheet.]

Institute for Local Self-Reliance
2425 18th Street NW
Washington, DC 20009
Phone: 202-232-4108
Fax: 202-332-0463

The Institute for Local Self-Reliance is a research, education, and technical assistance organization that focuses on environmentally sound economic development practices for U.S. urban and rural communities. [Description supplied by ILSR.]

International Planned Parenthood Federation
902 Broadway, 10th Floor
New York, NY 10010
Phone: 212-995-8800
Fax: 212-995-0225

IPPF is a multi-cultural, multi-lingual organization which provides technical assistance and financial support, helps facilitate information sharing, and advocates family planning rights on a regional and international level on behalf of its affiliates. [Quoted from an IPPF brochure.]

Izaak Walton League of America
707 Conservation Lane
Gaitherburg, MD 20878-2983
Phone: 301-548-0150
Fax: 301-548-0146

Established in 1922 by a group of concerned anglers, the respected Izaak Walton League of America (IWLA) is a national non-profit organization whose 53,000 members protect and enjoy the nation's soil, air, woods, waters, and wildlife. [Quoted from an IWLA brochure.]

Land Trust Alliance
1319 F Street NW, Suite 501
Washington, DC 20004
Phone: 202-638-4725
Fax: 202-638-4730

An organization that works with local and regional land trusts to help them preserve open space and natural habitats.

League of Conservation Voters
1707 L Street NW, Suite 750
Washington, DC 20036
Phone: 202-785-8683
Fax: 202-835-0491

The League of Conservation Voters is the bipartisan political action arm of the U.S. environmental movement. LCV helps elect members of Congress who will vote for the Earth, and produces the National Environmental Scorecard to hold them accountable. [Description provided by LCV.]

League of Women Voters Education Fund
1730 M Street NW
Washington, DC 20036
Phone: 202-429-1965
Fax: 202-429-0854

There are two branches of the League of Women Voters. League of Women Voters in U.S. is an advocacy organization which has historically been involved in environmental policy issues, among other things. The League of Women Voters Education Fund encourages the informed participation of citizens in government and works to increase understanding of public policy issues including nuclear energy waste disposal, conserving resources, and other environmental issues.

National Audubon Society
700 Broadway
New York, NY 10003-9501
Phone: 212-979-3000
Fax: 212-979-3188

Operates dozens of wildlife sanctuaries across the United States and supports a wide range of environmental and educational activities.

National Park Foundation
1101 17th Street NW, Suite 1102
Washington, DC 20036-4704
Phone: 202-785-4500
Fax: 202-785-3539

The National Park Foundation is the official nonprofit partner of the National Park Service. Dedicated to helping meet the needs of the country's 369 national parks, the Foundation was chartered by Congress in 1967 to channel private resources into the parks. The Foundation awards more than $2 million each year to support education, visitor services, NPS employees, and volunteer activities to preserve and enhance the parks. [Adapted from a description supplied by NPF.]

National Parks and Conservation Association
1776 Massachusetts Avenue NW
Washington, DC 20036
Phone: 202-223-6722
Fax: 202-659-0650

NPCA is a national nonprofit citizen organization dedicated to defending and improving the National Park System, as well as educating Americans about the National Park System. [Adapted from a NPCA flyer.]

National Wildlife Federation
1400 16th Street NW
Washington, DC 20036
Phone: 202-797-6800
Fax: 202-797-6646

A private conservation organization whose primary goal is education. NWF sponsors a conservation internship program directly primarily at recent college graduates.

Natural Resources Defense Council
40 West 20th Street
New York, NY 10011
Phone: 212-727-2700
Fax: 212-727-1773

NRDC, with 170,000 members worldwide, works to preserve the environment, protect the public health, and ensure the conservation of wilderness and natural resources. NRDC pursues its goals through research, advocacy, litigation and public education. Program areas include public health (air and water pollution, pesticide safety, environmental justice, urban environments); resource conservation (coastal protection, energy conservation, public lands protection); and stemming the proliferation of nuclear weapons. [Description provided by NRDC.]

Oxfam America
115 Broadway
Boston, MA 02116
Phone: 617-482-1211
Fax: [Not provided]

An organization that provides funding for projects that benefit poor persons around the world.

Physicians for Social Responsibility
1101 Fourteenth Street NW, Suite 700
Washington, DC 20005
Phone: 202-898-0150
Fax: 202-898-0172

Physicians for Social Responsibility is a leading organization of nearly 20,000 health professionals and supporters working in 80 U.S. chapters to reduce weapons of mass destruction, promote a sustainable environment, and address the root causes of violence, especially handgun violence. [Description supplied by PFSR.]

Planet Drum Foundation

P.O. Box 31251
San Francisco, CA 94131
Phone: 415-285-6556
Fax: 415-285-6563

Planet Drum was founded in 1973 to provide an effective grassroots approach to ecology that emphasizes sustainability, community self-determination and regional self-reliance. In association with community activists and ecologists, Planet Drum developed the concept of a bioregion: a distinct area with coherent and interconnected plant and animal communities, and natural systems, often defined by a water-shed. A bioregion is a whole "life-place" with unique requirements for human inhabitation so that it will not be disrupted and injured. Through its projects, Planet Drum helps local organizations and individuals find ways to live within the natural confines of bioregions. [Quoted from a PD brochure.]

Planned Parenthood Federation of America, Inc.

810 Seventh Avenue
New York, NY 10019-5882
Phone: 212-541-7800
Fax: 212-245-1845

The mission of Planned Parenthood is: to provide comprehensive reproductive and complementary health care services in settings which preserve and protect the essential privacy and rights of each individual; to advocate public policies which guarantee these rights and ensure access to such services; to provide educational programs which enhance understanding of individual and societal implications of human sexuality; to promote research and the advancement of technology in reproductive health care and encourage understanding of their inherent bioethical, behavioral, and social implications. [Quoted from the mission statement of PP.]

Population Action International

(formerly Population Crisis Committee)
Population and Environment Program
1120 19th Street NW, Suite 550
Washington, DC 20036
Phone: 202-659-1833
Fax: 202-293-1795

Population Action International works for universal access to family planning and reproductive health services for women and men and for early stabilization of world population. PAI seeks to develop and strengthen the commitment of governments to increased financial assistance for high quality, voluntary family planning and related programs in developing countries. PAI carries out its mission through broad dissemination of policy-oriented educational materials to decisionmakers, the media, and the general public. [Statement supplied by PAI.]

The Population Institute

107 2nd Street NE
Washington, DC 20002
Phone: 202-544-3300
Fax: 202-544-0068

An educational and public policy organization concerned with population growth, especially in the developing countries.

Population Reference Bureau

1875 Connecticut Avenue NW, Suite 520
Washington, DC 20009-5728
Phone: 202-483-1100
Fax: 202-328-3937

The Population Reference Bureau, Inc., is a leader in providing timely, objective information on U.S. and international population trends. PRB informs policymakers, educators, the media, and concerned citizens working in the public interest around the world through a broad range of activities including publications, information services, seminars and workshops, and technical support. PRB is a nonprofit, nonadvocacy organization. PRB efforts are supported by government contracts, foundation grants, individual and corporate contributions, and the sale of publications. [Description provided by PRB.]

Population Resource Center
1725 K Street NW
Washington, DC 20006
Phone: 202-467-5030
Fax: 202-467-5034

An organization that provides information, briefings, and seminars on population issues, both domestic and international.

Public Citizen
1600 20th Street, NW
Washington, DC 20009
Phone: 202-546-4996
Fax: 202-547-7392

Founded in 1971 by Ralph Nader, this political action organization has a number of suborganizations, including: Buyers Up, Congress Watch, Critical Mass, Health Research Group, and Litigation Group. The Critical Mass Energy Project advocates decreasing the reliance on nuclear and fossil fuels in order to promote safe, environmentally sound energy alternatives.

Public Interest Research Group (PIRG)
(See U.S. Public Interest Research Group)

Rachel Carson Council, Inc.
8940 Jones Mill Road
Chevy Chase, MD 20815
Phone: 301-652-1877
Fax: 301-951-7179

Rachel Carson Council is a non-profit environmental organization that focuses on chemical contaminants, especially pesticides. [Statement provided by RCC.]

Rainforest Action Network
450 Sansome Street, Suite 700
San Francisco, CA 94553
Phone: 415-398-4404
Fax: 415-398-2732

The Rainforest Action Network (RAN) works to protect the Earth's rainforests and support the rights of their inhabitants through education, grassroots organizing, and non-violent direct action. [Description supplied by RAN.]

Rainforest Alliance
65 Bleecker Street, 6th Floor
New York, NY 10012-2420
Phone: 212-677-1900
Fax: 212-677-2187

The Rainforest Alliance is an international nonprofit organization dedicated to the conservation of tropical forests for the benefit of the global community. The mission of RA is to develop and promote the economically viable and socially desirable alternatives to the destruction of this endangered, biologically diverse natural resource. This mission is pursued through education, research in the social and natural sciences, and the establishment of cooperative partnerships with business, governments, and local peoples. [Description supplied by RA.]

Renew America
1400 16th Street NW, Suite 710
Washington, DC 20036
Phone: 202-232-2252
Fax: 202-232-2617

Renew America coordinates a network of community groups, environmental organizations, businesses, governmental leaders and civic activists involved in environmental improvement. Founded in 1979, RA seeks out and promotes exemplary environmental programs, offering positive, constructive models to help inspire communities and businesses to meet environmental challenges. [Description supplied by RA.]

Resources for the Future
1616 P Street NW
Washington, DC 20036-1400
Phone: 202-328-5000
Fax: 202-939-3460

Resources for the Future (RFF) is an independent nonprofit organization engaged in research and public education on natural resources and environmental issues. Its mission is to create and disseminate knowledge that helps people to make better decisions about the conservation and use of their natural resources and the environment. [Quoted from RFF 1994 Annual Report.]

Rocky Mountain Institute
1739 Snowmass Creek Road
Snowmass, CO 81654-9199
Phone: 970-927-3851
Fax: 970-927-4178

The Rocky Mountain Institute is a nonprofit research and educational foundation that educates and informs the general public and private sector about energy and explains the hidden connections between resource efficiency and national security, economic renewal, and environmental well-being. Its mission is to foster the efficient and sustainable use of resources as a path to global security. The Institute creates and helps individuals and the private sector to practice new solutions to old problems—mainly be harnessing the problem-solving power of market economics and of advanced techniques for resource efficiency. [Description supplied by RMI.]

Rodale Institute
222 Main Street
Emmaus, PA 18098
Phone: 610-967-8405
Fax: 610-967-8959

Rodale Institute works with people worldwide to achieve a regenerative food system that renews environmental and human health. RI programs aim to find agricultural solutions to hunger, malnutrition, disease, and soil degradation. RI encourages growing organic food using regenerative principles. RI places primary emphasis on information exchange to affect changes in behavior, conditions, and thinking. Using education, communication, and research, RI shares success stories wherever RI finds them with farmers, consumers, food industry leaders, policymakers, and youth—the most powerful potential agents for change. [Adapted from the RI mission statement.]

Sea Shepherd Conservation Society
3107A Washington Boulevard
Marina del Rey, CA 90292
Phone: 310-301-7325
Fax: 310-574-3161

The Sea Shepherd Conservation Society is a non-profit organization involved with the investigation and documentation of violations of international laws, regulations, and treaties protecting marine wildlife species. The Society is committed to the goal of stopping illegal activities that are decimating marine species. Sea Shepherd is very concerned about protecting whales, dolphins, seals, and all other marine species, and strives to ensure that the heritage of our children's children will include these magnificent creatures. [Description supplied by SSCS.]

Sierra Club
730 Polk Street
San Francisco, CA 94109
Phone: 415-776-2211
Fax: [Not Provided]

The Sierra Club's Statement of Purpose is: "To explore, enjoy and protect the wild places of the Earth; to practice and promote the responsible use of the Earth's ecosystems and resources; to enhance and enlist humanity to protect and restore the quality of the natural and human environment; and to use all lawful means to carry out these objectives." [Description provided by SC.] The Sierra Club was established in 1892 and John Muir served as its first president.

Social Investment Forum
430 First Avenue North, Suite 290
Minneapolis, MN 55401
Phone: 612-333-8338
Fax: [Not provided]

A professional association for financial planners, investment advisors, fund managers, and others involved in investing, which helped to develop, and encourages, socially responsible investment.

Student Conservation Association, Inc.
P.O. Box 550
Charlestown, NH 03603-0550
Phone: 603-543-1700
Fax: 603-543-1828

The Student Conservation Association is the oldest and largest organization of its kind. Each year it sends nearly 2,000 students and adults into National Parks, Forests, Wildlife Refuges, and other natural areas to conduct professional-level conservation work. Projects include wildlife research, back-country patrol, habitat restoration, cultural resource management, cartography, interpretation, and much more. [Description supplied by SCA.]

Trust for Public Land
National Office
116 New Montgomery, 4th Floor
San Francisco, CA 94105
Phone: 415-495-4014
Fax: 415-495-4103

The Trust for Public Land is dedicated to protecting and preserving special lands and places throughout the United States, including saving threatened open spaces; creating parks, playgrounds, gardens, and greenways; and preserving historic places.

Union of Concerned Scientists
1616 P Street NW, Suite 310
Washington, DC 20036
Phone: 202-332-0900
Fax: 202-332-0905

The Union of Concerned Scientists is dedicated to advancing responsible public policies in areas where technology plays a critical role. Established in 1969, UCS has created a unique alliance between many of the nation's leading scientists and thousands of committed citizens. This partnership addresses the most serious environmental and security threats facing humanity. UCS is currently working to encourage responsible stewardship of the global environment and life-sustaining resources; promote energy technologies that are renewable, safe, and cost effective; reform transportation policy; advance sustainable agricultural practices; and curtail weapons proliferation. An independent non-profit organization, UCS conducts technical studies and public education, and seeks to influence government policy at the local, state, and international levels. [Description supplied by UCS.]

United Nations Environment Programme
(See under governmental listings.)

U.S. Public Interest Research Group (PIRG)
218 D Street SE
Washington, DC 20003
Phone: 202-546-9707
Fax: 202-546-2461

U.S. PIRG is the national legislative office of the State Public Interest Research Groups. PIRGs are non-profit, non-partisan organizations active in more than 30 states and on more than 100 college campuses. The PIRGs conduct research, public education and grassroots organizing along with lobbying in such areas as clean water, safe drinking water, pesticide reform, toxics use reduction, solid waste and energy policy. In addition to U.S. PIRG's environmental agenda, PIRGs are also active in areas of consumer protection and good government. [Description provided by U.S. PIRG.]

Water Environment Federation
601 Wythe Street
Alexandria, VA 22314-1994
Phone: 703-684-2400
Fax: 703-684-2492
A not-for-profit technical and educational organization, founded in 1928, dedicated to preserving and enhancing the global water environment.

The Wilderness Society
900 17th Street NW
Washington, DC 20006-2596
Phone: 202-833-2300
Fax: 202-429-3957
The Wilderness Society, founded in 1935, is a nonprofit membership organization devoted to preserving wilderness and wildlife, protecting America's prime forests, parks, rivers, deserts, and shorelands and to fostering an American Land Ethic. [Statement provided by WS.]

Wildlife Habitat Council
1010 Wayne Avenue, Suite 920
Silver Spring, MD 20910
Phone: 301-588-8994
Fax: 301-588-4629
The Wildlife Habitat Council is a non-profit, non-lobbying organization dedicated to the enhancement and preservation of wildlife habitats internationally. WHC works with companies, conservation groups, and communities to create solutions that balance the demands of economic growth with the requirements of a healthy and diversely endowed environment. [Description provided by WHC.]

Wildlife Management Institute
1101 14th Street NW, Suite 801
Washington, DC 20005
Phone: 202-371-1808
Fax: 202-408-5059
The Wildlife Management Institute is a private, nonprofit, scientific and educational organization dedicated to the restoration, sound management and wise use of natural resources in North America. It was founded in 1911 by farsighted businessmen/sportsmen concerned that wildlife was in serious trouble. [Quoted from a WMI brochure.]

Wildlife Society
5410 Grosvenor Lane
Bethesda, MD 20814-2197
Phone: 301-897-9770
Fax: 301-530-2471
The Wildlife Society is an international non-profit scientific and educational organization serving 9,400 professionals in all areas of wildlife conservation and resource management. The mission of The Wildlife Society is to enhance the scientific, technical, managerial, and educational capability of wildlife professionals in conserving diversity, sustaining productivity, and ensuring sound use of wildlife resources for the benefit of society. [Description provided by WS.]

World Resources Institute
1709 New York Avenue NW, Suite 700
Washington, DC 20006
Phone: 202-638-6300
Fax: [Not provided]

A research center that focuses on environmental and developmental issues. World Resources Institute publishes the standard reference *World Resources* biennially.

World Wildlife Fund
1250 24th Street NW
Washington, DC 20037-1175
Phone: [Not provided]
Fax: [Not provided]

World Wildlife Fund leads worldwide efforts to protect endangered wildlife and wildlands. WWF is the U.S. affiliate of the international WWF network, which has national organizations or representatives in more than 50 countries and works in more than 100 countries throughout the world. [Quoted from WWF flyer.]

Worldwatch Institute
1776 Massachusetts Avenue NW
Washington, DC 20036
Phone: 202-452-1999
Fax: 202-296-7365

Worldwatch Institute is a nonprofit, public-interest research institute concentrating on global environmental and environmentally related issues. Founded in 1974, the goal of the Institute is to raise public awareness of global environmental and environmentally related threats to the level where it will support an effective public policy response. Worldwatch produces many publications, including the annual *State of the World* and *Vital Signs* reports. [Description summarized from information provided by Worldwatch.]

WorldWIDE Network
1627 K Street NW, Suite 300
Washington, DC 20006
Phone: 202-347-1514
Fax: 202-496-0552

WorldWIDE (World Women in Development and Environment) Network, based in Washington, D.C., is an international, non-profit organization established in 1981 to help women at all levels of society participate in the protection of the environment and the promotion of sustainable development. WorldWIDE has an active Board of Trustees, National and International Advisory Councils, as well as a global network of women in the international arena who are concerned about environmental issues. [Description supplied by WorldWIDE.]

Zero Population Growth
1400 16th Street NW, Suite 320
Washington, DC 20036
Phone: 202-332-2200
Fax: 202-332-2302

The goal of Zero Population Growth "is to stop global population growth and overconsumption of our natural resources by changing U.S. public policies, attitudes and behavior." [Quoted from ZPG's "Statement of Policy" as revised May 4, 1991.]

Governmental Agencies

Bureau of the Census
U.S. Department of Commerce
Washington, DC 20233
Phone: 301-457-2422 (Phone number for population information)
Fax: 301-457-4714 (General fax number)

The primary source of information on the demography of the United States.

Bureau of Land Management

Public Affairs Office
U.S. Department of the Interior
1849 C Street NW
Washington, DC 20240
Phone: 202-452-5125
Fax: 202-452-5124

The Bureau of Land Management (BLM) is responsible for managing approximately 270 million acres of public land that are owned by the American people. [Statement supplied by BLM.]

Bureau of Mines

U.S. Department of the Interior
810 7th Street, NW., MS 1040
Washington, DC 20241
Phone: 202-501-9649
Fax: 202-219-2493

The U.S. Bureau of Mines (USBM) was founded in 1910 to address high death and injury rates among miners. Its mission was later expanded to include developing mining, metallurgical, and reclamation technologies; collecting statistics on mineral production and consumption; assessing mineral resources on Federal lands; and tracking the worldwide availability of minerals. [Description supplied by USBM.]

Bureau of Reclamation

U.S. Department of the Interior
Office of Public Affairs
18th and C Streets, NW
Washington, DC 20240
Phone: 202-208-4662
Fax: 202-208-3484

The Bureau of Reclamation is primarily a water conservation agency serving the Western states.

Council on Environmental Quality

Executive Office of the President
Old Executive Office Building, Room 360
Washington, D. C. 20501
Phone: 202-456-6224
Fax: 202-456-2710

Established by congress as part of the National Environmental Policy Act (1969), the Council on Environmental Quality oversees federal agency implementation of environmental impact assessment processes, acts as a referee in interagency disputes regarding environmental issues, provides advice to the President on environmental matters, and helps to lead interagency decision making that affects the environment. The Council does not administer specific environmental programs or execute environmental policy.

Department of Agriculture

14th and Independence Avenue SW
Washington, DC 20250
(See also listings for Forest Service and Soil Conservation Service.)

Department of Energy

Forrestal Building
1000 Independence Avenue SW
Washington, DC 20585
(See also the next listing.)

Department of Energy
Environmental Sciences Division
Office of Health and Environmental Research
Office of Energy Research
19901 Germantown Road
Germantown, MD 20874
Phone: 301-903-4902
Fax: 301-903-8519

Supports research and publishes information on a number of health related and environmental topics.

Environmental Protection Agency
Public Information Center
401 M Street NW
Washington, DC 20460
Phone: 202-260-2080
Fax: 202-260-6257

The Public Information Center provides non-technical information about environmental issues and the Environmental Protection Agency. Information is available on drinking water, air quality, pesticides, radon, indoor air, Superfund, water quality, and many other environmental topics. [Description supplied by PIC, EPA.]

Fish and Wildlife Service
U.S. Department of the Interior
1849 C Street NW
Washington, DC 20240
Phone: 202-208-4131
Fax: 202-208-7407

The mission of the U.S. Fish and Wildlife Service is to conserve, protect, and enhance fish and wildlife and their habitats for the continuing benefit of the American people. [Statement supplied by the FWS.]

Food and Drug Administration
U.S. Department of Health and Human Services
5600 Fishers Lane
Rockville, MD 20879
Phone: 1-800-532-4440
Fax: 301-443-9767

The mission of the FDA is to protect the public health; this is accomplished through inspection, regulation, and oversight of various aspects of the food supply, drugs, medical devices, and cosmetics.

Forest Service
U.S. Department of Agriculture
14th and Independence Avenue, SW
P.O. Box 96090
Washington, DC 20090-6090
Phone: 202-205-1760
Fax: 202-205-0885

This agency oversees the use, protection, and management of national forests, rangelands, and grasslands.

Geological Survey
U.S. Department of the Interior
Earth Science Information Center
507 National Center
Reston, VA 22092
Phone: 703-648-6045
Fax: 703-648-5548

The United States Geological Survey (USGS) was established by an act of Congress in 1879 to conduct scientific and systematic "classification of the public lands, and examination of the geological structure, mineral resources, and products of the national domain." Since that time the USGS has been collecting, analyzing, and publishing information about the country's land, mineral, and water resources. [Description adapted from information supplied by the USGS.]

National Oceanic and Atmospheric Administration

Office of Public and Constituent Affairs
14th Street and Constitution Avenue NW, Room 6013
Washington, DC 20230
Phone: 202-482-6090
Fax: 202-482-3154

NOAA is the nation's premier agency studying the oceans, the atmosphere, and their interactions. [Statement supplied by NOAA.]

National Park Foundation

(See National Park Foundation under Nongovernmental Organizations)

National Park Service

Office of Public Affairs
U.S. Department of the Interior
P.O. Box 37127 (Room 3424)
Washington, DC 20013-7127
Phone: 202-208-6843
Fax: 202-219-0910

The National Park Service manages 369 sites covering more than 80 million acres in 49 states, the District of Columbia, American Samoa, Guam, Puerto Rico, Saipan, and the Virgin Islands. [Statement supplied by the NPS.]

National Response Center

(formerly National Response Center for Water Pollution)
2100 2nd Street SW
Room 2611, (G-OFP-2)
Washington, DC 20593-0001
Phone: 1-800-424-2165
Fax: 202-267-2165

The National Response Center is the sole national point of contact for the initial reporting of oil and chemical/hazardous materials discharges, and biological, radiological and etiological incidents. The NRC does not actually respond to any incident—it collates information and provides immediate incident notifications to federal and state agencies that do respond near the incident site. [Description supplied by the NRC.]

Nuclear Regulatory Commission

Office of Public Affairs
Washington, DC 20555
Phone: 301-415-8200
Fax: 301-415-2234

The Nuclear Regulatory Commission is involved with many aspects of the construction and operation of nuclear power plants/facilities and related issues, including licensing, inspection and enforcement of safety regulations, and regulatory research and standards development.

Occupational Safety and Health Administration

U.S. Department of Labor
200 Constitution Avenue, NW, Room N3647
Washington, DC 20210
Phone: 202-219-8615
Fax: 202-219-5986

OSHA is responsible for assuring that every working American has safe and healthful working conditions. [Statement supplied by OSHA.]

Smithsonian Institution

Office of Environmental Awareness
S. Dillon Ripley Center, Suite 3123
Washington, DC 20560
Phone: 202-357-4797
Fax: [Not provided]

The Smithsonian Institution, composed of 16 museums and the National Zoo, includes an Office of Environmental Awareness that sponsors environmental and conservation activities and programs.

Soil Conservation Service

Natural Resources Conservation Service
Office of Public Affairs
U.S. Department of Agriculture
P.O. Box 2890
Washington, DC 20013
Phone: 202-720-3210; 1-800-THE SOIL
Fax: 202-720-1564

The Natural Resources Conservation Service (NRCS) is the federal agency that works with landowners on private lands to conserve natural resources. [Statement supplied by NRCS.]

United Nations Environment Programme

UNEP Regional Office, North America
Two United Nations Plaza, DC2-803
New York, NY 10017
Phone: 212-963-8098
Fax: 212-963-7341

The UNEP was created as a result of the United Nations Conference on the Human Environment convened at Stockholm in 1972. UNEP is "a programme which comprises all the activities undertaken within the United Nations system that relate to the environment." "UNEP is dedicated to bridging the gap between awareness and action. It has worked closely with other members of the UN system and forged new relationships among scientists and decision-makers, industrialists and environmental activists on behalf of the environment. It seeks the balance between national interests and the global good, aiming to unite nations to confront common environmental problems." [Quotes from Mostafa K. Tolba, Executive Director, UNEP, as printed in *UNEP: Two Decades of Achievement and Challenge* [Nairobi: Information and Public Affairs Branch, UNEP, 1992, pp. 7 and 5].)

ANSWERS TO ODD-NUMBERED STUDY QUESTIONS

CHAPTER 1

1. It is costly to our quality of life, to future generations, and in economic terms.
3. Movement of materials and energy through society
5. Population and traditional industrial technology
7. National Environmental Policy Act (1970)—requires environmental impact studies before land development projects. Endangered Species Act (1973)—enacted to preserve endangered species. Toxic Substances Control Act (1976)—limits the amount of poisonous chemicals made and sold in the United States.
9. Past conservation movements emphasized specific problems, whereas the current transition stage has led to a sustainability movement seeking long-term coexistence with the environment.
11. Environmental costs are imposed on future generations by actions of the present generation.
13. 1% was pledged to developing nations in 1961; 0.17% was spent on foreign aid in 1994.
15. 8.7 billion

CHAPTER 2

1. Lithosphere, hydrosphere, atmosphere, and biosphere
3. From the surface to the center of the Earth, one would encounter the atmosphere, possibly seawater, oceanic or continental crust, the uppermost mantle (together the crust and the uppermost mantle compose the lithosphere), asthenosphere, upper mantle, lower mantle, outer core, and inner core.
5. All familiar macroscopic matter is composed of elements. The elements themselves are composed of atoms, which in turn are made up of protons, neutrons, and electrons. On Earth, atoms combine together to form compounds and the various states of matter known as solids, liquids, and gases. The most common solid substances on Earth are rocks, composed primarily of minerals. Minerals are naturally occurring inorganic solids composed of atoms arranged in a regular structure—such as quartz or diamond.
7. The hydrologic cycle redistributes water and heat over the Earth's surface and causes the atmospheric changes humans generally think of as weather.
9. It will cool and lose its moisture as precipitation.
11. Earth's atmosphere is composed of about 78.1% N_2 and 20.9% O_2. The basic layers of the atmosphere, moving up from the Earth's surface, are the troposphere, stratosphere, mesosphere, and thermosphere. These layers are distinguished mainly by the changing temperature gradient encountered at progressively higher altitudes.
13. In terms of human lives lost and monetary damages incurred, among the most dangerous natural hazards are tropical cyclones (hurricanes and typhoons), earthquakes, and floods (see Table 2–1).
15. The earthquake's epicenter is about 1585 miles (about 2550 km) from the seismograph station.

CHAPTER 3

1. Cell
3. A group of individuals that can interbreed to produce fertile offspring
5. Mutation
7. Growth, stability, and decline
9. Potential for increase in a given population, r
11. The species richness of most groups decreases going away from the equator.
13. Growth is limited by the resource in the shortest supply.
15. 2 per day

CHAPTER 4

1. Carbon, hydrogen, oxygen, nitrogen, phosphorus, and sulfur
3. The ocean
5. Because of its extremely slow cycling time, phosphorus becomes locked up in deep-ocean sediments and the Earth's crust.
7. The carbon cycle, leading to global warming; the phosphorus cycle, with excessive amounts causing out-of-control plant growth in natural waters; and the nitrogren cycle, increasing smog.
9. Energy degrades with each use, becoming less capa-

ble of doing work (two laws of thermodynamics).

11. The Moon's gravitational pull, the Earth's internal geothermal energy

13. Moderate integration and high complexity

15. 80 generations

CHAPTER 5

1. The 1974 conference advocated the rapid industrialization of the developing countries. The 1984 conference emphasized increased access to modern family planning technologies and information. The 1994 conference focused on the interrelationships among population, poverty, inequality among individuals and nations, environmental decay, and sustainable development. A major focus of the 1994 conference was women's education and status.

3. There were perhaps only 125,000 human ancestors on Earth a million years ago. The population increased very, very slowly until it reached about 5–10 million about 10,000 years ago. With the development of agriculture and the domestication of animals starting about 8000 B.C. or earlier, the population began to increase more rapidly, reaching an estimated 150–300 million by A.D. 1. Thereafter, the world's human population has increased at an ever faster rate, reaching 500 million in 1650, 1.2 billion by 1850, 2.5 billion in 1950, and 5.7 billion in 1995.

5. Developments in technology affecting agriculture, medicine (for example, germ theory and vaccines), sanitation, food preservation and storage, and the cheap and efficient mass production of necessary commodities were all important. These developments have helped decrease infant mortality rates, increase life expectancies, and generally allow ever increasing numbers of humans to be fed, clothed, and housed.

7. If the world's population continues to grow at the recent annual rate of 1.7%, it could reach 28 billion by the year 2100. However, if family size stabilizes at two children by 2015, the population in 2100 might be 9–10 billion. Considering the current status of global family planning and extrapolating advances that can be reasonably expected, many demographers suggest that the global population may peak at 11 or 12 billion around 2100.

9. "Overpopulation" has been blamed for many of the world's environmental problems. The equation I = PT (Impact equals Population times Technology) sheds further light on this issue. As the equation describes, the environmental impact of a particular population is a function of both its size and the technology it uses. A large population using an environmentally friendly and sustainable technology (either a low-tech traditional technology or a high-tech environmentally benign technology) can have a less detrimental impact on the environment than a smaller population using an environmentally damaging, nonsustainable technology. When comparing the environmental effects of different populations, more than simply crude population size must be taken into account.

11. Indigenous peoples are sometimes killed in purposeful acts of genocide; large numbers of indigenous peoples have succumbed to diseases introduced from other parts of the world; invading conquerors may push indigenous peoples out of their prime territories; or the individuals of an indigenous population may become assimilated into the culture of a dominant invader such that the indigenous culture goes extinct even though its people do not physically die out.

13. It has been demonstrated many times that one of the best ways to decrease the growth rate of a particular population is to increase the average educational level and societal status of women.

15. El Salvador's annual growth rate was 1.9% over this period; at this rate, El Salvador's population will double in approximately 37 years.

CHAPTER 6

1. At the landscape level

3. Modern society has tended to ignore environmental costs. This has made resources seem "cheap" and made the ratio artificially high (exceed one) so the benefits of resource exploitation superficially appear to outweigh the costs.

5. Direct values are a resource's short-term economic values. These values are usually acquired by destructive harvesting of the resource such as mining or logging. Indirect values do not involve destruction of the resource. Examples include long-term (sustainable) economic value, esthetic, emotional, ethical, and environmental service values.

7. Matter resources are depleted through dispersion, as atoms are dispersed into less concentrated forms. Examples include soil erosion and mining and melting of ore deposits. Energy resources are depleted by transforming energy into a less usable form. For example, when fossil fuels are burned, much of the energy becomes "waste heat" that is less able to do work than gasoline or coal energy.

9. Very rapid (exponential) rates of exploitation and depletion

11. Equal to renewal rate. MSY is about one-half the carrying capacity.

13. Throughput is slowed down because resources are used more efficiently. Jobs are concentrated at the input end of the throughput, such as jobs in recycling and efficiency design.

15. It would be reduced by 50%, to a value of approximately 7.25 billion BTUs per $1 million GNP (0.0075 petajoules per $1 million GNP).

CHAPTER 7

1. Energy is the ability to do work, and work is defined as a force applied to a material object times

the distance that the material object is moved.

3. The first law of thermodynamics is the law of the conservation of energy: energy can be neither created nor destroyed; it is changed from one form to another. The second law of thermodynamics states that heat or energy cannot be transformed into work with 100% efficiency. When our machines (such as automobile engines or electrical generators) transform energy from one form to another, some potentially useful energy is always lost.

5. According to one estimate, slightly over 340,000 petajoules of energy are consumed each year; 73% of this energy is consumed in the industrialized countries, and more than 25% of the total energy is consumed in North America. Based on another approach, the world consumes energy at a rate of slightly over 13.1 terawatts (which would be equivalent to using over 400,000 petajoules of energy per year). The approximately 1.2 billion citizens of industrialized nations consume energy at a rate of about 7.5 kW per person on average while the over 4 billion citizens of the developing nations consume energy at a rate of only 1.0 kW per person on average—in other terms, the richest 25% of the world's population use over 60% of the world's energy.

7. A power plant is a large facility, usually operated by a private or semi-public company, dedicated to generating electricity that is fed into a power grid and thence distributed to consumers. Most operating power plants today use some sort of turbine to drive a generator that transforms mechanical energy into electrical energy. In fossil fuel–burning plants, nuclear power plants, and geothermal plants, the turbine is usually driven by steam; in hydroelectric plants, it is driven by falling water; and in wind-powered plants, the turbine is driven by wind turning a huge propeller.

9. The fossil fuels are a convenient (and for the moment plentiful) form of high-grade concentrated energy that can be easily stored, transported, and converted to many forms of useful work. Most researchers believe that we cannot indefinitely maintain our dependence on fossil fuels. The continued use of fossil fuels may irreparably damage the global environment (for instance, they may promote global warming); furthermore, the fossil fuels are a limited, nonrenewable resource.

11. Fast-moving water is used to turn a turbine that drives an electrical generator. Most often a natural river is dammed to create an artificial waterfall, and the falling water is used to turn the turbine.

13. Oil shale is a type of rock that contains the organic precursors of oil known as kerogen. If oil shale is mined and processed correctly, the kerogen can be artificially converted to oil.

15. The industrialized countries produce approximately 59.5% of the world's commercial energy, but consume approximately 73% of the total. About 10.8% of the world's proven oil reserves occur in the industrialized countries.

CHAPTER 8

1. Nuclear power, a generator of electricity, supplies roughly 5% of the world's commercial energy. In the United States, roughly 21% of all electricity is generated by nuclear power, and many countries (such as France, Belgium, and Hungary) rely heavily on nuclear power for electrical energy generation.

3. During fission a radioactive isotope of a heavy element, such as an uranium or plutonium atom, is split into daughter products, and energy is released. In a nuclear power plant, the energy released during the fission process is used to heat water; the resulting stream powers a turbine connected to an electrical generator.

5. Nuclear proliferation is the spreading of nuclear bomb and weapon technology from nations and organizations that possess it to those that do not. Many people are afraid that nuclear proliferation will increase the chances of nuclear weapons being used in a war or during an act of terrorism. Certain concentrated fissionable materials, which may be produced in some reactors or be isolated during reprocessing of spent nuclear fuel, can be used to manufacture nuclear weapons.

7. Advantages of nuclear power plants include the potentially vast supply of fuel if breeder technology is used, their relative safety record (despite a few well-publicized mishaps), and the fact that they produce very little standard air pollution and do not emit greenhouse gases. Disadvantages include the high cost of installing, maintaining, and eventually decommissioning a nuclear power plant; the radioactive emissions and thermal pollution usually associated with a nuclear power plant; the problem of disposing of spent nuclear fuel and other radioactive waste; nuclear weapon proliferation that may be associated with the spread of nuclear power technology; and the potential for a catastrophic disaster if a nuclear reactor malfunctions or is mishandled.

9. The Petkau effect involves damage to cell membranes exposed to very low intensity radiation over long periods of time. Low doses of radiation apparently produce O_2- free radicals that can initiate a series of reactions that cause a cell membrane to dissolve or break. Some have suggested that very small doses of radiation released by nuclear reactors and as fallout from bomb testing could have a serious detrimental long-term effect on all living organisms.

11. Radioactive wastes produced by nuclear power plants include spent fuel, radioactive products generated in the core of a reactor, contaminated materials and clothing, and radioactive mining wastes and tailings.

13. Global nuclear generating capacity will peak at slightly above 350 gigawatts before the year 2000, then stabilize during the first half of the twenty-first century. Although older reactors will be taken

off line in Europe and North America and replaced by fossil fuel plants and alternative energy sources, nuclear power will likely play an increasingly important role in the East (for instance, in Russia, Ukraine, Japan, China, and South Korea). By the middle or late twenty-first century, nuclear power may be a predominantly eastern European and Asian phenomenon.

15. After 19 days, 0.28125 ounces (approximately 7.97 g) of radon-222 will remain.

CHAPTER 9

1. The alternative energy sources are alternatives to the "big five" energy sources (coal, oil, natural gas, hydroelectric power, and nuclear power). Common alternative energy sources include solar power, wind power, geothermal power, ocean energy, and the burning of biomass. Generally, the alternative energy sources are viewed as "renewable" (although strictly speaking geothermal power is nonrenewable) and more environmentally friendly than the big five. Among the big five, hydroelectric power has the most in common with the alternative energy sources.

3. In most wind power systems, the blowing wind turns blades and a rotor that are connected to an electrical generator; essentially, wind power utilizes the centuries-old concept of a windmill.

5. Geothermal energy systems tap the natural heat from the Earth's interior and use this heat directly to heat buildings or in manufacturing processes or to generate electricity. Today hydrothermal fluid reservoirs are the most common form of geothermal energy used. Strictly speaking, geothermal energy is not a renewable energy source. On a small scale, convenient geothermal sources may be depleted, sometimes very quickly. Natural hydrothermal fluid reservoirs may be withdrawn more quickly than they are replenished. If heat is withdrawn quickly enough, ultimately any hot rocks will cool down.

7. In tidal plants the tides are used to drive mechanical systems that transform the mechanical energy into electrical energy. An ocean thermal energy conversion plant is a giant heat engine that uses the temperature gradient in the oceans to run a turbine and generate electricity.

9. Pumped hydroelectric storage (PHS), compressed air energy storage (CAES), batteries, fuel cells, spinning flywheels, and superconducting magnetic energy storage (SMES) systems are all ways of storing electrical energy. Of these six, batteries and PHS systems are the most widely used today. Fuel cells will probably become increasingly important in the future. Spinning flywheels and SMES systems are currently under development.

11. Three major ways of storing heat are through sensible heat storage (a material body absorbs heat and then releases it), latent heat storage (a substance absorbs or releases heat as it goes through a phase change), and thermochemical heat storage (reversible chemical reactions are used to store heat energy).

13. Natural gas is an abundant and clean (compared to coal and oil) fossil fuel. Most natural gas technologies and infrastructures can be relatively easily converted to hydrogen gas use. Some researchers suggest that we should initially substitute natural gas for other fossil fuels whenever and wherever possible, then develop a solar-hydrogen economy, and finally substitute hydrogen gas for natural gas.

15. Burning bituminous coal to generate 33 exajoules of electricity would require from 22,110 to 108,900 square kilometer–years (8,534.5 to 42,035 square mile–years).

CHAPTER 10

1. Mineral resources refers not only to minerals in a strict sense, but also to material substances that are composed of minerals or extracted from minerals.

3. Mineral resources, formed over long periods of time by geological processes, do not substantially increase on a human time scale. Thus, once a copper mine, for instance, is depleted, the copper-bearing minerals will not "grow" back. Mineral resources are finite and exhaustible.

5. An ore deposit is a mineral deposit that, at a certain time and place with a certain technology, can be economically mined.

7. A static reserve (expressed in years) is how long a mineral reserve will last given current consumption rates; an expotential reserve takes the growth rate of demand into account in estimating how long the reserve will last.

9. Two basic strategies have been used to deal with mineral scarcity and the demand for more minerals: (1) increasing the supply of minerals by locating new ore deposits (including improving technologies so that lesser-grade ores can be mined) and recycling old mineral-bearing materials, and (2) decreasing the demand for certain minerals by finding substitutes or eliminating the need for certain minerals through technological and cultural developments.

11. Traditionally, mineral exploration in remote territories was associated with national expansion and the "taming" of the frontier. During the nineteenth century, the U.S. government actively encouraged mining companies to explore undeveloped public lands so as to encourage development and settlement. Also, traditionally mining and heavy industry have been viewed as the mainstay of a healthy national economy. For many present-day developing countries, mineral exports are the primary means of earning currency to pay off their international debts. Additionally, mineral production has historically been associated with national security; metals are needed to build weapons to win wars.

13. Dematerialization is the systematic reduction in the size or weight of certain products such that they require less material, and therefore use fewer mineral resources, to manufacture.

15. To obtain one metric ton of copper, 250 metric tons (275.6 tons) of 0.4% grade ore would have to be mined and processed.

CHAPTER 11

1. The H_2O molecule has a net electric charge that is bipolar with a positive charge at one end and a negative charge on the other end. This helps explain why water boils at high temperatures and is a good solvent.

3. Water consumption means that the water is lost to the local part of the water cycle. Usually, this loss is through evaporation, which is much greater in farming due to open-ditch irrigation. Microirrigation greatly reduces this evaporation by transporting the water to the crops in pipes.

5. Riparian law is a common-law practice wherein the owner of land controls the water rights of the water running through it. This law is used mainly east of the Mississippi River. Appropriation law dictates that owners of the land may be denied water use by the government if a more appropriate use is found. This law is practiced mainly west of the Mississippi River.

7. Groundwater depletion, land subsidence, and saltwater intrusion are three withdrawal problems. Wetland destruction promotes these problems and groundwater pollution as well, because wetlands are major recharge areas and serve as the "kidneys" of the water cycle, purifying the water. About 50% of U.S. wetlands have been lost.

9. Toilet flushing, showers and baths, laundry, dishwashing. Americans accounted for 1400 gallons per day, compared to 1 gallon for biological needs.

11. Evapotransportation and precipitation. Evapotransportation is the transfer of water into the atmosphere by evaporation and transpiration. Precipitation occurs when water falls to the ground as rain, snow, sleet, or hail. In all, 9800 cubic miles (40,000 km³) of water return to the oceans as runoff.

13. Water conservation (input reduction) occurs via increased efficiency of use, recycling, and substitution. Ways to encourage this include stop subsidizing water use for agriculture and tax water use in industry and households.

15. 10 cubic miles × (4.1655 cubic km/1 cubic mile) = 41.655 cubic km.

CHAPTER 12

1. Yes. Areas with high local diversity also tend to have high regional diversity. The tropics, for example, have both high local and high regional diversity.

3. A species-area curve shows that the number of species living in an area initially rises rapidly as the area surveyed increases. As the area surveyed continues to expand, the total number of species found begins to level off, as fewer new species are encountered. The curve predicts that 50% of the species will become extinct if 90% of a habitat is destroyed.

5. Five, 2–10 species per year, hundreds of times higher

7. Habitat disruption, introduced species, overhunting, secondary extinctions. The last three are biological. Most extinctions involve more than one cause.

9. On islands. Species are isolated and poorly adapted to cope with new species. Hawaii and Guam are examples.

11. No. Species differ in their evolutionary and ecological importance, for example. Unique species tend to have much greater evolutionary potential than species with many closely related species.

13. A hot spot is an area of exceptionally high species richness, especially species that occur nowhere else. Hot spots can help because they represent preserves with high biodiversity, unlike many existing preserves, which were selected on the basis of scenic beauty or charismatic species.

15. In selective cutting (also known as "uneven-aged" management) only certain trees in the stand are cut down, so the land is not stripped bare. In clearcutting (also known as "even-aged" management) an entire stand of trees is completely removed.

17. 36,500 species; 3.65 million species; 36.5%

CHAPTER 13

1. Many researchers believe that with perfect management the world's current food production would feed the current global population; in the future, however, the increasing global population may outrun the available food supply.

3. Rice, wheat, and maize (corn) constitute approximately 65% of the world food supply.

5. Many people avoid eating meat and eat lower on the food chain, so that possibly more people in the world can be fed an adequate diet. Other people avoid eating meat for personal health reasons (many studies indicate that a diet overly rich in meats is less healthy than a diet containing more moderate amounts), and some people avoid meats based on ethical and moral principles (perhaps they do not believe that animals should be raised and slaughtered for human consumption).

7. The various species of fishes and other seafood harvested from the oceans are the major nonagricultural food source. Many researchers believe that we are overfishing the oceans.

9. Integrated Pest Management (IPM) deemphasizes the use of pesticides and attempts to control, rather than totally eliminate, agricultural pests by using biological predators, rotating fields, interplanting

crops, and using other "natural" means.

11. Quite simply, soil is necessary to raise agricultural food crops, and without food crops most people of the world would starve. Unfortunately, at present, soil is being allowed to erode from many agricultural lands faster than it is replenished by natural processes.

13. To increase world food production, two basic, but not mutually exclusive strategies have been proposed: increase the amount of land under cultivation and increase the yield per unit of land under cultivation.

15. An increase in the world population from 5.8 to 10 billion would be a 72.4% increase in the number of mouths to feed. Assuming current yields per unit land area, the amount of cultivated land would have to increase by about 72–73%—from 3.7 billion acres to 6.4 billion acres (2.6 billion hectares).

CHAPTER 14

1. LCA is a method used increasingly by engineers to pinpoint steps in production, manufacturing, or other activities that can be eliminated. This can reduce waste by reducing the number of steps and the waste generated per step. LCA is also called "cradle to grave" analysis.

3. Bioengineering, or transferring genes between organisms, is one solution. Also called "genetic engineering," it can produce organisms that digest the stock pollutant. Bacteria are among the organisms most commonly used in this manner.

5. Over 2% is spent each year.

7. Benefits and/or costs may be omitted or inaccurately estimated. This is common because placing values on environmental resources is very difficult. Benefit-cost ratios over 1 indicate that additional controls could result in a net overall gain to society.

9. The utility-based approach differs from rights-based and technology-based approaches of the past. The Contingent Valuation Method uses questionnaires.

11. Most directly released toxics are released in the air. The chemical industry is by far the major industrial source.

13. Because these nations often subsidize the use of fossil fuels and other natural resources, causing them to be used wastefully. Green technology can reduce overall economic costs because it often improves efficiency and reduces fuel use.

15. $3182 = .65(X)$ so $X = 4895$ million pounds. 4895 million pounds $\times$ (1 kg/2.205 lb) = 2220 million kg.

CHAPTER 15

1. Toxicology studies the effects of chemicals that are harmful or fatal when consumed by organisms in relatively small amounts. Paracelsus is often given that name.

3. ADMSE describes the pathway of toxic substances through the body: absorption by skin, ingestion, or inhaling; distribution by the blood; metabolism by cells; storage in fat, bone, or other tissues; and excretion out of the body.

5. Chlorinated hydrocarbons, organophosphates, and carbamates are the three kinds of synthetic organic pesticides. Chlorinated hydrocarbons, such as DDT and chlordane, are most persistent and easily bioconcentrated.

7. An environmental hormone is a pollutant that sends false signals to the complex hormonal systems that regulate reproduction, immunity, behavior, and growth. When any or all of these systems are affected, reproductive loss, disease, and behaviorial or growth abnormalities can occur.

9. Chemical interactions in the environment include antagonism, when chemicals cancel each other's effects; addivity, when toxic effects are added together; and synergism, when toxic effects are multiplied. Synergism is the most dangerous.

11. Evolved immunity is caused by natural selection: resistant individuals pass on their resistance to their offspring. Eventually, the entire population becomes immune to the pesticide.

13. The TSCA requires the industry to provide data on the environmental effects of the chemicals produced. The centerpiece is the "premanufacturing notice," which requires the industry to notify the EPA 90 days before a chemical is manufactured for sale. Chemicals produced before the act was enacted in 1976 were "grandfathered in," meaning that, with very few exceptions, they were never tested for toxicity.

15. $(.01)(1,000,000 \text{ gallons}) = 10,000 \text{ gallons} = 37,900 \text{ L}.$

CHAPTER 16

1. Three methods of treating water before distribution to taps are coagulation to cause suspended particles to settle, filtration by clay or sand filters, and disinfection, usually by chlorine.

3. Inorganic chemicals, organic chemicals, radioactive matter, and microbes

5. Oxygen-demanding wastes lead to a rapid increase in the rate of decomposition, causing an increased biological oxygen demand. This depletes oxygen available to aquatic life.

7. Metal atoms will chemically bind to protein molecules such as enzymes, interfering with their function. This is especially common with nervous system enzymes and causes disorders of the nervous system such as learning disabilities.

9. Increased temperatures may exceed the temperature tolerance of the organism and also cause the water to retain less dissolved oxygen.

11. Lakes are more easily polluted because lake water circulates more slowly, lakes form in basins that accumulate pollutants, and lakes often contain less water.

13. Microbes treat polluted groundwater by digesting pollutants. The process involves injecting microbes underground and/or injecting nutrients and oxygen to stimulate growth of preexisting microbe populations.

15. (600 tons/200 miles) = 3 tons/mile or 1.88 tons/km; (.64)(600 tons) = 384 tons.

CHAPTER 17

1. The variable gases are components of air that vary from place to place. These include water vapor, carbon dioxide, and ozone.

3. The five basic criteria pollutants are particulates, sulfur oxides, nitrogen oxides, volatile organic compounds, and carbon monoxide. The two main sources are fossil fuels and industrial processes.

5. On the pH scale, 1 means very acidic. The average pH of rainfall is 5.6. Game fishes are most sensitive to acid waters.

7. Oxygenation is a method of reformulating gasoline by adding oxygen-rich liquids. By adding oxygen, it promotes less carbon monoxide and VOC pollution because fuel is more completely "burned."

9. A PSI value of 100 means that at least one major air pollutant has exceeded its air quality standard. About 25% of U.S. vehicles are "clunkers."

11. The atmosphere is a commons because it is a shared resource that people will exploit or pollute as long as they are free to do so. Economic ways to promote payments of true costs include taxation, fees, and other charges on the amount of emissions or fuel burned.

13. The three main categories of sources of indoor air pollution are underground emissions, combustion, and underground diffusion. The harmful effects can usually be reduced by increased ventilation.

15. 20 dB = (10)(10) = 100 times greater.

CHAPTER 18

1. The Japanese, under the auspices of their Research Institute of Innovative Technology for the Earth, are working on developing new ozone-safe CFC substitutes, harnessing microorganisms to remove carbon dioxide from industrial gases, and developing selectively permeable membranes to filter carbon dioxide out of industrial gases.

3. The CFCs, or chlorofluorocarbons, are artificially produced compounds composed primarily of carbon, fluorine, and chlorine.

5. CFCs in the stratosphere break down in the presence of ultraviolet radiation, releasing atomic chlorine. The free chlorine reacts with an ozone molecule, removing an oxygen atom and converting the ozone to diatomic oxygen. The unstable chlorine monoxide molecule easily releases its oxygen atom, and the chlorine molecule can react with another ozone molecule.

7. Hydrochlorofluorocarbons (HCFCs), hydrofluorocarbons (HFCs), halons, methyl chloroform, methyl bromide, carbon tetrachloride, nitrogen oxides, chlorine monoxide, and stratospheric aerosols are some of the substances besides CFCs that can harm the ozone layer.

9. The major greenhouse gases are carbon dioxide, CFCs, methane, trophospheric ozone, and nitrogen oxides.

11. The United States, the countries of the former Soviet Union, China, Japan, and Brazil are currently the biggest contributors to potential global warming.

13. Some of the potential consequences of significant global warming include rising sea levels, increased incidences of violent weather patterns and storms, shifting of climatic zones, and decreases in biodiversity.

15. It would be a 42.8% increase.

CHAPTER 19

1. Instead of building an incinerator, East Hampton adopted an intensive recycling program for trash disposal. The recycling program has cost less than building and operating an incinerator and is also much more environmentally friendly.

3. Some, primarily poorer communities (or nations) have found that other richer communities (or nations) will pay a fee to any community that will receive and store their garbage and waste. Performing such "waste services" can bring much needed revenue and jobs to a poorer community in the short term, but in the long term the waste may pollute and degrade the community's environment. Eventually, the community may run out of room to dispose of waste, and "waste income" will end, and the community will be left with a store of waste.

5. Some environmentalists object to placing a heavy emphasis on recycling because it may reinforce the mentality of the "throwaway" society characterized by obscene levels of consumption. These critics suggest that reduction (using less) and reuse (as opposed to recycling) should be emphasized instead.

7. Currently, about 73% (by weight) of all municipal solid waste in the United States is disposed of in landfills, about 14% is incinerated, and about 13% is recycled.

9. Composting, in the simplest sense, consists of allowing natural microorganisms to decompose the organic matter of yard, food, and other wastes. The process can produce various grades of humus or topsoil. Topsoil and other forms of compost are in high demand for agricultural lands, gardens, land reclamation projects, landfill cover, reforestation projects, and so on.

11. An industrial ecosystem would mimic a natural ecosystem. Ideally, the industrial ecosystem would produce no waste; the effluents of one industrial

process would be raw materials for another industrial process. The ultimate goal would be for virtually all materials to be recycled or reused over and over again.

13. The Toxics Release Inventory is an annual report produced by the U.S. Environmental Protection Agency that compiles information on the production, use, and release of over three hundred potentially hazardous chemicals. The TRI allows citizens and communities, armed with data, to put pressure on companies to cut emissions of hazardous substances. Likewise, many industry officials, appalled by the amounts of toxic chemicals released by factories and businesses, have taken voluntary actions to reduce the amount of toxic and hazardous waste released into the environment.

15. The per capita daily garbage output of the average American is predicted to increase by about 22% between 1980 and 2000.

CHAPTER 20

1. Economics is concerned with resource scarcity and pollution. Economics takes a short-term view, puts priority on social needs, and uses incentives to solve problems. In contrast, environmental science takes a long-term view, its priority is on the environment, and it uses laws and persuasion to solve problems.

3. They produce so many jobs because they are labor-intensive. Greenmail, or job blackmail, is when a company threatens to close or relocate if it is forced to comply with environmental laws.

5. Traditional economics uses the Gross National Product (GNP). The ISEW (Index of Sustainable Economic Welfare) includes depletion of nonrenewable resources, loss of farmland and wetlands, damage from pollution, and long-term damage from global warming and ozone depletion.

7. Externalities are market failures wherein some costs of production are not included in the product's price. Instead, society as a whole pays the price. The tragedy of the commons refers to the way people deplete or pollute resources that are public goods or commons as long as they are free to do so.

9. A severance tax is levied on minerals as they are extracted. The purpose is to offset the high price of scarce supplies by increasing the tax as the resource becomes scarcer.

11. Persuasion asks people to stop depleting and polluting. Regulation combats these actions by passing laws against them. Economic methods use taxes, subsidies, fees, and other monetary incentives to stop depletion and pollution. Persuasion is generally least effective.

13. The net flow of money toward rich nations began in 1982. The fundamental cause of this net flow is that developing nations are not being paid the true costs for their resources. Examples include conservation of rare genes and species for agriculture and pharmaceuticals and conservation of rainforests to reduce global warming.

15. $(21)/(0.1) = 210$ jobs lost from falling demand for each job lost from environmental regulations.

CHAPTER 21

1. Ethics can be defined as the philosophical study of moral values. Environmental ethics is the application of ethical studies to environmental concerns.

3. Descriptive ethics concentrates on cataloging and describing the various ethical approaches used by different people around the world. Normative ethics prescribes appropriate ethical behavior and distinguishes good from bad or right from wrong, based upon a certain ethical system or philosophy. Philosophical ethics analyzes and evaluates the underlying bases and assumptions of normative judgments within and among various ethical systems and also places such judgments and systems within a larger philosophical context.

5. According to the teleological tradition, developed in large part by Aristotle, every being and every object in nature have a purpose, function, end, final cause, or utility in the overall natural design and order of the world or universe. A thing is "good" when it fulfills its natural function.

7. Deontology, especially as espoused by Immanuel Kant, is the study of moral obligations and duties. According to Kant, humans are free, rational beings who can choose their own actions and are responsible for those actions—at least as far as the consequences they can anticipate. Additionally, free, rational humans are morally obliged to treat their fellow humans as free, rational beings. Each person has the right to be treated as an autonomous, free, thinking being who pursues her or his own purposes and goals—no human is to be treated as a mere object.

9. The basic principle behind much of classic utilitarianism is that the overall good should be maximized. Modern benefit-cost analyses often adopt this utilitarian assumption and attempt to maximize "good" as quantified monetarily.

11. Biocentric ethics, which goes back at least to the ancient Greeks, views all living things as having inherent worth. Living things—upon which we depend—are good in their own right and deserve the consideration and respect of humans.

13. Deep ecology, a term first coined by the Norwegian environmental philosopher Arne Naess, takes a holistic and nonanthropocentric perspective that rejects the human versus environment dichotomy. Humans are considered at most to be one species among equal species, and even rivers, mountains, and the like may be considered to have intrinsic purpose, value, and moral rights.

15. Ecofeminism arose out of the general modern feminist movement. Ecofeminism identifies the

oppression of women by a traditional patriarchal society as a major form of social domination that has precipitated other forms of exploitation and domination, including the current large-scale exploitation of the environment.

CHAPTER 22

1. The Green movement is a political and social movement, with underpinnings in deep ecology, social ecology, and ecofeminist analyses, that has grown out of more traditional environmentalism. Many Greens believe that to solve the current global environmental crisis we need to make a revolutionary break from the past and establish new, Earth-amenable social institutions. Establishing such a new, planet-friendly social order is the general goal of the movement.

3. The most basic social institutions of Western society (and, indeed, of most societies) involve family organization and relationships, economic concerns, political concerns, educational concerns, and religious concerns. Some analysts have blamed Western social institutions for the current environmental crisis, but others point out that non-Western societies have also degraded their environments. It can be argued that Western social institutions may ultimately contain the solutions needed to end the current environmental crisis.

5. Classically, both conservationists and preservationists support environmentalism—they are interested in preserving the natural world—but take different approaches and have different goals. Conservationists traditionally adopt a utilitarian stance, believing that natural resources (such as forests) should be managed so as to obtain the most benefit for the greatest number of people—thus, a forest may be selectively harvested for lumber. Preservationists traditionally feel that at least certain natural resources, such as selected pristine forests, should be preserved intact and protected from any human intervention whatsoever.

7. The Great Depression may be attributable, in part, to soil exhaustion and land degradation; during the depression, the federal government attempted to restore the environment and create employment with such programs as the Civilian Conservation Corps; certain government programs of the time were seen as both conserving natural resources and promoting economic well-being. World War II led to a situation where conservation and resource management issues took a back seat to industrialization and technological efforts concentrating on military production.

9. Hard laws are legally binding and mandatory, whereas soft laws are not legally binding, but act more as a guide to policy.

11. Enforcing international environmental laws is difficult because there is no single "world government" with the power and authority for such enforcement. Rather, sovereign nations are expected to police themselves and live up to the agreements of international treaties—but in practice, they often fall short of their obligations. Nations can often be persuaded to comply with the provisions of environmental treaties, however, if peer pressure, moral persuasion, and public embarrassment are applied appropriately—most nations and their leaders consider their "public face" (how they are viewed by the rest of the world) to be very important.

13. The various ways that environmental decisions, especially public policy decisions, may be arrived at include relying on precedent, utilizing the judgment of experts, performing benefit-cost analyses, and taking ethical considerations into account.

15. Some critics have suggested that perceived panics and crises have been the immediate guiding factor behind some environmental policy decisions. For instance, money has been wasted on cleaning up high-profile hazardous sites when it might have been better spent on more important environmental issues.

GLOSSARY

abatement devices "End of the pipe" pollution control equipment.

abortion The termination of a pregnancy before the term is up (before the child is scheduled to be born).

absorptive ability The ability of a natural sink (such as a river, lake, or the atmosphere) to absorb pollutants or potential pollutants.

acid rain Precipitation (rain, snow, sleet, and so forth) that is more acidic than normal (generally due to human-produced air pollutants); also known as acid precipitation.

acoustical materials Sound-absorbing materials that can be used to reduce noise.

active solar techniques Mechanisms, such as flat-plate collectors, that are designed to actively collect the energy of sunlight and use it to heat a building or to heat water.

acute toxicity When toxic substances are harmful shortly after exposure.

additivity With reference to toxicology, when the toxic effects of two substances are added together.

ADMSE Acronym for absorption, distribution, metabolism, storage, and excretion—the five basic steps in the path of a toxic substance through the body.

aeration Exposing water to the air; often results in the release into the atmosphere of gaseous impurities found in polluted water.

aeration, zone of The zone above the water table where the voids in the soil or rock may contain water but are not fully saturated.

aerosol spray Products that are sprayed as a fine mist during use, such as canned spray paints, deodorants, and so forth. For many years such products used ozone-depleting CFCs as propellants.

age profile The population age structure profile is a graphic representation of the age structure of a population at a given time.

age structure The relative proportion of individuals in each age group in a population.

agricultural (Neolithic) revolution The advent of domestication and agriculture beginning around 10,000 years ago.

agriculture The cultivation or raising of plant crops and livestock.

alkaline The opposite of acidic; basic. Alkaline soil or rock may neutralize acid rain.

alpha particles A type of radiation essentially composed of energetic helium nuclei.

alternative energy sources Energy sources, such as solar power, wind power, and so forth, that are alternatives to the fossil fuels, nuclear power, and large-scale hydroelectric power.

amensalism A form of symbiosis where one species inhibits another while being relatively unaffected itself.

amino acids The complex molecules that are the "building blocks" of proteins.

animal rights The concept that nonhuman animals have inherent ethical moral status and rights.

annual growth rate How much a population grows in one year. *See also* percent annual growth.

antagonism With reference to toxicology, when substances work against each other and cancel each other's effects.

anthracite Hard coal.

anthropocentric Human-centered.

anthropogenic Formed, produced, or caused by humans.

appropriation law A law under which owners of land may be denied the right to withdraw water from a lake or stream if a more beneficial use for the water is found (government can appropriate the use of the water).

aquaculture Refers to aquatic organism farming in general and sometimes to freshwater organism farming in particular.

aquiclude A relatively impermeable rock layer that obstructs the flow of water.

aquifer A relatively permeable rock layer below the water table that contains a significant amount of water.

artesian well A well from which water flows freely without pumping due to water pressure built up in the recharge area.

asthenosphere A layer in the mantle that is relatively weak and viscous; lies directly underneath the solid lithosphere.

atmosphere The sphere or "layer" of gases that surrounds the Earth.

atmospheric cycles The large-scale movements in the Earth's atmosphere that give rise to the major wind belts and so forth.

atom The smallest particle of an element.

baghouses A series of fabric bags that act as filters to remove particulate matter from polluted air.

battery A device that when charged with electricity stores the energy in the form of chemical energy. When the battery is discharged, the energy is converted back into electrical energy.

behavioral toxicology The study of chemicals that cause disorders of behavior or learning.

benefit-cost analysis (BCA) A method of comparing the benefits of an activity to its cost; also known as risk-benefit analysis.

benthic Refers to the bottom-dwelling zone of the aquatic (specifically marine) biome.

beta particles A type of radiation, essentially high-speed electrons.

Bhopal The city in India where, in December 1984, a major leak occurred at the Union Carbide pesticide-producing plant, ultimately killing thousands and injuring tens of thousands more. The Bhopal incident helped inspire Congress to pass the Emergency Planning and Community Right-to-Know Act that established the Toxics Release Inventory. *See also* Toxics Release Inventory.

big five energy sources Coal, oil, natural gas, large-scale hydroelectric, and nuclear power.

bioassay An hierarchical sequence of procedures used to test the toxicity of a chemical substance. Initially, a relatively short, inexpensive test is administered; if harmful effects are indicated, then progressively more thorough tests are carried out.

biocentric Life-centered.

biochemical conversion The harnessing of microorganisms to convert biomass into certain fuels.

bioconcentration Bioaccumulation or biomagnification; the tendency for a substance to accumulate in living tissue. An organism may take in a substance, but not excrete or metabolize it; then, a predator eats the organism and ingests the substance already accumulated in the prey.

bioconcentration factor (BCF) A measure of the tendency for bioconcentration by a given substance.

biodegradable plastics Biodegradable generally refers to a substance that can be degraded, decomposed, or broken down by microorganisms into simple compounds such as water and carbon dioxide. A biodegradable plastic is a plastic that can be broken down in such a manner; traditionally, most plastics have been synthetic compounds that are not biodegradable.

bioengineering Genetic manipulations and engineering to produce new varieties and types of organisms.

biogas digester A special chamber or reactor used to promote biochemical conversion of biomass.

biogeochemical cycles The cycles of elements and compounds through the atmosphere, lithosphere, hydrosphere, and biosphere.

biological control *See* Integrated Pest Management.

biological environment The living world or biosphere.

biological impoverishment The loss of variety in the biosphere (even when species have not gone completely extinct).

biological oxygen demand (BOD) The amount of oxygen used by organisms in a particular stream, lake, or other body of water to carry out decomposition.

biomass The total weight of living tissue in a community.

biomass energy Energy produced by the burning of such biomass as wastes, standing forests, and energy crops.

biomass pyramid A graphic depiction of the amount of biomass that occurs at each trophic level in a particular community or ecosystem.

biome A large-scale category that includes many communities of a similar nature.

bioremediation The use of bacteria and other small organisms (such as single-celled and multicellular microbes and fungi) to clean up or reduce unwanted concentrations of certain substances; also know as biotreatment.

biosphere The sphere or "layer" of living organisms on Earth.

biotechnology The artificial use and manipulation of organisms toward human ends.

biotoxin A poisonous substance produced by an organism, often of high potency such that a small amount can kill an adult human.

birth control The artificial control, or prevention, of unwanted births.

bituminous coal Soft coal.

blackout When a region served by an electric power plant is left without power for an extended period of time, perhaps due to a major breakdown.

bootstrapping Basing new policies on the precedents of previous ones; sometimes referred to as "muddling along" or following the path of least resistance.

bottom-up approach The development and encouragement of sustainable uses of biodiversity that provides incentives to save species while also respecting the right of all people to support their families and have a decent quality of life.

breeder reactor A nuclear reactor that is especially designed to actively convert nonfissionable isotopes into fissionable isotopes that can then be used as fuel.

brownout When the capacity of a power plant is exceeded by a few percent and the voltage to consumers is inadequate such that lights often dim.

BTU British thermal unit; the amount of energy that when converted completely to heat will warm one pound of water by one degree Fahrenheit.

buffer zone In a preserve, an area of moderately utilized land that provides a transition into the unmodified natural habitat in the core preserve where no human disturbance is allowed.

calorie The amount of energy that when converted completely to heat will warm one gram of water by one degree Celsius.

carbamates A group of synthetic organic pesticides that are less persistent, but more toxic to humans, than chlorinated hydrocarbons; includes sevin.

carbon cycle The biogeochemical cycle of carbon.

carbon dioxide CO_2, the primary greenhouse gas.

carbon efficiency The amount of economic output per unit of carbon released. For instance, the United States as a whole produces less than $2 per pound of carbon released into the atmosphere from the burning of fossil fuels.

carbon emission The emission of carbon, primarily as carbon dioxide, into the atmosphere during the burning of fossil fuels and other organic matter and similar activities.

carbon tax A tax levied on fossil fuels (or any fuels) in proportion to the amount of carbon emitted during combustion.

carcinogen A cancer-producing substance.

carrying capacity The maximum population size that can be sustained by a certain environment for a long period of time (potentially indefinitely); often represented by the symbol K.

carryover grain stocks Stocks of grain that are saved from one harvest year and remain at the beginning of the next harvest year.

cassandras People who argue that humans have always altered the environment and managed things poorly; they maintain that ultimately exponential growth of populations and technologies will totally degrade the environment.

catalytic converter A device that carries out a number of chemical reactions that convert air pollutants to less harmful substances.

cataract A condition where the lens of the eye becomes opaque.

chain reaction In a nuclear reactor, when the fissioning of one atom releases neutrons that induce the fissioning of other atoms, and so forth.

channelization The artificial straightening of a river or stream.

charismatic species A high-profile endangered or threatened species that attracts broad public concern.

chemical prospecting The search for data on the chemical properties and potential of various species (such as for use in medicines, cosmetics, genetic engineering, and so forth).

chlorinated hydrocarbons A group of synthetic organic pesticides that includes chlordane and DDT.

chlorine A reactive element, found in chlorofluorocarbons and other substances, that has been implicated as a prime factor in the deterioration of the ozone layer.

chlorofluorocarbons (CFCs) Artificially produced compounds composed primarily of carbon, fluorine, and chlorine. CFCs have been implicated in the deterioration of the ozone layer.

chronic toxicity Long-term effects of toxic substances, especially relative to long exposures of low doses.

Clean Air Act A federal statute enacted in 1963 that was the first of a series of acts and amendments that exerted increasing federal pressure on air polluters to clean up their emissions.

Clean Water Act (CWA) A federal statute enacted in 1972 that has been very successful in improving the water quality of lakes and rivers.

clear-cutting The harvesting of trees such that an entire stand of trees is completely removed; also known as even-aged management

climate The average weather in a certain area over time ranges of decades to millennia to hundreds of millions of years.

climax community The last, relatively stable and diverse, community in the sequence of community succession.

closed-loop reclamation (water) Treating wastewater to the level needed before direct reuse.

closed-loop recycling The indefinite recycling of a material or substance without degradation or deterioration, such as the recycling of many metals and glasses.

closed system An isolated system that exchanges nothing with other systems.

coal A general term used to refer to various solid fossil fuels.

cogeneration A power plant produces several types of energy simultaneously, such as electricity and heat, that can be used locally.

cold fusion Promotion of fusion reactions at relatively low ("room temperatures") temperatures.

coliform bacteria Bacteria, such as *Escherichia coli*, that live in the human intestine in huge numbers. The abundance of coliform bacteria in water is a good indicator of how much human feces has recently entered the water.

combined cycle turbine plant A power plant that not only uses a gas turbine, but utilizes excess heat to heat water and power a steam turbine.

command economy A national economy where the central government tells individuals and companies what to produce and sets prices for the resultant products (for example, the economy of the former Soviet Union before its collapse). *See also* market economy for comparison.

commensalism A form of symbiosis where one species benefits and the other is not affected.

commercial extinction When a species becomes so rare that harvesting it is no longer economically viable.

common law A body of law based primarily on judicial rulings, custom, and precedent.

common law torts Basically "wrongs" or wrongful acts against a person, people, or institution.

community All of the populations of different species that inhabit a certain area.

community succession The sequential replacement of species in a community by immigration of new species and the local extinction of old species. The first stage is the pioneer community, and the last stage is the climax community.

competition Organisms competing ("fighting") for the same limited resource.

competitive exclusion A situation where niche overlap is very great and competition is so intense that one species eliminates another from a particular area.

complexity How many kinds of parts a system has.

composting The decomposition of organic materials by microorganisms; produces various forms of "soils."

compound Two or more atoms chemically bonded together. For instance, water is a compound of hydrogen and oxygen.

compressed air energy storage (CAES) Electricity is used to pump air under pressure into a storage reservoir; when the energy is needed, the pressurized air is released.

cone of depression The localized lowering of the water table around a well from which water is being withdrawn faster than it is replenished.

confined aquifer An aquifer bounded above and below by aquicludes.

conservation Refers to attempts to minimize the use of a natural resource.

conservation biology A subdiscipline of biology that draws on genetics, ecology, and other fields to find practical ways to save species from extinction and preserve natural habitats.

conservationism The classical view that forests and other natural resources should be managed to provide the most benefit for the greatest number of people.

conservation of matter and energy, law of The concept that matter and energy cannot be created or destroyed; they can only be transformed.

Contingent Valuation Method (CVM) A method that attempts to "objectively" measure the dollar values of changes in environmental quality; often uses questionnaires and other surveys that ask people what they would pay for various environmental improvements.

consumed water Water that is withdrawn and not returned to its original source.

contaminated water Water that is rendered unusable for drinking.

contraception The prevention of conception or impregnation.

convection cell A circulation pattern set up in a hot fluid, such as in the Earth's mantle or in the atmosphere. A hot liquid rises, flows laterally, and sinks as it cools.

Convention on Biological Diversity (CBD) A document signed at the 1992 Earth Summit that acknowledges that developing nations deserve a share of the profits generated from their genetic resources by agricultural activities and genetic technology.

Convention on International Trade in Endangered Species (CITES) An international convention that outlaws trade in endangered species and products made from endangered species.

core (a) The innermost portion of the Earth; thought to be composed primarily of an iron-nickel alloy. (b) The interior of a nuclear reactor containing the fuel, moderator, and control rods.

cornucopians People who argue that human ingenuity always has, and always will, overcome environmental limitations.

corrosive When used in reference to hazardous wastes, generally referring to liquids that are highly acidic, very alkaline, or otherwise chemically very reactive.

cowboy economics A way of thinking that views the environment as a source of endless space and riches (as the frontier in the Old West was once viewed).

criteria pollutants With reference to air pollution, the five basic criteria pollutants are particulates, sulfur oxides, nitrogen oxides, volatile organic compounds, and carbon monoxide.

critical mineral A mineral that is necessary for the production of essential goods.

crop rotation Planting different crops on a particular field in different years—the same crop is not planted on the same field year after year.

crude birth rate The number of births per year per 1000 members of a population.

crude death rate The number of deaths per year per 1000 members of a population.

crust The outermost layer of rock that forms the solid surface of our planet Earth; divided into continental crust and oceanic crust.

cultivable land Land that can be successfully cultivated to grow crops.

cultural extinction The extinction of a tribal people or indigenous culture.

cyclone An intense storm that typically develops over a warm tropical sea.

dams Structures that obstruct river or stream flow to form artificial lakes or reservoirs.

daughter products The atoms resulting from the splitting, or fission, of a large atom such as uranium or plutonium.

dead zone An area around a mine in which no vegetation or animal life can survive.

debt bomb The more than $1.3 trillion that the poor, developing countries (generally found in the Southern Hemisphere) owe the developed countries; sometimes referred to as the Third World debt crisis.

decentralization The movement away from large, centralized sources of power and production.

decibel (dB) scale A scale used to measure the loudness of sounds.

decommission To take out of service, dismantle, and dispose of a nuclear power plant.

deep ecology A philosophical outlook that takes a holistic and nonanthropocentric perspective, and rejects the human versus environment/nature dichotomy.

deep-well injection A method of disposing of liquid wastes, such as industrial or hazardous wastes, wherein they are pumped or injected down wells deep below the Earth's surface.

deficit areas (water) Areas that receive less precipitation than is needed by well-established vegetation.

deforestation The removal of forest cover from an area.

Delaney Clause A controversial provision, passed in 1958, of the Food, Drug and Cosmetics Act that explicitly prohibits even minuscule amounts of pesticides and other chemicals in processed foods if the chemicals are found to harm laboratory animals. Critics of the clause argue that the costs of regulating and removing such minuscule amounts of chemicals (which may cause little, if any, harm in humans) far outweigh any potential benefits.

dematerialization The reduction of the size of products, particularly as a way to conserve mineral resources.

demographic transition Essentially, the concept or theory that as a nation undergoes technological and economic development, its population growth rate will decrease.

demography The study of the size, growth, density, distribution, and other characteristics of human populations.

density-dependent regulation Biological interactions, such as competition and predation, acting to control the abundance of a population of organisms.

density-independent regulation Physical processes, such as droughts or volcanic eruptions, acting to control the abundance of a population of organisms.

deontology The study of moral obligations and duties.

depth diversity gradient The concept that among aquatic communities species richness generally increases with water depth down to about 6560 feet (2000 m) and then declines with further depth.

descriptive ethics The cataloging and description of the various ethical approaches that have been used by humans.

desertification The spread of desertlike conditions due to human exploitation and misuse of the land.

dilution The reduction in concentration of a pollutant when it is discharged into water.

diminishing returns, law of As the limits of a resource are encountered, increasing efforts to extract that resource produce progressively smaller amounts of the resource.

dioxin A group of more than two hundred related compounds that are extremely toxic, artificially produced chemicals. Dioxins can be inadvertently synthesized in incinerators when trash and garbage are burned.

direct value The value of utilizing a particular resource in such a way that it may be depleted or destroyed—for instance, the value of logging a forest.

discharge The volume of water carried by a channel.

discounting by distance Ignoring or not fully paying for the environmental costs of our actions on people living in another area.

discounting the future Focusing on the present and ignoring or discounting future costs of resource depletion and environmental degradation.

distillation A method of desalination whereby salt water is evaporated so as to remove the dissolved salts.

DNA Deoxyribonucleic acid, the material of which genes are composed.

dosage The amount of a substance, such as a poison, medicine, or vitamin, administered to an individual organism. Dosage is generally measured as the amount of a substance administered to an organism divided by the body weight of the organism.

doubling time The amount of time that a population of a given size at time zero, increasing at a fixed rate, will take to double in size.

drainage basin The region drained by a particular network of rivers and streams.

dump A place where trash, garbage, and other waste are piled—often in a relatively out-of-the-way area such as on the outskirts of a town.

durable goods Material goods or products that are designed to last a relatively long period of time.

duty A moral or required action or obligation.

earthquake Shock waves that originate when large masses of rocks, generally located below the surface of the Earth, suddenly move relative to each other.

Earth Summit The United Nations Conference on Environment and Development (UNCED), an international meeting held in Rio de Janeiro in June 1992 to discuss environmental and development issues; delegations from over 175 countries, including more than a hundred heads of state, attended.

ecocentric Ecological-centered.

ecofeminism Analyzes societal and cultural traits that may have led to the degradation of the environment; specifically concentrates on the oppression of women by a traditional patriarchal society as a major form of social domination that has precipitated other forms of exploitation and domination, including exploitation of the environment.

ecological extinction Occurs when a species, although not totally extinct in an area, has become so rare that it has essentially no role or impact on its ecosystem.

ecological release The population of a particular species increases greatly in size when a competitor is removed.

ecological succession The successive groups of plants and animals that will colonize a newly cleared patch of land or uncolonized body of water.

ecology The study of how organisms interact with each other and their environment.

ecology, first law of Garrett Hardin's concept that "we can never do merely one thing"; sometimes referred to as the "law of unintended consequences."

economics The study of the production, distribution, and consumption of goods and services; in an environmental context, economics is often defined as the study of scarcity and how humans can cope with scarcity.

economic take-off The point at which a poor country can presumably produce enough wealth to financially support itself, export manufactured goods, and eventually attain the living standards of a wealthy, industrialized country.

ecoscam *See* greenwashing.

ecosystem A biological community plus the surrounding physical environment.

ecosystem simplification Occurs when the number of species in an ecosystem declines.

ecoterrorism Committing terrorist-type acts, such as sabotage against property or people, in the defense of the environment and environmental issues and ideals.

ecotone A sharp boundary between adjacent biological communities.

ecotourism Responsible travel to natural areas, often to see wild flora and fauna, that conserves the local environment and supports the local people.

ecotoxicology The study of how chemicals affect entire ecosystems.

edge effects Disturbances from the surrounding area (perhaps dogs, housecats, humans, wind, temperature changes, pollution, and so forth) penetrate along the edges of a preserved area, resulting in habitat loss.

efficiency The useful work that is performed relative to the total energy input to a system.

efficiency improvements Innovations that reduce the flow of throughput by decreasing the per capita resource use.

effluent charges (water) Taxes or fees levied on the discharge of industrial wastewater.

effluent taxes Taxes charged on the basis of how much pollution (effluent) is discharged by a company, industry, or operation.

electricity An electric current or flow of electrons through a conductor.

electrostatic precipitator A device that uses a high voltage to remove charged particulates from polluted air (such as the smoke coming out of a smokestack).

element A fundamental substance that cannot be broken down further into other elements by standard chemical means. Gold, iron, hydrogen, and oxygen are examples of elements.

embodied energy The energy used in producing a product.

emissions offsets The concept that in order to receive a construction permit to build a factory or other industrial operation that may be a new source of air pollution in a particular area, ways must be found to reduce emissions from existing sources in that area.

Endangered Species Act of 1973 An act that directs the U.S. Fish and Wildlife Service to maintain a list of species that are endangered (in immediate danger of extinction) or threatened (likely to be endangered soon).

endemic species A very localized species that inhabits only a relatively small area.

energy The ability to do work.

energy budget The Earth's energy budget is, collectively, all of the various flow pathways of all energy on Earth.

energy conservation Decreasing the demand for energy.

energy efficiency The usable output per unit of energy.

energy farm A farm that produces biomass to be used as an energy source.

energy intensity index The energy consumption per gross national product of a nation.

energy minerals The fossil fuels (oil, coal, and natural gas) and uranium ore.

energy storage Storing energy in a form that is readily accessible to humans.

enrichment Increasing the percentage of fissionable uranium above that found in natural uranium as it is mined and processed.

entropy The amount of low-quality energy, or the amount of disorder and randomness, in a system.

environment In the broadest sense, all aspects of the natural environment plus human manipulations and additions to the natural environment.

environmental economics Economics with an emphasis on the study of the integration of jobs and environmental preservation.

environmental equity Treating all persons, regardless of color, creed, or social status, equally when developing environmental policies and enforcing environmental laws and regulations.

environmental hormones Pollutants that send false signals to the complex hormonal systems that regulate reproduction, immunity, behavior, and growth of organisms.

environmental justice The concept of implementing environmental equity and also reducing the environmental risks to all people.

environmental law Laws, statutes, regulations, treaties, agreements, declarations, reso-

lutions, and the like that have bearing on environmental issues.

environmental racism Racial discrimination in environmental policy making and the racially unequal enforcement of environmental laws and regulations.

environmental science The systematic study of all aspects of the environment and their interactions.

environmental wisdom The ability to sort through facts and information about the environment and make correct decisions and plan long-term strategies.

epidemiological statistics Statistics used to examine correlations between environmental factors and the health of humans and other organisms.

erosion The deterioration and weathering away of soil or rock.

ethanol Ethyl alcohol, a commonly used biomass-derived fuel.

ethics The philosophical study of moral values.

eukaryote A cell with a true nucleus, true chromosomes, and various specialized cellular organelles.

eutrophication A rapid increase in algae or plant growth in an aquatic system due to the influx of a limiting nutrient that was in short supply previously.

evaporite A mineral deposit formed when salt ions precipitate out of a natural body of water.

evapotranspiration The transfer of water into the atmosphere by evaporation and transpiration (the release of water vapor by plants).

executive branch The branch of the government charged with administering and enforcing the laws; the federal executive branch consists of the president, the vice president, and the president's appointees.

exotic species A nonnative species that is artificially introduced to an area.

explosion of life A phrase sometimes used to refer to the rapid diversification of life on Earth about 570 million years ago.

exponential growth The relatively rapid ("geometric") growth phase experienced by many populations during their history. Such growth can be expressed, at least approximately, using an exponential equation or curve.

exponential reserve How long a resource reserve, such as a mineral reserve, will last if demand changes (specifically, if it increases) over time.

externality Environmental, social, and other costs of production that are not included in the price of the product that causes the costs. *See also* market failure.

extinction The loss or death of a group of organisms.

extinction vortex Even if some individuals of a species or population survive disturbances, the population may never fully recover if it becomes too small. The species is said to fall into an extinction vortex and is doomed to eventual extinction.

extirpation The extinction of a species or other group of organisms in a particular local area.

extrinsic value Value of a resource that is external to the resource's intrinsic right to exist.

fallacy of enlightenment The idea or notion that education of people alone, without any other action, will solve the overpopulation and associated environmental problems of the world.

false dichotomy When a complex question inappropriately becomes polarized into an "either-or" issue (for instance, jobs or the environment).

Federal Insecticide, Fungicide, and Rodenticide Act (FIFRA) A law that requires anyone wishing to manufacture a pesticide to register that product with the EPA.

ferrous Referring to iron and related metals that are commonly alloyed with iron, such as nickel and chromium.

fertile isotope An isotope, such as U-238, that can absorb a neutron and form a new element/isotope (such as Pu-239) that is readily fissionable.

fertility rate The number of births in a population. The general fertility rate is the total number of births in a population in any given year as a function of the number of women in their reproductive years. The total fertility rate is the number of children a woman in a given population will have, on average, during her childbearing years.

fertilizer A substance, often an artificial chemical mixture, that is spread on or through the soil to make it more fertile.

filtration The percolation of water through sand and other settled sediment to remove suspended particles.

fission The splitting of an atom, such as uranium or plutonium, to release energy.

fissionable atom An atom that is easily split

by neutron penetration, such as U-235.

five e's The five potential values of environmental resources: esthetic (aesthetic), emotional, economic, environmental services, and ethical.

flat-plate collector A device that usually consists of a black metal plate that absorbs heat from the Sun; the heat can be transferred to a liquid and then used as desired (for instance, to heat a building).

flood A high flow of water that overruns its normal confinement area and covers land that is usually dry.

fluidized bed combustion A way to reduce air pollution by burning very small coal particles at very high temperatures in the presence of limestone particles (the limestone helps to capture sulfur and other pollutants).

flywheel energy storage system Uses a rapidly rotating flywheel to store energy.

food web A graphic depiction of the interrelationships by which organisms consume other organisms.

fossil fuels Coal, oil, natural gas, and related organic materials that have formed over geologic time.

Framework Convention on Climate Change A convention agreed to by many nations at the 1992 Earth Summit. Although the convention does not establish legal obligations or specific target dates, it requires signing countries to use their best efforts to control emissions of greenhouse gases.

frontier mentality The general concept that humans are separate from and above nature, that humans need to subdue the uninhabited wilderness, and that there are always plenty of fresh natural resources to exploit on the edge of the frontier.

fuel cell In a fuel cell electrons are removed from hydrogen atoms to form an electric current; the hydrogen ions combine with oxygen to form water.

fusion The combining or fusing of isotopes of light elements to form a heavier element—in the process, energy may be released.

future costs Environmental costs of a product or service that are not paid now, but rather are passed on to future generations.

Gaia hypothesis The hypothesis that the Earth is similar to an organism and its component parts are integrated analogously to the cells and organs in a living body.

gamma rays A type of radiation consisting of short-wavelength, high-energy electromag-

netic radiation.

garbage "Wet" and generally edible (perhaps by pigs or other animals) discarded matter, such as old food remains, yard clippings, dead animals, leftovers from meat packing operations and butcher shops, and so forth.

gene The basic unit of heredity.

General Circulation Models (GCMs) Complex mathematical models that, with the help of supercomputers, simulate the Earth's climatic patterns.

generator A machine that converts mechanical energy (rotational energy) into electrical energy.

genetic patent rights The patenting of genetic resources, often advocated as a way to allow native peoples to receive profits derived from pharmaceuticals, agriculture, and other uses of genetic resources found in their territories.

geothermal energy Energy (heat) originating from deep within the Earth.

grain Cereals and similar plants that are used for human or animal consumption, such as wheat, corn (maize), rice, barley, and so forth.

grassroots activism Local participation in environmental issues.

gray water Untreated or partially treated wastewater that is used for such purposes as watering golf courses and lawns or flushing toilets (rather than using cleaner water of drinkable quality).

green fees Fees or taxes (such as fees that increase the price of a resource) that are applied to generally reduce throughput (reduce the use of a resource and/or to reduce the production of pollutants).

greenhouse effect The warming up of the lower atmosphere due to the accumulation of greenhouse gases that trap heat near the surface of the Earth.

greenhouse gases Gases, such as carbon dioxide, methane, and CFCs, that are relatively transparent to the higher-energy sunlight, but trap lower-energy infrared radiation. Greenhouse gases that accumulate in the atmosphere promote global warming.

Green movement A political and social movement of the late twentieth century that addresses the root causes of environmental degradation and generally advocates a revolutionary break from the past and the establishment of new, Earth-amenable social institutions.

Green Revolution Modern, chemically based, usually mechanized agriculture that was first used on a large scale in the industrialized countries after World War II.

greenwashing Marketing that unscrupulously seeks to profit from environmental concerns; also known as ecoscams.

Gross National Product (GNP) A standard index that measures a nation's output of goods and services.

groundwater A general term for the water beneath the Earth's surface.

growth rate The rate at which a population is increasing (or decreasing, in the case of a negative growth rate) in size. *See also* percent annual growth.

habitat The general place or physical environment in which a population lives.

habitat fragmentation Habitat disruption where natural habitat is broken into small, relatively isolated fragments.

hard laws Statutes or legal instruments that are legally binding and mandatory.

hardness The amount of calcium, magnesium, and certain other ions in water; "hard water" contains high amounts of these ions.

hard technologies Energy technologies that depend on largescale, centralized, complex, and expensive plants and infrastructures.

hazardous waste Wastes that are particularly dangerous or destructive; specifically characterized by one or more of the following properties: ignitable, corrosive, reactive, or toxic.

heat Infrared radiation.

heavy metals Elements, such as lead, mercury, zinc, copper, cadmium, and so forth, that may be required in trace amounts by organisms, but can cause damage when ingested in larger quantities (such as binding with enzymes and thus impairing their functions).

herbicide A chemical substance used to kill plant weeds.

hidden costs Environmental costs of a product or service that we are initially unaware of, such as future environmental degradation from the full effects of pesticides or other pollutants.

holistic Seeking connections among all aspects of a problem, concern, or issue.

hot spot An area of exceptionally high species richness, especially of concentrations of localized rare species that occur nowhere else.

Hubbert's bubble In the 1950s the geologist M. King Hubbert accurately predicted that U.S. oil production would peak around 1970 and subsequently decline.

Human Suffering Index (HSI) An index

developed by the Population Crisis Committee in the 1980s. This index is a summation of a number of different ratings of a country, such as GNP per capita, food sufficiency, inflation, accessibility of clean drinking water, literacy, energy consumption, growth of the labor force, urbanization, and political freedom.

hunger Not having enough food to sustain oneself adequately; a weakened condition that is brought on by the lack of food.

hydrologic cycle Movement of water about the surface of the Earth, driven by energy from the Sun.

hydropower The use of artificial or natural waterfalls to generate electricity.

hydrosphere The liquid water sphere or "layer" on Earth; it includes the oceans, rivers, lakes, and so on.

hydrothermal fluid reservoir An area where hot rock occurs at relatively shallow depth and natural groundwater is heated, sometimes to extremely high temperatures.

hydrothermal processes Hot water dissolves, transports, and subsequently re-precipitates and concentrates elements and minerals into deposits.

ice ages Intervals in the history of the Earth, especially during the last two million years, when average global surface temperatures were lower than they are currently and continental ice sheets were much more extensive than they are today.

igneous rock A rock formed or crystallized from molten rock (magma).

ignitable A substance that will easily ignite and burn rapidly; a characteristic of some types of hazardous waste.

immigration The movement of people into a country or, more generally, the movement of individuals into a particular population.

immunotoxicology The examination of how chemicals affect the immune system.

incineration The burning of trash and garbage at high temperatures in a large furnace so as to get rid of as much as possible.

independent power producers (IPPs) IPPs construct electricity-generating plants and then sell the electricity to the large utilities.

Index of Sustainable Economic Welfare (ISEW) An alternative to the traditional Gross National Product, the ISEW measures sustainable growth. The ISEW includes environmental measures such as depletion of non-renewable resources, loss of farmland from erosion and urbanization, loss of wetlands,

damage from air and water pollution, and so forth.

indicator species A species in a community or ecosystem that is more susceptible to disturbances than most other species.

indirect value The way that a resource may be valued other than its direct value, such as the emotional and aesthetic values of a forest.

industrial ecosystem An industrial situation that mimics the principles of ecosystems in nature. No "waste" is produced; rather, the effluents of one industrial process form the raw materials for another industrial process.

industrial materials Nonmetallic materials/minerals necessary to industry, such as salts, fertilizer components, sulfur, asbestos, abrasive minerals, and so forth.

Industrial Revolution A series of industrial and technological inventions, beginning in England in the late eighteenth and early nineteenth centuries, that resulted in the cheap and efficient mass production of many commodities.

infant mortality The number of babies that die before their first birthday, given that they are born alive.

infrared radiation Low-energy, long-wavelength electromagnetic radiation that humans perceive as heat.

input reduction Reducing the flow of materials through society.

intangible costs Environmental costs of a product or service that include destruction of scenery or other subjective costs that are very difficult to measure because different people place different values on them.

Integrated Pest Management (IPM) Integrated Pest Management and the concept of biological control follow the basic philosophy that the farmer should not try to totally eliminate pests, but should simply attempt to control them so that they do not cause serious damage. IPM and biological control often use "natural" controls, such as the pests' natural biological predators. IPM seeks to reduce the use of artificial chemical pesticides.

integration The strength of the interactions among the parts of a system.

Intergovernmental Panel on Climate Change (IPCC) A large, international group of officials, scientists, and other researchers who, under the auspices of the United Nations, have been investigating the issue of global climate change, particularly potential future global warming.

intermittent power source A power source,

such as the Sun, that can only be used periodically (the Sun can only be used directly during daylight hours).

intrinsic factors The subtle ways that the complex biochemistries of even closely related species can differ such that a chemical that has no effect on one species may have acute or long-term effects on another species.

intrinsic rate of increase The potential for increase in a given population, often symbolized by r; in large part it is determined by the birth rate and death rate of the population.

intrinsic value The value of a resource unto itself, regardless of its value to humans; often considered the ethical value of a resource, or the right of the resource to exist.

introduction The release of species into new areas that they did not formerly (naturally) occupy, such as the introduction of African savanna species onto game preserves in Florida and Texas.

ionizing radiation Radiation that upon hitting electrically neutral atoms may cause the atoms to lose electrons and thus gain an electrical charge—that is, become ionized.

irrigation The artificial watering of land.

isotopes Atoms of the same element that differ from each other in weight because they have differing numbers of neutrons.

joule A basic unit of energy and work, equal to a force of one newton times one meter.

judicial branch The branch of a government that interprets the laws of the land; in the United States, this is the court system, and the highest federal level is the U.S. Supreme Court.

keystone species A certain species that one or more other species are dependent upon for food, reproduction, or some other basic need.

lag phase The relatively slow growth exhibited by many populations at the beginning of their history.

landfill In the simplest sense, a hole in the ground where solid waste is deposited. In a modern sanitary landfill, the hole is lined so that materials will not escape, and it is covered with layers of dirt as it is progressively filled. When completely filled, it is capped and sealed with more dirt and topsoil.

latent heat storage Heat storage based on phase changes in material objects, such as the melting of ice.

latitudinal diversity gradient The steady decrease in species richness in most groups as one moves away from the equator.

law of the minimum Holds that the growth of a population is limited by the resource in shortest supply.

leachate A liquid solution that forms as water percolates through waste, such as refuse in a landfill or old mining tailings. Leachate may contain any chemicals that can be dissolved, particles, and even live microorganisms.

legal instruments Laws, treaties, regulations, conventions, and the like.

legislative branch The branch of a government that is responsible for making basic laws; in the United States, the federal legislative body is the Congress, composed of the House of Representatives and the Senate.

less developed countries (LDCs) The less rich and less industrialized countries of the world; basically, the countries that are not considered to be more developed countries. *See also* more developed countries.

Lethal Dose-50 (LD-50) The dose of a toxic substance that will kill 50% of a certain population. LD-50 has become the standard reference for summarizing the toxicity of substances.

Life Cycle Analysis (LCA) Sometimes known as cradle to grave analysis, LCA analyzes the entire "life cycle" of a product, from procurement of the raw materials, through its use, to its eventual disposal and the possible reuse or recycling of its components.

life expectancy The average number of years that a typical person at a certain age can expect to live.

life history Age of sexual maturation, age of reproduction, age of death, and other important events in an individual's lifetime, particularly as they influence reproductive traits.

light water reactor (LWR) A common type of commercial reactor that uses ordinary (light) water as the moderator.

lignite A soft, dark brown, coal-like material.

limiting nutrient The nutrient in shortest supply in a particular ecosystem.

lithosphere The rock sphere or layer that forms the surface of the Earth; composed of the crust and uppermost portion of the mantle.

Little Ice Age A period in Earth history, beginning in late medieval/early renaissance times (ca. A.D. 1300) and ending only two or three hundred years ago, during which average global temperatures were slightly lower than before or after.

loss of life expectancy (LLE) The average amount that a life will be shortened by a particular risk under consideration.

Love Canal A site in the town of Niagara Falls, New York, that gained national attention in the late 1970s when hazardous chemicals that were buried in the area began to adversely affect the residents. The disaster of Love Canal helped to spur Congress to pass the Comprehensive Environmental Response, Compensation, and Liability Act of 1980.

magmatic processes Processes during which certain minerals may selectively crystallize out of a hot, molten body of rock.

mantle The thick, at least partially molten layer of rock found between the Earth's core and crust.

mariculture Saltwater seafood farming. *See also* aquaculture.

marine protected areas Areas of ocean that are set aside as preserves for marine life.

market economy A national economy in which production and costs are determined by competition among individuals. *See also* command economy for comparison.

market failure When market prices do not reflect all the true costs of a product or service (often referred to as an "externality").

mass extinction A catastrophic event in Earth history that kills large numbers of species. Some mass extinctions killed more than 60% of all living species on Earth at the time of the extinction.

maximum contaminant levels (MCLs) The highest concentrations allowed by the EPA in water designated for certain uses.

maximum sustainable yield (MSY) The concept that the optimum way to exploit a renewable resource is to harvest as much as possible up to the point where the harvest rate equals the renewal rate.

megacity A large city, generally with a population of more than 10 million.

megalopolis A single vast urban area formed by the expansion and merging of adjacent cities and their suburbs.

megawatt (MW) A million watts.

melanoma A condition of malignant skin cancer.

meltdown A major accident at a nuclear power plant where the core is damaged and begins to "melt."

membrane method A way of producing fresh water from salt water by forcing the salt water through a fine membrane; also known as the filter or reverse-osmosis method.

metallic minerals Minerals containing significant (and often minable) amounts of iron, aluminum, copper, zinc, lead, gold, silver, and so forth.

metamorphic rock A rock formed by modifying a preexisting rock, usually through high temperatures and/or pressures.

methane Natural gas, CH_4, a fossil fuel and potent greenhouse gas.

methanol Methyl alcohol; a fuel that can replace gasoline in many situations and can be produced from natural gas, coal, or biomass.

microirrigation Method of irrigation in which water is transported to crops through pipes and then dripped onto the plants through tiny holes in the pipes, which are installed on or below the surface of the soil; sometimes called drip irrigation.

milling process The process, including crushing, grinding, and leaching, during which a mineral, such as copper or uranium oxide (yellowcake), is removed from the raw ore and concentrated.

mineral A naturally occurring inorganic solid that has a regular crystalline internal structure and composition—for instance, the mineral quartz.

mineral deposit An area where a certain mineral has been concentrated by natural processes.

mineral resources Minerals and earth materials (sometimes including the energy minerals, such as fossil fuels and uranium ore) that form natural resources from which humans draw.

minimum viable population The smallest population size (for a certain population or species) that can stay above the extinction vortex.

moderator A substance, such as water, graphite, or beryllium, used in a nuclear reactor to slow down fast neutrons.

molecular toxicology The examination of the interaction of toxic chemicals with cellular enzymes.

monoculture A form of agriculture where only a single species is grown in a particular field, such as a field devoted entirely to wheat.

Montreal Protocol An agreement reached in 1987 at a meeting in Montreal, Canada, whereby a number of industrialized countries pledged to freeze CFC production at 1986 levels and then gradually decrease CFC production to 50% of 1986 levels by 1999.

moral/moral values Relating to the principles of right or wrong, good or bad behavior. Moral values involve distinguishing or discovering the principles of right and wrong and determining their relative importance and relations.

moral antirealists Persons who maintain that moral values are created by humans, either consciously or unconsciously.

moral realists Persons who believe that moral values are objective and real and can be discovered by humans.

moral status The question of who, or what, is to be considered worthy of having rights (or what level of rights) in an ethical system.

moral values *See* moral.

more developed countries (MDCs) The richer, industrialized countries of the world; basically, the countries of North America, Europe, Japan, Australia, New Zealand, and the former Soviet Union.

Mount Pinatubo The site of a 1991 volcanic eruption in the Philippines that spewed so much smoke and ash into the atmosphere that it temporarily depressed global temperatures (had a minor cooling effect that was experienced worldwide for several years).

muddling along *See* bootstrapping.

multiple-use principle When land is put to many uses at the same time, such as logging, mining, grazing, farming, oil exploration, hunting, fishing, and so forth.

multistage flash distillation (MSF) A method of distillation used to desalinate seawater; cold seawater is run through a series of coils in chambers that become progressively hotter.

municipal solid waste The solid waste produced by the residents and businesses of a city, town, or other municipality; includes old newspapers, packaging materials, empty bottles, leftover foods, leaves and grass clippings, and so forth.

mutagen A substance that causes genetic mutations in sperm or egg cells.

mutation A change in a gene, ultimately caused by a change in the DNA sequence.

mutualism A form of symbiosis that benefits both species.

National Marine Sanctuary A marine area that is protected under the auspices of the U. S. government.

natural environment The physical and biological environments independent of human technological intervention.

natural gas A term used for fossil fuels in the gaseous state, particularly methane.

natural hazard An "unpredictable" natural event, such as an earthquake, volcanic eruption, flood, avalanche, drought, fire, tornado, hurricane, and so forth.

natural selection The basic mechanism of evolutionary change, first formulated by Charles Darwin. Biological populations of organisms exhibit variations among the individuals, and the individuals with more advantageous traits tend to contribute more offspring (bearing the advantageous traits) to the next generation. Thus, this natural selection determines which individuals will contribute most to the next generation.

neo-Malthusian A term often used to refer to persons who believe that the modern rapid increase in the human population is extremely detrimental.

net primary productivity (NPP) The rate at which producer or primary, usually plant, biomass is created.

net yield The concept of net yield for nonrenewable resources holds that a resource can continue to be extracted as long as the resources used in extraction do not exceed the resources gained.

neutron A subatomic particle that has approximately the same mass as a proton, but does not bear an electric charge.

niche An organism's "occupation," or how it lives.

Nimbus-7 A NASA satellite that confirmed the depletion of the ozone layer over the South Pole in the 1980s.

nitrogen oxides NO_x, important components of both lower atmospheric pollution and the upper atmospheric greenhouse gases that promote global warming.

noise Unwanted sound.

nonferrous Metals such as gold, copper, silver, and so forth that are not commonly alloyed with iron. *See also* ferrous.

nonmetallic minerals Structural materials, such as sand, gravel, and building stone, and nonmetallic industrial minerals, such as salts, sulfur, fertilizer components, abrasives, gemstones, and so forth.

nonrenewable resource A resource, such as fossil fuels, that does not significantly regenerate itself on a human time scale.

normative ethics Drawing upon a certain ethical system, normative ethics renders ethical opinions and judgments of actions and prescribes appropriate behavior.

nuclear power The use of nuclear fission reactions to generate electricity.

nuclear proliferation The spread of atomic weapons.

ocean A large body of salt water on the Earth's surface, such as the Atlantic or Pacific Ocean; also refers to the entire body of salt water that covers much of the surface of our planet.

ocean energy Waves, tides, differential heat layers, and other sources of energy directly related to the world's oceans.

ocean thermal energy conversion (OTEC) A proposed way of extracting usable energy from the oceans based on the fact that in tropical areas the surface waters are warmer than the waters at depth.

oil Petroleum and related liquid fossil fuels.

oil shale A rock that contains the organic precursors of oil known as kerogen. Kerogen can be converted to oil by heating.

open-loop recycling A situation where a material or substance can be recycled once or a few times, but not indefinitely because the material is damaged or degraded each time it is recycled (for instance, paper fibers or some plastics).

openness Refers to whether a system is isolated from other systems.

open system A system that is not isolated in that it exchanges matter and/or energy with other systems.

ore A mineral deposit that can be economically mined at a certain time and place with a certain technology.

organophosphates A group of synthetic organic pesticides that are less persistent, but more toxic to humans, than chlorinated hydrocarbons; includes malathion and parathion.

overshoot When a population exceeds its carrying capacity.

oxygenation A method of reformulating gasoline by blending oxygen-rich liquids into it such that carbon monoxide will be converted to carbon dioxide and volatile organic compounds will be better oxidized.

ozonation The use of the reactive chemical ozone (O_3) to disinfect water.

ozone An O_3 molecule. Ozone contributes to air pollution in the troposphere, but is an important natural component of the stratosphere. The stratospheric ozone layer protects the Earth's surface from excessive levels of ultraviolet radiation.

ozone layer A layer of ozone in the stratosphere, most concentrated at an altitude between about 12 and 16 miles (20–25 km).

parasitism Occurs where one species (the parasite) lives off another species (the host) and may actively harm the host; often considered a form of symbiosis.

passive solar design A type of architecture that uses the inherent characteristics of a building to capture heat and light from the Sun.

peak load The amount of electricity needed at the time of highest demand.

peat A thick accumulation of partially decayed plant material.

pegmatite A rock type formed from residual magma that is often characterized by very large crystals that may contain high concentrations of otherwise relatively rare elements.

pelagic Refers to the water column zone of the aquatic (specifically, marine) biome.

percent annual growth The rate of natural increase expressed as a percentage of the given population.

persistence How long a pollutant stays in the environment in unmodified form.

pesticide A chemical substance used to destroy animal pests, such as insects, that might attack a crop. More generally, a pesticide can be any chemical manufactured to kill any organisms that humans consider undesirable.

pesticide treadmill The concept that to keep up with the rapid pace of evolving pesticide immunity, new pesticides must constantly be developed.

petajoule 10^{15} joules.

Petkau effect The general concept that sustained low doses of radiation may be more damaging to organisms than single large doses. More specifically, the Petkau effect documents how cell membranes are damaged by low but sustained doses of radiation.

petroleum Essentially, oil or liquid fossil fuel.

pH scale A scale that is used to measure acidity; 1 is very acidic, 7 is neutral, and 14 is very basic (alkaline).

pheromones Biochemical scents used by males or females to attract the opposite sex.

philosophical ethics The consideration of ethical controversies and underlying values, principles, and rules at an abstract level.

photic zone The upper part of the aquatic biome where light can penetrate the water.

photochemical pollutant A pollutant produced when sunlight initiates chemical reactions among NO_x, volatile organic compounds, and other substances found in the air.

photosynthesis The process by which organisms such as green plants convert light energy to chemical energy and synthesize organic compounds from water and carbon dioxide.

photovoltaics The use of semiconductor technology to generate electricity directly from sunlight.

physical environment The natural physical nonliving world, including the lithosphere, hydrosphere, and atmosphere.

Physical Quality of Life Index (PQLI) An index developed by the Overseas Development Council in the late 1970s that rates a country on the basis of the average life expectancy, infant mortality, and literacy rates of its citizens.

pioneer community The initial community of colonizing species in a particular area.

pioneer stage *See* pioneer community.

placer deposit Heavy mineral grains that have weathered from rocks, been transported, sorted, and finally settled in an ore deposit, such as gold nuggets in the bottom of a stream.

plate tectonics The concept or theory that the Earth's lithosphere is divided into numerous plates that are in motion relative to each other; the continents ride on the backs of the plates and thus move ("drift") over geologic time. Plate tectonics accounts for the distribution of most earthquakes, volcanoes, and other important geological phenomena.

plutonium A heavy element that contains 94 protons. Fissionable isotopes of plutonium can be used as fuel in nuclear reactors and can also be manufactured into bombs.

Pollutant Standards Index (PSI) An index that measures air quality, ranging from 0 (best air quality) to over 400 (worst air quality).

polluted water Water that is rendered unusable for its intended purpose.

pollution A term often used to refer to excess outputs by society into the environment. Depending on how the term is used, pollution can also refer to excess outputs by natural processes (such as "pollution" caused by a volcanic eruption).

population A group of individuals of the same species living in the same area.

population bomb A term used to refer to the fact that the vast majority of the world's population growth is currently taking place in the Southern Hemisphere.

positive feedback The process in which part of a system responds to change in a way that magnifies the initial change.

power Work (requiring energy) divided by

the time period over which the work is done.

power plant A plant that converts some form of energy, for instance, chemical energy found in coal, into electrical energy.

precautionary principle The principle that advises that, in the face of uncertainty, the best course of action is to assume that a potential problem is real and should be addressed ("better safe than sorry").

precipitation Removal of water from the atmosphere as rain, snow, sleet, or hail.

precycling The reduction of packaging materials by manufacturers.

predation The process in which certain organisms kill and consume other organisms.

preservation Refers to nonuse, such as a "preserve" that is set aside and protected in its pristine natural state.

preservationism The classical view that nature should be preserved for its own sake.

primary pollutants Pollutants that are directly emitted, such as SO_x by coal-burning power plants.

primary standards Under the drinking water standards of the Safe Drinking Water Act, primary standards specify contaminant levels based on health-related criteria.

primary treatment The use of physical processes, especially screening and settling, to remove materials from water.

privatization When a resource, such as an environmental resource, is transferred from the commons to an individual or company that has a vested interest in the particular resource.

progressive conservationism The view that the federal government in particular should take an active role in protecting forests and other natural resources for the public; popular during the late nineteenth and early twentieth centuries.

property rights Rights associated with ownership or use of material property, including land.

protocells Cell-like structures artificially produced by heating amino acids.

pumped hydroelectric storage (PHS) In PHS, electricity is used to drive pumps that transfer water from a lower reservoir to a higher one. Electricity can then be regenerated by allowing water to flow through a turbine on its way back to the lower reservoir.

quad A quadrillion BTUs.

radiation Electromagnetic radiation; includes visible light, heat, ultraviolet radiation, gamma rays, X rays, and so forth. The term radiation is also sometimes used to refer to the emission of particles (such as alpha and beta particles) from a radioactive atom.

radioactivity The emission of particles (such as alpha and beta particles) and rays (energy, such as gamma rays) from a nucleus as it disintegrates.

radionuclides Unstable atoms that undergo spontaneous disintegration and give off radiation in the process.

rate of natural increase The crude birth rate minus the crude death rate of a population.

reactive With reference to hazardous waste, materials that are very active chemically and can easily cause explosions and/or release harmful fumes.

reactor vessel In a nuclear power plant, a thick steel tank that usually contains the reactor core and primary water loop.

recharge area An area where rainfall can infiltrate into an aquifer.

recovery rate The amount of the original material that can actually be recovered and recycled.

recycling Using the same resource over and over, but in modified form.

recycling loop The use of a resource, followed by the discarding and reprocessing of the resource, and then the reuse of the resource.

refuse Refers to both trash and garbage. *See also* garbage; trash.

regulatory agencies Agencies that are part of the executive branch of the government and are responsible for administering and enforcing laws enacted by Congress.

reintroduction Release of plants and animals back into habitat that they formerly occupied, but in which they may have become locally scarce or extinct.

relativists Persons who believe that there is no objective or rational way to determine right or wrong, good or bad.

remediation Efforts to counteract some or all of the effects of pollution after it has been released into the environment.

renewable energy An energy source that, from an Earth perspective, is continually renewed (for example, solar energy).

renewable resource A resource that will regenerate within a human time scale; for example, crops and energy received from the Sun.

replacement level fertility The number of children needed to keep a population at a stable size; generally considered to be a total fertility rate of about 2.1 children per woman.

reprocessing facility A facility designed to reprocess spent nuclear fuel in order to recover fissionable materials.

reproductive rights Essentially, a woman's right to determine for herself if, and when, she will bear children.

reserve A resource that has been located and can be profitably extracted at the current market price. For minerals in particular, a reserve is an identified ore deposit that has yet to be exploited.

residence time (a) The amount of time that a certain atom or molecule spends, on average, in a certain portion of its biogeochemical cycle. (b) The time it takes for a pollutant to move through the environment.

resource A source of raw materials used by society.

resource recovery facility A plant where trash and garbage are burned and the heat generated is recovered and applied to some useful end, such as generating electricity.

respiration Biological combustion or the "burning" of food molecules in an organism. During respiration large organic molecules are broken down into simpler organic molecules, and energy is released.

restoration The process of returning a degraded resource to its natural state.

reuse Using the same resource over and over in the same form.

right Something to which one has a just, inherent, or natural claim—such as the right to life.

riparian law A law under which the owner of land has the right to withdraw water that is adjacent to the land, such as from a river or lake.

risk A dangerous element, or the chance of loss or peril to human life or other valuable entities; generally refers to any potential danger.

rock cycle The cycling of solid earth materials—rocks—from one form to another. Sedimentary rocks may be subjected to great pressures and be transformed into metamorphic rocks. Metamorphic rocks may be heated to the point where they melt, forming a magma that later crystallizes as igneous rocks. Igneous rocks may be weathered and broken down into grains that form the basis of a sedimentary rock.

rubbish A very general term that includes trash, garbage, and other items such as construction and demolition debris.

Safe Drinking Water Act (SDWA) A federal statute enacted in 1974 that aimed explicitly at improving the quality of drinking water by establishing primary and secondary standards for contaminant levels in water.

salinization An increase in soil salt content that sometimes occurs due to prolonged irrigation, especially in poorly drained arid regions.

sanitary landfill *See* landfill.

saturation, zone of The region below the water table where all voids in the soil and rock are fully filled with water.

scarcity With reference to natural resources, such as minerals, a lack of such resources as compared to demand for the resources.

scrubbers Devices that cleanse emissions, usually with water, before they are released into the air.

sea level rise Worldwide rises in sea level (sea level height increasing relative to the elevations of the continents), such as has been predicted as a result of global warming.

secondary pollutants Pollutants produced by reactions among other air pollutants, such as photochemical pollutants.

secondary standards Under the drinking water standards of the Safe Drinking Water Act, secondary standards specify contaminant levels based on nonhealth-related criteria (such as color or odor, which are not strictly health issues).

secondary treatment The use of biological (microbial) processes to remove materials from polluted water.

sedimentary processes Natural processes that may concentrate minerals through precipitation from a solution or by differential settling of grains in moving or still water.

sedimentary rock A rock formed on or near the Earth's surface by the settling or precipitation of materials. A sedimentary rock may be composed of grains or clasts of particulate matter (usually older rocks or mineral grains), or it may be formed from the chemical or organic precipitation of minerals from an aqueous solution (such as certain limestones formed in an ocean).

sedimentation The settling out of suspended particles from a body of water.

selective cutting The harvesting of trees such that only certain trees are cut down and the land is not stripped bare; also known as uneven-aged management.

sensible heat storage Allowing a material substance to heat up and then release its heat again.

septic tank A large concrete tank buried underground to receive household sewage. Septic tanks are used in areas without a sewer system.

severance tax A tax levied on minerals or other resources as they are extracted.

sick building syndrome Refers to ailments such as headaches, nausea, allergic reactions, and other symptoms that are caused by indoor air pollutants in a building where people work or live.

sinkhole A type of land subsidence, taking the form of a large depression in the ground, caused by water withdrawal. A sinkhole occurs when a thin layer of rock overlying an underground cavern collapses.

sinks Environmental reservoirs that receive the throughput of society.

six e's The six potential values of wild biological resources: esthetic (aesthetic), emotional, economic, environmental services, ethical, and evolutionary.

slash and burn agriculture A form of agriculture where trees and other vegetation are cut down and burned in order to clear the land and release nutrients into the soil.

smelting A process in which concentrated ore, such as copper ore, is roasted and subjected to high temperatures in a smelting furnace to produce crude metal (for instance, crude copper).

smog Originally referred to a mixture of smoke and fog, but now generally refers to the brown haze of photochemical pollutants found in some urban areas.

social ecology An approach to the environmental crisis that attempts to identify social factors that are the underlying causes of current environmental degradation.

social institutions Generally, the institutions or constructs that are important in regulating society, such as familial, political, educational, religious, and economic systems and institutions.

soft laws Legal instruments that are not legally binding, but act more as guides to policy.

soft technology Energy technologies that are generally small scale, relatively inexpensive, and localized.

soil A mixture of weathered rocks and minerals, decayed organic matter, living organisms, air, and water.

soil degradation The damaging or destruction of natural soils; often due to overuse, abuse, and neglect by humans.

soil fertility The ability of the soil to support plant life and associated fauna.

soil horizons Layers of soil that form approximately parallel to the surface of the land; may include the topsoil, subsoil, a layer of partially disintegrated rock, and finally the underlying bedrock.

solar-hydrogen economy An economy based primarily on solar power (in all its forms, including wind power and hydroelectric power) and using hydrogen as a convenient way to store and transport energy.

solar thermal technology The use of the Sun's energy to heat substances such as water to produce steam that drives a turbine and generates electricity.

solid waste Broadly defined, solid waste includes such items as household garbage, trash, refuse, and rubbish, as well as various semisolids, liquids (such as sludge or liquids in solid containers), and gases (often contained in solid containers, such as gas canisters), that result from mining, agricultural, commercial, and industrial activities.

source reduction As applied to solid waste, reducing the generation of waste in the first place (as opposed to later reusing or recycling waste).

sources The environmental resources (matter and energy) that are taken from nature and used by society.

species Often defined, at least for sexual organisms, as all of the organisms that can interbreed (or potentially interbreed) to produce fertile offspring. Different species are reproductively isolated from one another.

species-area curve A curve or graph that shows the number of different species found in a gradually enlarged area of sampling.

species richness The number of different species that occur in a given area.

species triage The concept that conservation efforts should be directed at those species that are at risk of extinction and can still be saved.

static reserve How long a resource reserve, such as a mineral reserve, will last if demand does not change with time.

stock pollutant Refers to synthetic materials that are not found in nature and tend to be among the most persistent pollutants.

strategic mineral A critical mineral that a particular country must import from areas that are potentially unstable politically, militarily, or socially.

stratosphere The thermal layer of the atmosphere above the troposphere in which temperature increases with altitude. The ozone layer occurs within the stratosphere.

strip-mining A form of surface mining, especially for coal, that is very destructive to the landscape.

structural materials Nonmetallic materials/minerals used in building, such as building stone, sand, gravel, and other components of cement and concrete.

substitution The use of one resource in place of another.

suburban sprawl The spreading of a city's population out into the surrounding countryside, forming suburbs.

superconductivity Superconductors are substances through which electrons can pass with virtually no friction or resistance, thus allowing almost 100% energy transmission.

superconducting magnetic energy storage (SMES) A system in which superconducting loops or coils would be used to store electrical energy by allowing the current to circulate around a closed loop of nearly zero resistance.

Superfund The common name for the federal Hazardous Substance Response Fund that is used for cleanup and related expenses associated with hazardous waste sites on the EPA's National Priorities List.

supertoxin A poisonous substance of such high potency that less than a drop can kill an adult human.

surplus areas (water) Areas that receive more precipitation than is needed by well-established vegetation, including crops.

sustainable development Development that focuses on making social, economic, and political progress to satisfy global human needs, desires, aspirations, and potential without damaging the environment; sometimes known as sustainable growth.

sustainable economy An economy that produces wealth and provides jobs for many human generations without degrading the environment.

sustainable growth See sustainable development.

sustainable harvesting The sustainable use/harvesting of nuts, fruits, and other products that can be extracted from an ecosystem without causing damage; sometimes known as extractive forestry.

sustainable technology Technology that permits humans to meet their needs with minimum impact on the environment.

sustainability Meeting the needs of today without reducing the quality of life for future generations.

symbiosis Organisms of different species living together; includes such relationships as amensalism, commensalism, mutualism, and parasitism.

synergism With reference to toxicology, when the toxic effects of different substances are multiplied through interaction.

syngas A mixture of hydrogen gas and carbon monoxide; also known as coal gas or town gas.

system A set of components functioning together as a whole.

tailings In mining, the residue after high-grade ore is extracted.

taxonomy In biology, the description, classification, and naming of groups of organisms.

teleological tradition According to this way of thinking, every being and object in nature (as well as among human artifacts) has a purpose, function, end, final cause, or utility in the overall natural design and order of the world and universe.

teratogen A substance that adversely affects fetal development, such as when a pregnant woman ingests harmful chemicals.

terawatt (TW) 10^{12} watts.

thermal inversion Occurs when a layer of warm air overlies cooler air in the troposphere (lower atmosphere), thus inverting the usual condition in which air becomes cooler as altitude increases.

thermochemical conversion The heating of biomass in an oxygen-deficient environment in order to produce substances that can be used as fuels.

thermochemical heat storage The use of reversible chemical reactions to store heat.

thermodynamics The study of energy and energy conversions.

thermodynamics, first law of States that energy can be neither created nor destroyed, but only transformed.

thermodynamics, second law of States that when energy is transformed from one form to another, it is degraded. This is sometimes known as the law of entropy because energy transformations increase the entropy of a closed system.

Third World debt crisis See debt bomb.

thorium An element that contains 90 protons; thorium-232 can be used in a breeder reactor to produce fissionable U-233.

three R's Return, repurify, and reuse (with reference to water).

threshold of exposure The smallest amount of a poison or other toxic substance that is necessary to cause harm.

throughput The movement of materials and energy through society.

throwaway society A society based on the one-way flow of matter; products are simply discarded after being used.

tidal power The harnessing of the tides to produce energy in a form that humans can readily utilize.

tokamak A large machine that uses magnetic fields to confine and promote controlled fusion reactions.

topsoil An upper layer of the soil, composed primarily of a mixture of organic matter and mineral matter; it is alive with microscopic and small macroscopic organisms.

tornado Typically consists of a rapidly rotating vortex of air that forms a funnel.

torts See common law torts.

toxic Toxic materials or substances are harmful or fatal when consumed by organisms in relatively small amounts.

toxicology The study of the effects of chemicals that are harmful or fatal when consumed by organisms in relatively small amounts.

Toxics Release Inventory (TRI) A report compiled annually by the Environmental Protection Agency on toxics released by U.S. industries based on data reported to the EPA by those industries under the Emergency Planning and Community Right-to-Know Act of 1986.

Toxic Substances Control Act (TSCA) A federal statute enacted in 1976 to regulate toxic substances not covered under other laws. The basic goals of the TSCA are to require industry to produce data on environmental effects of chemicals and to prevent harm to humans and the environment, while not creating unnecessary barriers to technology.

toxic threshold See threshold of exposure.

toxic tort A lawsuit against a manufacturer of a toxic substance for harm caused by that substance.

toxin A poisonous substance produced by an organism; the term is sometimes used to refer to any toxic substance in general.

transcendentalism A general philosophy espoused in the nineteenth century by such writers as Ralph Waldo Emerson and Henry David Thoreau. In many ways, transcendentalism emphasized the spiritual over the material, especially the materialism of society. This resulted in a concern for the natural environment and a mourning and decrying of the destruction of the natural environment by humans.

transgenic crops Genetically transformed crops; crops that have been artificially engineered using bioengineering.

trash Waste that is "dry" (as opposed to liquid or gas) and nonedible, such as newspapers, boxes, cans, containers, and so forth.

troposphere The lowermost thermal layer of the atmosphere, wherein temperatures normally decline with increasing altitude; the layer of the atmosphere in which most weather phenomena take place.

turbine A machine that converts the lateral motion of a liquid or gas into rotational motion.

ultraviolet (UV) radiation Relatively high-energy, short-wavelength, electromagnetic radiation (light). UV has wavelengths in the range of 200 to 400 nanometers (one nanometer equals a billionth of a meter).

umbrella species A large, charismatic species (e.g., the Florida panther). When the habitat for such a species is protected, many other species will be protected as well.

unequally distributed costs Environmental costs of a product or service that are not distributed evenly among socioeconomic groups of people, such as when poorer people either pay relatively more or absorb relatively more of the environmental costs (for instance, being forced by economics to live in more polluted areas).

unique species Species that are not closely related to any other living species.

uranium A heavy element that contains 92 protons. Fissionable isotopes of uranium can be used as fuel in nuclear reactors and can also be manufactured into bombs.

urbanization The trend toward increasing numbers of people living in cities.

utilitarianism A philosophy whose basic principle is that the overall good should be maximized ("the greatest good for the greatest number").

value The relative worth, utility, or importance of an object or idea. *See also* moral.

virgin ores or resources Original natural ores or resources that are extracted from the Earth or from "Nature."

volcano A place on the Earth's crust where hot, molten rock (magma) wells up to the surface.

waste-to-energy The burning of municipal solid waste to produce energy.

waterlogging The rising of the water table over time, and the soaking of soils, in areas where irrigated land is poorly drained. Waterlogging is often associated with salinization.

water table The boundary between the zones of aeration and saturation.

watt A common unit of power defined as one joule of work or energy per second.

weather Short-term, daily perturbations in the atmospheric/hydrologic cycles.

Wilderness Act of 1964 A federal statute that allowed for the designation of wilderness areas on federal lands that are to be managed so as to retain their primeval character.

wind farm A vast tract of land covered with wind-powered turbines that are used to drive generators that produce electricity.

wind power The harnessing of the wind's energy for human applications.

Wise Use movement A movement with the avowed goal of nullifying or eliminating most environmentally based laws and regulations. Wise Users generally see such laws as overly expensive, disruptive of free enterprise, and infringing on property rights.

withdrawn water Water that is taken from its source (such as a river, lake, or aquifer); it may be returned to its source after use.

work A force applied to a material object times the distance that the object is moved.

xeriscaping Landscaping designed to save water.

yellowcake Uranium oxide (U_3O_8) or "natural uranium."

INDEX

Energy crisis in United States, 185–186
Energy crops, 228–229
Energy efficiency, 249
 improving, 250–251
 at national level, 250
Energy farms, 228–229
Energy flow, 101–103
 human use of, 103
 through ecosystems, 85–87
Energy flow and productivity, human disturbance
  of, 89
Energy intensity, 250
Energy intensity index, 157
Energy minerals, 259
Energy Policy and Conservation Act (1975), C.3
Energy resources, depletion of, 152
Energy storage, 244
 electrical, 244–247
 heat, 247–248
  latent, 248
  sensible, 248
  thermochemical, 248
English/metric conversion table, B.1–2
English starling, 321
Entombment, 223
Entropy, 101, 170
Environment
 biological, 31
 concern about, 3–4
 economic incentives to sustain, 572–574
 human impact on, 15
 impact of people on, 2–3
 natural, 31
 physical, 31
Environmental advantages and disadvantages of
  biomass energy, 231–232
Environmental crisis, 607–608
 and Green movement, 606–607
 historical perspectives of, 608–619
 and North American bison, 610–611
 solving by refocusing Western political-
  economic structures, 622–625
 Western social values as cause of, 618–625
 and Wise Use movement, 616–617
Environmental degradation, 12, 191–192
 due to mineral exploitation, 266, 268–271
Environmental economics, 565–567. See also
  Economics
Environmental ethics, 585–586. See also Ethics
 animal rights in, 596–597
  versus freedom of religious expression,
   584–585
 biocentric, 594
 and civil disobedience, 600
 deep ecology, 598
 definition of, 586
 ecocentric, 594–595, 598
 ecofeminism, 599
 and ecoterrorism, 600
 importance of, 603
 non-western perspectives on, 599, 601
 social ecology, 598–599
Environmental externalities, internalizing,
  570–576
Environmental hormones, 415
Environmental impact
 definition of, 12–16

of energy use, 175
exponential growth of, 14
history of, 8–12
Environmentalism, 8, 64
 historical perspective on American, 608–618
Environmental issues
 choice of clothing as, 362–363
 public debates on, 6
Environmental justice, 589
Environmental laws, 625
 decision making in public arena, 632, 634–635
 in fighting environmentalism, 631
 international, 625–628
 selected major pieces of United States, C.1–3
 selected pieces of international, D.1–3
 in United States, 628, 631–632
Environmental literacy, 638–639
Environmental movements, history of, 8–12
Environmental organizations, selected, E.1–E.18
Environmental problems
 basic causes of, 7–8
 in China, 621
Environmental Protection Agency (EPA)
 and air pollution control, 464, 467, 478–483,
  484, 486
 creation of, 9
 establishment of, 615
 and landfill regulations, 537
 and racism, 588
 spending priorities of, 6
 and waste management, 539, 547
 and water pollution control, 431–432, 452–453,
  454, 456–457, 458
Environmental racism, 588–589
Environmental revolution, 21
Environmental science
 definition of, 8
 versus economics, 563–567
 as holistic, 5
 negative implication of, 638–639
Environmental services, 328
Environmental system
 definition of, 103
 key traits of, 103–106
 society in, 108, 110
Environmental technologies
 developing innovative, 493–494
 role of United States in, 568
Environmental wisdom, 5
Environmental worth, 570–571
Epidemiological statistics, 410
Erosion, 376
Erwin, Terry, 314
Esthetic value, 150
Ethanol, 228, 230, 464, 476
Ethics, 585–587, 635
 biocentric, 594
 definition of, 586
 descriptive, 587
 ecocentric, 594–595, 598
 and environmental crisis, 635
 and global population, 602
 major traditions in Western thought, 588
  deontology, 592–593
  Judeo-Christian environmental ethics,
   588–590
  property rights, 593–594

teleological tradition, 590–591
 utilitarianism, 591–592
 normative, 587
 philosophical, 587
Ethyl alcohol, 230
Eugenia psyllid, 406
Eukaryotes, 63
Eutrophication, 71, 435
Evaporite deposit, 264
Evapotranspiration, 284
Even-aged management, 347
Everglades
 ecosystems of, 300
 restoration of Florida's, 398
 saving, 302
Evolution
 of biosphere, 60–64
 community, 83–84
 through natural selection, 60–62
Evolved immunity, 423
Executive branch, 628
Exotic species, problems created by introduction
  of, 320–324
Experimental ecology, 90
Explosion of life, 63
Exponential depletion, 152
Exponential exploitation, 152
Exponential growth, 114, 115–118
 of environmental impact, 14
 of human population, 12–13
 of technology, 13
Exponential reserve, 272–273
Exposure assessment, 410, 414–416
Externalities, 274–275, 569–570
Extinction, 315
 causes of, 317–324
 characteristics of susceptibility, 330
 crisis in, 312, 316
 determining which species to save, 328–331
 methods of saving species, 331–333
 reasons to stop, 327–328
 secondary, 324
Extinction vortex, 325
Extirpations, 315
Extrinsic values, 150
Exxon Valdez oil spill, 183, 446, 567. *See also* Oil
  spills
 bioremediation in cleaning up, 556, 558

ℱ

Fallacy of enlightenment, 20
Fallow, 383
False dichotomy, 563
Farming. *See also* Agriculture
 fish, 377
 organic, 370–371
Farms, energy, 228–229
Fast neutrons, 200
Federal Aid in Wildlife Restoration (Pittman-
  Robertson) Act (1937), C.1
Federal Environmental Pesticide Control Act
  (1972), C.2
Federal government, consumption of energy by,
  252–253
Federal Hazardous Substances Act (1960), 399,
  C.2
Federal Insecticide, Fungicide, and Rodenticide

legal control of, 307
pollution of, 292, 457
problems with, 292–295
remediation of, 451–452
Growth rate, 113
Gulf War, 615
Gypsy moths, 320–324

H

Habitat, 67
disruption of, 318–320, 331
fragmentation of, 319
Habitat conservation plans (HCP), 339
Half-life, 210
Halons, 497
Hanford Nuclear Reservation, 222
Hardin, Garrett, 16, 108
Hard laws, 625
Hardness, 453
Hard technologies, 178
Hazardous Liquid Pipeline Safety Act (1979), C.3
Hazardous Materials Transportation Act (1974), C.3
Hazardous waste, 393, 549–561
and Bhopal disaster, 427–428, 553
categories of, 550
definition of, 549
and Love Canal, 10, 551–552, 615
new technologies for dealing with, 554, 556–558
and Superfund, 9, 398, 552–553, 633
and Toxics Release Inventory, 402–403, 553–554
Heat pollution, 389
Heat radiation, 504
Heat storage, 247–248
Heavy metals, 415
as source of water pollution, 440
Helium as atmospheric component, 465
Herbicides, 358, 417
agricultural techniques of, 366
pollution from, 369
Herculaneum, 50
Hickel, Walter, 282
Hidden costs, 570
Himalayas, 36
Hiroshima, 210
Holistic approach to environment, 5
Holton, Gerald, 6
Homes-from-pollution process, 568
Homestead Act (1862), 609, C.1
Hooker Chemical and Plastics Corporation, and Love Canal, 551–552, 615
Hoover Dam, 47, 613
Hormones, environmental, 415
Hot dry rock technology, 242
Hot molten rock, 241–242
Hot spots, 332
Household pollution, 391
Households, taxing water use for, 304–305
Hubbert, M. King, 152
Hubbert's bubble, 152
Humane Society of the United States, 585
Human impact
on biogeochemical cycles, 99–101
on matter cycling, 91–92
on population decline, 72–73
on population growth, 71–72
on population ranges, 74

Human overkill, 73
Human overpopulation as central issue in environmental science, 114
Humans
biodiversity losses before, 316
use of energy flows, 103
use of fossil fuels, 180–184, 186–188
Human Suffering Index (HSI), 126
Hunger, 354
Hunting, 8
Hurricanes, 51
Hydrocarbons, and indoor air pollution, 486
Hydrochlorofluorocarbons (HCFCs), 393, 496–497, 503
Hydroelectric power, 228
Hydrofluorocarbons (HFCs), 393
Hydrogen, 37
clean-burning, 244
Hydrogen oxides (HO_x), and ozone depletion, 497
Hydrogen sulfide, release of, in geothermal energy, 242
Hydrogeology, 443
Hydrologic cycle, 40, 283–284
inequalities in, 286
Hydropower, 192–194
Hydrosphere, 31
Hydrothermal fluid reservoirs, 241
Hydrothermally formed ore deposits, 263–264
Hydrothermal processes, 262–263
Hydrothermal vents, 35

I

Ice Ages, 510, 511–514
Igneous rocks, 38–39
Ignitable materials, 393
Immigration, 129
Immunity, evolved, 423
Immunotoxicology, 408
Inbreeding, genetic, 325
Incineration, 530–531, 539
problems with, 532–533
Independent power producers (IPPs), 228
Index of Sustainable Economic Welfare (ISEW), 567
India
alternative energy sources in, 227
population control in, 139–140
Indicator species, 326
Indirect values, 150, 327
Indoor air pollution, 464, 484
Indoor pollutants
chemical emissions as, 486
costs of, 486–487
radon as, 484, 485–486
smoking as, 486
sources and types of, 484, 486
Industrial accidents, 427–428
Industrial ecology, 388–389
Industrial ecosystems, 530, 547–549
Industrial hygiene, 389
Industrial materials, 259
Industrial pollution, 391
Industrial Revolution, 118
Industry
necessity of energy for development in, 167–168
recycling of water in, 306
taxing water use for, 304–305

wastes in, as source of water pollution, 439
water use in, 286
Infant mortality, 118
rate of, 119
Infectious agents as water pollutants, 435
Information overload, coping with, 4–5
Infrared radiation, 504
Inner core, 34
Inorganic chemicals as water pollutant, 437
Inorganic compounds as category of hazardous waste, 550
Inorganic pesticides, 418–419
Input reduction, 7, 397–398. See also Conservation
implementing, 401–402
Insecticides, 417
Intangible costs, 570
Integrated pest management (IPM), 370–371, 423–424
techniques in, 371
Integration, 103
Interbreeding, 328
Intergovernmental Panel on Climate Change (IPCC), 510, 515
Intermediate disturbance hypothesis, 82
Intermittent energy, 232, 234
International Bottled Water Association (IBWA), 455
International environmental law, 625–628
International Potato Center, 367
International Rice Research Institute, 367
International Soil Reference and Information Centre, 378
Intrinsic factors, 411
Intrinsic rate of increase, 65–66
Intrinsic value, 149
Introduced species, 320–324, 331
Investor Responsibility Research Center (IRRC), 575
Iodine-131, 210
Ionizing radiation, 209
Iron, 37
availability of, 261, 264, 275
as metallic mineral, 258–259
as ore, 263
reserves of, 262, 263
Iron Age, 258
Irrigation, 363
drip, 296, 370
effects of, 364–365
Isotopes, 37, 199
Ivory, 312

J

Japanese beetles, 320–324
Job blackmail, 564
Joule (J), 169
Judeo-Christian environmental ethics, 588–590
Judeo-Christian theology, 608
Judgments of experts, 632
Jupiter, 32n
Justice, environmental, 589

K

Kant, Immanuel, 593
Kennecott Copper, 268
Kennedy, John F., 576
Kent, Donald M., 407

Syngas, 229–230, 248
Synthetic growth hormones, 421
Synthetic organic chemicals (SOCs), 436
Synthetic organic pesticides, 419–420
System. *See also* Environmental system
   definition of, 103
Systems theory in studying complex systems, 107

T

Taiga, 78
Tailings, 260, 270
Tambora, 31, 42
Tantalum, 263
Taxes
   gasoline, 254
   green, 572–573
   severance, 570
Taxonomists, 313
Taxonomy, 62
Taylor Grazing Act (1934), C.1
Technology
   exponential growth of, 13
   green, 391, 402
   reducing impact of, 17–20
   sustainable, 17
Technology-based control of pollution, 394
Teleological tradition, 590–591
Temperate forests, 78
Temperature
   English/metric conversion table, B.1
   English/metric measures for, B.1, B.2
Teratogen, 409
Terawatt (TW), 169
Terawatt-years per year (TW), 174
Terborgh, John, 321
Terrestrial biomes, 76
Thalidomide, 413–414
Thermal inversion, 477
Thermal pollution as water pollutant, 437–438
Thermochemical conversion, 229–230
Thermochemical heat storage, 248
Thermodynamics, laws of, 169–170
   first, 101
   second, 101
Thermosphere, 39–40
Third world debt crisis, 579
Thoreau, Henry David, 5, 64, 598, 609
Thorium, 263
Thorium-232, 202
Three Mile Island nuclear power plant accident,
   10, 208, 212–214, 615
3M (Minnesota Mining and Manufacturing),
   Pollution Prevention Pays program at,
   388–389
Threshold of exposure, 209
Throughput, 14
   reducing, 16–22
Tidal power station, 242–243
Tiltmeters, 49
Timber Culture Act (1873), C.1
Tin, 263, 272, 276, 278
Tires, recycling, 534–535
Titanium, 263, 264, 275, 278
Tokamak, 202
Tongass National Forest, 348–349
Topsoil, 378, 379
Tornadoes, 52

Torts
   common law, 625
   toxic, 426–428
Total fertility rate (TFR), 119
Town gas, 229
Toxic identification, 410, 411
Toxicity
   acute, 409
   chronic, 409
   nontarget, 421–422
Toxic materials, 393
Toxicology
   behavioral, 408
   definition of, 407
   and effects of toxic substances, 408–409
   history and future of, 407–408
   molecular, 408
   and toxic risk assessment, 410–417
Toxic pollutants, 407
Toxics Release Inventory (TRI), 402–403, 553–554
Toxic risk assessment, 410
   characterization, 410, 416–417
   dose-response, 410, 411–414
   exposure, 410, 414–416
   identification, 410, 411
Toxic substances
   effects of, 408–409
   legal aspects of, 424, 426–428
   new, 458–459
Toxic Substances Control Act (1976), 9, C.3
Toxic Substances Control Act (1980), 399, 400,
   424, 426
Toxic threshold, 413
Toxic torts, 426–428
Toxic wastes
   cleaning up, 7, 633
   generation of, from solar energy, 234
Transgenic crops, 371–373
Trash. *See* Wastes
Treadmill, pesticide, 423
Tree harvesting, 147
Tributaries, 289
Trichlorofluoromethane, 496
Tropical rainforest, 78
Troposphere, 39, 40, 498
Tropospheric pollution, and ultraviolet light, 504
Truman, Harry, 576
Tsunami, 50
Tundra, 78
Tungsten, 264
Turbine, 176
Typhoons, 51

U

Ultraviolet (UV) radiation, 494
   effects of, on reaching Earth's surface, 501–503
   and tropospheric pollution, 504
Umbrella species, 331
Underground leakage, 443
Unequally distributed costs, 570–571
Uneven-aged management, 347–348
Union Carbide, and Bhopal disaster, 427–428, 553
Union of Concerned Scientists, 208
Unique species, 330–331
United Nations Conference on Environment and
   Development (UNCED), 341, 520, 578, 579,
   626

United Nations Convention on Biological
   Diversity, 626–627
United Nations Environment Programme, 510,
   538
United Nations Framework Convention on
   Climate Change, 626
United Nations Intergovernmental Panel on
   Climate Change (IPCC), 510, 515
United Nations population conference, 113–114
United States
   energy crisis in, 185–186
   environmental policy in, as misguided or
   enlightened, 633
   population of, 129–130
   sources and consumption of energy in, 172–173
   species preservation in, 333–337
U.S. Forest Service, 347
U.S. Geological Survey, 459
Unsustainable growth versus sustainable growth,
   566
Uraninite, 263
Uranium, 199, 200, 259, 263
Uranium Mill Tailings Act (1978), C.3
Uranium resources, 205
Uranus, 32n
Urbanization, 128–129
Urey, Harold, 60
Utilitarianism, 591–592
Utility-based approach to pollution, 396

V

Values, 23–24, 586
Vapor as atmospheric component, 465
Venus, 32, 32n
Virgin resources, 157, 262
Vitamin deficiencies, 354
Volatile organic compounds (VOCs), 400, 465
   and air pollution, 472–474
   biotreatment of, 556–557
   pollution trends in, 473–474
Volcanoes, 47
Volta, Alessandro, 244
Volume
   English/metric conversion table, B.1
   English/metric measures for, B.1, B.2

W

Wally's garden hose, 282
Waste management
   alternative paradigms for, 528–530
   for polychlorinated biphenyls (PCBs), 555
   traditional means of, 530–538
Wastes, 228. *See also* Hazardous wastes
   combustion of, 419
   disposal and recycling of, in United States,
   540–542
   disposal of nuclear fuels, 218–220, 222
Waste-to-energy facilities, 228
Wastewater
   reclamation of, 298–299, 302
   treatment of, 448–449
      advanced (tertiary), 451
      primary, 449–450
      secondary, 450
      septic tanks, 451
Wastewell injection, 291
Water